Contents

Published by the
National Garden Scheme
A company limited by guarantee.
Registered in England & Wales.
Charity No. 1112664.
Company No. 5631421

Registered & Head Office:
Hatchlands Park, East Clandon,
Guildford, Surrey, GU4 7RT.
01483 211535 www.ngs.org.uk

© The National Garden Scheme 2024

Foreword

How wonderful to start with the news that 2023 raised more funds than any year in the history of the National Garden Scheme. Some 3,500 gardens which opened during the year raised more than £4 million for the very first time. Achieving this meant that more funds were available for donation to our beneficiaries. What a wonderful achievement by all our garden owners and volunteers.

We all know that gardens give space and time to reflect in peace and bring one closer to nature. I think that the results of last year showed that the pleasure of visiting a garden was more important to people than ever before. And, as I know from having opened our garden for over 20 years, it is a shared pleasure. Owners share their passion and hard work to get the garden Open Day ready, and visitors share the joy, have a wonderful time - and with any luck there will be tea and cake!

Shared pleasure is an important part of the National Garden Scheme's increasingly successful community garden grants programme which saw 86 projects receive a total of £260,000 in grants of not more than £5,000. All over the country these community gardens bring together hugely diverse groups of people and spring up ingeniously in all kinds of unlikely places for the benefit of their local communities.

2024 has the potential to be a memorable year for the National Garden Scheme because for only the second time in its history the charity is putting on a show garden at the RHS Chelsea Flower Show. The garden has been fully funded by Project Giving Back and designed by the peerless Tom Stuart-Smith, who has opened his Hertfordshire garden with the National Garden Scheme for 30 years. It will be an occasion to showcase the wonderful talents and hospitality of our garden owners. I'm very much looking forward to seeing the National Garden Scheme Garden and the team will be there to welcome us.

Mary Berry

Dame Mary Berry
President

Who's who

Chairman's message

Once again, I would like to thank our President, Dame Mary Berry, for writing such an uplifting Foreword to this 2024 edition of the *Garden Visitor's Handbook*.

Readers will notice that we have arranged the contents by region rather than the simple county A to Z of previous years. Gardens are listed in their counties, but the counties are grouped together in nine regions: North East, North West, East Midlands, West Midlands, East, South East, South West, Wales and Northern Ireland. We hope that grouping neighbouring counties together will make planning a visit easier.

Otherwise, the contents remain largely as in previous years, refreshed by a total of more than 900 gardens which are either opening in support of the National Garden Scheme for the first time or returning to opening after a break of some years. A special welcome and thank you to all of them.

In the editorial pages in front of the garden listings you will find articles about the donations and other charitable activities which are only made possible by your visits and the generosity of our supporters who open their gardens. The National Garden Scheme was founded in 1927 to raise funds for district nurses and we are very proud that nearly 100 years later the majority of donations continue to go to nursing and health charities, also that more than 80% of funds raised at gardens are donated annually.

An article on page 22 describes a very generous collaboration to support our charity between two renowned retailers, David Austin Roses and Emma Bridgewater, while on page 10 you will find an article about how we are supported by people leaving the charity a gift in their will, with two uplifting stories of generous gifts from supporters who enjoyed a lifetime of visiting National Garden Scheme gardens.

There would be no National Garden Scheme without our wonderful visitors, as well as people generously making the commitment to open their gardens or to volunteer for the charity, highlighted on pages 24 and 25. Together they make a wonderful, dedicated army and we always welcome new recruits.

Rupert Tyler

Tips on using your Handbook

This book lists all the gardens opening for the National Garden Scheme between January 2024 and early 2025. It is arranged alphabetically in county sections within nine regions, each including a map, calendar of opening dates and details of each garden with illustrations of some.

Symbols explained

NEW Gardens opening for the first time this year or re-opening after a long break.

◆ Garden also opens on non-National Garden Scheme days. (Gardens which carry this symbol contribute to the National Garden Scheme either by opening on a specific day(s) and/or by giving a guaranteed contribution.)

♿ Wheelchair access to at least the main features of the garden.

🐕 Dogs on short leads welcome.

❋ Plants usually for sale.

•)) Card payments accepted.

NPC Plant Heritage National Plant Collection.

🛏 Gardens that offer accommodation.

☕ Refreshments are available, normally at a charge.

🪑 Picnics welcome.

D Garden designed by a Fellow, Member, Pre-registered Member, or Student of The Society of Garden Designers.

🚌 Garden accessible to coaches. Coach sizes vary so please contact the garden owner or County Organiser in advance to check details.

Group Visits Group Organisers may contact the County Organiser or a garden owner direct to organise a group visit to a particular county or garden. Otherwise contact the National Garden Scheme office on 01483 211535.

Children must be accompanied by an adult.

Photography is at the discretion of the garden owner; please check first. Photographs must not be used for sale or reproduction without prior permission of the owner.

Funds raised In most cases all funds raised at our open gardens comes to the National Garden Scheme. However, there are some instances where income from teas or a percentage of admissions is given to another charity.

Toilet facilities are not guaranteed at all gardens.

If you cannot find the information you require from a garden owner or County Organiser, call the National Garden Scheme office on 01483 211535.

Discovering the nation's best gardens

The National Garden Scheme gives visitors unique access to exceptional private gardens and raises impressive amounts of money for nursing and health charities through admissions, teas and cake.

Thanks to the generosity of garden owners, volunteers and visitors we have donated over £70 million to nursing and health charities since we were founded in 1927. In 2023 we made a record level of donations from our garden opening season of £3,403,960.

Originally established to raise funds for district nurses, we are now the most significant charitable funder of nursing in the UK and our beneficiaries include Macmillan Cancer Support, Marie Curie, Hospice UK, Parkinson's UK, The Queen's Nursing Institute and Carers Trust. Year by year,

the cumulative impact of our donations grows incrementally, helping our beneficiaries make their own important contribution to the nation's health and care.

The National Garden Scheme doesn't just open beautiful gardens for charity – we are passionate about the physical and mental health benefits of gardens too. We fund projects which promote gardens and gardening as therapy, support charities doing amazing work in gardens and health and give grants for community gardening projects. Our funding also supports the training of gardeners and offers respite to horticultural workers who have fallen on difficult times.

With over 3,500 gardens opening across England, Wales, Northern Ireland and the Channel Islands in 2023 there are plenty for you to explore. We hope you enjoy revisiting old favourites and discovering new horticultural gems. Most gardens open on one or more specific dates but many also open by arrangement, offering the facility for you to book a private visit.

YOUR GARDEN VISITS HELP CHANGE LIVES

In 2023 the National Garden Scheme donated £3,403,960 to our beneficiaries, providing critical support to nursing and health charities.

Marie Curie
£450,000

Macmillan Cancer Support
£450,000

Hospice UK
£450,000

Carers Trust
£350,000

The Queen's Nursing Institute
£425,000

Parkinson's UK
£350,000

SUPPORT FOR GARDENERS

- English Heritage £125,000
- Perennial £100,000
- National Botanic Garden, Wales £26,000
- Professional Gardeners' Trust £20,000
- Garden Museum £10,000

- Support for Community Gardens £260,000

GARDENS AND HEALTH CHARITIES

- Maggie's £100,000
- Horatio's Garden £90,000
- Army Benevolent Fund £80,000
- Mencap £50,000
- Sue Ryder £40,660
- Thrive £27,300

DONATE

Thank you!

To find out more visit **ngs.org.uk/beneficiaries**

Charity number: 1112664

The impact of our donations on nursing

Above: Sharon, Macmillan Gynaecology Clinical Nurse Specialist with patient, © Macmillan Cancer Support
Opposite: Marie Curie Senior Nurse, Halima, supports a patient during a home visit, © Philip Hardman/Marie Curie

Originally established to raise funds for district nurses, the National Garden Scheme is now the most significant charitable funder of nursing in the UK and our beneficiaries include Macmillan Cancer Support, Marie Curie, Hospice UK, Parkinson's UK, The Queen's Nursing Institute and Carers Trust.

Thanks to the generosity of garden owners, volunteers and visitors, we have donated over £70 million to nursing and health charities since we were founded in 1927. In 2023 the lion's share of our £3,403,960 donation went to our major long-term beneficiaries who are all leading providers of nursing and healthcare, in particular community and specialist nursing, cancer, palliative, and end of life care.

In the current state of the wider UK health and care landscape, the impact of our donations has never been more telling, ensuring that our beneficiary charities can continue to make a crucial contribution to the health of the nation. As a group our beneficiaries are a significant force, and our support helps them continue their individual and joint activities.

We have continued to have a special impact with some beneficiaries by funding specific projects that benefit both their staff and patients or other service users. With The Queen's Nursing Institute (QNI) we have continued to fund their Executive Nurse Leadership programme which trains and equips senior community nurses to take on some of the highest roles in the nursing profession. Previously these roles have rarely been filled by community nurses. Also, with the QNI we continue to fund their Elsie Wagg scholarships. These are named after the QNI Trustee who had the original idea to establish the National Garden Scheme in 1927. They fund nurses to develop garden projects at their place of work, such as a GP's surgery or a care home, for the benefit of patients and their families. And with Marie Curie we continue to support their Nightingale Challenge which funds Marie Curie nurses to gain qualifications which enable their career progression, thereby helping ensure that nurses stay in the profession and do not leave.

National Garden Scheme funding has also helped to fund 20 new nurse and allied health professional posts for Parkinson's UK to bring better care, treatments and quality of life to those living with the condition. Over 7,000 people living with Parkinson's who did not previously have access to specialist care are now reached thanks to our funding and we will continue to support Parkinson UK's ambitious strategy to support an additional 30 new nurse posts and 30 new allied health professional roles between 2023–2025.

Our funding in 2023 has helped:

- Support 270 inpatients at the Y Bwthyn NGS Macmillan Specialist Palliative Care Unit in Wales

- Provide the equivalent of 17,496 hours of Marie Curie nursing care

- Support 2,500 Queen's Nurses

- Provide specialist care for 7,000 people living with Parkinson's

Pass on your love of gardens with a gift in your Will

Leaving a gift in your Will to the National Garden Scheme will help us ensure that everyone can experience the joy of garden visiting and inspire a passion for gardens in future generations.

When we look back over our lives, we think about the things that matter most to us; our family, our friends and our community. After providing for those closest to you, a charitable gift is a very personal way to ensure the things that matter most to you live on, while inspiring your family and friends with the causes you hold most dear.

Legacies make an enormous difference to our work, and we are so grateful to everyone who chooses to support us by leaving a gift in their Will.

They wanted their legacy to enable future generations to experience the joy of garden visiting.

Di handled her sister and brother-in-law's estate when they passed away and she explained why they wanted to leave a gift to the National Garden Scheme: "My sister and brother-in-law were both avid supporters of the National Garden Scheme and loved nothing more than to visit open gardens. They wanted their legacy to benefit others in a field they were passionate about – and ultimately enable future generations to experience the joy of garden visiting, just like they did."

Visiting gardens throughout her lifetime was a much-loved pastime

Lynda's brother Martin told us: "I believe Lynda made the decision to donate her estate to the National Garden Scheme shortly after our mother's death in 2011. Never having married and living alone, Lynda began to think about her own funeral and making a Will – this was many years before the cancer diagnosis. As an enthusiastic gardener, visiting private gardens through the National Garden Scheme was a much-loved pastime. First visits were with our mother, also a gardener, and later, on her own. I also joined her on visits home, and it was therefore no surprise when Lynda told me last year that she was donating everything to the National Garden Scheme."

How your gifts can help

In addition to our annual donations to nursing and health charities, the National Garden Scheme awards grants to help community gardening projects. Thanks to the generosity of those who have contributed to our legacy fund with a gift in their Will, we were able to award 86 community garden grants with a total of £260,000 in 2023.

Included below are just a couple of examples of the amazing community garden projects which were made possible by generous legacies last year.

Danny Clarke, aka The Black Gardener (pictured), **and National Garden Scheme Ambassador says:**

"It's great to see this funding going to the heart of so many community projects. Projects that will help invigorate the people they support and introduce new audiences to the huge benefits that gardens, and gardening bring to their health and wellbeing and to the environment and communities around them."

Dig Killicomaine – transforming an eyesore into a thriving community allotment

Thanks to a £4,049 Community Garden Grant from the National Garden Scheme, a former fly-tipping site, described by residents in Portadown as an 'eyesore', has been transformed into a thriving community allotment by the Killicomaine Residents Group and the Housing Executive's maintenance staff. It is now home to a range of vegetable patches, and an outdoor kitchen and community space which benefits all the residents in the area making a safer, more welcoming and healthier community. Local people have really benefitted from the allotment, with residents receiving surplus produce free of charge.

Homerton University Hospital – bringing a garden to life

Homerton University Hospital received £4,989 from the National Garden Scheme to enable them to renovate a previously unused patch of land at the back entrance of the hospital. Now a beautiful harvest and growing garden for staff and patients, it serves as a space for connection with nature and with each other, for both patient groups (from diabetes, cardiology, stroke and rehabilitation) and staff from clinical and administrative teams across the site.

Find out more about leaving a gift in your Will to the National Garden Scheme or request our free Gift In Wills guide – visit our website: ngs.org.uk/get-involved/giftinwill

The art of sitting comfortably

Gardens and Health: people and communities

Our Gardens and Health programme raises awareness of the physical and mental health benefits of gardens and gardening for everyone. Celebrated in May each year with a dedicated Gardens and Health Week, we work to promote gardens and health throughout the year, linking service users from our beneficiaries with free garden visits, and funding gardens and health projects.

The charities we fund create gardens with health benefits and promote gardens and gardening as therapy. They include Horatio's Garden, which builds beautiful, accessible gardens in NHS spinal injury centres, and Maggie's which creates cancer support centres combining the best architects and landscape designers to build a strong connection between the outside and inside space. In 2023, over 100 inpatients were supported at the new Horatio's Garden, Wales and over 47,000 people affected by cancer were reached by Maggie's

centres supported by the National Garden Scheme. Our donation to the Army Benevolent Fund also supports the provision of horticultural-related assistance to soldiers, veterans and their immediate families to help improve their health and wellbeing and reaches over 600 people each year.

The National Garden Scheme also give grants for community gardening projects that support the wellbeing of local communities and groups. In 2023 we funded 86 projects with a total of £260,000.

The funding for 2023 was announced in April to mark Community Gardens Week. Commenting, Chief Executive, George Plumptre said: "The Covid-19 pandemic demonstrated the growing popularity and importance of community gardens, and our support has responded to this. Now, at a time when the cost-of-living crisis is forcing many people to find innovative ways to support themselves, their families and their communities our Community Garden Grants are providing even more of a helping hand to thousands of people across the UK."

Many of the 500 applications centred on the growing of food for communities, foodbanks and those helping others to learn to grow food. Applications also came from a broad spectrum of society, including a number of ethnic minorities.

"Community gardens can help reduce isolation and build friendships, so it is easy to see why people get involved and we are delighted to provide ongoing support to so many inspirational projects," adds George.

From social welfare and gardening projects that help the isolated, the disabled and the disenfranchised to support for community orchards, food banks and social prescribing projects at GP surgeries, the funding provides a much-needed boost to those working on, or initiating, community garden projects throughout England, Wales and Northern Ireland. Many of the funded community projects in turn open for the National Garden Scheme completing a virtuous circle of giving and giving back.

Above: Members of St Paul's Community Group, Bristol celebrate the completion of their garden project with the presentation of a National Garden Scheme plaque by County Organiser Su Mills. Opposite: Maggie's, Newcastle

Applications for 2025 grants open in autumn 2024, full details will be available on the website at **ngs.org.uk**

Our show garden at RHS Chelsea Flower Show

Above: Sketch view of the National Garden Scheme show garden
Opposite, top: Tom Stuart-Smith, Landscape Architect and Designer

The National Garden Scheme is thrilled to announce that it will have a show garden at the prestigious 2024 RHS Chelsea Flower Show in May

Designed by eight times RHS gold medal winner, Tom Stuart-Smith, and sponsored by Project Giving Back, the garden will exemplify the joy and associated health and wellbeing benefits of garden visiting that have been at the heart of the National Garden Scheme since 1927. Following the show, the garden will be relocated to Addenbrooke's Hospital, Cambridge, to become the garden of a new Maggie's Centre for people undergoing cancer treatment.

Tom Stuart-Smith, who last designed a show garden for the RHS Chelsea Flower Show in 2010, says: "The National Garden Scheme is a wonderfully unique charity, and I am proud to have opened my own garden at Serge Hill in Hertfordshire in aid of it for nearly 30 years. It's a very special honour for me to be helping bring the National Garden Scheme to an even wider audience through this new garden, that has been made possible with Project Giving Back support."

With a woodland edge theme, the garden's drift of gentle underplanting, made up of principally drought tolerant woodland plants laid out through an open hazel coppice, is designed to give a sense of calm and a connection to nature. With a selection of plants donated by National Garden Scheme garden owners incorporated into the design, the garden exemplifies the spirit of generosity that is woven through the relationship the charity has with its supporters.

George Plumptre, Chief Executive of the National Garden Scheme says: "We very much hope that our presence at the RHS Chelsea Flower Show and our show garden will inform more people and inspire them to visit our gardens through 2024, contributing further to our fundraising record." Exhibiting a show garden at the RHS Chelsea Flower Show is a unique privilege for the National Garden Scheme. It gives our charity the opportunity to celebrate our passion for gardens and our charitable activities with a worldwide audience of garden lovers and we look forward to sharing the garden with you in May. Do come and say hello if you are visiting the show.

For more information about the garden see: ngs.org.uk/our-chelsea-garden

---

We will be holding a plant sale featuring perennials from our RHS Chelsea Flower Show garden in June 2024. All plants have been grown in the UK especially for the National Garden Scheme show garden. Everything will be available to purchase on a first-come, first-served basis. All profits will support the National Garden Scheme. Venue and date to be announced – see our website for full details: ngs.org.uk/our-chelsea-garden

The beneficiary collection: garden openings in 2024

We all know that gardens are good for us, they provide respite from the chaos of our busy lives, exercise through gardening, buckets of fresh air and a real sense of achievement and calm. This heady mix of benefits can help us in our daily lives as well as those who are recovering from or living with life-threatening conditions.

The National Garden Scheme opens a diverse portfolio of gardens across the country to raise funds for some of the UK's best-loved nursing and health charities, but it doesn't just open private gardens. In the mix are a wonderful array of gardens owned by the beneficiaries that we work to support, gardens that provide therapy, solace, reflection, respite and purpose.

Above right: Maggie's, Manchester
Opposite: Horatio's Garden Salisbury, © Horatio's Garden
Below: Marie Curie Hospice Garden, Warwickshire
Bottom: Leckhampton Court Hospice, Gloucestershire

You can visit the gardens that the National Garden Scheme helps fund at Maggie's centres and Horatio's Gardens across the UK and experience first-hand the beautiful planting and thoughtful design that makes these gardens so special to the patients and their families who benefit from them. There are also fourteen hospices that open their gardens to National Garden Scheme visitors in 2024. Many are maintained by volunteers and opening their gates to the garden visiting public gives the hospice teams a wonderful opportunity not only to share their beautiful, restful spaces but to also integrate and connect with the local community.

Among those opening in 2024 are the gardens at the Marie Curie hospices in Newcastle, Hampstead and Solihull, Wigan & Leigh Hospice, Leckhampton Court Hospice in Gloucestershire and Skanda Vale Hospice in Dyfed.

Visiting these gardens not only helps support those they care for but also provides an insight into how beneficial to our health and wellbeing spending time in a garden can be.

To find out more use our Find A Garden tool on the **ngs.org.uk** website to search for a hospice, Maggie's or Horatio's Garden

The National Garden Scheme is looking for new gardens

Join a community of like-minded individuals passionate about gardens and open your garden to raise money for vital nursing and health charities.

Our garden portfolio is diverse: from gorgeous country estates to tropical urban extravaganzas, gardens planted for wildlife and allotments. So, whatever its size or style, if your garden has quality, character and interest we'd love to hear from you.

Call us on 01483 211 535 or email hello@ngs.org.uk

Griffin has been designing bespoke glasshouses since the early 1960s. With a history of innovating glasshouse design for the commercial sector, Griffin continues to be the choice of many estate managers and discerning professional gardeners today, with glasshouses installed in the UK and worldwide.

Traditionally...

The Gardener's Glasshouse

Each Griffin glasshouse is individually created for you, tailored to your individual requirements and unique surroundings whilst being both a pleasure for you to use and an enhancing feature of your property. Manufactured from powder coated aluminium in any colour of your choice, your glasshouse will have all the appeal of a traditional wooden structure but without the maintenance issues.

Unreservedly distinct *Glasshouses, Greenhouses* and *Orangeries*

For more information please call or visit our website.

GRIFFIN GLASSHOUSES

GREENHOUSES OF DISTINCTION

50 YEARS EXPERIENCE

www.griffinglasshouses.com

01962 772512

Partnering National Garden Scheme with our select range of free standing glasshouses

A charitable collaboration bursting with sunshine!

Emma Bridgewater   DAVID AUSTIN®

We are delighted to be part of an exciting charitable collaboration with Emma Bridgewater and David Austin®.

The iconic pottery company and famous rose grower have teamed up to create a charming 'Bring Me Sunshine' ½ Pint Mug, on sale to raise funds for the National Garden Scheme. Designed by Emma Bridgewater the mug is decorated with the vibrant English shrub rose *Bring Me Sunshine®* – named after the heart-warming tune made famous by comedy duo Morecambe and Wise.

Whether you are a seasoned rose enthusiast or just starting on your gardening journey, this mug and beautifully fragranced rose are perfect for bringing you sunshine whatever the weather. A £5 donation will be made to the National Garden Scheme for every mug purchased helping to make an even bigger difference to the nursing and health charities we support.

Emma Bridgewater

At Emma Bridgewater we like to make things that make every day a little bit nicer. Each design is inspired by what we love in the world around us, from people and places to flora and fauna, from the warmth of the home to the Great British outdoors. We believe the things we treasure most reflect the stories of our lives: they have the power to make every day lovely and fill our hearts and homes with spots of joy. www.emmabridgewater.co.uk

David Austin®

For over 60 years, we have been growing roses on our family farm in Shropshire, lovingly nurturing them by hand until they are ready to be passed onto you, and to be enjoyed in your own gardens. All our roses have beautiful blooms and in most cases wonderful fragrance held on graceful attractive stems. A garden of these outstanding roses is hard to beat for sheer exuberance of flower and fragrance. www.davidaustinroses.co.uk

Join our exclusive open weekend at David Austin®, on the 15th and 16th of June

As part of our collaboration, David Austin Roses are opening the garden gate, for the very first time, to Mr Austin Senior's private gardens where the business began with the launch of his first rose in 1961 – Constance Spry. Alongside also having the opportunity to explore his personal rose collection and the six themed public gardens, open weekend visitors will be treated to music, garden games and typically English tea-time treats amongst the roses. See page 204 for more details. Tickets can be booked in advance on the David Austin website www.davidaustinroses.co.uk/products/ngs-open-gardens and a £10,000 donation will be made to the National Garden Scheme.

Volunteering is at the heart of everything we achieve

GARDEN OPEN CHARITY

The success of the National Garden Scheme and the significant amounts of money it donates to its beneficiary charities would not be possible without the dedicated input of the charity's garden owners and volunteers.

In 2023, 3,389 gardens opened for the Scheme across England, Wales, Northern Ireland and the Channel Islands supported by 585 volunteers. The enthusiasm, expertise and generosity of our garden owners and volunteers is at the heart of everything the charity achieves.

Some gardens have been opening since 1927, and in 2023 three of them, The Garden at Miserden in Gloucestershire, Saint Paul's Walden Bury in Hertfordshire and Scotney Castle in Kent marked 90 years of opening for the National Garden Scheme. These, and other landmark openings, were all celebrated.

"Whether it opens once or over a number of decades every garden is important," says Chairman, Rupert Tyler, who has opened his own garden at 51 The Chase in Clapham since 2009. "We owe an enormous debt of gratitude to all of our garden owners and all the volunteers who support them. Without their combined dedication and passion, we would not have become the most significant funder of nursing charities in the UK or been able to give £3,403,960 to our beneficiaries in 2023. And, as we head towards our centenary year in 2027, we would like to thank everyone who has helped create such a vibrant, inspiring and enduring community that gives so much pleasure to visitors and raises so much money for good causes."

Confirming the importance of our volunteers, in 2023 we shared the wonderful news that one of our volunteers was awarded an MBE for her work with the National Garden Scheme. Susan Copeland (pictured opposite, top right), who first opened her garden in 1996 and went on to become County Organiser for Essex and a Regional Chair and Trustee, received the honour from The King, patron of the National Garden Scheme since 2002 at an investiture at Buckingham Palace in October. This prestigious honour recognises not only Susan's dedication to the charity but also illustrates the high esteem in which our volunteers are held.

If you would like to open your garden or volunteer to support the National Garden Scheme you can find out more at: ngs.org.uk/get-involved

Above and opposite: Just a few of the fabulous 585 volunteers who help us achieve so much for nursing and health charities every year

We're here for all seasons

We need the people behind the flowers, plants, trees and grass, and sometimes they need us. We're here for everyone, working now and if retired, to help grow their wellbeing physically, mentally and financially. Please support the people behind our beautiful gardens.

" Perennial's help is free and given in confidence. As a charity, it relies on the support of all those in the horticultural industry and also from all of us who enjoy the benefits of their hard work. We can all play a part. "

Alan Titchmarsh,
President, Perennial

Find out more or donate
perennial.org.uk

Helping people
in horticulture
Perennial

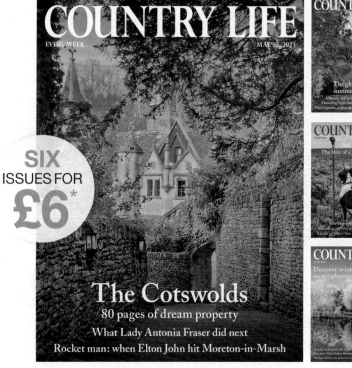

County Durham
Northumberland
Tyne and Wear
Yorkshire

NORTH EAST

Above: Lorbottle Hall, Northumberland

NORTH EAST

Stretching from the Scottish border to the Midlands, the North East region combines some of the largest expanses of English countryside with a selection of the country's most historic cities. From Berwick-on-Tweed south the coastline offers a range of iconic landmarks from Lindisfarne and Holy Island to the River Tyne, from Whitby to Flamborough Head.

Across Northumberland, parts of the Roman Hadrian's Wall survive as a reminder that this has always been border country and the region is rich in historical evidence, both ancient and more modern. It also has a majestic scale, exemplified in the two majestic cathedrals of Durham and York, found naturally in the famous landscapes of the northern Pennines in County Durham, the Yorkshire Dales and North York Moors, but also in great cities such as Newcastle-upon-Tyne, Leeds and Sheffield, each of which has evolved from their industrial past to modern vitality. In many areas gardening can be challenging with cold, often snowy winters and late springs, but this is compensated by outlooks to spectacular stretches of countryside or the protection of an urban setting.

Above, from top: Hill House, Northumberland; The Old Vicarage, Whixley Gardens, Yorkshire

Below: Swindon House Farm, Yorkshire

COUNTY DURHAM, NORTHUMBERLAND & TYNE AND WEAR

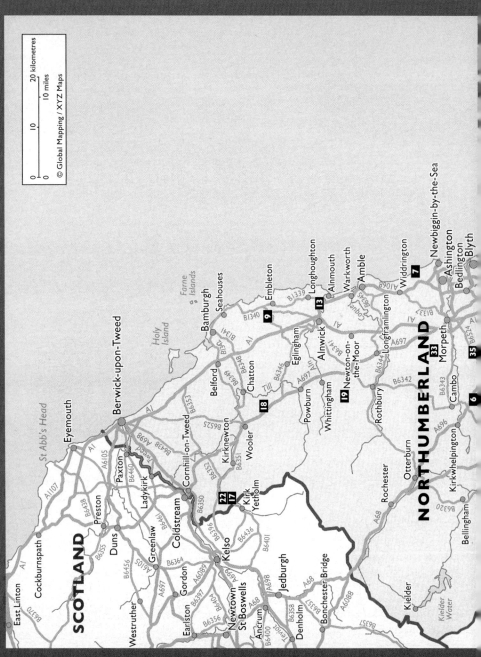

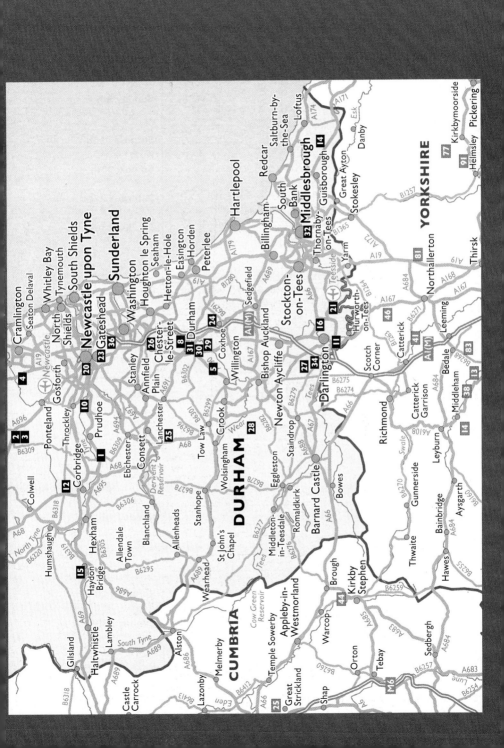

VOLUNTEERS

County Durham

County Organiser
Aileen Little
01325 356691
aileen.little@ngs.org.uk

County Treasurer
Monica Spencer
01325 286215
monica.spencer@ngs.org.uk

Publicity
Margaret Stamper
01325 488911
margaretstamper@tiscali.co.uk

Booklet Co-ordinator
Sue Walker
07849 451079
walker.sdl@gmail.com

Assistant County Organisers
Iain Anderson
01325 778446
iain.anderson@ngs.org.uk

Sarah Garbutt
sarah.garbutt@ngs.org.uk

Helen Jackson
helen.jackson@ngs.org.uk

Gill Knights
01325 483210
gillianknights55@gmail.com

Gill Naisby
01325 381324
gillnaisby@gmail.com

Margaret Stamper (see above)

Sue Walker (see above)

f @gardensopenforcharity
X @NGSNorthumberl1
@ngsnorthumber
@ngscountydurham

Northumberland & Tyne and Wear County Organiser & Booklet Coordinator
Maureen Kesteven 01914 135937
maureen.kesteven@ngs.org.uk

County Treasurer
David Oakley 07941 077594
david.oakley@ngs.org.uk

Publicity, Talks Co-ordinator & Social Media
Liz Reid 01914 165981
liz.reid@ngs.org.uk

Assistant County Organisers
Maxine Eaton 077154 60038
maxine.eaton@ngs.org.uk

Natasha McEwen 07917 754155
natashamcewengd@aol.co.uk

Liz Reid (as left)

Susie White 07941 077594
susie@susie-white.co.uk

David Young 01434 600699
david.young@ngs.org.uk

OPENING DATES

All entries subject to change.
For latest information check
www.ngs.org.uk
Map locator numbers are
shown to the right of each
garden name.

April

Sunday 28th
Blagdon   4

May

Saturday 18th
◆ Whalton Manor Gardens   35

Sunday 19th
Ferndene House   10

Thursday 30th
NEW ◆ Belsay Hall, Castle &
Gardens   2

June

Wednesday 5th
Thornton Hall Gardens   34

Thursday 6th
◆ Crook Hall & Gardens   8
NEW Hill House   15

Sunday 9th
NEW Lorbottle Hall   19
Oliver Ford Garden   25

Saturday 15th
Bichfield Tower   3

Sunday 16th
Halton Castle   12

Saturday 22nd
NEW Hawkhill House   13

Sunday 23rd
Kirky Cottage   17
Marie Curie Hospice   20
◆ Mindrum House Garden   22
Old Quarrington Gardens   24

Saturday 29th
Fallodon Hall   9

Sunday 30th
NEW ◆ Cresswell Pele Tower
Walled Garden   7
Stanton Fence   33

July

Saturday 6th
Capheaton Hall   6
NEW Historic Haughton-le-Skerne
Gardens   16

Sunday 7th
Capheaton Hall   6
NEW ◆ Cresswell Pele Tower Walled
Garden   7

Sunday 14th
NEW ◆ Cresswell Pele Tower
Walled Garden   7
NEW The Gardens of Carmel
Road South   11
St Margaret's Allotments   31

Saturday 20th
NEW Brancepeth Village Gardens 5

Sunday 28th
St Cuthbert's Hospice   30

August

Sunday 4th
Heather Holm 14

Saturday 17th
Middleton Hall Retirement
Village 21

September

Thursday 5th
NEW Hill House 15

Sunday 22nd
Ravensford Farm 28

By Arrangement

Arrange a personalised garden visit with your club, or group of friends, on a date to suit you. See individual garden entries for full details.

Capheaton Hall

THE GARDENS

1 THE BEACON

10 Crabtree Road, Stocksfield, NE43 7NX. Derek & Patricia Hodgson OBE, 01661 842518, patanddderek@btinternet.com. *12m W of Newcastle. From A69 follow signs into village. Stn & cricket ground on L. Turn R into Cadehill Rd then 1st R into Crabtree Rd (cul-de-sac) Park on Cadehill.* **Visits by arrangement 27 May to 15 Sept for groups of 5+. Home-made teas £6 pp. Adm £7, chd free.**
This garden illustrates how to make a cottage garden on a steep site with loads of interest at different levels. Planted with acers, roses and a variety of cottage garden and formal plants. Water runs gently through it and there are tranquil places to sit and talk or just reflect. Stunning colour and plant combinations. Wildlife friendly - numerous birds, frogs, newts, hedgehogs. Haven for butterflies and bees. Owner available for entertaining group talks. Comedy/piano recital available at By Arrangement visits (£4 per person in aid of NSPCC).

2 NEW ◆ BELSAY HALL, CASTLE & GARDENS

Belsay, nr Morpeth, NE20 0DX. English Heritage. *Off A696 at Belsay village. Follow the brown signs. SatNav: NE20 0DU.* **For NGS: Evening opening Thur 30 May (5.30-8). Adm £15. Pre-booking essential, please phone 07721 813442, email alison. makosch@english-heritage. org.uk or visit www.english-heritage.org.uk/visit/places/ belsay-hall-castle-and-gardens/ events for information & booking. Refreshments available to purchase from the café before the tour. For other opening times and information, please phone, email or visit garden website.**
Explore a rare surviving picturesque garden, with its informative gardening team. Follow the paths into the Quarry garden, transporting you to another world. These rocky walls offer shelter to a vast range of exotics all hidden within the Northumberland countryside. Enjoy the beautiful borders at Belsay Hall, newly created by garden designer Dan Pearson, and inspired by the past.

3 BICHFIELD TOWER

Belsay, Newcastle Upon Tyne, NE20 0JP. Lesley & Stewart Manners, 07511 439606, lesleymanners@gmail.com. *Private rd off B6309, 4m N of Stamfordham & SW of Belsay village.* **Sat 15 June (12-4). Adm £8, chd free. Home-made teas in the carriage house & garden.**
A 6 acre mature garden. Set around a Medieval Pele Tower, there is an impressive stone water feature, large trout lake, mature woodland, pear orchard, and 2 walled gardens. Extensive herbaceous borders, prairie borders and contemporary grass borders. Delicious home-made teas.

4 BLAGDON

Seaton Burn, NE13 6DE. Viscount Ridley. *5m S of Morpeth on A1. 8m N of Newcastle on A1, N on B1318, L at r'about (Holiday Inn) & follow signs to Blagdon. Entrance to parking area signed.* **Sun 28 Apr (1-4). Adm £6, chd free. Home-made teas.**
Unique 27 acre garden encompassing formal garden with Lutyens designed 'canal', Lutyens structures and walled kitchen garden. Valley with stream and various follies, quarry garden and woodland walks. Masses of daffodils in spring. Large numbers of ornamental trees and shrubs planted over many generations. National Collections of Acer, Alnus and Sorbus. Partial wheelchair access.

5 NEW BRANCEPETH VILLAGE GARDENS

Brancepeth, Durham, DH7 8EN. Alison Young. *5 m W of Durham City on A690. Take A690 to Brancepeth. Turn to golf club and enter gates to castle where parking is arranged.* **Sat 20 July (11-4.30). Adm £5, chd free. Home-made teas in village hall.**
Village gardens spread out over ½ mile in a picturesque historic setting.Refreshments available in the Village Hall. Proceeds to the Hall maintenance fund. Parking courtesy of the Castle. Dogs on leads please.

6 CAPHEATON HALL

Capheaton, Newcastle Upon Tyne, NE19 2AB. William & Eliza Browne-Swinburne, 01913 758152, estateoffice@capheatonhall.co.uk, www.capheatonhall.co.uk. *Off A696 24m N of Newcastle. From S turn L off A696 onto Silver Hill Rd signed Capheaton. From N, past Wallington/Kirkharle junction, turn R.* **Sat 6, Sun 7 July (10-5). Adm £10, chd free. Home-made teas.**
Set in parkland, Capheaton Hall has magnificent views over the Northumberland countryside. Formal ponds sit south of the house which has C19 conservatory and a walk to a Georgian folly of a chapel. The outstanding feature is the very productive walled kitchen garden, mixing colourful vegetables, espaliered fruit with annual and perennial flowering borders. Victorian glasshouse and conservatory Pre-booking recommended.

7 NEW ◆ CRESSWELL PELE TOWER WALLED GARDEN

Cresswell Road, Cresswell, Morpeth, NE61 5LE. Mr Steve Lowe, cresswellpeletower.org.uk. *10 m E of Morpeth. W of Cresswell Pele Tower, accessed through double gate. No parking on the village green. Public parking from seafront nearby.* **For NGS: Sun 30 June, Sun 7, Sun 14 July (1-4). Adm £3, chd free. Tea. For other opening times and information, please visit garden website.**
A newly restored C18 walled garden which was part of Cresswell Hall kitchen gardens, abandoned in the 1930's when the main house was demolished. With a grant from Heritage Lottery in 2022, the garden has been restored to inc borders, orchard, gazebo, wildlife pond and greenhouse. Work to increase plantings is underway. The garden is managed by volunteers. Wildlife Pond. Medieval Orchard and cordoned fruit. Raised beds for food growing. Diverse floral borders. Fern border. Medieval pele tower (restricted openings). Re-enactments. Interpretation History book in print. Beehives. Greenhouse. Short slope on lightly gravelled path initially, then level paths to Tower and Garden, which is fully accessible.

Riverside Lodge

8 ◆ CROOK HALL & GARDENS
Sidegate, Durham City, DH1 5SZ.
National Trust, 01913 831832,
crookhallgardens@nationaltrust.
org.uk, www.nationaltrust.org.
uk/visit/north-east/crook-hall-
gardens. *Centre of Durham City.
Crook Hall is short walk from
Durham's Market Place. Follow the
tourist info signs. Pay and display
parking available at entrance.* **For
NGS: Evening opening Thur 6
June (6-8.30). Adm £12. Pre-
booking essential, please visit
www.ngs.org.uk for information
& booking. Home-made teas
in outdoor covered Woodland
Glade area. Tea/coffee and
cakes available inc in ticket
price. For other opening times and
information, please phone, email or
visit garden website.**
Described in Country Life as having
'history, romance and beauty'.
Intriguing medieval hall and manor
houses surrounded by 5 acres of
fine gardens. Visitors can enjoy
magnificent cathedral views from
the 2 walled gardens. Other garden
'rooms' inc the silver and white
garden, an orchard and the moat
pond. The maze and Sleeping Giant
give added interest.

9 FALLODON HALL
Alnwick, NE66 3HF. Mr & Mrs
Mark Bridgeman, 07765 296197,
luciabridgeman@gmail.com,
www.bruntoncottages.co.uk. *5m
N of Alnwick, 2m off A1. From the
A1 turn R onto the B6347 signed
Christon Bank & Seahouses. Turn
into the Fallodon gates after exactly
2m, at Xrds. Follow drive for 1m.* **Sat
29 June (2-5). Adm £6, chd free.
Home-made teas. Visits also by
arrangement 20 Mar to 30 Oct for
groups of 5 to 30.**
Part of Northumberland's history.
Extensive, well established garden,
with a hot greenhouse beside the bog
garden. The late C17 kitchen garden
walls surround cutting and vegetable
borders and the fruit greenhouse.
Natasha McEwen replanted the
sunken garden (from 1898) and the
redesigned 30 metres border was
planted in 2019. Woodlands, pond
and arboretum with over 10 acres
to explore. Grave of Sir Edward
Grey, Foreign Secretary during
WW1, famous ornithologist and fly
fisherman, is in the woods near the
pond and arboretum. The walls of
the kitchen garden contain a fireplace
built to heat the fruit trees of the
Salkeld family, renowned for their
gardening expertise in the C17. Partial
wheelchair access.

10 FERNDENE HOUSE
2 Holburn Lane Court, Holburn
Lane, Ryton, NE40 3PN. Maureen
Kesteven, 01914 135937,
maureen.kesteven@ngs.
org.uk, www.facebook.com/
northeastgardenopenforcharity.
*In Ryton Old Village, 8m W of
Gateshead. Off B6317, on Holburn
Ln. Park on street or in Co-op car
park on High St, cross rd through
Ferndene Park following yellow signs.*
**Sun 19 May (12.30-4.30). Adm £6,
chd free. Light refreshments inc
pizza & prosecco. Visits also by
arrangement 15 Apr to 19 Aug for
groups of 10+.**
¾ acre garden surrounded by
trees. Informal areas of herbaceous
perennials, formal box bordered area,
wildlife pond, gravel and bog gardens
(with boardwalk). Willow work. Early
interest - hellebores, snowdrops,
daffodils, bluebells and tulips.
Summer interest from wide range of
flowering perennials. 1½ acre mixed
broadleaf wood with beck running
through. Driveway, from which main
borders can be seen, is wheelchair
accessible but phone for assistance.

GROUP OPENING

**11 NEW THE GARDENS OF
CARMEL ROAD SOUTH**
84 Carmel Road South, Darlington,
DL3 8DR. Grace Hunter. *All 6
gardens are within easy walking
distance of each other on Carmel
Rd South and Carmel Grove.* **Sun
14 July (11-5.30). Combined adm
£6, chd free. Home-made teas at
Dene Lodge, Linwood Grove.**

**NEW 48 CARMEL ROAD
SOUTH**
Mr Bryan & Mrs Paula Stapley.

**NEW 76 CARMEL ROAD
SOUTH**
Mrs Heather Scott.

**NEW 84 CARMEL ROAD
SOUTH**
Grace Hunter.

**NEW DENE LODGE, LINWOOD
GROVE**
Mr Paul & Mrs Julie Sheppard.

**NEW GREEN GABLES,
CARMEL ROAD SOUTH**
Mr Tony Ward.

**NEW THE WILLOWS, CARMEL
GROVE**
Mr Denys & Mrs Janet Orme.

The Carmel Road South Group
comprise of 6 interesting and varied
town gardens with some different
and unusual plants, all have colour
and interest. The smaller gardens
are delightful, the two larger ones
have views of the Tees and beyond.
The largest garden is a colourful 1½
acres with a sunken garden and
rockery and many shrubs. The garden
offering refreshments at Dene Lodge
is newly restored and is developing
with colourful planters but also has
wonderful views. Views of the River
Tees from Linwood Grove where the
teas, refreshments, chutneys, cakes
and plants are available for sale.

12 HALTON CASTLE
Corbridge, NE45 5PH. Hugh &
Anna Blackett. *2m N of Corbridge
turn E off the A68 onto the B6318
(Military Rd) towards Newcastle. Turn
R onto drive after ¼ m.* **Sun 16 June
(11.30-4.30). Adm £6, chd free.
Light lunches and cream teas
from 12pm.**
The terraced garden has stunning
views over the Tyne Valley. Massive
beech hedges give protection for
herbaceous borders, lawns and
shrubs. A box parterre is filled with
fruit, vegetables and picking flowers.
Paths lead through a wildflower
meadow garden. The Castle (not open)
is a C14 Pele tower with Jacobean
manor house attached beside a
charming chapel with Norman origins.
Partial wheelchair access.

13 NEW HAWKHILL HOUSE
Lesbury, Alnwick, NE66 3PG.
Dr Lily Fulton-Humble. *2 m E of
Alnwick. Driveway entrance is on the
main road opp Hawkhill Business
Park/Alnwick Brewery Co.* **Sat 22
June (2-5). Adm £5, chd free.
Light refreshments inc teas,
coffees and a selection of baked
goods for sale.**
A developing garden, Hawkhill House
restoration of the Victorian garden
combines traditional design with
romantic cottage garden planting.
Featuring a rose garden, lily pond,

mature shrubbery, large herbaceous and mixed perennial borders, to create avenues and rooms. The South facing aspect and planting enhances the beautiful views over the countryside. A woodland area is under development.

14 HEATHER HOLM
Stanghow Road, Stanghow, Saltburn-by-the-Sea, TS12 3JU. Arthur & June Murray. *Stanghow is 5km E of Guisborough on A171. Turn L at Lockwood Beck (signed Stanghow) Heather Holm is on the R past the Xrds.* **Sun 4 Aug (11-4). Adm £5, chd free. Home-made teas.**
Divided into several rooms, this is a garden of different aspects, formal, floral and architectural. The owners have a philosophy of colour throughout the year having hundreds of lilies flowering from March to October. Sheltered by mature hedges, hostas, hydrangeas and agapanthus thrive. There are fruit trees, soft fruit bushes, a greenhouse, summerhouse and a large pond attracting wildlife.

15 NEW HILL HOUSE
Haydon Bridge, Hexham, NE47 6HL. John and Mary Milford. *1½ m NW of Haydon Bridge. Hill House is marked on the OS map. Satnav will take visitors to car park.* **Thur 6 June, Thur 5 Sept (11-4). Adm £7.50, chd free. Pre-booking essential, please visit www.ngs. org.uk for information & booking.**
Unusual double Walled Garden, generously planted in Cottage Garden style. Circle of box hedges, yew square and topiary; aquilegia and lupins in early June and dahlias, roscoeas and annuals in early September provide much colour. The old orchard, with wildflowers, gives access to a mown walk through a sheep grazed meadow to a woodland area, affording good views across South Tyne valley.

GROUP OPENING

16 NEW HISTORIC HAUGHTON-LE-SKERNE GARDENS
Haughton Green, Darlington, DL1 2DD. *Approx 1.6m NE from town centre. From A1(M)S J57, A66 ring road until L at sign to A1(M)N, then L at next r'about. From A1(M) N leave at J59, follow A167 turn L at 1st r'about, R at next full r'about.* **Sat 6 July (1.30-5). Combined adm £5, chd free. Home-made teas at St Andrew's Church Hall 2-5pm.**

NEW THE COTTAGE AT BUTLER HOUSE
Barbara Roberts.

NEW SUNDIAL COTTAGE
Peter and Philippa Sinclair.

NEW WALNUT
Monica Spencer.

NEW WHITE HALL
Gina and Warren Blakemore-Murray.

Enjoy a range of secluded gardens, ancient and modern, set in this historic village: tranquil spaces which combine dense planting with a variety of styles and structures. Plenty of seating to relax and enjoy your surroundings. Teas (2-5) at the Church Hall provided by and proceeds to St Andrew's, the oldest church in Darlington. Accompanied children free. Assistance dogs only, please. Almost all parts wheelchair accessible.

17 KIRKY COTTAGE
12 Mindrum Farm Cottages, Mindrum, TD12 4QN. Mrs Ginny Fairfax, 01890 850246, ginny@mindrumgarden.co.uk, www.mindrumestate.co.uk/kirky-garden. *6m SW of Coldstream. 9m NW of Wooler on B6352. 4m N of Yetholm village.* **Sun 23 June (12-5). Combined adm with Mindrum House Garden £10, chd free. Home-made teas in nearby Mindrum Garden. Visits also by arrangement.**
Ginny Fairfax has created Kirky Cottage Garden in the beautiful Bowmont valley surrounded and protected by the Border Hills. A gravel garden in cottage garden style, old roses, violas and others jostle with favourites from Mindrum. A lovely, abundant garden and, with Ginny's new and creative ideas, ever evolving. All plants propagated from garden. Regional Finalist, The English Garden's The Nation's Favourite Gardens 2021.

19 NEW LORBOTTLE HALL
Whittingham, Alnwick, NE66 4TD. Ms Kate Donaghy. *What3words app - promises.struggle.variously. From Whittingham, 1½ m beyond Callaly, on L. From Rothbury, 4½ m. From Thropton, on the road to Whittingham, on R.* **Sun 9 June (1-5.30). Adm £8, chd free. Light refreshments.**
Garden and woodlands set in 20 acres with beautiful vistas, lovingly transformed over the last 8 years from considerable neglect. A Walled Garden contains wisteria arches, wild flowers and a long mixed border richly planted with shrubs, roses and herbaceous perennials. The wood continues to be transformed with woodland/shade loving plants and meandering paths leading to the large meadow. The lawns around the house, the walled and the pond gardens can be accessed by wheelchair users.

20 MARIE CURIE HOSPICE
Marie Curie Drive, Newcastle Upon Tyne, NE4 6SS. Marie Curie, www.mariecurie.org.uk/help/hospice-care/hospices/newcastle/about. *In W Newcastle just off Elswick Rd. At the bottom of a housing estate. Turning is between MA Brothers & Dallas Carpets.* **Sun 23 June (1.30-4). Adm by donation. Light refreshments in Garden Café.**
The landscaped garden of the purpose-built Marie Curie Hospice overlooks the Tyne and Gateshead and offers a beautiful, tranquil place for patients and visitors to sit and chat. Rooms open onto a patio garden with gazebo and fountain. There are climbing roses, evergreens and herbaceous perennials. The garden is well maintained by volunteers. Come and see the work NGS funding helps make possible. Plant sale. The Hospice and gardens are wheelchair accessible.

The National Garden Scheme searches the length and breadth of England, Wales, Northern Ireland and the Channel Islands for the very best private gardens.

21 MIDDLETON HALL RETIREMENT VILLAGE

Middleton St George, Darlington, DL2 1HA. Middleton Hall Retirement Village, www. middletonhallretirementvillage. co.uk. *From A67 D'ton/Yarm, turn at 2nd r'about signed to Middleton St George. Turn L at the mini r'about & immed R after the railway bridge, signed Low Middleton. Main entrance is ¼m on L.* **Sat 17 Aug (11-4). Adm £5, chd free. Light refreshments.**
Main features are natural woodland and parkland walks within the 45 acre estate. There is a Japanese themed garden, Mediterranean and butterfly gardens alongside wetland, ponds, a bird hide, fernery, a ceramic garden and allotments. There is also a residents' Putting Green and Golf course. For more information please visit our website. All wheelchair accessible and linked by a series of woodland walks.

22 ◆ MINDRUM HOUSE GARDEN

Mindrum, TD12 4QN. Mr & Mrs T Fairfax, 01890 850634, info@mindrumpartnership.com, www.mindrumestate.com. *6m SW of Coldstream, 9m NW of Wooler. Off B6352. Disabled parking close to house. Parking is available by both gardens.* **For NGS: Sun 23 June (12-5). Combined adm with Kirky Cottage £10, chd free. Home-made teas at Mindrum House. Plant Stall at Kirky Cottage. For other opening times and information, please phone, email or visit garden website.**
A magical combination of old-fashioned roses, hardy perennials and wildlife gardens in a natural setting. Lawns surround the house with borders of climbing roses, mature shrubs and trees throughout. Mindrum House has more extensive gardens inc a rose garden, limestone rock garden (steep slope), fish ponds with terraced walk, and woodland walk with mature pines.

23 ◆ NGS BUZZING GARDEN

East Park Road, Gateshead, NE9 5AX. Gateshead Council, maureen.kesteven@ngs.org.uk, www.gateshead.gov.uk/ article/11548/Growing-Gateshead-The-Buzzing-Garden. *Between Pets' Corner & Saltwell Towers.*
Pedestrian entrance E Park Rd/car park in Joicey Rd. Open all year as part of the 55 acre Saltwell Park, 'The People's Park'. **For opening times and information, please email or visit garden website.**
Unique collaboration between the National Garden Scheme North East, Trädgårdsresan, Region Västra Götaland and Gateshead Council. Planted in 2019, it was funded by sponsorship and is a tribute to the importance of international friendship. The Swedish design reflects the landscape of West Sweden, with coast, meadow and woodland areas. Many of the plant species grow wild in Sweden, providing a welcoming vision for visitors and a feast for pollinators. Donate at https://www.justgiving. com/ngs. Refreshments at Saltwell Towers Café. Wide tarmac path around the garden and mown grass paths through the meadow, but much of the garden is loose gravel.

GROUP OPENING

24 OLD QUARRINGTON GARDENS

The Stables, Old Quarrington, Durham, DH6 5NN. John Little, 07967 267864, johndlittle10@gmail.com, www. facebook.com/thestablesOQ. *1m from J61 of A1(M). All vehicle access from Crow Trees Ln, Bowburn. SatNav may be misleading.* **Sun 23 June (11-4). Combined adm £6, chd free. Home-made teas at The Stables - also picnics and WC. Visits also by arrangement Apr to Oct for groups of 10+.**

13 HEUGH HALL ROW
Jacqueline Robson, www.facebook.com/ OldQuarringtonGardens.

NEW **ORCHARD COTTAGE**
Chrissy and Steve Skinner.

ROSE COTTAGE
Mr Richard Cowen.

THE STABLES
John & Claire Little, 07967 267864, johndlittle10@gmail.com, www.facebook.com/thestablesOQ. **Visits also by arrangement Apr to Oct for groups of 12+.**

Four very distinct gardens in the hamlet of Old Quarrington. The Stables is a large family garden full
of hidden surprises and extensive views. The main garden is about an acre inc gravel garden, orchard, play area, lawn and woodland gardens. There is a further 4 acres to explore which inc wildlife ponds, woodlands, meadows, hens, ducks and alpacas. Number 13 has many small garden rooms inc a rose garden, a white garden, a small link garden which contains ferns, viburnum, birch trees and a Cercidiphyllum japoniocum. There is a pond and herbaceous beds with perennials and grasses. Many roses can be seen throughout the garden. The main garden at Rose Cottage is planted with wildlife friendly flowers and a pond that attracts 2 species of newts. To the rear there is a Mediterranean area and a woodland garden with stream beyond. Orchard Cottage has a strong focus on self sufficiency, re use and recycling, with a large vegetable plot growing a wide range of interesting edibles. Plant sales at 13 Heugh Hall Row.

25 OLIVER FORD GARDEN

Longedge Lane, Rowley, Consett, DH8 9HG. Bob & Bev Tridgett, www.gardensanctuaries.co.uk. *5m NW of Lanchester. Signed from A68 in Rowley. From Lanchester take rd towards Sately. Garden will be signed as you pass Woodlea Manor.* **Sun 9 June (1-5). Adm £5, chd free. Home-made teas.**
A peaceful, contemplative 3 acre garden developed and planted by the owner and BBC Gardener of the Year as a space for quiet reflection. Arboretum specialising in bark, stream, wildlife pond and bog garden. Semi-shaded Japanese maple and dwarf rhododendron garden. Rock garden and scree bed. Insect nectar area, orchard and 1½ acre meadow. David Austin rose bed. Terrace and ornamental herb garden. The garden is managed to maximise wildlife and there are a number of sculptures around the garden. Finalist, North, The English Garden Magazine's The Nation's Favourite Gardens 2023

26 25 PARK ROAD SOUTH

Chester le Street, DH3 3LS. Mrs A Middleton, 01913 883225, midnot2@gmail.com. *4m N of Durham. Located at S end of A167 Chester-le-St bypass rd. Precise directions provided when booking visit.* **Visits by arrangement May to**

The Cottage at Butler House, Historic Haughton-Le-Skerne Gardens

July for groups of up to 20. **Adm £4, chd free. Light refreshments.** A stunning town garden with year-round interest. Herbaceous borders with unusual perennials, grasses, shrubs surrounding lawn and paved area. Courtyard planted with foliage and small front gravel garden. The garden owner is a very knowledgeable plantswoman who enjoys showing visitors around her inspiring garden. Plants for sale.

♿ ✳ ☕

27 QUARRY END
Walworth, Darlington, **DL2 2LY. Iain & Margaret Anderson, 01325 778446, quarryend@btinternet.com.** *Approx 5m W of Darlington on A68 or ½ m E of Piercebridge on A67. Follow brown signs to Walworth Castle Hotel. Just up the hill from the Castle entrance, follow NGS yellow signs down private track.* **Visits by arrangement May to Sept for groups of 8 to 25. Adm £5, chd free. Tea or coffee, scones and**

cakes will be provided for an additional charge of £4.00pp. Woodland garden in an ancient quarry setting. Redeveloped over 21 yrs the garden has a C18 ice house, a wide variety of trees, shrubs and perennials, a fernery and ornamental vegetable plot. Spectacular late summer display but something of interest throughout the year inc an acre of reclaimed naturalised woodland in the adjacent quarry. Extensive views over South Durham. Only partial wheelchair access to woodland area especially if wet. Main garden includes some rough steps and gravel paths.

♿ 🐎 ✳ ☕)

28 RAVENSFORD FARM
Hamsterley, Bishop Auckland, **DL13 3NH. Jonathan & Caroline Peacock.** *7m W of Bishop Auckland. From A68 between Witton-le-Wear & Toft Hill, turn W to Hamsterley. Follow yellow NGS signs.* **Sun 22 Sept (2-5). Adm £5, chd free. Light refreshments.**

In 1984 Ravensford Farm was a ruin in a field full of weeds, with one tree. Today it is surrounded by a richly varied garden, a wood, two ponds, orchard, rhododendron dell and extensive flowerbeds. 2024 is our 25th opening for the NGS. Regretfully it'll be our last. We shall continue with By Arrangement visits, so please come for this final opening to celebrate in style as we go out with a bang. While children hunt for hidden animal figures, gardeners can discover unusual shrubs and trees. Visitors will enjoy tea, home-made cakes and local music. Some gravel, so assistance will be needed for wheelchairs. Assistance dogs only, please.

♿ ✳ ☕

Our donation to Marie Curie this year equates to 17,496 hours of nursing care

29 NEW 1 RIVERSIDE LODGE

Darlington Road, Durham, DH1 3SS. Iain and Christine Forsyth, 07478 944495, oneriversidedurham@outlook. com. *3m S of Durham. The garden is situated within the private Burn Hall estate. Park in the large lay-by off the north bound carriageway of the A167, just north of The Honest Lawyer.* **Visits by arrangement 1 May to 8 Sept for groups of 10 to 40. Please speak to us about parking and access arrangements. Adm £5, chd free. Light refreshments. Other dietary requirements may be catered for upon request.**

Once part of the walled garden of Burn Hall, the garden was redesigned in 2020 to reflect the symmetrical layout of a traditional kitchen garden. Within this formal structure, the planting is relaxed and exuberant. There's always something of interest from tulips in Spring to roses and, in late Summer, dahlias and the prairie garden. In front of the house is an impressive Victorian glasshouse.

30 ST CUTHBERT'S HOSPICE

Park House Road, Durham, DH1 3QF. St Cuthbert's Hospice, www.stcuthbertshospice.com. *1ml SW of Durham City on A167. Turn into Park House Rd, the hospice is on L after the Merryoaks Community Hub building and play park. Parking available.* **Sun 28 July (10-4). Adm £5, chd free. Light refreshments. Café open 10am-4pm for light refreshments.**

5 acres of mature gardens surround this CQC outstanding-rated Hospice. In development since 1988, the gardens are cared for by volunteers inc a Victorian-style greenhouse and large vegetable, fruit and cut flower area. Lawns surround smaller scale specialist planting, and areas for patients and visitors to relax. Woodland area with walks, sensory garden, and an 'In Memory' garden with stream. Plants and produce for sale. We are active participants in Northumbria in Bloom and Britain in Bloom, with several awards in recent years, inc overall winner in 2015, 2018, 2019 and 2023 for the Care/Residential/Convalescent Homes/Day Centre/Hospices category. Almost all areas are accessible for wheelchairs.

31 ST MARGARET'S ALLOTMENTS

Margery Lane, Durham City, DH1 4QU. St Margaret's Allotments Association, www. stmargaretsallotments.com. *Close to Durham City Centre, S side; limited free on-street parking; car parks in city centre. From A1(M), take A690 to City Centre/Crook; straight ahead at T-lights after 4th r'about. From A167, turn R along A690, and R at next T-lights. 10mins walk from bus /rail stn.* **Sun 14 July (1.30-5). Adm £5, chd free. Home-made teas in St Margaret's Centre adjacent to allotments.**

Five acres of over 100 allotments against the spectacular backdrop of Durham Cathedral. Enthusiastic gardeners, many using organic methods, cultivate plots which display a great variety of fruit, vegetables and flowers. One of the most attractive allotments-site anywhere. Visitors may also visit the adjacent St Margaret's Churchyard, with its interesting graves and natural history. Experienced gardeners will answer visitors' questions, on the plots and also in a Gardeners' Question Time session for those new to gardening

Middleton Hall Retirement Village

and allotment gardening; Tours of the plots; Historical and natural history tours; Musical events; Home-made refreshments, plants and produce for sale.

🐐 ✳ ☕))

32 NEW ST OSWALDS CHURCH
Middlesbrough, TS4 2FJ. Sally Middleton, 07719 938149, smgs56@outlook.com. *Look for the large red brick church opp postcode, and a welcomer will greet you.* **Visits by arrangement May to Sept for groups of 15 to 30. Adm £8, chd free. Light refreshments inc tea, coffee and cake. Admission charge includes a cake.**
A private community garden, born out of a vision to provide an oasis of green space in a neglected area. Browse the raised vegetable beds, watch the wildlife pond. Enjoy spring bulbs, followed by a procession of different blooms through summer and autumn. The garden started in October 2020, and now has borders with flowers and produce, willow pergola and arch, seating areas, and a story to tell. There is wheelchair access on the main paths, some paths may be too narrow for large wheelchairs.

♿ 🐐 ✳ 🚗 ☕))

33 STANTON FENCE
Stanton, Morpeth, NE65 8PP. Sir David Kelly. *5m NW of Morpeth. Nr Stanton on the C144 between Pigdon & Netherwitton.* **Sun 30 June (1-5). Adm £8, chd free. Home-made teas. Donation to St Giles Church Netherwitton.**
Contemporary 4.7 acre country garden designed by Chelsea Gold Medal winner, Arabella Lennox-Boyd, in keeping with its rural setting. A strong underlying design unites the different areas from formal parterre and courtyard garden to orchard, wildflower meadows and woodland. Romantically planted rose covered arbours and long clematis draped pergola walk. Nuttery, greenhouse and greenhouse garden. Delightful views. Robert Iley, the garden builder, and Steve Grimwood, the gardener, present. Wheelchair access for chairs that can use mown paths as well as hard paving.

♿ 🐐 ✳ Ⓓ ☕

34 THORNTON HALL GARDENS
Staindrop Road, Darlington, DL2 2NB. Michael & Sue Manners, www.thorntonhallgardens. co.uk. *2 m W of Darlington on B6279 Staindrop Rd.* **Wed 5 June (10-4). Adm £10, chd free. Light refreshments.**
3 acre walled gardens wrapped around a Grade I listed C16 Hall previously grazed by cattle and sheep lovingly restored from a blank canvas, with no plan and Sue's gardening passion. Inc separate vegetable garden, wildlife and waterfall ponds, meadow and colour-themed borders with unusual perennials interspersed with interesting trees and shrubs with quirky seats, statuary and sculpture. For other opening times and information, please visit the garden website www.thorntonhallgardens. co.uk. Whilst we welcome and do have access for wheelchairs please be aware that the majority of the garden is on grass with some steep banks and gravel.

♿ ✳ 🚗 ☕

35 ♦ WHALTON MANOR GARDENS
Whalton, Morpeth, NE61 3UT. Mr T R P S Norton, pn@whaltonmanor.com, www.whaltonmanor.co.uk. *5m W of Morpeth. On the B6524, the house is at E end of the village & will be signed.* **For NGS: Sat 18 May (11-4). Adm £8, chd free. Home-made teas in The Game Larder. For other opening times and information, please email or visit garden website.**
The historic Whalton Manor, altered by Sir Edwin Lutyens in 1908, is surrounded by 3 acres of magnificent walled gardens, designed by Lutyens with the help of Gertrude Jekyll. The gardens, developed by the Norton family since the 1920s inc extensive herbaceous borders, spring bulbs, 30yd peony border, rose garden, listed summerhouses, pergolas and walls festooned with rambling roses and clematis. Partial wheelchair access to main area but otherwise stone steps and gravel paths.

♿ ✳ 🚗 🚐 ☕

36 WOODLANDS
Peareth Hall Road, Springwell Village, Gateshead, NE9 7NT. Liz Reid, 07719 875750, liz.reid@ngs.org.uk, www. facebook.com/visitgarden. *3½ m N Washington Galleries. 4m S Gateshead town centre. On B1288 turn opp Guide Post pub (NE9 7RR) onto Peareth Hall Rd. Continue for ½ m passing 2 bus stops on L. 3rd drive on L past Highbury Ave.* **Visits by arrangement 10 June to 27 July for groups of 10 to 30. Adm £8, chd free. Home-made teas. Beer & wine also available.**
Mature garden on a site of approx one seventh acre - quirky, with tropical themed planting and Caribbean inspired bar. Also an area of cottage garden planting. A fun garden with colour year-round, interesting plants, informal beds and borders and pond area.

✳ ☕

WOODSIDE, KILLERBY
North Lane, Killerby, Darlington, DL2 3UH. Dr Satinder Faulkner, 07789 640421, satinderreborn@gmail.com. *Between Summerhouse & Ingleton. Parking offered in fields if ground very wet, vehicles can also park on the main road in Killerby village & walk the ¼ m up North Ln.* **Visits by arrangement June to Aug for groups of up to 15. Adm £8, chd free. Light refreshments inc in adm price.**
Woodside is set in 12 acres of which 2 acres have been developed into garden. The owner had a stroke 32 years ago yet has designed and executed the works mostly single handed. The garden includes prairie bed, woodland beds, rose garden, bog garden over 100 trees, a wood, wildlife pond, vegetable and cut flower beds and runs horticultural therapy for adults with disability. The garden sits mostly on one level although paths in the woods are narrow for wheelchair access.

♿ ✳ ☕

100 inpatients and their families are being supported at the newly opened Horatio's Garden Wales, thanks to the National Garden Scheme donations

YORKSHIRE

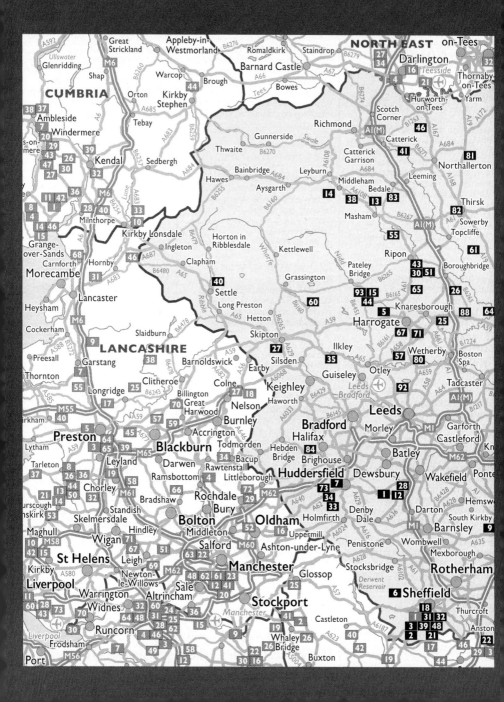

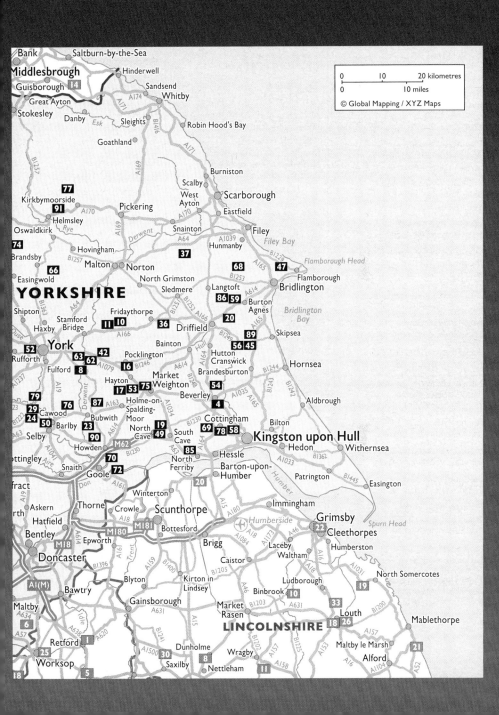

VOLUNTEERS

County Organisers

East Yorks
Helen Marsden 07703 529112
helen.marsden@ngs.org.uk

North Yorks
Dee Venner 01765 690842
dee.venner@ngs.org.uk

South & West Yorks
Elizabeth & David Smith
01484 644320
elizabethanddavid.smith@ngs.org.uk

County Treasurer
Angela Pugh 01423 330456
angela.pugh@ngs.org.uk

Publicity & Social Media
Sally Roberts 01423 871419
sally.roberts@ngs.org.uk

Booklet Advertising
Sally Roberts (as above)

Group Visits Co-ordinator
Mandy Gordon 01423 331643
mandy.gordon@ngs.org.uk

Assistant County Organisers

East Yorks
Ian & Linda McGowan 01482 896492
ianandlinda.mcgowan@ngs.org.uk

Hazel Rowe 01430 861439
hazel.rowe@ngs.org.uk

Natalie Verow 01759 368444
natalieverow@aol.com

North Yorks
Annabel Alton 07803 907042
annabel.alton@ngs.org.uk

Veronica Brook 01423 340875
veronica.brook@ngs.org.uk

Jo Gaunt 07443 505291
jo.gaunt@ngs.org.uk

South & West Yorks
Felicity Bowring 07773 647943
felicity.bowring@ngs.org.uk

Jane Hudson 01484 866697
jane.hudson@ngs.org.uk

Peter Lloyd 07958 928698
peter.lloyd@ngs.org.uk

f @YorkshireNGS
X @YorkshireNGS
@YorkshireNGS

OPENING DATES

All entries subject to change. For latest information check **www.ngs.org.uk**
Map locator numbers are shown to the right of each garden name.

February

Snowdrop Openings

Saturday 24th
Skipwith Hall ... 76

Sunday 25th
Devonshire Mill ... 16

March

Sunday 24th
Fawley House ... 19

April

Monday 1st
Holmfield ... 36

Sunday 7th
Clifton Castle ... 13
Ellerker House ... 17
Goldsborough Hall ... 25

Sunday 21st
Langton Farm ... 41
♦ RHS Garden Harlow Carr ... 67

Saturday 27th
249 Barnsley Road ... 1

Sunday 28th
249 Barnsley Road ... 1
23 The Paddock ... 58
NEW Southwood Hall ... 78

May

Sunday 5th
Low Hall ... 44
Saltmarshe Hall ... 72
Scape Lodge ... 73
Warley House Garden ... 84

Wednesday 8th
Warley House Garden ... 84

Sunday 12th
♦ Jackson's Wold ... 37
The Poplars ... 62
Scape Lodge ... 73
♦ Stillingfleet Lodge ... 79
Thirsk Hall ... 82
Whixley Gardens ... 88

Wednesday 15th
Primrose Bank Garden and Nursery ... 63

Sunday 19th
Grafton Gardens ... 26
Rudding Park ... 71

Friday 24th
Thimbleby Hall ... 81

Sunday 26th
Bramblewood Cottage ... 6
115 Millhouses Lane ... 48
The Ridings ... 68
Rosemary Cottage ... 70

Monday 27th
Holmfield ... 36
Pilmoor Cottages ... 61

Wednesday 29th
5 Hill Top ... 35

June

Saturday 1st
Shiptonthorpe Gardens ... 75

Sunday 2nd
Galehouse Barn ... 24
5 Hill Top ... 35
New House Farm ... 50
Shiptonthorpe Gardens ... 75

Tuesday 4th
NEW The Manor ... 46

Thursday 6th
Skipwith Hall ... 76

Friday 7th
♦ Shandy Hall Gardens ... 74
Thorp Perrow ... 83

Saturday 8th
Old Sleningford Hall ... 55

The Orchards

Holmfield

THE GARDENS

1 249 BARNSLEY ROAD

Flockton, Wakefield, WF4 4AL.
Nigel & Anne Marie Booth,
01924 848967, nigel.booth1@
btopenworld.com. *On A637
Barnsley Rd. M1 J38 or J39 follow
signs for Huddersfield. Parking
on Manor House Rd (WF4 4AL) &
Hardcastle Ln. Please park with
consideration. Park on Hardcastle
Ln if possible.* **Sat 27, Sun 28 Apr,
Sat 27, Sun 28 July (1-5). Adm £5,
chd free. All cakes home made.
Visits also by arrangement 29
Apr to 27 Sept for groups of 15+.
Refreshments at an additional
cost of £4 per person.**
An elevated $\frac{1}{3}$ acre, south-facing
garden with panoramic views. The
garden is packed with an abundance
of spring colour, created from 1000s
of bulbs, perennials, shrubs and trees.
Make a return visit in the summer to
view a transformation, with up to 60
hanging baskets and over 150 pots,
creating the 'wow factor' summer
garden. Massive plant sale with over
100 different varieties of plants on
sale. A local ukulele group playing live
in the garden on 28 July. Disabled
drop-off point at the bottom of the
drive.

2 NEW 74 BENTS ROAD

Sheffield, S11 9RL. Mr &
Mrs G Saxon, 07912 251905,
lucy@lucywoodhouse.com. *3m SW
of Sheffield via Ecclesall Rd/A625.
Bents Rd approx 3m on R.* **Visits by
arrangement 20 July to 18 Aug
for groups of up to 40. Also by
arrangement is 90 Bents Road.
Adm £4, chd free. Home-made
teas.**
A charming garden which has evolved
over time. A meandering path leads
you past specimen trees, acers in
agricultural pots, a tub pond, stone
troughs with dwarf conifers and
mixed herbaceous planting to reveal
another part of the garden which inc
a glasshouse, seating areas and a
wildlife pond.

3 90 BENTS ROAD

Bents Green, Sheffield, S11 9RL.
Mrs Hilary Hutson, 01142 258570,
h.hutson@paradiseregained.net.
*3m SW of Sheffield. From inner
ring road nr Waitrose, follow A625
(Ecclesall Rd). Bents Rd approx 3m
on R.* **Visits by arrangement 20
July to 18 Aug for groups of up
to 40. Adm £4, chd free. Also by
arrangement is 74 Bents Road. If
you have arranged to visit both
gardens refreshments will be at
74 Bents Road.**
Plantswoman's north east facing
garden with many unusual and
borderline hardy species. Patio with
alpine troughs for year-round interest
and pots of colourful tropical plants
in summer. Mixed borders surround
a lawn which leads to mature trees
underplanted with shade-loving plants
at end of garden. Front garden peaks
in late summer with hot-coloured
blooms. Front garden and patio are
wheelchair accessible. Back garden
accessed via 6 steps with handrail, so
unsuitable for wheelchairs.

GROUP OPENING

4 BEVERLEY GARDENS

Minster Parish Centre, 38
Highgate, Beverley, HU17 0DN.
*Garden Lodge on Wylies Rd outside
walls at North Bar. Minster Secret
Garden on Minster Moorgate.
30 St Giles Croft, cul-de-sac off
The Leases, 15 min walk from
The Minster to W.* **Sun 30 June
(10.30-4.30). Combined adm £8,
chd free. Home-made teas at
The Minster Secret Garden and
Garden Lodge.**

NEW GARDEN LODGE
Mr James Marritt.

**THE MINSTER SECRET
GARDEN**
Beverley Minster.

NEW 30 ST GILES CROFT
Mr and Mrs McIntyre.

The Minster Secret Garden is a
woodland oasis created from an old
orchard, animal yard and associated
buildings in the lee of Beverley
Minster, maintained by volunteers for
community use. It supplies produce
and cut flowers for the Minster.
Garden Lodge offers unexpected
tranquillity behind high town walls
with a satisfying mix of old and new
styles. 30 St Giles Croft is a modern
lawn-free walled garden with colourful
borders, magnolias and wall shrubs.

5 BIRSTWITH HALL

High Birstwith, Harrogate,
HG3 2JW. Sir James & Lady
Aykroyd, 01423 770250,
ladya@birstwithhall.co.uk.
*5m NW of Harrogate. Between
Hampsthwaite & Birstwith villages,
close to A59 Harrogate/Skipton
road.* **Sun 23 June (2-5). Adm £5,
chd free. Home-made teas. Visits
also by arrangement June & July
for groups of 10 to 50.**
Charming and varied four acre garden
nestling in secluded Yorkshire dale.
Formal garden and ornamental
orchard, extensive lawns leading
to picturesque stream and large
pond. Walled garden and Victorian
greenhouse.

SPECIAL EVENT

6 BRAMBLEWOOD COTTAGE

Old Coach Road, Bradfield,
Sheffield, S6 6HX. Nigel Dunnett,
www.instagram.com/nigel.dunnett.
*6m from Sheffield City centre. Follow
Loxley Rd (B6077) turn L onto New
Rd before Damflask reservoir. Follow
alongside reservoir until Old Coach
Rd.* **Sun 26 May, Sun 16 June,
Sun 7 July (10.30-5). Adm £15,
chd free. Pre-booking essential,
please visit www.ngs.org.uk for
information & booking. Adm inc
light refreshments.**
The experimental, hillside home
garden of renowned horticulturist
and designer Nigel Dunnett, which
is based on strong ecological and
sustainable principles, with extensive
areas of naturalistic perennial planting.
The front garden is designed around a
pool, rain gardens and bioswales that
collect rainwater runoff. Each time
slot will have an introduction from
Nigel. To the rear, a range of different
designed annual and perennial
meadows, large-scale log pile and
habitat sculptures, bluebell woodland,
vegetable garden, naturalistic
planting.

*Our donation in 2023 has
enabled Parkinson's UK to
fund 3 new nursing posts
this year, directly supporting
people with Parkinson's*

⁊ 12 BRENDON DRIVE

Birkby, Huddersfield, HD2 2DF. **Jon Caddick.** *Off Birkby Rd.* **Sat 6 July (11-5). Adm £3, chd free. Pre-booking essential, please visit www.ngs.org.uk for information & booking. Light refreshments.** The inspiration for the garden is to create a family space with an atmosphere of relaxation and sensory experiences. Small but practical, the garden is packed with striking blooms, colour and interest. Meandering paths, a pond and idyllic views are complemented by the sound of water and wildlife attracted to the garden. Architectural plants and wide borders create colour, drama and variety.

⁸ BRIDGE HOUSE

Main Street, Elvington, York, YO41 4AA. **Mrs W C Bundy,** 07974 277792, wendy@bundy.co.uk. *6m E from York ring road (A64). On B1128 from York, last house on R before bridge.* **Visits by arrangement 21 May to 31 Aug for groups of up to 40. Adm £5, chd free. Tea.** Two acre garden carved out of the River Derwent's floodplain 40 years ago. It survives annual winter flooding of the river which can last up to 2 months. Formal rose garden, mixed borders,shrubbery, large pond surrounded by hostas and ferns. Productive kitchen garden and orchard. Various devices in kitchen garden used to keep above water level. Groups may book a talk about flooding with garden tour and lunch. Slopes to main garden are steep.

⁹ NEW ◆ BRODSWORTH HALL

Brodsworth, Doncaster, DN5 7XJ. **English Heritage.** *In Brodsworth, 5m NW of Doncaster off A635 Barnsley Rd; from J37 of A1(M). Please follow brown tourist signs to Brodsworth, do not rely on SatNav directions.* **For NGS: Evening opening Wed 14 Aug (5.30-8). Adm £15. Pre-booking essential, please phone 07721 813442, email alison. makosch@english-heritage.org. uk or visit www.english-heritage. org.uk/visit/places/brodsworth-hall-and-gardens for information & booking. Refreshments will be available from the on-site café before the start of the tour. For other opening times and information, please phone, email or** visit garden website.

Step back in time to the 1860s in the extraordinary surroundings of Brodsworth Hall, exquisitely restored to their Victorian splendour. Awe-inspiring displays of colourful Victorian bedding surrounded by a vast collection of formal topiary and the wonders of the Fern Dell all await.

GROUP OPENING

⅒ BUGTHORPE GARDENS

Bugthorpe, York, YO41 1QG. *Bugthorpe. 4m E of Stamford Bridge, A166, village of Bugthorpe.* **Sun 23 June (10-4). Combined adm £8, chd free. Light refreshments at 3 Church Walk.**

3 CHURCH WALK
Barrie Creaser & David Fielding. (See separate entry)

THE OLD RECTORY
Dr & Mrs P W Verow.

Two gardens in Bugthorpe with contrasting styles with different views of the countryside. Several changes in each since previous openings. 3 Church Walk, created in 2000, has surprisingly mature trees and borders amalgamated in quirky way to give depth and intrigue. The owners have developed a keen interest in growing from seed, resulting in plants for sale. Recently acquired old oak stump made into a table. Plenty of seating to appreciate the views. The Old Rectory is ¾ acre country garden of mixed borders, ponds, terrace, mature trees, summerhouse, courtyard & raised veg beds. Seating to view The Wolds. Gravel drive with lawn access to garden.

⑪ 3 CHURCH WALK

Bugthorpe, York, YO41 1QL. **Barrie Creaser & David Fielding.** *E of Stamford Bridge. On A166, 4m E of Stamford Bridge. Park outside Bugthorpe Church.* **Sun 1 Sept (2-8). Adm £4, chd free. Light refreshments. Hot savoury supper served from 6.00pm (not included in adm price). Opening with Bugthorpe Gardens on Sun 23 June.** Created in 2000, this garden has surprisingly mature trees and borders amalgamated in a quirky way to give depth and intrigue. The owners have developed a keen interest in growing from seed, resulting in plants for sale. Recently acquired old oak stump made into a table. Plenty of seating to appreciate the views. Garden wheelchair accessible, but gravel in courtyard. Please contact owners prior to arrival to ensure access to garden by car.

⑫ THE CIRCLES GARDEN

8 Stocksmoor Road, Midgley, nr Wakefield, WF4 4JQ. **Joan Gaunt,** mandy.gordon@ngs.org.uk. *Equidistant from Huddersfield, Wakefield & Barnsley, W of M1. Turn off A637 in Midgley at the Black Bull Pub (sharp bend) onto B6117 Stocksmoor Rd. Park on road.* **Visits by arrangement Apr to June for groups of 5 to 20. Not Sundays. Adm £4, chd free.** An organic and self-sustaining plantswoman's ½ acre garden on gently sloping site overlooking fields, woods and nature reserve opposite. Designed and maintained by owner. Herbaceous, bulb and shrub plantings linked by grass and gravel paths, woodland area with mature trees, meadows, fernery, greenhouse, fruit trees, viewing terrace with pots. About 100 hellebores propagated from owner's own plants. South African plants, hollies, and small bulbs of particular interest. This garden is proud to provide plants for the National Garden Scheme's Show Garden at Chelsea Flower Show 2024.

⑬ CLIFTON CASTLE

Ripon, HG4 4AB. **Lord & Lady Downshire.** *2m N of Masham. On road to Newton-le-Willows & Richmond. Gates on L just before turn to Charlcot.* **Sun 7 Apr, Sun 7 July (2-5). Adm £7, chd free. Home-made teas.** Impressive gardens and parkland with fine views over lower Wensleydale. Formal walks through the wooded 'pleasure grounds' feature bridges and follies, cascades and abundant wildflowers. The walled kitchen garden is similar to how it was set out in the C19. Recent wildflower meadows have been laid out with modern sculptures. Gravel paths and steep slopes to river.

Southwood Hall

I4 COVERHAM ABBEY
Middleham, Leyburn, DL8 4RL.
Mr & Mrs Nigel Corner,
www.coverhamchurch.com. *A6108 to Middleham then Coverdale Rd out of Middleham following signs to 'The Forbidden Corner', past pond on R. Drive at bottom of steep bank on L before Church. Do not follow satnav.* **Sat 3 Aug (10-4). Adm £5, chd £1. Home-made teas.**
Stunning gardens set in the heart of tranquil Coverdale. Within the grounds of C13 Premonstratensian Abbey ruins, a large intricate knot garden, mixed borders, parterre and yew rondel with rose arches. Some new areas being developed. Wildflower meadow at front of house.

GROUP OPENING

I5 DACRE BANKS GARDENS
Nidderdale, HG3 4EW.
www.yorkehouse.co.uk. *4m SE Pateley Bridge, 10m NW Harrogate, 10m N Otley, on B6451. On-site parking at both gardens.* **Sun 7 July (12-4.30). Combined adm £8, chd free. Home-made teas at Yorke House and Low Hall.** Visitors are welcome to

picnic in the orchard at Yorke House.

LOW HALL
Mrs P A Holliday.
(See separate entry)

YORKE HOUSE & WHITE ROSE COTTAGE
Tony, Pat, Mark & Amy Hutchinson.
(See separate entry)

Dacre Banks Gardens are located in the beautiful countryside of Nidderdale and are designed to take advantage of the scenic Dales landscape. The gardens are linked by an attractive level walk along the valley, but each may be accessed individually by car. Low Hall has a romantic walled garden set on different levels around the historic C17 family home (not open) with herbaceous borders, shrubs, climbing roses, productive vegetable area and a tranquil water garden. Yorke House has extensive colour-themed borders and water features with beautiful waterside plantings together with plentiful seating areas. The newly developed garden at White Rose Cottage is specifically designed for wheelchair users and features a colourful cottage garden, woodland

plantings and large collection of hostas. Full wheelchair access at White Rose Cottage. Main features accessible at Low Hall and Yorke House.

I6 DEVONSHIRE MILL
Canal Lane, Pocklington,
York, YO42 1NN. Sue & Chris Bond, 01759 302147, chris.
bond.dm@btinternet.com,
www.devonshiremill.co.uk. *1m S of Pocklington. Canal Ln, off A1079 on opp side of the road from the canal towards Pocklington.* **Sun 25 Feb (11-4.30). Adm £6, chd free. Home-made teas. Visits also by arrangement. £10 includes refreshments.**
Drifts of double snowdrops, hellebores and ferns surround the historic Grade II listed watermill (not open). Explore the two acre garden with mill stream, orchards, woodland, herbaceous borders, hen run and greenhouses. The old mill pond is now a vegetable garden with raised beds and polytunnel. Over the past 30 years the owners have developed the garden on organic principles to encourage wildlife.

17 ELLERKER HOUSE

Everingham, York, YO42 4JA. Mr & Mrs M Wright, www.ellerkerhouse. weebly.com. *15m SE of York. 5½m from Pocklington. Just out of Everingham towards Harswell on R.* **Sun 7 Apr (10-4). Adm £7, chd free. Home-made teas inc savouries.**

This 5 acre garden is a plant lovers delight. Planted for all seasons with colour themed borders and many fine old trees. Daffodils, spring bulbs and alpines planted around the lake in a stumpery. A woodland walk of bluebells, thatched oak hut and intimate seating. Shady borders planted with shrubs, ferns and hostas. Rose arbours planted with old English roses. Topiary garden. Entry inc rare plant fair with many plant stalls. See website for details. Most of the garden is accessible by wheelchair.

18 3 EMBANKMENT ROAD

Broomhill, Sheffield, S10 1EZ. Charlotte Cummins. *1½m W of city centre. A61 ring roadd follow A57 to Manchester. In Broomhill turn R onto Crookes Rd, 1st R onto Crookesmoor Rd. Embankment Rd is 2nd on L.* **Sun 9 June (10.30-4). Adm £4, chd free. Light refreshments and a good selection of home-made cakes.**

Immaculate, compact, city garden with cottage style planting. Well stocked borders of interesting, carefully selected herbaceous perennials. Front garden features clipped box, hostas and a lavender bed. Rear garden with steep steps to small, elevated lawn, herbaceous borders and many pots. Collection of over 50 Astrantias and more than 170 varieties of hosta. Many homegrown plants for sale.

19 FAWLEY HOUSE

7 Nordham, North Cave, nr Brough, Hull, HU15 2LT. Mr & Mrs T Martin, 07951 745033, louisem200@hotmail.co.uk, www.nordhamcottages.co.uk. *15m W of Hull. Leave M62E at J38. L at '30' & signs: Wetlands & Polo. At L bend, turn R into Nordham. From Beverley, B1230 to N Cave. R after church & over bridge.* **Sun 24 Mar (12-5). Adm £6, chd free. Home-made teas in beamed cottage tea room with log burners near garden entrance. Visits also by arrangement 16 Feb to 14 June for**

groups of 10 to 50.
Tiered, 2½ acre formal garden with lawns, mature trees, hedging, gravel pathways. Lavender beds, mixed shrub and hot double herbaceous borders. Apple espaliers, pears, soft fruit, produce and herb gardens. Terrace with pergola and vines. Sunken garden with white border. Further woodland area with naturalistic planting and spring bulbs. Quaker well, stream and spring with three bridges, ferns and hellebores near mill stream. Snowdrops and aconites early in year. Treasure hunt for children. Self catering, accessible accommodation at Nordham Cottages. Wheelchairs welcome on pea gravelled terrace for views & teas, but no accessible WC available.

20 FERN HOUSE, 5 WOLD ROAD

Nafferton, Driffield, YO25 4LB. Peter & Jennifer Baker, 01377 255224. *N Nafferton. Follow directions rather than SatNav: From Driffield bypass to Nafferton on A614. Then 1st L & 1st L on Wold Rd. Park on street.* **Sun 30 June, Sun 4 Aug (10-4). Adm £4, chd free. Light refreshments. Visits also by arrangement 1 May to 9 Sept for groups of up to 30.**

Designed and developed by owners since 2019, this small garden feels spacious with over 50 varieties of fern amongst many other plants in the borders. Mixed planting is also in quirky containers and up trellises and walls. A pond, a living wall and two greenhouses, one entirely full of ferns. Seats to view different aspects of a constantly evolving garden.

21 FERNLEIGH

9 Meadowhead Avenue, Meadowhead, Sheffield, S8 7RT. Mr & Mrs C Littlewood, 01142 747234, littlewoodchristine@gmail.com. *4m S of Sheffield. From city centre. A61, A6102, B6054 r'about, exit B6054. 1st R Greenhill Ave, 2nd R. From M1 J33, A630 to A6102, then as above.* **Sun 30 June, Sun 25 Aug (11-5). Adm £3.50, chd free. Visits also by arrangement Apr to Aug for groups of 10 to 30. Refreshments to be confirmed for by arrangement visits.**

Plantswoman's ⅓ acre cottage style suburban garden. Large variety of unusual plants set in different areas

provide year-round interest. Several seats to view different aspects of garden. Auricula theatre, patio, gazebo and greenhouse. Miniature log cabin with living roof and cobbled area with unusual plants in pots. Sempervivum, alpine displays, collection of Epimedium and wildlife hotel. Over 30 peonies end of May. Wide selection of homegrown plants for sale. Animal Search for children.

22 FIRVALE PERENNIAL GARDEN

Winney Hill, Harthill, nr Worksop, S26 7YN. Don & Dot Witton, 01909 771366, donshardyeuphorbias@ btopenworld.com. www. donseuphorbias.webador.co.uk. *12m SE of Sheffield, 6m W of Worksop. M1 J31 A57 to Worksop. Turn R to Harthill. Allotments at S end of village, 26 Casson Dr at N end on Northlands Estate.* **Visits by arrangement 1 Apr to 16 June. Adm £4, chd free. Home-made teas at 26 Casson Drive, Harthill S26 7WA.**

Interesting and unusual large allotment with 13 island beds displaying 500+ herbaceous perennials inc the National Collection of hardy euphorbias with over 100 varieties flowering between March and October. Organic vegetable garden. Refreshments, WC and plant sales at 26 Casson Drive, a small garden with mixed borders, shade and seaside garden.

23 FROG HALL BARN

Breighton, Selby, YO8 6DH. Mr & Mrs Clarke, 07511 821353, sarahclarke100@btinternet. com. *From Bubwith, pass sign for Breighton, 3rd house on R.* **Sat 29, Sun 30 June (10.30-4.30). Adm £4, chd free. Home-made teas. Visits also by arrangement June to Aug. Price includes refreshments.**

Bee friendly flower and vegetable garden in ¾ acre around a converted threshing barn. At the front, a walled courtyard garden of perennials and annuals. To the rear the garden reaches down to water feeding the River Derwent. Borders full of cottage garden flowers selected to encourage wildlife. A small meadow, fruit trees, beehives and chickens. Kitchen garden with traditional greenhouse.

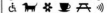

24 GALEHOUSE BARN

Bishopdyke Road, Cawood, Selby, YO8 3UB. Mr & Mrs P Lloyd, 07768 405642, junelloyd042@gmail.com. *On B1222 out of Cawood towards Sherburn-in-Elmet. On B1222 1m out of Cawood towards Sherburn in Elmet.* **Sun 2 June (12-5). Combined adm with New House Farm £6, chd free. Home-made teas. Visits also by arrangement 22 Apr to 29 Sept for groups of up to 15.**

The Barn: A plantaholic's informal cottage garden, created in 2015, to encourage birds and insects. Raised beds with tranquil seating area. The Farm: South facing, partly shaded varied herbaceous border. North facing exposed shaded border redeveloped 2017, ongoing for spring and autumn interest. Small experimental white garden. Raised beds for vegetables Partial wheelchair access. Help available.

25 GOLDSBOROUGH HALL

Church Street, Goldsborough, HG5 8NR. Mr & Mrs M Oglesby, 01423 867321, info@goldsboroughhall.com, www.goldsboroughhall.com. *2m SE of Knaresborough. 3m W of A1(M). Off J47 (A59 York-Harrogate). Spring: parking at Hall top car park. Summer: parking E of village in field off Midgley Ln. Disabled parking only at front of Hall.* **Sun 7 Apr (11-4); Sun 21 July (11-5). Adm £7.50, chd free. Light refreshments inc sandwiches, scones and cakes along with tea and coffee. Donation to St Mary's Church, Goldsborough.**

Historic 12 acre garden and formal landscaped grounds in parkland setting around Grade II*, C17 house, former residence of HRH Princess Mary, daughter of George V and Queen Mary. Gertrude Jekyll inspired 120ft double herbaceous borders, rose garden and woodland walk. Large restored kitchen garden with rill, fountain and large glasshouse which produces fruit and vegetables for the Hall's commercial kitchens. ¼ Lime tree walk planted by royalty in the 1920s, orchard and flower borders featuring 'Yorkshire Princess' rose, named after Princess Mary. Gravel paths and some steep slopes.

GROUP OPENING

26 GRAFTON GARDENS

Marton Cum Grafton, York, YO51 9QJ. Mrs Glen Garnett. *2½ m S of Boroughbridge. Turn off the A168 or B6265 to Marton or Grafton, S of Boroughbridge.* **Sun 19 May, Sun 9 June (1-5). Combined adm £8, chd free.**

NEW ► ORCHARD HOUSE
Mr Rob & Mrs Lizzie Shepherd.

PADDOCK HOUSE
Tim & Jill Smith.

WELL HOUSE
Glen Garnett, 07901 592768, gwg01@talktalk.net.
Visits also by arrangement May & June for groups of 10 to 30.

Three gardens in two adjacent rural villages within walking distance of each other. In Marton, Paddock House is on an elevated site with extensive views and sloping lawn to wildlife pond. The house is encircled by a profusion of pots combining cottage garden and Mediterranean styles. A terrace of Yorkshire stone and steps using gravel and wood sleepers leads to seating areas and cutting garden with small greenhouse. Orchard House is a contemporary village garden with an abundance of features inc gravel garden, raised beds and extensive views across alpaca paddock. Well House in Grafton nestles under the hillside. A traditional English cottage garden with herbaceous borders, climbing roses and ornamental shrubs with a variety of interesting species. Paths meander through the borders to an orchard with chickens. Parking in Grafton. Refreshments at The Punch Bowl PH, Marton 01423 322519. Reservations advisable.

National Garden Scheme gardens are identified by their yellow road signs and posters. You can expect a garden of quality, character and interest, a warm welcome and plenty of home-made cakes!

27 THE GRANGE

Carla Beck Lane, Carleton in Craven, Skipton, BD23 3BU. Mr & Mrs R N Wooler, 07740 639135, margaret.wooler@hotmail.com. *1½ m SW of Skipton. Turn off A56 (Skipton-Clitheroe) into Carleton. Keep L at Swan Pub, continue to end of village then R into Carla Beck Ln.* **Wed 24 July, Wed 14 Aug (12-4.30). Adm £5, chd free. Home-made teas. Visits also by arrangement July & Aug for groups of 20+. Donation to Sue Ryder Care Manorlands Hospice.**

Over four acres of wonderfully varied garden set in the grounds of Victorian house (not open) with mature trees and panoramic views towards The Gateway to the Dales. The garden has been restored and expanded by the owners over the past three decades. Bountiful herbaceous borders with many unusual species, rose walk, parterre, mini-meadows and water features. Topiary and large greenhouse. Extensive vegetable and cut flower beds. Oak seating placed throughout the garden invites quiet contemplation - a place to 'lift the spirits'. Gravel paths and steps in some areas.

28 GREAT CLIFF EXOTIC GARDEN

Cliff Drive, Crigglestone, Wakefield, WF4 3EN. Kristofer Swaine, www.greatcliffexoticgarden.co.uk. *1m from J39 M1. From M1 (J39) take A636 towards Denby Dale, past Cedar Court Hotel then L at British Oak pub onto Blacker Ln. Parking on Cliff Rd m'way bridge a 3 min walk from the garden.* **Sat 10, Sun 11 Aug (10-4). Adm £4, chd free. Pre-booking essential, please visit www.ngs.org.uk for information & booking. Light refreshments inc vegan options and home-made tray bakes.**

An exotic garden on a long narrow plot. Possibly the largest collection of palm species planted out in Northern England inc a large Chilean wine palm. Colourful and exciting borders with zinnias, cannas, ensete, bananas, tree ferns, agaves, aloes, colcasias and bamboos. Jungle hut, winding paths and a pond that traverses the full width of the garden.

29 21 GREAT CLOSE
Cawood, Selby, YO8 3UG. David & Judy Jones, 01757 268571, davidjones051946@gmail.com. *On B1223 5m N of Selby & 7m SE of Tadcaster. Between York & A1 on B1222* **Sat 13, Sun 14 July (12-5). Adm £5, chd free. Home-made teas. Visits also by arrangement in July for groups of 10 to 30.**
A flower arranger's garden designed and built by the owners over 50 years. Interesting trees and shrubs combine with herbaceous borders, a collection of dierama and a cutting garden. Two ponds linked by a stream lead to a summerhouse, rose and clematis pergola and colourful terrace with exotic plants and views of the countryside beyond. Partial wheelchair access.
&♿ ✿ ☕

30 GREENCROFT
Pottery Lane, Littlethorpe, Ripon, HG4 3LS. David & Sally Walden, 01765 602487, s-walden@outlook.com. *1½ m SE of Ripon town centre. Off A61 Ripon bypass, signs to Littlethorpe, R at church. From Bishop Monkton take Knaresborough Rd towards Ripon then R to Littlethorpe.* **Sun 4 Aug (12-4). Adm £5, chd free. Home-made teas. Visits also by arrangement 15 July to 4 Aug for groups of 20+.**
½ acre country garden with long herbaceous borders packed with colourful late summer perennials, annuals and exotics. Circular garden with views through to large wildlife pond and surrounding countryside. Ornamental features inc gazebo, temple pavilions, formal pool, stone wall with mullions, gate to pergola and a water cascade.
& 🐕 ✿ 🚗 ☕ ⛱

31 NEW **128 GREYSTONES ROAD**
Greystones Road, Sheffield, S11 7BR. Tricia and Geoff Anderson. *2m S of Sheffield city centre. From Sheffield inner Ring Rd, W on A625 (Ecclesall Rd) for 1.8m; R onto Greystones Rd.* **Sun 25 Aug (10-4). Combined adm with 138 Greystones Road £6, chd free. Refreshments and plants available at 138 Greystones Road.**
A suburban, north facing garden on a steep hill. Natural springs create a damp habitat perfect for candelabra primulas, astilbes and meadowsweet and woodland plants inc ferns, Epimedium and foxgloves. Exposed spring, bespoke water feature and small wildlife pond. Cottage garden style. Collections of roses, geraniums and hostas mingle with Astrantia, Thalictrum, Achillea and Campanula.

Langcliffe Hall

32 138 GREYSTONES ROAD

Sheffield, S11 7BR. Mr Nick Hetherington, nick.hetherington@outlook.com. *From Sheffield inner Ring Rd, W on A625 (Ecclesall Rd) for 1.8m; R onto Greystones Rd.* **Sun 25 Aug (10-4). Combined adm with 128 Greystones Road £6, chd free. Sun 1 Sept (10-4). Adm £4, chd free. Light refreshments. Visits also by arrangement in Aug.**
This typical, small suburban plot has been developed into a lovely garden over 20 yrs. It features many trees and acers combined with stunning late tender perennials inc banana plants, Ricinus, Canna, Agapanthus, Colocasia and dahlias. Several sculptures created by the owner are displayed amongst the plants. The garden has a tropical feel with splashes of colour, mainly orange and purple.

33 HAWTHORNE COTTAGE

21 Healey Houses, Netherton, Huddersfield, HD4 7DG. Mr & Mrs Peter Sargent. *Off Crosland Factory Ln, off the B6108 between Netherton & Meltham. From Meltham follow the B6108 N. Sharp R turn down to the valley on Crosland Factory Ln, take the next L after Siskin Gdns onto Healy Houses.* **Sun 9 June, Sun 21 July (12-4). Adm £5, chd free. Pre-booking essential, please visit www.ngs.org.uk for information & booking. Light refreshments. Donation to The Welcome Centre (Huddersfield).**
Hawthorne Cottage sits in Magdale with views toward Emley Moor in the far distance. There is a small front lawned area with a stream, herb garden and mixed planting of shrubs. The main lawn at the rear of the property is bordered by mixed beds of herbaceous plants and shrubs. The lawn extends into a small orchard on two levels. There is a stream and trough fountain with a number of sculptures by Mick Kirkby-Geddes. The dry stone walling is by Richard Clegg who has worked at RHS Chelsea. There is a slope into the garden. There is level access to most areas inc part of the allotment area.

34 NEW 33 HEIGHTS DRIVE

Linthwaite, Huddersfield, HD7 5SU. Dawn & Roy Meakin, 07825 184919, roymeakin7@btinternet.com. *4m SW of Huddersfield. From Huddersfield on A62 Manchester Rd for about 2m then fork L at T-lights, Cowlersley Ln, then Gillroyd Ln, all one road for 2m, parking by bus shelter opp Heights Dr.* **Sat 13 July (10-4). Adm £5, chd free. Cream teas inc a selection of home-made cakes with allergen labelling. Visits also by arrangement Apr to Sept for groups of 15+. Additional charge for cream teas. Donation to Royal National Lifeboat Institute (RNLI).**
Situated on a Pennine hillside in a quirky garden overlooking the Colne Valley. The plot has been carefully designed with a flower arranger's eye and offers many handmade bespoke features. The meandering paths draw the visitor's eye around the garden, within a wide range of different room settings. The garden has a range of modern and quirky twists, with a wonderful nod to tradition. Bespoke handmade creations nestled around the garden complementing the colour schemes of the plants, creating traditional and contemporary settings. Flower arranging demonstrations could be offered, please ask for details.

35 5 HILL TOP

Westwood Drive, Ilkley, LS29 9RS. Lyn & Phil Short. *½ m S of Ilkley town centre, steep uphill. Turn S at town centre T-lights up Brook St, cross The Grove taking Wells Rd up to the Moors where road becomes Westwood Dr.* **Wed 29 May, Sun 2 June (11-4). Adm £4.50, chd free. Home-made teas.**
Delightful ⅔ acre steep garden on edge of Ilkley Moor. Sheltered woodland underplanted with naturalistic, flowing tapestry of foliage, shade-loving flowers, shrubs and ferns amongst large moss-covered boulders. Many Japanese maples, natural rocky stream and bridges. Meandering gravel paths and steps lend magic to 'Dingley Dell'. Lawns, large rockery, and summerhouse with stunning views. Some steep steps.

36 HOLMFIELD

Fridaythorpe, YO25 9RZ. Susan & Robert Nichols, 07449 846236, snicholswire@gmail.com. *9m W of Driffield. From York A166 through Fridaythorpe. After 1m turn R by small copse of trees. 1st house on lane.* **Mon 1 Apr, Mon 27 May (12-5). Adm £6, chd free. Home-made teas. Visits also by arrangement Apr to June for groups of 10+.**
Informal two acre country garden on gentle south facing slope, developed from a field since 1988. Family friendly garden with mixed borders, bespoke octagonal gazebo, 'Hobbit House', sunken trampoline, large lawn, tennis court and hidden paths for hide and seek. Productive fruit cage, vegetable and cut flower area. Collection of Phlomis. Display of wire sculptures. Bee friendly planting. Some gravel areas, sloping lawns. Wheelchair access possible with help.

37 ◆ JACKSON'S WOLD

Sherburn, Malton, YO17 8QJ. Mr & Mrs Richard Cundall, 07966 531995, jacksonswoldgarden@gmail.com, www.jacksonswoldgarden.com. *11m E of Malton, 10m SW of Scarborough. Signs from A64. A64 E to Scarborough. R at T-lights in Sherburn, take the Weaverthorpe Rd, after 100 metres R fork to Helperthorpe & Luttons. 1m to top of hill, turn L at garden sign. Do not use SatNav.* **For NGS: Sun 12 May, Sun 16 June (1-5). Adm £5, chd free. Home-made teas in the chalk barn. For other opening times and information, please phone, email or visit garden website.**
Spectacular two acre country garden. Many old shrub roses underplanted with unusual perennials in walled garden. Woodland paths lead to further shrub and perennial borders. Lime avenue with wildflower meadow. Traditional vegetable garden inc roses and flowers with a Victorian greenhouse. Adjoining nursery. Tours by appointment.

Our donation to the Army Benevolent Fund supported 608 individuals with front line services and horticultural related grants in 2023

38 JERVAULX HALL
Jervaulx, Ripon, HG4 4PH. Mr & Mrs Phillip Woodrow. *Parking in the grounds of Jervaulx Abbey accessed from the A1608.* **Wed 12 June, Wed 7 Aug (12-5). Adm £7, chd free. Light refreshments.**
Eight acre garden adjacent to ruins of Jervaulx Abbey and inc Abbey Mill ruins with views of River Ure. Mixed borders and beds, croquet lawn, parterre, glasshouse. A small vegetable garden and fernery. Magnificent older trees and woodland areas with choice trees and shrubs planted in last seven years, inc magnolia, acer, Sorbus and Betula. Collection of contemporary sculptures.
✿ ☕))

39 THE JUNGLE GARDEN
124 Dobcroft Road, Millhouses, Sheffield, S7 2LU. Dr Simon & Julie Olpin, 07710 559189, simonolpin@blueyonder.co.uk. *3m SW of city centre. Dobcroft Rd runs between A625 & A621.* **Visits by arrangement 1 July to 15 Oct for groups of up to 25. Adm £5, chd free. Adm with good home-made cakes and tea is available at £12 per head. Donation to Sheffield Children's Hospital.**
Not a traditional garden, but a fascinating mature space of specialist interest using mainly hardy exotics creating a jungle effect. Long (250ft) narrow site, densely planted with mature trees and shrubs inc many Trachycarpus, European fan palms, large bamboos, several tree ferns, mature Eucalyptus and a number of species of mature Scheffleras. The planting has a South East Asian theme.
☕

40 LANGCLIFFE HALL
Langcliffe, Settle, BD24 9LY. *1m N of Settle. Take B4679 from Settle up the hill for ½ m. Take RH turning onto Langcliffe Main St (signposted to Malham). Langcliffe Hall is on R.* **Sun 30 June (11-4). Adm £5, chd free. Home-made teas.**
Rambling gardens in the grounds of a historic, grade II listed Jacobean hall (not open). With a picturesque backdrop of the Yorkshire Dales, explore winding paths leading you from the front of the house through secluded nooks filled with tumbling roses and fairytale charm. Wildflowers spill out of the formally structured garden, overflowing into

the paths, lawns and steps. Features herbaceous borders, native wildflower meadows, a woodland walk, and a large walled garden filled with organic vegetables, cutting flowers and an apothecary garden growing native medicinal herbs.
☕))

41 LANGTON FARM
Great Langton, Northallerton, DL7 0TA. Richard & Annabel Fife. *5m W of Northallerton. B6271 in Great Langton between Northallerton & Scotch Corner.* **Sun 21 Apr (2-5), Sun 23 June (12-5). Adm £5, chd free. Home-made teas.**
Garden designer's organic garden created since 2000. Romantic flower garden with mixed borders, roses, poppies, Astrantias, delphiniums, white lilies and pebble pool. Formal and informal gravel areas, nuttery. Pear avenue underplanted with double helix of white daffodils.
♿ 🐎 ✿ ☕))

42 LINDEN LODGE
Newbridge Lane, nr Wilberfoss, York, YO41 5RB. Robert Scott & Jarrod Marsden, 07900 003538, rdsjsm@gmail.com. *Equidistant between Wilberfoss, Bolton & Fangfoss. From York on A1079, ignore signs for Wilberfoss, take nxt turn to Bolton village. After 1m at Xrds, turn L onto Newbridge Ln.* **Visits by arrangement 2 Jan to 14 June for groups of 10 to 50. We are happy to offer cream teas, cakes & refreshments for by arrangement openings.**
A one acre garden with five acres of developing meadow, trees, pathways, hens and vegetable garden. Owner designed and constructed since 2000. Gravel paths edged with brick or lavender, many borders with unusual mixed herbaceous perennials, shrubs and feature trees. Wildlife pond, summerhouse, nursery, glasshouse and fruit cage. Orchard and woodland area. Formal garden with pond and water feature. Far-reaching views towards the Yorkshire Wolds. Plant sales.
🐎 ✿ 🚗 ☕

43 LITTLETHORPE MANOR
Littlethorpe Road, Littlethorpe, Ripon, HG4 3LG. Mrs J P Thackray, www.littlethorpemanor.com. *Outskirts of Ripon nr racecourse. Ripon bypass A61. Follow*

Littlethorpe Rd from Dallamires Ln r'about to stable block with clock tower. Map supplied on application. **Sun 8 Sept (1.30-5). Adm £7, chd free. Home-made teas in marquee.**
11 acres. Walled garden with herbaceous planting, roses and gazebo. Sunken garden with ornamental plants and herbs. Brick pergola with wisteria, blue and yellow borders. Formal lawn with fountain pool, hornbeam towers, yew hedging. Box-headed hornbeam drive with Aqualens. Large pond with classical pavilion and boardwalk. New contemporary physic garden with rill, raised beds and medicinal plants. Wheelchair access - gravel paths, some steep steps.
♿ ✿ ☕))

44 LOW HALL
Dacre Banks, Nidderdale, HG3 4AA. Mrs P A Holliday. *10m NW of Harrogate. On B6451 between Dacre Banks & Darley.* **Sun 5 May (1-5). Adm £5, chd free. Home-made teas. Opening with Dacre Banks Gardens on Sun 7 July.**
Romantic walled garden set on differing levels designed to complement historic C17 family home (not open). Spring bulbs, rhododendrons and azaleas round tranquil water garden. Asymmetric rose pergola underplanted with auriculas and lithodora links the orchard to the garden. Vegetable garden and conservatory. Extensive herbaceous borders, shrubs and climbing roses give later interest. Bluebell woods, lovely countryside and farmland all around, overlooking the River Nidd. 80% of the garden can be seen from a wheelchair but access involves 3 stone steps.
♿ 🐎 ✿ 🚗 ☕

45 NEW   42 MAIN STREET
North Frodingham, Driffield, YO25 8LG. Ms Beryl Fallows, 01262 481650, wsmith67@btinternet.com. *6m SE of Driffield. From Driffield take B1249 E for 6m. Garden on the R, halfway through the village. Street parking.* **Sun 30 June (10-4). Adm £4, chd free. Open nearby The Old Vicarage. Visits also by arrangement 14 June to 14 July for groups of up to 10.**
Welcoming garden. Side path bordered with mix of herbs and flowers. Main garden created since

2019 designed with wildlife in mind. Paths wind through borders of shrubs, veg, herbs, fruit, herbaceous and trees. *Tibouchina granulosa*, peonies, roses, *Astilboides tabularis* and irises. Secluded sitting area by wall covered in wisteria, wild roses and clematis greenhouse. Pots inc eucomis, abutilon 'Kentish Belle'. Wheelchair access via path to rear garden. Further access across lawns.

🚻 🐕 ✳ ☕

46 NEW THE MANOR

Birkby, Birkby Lane, Northallerton, DL7 0EF. Ginny and Jonathan McCloy. *7m NNW of Northallerton. On the A167, 5½m N of Northallerton turn L into Birkby Ln. ½m along lane next to St. Peter's Church.* **Tue 4 June, Tue 20 Aug (11-4.30). Adm £6, chd free. Light refreshments.**
C18 manor (not open) former rectory to adjacent church. 2½ acre gardens surrounded by mature trees. Extensive lawns, croquet lawn, mixed shrub and flower borders. Current owners have added new features –specimen trees, glasshouse, unusual orchard in the shape of an amphitheatre with central corten steel planters for vegetables. Meandering woodland path with curiosities for the observant. WC access for wheelchair users.

🚻 🐕 ✳ ☕ 🔊

47 MANSION COTTAGE

8 Gillus Lane, Bempton, Bridlington, YO15 1HW. Polly & Chris Myers, 07749 776746, chrismyers0807@gmail.com. *2m NE of Bridlington. From Bridlington take B1255 to Flamborough. 1st L at T-lights - Bempton Ln, continue and turn R into Short Ln then L at end. L fork at church.* **Sat 10, Sun 11 Aug (10-4). Adm £4.50, chd free. Light refreshments. Visits also by arrangement 11 June to 9 Aug for groups of 10 to 35.**
A truly hidden, private and secret garden with exuberant, packed, vibrant borders. Visitors' book says 'a veritable oasis', 'the garden is inspirational', with a surprise around every corner. Japanese influenced area, mini hosta walk, 100ft border, summerhouse and art studio. Vegetable plot, cuttery, late summer border, bee and butterfly border, deck and lawns. Sweet and savoury small plates served from the conservatory. Produce, plants and home made soaps for sale.

🐕 ✳ 🚗 ☕

48 115 MILLHOUSES LANE

Sheffield, S7 2HD. Sue & Phil Stockdale, 01142 365571, phil.stockdale@gmail.com. *SW Sheffield nr Derbyshire border. Approx 4m SW of Sheffield City Centre. Follow A625 Castleton/ Dore Rd, 4th L after Prince of Wales pub, 2nd L. Alternatively take A621 Baslow Rd. After Tesco garage take 2nd R, then 1st L.* **Sun 26 May (11-4.30). Adm £4, chd free. Light Refreshments. Visits also by arrangement 4 May to 1 Sept for groups of up to 25.**
Plantswoman's ⅓ acre south facing level cottage style garden with many choice and unusual perennials and bulbs, providing year-round colour and interest. Large collection of 60+ hostas, roses, peonies, iris and clematis with many tender and exotic plants inc aeoniums, echeverias, aloes, bananas and echiums. Seating areas around the garden. Many home-propagated plants for sale. Most of the garden is accessible for wheelchairs.

🚻 🐕 ✳ 🚗 ☕ 🔊

Frog Hall Barn

49 MIRES BECK NURSERY
Low Mill Lane, North Cave,
Brough, HU15 2NR. Graham
Elliott, www.miresbeck.co.uk.
*Between N & S Cave. Do not follow
SatNav if entering N Cave from the
A63/M62. Through village, take S
Cave Rd and reset SatNav.* **Wed 3
July (10-4). Adm £5, chd free.**
Charity that provides horticultural
work experience for adults with
learning disabilities. 14 acre site
features herbaceous borders, veg
beds, dementia garden and Hull's
official Garden of Sanctuary. We
grow 400 herbaceous perennials, 50
herbs, 100 wildflowers for regional
garden centres and heritage sites. For
NGS visitors there are talks about the
history and workings of MB, tours and
woodland walk. Tarmac main paths,
and compressed gravel side paths.

50 NEW HOUSE FARM
Lordship Lane, Wistow Lordship,
Selby, YO8 3RR. Prof Chris
Thomas and Dr Helen Billington,
helen.billington@gmail.com. *1m
E of Wistow and 2m NNE of Selby.
From B1223 in Wistow take Lordship
Ln out of village for 1m. From B1223
in Selby turn R at mini r'about on
Monk Ln, onto Lordship Ln for 2m.*
**Sun 2 June (12-5). Combined adm
with Galehouse Barn £6, chd free.
Refreshments at Galehouse Barn.
Visits also by arrangement 2 June
to 13 Sept for groups of up to 20.**
Two hectares of wildlife garden,
developed since 2000 by professional
ecologists, incorporating wildflower
meadows, mixed species shelterbelt,
ponds, courtyard garden, bee-friendly
border, vegetable gardens and a
banana-filled subtropical glasshouse.
Partial wheelchair access.

51 ◆ NEWBY HALL & GARDENS
Ripon, HG4 5AE. Mr R C Compton,
01423 322583,
info@newbyhall.com,
www.newbyhall.com. *4m SE of
Ripon. (HG4 5AJ for SatNav). Follow
brown tourist signs from A1(M)
or from Ripon town centre.* **For
opening times and information,
please phone, email or visit garden
website.**
40 acres of award-winning
gardens and woodland laid out in
the1920s. Full of rare and beautiful
plants. Formal seasonal gardens
and stunning double herbaceous
borders slope down to River Ure.

National Collection of cornus. Newly
refurbished rock garden. Miniature
railway and adventure gardens for
children. Free parking. Licensed
restaurant, shop and plant nursery.
Wheelchair map available. Disabled
parking. Manual and electric
wheelchairs available on loan, please
call to reserve.

52 THE NURSERY
15 Knapton Lane, Acomb, York,
YO26 5PX. Tony Chalcraft &
Jane Thurlow, 01904 781691,
janeandtonyatthenursery@hotmail.
co.uk. *2½ m W of York. From A1237
take B1224 towards Acomb. At
r'about turn L (Beckfield Ln). After
150 metres turn L.* **Sun 21, Mon 22,
Tue 23 July (1-6). Adm £4, chd
free. Home-made teas. Visits also
by arrangement May to Sept for
groups of 12+.**
A former suburban commercial
nursery, now an attractive and
productive one acre organic, private
garden. Over 100 fruit trees, many
in trained form. Many different
vegetables grown both outside and
under cover in 20 metres greenhouse.
Productive areas interspersed with
informal ornamental plantings and
cut flower areas to provide colour
and habitat for wildlife. Group visits
by arrangement particularly welcome
and can be themed depending on the
time in the season to inc tastings.

53 THE OLD PRIORY
Everingham, YO42 4JD. Dr J D &
Mrs H J Marsden, 01430 860222,
helen.marsden@ngs.org.uk. *15m
SE of York, 6m from Pocklington.
2m S of A1079. On E side of
village.* **Visits by arrangement 21
Apr to 30 June. Price includes
refreshments. Adm £10, chd free.
Home-made teas. Wine and beer
can be served at evening visits if
requested.**
Two acre rural garden. Created in
1990s to enable self-sufficiency in
veg, meat, most fruit, logs and timber.
Walled veg garden, polytunnel and
greenhouse. Borders planted to cope
with sandy loam. Garden slopes
down to natural bog garden. Dove
tree, variegated tulip tree and various
willows. Roughly mown pathway
through woodland, along ponds, lake
and lightly grazed pasture. Plenty wild
flora and fauna.

54 THE OLD RECTORY
Arram Road, Leconfield,
Beverley, HU17 7NP. David
Baxendale, 01964 502037,
davidbax@newbax.co.uk. *Garden
entrance on L 80yds along Arram
Rd next to double bend sign before
the church.* **Visits by arrangement
Jan to May for groups of up to 15.
Adm £7.50.**
Approx three acres of garden and
paddock. The garden is particularly
attractive from early spring until
mid summer. Notable for aconites,
snowdrops, crocuses, daffodils and
bluebells. Later hostas, irises, lilies
and roses. There is a small wildlife
pond with all the usual residents inc
grass snakes. Well established trees
and shrubs, with new trees planted
when required. No refreshments
available but visitors are welcome to
bring a picnic.

55 OLD SLENINGFORD HALL
Mickley, nr Ripon, HG4 3JD. Jane
& Tom Ramsden. *5m NW of Ripon.
Off A6108. After N Stainley turn L,
follow signs to Mickley. Gates on R
after 1½ m opp cottage.* **Sat 8, Sun
9 June (12-4). Adm £7.50. Home-
made teas. Donation to other
charities.**
A large English country garden and
award winning permaculture forest
garden. Early C19 house (not open)
and garden with original layout.
Wonderful mature trees, woodland
walk and Victorian fernery, romantic
lake with islands, watermill, walled
kitchen garden, beautiful long
herbaceous border, yew and huge
beech hedges. Several plant and
other stalls. Picnics around the mill
pond very welcome. Of particular
interest to anyone interested in
permaculture. Reasonable wheelchair
access to most parts of garden.
Disabled WC at Old Sleningford Farm
next to the garden.

56 THE OLD VICARAGE
North Frodingham, Driffield,
YO25 8JT. Professor Ann
Mortimer. *From Driffield take B1249
E for approx 6m, garden on R opp
church. Entrance at T-junc of road
to Emmotland & B1249. From N
Frodingham take B1249 W for ½ m.
Park in farmyard 50yds E opp side
B1249.* **Sun 30 June (10.30-4.30).
Adm £5, chd free. Home-made
teas. Open nearby 42 Main Street.**
1½ acre plantsman's garden,

developed by owner over 27 years. Many themed areas inc rose garden, jungle, desert, fountain, scented, kitchen gardens, glasshouses. Classical statues, unusual trees and shrubs, large and small ponds, orchard, nuttery. Children's interest: 'Jungle Book', dinosaur and wild animals in the jungle. Neo-Jacobean revival house, built 1837, mentioned in Pevsner (not open). The land occupied by the house and garden was historically owned by the family of William Wilberforce.

&. ⛺ ❀ ☕ 🧺

57 NEW THE ORCHARDS

Crag Lane, Huby, Leeds, LS17 0BW. Joanne McCudden, www.instagram.com/ harrogategardening. *Between Harrogate (8m) and Leeds (13m). Serviced well by Weeton train stn. From Harrogate Rd, in village of Huby, turn up Crag Ln or Strait Ln. The Orchards is near the top of the hill, opp the junc to Almscliffe Dr. 8min walk from train stn.* **Thur 29, Fri 30 Aug (11-3). Adm £5, chd free. Home-made teas inc cakes, tea and coffee in aid of North Rigton Primary School PTA. Square and Compass pub nearby for larger meals (please book).** Relaxed 2 acre family garden set into a hillside, has an Arts and Crafts structure, with more recent contemporary garden design by the award winning designer, Lizzie Tulip. Subtropical zone and greenhouse further down hill, growing a range of interesting plants and edibles. Arts and Crafts terracing, stone staircase, woodland glade and giant planters are key features. Plant sale by Cliffbank Nursery.

⛺ ❀ D ☕ 🔊

58 23 THE PADDOCK

Cottingham, HU16 4RA. Jill & Keith Stubbs, 07932 713281, keith@ cottconsult.karoo.co.uk. *Between Beverley & Hull. From Humber Br A164 towards Beverley. R onto Castle Rd, past hospital. From Beverley A164 towards Humber Br, L onto Harland Way 1st r'about. Over L/x-ings and Garden at S of village.* **Sun 28 Apr, Sun 7 July (10.30-4.30). Adm £5, chd free. Home-made teas. Open nearby Southwood Hall. Visits also by arrangement May to July for groups of 8 to 15. Price includes refreshments.** A secret garden behind a small mixed frontage. Archway to themed areas

within the garden inc Japanese, Mediterranean, fairy and mixed herbaceous areas with patios and lawns. Two ponds, a rill, ornamental and tree sculptures. Re-landscaped areas and new sculptures. Art work, blacksmith's garden ornaments and sculptures for sale. Assisted access for disabled through front gate.

&. ⛺ ❀ ☕ 🔊

59 NEW PADDOCK WOOD

Driffield Road, Kilham, YO25 4SP. Chris and Emma Hobbs, www.instagram.com/ paddockwoodgarden. *Next to Kilham Primary School.* **Sat 15 June (11-5). Combined adm with 3 West Garth £8, chd free. Light refreshments.** 1¼ acre garden bordered by mature trees and beech hedges. Garden is a blend of established and recent planting. House surrounded by perennial borders. Lawn leads to mixed borders and ornamental pond created using unearthed old rockery. Beyond beech hedge, gravel herb garden, 50 year old greenhouse, rose garden and paved kitchen garden. Refreshments, plants and pottery for sale. WC facilities provided in local church. Most areas of the garden are accessible by wheelchair.

&. ⛺ ❀ 🚗 ☕ 🔊

60 ♦ PARCEVALL HALL GARDENS

Skyreholme, Skipton, BD23 6DE. Walsingham College, 01756 720311, parcevallhallgarden@gmail.com, www.parcevallhallgardens.co.uk. *9m N of Skipton. Signs from B6160 Bolton Abbey-Burnsall rd or off B6265 Grassington-Pateley Bridge & at A59 Bolton Abbey r'about.* **For NGS: Wed 11 Sept (10-4.30). Adm £8, chd free. Light refreshments. For other opening times and information, please phone, email or visit garden website.** The only garden open daily in the Yorkshire Dales National Park. 24 acres on a sloping south facing hillside in Wharfedale sheltered by mixed woodland. Terrace garden, rose garden, rock garden and ponds. Mixed borders, spring bulbs, tender shrubs and autumn colour.

⛺ ❀ ☕ 🧺

61 PILMOOR COTTAGES

Pilmoor, nr Helperby, YO61 2QQ. Wendy & Chris Jakeman, 01845 501848, cnjakeman@aol.com. *20m N of York. From A1M J48. From B'bridge follow rd towards Easingwold. From A19 follow signs to Hutton Sessay then Helperby. Garden next to mainline railway.* **Mon 27 May, Mon 26 Aug (11-5). Adm £5, chd free. Light refreshments. Visits also by arrangement Apr to Sept.** A year-round garden for rail enthusiasts and garden visitors alike. A ride on the 7¼" gauge railway runs through two acres of gardens and gives you the opportunity to view the garden from a different perspective. The journey takes you across water, through a little woodland area, past flower filled borders, and through a tunnel behind the rockery and water cascade. 1½ acre wildflower meadow and pond. Clock-golf putting green.

&. ⛺ ❀ ☕ 🧺

62 THE POPLARS

Main Street, Newton upon Derwent, York, YO41 4DA. Peter & Christina Young, young.at.poplars@gmail.com, www.vimeo.com/ showcase/10043886. *9m E of York. From A1079 at Wilberfoss, turn S towards Sutton upon Derwent. After ¾m, turn R into Newton, then L. Garden on R past pub.* **Sun 12 May (1-5). Adm £5, chd free. Home-made teas in Village Community Centre. Visits also by arrangement 13 May to 31 May.** A plant-lover's paradise. Over 100 different trees and shrubs around a Victorian house and barns provide structure and shelter for a succession of flowers through the seasons. Glasshouses full of tender plants that spill out into the gardens in summer. Meadow walk leads to two acre arboretum with over 200 woody species around a wildlife pond. Ceramic sculptures.

❀ ☕

47,000 people affected by cancer were reached by Maggie's centres supported by the National Garden Scheme over the last 12 months

63 PRIMROSE BANK GARDEN AND NURSERY
Dauby Lane, Kexby, York, YO41 5LH. Sue Goodwill & Terry Marran, www.primrosebank.co.uk. *4m E of York. At Junc of A64 & A1079 take rd signed to Hull. After 3m, just as entering Kexby, turn R onto Dauby Ln, signed for Elvington. From the E travel on A1079 towards York. Turn L in Kexby.* **Wed 15 May (11-4). Adm £5, chd free. Home-made teas.**
Two acres of rare and unusual plants, shrubs and trees. Bulbs, hellebores and flowering shrubs in spring, followed by planting for year-round interest. Extensive eranthis collection. Courtyard garden, mixed borders, summerhouse and pond. Lawns, contemporary rock garden, shade and woodland garden with pond, stumpery and shepherd's hut. Adjoining award-winning nursery. Poultry and Hebridean sheep. Dogs allowed on a short lead in car park and at designated tables outside the tearoom. CL Caravan Site (CAMC members only) adjoining the nursery. Most areas of the garden are level and are easily accessible for wheelchairs. Accessible WC available.

64 THE PRIORY, NUN MONKTON
York, YO26 8ES. Mrs K Harpin. *9m W of York, 12m E of Harrogate. E of A1M J47 off A59 signed Nun Monkton.* **Thur 13 June (11-4). Adm £7.50, chd free. Home-made teas in greenhouse.**
Large and varied country garden surrounding William and Mary house (not open) at the confluence of the River Nidd and River Ouse. Featuring species trees, calm swathes of lawn, clipped yew, beech and box, formal rose garden and mixed borders. Area of soft perennial planting and informal parkland. Gravel paths.

65 PROSPECT HOUSE
Scarah Lane, Burton Leonard, Harrogate, HG3 3RS. Cathy Kitchingman, 07989 195773, cathyrk@icloud.com, www.abrightprospect.co.uk. *5m S of Ripon 5½m from A1, J48. Exit A61 signed Burton Leonard. Parking marshals on Station Ln. Drop off only for those with mobility issues outside Prospect House.* **Sun 16 June (12.30-4.30). Adm £5, chd free. Home-made teas. Visits also by**
arrangement 8 Apr to 14 Sept for groups of 15+.
One acre walled, landscaped garden with ornamental pond, pergola, large oval lawned area, cutting garden beds. Colour-themed herbaceous long border, 'hot' border, physic bed, woodland area. Also mature hedging, trees and seasonal interest throughout. Additional new planting areas are being established. A renovated outhouse now converted into a potting area used for garden workshops.

66 REWELA COTTAGE
Skewsby, YO61 4SG. John Plant & Daphne Ellis, 07711 555665, rewelacottage@gmail.com, www.rewelahostas.com. *4m N of Sheriff Hutton, 15m N of York. After Sheriff Hutton, towards Terrington, turn L towards Whenby & Brandsby. Turn R just past Whenby to Skewsby. Turn L into village. 500yds on R.* **Visits by arrangement May to Aug for groups of 10+. Adm £12, chd free. Home-made teas.**
Situated in a lovely quiet country village, Rewela Cottage was designed from an empty paddock, to be as labour saving as possible using unusual trees and shrubs for year-round interest. Their foliage, bark and berries enhance the well-designed structure of the garden. The garden owner now specialises in growing and selling hostas. Over 650 varieties of hostas in the garden. Some gravel paths may make assistance necessary.

67 ◆ RHS GARDEN HARLOW CARR
Crag Lane, Harrogate, HG3 1QB. Royal Horticultural Society, 01423 565418, harlowcarr@rhs.org.uk, www.rhs.org.uk/harlowcarr. *1½m W of Harrogate town centre. On B6162 (Harrogate - Otley).* **For NGS: Sun 21 Apr (9.30-5). Standard adm charges subject to change. Children under 5 free. For other opening times and information, please phone, email or visit garden website.**
Harlow Carr offers a variety of growing landscapes, from running and still water, to woodland and wildflower meadows. Highlights inc the lavish main borders, bursting with generous prairie-style planting and the lush, moisture-loving plants around Streamside. Betty's Cafe Tearooms,
gift shop, plant centre and children's play area inc treehouse and log ness monster. Wheelchairs and mobility scooters available, advanced booking recommended.

68 THE RIDINGS
South Street, Burton Fleming, Driffield, YO25 3PE. Roy & Ruth Allerston, 01262 470489. *11m NE of Driffield. 11m SW of Scarborough. From Driffield B1249, before Foxholes turn R to Burton Fleming. From Scarborough A165 turn R to Burton Fleming.* **Sun 26 May, Sun 7 July (12-4). Adm £4, chd free. Home-made teas. Visits also by arrangement Apr to July.**
Secluded cottage garden with colour-themed borders surrounding neat lawns. Grass and paved paths lead to formal and informal areas through rose and clematis covered pergolas and arbours. Box hedging defines well-stocked borders with roses, herbaceous plants and trees. Seating in sun and shade offers vistas and views. Greenhouse and summerhouse. Terrace with water feature. Indoor model railway. Finalist, North Region, The English Garden Magazine's The Nation's Favourite Gardens 2023. Terrace, tea area and main lawn accessible via ramp.

249 Barnsley Road

138 Greystones Road

69 NEW **18 RIPLINGHAM ROAD**
Skidby, Cottingham, HU16 5TR.
Mrs Mary Caldwell. *Between Beverley and Hull. From Humber Br A164 to Beverley L at Skidby r'about. From Beverley A164 to Humber Br R at Skidby r'about. Follow Main St past church then sch on L. Riplingham Rd straight ahead.* **Evening opening Thur 27 June (5-8.30); Thur 5 Sept (5-8). Adm £5, chd free. Light refreshments inc wine, soft drinks and cakes.**
A small garden created by owner. The front has colour themed borders with dozens of pots. The rear planting creates a feeling of seclusion. From an octagonal lily pond paths radiate outwards under arches festooned in clematis leading to hidden corners. Borders overflow with trees, flowering shrubs, perennials, dozens of roses and hidden statues and ornaments. Productive greenhouse with soft fruit. Rear garden can be viewed in part from lower patio. Front garden accessible.
& ❀ ☕ »))

70 **ROSEMARY COTTAGE**
163 High Street, Hook, Goole, DN14 5PL. **Justine Dixon, www.rosemarycottagehook.co.uk.** *Between Goole, Howden & Airmyn, close to M62 J36. Approach Hook from Boothferry Rd r'about 300yds S of Boothferry Bridge. Follow signs for Hook at Xrds turn L. Garden 550yds on L. Garden entry from rear through free car park.* **Sun 26 May (12-4). Adm £4, chd free. Light refreshments. Home baking & preserves for sale.**
Delightful combination of traditional cottage garden with themed planting overlooking open fields. Garden rooms link to a small orchard and on through a living willow arch to herbaceous perennial borders and an edible garden. Variety of stalls for local groups and businesses. Wheelchair access is available to most of the garden from rear car park. Ground is a little uneven. One part of the garden has stepped access.
& 🐄 ❀ 🚌 ☕ »))

71 **RUDDING PARK**
Follifoot, Harrogate, HG3 1JH. **Mr & Mrs Simon Mackaness, 01423 871350, simon.mackaness@ruddingpark.com, www.ruddingpark.co.uk.** *3m S of Harrogate off the southern bypass A658. Follow brown tourist signs. Use hotel entrance.* **Sun 19 May (1-4). Adm £6, chd free. Home-made teas.**
20 acres of attractive formal gardens, kitchen gardens and lawns around a Grade I Regency House extended and now used as an hotel. Humphry Repton parkland. Formal gardens designed by Jim Russell with extensive rhododendron and azalea planting. Contemporary designs by Matthew Wilson featuring grasses and perennials.
& 🐄 D 🚌 ☕ 🎪 »))

72 **SALTMARSHE HALL**
Saltmarshe, Howden, DN14 7RX. **Mark Chittenden, 01430 434920, info@saltmarshehall.com, www.saltmarshehall.com.** *6m E of Goole. From Howden (M62, J37) follow signs to Howdendyke & Saltmarshe.* **Sun 5 May (10-4). Adm £5, chd free. Light refreshments available outside. Afternoon teas in Hall and picnic hampers available via pre-booking.**
Saltmarshe Hall sits within a 17 acre estate. Five acres of ornamental gardens, the remainder consisting of parkland and woodland. The gardens consist of herbaceous borders, an ornamental pond, walled garden, small orchard and lime avenue. Enjoy a pre-booked afternoon tea in the River Garden with its beautiful white floral palette. Wheelchair to the house via a ramp. Garden is accessed via gravel paths, narrow walkways and shallow steps.
& 🐄 ❀ 🚌 ☕ »))

73 **SCAPE LODGE**
11 Grand Stand, Scapegoat Hill, Golcar, Huddersfield, HD7 4NQ. **Elizabeth & David Smith, 01484 644320, elizabethanddavid.smith@ngs.org.uk, www.instagram.com/elizabethatscapelodge.** *5m W of Huddersfield. From J23 or 24 M62, follow signs to Rochdale. From Outlane village, 1st L. At top of hill, 2nd L. Park at Scapegoat Hill Baptist Church (HD7 4NU) or in village. 5 mins walk to garden. 303/304 bus.* **Sun 5, Sun 12 May (1.30-4.30). Adm £5, chd free. Home-made teas. Visits also by arrangement 6 May to 9 June. Donation to Mayor of Kirklees Charity Appeal.**
⅓ acre contemporary country garden at 1000ft in the Pennines on a steeply sloping site with far-reaching views. Gravel paths lead between mixed borders on many levels. Colour-themed informal planting sits comfortably in the landscape and gives year-round interest. Steps lead to a terraced kitchen and cutting garden. Gazebo, pond, shade garden, large collection of pots and tender plants.
❀ 🚌 ☕ »))

74 ◆ **SHANDY HALL GARDENS**
Thirsk Bank, Coxwold, York, YO61 4AD. **The Laurence Sterne Trust, 01347 868465, info@laurencesternetrust.org.uk, www.laurencesternetrust.org.uk.** *N of York. From A19, 7m from both Easingwold & Thirsk, turn E signed Coxwold. Park on rd.* **For NGS: Evening opening Fri 7, Fri 21 June (6.30-8). Adm £4, chd free. For other opening times and information, please phone, email or visit garden website.**
Home of C18 author Laurence Sterne. Two walled gardens, one acre of unusual perennials interplanted with tulips and old roses in low walled beds. In old quarry another acre of trees, shrubs, bulbs, climbers and wildflowers encouraging wildlife, inc over 450 recorded species of moths. Moth trapping demonstration. Partial wheelchair access. Gravel car park, steps down to Wild Garden.
& 🐄 ❀ 🎪

Our 2023 donation to the Queen's Nursing Institute now helps support over 2,500 Queen's Nurses working in the community in England, Wales, Northern Ireland, the Channel Islands and the Isle of Man

GROUP OPENING

75 SHIPTONTHORPE GARDENS
Shiptonthorpe, York, YO43 3PQ. *2m NW of Market Weighton. Halfway betw York & Hull on A1079, 2m NW of Mkt Weighton. Parking on playing fields car park off Station Rd. York Ho (opp village hall) & Langdale End on Station Rd. Oranmore & Wayside on Town St near church.* **Sat 1, Sun 2 June (11-5). Combined adm £7.50, chd free. Home-made teas in village hall & local garden centre.**

LANGDALE END
Mr & Mrs Thompson.

ORANMORE COTTAGE
Susan & Paul Kraus.

WAYSIDE
Susan Sellars.

YORK HOUSE
Tracey Baty.

Four contrasting gardens with different gardening styles. Langdale End is an eclectic maze-like garden with a mix of contemporary and cottage garden styles, featuring tropical plants, an Asian inspired garden, water features and a pond. Wayside has interesting planting in a variety of garden areas, with developing vegetable and fruit growing areas. Oranmore cottage is a surprising 'hidden garden' divided into two distinct areas featuring decorative architectural plants and carefully chosen herbaceous perennials. Finally, there is York House, a wildlife-friendly garden with a bit of everything inc prairie-style and cottage garden planting, an edible garden and the chatter of chickens. Wheelchairs possible in some gardens.

& 🚗 🍵

76 SKIPWITH HALL
Skipwith, Selby, YO8 5SQ. Sir Charles and Lady Forbes Adam, 07976 821903, rosalind@escrick.com, www.escrick.com/hall-gardens. *9m S of York, 6m N of Selby. From York A19 Selby, L in Escrick, 4m to Skipwith. From Selby A19 York, R onto A163 to Market Weighton, then L after 2m to Skipwith.* **Sat 24 Feb (11-2). Light refreshments. Thur 6 June (1-4). Home-made teas. Adm £6, chd free. 2025: Sat 22 Feb.** Visits also by arrangement 27 May to 7 July for groups of 10 to 30. Mon, Tues, Thurs preferred between 10am and 5pm.
Four acre walled garden of Queen Anne house (not open). Mixture of historic formal gardens in part designed by Cecil Pinsent, woodmeadow, wildflower walks and lawns. 'No-dig' kitchen garden with herb maze, Italian garden, collection of old-fashioned shrub roses and climbers. No dig veg, meadows, espaliered and fan trained fruit. Arboretum/woodland and a variety of specimen trees. Gravel paths.

& 🌸 🚗 🍵))

77 SLEIGHTHOLMEDALE LODGE
Fadmoor, YO62 7JG. Patrick & Natasha James. *6m NE of Helmsley. Parking limited in wet weather. Garden is 1st property in Sleightholmedale, 1m from Fadmoor.* **Sun 30 June (1.30-5.30). Adm £5, chd free. Home-made teas.**
A glorious south facing, three acre hillside garden with views over a peaceful valley in the North York Moors. Cultivated for over 100 years, wide herbaceous borders and descending terraces lead down the valley with beautiful, informal planting within the formal structure of walls and paths. The garden features roses, delphiniums and other classic English country garden perennials.

🐂 🍵

78 NEW SOUTHWOOD HALL
Burton Road, Cottingham, HU16 5AJ. Kevin and Janet Barnes, 07976 605669, kevingasbarnes@icloud.com. *Two entrances: Burton Rd and from Southwood Rd, along Southwood Gardens. On street parking only.* **Sun 28 Apr, Sun 7 July (10-4.30). Adm £6, chd free. Home-made teas. Open nearby 23 The Paddock.** Visits also by arrangement 15 Apr to 30 Sept for groups of 5 to 25. Tours by head gardener Justin Lowe, history of the Hall by Mr Kevin Barnes.
Explore 1½ acres of secluded grounds surrounding this historic property. Spot the Alice in Wonderland sculptures in the Secret Walled Garden around a dipping pool and fountain. Enjoy teas in the formal front garden and parterre. View extensive driveway flowerbeds. Meander through the orchard, meadow, greenhouse and raised beds and marvel at the extensive composting area! Gardens continually developing under head gardener Justin Lowe. Wheelchair access possible in the grounds with assistance, all paths are gravel/grass, ramp available to access walled garden (2 steps).

& 🐂 🌸 🍵

79 ◆ STILLINGFLEET LODGE
Stewart Lane, Stillingfleet, York, YO19 6HP. Mr & Mrs J Cook, 01904 728506, vanessa.cook@stillingfleetlodgenurseries.co.uk, www.stillingfleetlodgenurseries.co.uk. *6m S of York. From A19 York-Selby take B1222 towards Sherburn in Elmet Ln village turn opp church.* **For NGS: Sun 12 May, Sun 15 Sept (1-5). Adm £7, chd £2. Home-made teas. For other opening times and information, please phone, email or visit garden website.**
Organic, wildlife garden subdivided into smaller gardens, each based on a colour theme with emphasis on use of foliage plants. Wildflower meadow, natural pond, 55yd double herbaceous borders and modern rill garden. Rare breeds of poultry wander freely in garden. Adjacent nursery. Garden courses run all summer (see garden website.) Art exhibitions in the cafe. Gravel paths and lawn. Ramp to cafe if needed. No disabled WC.

& 🌸 🚗 🍵))

80 SWINDON HOUSE FARM
Spring Lane, Kirkby Overblow, Harrogate, HG3 1HT. Penny Brook, 07770 916666, pennybrook65@gmail.com. *1m S of Kirkby Overblow village. From Spring Ln/Swindon Ln junc, the drive is exactly ½ m on R.* **Fri 12 July (11-4). Adm £5, chd free. Home-made teas.**
An English country garden surrounded by farmland, with mixed perennial borders, a pond garden, orchard, roses, mature trees and native hedges, with wildlife at its heart. Wildflower areas have been created in the paddock together with re-wilding areas and paths mown through. A potager with espaliers, raised willow hurdle beds for vegetables and cut flowers, thyme path and small camomile lawn. Parking for wheelchair users so that all areas are accessible.

81 THIMBLEBY HALL

Thimbleby, Northallerton, DL6 3PY.
Mr & Mrs A Shelley. *From A19,
follow signs for Osmotherly then R in
the village centre onto South End Rd
towards Thimbleby. Proceed through
the ford and entrance lodges are on
the L.* Fri 24 May (1-5). Adm £8,
chd free. Home-made teas.
Country estate on the western edge
of the North York Moors. A number
of formal garden areas inc terraced
gardens, herbaceous garden and
lake within an extensive parkland
setting with sweeping views of the
surrounding countryside. The gardens
have been substantially extended by
the owner with formal planting and a
large banked area to the west of the
house with spring flowering shrubs.
Mature trees feature on the estate and
especially impressive is an avenue of
redwoods framing views across the
lake to the south of the Hall.

82 THIRSK HALL

Kirkgate, Thirsk, YO7 1PL.
Willoughby & Daisy Gerrish,
01845 444455, info@thirskhall.com,
www.thirskhall.com. *In the centre of
Thirsk. On Kirkgate, next to St Mary's
Church.* Sun 12 May (11-4). Adm
£6.50, chd free. Home-made teas.
Pimms bar.
Thirsk Hall is a Grade II* listed
townhouse completed by John Carr
in 1777 (not open). Behind the house
the unexpected 20 acre grounds inc
lawns, herbaceous borders, kitchen
gardens, walled paddocks and
parkland. The present layout and
planting are the result of a sensitive
restoration, blending formal and
informal beds, shrubbery and mature
trees. Sculpture Park.

83 THORP PERROW

Bedale, DL8 2PR. Sir Henry
Ropner, www.thorpperrow.com.
*For satnav use DL8 2PS. From
Bedale follow signs towards Masham
(B6268), ignore signs for Thorp
Perrow along Firby Rd and continue
for approx 1m. L after signs for
Snape. Arboretum approx ¼ m
on L.* Fri 7 June (11-4). Adm £5,
chd free. Light refreshments.
Refreshments also available in
Arboretum tearoom. Donation to
Yorkshire Air Ambulance.
The four acres of Thorp Perrow
Gardens are adjacent to the 100 acre
Arboretum, laid out in the 1800s.
The gardens surround the Hall (not

open) with formal lawns, herbaceous
borders and the remnants of the
Italian renaissance style topiary
all overlooked by the traditional
summerhouse. Historical woodland
with a natural spring. The gardens
and greenhouses are in the stages of
restoration. A new vegetable patch,
peach house and a young orchard
have been added to grounds. Some
steps but most of the garden is
wheelchair accessible.

84 WARLEY HOUSE GARDEN

Stock Lane, Warley, Halifax,
HX2 7RU. Mr & Mrs Cooke,
www.warleyhousegardens.com.
*2m W of Halifax. Take A646 (towards
Burnley) from Halifax centre. Go
through large intersection after
approx 1m. Approx 1m, turn R up
Windle Royd Ln. Disabled parking on
site, for 4/5 vehicles.* Sun 5, Wed 8
May (1.30-4.30). Adm £5, chd free.
Home-made teas.
Partly walled 2½ acre garden of
demolished C18 House. Rocky
paths and Japanese style planting
lead to lawns and lovely south facing
views. Alpine ravine planted with
ferns and fine trees give structure
to the woodland area. Drifts of
shrubs, herbaceous plantings,
wild flowers and heathers maintain
constant seasonal interest. This is
an historic garden, renovated after
total neglect from 1945 to 1995.
Spring planting is enhanced by many
new rhododendrons and woodland.
Most of the garden is accessible to
wheelchairs. Lawns usually suitable
unless very wet. Disabled access to
WCs and tearoom.

85 WELTON LODGE

Dale Road, Welton, Brough,
HU15 1PE. Brendon
Swallow, 07792 345858,
manager@weltonlodge.co.uk. *11
m W of Hull nr A63. From A63 take
exit for Welton, Elloughton & Brough.
Immed turn R at junc. Garden on R
just after Xrds.* Sun 28 July (10-4).
Adm £5, chd free. Cakes, cream
teas and coffee / tea available.
Welton Lodge is a Grade II listed
house occupying 1½ acres in
the beautiful village of Welton and
features a series of tiered gardens.
The top lawn features topiary bay
balls, leading to a tranquil formal pond
with box hedging and shaded semi-
circular seating. The renovated walled
kitchen gardens have espaliers of fruit

trees and vines around formal lawns
and flower beds and a 20m orangery.
Block paved ramp leads to gravelled
access to lower and upper gardens
without steps. Steep upper garden.

86 NEW 3 WEST GARTH

Kilham, YO25 4RD. Ian and
Teresa Maggs. *Cul-de-sac off West
End, Kilham.* Sat 15 June (11-5).
Combined adm with Paddock
Wood £8, chd free.
Plantaholic's ⅓ acre garden
developed over the last 20 years.
Large variety of unusual plants trees
and shrubs set out in different areas
to provide year-round interest. Roses,
herbaceous perennials, hostas,
clematis, ferns and grasses. Arbours,
summerhouse, two ponds, several
water features linked by lawn and
gravel areas with plenty of seating to
view garden. Some gravel areas.

87 WHITE WYNN

Ellerton, York, YO42 4PN.
Cindy & Richard
Hutchinson, 01757 289495,
richardahutchinson@btinternet.
com. *From York B1228 through
Sutton, turn R towards Howden.
From Selby A19 N turn R along A163
towards Market Weighton. Turn L
at Bubwith Xrds. ½ m up Shortacre
Ln (no through road).* Visits by
arrangement May to Sept for
groups of 8 to 30. Parking limited
to about 12 cars. Adm £5, chd
free. Light refreshments.
1½ acre country garden with many
mature trees. Lawns and patios
adjoin 60m long border, heather bed,
orchard, rose garden with arbour.
Vegetable beds, woodland, wildflower
meadow and shade beds. Secret
garden contains less usual plantings
to give a tropical feel. Wildlife-friendly
with two ponds, blackthorn and
damson copses and stored logs
providing shelter for hedgehogs
and toads. Very good, level access,
mostly on grass. Very wet weather
can make things difficult.

GROUP OPENING

88 WHIXLEY GARDENS
York, YO26 8AR. *8m W of York, 8m E of Harrogate, 6m N of Wetherby. 3m E of A1(M) off A59 York-Harrogate. Signed Whixley.* **Sun 12 May, Wed 12 June (11-5). Combined adm £8, chd free. Home-made teas and light refreshments at The Old Vicarage.**

COBBLE COTTAGE
John Hawkridge & Barry Atkinson, 01423 331419, cobblecottage@outlook.com. **Visits also by arrangement May to July.**

NEW LABURNUM FARM
David & Rachel Lindley.

THE OLD VICARAGE
Mr & Mrs Roger Marshall, biddymarshall@btinternet.com. **Visits also by arrangement May to July.**

Attractive rural yet accessible village nestling on the edge of the York Plain with beautiful historic church and Queen Anne Hall (not open). The gardens span the village with good footpaths. A plantsman's and flower arranger's garden at Cobble Cottage has views to the Hambleton Hills. In the centre of the village the garden at Laburnum Farm has been developed over the last eight years with formal parterre at the front and mixed herbaceous borders and a small courtyard leading to an orchard and paddock to the rear. Close to the church is The Old Vicarage with a ¾ acre walled flower garden overlooking the old deer park. The walls, house and various structures are festooned with climbers creating the atmosphere of a romantic English garden. Wheelchair access to The Old Vicarage only.

89 WOODHOUSE FARM
Foston-on-the-Wolds, Driffield, YO25 8BH. Dave and Diana Blanchard. *7 m SE of Driffield. On road between Foston & Beeford. 1m from each. Down long tarmac drive.* **Sun 16 June (11-4). Adm £5, chd free. Light refreshments.**
One acre, partly walled garden surrounding Grade II listed farmhouse (not open). Created from dereliction 16 years ago. Mainly south facing with extensive views over surrounding countryside. Mixed borders, garden rooms, Mediterranean themed sun patio with lily pond, courtyard garden, polytunnel. Eclectic range of plants, with many unusual species. Mainly paved but some gravel paths.

90 NEW WRESSLE BRICKYARD FARM
Newsholme, Goole, DN14 7JX. Ms Elizabeth Shutt. *3m from Howden M62 Junction, 10m from Selby. From M62 follow signs to Selby on A63. In 3m turn R to Wressle. From York/ Selby on A19 take A63 signed Hull. In 7m turn L to Wressle.* **Sun 14 July (11-5). Adm £5, chd free. Light refreshments.**
One acre garden with EW&B standard gauge railway and 1930s station. Formal garden with lawns, mature trees, borders and pots of summer colour. Old orchard leads to fountain garden. Two large natural ponds, bog garden and mature trees inc weeping copper, beech and spindle. Bandstand, polytunnel and greenhouse for fruit/vegetable and species geraniums. Botanical illustrations in studio.

91 WYTHERSTONE GARDENS
Pockley, York, YO62 7TE. Damien & Martha Byrne Hill. *2m NE of Helmsley. Signed from A170. Turn L into Wytherstone House, before the church in Pockley. Severely restricted parking. Disabled parking on drive & all other parking in field opp.* **Sun 9 June (11-4.30). Adm £5, chd free. Home-made teas in village hall, a short walk from garden & parking.**
Plantsman's garden set in eight acres of rolling countryside on edge of North York Moors. Interlinked areas behind huge beech hedges inc spring ericaceous, terraced, fern, peonia, foliage and bamboo gardens and small arboretum. Plants not thought hardy in northern England thrive in well-mulched free draining soil. Finalist, North Region, The English Garden Magazine's The Nation's Favourite Gardens 2023. Some steep slopes, but most of the garden is accessible for wheelchairs.

92 ♦ YORK GATE
Back Church Lane, Adel, Leeds, LS16 8DW. Perennial, 01132 678240, yorkgate@perennial.org.uk, www.yorkgate.org.uk. *5m N of Leeds. A660 to Adel, turn R at lights after the Co-op. L on to Church Ln. After church, R onto Back Church Ln. Garden on L.* **For opening times and information, please phone, email or visit garden website.**
An internationally acclaimed one acre jewel of a garden with 14 individual garden 'rooms'. Many unusual plants and architectural topiary. Exciting recent additions include a new café, gift shop and heritage exhibition as well as new gardens and plant nursery. Owned by Perennial, the charity that looks after horticulturists and their families in times of need.

93 YORKE HOUSE & WHITE ROSE COTTAGE
Dacre Banks, Nidderdale, HG3 4EW. Tony, Pat, Mark & Amy Hutchinson, 01423 780456, pat@yorkehouse.co.uk, www.yorkehouse.co.uk. *4m SE of Pateley Bridge, 10m NW of Harrogate, 10m N of Otley. On B6451 near centre of Dacre Banks. Car park on site.* **Sun 23 June (11-4.30). Adm £5, chd free. Cream teas. Visitors welcome to use picnic area in orchard. Opening with Dacre Banks Gardens on Sun 7 July. Visits also by arrangement 15 June to 21 July for groups of 10+.**
Award-winning English country garden in the heart of Nidderdale. A series of distinct areas flowing through two acres of ornamental garden. Colour-themed borders, natural pond and stream with delightful waterside plantings. Secluded seating areas and attractive views. Adjacent cottage has a recently developed garden designed for wheelchair access. Large collection of hostas. Orchard picnic area. All main features and car parking accessible to wheelchair users.

Cheshire & Wirral
Cumbria
Lancashire,
Merseyside
& Greater Manchester

NORTH WEST

Above: The Growth Project, Lancashire

NORTH WEST

Like its counterpart across the Pennines, the North West region of England combines some of the country's most revered landscapes with some of its greatest cities, contrasting areas of rural tranquillity with areas of dense population.

Nowhere has been more celebrated in literature than the Lake District, far more secretive is the wonderful countryside to be discovered in Lancashire's Forest of Bowland. From the Solway Firth which marks the border with Scotland to the Wirral which marks the border with Wales, the coastline includes Morecambe Bay and the River Mersey, as well as a selection of golfing meccas. The cities of Liverpool and Manchester may have lost much of the industrial heritage which made them two of the greatest mercantile centres in modern history, but they have found new ways to prosper and energise their communities. Liverpool is famous for its group of Victorian public parks, although it has to concede the oldest to neighbouring Birkenhead across the Mersey, designed by Joseph Paxton in the 1840s. Liverpool has England's largest cathedral, built during the 20th century, the region also boasts the country's smallest, originally built some 800 years earlier at Carlisle just a few miles from the Scottish border.

Above, from top: Maggie's Oldham, Oldham Gardens, Lancashire; Crumble Cottages, Cumbria

Below: 15 Park Crescent, Cheshire & Wirral

CHESHIRE & WIRRAL

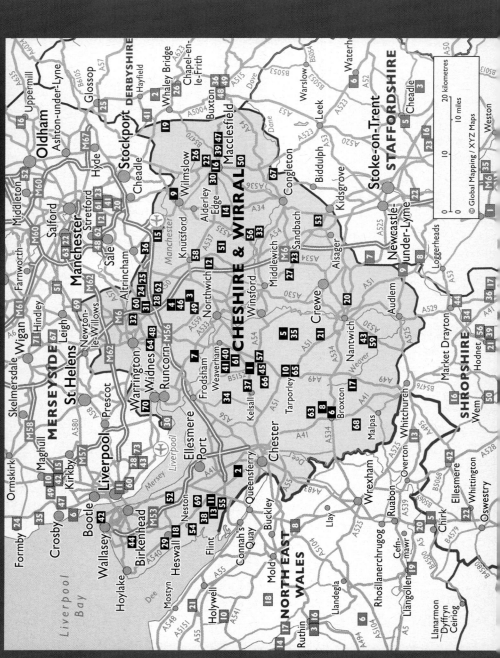

VOLUNTEERS

County Organiser
Janet Bashforth
07809 030525
jan.bashforth@ngs.org.uk

County Treasurer
John Hinde
0151 353 0032
johnhinde059@gmail.com

Booklet Co-ordinator
Sharon Maher
0151 837 1321
sharon.maher@ngs.org.uk

Booklet Advertising
Richard Goodyear
richard.goodyear@ngs.org.uk

Social Media & Publicity
Jacquie Denyer
jacquie.denyer@ngs.org.uk

Photographer
Liz Mitchell 01260 291409
liz.mitchell@ngs.org.uk

Talks
Mike Porter 07951 606906
porters@mikeandgailporter.co.uk

Assistant County Organisers
Sue Bryant 01619 283819
suewestlakebryant@btinternet.com

Jean Davies 01606 892383
mrsjeandavies@gmail.com

Linda Enderby 07949 496747
linda.enderby@ngs.org.uk

Sandra Fairclough 0151 342 4645
sandrafairclough51@gmail.com

Richard Goodyear (see above)

Juliet Hill 01829 732804
t.hill573@btinternet.com

Romy Holmes 01829 732053
romy@holmes-email.co.uk

Mike Porter (see above)

---

f **@National Garden Scheme**
 Cheshire & Wirral

X **CheshireWirrNGS**

◎ **@ngscheshirewirral**

OPENING DATES

All entries subject to change. For latest information check **www.ngs.org.uk**

Map locator numbers are shown to the right of each garden name.

February

Snowdrop Openings

Friday 9th
Briarfield 11

Friday 16th
Briarfield 11

Friday 23rd
Briarfield 11

Sunday 25th
Bucklow Farm 12

March

Friday 1st
Briarfield 11

Saturday 30th
◆ Poulton Hall 52

Sunday 31st
◆ Poulton Hall 52

April

Saturday 6th
Adswood 2

Sunday 7th
Adswood 2
Parm Place 49

Sunday 14th
Briarfield 11

Monday 15th
◆ Arley Hall & Gardens 4

Sunday 21st
Hill Farm 27

Saturday 27th
10 Statham Avenue 60

Sunday 28th
Somerford 58
10 Statham Avenue 60

May

Thursday 2nd
◆ Cholmondeley Castle
 Gardens 17

Saturday 4th
All Fours Farm 3

Sunday 5th
All Fours Farm 3
Laskey Farm 32
◆ Stonyford Cottage 61

Monday 6th
All Fours Farm 3
Laskey Farm 32

Friday 10th
Bolesworth Castle 8

Saturday 11th
Bolesworth Castle 8
Hathaway 22
Highbank 23
◆ Lane End Cottage Gardens 31

Sunday 12th
Hathaway 22
Highbank 23
Hill Farm 27
◆ Lane End Cottage Gardens 31
Norley Court 41
Tiresford 65
Tirley Garth Gardens 66

Saturday 18th
Bankhead 6
64 Carr Wood 15
Parvey Lodge 50
◆ Peover Hall Gardens 51

Sunday 19th
Manley Knoll 34
◆ Peover Hall Gardens 51
NEW Swineyard Hall 62

Saturday 25th
The Old Parsonage 46

Sunday 26th
Laskey Farm 32
Norley Court 41
The Old Parsonage 46
Rowley House 56

Monday 27th
Laskey Farm 32

June

Saturday 1st
10 Statham Avenue 60

Sunday 2nd
◆ Mount Pleasant 37
10 Statham Avenue 60
Tattenhall Hall 63

Thursday 6th
15 Park Crescent 48

Saturday 8th
Drake Carr 19

Sunday 9th
Drake Carr 19
NEW 24 Eastern Road 20
NEW 166 Higher Lane 25
Hill Farm 27
60 Kennedy Avenue 30
Sandymere 57
The Wonky Garden 70

Wednesday 12th
NEW ◆ Capesthorne Hall 14

Saturday 15th
NEW Chinook Cottage 16
New Inn Farm 39
One House Walled Garden 47
Willaston Grange 69

Sunday 16th
18 Dee Park Road 18
New Inn Farm 39
One House Walled Garden 47
NEW Swineyard Hall 62

Wednesday 19th
18 Dee Park Road 18
10 Statham Avenue 60

Saturday 22nd
18 Highfield Road 26

Sunday 23rd
18 Dee Park Road 18
18 Highfield Road 26
The Homestead 28
24 Old Greasby Road 44

Saturday 29th
All Fours Farm 3
NEW The Old Parsonage 45
NEW Toft Green Farm 67

Sunday 30th
◆ Abbeywood Gardens 1
All Fours Farm 3
Burton Village Gardens 13
NEW The Mill House 36
NEW The Old Parsonage 45
15 Park Crescent 48
NEW Toft Green Farm 67

July

Friday 5th
10 Statham Avenue 60

Saturday 6th
◆ Bluebell Cottage Gardens 7
10 Statham Avenue 60

Sunday 7th
◆ Bluebell Cottage Gardens 7
Parm Place 49
Rowley House 56
Somerford 58

Saturday 13th
Milford House Farm 35
The Old Byre 43
Sound Manor 59

Sunday 14th
The Old Byre 43
Sound Manor 59
The Wonky Garden 70

Saturday 20th
Laskey Farm 32

Sunday 21st
The Homestead 28
Laskey Farm 32
Norley Bank Farm 40
Rose Brae 54

Saturday 27th
NEW 2 Ashcroft Cottages 5

Sunday 28th
NEW 2 Ashcroft Cottages 5
Norley Bank Farm 40

August

Saturday 3rd
NEW 2 Ashcroft Cottages 5
Thorncar 64

Sunday 4th
NEW 2 Ashcroft Cottages 5
The Firs 21

Monday 5th
Norley Bank Farm 40

Saturday 10th
◆ Lane End Cottage Gardens 31

Sunday 11th
◆ Lane End Cottage Gardens 31

Sunday 25th
Laskey Farm 32

Monday 26th
Laskey Farm 32

September

Sunday 1st
◆ Mount Pleasant 37

Saturday 7th
NEW 2 Ashcroft Cottages 5

Sunday 8th
NEW 2 Ashcroft Cottages 5

Tuesday 17th
◆ Ness Botanic Gardens 38

Sunday 22nd
◆ Abbeywood Gardens 1

October

Sunday 6th
Bucklow Farm 12

Sunday 13th
◆ The Lovell Quinta Arboretum 33

Saturday 19th
Parvey Lodge 50

February 2025

Sunday 23rd
Bucklow Farm 12

By Arrangement

Arrange a personalised garden visit with your club, or group of friends, on a date to suit you. See individual garden entries for full details.

Adswood 2
NEW 2 Ashcroft Cottages 5
Bankhead 6
Bolesworth Castle 8
Bollin House 9
Bowmere Cottage 10
Briarfield 11
18 Dee Park Road 18
213 Higher Lane 24
Hill Farm 27
The Homestead 28
Inglewood 29
Laskey Farm 32
Milford House Farm 35
Norley Bank Farm 40
Norley Court 41
6 Oakland Vale 42
Parm Place 49
Parvey Lodge 50
Rosewood 55
Sandymere 57
10 Statham Avenue 60
Tattenhall Hall 63
Thorncar 64
The Well House 68
The Wonky Garden 70

THE GARDENS

1 ◆ ABBEYWOOD GARDENS
Chester Road, Delamere, Northwich, CW8 2HS. The Rowlinson Family, 01606 889477, info@abbeywoodestate.co.uk, www.abbeywoodestate.co.uk. *11m E of Chester. On the A556 facing Delamere Church.* **For NGS: Sun 30 June, Sun 22 Sept (9-4). Adm £6.50, chd free. Light refreshments. Restaurant in Garden. For other opening times and information, please phone, email or visit garden website.**
Superb setting near Delamere Forest. Total area 45 acres inc mature woodland, new woodland and new arboretum all with connecting pathways. Approx 4½ acres of gardens surrounding large Edwardian house. Vegetable garden, exotic garden, chapel garden, pool garden, woodland garden, lawned area with beds.
&. 🐎 ✿ 🚗 🚌 ☕

2 ADSWOOD
Townfield Lane, Mollington, CH1 6LB. Ken & Helen Black, 01244 851327, keneblack@outlook.com, www.kenblackclematis.com. *3m N of Chester. From Wirral take A540 towards Chester. Cross A55 at r'about, past Wheatsheaf pub, turn L into Overwood Lane. At T junction turn R into Townfield Lane. NGS sign 100 yds on the L.* **Sat 6, Sun 7 Apr (9-5). Adm £5, chd free. Pre-booking essential, please visit www.ngs.org.uk for information & booking. Light refreshments. Pls note the garden will be closed between 12 - 2 pm each day. Visits also by arrangement May to July for groups of 6 to 30.**
A cottage garden with perennials, climbers and English roses. The garden has over 150 varieties of clematis, providing colour throughout the year. There are several seating areas inc a pavilion and a summerhouse. Book on April dates for tours of early spring flowering clematis - as featured on Gardeners' World, or contact us for a small group visit, by arrangement. Packs of young spring clematis to start your own collection can be purchased. There are no steps but the front drive and some of the garden paths are gravelled and the side access to the rear garden is quite narrow.
&. 🐎 ✿ 🚗 ☕))

3 ALL FOURS FARM
Colliers Lane, Aston by Budworth, Northwich, CW9 6NF. Mr & Mrs Evans, www.curbishleysroses.co.uk. *M6 J19, take A556 towards Northwich. Turn immed R, past The Windmill pub. Turn R after approx 1m, follow rd, garden on L after approx 2m. Direct access available for drop off & collection for those with limited mobility.* **Sat 4, Sun 5, Mon 6 May, Sat 29, Sun 30 June (10-4). Adm £5, chd free. Home-made teas.**
A traditional and well established country garden with a wide range of roses, hardy shrubs, bulbs, perennials and annuals. You will also find a small vegetable garden, pond and greenhouse as well as vintage machinery and original features from its days as a working farm. The garden is adjacent to the family's traditional rose nursery. The majority of the garden is accessible by wheelchair.
&. ✿ 🚗 ☕

4 ◆ ARLEY HALL & GARDENS
Arley, Northwich, CW9 6NA. Viscount Ashbrook, 01565 777353, enquiries@arleyhallandgardens.com, www.arleyhallandgardens.com. *10m from Warrington. Signed from J9 & 10 (M56) & J19 & 20 (M6) (20 min from Tatton Park, 40 min to Manchester). Please follow the brown tourist signs.* **For NGS: Mon 15 Apr (10-5). Adm £12, chd £5. For other opening times and information, please phone, email or visit garden website.**
Within Arley's 8 acres of formal garden there are many different areas, each with its own distinctive character. Beyond the Chapel is The Grove, a well established arboretum and a woodland walk of about another 6 or 7 acres. Gardens are mostly wheelchair accessible (steps in some areas). Parts of the estate have cobbles which can prove difficult for manual wheelchairs.
&. 🐎 ✿ 🚗 🚌 ☕ 🪑))

5 NEW 2 ASHCROFT COTTAGES
Wettenhall, Winsford, CW7 4DQ. Steve & Sue Redmond, 07763 923005, sredmond24707825@aol.com. *Between Winsford & Tarporley. From Winsford follow Hall Lane for approx 2m. From Tarporley direction, follow signs for Eaton, pick up Hickhurst Lane until it meets Winsford Rd,* *turn L. We are 500 metres on L.* **Sat 27, Sun 28 July, Sat 3, Sun 4 Aug (11.30-6); Sat 7, Sun 8 Sept (11.30-5). Adm £6, chd free. Light refreshments. Visits also by arrangement 30 June to 16 Sept for groups of 6 to 26.**
A beautiful ¾ acre garden with large herbaceous borders, mature shrubs and grasses and a large wildlife pond with waterfall. Within the garden there are paths that lead you around with something new at every turn. This a garden full of colour and interest, a quirky garden mixing both kitchen and ornamental and animals. If you want to see something different this is the garden for you. Good access for wheelchairs.
&. 🐎 ✿ 🚗 ☕ 🪑))

6 BANKHEAD
Old Coach Road, Barnhill, Chester, CH3 9JL. Simon & Sian Preston, 07970 794456, sian@simonpreston.org. *10 m S of Chester. At the top end of Old Coach Road just by the junction with A534.* **Sat 18 May (1-5). Adm £7, chd free. Home-made teas. Visits also by arrangement 6 May to 30 June for groups of 10 to 20. Refreshments on request.**
Two acres of terraced gardens developed from Victorian times with spectacular views south and west over the Dee valley towards the Welsh hills. Rose garden, herbaceous borders, large pond with Japanese style garden, rhododendrons and azaleas. Small orchard and vegetable garden. Shetland ponies and chickens. Some steps to the main terrace but can reach most areas on paths with slight inclines. Parking close to the garden for disabled access.
&. ☕))

7 ◆ BLUEBELL COTTAGE GARDENS

Lodge Lane, Dutton, WA4 4HP.
Sue Beesley, 01928 713718,
info@bluebellcottage.co.uk,
www.bluebellcottage.co.uk. *5m
NW of Northwich. From M56 (J10)
take A49 to Whitchurch. After 3m
turn R at T-lights towards Runcorn/
Dutton on A533. Then 1st L. Signed
with brown tourism signs from A533.*
**For NGS: Sat 6, Sun 7 July (10-5).
Adm £5, chd free. Home-made
teas. For other opening times and
information, please phone, email or
visit garden website.**
South facing country garden wrapped
around a cottage on a quiet rural
lane in the heart of Cheshire. Packed
with thousands of rare and familiar
hardy herbaceous perennials, shrubs
and trees. Unusual plants available
at adjacent nursery. New walled
garden with greenhouse and raised
vegetable beds. The opening dates
coincide with the peak of flowering
in the herbaceous borders. Visitors
are welcome to picnic in the meadow
area adjacent to the car park or at the
benches in the nursery. The garden
is on a gentle slope with wide lawn
paths. All areas are accessible. We
have a wider access accessible toilet.

8 BOLESWORTH CASTLE

Tattenhall, CH3 9HQ. Mrs
Anthony Barbour, 01829 782210,
dcb@bolesworth.com,
www.bolesworth.com. *8m S of
Chester on A41. Enter via Production
Gate A in Old Coach Rd CH3
9JJ & follow signs to park on the
Showground. There is a short
walk up the Bridge Walk to access
the start of the Rock Walk.* **Fri 10,
Sat 11 May (10-5). Adm £10, chd
free. Visits also by arrangement
15 Apr to 31 May for groups of 10
to 40.**
The Rock Walk, which stretches
for half a mile above Bolesworth
Castle has stunning views across
to the Welsh Hills and Liverpool.
It was originally planted up by
Anthony Barbour in 1986. Many new
camellias, rhododendrons, azaleas
and other spring plants have been
added to the collection. New paths
have been created and original stone
features restored. The walk will take
you up the Bridge Walk before the
climb up to The Rock Walk. This is
a strenuous walk (steep at times)
and only suitable for keen walkers.
No children under 12 owing to steep

drops down to the drive. The walk
then continues through the castle
gardens and round the lake. Dogs to
be on leads at all times (please pick
up after them).

9 BOLLIN HOUSE

Hollies Lane, Wilmslow,
SK9 2BW. Angela Ferguson &
Gerry Lemon, 07828 207492,
fergusonang@doctors.org.uk.
*From Wilmslow past stn & proceed
to T-junction. Turn L onto Adlington
Rd. Proceed for ½m, then turn R
into Hollies Ln (just after One Oak
Ln). Drive to the end of Hollies Ln
& follow yellow signage. Park on
Browns Ln (other side Adlington
Rd) or Hollies Ln.* **Visits by
arrangement for groups of 8+.
Tea & cake/biscuits. Cold drinks
also available.**
The garden has deep borders full
of perennials, a wildflower meadow
and a formal area with parterres and
central water feature. The perennial
wildflower meadow (with mown
pathways and benches) attracts lots
of bees, dragonflies and other insects
and butterflies. There are views over
the Bollin river valley and the Edge to
the south and over to White Nancy in
the east. Bollin House is in an idyllic
location with the garden, orchard
and meadow dropping into the Bollin
valley. The River Bollin flows along this
valley and on the opp side the fields
lead up to views of Alderley Edge.
Ramps to gravel lined paths to most
of the garden. Some mown pathways
in the meadow.

10 BOWMERE COTTAGE

5 Bowmere Road, Tarporley,
CW6 0BS. Romy & Tom
Holmes, 01829 732053,
romy@holmes-email.co.uk. *10m
E of Chester. From Tarporley High
St (old A49) take Eaton Rd signed
Eaton. After 100 metres take R fork into
Bowmere Rd, Garden 100 metres on L.*
**Visits by arrangement 10 June to 31
July for groups of 5+. Adm £5, chd
free. Home-made teas.**
A colourful and relaxing 1 acre
country style garden around a
Grade II listed house. The lawns
are surrounded by well-stocked
herbaceous and shrub borders and
rose covered pergolas. There are 2
plant filled courtyard gardens and
a small vegetable garden. Shrubs
and rambling roses, clematis, hardy
geraniums and a wide range of hardy

herbaceous plants make this a very
traditional English garden.

11 BRIARFIELD

The Rake, Burton, Neston,
CH64 5TL. Liz Carter,
07711 813732, carter.burton@
btinternet.com. *9m NW of Chester.
Turn off A540 at Willaston-Burton
Xrds T-lights & follow road for 1m to
Burton village centre.* **Every Fri 9
Feb to 1 Mar (10-4). Sun 14 Apr (1-
5). Home-made teas in the church
just along the lane from the garden
on 14 April ONLY. Adm £5, chd
free. There are NO refreshments at
the Feb & Mar openings. Opening
with Burton Village Gardens
on Sun 30 June. Visits also by
arrangement 10 Feb to 7 Oct.**
Tucked under the south side of
Burton Wood the garden is home to
many specialist and unusual plants,
some available in plant sale. This 2
acre garden is on two sites, a short
walk along an unmade lane. Trees,
shrubs, colourful herbaceous, bulbs,
alpines and water features compete
for attention. Deliberately left untidy
through the winter for wildlife, the
snowdrops love it. Erythronium are
a feature of the garden in April and
May. Always changing, Liz can't
resist a new plant! Rare and unusual
plants sold (70% to NGS) from the
drive each Friday from 10am to
4pm, Feb to Oct. Check updates
on Briarfield Gardens Facebook
page: www.facebook.com/people/
Briarfield-Gardens-National-Garden-
Scheme/100063468283490/.

12 BUCKLOW FARM

Pinfold Lane, Plumley, Knutsford,
WA16 9RP. Dawn & Peter
Freeman. *2m S of Knutsford. M6
J19, A556 Chester. L at 2nd set of
T-lights. In 1¼m, L at concealed
Xrds. 1st R. From Knutsford A5033,
L at Sudlow Ln, becomes Pinfold Ln.*
**Sun 25 Feb, Sun 6 Oct (12.30-
4.30). Adm £4, chd free. Light
refreshments. Mulled wine in
Feb & Oct, with usual tea, coffee
& biscuits. 2025: Sun 23 Feb.
Donation to The Ticker Club.**
Country garden with shrubs, perennial
borders, rambling roses, herb garden,
vegetable patch, meadow, wildlife
pond/water feature and alpines.
Landscaped and planted over the last
30 yrs with recorded changes. Free
range hens. Carpet of snowdrops
and spring bulbs. Leaf, stem and

Burton Manor Walled Garden, Burton Village Gardens

© Liz Mitchell

berries to show colour in autumn and winter. Cobbled yard from car park, but wheelchairs can be dropped off near gate.

GROUP OPENING

13 BURTON VILLAGE GARDENS
Burton, Neston, CH64 5SJ. *9m NW of Chester. Turn off A540 at Willaston-Burton Xrds T-lights & follow road for 1m to Burton. Parking well signed. Maps given to visitors. Buy your ticket at 1st garden & keep it for entry to other gardens.* **Sun 30 June (11-5). Combined adm £6, chd free. Home-made teas in the Sport and Social Club behind the village hall.**

BRIARFIELD
Liz Carter.
(See separate entry)

◆ BURTON MANOR WALLED GARDEN
Friends of Burton Manor Gardens CIO, 0151 336 6154, www.burtonmanorgardens.org.uk.

THE COACH HOUSE
Jane & Mike Davies,
0151 353 0074,
burtontower@googlemail.com.

TRUSTWOOD
Peter & Lin Friend, 0151 336 7118, lin.friend@icloud.com, www.trustwoodbnb.uk.

With our light sandy soil, often on a south facing slope, we are focussing on drought tolerant planting and copious mulching. The Coach House has stunning views of the Welsh hills. The garden is full of colour with herbaceous borders, a cut flower area plus a productive fruit and vegetable patch. Using terracing to retain water, it has been successfully extended up the hillside. Briarfield is home to many unusual plants, some available in the plant sale at the house. The 1½ acre main garden invites exploration not only for its variety of plants but also for the imaginative use of ceramic sculptures. Period planting with a splendid vegetable garden surrounds the restored Edwardian glasshouse in Burton Manor's walled garden.

Paths lead past a sunken garden and terraces to views across the Cheshire countryside. Trustwood is a relaxed country garden, a haven for wildlife with emphasis on British native trees planted along the drive, the use of insect friendly plants and wildlife ponds. Briarfield & The Coach House are too hilly for wheelchairs, with steep slopes and steps.

152,684 people were able to access guidance on what to expect when a person is dying through the National Garden Scheme support for Hospice UK this year

14 NEW ◆ CAPESTHORNE HALL
Congleton Road, Siddington,
Macclesfield, SK11 9JY.
Sir William & Lady Bromley-
Davenport, 01625 861221,
info@capesthorne.com,
capesthorne.com/the-grounds-
and-gardens/. *5m W of
Macclesfield. 7m S of Wilmslow. On
A34. Free parking.* **For NGS: Wed
12 June (11-4.30). Adm £8.50.
Lakeside Café offers delicious
home-made light refreshments.
Afternoon teas are available,
pre-booking is required. For other
opening times and information,
please phone, email or visit garden
website.**
Varied garden with daffodil lawn,
azaleas, rhododendrons, herbaceous
border, woodland walk and
arboretum. The tranquil gardens
at Capesthorne Hall alongside the
adjoining lakes are full of colourful
perennials merging with the more
unusual C18 plants, shrubs and
trees. A family Georgian Chapel, ice
house, cascade and memorial garden
are located within the grounds. Our
landmark trail gives details of all the
main architectural features within
the grounds. A copy of the map and
feature descriptions will be given out
to each visitor. Uneven ground on
the Woodland Walk, Wilderness Trail
and the narrow pathway around the
lower pool may be inaccessible to
wheelchairs users.
&. ⌐ 🚗 🛏 🍵 ›)

15 64 CARR WOOD
Hale Barns, Altrincham, WA15 0EP.
Mr David Booth. *10m S of
Manchester city centre. 2m from J6
M56: Take A538 to Hale Barns. L at
'triangle' by church into Wicker Lane
& L at mini r'about into Chapel Lane
& 1st R into Carr Wood.* **Sat 18 May
(1-5). Adm £5, chd free. Home-
made teas.**
²⁄₃ acre landscaped, south facing
garden overlooking Bollin valley laid
out in 1959 by Clibrans of Altrincham.
Gently sloping lawn, woodland
walk, seating areas and terrace,
extensive mixed shrub and plant
borders. Ample parking on Carr
Wood. Wheelchair access to terrace
overlooking main garden.
&. ❋ 🍵 🕑 ›)

16 NEW CHINOOK COTTAGE
96 Westminster Road,
Macclesfield, SK10 3AJ. Miss Sara
Wreford. *1m NW of Macclesfield.*

From Sainsburys r'about, turn L
directly after Sainsburys entrance.
*The garden is down on the R, opp
West Park/ Cemetery. There is more
free parking at Bollinbrook shops
just further along.* **Sat 15 June
(12-4.30). Adm £4, chd free. Light
refreshments. Pimms & wine.**
A mature enclosed cottage garden
of flowers, edibles and fruit trees.
Patio screened by bamboo, ferns,
crocosmia, foxgloves, poppies,
pieris, lychnis and many pots. Lawn
surrounded by mature trees and
perennials. Mediterranean themed
summerhouse. Long border of
rhubarb, currants and berries. Front
beds inc astrantia, iris, daphne,
campsis. Small greenhouse enables
propagation for 2 raised beds in side
garden. Lots of seating areas to enjoy
refreshments and Pimms. Mainly lawn
with some inclines.
&. ❋ 🍵

17 ◆ CHOLMONDELEY CASTLE
GARDENS
Cholmondeley, Malpas,
SY14 8AH. The Cholmondeley
Gardens Trust, 01829 720203,
eo@chol-estates.co.uk,
www.cholmondeleycastle.com.
*4m NE of Malpas SatNav SY14
8ET. Signed from A41 Chester-
Whitchurch road & A49 Whitchurch-
Tarporley road.* **For NGS: Thur
2 May (10-5). Adm £9, chd £5.
For other opening times and
information, please phone, email or
visit garden website.**
Discover the romantic Temple
and Folly Water Gardens, Glade,
Arboretum, 100m long double
herbaceous border walkway Lavinia
Walk, ornamental woodland upon
Tower Hill and the newly created
Cholmondeley Rose Garden with
250 rose varieties. Large display of
daffodils. Magnificent magnolias.
One of the finest features of the
gardens are its trees, many of which
are rare and unusual, Cholmondeley
Gardens is home to over 40 county
champion trees. Fresh coffee, lunches
and cakes daily with locally sourced
products located in the heart of the
Gardens. Partial wheelchair access.
&. ⌐ 🚗 🍵 🛏 ›)

18 18 DEE PARK ROAD
Dee Park Road, Wirral,
CH60 3RQ. Mrs Shay & Mr Les
Whitehead, 07778 309671,
shaywhitehead@gmail.com.
*Heswall. J4 off M53. Follow signs for
Brimstage, Heswall, follow to end.*

Turn L at r'about, take 1st L onto
A540 to Chester, 1st R down Gayton
Lane. Dee Park is on the bottom L.
**Sun 16, Wed 19, Sun 23 June (11-
5). Adm £5, chd free. Home-made
teas. Visits also by arrangement
10 June to 12 July. Refreshments
will be available.**
A long suburban garden backing onto
private woodland. Mature garden
laid to lawns, with mixed borders,
leading on to numerous seating
areas. The garden features a very
unusual triple hexagonal greenhouse,
which was originally purchased from
the Liverpool Garden Festival site,
c1984, before taking you through to
a shaded wooded area where there
are numerous different types of hosta
on display. Wheelchair accessible with
one step to negotiate.
&. ⌐ ❋ 🍵

19 DRAKE CARR
Mudhurst Lane, Higher Disley,
SK12 2AN. Alan & Joan Morris.
*8m SE of Stockport, 10m NE of
Macclesfield. From A6 in Disley
centre turn into Buxton Old Rd, go
up hill 1m & turn R into Mudhurst
Lane. After ¹⁄₃ m park on layby or
grass verge. No parking at garden.
Approx 150 metre walk.* **Sat 8, Sun
9 June (11-5). Adm £5, chd free.
Home-made teas and gluten-free
cakes.**
¹⁄₂ acre cottage garden in beautiful
rural setting with natural stream
running into wildlife pond with many
native species. Surrounding C17
stone cottage, the garden, containing
borders, shrubs and vegetable plot, is
on several levels divided by grassed
areas, slopes and steps. This blends
into a boarded walk through bog
garden, mature wooded area and
stream-side walk into a wildflower
meadow.
❋ 🍵 ›)

20 NEW 24 EASTERN ROAD
Willaston, Nantwich, CW5 7HT. Mr
Roger & Mrs Rosemary Murphy.
*1m E of Nantwich. From A51
Nantwich bypass follow sign into
Willaston at Crewe Rd R'about. At
the T junction turn R over the level
Xing then immed turn L into Eastern
Rd, garden is approx 100yds on R.*
**Sun 9 June (11-4). Adm £4.50, chd
free. Home-made teas.**
South facing garden evolved over
the last 4yrs, mixed herbaceous
borders include trees, shrubs and
climbers, raised bed, small vegetable
plot, seating areas, summerhouse,

greenhouse with succulent collection, pots and containers and other features.

21 THE FIRS

Old Chester Road, Barbridge, Nantwich, CW5 6AY. Richard & Valerie Goodyear. *3m N of Nantwich on A51. After entering Barbridge turn R at Xrds after 100 metres. The Firs is 2nd house on L.* **Sun 4 Aug (11-4). Adm £5, chd free. Light refreshments.**
Canalside garden set idyllically by a wide section of the Shropshire Union Canal with long frontage. Garden alongside canal with varied trees, shrubs and herbaceous beds, with some wild areas. All leading down to an observatory and Japanese torii gate at the far end of the garden with views across fields. Usually have nesting friendly swans with cygnets May to September. Wheelchair access to main areas and to all unless the lawns are wet/soft.

22 HATHAWAY

1 Pool End Road, Tytherington, Macclesfield, SK10 2LB. Mr & Mrs Cordingley. *2m N of Macclesfield, ½ m from The Tytherington Club. From Stockport follow A523 past the Butley Ash pub, at r'about turn R on A538 for Tytherington. From Knutsford follow A537 at A538, L for Tytherington. From Leek follow A523 at A537 L & 1st R A538.* **Sat 11, Sun 12 May (10.30-4). Adm £5, chd free. Light refreshments. Teas, coffee, cordial & cakes.**
South-west facing garden of approx ⅕ acre, laid out in two parts. Lawn area surrounded by mature, colourful perennial borders. Rose arbour. Our small pond has now become a large one, located in the lawn, with goldfish. Larger patio. Small mature wooded area with winding paths on a lower level. Front laid to lawn with 2 main borders separated by a small grass area. Good wheelchair access to most of garden except wood area.

23 HIGHBANK

110 Bradwall Road, Sandbach, CW11 1AW. Peter & Coral Hulland. *Approx 1m N of Sandbach town centre. The garden runs between Bradwall Rd & Twemlow Ave, but access & limited parking are on Twemlow Ave only (CW11 1GL).*

Sat 11, Sun 12 May (11-4). Adm £5, chd free. Light refreshments.
Beautiful town garden, designed by Peter an RHS Gold Medalist, originally a builders yard of approximately ⅓ acre. The current owners of 37 yrs have planted trees, many unusual shrubs and perennials, some being allowed to naturalise, encouraging biodiversity, wildlife and nesting birds. The garden is on different levels featuring lawns, a pond, water features, greenhouse and many seating areas.

24 NEW 166 HIGHER LANE

Lymm, WA13 0RG. Trevor Holland & Marian Bingham. *6m ESE of Warrington on E edge of Lymm, just off the A56. From M6, exit at J20, from M56 exit at J9 & follow signs to Lymm (B5158), R at T-junction onto A56 heading SE for 1.6m on Higher Lane. Park on Higher Ln, garden 50yds on Whiteleggs Ln.* **Sun 9 June (11-4.30). Adm £5, chd free. Home-made teas. Barista coffees, sweet & savoury baked goods.**
Garden plot 110'x 80' on Whiteleggs Lane off Higher Lane with summerhouse and orangery. Habitats and flowers for bees and wildlife. Wooded area of silver birch, maples, shrubs and pond, patio area with vine arbour and gravel garden, cottage garden with lawn and less mowed area for wild flowers. No parking on Whiteleggs Lane, parking only on Higher Lane on the side of the cottages.

25 213 HIGHER LANE

Lymm, WA13 0RN. Mark Stevenson, 07470 715007, mjs.stevenson@btinternet.com. *From M56 J7 follow signs for Lymm A56. The garden is approx 300 metres from the Jolly Thresher pub towards Lymm on R.* **Visits by arrangement 1 Apr to 27 Oct for groups of up to 20. Adm £4, chd free. Home-made teas.**
Established on an acre of grounds, segregated into various planting schemes. Herbaceous borders, specimen rhododendrons, hydrangeas, ferns and grasses, gingers and subtropical plants, along with so much more. A pond complete with fish and waterfalls surrounded by Japanese acers with far reaching views across fields and woodland. Many rare and unusual plants and

shrubs with wooded pathways. 70% of the garden is accessible to wheelchair users.

26 18 HIGHFIELD ROAD

Bollington, Macclesfield, SK10 5LR. Mrs Melita Turner. *3m N of Macclesfield. A523 to Stockport. Turn R at B5090 r'about signed Bollington. Pass under viaduct. Take next R (by Library) up Hurst Lane. Turn R into Highfield Rd. Property on L. Park on wider road just beyond.* **Sat 22, Sun 23 June (10-4.30). Adm £4.50, chd free. Home-made teas.**
This small terraced garden packed with plants was designed by Melita and has evolved over the past 16 yrs. This plantswoman is a plantaholic and RHS Certificate holder. An attempt has been made to combine formality through structural planting which is softened by cottage style planting of perennials.

27 HILL FARM

Mill Lane, Moston, Sandbach, CW11 3PS. Mrs Chris & Mr Richard House, 01270 526264, housecr2002@yahoo.co.uk. *2m NW of Sandbach. From Sandbach town centre take A533 towards Middlewich. After Fox pub take next L (Mill Lane) to a canal bridge & turn L. Hill Farm 400m on R just before post box.* **Sun 21 Apr, Sun 12 May, Sun 9 June (11-5). Adm £5, chd free. Home-made teas. Visits also by arrangement 1 Apr to 29 Sept.**
The garden extends to approx ½ acre and is made up of a series of gardens inc a formal courtyard with a pond and vegetable garden with south facing wall. An orchard and wildflower meadow were established about 6 yrs ago. A principal feature is a woodland garden which supports a rich variety of woodland plants. This was extended in April 2020 to include a pond and grass/herbaceous borders. A level garden, the majority of which can be accessed by wheelchair.

28 THE HOMESTEAD

2 Fanners Lane, High Legh, Knutsford, WA16 0RZ. Janet Bashforth, 07809 030525, janbash43@sky.com. *J20 M6/J9 M56 at Lymm interchange take A50 for Knutsford, after 1m turn R into Heath Lane then 1st R into Fanners Lane. Follow parking signs.* **Sun 23 June, Sun 21 July (11-4). Adm £5, chd free. Home-made teas. Visits also by arrangement 1 May to 30 Aug for groups of 10 to 40. Evening visits can be arranged with refreshments.**

This compact gem of a garden has been created over the last 8yrs by a keen gardener and plantswoman. Enter past groups of liquidambar and white stemmed birch. Colour themed areas with many perennials, shrubs and trees. Past topiary and obelisks covered with many varieties of clematis and roses, enjoy the colours of the hot border, a decorative greenhouse and pond complete the picture.

29 INGLEWOOD

4 Birchmere, Heswall, CH60 6TN. Colin & Sandra Fairclough, 07715 546406, sandrafairclough51@gmail.com. *6m S of Birkenhead. From A540 Devon Doorway/Clegg Arms r'about go through Heswall. ¼ m after Tesco, R into Quarry Rd East, 2nd L into Tower Rd North & L into Birchmere.* **Visits by arrangement for groups of 12 to 25. Adm £5, chd free. Home-made teas.**

Beautiful ½ acre garden with stream, large koi pond, 'beach' with grasses, wildlife pond and bog area. Brimming with shrubs, bulbs, acers, conifers, rhododendrons, herbaceous plants and hosta border. Interesting features inc hand cart, wood carvings, bug hotel and Indian dog gates leading to a secret garden. Lots of seating to enjoy refreshments.

30 60 KENNEDY AVENUE

Macclesfield, SK10 3DE. Bill North. *5min NW of Macclesfield town centre. Take A537 Cumberland St, 3rd r'bout (West Park) take B5087 Prestbury Rd. Take 5th turn on L into Kennedy Ave, last house on L before Brampton Ave opp Belong Care Home.* **Sun 9 June (12-5). Adm £5, chd free. Home-made teas.**

Small suburban garden which certainly packs a punch. The main part of the garden features herbaceous borders specifically to attract insects and pollinators. The upper part of the garden, redesigned over the past year, now features a generous waterfall, a number of Acers and a seating area where you can watch the birds feed and observe the 2 working bee hives. In addition visitors will be treated to music from American Country and Western Singer and Film Star Michael James. Wheelchair access will require a carer to guide up the drive and will only provide access to part of the garden.

2 Ashcroft Cottages

31 ◆ LANE END COTTAGE GARDENS

Old Cherry Lane, Lymm, WA13 0TA. Imogen Sawyer, 01925 752618, imogen@laneendcottagegardens.co.uk, www.laneendcottagegardens.co.uk. *1m SW of Lymm. J20 M6/J9 M56/A50 Lymm interchange. Take B5158 signed Lymm. Turn R 100 metres into Cherry Corner, turn immed R into Old Cherry Lane.* **For NGS: Sat 11, Sun 12 May, Sat 10, Sun 11 Aug (10-5). Adm £5, chd £2.50. Home-made teas. For other opening times and information, please phone, email or visit garden website.**

Formerly a nursery, this 1 acre cottage garden is densely planted for year-round colour with many unusual plants. Features include deep mixed borders, scented shrub roses, ponds, herb garden, walled orchard with trained fruit, shady woodland walk, sunny formal courtyard, vegetable garden and chickens. Wheelchair accessible WC. Park by garden entrance. Flat garden. Some bark paths may be difficult if wet.

&. ✿ 🚗 ☕ 🛋

32 LASKEY FARM

Laskey Lane, Thelwall, Warrington, WA4 2TF. Howard & Wendy Platt, 07785 262478, howardplatt@lockergroup.com, www.laskeyfarm.com. *2m from M6/M56. From M56/M6 follow directions to Lymm. At T-junction turn L onto the A56 in Warrington direction. Turn R onto Lymm Rd. Turn R onto Laskey Lane.* **Sun 5, Mon 6, Sun 26, Mon 27 May, Sat 20, Sun 21 July, Sun 25, Mon 26 Aug (11-4). Adm £6, chd £1. Home-made teas. Visits also by arrangement May to Aug for groups of 20 to 50. Joint group visits may be arranged with 10 Statham Avenue.**

1½ acre garden inc herbaceous and rose borders, vegetable area, a greenhouse, parterre and a maze showcasing grasses and prairie style planting. Interconnected pools for wildlife, specimen koi and terrapins form an unusual water garden which features a swimming pond. There is a treehouse plus a number of birds and animals. Family friendly, we offer a treasure hunt, and a mini menagerie consisting of chickens, guinea fowl and guinea pigs. Most areas of the garden may be accessed by wheelchair.

&. 🐕 ✿ 🚗 ☕ 🛋

33 ◆ THE LOVELL QUINTA ARBORETUM

Swettenham, CW12 2LF. Tatton Garden Society, 01565 831981, admin@tattongardensociety.org.uk, www.lovellquintaarboretum.co.uk. *4m NW of Congleton. Turn off A54 N 2m W of Congleton or turn E off A535 at Twemlow Green, NE of Holmes Chapel. Follow signs to Swettenham. Park at Swettenham Arms. What3words app - twins.sheds.keepers.* **For NGS: Sun 13 Oct (2-4). Adm £5, chd free. For other opening times and information, please phone, email or visit garden website.**

This 28 acre arboretum has been established since the1960s and contains around 2,500 trees and shrubs, some very rare. National Collections of Quercus, Pinus and Fraxinus. A large selection of oak, a private collection of hebes plus autumn flowering, fruiting and colourful trees and shrubs. Waymarked walks. Refreshments at the Swettenham Arms during licensed hours or by arrangement. With care wheelchairs can access much of the arboretum on the mown paths.

&. 🐕 🚗 NPC

34 MANLEY KNOLL

Manley Road, Manley, WA6 9DX. Mr & Mrs James Timpson. *3m N of Tarvin. On B5393, via Ashton & Mouldsworth. 3m S of Frodsham, via Alvanley.* **Sun 19 May (12-5). Adm £5, chd free. Home-made teas.**

Arts & Crafts garden created in the early 1900s. Covering 6 acres, divided into different rooms encompassing parterres, clipped yew hedging, ornamental ponds and herbaceous borders. Banks of rhododendron and azaleas frame a far-reaching view of the Cheshire Plain. Also a magical quarry/folly garden with waterfall and woodland walks.

🐕 ✿ ☕ 🛋

35 MILFORD HOUSE FARM

Long Lane, Wettenhall, Winsford, CW7 4DN. Chris & Heather Pope, 07887 760930, hclp@btinternet.com. *3m E of Tarporley. From A51 at Alpraham turn R into Long Lane. Proceed for 2½m to St David's Church on L. Milford House Farm is 150 metres further on L. Park at church or those with limited mobility can park at house.* **Sat 13 July (12-5). Adm £4, chd free. Home-made teas in marquee at garden. Gluten free,**

dairy free, vegan options. Visits also by arrangement 17 June to 12 July for groups of 5 to 35. Group refreshments, lunches etc, by arrangement.

A large country garden created over 21 yrs with lawn, mixed borders, hot, white, pastel and Zen areas. Modern walled garden for vegetables and fruit, greenhouse, potting shed, dahlias, wall shrubs and exotics, succulents, tender plants, water feature. Orchard for fruit, native, ornamental trees. Wildlife pond with toads and newts. Gardened on organic lines to increase biodiversity and attract wildlife. Picnics in orchard. Visits by arrangement can inc woodland walks (weather dependent) Children's activities. Walled garden has gravel and flags. Accessible WC at church.

&. 🐕 ✿ 🚗 ☕ 🛋 🍴 🔊

36 NEW THE MILL HOUSE

South Downs Drive, Hale, Altrincham, WA14 3HS. Mr Anthony & Mrs Margaret Preston. *The Mill House is on L at the end of a short cul-de-sac.* **Sun 30 June (10-4). Adm £5, chd free. Light refreshments. No picnics.**

An urban garden of ¾ acre, established in 2019. Herbaceous border to the west, rose pergolas, enclosed yard with greenhouse and potager garden. Designed by Jane Fearnley-Whttingstall. Site is mainly level with some gravel paths and ramped steps.

&. ☕

The National Garden Scheme's final instalment to support the building of the Y Bwthyn NGS Macmillan Specialist Palliative Care Unit in Wales, enabled 270 inpatients to be supported this year

37 ◆ MOUNT PLEASANT
Yeld Lane, Kelsall, CW6 0TB.
Dave Darlington & Louise
Worthington, 01829 751592,
louisedarlington@btinternet.com,
www.mountpleasantgardens.co.uk.
*8m E of Chester. Off A54 at T-lights
into Kelsall. Turn into Yeld Lane opp
Farmers Arms pub, 200yds on L. Do
not follow SatNav directions.* **For NGS:
Sun 2 June, Sun 1 Sept (11-4). Adm
£7, chd £5. Tea. For other opening
times and information, please phone,
email or visit garden website.**
10 acres of landscaped garden
and woodland started in 1994
with impressive views over the
Cheshire countryside. Steeply
terraced in places. Specimen trees,
rhododendrons, azaleas, conifers,
mixed and herbaceous borders; 4
ponds, formal and wildlife. Vegetable
garden, stumpery with tree ferns,
sculptures, wildflower meadow and
Japanese garden. Bog garden, tropical
garden. Sculpture trail and exhibition.
✿ 🚗 ☕

38 ◆ NESS BOTANIC GARDENS
Neston Road, Ness, Neston,
CH64 4AY. The University of
Liverpool, 0151 795 6300,
nessgdns@liverpool.ac.uk, www.
liverpool.ac.uk/ness-gardens. *10m
NW of Chester. Off A540. M53 J4,
follow signs M56 & A5117 (signed
N Wales). Turn onto A540 follow
signs for Hoylake. Ness Gardens
is signed locally. 487 bus takes
visitors travelling from Liverpool,
Birkenhead etc.* **For NGS: Tue
17 Sept (10-5). Adm £7.50, chd
£3.50. Light refreshments in Café
in the Visitor Centre. For other
opening times and information,
please phone, email or visit garden
website.**
Looking out over the dramatic
views of the Dee estuary from a
lofty perch on the Wirral peninsula,
Ness Botanic Gardens boasts 64
acres of landscaped and natural
gardens overflowing with horticultural
treasures. With a delightfully peaceful
atmosphere, a wide array of events
taking place, plus a café and
gorgeous open spaces it is a great
fun-filled day out for all the family.
National Collections of Sorbus and
Betula. Herbaceous borders, Rock
Garden, Mediterranean Bank, Potager
and conservation area. Wheelchairs
are available free to hire (donations
gratefully accepted) but advance
booking is highly recommended.
♿ ✿ 🚗 NPC ☕

39 NEW INN FARM
Buxton New Road, Rainow,
Macclesfield, SK11 0AD. Mark
& Louise Simms. *2½m NE
Macclesfield on A537 Macclesfield
to Buxton road. Car parking at One
House Walled Garden, 500m walk
to New Inn Farm. Drop off possible,
disabled parking for 2-3 cars.* **Sat
15, Sun 16 June (9.30-5). Adm £5,
chd free. Home-made teas.**
Beautiful cottage style garden
constructed on hillside with
spectacular views to the Welsh Hills
and Cheshire Plain, ⅓ acre garden
leading from stone flagged patio, with
natural stone trough to lawned area.
Established herbaceous borders inc
rhododendrons, azaleas and mature
trees. Paths leading to wildlife pond,
greenhouse and newly planted wildlife
garden inc folly and cairn.
☕))

40 NORLEY BANK FARM
Cow Lane, Norley, Frodsham,
WA6 8PJ. Margaret & Neil
Holding, 07828 913961,
neil.holding@hotmail.com. *Near
Delamere forest. From the Tigers
Head pub in the centre of Norley
village keep the pub on L, carry
straight on through the village for
approx 300 metres. Cow Lane is on
the R.* **Sun 21, Sun 28 July, Mon
5 Aug (11-5). Adm £6, chd free.
Home-made teas. Some allergy
free refreshments available. Visits
also by arrangement 15 July to 11
Aug for groups of 10+.**
Wander past a flower meadow before
entering the main garden. Here
well-stocked herbaceous borders
wrap around this traditional Cheshire
farmhouse. Within an orchard are
enclosed cut flower borders that
surround a greenhouse and just
beyond the house lies a vegetable
garden. Wander past this to 2 wildlife
ponds with a backdrop of pollinating
flowers and stumpery. All set in 2
acres. Free range hens, donkeys
and Coloured Ryeland sheep. WC
available. Access in the main is
possible for wheelchairs (though not
the WC). There are some stone steps
and a small number of narrow paths.
♿ 🐴 ✿ 🚗 ☕))

41 NORLEY COURT
Marsh Lane, Norley,
Frodsham, WA6 8NY. Clare
Albinson, 07717 447465,
Albinsonc@hotmail.com. *20 mins
E of Chester. Close to Delamere
Forest. A556 - Stoneyford Ln/*
*Cheese Hill/Cow Ln - L then R. A49
Acton Ln/Station Rd L at church next
R into Marsh Ln. Norley Ct is top of
hill. Parking on nearby roads or in
field at bottom of steep hill.* **Sun 12,
Sun 26 May (11-5). Adm £6, chd
free. Home-made teas. Visits also
by arrangement 27 Apr to 23 June
for groups of 5 to 15. Visits from
2pm onwards. Nibbles/soft drinks/
wine served.**
Norley Court is a large spring garden
with rhododendrons, azaleas, pieris,
a bluebell wood and embothyriums
flowering against a backdrop of North
Cheshire views. A variety of trees are
planted along the banks, inc cornus,
a handkerchief tree, Judas trees,
sorbus, an *Arbutus unedo* and others.
There is sloped access to most areas
of the garden, though some are quite
steep and grassed. Drop off at house
for those with limited mobility.
♿ ✿ ☕))

42 6 OAKLAND VALE
New Brighton, Wallasey,
CH45 1LQ. Ian Butler & Charles
Stringer, 07808 162697,
ianbut@btinternet.com. *On
Magazines Promenade, New
Brighton. J1 M53 , signs to New
Brighton attractions on A554. R at
Morrisons r'about, up hill on A554.
L at Vaughan Rd, down to river.
Park before river. No cars on prom.
Oakland Vale on L facing river.* **Visits
by arrangement 20 Aug to 31
Aug for groups of up to 15. Open
only on last two Tuesdays and
Saturdays of August. Individuals
welcome. Adm £4, chd free.
Home-made teas.**
A very small walled town garden
densely filled with tropical and exotic
style plants. Bananas, tree ferns,
cordylines and bamboo along with
tetrapanax and paulownia form the
backdrop to more unusual 'exotic'
plants and a pond. The terraced front
garden overlooking the Mersey is filled
with grasses, ferns, phormiums and
echiums along with drought tolerant
plants. Located on Magazines
Promenade offering interesting river/
beach walks with dockland and
Liverpool views; close to Vale Park.
☕

43 THE OLD BYRE
Sound Lane, Sound, Nantwich,
CW5 8BE. Gill Farrington. *11m
from J16 from Nantwich signs for
A530 Whitchurch. At Sound School
take 1st R Wrenbury Heath Rd.
Parking at garden for visitors with*

limited mobility. Additional parking at Sound Manor a short walk away. **Sat 13, Sun 14 July (10-4). Adm £4, chd free. Home-made teas. Open nearby Sound Manor.**
5 acre working smallholding. 4 acres used for grazing and beehives, the rest is garden with a large cider apple orchard, wildlife pond, vegetable and cutting garden patch, herbaceous borders, poultry and sheep. We aim to be wildlife friendly and re-use and recycle everything we can, hence some weedy and untidy areas where items are stored ready to be re-used or incorporated into a new project. We produce up to 2 tons of cider apples a year which are used by a local cider maker just 3 miles away. Homemade crafts using recycled materials will be on sale inc yarn made from the fleece of our Ouessant sheep.

44 24 OLD GREASBY ROAD
Upton, Wirral, CH49 6LT. Lesley Whorton & Jon Price. *Approx 1m from J2A M53 (Upton bypass). M53 J2 follow Upton sign. At r'about (J2A) straight on to Upton bypass. At 2nd r'about, turn L by Upton Cricket Club. 24 Old Greasby Rd is on L.* **Sun 23 June (11-4). Adm £4, chd free. Home-made teas.**
A multi-interest and surprising suburban garden. Both front and rear gardens incorporate innovative features designed for climbing and rambling roses, clematis, underplanted with cottage garden plants with a very productive kitchen garden. Garden transformed from a boggy, heavily-clayed and flood-damaged suburban garden to a peaceful and productive location.

45 NEW THE OLD PARSONAGE
Stable Lane, Cotebrook, Tarporley, CW6 0JL. Nick Parker & Lesley Boyle. *2m N of Tarporley on A49. From A49 turn into Utkinton Lane. After 150 yds turn L onto Stable Lane. After 150 yds turn into Cotebrook Village Hall car park situated on R. Gardens are directly opp.* **Sat 29, Sun 30 June (10.30-4.30). Adm £7, chd free. Home-made teas at Cotebrook Village Hall. WC at the hall.**
Presented as a collaboration between owners and RHS Award winning garden designer, Jane Bingham. The garden intends to give false perspective and incorporates

meandering lawned and gravel paths between borders with rare and unusual plants. Incorporating wildlife and koi ponds surrounded by aquatic planting, lilies, hostas and gunnera. A veranda and 3 gazebos with roses and climbers. Main driveway and access is gently sloping gravel. Access to the lawned area is by a steeper but manageable grassed area.

46 THE OLD PARSONAGE
Back Lane, Arley Green, Northwich, CW9 6LZ. The Hon Rowland & Mrs Flower, www.arleyhallandgardens.com. *5m NNE of Northwich. 3m NNE of Great Budworth. M6 J19 & 20 & M56 J10. Follow signs to Arley Hall & Gardens. From Arley Hall follow signs to Old Parsonage which lies across park at Arley Green (approx 1m).* **Sat 25, Sun 26 May (2-5). Adm £6, chd free. Home-made teas.**
2 acre garden in attractive and secretive rural setting in secluded part of Arley Estate, with ancient yew hedges, herbaceous and mixed borders, shrub roses, climbers, leading to woodland garden and unfenced pond with gunnera and water plants. Rhododendrons, azaleas, meconopsis, cardiocrinum, some interesting and unusual trees. Wheelchair access over mown grass, some slopes and bumps and rougher grass further away from the house.

47 ONE HOUSE WALLED GARDEN
off Buxton New Road, Rainow, SK11 0AD. Louise Baylis. *2½m NE of Macclesfield. Just off A537 Macclesfield to Buxton road. 2½m from Macclesfield Station.* **Sat 15, Sun 16 June (10-5). Adm £5, chd free. Home-made teas.**
An historic early C18 walled kitchen garden, hidden for 60 yrs and restored by volunteers. This romantic and atmospheric garden has a wide range of vegetables, flowers and old tools. There is an orchard with friendly pigs, a wildlife area and pond, woodland walk with wildflowers and foxgloves and views and a traditional greenhouse with ornamental & edible crops. Small plant nursery.

48 15 PARK CRESCENT
Appleton, Warrington, WA4 5JJ. Linda & Mark Enderby. *2½m S of Warrington. From M56 J10 take A49 towards Warrington for 1½m. At 2nd set of lights turn R into Lyons Lane, then 1st R into Park Crescent. No15 is last house on R.* **Thur 6, Sun 30 June (11.30-5). Adm £5, chd free. Home-made teas. Prosecco.**
An abundant garden containing many unusual plants, trees and a mini orchard. A cascade, ponds and planting encourage wildlife. There are raised beds, many roses in various forms and herbaceous borders. The garden has been split into distinct areas on different levels each with their own vista drawing one through the garden. You never know what is around the next hedge! Many unusual plants and a good example of planting under a lime tree in clay soil and shade.

49 PARM PLACE
12 High Street, Great Budworth, CW9 6HF. Jane Fairclough, 07770 612915, janefair@btinternet.com. *3m N of Northwich. Great Budworth on E side of A559 between Northwich & Warrington, 4m from J10 M56, also 4m from J19 M6. Parm Place is W of village on S side of High St.* **Sun 7 Apr, Sun 7 July (1-5). Adm £5, chd free. Visits also by arrangement. Donation to Great Ormond Street Hospital.**
Well-stocked ½ acre plantswoman's garden with stunning views towards south Cheshire. Curving lawns, parterre, shrubs, colour coordinated herbaceous borders, roses, water features, rockery, gravel bed with some grasses. Fruit and vegetable plots. In spring large collection of bulbs and flowers, camellias, hellebores and blossom.

The National Garden Scheme donated £3,403,960 to our nursing and health beneficiaries from money raised at gardens open in 2023

50 PARVEY LODGE
Parvey Lane, Sutton, Macclesfield, SK11 0HX. Mrs Tanya Walker, 07789 528093, tanya.v.walker@gmail.com. *In the heart of the village of Sutton, we are close to Fairways Garden Centre, Sutton Hall & Sutton PO.* **Sat 18 May, Sat 19 Oct (11-4). Adm £5, chd free. Home-made teas. Light refreshments. Visits also by arrangement for groups of 10+.** A beautiful privately owned 3 acre garden with different areas to explore. Formal garden, Himalayan Cedar majestically situated at the front of the house, plenty of acer, fruit trees, shaped box hedge, tennis court lawn, lots of bulbs, snowdrops, daffodils. rhododendron and camellia, birds and wildlife (deer). Best to visit in spring and late autumn. Most of the garden is wheelchair friendly.

&. 🐾 🍵))

51 ◆ PEOVER HALL GARDENS
Over Peover, Knutsford, WA16 9HW. Mr & Mrs Brooks, 01565 654107, bookings@peoverhall.com, www.peoverhall.com. *4m S of Knutsford. Do not rely on SatNav. From A50/Holmes Chapel Rd at Whipping Stocks pub turn onto Stocks Lane. Follow R onto Grotto Ln ¼ m turn R onto Goostrey Ln. Main entrance on R on bend through white gates.* **For NGS: Sat 18, Sun 19 May (2-5). Adm £7, chd free. Cream teas in the Park House Tea Room. For other opening times and information, please phone, email or visit garden website.** The extensive formal gardens to Peover Hall feature a series of 'garden rooms' filled with clipped box, water garden, Romanesque loggia, warm brick walls, unusual doors, secret passageways, beautiful topiary work and walled gardens, rockery, rhododendrons and pleached limes. Peover Hall, a Grade II* listed Elizabethan family house dating from 1585, provides a fine backdrop. The Grade I listed Carolean Stables, which are of significant architectural importance, will be open to view. Tours of Peover Hall will also be available over the weekend with Mr & Mrs Brooks. Partial wheelchair access to garden - wheelchair users please ask the car-park attendant for parking on hard standing rather than on the grass.

&. 🐾 ✿ 🚗 🍵))

52 ◆ POULTON HALL
Poulton Lancelyn, Bebington, Wirral, CH63 9LN. The Poulton Hall Estate Trust & Poulton Hall Walled Garden Charitable Trust, 07836 590875, info@poultonhall.co.uk, www.poultonhall.co.uk. *2m S of Bebington. From M53, J4 towards Bebington; at T-lights R along Poulton Rd; house 1m on R.* **For NGS: Sat 30, Sun 31 Mar (2-5). Adm £6, chd free. Cream teas may be booked in advance via our website. For other opening times and information, please phone, email or visit garden website.** A quirky garden which children love. 3 acres, lawns fronting house, wildflower meadow. Surprise approach to walled garden, with reminders of Roger Lancelyn Green's retellings, Excalibur, Robin Hood and Jabberwock. Memorial sculpture for Richard Lancelyn Green by Sue Sharples. Rose, nursery rhyme, witch, herb and oriental gardens and Memories Reading room. Restored Excalibur garden. Level gravel paths. Separate wheelchair access (not across parking field). Disabled WC.

&. 🐾 ✿ 🍵))

> National Garden Scheme gardens are identified by their yellow road signs and posters. You can expect a garden of quality, character and interest, a warm welcome and plenty of home-made cakes

53 ◆ RODE HALL
Church Lane, Scholar Green, ST7 3QP. Randle & Amanda Baker Wilbraham, 01270 873237, enquiries@rodehall.co.uk, www.rodehall.co.uk. *5m SW of Congleton. Between Scholar Green (A34) & Rode Heath (A50).* **For opening times and information, please phone, email or visit garden website.** Nesfield's terrace and rose garden with stunning view over Humphry Repton's landscape is a feature of Rode, as is the woodland garden with terraced rock garden and grotto. Other attractions inc the walk to the lake with a view of Birthday Island complete with heronry, restored ice house, working 2 acre walled kitchen garden and Italian garden. Fine display of snowdrops in Feb and bluebells in May. Snowdrop walks in February. Bluebell walks in May. Summer: Weds and Bank Hol Mons until end of Sep, 10-5. Courtyard Kitchen offering wide variety of homemade cakes and lunches.

🐾 ✿ 🚗 🍵

54 ROSE BRAE
Earle Drive, Parkgate, Neston, CH64 6RY. Joe & Carole Rae. *11m NW of Chester. From A540 take B5134 at the Hinderton Arms towards Neston. Turn R at the T- lights in Neston & L at the Cross onto Parkgate Rd, B5135. Earle Drive is ½ m on R.* **Sun 21 July (1.30-4.30). Adm £5, chd free. Home-made teas.** An all season, half acre garden comprising bulbs, trees, shrubs, perennials and climbers. In July roses, clematis, hydrangeas, phlox and agapanthus predominate together with ferns, grasses, flowering trees, topiary, a bulb lawn and a formal pool with water lilies.

✿ 🍵))

55 ROSEWOOD
Old Hall Lane, Puddington, Neston, CH64 5SP. Mr & Mrs C E J Brabin, 0151 353 1193, angela. brabin@btinternet.com. *8m N of Chester. From A540 turn down Puddington Lane, 1½ m. Park by village green. Walk 30yds to Old Hall Lane, turn L through archway into garden.* **Visits by arrangement 1 Jan to 28 Dec for groups of up to 40. Adm £4, chd free. Tea.** Year-round garden; thousands of snowdrops in Feb, camellias in autumn, winter and spring.

The Mill House

Rhododendrons in April/May and unusual flowering trees from March to June. Autumn cyclamen in quantity from Aug to Nov. Perhaps the greatest delight to owners are 2 large *Cornus capitata*, flowering in June. Bees kept in the garden. Honey sometimes available.

56 ROWLEY HOUSE

Forty Acre Lane, Kermincham, Holmes Chapel, CW4 8DX. Tim & Juliet Foden. *3m ENE from Holmes Chapel. J18 M6 to Holmes Chapel, then take A535 (Macclesfield). Take R turn in Twemlow (Swettenham) at Yellow Broom restaurant. Rowley House ½m on L.*

Sun 26 May, Sun 7 July (11-4.30). Adm £6, chd free. Home-made teas.
Our aim is to give nature a home and create a place of beauty. There is a formal courtyard garden and informal gardens featuring rare trees, and herbaceous borders, a pond with swamp cypress and woodland walk with maples, rhododendrons, ferns and shade-loving plants. Beyond the garden there are wildflower meadows, natural ponds and a wood with ancient oaks. Also wood sculptures by Andy Burgess. Many unusual plants and trees, also many areas dedicated to wildlife. Leaflet provided with map and details of garden.

57 SANDYMERE

Middlewich Road, Cotebrook, CW6 9EH. Sir John Timpson, rme2000@aol.com. *5m N of Tarporley. On A54 approx 300yds W of T-lights at Xrds of A49/A54.* **Sun 9 June (12-4). Adm £7, chd free. Home-made teas. Visits also by arrangement 29 Apr to 31 July.**
16 landscaped acres of beautiful Cheshire countryside with terraces, walled garden, extensive woodland walks and an amazing hosta garden. Turn each corner and you find another gem with lots of different water features inc a rill built in 2014, which links the main lawn to the hostas. Look out for our new Japanese themed garden. Partial wheelchair access.

58 SOMERFORD

19 Leycester Road, Knutsford, WA16 8QR. Emma Dearman & Joe Morris. *1m from centre of Knutsford. Somerford is opp Leycester Close. Park on Leycester Rd or Legh Rd with consideration to local residents.* **Sun 28 Apr (11-4); Sun 7 July (10-4). Adm £5, chd free. Home-made teas.**

Majestic trees surround this 1½ acre garden. Hard landscaping and sculptures complement lush herbaceous and perennial borders. Lawns are separated by a magnificent oak pergola. Cube-headed hornbeams lead into the snail-trail walk and informal lawn and fernery. Most of the garden is accessible by wheelchair. Phone 07984 311352 for further information.

59 SOUND MANOR

Wrenbury Heath Road, Sound, Nantwich, CW5 8BT. Gill & Richard Ratcliffe. *5 minutes drive from the A530 Nantwich to Whitchurch road. Our drive is next to a line of bollards.* **Sat 13, Sun 14 July (10-4). Adm £5, chd free. Open nearby The Old Byre. Refreshments avail at The Old Byre, a 5 minute walk away.**

Our 0.4 acre country garden is within our 10 acre equestrian property. The garden wraps around an old farmhouse festooned with climbers. The part cobbled yard is lined with pots of summer bedding and tender perennials. There is a raised alpine bed, a large ornamental pond and a bog garden. The overflowing mixed borders have specimen trees, shrubs, perennials and magnificent *Stipa gigantea* grasses.

60 10 STATHAM AVENUE

Lymm, WA13 9NH. Mike & Gail Porter, 07951 606906, porters@mikeandgailporter. co.uk, www.youtube.com/watch?v=53zmVWfZa-s. *Approx 1m from J20 M6 /M56 interchange. From M/way follow B5158 to Lymm. Take A56 Booth's Hill Rd, L towards Warrington, R on to Barsbank Lane, pass under bridge, 50mtrs turn R onto Statham Ave. No 10 is 100mtrs on R. What 3 Words app - smallest. plump.snooze.* **Sat 27, Sun 28 Apr, Sat 1, Sun 2, Wed 19 June (11-4). Home-made teas. Fri 5 July (2-8). Wine. Sat 6 July (11-4). Home-made teas. Adm £5, chd free.**

Enjoy Gail's famous meringues with fresh fruit & cream. Visits also by arrangement 30 Apr to 31 Aug for groups of 10 to 30. Coach parking in front of the garden. Beautifully structured ¼ acre south facing terraced garden rising to the Bridgewater towpath. Hazel arch opens to clay paved courtyard with peach trees and kitchen herb bed. Rose pillars lead to lush herbaceous beds and tranquil shaded areas, vibrant azaleas and rhododendrons in spring, peaceful, pastel shades in early summer and hydrangeas, fuchsias in late summer. Interesting garden buildings. A treasure hunt/quiz to keep the children occupied. Delicious refreshments to satisfy the grown ups. On Friday July 5th there will be tasty savouries & a glass of wine.

61 ◆ STONYFORD COTTAGE

Stonyford Lane, Oakmere, CW8 2TF. Janet & Tony Overland, 01606 888970, info@stonyfordcottagegardens.co.uk, www.stonyfordcottagegardens.co.uk. *5m SW of Northwich. From Northwich take A556 towards Chester. ¾m past A49 junction turn R into Stonyford Lane. Entrance ½m on L.* **For NGS: Sun 5 May (11-4). Adm £5, chd free. Home-made teas in our Tea Room. For other opening times and information, please phone, email or visit garden website.**

Set around a tranquil pool, this Monet style landscape has a wealth of moisture loving plants, inc iris and *Candelabra primulas*. Drier areas feature unusual perennials, rarer trees and shrubs. Woodland paths meander through shade and bog plantings, along boarded walks, across wild natural areas with views over the pool to the cottage gardens. Unusual plants available at the adjacent nursery. Open Tues - Fri, Apr - Oct 10-5pm. Some gravel paths.

62 NEW SWINEYARD HALL

Swineyard Lane, High Legh, Knutsford, WA16 0RY. Mr John & Mrs Victoria Fenton. *Between Knutsford & Lymm. Swineyard Lane is off the A50 opp the Bears Paw pub. Swineyard Hall is on L left after 1km.* **Sun 19 May, Sun 16 June (11-4). Adm £4, chd free. Light refreshments.**

The gardens extend to 2 acres including the Moat, listed as a national monument dating back to C13. Our priorities with this ongoing project have been to include English country garden borders and specimen trees alongside the old roses, rhododendron, azaleas and horizontal willow trees. Established oak trees, hornbeam, chestnut and copper beach to name a few complete the scene.

63 TATTENHALL HALL

High Street, Tattenhall, Chester, CH3 9PX. Jen & Nick Benefield, Chris Evered & Jannie Hollins, 01829 770654, janniehollins@gmail.com. *8m S of Chester on A41. Turn L to Tattenhall, through village, turn R at Letters pub, past War Memorial on L through sandstone pillared gates. Park on road or in village car park.* **Sun 2 June (2-5). Adm £6, chd free. Home-made teas. Visits also by arrangement 1 Apr to 30 July.**

Plant enthusiasts' garden around Jacobean house (not open). 4½ acres, wildflower meadows, interesting trees, large pond, stream, walled garden, colour themed borders, succession planting, spinney walk with shade plants, yew terrace overlooking meadow, views to hills. Glasshouse and vegetable garden. Wildlife friendly, sometimes untidy garden, interest year-round, always developing. Extensive collection of plants. Partial wheelchair access due to gravel paths, cobbles and some steps.

64 THORNCAR

Windmill Lane, Appleton, Warrington, WA4 5JN. Mrs Kath Carey, 01925 267633, john. carey516@btinternet.com. *South Warrington. From M56 J10 take A49 towards Warrington for 1½m. At 2nd set of T-lights turn L into Quarry Ln, as the road swings R it becomes Windmill Ln. Thorncar is 4th house on R.* **Sat 3 Aug (10-4). Adm £4.50, chd free. Visits also by arrangement 31 Mar to 31 Oct for groups of 5 to 15.**

⅓ acre plantwoman's suburban garden planted since 2011 within the framework of part of an older garden to provide year-round interest. Each month has its plants of interest. The plants grown have to survive in poor sandy soil with no watering even during hot spells. An area in shade has been given a makeover and planted up with trilliums and other shade lovers.

65 TIRESFORD

Tarporley, CW6 9LY. Susanna Posnett, 07989 306425. *Tiresford is on an A49 Tarporley bypass. It is adjacent to the farm on R leaving Tarporley in the direction of Four Lane Ends T-lights.* **Sun 12 May (2-5). Adm £5, chd free. Home-made teas. Ice-Cream.**
Established 1930s garden undergoing a major restoration project to reinstate it to its former glory. Fabulous views of both Beeston and Peckforton Castles offer a wonderful backdrop in which to relax and enjoy a delicious tea. This year we hope to realise our long term plan to recreate the kitchen garden and to repair the fountain amongst the new hot borders of the sunken garden. The house has been transformed into a stylish 6 bedroom B&B. There is parking for wheelchair users next to the house and access to a disabled WC in the house.

66 TIRLEY GARTH GARDENS

Mallows Way, Willington, Tarporley, CW6 0RQ. *2m N of Tarporley. 2m S of Kelsall. Entrance 500yds from village of Utkinton. At N of Tarporley take Utkinton road.* **Sun 12 May (1-5). Adm £5, chd free. Home-made teas.**
40 acre garden, terraced & landscaped, designed by Thomas Mawson who is considered the leading exponent of garden design in early C20. It is the only Grade II* Arts & Crafts garden in Cheshire that remains complete and in excellent condition. The gardens are an important example of an early C20 garden laid out in both formal and informal styles. By early May the garden is bursting into flower with almost 3000 rhododendron and azalea, many 100 yrs old. Art Exhibition by local Artists.

67 NEW TOFT GREEN FARM

Toft Green, Congleton, CW12 3QE. Mr John & Mrs Clare Pollard. *3½ m E of Congleton. Take A54 from Congleton. After 2.4m go over canal and R onto Middle Lane. Follow for 0.7m, past Key Green Chapel onto Pedley Lane. Go to top, L onto Tunstall road. Follow 0.8 m down hill,* garden on L. **Sat 29, Sun 30 June (11-4). Adm £6, chd free. Light refreshments.**
A country garden of 1½ acres surrounding an old farmhouse. A south facing garden to the front, lawns divided by herbaceous borders and a gravel path. Shrubs and grasses on the east and a vegetable garden with raised beds and soft fruit to the west. The old farmyard has an ornamental pond, a gravel garden and raised beds. The orchard is in a field with mown paths and a pond. Generally accessible. A few steps which can be avoided. Some grass and gravel paths but also large paved areas.

68 THE WELL HOUSE

Wet Lane, Tilston, Malpas, SY14 7DP. Mrs S H French-Greenslade, 01829 250332. *3m NW of Malpas. On A41, 1st R after Broxton r'about, L on Malpas Rd through Tilston. House on L.* **Visits by arrangement. Open in February for snowdrops and then until September. Adm £5, chd free. Pre-booked refreshments for small groups only.**
1 acre cottage garden, bridge over natural stream, spring bulbs, perennials, herbs and shrubs. Triple ponds. Adjoining ¾ acre field made into wildflower meadow; first seeding late 2003. Large bog area of kingcups and ragged robin. February for snowdrop walk. Victorian parlour and collector's items on show. Dogs on leads only.

69 WILLASTON GRANGE

Hadlow Road, Willaston, Neston, CH64 2UN. Anita & Mark Mitchell. *On A540 (Chester High Rd) take the B5151 into Willaston. From the village green in the centre of Willaston turn onto Hadlow Rd, Willaston Grange is ½ m on L.* **Sat 15 June (12-5). Adm £6, chd free. Home-made teas.**
Willaston Grange is an Arts & Craft property. 14 yrs ago the house and gardens had been derelict for 3 yrs. After months of detailed planning, the significant restoration work began. The gardens extend to 6 acres with a small lake, wide range of mature and rare tree species, herbaceous border, woodland and vegetable gardens, orchard and magical treehouse. The fully restored Arts & Crafts house provides the perfect backdrop for a summer visit, along with afternoon tea and live music. Most areas accessible by wheelchair.

70 THE WONKY GARDEN

Ditton Community Centre, Dundalk Road, Widnes, WA8 8DF. Mrs Angela Hayler, 07976 373979, thewonkygarden@gmail.com, en-gb.facebook.com/thewonkygarden/. *From the Widnes exit of the A533 turn L (Lowerhouse La) then L at the r'about. The Community Centre is ½ m up on the R. The garden is behind the Centre.* **Sun 9 June, Sun 14 July (11.30-3.30). Adm £5, chd free. Home-made teas. Visits also by arrangement Apr to Oct.**
The flower garden is our show garden, the focus for horticultural therapy/nature based activities. It has large herbaceous borders, trees and shrubs, planting focussing on the senses and wildlife. We grow masses of edibles and cut flowers in the allotment garden, 80% is donated to support food poverty. The children's 'explorify' garden nestles between the two and is used to support young families. The garden is designed and managed by a wonderful group of volunteers. We support many community groups and individuals of all ages and abilities inc schools, colleges and work experience. Our focus is on supporting physical and mental health, isolation and loneliness. An accessible path (1½ metres wide) extends from the car park through the herbaceous and children's nature garden and into the allotment.

In 2023 we awarded over £260,000 in Community Garden Grants, supporting 86 community garden projects

CUMBRIA

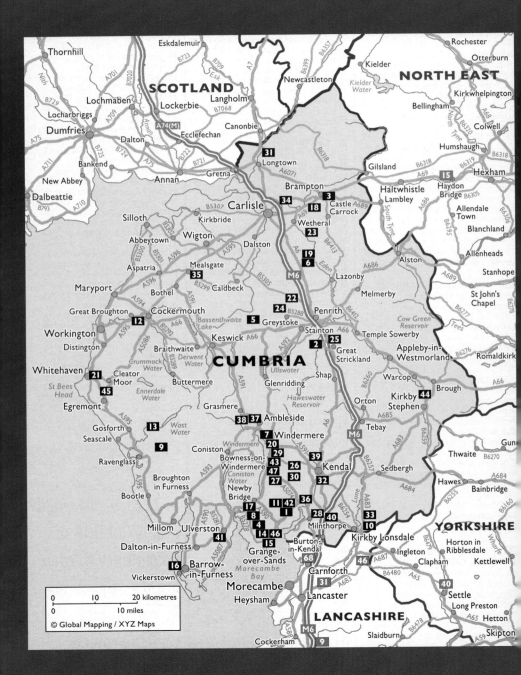

VOLUNTEERS

County Organiser
Alannah Rylands
01697 320413
alannah.rylands@ngs.org.uk

County Treasurer
Cate Bowman
01228 573903
cate.bowman@ngs.org.uk

Publicity – Social Media
Gráinne Jakobson
01946 813017
grainne.jakobson@ngs.org.uk

Booklet Co-ordinator
Cate Bowman
01228 573903
cate.bowman@ngs.org.uk

Assistant County Organisers
Carole Berryman
07808 974877
carole.berryman@outlook.com

Bruno Gouillon
01539 532317
brunog45@hotmail.com

Sarah Byrne
015395 34405
sarah.byrne@ngs.org.uk

Gráinne Jakobson (as above)

Christine Davidson
07966 524302
christine.davidson@ngs.org.uk

Belinda Quigley
07738 005388
belinda.quigley@ngs.org.uk

f @CumbriaNGS
@CumbriaNGS
@ngscumbria

OPENING DATES

All entries subject to change.
For latest information check
www.ngs.org.uk
Map locator numbers are
shown to the right of each
garden name.

March

Friday 1st
◆ Swarthmoor Hall 41

Sunday 24th
◆ Holehird Gardens 20
◆ Rydal Hall 37
NEW ◆ Rydal Mount and
Gardens 38

Tuesday 26th
Haverthwaite Lodge 17

Saturday 30th
Hazel Cottage 19

Sunday 31st
Hazel Cottage 19

April

Monday 1st
NEW ◆ Rydal Mount and
Gardens 38

Tuesday 2nd
NEW ◆ Rydal Mount and
Gardens 38

Wednesday 3rd
NEW ◆ Rydal Mount and
Gardens 38

Saturday 20th
Park House 33

Sunday 21st
Park House 33
◆ Rydal Hall 37

Sunday 28th
Summerdale House 40

May

Saturday 4th
Coombe Eden 6

Sunday 5th
Coombe Eden 6
Low Fell West 27

Monday 6th
Low Fell West 27

Sunday 12th
Low Crag 26

Sunday 19th
Hayton Village Gardens 18
Matson Ground 29

Thursday 23rd
Haverthwaite Lodge 17

Saturday 25th
Galesyke 13
27 Haverigg Gardens 16
Hazel Cottage 19
Lower Rowell Farm & Cottage 28

Sunday 26th
Galesyke 13
27 Haverigg Gardens 16
Hazel Cottage 19
Lower Rowell Farm & Cottage 28
Sprint Mill 39
Summerdale House 40

June

Sunday 2nd
Brampton East Gardens 3
Quarry Hill House 35
Sprint Mill 39
Windy Hall 43
Yewbarrow House 46

Tuesday 4th
Cragwood Country House Hotel 7

Sunday 9th
Chapelside 5
Fernhill Coach House 11
NEW ◆ Rydal Mount and
Gardens 38
NEW Vicarage House East 42

Monday 10th
NEW ◆ Rydal Mount and
Gardens 38

Tuesday 11th
NEW ◆ Rydal Mount and
Gardens 38

Wednesday 12th
NEW ◆ Rydal Mount and
Gardens 38

Friday 14th
◆ Swarthmoor Hall 41

Saturday 15th
◆ Swarthmoor Hall 41

Sunday 16th
Askham Hall   2
◆ Hutton-In-The-Forest   22
◆ Swarthmoor Hall   41
Yews   47

Saturday 22nd
Esk Bank   9

Sunday 23rd
Esk Bank   9
Ivy House   23

Sunday 30th
5 Primrose Bank   34

July

Thursday 4th
◆ Holehird Gardens   20

Sunday 7th
Chapelside   5
Winton Park   44
Yewbarrow House   46

Thursday 11th
Larch Cottage Nurseries   25

Saturday 20th
27 Haverigg Gardens   16
Haverthwaite Lodge   17

Sunday 21st
NEW Cartmel Gardens   4
27 Haverigg Gardens   16
◆ Rydal Hall   37

August

Saturday 3rd
Holly House   21

Sunday 4th
Grange Fell Allotments   14
Holly House   21
Yewbarrow House   46

Monday 5th
Cragwood Country House Hotel   7

Thursday 8th
Larch Cottage Nurseries   25

Sunday 11th
Abi and Tom's Garden Plants   1
Ivy House   23

Saturday 17th
Galesyke   13

Sunday 18th
Fell Yeat   10
Galesyke   13
◆ Rydal Hall   37

Monday 19th
Fell Yeat   10

Tuesday 20th
Fell Yeat   10

Wednesday 21st
Fell Yeat   10

Thursday 22nd
Fell Yeat   10

Friday 23rd
Fell Yeat   1(

Saturday 24th
Fell Yeat   1(

Monday 26th
◆ Netherby Hall   3

Saturday 31st
Middle Blakebank   3(
Woodend House   4!

September

Sunday 1st
Woodend House   4!
Yewbarrow House   4(

Thursday 5th
Larch Cottage Nurseries   2!

Saturday 14th
Haverthwaite Lodge   1

October

Sunday 20th
Low Fell West   2

By Arrangement

Arrange a personalised garden visit
with your club, or group of friends,
on a date to suit you. See individua
garden entries for full details.

Coombe Eden
Crumble Cottages   8
Esk Bank
Fernhill Coach House   1
NEW Foinhaven   1:
Galesyke   1:
Grange Fell Allotments   1
Grange over Sands Hidden
   Gardens   1!
Haverthwaite Lodge   1
Ivy House   2
NEW Johnby Hall   2
Low Fell West   2
Lower Rowell Farm & Cottage   2
Matson Ground   2!
Middle Blakebank   3
8 Oxenholme Road   3:
5 Primrose Bank   3
Rose Croft   3
Sprint Mill   3
Woodend House   4!
Yewbarrow House   4
Yews   4

Johnby Hall

THE GARDENS

1 ABI AND TOM'S GARDEN PLANTS

Halecat, Witherslack, Grange-over-Sands, LA11 6RT. Abi & Tom Attwood, www.abiandtom.co.uk. *20 mins from Kendal. From A590 turn N to Witherslack. Follow brown tourist signs to Halecat. Rail Grange-over-sands 5m, Bus X6 2m, NCR 70.* **Sun 11 Aug (10-5). Adm £4.50, chd free. Home-made teas.**
The 1 acre nursery garden is a fusion of traditional horticultural values with modern approaches to the display, growing and use of plant material. Our full range of perennials can be seen growing alongside one another in themed borders be they shady damp corners or south facing hot spots. The propagating areas, stock beds and family garden, normally closed to visitors, will be open on the NGS day. More than 1,000 different herbaceous perennials are grown in the nursery, many that are excellent for wildlife. For other opening times and information please visit our website. Sloping site that has no steps but steep inclines in places.

2 ASKHAM HALL

Askham, Penrith, CA10 2PF. Charles Lowther, 01931 712350, askhamhall@askhamcollection. co.uk, www.askhamhall.co.uk. *5m S of Penrith. Turn off A6 for Lowther & Askham.* **Sun 16 June (11.30-7). Adm £6, chd free. Light refreshments. Donation to Askham & Lowther Churches.**
Askham Hall is a Pele Tower incorporating C14, C16 and early C18 elements in a courtyard plan. Opened in 2013 with luxury accommodation, a restaurant, outdoor heated pool and wedding barn. Splendid formal garden with terraces of herbaceous borders and topiary, dating back to C17. Meadow area with trees and pond, kitchen gardens and animal trails. Café serving wood-fired pizzas, cakes, hot & cold drinks with indoor & outdoor seating.

GROUP OPENING

3 BRAMPTON EAST GARDENS

Brampton, CA8 1EX. *Gardens located at the eastern side of Brampton, between the Co-op. & the top of Station Rd. Parking around the Sands & Lanercost Rd area of Brampton. Community garden & Sands Terrace are to the W of the sands. A map will be provided on entry to the first garden.* **Sun 2 June (1-5). Combined adm £5, chd free. Visitors can picnic at the Community Garden, weather permitting. The Sands grassed area can also be used for picnics which also has a roofed shelter.**

NEW   25 EDMONDSON CLOSE
CA8 1GH. Mrs Penny Young.

LOVER'S LANE COMMUNITY GARDEN
CA8 1TN. Ms Julia Turnton, www.facebook.com/ Loverslanecommunitygarden.

NEW   RIDGE HOUSE
CA8 1EN. Mrs Vita Collins.

NEW   6 SANDS COTTAGES
CA8 1UQ. Ms Jane Streames.

NEW   WOODLANDS
CA8 1EX. Mr & Mrs Potter.

A selection of gardens of differing sizes and styles. 25 Edmondson Close, created from scratch 12 yrs ago, features a productive organic veg area, espaliered apples, soft fruit, area set aside for wildlife inc small pond, greenhouse, ornamental pond and herbaceous borders. Ridge House is well established, with mature trees around a house built in 1833; in a traditional setting with relaxed naturalistic planting with self-seeders positively encouraged. Lover's Lane is a Community Garden currently with around 40 members. Their aim is to be inclusive and organic, and experiment with new ways of gardening in trial beds. 6 Sands Cottages is a communal back lane behind terraced cottages which has been transformed into a lovely space. Woodlands is a unique 3/4 acre sloped garden with far reaching views and has been newly developed over the last 3 yrs.

GROUP OPENING

4 NEW   CARTMEL GARDENS

Barn Garth, Cartmel, Grange-over-Sands, LA11 6PP. Linda Crabtree. *Gardens in the village of Cartmel approx 2m from Grange Over Sands & approx 3m from the A590 eastbound. Free parking at Cartmel Primary School, Aynsome Rd, LA11 6PR.* **Sun 21 July (10.30-4.30). Combined adm £7.50, chd free. Home-made teas at Laburnum Cottage.**

NEW   GREENCROFT
LA11 6PT. Charles & Bunty Godwin.

NEW   LABURNUM COTTAGE
LA11 6PP. David & Linda Crabtree.

NEW   THE ROWANS
LA11 6PH. Philip & Sandra Pascall.

A group of 3 diverse gardens in the lovely medieval village of Cartmel, all within easy reach of one another. Greencroft is a garden of parkland with various species of trees with herbaceous borders. Lawns divided by the River Ea with a backdrop to the stunning C12 Priory Church. At the rear of the house is the coach house courtyard showcasing urns and evergreen plants. Laburnum Cottage is a small, compact walled garden with views of the C12 Priory Church. The garden is in 3 parts; small front to the roadside, rear garden planted with a cottage style approach and a side garden with raised cutting flower beds and vegetables. Shrubs, clematis, perennials and a variety of pots with a collection of hostas. The Rowans is a beautiful garden of shrubs and herbaceous plants around 4 lawns with a large selection of pots many containing hostas. The Flow Beck bisects the rear garden. Various seating areas and a summerhouse take advantage of the sun and views to the fells.

5 CHAPELSIDE
Mungrisdale, Penrith, CA11 0XR. Tricia & Robin Acland. *12m W of Penrith. On A66 take minor rd N signed Mungrisdale (no NGS sign till turned!). After 2m, sharp bends, garden on L after tiny church on R. Use church car park at foot of our short drive.* **Sun 9 June, Sun 7 July (1-5). Adm £5, chd free.**
1 acre, windy garden below fell, round C18 farmhouse and outbuildings. Fine views. Tiny stream, large pond. Herbaceous, gravel, alpine and shade areas, bulbs in grass. Wide range of plants, many unusual. Relaxed planting regime, lively plant combinations. Run on organic lines. Art constructions in and out, local stone used creatively. Good teas available nearby.

6 COOMBE EDEN
Armathwaite, Carlisle, CA4 9PQ. Belinda & Mike Quigley, 07738 005388, Belinda.quigley@ngs.org.uk. *8m SE of Carlisle. Turn off A6 just S of High Hesket signed Armathwaite. Continue to bottom of hill where garden can be found on R turn for Lazonby.* **Sat 4, Sun 5 May (12-5). Adm £5, chd free. New to Coombe Eden, cream teas & home-made cakes. Visits also by arrangement 4 May to 30 June. Refreshments for groups must be pre-booked and are limited to 20.**
A large, 1 acre garden of traditional and contemporary beds. A pretty beck runs through the lower garden with a Japanese style bridge and large rhododendrons. Many choice trees can be seen throughout the garden, Japanese acers, white birches and a growing rowan collection. A long herbaceous border, grassed areas and gravelled paths lead to a formal garden and potager.

7 CRAGWOOD COUNTRY HOUSE HOTEL
Ecclerigg, Windermere, LA23 1LQ. David Williams, 015394 88177, info@cragwoodhotel.co.uk. www.lakedistrictcountryhotels.co.uk/cragwood-hotel. *Leave the M6 at J36 & follow the A591 for 15m until you see Cragwood signed on the L. Cragwood is immed before the National Park Visitor Centre at Brockhole.* **Tue 4 June, Mon 5 Aug (11-4.30). Adm £5, chd free. Light refreshments can be enjoyed** either in one of our lounges or outside on our terrace.
The gardens at Cragwood Country House are an integral part of the property's rich history and charm. The gardens were originally designed in the late C19 by the renowned landscape architect Thomas Hayton Mawson, who was known for his work in the Lake District and other parts of England. Mawson created a beautiful formal garden with carefully manicured lawns, elegant flower beds, and striking topiary, as well as a peaceful woodland walk and a charming rock garden. Over the years, the gardens have been carefully maintained and developed, with new features and plantings added to enhance their beauty and appeal. Today, the gardens at Cragwood are a highlight of any visit to the property, offering a tranquil and picturesque setting in which to relax and explore. There is a gradual slope to the left of reception. Also some gravel paths.

8 CRUMBLE COTTAGES
Beckside, Cartmel, LA11 7SP. Sarah Byrne & Stewart Cowe, 015395 34405, sarah@crumblecottages.co.uk, www.crumblecottages.co.uk. *Beckside Cartmel. 1m from Cartmel up past the racecourse on the Haverthwaite Rd. Car Sat Nav brings you directly here but best to avoid mobile phone Sat Nav which may take you up the wrong lane.* **Visits by arrangement May to Sept for groups of 20+. Home-made teas.**
Ornamental cottage garden using a variety of different colour schemes with topiary surround our C17 listed Cumbrian Longhouse. The remaining 4 acres are divided into a Water garden with ponds and rewilded areas designed to improve biodiversity, Kitchen garden using companion planting within listed bee bole wall, wildflower meadows, butterfly borders, cut flower beds and woodland walks. Wheelchair access to ornamental areas by house and outlying areas of garden but only by a wheelchair that can cope with uneven ground.

9 ESK BANK
Eskdale Green, Holmrook, CA19 1UE. Pooja & Adrian Norton, 07947 146737, esk.bank@btinternet.com. *Take the A595 to Holmrook, turn off on the rd to Eskdale Green. Park at the Green Station. By train to Ravenglass for Eskdale, then take La'al Ratty steam train to the Green Station.* **Sat 22 June (11-5); Sun 23 June (11-4). Adm £5, chd free. Home-made teas. Visits also by arrangement 1 June to 1 Sept for groups of 10 to 30.**
Nestled in Eskdale, the ¾ acre cottage-style garden is on a south-facing slope with 360 panoramic views of the valley. There is a mix of perennial beds and herbaceous borders with many roses and shrubs inc rhododendrons, magnolia and azaleas. There is a summerhouse and a large kitchen garden with a greenhouse. The sloping lawns have an orchard, wildflower borders and a small pond. Public WC available in Eskdale Green village next to shop.

10 FELL YEAT
Casterton, Kirkby Lonsdale, LA6 2JW. Mrs A E Benson. *1m E of Casterton village. On the road to Bull Pot. Leave A65 at Devils Bridge, follow A683 for 1m, take the R fork to High Casterton at golf course, straight across at 2 sets of Xrds, house on L, ¼m from no-through-rd sign.* **Sun 18 Aug (11-5). Daily Mon 19 Aug to Sat 24 Aug (11-4.30). Adm £4, chd free.**
One acre garden the largest part of which was started 35 yrs ago. Planted with many unusual trees, shrubs and large collection of hydrangeas. Increasingly the emphasis is on encouraging wildlife and creating a wilder feel. A wonderful breeding ground for owls, sparrow hawks and buzzards. Enjoy the meandering paths, fernery, maturing stumpery and new grotto house with rocks and ferns. Adjoining nursery specialising in ferns, hostas, hydrangeas and many unusual plants.

11 FERNHILL COACH HOUSE
Bleacragg Road, Witherslack, Grange-over-Sands, LA11 6RX. Adele & Mike Walford, 015395 52102, mwandaj@icloud.com. *Country road, ½m beyond Halecat & Abi and Tom's Garden Plants. From A590 turn N to Witherslack. Follow brown signs to Halecat, continue along Bleacragg Rd for ½m. Fernhill on L. Rail to Grange-over-sands Bus X6 - 2m walk, NCR 70. Roads & parking are not suitable for coaches.* **Sun 9 June (10-4). Combined**

adm with Vicarage House East £6, chd free. Home-made teas at Vicarage House East. Tea, coffee, apple juice, scones and bicuits at Fernhill. Visits also by arrangement 9 June to 30 Sept for groups of up to 20. Not suitable for coaches.

Cottage garden; mixed borders, vegetables, greenhouse, orchard, small ponds, roses. Organic and biodiverse. We propagate cottage garden plants and grow and sell heritage and northern fruit trees and produce apple juice. Witherslack Orchard Group apple juice, damson and apple juice. Numerous apple trees for sale. Wheelchair access to flower garden only. Paths are uneven and on sloping ground.

12 NEW FOINHAVEN
Brigham, Cockermouth, CA13 0SY. Bill Wheeler, 01900 827921, junebill1@gmail.com. *2m W Cockermouth. Leave Cockermouth on A5086 & turn R at r'about on A66. 1st L for Brigham, Foinaven 100y on L after 30mph sign.* **Visits by arrangement May to Sept for groups of up to 10. Adm £4, chd free. Light refreshments.**

Cottage style, small garden in a village location. Densely planted around a chalet bungalow on sloping, half-acre site. Wide range of small trees, shrubs and perennials. Pond, bog garden, rockeries and camomile lawn. Parking on site. Partial wheelchair access.

&. ☕

13 GALESYKE
Wasdale, CA20 1ET. Christine McKinley, 01946 726267, mckinley2112@sky.com. *In Wasdale valley, between Nether Wasdale village & the lake. From Gosforth, follow signs to Nether Wasdale & then to lake, approx 5m. From Santon Bridge follow signs to Wasdale then to lake, approx 2¼ m.* **Sat 25, Sun 26 May, Sat 17, Sun 18 Aug (10-5). Adm £5, chd free. Cream teas. Visits also by arrangement 11 May to 31 Aug.**

4 acre garden combining formal areas, shrubberies and woodland, dissected by the River Irt which can be crossed by a suspension bridge. In spring the garden is vibrant with azaleas and rhododendrons, in summer by an impressive collection of colourful hydrangeas. Set in the heart of the Wasdale valley the garden has an unforgettable backdrop of

the Screes and the high Lakeland fells. There is a magnificent Victorian sandstone sundial in the garden.

14 GRANGE FELL ALLOTMENTS
Fell Road, Grange-over-Sands, LA11 6HB. Mr Bruno Gouillon, 01539 532317, brunog45@hotmail.com. *Opp Grange Fell Golf Club. Rail 1.3m, Bus 1m X6, NCR 70.* **Sun 4 Aug (11-4). Adm £4.50, chd free. Light refreshments. Visits also by arrangement 1 May to 30 Aug for groups of 10 to 40.**

The allotments are managed by Grange Town Council. Opened in 2010, 30 plots are now rented out and offer a wide selection of gardening styles and techniques. The majority of plots grow a mixture of vegetables, fruit trees and flowers. There are a few communal areas where local fruit tree varieties have been donated by plot holders with herbaceous borders and annuals.

GROUP OPENING

15 GRANGE OVER SANDS HIDDEN GARDENS
Grange-over-Sands, LA11 7AF. Bruno Gouillon, 01539 532317, brunog45@hotmail.com. *Off Kents Bank Rd, 3 gardens on Cart Lane then last garden up Carter Rd for Shrublands. Rail 1.4m; Bus X6; NCR 70.* **Visits by arrangement May to Aug for groups of 10 to 40. Combined adm £5.50, chd free. Tea. Donation to St Mary's Hopsice.**

21 CART LANE
Veronica Cameron.

ELDER COTTAGE
Bruno Gouillon & Andrew Fairey.

HAWTHORNE COTTAGE
Mrs Carroll Ashton.

SHRUBLANDS
Jon & Avril Trevorrow.

4 very different gardens hidden down narrow lanes off the road south out of Grange. Off Kents Bank Road, 3 gardens on Cart Lane all back onto the railway embankment, providing shelter from the wind but also creating a frost pocket. The garden at 21 Cart Lane is a series of rooms designed

to create an element of surprise with fruit and vegetables in raised beds. Elder Cottage is an organised riot of fruit trees, vegetables, shrubby perennials and herbaceous plants. Productive and peaceful. Hawthorne Cottage has been redesigned and replanted over the last 2 yrs to create a garden with colour and interest. Up the hill on Carter Rd, Shrublands is a ¾ acre garden situated on a hillside overlooking Morecambe Bay. Visitors with mobility issues can access Shrublands & 21 Cart Ln, but can only view Elder Cottage from the roadside & Hawthorne Cottage from the gate.

&. ☕ ♪))

16 27 HAVERIGG GARDENS
North Scale, Walney, Barrow-in-Furness, LA14 3TH. Jo & Brendan Sweeney. *North end of Walney Island. A590 to Walney Island, R at end of the bridge, continue on through N Scale. We are the last road before the airport. Additional parking at N Scale Community Centre.* **Sat 25, Sun 26 May, Sat 20, Sun 21 July (11-4). Adm £4, chd free. Light refreshments.**

Relaxing 300ft cottage style garden backing on to sheep fields with views to Blackcombe and the Coniston hills. Designed to be wildlife friendly and cope with the exposed site and salt laden winds for which Walney is renowned. Wildlife pond, woodland area, herbaceous borders, vegetable and fruit beds, two summerhouses and many seating areas; plus a slate scree front garden.

&. ☕ ♪))

The National Garden Scheme searches the length and breadth of England, Wales, Northern Ireland and the Channel Islands for the very best private gardens.

Coombe Eden

17 HAVERTHWAITE LODGE
Haverthwaite, LA12 8AJ. David
Snowdon, 015395 30022,
office@dstrust.org.uk. *100yds off
A590 at Haverthwaite. Turn S off
A590 opp Haverthwaite train stn.
Bus 6, NCR 70. Parking on the
roadside at the top of the drive. No
vehicle access on the drive except
for those with mobility aids.* **Tue 26
Mar, Thur 23 May, Sat 20 July, Sat
14 Sept (11-4). Adm £5, chd free.
Visits also by arrangement.**
Traditional Lake District garden that
has been redesigned and replanted.
A series of terraces lead down to the
River Leven and wooded area. Inc a
rose garden, cutting garden, dell area,
rock terrace, herbaceous borders
and many interesting mature shrubs.
Although unsuitable for wheelchairs
or those using mobility aids, visitors
may view the garden from the terrace.
In a stunning setting the garden is
surrounded by oak woodland and
was once a place of C18 and C19
industry.

GROUP OPENING

18 HAYTON VILLAGE GARDENS
Hayton, Brampton, CA8 9HR.
Facebook.HaytonOpenGardens.
*5m E of M6 J43 at Carlisle, ½ m S
of A69. 3m W of Brampton. Signed
to Hayton off A69. Narrow roads:
Please park 1 side only & if poss
park less centrally leaving space
for less able near pub. Tickets
sold in E of village (Townhead),
W & middle with map. Map also
available on Facebook.* **Sun 19
May (12-5). Combined adm £5,
chd free. Home-made teas at
Hayton Village Primary School,
often with live music. Also
cold refreshments in one of
the gardens outside if suitable.
Donation to Hayton Village Primary
School.**

ARNWOOD
Joanne Reeves-Brown.

BECK COTTAGE
Fiona Cox.

THE GARTH
Frank O'Connor & Linda Mages.

**HAYTON C OF E PRIMARY
SCHOOL**
Hayton C of E Primary School,
www.hayton.cumbria.sch.uk.

HEMPGARTH
Sheila & David Heslop.

HOPE COTTAGE
Adam & Samantha Grant.

KINRARA
Tim & Alison Brown,
Facebook.KinraraOpenGardens.

MILLBROOK
M & J Carruthers.

TOWNFOOT HOUSE
Alison Springall.

TOWNHEAD COTTAGE
Chris & Pam Haynes.

A valley of quality gardens of very
varied size and styles mostly around
old stone cottages. Smaller and

larger cottage gardens, courtyards and containers, woodland walks, exuberant borders, frogs, pools, colour and texture throughout. Spring bluebells, azaleas and wisteria. Home-made teas and sometimes live music at the school where the children create gardens annually within the main school garden (RHS award). Gardens additional to those listed also generally open or visible. Kinrara is designed by an artist and an architect with multiple garden design experience. Accessibility ranges from full to none. Furthest gardens require a half-mile walk (and back) or extra driving. Come early or late for easier parking.

& ✳ ☕

19 HAZEL COTTAGE
Armathwaite, Carlisle, CA4 9PG. Mr D Ryland & Mr J Thexton. *8m SE of Carlisle. Turn off A6 just S of High Hesket signed Armathwaite, after 2m house facing you at T-junction. $1^1/_4$ m walk from Armathwaite train stn.* **Sat 30, Sun 31 Mar, Sat 25, Sun 26 May (12-5). Adm £5, chd free. Home-made teas.**

Flower arrangers and plantsman's garden. Extending to approx 5 acres. Inc mature herbaceous borders, pergola, ponds and planting of disused railway siding providing home to wildlife. Many variegated and unusual plants. Varied areas, planted for all seasons, south facing, some gentle slopes, ever changing. Partial access for wheelchair users, small steps to WC area. Main garden planted on gentle slope.

& 🐕 ✳ 🚗 ☕

20 ◆ HOLEHIRD GARDENS
Patterdale Road, Windermere, LA23 1NP. Lakeland Horticultural Society, 015394 46008, enquiries@ holehirdgardens.org.uk, www.holehirdgardens.org.uk. *1m N of Windermere. On A592, Windermere to Patterdale road.* **For NGS: Sun 24 Mar, Thur 4 July (10-4). Adm by donation. Self-service hot drinks available for July opening only, not spring. For other opening times and information, please phone, email or visit garden website. Donation to Plant Heritage.**

Run by volunteers of the Lakeland Horticultural Society to promote knowledge of gardening in Lakeland conditions. On fellside overlooking Windermere, the 10 acres provide year-round interest. 6 National Collections plus collections of hydrangeas and roses. Walled garden hosts colourful mixed borders and island beds. Rock garden, alpine beds and display houses. Streamside garden. Spring bulbs. Regional Finalist, The English Garden Magazine's The Nation's Favourite Gardens 2023 Wheelchair access to walled garden and parts of fellside via accessible paths.

& ✳ NPC ☕ 🏓

21 HOLLY HOUSE
37 Holly Terrace, Hensingham, Whitehaven, CA28 8RF. Dave & Lynne Todhunter. *1m from Whitehaven Town Centre. A595 from N turn L at T-lights signed Hensingham follow B5295 to mini-r'about in Hensingham Sq take 1st exit, Holly House on L across road from Globe pub. Car park in Square/ Main St.* **Sat 3, Sun 4 Aug (12-5). Adm £5, chd free. Home-made teas.**

Tucked behind a large Grade II listed Georgian house, the gardens of Holly House are a hidden gem. Split into 3 sections they comprise the top garden with terrace, lawn and herbaceous borders. The middle garden has a hydrangea walk, formal rose garden, wildflower/orchard area, fruit and vegetable beds and large greenhouse. The woodland garden has some steep paths which may be muddy/slippy at times. Wheelchair access to most of the garden, apart from the woodland garden which is not suitable. 'Keep Clear' section at the front for drop off only.

& ✳ ☕

22 ◆ HUTTON-IN-THE-FOREST
Penrith, CA11 9TH. Lord & Lady Inglewood, 01768 484449, info@ hutton-in-the-forest.co.uk, www. hutton-in-the-forest.co.uk. *6m NW of Penrith. On B5305, 2m from exit 41 of M6 towards Wigton.* **For NGS: Sun 16 June (10-5). Adm £9, chd £2. Home-made teas. For other opening times and information, please phone, email or visit garden website.**

Hutton-in-the-Forest is surrounded on two sides by distinctive yew topiary and grass terraces - which to the south lead to C18 lake and cascade. 1730s walled garden is full of old fruit trees, tulips in spring, roses and an extensive collection of herbaceous plants in summer. Our gravel paths can make it difficult to push a wheelchair in places.

& 🐕 ✳ 🚗 ☕ 🏓

23 IVY HOUSE
Cumwhitton, CA8 9EX. Martin Johns & Ian Forrest, 01228 561851, martinjohns193@btinternet.com. *6m E of Carlisle. At the bridge at Warwick Bridge on A69 take turning to Great Corby & Cumwhitton. Through Great Corby & woodland until you reach a T-junction. Turn R into village.* **Sun 23 June, Sun 11 Aug (1-5). Adm £5, chd free. Light refreshments. Visits also by arrangement 1 Apr to 1 Sept.**

Approx 2 acres of sloping fellside garden with meandering paths leading to a series of 'rooms': inc pond, fern garden, Acer terrace, shrubberies, herbaceous borders and a vegetable and herb garden. Copse with meadow leading down to beck. Trees, shrubs, ferns, grasses, bamboos, evergreens and perennials planted with emphasis on variety of texture and colour. Sadly unsuitable for wheelchairs. WC available.

🐕 🚗 ☕

24 NEW JOHNBY HALL
Johnby, Penrith, CA11 0UU. Henry & Anna Howard, 01768 483257, bookings@johnbyhall.com, www.johnbyhall.com. *Greystoke, Penrith. From Greystoke village green follow signs to Johnby, forking L as you leave the village. Gateway signed Johnby Hall after 1m on the L.* **Visits by arrangement 13 May to 18 June for groups of 10+. Mondays and Tuesdays. Max 15 cars. Coach parties possible; pls enquire. Light refreshments. Tea, coffee & cakes or biscuits.**

Large, very informal and natural mature garden around an ancient manor house. Intriguing courtyards are full of wild flowers and old roses; the 1683 walled garden is now an orchard. Wildflower lawns and meadows in summer, a bluebell walk through the beginnings of a pinetum with some unusual young specimens, and a field of free-range rare-breed pigs.

🐕 🏛 ☕

Our donation to Marie Curie this year equates to 17,496 hours of nursing care

25 LARCH COTTAGE NURSERIES
Melkinthorpe, Penrith, CA10 2DR. Peter Stott, www.larchcottage.co.uk. *From N leave M6 J40 take A6 S. From S leave M6 J39 take A6 N signed off A6.* **Thur 11 July, Thur 8 Aug, Thur 5 Sept (1-4). Adm £5, chd free.**
A unique nursery and garden designed and built over the past 35 yrs. The gardens include lawns, flowing perennial borders, rare and unusual shrubs, trees, a small orchard and a kitchen garden. A natural stream runs into a small lake, a haven for wildlife and birds. At the head of the lake stands a small frescoed chapel designed and built by the owner for family use. Japanese dry garden, ponds and Italianesque columned garden specifically for shade plants. The Italianesque tumbled down walls are draped in greenery, acting as a backdrop for the borders filled with stock plants. Newly designed and constructed lower gardens and chapel. Accessible to wheelchair users although the paths are rocky in places.

26 LOW CRAG
Crook, Kendal, LA8 8LE. Chris Dodd & Liz Jolley. *Turn off B5284 opp Sun Inn. Pass Ellerbeck Farm on R, continue for ¼ m. Take the 3rd drive on L. Steep drive to large, flat yard. Note - SatNav takes you to Ellerbeck Farm.* **Sun 12 May (10-5). Adm £5, chd free. Light refreshments.**
A relaxed, wildlife friendly 2 acre farmhouse garden, designed and maintained on organic principles. Transitions from a formal garden, featuring yew hedges and herbaceous planting, through to a wildlife pond, arboretum, small vegetable garden, and an orchard, and out to meadows and the greater landscape. Long views with seating and viewpoints throughout. Some steep slopes and steps.

27 LOW FELL WEST
Crosthwaite, Kendal, LA8 8JG. Barbie & John Handley, 015395 68297, barbie@handleyfamily.co.uk. *4½ m S of Bowness. Off A5074, turn W just S of Damson Dene Hotel. Follow lane for ½ m.* **Sun 5 May (2-5); Mon 6 May (11-2); Sun 20**

Oct (11-4). Adm £5, chd free. Light refreshments. Visits also by arrangement for groups of up to 30. Coach park ½ a hilly mile away. Any group size down to singles welcome.
This 2 acre woodland garden in the tranquil Winster valley has extensive views to the Pennines. The four season garden, restored since 2003, inc expanses of rock planted sympathetically with grasses, unusual trees and shrubs, climaxing for autumn colour. There are native hedges and areas of plant rich meadows. A woodland area houses a gypsy caravan and there is direct access to Cumbria Wildlife Trust's Barkbooth Reserve of Oak woodland, bluebells and open fellside. Wheelchair access to much of the garden, but some rough paths and steep slopes.

28 LOWER ROWELL FARM & COTTAGE
Milnthorpe, LA7 7LU. John, Mavis & Sophie Robinson & Julie Welton, 015395 62270. *Approx 2m from Milnthorpe, 2m from Crooklands. Signed to Rowell off B6385, Milnthorpe to Crooklands Rd. Garden ½ m up lane on L.* **Sat 25, Sun 26 May (1-5). Adm £5, chd free. Light refreshments. Visits also by arrangement 3 June to 7 July for groups of 10 to 30.**
Approx 1¼ acre garden with views to Farleton Knott and Lakeland hills. Unusual trees and shrubs, plus perennial borders. Architectural pruning, greenhouse, polytunnel with tropical plants, cottage gravel garden and vegetable plot. Fabulous display of colour most of the year. New for 2024, NorthStar Botanical Flower Farm with a polytunnel and greenhouse.

29 MATSON GROUND
Windermere, LA23 2NH. Matson Ground Estate Co Ltd, 07831 831918, sam@matsonground.co.uk. *⅔ m E of Bowness. Turn N off B5284 signed Heathwaite. From E 100yds after Windermere Golf Club, from W 400yds after Windy Hall Rd. Rail 2½ m; Bus 1m, 6, 599, 755, 800; NCR 6 (1m).* **Sun 19 May (1-5). Adm £6.50, chd free. Home-made teas. Visits also by arrangement 8 Jan to 23 Dec for groups of 5 to 25. WC and parking available**

but no refreshments for groups. Picnics welcome.
2 acres of mature, south facing gardens. A good mix of formal and informal planting inc topiary features, herbaceous and shrub borders, wildflower areas, stream leading to a large pond and developing arboretum. Rose garden, rockery, topiary terrace borders, ha-ha. Productive, walled kitchen garden c1862, a wide assortment of fruit, vegetables, cut flowers, cobnuts and herbs. Greenhouse.

30 MIDDLE BLAKEBANK
Underbarrow, Kendal, LA8 8HP. Mrs Hilary Crowe, 07713 608963, hfcmbb@aol.com. *Lyth valley between Underbarrow & Crosthwaite. From Underbarrow take A5074 to Crosthwaite. The garden is on Broom Lane, a turning between Crosthwaite & Underbarrow signed Red Scar & Broom Farm What 3 words app - hampers.speedily. budget.* **Sat 31 Aug (11-4). Adm £5, chd free. Home-made teas. Visits also by arrangement 15 Apr to 31 Oct.**
The garden extends to 4½ acres and overlooks the Lyth valley with extensive views south to Morecambe Bay and east to the Howgills. We have orchards, a wildflower meadow and more formal garden with a range of outbuildings. Over the last 8 yrs the garden has been developed with plantings that provide varying colour and texture year-round. Some parts of the garden are accessed by steps. We enjoy providing home-made cakes and sandwiches - under cover in large barn if necessary!

31 ◆ NETHERBY HALL
Longtown, Carlisle, CA6 5PR. Mr Gerald & Mrs Margo Smith, 01228 792732, events@netherbyhall.co.uk, netherbyhall.co.uk/. *2m N of Longtown. Take Junction 44 from the M6 & follow the A7 to Longtown. Take Netherby Rd & follow it for about 2m. Netherby Hall is on L.* **For NGS: Mon 26 Aug (10-4). Adm £6, chd free. For other opening times and information, please phone, email or visit garden website.**
Netherby Hall Garden is 36 acres, consisting of a 1½ acre walled kitchen garden which produces fruit, vegetables and herbs for the Pentonbridge Inn restaurant, as well

as herbaceous borders, traditional kidney beds amongst wonderful lawns, woodlands with many fine specimen trees, azaleas and rhododendrons, all set in a designed landscape bordering the River Esk. Ample parking. Carriage paths allow access around the Victorian pleasure grounds & walled garden.

Nertherby Hall

© GJ May

32 8 OXENHOLME ROAD
Kendal, LA9 7NJ. **Mr John & Mrs Frances Davenport, 07496 029842, frandav8@btinternet.com.** *SE Kendal. From A65 (Burton Rd, Kendal/Kirkby Lonsdale) take B6254 (Oxenholme Rd). No.8 is 1st house on L beyond red post box.* **Visits by arrangement 11 May to 29 Sept for groups of 10+. Adm £5. Home-made teas.**
Artist and potter's garden of approx ½ acre of mixed planting designed for year-round interest, inc two linked small ponds. Roses, grasses and colour themed borders surround the house, with a gravel garden at the front, as well as a number of woodland plant areas, some vegetables, fruit and orchard areas and lots of sitting spaces. Designed to attract birds and insects. John is a ceramic artist and Frances is a painter and paintings and pots are a feature of the garden display. We offer tea, coffee, biscuits and cakes to eat at seating around garden. Garden essentially level, but access to WC is up steps.

33 PARK HOUSE
Barbon, Kirkby Lonsdale, LA6 2LG. **Mr & Mrs P Pattison.** *2½ m N of Kirkby Lonsdale. Off A683 Kirkby Lonsdale to Sedburgh road. Follow signs into Barbon Village.* **Sat 20, Sun 21 Apr (10.30-4.30). Adm £5, chd free. Cream teas.**
Romantic Manor House (not open). Extensive vistas. Formal tranquil pond encased in yew hedging. Meadow with meandering pathways, water garden filled with bulbs and ferns. Formal lawn, gravel pathways, cottage borders with hues of soft pinks and purples, shady border, kitchen garden. An evolving garden to follow.

34 5 PRIMROSE BANK
Crosby-on-Eden, Carlisle, CA6 4QT. **Mark & Cate Bowman, 01228 573903, cate.bowman@ngs.org.uk.** *3m NE of Carlisle off A689. From M6 J44 take A689 towards Hexham. At the next r'about take the 1st turn towards Brampton/Hexham. Take the 2nd turn on R to Crosby on Eden. Park at the village hall.* **Sun 30 June (12.30-4.30). Adm £4.50, chd free. Home-made teas. Visits also by arrangement 24 June to 15 July for groups of 10 to 40.**
A beautiful village garden overlooking the river Eden and Hadrian's Wall footpath. Gravel paths take you through several garden rooms featuring extensive vegetable garden, small orchard, rose garden, wildlife pond, wide mixed borders with espaliered crab apples on the boundary, rose clad pergolas and arches. Designed to be wildlife friendly. Gravel paths unsuitable for wheelchairs.

35 QUARRY HILL HOUSE
Boltongate, Mealsgate, Wigton, CA7 1AE. **Mr Charles Woodhouse & Mrs Philippa Irving.** *⅓ m W of Boltongate, 6m SSW of Wigton, 13m NW of Keswick, 10m E Cockermouth. M6 J41, direction Wigton, through Hesket Newmarket, Caldbeck & Boltongate on B5299, entrance gates to drive on R. On A595 Carlisle to Cockermouth turn L for Boltongate, Ireby.* **Sun 2 June (1.30-6). Adm £5, chd free. Home-made teas. Donation to Cumbria Community Foundation: Quarry Hill Grassroots Fund.**
3 acre parkland setting, country house (not open), woodland garden with marvellous views of Skiddaw, Binsey and the Northern Fells and also the Solway and Scotland. Outstanding trees, some ancient and rare and many specimen, shrubs, herbaceous borders, potager vegetable garden.

36 ROSE CROFT

Levens, Kendal, LA8 8PH.
Enid Fraser, 07976 977018,
fraserenid@gmail.com. *Approx 4m
from J36 on M6. From J36 take A590
toward Barrow. R turn Levens, L at
pub, follow road to garden on L. From
A6, into Levens, past shop, bear L,
over Xrds, downhill. L turn signed 'PV
Dobson'. Garden on R after Dobsons.*
**Visits by arrangement 1 June to 7
Sept for groups of up to 20. Adm
£5, chd free. Light refreshments.
Tea, soft drinks, biscuits.**
This 'secret' garden's richness in
herbaceous plants, grasses, shrubs
and trees belies the twin challenges
of thin topsoil and an acutely sloping
site. With grand views across the
Lyth valley, steps and pathways carry
down to lower-level lawns, streamside
summerhouse and wild flowers. Long
season of interest with designed
elements providing bountiful displays
well into late summer.

✿ ☕ ⋙))

37 ◆ RYDAL HALL

Ambleside, LA22 9LX. Diocese
of Carlisle, 01539 432050,
gardens@rydalhall.org,
www.rydalhall.org. *2m N of
Ambleside. E from A591 at Rydal
signed Rydal Hall. Bus 555, 599,
X8, X55; NCR 6.* **For NGS: Sun 24
Mar, Sun 21 Apr, Sun 21 July, Sun
18 Aug (9-4). Adm by donation.
Light refreshments in tea shop on
site. For other opening times and
information, please phone, email or
visit garden website.**
Forty acres of park, woodland and
gardens to explore. The formal
Thomas Mawson garden has fine
examples of herbaceous planting,
seasonal displays and magnificent
views of the Lakeland Fells. Enjoy the
peaceful atmosphere created in the
Quiet Garden with informal planting
around the pond and stunning views
of the waterfalls from The Grot, the
UK's first viewing station. Partial
wheelchair access, top terrace only.

♿ 🐕 🚐 🚌 ☕

38 NEW ◆ RYDAL MOUNT AND GARDENS

Rydal, Ambleside, LA22 9LU.
Helen Green, 01539 433002,
info@rydalmount.co.uk,
www.rydalmount.co.uk. *Rydal
Mount is located between Ambleside
& Grasmere. Visitors will turn L
up Rydal Hill to arrive at the Rydal
Mount car park where there is
limited parking.* **For NGS: Sun 24**

Mar, Mon 1, Tue 2, Wed 3 Apr,
Sun 9, Mon 10, Tue 11, Wed 12
June (10.30-4.30). Adm £5, chd
free. Visitors can buy home-
made scones & soup as well as
tea, coffee & cold drinks in our
tearoom. For other opening times
and information, please phone,
email or visit garden website.
Rydal Mount was the family home
of William Wordsworth. Wordsworth
considered himself as good a
landscape gardener as a poet, and
the Rydal Mount garden is the largest
example of his design. The garden
stretches over 5 acres and includes
the terraces that Wordsworth built,
informal herbaceous borders, trees
planted by the poet and a wonderful
range of traditional lakeland plants.

☕ 🧺

39 SPRINT MILL

Burneside, Kendal, LA8 9AQ.
Edward & Romola Acland,
01539 725168 or 07806 065602,
mail@sprintmill.uk. *2m N of Kendal.
From Burneside follow signs towards
Skelsmergh for ½ m, then L into drive
of Sprint Mill. Or from A6, about 1m
N of Kendal follow signs towards
Burneside, then R into drive.* **Sun 26
May, Sun 2 June (10.30-5). Adm £4,
chd free. Light refreshments. Visits
also by arrangement Apr to Sept.**
Unorthodox organically run
garden,the wild and natural alongside
provision of owners' fruit, vegetables
and firewood. Idyllic riverside setting,
5 acres to explore inc wooded
riverbank with hand-crafted seats.
Large vegetable and soft fruit area,
following no dig and permaculture
principles. Hand tools prevail. Historic
water mill with original turbine. The
3 storey building houses owner's
art studio and personal museum,
inc collection of old hand tools
associated with rural crafts. Goats,
hens, ducks, rope swing, very family
friendly. Short walk to our flower-
rich hay meadows. Access for
wheelchairs to some parts of both
garden and mill.

♿ 🐕 ☕ 🧺

40 SUMMERDALE HOUSE

Cow Brow, Nook, Lupton,
LA6 1PE. David & Gail Sheals,
www.summerdalegardenplants.
co.uk. *7m S of Kendal, 5m W of
Kirkby Lonsdale. From J36 M6 take
A65 towards Kirkby Lonsdale, at Nook
take R turn Farleton. Location not
signed on highway. Detailed directions
available on our website.* **Sun 28 Apr,**

Sun 26 May (11-4.30). Adm £5, chd
free. Home-made teas.
1½ acre part-walled country garden
set around C18 former vicarage.
Several defined areas have been
created by hedges, each with its own
theme and linked by intricate cobbled
pathways. Relaxed natural planting
in a formal structure. Rural setting
with fine views across to Farleton
Fell. Large collection of auriculas with
displays during the season.

🐕 ✿ ☕ ⋙))

41 ◆ SWARTHMOOR HALL

Swarthmoor Hall Lane, Ulverston,
LA12 0JQ. 01229 583204,
info@swarthmoorhall.co.uk,
www.swarthmoorhall.co.uk. *1½ m
SW of Ulverston. A590 to Ulverston.
Turn off to Ulverston railway stn.
Follow Brown tourist signs to Hall.
Rail 0.9m. NCR70 & 700 (1m).* **For
NGS: Fri 1 Mar, Fri 14, Sat 15, Sun
16 June (10-4). Adm £2.50, chd
free. Light refreshments. For other
opening times and information,
please phone, email or visit garden
website.**
Traditional English country garden
surrounding a Grade II* C17 hall.
Cottage style borders, woodland
garden. Quiet Garden dedicated to
peaceful contemplation, ornamental
vegetable garden and hay meadow.
Please check the website for opening
times for the historic hall.

✿ 🚐 🚌 ☕ 🧺 ⋙))

42 NEW VICARAGE HOUSE EAST

Witherslack, Grange-over-
Sands, LA11 6RS. Steve &
Jackie Ratcliffe. *Turn off A590 at
Witherslack junction, past Derby
Arms pub. In village turn L on to
Church Rd (following brown signs
to Halecat Garden Nursery) and
stay on road for 1m. Pass Dean
Barwick School.* **Sun 9 June (11-4).
Combined adm with Fernhill
Coach House £6, chd free. Home-
made teas.**
A secret haven, surrounded by stone
walling and woodland, the backbone
of which is a wildlife pond and walled
garden. A series of connecting
rooms create a sequence of gardens,
each with their own distinctive
character. Includes a flower and
herbaceous formal garden planted
by colour schemes, a vegetable
garden, orchard with mown paths, a
woodland garden with hellebores and
a hosta collection. Please park on
road between Dean Barwick School

and the church, apart from those with disabilities who can access via drive adj to Church Green.

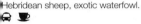

43 WINDY HALL
Crook Road, Windermere, LA23 3JA. Luke Evans & Sophie Bryde. ½m S of Bowness-on-Windermere. On western end of B5284, pink house up Linthwaite House Hotel driveway. Rail 2.6m; Bus 1m, 6, 599, 755, 800; NCR 6 (1m). **Sun 2 June (10-5). Adm £5, chd free. Light refreshments. Teas and home-made cake.**
Crafted and nurtured by David and Diane Kinsman over 40 years, the 6 acre gardens are eclectic and unique within the lakeland landscape. Carved out of the fellside this garden is steeped in character and charm. Sophie and Luke are now caring for the garden and continuing David and Diane's legacy. Mosses and ferns, rare Hebridean sheep, exotic waterfowl.

44 WINTON PARK
Appleby Road, Kirkby Stephen, CA17 4PG. Mr Anthony Kilvington, www.wintonparkgardens.co.uk. 2m N of Kirkby Stephen. On A685 turn L signed Gt Musgrave/Warcop (B6259). After approx 1m turn L as signed. **Sun 7 July (11-4). Adm £6, chd free. Light refreshments.**
5 acre country garden bordered by the banks of the River Eden with stunning views. Many fine conifers, acers and rhododendrons, herbaceous borders, hostas, ferns, grasses, heathers and several hundred roses. Four formal ponds plus rock pool. Partial wheelchair access.

45 WOODEND HOUSE
Woodend, Egremont, CA22 2TA. Grainne & Richard Jakobson, 019468 13017, gmjakobson22@gmail.com. 2m S of Whitehaven. Take A595 from Whitehaven towards Egremont. On leaving Bigrigg take 1st turn L. Go down the hill. Garden is at the bottom of the road opp Woodend Farm. **Sat 31 Aug, Sun 1 Sept (11-5). Adm £5, chd free. Home-made teas. Visits also by arrangement 31 May to 30 Sept for groups of up to 20.**
A beautiful garden tucked away in a small hamlet. Meandering gravel paths lead around the garden with imaginative, colourful planting and quirky features. Take a look around a productive, organic potager using no-dig methods, wildlife pond, mini spring and summer meadows and sit in the pretty summerhouse. Designed to be beautiful year-round and wildlife friendly. Children's trail with prizes. The gravel drive and paths are difficult for wheelchairs but more mobile visitors can access the main seating areas in the rear garden.

46 YEWBARROW HOUSE
Hampsfell Road, Grange-over-Sands, LA11 6BE. Jonathan & Margaret Denby, 07733 322394, jonathan@bestlakesbreaks.co.uk, www.yewbarrowhouse.co.uk. ¼m from town centre. Proceed along Hampsfell Rd passing a house called Yewbarrow to brow of hill then turn L onto a lane signed 'Charney Wood/Yewbarrow Wood' & sharp L again. Rail 0.7m, Bus X6, NCR 70. **Sun 2 June, Sun 7 July, Sun 4 Aug, Sun 1 Sept (11-4). Adm £5, chd free. Light refreshments. Visits also by arrangement Mar to Oct for groups of 10 to 60.**
More Cornwall than Cumbria, according to Country Life, a colourful 4 acre garden filled with exotic and rare plants, with dramatic views over Morecambe Bay. Outstanding features inc the Orangery, the Japanese garden with infinity pool, the Italian terraces and the restored Victorian kitchen garden. Dahlias, cannas and colourful exotica are a speciality. Find us on YouTube.

47 YEWS
Storrs Park, Bowness-on-Windermere, LA23 3JR. Sir Christopher & Lady Scott, 07771553704, blenheimcrescent@icloud.com, www.yewsestate.com. 1.4m S of Bowness-on-Windermere. On A5074 about 0.3m N of Blackwell, The Arts & Crafts House. Rail Windermere 3m, What3words app - ballots.speak.fractions. **Sun 16 June (11-4.30). Adm £6.50, chd free. Home-made teas. Visits also by arrangement.**
7 acre garden overlooking Windermere which has undergone extensive redevelopment since 2018. Formal gardens designed by Mawson and Avray Tipping inc sunken borders, rose garden and croquet lawn. Newly planted woodland walk, bog garden and renovated Yew maze. Naturalistic planting, areas left for wildlife and many fine trees. New kitchen garden built 2022 and original Messenger glasshouse. There is some level access to formal areas of the garden but only via gravel paths.

Ivy House

LANCASHIRE
Merseyside, Greater Manchester

VOLUNTEERS

County Organiser
Marian & Brian Jones
01695 574628
marianandbrian.jones@ngs.org.uk

County Treasurer
Peter Curl
01704 893713
peter.curl@ngs.org.uk

Publicity
Christine Ruth
07740 438994
caruthchris@aol.com

Social Media
Carole Ann Powers
01254 824903
chows3@icloud.com

John Spendlove
07746 378194
john.spendlove@ngs.org.uk

Radio
Tania Craine
tania.craine@ngs.org.uk

Photographer
Norman Rigby
01704 840329
norman.rigby@ngs.org.uk

Booklet Co-ordinator
Brian Jones
(see above)

Booklet Distribution
Claire Spendlove
01524 727770
claire@lavenderandlime.co.uk

John & Jennifer Mawdsley
01704 564708

Visits by Arrangement
Roger Craine
07595 229700
roger.craine@ngs.org.uk

Talks
Maureen Sawyer & Sue Beacon
01695 574628

Assistant County Organisers
Sue Beacon 077092 43986
suedrake@btinternet.com

Laura Carstensen 07784 221919
laura@ngs.org.uk

Sandra Curl 01704 893713
peter.curl@btinternet.com

Margaret & Geoff Fletcher
01704 567742
margaret.fletcher@ngs.org.uk

John & Jennifer Mawdsley
(see left)

Carole Ann & Stephen Powers
(see left)

Claire & John Spendlove
(see left)

OPENING DATES

All entries subject to change.
For latest information check
www.ngs.org.uk
Map locator numbers are
shown to the right of each
garden name.

February

Snowdrop Openings

Sunday 11th
Weeping Ash Garden — 69

Sunday 18th
Weeping Ash Garden — 69

Sunday 25th
Weeping Ash Garden — 69

April

Saturday 13th
Dale House Gardens — 17

Sunday 14th
Dale House Gardens — 17

Sunday 28th
Plant World — 55

May

Sunday 5th
Kington Cottage — 40

Monday 6th
◆ The Ridges — 58

Sunday 12th
Derian House Children's
Hospice — 19

Saturday 18th
Halton Park House — 31
NEW 33 Pershore Grove — 54

Sunday 19th
Halton Park House — 31
Woolton Village Gardens — 73

Saturday 25th
Mill Barn — 45

Sunday 26th
Bretherton Gardens — 8
Mill Barn — 45

June

Saturday 1st
Higher Bridge Clough House — 34
Mill Barn — 45

Sunday 2nd
NEW The Hawes — 33
Higher Bridge Clough House — 34
Hightown Gardens — 35
Kington Cottage — 40
Mill Barn — 45
NEW 87 Todd Lane North — 64
NEW 101 Todd Lane North — 65

Saturday 8th
136 Buckingham Road — 10
31 Cousins Lane — 13
Ellesmere Park Gardens — 22
The North Tithebarn — 49
Oaklands — 50

Sunday 9th
Bretherton Gardens — 8
136 Buckingham Road — 10
31 Cousins Lane — 13
Didsbury Village Gardens — 20
Holly House — 36
Meresands Kennels & Cattery — 44
The North Tithebarn — 49
Oaklands — 50
Sefton Park Gardens — 60

Saturday 15th
Dale House Gardens — 17
Giles Farm — 25
Warton Gardens — 68

f @Lancsngs   ✕ @lancsngs   ◎ @ngslancashire

Sunday 16th

Ainsdale & Birkdale Gardens	1
79 Crabtree Lane	14
Dale House Gardens	17
Giles Farm	25
Greenfield Hall	27
Maggie's, Manchester	41
Warton Gardens	68

Saturday 22nd

Jack Green Cottage	39
Turton Tower Kitchen Garden	66

Sunday 23rd

NEW Canning and Toxteth Gardens	11
Chorlton Gardens	12
Jack Green Cottage	39

Saturday 29th

Arevinti	4
NEW Bryn Mor	9
5 Crib Lane	16
Hale Village Gardens	30
The Old Vicarage	51

Sunday 30th

Arevinti	4
5 Crib Lane	16
Hale Village Gardens	30
The Old Vicarage	51
Ormskirk and Aughton Gardens	53

July

Saturday 6th

NEW The Shakespearean Garden, Platt Fields Park	61

Sunday 7th

Freshfield Gardens	24
Glynwood House	26
NEW 3 Harrock View	32
Kington Cottage	40
NEW The Shakespearean Garden, Platt Fields Park	61

Saturday 13th

47 The Crescent	15
NEW 85 Ribchester Road	57

Sunday 14th

NEW 16 Beach Lawn	6
Bretherton Gardens	8
NEW Drummersdale Crossing Cottage	21
33 Greenhill Road	28
NEW Maghull Gardens	42
146 Mather Avenue	43
NEW 18 Moor Drive	47
Moss Park Allotments	48
NEW Oldham Gardens	52
NEW 85 Ribchester Road	57

NEW 280 Warrington Road	67
Wigan & Leigh Hospice	71
NEW 32 Wood Hey Grove	72

Sunday 21st

Ainsdale & Birkdale Gardens	1
79 Crabtree Lane	14
Southlands	62

Saturday 27th

NEW 30 Bonds lane	7
NEW Whalley and District Gardens	70

Sunday 28th

NEW 30 Bonds lane	7
The Growth Project	29
NEW Whalley and District Gardens	70

August

Saturday 3rd

NEW Ambledene, Moss Lane	3
NEW Fallowfield & Ladybarn Gardens	23

Sunday 4th

NEW 3 Alexander Mews	2
NEW Fallowfield & Ladybarn Gardens	23
NEW 46 Holmdale Avenue	37
Kington Cottage	40
Plant World	55

Saturday 10th

NEW Rishton Tropical Garden	59

Sunday 11th

NEW Rishton Tropical Garden	59
Weeping Ash Garden	69

Saturday 17th

NEW 28 Stafford Road	63

Sunday 18th

Derian House Children's Hospice	19

Monday 26th

♦ The Ridges	58

Saturday 31st

Rainbag Cottage	56

September

Sunday 1st

33 Greenhill Road	28
146 Mather Avenue	43
Rainbag Cottage	56

Saturday 7th

Ashton Walled Community Gardens	5

Sunday 8th

Weeping Ash Garden	69

October

Saturday 19th

NEW 33 Pershore Grove	54

By Arrangement

Arrange a personalised garden visit with your club, or group of friends, on a date to suit you. See individual garden entries for full details.

Arevinti	4
NEW 16 Beach Lawn	6
Briar Cottage, Warton Gardens	68
79 Crabtree Lane	14
Dent Hall	18
Derian House Children's Hospice	19
Giles Farm	25
The Growth Project	29
Hazel Cottage, Bretherton Gardens	8
The Inn at Whitewell	38
Kington Cottage	40
72 Ludlow Drive, Ormskirk and Aughton Gardens	53
NEW 15 Lynton Green, Woolton Village Gardens	73
111 Main Street, Warton Gardens	68
Mill Barn	45
Mill Croft	46
Moss Park Allotments	48
NEW 1A Moss Side, Freshfield Gardens	24
The Old Vicarage	51
NEW 33 Pershore Grove	54
NEW Ruloe, 89 Derby Street, Ormskirk and Aughton Gardens	53
14 Saxon Road, Ainsdale & Birkdale Gardens	1
Southlands	62
NEW 28 Stafford Road	63

THE GARDENS

GROUP OPENING

1 AINSDALE & BIRKDALE GARDENS
14 Saxon Road, Southport, PR8 2AX. Mrs Margaret Fletcher. *1-4m S of Southport. Gardens signed from A565 & A5267.* **Sun 16 June, Sun 21 July (11-5). Combined adm £6, chd free. Home-made teas at 12 & 14 Saxon Rd, 45 Stourton Rd, 115 Waterloo Rd & 22 Hartley Crescent.**

23 ASHTON ROAD
PR8 4QE. John & Jennifer Mawdsley.
Open on all dates

22 HARTLEY CRESCENT
PR8 4SG. Sandra & Keith Birks.
Open on Sun 21 July

12 SAXON ROAD
Karen & Douglas Traynor.
Open on Sun 16 June

14 SAXON ROAD
PR8 2AX. Margaret & Geoff Fletcher, 01704 567742, margaret.fletcher@ngs.org.uk.
Open on all dates
Visits also by arrangement 1 May to 1 Aug for groups of 10 to 50.

45 STOURTON ROAD
PR8 3PL. Pat & Bill Armstrong.
Open on all dates

115 WATERLOO ROAD
PR8 4QN. Antony & Rebecca Eden.
Open on Sun 16 June

A group formed to showcase some of the beautiful gardens to visit around the Victorian seaside town of Southport. They range in size and design from a walled garden featuring tender perennials, a mature tranquil ever evolving garden, a flower arranger's garden of infinite detail and surprises and a garden of rooms leading to a spectacular fruit and vegetable plot. A family garden reclaimed from neglect featuring unusual shrubs and perennials and we welcome the return of an L shaped plantswoman's garden containing a kaleidoscope of flowers. Not all gardens are wheelchair friendly due to narrow paths or gravel.

2 3 ALEXANDER MEWS
Queens Road, Southport, PR9 9JH. Ian Whitaker. *½ m N of Southport. M6 J26 join M58 for Liverpool M58 J3 A570 to Ormskirk & then Southport. Turn R onto A565 over r'about 2nd exit 2nd R onto Alexandra Rd. Garden is at the next junction.* **Sun 4 Aug (10-5). Combined adm with 46 Holmdale Avenue £5, chd free. Cream teas at 46 Holmdale Ave.**
Large corner plot with deep colourful cottage style beds transformed from an area totally covered in slate. A small wildlife pond that overflows into a bog garden. 2 pergolas with climbing roses, honeysuckle and jasmine. Small enclosed seating area, another seating area in sunny position. Future plans for a summerhouse and large water feature.

3 AMBLEDENE, MOSS LANE
Penwortham, Preston, PR1 9TX. Teressa Ryan. *From Bee Lane, turn R onto Moss Ln. Ambledene is the white house on the R at the end of the single track lane. Park on the grass field opp the house. What 3 Words app - ready.worms. scouts.* **Sat 3 Aug (10.30-5). Adm £4, chd free. Home-made bakes & biscuits with a choice of hot & cold beverages.**
There are gardens to both the front and back of the house with views over fields. Some mature trees create woodland like areas and there are also areas in full sun with planting to suit each aspect. A large patio at the back has gazebos and seating. Other features include a slate bed with fountain, pond, greenhouse and containers for alpines, vegetables, herbs etc. Planting style is naturalistic. The garden is flat with some areas covered in gravel.

4 AREVINTI
1 School Court, Ramsbottom, Bury, BL0 0SD. Lavinia Tod, 01706 822474, arevintgarden@gmail.com. *4m N of Bury. Exit at J1 turn R onto A56 signed Ramsbottom continue straight until yellow signs.* **Sat 29, Sun 30 June (11-5). Adm £4, chd free. Light refreshments. Visits also by arrangement May to Sept for groups of 5 to 20. Pls order**

refreshments on booking.
The main garden has a roofed pergola with clematis growing around it and a raised pond. The Chinese garden laid with gravel has two water features, stone dragons and buddha. There is a working miniature railway in the garden shed. The churchyard contains a wildlife pond, colourful herbaceous borders and a fairy house for children. Talk on the history of the area by the garden owner at 1pm. History walk at 2pm - please meet at the Porrits Tomb in the churchyard.

5 ASHTON WALLED COMMUNITY GARDENS
Pedders Lane, Ashton-on-Ribble, Preston, PR2 1HL. Let's Grow Preston, www.letsgrowpreston.org. *W of Preston. From M6 J30 head towards Preston turn R onto Blackpool Rd, continue for 3.4m, turn L onto Pedders Lane & next R onto the park. Entrance to walled garden is 50 metres on L.* **Sat 7 Sept (10-3). Adm £5, chd free. Light refreshments. Vegan & gluten free options. Pls tell us about any allergies when purchasing refreshments.**
Formal raised beds within a walled garden, a peace garden and an edible garden. The formal part of the garden uses plants predominantly from just 3 families, rose, geranium and aster. It is punctuated by grasses and has been designed to demonstrate how diverse and varied plants can be from just the one family. Practical demonstrations and talking tour about the work that Let's Grow Preston does within the PR postcode inc improving mental and physical wellbeing and working with the 41 food hubs of Preston.

100 inpatients and their families are being supported at the newly opened Horatio's Garden Wales, thanks to the National Garden Scheme donations

6 **NEW** **16 BEACH LAWN**
Waterloo, Liverpool,
L22 8QA. Ms Claire Curtis
Thomas, 07852 982991,
cctsenior@gmail.com. *What 3*
Words app - novel.given.simple.
Access on foot from end of Beach
Lawn & Harbord Rd. No 53 Bus
stops nearby. **Sun 14 July (11-4).**
Combined adm with 18 Moor
Drive £5, chd free. Home-made
teas. Visits also by arrangement
June & July for groups of 5 to 20.
Originally this coastal garden was
little more than a 30m long, 7m wide
and 1m tall sand dune, now, some
ten years later the garden is full of
colour for 8 months of the year.
There are quiet immersive places to
sit and always something beautiful
to catch the eye. Despite many
failures everything in this garden has
been grown by the owner who will
be happy to answer any questions.

The public sculpture installation,
Another Place by Anthony Gormley,
is less than 10 mins walk from the
garden. Crosby Coastal Park is a very
short walk away and is designated
both Site of Local Biological interest
and Sefton Coast Special Area of
Conservation. The garden has wide
paths built for wheelchair users.

& 🐕 ❀ ☕))

7 **NEW** **30 BONDS LANE**
Garstang, Preston, PR3 1ZB. Mr
Alan & Mrs Liz Pearson. *½ m S*
of Garstang town centre. From the
South; follow the B6430 N from
the A6 (signed Garstang). From the
North; follow the B6430 S through
the town & follow the signs for
Preston. Parking adjacent to the
property. **Sat 27, Sun 28 July (11-**
5). Adm £5, chd free. Cream teas.
A 90 yr old garden, which has been
in the hands of the current owners for

30 yrs. To the front are formal lawns
and beds of annuals with topiary and
a side bed of perennials and gatepost
features To the rear are 3 lawned
areas with the one now being left as
meadow and orchard. A varied planting
throughout with a lot of hostas, a
year-round garden with lots of features,
seating and vistas. A steep gradient to
the drive otherwise mainly accessible.

& ❀ ☕

GROUP OPENING

8 **BRETHERTON GARDENS**
Bretherton, Leyland, PR26 9AD.
8m SW of Preston. Between
Southport & Preston, from A59,
take B5247 towards Chorley for
1m. Gardens signed from South Rd
(B5247) & North Rd (B5248). Maps
& tickets at all gardens. **Sun 26 May**
(12-5). Combined adm £5, chd

8 Copley Road, Chorlton Gardens

free. Sun 9 June, Sun 14 July (12-5). Combined adm £6, chd free. Home-made teas at Bretherton Congregational Church from 12 noon on all dates.

HAZEL COTTAGE
PR26 9AN. John & Kris Jolley, 01772 600896, jolley@johnjolley.plus.com.
Open on all dates
Visits also by arrangement May to Sept for groups of 10 to 30.

◆ HAZELWOOD
PR26 9AY. Jacqueline Iddon & Thompson Dagnall, 01772 601433, jacquelineiddon@gmail.com, www.jacquelineiddon.co.uk.
Open on Sun 9 June, Sun 14 July

NEW **LANESIDE, 10 BAMFORDS FOLD**
PR26 9AL. Robert & Ann Alty.
Open on all dates

OWL BARN
PR26 9AD. Richard & Barbara Farbon.
Open on all dates

PALATINE, 6 BAMFORDS FOLD
PR26 9AL. Alison Ryan.
Open on all dates

A group of contrasting gardens spaced across an attractive award winning village with a conservation area. Hazelwood is a 1½ acre plant lover's paradise with herbaceous and mixed borders, kitchen and cutting garden, alpine house, sculpture gallery, pond and plant nursery. At the sculpture gallery there are usually demonstrations at 2pm. Hazel Cottage's former Victorian orchard plot has evolved into a series of themed spaces while the adjoining land has a natural pond, meadow and developing native woodland. Owl Barn has herbaceous borders filled with cottage garden and hardy plants, a productive kitchen garden with fruit, vegetables and cut flowers. There are two ponds with water features and secluded seating areas. Palatine is a garden of 3 contrasting spaces started in 2019 around a modern bungalow to attract wildlife and give year-round interest. In the same cul-de-sac Laneside is still a work in progress, the garden is on 3 sides of the bungalow, with mature shrubs and trees, a rose garden, perennials and a small fruit growing area. Also an inherited Woodland Walk which is a current project. Home-made preserves for sale. Full wheelchair access at Palatine, the majority of Hazelwood is accessible, other gardens have narrow paths or gravel limiting accessibility.

♿ 🐕 ✿ 🚌 ☕ 🔊

9 NEW **BRYN MOR**
Long Lane, Scorton, Preston, PR3 1DB. Mrs Elizabeth Ward. *What 3 Words app - slopes.faster. elevated. 1m N of Scorton village. Carry on past the turning for Scorton picnic site. Car park 500 metres on the L. Travelling south on Long Lane pass the white metal railings Car park on the R.* **Sat 29 June (11-5). Adm £5, chd free. Home-made teas.**
A mature garden of ¾ of an acre. A mixture of perennial beds, shrubs and mature trees and box hedge parterres. Vegetable garden and paddock, with unusual trees, to walk through.

🐕 ✿ ☕ 🔊

10 136 BUCKINGHAM ROAD
Maghull, L31 7DR. Debbie & Mark Jackson. *7m N of Liverpool. End M57/M58, take A59 towards Ormskirk. Turn L after Aldi onto Liverpool Rd Sth, cont' on past Meadows pub, 3rd R into Sandringham Rd, L into Buckingham Rd.* **Sat 8, Sun 9 June (12-5). Combined adm with The North Tithebarn £5, chd free. Home-made teas. Donation to MS Society UK.**
A delightful suburban garden overflowing with cottage garden plants creating a haven for bees and butterflies. Wisteria covered pergola provides shade and roses complement the planting. A pond and water feature along with an array of planters complete the garden.

♿ ✿ ☕

GROUP OPENING

11 NEW **CANNING AND TOXTETH GARDENS**
27 Canning Street, Liverpool, L8 7NN. *No 86 bus runs every 12 mins from city centre. Ask for bus stop Back Canning St* **Sun 23 June (1-5). Combined adm £6. Light refreshments.**

27 CANNING STREET
L8 7NN. Mrs Waltraud Boxall.

EL JARDIN DE LA NUESTRA SENORA
L8 7NL. R.C. Archdiocese of Liverpool.

10 GAMBIER TERRACE
L1 7BG. Mr Paul Murphy.

NEW **GRANBY BACK ALLEY GARDEN**
L8 2UW.

NEW **GRANBY WINTER GARDEN**
L8 2UW.

GRAPES COMMUNITY FOOD GARDEN
L8 1XE. Squash Liverpool, admin@squashliverpool.co.uk.

PAKISTAN ASSOCIATION LIVERPOOL WELLBEING GARDEN
L8 2TF. Pakistan Association Liverpool.

The Canning Georgian Quarter gardens have extended their reach further into Toxteth this year, with the new opening of the beautiful Granby Winter Garden and an innovative back alley garden recently featured on Gardeners' World. The winter garden was created out of two derelict houses, in an area being beautifully regenerated thanks to the efforts of the local residents. They join 2 contrasting private gardens behind the grand homes in Liverpool's Georgian Quarter, and the unusual classically designed Spanish garden of St Philip Neri church. El Jardin de la Nuestra Senora was created on a bomb site after WW2. The church's exquisite Byzantine interior, designed by PS Gilby, will also be open. In contrast to all the Georgian Quarter classicism are the vibrant Grapes Community Food Garden and Squash cafe garden in Windsor Street, plus the Wellbeing garden in the grounds of the Liverpool Pakistan Association. It's a fascinating group, all within the historic heart of Liverpool, with many architecturally important buildings. These include Liverpool's Anglican cathedral, the largest cathedral and religious building in Britain right opposite the Georgian Gambier Terrace garden.

✿ 🔊 ☕

GROUP OPENING

12 CHORLTON GARDENS

Chorlton, Manchester, M21 8UZ. *Chorlton is a short drive off the M60 (J6/7) through Stretford. There are 2 tram stops or parking in some of the side streets or a paying carpark in Chorlton precinct - We will provide maps if you need them.* **Sun 23 June (11-4). Combined adm £8, chd free. Light refreshments at Hattergreen Alley, Edge Lane & Whitelow Road. Drinks may be available at other gardens on the day.**

NEW   6 COPLEY ROAD
M21 9WT. Miss Katie Moss.

NEW   8 COPLEY ROAD
M21 9WT. Mr Roy Bickley.

20 DARTMOUTH ROAD
M21 8XJ. Ms Sarah Rycroft.

NEW   57 EDGE LANE
M21 9JU. David Benson.

NEW   118 EGERTON ROAD SOUTH
M21 0XJ. Peter Hughes.

23 HARTINGTON ROAD
M21 8UZ. Ms Emma Dibb, www.instagram.com/ compostwoman.

NEW   HATTERGREEN ALLEY
M21 9FT. The Residents.

NEW   19 REDLAND CRESCENT
M21 8DL. Sally Geldard.

NEW   58 SOUTH DRIVE
M21 8FB. Alison Wainwright.

NEW   16 WHITELOW ROAD
M21 9HQ. Laura Carstensen.

Chorlton is a suburb of Manchester with great food shops, bars, cafes, and a bohemian atmosphere. Our gardens reflect what you can do with urban spaces both small, large and in one case a long alleyway . We have a range of styles and planting to enjoy, from exotic tropical schemes to more traditional mixed herbaceous and cottage garden planting, formal rose gardens to an alley garden with fruit and vegetables. There are small immersive spaces, unexpected views over open parkland, to neighbourly adjoining gardens, and a community alleyway.

☕))

13 31 COUSINS LANE

Ardilea 31 Cousins Lane, Rufford, Ormskirk, L40 1TN. Brenda & Roy Caslake. *From M6 J27, follow signs for Parbold then Rufford. Turn L onto the A59. Turn R at Hesketh Arms pub. 4th turn on L.* **Sat 8, Sun 9 June (10-4). Combined adm with Oaklands £5, chd free. Home-made teas at Rufford Cricket Club adjacent to garden.**
Rooms within rooms, discreet corners punctuated with an open vista to the cricket ground. This cottage garden welcomes the bees and butterflies. Frogs, toads and newts are resident and the blackbird and thrush lead a vocal chorus whilst wren and robin flit. A potpourri of planting with scents pleasing to the senses. A small, tranquil oasis. Take time to re-energise with a glass of prosecco and a cream tea whilst enjoying the best of English pastimes.

✿ ☕))

14 79 CRABTREE LANE

Burscough, L40 0RW. Sandra & Peter Curl, 01704 893713, peter.curl@btinternet.com, www. youtube.com/watch?v=CW7S8nB_ iX8. *3m NE of Ormskirk. A59 Preston - Liverpool Rd. From N before bridge R into Redcat Lane signed for Martin Mere. From S over 2nd bridge L into Redcat Lane after 3/4 m L into Crabtree Lane.* **Sun 16 June, Sun 21 July (11-4). Adm £5, chd free. Visits also by arrangement June & July. Includes introductory talk on the garden and how it was developed.**
3/4 acre year-round plantsperson's garden with many rare and unusual plants. Herbaceous borders and island beds, pond, rockery, rose garden, and autumn hot bed. Many stone features built with reclaimed materials. Shrubs and rhododendrons, Koi pond and waterfall, hosta and fern walk. Gravel garden with Mediterranean plants. Patio surrounded by shrubs and raised alpine bed. Trees give areas for shade loving plants. Many beds replanted recently. Many stone buildings and features. Flat grass paths.

♿ 🐕 ✿ 🚗 ☕))

15 47 THE CRESCENT

Maghull, Liverpool, L31 7BL. Mr Ian & Mrs Nikki Fennah. *7m N of Liverpool. End M57/M58, take A59 Ormskirk. L at Aldi onto Liverpool Rd South, then 2nd into The Crescent.*

From Ormskirk, follow A59 to Maghull, turn R at town hall L at Meadows pub, 4th R. **Sat 13 July (11-4). Adm £3, chd free. Home-made teas. Opening with Maghull Gardens on Sun 14 July.**
A garden with full borders, cleverly split into 'rooms', inc a gravel garden by the summerhouse and wildlife pebble pond, surrounded by heleniums and other perennials, a corner arbour overlooking the fish pond, a cut flower garden inc a secluded seat and small natural pond, greenhouse, courtyard garden and apple tree/passion flower walkway, edged with successional perennial planting. Main paths are paved. Some uneven surfaces not accessible.

♿ ✿ ☕))

16 5 CRIB LANE

Dobcross, Oldham, OL3 5AF. Helen Campbell. *5m E of Oldham. From Dobcross head towards Delph on Platt La. Crib La opp Dobcross Band Club. Limited parking for disabled visitors only up steep lane. All other visitors to park in the village.* **Sat 29, Sun 30 June (12.30-4.30). Adm £4, chd free. Home-made teas.**
A challenging garden as on a high terraced hillside on tip site. Visited by deer, hares and the odd cow! One elderly gardener. An example of an ordinary family Pennine garden. Of additional interest are wildlife ponds, wildflower areas, a polytunnel, four beehives with 250,000 bees, an art gallery and garden sculptures. Areas re thought annually, dug up and changed. Local honey, cards and art work for sale.

☕ 🛋

In 2023, National Garden Scheme funding for Perennial supported a helpline service which provided advice, information and frontline support to around 800 people working in horticulture

Moss Park Allotments

Bed 7
Alliums
Front 8
Annie

Bed 8
Roots
Gail

© Linda Viney

17 DALE HOUSE GARDENS

off Church Lane, Goosnargh, Preston, PR3 2BE. Caroline & Tom Luke. *2½ m E of Broughton. M6 J32 signed Garstang Broughton, T-lights R at Whittingham Lane, 2½m to Whittingham. At PO turn L into Church Lane. Garden between nos 17 & 19.* **Sat 13, Sun 14 Apr, Sat 15, Sun 16 June (10-4). Adm £3.50, chd free. Home-made teas. Donation to St Francis School, Goosnargh.**
½ acre tastefully landscaped gardens comprising limestone rockeries, well-stocked herbaceous borders, raised alpine beds with 100 new plants, well-stocked koi pond, lawn areas, greenhouse and polytunnel, patio areas, specialising in alpines, rare shrubs and trees, large display of unusual spring bulbs. Secret Garden and year-round interest. Large indoor budgerigar aviary with 300+ budgies. Gravel path, lawn areas.

18 DENT HALL

Colne Road, Trawden, Colne, BB8 8NX. Chris Whitaker-Webb & Joanne Smith, 01282 861892, denthall@tiscali.co.uk. *10 min from end of M65. Turn L at end of M65. Follow A6068 for 2m; just after 3rd r'about turn R down B6250. After 1½m, in front of church, turn R, signed Carry Bridge. Keep R, follow road up hill, garden on R after 300yds.* **Visits by arrangement 1 June to 29 Sept for groups of 10+. Adm £7.50, chd free. Home-made teas.**

Nestled in the oldest part of Trawden village and rolling Lancashire countryside, this mature and evolving country garden surrounds a 400 yr old grade II listed property (not open); featuring a parterre, lawns, herbaceous borders, shrubbery, wildlife pond with bridge to seating area and a hidden summerhouse in a woodland area. Plentiful seating throughout. Some uneven paths and gradients.

19 DERIAN HOUSE CHILDREN'S HOSPICE

Chancery Road, Chorley, PR7 1DH. Gareth Elliott, 01257 271271, ellie.smith@derianhouse.co.uk, www.derianhouse.co.uk/. *2m from Chorley town centre. From B5252*

Ambledene, Moss Lane

pass Chorley Hospital on L, at r'about 1st exit to Chancery Lane. Hospice on L after 0.4 m. Parking is available around the building & on the road. SatNav directions not always accurate. **Sun 12 May, Sun 18 Aug (10-4). Adm £3, chd free. Light refreshments. Visits also by arrangement.**

The Chorley-based children's hospice provides respite and end-of-life care to more than 400 children and young people from across the North West and South Cumbria. The gardens at the hospice help to create an atmosphere of relaxation, tranquillity and joy. Distinct areas including the seaside garden, the sensory garden, the memorial garden and the Smile Park adventure playground. Family activities. Home-made cakes and plant sale. Gardens and refreshments area are wheelchair friendly, accessible parking and WC facilities also available.

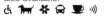

GROUP OPENING

🟦20 DIDSBURY VILLAGE GARDENS
Tickets from 68 Brooklawn Drive M20 3GZ or any garden, Didsbury, Manchester, M20 6RW. *5m S of Manchester. From M60 J5 follow signs to Northenden. Turn R at T-lights onto Barlow Moor Rd to Didsbury. From M56 follow A34 to Didsbury.* **Sun 9 June (12-5). Combined adm £6, chd free. Home made teas at 68 Brooklawn Drive.**

68 BROOKLAWN DRIVE
M20 3GZ. Anne & Jim Britt, www.annebrittdesign.com.

3 THE DRIVE
M20 6HZ. Peter Clare & Sarah Keedy, www.theshadegarden.com.

1 OSBORNE STREET
M20 2QZ. Richard & Teresa Pearce-Regan.

5 PARKFIELD ROAD SOUTH, FLAT 1
M20 6DA. Kath & Rob Lowe.

40 PARRS WOOD AVENUE
M20 5ND. Tom Johnson.

🆕 46 PARRS WOOD AVENUE
M20 5NB. Mr Mike Taylor.

38 WILLOUGHBY AVENUE
M20 6AS. Simon Hickey.

We have added a new contemporary garden this year to make a wonderful collection of 7 very beautiful and individual gardens to visit in the attractive suburb of Didsbury. There is so much to see and inspire in these gardens, from our traditional cottage gardens with alliums, roses, clematis and topiary, to the crisp lines of two beautifully planted contemporary gardens with white rendered walls, pale porcelain paving and stylish outdoor living and dining ideas. Other gardens offer a diverse range of water features, inspirational shade planting and organic wildlife friendly planting ideas - all within our relatively small garden spaces which are a feast to the eye and full of detail to imitate at home. Wheelchair access to some gardens.

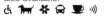

🟦21 🆕 DRUMMERSDALE CROSSING COTTAGE
Wholesome Lane, Scarisbrick, Ormskirk, L40 9SW. Mrs Janet & Mr Mike Hinton. *500 yds SE of Bescar Ln Railway Stn. There is no parking at this address. Parking in adjacent meadow accessed via junction of Drummersdale Ln & Wholesome Ln also known as Midge Hall Ln.What 3 Words app - Wedge. Flock.Blemishes. OS Grid SD 399 14.* **Sun 14 July (11-5). Adm £4, chd free. Light refreshments.**
Beautiful ½ acre country garden with open views to adjacent farmland. Colour themed beds with herbaceous perennials set within lawned area. Various trees & shrubs. Wildlife ponds, summerhouse with viewing window overlooking beehives. Shaded areas with ferns and hostas. Polytunnel with variety of fruit and veg. Meadow, orchard and woodland walks. Veg patch and wildflower areas are under development.

GROUP OPENING

🟦22 ELLESMERE PARK GARDENS
35 Westminster Road, Eccles, Manchester, M30 9FE. Enid Noronha. *4m S from central Manchester. From A56 Stretford take Edge Lane (A5154) ¾ m then bear L onto Wilbraham Rd (A6010) for ¾ m then L onto Westminster Rd.* **Sat 8 June (11.30-4). Combined adm £6, chd free. Cream teas at** 35 Ellesmere Rd, hot dogs at 20 Stafford Rd and tea & biscuits at 11 Westminster Rd.

35 ELLESMERE ROAD
M30 9FE. Enid Noronha.

20 STAFFORD ROAD
M30 9HW. Mrs Paula Gibson.

11 WESTMINSTER ROAD
M30 9HF. George & Lynne Meakin.

The group consists of 3 diverse suburban gardens in adjoining streets in Eccles. 35 Ellesmere Road is a cottage style garden with walkways, palisade, greenhouse and raised beds with vegetables and herbs. Lawns with box hedges. Mature fruit and other trees. At 11 Westminster Road there is a pretty front garden with topiary chickens, well-stocked with perennials, mature trees, and box hedging. The garden is divided by a trellis and rose arch which separates the flower beds and lawn from the fruit growing area, and there are a large number of fuchsias grown in pots. Finally at 20 Stafford Road the garden features mature trees and shrubs alongside many recent additions. An ongoing project involves upcycling items the garden owners find interesting that others have discarded. The owners like to put bold colours and statements in wherever they can to enable colour year-round. Some areas with only partial access.

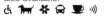

GROUP OPENING

23 NEW FALLOWFIELD & LADYBARN GARDENS
27 Clifton Avenue, Manchester, M14 6UD. Mrs Kattie Kincaid. *Trail runs from M14 6UD to M14 6YR. Approaching Fallowfield from Withington on Wilmslow Rd, turn R just after the Shell garage into Whiteoak Rd and you can park on the streets around there.* **Sat 3, Sun 4 Aug (11-5). Combined adm £6, chd free. Light refreshments at Tatton Villa, 3 Brook Road.**

NEW 1 BESFORD CLOSE
M14 6NF. Mr Matthew Baddeley.

NEW 6 CLIFTON AVENUE
M14 6UB. Mrs Lesley Bowers.

NEW 12 CLIFTON AVENUE
M14 6UB. Sue Hare.

NEW 27 CLIFTON AVENUE
M14 6UD. Mrs Kattie Kincaid.

NEW 11 EGERTON TERRACE
M14 6RL. Sue Bell.

NEW 7 ROSE COTTAGES, LADYBARN LANE
M14 6YR. Gillian Smithson.

NEW TATTON VILLA, 3 BROOK ROAD
M14 6UJ. Sian Astley.

Each garden on this short trail has something different to offer. They comprise a quintessentially, English cottage garden, a garden owned by professional designers who have created, amongst everything else, a highly imaginative outside entertaining space for their glorious old villa, a small, pretty garden which makes perfect use of its limited space, 2 beautifully mature Victorian gardens with thoughtful planting, mixed borders and lovely seating areas, a perfectly designed, modern garden with a stunning array of borders around circular lawns and, finally, a corner garden divided into 'rooms'. Fallowfield and Ladybarn suburbs grew rapidly from the mid 19th Century, the oldest garden on our trail belongs to a listed Georgian cottage and evokes an era when the area was nothing but farmland, the newest belongs to a smart, modern town house built for a bustling suburb. Along a large part of the trail you will pass some beautiful tree bases, planted and tended by local residents. Most of the gardens on this trail have easy wheelchair access and are on flat terrain.

&. 🍵))

GROUP OPENING

24 FRESHFIELD GARDENS
Formby, L37 7BA. *6m S of Southport. From Formby Bypass (A565) Filling Station r'about: Cable St & Moss Side are close together & situated 1m S, Brewery Ln is 1m N, Ennerdale Rd is 1.7m W.* **Sun 7 July (11-4). Combined adm £5, chd free. Home-made teas at Buttermere Close & Brewery Lane.**

33 BREWERY LANE
L37 7DY. Sue & Dave Hughes.

4 BUTTERMERE CLOSE
L37 2YB. Marilyn & Alan Tippett.

60 CABLE STREET
L37 3LX. Mrs Kate Crook.

NEW 1A MOSS SIDE
L37 3JY. John & Dina Nixon, dina_cuthbertson@hotmail.com, www.gardensandwildlife.com. **Visits also by arrangement 21 June to 7 July.**

4 coastal suburban gardens near to Formby sand dunes and NT Nature Reserve, home to the red squirrel. Soil is sandy and well drained. All the gardens feature colourful herbaceous borders with a mixture of shrubs, perennials roses and hydrangeas. The group gardens demonstrate a variety of styles and designs and some with fruit and vegetables areas. Features include raised beds, greenhouses, rockeries, ponds, arches, pergolas and basket/container displays.

❀ 🍵))

25 GILES FARM
Four Acre Lane, Thornley, Preston, PR3 2TD. Kirsten & Phil Brown, 07925 603246, phil.brown32@aol.co.uk. *3m NE of Longridge. Pass through Longridge & follow signs for Chipping. After 2m turn R at the old school up Hope Lane. Turn L at the top and continue to the farm where there is ample parking.* **Sat 15, Sun 16 June (12-5). Adm £5, chd free. A wide selection of home-made cakes & sandwiches. Visits also by arrangement 1 June to 14 July for groups of 15+. Guided tour with hand drawn map.**
Nestled high on the side of Longridge Fell, with beautiful long-reaching views across the Ribble Valley, the gardens surround the old farmhouse

and buildings. The gardens are ever evolving and inc an acre of perennial wildflower meadows, wildlife ponds, woodland areas and cottage gardens. There are plentiful areas to sit and take in the views. There are steps and uneven surfaces in the gardens.

🐕 ❀ 🍵

26 GLYNWOOD HOUSE
Eyes Lane, Bretherton, Leyland, PR26 9AS. Terry & Sue Riding. *Once in Bretherton, turn onto Eyes Lane by the War Memorial. After 50 yds take the R fork, after 100 yds follow the road around to the L. Glynwood House is a further 200 yds on the L.* **Sun 7 July (11-5). Adm £4, chd free. Home-made teas.**
Set in a peaceful rural location with spectacular views. Highlights of this ¾ acre garden inc colour themed mixed borders with rare and unusual plants, wildlife pond with cascade water feature and meandering paths through a woodland shaded area. A patio garden, surrounded by a large pergola, features a kinetic sycamore seed sculpture. Access available to most of the garden apart from paths in the woodland walk area.

&. 🐕 ❀ 🚗 🍵 🧺))

27 GREENFIELD HALL
Greenfield Road, Colne, BB8 9PE. Dr Mike & Mrs Lesley Pusey. *Close to the end of the M65 motorway. From end of M65 take A6068 signed Nelson & Colne. Take 1st exit A56 then 2nd L down Phillips Lane, follow to R into Greenfield Rd. Parking opp Industrial Units. What3words: landlords.tides.outline.* **Sun 16 June (1-5). Adm £4, chd free. Home-made teas.**
Set in a green oasis on the edge of Colne, C16 Greenfield Hall (not open) has a quirky informal garden featuring old and English roses and a wide variety of perennials, shrubs and young trees. A new pond is home to ghost carp and goldfish. The garden has several different planting areas. It is divided by the beck, crossed by a medieval bridge, and showcases work by renowned sculptor Clare Bigger.

28 33 GREENHILL ROAD

Mossley Hill, Liverpool, L18 6JJ.
Tony Rose. *From L lane at end of M62 follow Ring Road A5058 (S). Follow A5058 through 1st island. Keep to L lane through 2nd island then take B5180 for about ½ m to signage.* **Sun 14 July, Sun 1 Sept (12-5). Combined adm with 146 Mather Avenue £5, chd free. Light refreshments at 146 Mather Avenue.**
The central attraction in the garden is a raised water stream over cobbles running into a raised pond (reservoir). On two sides planted into the ground are mature bamboo and other plants around a golden Buddha statue. The remainder of the garden is hard paved in varying materials. There is no lawn. Throughout the garden the embellishment is with many types of plants in pots, exotic and unusual.

29 THE GROWTH PROJECT

Kellett Street Allotments, Kellett St, Rochdale, OL16 2JU. Karen Hayday, 07464 546962, k.hayday@hourglass.org.uk, www.facebook.com/Hourglass.org.uk. *From A627 M. R A58 L Entwistle Rd then R Kellett St.* **Sun 28 July (11.30-3). Adm £3.50, chd free. Home-made teas. Visits also by arrangement 26 June to 26 Sept. Open on Wednesdays & Thursdays each week. Donation to The Growth Project.**
The project covers over an acre inc a huge variety of organic veg, wildlife pond, insect hotels, formal flower and Japanese garden, potager, cut flower and woodland garden. See the mock Elizabethan strawbale build, the witch's hat, & railway station. Stroll down the pergola walk to the secret annual wildflower meadow, orchard & theatre. The new attractions this year are the development of the Japanese garden and the 'Witch's hat'. Home-made tea & lunch on the lawn, produce, jams & flowers for sale. No disabled WC, ground can be uneven.

GROUP OPENING

30 HALE VILLAGE GARDENS

2 Pheasant Field, Hale Village, Liverpool, L24 5SD. Roger & Tania Craine. *6m S of M62 J6. Take A5300, A562 towards L'pool, then A561 and then L for Hale. From S L'pool head for the airport then L sign for Hale.*

The 82A bus from Widnes/Runcorn to L'pool has village stops. **Sat 29, Sun 30 June (12-5). Combined adm £5, chd free. Cream teas at 2 Pheasant Field & cold drinks & cakes at 33 Hale Rd.**

4 CHURCH ROAD
L24 4BA. Ms Chris Chesters.

54 CHURCH ROAD
L24 4BA. Norma & Ray Roe.

66 CHURCH ROAD
L24 4BA. Liz Kelly-Hines & David Hines.

2 PHEASANT FIELD
L24 5SD. Roger & Tania Craine.

WHITECROFT, 33 HALE ROAD
L24 5RB. Donna & Bob Richards.

The delightful village of Hale is set in rural South Merseyside between Widnes and Liverpool Airport. It is home to the cottage, sculpture and grave of the famous giant known as the Childe of Hale. Five gardens of various sizes have been developed by their present owners. There are 2 gardens (a large skilfully landscaped one and a beautiful contemporary one) to the west of the village and 3 delightful gardens in Church Rd to the east of the village.

31 HALTON PARK HOUSE

Halton Park, Halton, Lancaster, LA2 6PD. Mr & Mrs Duncan Bowring. *7min drive from both J34 & 35 M6. On Park Lane, approx 1½ m from Halton or Caton. Park Lane accessed either from Low Rd or High Rd out of Halton. From Low Rd turn into Park Lane through pillars over cattle grid.* **Sat 18, Sun 19 May (11-4). Adm £5, chd free. Home-made teas. Barbecue over lunch time.**
Approx 6 acres of garden, with gravel paths leading through large mixed herbaceous borders, terraces, orchard and terraced vegetable beds. Wildlife pond and woodland walk in dell area, extensive lawns, greenhouse and herb garden. Plenty of places to sit and rest. Gravel paths (some sloping) access viewing points over the majority of the garden. Hard standing around the house.

32 NEW 3 HARROCK VIEW

Barmskin Lane, Heskin, Chorley, PR7 5PZ. Tony & Janet Trafford. *From M6 J27 take 1st exit and go past Crow Orchard petrol station for ¼ m. Turn R onto Moss Ln. After ¾ m turn R onto Courage Low Ln. Garden is on R after 1.2m.* **Sun 7 July (12-5). Adm £4, chd free. Light refreshments. Wine.**
Surprises galore in this long, narrow garden split into several themed areas with mature specimen trees and shrubs. Lots of unique animal sculptures, fun topiaries, luxury bug hotel, ornamental fish pond and wildlife ponds. There is a summerhouse and BBQ area with seating and many other interesting features. Gentle slope and steps from halfway therefore wheelchair access is limited.

33 NEW THE HAWES

Sandringham Road, Ainsdale, Southport, PR8 2NZ. Niall & Joan Roy. *5m S of Southport. From A565, at r'about turn R into Station Rd through Ainsdale Village. Take 1st R after level crossing and drive to far end of Sandringham Rd.* **Sun 2 June (11-4). Adm £5, chd free. Light refreshments.**
A 6 acre woodland garden plus numerous lawns and borders with stunning summer colour as well as several water features . The formal garden is designed with an arts and crafts theme. A long woodland walk leads you through rhododendron and pinewoods where red squirrels play. The garden has several wilding areas and there are 5 bee hives.

Our donation to the Army Benevolent Fund supported 608 individuals with front line services and horticultural related grants in 2023

34 HIGHER BRIDGE CLOUGH HOUSE

Coal Pit Lane, Rossendale, BB4 9SB. Karen Clough. *4m from Rawtenstall. Take A681 into Waterfoot. Turn L onto the B6238. Approx $\frac{1}{2}$ m turn R onto Shawclough Rd. Follow the road up until you reach the yellow signs.* **Sat 1, Sun 2 June (12-5). Adm £4, chd free. Cream teas, selection of cakes & drinks available.**
Nestled within Rossendale farmland in an exposed site the garden is split by a meandering stream. There are raised mixed borders with shrubs and perennials enclosed by a stone wall, with loose planting of shrubs and water loving plants around the stream. A local farmer once told me 'you won't grow 'owt up 'ere...' so the challenge is on. The Rossendale area provides some excellent walking and rambling sites. Rawtenstall has the famous East Lancashire railway, which is worth a visit.

🐕 ✱ ☕)))

GROUP OPENING

35 HIGHTOWN GARDENS

Alt Road, Hightown, Liverpool, L38 3RH. Dr Jan Proctor. *11m N of Liverpool & 11m S of Southport. M 57/58 Join A5758 keep L, at r'about take 2nd exit A565. Turn 2nd L onto B5193/Orrell Hill Lane Turn R Moss Lane. Turn L onto Alt Rd, then R to Kerslake Way & follow NGS signs from here.* **Sun 2 June (1-5). Combined adm £5, chd free. Home-made teas at The Cross House.**

11 BLUNDELL AVENUE
L38 9ED. Karen Rimmer.

THE CROSS HOUSE
L38 3RH. Dr Jan Proctor.

NEW 10 SANDHILLS
L38 9EP. Tracy Lewis.
07714 087736
rustyrose146@gmail.com

A welcoming group of 3 gardens in the village of Hightown. Visit a plantswoman's quirky garden full of surprises, a traditional garden surrounding a Victorian villa with herbaceous borders, and a sunken garden and a newly listed garden overlooking spectacular dunes housing the 2015 shed of the year. Sandhills is now a quirky Airbnb property. There is wheelchair access to the garden in Sandhills.

♿ ☕)))

36 HOLLY HOUSE

289 Moor Road, Croston, Leyland, PR26 9HP. Mrs Elaine Raper. *Situated on the A581, approx 200 metres after the Highfield pub if coming from Leyland area.* **Sun 9 June (11-5). Adm £4, chd free. Home-made teas.**
Large garden, approx an acre of perennial beds with mature trees. Pond with decking area leading to wooded area beyond with rill. Two wisteria clad pergolas, parterre with adjacent gazebo. Mostly accessible to the main parts of the garden. Wood behind pond not accessible.

♿ 🐕 ☕ 🛋)))

37 NEW 46 HOLMDALE AVENUE

Southport, PR9 8PS. Ms June Slater. *3½ m N of Southport. By car signed from A565 or by bus no 49 or X2 to Preston New Rd, alight at the Mormon church, into North Rd, take 1st L to Holmdale Ave.* **Sun 4 Aug (10-4). Combined adm with 3 Alexander Mews £5, chd free. Cream teas.**
A small and pretty garden filled with love for a peaceful experience. Borders filled with shrubs and plants in season. The lawn area incorporates a small pond, greenhouse and leads to a beach garden. In the autumn season hops flourish into fruition, these are a passion of the owner who comes from a hop picking family. The front garden is flagged from a central display with an abundance of flowering tubs.

☕

38 THE INN AT WHITEWELL

Dunsop Road, Whitewell, nr Clitheroe, BB7 3AT. Louise Bowman, 01200 448222, louise@innatwhitewell.com, www.innatwhitewell.com. *The garden is situated within a 3 min drive from the M55 exit. Please see website for directions under the 'contact us' page.* **Visits by arrangement 2 Apr to 30 Sept for groups of 10 to 50. Guided tours of garden. Adm £12, chd £4. Light refreshments. Tea, coffee & cakes.**
The Inn at Whitwell is a charming C17 wedding venue, hotel, gastro pub and restaurant on the banks of the River Hodder. The kitchen garden with an Alhambra style rill is a sight to behold with seasonal fruit, vegetables, cut flowers and herbs grown for the hotel. The piggery garden is a quintessential cottage garden with daffodils, tulips, wisteria, climbing roses, hydrangea and lavender. Beautiful fells and woodlands surround the property,

creating a gorgeous, tranquil backdrop for any occasion.

🐕 ✱ � 🛋 ☕)))

39 JACK GREEN COTTAGE

Mill House Lane, Brindle, Chorley, PR6 8NS. Aurelia & Peter McCann. *5m N Chorley. From Chorley A6 turn R at r'about on B5256 Westwood Rd then L at r'about on B5256 Sandy Lane through Brindle for 2m, then L on Hill House Lane for $\frac{3}{4}$ m. Turn L on Oram Rd for 200yd.* **Sat 22, Sun 23 June (11-4). Adm £5, chd free. Home-made teas.**
This $2\frac{3}{4}$ acre garden has been lovingly restored, developed and improved in the last 13 yrs. With long borders of cottage style plants, Japanese style garden, herb garden, orchards, fruit cage and vegetable plots, there is a surprise around every corner. Chicken pen, secluded BBQ area, Victorian-style greenhouse, a recycled bottle greenhouse and a willow tunnel are but few of the delights awaiting. Not all areas are suitable for wheelchair use, users should ideally be accompanied as some parts of the garden may be difficult to navigate.

♿ 🐕 ✱ ☕ 🛋)))

40 KINGTON COTTAGE

Kirkham Road, Treales, Preston, PR4 3SD. Mrs Linda Kidd, 01772 683005, www.littlekyoto. co.uk/gallery. *M55 J3. Take A585 to Kirkham, exit Preston St, L into Carr Lane to Treales village. Cottage on L.* **Sun 5 May, Sun 2 June, Sun 7 July, Sun 4 Aug (10-5). Adm £4, chd free. Home-made teas. Visits also by arrangement 1 May to 1 Sept for groups of 8 to 30. Escorted tours by garden owner.**
Nestling in the beautiful village of Treales this generously sized Japanese garden has many authentic and unique Japanese features, alongside its 2 ponds linked by a stream. The stroll garden leads down to the tea house garden. The planting and the meandering pathways blend together to create a tranquil meditative garden in which to relax. New additions complete four Japanese garden styles. Wheelchair access to some areas, uneven paths.

♿ 🐕 ✱ 🚗 ☕

41 MAGGIE'S, MANCHESTER

Kinnaird Road, Manchester, M20 4QL. Ruth Tobi, www. maggies.org/our-centres/maggies-manchester/. *At the end of Kinnaird Rd which is off Wilmslow Rd opposite the Christie Hospital.* **Sun 16 June (12-4). Adm £5, chd free. Cream teas. Light refreshments.**
The architecture of Maggie's Manchester, designed by world-renowned architect Lord Foster, is complemented by gardens designed by Dan Pearson, Best in Show winner at Chelsea Flower Show. Combining a rich mix of spaces, inc the working glasshouse and vegetable garden, the garden provides a place for both activity and contemplation. The colours and sensory experience of nature becomes part of the Centre through micro gardens and internal courtyards, which relate to the different spaces within the building. Wheelchair access to most of the garden from the front entrance.
& ✿ Ⓓ ☕ ᴗ))

GROUP OPENING

42 NEW MAGHULL GARDENS

The Crescent, Maghull, Liverpool, L31 7BL. Mr Ian & Mrs Nikki Fennah. *7m N of Liverpool. Gardens accessed via A59 Ormskirk to Maghull. R at Town Hall. Maghull stn approx ½ m over canal bridge. Summerville Dr & The Crescent within short drive of stn. Follow NGS signs. Cashless payments at 47 The Crescent.* **Sun 14 July (11-4). Combined adm £5, chd free. Home-made teas at 47 The Crescent & 44 Summerhill Dr.**

47 THE CRESCENT
Mr Ian & Mrs Nikki Fennah.
(See separate entry)

MAGHULL STATION
Merseyrail.

NEW **44 SUMMERHILL DRIVE**
Laura Brislin.

A small group of diverse and contrasting gardens on the outskirts of Liverpool. 47 The Crescent is a suburban garden with gravel, cut flower and courtyard areas. Relax and unwind in the lovely summerhouse surrounded by beautiful perennial planting. Several ponds encourage a variety of wildlife. Maghull Station gardens, voted RHS Britain in Bloom Best Station in 2021, feature borders with herbaceous perennials & shrubs. Rockery and secret garden with areas to encourage wildlife. Beautifully planted troughs and hanging baskets. 44 Summerhill Drive is a developing cottage style suburban garden with an extremely colourful and unusual variety of planting aimed at encouraging pollinators. There is a small Japanese inspired area with a collection of Bonsai. Lovely seating areas framing different views of the garden. A lovely reflective space in which to relax. Plants for sale at each of the gardens. Frank Hornby is said to have been inspired by Maghull Railway Station when creating his model buildings as he lived within sight of the station. His family grave is to be found in the grounds of St. Andrew's Church & The Maghull Ancient Chapel, which appears in the 1066 Magna Carta. Partial access at Maghull Stn & 47 The Crescent due to uneven/narrow paths.
& ✿ ☕ ᴗ))

7 Rose Cottages, Fallowfield & Ladybarn Gardens

43 146 MATHER AVENUE
Allerton, Liverpool, L18 7HB.
Barbara Peers. *3m S from end
of M62. On the R of Mather Ave
heading out of town: on the same
side as Tesco and 800 metres
beyond.* **Sun 14 July, Sun 1 Sept
(12-5). Combined adm with 33
Greenhill Road £5, chd free. Light
refreshments.**
A small tree fringed town garden
with two ponds, one for fish and
one for wildlife. A large woodpile is
left to encourage insects as are the
nettles along the back wall. One bed
allowed to self seed with wildflowers.
No pesticides and only home-made
compost used. A multitude of plants
encroach on the ever decreasing
patch of lawn. Paths around give
access.

**44 MERESANDS KENNELS &
CATTERY**
Holmeswood Rd, Rufford,
Ormskirk, L40 1TG. Mrs Bridget
Street. *6m N of Ormskirk. From
the A59 Rufford, turn L on to
Holmeswood Rd, past the Hesketh
Arms on R. 1m on L Signed to
Meresands Kennels & Cattery.* **Sun 9
June (10-4.30). Adm £5, chd free.
Tea, coffee & cake.**
An enchanting woodland garden of
approx 4 acres with formal gardens
and colourful koi pond. Walking
through the laburnum arch you
can explore the woodland area.
Winding paths lead you through
rhododendrons and mature trees,
with areas for sitting, a hobbit house
and wildflower area. There is a natural
pond overlooked by a pavilion, with
lovely views and an abundance
of wildlife. Not all the garden is
accessible by wheelchair.

45 MILL BARN
Goosefoot Close, Samlesbury,
Preston, PR5 0SS. Chris
Mortimer, 07742 924124,
millbarnchris@gmail.com. *6m E
of Preston. From M6 J31 2½m on
A59/A677 B/burn. Turn S. Nabs
Head Ln, then Goosefoot Ln.* **Sat
25, Sun 26 May, Sat 1, Sun 2 June
(11.30-5). Adm £5, chd free. Light
refreshments. Picnics welcome.
Visits also by arrangement 27 Apr
to 4 Aug for groups of 6 to 30.**
The unique and quirky garden at Mill
Barn is a delight, or rather a series
of delights. Along the River Darwin,
through the tiny secret grotto, past

the suspension bridge and view of
the fairytale tower, visitors can stroll
past folly, sculptures, lily pond, and
lawns, enjoy the naturally planted
flowerbeds, then enter the secret
garden and through it the pathways
of the wooded hillside beyond. A
garden developed on the site of old
mills gives a fascinating layout which
evolves at many levels. The garden
jungle provides a smorgasbord of
flowers to attract insects throughout
the season. Children enjoy the garden
very much. Partial wheelchair access.

46 MILL CROFT
Spout Lane, Wennington,
Lancaster, LA2 8NX.
Linda Ashworth & Carl
Hunter, 07811 347785,
linda.ashworth1@outlook.com.
*10m NE of Lancaster. From J34
of M6 take A683 towards Kirkby
Lonsdale. Turn R on B6480 towards
Bentham. Pass through Wray & the
narrowing in the road at Wennington,
then take the 1st L onto Spout Lane.*
**Visits by arrangement 25 Feb to
28 July for groups of 12 to 24.
Due to single track access no
coaches but minibus welcome.
Light refreshments. Home-made
cakes, inc gluten-free & vegan
options.**
A rural garden extending to about
3¼ acres with a summer flowering
meadow, stream, trees, shrubs,
herbaceous planting, vegetable plot
and stumpery. Various seating areas
to rest and enjoy local wildlife and
the surrounding views. Winter/spring
interest from snowdrops, hellebores,
daffodils and tulips. New projects
always underway.

47 NEW 18 MOOR DRIVE
Crosby, Liverpool,
L23 2UP. Mrs Vicki Hall,
vickihallhome@gmail.com. *12m
S of Southport & 7m N of Liverpool
close to Crosby village. A565 from
Southport. Formby bypass becomes
Southport Rd. Continues onto Moor
Ln Turn into Moor Drive, turn R at
junction, then R into cul de sac.
House on L. What 3 Words app -
rush.shades.quest.* **Sun 14 July
(11-4). Combined adm with 16
Beach Lawn £5, chd free. Home-
made teas.**
Wonderfully planted, picturesque
urban garden with numerous trees,
shrubs and climbers developed
over several years. Emphasis on

encouraging wildlife and organic
gardening practices. Lawned areas,
mixed perennial planting, small
veg garden with crop rotation.
Greenhouse. Ornamental & wildlife
ponds. Seating areas surrounded by
scented climbers and roses. Several
frogs and a tortoise live here! Crosby
beach is a short drive away where
it's possible to visit the art installation
'Another Place' by renowned sculptor
Anthony Gormley. Good access front
garden, seating areas & most of rear
garden. Some uneven pebble paths
around greenhouse area.

48 MOSS PARK ALLOTMENTS
Lesley Road, Stretford,
Manchester, M32 9EE. Allison
Sterlini, 07778 931029,
mossparksecretary@gmail.com.
*3m SW of Manchester. From M60
J7 (Manchester), A56 (Manchester),
A5181 Barton Rd, L onto B5213
Urmston Lane, ½m L onto Lesley
Rd signed Stretford Cricket Club.
Parking at 2nd gate.* **Sun 14
July (11-4). Adm £5, chd free.
Gorgeous array of home-made
cakes. Visits also by arrangement.**
Moss Park is a stunning, award
winning allotment site in Stretford,
Manchester. Wide grass paths
flanked by pretty flower borders give
way to a large variety of well-tended
plots bursting with ideas to try at
home, from insect hotels to unusual
fruits and vegetables. Take tea and
cake on the lawn outside the quirky
society clubhouse that looks like a
beamed country pub. WC facilities.
Partial wheelchair access.

49 THE NORTH TITHEBARN
Lunt Lane, Lunt, Liverpool,
L29 7WL. Mrs Janis & Mr Howard
Sleeman. *Between Maghull & Ince
Blundell. 1m from Sefton Parish
Church & The Punch Bowl. From
Switch Island follow A5758 R onto
B5422 Brickwall Lane signed Sefton.
In Sefton turn L onto Lunt Rd & cont
into Lunt Village. Barn is signposted
in village.* **Sat 8, Sun 9 June
(12-5). Combined adm with 136
Buckingham Road £5, chd free.
Home-made teas.**
Nestled in the village of Lunt this
2 acre garden comprises of ½ an
acre of woodland, and an impressive
25 metre pond surrounded by
perennial planting. Several other
ponds, orchard, wildflower area and

vegetable beds along with mature trees, rhododendrons and 'hosta hill' provide plenty of interest in a tranquil setting.

50 OAKLANDS
Flash Lane, Rufford, Ormskirk, L40 1SW. Mr John & Mrs Jane Hoban. *Pls park in the village hall car park which is situated on the L at the end of Flash Lane.* **Sat 8, Sun 9 June (10-4). Combined adm with 31 Cousins Lane £5, chd free. Home-made teas at Rufford Cricket Club.**
Oaklands is a woodland garden full of mature trees, acers, camellias and rhododendrons. We have over the years created beautiful pathways and seating areas flanked with ferns and hostas. The garden also has several water features and large areas of lawn. Most areas of our garden are wheelchair accessible but most of the pathways are through the woodlands so it can be quite uneven.

51 THE OLD VICARAGE
Church Road, Astley, Manchester, M29 7FS. Susan & Neil Kinsella, 07748 323222, susan.kinsella@ hotmail.co.uk. *Halfway between Leigh & Worsley off A580 East Lancs Rd. Opp the site of the old St Stephens Astley CE Church & next to Dam House, 250 yds from the mini r'about junction at Church Rd (A5082) & Manchester Rd (A572). Close to the Bull's Head.* **Sat 29, Sun 30 June (10-4). Adm £4, chd free. Home-made teas. Visits also by arrangement 1 June to 20 Sept for groups of 15 to 30.**
Recently restored medium sized gardens of Grade II* vernacular Georgian vicarage comprising both formal and informal planting and statuary as the garden narrows to follow the woodland stream which runs through it. There are 6 separate areas/rooms which gradually merge into the surrounding trees ending several hundred yards from the frontage to the property. Most of the garden is flat with some gravel paths.

GROUP OPENING

52 NEW OLDHAM GARDENS
Lark Rise 515 Burnley Lane, Chadderton, Oldham, OL9 0BW. Wendy & Ian Connor. *Green Ln leave M60 J22 towards Manchester. 1st exit L (Hollins Rd). In 1m turn R into Garden Suburb. Lark Rise leave A627(M) at J1 Elk Mill R'about taking Middleton exit. House is ½ m on L. Maggie's is in Royal Oldham Hospital grounds next to A&E. Maps at all gardens.* **Sun 14 July (12-5). Combined adm £5, chd free. Home-made teas at each garden.**

NEW 76 GREEN LANE
OL8 3BA. Susan & John Clegg.

LARK RISE
OL9 0BW. Wendy & Ian Connor.

MAGGIE'S, OLDHAM
OL1 2JH. Maggie's Centres, www.maggies.org/oldham.

3 gardens less than 3m from Oldham town centre, all different in style. 76 Green Lane is entered through a wooden pergola past a cutting garden. Steps lead through a rose arch onto a path past 2 greenhouses down to another cutting patch. The garden consists of large mature trees & borders containing many cottage garden favourites inc roses, clematis, sweet peas and foxgloves. Lark Rise is a ½ acre suburban garden with borders surrounding the garden planted with perennials, shrubs and small decorative trees. Its features inc an apple archway leading to a box parterre with a decorative ironwork water feature. There is a beehive in a wild area at the bottom of the garden. Maggie's Oldham is a one storey building supported over its garden by steel legs. The building 'floats' aloft like a drop curtain to the scene creating a picture window effect. The garden flows below the building into a walled & secluded woodland sanctuary. Designed by Rupert Muldoon, it has featured on Gardeners' World. Wheelchair access is available at Lark Rise and Maggie's.

GROUP OPENING

53 ORMSKIRK AND AUGHTON GARDENS
Ormskirk, L39 1LF. Brian & Marian Jones. *13m N of Liverpool. From the end of M57 take A59 & follow signs for Ormskirk or from M58 J3 take A570 to Ormskirk.* **Sun 30 June (11-4). Combined adm £5, chd free. Home-made teas.**

GORSE HILL NATURE RESERVE
Holly Lane, Ormskirk, L39 7HB. Jonathan Atkins (Reserve Manager), www.nwecotrust.org.uk.

72 LUDLOW DRIVE
L39 1LF. Marian & Brian Jones, 01695 574628, 72ludlow@gmail.com. **Visits also by arrangement 9 June to 28 July for groups of 6 to 20.**

NEW RULOE, 89 DERBY STREET
L39 2BW. Mr Ian Murray, 07976 606157, ian@4dgardendesign.co.uk. **Visits also by arrangement 1 June to 1 Aug.**

Ormskirk is an historic market town in W Lancashire. The gardens are very diverse with something for everyone. Gorse Hill Nature Reserve situated on a sandstone ridge offers spectacular views across the Lancashire Plain. There is a 5 acre wildflower meadow in summer brimming with a wide variety of wildflowers and grasses. The meadows pond is patrolled by dragonflies and damselflies. 72 Ludlow Drive is a beautiful town garden overflowing with exuberant planting. Comprising a gravel garden, colourful herbaceous and shrub borders, raised shade and rose borders with many old and new roses and clematis. A large glasshouse with a collection of succulents, aeoniums, cacti and pelargoniums. There is also a raised pond and alpine troughs. Ruloe, 89 Derby St is a Georgian property with a medium sized garden with a large koi pond, tulip tree, specimen oak tree and mixed beds. Gorse Hill woodland walk leading to the wildflower meadow has wheelchair accessible paths. Ruloe has 2 steps leading to lawn/ patio area.

111 Main Street

54 NEW 33 PERSHORE GROVE
Ainsdale, Southport, PR8 2SY. Mr
Francis Proctor, 07866 667066,
francisandbarbara33@gmail.com.
*4.9 m S of Southport. Disabled
parking on the garden driveway.
Other parking pls use Westminster
Drive.* **Sat 18 May, Sat 19 Oct
(10-4.30). Adm £5, chd free. Pre-
booking essential, please visit
www.ngs.org.uk for information
& booking. Tea. Visits also by
arrangement 18 May to 19 Oct.**
Small private garden, which includes
bridge, romantic ruin and man
made caves. Entrance via side
gate. Entrance to caves may not be
suitable for those with mobility issues.
☕

55 PLANT WORLD
Myerscough College, St
Michaels Road, Bilsborrow,
Preston, PR3 0RY. 01995 642264,
tmelia@myerscough.ac.uk, www.
myerscough.ac.uk/commercial-
services-equine-events/plant-
world-gardens/. *From M6 take J32
and head N for 5m up the A6. Turn
L onto St Michaels Rd take 2nd
entrance into the college signed
Plant World.* **Sun 28 Apr, Sun 4 Aug
(10-4). Adm £4.50, chd free. Light
refreshments in the tearoom with
a range of sandwiches & cakes
on offer.**
A gardener's paradise within an
acre of RHS Gold Award winning
gardens and glasshouses, inc
Tropical, Temperate and Desert
Zones. Themed and herbaceous
borders, roses, pinetum, bog garden
and pond. Plant sales of many
rare unusual specimens. Tearooms
overlook stunning gardens serving
a wide range of delicious locally
produced cakes and sandwiches.
Indoor and outdoor seating. Dogs
welcome in the gardens, sales area
and café. Wonderful pollinator friendly
herbaceous borders in the spring,
summer and autumn months - a
photographer's dream! Partial access
for wheelchairs. Paths are grass and it
can be wet in some areas.
& 🐕 ✳ 🚐 🛏 ☕

56 RAINBAG COTTAGE
Carr Moss Lane, Halsall, Ormskirk,
L39 8RZ. Sue & Mick Beacon. *8m
NW of Ormskirk. What 3 Words app
doll.talkative.hamsters. A570 from
Ormskirk to Southport after 4m,
L into Gorsuch Lane A5147. After
1½m pass church R into Carr Moss*

*Ln which becomes single track,
house sign on L after 2m.* **Sat 31
Aug, Sun 1 Sept (11-4.30). Adm
£4, chd free. Home-made teas.**
A magical ½ acre garden in a
rural setting with open views to the
surrounding countryside. Oriental
themed stroll garden with wildlife
ponds and moon gate. Herbaceous
borders and woodland walk.
Small flower meadow, fruit trees,
greenhouse, wormery and bug pad.
Various seating areas. Fairies, a
scarecrow and an angel live here.
Projects under development inc
vegetable and cut flower garden.
✳ ☕ 🛏

57 NEW 85 RIBCHESTER ROAD
Clayton Le Dale, Blackburn,
BB1 9HT. Mrs Elizabeth Seed.
*1m N of Blackburn. From Preston/
Clitheroe take B6245 off A59 for
0.8m and from B/burn take A666,
turn L on B6245 for 0.5m. Garden
opp. St. Peters Church, Salesbury.
Parking at Salesbury School, Lovely
Hall Lane, 0.2m.* **Sat 13, Sun 14
July (12-4). Adm £3. Home-made
teas.**
Year-round interest is provided in this
small suburban garden. Herbaceous
borders inc. a mix of perennials,
shrubs, roses, climbers, and grasses.
Decorative ironwork arches and
pergola complement the planting.
Two raised ponds with water features,
fruit trees, a small vegetable area and
greenhouse complete the garden.
Seating available and home-made
cakes. Some uneven paths and steps.
✳ ☕ 🔊

58 ◆ THE RIDGES
Weavers Brow (cont of
Cowling Rd), Limbrick,
Chorley, PR6 9EB. Mr & Mrs
J M Barlow, 01257 279981,
barbara@barlowridges.co.uk,
www.bedbreakfast-gardenvisits.
com. *2m SE of Chorley town centre.
From M6 J27 & M61 J8. Follow signs
for Chorley A6 then signs for Cowling
& Rivington. Passing Morrison's
up Brook St, mini r'about 2nd exit,
Cowling Brow. Pass Spinners Arms
on L. Garden on R.* **For NGS: Mon
6 May, Mon 26 Aug (11-5). Adm
£5, chd free. Light refreshments.
For other opening times and
information, please phone, email or
visit garden website.**
3 acres, inc old walled orchard
garden, cottage-style herbaceous
borders, with perfumed rambling
roses and clematis through fruit trees.

Arch leads to formal lawn, surrounded
by natural woodland, shrub borders
and specimen trees with contrasting
foliage. Woodland walks and dell.
Natural looking stream, wildlife ponds.
Walled water feature with Italian
influence, and walled herb garden.
Classical music played. Some gravel
paths and woodland walks not
accessible.
& 🐕 ✳ 🛏 ☕

**59 NEW RISHTON TROPICAL
GARDEN**
52 Tomlinson Place, Rishton,
Blackburn, BB1 4AZ. Mr Tez
Donnelly, www.facebook.com/
LancsTropicalGarden. *Junction
7 M65, then Clitheroe exit on the
r'about, then turn L to Rishton.
Turn L into Parker St, then L into
Wheatfield St. Please note there is
no parking available at the address.*
**Sat 10, Sun 11 Aug (12.30-4). Adm
£4, chd free. Light refreshments.**
A recently created Tropical style
garden, with palm trees, bananas,
cannas, gingers and a wide range of
other exotic style plants. The garden
is located next to the Leeds Liverpool
canal.
✳ ☕ 🔊

Our donation in
2023 has enabled
Parkinson's UK to
fund 3 new nursing
posts this year,
directly supporting
people with
Parkinson's

GROUP OPENING

60 SEFTON PARK GARDENS
Liverpool, L17 1AS. Sefton Park Allotments Society. *From end of M62 take A5058 Queens Drive S through Allerton to Sefton Park. Circle the park and use postcodes. Maps available at all gardens.* **Sun 9 June (12-5). Combined adm £6, chd free. Home-made teas.**

6 CROXTETH GROVE
L8 0RX. Stuart Speeden.

FERN GROVE COMMUNITY GARDEN
L8 0RY. Liverpool City Council.

PARKMOUNT
L17 3BP. Jeremy Nicholls.

37 PRINCE ALFRED ROAD
L15 8HH. Jane Hammett.

SEFTON PARK ALLOTMENTS
Greenbank Drive, Liverpool, L17 1AS. Sefton Park Allotments Society.

SEFTON VILLA
L8 3SD. Patricia Williams.

17 SYDENHAM AVENUE
L17 3AU. Fatima Aabbar-Marshall.

Seven glorious examples of inner city gardening are on offer from the Sefton Park group this year. The opening is timed for the gardens' stunning rose displays. There are five private gardens, all beautifully planted, varying from the small colourful back garden in Croxteth Grove, to the spacious grandeur of Park Mount, backing on to Sefton Park itself. The gardens of Sefton Villa and Sydenham Avenue have exquisite planting schemes. The secret walled garden in Prince Alfred Road has much to delight and charm visitors. At Sefton Park Allotments, some of the best kept plots in the city are on display. And there's fun for all the family at Fern Grove Community Garden. Look out for the Liverpool City's 'Allotment of the Year 2022' at Sefton Park Allotments, along with a developing orchard and children's plot. Children's activities and bee demonstration at Fern Grove Community Garden. Classical music 2-4pm at Sefton Park Allotments.

61 NEW THE SHAKESPEAREAN GARDEN, PLATT FIELDS PARK
Manchester, M14 6LA. Manchester City Council, www.facebook.com/ShakespeareanGarden. *The garden is situated off Wilmslow Rd, down Mabfield Rd. There is a car park in the park nr the Mabfield Rd entrance, if that is full people can park on the streets near the park entrance.* **Sat 6, Sun 7 July (11.30-5). Adm £5, chd free. Light refreshments.**
The concept of a Shakespearean Garden was first developed in Victorian England with the idea of creating a garden with some or all, of the trees and flowers mentioned in the bard's works. With strong links to the suffrage movement and Edwardian Manchester society our garden opened in 1922 and was rescued from near obscurity over 3yrs by volunteers. Few public Shakespearean Gardens remain in the UK. There is a simple Elizabethan knot and a human sunclock. There are two entrances into the garden; one down steps, but the entrance on the east side is sloped. There are wide paths inside the garden.

62 SOUTHLANDS
12 Sandy Lane, Stretford, M32 9DA. Maureen Sawyer & Duncan Watmough, 0161 283 9425, moe@southlands12.com, www.southlands12.com. *3m S of Manchester. Sandy Lane (B5213) is situated off A5181 (A56) ¼m from M60 J7.* **Sun 21 July (12-5.30). Adm £5, chd free. Home-made teas. Cake-away service (take a slice of your favourite cake home). Visits also by arrangement June to Aug for groups of up to 30. We can offer early evening visits by arrangement.**
This beautiful multi-award winning garden inc a newly planted Mediterranean terrace, an ornamental garden with stunning herbaceous borders, organic kitchen potager with large greenhouse and tranquil woodland garden. Fabulous container plantings throughout add to its continued appeal as a garden that is 'Absolutely wonderful to walk through' and 'an unforgettable experience' for visitors. Artist's work on display.

63 NEW 28 STAFFORD ROAD
Eccles, Manchester, M30 9HW. Mr Tony Shepherd, 07834 452180, shepsurf@gmail.com, www.instagram.com/monton_garden/. *M602 Eccles exit, take the 1st exit then at the lights, turn L. Follow the road for 1m heading towards Monton, go over small r'about, next R is Stafford Rd.* **Sat 17 Aug (9-5). Adm £5, chd free. Light refreshments. Visits also by arrangement 10 June to 1 Nov.**
A large garden in Manchester with large borders full of woodland jungle plants. Mature bamboos, inc a magnificent *Borinda papyrifera*, large palm trees and a collection of rare, hardy plants from around the world inc a number of hardy Schefflera plants. There is a small gravel area over which a wheel chair will have to pass.

64 NEW 87 TODD LANE NORTH
Lostock Hall, Preston, PR5 5UP. Sue & Steve Green. *3m S of Preston. From J29 off the M6 nr Preston follow signs to Lostock Hall. Entrance is through the front gate. Street parking mainly, additional parking may be available at 85 Todd Lane North.* **Sun 2 June (10.30-4.30). Combined adm with 101 Todd Lane North £5, chd free. Light refreshments.**
The front & side gardens have a number of raised beds, a large Buddha and a relaxation pod. The main garden at the rear of the property takes you through a number of 'garden rooms' including a cut flower section, an orchard, a large lawned garden with a number of stone features, a BBQ area, summerhouse and greenhouse, a ying-yang woodland, and a child's play area. Most parts of the garden are on level ground. The front garden has steps but this can also be accessed via an adjacent sloping drive.

65 NEW 101 TODD LANE NORTH
Lostock Hall, Preston, PR5 5UP. Peter & Pauline Broadbent. *Nr Preston J29 off M6. Follow signs for Lostock Hall.* **Sun 2 June (10.30-4.30). Combined adm with 87 Todd Lane North £5, chd free. Light refreshments.**
A hidden gem, ¾ of an acre of well established flower borders, grassed areas, winding paths and a few surprises. Includes a koi pond and a wildlife pond. The garden encourages bees and wildlife.

66 TURTON TOWER KITCHEN GARDEN

Tower Drive, Turton, Bolton, BL7 0HG. Nancy Walsh, www. turtontower-kitchengarden.co.uk. *1½ m from Edgworth. Turton Tower is signed off the B6391 between Bolton & Edgworth.* **Sat 22 June (11-4). Adm £3, chd free.**

The garden is set in the historic Turton Tower grounds and was originally the kitchen garden in Victorian times. A group of enthusiastic volunteers began to restore the heavily overgrown ⅔ of an acre garden in 2008. Over the years the volunteers have created a tranquil and much visited garden. The garden today consists of raised vegetable beds and soft fruit areas but most of the garden is divided into smaller feature gardens. Turton Tower's history is reflected in its Tudor and Victorian beds. More contemporary gardens inc The White Garden and Japanese Garden. There are also two long herbaceous borders with a large variety of perennials. An area of the garden is shaded and we have an interesting variety of ferns and shade loving plants in our stumperies. Plants, cards and jam will be for sale. The paths are wheelchair friendly but in some places are moderately sloped.

67 NEW 280 WARRINGTON ROAD

Abram, Wigan, WN2 5RJ. Andy & Paula Prescott. *2m S of Wigan. Pls park at Abram Village Club, opp house. Look out for yellow signs.* **Sun 14 July (11-4). Combined adm with Wigan & Leigh Hospice £4, chd free. Light refreshments. Tea, coffee & cake.**

The garden is about ¾ of an acre of back land behind our property. It is our little haven which we have transformed into a garden from overgrown land with brambles, nettles and self seeding trees. It now has colourful borders, both shade and full sun, trees, shrubs, a large pond with ducks and fish. We are self taught gardeners and still learning, with a love for saving plants and being outdoors. Pond, summerhouse, potting shed, greenhouse.

GROUP OPENING

68 WARTON GARDENS

Warton, LA5 9PJ. 01524 727770, claire@lavenderandlime.co.uk, www.facebook.com/6WartonGardensNGS/. *3m J35 M6, 1m N of Carnforth. 5 gardens on Main St span approx ¾ m, 1 garden is just off Main St in Church Hill Ave. Allotments off Back Lane nr school down footpath.* **Sat 15, Sun 16 June (11-5). Combined adm £6, chd free. Home-made teas at 9 Main Street and 111 Main Street.**

BRIAR COTTAGE
LA5 9PT. Mr Bendall, 01524 733836, richardbendall@hotmail.co.uk.
Visits also by arrangement 14 June to 17 June for groups of 5 to 15.

2 CHURCH HILL AVENUE
LA5 9NU. Mr & Mrs J Street.

9 MAIN STREET
LA5 9NR. Mrs Sarah Baldwin.

80 MAIN STREET
LA5 9PG. Mrs Yvonne Miller.

107 MAIN STREET
LA5 9PJ. Becky Hindley, www.erdabotanicals.co.uk.

111 MAIN STREET
LA5 9PJ. Mr & Mrs J Spendlove, 01524 727770, claire@onezeronine.co.uk.
Visits also by arrangement 19 June to 13 Sept for groups of 10 to 30. Please note that there are steps and paths leading up the garden.

WARTON ALLOTMENT HOLDERS
LA5 9QU. Mrs Jill Slaughter.

The 6 gardens are spread across the village and offer a wide variety of planting and design ideas. They comprise of a contemporary garden skilfully planted on limestone pavement, a flower picking garden, a plantsman's garden with unusual herbaceous planting, trees and productive vegetable/soft fruit section, a large garden with a series of rooms each with a different atmosphere, a garden with the epitome of country style and a recently created garden designed to encourage pollinators. A group of allotments complete your visit. Families are encouraged and we will be offering children's activities at some gardens. Warton is the birthplace of the medieval ancestors of George Washington.

The ruins of the Old Rectory (English Heritage) is the oldest surviving building in the village. Ascent of Warton Crag (AONB), provides panoramic views across Morecambe Bay to the Lakeland hills beyond. 111 Main Street Regional Winner (North), The English Garden Magazine's The Nation's Favourite Gardens 2023

69 WEEPING ASH GARDEN

Bents Garden & Home, Warrington Road, Glazebury, WA3 5NS. John Bent, www.bents.co.uk. *15m W of Manchester. Next to Bents Garden & Home, just off the A580 East Lancs Rd at Greyhound r'about nr Leigh. Follow brown 'Garden Centre' signs.* **Sun 11, Sun 18, Sun 25 Feb, Sun 11 Aug, Sun 8 Sept (10-4). Adm by donation.**

Created by retired nurseryman and photographer John Bent, Weeping Ash is a garden of year-round interest with a beautiful display of early snowdrops. Broad sweeps of colour lend elegance to this stunning garden which is much larger than it initially seems with hidden paths and wooded areas creating a sense of natural growth. Bents Garden & Home offers a choice of dining destinations inc The Fresh Approach Restaurant, Caffe nel Verde and a number of al fresco dining options.

The National Garden Scheme's final instalment to support the building of the Y Bwthyn NGS Macmillan Specialist Palliative Care Unit in Wales, enabled 270 inpatients to be supported this year

GROUP OPENING

70 NEW WHALLEY AND DISTRICT GARDENS

Whalley, Billington and Old Langho, Clitheroe, BB7 9UG. Mrs Carole Ann Powers, www.facebook.com/groups/783913449708147. *4m S of Clitheroe. From M6 J31 take A59 to Clitheroe. After 9m take 2nd exit at r'about for Whalley. After 2m reach village & follow yellow signs. Tickets sold at all gardens, cashless payments at 5 Woodlands Pk, English Martyrs' Church & NGS Info Desk at Whalley Methodist Church.* **Sat 27, Sun 28 July (12-5). Combined adm £8, chd free. Home-made teas at Whalley Methodist Church, English Martyrs Church, Whalley Abbey, Ebenezers Chapel in Billington & The Parish Church of St Mary & All Saints.**

NEW THE ALLOTMENTS
BB7 9SY. Miss Judith Davies.

2 BROOKSIDE
BB6 8AP. Mr Peter Lumsden.

CASA LAGO
BB7 9UG. Mr Stephen & Mrs Carole Ann Powers.

NEW 33 DEER PARK CRESCENT
BB7 9XH. Mrs Sheila Maw.

NEW EBENEZERS CHAPEL
BB7 9NN. Mr Graham Vernon.

NEW ENGLISH MARTYRS' CHURCH
BB7 9TN. Mrs Alison Butler alison.butler@dioceseofsalford.org.uk

NEW THE HOLLIES
BB7 9AA. Mrs Linzee Greenhalgh.

NEW POOLE HOUSE
BB7 9SU. Mr David Ridehalgh.

NEW ST MARY AND ALL SAINTS CHURCH
BB7 9SY. Mrs Catherine Duckworth, www.whalleypc.org.uk.

NEW WARWICK HOUSE
BB7 9LS. Mr Basheer Butt.

NEW WHALLEY ABBEY
BB7 9SS. Rev Anna Walker, www.whalleyabbey.org.

NEW 5 WOODLANDS PARK
BB7 9UG. Mr Denis & Mrs Marion Teulon.

The gardens are predominantly spread across Whalley, one in Old Langho, two in Billington, varying in both size and design ideas. Our group offers a front garden planted to complement the home's heritage, whilst others showcase water features, koi ponds, bonsai collection, acers, beehives, wildlife friendly planting schemes, Grow Your Own food, developing allotments and a sensory community garden, secluded ⅓ of an acre wilder wooded area with fruit trees, historic Whalley Abbey founded in 1296 set in 12 acres of naturalistic planting. The English Martyrs Church with fragrant flowers and roses and The Parish Church of St Mary and All Saints with a plethora of historical interest. Whalley and District Gardens is a start up Community Project, with garden themed activities, linking Mental Health/Wellbeing to therapeutic horticulture.

🐕 ❀ ☕))

71 WIGAN & LEIGH HOSPICE

Kildare Street, Hindley, Wigan, WN2 3HZ. Wigan & Leigh Hospice, www.thehospicegardener.com. *1½m SW of Wigan. From Wigan on A577 Leigh/Manchester Rd. In Hindley turn R at St Peter's Church onto Liverpool Rd A58. After 250 metres turn R into Kildare St.* **Sun 14 July (11-4). Combined adm with 280 Warrington Road £4, chd free. Home-made teas.**
Large attractive gardens surround the Hospice creating a place of tranquillity. At the front are raised beds and a courtyard garden, at the rear 3 large ponds and a 'rainbow' bridge. Outside patients' rooms are colourful mixed borders. A memorial daisy garden. A wildflower garden has been created which is a haven for wildlife. Awarded 'Gold' in NW in Bloom, featured on NW Tonight and RHS Tatton. Fully accessible, including WC.

♿ 🐕 ❀ 🚗 ☕))

72 NEW 32 WOOD HEY GROVE

Syke, Rochdale, OL12 9UA. Mr Graham & Mrs Janine Bullas. *Around 2m N of Rochdale town centre. Follow the A671 (Whitworth Rd) out of Rochdale towards Burnley and turn R at the 2nd r'about (Fieldhouse Ln) At the next junction turn L & Wood Hey Grove will be 1m on L.* **Sun 14 July (10-4). Adm £3.50, chd free. Light refreshments.**
The garden was Graham's retirement landscape project and continues to evolve 10 yrs on. The planting only really started when Janine also retired 4 yrs ago and the garden is now taking shape. The hard landscaping is a mix of complex curves over 4 levels with paved patios, hardwood decking, lawns, trees and herbaceous borders complementing the overall scheme. We plan to offer home made bread and craft items for sale as well as cakes and tea & coffee for consumption in the garden. The steps within the garden would prevent access to the whole plot but most of the garden is visible due to the slope of the garden.

♿ 🐕 ❀ ☕))

GROUP OPENING

73 WOOLTON VILLAGE GARDENS

Hillside Drive, Woolton, Liverpool, L25 5NR. *6m SE of Liverpool city centre. Gardens are best accessed by car or bus (75, 78, 81, 89). Nearest train stn is Hunts Cross.* **Sun 19 May (12-5). Combined adm £5, chd free. Light refreshments.**

GREEN RIDGES, RUNNYMEDE CLOSE
L25 5JU. Sarah & Michael Beresford.

23 HILLSIDE DRIVE
L25 5NR. Bruce & Fiona Pennie.

NEW 15 LYNTON GREEN
L25 6JB. Gill & Danny O'Donoghue, 0151 281 1028, Gill0527@hotmail.com.
Visits also by arrangement Apr to Sept for groups of up to 30.

MERRICK, 4 HILLSIDE DRIVE
Liverpool, L25 5NS. Kerry & Tony Marson.

Four suburban gardens located in the beautiful historic village of Woolton featuring C17 buildings that act as a backdrop to the public space plant displays maintained by Woolton in Bloom, for whom the gardens also open. The gardens feature herbaceous borders, water features, tropical plants, greenhouses, kitchen garden, and garden sculptures.

🐕 ❀ 🚗 ☕))

Derbyshire
Leicestershire & Rutland
Lincolnshire
Northamptonshire
Nottinghamshire

EAST MIDLANDS

Above: Glebe Steading, Nottinghamshire

EAST MIDLANDS

From the busy urban clusters of Derby, Leicester and Nottingham, to the remote coast of Lincolnshire stretching from the Wash to the Humber, this is a region of great natural variety and throughout the region there is a good mix of rural and urban gardens.

Areas of renowned landscape beauty, such as Derbyshire's famous Peak District which became England's first National Park in 1951, Nottinghamshire's Sherwood Forest, and the gentle, undulating Lincolnshire Wolds, provide havens of unspoilt countryside to which people have flocked for decades. Through the middle of the region the invasive coal mines of Derbyshire and Nottinghamshire have been quiet for decades, their great tips of coal waste which were so prevalent now gently restored as rolling green hills in a new landscape. Cathedrals reflect the variety, from unforgettable medieval Lincoln which can be seen towering over the city from miles around, to Nottinghamshire's more modest and lesser-known Southwell Minster. In the south of the region, Northamptonshire villages with houses built of the distinctive local stone are popular destinations for visiting groups of gardens which open together.

Above, from top: Easton Walled Gardens, Lincolnshire; 7 Burnham Way, Long Buckby Gardens, Northamptonshire

Below: 9 Hawkins Drive, Derbyshire

DERBYSHIRE

VOLUNTEERS

County Organiser
Hildegard Wiesehofer
07809 883393
hildegard@ngs.org.uk

County Treasurer
Ann Wilkinson
07831 598396
anne.wilkinson@ngs.org.uk

Social Media
Tracy & Bill Reid
07932 977314
billandtracyreid@ngs.org.uk

Booklet Co-ordinator
Dave & Valerie Booth
07891 436632
valerie.booth1955@gmail.com

Group Visit Co-ordinator
Pauline Little
01283 702267
plittle@hotmail.co.uk

Assistant County Organisers
Gill & Colin Hancock
01159 301061
gillandcolinhancock@gmail.com

Jane Lennox
07939 012634
jane@lennoxonline.net

Pauline Little
(See above)

Christine & Vernon Sanderson
01246 570830
christine.r.sanderson@uwclub.net

Kate & Peter Spencer
01629 822499
pandkspencer@gmail.com

Paul & Kathy Harvey
01629 822218
pandk.harvey@ngs.org.uk

f @ngsderbyshire
X @DerbyshireNGS
O @derbyshirengs

OPENING DATES

All entries subject to change.
For latest information check
www.ngs.org.uk
Map locator numbers are
shown to the right of each
garden name.

February

Snowdrop Openings

Saturday 10th
The Dower House   16

Sunday 11th
The Dower House   16

Sunday 18th
10 Chestnut Way   11

March

Friday 22nd
◆ Cascades Gardens   10

Saturday 23rd
Chevin Brae   12

April

Wednesday 17th
Greenacres   21

Saturday 20th
◆ Cascades Gardens   10

Sunday 21st
NEW Dronfield Heritage Trust   17
The Paddock   44
26 Stiles Road   52
Yew Tree Bungalow   58

Wednesday 24th
Brierley Farm   6

May

Wednesday 1st
◆ Meynell Langley Trials Garden   38
◆ Renishaw Hall & Gardens   46

Saturday 4th
12 Ansell Road   1

Sunday 5th
12 Ansell Road   1
The Hollies   29
◆ Meynell Langley Trials Garden   38

Monday 6th
12 Ansell Road   1
◆ Tissington Hall   53

Sunday 12th
26 Stiles Road   52
27 Wash Green   54

Friday 17th
◆ Cascades Gardens   10

Saturday 18th
334 Belper Road   4
2 Haddon View   23

Sunday 19th
Broomfield Hall   7
Fir Croft   19
2 Haddon View   23
Littleover Lane Allotments   32

Saturday 25th
12 Ansell Road   1

Sunday 26th
12 Ansell Road   1
13 Chiltern Drive   13
88 Church Street West   14
Moorfields   39

Monday 27th
12 Ansell Road   1
Moorfields   39
Repton NGS Village Gardens   47

Wednesday 29th
Fir Croft   19

June

Saturday 1st
12 Ansell Road   1

Sunday 2nd
12 Ansell Road   1
Higher Crossings   26
Highfield House   27

Wednesday 5th
The Hollies   29

Sunday 9th
334 Belper Road   4
Fir Croft   19
NEW Gorsey Bank Gardens   20
The Smithy   49
15 Windmill Lane   56

Wednesday 12th
Brierley Farm   6
The Hollies   29

Saturday 15th
Elmton Gardens   18
Holmlea   30
Longford Hall Farm   33
The Smithy   49

Sunday 16th
Ashen Clough   2
◆ Cascades Gardens   10
Elmton Gardens   18
Fir Croft   19
Holmlea   30
The Smithy   49
13 Westfield Road   55

Wednesday 19th
◆ Bluebell Arboretum and
   Nursery   5

Friday 21st
330 Old Road   43

Saturday 22nd
The Dower House   16
◆ Melbourne Hall Gardens   37
330 Old Road   43

Sunday 23rd
The Dower House   16
58A Main Street   35
◆ Melbourne Hall Gardens   37

Sunday 30th
High Roost   25
◆ Meynell Langley Trials Garden   38
Yew Tree Bungalow   58

July

Wednesday 3rd
◆ Renishaw Hall & Gardens   46

Saturday 6th
NEW Marlborough Cottage   36

Sunday 7th
Hill Cottage   28
NEW Marlborough Cottage   36

Saturday 13th
Barlborough Gardens   3
New Mills School   41

Sunday 14th
Barlborough Gardens   3
New Mills School   41

Wednesday 17th
◆ Bluebell Arboretum and
   Nursery   5

Sunday 21st
◆ Cascades Gardens   10
◆ Meynell Langley Trials Garden   38
Repton NGS Village Gardens   47
26 Windmill Rise   57

Thursday 25th
72 Burnside Avenue   8

Saturday 27th
Byways   9
Stanton in Peak Gardens   51

Sunday 28th
Byways   9
The Paddock   44
Stanton in Peak Gardens   51

Wednesday 31st
NEW 9 Hawkins Drive   24

August

Friday 2nd
NEW Grow Outside Garden   22

Saturday 3rd
NEW Grow Outside Garden   22

Sunday 4th
9 Main Street   34
13 Westfield Road   55

Sunday 11th
NEW 9 Hawkins Drive   24

Monday 12th
◆ Tissington Hall   53

Saturday 17th
◆ Cascades Gardens   10
Chevin Brae   12

Monday 19th
◆ Tissington Hall   53

Wednesday 21st
◆ Bluebell Arboretum and
   Nursery   5
Greenacres   21

Saturday 24th
NEW Landown Farm   31

Sunday 25th
72 Burnside Avenue   8
The Hollies   29
NEW Landown Farm   31
◆ Meynell Langley Trials Garden   38
27 Wash Green   54

Monday 26th
72 Burnside Avenue   8
Repton NGS Village Gardens   47
◆ Tissington Hall   53

Saturday 31st
NEW The Nightingale Centre   42

September

Sunday 1st
Broomfield Hall   7
NEW The Nightingale Centre   42
Yew Tree Bungalow   58

Saturday 7th
Holmlea   30

Sunday 8th
Coxbench Hall   15
Holmlea   30
Littleover Lane Allotments   32

Sunday 15th
◆ Meynell Langley Trials Garden   38

By Arrangement

Arrange a personalised garden visit
with your club, or group of friends,
on a date to suit you. See individual
garden entries for full details.

Askew Cottage, Repton NGS
   Village Gardens   47
334 Belper Road   4
Byways   9
10 Chestnut Way   11
Chevin Brae   12
88 Church Street West   14
Coxbench Hall   15
The Dower House   16
Greenacres   21
High Roost   25
NEW 34 High Street, Repton NGS
   Village Gardens   47
Highfield House   27
Hill Cottage   28
The Hollies   29
Holmlea   30
Littleover Lane Allotments   32
9 Main Street   34
58A Main Street   35
Nether Moor House   40
330 Old Road   43
The Paddock   44
Park Hall   45
Riversvale Lodge   48
Snitterton Hall   50
27 Wash Green   54
Yew Tree Bungalow   58

Birchenlee, Stanton in Peak Gardens

THE GARDENS

1 12 ANSELL ROAD

Ecclesall, Sheffield, S11 7PE. Dave Darwent. *Approx 3m SW of City Centre. Travel to Ringinglow Rd (88 bus), then Edale Rd (opp Ecclesall CofE Primary School). 3rd R - Ansell Rd. No 12 on L ¾ way down.* **Sat 4, Sun 5, Mon 6, Sat 25, Sun 26, Mon 27 May, Sat 1, Sun 2 June (11-5). Adm £4, chd free. Light refreshments inc vegan & GF options.**

Now in its 96th year since being created by my grandparents, this is a suburban mixed productive and flower garden retaining many original plants and features as well as the original layout but with the addition of seven water features and a small winter garden. Original rustic pergola with 90+ year old roses. Then and now pictures of the garden in 1929 and 1950's vs present. Map of landmarks up to 55m away which can be seen from garden. Seven water features. Wide variety of unique-recipe home-made cakes available.

✿ ☕

2 ASHEN CLOUGH

Maynestone Road, Chinley, High Peak, SK23 6AH. Adrian & Maggie Porteous. *From A6 turn onto A624, then B6062 into Chinley village. Turn R over railway and immed R into Maynestone Rd. Follow the road for 1¼ m. The garden can be found on the L.* **Sun 16 June (11-4). Adm £5, chd free. Teas, coffee and cakes and Prosecco. Craft beer from the onsite micro brewery.**

Located in a beautiful Peak District valley this large garden has stunning views of Cracken Edge and South Head. The garden is split into a number of different areas inc a Japanese influenced rockery, a long herbaceous border, a wilderness area with naturalised bulbs and wildflowers, a formal kitchen garden and a greenhouse and polytunnel. In June when the garden will be open, many of the rhododendrons and azaleas are in bloom. The garden is on a hillside with some steps and some steep pathways. Care also needs to be taken near the beehive which is situated in the rockery.

🐕 ✿ ☕ 🧺))

GROUP OPENING

3 BARLBOROUGH GARDENS

Clowne Road, Barlborough, Chesterfield, S43 4EH. Christine Sanderson, 07956 203184, christine.r.sanderson@uwclub. net, www.facebook.com/ barlboroughgardens. *7m NE of Chesterfield. Off A619 between Chesterfield & Worksop. ½ m E M1, J30. Follow signs for Barlborough then yellow NGS signs. At De Rhodes Arms r'about take 3rd exit onto Clowne Rd S43 4EH - where 2 gardens located.* **Sat 13, Sun 14 July (11.30-4.30). Combined adm £6, chd free. Home-made teas. Cool drinks will also be available at 90 Boughton Lane.**

NEW **90 BOUGHTON LANE**
S43 4QF. Angela and Ian Cross.

NEW **GREYSTONES BARN**
S43 4EN. Kathryn and John Hardwick.

THE HOLLIES
Vernon & Christine Sanderson. (See separate entry)

Meynell Langley Trials Garden

NEW 19 WEST VIEW

S43 4HT. Mrs Pat Cunningham.

Barlborough is an ancient village, steeped in history, perched on the top of yellow limestone scarp in the furthest North East corner of Derbyshire. A range of interesting buildings can be seen all around the village centre inc St James The Greater Church, an ancient place of worship which will be open to visitors both afternoons of the July opening weekend. Four colourful gardens of different sizes and styles will be opening their garden gates, inc three new gardens. A map detailing the location of all four gardens plus a community garden will be issued with adm ticket. More information about Barlborough Gardens can be found by visiting our Facebook page - see details above. The Hollies inc an area influenced by the Majorelle Garden in Marrakech. This makeover was achieved using upcycled items together with appropriate planting. It was featured in an episode of TVs "Love Your Garden". Packets of feed can be purchased at 90 Boughton Lane to feed the poultry. Partial wheelchair access at The Hollies.

4 334 BELPER ROAD

Stanley Common, DE7 6FY. Gill & Colin Hancock, 01159 301061, gillandcolinhancock@gmail.com. 7m N of Derby. 3m W of Ilkeston. On A609, ¾ m from Rose & Crown Xrds (A608). Please park in field up farm drive. **Sat 18 May, Sun 9 June (11.30-4.30). Adm £4, chd free. Light refreshments inc gluten and dairy free options. Visits also by arrangement 1 Apr to 21 June for groups of 5 to 30.**
Beautiful country garden with many attractive features inc a laburnum tunnel, rose and wisteria domes, old workmen's hut, wildlife pond. Take a walk through the 10 acres of woodland and glades to a ½ acre lake. Organic vegetable garden. See the lovely wisteria pergola in May and wild orchids and rose meadow in June. Plenty of seating to enjoy home-made cakes. Children welcome with plenty of activities to keep them entertained. Abundant wildlife.

5 ◆ BLUEBELL ARBORETUM AND NURSERY

Annwell Lane, Smisby, Ashby de la Zouch, LE65 2TA. Robert Vernon, 01530 413700, sales@bluebellnursery.com, www.bluebellnursery.com. *1m NW of Ashby-de-la-Zouch. Arboretum is clearly signed in Annwell Ln (follow brown signs), ¼ S, through village of Smisby off B5006, between Ticknall & Ashby-de-la-Zouch. Free parking.* **For NGS: Wed 19 June, Wed 17 July, Wed 21 Aug (9-4). Adm £6, chd free. For other opening times and information, please phone, email or visit garden website.**
Beautiful 9 acre woodland garden with a large collection of rare trees and shrubs. Interest throughout the year with spring flowers, cool leafy areas in summer and sensational autumn colour. Many information posters describing the more obscure plants. Adjacent specialist tree and shrub nursery. Please be aware this is not a wood full of bluebells, despite the name. The woodland garden is fully labelled and the staff can answer questions or talk at length about any of the trees or shrubs on display. Please wear sturdy, waterproof footwear during or after wet weather. Full wheelchair access however grass paths can become inaccessible after heavy rain.

6 BRIERLEY FARM

Mill Lane, Brockhurst, Ashover, Chesterfield, S45 0HS. Anne & David Wilkinson. *6m SW of Chesterfield, 4m NE of Matlock, 1½ m NW of Ashover. From the A632 turn W into Alicehead Rd, L into Swinger Ln, 2nd L into Brockhurst Ln & R into Mill Ln. Brierley Farm is the only house on the L.* **Wed 24 Apr, Wed 12 June (12-4). Adm £6. Home-made teas.**
This hillside site features a 2 acre garden and 3 acre woodland with paths, with a bridge over a stream connecting the two. There are three linked ponds and raised stone-walled beds feature bulbs, hellebore, geum, azaleas and rhododendron in the spring followed by seasonal perennial and annual flowering plants into the autumn.

7 BROOMFIELD HALL

Morley, Ilkeston, DE7 6DN. Derby College, www.facebook.com/BroomfieldPlantCentre. *4m N of Derby. 6m S of Heanor on A608, N of Derby.* **Sun 19 May (10-4). Sun 1 Sept (10-4). Light refreshments in a pop-up volunteer run, café. Adm £5, chd free. Home-made cakes, hot drinks and squash.**
25 acres of constantly developing educational Victorian gardens/woodlands maintained by volunteers and students. Herbaceous borders, walled garden, themed gardens, rose garden, potager, prairie plantings, Japanese garden, tropical garden, winter garden, plant centre. Light refreshments, entertainment, cacti, carnivorous, bonsai, fuchsia specialists and craft stalls. A gem of Derbyshire. Most of garden is accessible to wheelchair users and we are all on hand to help.

8 72 BURNSIDE AVENUE

Shirland, Alfreton, DE55 6AE. A & S Wilson-Hunt. *2½ m from Alfreton. 3½ m from Clay Cross on A61. Signed from, A61onto Hallfieldgate Ln, R onto Byron St then R onto Burnside Ave. Follow the road & garden is last bungalow on L.* **Thur 25 July, Sun 25, Mon 26 Aug (12.30-5). Adm £3, chd free. Pre-booking essential, please visit www.ngs.org.uk for information & booking. Light refreshments.**
Delightful small garden packed with herbaceous borders and some tropical planting. Dahlias, Cannas and Phlox give colour with hanging baskets, tree ferns and sedum roof offer plenty of interest. Level garden with paved seating area offering a peaceful haven to enjoy refreshments. Wide variety of plants to see. Animal safari around the garden. Can you find them all? Ask about hot composting.

47,000 people affected by cancer were reached by Maggie's centres supported by the National Garden Scheme over the last 12 months

9 BYWAYS

7A Brookfield Avenue, Brookside, Chesterfield, S40 3NX. Terry & Eileen Kelly, 07414 827813, telkel1@aol.com. *1½ m W of Chesterfield. Follow A619 from Chesterfield towards Baslow. Please park carefully in Brookfield Sch Car Park or neighbouring roads. Brookfield Ave is 2nd on R after sch.* **Sat 27, Sun 28 July (11.30-4.30). Adm £3.50, chd free. Home-made teas inc gluten free option. Visits also by arrangement 30 June to 16 Aug for groups of 10 to 25. Visitor numbers must be confirmed 1 week prior to visit. Donation to Ashgate Hospice.**

Three times winners of the Best Back Garden over 80 sqm, and also twice winners of Best Front Garden, Best Container Garden and Best Hanging Basket in Chesterfield in Bloom. Well established perennial borders inc helenium, monardas, phlox, grasses, acers. Rockery and many planters containing acers, pelargoniums, ferns and hostas. Large shady pergola with acers, hostas and ferns.

❄ ☕

10 ◆ CASCADES GARDENS

Clatterway, Bonsall, Matlock, DE4 2AH. Alan & Alesia Clements, 07967 337404, alan.clements@ cascadesgardens.com, www.cascadesgardens.com. *5m SW of Matlock. From Cromford A6 T-lights turn to Wirksworth. Turn R along Via Gellia, signed Buxton & Bonsall. After 1m turn R up hill towards Bonsall. Garden entrance at top of hill. Park in village car park.* **For NGS: Fri 22 Mar, Sat 20 Apr, Fri 17 May, Sun 16 June, Sun 21 July, Sat 17 Aug (12-4). Adm £8, chd £4. Home-made teas. For other opening times and information, please phone, email or visit garden website.**

The Meditation Garden and Bonsai centre: Fascinating 4 acre peaceful garden in spectacular natural surroundings with woodland, cliffs, stream, pond and an old limestone quarry. Inspired by Japanese gardens and Buddhist philosophy, secluded garden rooms for relaxation and reflection. Beautiful landscape with a wide collection of unusual perennials, conifers, shrubs and trees. Plants for sale. Hellebore month in March. Launching new authentic Japanese Tea House and garden this year. Mostly wheelchair accessible. Gravel paths, some steep slopes.

♿ 🐕 ❄ 🚗 🛏 ☕ ᵈ))

11 10 CHESTNUT WAY

Repton, DE65 6FQ. Pauline Little, 01283 702267, plittle@hotmail.co.uk. *6m S of Derby. From A38/A50, S of Derby, follow signs to Willington, then Repton. In Repton turn R at r'about. Chestnut Way is ¼ m up hill, on L.* **Sun 18 Feb (11-3). Adm £5, chd free. Light refreshments at Chestnut Way for February opening inc home-made soup. Opening with Repton NGS Village Gardens on Mon 27 May, Sun 21 July, Mon 26 Aug. Visits also by arrangement 10 Feb to 31 Oct for groups of 5 to 25.**

A large and wonderfully diverse garden with lots of separate areas of interest and thoughtful planting throughout. The unusual sculptures and renowned home-made teas make for a memorable visit. Overflowing borders and a surprise round every corner. Come in May for the best selection of plants for sale from the garden. Special interest in woodland/shade plants and composting. Finalist, Midlands, The English Garden Magazine's The Nation's Favourite Gardens 2023. Level garden, good solid paths to main areas. Some grass/bark paths.

♿ 🐕 🐾 ❄ 🚗 ☕ ᵈ))

12 CHEVIN BRAE

Chevin Road, Milford, Belper, DE56 0QH. Dr David Moreton, 07778 004374, davidmoretonchevinbrae@gmail. com. *1½ m S of Belper. Coming from S on A6 turn L at Strutt Arms & cont up Chevin Rd. Park on Chevin Rd. After 300yds follow arrow to L up Morrells Ln. After 300yds Chevin Brae on L with silver garage.* **Sat 23 Mar, Sat 17 Aug (1-5). Adm £3, chd free. Home-made teas. Visits also by arrangement for groups of up to 16.**

A large garden, with swathes of daffodils in the orchard a spring feature. Extensive wildflower planting along edge of wood features aconites, snowdrops, wood anemones, fritillaries and dog tooth violets. Other parts of garden will have hellebores and early camelias. In the summer, the large flower borders and rose trellises give much colour, and the vegetable and fruit gardens are at their peak. A steep drive and two flights of steps need to be climbed to access the garden. Tea and home-made cakes, pastries and biscuits, many of which feature fruit and jam from the garden.

🐕 ❄ ☕ ᵈ))

13 13 CHILTERN DRIVE

West Hallam, Ilkeston, DE7 6PA. Jacqueline & Keith Holness. *Approx 7m NE of Derby. From A609, 2m W of Ilkeston, nr The Bottle Kiln, take St Wilfreds Rd. Take 1st R onto Derbyshire Av, Chiltern Drive is 3rd turning on L.* **Sun 26 May (10.30-4.30). Adm £3, chd free. Home-made teas. Gluten free options available.**

A small walled garden on an estate with a woodland feel. A true plant lover's garden, brimming with plants, many rare and unusual. Paris, beesia, schefflera, podophyllum, to name but a few. There's a pretty summerhouse, a small pond and fernery, together with over 50 different acers, over 30 varieties of hosta and a good collection of rarely seen ferns. A secret hidden gem.

❄ ☕ ᵈ))

14 88 CHURCH STREET WEST

Pinxton, Derbyshire, NG16 6PU. Rosemary Ahmed, 07842 141210. *Pinxton is approx 1m from J28 of the M1. At motorway island take B6019 towards Alfreton & take the 1st L Pinxton Ln which turns into Alfreton Rd, the garden is signposted from there.* **Sun 26 May (1-5). Adm £3.50, chd free. Light refreshments. Visits also by arrangement 27 Apr to 6 Oct for groups of 5 to 15. Please be aware their are steep steps and uneven paths.**

Plantwomens garden, developed over 25 years to inc collections of hardy geraniums, agaves, ferns, persicaria and grasses. The garden has a quirky mix of salvage items. A wildflower lawn is a work in progress, a small rockery, upcycled garden room with mature grapevine, mixed borders and a large patio with pot displays.

❄ ☕ 🪑

15 COXBENCH HALL

Alfreton Road, Coxbench, Derby, DE21 5BB. Mr Brian Ballin, 01332 880200, office@coxbench-hall.co.uk, www.coxbench-hall.co.uk. *4m N of Derby close to A38. After going through Little Eaton, turn L onto Alfreton Rd for 1m, Coxbench Hall is on L next to Fox & Hounds pub between Little Eaton & Holbrook. From A38 take Kilburn turn & go towards Little Eaton.* **Sun 8 Sept (2.30-4.30). Adm £3, chd free. Light refreshments inc home-made GF cakes. Visits also by arrangement for groups of up to 15.**

Former ancestral Georgian Home of the Meynell family, the gardens focus on sustainability, organic and wildlife friendly themes. There is a tropical style garden, ponds, hosta's, vegetables, C18 potting shed, veteran yew tree, kitchen garden and hillside rhododendron garden with a stoned path by the upper woodland overlooking the gardens below. We grow vegetables next to the C18 potting shed, have a veteran (500-800 year old) yew tree, tropical style garden, hosta's, rhododendrons and woodland walks. Our wheelchair accessible gardens are developed to inspire the senses of our residents via different colours, textures and fragrances of plants. Block paved path around the edges of the main lawn. We regret no wheelchair access to woodland area.

♿ 🐕 ❋ ☕

16 THE DOWER HOUSE
Church Square, Melbourne, DE73 8JH. William & Griselda Kerr, 07799 883777, griseldakerr@btinternet.com. *6m S of Derby. 5m W of J23A M1. 4m N of J13 M42. When in Church Sq, turn R just before the church by a blue sign giving service times. Gates are 50 yds ahead.* **Sat 10, Sun 11 Feb (10-4); Sat 22, Sun 23 June (10-5). Adm £8, chd free. Light refreshments. Visits also by arrangement Feb to Oct for groups of 10 to 40. Please email for dates and booking form.**
Beautiful view of Melbourne Pool from balustraded terrace running length of 1829 house. Garden drops steeply by paths or steps to lawn with herbaceous borders and bank of some 60 shrubs. Numerous paths lead to different areas of the garden, providing varied planting opportunities inc a bog garden, glade, shrubbery, grasses, herb and kitchen garden, rose tunnel, arbour, orchard and small woodland. Hidden paths and different areas entice children to explore the garden with various animals such as a bronze crocodile and stone dragons to find. Children must be supervised by an adult at all times due to the proximity of water. This garden is proud to provide plants for the National Garden Scheme's Show Garden at Chelsea Flower Show 2024. Wheelchair access to top half of the garden only. Shoes with a good grip are highly recommended as slopes are steep. No parking within 50 yds.

♿ 🐕 ❋ 🚗 ☕

---

17 NEW DRONFIELD HERITAGE TRUST
High Street, Dronfield, S18 1PX. Mr Sam Reavy, 07814 140034, sam@dronfieldhallbarn.org, www.dronfieldhallbarn.org. *Dronfield. The Barn is located in the centre of Dronfield. There are 2 accessible spaces at front (High St). There is free, unlimited parking at Sainsburys (S18 1NW) at the back of site.* **Sun 21 Apr (10-4). Adm £3, chd £1. Pre-booking essential, please visit www.ngs.org.uk for information & booking.**
The garden is part of the Dronfield heritage centre, situated in the grounds of the original manor house of Dronfield. It was transformed from a muddy field to a much loved community space with mixed native flower beds, veteran trees, woodland border, small herb garden and a lawned play/ picnic area. Children must be accompanied by an adult. Coffee shop, exhibition space and toilets. Children's activities include a bug safari, creating seed bombs and a garden quiz. Please contact garden to pre-book children's activities. The garden and Barn are on one level. The garden is situated on a slope, but there is a hard standing path that runs top to bottom.

♿ ❋ ☕

GROUP OPENING

18 ELMTON GARDENS
Elmton, Worksop, S80 4LS. *2m from Creswell, 3m from Clowne, 5m from J30, M1. From M1 J30 take A616 to Newark. Follow approx 4m. Turn R at Elmton signpost. At junc turn R, the village centre is in ½m.* **Sat 15, Sun 16 June (1-5). Combined adm £6, chd free. Cream teas at the Old Schoolroom next to the church. Food also available all day at the Elm Tree Inn.**

THE BARN CHALICO FARM
S80 4LS. Mrs Anne Merrick.

THE COTTAGE
S80 4LX. Judith Maughan & Roy Reeves.

ELM TREE COTTAGE
S80 4LS. Mark & Linda Hopkinson.

ELM TREE FARM
S80 4LS. Angie & Tim Caulton.

NEW THE ELMS
S80 4LS. Mrs Karen Henderson.

PEAR TREE COTTAGE
S80 4LS. Geoff & Janet Cutts.

PINFOLD
S80 4LS. Nikki Kirsop & Barry Davies.

ROSE COTTAGE
S80 4LX. Andrew & Ruth Saxton.

Elmton is a lovely little village situated on a stretch of rare unimproved Magnesian limestone grassland with quaking grass, bee orchids and harebells all set in the middle of attractive, rolling farm land. It has a pub, which serves food all day, a church and a village green with award winning wildlife conservation area and a village Pinfold. The very colourful but different open gardens have wonderful views. They show a range of gardening styles, themed beds and several have a commitment to fruit and vegetable growing. Elmton received a gold award and was voted best small village for the 7th time and best wildlife and conservation area in the East Midlands in Bloom competition in 2019. Village trail with interpretation boards.

♿ 🐕 ❋ 🚗 ☕ 🔊

---

19 FIR CROFT
Froggatt Road, Calver, S32 3ZD. Dr S B Furness, www.alpineplantcentre.co.uk. *4m N of Bakewell. At junc of B6001 with A625 (formerly B6054), adjacent to Froggat Edge Garage.* **Sun 19, Wed 29 May, Sun 9, Sun 16 June (1-4). Adm by donation.**
Massive scree with many varieties. Plantsman's garden; rockeries, water garden, extensive collection (over 3000 varieties) of alpines, conifers and sempervivums. Many new varieties not seen anywhere else in the UK. Huge new tufa wall planted with many rare Alpines and sempervivums. Superb views over the Dales. Two National Collections. Wheelchair access to part of garden only.

♿ ❋ NPC

In 2023, our donations to Carers Trust meant that 26,118 unpaid carers were supported across the UK

GROUP OPENING

20 NEW GORSEY BANK GARDENS

Brooklands Avenue, Wirksworth, Matlock, DE4 4AB. Miss Philippa Cooper. *At the southern edge of Wirksworth. From Duffield on B5023. R onto Water Ln immed after mini r'about, signed Hannage Brook Medical Centre. From Cromford on B5036/B5023 3rd L after pelican crossing. Park nr Medical Centre. Parking in designated areas. Follow signs.* **Sun 9 June (11-4). Combined adm £7, chd free. Home-made teas. Selection of sandwiches made to order (gluten free on request) and home-made cakes at Watts House. Light refreshments at Fern Bank.**

NEW **2 BROOKLANDS AVENUE**
DE4 4AB. Miss Philippa Cooper.

NEW **FERN BANK**
DE4 4AD. Scott Thompson and Beccy Owen.

NEW **MILL COTTAGE**
DE4 4AB. Kirstie and Andy Lyne.

NEW **WATTS HOUSE**
DE4 4AR. Sue and Robert Watts.

Gorsey Bank is a charming hillside hamlet at the southern edge of the historic market town of Wirksworth, set in the beautiful Derbyshire Dales. This group features 4 gardens which demonstrate contrasting design responses to challenging terrain with a wide variety of planting; 2 Brooklands Ave has been developed since 2019, using a naturalistic planting style, with many interesting and unusual plants. Fern Bank is a cottage garden set in a small former quarry, surrounded by farmland, with beautiful views. Mill Cottage is a secluded cottage style garden with mill stream and architectural features, with seating areas to enjoy the different aspects. Watts House is a delightful tranquil cottage garden. Ticket sales at 2 Brooklands Ave. The four gardens are within comfortable walking distance, although it is a steep uphill walk on tarmac to Mill Cottage and Fern Bank, but the gardens and spectacular views are well worth the effort. The walk to Watts House is relatively flat. Watts House features Robert's sculptures, some previously exhibited at RHS Chatsworth.

21 GREENACRES

Makeney Road, Holbrook, Belper, DE56 0TF. Veronica Holtom, 07749 277927, veronica.cooke1@icloud.com. *5m N of Derby. Approach via Makeney Rd. Turn into the private drive for Holbrook Hall Care Home. Please park on St Michael's FC car park. Parking for disabled visitors is available at the house.* **Wed 17 Apr, Wed 21 Aug (1.30-5). Adm £6, chd free. Home-made teas. Visits also by arrangement 13 Apr to 29 Sept for groups of 10 to 35. GF and vegan options are available upon request for by arrangement visits.** Beautiful large garden in rural Derbyshire, wonderful countryside views. Wander among the pines, weeping birches, acers, oaks and beeches. Many camellias, shrubs, hellebores and spring bulbs. Spectacular mixed beds and borders, ornamental grasses, lily pond, rock garden, cascades and alpines. Colourful patio plants, sweeping lawns, lots of seating areas and walkways. There are few steps and the majority of the site is level.

The Dower House

22 NEW **GROW OUTSIDE GARDEN**
Butterley Station, Ripley, DE5 3QZ. Grow Outside CIC, 07960 249816, hello@growoutside.co.uk, growoutside.co.uk. *Adj to Butterley Stn on B6179. Follow brown tourist signs for car park. ½m from Ripley. Along B6179. 3m from Oakerthorpe: Follow B6013. Turn R at Xrds with B6179. Park in Midland Railway car park. Garden at end of platform, turn L at the station building.* **Fri 2, Sat 3 Aug (11-4). Adm £3, chd £1. Pre-booking essential, please visit www.ngs.org.uk for information & booking. Light refreshments.**
A community focused horticultural social enterprise, the garden is based on no-dig, organic and regenerative principles. Range of raised beds growing cut-flowers, showcasing sustainable gardening techniques, and what is achievable in small spaces using minimal resources. Family friendly nature based activities and games. Please contact garden to pre-book children's activities. Flat pathways surfaced with gravel, bark and grass.

23 **2 HADDON VIEW**
Birchover Road, Stanton-in-the-Peak, Matlock, DE4 2LR. Steve Tompkins. *At the top of the hill in Stanton in Peak, on the rd to Birchover. Stanton in Peak is 5m S of Bakewell. Turn off the A6 at Rowsley, or at the B5056 & follow signs up the hill.* **Sat 18, Sun 19 May (12.30-4.30). Adm £4, chd free. Home-made teas. Opening with Stanton in Peak Gardens on Sat 27, Sun 28 July.**
The thirty rhododendrons and azaleas make a lovely spring display. They wrap around the summerhouse and are part of the herbaceous borders. Other spring flowers inc marsh marigolds around the ponds, and dog's-tooth violets in pink and yellow. Dramatic agaves, aeoniums, tulips and bedding plants fill the diverse range of pots on the patios. Home-made cakes, teas and coffees will be waiting!

24 NEW **9 HAWKINS DRIVE**
Ambergate, Belper, DE56 2JN. Carol and Martyn Taylor-Cockayne. *Just off the A610 at Ambergate between Belper & Matlock. From Derby at the A6 and A610 inter-section by the Hurt Arms, turn R onto the A610. After ½m turn R onto New Rd. After 100yds turn R onto Crich Ln. After 100yds turn R onto Hawkins Dr.* **Wed 31 July, Sun 11 Aug (11-4). Adm £3.50, chd free. Cream teas.**
A small yet busy garden with flowering shrubs and evergreens, perennials and annuals. Fern and heuchera beds provide a splash of colour. Terraced patio with planters containing snapdragons, dwarf calendulas and vibrant begonias. Two small wildlife ponds with log pile lodges, home to resident toads and frogs. Elevated view over the rooftops to Crich Chase.

25 **HIGH ROOST**
27 Storthmeadow Road, Simmondley, Glossop, SK13 6UZ. Peter & Christina Harris, 01457 863888, harrispeter448@gmail.com. *¾m SW of Glossop. From Glossop A57 to Manche' L at 2nd r'about, up Simmondley Ln nr top R turn. From Marple A626 to Glossop, in Ch'worth R up Town Ln past Hare & Hound pub 2nd L.* **Sun 30 June (12-4). Adm £4, chd free. Visits also by arrangement 27 May to 31 July for groups of up to 30. Donation to Donkey Sanctuary.**
Garden on terraced slopes, views over fields and hills. Winding paths, archways and steps explore different garden rooms packed with plants, designed to attract wildlife. Alpine bed, gravel gardens; vegetable garden, water features, statuary, troughs and planters. A garden which needs exploring to discover its secrets tucked away in hidden corners. Craft stall, children's garden quiz and lucky dip.

26 **HIGHER CROSSINGS**
Crossings Road, Chapel-en-le-Frith, High Peak, SK23 9RX. Malcolm & Christine Hoskins. *Chapel-en-le-frith. Turn off B5470 N from Chapel-en-le-Frith on Crossings Rd signed Whitehough/Chinley. Higher Crossings is 2nd house on R beyond 1st xrds. Park best before xrds on Crossings Rd or L on Eccles Rd.* **Sun 2 June (2-5.30). Adm £5, chd free. Light refreshments inc tea, biscuits and cakes.**
Nearly 2 acres of formal terraced country garden, sweeping lawns and magnificent Peak District views. Rhododendrons, acers, azaleas, hostas, herbaceous borders, Japanese garden. Mature specimen trees and shrubs leading through a dell. Beautiful stone terrace and sitting areas. Garden gate leading into meadow. Wheelchair access around the house and upper terrace and gravel garden.

27 **HIGHFIELD HOUSE**
Wingfield Road, Oakerthorpe, Alfreton, DE55 7AP. Paul & Ruth Peat / Janet & Brian Costall, 01773 521342, highfieldhouseopengardens@hotmail.co.uk, www.highfieldhouse.weebly.com. *Rear of Alfreton Golf Club. A615 Alfreton-Matlock Rd.* **Sun 2 June (10.30-5). Adm £3, chd free. Home-made teas. Visits also by arrangement 20 May to 28 June for groups of 15+. Snowdrop group visits between 19th-25th Feb with afternoon tea/lunch.**
Lovely country garden of approx 1 acre, incorporating a shady garden, woodland, pond, laburnum tunnel, orchard, herbaceous borders and vegetable garden. Fabulous AGA baked cakes and lunches. Lovely walk to Derbyshire Wildlife Trust nature reserve to see Orchids in June. Some steps, slopes and gravel areas.

28 **HILL COTTAGE**
Ashover Road, Littlemoor, Ashover, nr Chesterfield, S45 0BL. Jane Tomlinson & Tim Walls, 07946 388185, lavenderhen@aol.com. *Littlemoor. 1.8m from Ashover village, 6.3m from Chesterfield & 6.1m from Matlock. Hill Cottage is on Ashover Rd (also known as Stubben Edge Ln). Opp the end of Eastwood Ln).* **Sun 7 July (11-4). Adm £4, chd free. Home-made teas. Visits also by arrangement 8 July to 28 July for groups of up to 15.**
Hill Cottage is a lovely example of an English country cottage garden. Whilst small, the garden has full, colourful and fragrant mixed borders along with a heart shaped lawn. A greenhouse full of chillies and scented pelargoniums and a small Potager. Views over a pastoral landscape to Ogston reservoir. A wide variety of perennials and annuals grown in pots and containers.

29 THE HOLLIES

87 Clowne Road, Barlborough, Chesterfield, S43 4EH. Vernon & Christine Sanderson, 07956 203184, christine.r.sanderson@uwclub.net, www.facebook.com/barlboroughgardens. *7m NE of Chesterfield. Off A619 midway between Chesterfield & Worksop. ½m E M1, J30. Follow signs for Barlborough then yellow NGS signs. At De Rhodes Arms r'about take 3rd exit onto Clowne Rd. Garden at far end on L.* **Sun 5 May (12-4.30). Light refreshments inc home-made cakes. Sweet & savoury cream teas available in June. Wed 5, Wed 12 June (1.30-4.30); Sun 25 Aug (12-4.30). Adm £3.50, chd free. Opening with Barlborough Gardens on Sat 13, Sun 14 July. Visits also by arrangement May to Aug for groups of 10 to 30.**

The Hollies maximises the unusual garden layout and inc shade area, patio garden with Moroccan corner, cottage border plus fruit trees. A wide selection of home-made cakes on offer inc gluten free, sugar free and vegan options. Home-made preserves for sale. Extensive view across arable farmland. An area of the garden, influenced by the Majorelle Garden in Marrakech, was achieved using upcycled items together with appropriate planting. This garden project was featured on an episode of "Love Your Garden". Partial wheelchair access.

30 HOLMLEA

Derby Road, Ambergate, Belper, DE56 2EJ. Bill & Tracy Reid, 07932 977314, billandtracy.reid@gmail.com. *On the A6 in Ambergate - between Belper & Matlock. 9m N of Derby, 6m S of Matlock. Easy access from M1 J28. On A6 next to Bridge House Cafe. Additional Parking at Anila Restaurant opp Hurt Arms. Short walk from Ambergate Station.* **Sat 15, Sun 16 June, Sat 7, Sun 8 Sept (11-4). Adm £4, chd free. Home-made teas. Refreshments self-service with honesty box. Gluten Free and Vegan options. Visits also by arrangement 11 Sept to 2 Oct for groups of 10 to 20. Afternoons only.**

Discover the 1½ acre garden, described by many visitors as unique. Formal garden, kitchen garden, gravel garden, boules court, 'Disused Railway', canal lock water feature, riverside walk and more. Home-made teas in 'The Pavilion'. Family friendly with activities for kids, dogs on leads welcome - beware of the free ranging poultry. Adjacent to Shining Cliff Woods, SSI. Find us on Facebook at 'Holmlea Gardens'. Wheelchair route around main features of the garden. Unfortunately the Riverside Walk is not suitable for wheelchairs.

31 NEW LANDOWN FARM

Bakeacre Lane, Findern, Derby, DE65 6BH. Mr Dean Froom, www.facebook.com/FroomsDahlias. *Exit A38 at Findern Interchange. Follow signs to Bakeacre Ln. Park in the car park & enjoy the garden with its planted borders and potted flowers before heading 200 metres up the track where you will find Frooms Dahlias.* **Sat 24, Sun 25 Aug (10.30-3.30). Adm £6, chd free. Light refreshments.**

The garden is located in an equestrian setting and is mainly laid to lawn, with raised beds and borders brimming with 100 dahlia varieties in the spectacular showcase beds. There is a pond and seating areas. We offer a 'make your own eco vase' activity and a wide selection of dahlia cuttings/plants. A horse trailer café sets the scene enabling you to enjoy refreshments watching the horses. Mature farm garden surrounded by horses grazing in the paddocks. Quirky features to enjoy.

32 LITTLEOVER LANE ALLOTMENTS

19 Littleover Lane, Normanton, Derby, DE23 6JF. Ms Amanda Sawford, 07883 010924, amanda.sawford@sky.com, www.littleoverlaneallotments.org.uk. *On Littleover Ln opp the junc with Foremark Ave. Off the Derby Outer Ring Rd (A5111). At the Normanton Park r'about turn into Stenson Rd then R into Littleover Ln. The main gates are on the L as you travel down the road.* **Sun 19 May, Sun 8 Sept (11-3). Adm £5, chd free. Light refreshments. Visits also by arrangement 1 Apr to 20 Oct.**

A quiet oasis just off Derby's Outer Ring Road, hidden away in a residential area. A private site of nearly 12 acres, established in 1920, cultivated in a variety of ways, inc organic, no dig and potager style. Come and chat with plot holders about their edibles and ornamentals. Many exotic and Heritage varieties cultivated. Later in the year produce can be available to sample. On site disabled parking available. All avenues have been stoned but site is on a slope and extensive so some areas not accessible.

33 LONGFORD HALL FARM

Longford, Ashbourne, DE6 3DS. Liz Wolfenden, Longfordhallfarmholidaycottages.com. *From A52 take turn to Hollington. At T-junc (Long Ln) turn R & follow signs. Use drive with Longford Hall Farm sign at the entrance.* **Sat 15 June (1.30-5.30). Adm £5, chd free. Home-made teas.**

The large front garden is mainly shrubs hydrangeas, roses, ferns, grasses and hostas beds. These surround a modern pond and fountain. there is also a large pond with pontoon. The walled garden has traditional herbaceous borders. Most of the garden is on one level.

34 9 MAIN STREET

Horsley Woodhouse, Ilkeston, DE7 6AU. Ms Alison Napier, 01332 881629, ibhillib@btinternet.com. *3m SW of Heanor. 6m N of Derby. Turn off A608 Derby to Heanor Rd at Smalley, towards Belper, (A609). Garden on A609, 1m from Smalley turning.* **Sun 4 Aug (1.30-4.30). Adm £4, chd free. Cream teas. Water provided and soft drinks available to purchase. Visits also by arrangement 8 Apr to 15 Sept for groups of 12+.**

⅓ acre hilltop garden with lovely farmland views. Terracing, borders, lawns and pergola create space for an informal layout with planting for colour effect. Features inc large wildlife pond with water lilies, bog garden and small formal pool. Emphasis on carefully selected herbaceous perennials mixed with shrubs and old fashioned roses. Gravel garden for sun loving plants and scree garden, both developed from former drive. Please ensure you bring your own carrier bags for the plant stall. Wide collection of homegrown plants for sale. All parts of the garden accessible to wheelchairs. Wheelchair adapted WC.

35 58A MAIN STREET

Rolleston, Swadlincote, DE12 8JW. Paul Marbrow, 07596 629886, paulmarbrow@hotmail.co.uk. *Rolleston. If exiting the M42, J11 onto the A444 to Overseal follow signs Linton then Rolleston. From A38, exit to Walton on Trent, then follow Rolleston signs.* **Sun 23 June (12.30-4). Adm £5, chd free. Light refreshments inc scones, cake, tea and coffee. Visits also by arrangement 19 June to 18 Aug for groups of 5 to 30.**

¾ acre garden formed from a once open field over the last few years. The garden has developed into themed areas and is changing and maturing. Japanese, arid beach, bamboo grove with ferns, water gardens etc. The 100 sq metre indoor garden for cacti, exotic and tender plants, is now becoming established as a mini Eden. There are also vegetable gardens. Areas are easily accessible, although some are only for the sure of foot, advice signs will be situated on non suitable routes.

36 NEW MARLBOROUGH COTTAGE

Corbar Road, Buxton, SK17 6RQ. Sandra and Graham Jowett. *On N side of Corbar Rd. Directly opp junc with Marlborough Rd. Free on-street parking is readily available on Corbar Rd.* **Sat 6, Sun 7 July (10.30-4.30). Adm £4, chd free. Home-made teas.**

Victorian gardener's cottage close to the centre of Georgian Buxton. A fifth of an acre organic garden, reclaimed in the last six years. It is 1100ft above sea level, surrounded by mature trees and a tranquil haven for wildlife. It has front and rear borders, herbs and a variety of containers and ornaments. It has a small wildlife pond, wildflowers, vegetable beds, soft fruit and a greenhouse.

37 ◆ MELBOURNE HALL GARDENS

Church Square, Melbourne, Derby, DE73 8EN. Melbourne Gardens Charity, 01332 862502, info@melbournehall.com, www.melbournehall.com. *6m S of Derby. At Melbourne Market Place turn into Church St, go down to Church Sq. Garden entrance across visitor centre next to Melbourne Hall tea room.* **For NGS: Sat 22, Sun 23 June (1-5). Adm £10,**

chd £5. Sitooterie - Coffee/Ice Cream Takeaway - Melbourne Hall Courtyard. For other opening times and information, please phone, email or visit garden website.

A 17 acre historic garden with an abundance of rare trees and shrubs. Woodland and waterside planting with extensive herbaceous borders. Meconopsis, candelabra primulas, various Styrax and Cornus kousa. Other garden features inc Bakewells wrought iron arbour, a yew tunnel and fine C18 statuary and water features. 300yr old trees, waterside planting, feature hedges and herbaceous borders. Fine statuary and stonework. Don't forget to visit the pigs, alpacas, goats and various other animals in their garden enclosures. Gravel paths, uneven surface in places, some steep slopes.

38 ◆ MEYNELL LANGLEY TRIALS GARDEN

Lodge Lane (off Flagshaw Lane), Kirk Langley, Ashbourne, DE6 4NT. Robert & Karen Walker, 01332 824358, enquiries@meynellgardens.com, www.meynellgardens.com. *4m W of Derby, nr Kedleston Hall. Head W out of Derby on A52. At Kirk Langley turn R onto Flagshaw Ln (signed to Kedleston Hall) then R onto Lodge Ln. Follow Meynell Langley Gardens signs.* **For NGS: Wed 1, Sun 5 May, Sun 30 June, Sun 21 July, Sun 25 Aug, Sun 15 Sept (10-4). Adm £5, chd free. For other opening times and information, please phone, email or visit garden website.**

Completely re-designed during 2020 with new glasshouse and patio area incorporating water rills and small ponds. New wildlife and fish ponds also added. Displays and trials of new and existing varieties of bedding plants, herbaceous perennials and vegetable plants grown at the adjacent nursery. Over 180 hanging baskets and floral displays. Adjacent tearooms serving lunches and refreshments daily. Plant sales from adjacent nursery. Level ground and firm grass and some hard paths.

39 MOORFIELDS

261 Chesterfield Road, Temple Normanton, Chesterfield, S42 5DE. Peter, Janet & Stephen Wright. *4m SE of Chesterfield. From Chesterfield take A617 for 2m, turn on to B6039 through Temple Normanton, taking R fork signed Tibshelf, B6039. Garden ¼ m on R. Limited parking.* **Sun 26, Mon 27 May (1-5). Adm £4, chd free. Light refreshments inc gluten free options.**

Two adjoining gardens, each planted for seasonal colour, which during the late spring and early summer feature perennials inc alliums, lupins, camassias and bearded irises. The larger garden has mature, mixed island beds and borders, a gravel garden to the front, a small wildflower area, large wildlife pond, orchard, soft fruit beds and vegetable garden. Seasonal colour. Large wildlife pond. Open aspect with extensive views to mid Derbyshire.

🌸 ☕

40 NETHER MOOR HOUSE

Granby Road, Bradwell, Hope Valley, S33 9HU. Anna & Rod Smallwood, 07973 738846, annamsmallwood@gmail.com, www.nethermoorgarden.uk. *15m W of Sheffield on the B6049 off the Hope Valley (A6187). From N via A6187 & B6049 R at playing field (Gore Ln), up Smalldale. From S via B6049 L at playing field, (Town Ln) up Smalldale. Turn L onto Granby Rd. Park on L side of rd, well tucked in.* **Visits by arrangement 16 Feb to 7 July for groups of 6 to 20. The garden is open in mid February for snowdrops, weather permitting. Adm £6, chd free. Light refreshments inc tea & biscuits.**

A country garden with views of Hope Valley. Mature trees. Front terraces with colourful planting and box hedges, below lawn and mixed borders, unusual plants. Japanese patio garden: small pond, pools of planting, massive arches, mix of Japanese and traditional plants. At the back, a Japanese walk, long border, sloping grass, sculptures, wild flowers, vegetables. Sit and take in the views. Snowdrops, hellebores, daffodils, peonies, Japanese Tai Haku, Ginkgo and handkerchief trees, rambling and shrub roses.

41 NEW MILLS SCHOOL

Church Lane, New Mills,
High Peak, SK22 4NR.
Mr Craig Pickering,
www.newmillsschool.co.uk. *12m
NNW of Buxton. From A6 take
A6105 signed New Mills, Hayfield.
At C of E Church turn L onto Church
Ln. Sch on L. Parking on site.* **Sat
13, Sun 14 July (2-5). Adm £4,
chd free. Light refreshments in
School Library.**
Mixed herbaceous perennials/shrub
borders, with mature trees and lawns
and gravel border situated in the
semi rural setting of the High Peak
inc a Grade II listed building with
four themed quads. The school was
awarded highly commended in the
School Garden 2019 RHS Tatton
Show and won the Best High School
Garden and the People's Choice
Award. Hot and cold beverages and
cakes are available. Ramps allow
wheelchair access to most of outside,
flower beds and into Grade II listed
building and library.

42 THE NIGHTINGALE CENTRE

Great Hucklow, Buxton,
Buxton, SK17 8RH. Ms Marion
Baker, 01298 871218, info@
thenightingalecentre.org.uk, www.
thenightingalecentre.org.uk. *12
miles NE of Buxton. For SatNav:
use SK17 8RG. Parking: main car
park and overflow (car park at rear
of Centre, accessed via entrance
opposite Old Unitarian Chapel).* **Sat
31 Aug (10.30-3.30); Sun 1 Sept
(10.30-4.30). Adm £3, chd £1. Pre-
booking required, please visit
www.ngs.org.uk for information &
booking. Teas, coffee and home-
made cakes.**
Charity conference Centre in the heart
of the Peak National Park. 1½ acre
garden, with views of surrounding
countryside. Inc herbaceous borders,
living willow structures, rock garden, a
small vegetable plot and greenhouse
to supply produce to the kitchen
and educate visiting school groups
about growing food. Plants for sale.
The weekend's focus is on activities
for children, inc making a bug hotel
and seed bombs and a garden quiz.
Please contact garden to pre-book
children's activities.

43 330 OLD ROAD

Brampton, Chesterfield,
S40 3QH. Christine Stubbs &
Julia Stubbs, 07919 217559,
julia.stubbs@aecom.com. *Approx
1½ m from town centre. 50 yds from
junc with Storrs Rd. 1st house next
to grazing field; on-road parking
available adjacent to tree-lined
roadside stone wall.* **Fri 21, Sat 22
June (10.30-5). Adm £4, chd free.
Home-made teas. Visits also by
arrangement 24 June to 9 Sept.**
Deceptive ⅓ acre plot of mature
trees, landscaped lawns, orchard
and cottage style planting. Unusual
perennials, species groups such
as astrantia, lychnis, thalictrum,
heuchera and 40+ clematis. Acers,
actea, hosta, ferns and acanthus lie
within this interesting garden. Through
a hidden gate, another smaller plot
of similar planting, with delphinium,
helenium, Echinacea, acers and
hosta. Winner Chesterfield in Bloom
Best Large Garden.

44 THE PADDOCK

12 Manknell Rd, Whittington
Moor, Chesterfield, S41 8LZ. Mel
& Wendy Taylor, 07816 284329,
debijt9276@gmail.com. *2m N
of Chesterfield. Whittington Moor
just off A61 between Sheffield &
Chesterfield. Parking at Victoria
Working Mens Club, garden signed
from here.* **Sun 21 Apr, Sun 28
July (11-5). Adm £3.50, chd
free. Cream teas. Visits also by
arrangement 21 Apr to 30 Sept for
groups of 10+.**
½ acre garden incorporating small
formal garden, stream and koi filled
pond. Stone path over bridge, up
some steps, past small copse, across
the stream at the top and back
down again. Past herbaceous border
towards a pergola where cream teas
can be enjoyed.

45 PARK HALL

Walton Back Lane, Walton,
Chesterfield, S42 7LT. Kim
Staniforth, 07785 784439, kim.
staniforth@btinternet.com. *2m SW
of Chesterfield centre. From town on
A619 L into Somersall Ln. On A632
R into Acorn Ridge. Park on field
side only of Walton Back Ln.* **Visits
by arrangement Apr to July for
groups of 10+. Adm £7, chd free.**
Romantic 2 acre plantsmans
garden, in a stunningly beautiful
setting surrounding C17 house (not

open) four main rooms, terraced
garden, parkland area with forest
trees, croquet lawn, sunken garden
with arbours, pergolas, pleached
hedge, topiary, statuary, roses,
rhododendrons, camellias, several
water features. Runner-up in Daily
Telegraph Great British Gardens
Competition 2018. Two steps down
to gain access to garden.

46 ◆ RENISHAW HALL & GARDENS

Renishaw Park, Sheffield,
S21 3WB. Alexandra Hayward,
01246 432310, enquiries@
renishaw-hall.co.uk,
www.renishaw-hall.co.uk. *10m
from Sheffield city centre. By car:
Renishaw Hall only 3m from J30
on M1, well sign posted from junc
30 r'about. What3words app -
bungalows.relished.staining.* **For
NGS: Wed 1 May, Wed 3 July
(10.30-4.30). Adm £10, chd free.
Takeaway kiosk at the Gardens
entrance. For other opening times
and information, please phone,
email or visit garden website.**
Renishaw Hall and Gardens boasts
7 acres of stunning gardens created
by Sir George Sitwell in 1885. The
Italianate gardens feature various
rooms with extravagant herbaceous
borders. Rose gardens, rare trees and
shrubs, National Collection of Yuccas,
sculptures, woodland walks and
lakes create a magical and engaging
garden experience. The National
Garden Scheme openings coincide
with the bluebells being in flower on
Wednesday1st May and the roses
blooming on Wednesday 3rd July.
For a sumptuous Afternoon Tea in the
Courtyard Café, on the day of your visit,
prebooking is required. Please phone
the office on 01246 432310. Mobility
scooter and wheelchairs available to
hire free of charge. Pre-booking is
strongly advised. Wheelchair route &
map around the formal gardens.

GROUP OPENING

47 REPTON NGS VILLAGE GARDENS

Repton, Derby, DE65 6FQ. *6m S of
Derby. From A38/A50, S of Derby,
follow signs to Willington, then
Repton, then R at r'about towards
Newton Solney to reach 10 Chestnut
Way, other gardens signposted from
the r'about.*

Mon 27 May, Sun 21 July, Mon 26 Aug (11-4). Combined adm £6, chd free. Light refreshments at 10 Chestnut Way in May, Askew Cottage in July, High Street in August.

ASKEW COTTAGE
DE65 6FZ. Louise Hardwick, 07970 411748, louise.hardwick@hotmail.co.uk, www.hardwickgardendesign.co.uk. Open on Mon 27 May, Sun 21 July

Visits also by arrangement May to July for groups of up to 25.

10 CHESTNUT WAY
Pauline Little.
Open on all dates
(See separate entry)

NEW **34 HIGH STREET**
DE65 6GD. Adrian and Natalie Argyle, 01283 701277, nargyle@argylefrics.co.uk. Open on all dates

Visits also by arrangement 18 May to 1 Sept for groups of 5 to 15. Adm inc home-made teas.

22 PINFOLD CLOSE
DE65 6FR. Mr & Mrs O Jowett.
Open on Mon 27 May, Mon 26 Aug

REPTON ALLOTMENTS
DE65 6FX. Mr A Topping.
Open on Sun 21 July, Mon 26 Aug

Repton is a thriving village dating back to Anglo Saxon times. The village gardens are all very different, ranging from the very small to very large, several of them have new features for 2024. Askew Cottage is a professionally designed garden and has many structural features linked together by curving paths. 34 High Street is a traditional old-established garden at the rear of one of the historic village properties. 10 Chestnut Way is a plantaholic's garden much changed over winter - be prepared to be surprised. 22 Pinfold Close is a small garden but is packed full with a special interest in tropical plants and has a new orchid house. Repton Allotments is a small set of allotments currently undergoing a revival with community area, new polytunnel and attractive views across Derbyshire. All gardens have plenty of seats. Some gardens have grass or gravel paths but most areas wheelchair accessible.

Ashen Clough

48 RIVERSVALE LODGE
Riversvale, Buxton, SK17 6UZ.
Dena Lewis, 01298 70504, lewis.riversvale@btinternet.com. *½ m from Buxton town centre just off the A53 to Leek. Turn R off St John's Rd, down Gadley Ln. This becomes single track so cars need to park at the top of the lane. Short walk down to the garden, following the NGS signs.* **Visits by arrangement Apr to Sept for groups of 10 to 15. Adm £6, chd free. Home-made teas inc tea/coffee & cake.**

The garden is small but full of plants collected over nearly 30 yrs. The aim is for interest throughout the seasons, based on foliage, texture and unusual plants which will flourish at over 1000ft. A wide range of insects has resulted. The site provides a clay loam soil and a range of aspects so that many plant groups thrive. Firm paths around the house but many narrow bark paths around the garden. The main features are visible.

49 THE SMITHY

Church Street, Buxton, SK17 6HD. Roddie & Kate MacLean. *200 metres S of Buxton Market Place, in Higher Buxton. Located on access-only Church St, which cuts corner between B5059 & A515. Walk S from Buxton Market Place car park. Take slight R off A515, between Scriveners Bookshop & The Swan Inn.* **Sun 9, Sat 15, Sun 16 June (10.30-5). Adm £4, chd free.** Small oasis of calm in the town centre, designed by its architect-owners. Pretty colour-themed borders and dappled tree cover. Many visitors comment about how the owners have optimised the use of the space without appearing to cram it all in. Herbaceous borders, wildlife pond, octagonal greenhouse, raised vegetable beds and several different seating areas for eating outdoors.

50 SNITTERTON HALL

Snitterton, Matlock, DE4 2JG. Simon Haslam & Kate Alcock, simon@snitterton.org. *1m NW of Matlock. Follow signs from Matlock to Winster, heading up the hill past Sainsbury's. Ignore SatNav if it sends you to Matlock Meadows Ice creams & stay on the road for ½ m until you see our signs.* **Visits by arrangement Feb to Sept for groups of up to 20. Adm £10, chd free. Light refreshments.** Snitterton Hall is a Grade I listed late Elizabethan manor house, and its gardens extend to over 4 acres. While little of the original C16 and C17 gardens remain, there are areas of formal planting, a productive vegetable garden and more naturally planted areas extending into the surrounding countryside - with a delightful collection of sculptures. The gardens are a real haven. Lots of garden sculptures - particularly driftwood sculptures by James Doran-Webb and bronzes by Helen Sinclair.

GROUP OPENING

51 STANTON IN PEAK GARDENS

Stanton-in-the-Peak, Matlock, DE4 2LR. *At the top of the hill in Stanton in Peak. Stanton in Peak is 5m S of Bakewell. Turn off the A6 at Rowsley, or at the B5056 & follow signs up the hill.* **Sat 27, Sun 28 July (12.30-4.30). Combined adm £5, chd free. Home-made teas at 2 Haddon View. At Woodend Cottage, a pop-up pub serves real ale from the barrel.**

NEW BIRCHENLEE
DE4 2LS. Mr Julian Corner.

2 HADDON VIEW
Steve Tompkins.
(See separate entry)

WOODEND COTTAGE
DE4 2LX. Will Chandler.

Stanton in Peak is a hillside, stone village which is a Conservation Area in the Peak District National Park. Three gardens are open, all with glorious views. Steve's garden at 2 Haddon View is at the top of the village and is crammed with plants. Follow the winding path up the garden with a few steps. There are cacti flowering in the greenhouse, lots of pots, herbaceous borders, three wildlife ponds with red and pink water lilies, a koi pond, lots of rhododendrons and a cosy summerhouse. Enjoy home-made cakes and refreshments on one of the patios. Just down the hill is Woodend where Will has constructed charming roadside stone follies on a strip of raised land along the road. The hidden rear garden has diverse planting, and an extended vegetable plot. A pop-up 'pub' will have draught beer from a local brewery. Julian's garden at Birchenlee wraps around the house with drifts of perennials, varied shrubs, a wildflower meadow area, and flowers grown for cutting.

Mill Cottage, Gorsey Bank Gardens

52 26 STILES ROAD

Alvaston, Derby, DE24 0PG. Mr Colin Summerfield & Karen Wild. *Alvaston, Derby. 2m SE of Derby city centre. From city take A6 (London Rd) towards Alvaston. At Blue Peter Island take L into Beech Ave 1st R into Kelmoor Rd & 1st L into Stiles Rd.* **Sun 21 Apr, Sun 12 May (12-4). Adm £3, chd free. Home-made teas.**

A small town garden full of surprises. New for 2024 Tulip display. Pass through our ever growing wisteria tunnel and fernery to find ponds, a stream, mini woodland walk, seating areas, an eclectic mix of plants, veg plot and mature fruit trees, over 30 clematis, 10 acers, 3 wisteria. Front garden features an aubrietia wall, azaleas and clematis plus much more. Close to Elvaston Castle. Half of garden is wheelchair accessible, most can be seen from patio area.

53 ◆ TISSINGTON HALL

Tissington, Ashbourne, DE6 1RA. Sir Richard & Lady FitzHerbert, 01335 352200, sirrichard@tissingtonhall.co.uk, www.tissingtonhall.co.uk. *4m N of Ashbourne. E of A515 on Ashbourne to Buxton Rd in centre of the beautiful Estate Village of Tissington.* **For NGS: Mon 6 May, Mon 12, Mon 19, Mon 26 May (12-3). Adm £8, chd £4. Tea at Award winning Herbert's Fine English Tearooms. Tel 01335 350501. For other opening times and information, please phone, email or visit garden website.**

Large garden celebrating over 85yrs in the National Garden Scheme, with stunning rose garden on west terrace, herbaceous borders and 5 acres of grounds. Herbert's Tearooms Andrew Holmes Butchers and Onawick Candle workshop also open in the village. Wheelchair access advice from ticket seller. Please seek staff and we shall park you nearer the gardens.

54 27 WASH GREEN

Wirksworth, Matlock, DE4 4FD. Paul & Kathy Harvey, 01629 822218, pandkharvey@btinternet.com. *⅓m E of Wirksworth centre. From Wirksworth centre, follow B5035 towards Whatstandwell. Cauldwell St leads over railway bridge to Wash Green, 200 metres up steep hill on L. Park in town or uphill from garden entry.* **Sun 12 May, Sun 25 Aug (11-4). Adm £4, chd free. Home-made teas inc gluten free options. Visits also by arrangement 1 Apr to 11 Oct for groups of 10 to 30.**

Secluded 1 acre garden, with outstanding 360° views. Inner enclosed area has topiary, pergola and lawn surrounded by mixed borders, with paved seating area. The larger part of the garden has sweeping lawns, with large borders, beds, wildlife pond with summerhouse, bog garden, areas of woodland and specimen trees. A quarter of the plot is a productive fruit and vegetable garden with polytunnel. Drop off at property entry for wheelchair access. The inner garden has flat paths with good views of whole garden.

55 13 WESTFIELD ROAD

Swadlincote, DE11 0BG. Val & Dave Booth. *5m E of Burton-on-Trent, off A511. Take A511 from Burton-on-Trent. Follow signs for Swadlincote. Turn R into Springfield Rd, take 3rd R into Westfield Rd.* **Sun 16 June, Sun 4 Aug (12-5). Adm £3.50, chd free. Home-made teas.**

A deceptive country-style garden in Swadlincote, a real gem. The garden is on two levels of approx ½ acre. Packed herbaceous borders designed for colour. Shrubs, baskets and tubs. Lots of roses. Greenhouses, raised-bed vegetable area, fruit trees and two ponds. Free range chicken area. Plenty of seating to relax and take in the wonderful planting from two passionate gardeners.

56 15 WINDMILL LANE

Ashbourne, DE6 1EY. Jean Ross & Chris Duncan. *Take A515 (Buxton Rd) from the market place & at the top of the hill turn R into Windmill Ln; house by 4th tree on L.* **Sun 9 June (1.30-5). Adm £3, chd free.**

Densely planted town garden providing ideas others may wish to develop. Using a limited palette (mainly white, pink, mauve and burgundy) and emphasising leaf shape and colour, the key aims in establishing this garden were all-year interest, low maintenance, attraction of pollinators, and growing some soft fruit and veg. Garden now contains many drought-resistant plants. Extensive views.

57 26 WINDMILL RISE

Belper, DE56 1GQ. Kathy Fairweather. *From Belper Market Place take Chesterfield Rd towards Heage. Top of hill, 1st R Marsh Ln, 1st R Windmill Ln, 1st R Windmill Rise - limited parking on Windmill Rise - disabled mainly.* **Sun 21 July (11.30-4). Adm £3, chd free. Light refreshments inc gluten free & vegan options.**

Behind a deceptively ordinary façade, lies a real surprise. A lush oasis, much larger than expected, with an amazing collection of rare and unusual plants. A truly plant lovers' organic garden divided into sections: woodland, Japanese, secret garden, cottage, edible, ponds and small stream. Many seating areas, inc a new summerhouse in which to enjoy a variety of refreshments. Home made delicious cakes and light lunches available.

58 YEW TREE BUNGALOW

Thatchers Lane, Tansley, Matlock, DE4 5FD. Jayne Conquest, 07745 093177, jayneconquest@btinternet.com. *2m E of Matlock. On A615, 2nd R after Tavern at Tansley. Parking available in Charles Gregory & Sons Timber yard car park opp. Tavern Inn.* **Sun 21 Apr, Sun 30 June, Sun 1 Sept (11.30-4). Adm £5, chd free. Home-made teas. Visits also by arrangement 22 Apr to 30 Aug for groups of 6 to 30.**

Plants women's ½ acre cottage style garden on a slope created by the present owners over 30 years. Many mixed borders planted with many choice and unusual trees, shrubs, herbaceous perennial, bulbs and annuals to provide year-round interest. Several seats to view different aspects of the garden. Shady area planted with a wide range of ferns. Vegetable and fruit garden. The garden is sloping but most of garden can be seen from patio.

In 2023 we awarded over £260,000 in Community Garden Grants, supporting 86 community garden projects

LEICESTERSHIRE & RUTLAND

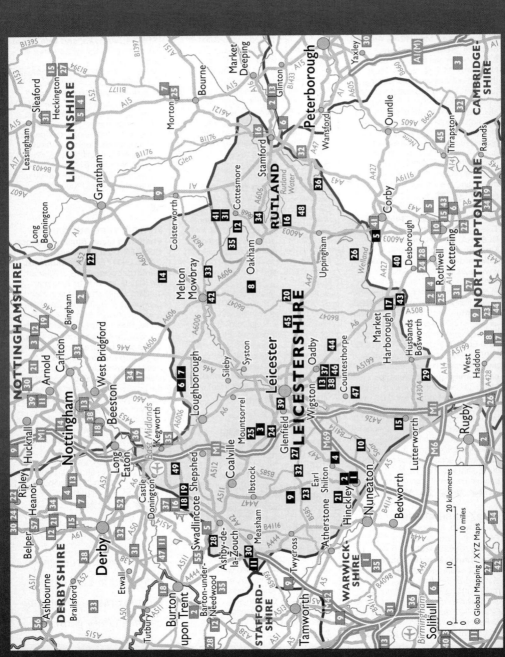

VOLUNTEERS

Leicestershire

County Organiser
Pamela Shave 01858 575481
pamela.shave@ngs.org.uk

County Treasurer
Martin Shave 01455 556633
martin.shave@ngs.org.uk

Publicity
Carol Bartlett 01616 261053
carol.bartlett@ngs.org.uk

Booklet Co-ordinator
(Leicestershire & Rutland)
Carole Troake 07580 500261
carole.troake@ngs.org.uk

Social Media
Zoe Lewin 07810 800 007
zoe.lewin@ngs.org.uk

Photographer
Rosie Furniss 07837 793321
rosie.furniss@ngs.org.uk

Talks
Karen Gimson 07930 246974
k.gimson@btinternet.com

John Fraser 07502 051663
john.fraser@ngs.org.uk

Group Visit Co-ordinator
Judith Boston 07740 945332
judith.boston@ngs.org.uk

Assistant County Organisers
Janet Rowe 01162 597339
janetnandrew@btinternet.com

Gill Hadland 01162 592170
gillhadland1@gmail.com

Rutland

County Organisers
Sally Killick 07799 064565
sally.killick@ngs.org.uk

Lucy Hurst 07958 534778
lucy.hurst@ngs.org.uk

County Treasurer
Sandra Blaza 01572 770588
sandra.blaza@ngs.org.uk

Publicity
Lucy Hurst (as above)

Social Media
Nicola Oakey 07516 663358
nicola.oakey@ngs.org.uk

OPENING DATES

All entries subject to change. For latest information check
www.ngs.org.uk

Extended openings are shown at the beginning of the month.

Map locator numbers are shown to the right of each garden name.

February

Snowdrop Openings

Sunday 18th
The Acers	1
Oak Cottage	28

Saturday 24th
Hedgehog Hall	20
Westview	44

Sunday 25th
Hedgehog Hall	20
Westview	44

March

Sunday 3rd
Tresillian House	42

Sunday 17th
Gunthorpe Hall	16

April

Sunday 28th
Tresillian House	42
Westbrooke House	43

May

Sunday 5th
Burrough Hall	8

Sunday 12th
Carlton Gardens	9
The Old Vicarage, Whissendine	35

Saturday 18th
Hedgehog Hall	20
8 Hinckley Road	21
The New Barn	27

Sunday 19th
1 The Dairy, Hurst Court	11
Fox Cottage	12
Goadby Marwood Hall	14
Hedgehog Hall	20
8 Hinckley Road	21
The New Barn	27
NEW The Old Rectory, Goadby Marwood	33

Saturday 25th
Westview	44

Sunday 26th
The Old Vicarage, Burley	34
Westbrooke House	43

Monday 27th
Westview	44

June

Every day from Tuesday 11th to Sunday 16th
Nevill Holt Hall	26

Every Wednesday
Stoke Albany House	40

Saturday 1st
28 Gladstone Street	13

Sunday 2nd
28 Gladstone Street	13

Saturday 8th
88 Brook Street	6
109 Brook Street	7
The Secret Garden at Wigston Framework Knitters Museum	38

Sunday 9th
88 Brook Street	6
109 Brook Street	7
Dairy Cottage	10
The Secret Garden at Wigston Framework Knitters Museum	38

Saturday 15th
The Old Rectory	32

Sunday 16th
The Old Rectory	32
59 Thistleton Road	41

 @NGSLeicestershire

 @LeicsNGS

 @leicestershire_ngs

 @rutlandngs

 @RutlandNGS

 @rutlandngs

Saturday 22nd
The Secret Garden, Glenfield
   Hospital   39

Sunday 23rd
Westbrooke House   43
Wing Gardens   48
15 The Woodcroft   49

Friday 28th
Brickfield House   5

Saturday 29th
Oak Tree House   29

Sunday 30th
Oak Tree House   29
Tresillian House   42

July

Every Wednesday
Stoke Albany House   40

Wednesday 3rd
The Old Hall   31

Saturday 6th
12 Hastings Close   18
NEW 22 Hastings Close   19

Sunday 7th
Market Bosworth Gardens   23

Saturday 13th
8 Hinckley Road   21
Wigston Gardens   46

Sunday 14th
Green Wicket Farm   15
8 Hinckley Road   21
Wigston Gardens   46
Willoughby Gardens   47

Wednesday 17th
Green Wicket Farm   15

Saturday 20th
The Secret Garden, Glenfield
   Hospital   39

Sunday 21st
St Wolstan's House   37

August

Every Sunday
Honeytrees Tropical Garden   22

**Every day from Saturday
10th to Sunday 18th**
221 Markfield Road   24

Saturday 3rd
182 Ashby Road   2

Sunday 4th
182 Ashby Road   2

Saturday 17th
The Old Barn   30

Sunday 18th
The Old Barn   30

Sunday 25th
Tresillian House   42

September

Thursday 12th
Redhill Lodge   36

Saturday 14th
Westview   44

Sunday 15th
Westview   44

Saturday 21st
St Wolstan's House   37

October

Sunday 6th
Hammond Arboretum   17

Sunday 27th
Tresillian House   42

By Arrangement

Arrange a personalised garden visit
with your club, or group of friends,
on a date to suit you. See individual
garden entries for full details.

The Acers   1
Bank Cottage   3
Barracca   4
88 Brook Street   6
109 Brook Street   7
1 The Dairy, Hurst Court   11
Farmway, Willoughby Gardens   47
Goadby Marwood Hall   14
Green Wicket Farm   15
Honeytrees Tropical Garden   22
221 Markfield Road   24
Mountain Ash   25
The Old Barn   30
Stoke Albany House   40
Tresillian House   42
Westview   44
The White House Farm   45

Hedgehog Hall

THE GARDENS

1 THE ACERS

10 The Rills, Hinckley, LE10 1NA. Mr Dave Baggott, 01455 617237, davebaggott18@hotmail.com. *10 mins from J1 of the M69. Off B4668 out of Hinckley. Turn into Dean Rd then 1st R into The Rills. Last house on the R.* **Sun 18 Feb (10.30-4). Adm £5, chd free. Visits also by arrangement Sept & Oct.** Medium sized garden, with a Japanese theme inc a zen garden, Japanese tea house, koi pond, more than 20 different varieties of acers, many choice alpines, trilliums, cyclamen, erythroniums, cornus, hamamelis and dwarf conifers. Approximately 200 different varieties of snowdrops in spring. Large greenhouse.

2 182 ASHBY ROAD

Hinckley, LE10 1SW. Ms Lynda Blower. *Hinckley is SW Leics near to the border with Warks, with access off the M69 or A5. From Hinckley town centre on the B4667 on R 400yds before the A47/A447 jnc. Parking in the road nearby.* **Sat 3, Sun 4 Aug (11-4). Adm £3.50, chd free. Light refreshments.** 120ft cottage style garden packed with lots of colourful perennials and annuals. Many pots and containers full of cannas, agapanthus, banana plants and dahlias. A small pond and bog garden planting. A garden room and plenty of comfortable seating to sit and view different aspects of the garden. Many salvage collectables cited around the garden which provide further interest.

3 BANK COTTAGE

90 Main Street, Newtown Linford, Leicester, LE6 0AF. Jan Croft, 07429 159910, gardening91@icloud.com. *6m NW Leicester. 2½m from M1 J22. From Leicester via Anstey Bank cottage is on the L after Markfield Ln, just before a public footpath sign. If coming via Warren Hill cottage is on the R just after public footpath sign.* **Visits by arrangement Mar to Aug. Home-made teas or bring your own picnic to sit and relax by the River Lin. Adm £3, chd free. Home-made teas.**

Celebration parties can be accommodated. The owner sets up appropriately by the river. Traditional cottage garden set on different levels leading down to the River Lin. Providing colour all year-round but at its prettiest in the spring. Aconites, snowdrops, blue and white bells, primroses, alliums, aquilegia, poppies, geraniums, roses, honeysuckle, Philadelphia, acers, wisteria, autumn crocus, perennial sweet pea, perennial sunflowers, some fruit trees, small pond. Full of wildlife.

4 BARRACCA

Ivydene Close, Earl Shilton, LE9 7NR. Mr John & Mrs Sue Osborn, 01455 842609, susan.osborn1@btinternet.com. *10m W of Leicester. From A47 after entering Earl Shilton, Ivydene Cl is 4th on L from Leicester side of A47.* **Visits by arrangement 21 Feb to 31 July for groups of up to 50. Adm £9, chd free. Refreshments included in admission price.** 1 acre garden with lots of different areas, silver birch walk, wildlife pond with seating, apple tree garden, Mediterranean planted area and lawns surrounded with herbaceous plants and shrubs. Patio area with climbing roses and wisteria. There is also a utility garden with greenhouses, vegetables in beds, herbs and perennial flower beds, lawn and fruit cage. Part of the old gardens owned by the Cotton family who used to open approx 9 acres to the public in the 1920's. Partial wheelchair access.

5 BRICKFIELD HOUSE

Rockingham Road, Cottingham, Market Harborough, LE16 8XS. Simon & Nicki Harker. *SatNav will take you into Cottingham Village but garden is ½m from Cottingham on Rockingham Rd/B670 towards Rockingham.* **Fri 28 June (12-4). Adm £5, chd free. Home-made teas.** Lovely views overlooking the Welland Valley, this 2 acre garden has been developed from a sloping brickyard rubbish plot over 36 yrs. There is a kitchen garden, orchard, herbaceous borders filled with roses, perennials and shrubs, paths and many pots, filled with succulents, herbs and colourful annuals.

6 88 BROOK STREET

Wymeswold, LE12 6TU. Adrian & Ita Cooke, 01509 880155, itacooke@btinternet.com. *4m NE of Loughborough. From A6006 Wymeswold turn S by church onto Stockwell, then E along Brook St. Roadside parking on Brook St.* **Sat 8, Sun 9 June (2-5). Combined adm with 109 Brook Street £6, chd free. Home-made teas at 109 Brook Street. Visits also by arrangement May to July for groups of 10 to 40.** The garden is set on a hillside with lovely views across the village. It comprises a cottage style garden; then a series of water features inc a stream and a 'champagne' pond; and finally a vegetable garden, small orchard and wildflower meadow. Artistic touches run throughout and local artwork is featured. The ponds attract great crested and common newts, frogs, toads and grass snakes.

7 109 BROOK STREET

Wymeswold, LE12 6TT. Maggie & Steve Johnson, 07973 692931, steve@brookend.org, www.brookend.org. *4m NE of Loughborough. From A6006 Wymeswold turn S onto Stockwell, then E along Brook St. Roadside parking along Brook St. Steep drive with limited disabled parking at house.* **Sat 8, Sun 9 June (2-5). Combined adm with 88 Brook Street £6, chd free. Home-made teas inc gluten free and vegetarian options. Visits also by arrangement May to July.** South facing, ¾ acre, gently sloping garden with views over open countryside. Modern garden with mature features. Patio with roses and clematis, wildlife and fish ponds, mixed borders, vegetable garden, orchard, hot garden and woodland garden. Something for everyone. Optional tour of rain water harvesting. Some gravel paths. Drive to top of drive and ask for assistance.

152,684 people were able to access guidance on what to expect when a person is dying through the National Garden Scheme support for Hospice UK this year

8 BURROUGH HALL
Somerby Road, Burrough on the Hill, Melton Mowbray, LE14 2QZ. Richard & Alice Cunningham. *Somerby Rd, Burrough on the Hill. Close to B6047. 10 mins from A606. 20 mins from Melton Mowbray.* Sun 5 May (2-5). Adm £5, chd free. Home-made teas.
Burrough Hall was built in 1867 as a classic Leicestershire hunting lodge. The garden, framed by mature trees and shrubs, was extensively redesigned by garden designer George Carter in 2007. The garden continues to develop. This family garden designed for all generations to enjoy is surrounded by magnificent views across High Leicestershire. In addition to the garden there will be a small collection of vintage and classic cars on display. Gravel paths and lawn.

GROUP OPENING

9 CARLTON GARDENS
64, Main Street, Carlton, Nuneaton, CV13 0EZ. Mr & Mrs Boston. *Carlton is 2m N of Market Bosworth & 5m S of Ibstock. All the gardens are either on or close to Main St. There is plenty of on-street parking.* Sun 12 May (11-4.30). Combined adm £5, chd free. Light refreshments in St Andrew's Parish Church, Main Street, Carlton.

BUMBLE COT
Murray & Pat Lockwood.

HOME FARM HOUSE
Mr & Mrs C J Peat.

64 MAIN STREET
Paul & Judith Boston.

NEW **PENWOOD COTTAGE**
Simon and Jill Cooper.

WOODMILL
Tom & Liz Alun-Jones.

Five very different and interesting gardens displaying a variety of styles and a range of spring flowers. Bumble Cot is a small courtyard style garden, 64, Main Street is planted to encourage wildlife with views to open countryside with a variety of trees. Woodmill is a recently redeveloped garden with areas planted in both traditional and modern styles. Penwood is a small, pretty cottage garden and Home Farm is an informal, family garden with a beautiful

spring woodland of 1½ acres, planted in 2000. All of the gardens are partially wheelchair accessible, although some have gravel paths. Inaccessible areas will be clearly labelled.

10 DAIRY COTTAGE
15 Sharnford Road, Sapcote, LE9 4JN. Mrs Norah Robinson-Smith. *9m SW of Leicester. Sharnford Rd joins Leicester Rd in Sapcote to B4114 Coventry Rd. Follow NGS signs.* Sun 9 June (11-4). Adm £5, chd free. Home-made teas.
Peaceful garden with places to sit and enjoy the old cottage setting. The garden is over half an acre which inc a walled cottage garden, stumpery, potager, fernery and woodland walk. The planting consists of many unusual shrubs and trees and over 90 clematis, climbing roses and colourful herbaceous borders. The garden has been featured in Garden News and Garden Answers. May need to access over a gravel drive.

11 1 THE DAIRY, HURST COURT
Netherseal Road, Chilcote, Swadlincote, DE12 8DU. Alison Dockray, alisondockray56@gmail.com. *3m from J11 of the M42. 10m from Tamworth & Ashby de la Zouch. Hurst Court is situated on Netherseal Rd but SatNav show it as Church Rd. Due to limited parking it is advisable to park on Netherseal Rd. Chilcote is on the border of four counties.* Sun 19 May (1-5). Adm £5, chd free. Light refreshments. Visits also by arrangement 19 May to 31 Aug for groups of up to 20. Adm inc tea and coffee. Cakes may be purchased.
Developed over the last 17 years from a muddy ¼ acre patch attached to a barn conversion, the garden now contains a large Japanese Koi Carp pond, goldfish pond and a stream with planting having a Japanese connection viewed from winding paths. With many rhododendrons, camellias and azaleas combined with cloud pruning and a variety of other plants, an air of peace pervades the garden.

12 FOX COTTAGE
Woodside, Ashwell, Oakham, LE15 7LX. Mr & Mrs D Pettifer. *No access via Woodside. Follow signs for parking.* Sun 19 May (11.30-4.30). Adm £5, chd free. Light refreshments.
A 2 acre country garden on the edge of the village with sweeping views across the surrounding open fields. Walks through the wonderful ancient oaks and ash underplanted with spring bulbs and lawns surrounded by rampant cow parsley. South facing terrace with seasonal planting. Teas and light lunches in garden, live music from Happy Jazz Band.

13 28 GLADSTONE STREET
Wigston Magna, LE18 1AE. Chris & Janet Huscroft. *4m S of Leicester. Off Wigston by-pass (A5199) follow signs off McDonalds r'about.* Sat 1, Sun 2 June (11-5). Adm £3.50, chd free. Home-made teas. Opening with Wigston Gardens on Sat 13, Sun 14 July.
The mature 70'x15' town garden is divided into rooms and bisected by a pond with a bridge. It is brimming with unusual hardy perennials, inc collections of ferns and hostas. David Austin roses chosen for their scent feature throughout, inc a 30' rose arch. A shade house with unusual hardy plants and a Hosta Theatre. Regular changes to planting. Wigston Framework Knitters Museum and Secret garden nearby - open Sunday afternoons. Parts of the garden can be viewed, narrow paths and step limit full access.

14 GOADBY MARWOOD HALL
Goadby Marwood, Melton Mowbray, LE14 4LN. Mr & Mrs Westropp, 01664 464202, vwestropp@gmail.com. *4m NW of Melton Mowbray. Between Waltham-on-the-Wolds & Eastwell, 8m S of Grantham. Plenty of parking.* Sun 19 May (10.30-5). Combined adm with The Old Rectory, Goadby Marwood £10, chd free. Light refreshments in village hall. Visits also by arrangement Apr to Oct.
Redesigned in 2000 by the owner based on C18 plans. A chain of five lakes (covering 10 acres) and several ironstone walled gardens all interconnected. Lakeside woodland walk. Planting for year-round interest. Landscaper trained under plantswoman Rosemary Verey at

Barnsley House. Beautiful C13th church open. Gravel paths and lawns.

🚻 🐕 🚌 🚐 ☕

15 GREEN WICKET FARM
Ullesthorpe Road, Bitteswell, Lutterworth, LE17 4LR. Mrs Anna Smith, 01455 552646, greenfarmbitt@hotmail.com. *2m NW of Lutterworth J20 M1. From Lutterworth follow signs through Bitteswell towards Ullesthorpe. Garden situated behind Bitteswell Cricket Club. Use this as a landmark rather than relying totally on SatNav.* **Sun 14, Wed 17 July (2-5). Adm £5, chd free. Light refreshments. Visits also by arrangement 24 June to 31 Aug for groups of up to 25.**
A fairly formal garden on an exposed site surrounded by open fields. Mature trees enclosing the many varied plants chosen to give all round year interest. Many unusual hardy plants grown along side good

reliable old favourites present a range of colour themed borders. Grass and gravel paths allow access to the whole garden. Disabled parking areas.

🚻 ✿ ☕ 🔊

16 GUNTHORPE HALL
Gunthorpe, Oakham, LE15 8BE. Tim Haywood. *A6003 between Oakham & Uppingham; 1½ m S of Oakham, up drive between gate lodges.* **Sun 17 Mar (2-5). Adm £5, chd free. Home-made teas.**
Large garden in a country setting with extensive views across the Rutland landscape with the carpets of daffodils being a key seasonal feature. The Stable Yard has been transformed into a series of parterres. The kitchen garden and borders have all been rejuvenated over recent years. Gravel path allows steps to be avoided.

🚻 ✿ ☕ 🔊

17 HAMMOND ARBORETUM
Burnmill Road, Market Harborough, LE16 7JG. The Robert Smyth Academy, www.hammondarboretum.org.uk. *15m S of Leicester on A6. From High St, follow signs to The Robert Smyth Academy via Bowden Ln to Burnmill Rd. Park in 1st entrance on L.* **Sun 6 Oct (2-4.30). Adm £6, chd free. Home-made teas.**
A site of just under 2½ acres containing an unusual collection of trees and shrubs, many from Francis Hammond's original planting dating from 1913 to 1936 whilst headmaster of the school. Species from America, China and Japan with malus and philadelphus walks and a moat. Proud owners of three champion trees identified by national specialist and 37 which are the best in Leicestershire. Walk plans available. Some steep slopes.

🚻 🐕 ☕

Brickfield House

18 12 HASTINGS CLOSE
Breedon-on-the-Hill, Derby,
DE73 8BN. Mr & Mrs P Winship.
*5m N from Ashby de la Zouch.
Follow NGS signs in the Village.
Parking around the Village Green.
Please do not park in the close due
to limited parking.* **Sat 6 July (1-5).
Combined adm with 22 Hastings
Close £5, chd free.**
A medium sized prairie garden,
organically managed and planted
in the Piet Oudolf style. Also many
roses and a wide range of perennials.
The back garden has a small 'white'
garden with box hedging and more
colourful style perennial borders.
❀))

19 NEW 22 HASTINGS CLOSE
Breedon-on-the-Hill, Derby,
DE73 8BN. John and Kathy
Newall. *5m N from Ashby de la
Zouch. Follow NGS signs in the
village. Parking around the Village
Green. Please do not park in the
close due to limited parking.* **Sat 6
July (1-5). Combined adm with 12
Hastings Close £5, chd free. Light
refreshments.**

Set on a slight incline the south facing
medium sized garden has stunning
views of Breedon Priory church.
There are three distinct rooms within
the rear garden. Firstly, there is the
sundial garden containing a mixture
of alpines and acers leading through
into a seating area with raised beds
culminating in a traditional styled
garden with wide borders.
☕))

20 HEDGEHOG HALL
Loddington Road, Tilton on the
Hill, LE7 9DE. Janet & Andrew
Rowe. *8m W of Oakham. 2m N
of A47 on B6047 between Melton
& Market Harborough. Follow
yellow NGS signs in Tilton towards
Loddington. Disabled parking on
road outside the White House 20
yds past our entrance.* **Sat 24,
Sun 25 Feb (11-4), open nearby
Westview. Sat 18, Sun 19 May
(11-4). Adm £5, chd free. Home-
made teas in the church for
February opening. In the garden
for May opening.**
½ acre organically managed plant
lover's garden. Steps leading to three

stone walled terraced borders filled
with shrubs, perennials, bulbs and a
patio over looking the valley. Lavender
walk, herb border, beautiful spring
garden, colour themed herbaceous
borders. Courtyard with collection of
hostas and acers and terrace planted
for year-round interest with topiary
and perennials. Snowdrop collection.
Regret, no wheelchair access to
terraced borders.
♿ ❀ ☕))

21 8 HINCKLEY ROAD
Stoke Golding, Nuneaton,
CV13 6DU. John & Stephanie
Fraser. *3m NW of Hinckley.
Approach from any direction into
village then follow NGS signs. Please
park roadside with due consideration
to other residents properties.* **Sat
18 May (12-4); Sun 19 May (12-3);
Sat 13 July (12-4); Sun 14 July
(12-3). Adm £4, chd free. Light
refreshments.**
A small SSW garden with water
features to add interest to the
colourful and some unusual
perennials inc climbers to supplement
the trees and shrubs in May and July.

Kapalua, Willoughby Gardens

Garden established and recently re-established by current owner to provide seating for a variety of views of the garden. Many perennials in the garden are represented in the plants for sale. Wheelchair access to garden room patio which provides a view of the lower part of the garden.

22 HONEYTREES TROPICAL GARDEN

85 Grantham Road, Bottesford, NG13 0EG. Julia Madgwick & Mike Ford, 01949 842120, Julia_madgwick@hotmail.com, www.facebook.com/ HoneytreesTropicalGarden. *Bottesford, Leicestershire. 7m E of Bingham on A52. Turn into village. Garden is on L on slip road behind hedge going out of village towards Grantham. Parking on grass opposite property.* **Every Sun 4 Aug to 25 Aug (11-4). Adm £5, chd free. Home-made teas. Visits also by arrangement July & Aug for groups of 10+.**

Tropical and exotic with a hint of jungle! Raised borders with different themes from lush foliage to arid cacti. Exotic planting as you enter the garden gives way on a gentle incline to surprises, inc glasshouses dedicated to various climatic zones interspersed with more exotic planting, ponds and a stream. Representation of over 20 yrs plant hunting. Treehouse and viewing platform to view tree ferns from above whilst being among the canopy of the trees. Fernery new for 2024. There are some steps and ramps. Gravel and bark in certain areas but wheelchair access to most parts of the garden.

GROUP OPENING

23 MARKET BOSWORTH GARDENS

Market Bosworth, CV13 0LE. www.bosworthinbloom.co.uk. *13m W of Leicester; 8m N of Hinckley. 1m W off A447 Coalville to Hinckley Rd, 3m E off A444. Burton to Nuneaton Rd.* **Sun 7 July (11-5). Combined adm £7.50, chd free. Light refreshments at 13 Spinney Hill, 10 Weston Drive and 37 Heath Road. Donation to Bosworth in Bloom.**

GLEBE FARM HOUSE
Mr Peter Ellis & Ms Ginny Broad.

 37 HEATH ROAD
Jacquie Davis.

4 LANCASTER AVENUE
Mr Peter Bailiss.

26 NORTHUMBERLAND AVENUE
Mrs Kathy Boot.

NEW 157 THE PARK
Brian and Sandra Claybrook.

22 PARK STREET
Mr John Henderson.

30 PARK STREET
Lesley Best.

13 SPINNEY HILL
Mrs J Buckell.

138 STATION ROAD
Sheila & Peter Loseby.

NEW 2 TUDOR CLOSE
Dave and Helen Morris.

10 WESTON DRIVE
Ms Diane Shepherd.

Market Bosworth is an attractive market town, with an enviable record for the quality of its regular entry in the annual East Midlands in Bloom competition. There are a number of gardens open, all within walking distance of the Market Square. The gardens show various planting styles and different approaches to small and intimate spaces in the historic town centre, as well as larger plots in more recent developments. Tickets and descriptive maps obtainable in the Market Place, with refreshments available there and at some of the gardens. Plants will be on sale at a number of gardens. A proportion of the proceeds from the Gardens Open Day will be used to support Bosworth in Bloom, the voluntary group responsible for the town's floral displays.

24 221 MARKFIELD ROAD

Groby, Leicester, LE6 0FT. Jackie Manship, 01530 249363, jackiemanship@btinternet.com. *From M1 J22 take A50 towards Leicester. In approx 3m at the T-lights junction with Lena Dr turn L. Parking available along this road, no parking on A50.* **Daily Sat 10 Aug to Sun 18 Aug (10-4). Adm £5, chd free. Light refreshments. Visits also by arrangement 5 Aug to 9 Aug for groups of 20+.**

A south facing plot of land nestled between the village of Groby and Markfield approx 1 acre in size. The hidden treasures are deceptive from the front of the property which sits on one of the main trunk roads out of Leicester. Packed with interest and created over the last 20 yrs from a dishevelled overgrown plot you will be presented with a garden full of delight.

25 MOUNTAIN ASH

140 Ulverscroft Lane, Newtown Linford, LE6 0AJ. Mike & Liz Newcombe, 01530 242178, mjnew12@gmail.com. *7m SW of Loughborough, 7m NW of Leicester, 1m NW of Newtown Linford. Head ½ m N along Main St towards Sharpley Hill, fork L into Ulverscroft Ln & Mountain Ash, is about ½ m along on the L. Parking is along the opp verge.* **Visits by arrangement May to Sept for groups of 15 to 50. Adm £9, chd free. Home-made teas. Refreshments included in the entry price.**

2 acre garden with stunning views across Charnwood countryside. Near the house are patios, lawns, water feature, flower and shrub beds, fruit trees, soft fruit cage, greenhouses and vegetable plots. Lawns slope down to gravel garden, large wildlife pond and small areas of woodland with walks through many species of trees. Over 50 garden statues and ornaments. Many places to sit and relax. We allow dogs on leads.

National Garden Scheme gardens are identified by their yellow road signs and posters. You can expect a garden of quality, character and interest, a warm welcome and plenty of home-made cakes!

26 NEVILL HOLT HALL

Drayton Road, Nevill Holt, Market Harborough, LE16 8EG. Mr David Ross. *5m NE of Market Haborough. Signed off B664 at Medbourne.* **Daily Tue 11 June to Sun 16 June (12-4). Adm £6, chd free. Light refreshments in restaurant marquee, provided and served by Nevill Holt Opera. Donation to another charity.**

Nevill Holt Hall dates from the C13. Spacious and well proportioned, 10 acres of gardens are designed by Chelsea gold medal winner Rupert Golby. Highlights inc 3 distinctive walled gardens and generous herbaceous borders showing off an ancient Cedar of Lebanon. Nevill Holt Festival is a monthlong programme of exceptional events featuring world class musicians, performers, and speakers. Full details of the festival programme will be announced in January on www.nevillholtopera.co.uk - where tickets will be available for purchase. Walk-up tickets will also be available for purchase on the day of your visit subject to availability.

27 THE NEW BARN

Newbold Road, Desford, Leicester, LE9 9GS. A Nichols & R Pullin. *8m from J21 M1 & 12m from J22 M1.* **Sat 18, Sun 19 May (11-4). Adm £5, chd free. Light refreshments. Donation to Plant Heritage.**

A large, sloping garden of ³⁄₄ acre with wonderful views. Enter via a side gate and follow a narrow path opening up into what feels like a large secret garden, different levels and spaces add to this illusion enabling you to admire the planting and views. This is a well established plantsman's garden with many unusual plants, inc a collection of Asters and Benton irises.

28 OAK COTTAGE

Well Lane, Blackfordby, Swadlincote, DE11 8AG. Colin & Jenny Carr. *Blackfordby, just over 1m from (& between) Ashby-de-la-Zouch or Swadlincote. From Ashby-de-la-Zouch take Moira Rd, turn R on Blackfordby Ln. As you enter Blackfordby, turn L to Butt Ln & quickly R to Strawberry Ln. Park then it is a 2 min walk to Well Ln entrance.* **Sun 18 Feb (10-4). Adm £5, chd free.**

½ acre garden set around Blackfordby's 'hidden' listed thatched cottage, which itself is more than 300 years old. In total there are 3.4 acres of paddocks, front and rear gardens to explore with an extensive display of snowdrops (inc a named collection in rear garden) as well as Hellebores throughout. Later in spring the display changes to Snakes Heads and mature Magnolias. The lower paddock has been planted with 450 native trees as part of the National Forest Freewoods scheme, with a drainage pond created at its base. The central swathe is being developed with wildflowers. At the top of the rear garden there is a chicken run, old and new orchards and a peach house.

29 OAK TREE HOUSE

North Road, South Kilworth, LE17 6DU. Pam & Martin Shave. *15m S of Leicester. From M1 J20, take A4304 towards Market Harborough. At North Kilworth turn R, signed South Kilworth. Garden on L after approx 1m.* **Sat 29 June (11-5); Sun 30 June (11-2). Adm £5, chd free. Home-made teas.**

²⁄₃ acre beautiful country garden full of colour, formal design, softened by cottage style planting. Modern sculptures. Large herbaceous borders, vegetable plots, pond, greenhouse, shady area, colour-themed borders. Extensive collections in pots, home to everything from alpines to trees. Trees with attractive bark. Many clematis and roses. Dramatic arched pergola. Constantly changing garden. Access to patio and greenhouse via steps.

30 THE OLD BARN

Rectory Lane, Stretton-en-le-Field, Swadlincote, DE12 8AF. Gregg & Claire Mayles, 07870 160318, greggmayles@gmail.com. *On A444, 1½m from M42/A42 J11. Rectory Ln is a concealed turn off the A444, surrounded by trees. Look out for brown 'church' signs. Postcode in SatNav usually helps.* **Sat 17, Sun 18 Aug (10-4). Adm £5, chd free. Cream teas. Made by local WI. Visits also by arrangement in Aug for groups of 10+.**

2 acres in secluded hamlet, lots of interest. Lawned garden with colourful shrubs and tree-lined cobbled paths. Walled garden has fishpond, pergola with climbers and cottage garden planting. Large open views, rewilding meadow. A laid back peaceful garden to stroll around and relax. Lots of wildlife, inc our Peafowl. Plenty of drinks, cakes and seats. Redundant old church close, open to visitors. Tombola and a treasure hunt around the garden for children. Main garden fully wheelchair accessible. Walled garden partial access due to gravel. Meadow is accessible, but uneven.

31 THE OLD HALL

Main Street, Market Overton, LE15 7PL. Mr & Mrs Timothy Hart. *6m N of Oakham. 6m N of Oakham; 5m from A1via Thistleton. 10m E from Melton Mowbray.* **Evening opening Wed 3 July (5.30-8.30). Adm £10, chd free. Pre-booking essential, please visit www.ngs.org.uk for information & booking. Wine and Hambleton Bakery savouries.**

Set on a southerly ridge. Stone walls and yew hedges divide the garden into enclosed areas with herbaceous borders, shrubs, and young and mature trees. There are interesting plants flowering most of the time. In 2020 a Japanese Tea House was added at the bottom of the garden. Large plant stall. Partial wheelchair access. Gravel and mown paths. Return to house is steep. It is, however, possible to just sit on the terrace.

32 THE OLD RECTORY

Main Street, Newbold Verdon, Leicester, LE9 9NN. Gianni and Kate De Fraja. *10m W of Leicester. On the village Main St, just before the turning for the church. Bus stop 'Old White Swan' on lines 152 153 159.* **Sat 15 June (12-7); Sun 16 June (10-4). Adm £5.50, chd free. Home-made teas.**

The garden surrounds the Georgian Old Rectory. It contains many species of trees, ranging in age from centuries-old to very young saplings. This year we open when the roses are at their best, other attractions are the wisteria, the hostas, and the woods around the gravel paths. Recent additions are a greenhouse and a box parterre. The garden is accessed via a gravel drive. Wheelchair access is possible with some attention.

33 NEW ▶ THE OLD RECTORY, GOADBY MARWOOD

30 Main Street, Goadby Marwood, Melton Mowbray, LE14 4LN. **Mr & Mrs N Allen.** *6m NE of Melton Mowbray. Adjacent to the Church in the village of Goadby Marwood.* **Sun 19 May (10.30-5). Combined adm with Goadby Marwood Hall £10, chd free. Light refreshments in Goadby Marwood Village Hall. Tea, coffee, soft drinks, cakes and savouries.**
A walled garden surrounds the listed Georgian Old Rectory. The front facade is clad with wisteria which flowers in May. Of special interest are the Courtyard Garden, Cotinus Border and Coach House Walk recently designed by Bunny Guinness. Also features a parterre, wildflower meadow and woodland border with a fine, centuries old copper beech tree. Plant stall by local nursery. Wheelchair access to upper level of the garden is via a ramp.

& ✳ D ☕))

34 THE OLD VICARAGE, BURLEY

Church Road, Burley, Oakham, LE15 7SU. **Jonathan & Sandra Blaza, www.theoldvicarageburley. com.** *1m NE of Oakham. In Burley just off B668 between Oakham & Cottesmore. Church Rd is opp village green.* **Sun 26 May (11-5). Adm £6, chd free. Light refreshments.**
The Old Vicarage is a relaxed country garden, planted for year-round interest and colour. There are lawns and borders, a lime walk, rose gardens and a sunken rill garden. The walled garden produces fruit, herbs, vegetables and cut flowers. There are two orchards, an acer garden and areas planted for wildlife inc mature woodland, a meadow and a pond. Some gravel paths and steps between terraced areas.

& 🐏 ✳ 🚗 ☕))

35 THE OLD VICARAGE, WHISSENDINE

2 Station Road, Whissendine, LE15 7HG. **Prof Peter & Dr Sarah Furness, www. rutlandlordlieutenant.org/garden.** *Up hill from St Andrew's church, first L in Station Rd.* **Sun 12 May (2-5). Adm £6, chd free. Home-made teas in St Andrew's Church, Whissendine (next door).**
²/₃ acre packed with variety. Terrace with topiary, a formal fountain

courtyard and raised beds backed by gothic orangery. Herbaceous borders surround main lawn. Wisteria tunnel leads to raised vegetable beds and large ornate greenhouse, four beehives, Gothic hen house plus rare breed hens. Hidden white walk, unusual plants. New Victorian style garden room. Pebble mosaics, woodwork, doves and hens. The gravel drive is hard work for wheelchair users. Some areas are accessible only by steps.

& 🐏 ✳ ☕))

36 REDHILL LODGE

Seaton Road, Barrowden, Oakham, LE15 8EN. **Richard & Susan Moffitt, www.m360design.co.uk.** *Redhill Lodge is 1m from village of Barrowden along Seaton Rd.* **Evening opening Thur 12 Sept (5.30-8.30). Adm £6, chd free. Light refreshments and wine.**
A bold contemporary garden on varying levels. The formal structure inc landform and water in the form of a modern rill and a natural swimming pond. Planting is colourful and varied. The prairie style garden is naturalistic and vibrant especially in autumn. Natural swimming pond, turf amphitheatre, modern sculpture.

🐏 ✳ 🚗 ☕))

37 ST WOLSTAN'S HOUSE

Church Nook, Wigston Magna, LE18 3RA. **Mr Kevin De-Voy & Mr Stephen Walker.** *On corner of Church Nook & Bull Head St opp St Wistan's church. No parking or garden. Public car parks, all within 5 min walk on Frederick St, Junction Rd & Paddock St.* **Sun 21 July (11-5). Adm £5, chd free. Home-made teas. Evening opening Sat 21 Sept (6.30-9). Adm £5. Light refreshments.**
Approx ½ acre divided into garden rooms with formal and informal planting plus specimen trees. Incl. formal white garden, rose garden, sunken Italian garden, rose and wisteria pergola and laburnum arch, Edwardian conservatory, terracotta garden and well garden with raised beds. Sept opening to view garden lit up at night.

☕))

Our donation to Marie Curie this year equates to 17,496 hours of nursing care

The Old Rectory, Goadby Marwood

38 THE SECRET GARDEN AT WIGSTON FRAMEWORK KNITTERS MUSEUM

42-44 Bushloe End, Wigston, LE18 2BA. Wigston Framework Knitters Museum, www. wigstonframeworkknitters.org. uk. *4m S of Leicester. On A5199 Wigston bypass, follow yellow signs to Paddock St public car park. yellow signs onto Long St to All Saints Church turn R onto Bushloe End, Museum on R.* **Sat 8, Sun 9 June (11-5). Adm £3.50, chd free. Home-made teas.**
Victorian walled garden approx 70'x80' with traditional cottage garden planting, referred to as Higgledy Piggledy because of the random planting. Managed by a group of volunteers with much replanting during past 3 years. Garden located in the grounds of a historic museum, (an extra charge applies). A unique garden in the centre of Wigston which still retains an air of tranquillity. Cobbled area before garden, gravel paths through main parts of the garden.

&. ✿ ☕

39 THE SECRET GARDEN, GLENFIELD HOSPITAL

Groby Road, Leicester, LE3 9QP. **Karen James.** *Upon arrival to the Glenfield Hospital, please follow the blue directional signage.* **Sat 22 June, Sun 20 July (10-3). Adm £3.50, chd free. Light refreshments at The Secret Garden Cafe.**
Set within the grounds of the Glenfield Hospital, the Secret Garden is 1 acre in size, hidden behind the walls of a Victorian Walled garden which has been lovingly designed and restored for the benefit of all those who visit it and in consideration of the rich history and heritage of the garden and the wider Leicester Frith site. All main pathways are wheelchair accessible.

&. 🐃 ✿ 🚗 ☕))

40 STOKE ALBANY HOUSE

Desborough Road, Stoke Albany, Market Harborough, LE16 8PT. Mr & Mrs A M Vinton, 01858 535227, del.jones7@googlemail.com, www.stokealbanyhouse.co.uk. *4m E of Market Harborough. Via A427 to Corby, turn to Stoke Albany, R at the White Horse (B669) garden ½m on the L.* **Every Wed 5 June to 31 July (2-4.30). Adm £6, chd free. Visits also by arrangement 5 June to 31 July. Wednesday afternoons only.**

Donation to Marie Curie Cancer Care.
4 acre country house garden; fine trees and shrubs with wide herbaceous borders and sweeping striped lawn. Good display of bulbs in spring, roses June and July. Walled grey garden; nepeta walk arched with roses, parterre with box and roses. Mediterranean garden. Heated greenhouse, potager with topiary, water feature garden and sculptures.

&. 🐃 ✿ 🚗 🎡

41 59 THISTLETON ROAD

Market Overton, Oakham, LE15 7PP. **Wg Cdr Andrew Stewart JP.** *Market overton. 6m NE of Oakham.* **Sun 16 June (12-5). Adm £5, chd free. Home-made teas at local bowls club.**
Over the last 15 yrs, the owners have transformed 1.8 acres of bare meadow into a wildlife friendly garden full of colour and variety. Against a backdrop of mature trees, the garden inc a small kitchen garden, rose pergola, large pond, shrubbery with 'Onion Day Bed', orchard, wildflower meadow, a small arboretum, a woodland walk and large perennial borders a riot of colour. Small area of shingle to access main path, woodland walk inaccessible to wheelchairs.

&. ✿ ☕

42 TRESILLIAN HOUSE

67 Dalby Road, Melton Mowbray, LE13 0BQ. Mrs Alison Blythe, 01664 481997, alisonblythe@tresillianhouse. com, www.tresillianhouse.com. *½m S of Melton Mowbray centre. Situated on B6047 Dalby Rd, S of Melton town centre. (Melton to Gt Dalby/Market Harborough rd). Parking on site.* **Sun 3 Mar, Sun 28 Apr, Sun 30 June, Sun 25 Aug, Sun 27 Oct (11-4). Adm £5.50, chd free. Light refreshments inc cream teas, ploughmans' lunches, soup in winter, stew & dumplings in October. Visits also by arrangement 19 Feb to 25 Oct for groups of up to 40. Coach parking near by.On site parking for 14 cars/small mini bus.**
¾ acre garden re-established by current owner. Beautiful blue cedar trees, specimen tulip tree. Variety of trees, plants and bushes reinstated. Original bog garden and natural pond. Koi pond; glass garden room holds exhibitions and recitals. Vegetable plot. Cowslips and bulbs

in springtime. Wide variety of unusual plants, trees and shrubs. Quiet and tranquil oasis. Small Art Exhibition by local artists. The natural pond has been replanted by pond specialists, Wild Water Ponds. Replanted the natural pond at Tresillian House. Relax in June and August with cream tea listening to live traditional jazz. Keep warm in October with stew and dumplings or soup. Slate paths, steep in places but manageable.

&. 🐃 ✿ 🚗 🚌 ☕ 🎡))

43 WESTBROOKE HOUSE

52 Scotland Road, Little Bowden, Market Harborough, LE16 8AX. **Bryan & Joanne Drew.** *½m S Market Harborough. From Northampton Rd follow NGS arrows & park in public car park or on nearby roads - not on the road directly opp the entrance. No parking at property.* **Sun 28 Apr, Sun 26 May, Sun 23 June (10-4.30). Adm £5, chd free. Cream teas.**
Westbrooke House is a late Victorian property built in 1887. The gardens comprise 6 acres in total and are approached through a tree lined driveway of mature limes and giant redwoods. Key features are walled flower garden, walled kitchen garden, fernery, lower garden, wildlife pond, spring garden, lawns, woodland paths and a meadow with a wildflower area, ha-ha and hornbeam avenue.

🐃 ✿ 🅳 ☕))

44 WESTVIEW

1 St Thomas's Road, Great Glen, Leicester, LE8 9EH. **Gill & John Hadland,** 01162 592170, gillhadland1@gmail.com. *7m S of Leicester. Take either r'about from A6 into village centre then follow NGS signs. Please park in Oaks Rd.* **Sat 24, Sun 25 Feb (11-4). Light refreshments. Open nearby Hedgehog Hall. Sat 25, Mon 27 May, Sat 14, Sun 15 Sept (11-4). Home-made teas. Adm £3.50, chd free. Home-made soup & rolls served at the Feb openings. Visits also by arrangement Feb to Sept for groups of up to 20.**
Organically managed small walled cottage garden with year-round interest. Rare and unusual plants, many grown from seed. Formal box parterre, courtyard garden, alpines, herbaceous borders, woodland areas with unusual ferns, small wildlife pond, greenhouse, vegetables, fruit and herbs. Collection of Snowdrops. Recycled materials used to make

quirky garden ornaments and water feature. Restored Victorian outhouse functions as a garden office and houses a collection of old garden tools and ephemera. This garden is proud to provide plants for the National Garden Scheme's Show Garden at Chelsea Flower Show 2024.

45 THE WHITE HOUSE FARM

Billesdon Road, Ingarsby, Leicester, LE7 9JD. Pam & Richard Smith, 01162 595448, Pamsmithtwhf@gmail.com. *7m E of Leicester. From A47 bet Billesdon and Houghton on the Hill, take the turn signed to Quenby Hall. After 1m, take 1st L, signed to Ingarsby; garden is 1m further on.* **Visits by arrangement 1 June to 15 Sept for groups of 20 to 40. Adm £6, chd free. Home-made teas.** Former Georgian farm in 2 acres of country garden. Beautiful views. Box, yew and beech hedges divide a cottage garden of gaily coloured perennials and roses; a formal herb garden; a pergola draped with climbing plants; an old courtyard with roses, shrubs and trees. Herbaceous borders lead to pools with water lilies and informal cascade. Orchard, wild garden and lake. Home for lots of wildlife. Most of the formal parts of the garden can be accessed without steps.

GROUP OPENING

46 WIGSTON GARDENS

Wigston, LE18 3LF. Zoe Lewin. *Just S of Leicester off A5199.* **Sat 13, Sun 14 July (11-5). Combined adm £6, chd free. Home-made teas at Little Dale Wildlife Garden and 28 Gladstone Street.**

28 GLADSTONE STREET
Chris & Janet Huscroft.
(See separate entry)

2A HOMESTEAD DRIVE
Mrs Sheila Bolton.

LITTLE DALE WILDLIFE GARDEN
Zoe Lewin & Neil Garner,
www.facebook.com/
zoesopengarden.

'VALLENVINA' 6 ABINGTON CLOSE
Mr Steve Hunt.

Wigston Gardens consists of four relatively small gardens all within a 2m radius of each other. There is something different to see at each garden from traditional and formal to a taste of the unusual via wildflowers, upcycling, interesting artefacts and prairie style planting. A couple of the gardens are within walking distance of one another but you will need to travel by car to visit all of the gardens in the group or it will make for quite a long walk and you'll need your comfy shoes.

GROUP OPENING

47 WILLOUGHBY GARDENS

Willoughby Waterleys, LE8 6UD. *9m S of Leicester. From A426 heading N turn R at Dunton Bassett lights. Follow signs to Willoughby. From Blaby follow signs to Countesthorpe. 2m S to Willoughby.* **Sun 14 July (11-5). Combined adm £6, chd free. Light refreshments in the Village Hall.**

2 CHURCH FARM LANE
Valerie & Peter Connelly.

FARMWAY
Eileen Spencer, 07795 058582, eileenfarmway9@msn.com.
Visits also by arrangement 23 June to 25 Aug for groups of up to 25.

HIGH MEADOW
Phil & Eva Day.

JOHN'S WOOD
John & Jill Harris.

KAPALUA
Richard & Linda Love.

3 ORCHARD ROAD
Diane Brearley.

3 YEW TREE CLOSE
Emma Clanfield.

Willoughby Waterleys lies in the South Leicestershire countryside. 7 gardens will be open. John's Wood is a 1½ acre nature reserve planted to encourage wildlife. 2 Church Farm Lane has been professionally designed with many interesting features. Farmway is a plant lovers garden with many unusual plants in colour themed borders. 3, Orchard Road is a small south facing garden packed with interesting features. High Meadow has been evolving over 14yrs. Inc mixed planting and ornamental vegetable garden.

Kapalua has an interesting planting design incorporating views of open countryside. 3 Yew Tree Close is a wrap around garden that naturally creates a series of rooms with cottage garden style borders.

GROUP OPENING

48 WING GARDENS

Wing, Oakham, LE15 8SA. *2m S of Rutland Water. Off A6003 between Oakham & Uppingham.* **Sun 23 June (2-6). Combined adm £6, chd free. Home-made teas in Wing Village Hall.**

NEW SOL HOUSE
Mr & Mrs John Dejardin.

TOWNSEND HOUSE
David & Jeffy Wood.

Two very different gardens in pretty stone village of Wing with medieval church and turf maze. Townsend House, located opp Village Hall, is a cottage garden, full of roses and herbaceous borders. Sol House, further along Top St (follow signs) is a contemporary garden surrounding a PassivHaus with a serpentine yew hedge, trees, mixed borders, a woodland and meadow.

49 15 THE WOODCROFT

Diseworth, Derby, DE74 2QT. Nick & Sue Hollick. *The Woodcroft is off The Green, parking on The Woodcroft.* **Sun 23 June (11-4). Adm £4, chd free. Home-made teas.**
⅓ acre garden developed over 44 yrs with mature choice trees and shrubs, old and modern shrub roses, fern garden, wildlife garden, alpine troughs and mixed herbaceous borders, planted with a garden designer's eye and a plantsman's passion. Comfortable gazebo overlooking recently planted wildlife pond. New for 2024; the large border at the bottom of the garden has been refreshed. Three steps from the upper terrace to the main garden.

LINCOLNSHIRE

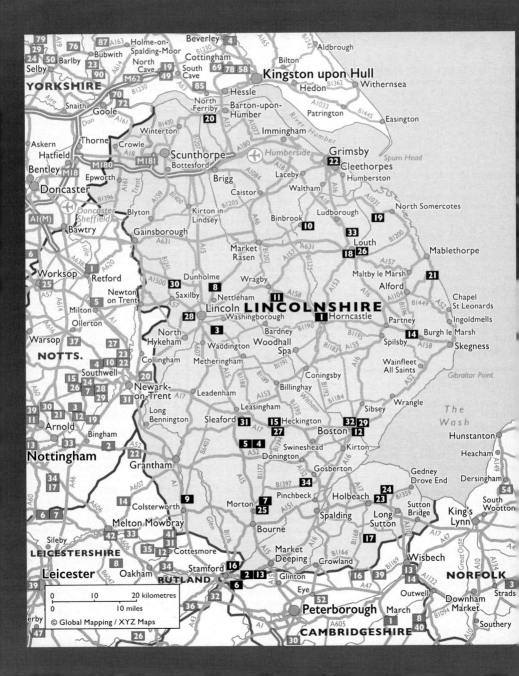

VOLUNTEERS

County Organisers
Lesley Wykes
01673 860356
lesley.wykes@ngs.org.uk

County Treasurer
Kate Richardson
07496 550516
kate.richardson@ngs.org.uk

Social Media
Diane Puncheon
01427 800008
dianepuncheon@yahoo.com

Publicity
Margaret Mann
01476 585905
marg_mann2000@yahoo.com

Tricia Elliott 01427 788517
t.elliott575@gmail.com

Assistant County Organisers
Karen Bourne 07860 504047
karen@karenwrightpr.com

Sally Grant 01205 750486
sallygrant50@btinternet.com

Sylvia Ravenhall 01507 526014
sylvan@btinternet.com

Robert Bailey- Scott 07860 833905
rbaileyscott@aol.com

Talks Co-ordinator
Neil Timm
01472 398092
neilfernnursery@gmail.com

f @LincolnshireNGS
✖ @LincsNGS

OPENING DATES

All entries subject to change.
For latest information check
www.ngs.org.uk
Map locator numbers are
shown to the right of each
garden name.
Extended openings are shown
at the beginning of each month.

February

Snowdrop Opening
Sunday 18th
Woodlands   33

March

Friday 29th
◆ Easton Walled Gardens   9
Saturday 30th
Oasis Garden - Your Place   22
Sunday 31st
Woodlands   33

April

Saturday 6th
◆ Burghley House Private South
Gardens   6
Sunday 7th
◆ Burghley House Private South
Gardens   6
Sunday 14th
Ashfield House   3

May

Sunday 5th
Dunholme Lodge   8
66 Spilsby Road   29
Woodlands   33
Saturday 11th
23 Accommodation Road   1
Oasis Garden - Your Place   22
Sunday 12th
23 Accommodation Road   1
Fydell House   12
Saturday 18th
Willoughby Road Allotments   32

Saturday 25th
NEW Greatford Mill   13
Sunday 26th
Aswarby House   4
Aswarby Park   5
The Fern Nursery and Bowling
Club   10

June

Every Sunday
NEW Ashcroft House   2
Saturday 1st
23 Accommodation Road   1
Sunday 2nd
23 Accommodation Road   1
NEW Firs Farm   11
Manor Farm   20
Sunday 9th
NEW 23 Linden Walk   18
West Syke   31
Tuesday 11th
NEW 23 Linden Walk   18
Sunday 16th
Shangrila   27
Woodlands   33
Sunday 23rd
The Old Vicarage   23
Old White House   24
Saturday 29th
Home Farm   16
Sunday 30th
Dunholme Lodge   8
Home Farm   16
Ludney House Farm   19
NEW Walnut Lodge   30

July

Every Sunday
NEW Ashcroft House   2
Saturday 13th
21 Chapel Street   7
Sunday 14th
21 Chapel Street   7
Saturday 27th
◆ Gunby Hall and Gardens   14
Sunday 28th
Yew Tree Farm   34

August

Every Thursday and Sunday
The Secret Garden of Louth   26

Sunday 4th
The Fern Nursery and Bowling
   Club   10
Fydell House   12

Sunday 11th
Woodlands   33

Saturday 31st
Willoughby Road Allotments   32

September

Sunday 1st
Skellingthorpe Hall   28

Saturday 14th
21 Chapel Street   7

Sunday 15th
21 Chapel Street   7
Woodlands   33

Saturday 21st
Inley Drove Farm   17

Sunday 22nd
NEW Firs Farm   11
Inley Drove Farm   17

By Arrangement

Arrange a personalised garden visit
with your club, or group of friends,
on a date to suit you. See individual
garden entries for full details.

23 Accommodation Road   1
Ashfield House   3
Fydell House   12
23 Handley Street   15
Home Farm   16
Inley Drove Farm   17
Ludney House Farm   19
Marigold Cottage   21
The Old Vicarage   23
The Plant Lover's Garden   25
The Secret Garden of Louth   26
Woodlands   33

The National Garden Scheme donated £3,403,960 to our nursing and health beneficiaries from money raised at gardens open in 2023

Aswarby House

THE GARDENS

1 23 ACCOMMODATION ROAD
Horncastle, LN9 5AS. Mr & Mrs
D Chapman, 01507 527797,
davechapman1953@outlook.com.
*Horncastle. From turning off Lincoln
Rd A158 onto Accommodation Rd
we are situated approx 600yds on R.*
**Sat 11, Sun 12 May, Sat 1, Sun 2
June (11-4). Adm £3.50, chd free.
Visits also by arrangement 4 May
to 1 June for groups of 6 to 20.**
We have a medium sized garden
which mixes flowers with fruit, places
to sit and admire the fish pond and
flowers. We have a range of iris,
perennials, auriculas and alpines.
Plenty to see and enjoy. Come and
sit and watch the fish, take your time
to look at the flowers and talk to the
owners, there's also garden plaques
and plants to purchase always a lot
of iris we have over 60 different plants
dwarf to tall it all makes a enjoyable
experience. Partial wheelchair access
to decking area.
&. 🐕 ✻

2 NEW ASHCROFT HOUSE
5 Red House Paddock, Tallington,
Stamford, PE9 4RG. Vivienne
Swift. *4 m E of Stamford on A1175.
Ashcroft House is in a private road
(foot access only) just off of the Main
Rd (A1175) opp West Rd. Parking
ltd to nearby side roads (West Rd,
Mill Ln, Bainton Rd) or as signed
within village.* **Every Sun 2 June to
28 July (11-4). Adm £4, chd free.
Light refreshments.**
A beautiful compact garden with
interest all year-round. Mature trees,
shrubs and screening separates the
wrap around plot into 'rooms' creating
a lush sense of seclusion. Informal
beds overflow with shrubs, perennials,
climbers, cottage garden traditionals,
bulbs and tropical specimens all
nestling alongside each other. There
are also multiple seating areas, a green
wall and several water features.
☕ ••)

3 ASHFIELD HOUSE
Lincoln Road, Branston,
Lincoln, LN4 1NS. John &
Judi Tinsley, 07977 505682,
john@tinsleyfarms.co.uk. *3m S
of Lincoln on B1188. N outskirts of
Branston on the B1188 Lincoln Rd.
Signed 'Tinsley Farms - Ashfield'. Nr
bus stop, follow signs down drive.*
**Sun 14 Apr (11-4). Adm £5, chd
free. Light refreshments. Visits
also by arrangement Apr to Oct for
groups of 20 to 30.**
See 140 flowering cherries and 30
magnolias. Many thousands of spring
bulbs, sweeping lawns and lake.
Beautiful naturally landscaped garden
with some superb mature trees as
well as a fascinating arboretum. One
of the best flowering cherry displays
in the area. Fairly level garden.
Wheelchair access via grass paths.
&. 🐕 ✻ ☕

4 ASWARBY HOUSE
Aswarby, Sleaford, NG34 8SE.
Penny & James Herdman. *Past
church on R of road. 300 yds from
the gates of Aswarby Park. Plenty of
parking available on the roadside &
gravel paths around the garden.* **Sun
26 May (2-5). Combined adm with
Aswarby Park £8, chd free. Home-
made teas in Aswarby Park.**
New garden of an acre planted
five years ago in the grounds
of a handsome C18 house and
coachhouse. It has a partial walled
garden, wildflower meadow
surrounded by ornamental grasses
and a 30 metre long herbaceous
border. With two box parterres, and
woodland shrubs, it has stunning
views over ancient ridge and furrow
grassland. This garden would
complement your visit to Aswarby
Park.
&. ✻ ☕ ••)

5 ASWARBY PARK
Aswarby, Sleaford, NG34 8SD.
Mr & Mrs George Playne,
www.aswarbyestate.co.uk. *5m S
of Sleaford on A15. Take signs to
Aswarby. Entrance is straight ahead
by church through black gates.* **Sun
26 May (2-5). Combined adm
with Aswarby House £8, chd free.
Home-made teas at Aswarby Park.
Home-made cakes available.**
Formal and woodland garden in a
parkland setting of approx 20 acres.
Yew trees form a backdrop to borders
and lawns surrounding the house
which is a converted stable block.
Walled garden contains a greenhouse
with a muscat vine, which is over 300
years old. Large display of daffodils,
snowdrops and climbing roses in
season. New cutting garden created
in 2022 and a wildflower border
created for 2024. Partial wheelchair
access on gravel paths and drives.
&. ✻ ☕ ••)

6 ◆ BURGHLEY HOUSE PRIVATE SOUTH GARDENS
Stamford, PE9 3JY. Burghley
House Preservation Trust,
01780 752451,
burghley@burghley.co.uk,
www.burghley.co.uk. *1m E of
Stamford. From Stamford follow
signs to Burghley via B1443.* **For
NGS: Sat 6, Sun 7 Apr (10-4.30).
Adm £10, chd £8.50. Pre-booking
essential, please visit www.
ngs.org.uk for information &
booking. Cream teas in The
Orangery Restaurant, Garden
Café and Muddy Mole. For other
opening times and information,
please phone, email or visit garden
website.**
The Private South Gardens at
Burghley House will open for the
NGS with spectacular spring bulbs
in a park like setting with magnificent
trees. Relish the opportunity to enjoy
Capability Brown's famous lake and
summerhouse. Entry via Garden
Kiosks. Fine Food Market and TVR
Car Rally. Admission charge is a
special pre-book price only via NGS
website. Visitors paying at the gate
on the day will be charged a Gardens
ticket price. Wheelchair access via
gravel paths.
&. ✻ 🚌 ☕ 🧺 ••)

7 21 CHAPEL STREET
Haconby, Bourne, PE10 0UL. Joan
Curtis, Sharron White and Paul
Cutler. *3m N of Bourne. A15, turn
E at Xrds into Hacconby, L at village
green.* **Sat 13, Sun 14 July, Sat 14,
Sun 15 Sept (11-4). Adm £6, chd
free. Home-made teas.**
The beautiful cottage garden created
by Cliff and Joan is being lovingly
maintained by the next generation.
The cottage garden overflows with a
wide range of hardy and tender plants
within borders and pot displays. The
extended garden inc a grass area
surrounded by woodland bed and
meadow areas. The newest feature
is a gravel garden incorporating wide
range of drought resistant plants.
✻ ☕

*Our donation in 2023 has
enabled Parkinson's UK to fund
3 new nursing posts this year,
directly supporting people
with Parkinson's*

Greatford Mill

8 DUNHOLME LODGE
Dunholme, Lincoln, LN2 3QA.
Hugh & Lesley Wykes. *4m NE
of Lincoln. Turn off A46 towards
Welton at the r'about. After ½ m
turn L up long private road. Garden
at top.* Sun 5 May, Sun 30 June
(11-5). Adm £5, chd free. Light
refreshments.
A five acre garden with mature trees,
spring bulbs and ferns, shrubs,
roses, natural pond, wildflower walk,
orchard and vegetable garden. Young
arboretum. RAF Dunholme Lodge
Museum and War Memorial within
the grounds. Craft stalls. Ukulele
Band. Vintage vehicles. Most areas
wheelchair accessible but some loose
stone and gravel.
♿ 🐕 ✿ 🚌 ☕))

9 ◆ EASTON WALLED GARDENS
Easton, NG33 5AP. Sir Fred &
Lady Cholmeley, 01476 530063,
info@eastonwalledgardens.co.uk,
www.visiteaston.co.uk. *7m S of
Grantham. 1m from A1, off B6403.*
For NGS: Fri 29 Mar (11-4). Adm
£9.50, chd £5. Light refreshments.
For other opening times and
information, please phone, email or
visit garden website.
A 400 year old, restored, 12 acre
garden set in the heart of Lincolnshire.
Home to snowdrops, sweet peas,
roses and meadows. The River
Witham meanders through the
gardens, teeming with wildlife. Other
garden highlights inc a yew tunnel,
turf maze and cut flower gardens.
The Courtyard offers shopping,
plant sales, a coffee room offering
a selection of teas and coffees and
beauty salon. Applestore Tearoom
and Coffee Room offers hot and cold
drinks, savoury snacks, homemade
cakes. Public Garden Finalist, The
English Garden Magazine's The
Nation's Favourite Gardens, 2023
Regret no wheelchair access to
lower gardens but tearoom, shop,
upper gardens and facilities are all
accessible.
♿ ✿ 🚌 🛏 ☕))

10 THE FERN NURSERY AND BOWLING CLUB
Grimsby Road, Binbrook, Market
Rasen, LN8 6DH. Neil Timm,
www.fernnursery.co.uk. *On B1203
from Market Rasen. On the Grimsby
rd from Binbrook Square, 400m.* Sun
26 May, Sun 4 Aug (11-4). Adm
£4, chd free. Light refreshments
in the bowling pavilion. Tea,
coffee and cake are provided by
Binbrook Bowling Club.
The garden has been designed as
a wildlife garden with a number of
features of interest to both visitors
and wildlife, helped by having a
natural stream running through the
garden, which supplies water to a
pond and water features. Visitors can
also enjoy rock features, acid beds,
and a sheltered winter garden with
a sundial at its centre. From which
a path leads to a small wood with
the main fern collection. In addition
there is a semi formal herb garden
and bowling green, where they will
often see a game being played, large
shrubs, a bank of drought tolerant
plants and herbaceous perennials,
while steps, seats, a gazebo, bridge
and many other features. Partial
wheelchairs access, gravel paths.
♿ 🐕 ✿ ☕ 🍴

11 NEW FIRS FARM
Hoop Lane, Langton-by-Wragby,
Market Rasen, LN8 5QB. Jean and
Malcolm Clarke. *2m SE of Wragby.
Approx 2m from Wragby on A158,
turn R on sharp bend into Hoop Ln.
Continue for approx 1m. Turn R at
yellow signs into car park.* Sun 2
June, Sun 22 Sept (10-4). Adm £5,
chd free. Home-made teas.
Discover this medium sized garden
with herbaceous borders featuring
dahlias. There is a pond, large
vegetable patch and a wooded area
with beautiful woodland walks. The
perimeter walk is 1m and suitable

for well behaved dogs on leads. Chambers Farm Wood is approx ½ m away. Its one of Lincolnshire's ancient limewoods, important for wildlife. Much of Hoop Lane is a roadside nature reserve.

 ♿ 🐕 ✿ ☕

🄲 FYDELL HOUSE

South Square, Boston, PE21 6HU. Boston Preservation Trust, 01205 351520, info@fydellhouse.org.uk. *Central Boston down South St. Through the Market Sq, past Boots. One way street by Guildhall. There are 3 car parks within 200 yds of the house. Disabled parking in council car park opp the house.* **Sun 12 May, Sun 4 Aug (10-4). Adm £4, chd free. Light refreshments. Home-made light bites on offer made by our volunteers. Visits also by arrangement.**

Within three original red brick walls a formal garden was been created in 1995. Yew buttresses, arbours and four parterres use Dutch themes. The borders contain herbaceous plants and shrubs. The north facing border holds shade loving plants. There is a mulberry and walnut tree. The astrolabe was installed in 1997. A Victorian rockery is built from slag from ironworks in Boston. Walled garden Astrolabe Parterres formal borders topiary of box and yew. Wheelchair access is the south alleyway from the front to the back garden.

 ♿ ✿ ☕))

🄳 NEW GREATFORD MILL

Greatford, PE9 4QA. Mr & Mrs D Lygo, www.instagram.com/ greatfordmillgarden/. *4m E of Stamford. At T-junc in village nr Hare & Hounds pub, take route to Carlby & Braceborough. Garden is opp village hall playing field.* **Sat 25 May (11-4). Adm £5, chd free. Home-made teas.**

One acre village garden overlooking St Thomas' church over the mill pond. Situated on the River Glen, restored water wheel and open, unfenced mill pond. Traditional English country style borders with special interest which inc various garden areas: wildflower, prairie, dry, shady, cutting, vegetable and bonsai. Wheelchair access via gravel paths. Extra care needed with steep banks each side of the water. WC facilities in the village hall.

 ♿ ✿ ☕))

🄴 ◆ GUNBY HALL AND GARDENS

Spilsby, PE23 5SS. National Trust, 01754 890102, gunbyhall@nationaltrust.org.uk, www.nationaltrust.org.uk/gunby-hall. *2½ m NW of Burgh-le-Marsh. 7m W of Skegness. On A158. Signed off Gunby r'about.* **For NGS: Sat 27 July (10-4). Adm £9.50, chd £4.75. Cream teas in the Gunby tea-room. For other opening times and information, please phone, email or visit garden website.**

Eight acres of formal and walled gardens. Old roses, herbaceous borders, herb garden and kitchen garden with fruit trees and vegetables. Greenhouses, carp pond and sweeping lawns. Tennyson's Haunt of Ancient Peace. House built by Sir William Massingberd in 1700. Enjoy a sweet treat from the tea-room, or visit one of the many craft and trade stalls which will spread out across the courtyard. Wheelchair access in gardens and with Gunby's dedicated wheelchair on ground floor of house. There are steps into the house.

 ♿ 🐕 ✿ 🛏 ☕ 🪑))

🄵 23 HANDLEY STREET

Heckington, nr Sleaford, NG34 9RZ. Stephen & Hazel Donnison, 01529 460097, donno5260@gmail.com. *A17 from Sleaford, turn R into Heckington. Follow rd to the Green. L, follow rd past Church, R into Cameron St. At end of this rd L into Handley St.* **Visits by arrangement 23 May to 24 Aug for groups of 8 to 30. Adm £3.50, chd free. Home-made teas.** Compact, quirky garden, large fish pond. Further five small wildlife ponds. Small wooded area and Jurassic style garden with tree ferns. Densely planted flower borders featuring penstemons. Large patio with seating.

 ✿ ☕

🄶 HOME FARM

Little Casterton Road, Ryhall, Stamford, PE9 4HA. Steve & Karen Bourne, 07860 504047, karen@karenwrightpr.com. *1½ m N of Stamford. Just off the A6121 Stamford to Bourne rd. 1½ m N of Stamford. At mini-r'about turn towards Little Casterton & Tolethorpe Hall. Car park 50 yards on the L.* **Sat 29, Sun 30 June (2-5). Adm £5, chd free. Home-made teas. Visits also by arrangement in June for groups of 10 to 40.**

More than 100 roses, inc many old English fragrant varieties, lavender avenues and herbaceous borders with delphiniums, fill the formal part of this nine acre garden. A wildflower meadow, now two years old, and the woodland walk encourage wildlife. The south east facing terrace overlooks the garden giving far-reaching views and provides the perfect place to enjoy a cup of tea. Most areas accessible by wheelchair.

 ♿ 🐕 ☕))

🄷 INLEY DROVE FARM

Inley Drove, Sutton St James, Spalding, PE12 0LX. Francis & Maisie Pryor, 01406 540088, maisietaylor7@gmail.com, www. pryorfrancis.wordpress.com/. *5m S of Holbeach. Just off road from Sutton St James to Sutton St Edmund. 2m S of Sutton St James. Look for yellow NGS signs on double bend.* **Sat 21, Sun 22 Sept (11-5). Adm £6, chd free. Home-made teas. Visits also by arrangement June & July for groups of 10 to 30.**

Garden developed over 27years for colour, scent and wildlife (inc butterflies, moths and dragonflies). Three acres of predominantly flower gardens with formal and informal areas, all framed by hornbeam hedges. Wide variety of traditional and unusual plants, shrubs and trees (inc Black Poplars), meadow, vegetable garden and orchard. Walks through seven acre wood. Wheelchair access, some gravel and a few steps but mostly flat, firm turf. Steps to wc.

 ♿ ✿ ☕ 🛏 🪑

In 2023, National Garden Scheme funding for Perennial supported a helpline service which provided advice, information and frontline support to around 800 people working in horticulture

The Secret Garden of Louth

18 NEW **23 LINDEN WALK**
Louth, LN11 9HT. Darren & Jane
Cunningham. *½m S from Louth
town centre. Free car park at Louth
Cattle Market LN11 9HF. Entrance
is on Linden Walk between Boars
Head Pub and Pedestrian crossing
close to petrol stn. Garden is a 3 min
walk S on Linden Walk.* **Sun 9 June
(1.30-4); Tue 11 June (11-2.30).
Adm £4, chd free. Home-made
teas. Gluten free option available.**
This garden was created six years
ago from bare earth by the current
owners, retaining just a few of the
original specimen trees. The front
garden is laid out in formal Victorian
style. The enclosed rear garden is on
two levels with lawn areas and and a
water feature bordered by Victorian
brick walls and herbaceous perennial
borders. There are seating areas
throughout to enjoy your tea and
cakes.

19 LUDNEY HOUSE FARM
Ludney, Louth, LN11 7JU.
Jayne Bullas, 07733 018710,
jayne@theoldgatehouse.com.
Between Grainthorpe & Conisholme.
**Sun 30 June (1-4). Adm £7, chd
free. Home-made teas. Cakes inc
in adm. Visits also by arrangement
12 May to 4 Aug for groups of 10
to 30.**
A beautiful large garden lovingly
developed over the last 20 years
with several areas of formal and
informal planting inc a pond which
attracts a wonderful variety of wildlife.
There is an excellent mix of trees,
shrubs, perennials, rose garden and
wildflower area. There are plenty of
seats positioned around to sit and
enjoy a cuppa and piece of cake.
Wheelchair access to most of garden.

20 MANOR FARM
Horkstow Road, South Ferriby,
Barton-upon-Humber, DN18 6HS.
Geoff & Angela Wells. *3m W of
Barton-upon-Humber. On A1077
turn L onto B1204, opp Village Hall.*
**Sun 2 June (11-4.30). Adm £6, chd
free. Home-made teas.**
A formal garden with many seating
areas which is much praised by
visitors. Set within approx two acres
with mature shrubberies, herbaceous
borders, gravel garden and pergola
walk. Roses and white garden
and fernery. Many old trees with
preservation orders. Wildlife pond set

within a paddock. Also on the day
there will be a classic car display and
various stalls.

21 MARIGOLD COTTAGE
Hotchin Road, Sutton-on-Sea,
LN12 2NP. Stephanie Lee &
John Raby, 01507 442151,
marigoldlee@btinternet.com,
www.rabylee.uk/marigold/. *16m N
of Skegness on A52. 7m E of Alford
on A1111. 3m S of Mablethorpe
on A52. Turn off A52 on High St at
Cornerhouse Cafe. Follow road past
playing field on R. Road turns away
from the dunes. House 2nd on L.*
**Visits by arrangement 1 May to
1 Sept for groups of 10 to 30.
Group visits adm (£7) inc home-
made teas. Adm for non-groups
is by donation.**
Slide open the Japanese gate to
find secret paths, lanterns, a circular
window in a curved wall, water
lilies in pots and a gravel garden,
vegetable garden and propagation
area. Take the long drive to see the
sea. Back in the garden, find a seat,
enjoy the birds and bees. We face
the challenges of heavy clay and salt
ladened winds but look for unusual
plants not the humdrum for these
conditions. Most of garden accessible
to wheelchairs along flat, paved
paths.

**22 OASIS GARDEN - YOUR
PLACE**
Rear of Your Place, 236 Wellington
Street, Grimsby, DN32 7JP.
Grimsby Neighbourhood Church,
www.yourplacegrimsby.com. *Enter
Grimsby (M180) over flyover, along
Cleethorpes Rd. Turn R into Victor
St, Turn L into Wellington St. Your
Place is on R on junc of Wellington
St & Weelsby St.* **Sat 30 Mar, Sat 11
May (11-3). Adm £3, chd free.**
The multi-award winning Oasis
Garden, Your Place, has been
described as one of the 'Most
inspirational garden in the six
counties of the East Midlands', is
approximately 1½ acres and nestles
in the heart of Great Grimsby's East
Marsh Community. A working garden
producing 15k plants per year, grown
by local volunteers of all ages and
abilities. Lawns, fruit, vegetable,
perennial and annual beds.

23 THE OLD VICARAGE
Low Road, Holbeach Hurn,
PE12 8JN. Mrs Liz Dixon-
Spain, 01406 424148,
lizdixonspain@gmail.com. *2m
NE of Holbeach. Turn off A17 N
to Holbeach Hurn, past post box
in middle of village, 1st R at war
memorial into Low Rd. Old Vicarage
is on R approx 400yds Parking in
grass paddock.* **Sun 23 June (1-5).
Combined adm with Old White
House £7.50, chd free. Home-
made teas at Old White House.
Visits also by arrangement 1 Mar
to 1 Oct for groups of 5 to 30.**
A two acre garden with 150 year old
tulip, plane and beech trees: borders
of shrubs, roses, herbaceous plants.
Shrub roses and herb garden in old
paddock area, surrounded by informal
areas with pond and bog garden,
wildflowers, grasses and bulbs.
Small fruit and vegetable gardens.
Flower and grass meadow. Kids love
exploring winding paths through the
wilder areas. Garden is managed
environmentally. Wheelchair access
via gravel drive. Some hard paths but
mostly grass.

24 OLD WHITE HOUSE
Baileys Lane, Holbeach Hurn,
PE12 8JP. Mrs A Worth. *2m N
of Holbeach. Turn off A17 N to
Holbeach Hurn, follow signs to
village, cont through, turn R after
Rose & Crown pub at Baileys Ln.*
**Sun 23 June (1-5). Combined adm
with The Old Vicarage £7.50, chd
free. Home-made teas.**
A mature garden of 1½ acres
featuring herbaceous borders, roses,
patterned garden, herb garden and
walled kitchen garden. Large Catalpa,
tulip tree that flowers, ginko and other
specimen trees. Wheelchair access to
all areas without using steps.

The National Garden
Scheme searches the
length and breadth of
England, Wales, Northern
Ireland and the Channel
Islands for the very best
private gardens.

25 THE PLANT LOVER'S GARDEN

Bourne, PE10 0XF. Danny & Sophie, 07850 239393, plantloversgarden@outlook.com. *2m N of Bourne off the A15. Situated on the edge of S Lincolnshire, bordering Cambridgeshire & Rutland d.* **Visits by arrangement 4 Mar to 2 Sept for groups of up to 35. Garden tour or talk inc. Discuss refreshments when booking. Adm £4.50, chd free.**

Make an arrangement to visit the Plant Lovers Garden for a friendly welcome and informative visit. Be inspired by a garden packed with plants showcasing colour, form, texture, various planting combinations and conditions. Elements of garden design and structures throughout. With a guided tour inc to tell the stories behind the design and planting. Large variety of plants for sale. Most areas accessible by wheelchair.

&. ✿ ☕))

26 THE SECRET GARDEN OF LOUTH

68 Watts Lane, Louth, LN11 9DG. Jenny & Rodger Grasham *½m S of Louth town centre. For SatNav & to avoid gate on Watts Ln, use postcode LN119DJ- Mount Pleasant Ave, leads straight to our house.* **Every Thur and Sun 1 Aug to 29 Aug (11-4). Adm £4, chd free. Pre-booking essential, please phone 07977 318145, email sallysing@hotmail. co.uk or visit www.facebook. com/thesecretgardenoflouth for information & booking. Home-made teas. Visits also by arrangement in Aug.**

Blank canvas of ⅕ acre in early 90s. Developed into lush, colourful, exotic plant packed haven. A whole new world on entering from street. Exotic borders, raised exotic island, long hot border, ponds, stumpery. Intimate seating areas along garden's journey. Can children find where the frogs are hiding? Butterflies and bees but how many different types? Feed the fish, find Cedric the spider, Simon the snake, Colin the Crocodile and more. Main areas wheelchair accessible with care. Narrow paths.

&. ✿ ☕

27 SHANGRILA

Little Hale Road, Great Hale, Sleaford, NG34 9LH. Marilyn Cooke & John Knight. *On B1394 between Heckington & Helpringham.* **Sun 16 June (11-5). Adm £4.50, chd free. Home-made teas.**

Approx three acre garden with sweeping lawns long herbaceous borders, colour themed island beds, hosta collection, lavender bed with seating area, topiary, acer collection Japanese garden. Wheelchair access to all areas.

&. ✿ ☕

28 SKELLINGTHORPE HALL

Lincoln Road, Skellingthorpe, Lincoln, LN6 5UU. Charlie & Anne Coltman. *4m W of Lincoln, 500 yds from A46 Lincoln relief road. At the r'about (mid way between A57 & B1190) signed Skellingthorpe take NW exit. Skellingthorpe Hall entrance is circa. 500yds on R opp Waterloo Ln.* **Sun 1 Sept (10.30-4.30). Adm £4, chd free. Home-made teas. Some allergies are not catered for. Please ask for details.**

A 3½ acre landscaped garden with long views across the ha-ha to the park and beyond. Extensive lawns with mature trees. Shrubs and perennial borders created over the last 25 years. Spring bulbs naturalised in the grass and tulips in the borders. Pond and paved area by the small conservatory and a larger one in the main garden, A large vegetable garden with greenhouses. Added pinnacle made from stones removed from Henry VI's chapel at Eton. Some paths can be an effort to navigate for wheelchair users.

&. 🐎 ✿ ☕))

29 66 SPILSBY ROAD

Boston, PE21 9NS. Rosemary & Adrian Isaac. *From Boston town take A16 towards Spilsby. On L after Trinity Church. Parking on Spilsby Rd.* **Sun 5 May (11-4). Adm £5, chd free. Home-made teas.**

1⅓ acre with mature trees, moat, Venetian Folly, summerhouse and orangery, lawns and herbaceous borders. Children's Tudor garden house, gatehouse and courtyard. Wide paths most paths suitable for wheelchairs.

&. ✿ ☕

30 NEW WALNUT LODGE

Bransby, Lincoln, LN1 2PH. David Lunt. *7m NW of Lincoln. From Saxilby on the A57 take the B1241 to Sturton. From the A1500 look for the yellow sign to Bransby 3m E of Sturton. Please park in Bransby Horses car parks.* **Sun 30 June (10-4.30). Adm £4, chd free. Home-made teas.**

Rural garden of ½ acres established by the owners over the past ten years on clay. Herbaceous borders extending to 60m. Mature trees comprise elms, walnut and false acacia. Raised vegetable garden. Outstanding views to the Wolds in the east. The charity Bransby Horses, is located in the village and the visitor centre is well worth a visit.

&. 🐎 ✿ ☕

31 WEST SYKE

38 Electric Station Road, Sleaford, NG34 7QJ. Ada Trethewey. *From A17, A15 & A153 take bypass exit at r'about to Sleaford Town centre. At banks turn R into Westgate. Turn R, on to Electric Station Rd, garden at end of road. Ample parking.* **Sun 9 June (12-5). Adm £6, chd free. Light refreshments.**

Over an acre, comprising bog gardens, rockeries, three large ponds, wildflower meadow, lawns and cottage garden planting. Rambling roses a feature and two acres of wildlife habitats. Sustainable principles and a wealth of native species which inc six species of native orchids. Lawned paths. WC wheelchair accessible.

&. 🐎 ✿ ☕

32 WILLOUGHBY ROAD ALLOTMENTS

Willoughby Road, Boston, PE21 9HN. Willoughby Road Allotments Association. *Entrance is adjacent to 109 Willoughby Rd. Street parking only.* **Sat 18 May, Sat 31 Aug (12-4). Adm £4, chd free. Light refreshments.**

Set in five acres the allotments comprise 60 plots growing fine vegetables, fruit, flowers and herbs. There is a small orchard and wildflower area and a community space adjacent. Grass paths run along the site. Several plots will be open to walk round. There will be a seed and plant stall. Artwork created by Bex Simon situated on site. A small cafe is now open to the public onsite. Small orchard and wildflower

Ashcroft House

beds. Community area with kitchen and disabled WC. Large polytunnel with raised beds inside and out. Accessible for all abilities.

33 WOODLANDS
Peppin Lane, Fotherby, Louth, LN11 0UW. Ann & Bob Armstrong, 01507 603586, annbobarmstrong@btinternet.com, www.woodlandsplants.co.uk. *2m N of Louth off A16 signed Fotherby. Please park on R verge opp allotments & walk approx 350 rds to garden. If full, please park considerately in the village. No parking at garden.* **Sun 18 Feb (10.30-3); Sun 31 Mar, Sun 5 May, Sun 16 June, Sun 11 Aug, Sun 15 Sept (10.30-4.30). Adm £5, chd free. Visits also by arrangement Feb to Oct.**
Renowned for its rich planting of shaded beds, but plenty to interest sun lovers too, especially salvias. A good selection available in the RHS listed nursery. A new attraction this year is a crevice garden. For the first time we have a winter opening featuring drifts of snowdrops and aconites amongst winter flowering shrubs. There is a small, but expanding collection of named snowdrops. Award winning professional artist's studio open to visitors. Specialist collection of Codonopsis with Plant Heritage status. Wheelchair access possible to some areas with care. Limited parking at the house for those with limited mobility.

In 2023, our donations to Carers Trust meant that 26,118 unpaid carers were supported across the UK

34 YEW TREE FARM
Westhorpe Road, Gosberton, Spalding, PE11 4EP. Robert & Claire Bailey-Scott. *Nr Spalding. Enter the village of Gosberton. Turn into Westhorpe Rd, opp The Bell Inn, cont for approx. 1½ m. Property is 3rd on R after bridge.* **Sun 28 July (11-5). Adm £5, chd free. Homemade teas.**
A lovely country garden, 1½ acres. Large herbaceous and mixed borders surround well kept lawns. Wildlife pond with two bog gardens, woodland garden, shaded borders containing many unusual plants. Stunning reflective pool surrounded by ornamental grasses. Orchard, wildflower meadow and vegetable plot. Regional Finalist, The English Garden Magazine's The Nation's Favourite Gardens, 2023

NORTHAMPTONSHIRE

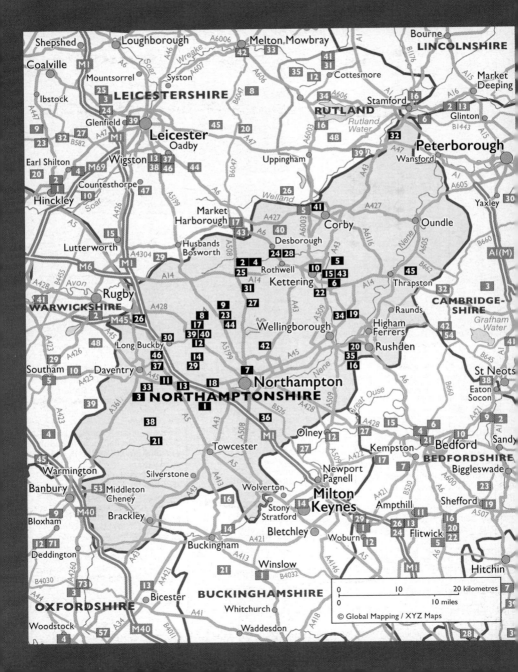

VOLUNTEERS

County Organisers
David Abbott
01933 680363
david.abbott@ngs.org.uk

Gay Webster
01604 740203
gay.webster@ngs.org.uk

County Treasurer
David Abbott (as above)

Publicity
David Abbott (as above)

Photographer
Snowy Ellson
07508 218320
snowyellson@googlemail.com

Booklet Coordinator
William Portch
01536 522169
william.portch@ngs.org.uk

Talks
Elaine & William Portch
01536 522169
elaine@ngs.org.uk

Assistant County Organisers
Amanda Bell
01327 860651
amanda.bell@ngs.org.uk

Lindsey Cartwright
01327 860056
lindsey.cartwright@ngs.org.uk

Jo Glissmann-Hill
07725 258755
joanna.glissmann-hill@ngs.org.uk

Philippa Heumann
01327 860142
pmheumann@gmail.com

Elaine & William Portch
(as above)

f @Northants Ngs
X @NorthantsNGS
@ @northantsngs

OPENING DATES

All entries subject to change.
For latest information check
www.ngs.org.uk
Map locator numbers are
shown to the right of each
garden name.

February

Snowdrop Openings

Sunday 18th
The Old Vicarage — 37

Sunday 25th
◆ Boughton House — 5
67-69 High Street — 19

March

Sunday 24th
Woodcote Villa — 46

April

Monday 1st
Titchmarsh House — 45

Sunday 7th
The Old Vicarage — 37

Sunday 14th
Flore Gardens — 13

Sunday 21st
Briarwood — 6
◆ Cottesbrooke Hall Gardens — 9
◆ Holdenby House & Gardens — 23
Rosi's Taverna — 43

Sunday 28th
Guilsborough Gardens — 17

May

Sunday 5th
Great Brington Gardens — 14
136 High Street — 20

Monday 6th
Titchmarsh House — 45

Friday 10th
Ravensthorpe Nursery — 40

Saturday 11th
Ravensthorpe Nursery — 40

Sunday 12th
Greywalls — 16
Ravensthorpe Nursery — 40

Sunday 19th
Badby Gardens — 3
Dene Lodge — 10
1 Hinwick Close — 22
Little Brington Gardens — 29
Maidwell Gardens — 31
83 Main Road — 32
Oaklea — 35

Sunday 26th
Newnham Gardens — 33

Monday 27th
East Haddon Gardens — 12
Titchmarsh House — 45

Friday 31st
Ravensthorpe Nursery — 40

June

Saturday 1st
Ravensthorpe Nursery — 40

Sunday 2nd
67-69 High Street — 19
Ravensthorpe Gardens — 39

Saturday 8th
◆ Lamport Hall — 27

Sunday 9th
Harpole Gardens — 18
Hostellarie — 24
◆ Kelmarsh Hall & Gardens — 25
16 Leys Avenue — 28
Old Rectory, Quinton — 36
Spratton Gardens — 44

Sunday 16th
NEW Dodford Gardens — 11
Rosearie-de-la-Nymph — 42

Saturday 22nd
Flore Gardens — 13

Sunday 23rd
Flore Gardens — 13
Long Buckby Gardens — 30
Rosearie-de-la-Nymph — 42

Tuesday 25th
◆ Rockingham Castle — 41

Sunday 30th
Arthingworth Open Gardens — 2
67-69 High Street — 19
Kilsby Gardens — 26

July

Friday 5th
Ravensthorpe Nursery 40

Saturday 6th
Ravensthorpe Nursery 40

Sunday 7th
Ravensthorpe Nursery 40

Sunday 14th
Oaklea 35

Sunday 21st
NEW C2C Grows - Community
Allotment Garden 7
Maidwell Gardens 31
Woodcote Villa 46

Sunday 28th
The Green Patch 15
Nonsuch 34

August

Sunday 4th
136 High Street 20

Sunday 18th
Highfields 21

September

Sunday 1st
Woodcote Villa 46

Friday 6th
Ravensthorpe Nursery 40

Saturday 7th
Ravensthorpe Nursery 40

Sunday 8th
Briarwood 6
Ravensthorpe Nursery 40
Rosi's Taverna 43

Sunday 15th
◆ Coton Manor Garden 8

October

Sunday 20th
◆ Boughton House 5

February 2025

Friday 14th
136 High Street 20

Saturday 15th
136 High Street 20

Sunday 16th
136 High Street 20

By Arrangement

Arrange a personalised garden visit
with your club, or group of friends,
on a date to suit you. See individual
garden entries for full details.

16 Ace Lane 1
Bosworth House 4
Briarwood 6
23 Cotton End, Long Buckby
Gardens 30
Dene Lodge 10
Greywalls 16
67-69 High Street 19
136 High Street 20
Hostellarie 24
83 Main Road 32
Old West Farm 38
Ravensthorpe Nursery 40
Titchmarsh House 45
Wisteria House, Long Buckby
Gardens 30
Woodcote Villa 46

Flore Gardens

THE GARDENS

1 16 ACE LANE

Bugbrooke, Northampton, NN7 3PQ. Steve & Kate, 01280 860811, kate@qdl.co.uk, www.instagram.com/kate_white_ architects. *Located 1m E of the A5, 3m S of M1 J16. Parking at church car park nearby, SatNav for parking NN7 3RG.* **Visits by arrangement Apr to Sept for groups of up to 20. Adm £5, chd free. Light refreshments on request.**
Over the last 14 yrs we have evolved our enclosed garden from what was previously extensively laid to lawn with traditional borders, to a varied characterful garden structured by hedges, paths and herbaceous borders. Topiary, creative planting and water features give emphasis and contrast with the lavender rill, pyramid and globe gardens. The lawn has gradually disappeared!

GROUP OPENING

2 ARTHINGWORTH OPEN GARDENS

Arthingworth, nr Market Harborough, LE16 8LA. *6m S of Market Harborough. From Market Harborough via A508, after 4m take L to Arthingworth. From Northampton, A508 turn R just after Kelmarsh. Park cars in Arthingworth village & tickets for sale in the village hall.* **Sun 30 June (1.30-6). Combined adm £7, chd free. Home-made teas by residents of the village at Bosworth House & village hall.**
Eight open gardens, four new in 2024. You will see a combination of small and large gardens, young and old gardeners. We promise you a variety of style from parkland to tiny village gardens, flowers to vegetables, wild and manicured, herbaceous to annuals; all open to give you joy and an afternoon of discovery. St Andrew's Church, Grade II* listed will be open and the village is next to the national cycle path. Wheelchair access to some gardens.

GROUP OPENING

3 BADBY GARDENS

Badby, Daventry, NN11 3AR. *3m S of Daventry on E-side of A361.* **Sun 19 May (1-5). Combined adm £6, chd free. Home-made teas in St Mary's Church.**

CORNER HOUSE
Philip Turvil.

THE GLEBE
Linda Clow.

SHAKESPEARES COTTAGE
Jocelyn Hartland-Swann & Pen Keyte.

SOUTHVIEW COTTAGE
Alan & Karen Brown.

SPRINGFIELD HOUSE
Chris & Linda Lofts.

Delightful hilly village with attractive old houses of golden coloured Hornton stone, set around a C14 church and two village greens (no through traffic). There are five gardens of differing sizes and styles; a wisteria-clad thatched cottage with a sloping garden and modern sculptures; an elevated garden with views over the village and beyond; a ¼ acre garden with mature planting and extensive new landscaping and planting in an informal formality; a new garden with a comparatively modern house that will develop over the next few yrs as the owner continues working with it; a garden which has been remodelled over the last 2 yrs with lawns, herbaceous beds, a pond, and a small vegetable and soft fruit area. We look forward to welcoming you to our lovely village!

4 BOSWORTH HOUSE

Oxendon Road, Arthingworth, nr Market Harborough, LE16 8LA. Mr & Mrs C E Irving-Swift, 01858 525202, cirvingswift@gmail.com. *When in Oxendon Rd, take the little lane with no name, 2nd to the R.* **Visits by arrangement May to July for groups of 15 to 25. Adm £12, chd free. Annual pass for 9 Apr, 11 Jun & 10 Sept (2-4). Adm £25, chd free.**
New for 2024, a yr at Bosworth House. The garden differs through the seasons. We propose three visits on 9 April for tulips and daffodils, 11 June for roses and herbaceous and 10 Sept to prepare for the winter. All conducted by Cécile Irving-Swift and finishing with a cup of tea and biscuits. The garden is also open May to end July for by arrangement visits. Partial wheelchair access.

5 ◆ BOUGHTON HOUSE

Geddington, Kettering, NN14 1BJ. Duke of Buccleuch & Queensberry, KT. *3m NE of Kettering. From A14, 2m along A43 Kettering to Stamford, turn R into Geddington, house entrance 1½ m on R. What3words app - crispier. sensible.maps.* **For NGS: Sun 25 Feb, Sun 20 Oct (1-5). Adm £8, chd £4. Pre-booking essential, please phone 01536 515731, email info@boughtonhouse.co.uk or visit www.boughtonhouse.org. uk for information & booking. Tea. For other opening times and information, please phone, email or visit garden website.**
The Northamptonshire home of the Duke and Duchess of Buccleuch. The garden opening inc opportunities to see the historic walled garden and herbaceous border, and the sensory and wildlife gardens. The wilderness woodland will open for visitors to view the spring flowers or the autumn colours. As a special treat the garden originally created by Sir David Scott (cousin of the Duke of Buccleuch) will also be open. Designated disabled parking. Gravel around house, please see our accessibility document for further information.

Our 2023 donation to the Queen's Nursing Institute now helps support over 2,500 Queen's Nurses working in the community in England, Wales, Northern Ireland, the Channel Islands and the Isle of Man

6 BRIARWOOD

4 Poplars Farm Road, Barton Seagrave, Kettering, NN15 5AF. William & Elaine Portch, 01536 522169, elaine@ngs.org.uk, www.briarwoodgarden.com. *1½m SE of Kettering Town Centre. J10 off A14 turn onto Barton Rd (A6) towards Wicksteed Park. R into Warkton Ln, after 200 metres R into Poplars Farm Rd.* **Sun 21 Apr, Sun 8 Sept (10-4). Combined adm with Rosi's Taverna £6.50, chd free. Light lunches & refreshments. Visits also by arrangement Apr to Sept for groups of 10 to 30.**

A garden for all seasons with quirky original sculptures and many faces. Firstly, a south aspect lawn and borders containing bulbs, shrubs, roses and rare trees with year-round interest; hedging, palms, climbers, a wildlife, fish and lily pond, terrace with potted bulbs and unusual plants in odd containers. Secondly, a secret garden with garden room, small orchard, raised bed potager and greenhouse. Good use of recycled and repurposed materials throughout the garden, inc a unique self-build garden cabin, sculpture and planters.

♿ ✻ ☕))

7 NEW C2C GROWS - COMMUNITY ALLOTMENT GARDEN

Kingsthorpe Park Allotments, off Tollgate Close, Northampton, NN2 6RP. www.c2csocialaction.com/general-8-2. *Off Mill Ln, towards Kingsthorpe. On arrival into Tollgate Cl, bear L at the T-junction & drive along to a free car park. Cross over the grass in the park following a line of wooden bollards up to the metal allotment gate.* **Sun 21 July (12-4). Adm £4, chd free. Pre-booking essential, please visit www.ngs.org.uk for information & booking. Light refreshments.**

C2C Grows is a community allotment project run by the charity C2C Social Action. The project offers social and therapeutic horticultural sessions for women referred to us who may be experiencing poor health and social disadvantage. The project takes place on a triple sized allotment with several polytunnels, a greenhouse, fruit cages, no dig raised beds and a peaceful wildlife area with pond. Art exhibited from an art project which took place at the allotment. Allotment site is next to Thornton Park.

Accessible, but contact garden on 07885 685781 for further details.

♿ ✻ ☕))

8 ◆ COTON MANOR GARDEN

Coton, Northampton, NN6 8RQ. Mr & Mrs Ian Pasley-Tyler, 01604 740219, pasleytyler@cotonmanor.co.uk, www.cotonmanor.co.uk. *10m N of Northampton, 11m SE of Rugby. From A428 & A5199 follow tourist signs.* **For NGS: Sun 15 Sept (11.30-5). Adm £10, chd £3.50. Light refreshments & home-made teas at Stableyard Café. For other opening times and information, please phone, email or visit garden website.**

10 acre garden set in peaceful countryside with old yew and holly hedges and extensive herbaceous borders, containing many unusual plants. One of Britain's finest throughout the season, the garden is at its most magnificent in Sept and is an inspiration as to what can be achieved in late summer. Adjacent specialist nursery with over 1000 plant varieties propagated from the garden. This garden is proud to

Kingsley House, Harpole Gardens

provide plants for the National Garden Scheme's Show Garden at Chelsea Flower Show 2024. Partial wheelchair access as some paths are narrow and the site is on a slope.

♿ ✿ 🚗 ☕ 🔊

9 ◆ COTTESBROOKE HALL GARDENS
Cottesbrooke,
Northampton, NN6 8PF.
Mr & Mrs A R Macdonald-Buchanan, 01604 505808,
welcome@cottesbrooke.co.uk,
www.cottesbrooke.co.uk.
Cottesbrooke Hall is 3m off A14, J1. Follow brown signs S towards Northampton & in Creaton turn L onto Violet Ln. What3words app - expand.allow.curly. **For NGS: Sun 21 Apr (2-5.30). Adm £13, chd £4. Home-made teas. Please visit garden website to pre-book tickets. For other opening times and information, please phone, email or visit garden website. Donation to All Saints Church, Cottesbrooke.**
Award-winning gardens by Geoffrey Jellicoe, Dame Sylvia Crowe, James Alexander-Sinclair, and more recently Arne Maynard and Angel Collins. Formal gardens and terraces surround Queen Anne house with extensive vistas onto the lake and C18 parkland containing many mature trees. Wild and woodland gardens, a short distance from the formal areas, are exceptional in spring. Partial wheelchair access as paths are grass, stone and gravel, please call ahead to discuss. Access map identifies best route.

♿ ✿ 🚗 ☕ 🪑

10 DENE LODGE
257 Rockingham Road,
Kettering, NN16 9JE. Mr & Mrs R Pooley, 01536 481012,
denelodge@btinternet.com. *N of Kettering Town Centre on A6003. From J7 of A14 take A43 towards Stamford, at next r'about take A6003 to town centre, then over r'about. Entrance opp Cotswold Ave. No parking on Rockingham Rd, road side parking by Beeswing Pub.* **Sun 19 May (11-5). Adm £5, chd free. Home-made teas & cream teas with gluten free option. Visits also by arrangement 1 May to 29 Sept for groups of 10 to 30. Day or eve visits. Various refreshment options.**
An established garden sloping downward from east to west with

many trees, shrubs, roses, perennials and bulbs. Small pond, terrace with wisteria covered pergola leads past the rock garden to the lower patio, a larger pond with pergola, decking, climbing roses, jasmine and clematis. A further lawn leads through an arch to the vegetable garden with fruit trees and soft fruit, bushes and climbers. Wheelchair access over concrete, paved patios and paths.

♿ 🐴 ✿ ☕ 🔊

GROUP OPENING

 DODFORD GARDENS
Dodford House, Dodford, Northampton, NN7 4SX. Paul & Stephanie Russell. *Off the A5 or A45 nr Weedon. The garden of Dodford House is located at the lower end of the village on a no through road lane.* **Sun 16 June (2-5.30). Combined adm £7.50, chd free. Pre-booking essential, please visit www.ngs.org.uk for information & booking. Light refreshments.**
Dodford is a charming small village in a very peaceful location. This new and evolving group, based around the beautiful 1½ acre garden at Dodford House which inc productive kitchen and cut flower garden, rose walkway, long borders, formal lawns and topiary, and a box parterre. There will be several gardens open on the day of contrasting types and styles, more information will be added to the website closer to the open day.

✿ ☕ 🔊

GROUP OPENING

12 EAST HADDON GARDENS
East Haddon, Northampton, NN6 8BT. *A few hundred yds off the A428 (signed) between M1 J18 (8m) & Northampton (8m). On-road parking. Strictly no parking in Priestwell Court, St Andrews Rd or on the properties.* **Mon 27 May (1-5). Combined adm £6, chd free. Home-made teas at St Mary's Church.**

BRAEBURN HOUSE
Judy Darby.

◆ HADDONSTONE, THE JUBLIEE GARDENS
Haddonstone Ltd, 01604 770711, info@haddonstone.co.uk, www.haddonstone.com.

LIMETREES
Barry & Sally Hennessey.

LINDEN HOUSE
Hilary Van den Boogaard.

9 PRIESTWELL COURT
Emma Forbes.

SADDLER'S COTTAGE
Val Longley.

THARFIELD
Julia Farnsworth.

TOWER COTTAGE
John Benson.

The pretty village of East Haddon dates back to the Norman invasion. The oldest surviving building is St Mary's, a C12 church. The village has many thatched cottages built in the local honey-coloured ironstone. Other features inc a thatched village pump and fire station which used to house a hand drawn pump and is now used as the bus shelter. The gardens opening this yr are a mixture of small, mature and family gardens with some having beautiful views across rolling hills. They are bursting with rare and unusual plants, various shrubs, climbers, roses and perennials. Borders galore, vegetable beds, espaliered fruit trees, and woodland areas. Tickets and refreshments will be available at the church and plants propagated from the gardens and raised from seed will be on sale inc some rarities at Limetrees. The village is less than 10 mins from Coton Manor Gardens. Partial wheelchair access at Tower Cottage and access to some gardens via gravel drives.

♿ ✿ ☕ 🔊

The National Garden Scheme's final instalment to support the building of the Y Bwthyn NGS Macmillan Specialist Palliative Care Unit in Wales, enabled 270 inpatients to be supported this year

GROUP OPENING

🔢 FLORE GARDENS

Flore, Northampton, NN7 4LQ.
Situated between the towns of Daventry & Northampton. 2m from J16 of the M1. **Sun 14 Apr (2-6). Combined adm £6, chd free. Sat 22, Sun 23 June (11-6). Combined adm £8, chd free. Home-made teas in Chapel School Room (Apr). Morning coffee & teas in Church & light lunches & teas in Chapel School Room (June). Donation to All Saints Church & United Reform Church, Flore (June).**

THE CROFT
John & Dorothy Boast.
Open on all dates

THE GARDEN HOUSE
Gary & Julie Moinet.
Open on Sat 22, Sun 23 June

NEW 25 LARBOURNE PARK ROAD
Jaqui Hoyle & Julian Hendon.
Open on Sat 22, Sun 23 June

THE OLD BAKERY
John Amos & Karl Jones.
Open on all dates

PRIVATE GARDEN OF BLISS LANE NURSERY
Christine & Geoffrey Littlewood.
Open on all dates

ROCK SPRINGS
Tom Higginson & David Foster.
Open on all dates

RUSSELL HOUSE
Peter Pickering & Stephen George, 01327 341734,
peterandstephen@btinternet.com,
www.RussellHouseFlore.com.
Open on all dates

NEW THREE CORNERS
Marg & Fabian Blamires.
Open on Sat 22, Sun 23 June

1 YEW TREE GARDENS
Mr & Mrs Martin Millard.
Open on all dates

Flore gardens have been open since 1963 as part of the Flore Flower Festival. The partnership with the NGS started in 1992 with openings every yr since. Flore is an attractive village with views over the Upper Nene Valley. We have a varied mix of gardens, large and small. They have all been developed by friendly, enthusiastic and welcoming owners who are in their gardens when open. Our gardens range from the traditional to the eccentric providing year-round interest. Some have been established over many yrs and others have been developed more recently. There are greenhouses, gazebos, summerhouses, water features and seating opportunities to rest while enjoying the gardens. The village Flower Festival is our main event on the same two days as the June opening and garden tickets will be valid for both days. Partial wheelchair access to most gardens, some assistance may be required.

GROUP OPENING

🔢 GREAT BRINGTON GARDENS

Northampton, NN7 4JJ. *7m NW of Northampton. Off A428 Rugby Rd. From Northampton, turn 1st L past main gates of Althorp. Details & maps available at free car park, NN7 4HY.* **Sun 5 May (11-4). Combined adm £7, chd free. Home-made teas.**

FOLLY HOUSE
Sarah & Joe Sacarello.

NEW 2 THE POUND
Mrs Sue Saunders.

RIDGEWAY HOUSE
Janet & Keith White.

ROSE COTTAGE
David Green & Elaine MacKenzie.

THE STABLES
Mrs J George.

SUNDERLAND HOUSE
Mrs Margaret Rubython.

YEW TREE HOUSE
Mrs Joan Heaps.

Great Brington is proud of over 28 yrs association with the NGS and arguably one of the most successful one day scheme events in the county. The gardens are situated in a circular and virtually flat walk around the village. Our gardens provide inspiration and variety; continuing to evolve each yr and designed, planted and maintained by their owners. The village on the Althorp Estate is particularly picturesque and well worth a visit, predominantly local stone with thatched houses, a church of historic interest, and walkers can extend their walk to view Althorp House. Visitors will enjoy a warm welcome with plants for sale, tea, coffee and cake available from 11am-4pm. There are also secluded spots for artists to draw, sketch and paint. Small coaches for groups welcome by prior arrangement only, please email friends_of_stmarys@btinternet.com. Wheelchair access to some gardens.

🔢 THE GREEN PATCH

Valley Walk, Kettering, NN16 0LU. Grey Lindley, www.greenpatch.org.uk. *NE of Kettering Town Centre. Signed from A4300 Stamford Rd, on the junction of Valley Walk & Margaret Rd.* **Sun 28 July (10-3). Adm £5, chd free. Tea, coffee, biscuits & cake.**
The Green Patch is a $2\frac{1}{2}$ acre, Green Flag award-winning community garden, nestled in the heart of England. We have hens, ducks, beehives, ponds, children's play area, orchard and so much more. We rely on our wonderful volunteers to make our friendly and magical garden the warm and welcoming place it is. Run by the environmental charity Groundwork Northamptonshire. Vegetable seedlings, herbs, and apple trees for sale. Bring a blanket for a picnic. Wheelchair access and disabled WC.

🔢 GREYWALLS

Farndish, nr Wellingborough, NN29 7HJ. Mrs P M Anderson, 01933 353495, greywalls@dbshoes.co.uk. *$2\frac{1}{2}$m SE of Wellingborough. A609 from Wellingborough, B570 to Irchester, turn to Farndish by cenotaph. House adjacent to church.* **Sun 12 May (12-4). Adm £5, chd free. Light refreshments. Visits also by arrangement 1 Feb to 1 Dec for groups of 10 to 30.**
Greywalls is an old vicarage set in 2 acres of relaxed country gardens planted for year-round interest. Featuring mature specimen trees, an impressive Banksia rose, three large ponds, many stone features, wildflower meadow and a Highgrove inspired stumpery. The borders feature unusual plants and there is an outside aviary. Strictly no dogs.

GROUP OPENING

🔟 GUILSBOROUGH GARDENS

Guilsborough, NN6 8RA. www.
instagram.com/gardenatfouracres.
*10m NW of Northampton. 10m E
of Rugby. Between A5199 & A428.
J1 off A14. Parking in field on Cold
Ashby Rd NN6 8QN. Please park
in car park to avoid congestion
in the village centre.* **Sun 28 Apr
(1.30-5.30). Combined adm £7.50,
chd free. Home-made teas in the
village hall.**

FOUR ACRES
Mark & Gay Webster.

THE GATE HOUSE
Mike & Sarah Edwards.

NEW HOLLY COTTAGE
Mr Mark & Mrs Beverley Brennan.

THE OLD HOUSE
Vanessa Berry.

THE OLD VICARAGE
John & Christine Benbow.

NEW ROSE COTTAGE
Mr Ian & Mrs Amanda Miller.

Enjoy a warm welcome in this village
with its very attractive rural setting of
rolling hills and reservoirs. We have a
group of contrasting gardens for you
to visit this yr inc two new cottage
style gardens. Several of us are
passionate about growing fruit and
vegetables, a kitchen garden and a
potager are an important part of our
gardening. No wheelchair access at
Rose Cottage, Holly Cottage or The
Gate House.

GROUP OPENING

🔟 HARPOLE GARDENS

Harpole, NN7 4BX. *On A45 4m W
of Northampton towards Weedon.
Turn R at The Turnpike Hotel into
Harpole. Village maps given to
all visitors.* **Sun 9 June (1-6).
Combined adm £5, chd free.
Home-made teas at The Close.**

CEDAR COTTAGE
Spencer & Joanne Hannam.

THE CLOSE
Michael Orton-Jones.

NEW KINGSLEY HOUSE
Gregory Hearne & Caroline
Fisermanis.

19 MANOR CLOSE
Caroline & Eamonn Kemshed.

THE OLD DAIRY
David & Di Ballard.

Harpole is an attractive village nestling
at the foot of Harpole Hills with many
houses built of local sandstone.
Visit us and delight in a wide variety
of gardens of all shapes, sizes and
content. You will see luxuriant lawns,
mixed borders with plants for sun and
shade, mature trees, shrubs, herbs,
alpines, water features and tropical
planting. We have interesting and
quirky artifacts dotted around, garden
structures and plenty of seating for
the weary.

🔟 67-69 HIGH STREET

Finedon, NN9 5JN. Mary &
Stuart Hendry, 01933 680414,
sh_archt@hotmail.com. *6m SE
Kettering. Garden signed from A6 &
A510 junction.* **Sun 25 Feb (11-3);
Sun 2, Sun 30 June (2-5.30). Adm
£3.50, chd free. Soup & roll in Feb
(inc in adm). Home-made teas in
June. Visits also by arrangement
Feb to Sept.**
1/3 acre rear garden of C17 cottage
(not open). Early spring garden with
snowdrops and hellebores, summer
and autumn mixed borders, many
obelisks and containers, kitchen
garden, herb bed, rambling roses and
at least 60 different hostas. All giving
varied interest from Feb through to
Oct. Large selection of home-raised
plants for sale (all proceeds to NGS).

🔟 136 HIGH STREET

Irchester, NN29 7AB. Ade & Jane
Parker, jane692@btinternet.com.
*200yds past the church on the
bend as you leave the village going
towards the A45. Please park on
High St. Disabled parking only in
driveway.* **Sun 5 May, Sun 4 Aug
(11-4). Adm £4, chd free. Light
refreshments. 2025: Fri 14, Sat
15, Sun 16 Feb. Visits also by
arrangement 15 Feb to 31 Aug.**
Large garden developed by the
current owners over the past 20 yrs.
Various different planting habitats inc
areas designed for shade, sun and
pollinator friendly sites. Wildlife pond
attracting large range of birds, insects
and other creatures into the garden.
Alpine houses, planted stone sinks
and raised beds. Seasonally planted

tubs adding bold summer colour.
Wildflower meadow. Wheelchair
access mainly over grass with some
gravel pathways.

🔟 HIGHFIELDS

Adstone, Towcester, NN12 8DS.
Rachel Halvorsen. *7m W of
Towcester. The village of Adstone
is midway between Banbury &
Northampton, about 15m from each.*
**Sun 18 Aug (2-5.30). Adm £5, chd
free. Cream teas.**
Two sheltered mixed courtyard
gardens with vibrant colours; granite
path winds between lawn borders;
formal walled garden with central
aquaglobe. Plantsman's garden.
Collection of succulents. Cream
teas on patio overlooking panoramic
views with ha-ha to 15m of unbroken
countryside, lake and 100 acre
Plumpton Wood. Walk down to
lake across a couple of fields to
see wildlife, beds, and water lilies.
Wheelchair access with a few single
steps.

🔟 1 HINWICK CLOSE

Kettering, NN15 6GB. Mrs Pat
Cole-Ashton. *J9 A14 A509
Kettering. At Park House r'about
take exit signed to Holdenby. Hinwick
Cl 3rd exit on R.* **Sun 19 May (12-4).
Adm £3.50, chd free. Home-made
teas & savouries.**
In the past 15 yrs Pat and Snowy
have transformed this space into
a wildlife haven. The garden has
numerous influences; seaside,
woodland and English country
garden. Ponds and waterfalls add to
the delights. Vintage signs, numerous
figures and seating areas at different
vantage points are dotted throughout
the garden.

100 inpatients and
their families are being
supported at the newly
opened Horatio's Garden
Wales, thanks to the
National Garden Scheme
donations

23 ◆ **HOLDENBY HOUSE & GARDENS**
Holdenby House, Holdenby, Northamptonshire, NN6 8DJ. Mr & Mrs James Lowther, 01604 770074, office@holdenby.com, www.holdenby.com. *7m NW of Northampton. Off A5199 or A428 between East Haddon & Spratton.* **For NGS: Sun 21 Apr (11-4). Adm £9, chd £5. Home-made teas & light refreshments. For other opening times and information, please phone, email or visit garden website.**
Holdenby has a historic Grade I listed garden. The inner garden inc Rosemary Verey's renowned Elizabethan Garden and Rupert Golby's Pond Garden and long borders. There is also a delightful walled kitchen garden. Away from the formal gardens, the terraces of the original Elizabethan Garden are still visible, one of the best preserved examples of their kind. Accessible, but contact garden for further details. Assistance dogs only.

24 **HOSTELLARIE**
78 Breakleys Road, Desborough, NN14 2PT. Stella Freeman, 01536 760124, stelstan78@outlook.com. *6m N of Kettering. 5m S of Market Harborough. From church & war memorial turn R into Dunkirk Ave, then 3rd R. From cemetery L into Dunkirk Ave, then 4th L.* **Sun 9 June (2-5). Combined adm with 16 Leys Avenue £4, chd free. Home-made teas & a gluten-free option. Visits also by arrangement 1 June to 27 July for groups of 10 to 25.**
Hostellarie is a long town garden divided into rooms. Lawns and grass paths lead you through varied colour borders, ponds and water features. Courtyard garden shaded by an old clematis has over 40 different hostas, there are even more mature specimen hostas in the north facing beds and other shady spots. Roses, clematis, cottage and gravel borders, and a welcoming relaxing atmosphere.

25 ◆ **KELMARSH HALL & GARDENS**
Main Road, Kelmarsh, Northampton, NN6 9LY. The Kelmarsh Trust, 01604 686543, marketing@kelmarsh.com, www.kelmarsh.com. *Kelmarsh is 5m S of Market Harborough &*

11m N of Northampton. From A14, exit J2 & head N towards Market Harborough on the A508. **For NGS: Sun 9 June (10-3). Adm £8, chd £4.50. Light lunches, cream teas & cakes in Sweet Pea's Tearoom. For other opening times and information, please phone, email or visit garden website.**
Kelmarsh Hall is an elegant Palladian house set in glorious Northamptonshire countryside with highly regarded gardens, which are the work of Nancy Lancaster, Norah Lindsay and Geoffrey Jellicoe. Hidden gems inc an orangery, sunken garden, long border, rose gardens and, at the heart of it all, a historic walled garden. Highlights throughout the seasons inc fritillaries, tulips, roses and dahlias. Beautiful interiors brought together by Nancy Lancaster in the 1930s, in a Palladian style hall designed by James Gibbs. The recently restored laundry and servants' quarters in the Hall are open to the public, providing visitors the incredible opportunity to experience life 'below stairs'. This garden is proud to provide plants for the National Garden Scheme's Show Garden at Chelsea Flower Show 2024. Blue badge disabled parking close to the Visitor Centre entrance. Paths are loose gravel, wheelchair users advised to bring a companion.

GROUP OPENING

26 **KILSBY GARDENS**
Middle Street, Kilsby, Rugby, CV23 8XT. *5m SE of Rugby. 6m N of Daventry on A361.* **Sun 30 June (1-5.30). Combined adm £7, chd free. Home-made teas at Kilsby Village Hall (1-5).**

BOLBERRY HOUSE
Mr & Mrs Richard Linnell.

LYNN COTTAGE
Alison Harrison.

RAINBOW'S END
Mr & Mrs J Madigan.

12 RUGBY ROAD
Mr & Mrs T Hindle.

SUMMERHILL
Diana & Ron Smith.

NEW **9 WATLING STREET**
Tracey Fisher.

Kilsby's name has long been associated with Stephenson's famous railway tunnel and an early skirmish in the Civil War. The houses and

gardens of the village offer a mixture of sizes and styles, which reflect its development through time. We welcome you to test the friendliness for which we are renowned and visit the gardens opening in the village this year! No wheelchair access at 9 Watling Street.

27 ◆ **LAMPORT HALL**
Lamport, Northampton, NN6 9HD. Lamport Hall Preservation Trust, 01604 686272, engagement@lamporthall.co.uk, www.lamporthall.co.uk. *For SatNav please use postcode NN6 9EZ. Exit J2 of the A14. Entry through the gate flanked by swans on the A508. What3words app - miracles. unusable.botanists.* **For NGS: Sat 8 June (10-4). Adm £8, chd £4. Light refreshments in The Stables Café. For other opening times and information, please phone, email or visit garden website.**
Home of the Isham family for over 400 yrs, the extensive herbaceous borders complement the Elizabethan bowling lawns, together with topiary from the 1700s. The 2 acre walled garden is full of colour, with 250 rows of perennials. Another highlight is the famous Lamport rockery, among the earliest in England and home of the world's oldest garden gnome. Wheelchair access on gravel paths within the gardens.

28 **16 LEYS AVENUE**
Desborough, NN14 2PY. Keith & Beryl Norman. *6m N of Kettering. 5m S of Market Harborough. From church & War Memorial turn R into Dunkirk Ave & 5th R into Leys Ave.* **Sun 9 June (2-5). Combined adm with Hostellarie £4, chd free. Tea.**
A town garden with two water features, plus a stream and a pond flanked by a 12ft clinker-built boat. There are six raised beds and an area of sweet peas. A patio lined with acers has two steps down to a gravel garden with paved paths. Mature trees and acers give the garden year-round structure and interest. Wheelchair access down two steps from patio to main garden.

GROUP OPENING

29 LITTLE BRINGTON GARDENS
Main Street, Little Brington, Northampton, NN7 4HS. *Off road parking can be found at the end of Folly Ln, Little Brington, NN7 4JR.* **Sun 19 May (11-4.30). Combined adm £7.50, chd free. Light refreshments.**

1 FERMOY COURT
Hilary & Chris Moore.

IVY COTTAGE
Mr David & Dirk Toulmin-Van Sittert.

MANOR COTTAGE
Derek & Carol Bull.

MANOR FARM HOUSE
Rob Shardlow.

14 PINE COURT
Chris & Judy Peck.

ROCHE COTTAGE
Malcolm & Susan Uttley.

STONECROFT
Peter & Jenny Holman.

Seven wonderful gardens in the historic village of Little Brington, nestled in the Northamptonshire farmlands will open for the NGS. They offer a variety of shapes, sizes and styles, from more formal planting to relaxed cottage gardens, along with a variety of vegetable gardens on show too. Lots of colours on display with a mix of both familiar and unusual plants and flowers. Refreshments will be served and the village pub Saracens Head will also be open, book early as the pub is very popular. Come and enjoy the wonderful gardens and the pretty village setting. Full or partial wheelchair access to most gardens. Some have gravel driveways.

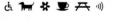

GROUP OPENING

30 LONG BUCKBY GARDENS
Northampton, NN6 7RE. *8m NW of Northampton, midway between A428 & A5. Long Buckby is signed from A428 & A5. 10 mins from J18 M1. Long Buckby Train Stn is ½ m from centre of the village. Free car park at Cotton End on B5385. Shuttle bus between farthest gardens.* **Sun 23 June (1-6). Combined adm £8, chd free. Home-made teas, ice creams, cold drinks & Pimms.**

NEW 7 BURNHAM WAY
Shelley & Wayne Byles.

3 COTTON END
Roland & Georgina Wells.

4 COTTON END
Sue & Giles Baker.

23 COTTON END
Lynnette & Malcolm Cannell, 01327 844069, lynnettecannell68@gmail.com. Visits also by arrangement May to July.

NEW 53 EAST STREET
Alison & Phil Weston.

THE GROTTO
Andy & Chrissy Gamble.

NEW LONG BARN, GRANGE FARM
Jenni McDonnell MBE.

15 SYERS GREEN CLOSE
Shona Mcnamee.

WISTERIA HOUSE
David & Clare Croston, 07771 911892, dad.croston@gmail.com. Visits also by arrangement 1 May to 15 July for groups of up to 30. Combined visit with Woodcote Villa and/or 23 Cotton End.

Nine gardens in the historic village of Long Buckby inc three new gardens. We have been busy creating new borders, features and extensively replanting, offering our visitors something new to enjoy. We welcome visitors old and new to see our wonderful variety of gardens which offer something for everyone. The gardens in the group vary in size and style, from old established gardens, cottage gardens, newly established gardens, terraced back gardens and plantsman's gardens. Some are well established, whilst others are totally new, redesigns or constantly evolving. They inc water features, pergolas, garden structures, but the stars are definitely the plants. Bursting with colour, visitors will find old favourites and the unusual, used in a variety of ways inc trees, shrubs, perennials, climbers, annuals, fruit and vegetables. Of course, there will be teas and plants for sale to complete the visit. Come and see us for a friendly welcome and a great afternoon out. Refreshments from volunteers of Long Buckby Library and Hub, Pimms at Wisteria House from Long Buckby & District Gardening Club. Full or partial wheelchair access to all gardens.

GROUP OPENING

31 MAIDWELL GARDENS
Draughton Road, Maidwell, Northampton, NN6 9JF. *From Market Harborough turn L off the A508 (or from Northampton turn R) & look for the yellow signs.* **Sun 19 May, Sun 21 July (10-5). Combined adm £6, chd free. Light refreshments at Wyatts.**

NIGHTINGALE COTTAGE
Ken & Angela Palmer.

WYATTS
Mr Colin & Mrs Amanda Goddard.

A friendly village with horses exercising daily and often sheep being herded through. The gardens opening are varied with many flowering plants and shrubs. Nightingale Cottage, a small cottage garden has been designed by the owners and surrounds an old barn. There are many pots and cottage type planting inc some vegetables. There are also some surprises of wooden animals made from pruning, steps and hidden seating areas, but no grass. It is a garden which is always evolving as different species self-seed and are often left to grow. In contrast Wyatts, is a large wrap-around garden featuring borders with many varied shrubs and mature trees providing year-round interest inc acers and hydrangeas. There are varying levels and many seating areas with a summerhouse in one corner. More gardens may open on the day, check the website closer to the time for further information! Partial wheelchair access to Nightingale Cottage.

Our donation to the Army Benevolent Fund supported 608 individuals with front line services and horticultural related grants in 2023

32 83 MAIN ROAD

Collyweston, Stamford, PE9 3PQ. Rosemary & Robert Fromm, 07597 684816, rrfromm@msn.com. *On A43 3½ m SW of Stamford. 1m from A43/A47 r'about. Three doors from The Collyweston Slater Pub.* **Sun 19 May (12.30-5). Adm £4, chd free. Home-made teas. Visits also by arrangement 1 Apr to 28 Sept for groups of 5 to 15.**

Wildlife friendly garden with many small trees, bushes and perennials. Spring bulbs and primroses proliferate underneath the trees, also a laburnum arch. Gravel paths and stone steps give access to the sloping site which is just under a ¼ acre. The garden is in the process of being made even more wildlife friendly, with many more plants being added to feed bees, moths and butterflies. Refreshments with be available on the patio with seating. Some plants will be on sale.

✿ ☕)))

GROUP OPENING

33 NEWNHAM GARDENS

Newnham, Daventry, NN11 3HF. *2m S of Daventry on B4037 between the A361 & A45. Continue to the centre of the village & follow signs for the car park, just off the main village green.* **Sun 26 May (11-5). Combined adm £6, chd free. Light lunches & cakes in village hall.**

THE BANKS
Sue & Geoff Chester.

NEW 1 CHURCH STREET
Joan & Harry Ferguson.

THE COTTAGE
Jacqueline Minor,
www.instagram.com/newnhamngs.

HILLTOP
David & Mercy Messenger.

WREN COTTAGE
Mr & Mrs Judith Dorkins.

You are so welcome to Newnham. Five plant-lover gardens inc a new garden opening this yr, all set in our beautiful old village nestled in the unspoilt Northamptonshire Uplands. The gardens, from large to small, are packed with spring colour, horticultural delights, lots of inspiration and lovely views. There is something to delight everyone. Spend the day with us enjoying the gardens, buying at our ever-popular plant sale, strolling around the village lanes and visiting our C14 church. Treat yourself to a tasty light lunch and scrumptious cakes and refreshments in the village hall (several times!). We look forward to seeing you. The old village is hilly in parts. While most gardens are accessible for wheelchairs, some have steps or narrow paths.

& ✿ ☕)))

34 NONSUCH

11 Mackworth Drive, Finedon, Wellingborough, NN9 5NL. Carrie Whitworth. *Off Wellingborough Rd (A510) onto Bell Hill, then to Church Hill, 2nd L after church, entrance on the L as you enter Mackworth Dr.* **Sun 28 July (1-5). Adm £4, chd free. Drinks, cakes & biscuits.**

⅓ acre country garden within a conservation boundary stone wall. Mature trees, enhanced by many rare and unusual shrubs and perennial plants. A garden for all seasons with several seating areas. Wheelchair access on a level site with paved and gravel paths.

& ✿ ☕)))

35 OAKLEA

84 Wollaston Road, Irchester, NN29 7DF. Mr Keith Wilson & Mrs Nicola Wilson-Brown. *3m SE of Wellingborough. Leave Wellingborough via A509 heading towards Wollaston, turn L at r'about onto B570 signed Irchester Country Park. Continue to end of road, turn L at r'about into Wollaston Rd.* **Sun 19 May, Sun 14 July (12-5). Adm £4, chd free. Light refreshments.**

An interesting and deceptive garden featuring courtyard area with succulents, seasonal pots, troughs and baskets. Borders well-stocked with shrubs and herbaceous perennials together with climbing plants and roses giving colour throughout the growing season. Two lawned areas, a pond planted with plants and stocked with fish. Several seating areas and a vegetable garden with potting shed. Wheelchair access over level garden.

& ✿ ☕)))

36 OLD RECTORY, QUINTON

Preston Deanery Road, Quinton, Northampton, NN7 2ED. Alan Kennedy & Emma Wise, www.garden4good.co.uk. *M1 J15, 1m from Wootton towards Salcey Forest. House is next to the church. On-road parking in village.* *Please note parking on village green is prohibited.* **Sun 9 June (10-4). Adm £10, chd free. Pre-booking essential, please visit www.ngs. org.uk for information & booking. Two hour timed slots at 10am, 12pm & 2pm. Hot drinks & cake (all day). Lunches to pre-order via garden website (11am-2pm).**

A contemporary 3 acre rectory garden designed by multi-award-winning designer, Anoushka Feiler. Taking the Old Rectory's C18 history and its religious setting as a key starting point, the main garden at the back of the house has been divided into six parts; a kitchen garden, glasshouse and flower garden, a woodland menagerie, a pleasure garden, a park and an orchard. Elements of C18 design such as formal structures, parterres, topiary, long walks, occasional seating areas and traditional craft work have been introduced, but with a distinctly C21 twist through the inclusion of living walls, modern materials and features, new planting methods and abstract installations. Pop-up shop selling plants, garden produce, local honey, home-made bread and organic gifts. Wheelchair access with gravel paths.

& ✿ 🚗 ☕

37 THE OLD VICARAGE

Daventry Road, Norton, Daventry, NN11 2ND. Barry & Andrea Coleman. *Norton is approx 2m E of Daventry, 11m W of Northampton. From Daventry follow signs to Norton for 1m. On A5 N from Weedon follow road for 3m, take L turn signed Norton. On A5 S take R at Xrds signed Norton, 6m from Kilsby. Garden is R of All Saints Church.* **Sun 18 Feb (11-1); Sun 7 Apr (1-5). Adm £5, chd free. Soup & bread in Feb (inc in adm). Home-made teas in orangery (Apr).**

The vicarage garden was once the centre of village life. Fifty yrs on, garden life is different with unexpected trees, bulbs, shrubs, perennials bursting year-round with birdlife, wildlife and life in general. A warm welcome awaits. The interesting and beautiful C14 church of All Saints will be open to visitors.

🐾 ☕)))

Rose Cottage, Great Brington Gardens

38 OLD WEST FARM
Little Preston, Daventry,
NN11 3TF. Mr & Mrs G Hoare,
caghoare@gmail.com. *7m SW
Daventry, 8m W Towcester, 13m NE
Banbury. ³⁄₄ m E of Preston Capes
on road to Maidford. Last house on
R in Little Preston with white flagpole.
Beware, the postcode applies to all
houses in Little Preston. Off road
parking.* **Visits by arrangement 15
May to 29 June for groups of up
to 30. Home-made teas.**
Large rural garden lovingly developed
over the past 43 yrs on a very
exposed site, planted with hedges
and shelter for wildlife and birds.
Roses, shrubs and borders aiming
for year-round interest. Particularly
attractive in May and June. A peaceful
place to sit and listen to birdsong.
Home-made teas served (weather
permitting) on the terrace. Partial
wheelchair access over grass.

GROUP OPENING

39 RAVENSTHORPE GARDENS
Ravensthorpe, NN6 8ES. *7m NW
of Northampton. Signed from A428.
Please start & purchase tickets at
Ravensthorpe Nursery.* **Sun 2 June
(1.30-5.30). Combined adm £7.50,
chd free. Home-made teas in
village hall.**

NEW **1 CHURCH GARDENS**
Tricia & Chris Freeman.

CORNERSTONE
Lorna Jones.

MANOR VIEW
Viv & David Rees.

RAVENSTHORPE NURSERY
Mr & Mrs Richard Wiseman.
(See separate entry)

Attractive village in Northamptonshire
uplands near to Ravensthorpe
reservoir and Top Ardles Wood
Woodland Trust which have bird
watching and picnic opportunities.
Established and developing gardens
set in beautiful countryside displaying
a wide range of plants, many
available from the nursery that now
only opens on NGS open days.
Offering inspirational planting, quiet
contemplation, beautiful views, water
features and gardens encouraging
wildlife. As a late addition, access to
a neighbour's vegetable garden only
from Manor View. Disabled WC in
village hall.

40 RAVENSTHORPE NURSERY
6 East Haddon Road,
Ravensthorpe, NN6 8ES. Mr & Mrs
Richard Wiseman, 01604 770548,
ravensthorpenursery@hotmail.com.
*7m NW of Northampton. 1st
property on L approaching from
A428.* **Fri 10, Sat 11, Sun 12, Fri
31 May, Sat 1 June, Fri 5, Sat
6, Sun 7 July, Fri 6, Sat 7, Sun 8
Sept (11-5). Adm £6, chd free.
Home-made teas. Opening with
Ravensthorpe Gardens on Sun 2
June. Visits also by arrangement
8 Apr to 30 Sept for groups of 10
to 40.**
Approx 1 acre garden wrapped
around the nursery with beautiful
views. Planted with many unusual
shrubs and herbaceous perennials
over the last 30+ yrs to reflect the
wide range of plants produced. Plants
for sale. Wheelchair access with
gradual slope to garden and nursery.

41 ◆ ROCKINGHAM CASTLE
Rockingham Castle Estate,
Rockingham, Market
Harborough, LE16 8TH.
www.rockinghamcastle.com. *1m
N of Corby. Off the A6003, 1m N
of Corby; 24m from Peterborough,
Northampton & Leicester; 30 mins
from the A1 & the M1 & 10 mins from
the A14 at Kettering.* **For NGS: Tue
25 June (11-7). Adm £8.50, chd
£2.50. Home-made teas. For other
opening times and information,
please visit garden website.**

Rockingham Castle

Rockingham Castle was built on the orders of William the Conqueror and offers a spectacular view over the Welland Valley. The original Motte and Bailey design still influences the sweeping formal gardens you see today. These inc a wealth of roses from hybrid teas to climbers covering every wall and features five key areas covering 13 acres, they are the terrace, the cross, rose garden, jewel borders and the dramatic wild garden. Light refreshments, cream teas, home-made cakes, coffee and wine in Walker's House Tearoom. Tickets can be booked online in advance through garden website or purchased on arrival at the ticket office. Disabled parking. Ramps provided. Accessible WC.

42 ROSEARIE-DE-LA-NYMPH
55 The Grove, Moulton, Northampton, NN3 7UE. Peter Hughes, Mary Morris, Irene Kay, Steven Hughes & Jeremy Stanton. *N of Northampton town. Turn off A43 at small r'about to Overstone Rd. Follow NGS signs in village. The garden is on the Holcot Rd out of Moulton.* **Sun 16, Sun 23 June (11-5). Adm £5, chd free. Home-made teas.**
We have been developing this romantic garden for about 20 yrs and now have over 1800 roses, inc English, French and Italian varieties. Many unusual water features and specimen trees. Ferns, inc tree ferns over 8ft high. Roses, scramblers and ramblers climb into trees, over arbours and arches. Collection of 140 Japanese maples. Mostly flat wheelchair access via a standard width doorway.

43 ROSI'S TAVERNA
20 St Francis Close, Barton Seagrave, Kettering, NN15 5DT. Rosi & David Labrum. *Approx 2m from J10 of the A14. Head towards Barton Seagrave, going through 3 sets of T-lights. At the 4th set turn R onto Warkton Ln. At the r'about turn L. Take the next 2 R turns into St Francis Cl.* **Sun 21 Apr, Sun 8 Sept (10-4). Combined adm with Briarwood £6.50, chd free. Light refreshments at Briarwood.**
An established medium south facing town garden. Kitchen garden intermingles with flowers, shrubs, plenty of fruit trees, soft fruits and vegetables in raised beds. Cacti and succulents hold high importance in the greenhouse. A new bog garden and a pyramid water feature are key elements in the garden. A unique taverna with mosaic flooring offers perfect shelter from sun, wind and drizzle.

GROUP OPENING

44 SPRATTON GARDENS
Smith Street, Spratton, NN6 8HP. *6½ m NNW of Northampton. Parking in Spratton Hall School car park, please follow yellow NGS signs from outskirts of village from A5199 or Brixworth Rd.* **Sun 9 June (11-5). Combined adm £7, chd free. Home-made teas.**

COTFIELD
Christina Warner-Keogh.

THE COTTAGE
Mrs Judith Elliott.

DALE HOUSE
Fiona & Chris Cox.

28 GORSE ROAD
Lee Miller.

11 HIGH STREET
Philip & Frances Roseblade.

MULBERRY COTTAGE
Kerry Herd.

OLD HOUSE FARM
Susie Marchant.

STONE HOUSE
John Forbear.

VALE VIEW
John Hunt.

25 YEW TREE LANE
Mrs Lise Beynon.

As well as attractive cottage gardens alongside old Northampton stone houses, Spratton also has unusual gardens, inc those showing good use of a small area; those dedicated to encouraging wildlife with views of the surrounding countryside; renovated gardens and those with new planting; courtyard garden; gravel garden with sculpture; no dig vegetable gardens; mature gardens with fruit trees and herbaceous borders. Refreshments in the Norman St Andrew's Church. The King's Head Pub will be open, lunch reservations recommended.

45 TITCHMARSH HOUSE
Chapel Street, Titchmarsh, NN14 3DA. Sir Ewan & Lady Harper, 01832 732439, ewan@ewanh.co.uk, www.titchmarsh-house.uk. *2m N of Thrapston. 6m S of Oundle. Exit A14 at junction signed A605, Titchmarsh signed as turning E towards Oundle & Peterborough.* **Mon 1 Apr, Mon 6 May (12-5); Mon 27 May (2-5). Adm £6, chd free. Visits also by arrangement 1 Apr to 22 June for groups of 10+.**
The gardens are spread over 4½ acres with formal and wild areas, a hedged quiet garden, and inc collections of naturalised bulbs, irises, peonies, magnolias, shrub roses, cherries, malus and a number of rare trees, expanded and planted by the existing owners over the past 55 yrs. Refreshments inc BBQ 12-2pm and teas 2-4.30pm (April and 6 May). Teas only 2-4.30pm (27 May). Wheelchair access to most of the garden without using steps. Sorry, no dogs.

46 WOODCOTE VILLA
Old Watling Street, Long Buckby Wharf, Long Buckby, Northampton, NN6 7EW. Sue & Geoff Woodward, geoff.and.sue@ btinternet.com. *2m NE of Daventry, just off A5. From M1 J16, take Flore by-pass, turn R at A5 r'about for approx 3m. From Daventry follow Long Buckby signs but turn L at A5 Xrds. From M1 J18 signed Kilsby, follow A5 S for approx 6m.* **Sun 24 Mar (1-5); Sun 21 July, Sun 1 Sept (11-5). Adm £4, chd free. Home-made teas. Gluten free option. Visits also by arrangement 5 Apr to 23 Aug for groups of 18 to 36. Tea & cake inc.**
In a much admired location, this stunning canal side garden has a large variety of plants, styles, structures and unusual bygones. Bulbs and hellebores abound in Mar, colourful planting in July/ Sept, many pots, all set against a backdrop of trees and shrubs in themed areas. Places to sit and watch the narrowboats and wildlife. Plants for sale (cash only). Sorry no WC. Wheelchair access via ramp at entrance to garden.

NOTTINGHAMSHIRE

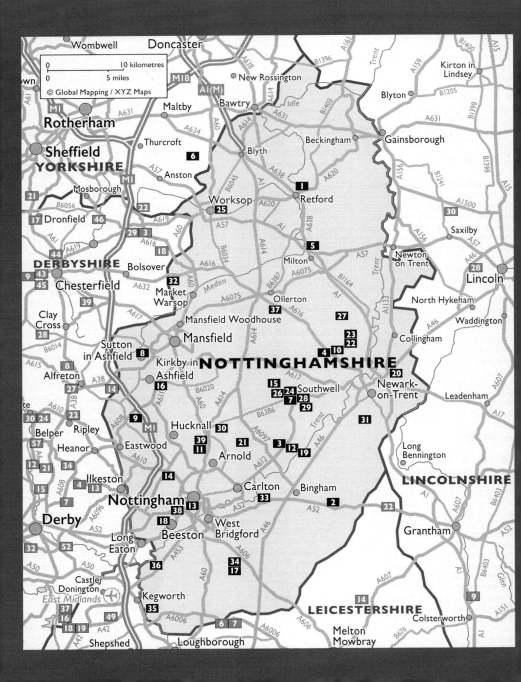

VOLUNTEERS

County Organiser
Georgina Denison
01636 821385
georgina.denison@ngs.org.uk

County Treasurer
Nicola Cressey
01159 655132
nicola.cressey@gmail.com

Publicity
Julie Davison
01302 719668
julie.davison@ngs.org.uk

Social Media
Malcolm Turner
01159 222831
malcolm.turner14@btinternet.com

Booklet Co-ordinator
Martyn Faulconbridge
01949 850942
mjfaulconbridge@gmail.com,

Assistant County Organisers
Linda Pacey
07972 480651
linda.pacey@ngs.org.uk

Beverley Perks
01636 812181
perks.family@talk21.com

Mary Thomas
01509 672056
nursery@piecemealplants.co.uk

Andrew Young
01623 863327
andrew.young@ngs.org.uk

@National Garden
Scheme Nottinghamshire

@ngs_nottinghamshire

OPENING DATES

All entries subject to change.
For latest information check
www.ngs.org.uk

Map locator numbers are
shown to the right of each
garden name.

February

Snowdrop Openings

Friday 2nd
1 Highfield Road   14

Sunday 4th
1 Highfield Road   14

Sunday 18th
Church Farm   5
Norwood Park   24

April

Saturday 20th
Capability Barn   3

Sunday 21st
Capability Barn   3
♦ Felley Priory   9

Saturday 27th
Oasis Community Gardens   25

May

Sunday 12th
NEW The Poplars   31

Thursday 16th
Rhubarb Farm   32

Saturday 18th
The Old Vicarage   26

Sunday 19th
10 Harlaxton Drive   13
6 Hope Street   18
38 Main Street   21
♦ Norwell Nurseries   23

Sunday 26th
The Palace Garden of Southwell
    Minster   28

June

Saturday 8th
Hill's Farm   15
The Old Vicarage   26

Sunday 9th
Home Farm House, 17 Main
    Street   17
NEW Hoveringham Gardens   19
Rose Cottage   34

Sunday 16th
Patchings Art Centre   30
Thrumpton Hall   36

Thursday 20th
Rhubarb Farm   32

Saturday 22nd
Clyde House   7
NEW Langford Hall   20

Sunday 23rd
Hollinside   16

Sunday 30th
10 Harlaxton Drive   13
Norwell Gardens   22
Ossington House   27

July

Wednesday 3rd
Norwell Gardens   22

Saturday 6th
Sutton Bonington Gardens   35

Sunday 7th
5 Burton Lane   2
Caunton Manor   4
Sutton Bonington Gardens   35

Saturday 13th
Floral Media   10

Sunday 14th
8 Church Lane   6
East Meets West   8

Thursday 18th
Rhubarb Farm   32

Saturday 20th
Park Farm   29

Sunday 21st
The Old Vicarage   26

August

Saturday 10th
NEW Glebe Steading   12

Sunday 11th
Gaunts Hill   11
NEW Glebe Steading   12

Thursday 15th
Rhubarb Farm   32

Sunday 18th
NEW The Poplars   31
University Park Gardens   38

Saturday 24th
Oasis Community Gardens   25

Sunday 25th
The Old Vicarage   26

Monday 26th
5 Burton Lane   2

September

Sunday 22nd
◆ Norwell Nurseries   23

By Arrangement

Arrange a personalised garden visit with your club, or group of friends, on a date to suit you. See individual garden entries for full details.

Bolham Manor   1
5 Burton Lane   2
8 Church Lane   6
10 Harlaxton Drive   13
Home Farm House, 17 Main
   Street   17
6 Hope Street   18
38 Main Street   21
Oasis Community Gardens   25
The Old Vicarage   26
Park Farm   29
Patchings Art Centre   30
NEW The Poplars   31
Riseholme, 125 Shelford Road   33
Rose Cottage   34
Tithe Barn   37
Waxwings & Goldcrest   39

Caunton Manor

THE GARDENS

1 BOLHAM MANOR

Bolham Way, Bolham, Retford, DN22 9JG. Pam & Butch Barnsdale, 07790 896022, pamandbutch@hotmail.co.uk. *1m from Retford. A620 Gainsborough Rd from Retford, turn L onto Tiln Ln, signed 'A620 avoiding low bridge'. At sharp R bend take rd ahead to Tiln then L Bolham Way.* **Visits by arrangement 10 Feb to 21 Sept for groups of up to 25. Adm £5, chd free. Light refreshments.**
This 3 acre mature garden provides year-round interest. In February, swathes of snowdrops greet you, followed by daffodils and other spring bulbs. Topiary features and sculptures guide you through the different areas of the garden, with its mixed planted terraces and herbaceous borders, ponds, orchard and wildflower areas. Partial wheelchair access to parts of garden.

2 5 BURTON LANE

Whatton in the Vale, NG13 9EQ. Ms Faulconbridge, 01949 850942, jpfaulconbridge@hotmail.co.uk, www.ayearinthegardenblog. wordpress.com. *3m E of Bingham. Follow signs to Whatton from A52 between Bingham & Elton. Garden nr Church in old part of village. Follow yellow NGS signs.* **Sun 7 July, Mon 26 Aug (11-4). Adm £4, chd free. Home-made teas. Drinks and cakes suitable for special dietary requirements are available. Visits also by arrangement 1 June to 14 Sept for groups of up to 25.**
Organic cottage style garden which is productive, highly decorative and wildlife friendly. It is full of colour and scent from spring to autumn. Several distinct areas inc fruit and vegetables. Large beds filled with over 600 varieties of plants with paths you can wander and get close. Also features seating, gravel garden, pond, shade planting, pergola with grapevine, wildflower lawn. Attractive village with walks.

3 CAPABILITY BARN

Gonalston Lane, Hoveringham, NG14 7JH. Malcolm & Wendy Fisher, www.capabilitybarn.com. *8m NE of Nottingham. A612 from Nottingham through Lowdham. Take 1st R into Gonalston Ln. Garden is 1m on L.* **Sat 20, Sun 21 Apr (11-4.30). Adm £5, chd free. Home-made teas. Opening with Hoveringham Gardens on Sun 9 June.**
Imaginatively planted large country garden with something new each year. April brings displays of daffodils, hyacinths and tulips along with erythroniums, brunneras and primulas. Wisteria, magnolia, rhodos and apple blossom greet May/June. A backdrop of established trees, shrubs and shady paths give a charming country setting. Large vegetable/fruit gardens with orchard/meadow completes the picture.

4 CAUNTON MANOR

Manor Road, Caunton, Newark, NG23 6AD. Sir John & Lady Peace. *6m from Newark & Southwell. Approach off the A616 signposted Caunton. Entry is through 2 large wrought iron gates opp the playing field next to Dean Hole sch.* **Sun 7 July (1-4). Adm £6, chd free. Tea.**
The fine gardens date from C18 but are in vivid C21 development. Kitchen garden, glasshouses, well garden, orchard, arboretum. A walled garden with generous borders still shelters two climbing roses introduced by Dean Hole the famous Victorian rose grower who once lived at Caunton Manor.

5 CHURCH FARM

Church Lane, West Drayton, Retford, DN22 8EB. Robert & Isabel Adam. *5m S of Retford. A1 exit Markham Moor. A638 Retford 500 yds signed West Drayton. ¾m, turn R, into Church Ln, 1st R past church. Ample parking in farm yard.* **Sun 18 Feb (10.30-4). Adm £4, chd free. Light refreshments. Served from 11.30am.**
Essentially a spring garden with a woodland area carpeted with snowdrops, aconites and cyclamen which have seeded also into the adjoining churchyard. Approximately180 named snowdrops flourish in island beds, along with hellebores and daffodils. Natural planting contrasts with elegant topiary. Refreshments available.

6 8 CHURCH LANE

Letwell, Worksop, S81 8DE. Vicky Bennett, 07795 058490, yvv.bennett64@gmail.com. *approx midway between Tickhill and Worksop. Turn off B6463 to Ramper Rd (signposted Letwell). At the end follow 90 degree bend to the R. Then Church Ln forks off to R. No 8 is the last property on the L, opp the church.* **Sun 14 July (1-5). Adm £6, chd free. Pre-booking essential, please visit www.ngs. org.uk for information & booking. Home-made teas. Visits also by arrangement 10 July to 10 Aug for groups of 10 to 36. £10 adm inc refreshments.**
An award-winning, professionally designed garden in ⅓ acre. The free-flowing lawn is surrounded by colourful, naturalistic borders with trees, shrubs, grasses and perennials. An informal path runs through a colourful gravel garden, planted with aromatics and grasses leading to the wildlife pond and sunken garden with oak pergola. Short woodland walk. Ample seating. Disabled parking on drive. Grade II listed church also open. Contact owner if difficulty with online booking.

7 CLYDE HOUSE

23 Westgate, Southwell, NG25 0JN. John & Lucy Murkett. *Near centre of Southwell. Pass Southwell Minister on L on Westgate. Garden entrance signed with NGS yellow arrow on L into a footpath between 21 & 23 Westgate. 1st gate on the R.* **Sat 22 June (1-5). Adm £5, chd free. Home-made teas.**
Secret, intriguing, organic walled garden in the centre of Southwell, first opened for NGS 1983 now reopened. Formal area rear of house mirrors wisteria clad Georgian house with C13/14 listed stone arch. Sweeping lawn bottom of broad steps with long and circular herbaceous borders. Through to beautiful wildflower meadow, wildlife pond, fruit, veg, cut flower beds with greenhouse and compost bins.

8 EAST MEETS WEST

85 Cowpes Close, Sutton-in-Ashfield, NG17 2BU. Kate & Mel Calladine. *Close to Quarrydale Sch entrance to Carsic Housing Estate. Passing Quarrydale Sch on B6028 on R, take 2nd L onto Carsic Rd then 1st L to Cowpes Cl. Please park thoughtfully so not to interfere with our neighbours access.* **Sun 14 July (12-4). Adm £3, chd free. Pre-booking essential, please visit www.ngs.org.uk for information & booking.**

Our very small but lovely garden combines the tranquillity of the Orient with the colour of a traditional English cottage garden. East: We have a number of sizable acers, bamboos and Japanese lanterns. A stream flows past a cloud pruned shrub into a pond with goldfish and water lilies. West: A trompe l'oeil arch creates a magical garden illusion. A 'rainbow' flower bed.
❀

9 ◆ FELLEY PRIORY

Underwood, NG16 5FJ. The Brudenell Family, 01773 810230, michelle@felleypriory.co.uk, www.felleypriory.co.uk. *8m SW of Mansfield. Off A608 ½m W M1 J27.* **For NGS: Sun 21 Apr (10-4). Adm £6.50, chd free. Light refreshments. For other opening times and information, please phone, email or visit garden website.**

Garden for all seasons with yew hedges and topiary, snowdrops, hellebores, herbaceous borders and rose garden. There are pergolas, a white garden, small arboretum and borders filled with unusual trees, shrubs, plants and bulbs. The grass edged pond is planted with primulas, bamboo, iris, roses and eucomis. Bluebell woodland walk. Orchard with extremely rare daffodils. This garden is proud to provide plants for the National Garden Scheme's Show Garden at Chelsea Flower Show 2024.
♿ ❀ 🚗 ☕))

10 FLORAL MEDIA

Norwell Road, Caunton, Newark, NG23 6AQ. Mr & Mrs Steve Routledge, 07811 399113, info@floralmedia.co.uk, www.floralmedia.co.uk. *Take Norwell Rd from Caunton. Approx ½m from Caunton on L.* **Sat 13 July (10-4). Adm £4, chd free. Home-made teas.**

A beautifully maintained country garden. Beds overflowing with a variety of roses, shrubs and flowers. A gravel/oriental garden, cutting gardens, vegetable beds, Flower Farm supplying British grown stems to florists/farm shops. Long sweeping borders surrounding the main lawn leading to the wildflower meadows where you will find an interesting garden retreat. A horticulturalist's haven. Excellent facilities, refreshments, plenty of parking. Often live music in the garden from a local folk group of musicians. A good range of plants available for sale. Full wheelchair access inc disabled WC.
♿ 🐕 ❀ 🚗 ☕))

Clyde House

1 GAUNTS HILL

Bestwood Lodge, Arnold, NG5 8NF. Nigel & Penny Lymn Rose. *5m N of Nottingham. Take Bestwood Lodge Dr up to the Bestwood Lodge Hotel, then turn R & continue until you see a sign saying vehicle access to stables only. Then turn R down the drive through the gates.* **Sun 11 Aug (11-3). Adm £5, chd free. Light refreshments.**
A large country garden with ponds, mature woodlands, greenhouse, borders, lawns and vegetable plot. Car parking available in an adjacent field. Enclosed within a listed Victorian wall. This was the walled kitchen garden built for the 10th Duke of St Albans. There is a mulberry tree planted by the then Prince of Wales. Livestock inc peacock, chickens and doves. Original Victorian circular pond, French fountain, two gazebos. Some gravel paths and lawns. There are some steps but these can be avoided.

2 NEW GLEBE STEADING

Gonalston, Nottingham, NG14 7JA. Smita and Craig Jobling. *Gonalston. 1st R off A612 from Southwell into village, 1st house on R. Green outbuildings and barn conversion. Signs on Gate post and by roadside turn off.* **Sat 10, Sun 11 Aug (2-5). Adm £5, chd free. Home-made teas.**
Welcome to a garden designed around a small pool, with full brightly coloured borders and plants reminiscent of the owner's childhood in Kenya, mingled with grasses for a looser feel. Flowering perennials attract pollinators and are left standing tall. A hillside of 35 trees with coppice/orchard and small kitchen garden. A small stream runs down the slope with a botanical medicinal border. Small natural pool with a summerhouse.

3 10 HARLAXTON DRIVE

Lenton, Nottingham, NG7 1JA. Jan Brazier, 07968 420046, jan-28b@hotmail.com, www. instagram.com/citygarden_oasis. *W of Nottingham city centre. From Nottingham centre, follow Derby Rd signs (A52), past St Barnabas Cathedral & just after Canning Circus, take 3rd L. From M1 J25, take A52 Nottingham & after 7m, 5th R after Savoy cinema.* **Sun 19 May, Sun 30 June (11-4). Adm £5, chd free. Home-made teas. Visits also by arrangement 19 May to 31 Aug**

for groups of 15+. Adm £5.00. Tea and biscuits extra.
City centre oasis, a short walk from the centre of Nottingham. Garden presented on three levels, separated by steep steps with handrails. The top terrace overlooks a large koi pond surrounded by bog plants, marginals and herbaceous perennials. Seating areas on second terrace under mature beech trees. On third level, a summerhouse as well as a small pond and densely-planted borders. Free on-street parking.

4 1 HIGHFIELD ROAD

Nuthall, Nottingham, NG16 1BQ. Richard & Sue Bold. *4 mins from J26 of the M1- 4m NW of Nottingham City. From J26 of the M1 take the A610 towards Notts. R lane at r'about, take turn-off to Horsendale. Follow rd to Woodland Dr, then 2nd R is Highfield Rd.* **Fri 2, Sun 4 Feb (10-3.30). Adm £5, chd free. Light refreshments. Tea, coffee, fruit teas and squash. Bacon rolls, sausage rolls, a variety of home-made cakes will be available including a gluten free option.**
Visit in Feb to see the collection of 700+ snowdrop varieties, with 300 varieties in the garden and many more in show benches. The spring garden has lots of colour with many rare and unusual plants - miniature narcissus, acers, aconites and hellebores A good selection of unusual pots and garden ornaments. Many snowdrop varieties and other plants available for sale.

5 HILL'S FARM

Edingley, NG22 8BU. John & Margaret Hill. *1 m drive or walk W. Hill's Farm wildflower meadow is a short drive of 1/2 m towards Edingley & turn R at brow of the hill as signed into tarmac farmyard for parking. Adm tickets at Old Vicarage.* **Sat 8 June (1-4.30). Combined adm with The Old Vicarage £6, chd free. Home-made teas at The Old Vicarage as usual in Halam (next door village).**
Created with passion to produce a delightful walk - 6 acres of Nottinghamshire hay meadow carpeted with colourful wildflowers - ragged robin, yellow rattle, pyramidal orchids. 40+ acres of this mixed organic farm were taken out of arable production 2006 to create traditional hay meadows - hay taken in July is fed

to the native beef shorthorn cattle. See some of the cows in adjoining fields.

6 HOLLINSIDE

252 Diamond Avenue, Kirkby-in-Ashfield, Nottingham, NG17 7NA. Sue & Bob Chalkley. *1m E of Kirkby in Ashfield at the Xrds of the A611 & B6020. Please park away from the busy junction.* **Sun 23 June (1-5). Adm £3, chd free. Home-made teas.**
A formal front garden with terraced lawns and borders lead to a shaded area with ferns, camellias, roses, hydrangeas and other flowering shrubs. The rear garden has a wildlife pond, a wildflower meadow, a summerhouse and a Victorian style greenhouse. There are topiary box and yews and a box parterre planted with roses. Majority of garden is suitable for wheelchairs. Disabled parking near house by prior arrangement.

7 HOME FARM HOUSE, 17 MAIN STREET

Keyworth, Nottingham, NG12 5AA. Graham & Pippa Tinsley, 07780 672196, Graham_Tinsley@yahoo.co.uk, www.homefarmgarden.wordpress. com. *7m S of Nottingham. Follow signs for Keyworth from A60 or A606 & head for church. Garden about 50yds down Main St. Parking on the street or at village hall or Bunny Ln car parks.* **Sun 9 June (12-5). Combined adm with Rose Cottage £5, chd free. Home-made teas. Visits also by arrangement May to Sept for groups of up to 30.**
Large garden behind old farm near village centre. The old paddock is an ornamental wilderness of unmown grass with perennials, a turf mound and wildlife ponds with clipped yew hedges surrounded by maturing trees. The cart shed is rebuilt as a pergola with roses and the old garden with more roses and perennial borders is divided from the orchard by high hedges creating hidden places to explore. Interesting and unusual perennials for sale by Piecemeal Plants (www.piecemealplants.co.uk).

18 6 HOPE STREET

Beeston, Nottingham, NG9 1DR.
Elaine Liquorish, 01159 223239,
eliquorish@outlook.com. *From
M1 J25, A52 for Nottm. After 2
r'abouts, turn R for Beeston at
The Nurseryman (B6006). Beyond
hill, turn R into Bramcote Dr. 3rd
turn on L into Bramcote Rd, then
immed R into Hope St.* **Sun 19 May
(1.30-5). Adm £4, chd free. Light
refreshments inc a selection of
cakes, cream scones, tea, coffee
and cold drinks. Visits also by
arrangement 19 May to 9 Aug for
groups of 5 to 20.**
A small garden packed with a wide
variety of plants providing flower
and foliage colour year-round.
Collections of alpines, bulbs, mini,
small and medium size hostas (60+),
ferns, grasses, carnivorous plants,
succulents, perennials, shrubs and
trees. A pond and a greenhouse with
subtropical plants. Troughs and pots.
Home-made crafts. Shallow step into
garden, into greenhouse and at rear.
No wheelchair access to plant sales
area or the back garden.

GROUP OPENING

19 NEW HOVERINGHAM GARDENS

Hoveringham, NG14 7JP. *Between
Nottingham and Southwell.
Hoveringham is S of A612, 2 m E
of Lowdham. All 7 gardens clearly
marked. 3 entry roads inc at least
1 garden. Park in village and walk
to many. Tickets purchased at
all gardens.* **Sun 9 June (11-
4.30). Combined adm £6, chd
free. Home-made teas in the
Village Hall. Pimms served at
Hoveringham Hall (not Village
Hall).**

NEW BIRCH END
Diane Roberts.

CAPABILITY BARN
Malcolm & Wendy Fisher.
(See separate entry)

CHURCH HOUSE
Alex & Sue Allan.

NEW HOVERINGHAM HALL

NEW MYRTLE COTTAGE
Mrs Val Parker.

NEW ROSE BANK
Nicholas and Clare Litherland.

NEW WATER'S EDGE
Chris and Pauline Bulpitt.

We would love you to visit
Hoveringham - a pretty village by the
River Trent which inc a church, a pub
and Village Hall, where teas will be
served. There are seven gardens, two
of which are beautiful, contrasting well
established NGS gardens. The two
small group gardens are exquisitely
planted and inc a Bonsai collection.
The three larger traditional gardens
inc the rambling grounds of the Hall
where Pimms will be served under
elegant mature trees on the lawn
with sweeping views and a riverside
property which boasts a rose garden
and Orchid house - the large gardens
inc herbaceous borders, rock
gardens, ornamental trees, growing
areas and greenhouses. There will
be Bric-a-Brac/Plant stalls and Clog
Dancing arranged for 2.15pm and
3.30pm. Be sure to look out for a
Victorian Orchard, Victorian Water
Tower and Greenhouse and, probably,
the oldest swing in Notts.

20 NEW LANGFORD HALL

Langford, Newark, NG23 7RS.
James and Beth Sumsion. *3m N of
Newark Upon Trent. From S, take the
A46 N to Lincoln. Langford Hall is 150
metres N of the A46/A1133 Newark
Showground r'about, the entrance is
straight off the A46 N bound carriage
way.* **Sat 22 June (1-5). Adm £6, chd
free. Light refreshments provided
by Winthorpe WI.**
Langford Hall is a Grade II listed country
house, built in 1774 by John Carr of
York. The large garden showcases
vibrant perennial flower beds, the rose
garden boasts a central lily pond and in
the courtyard, a majestic mulberry tree
stands tall. There is a highly productive
orchard and vegetable garden and
for those who appreciate nature, a
woodland trail to explore. In dry weather
most of the garden is accessible to
wheelchairs.

21 38 MAIN STREET

Woodborough, Nottingham,
NG14 6EA. Martin Taylor & Deborah
Bliss, 07999 786097. *About 8m NE of
Nottingham centre. Turn off Mapperley
Plains Rd at sign for Woodborough.
Alternatively, follow signs to
Woodborough off A6097 (Epperstone
bypass). Property is between Park Av
& Bank Hill.* **Sun 19 May (1-5). Adm
£4, chd free. Home-made teas
inc home made cake, tea, coffee,
squash. £4 for cake and drink.**

**Visits also by arrangement 1 May to
16 June for groups of 8 to 15.**
Started as a lawn at the front and
the back and 125 junipers and one
rosebush. Now a varied ⅓ acre.
Bamboo fenced Asian species area
with traditional outdoor wood fired
Ofuro bath, herbaceous border, raised
species rhododendron bed, vegetables,
greenhouse, pond area and art studio
and terrace. The art studio will be open.

GROUP OPENING

22 NORWELL GARDENS

Newark, NG23 6JX. *6m N of
Newark. Halfway between Newark
& Southwell. Off A1 at Cromwell
turning, take Norwell Rd at bus
shelter. Or off A616 take Caunton
turn.* **Sun 30 June (1-5). Evening
opening Wed 3 July (6-8.30).
Combined adm £6, chd free.
Home-made teas in Village Hall
(30 June) and Norwell Nurseries
(3 July).**

CHERRY TREE HOUSE
Simon & Caroline Wyatt.

FAUNA FOLLIES
Lorraine & Roy Pilgrim.

**NORWELL ALLOTMENTS /
PARISH GARDENS**
Norwell Parish Council.

◆ NORWELL NURSERIES
Andrew & Helen Ward.
(See separate entry)

PINFOLD COTTAGE
Mrs Pat. Foulds.

ROSE COTTAGE
Mr Iain & Mrs Ann Gibson.

This is the 28th year that Norwell
has opened a range of different, very
appealing gardens all making superb
use of the beautiful backdrop of a
quintessentially English countryside
village. Inc a garden and nursery of
national renown. To top it all there
are a plethora of breathtaking village
gardens showing the diversity that
is achieved under the umbrella of
a cottage garden description. The
beautiful medieval church and its
peaceful churchyard with grass
labyrinth will be open for quiet
contemplation.

23 ◆ NORWELL NURSERIES

Woodhouse Road, Norwell, NG23 6JX. Andrew & Helen Ward, 01636 636337, wardha@aol.com, www.norwellnurseries.co.uk. *6m N of Newark halfway between Newark & Southwell. Off A1 at Cromwell turning, take rd to Norwell at bus stop. Or from A616 take Caunton turn.* **For NGS: Sun 19 May, Sun 22 Sept (2-5). Adm £4, chd free. Home-made teas in Norwell Village Hall, Carlton Ln, on Sunday 30th June, other dates at the nurseries. Opening with Norwell Gardens on Sun 30 June, Wed 3 July. For other opening times and information, please phone, email or visit garden website.**

Jewel box of over 3,000 different, beautiful and unusual plants sumptuously set out in a one acre plantsman's garden inc shady garden with orchids, woodland gems, cottage garden borders, alpine and scree areas. Pond with opulently planted margins. Extensive herbaceous borders and effervescent colour themed beds. Sand beds showcase Mediterranean, North American and alpine plants. Nationally renowned nursery open with over 1,500 different rare plants for sale. Autumn opening features UK's largest collection of hardy chrysanthemums for sale and the National Collection of Hardy Chrysanthemums. New borders inc the National Collection Of Astrantias. Innovative sand beds. Grass paths, no wheelchair access to woodland paths.

&. ❀ 🚗 [NPC] ☕

24 NORWOOD PARK

Halam Road, Southwell, NG25 0PF. Sir John Starkey, 01636 302099, events@norwoodpark.co.uk, www.norwoodpark.co.uk. *NW edge of Southwell. From Southwell follow brown signs to Norwood Park.* **Sun 18 Feb (11-4). Adm £7.50, chd free. Light refreshments at Norwood Park Golf Club. Hot apple punch served at the Temple.**

The grounds of Norwood Park date back to medieval times when they were part of a series of deer parks. A new garden on the south front of the C18 house was created in 2021 to showcase plants for all seasons. To the west a lime avenue lined with snowdrops and daffodils leads on to Mrs Delaney's Path to the ornamental temple.

&. 🐎 ❀ 🚗 🛏 ☕))

25 OASIS COMMUNITY GARDENS

2a Longfellow Drive, Kilton Estate, Worksop, S81 0DE. Steve Williams, 07795 194957, Stevemark126@hotmail.com, www.oasiscommunitycentre.org. *Nottinghamshire. From Kilton Hill (leading to the Worksop hospital), take 1st exit to R (up hill) onto Kilton Cres, then 1st exit on R Longfellow Dr. Car Park off Dickens Rd (1st R).* **Sat 27 Apr, Sat 24 Aug (10-3). Adm £4, chd free. Visits also by arrangement 1 Mar to 1 Oct for groups of up to 30.**

Oasis Gardens is a community project transformed from abandoned field to an award winning garden. Managed by volunteers the gardens boast over 30 project areas, several garden enterprises and hosts many community events. Take a look in the Cactus Kingdom, the Liquorice Garden, Pre-school play village, Wildlife Wonderland and the wonderful variety of trees, plants, seasonal flowers and shrubs. The Oasis Gardens hosts the first Liquorice Garden in Worksop for 100 years. The site hosts the 'Flowers for Life' project which is a therapeutic gardening project growing and selling cut flowers and floristry. There is disabled access from Longfellow Drive. From the town end there is a driveway after the first fence on the right next to house number 2.

&. ❀ ☕))

26 THE OLD VICARAGE

Halam Hill, Halam, NG22 8AX. Mrs Beverley Perks, 01636 812181, perks.family@talk21.com. *1m W of Southwell, 1st house on L as entering Halam village. Please park diagonally into beech hedge on verge with speed interactive sign or in village - a busy road so no parking on roadside.* **Sat 18 May (1-4.30). Adm £5, chd free. Sat 8 June (1-4.30). Combined adm with Hill's Farm £6, chd free. Sun 21 July, Sun 25 Aug (1-4.30). Adm £5, chd free. Home-made teas at The Old Vicarage for all openings. Visits also by arrangement 20 May to 16 Aug for groups of 15 to 30. Welcome talk and accompanied tour included for by arrangement visits.**

An artful eye for design/texture/colour/love of unusual plants/trees makes this a welcoming gem to visit. One time playground for 4 children, this 2 acre organic hillside garden has matured over 27yrs into a much admired, popular, landscape garden with beautiful views. New garden

planting/design at the bottom - pond attracts diverse wildlife to complement plantings. A garden in its penultimate year of opening. Beautiful C12 Church open only a short walk into the village or across field through attractively planted churchyard - rare C14 stained glass window. Guitar Duo Paul & Paul may play live at one of the July/Aug openings. Short gravel drive at entrance - undulating levels as on a hillside - plenty of cheerful help available.

&. 🐎 ❀ 🚗 ☕))

27 OSSINGTON HOUSE

Moorhouse Road, Ossington, Newark, NG23 6LD. Georgina Denison. *10m N of Newark, 2m off A1. From A1 N take exit marked Carlton, Sutton-on-Trent, Weston etc. At T-junc turn L to Kneesall. Drive 2m to Ossington. Roadside parking on Main St and Moorhouse Rd.* **Sun 30 June (2-5). Adm £6, chd free. Home-made teas in The Hut, Ossington.**

Vicarage garden redesigned in 1960 and again in 2014. Chestnuts, lawns, formal beds, woodland walk, poolside planting, orchard. Terraces, yews, grasses. Ferns, herbaceous perennials, roses and kitchen garden. Disabled parking available in drive to Ossington House.

&. ❀ 🚗 [D] ☕

28 THE PALACE GARDEN OF SOUTHWELL MINSTER

Church Street, Southwell, NG25 0HD. Southwell Minster, www.southwellminster.org/theme/palace-gardens. *Centre of Southwell, Notts. Once at The Minster make your way to the South Door, opp the Archbishop's Palace, & follow the NGS yellow arrow & sign post down the footpath L for approx 40m to the garden entrance.* **Sun 26 May (11-4). Adm £5, chd free. Home-made teas in the Octagon Minster Palace Gardens or The Minster if available. Tea/coffee and home-made cakes.**

Set amongst magnificent ruins of The Archbishop's Palace the garden is packed with shrubs, flowering plants, mature trees, lawns and medieval herb garden. Sculptures/literature provide links to the 'Leaves of Southwell', C13 stone leaf carvings - Minster's Chapter House. Separate grasslands (short walk) to Potwell Dyke are not to be missed - a spectacular array of wild flowers and many orchids. The Minster, churchyard & garden are accessible to wheelchairs. The grasslands are not accessible.

&. 🐎 ❀ 🚗 ☕))

29 PARK FARM

Crink Lane, Southwell, NG25 0TJ.
Ian & Vanessa Johnston,
01636 812195,
v.johnston100@gmail.com. *1m SE
of Southwell. From Southwell town
centre go down Church St, turn R on
to Fiskerton Rd & 200yds up hill turn
R into Crink Ln. Park Farm is on 2nd
bend.* **Sat 20 July (1-4.30). Adm
£5, chd free. Home-made teas.
Visits also by arrangement 20 Apr
to 26 July for groups of up to 30.
Guided visits (min 10 visitors) £1
extra per person.**
3 acre garden noted for its extensive
variety of trees, shrubs and
perennials, many rare or unusual.
Long luxuriant herbaceous borders,
rose arches, alpine/scree garden,
large wildlife pond and area of
woodland and acid loving plants.
Spectacular views of the Minster
across a wildflower meadow and
ha-ha.

30 PATCHINGS ART CENTRE

Oxton Road, Calverton, Nottingham,
NG14 6NU. Chas & Pat Wood,
01159 653479,
Chas@patchingsartcentre.co.uk,
www.patchingsartcentre.co.uk. *N
of Nottingham city take A614 towards
Ollerton. Turn R on to B6386 towards
Calverton & Oxton. Patchings is on
L before turning to Calverton. Brown
tourist directional signs.* **Sun 16 June
(10.30-3). Adm £3, chd free. Light
refreshments at Patchings Café.
Visits also by arrangement June to
Aug. The visit will include a short
illustrative talk about Patchings.**
Promoting the enjoyment of art.
Established in 1988, Patchings is set
in 50 acres with a visitor centre and
galleries - a haven for artists and a
tranquil setting for visitors. Visitors
may watch artists at work on the
surrounding views. An exhibition of
recent work in oil and watercolour
by David Curtis ROI, RSMA will be
on show in the Barn Gallery. The
Patchings Artists' Trail - a walk
through art history, famous paintings
presented in glass takes visitors
through the centuries. Artists painting
in the grounds during NGS Day. Grass
and compacted gravel paths with
some undulations and uphill sections
accessible to wheelchairs with help.
Please enquire for assistance.

31 NEW THE POPLARS

Cotham Lane, Hawton, Newark,
NG24 3RL. Ian Brownhill &
Michael Hirschl, 07970 126318,
ian@staghill.co.uk. *Hawton village
is approx 2m S of Newark-on-Trent.
House is 2nd turning on the L past
All Saint's church in Hawton village.
Parking in All Saint's church car park.*
**Sun 12 May, Sun 18 Aug (2-5.30).
Adm £5, chd free. Home-made
teas. Visits also by arrangement
10 June to 27 Sept for groups of
10 to 25.**
1.2 acre garden being extensively
remodeled and replanted by its current
owners. Garden wraps around an
early Georgian farmhouse (not open).
Explore a number of distinct areas inc a
formal garden planted with ornamental
grasses and white-flowering plants,
a large Mediterranean-style gravel
patio, productive garden, new orchard,
wildflower areas and courtyard.
Masses of spring bulbs. The garden
is wheelchair accessible (driveways,
lawned areas) apart from the gravel
patio.

32 RHUBARB FARM

Hardwick Street, Langwith, nr
Mansfield, NG20 9DR. Rhubarb
Farm, www.rhubarbfarm.co.uk.
*On NW border of Nottinghamshire
in village of Nether Langwith. From
A632 in Langwith, by bridge (single
file traffic) turn up steep Devonshire
Dr. Then turn off SatNav. Take 2nd L
into Hardwick St. Rhubarb Farm at
end. Parking to R of gates.* **Thur 16
May, Thur 20 June, Thur 18 July,
Thur 15 Aug (10.30-3). Adm £3,
chd free. Light refreshments in
on-site café, made by Rhubarb
Farm volunteers.**
This 2 acre horticultural social enterprise
provides training and volunteering
opportunities to 60 ex-offenders, drug
and alcohol misusers, older people,
school students, people with mental
and physical ill health and learning
disabilities. Eight polytunnels, 100
hens, pigs, donkey and a Shetland
pony. Forest school barn, willow dome
and arch, large Keder polytunnel
(bubblewrap walls), flower borders,
Farm shop, pond, raised beds, comfrey
bed and comfrey fertiliser factory, junk
sculpture, Heath Robinson Feature.
Chance to meet and chat with
volunteers and staff. Main path suitable
for wheelchairs but bumpy. Not all site
accessible. Cafe & composting toilet
wheelchair-accessible.

33 RISEHOLME, 125 SHELFORD ROAD

Radcliffe on Trent, NG12 1AZ.
John & Elaine Walker,
01159 119867, elaine.walker10@
hotmail.co.uk. *4m E of Nottingham.
From A52 follow signs to Radcliffe.
In village centre take turning for
Shelford (by Co-op). Approx 3/4m
on L.* **Visits by arrangement June
& July for groups of 15 to 50.
Adm £5, chd free. Home-made
teas. Cost of refreshments to be
discussed when booking with the
garden owner.**
Imaginative and inspirational is how
the garden has been described by
visitors. A huge variety of perennials,
grasses, shrubs and trees combined
with an eye for colour and design.
Jungle area with exotic lush planting
contrasts with tender perennials
particularly salvias thriving in raised
beds and in gravel garden with
stream. Unique and interesting
objects complement planting.
Artwork, fairies and dragons feature in
the garden!

34 ROSE COTTAGE

81 Nottingham Road, Keyworth,
Nottingham, NG12 5GS. Richard
& Julie Fowkes, 01159 376489,
richardfowkes@yahoo.co.uk.
*7m S of Nottingham. Follow signs
for Keyworth from A606. Garden
(white cottage) on R 100yds after
Sainsburys. From A60, follow
Keyworth signs & turn L at church,
garden is 400yds on L.* **Sun 9 June
(12-5). Combined adm with Home
Farm House, 17 Main Street £5,
chd free. Home-made teas. Visits
also by arrangement 1 May to 30
Aug for groups of 8 to 30.**
As featured in Garden News
magazine, and described as "A
heavily planted heaven", with colourful
wildlife-friendly plants. This is a small
cottage garden with features such as
a sedum roof, decked seating area,
summerhouse and water features.
Different planting zones add unique
interest. A wildlife stream meanders
down between ponds and bog
areas. Art studio open. Paintings and
crafts by Julie will be on sale. Plants
available from local nurseryman.

Piecemeal

GROUP OPENING

35 SUTTON BONINGTON GARDENS

Main Street, Sutton Bonington, Loughborough, LE12 5PE. *2m SE of Kegworth (M1 J24). 6m NW of Loughborough. From A6 Kegworth, past University of Nottingham Sutton Bonington campus. From Loughborough, A6 then A6006. From Nottingham, A60 then A6006.* **Sat 6, Sun 7 July (2-6). Combined adm £6, chd free. Home-made teas at Forge Cottage and 118 Main Street.**

FORGE COTTAGE
Judith & David Franklin.

118 MAIN STREET
Alistair Cameron & Shelley Nicholls.

PIECEMEAL
Mary Thomas.

All 3 gardens are located at the north end of the village, near St Michael's Church and just a few minutes' walk apart. Piecemeal has a tiny walled garden featuring a wide range of unusual shrubs, most in terracotta pots bordering narrow paths. Also climbers, perennials and even a few trees! Focus is on distinctive form, foliage shape and colour combination. Half-hardy and tender plants fill the conservatory. Forge Cottage garden, a little larger and reclaimed from a blacksmith's yard, has vibrant, curved herbaceous borders extending into a woodland path. 118 Main Street is a large garden with well established trees and varied planting as well as an orchard/wildflower meadow. Varied features inc Japanese-inspired seating area, redesigned patio with water feature, as well as more traditional established borders surrounding lawn and pond. Attractive greenhouse.

36 THRUMPTON HALL

Thrumpton, NG11 0AX. Miranda Seymour, www.thrumptonhall.com. *7m S of Nottingham. M1 J24 take A453 towards Nottingham. Turn L to Thrumpton village & cont to Thrumpton Hall.* **Sun 16 June (1.30-4.30). Adm £6, chd free. Home-made teas.**
2 acres inc lawns, rare trees, flower borders, rose garden, new pagoda, and box-bordered sunken herb garden, all enclosed by C18 ha-ha and encircling a Jacobean house. Garden is surrounded by C18 landscaped park bordered by a river. Rare opportunity to visit Thrumpton Hall (separate ticket). Jacobean mansion, unique carved staircase, Great Saloon, State Bedroom, Priest's Hole.

37 TITHE BARN

Potter Lane, Wellow, Newark, NG22 0EB. Andrew & Carrie Young, 01623 863327, andrew.young@ngs.org.uk. *12 m NW of Newark on A616 about 1m SE from Ollerton on A616. Potter Ln is 1st L after the 30mph limit from Newark or 50yd past Maypole hotel on R from Ollerton, Tithe Barn is the long drive on R after churchyard and Lodge Farm Bungalow.* **Visits by arrangement 1 May to 2 June for groups of 15+. Adm inc tea/coffee and cake.**
The grass-lined approach to this garden between yew hedges sets the tone to the wide sweeps of lawn and generous terrace. Herbaceous beds, irises, roses and rambling roses scrambling into fruit trees. The mature planting of shrubs and weeping trees enhances this pretty barn conversion on the edge of the Wellow Dyke. Woodland garden along the edge of Wellow Dyke open. Patio not accessible by wheelchair without assistance. Woodland path not wheelchair accessible.

38 UNIVERSITY PARK GARDENS

Nottingham, NG7 2RD. University of Nottingham, www.nottingham.ac.uk/estates/grounds. *Approx 4m SW of Nottingham city centre & opp Queens Medical Centre. Purchase adm tickets online or on arrival in the Millennium Garden (in centre of campus), signed from N & W entrances to University Park & within internal road network.* **Sun 18 Aug (11.30-4). Adm £5, chd free. Light refreshments in Pavilion Café, Lakeside Arts Centre. Also adjacent to the Millennium Garden.**
University Park has many beautiful gardens inc the award-winning Millennium Garden with its dazzling flower gardens, timed fountains and turf maze. Also the huge Lenton Firs rock garden, and the Jekyll garden. For the NGS, the Walled Garden is also open and alive with exotic plantings. In total, 300 acres of landscape and gardens. Picnic area, café, walking tours, information desk, workshop, accessible minibus only to feature gardens within campus. Car parking next to the Millennium Garden where tickets and plants are for sale. Some gravel paths and steep slopes. Very large site.

39 WAXWINGS & GOLDCREST

Lamins Lane, Bestwood Village, Nottingham, NG6 8WS. Rob & Jill Carlyle, 07495 934449, robcarlyle@me.com, www.sustainablegarden.blogspot.com. *A60 N of Redhill r'about. Take Lamins Ln. Single track road, limited visibility & passing places. The properties are 1m along the lane on the L.* **Visits by arrangement 12 July to 26 July for groups of 20 to 50. Adm £7, chd free. Home-made teas.**
The six acre gardens for wildlife are open by invitation for groups. Orchard, meadows, prairie beds, woodland, stumpery, vegetable and fragrant gardens.

In 2023 we awarded over £260,000 in Community Garden Grants, supporting 86 community garden projects

Herefordshire
Shropshire
Staffordshire,
Birmingham
& West Midlands
Warwickshire
Worcestershire

WEST MIDLANDS

Above: David Austin Roses, Shropshire

WEST MIDLANDS

The West Midlands is the only region where all counties are completely landlocked. They are also full of contrasts: from the pastoral serenity of Herefordshire and Shropshire along the Welsh border; to the conurbation of Birmingham and West Midlands; while both Worcestershire and Warwickshire stretch from the rural glories of their southern boundaries within the Cotswolds to their busy, urban northern boundaries.

And what could be more different than Worcester's medieval cathedral, perched above the River Severn, and the modernist post-war majesty of Coventry's completed in 1962, where the cathedral symbolises the city overcoming the ravages of Second World War bombing. From Birmingham to Ironbridge and Stoke-on-Trent, this region was the cradle of the Industrial Revolution and today, while much reduced, there remain survivors from that great heritage, both visual landmarks and continuing businesses. The region's gardens reflect its rich variety in their sizes and different rural and urban settings.

Above, from top: Ilmington Manor, Ilmington Gardens, Warwickshire; Cherry Tree Barn, Worcestershire

Below: Dorothy Clive Garden, Staffordshire

HEREFORDSHIRE

© Global Mapping / XYZ Maps

VOLUNTEERS

County Organiser
Lavinia Sole
07880 550235
lavinia.sole@ngs.org.uk

County Treasurer
Angela Mainwaring
01981 251331
angela.mainwaring@ngs.org.uk

Booklet Coordinator
Chris Meakins
01544 370215
christine.meakins@btinternet.com

Booklet Distribution
Lavinia Sole (As above)

Social Media
Position vacant

Assistant County Organisers
Angela O'Connell
07970 265754
angela.oconnell@icloud.com

Graham O'Connell
07788 239750
graham.oconnell22@gmail.com

Penny Usher
01568 611688
pennyusher@btinternet.com

f @NGSHerefordshire
@ngsherefordshire

OPENING DATES

All entries subject to change.
For latest information check
www.ngs.org.uk
Extended openings are shown at the beginning of the month.
Map locator numbers are shown to the right of each garden name.

January

Thursday 25th
Ivy Croft 16

February

Snowdrop Openings

Every Thursday
Ivy Croft 16

Saturday 17th
Wainfield 37

Sunday 18th
Wainfield 37

Saturday 24th
Wainfield 37

Sunday 25th
◆ The Picton Garden 27
Wainfield 37

March

Thursday 7th
Ivy Croft 16

Friday 15th
◆ The Picton Garden 27

Saturday 16th
◆ Ralph Court Gardens 29

Sunday 17th
◆ Ralph Court Gardens 29

Sunday 24th
Whitfield 40

Monday 25th
◆ Moors Meadow Gardens . 23

Wednesday 27th
Ivy Croft 16

Friday 29th
Coddington Vineyard 7

Saturday 30th
Coddington Vineyard 7

April

Every Wednesday
Ivy Croft 16

Wednesday 3rd
◆ Stockton Bury Gardens .. 35

Saturday 6th
Aulden Farm 2
Ivy Croft 16

Sunday 7th
Aulden Farm 2
Ivy Croft 16

Sunday 14th
Lower Hope 19
Lower House Farm 20

Monday 15th
◆ Moors Meadow Gardens . 23

Friday 19th
◆ The Picton Garden 27

Saturday 27th
Wainfield 37

Sunday 28th
Wainfield 37

May

Every Wednesday
Ivy Croft 16

Saturday 4th
Southbourne & Pine Lodge . 34

Sunday 5th
NEW Hillcroft at Dilwyn 13
Lower House Farm 20
Southbourne & Pine Lodge . 34

Monday 6th
NEW Hillcroft at Dilwyn 13

Friday 10th
Coddington Vineyard 7

Saturday 11th
Coddington Vineyard 7

Friday 17th
◆ The Picton Garden 27

Saturday 18th
NEW Eaton Bishop Gardens . 8

Sunday 19th
Broxwood Court 4
NEW Eaton Bishop Gardens . 8
Lower Hope 19

Monday 20th
◆ Moors Meadow Gardens 23

Sunday 26th
Sheepcote 32
Wainfield 37

Monday 27th
Wainfield 37

Tuesday 28th
Aulden Farm 2

Wednesday 29th
Aulden Farm 2

Thursday 30th
Aulden Farm 2

June

Every Wednesday
Ivy Croft 16

Sunday 2nd
NEW Archways 1
Brockhampton Cottage 3
Grendon Court 10

Saturday 15th
◆ The Picton Garden 27

Sunday 16th
Lower House Farm 20
Whitfield 40

Monday 17th
◆ Moors Meadow Gardens 23

Tuesday 18th
Hillcroft 14

Wednesday 19th
Hillcroft 14

Thursday 20th
Hillcroft 14

Friday 21st
◆ Hereford Cathedral Gardens 12
Kentchurch Court 17

Saturday 22nd
Well House 38

Sunday 23rd
The Hurst 15
Well House 38

Saturday 29th
The Laskett Gardens 18
Wainfield 37

Sunday 30th
Wainfield 37

July

Every Wednesday
Ivy Croft 16

Saturday 6th
The Laskett Gardens 18

Sunday 14th
Poole Cottage 28

Monday 15th
◆ Moors Meadow Gardens 23

Wednesday 17th
◆ The Picton Garden 27

Thursday 18th
Herbfarmacy 11

Friday 19th
Coddington Vineyard 7
Herbfarmacy 11

Saturday 20th
Herbfarmacy 11
◆ Ralph Court Gardens 29

Sunday 21st
◆ Ralph Court Gardens 29
◆ Rhodds Farm 31

August

Every Wednesday
Ivy Croft 16

Saturday 3rd
NEW Marden Village Gardens 21
The Vine 36

Sunday 4th
NEW Marden Village Gardens 21

Saturday 10th
Millfield House 22

Sunday 11th
Millfield House 22

Monday 12th
◆ Moors Meadow Gardens 23

Wednesday 14th
◆ The Picton Garden 27

Friday 16th
Aulden Farm 2
Ivy Croft 16

Saturday 17th
Aulden Farm 2
Ivy Croft 16

Saturday 24th
◆ The Garden of the Wind at
   Middle Hunt House 9

Sunday 25th
◆ The Garden of the Wind at
   Middle Hunt House 9
Old Grove 24

September

Every Wednesday
Ivy Croft 16

Saturday 7th
NEW 30 Orchard Green 25

Sunday 8th
Lower Hope 19
NEW 30 Orchard Green 25

Sunday 15th
Brockhampton Cottage 3
Grendon Court 10

Monday 16th
◆ The Picton Garden 27

Saturday 21st
Ivy Croft 16

Sunday 22nd
Ivy Croft 16
◆ Perrycroft 26

October

**Every Wednesday to
Wednesday 9th**
Ivy Croft 16

Saturday 5th
◆ Ralph Court Gardens 29

Sunday 6th
◆ Ralph Court Gardens 29

Friday 11th
Coddington Vineyard 7

Saturday 12th
Coddington Vineyard 7

Monday 14th
◆ The Picton Garden 27

November

Saturday 16th
◆ Ralph Court Gardens 29

Sunday 17th
◆ Ralph Court Gardens 29

February 2025

Friday 21st
◆ The Picton Garden 27

By Arrangement

Arrange a personalised garden visit with your club, or group of friends, on a date to suit you. See individual garden entries for full details.

Lower House Farm

THE GARDENS

❶ NEW ARCHWAYS
St. Owens Cross, Hereford, HR2 8LG. Mrs Christine Mayne.
3m N of Ross-on-Wye. From N or S on A49 take B4521 to Abergaveny - garden 400 yds on L. Travelling E on B4521 from Abergaveny or N on the B4137 from the A40 look for sign at the x-roads by New Inn pub. **Sun 2 June (10-4). Adm £4, chd free. Light refreshments. Tea, coffee, cordials and cakes available.**
Started in 2019 this garden has been designed with wildlife and nature in mind. A relatively small garden divided into areas; flower-filled borders, wildlife woodland area, meadow area, pond and waterfall. Also inc a corner of Japan, a taste of Italy, a wisteria tunnel, herb garden, shrubs and trees. Parking for 10 cars opp. Level access to most of the garden via normal size gate entrance.

  ♿ ❋ ☕))

❷ AULDEN FARM
Aulden, Leominster, HR6 0JT. Alun & Jill Whitehead, 01568 720129, web@auldenfarm.co.uk, www.auldenfarm.co.uk. *4m SW of Leominster. From Leominster take Ivington/Upper Hill Rd, ¾m after Ivington church turn R signed Aulden. From A4110 signed Ivington, take 2nd R signed Aulden.* **Sat 6, Sun 7 Apr, Tue 28, Wed 29, Thur 30 May, Fri 16, Sat 17 Aug (11-5). Adm £5, chd free. Home-made teas. Visits also by arrangement Apr to Sept.**
Informal country garden, thankfully never at its Sunday best! Three acres planted with wildlife in mind. Emphasis on structure and form, with a hint of quirkiness, a garden to explore with eclectic planting. Irises thrive around a natural pond, shady beds and open borders, seats abound, feels mature but ever evolving. Our own ice cream and home-burnt cakes, Lemon Chisel a speciality.

  ❋ ☕ ☕))

❸ BROCKHAMPTON COTTAGE
Brockhampton, HR1 4TQ. Peter Clay & Catherine Connolly. *8m SW of Hereford. 5m N of Ross-on-Wye on B4224. In Brockhampton take road signed to B Court nursing home, pass N Home after ¾m, go down hill & turn L. Car park 500yds downhill on L in orchard.* **Sun 2 June (11-4). Sun 15 Sept (11-4), open nearby Grendon Court. Adm £5, chd free. Picnics welcome by the lake.**
Created from scratch in 1999 by the owner and Tom Stuart-Smith, this beautiful hilltop garden looks south and west over unspoilt countryside. Enjoy a woodland garden, five acre wildflower meadow, a Perry pear orchard and in valley below: lake, stream and arboretum. The extensive borders are planted with drifts of perennials in the modern romantic style. Steep walk from car park. Visit Grendon Court (11-4) after your visit to us.

  🐄 ☕ Ⓓ ⛱))

❹ BROXWOOD COURT
Broxwood, nr Pembridge, Leominster, HR6 9JJ. Richard Snead-Cox & Mike & Anne Allen. *From Leominster follow signs to Brecon A44/A4112. After approx 8m, just past Weobley turn off, go R to Broxwood/Pembridge. After 2m straight over Xrds to Lyonshall. 500yds on L over cattle grid.* **Sun 19 May (2-5.30). Adm £5, chd free. Home-made teas.**
Impressive 29 acre garden and arboretum, designed in 1859 by W. Nesfield. Magnificent yew hedges, long avenue of cedars and Scots pines. Spectacular view of Black Mountains, sweeping lawns, rhododendrons, gentle walks to summerhouse, chapel and lakes. Rose garden, mixed borders, rill, gazebo, sculpted benches and fountain. White and coloured peacocks, ornamental duck. Wildlife meadow in progress. Wheelchair access some gravel, but mostly lawn. Gentle slopes. Disabled WC.

  ♿ ❋ ☕ ☕ ⛱

❺ BURY COURT FARMHOUSE
Ford Street, Wigmore, Leominster, HR6 9UP. Margaret & Les Barclay, 01568 770618, l.barclay@zoho.com. *10m from Leominster, 10m from Knighton, 8m from Ludlow. On A4110 from Leominster, at Wigmore turn R just after shop & garage. Follow signs to parking & garden.* **Visits by arrangement Feb to Oct for groups of up to 30. Adm £5, chd free. Home-made teas.**
¾ acre garden surrounds the 1820's stone farmhouse (not open). The courtyard contains a pond, mixed borders, fruit trees and shrubs, with steps up to a terrace which leads to lawn and vegetable plot. The main garden (semi-walled) is on two levels with mixed borders, greenhouse, pond, mini-orchard, many spring flowers, and wildlife areas. Year-round colour. Mostly accessible for wheelchairs by arrangement.

  ♿ 🐄 ❋ ☕ ☕

❻ CASTLE MOAT HOUSE
Dilwyn, Hereford, HR4 8HZ. Mr T & Mrs M J Voogd, 01544 318 644, mjvoogd@outlook.com. *6m W of Leominster. A44, after 4m take A4112 to Dilwyn. Garden by the village green.* **Visits by arrangement 1 Apr to 7 Oct for groups of 10 to 30. Light refreshments.**
A two acre plot consisting of a more formal cottage garden that wraps around the house. The remaining area is a tranquil wild garden with paths to a Medieval castle motte, part filled moat and Medieval fish and fowl ponds. A haven for wildlife and people alike. The garden contains some steep banks and deep water, with limited access to motte, moat and ponds.

  🐄 ☕ ☕

❼ CODDINGTON VINEYARD
Coddington, HR8 1JJ. Sharon & Peter Maiden, 01531 641817, sgmaiden@yahoo.co.uk, www.coddingtonvineyard.co.uk. *4m NE of Ledbury. From Ledbury to Malvern A449, follow brown signs to Coddington Vineyard.* **Fri 29, Sat 30 Mar, Fri 10, Sat 11 May (11-3). Adm £5, chd free. Evening opening Fri 19 July (6-8). Adm £8. Wine. Fri 11, Sat 12 Oct (11-3). Adm £5, chd free. Wine, home-made ice cream & our own apple juice available. Visits also by arrangement 19 Feb to 30 Oct for groups of 10+.**
Five acres inc a two acre vineyard, listed farmhouse, threshing barn and cider mill. Garden with terraces, wildflower meadow, woodland with massed spring bulbs, large pond with wildlife, stream garden with masses of primula and hosta. Hellebores and snowdrops, Hamamelis and parrotia. Azaleas followed by roses and perennials. Lots to see all year. Developing year on year, planting for autumn colour. In spring, the gardens are a mass of bulbs.

  ♿ 🐄 ❋ ☕ ⛱ ☕))

GROUP OPENING

8  **EATON BISHOP GARDENS**
Martins Croft, Eaton Bishop, HR2 9QD. Dr Tim Coleman. *6m SW of Hereford. Take A465 SW from Hereford. After 3m turn R onto B4349. After 2½m continue onto B4352 for 1m and turn R towards Eaton Bishop. Parking and toilet facilities available at the Village Hall.* **Sat 18, Sun 19 May (11-4.30). Combined adm £7.50, chd free. Home-made teas.**

 MARTINS CROFT
THE OLD POST OFFICE
WHITE HOUSE

The Old Post Office extends to around ¾ acre with views mainly to the east and is designed as an wildlife friendly informal garden emphasising plant movement. Martins Croft has an area of between ¼ and ⅓ acre and faces south. It is a well planted, semi formal garden. The White House offers about three acres of lawns, flower beds and managed woodland with the house located centrally in the garden. The garden is under active development by the present owners. Tickets sold from the barn in The White House where plant sales and refreshments can also be purchased.

9 ✦ **THE GARDEN OF THE WIND AT MIDDLE HUNT HOUSE**
Walterstone, Hereford, HR2 0DY. Rupert & Antoinetta Otten, 01873 860600, gardenofthewind@gmail.com, www.gardenofthewind.co.uk. *4m W of Pandy, 17m S of Hereford, 10m N of Abergavenny. A465 to Pandy, W towards Longtown, turn R at Clodock Church, 1m on R. Disabled parking available. SatNav may take you via a different route but indicates arrival at adjacent farm.* **For NGS: Sat 24, Sun 25 Aug (2-5.30). Adm £6, chd free. Home-made teas. For other opening times and information, please phone, email or visit garden website.**
A modern garden using swathes of herbaceous plants and grasses, surrounding stone built farmhouse and barns with stunning views of the Black Mountains. Special features: rose border, hornbeam alley,

formal parterre and water rill and fountains, William Pye water feature, architecturally designed greenhouse and RIBA bridge, vegetable gardens. Carved lettering and sculpture throughout, garden covering about four acres. Garden seating throughout the site on stone, wood and metal benches inc some with carved lettering. Spectacular views. Partial wheelchair access but WC facilities not easily accessible due to gravel.

10 **GRENDON COURT**
Upton Bishop, Ross-on-Wye, HR9 7QP. Mark & Kate Edwards. *3m NE of Ross-on-Wye. M50, J3. Hereford B4224 Moody Cow Pub, 1m open gate on R. From Ross. A40, B449, Xrds R Upton Bishop. 100yds on L by cream cottage.* **Sun 2 June, Sun 15 Sept (11-4). Adm £5, chd free. Home-made teas. Open nearby Brockhampton Cottage. Picnics welcome in car park field.**
A contemporary garden designed by Tom Stuart-Smith. Planted on two levels, a clever collection of mass-planted perennials and grasses of different heights, textures and colour give all year interest. The upper walled garden with a sea of flowering grasses makes a highlight. Wheelchair access possible but some gravel.

11 **HERBFARMACY**
The Field, Eardisley, Hereford, HR3 6NB. Paul Richards, www.herbfarmacy.com. *Take A438 from Hereford to Willersley where Brecon Rd turns L, cont straight on for 1m on A4111 to Eardisley & Kington. Turn off by Tram Inn then turn R 3 times. Follow directional signs to carpark.* **Thur 18, Fri 19, Sat 20 July (10-4). Adm £5, chd free. Light refreshments.**
A four acre organic herb farm overlooking the Wye valley with views to the Black Mountains. Featured on BBC Countryfile, crops are grown for use in herbal skincare and medicinal products. Colourful plots of Echinacea, marshmallow, mullein and Calendula will be on show as well as displays on making products. Herbfarmacy products on sale in the shop. Wheelchair access possible with assistance when dry but parts of ground rough and some slopes.

12 ✦ **HEREFORD CATHEDRAL GARDENS**
Hereford, HR1 2NG. Dean of Hereford Cathedral, 01432 374251, events@herefordcathedral.org, www.herefordcathedral.org/events. *Centre of Hereford. The ticket desk is in the cathedral car park, please approach the desk to sign in with staff.* **For NGS: Fri 21 June (10-3). Adm £6, chd free. For other opening times and information, please phone, email or visit garden website.**
Explore the Chapter House garden, Cloister garden, the Canon's garden with plants with ecclesiastical connections and roses, the private Dean's Garden and the Bishop's Garden with fine trees and an outdoor chapel. These are open session where visitors can explore the gardens at their own pace, with Gardeners and Guides based within the gardens to share the history of the site. Partial wheelchair access. For more information please visit website or contact the team in advance.

14 **HILLCROFT**
Coombes Moor, Presteigne, LD8 2HY. Liz O'Rourke & Michael Clarke, 01544 262795, lorconsulting@hotmail.co.uk. *N Herefordshire, 10m from Leominster. Coombes Moor is under Wapley Hill on the B4362, between Shobdon & Presteigne. Garden on R just beyond Byton Cross when heading W.* **Tue 18, Wed 19, Thur 20 June (11-5). Adm £4, chd free. Home-made teas. Visits also by arrangement 24 June to 26 July for groups of up to 40. No coach parking. Coach drop off at lay-by only.**
The garden is part of a five acre site on the lower slopes of Wapley Hill in the beautiful Lugg Valley. The highlight in mid summer is the romantic Rose Walk, featured on Gardeners' World in 2023. It combines over sixty roses with mixed herbaceous planting set in an old cider apple orchard. In addition to the garden around the house, there is a secret garden, wildflower meadow and a vegetable area. Our delicious home-made cakes have always been very popular and we aim to make the selection for our final opening especially memorable.

13 **NEW** **HILLCROFT AT DILWYN**
Dilwyn, Hereford, HR4 8JF.
Rhonda Wood & Steven Brown.
6m W of Leominster on A44. Turn R opp turning for Dilwyn village. Then immed take L fork and follow lane for 0.3m. Parking in field adj to garden. Follow yellow signs. **Sun 5, Mon 6 May (10-4). Adm £5, chd free. Home-made teas.**
The garden is approximately 1.3 acres with an organic vegetable plot and polytunnel. Main garden has lawn with perennial beds either side containing small shrubs and trees. Paths reveal a wooded area to the rear to containing magnolias, camellias, rhododendrons, eucalyptus and other large trees. Informal and relaxed planting. Not wheelchair friendly. Visit the on-site pottery studio - Steven Brown Ceramics.

🐕 ☕ 🔊

15 **THE HURST**
Bosbury Road, Cradley, Malvern, WR13 5LT. Clare Gogerty. *16m E of Hereford, 11m W of Worcester. 'The Hurst' is situated directly on the Bosbury Rd. From the junc of A4103 & B4220, garden is 0.7m towards Bosbury on the L. On-road parking.* **Sun 23 June (12-4). Adm £5, chd free. Home-made teas.**
A garden based on the five elements: fire, water, earth, air and spirit, which is the subject of the garden owner's book 'Your Magical Garden'. At the heart of the garden is a cosmic spiral made from turf with a reflecting steel bowl at its centre. Borders are coloured themed to tie in with the elements. It is also a productive smallholding with a cutting garden, veg beds, hens and sheep. Gently sloping gravel and grass track to lower area. Orchard not suitable for wheelchairs.

♿ 🐕 ❀ ☕ 🏓 🔊

16 **IVY CROFT**
Ivington Green, Leominster, HR6 0JN. Roger Norman, 01568 720344, ivycroft@homecall.co.uk, www.ivycroftgarden.co.uk. *3m SW of Leominster. From Leominster take Ryelands Rd to Ivington. Turn R at church, garden ¾m on R. From A4110 signed Ivington, garden 1¾m on L.* **Every Thur 25 Jan to 7 Mar (10-4). Home-made teas. Every Wed 27 Mar to 9 Oct (10-4). Sat 6, Sun 7 Apr, Fri 16, Sat 17 Aug (11-5). Home-made teas. Open nearby Aulden Farm. Sat 21, Sun**

22 Sept (11-5). Home-made teas. Adm £5, chd free. Visits also by arrangement.
Now over 25 years old, the garden shows signs of maturity, inc some surprising trees. A very wide range of plants is displayed, blending with countryside and providing habitat for wildlife. The cottage is surrounded by borders, snowdrops, raised beds, trained pear trees and containers giving all year interest. Paths lead to the wider garden inc mixed borders, vegetables framed with espalier apples. Partial wheelchair access.

♿ ❀ 🐕 ☕ 🏓

17 **KENTCHURCH COURT**
Kentchurch, HR2 0DB.
Mr J Lucas-Scudamore, www.kentchurchcourt.co.uk. *12m SW of Hereford. From Hereford A465 towards Abergavenny, at Pontrilas turn L signed Kentchurch. After 2m fork L, after Bridge Inn. Garden opp church.* **Fri 21 June (11-4). Adm £7.50, chd free. Home-made teas. Refreshments also at The Bridge Inn, Kentchurch.**
Kentchurch Court is situated close to the Welsh border. Formal garden and traditional vegetable garden redesigned with colour, scent and easy access. Walled garden and herbaceous borders, rhododendrons and wildflower walk. Extensive collection of mature trees and shrubs. Stream with habitat for spawning trout and views into deer park at the heart of the estate. First opened for the NGS in 1927. Wheelchair access, some slopes, shallow gravel.

♿ 🐕 ❀ 🐕 ☕

18 **THE LASKETT GARDENS**
Much Birch, HR2 8HZ. Perennial, www.perennial.org.uk. *Approx 7m from Hereford; 7m from Ross. On A49, midway between Ross-on-Wye & Hereford, turn into Laskett Ln towards Hoarwithy. The drive is approx 350yds on L.* **Sat 29 June (10.30-4.30). Home-made teas. Sat 6 July (10.30-4.30). Light refreshments. Adm £12, chd free.**
The Laskett, Britain's great autobiographical gardens, created in celebration of their life and times, by Sir Roy Strong CH and his late wife Julia Trevelyan Oman CBE. The gardens were begun in 1974 and have continued to evolve ever since. They are the creative fruit of a happy marriage between two people who were at the centre of the arts for much of the latter half of the C20.

The garden's uneven surfaces, grassed areas, narrow paths and gravel walkways make many areas unsuitable for wheelchair access.

♿ ❀ 🐕 ☕ 🔊

19 **LOWER HOPE**
Lower Hope Estate, Ullingswick, Hereford, HR1 3JF. Mrs Sylvia Richards, www.lowerhopegardens.co.uk. *5m S of Bromyard. A465 N from Hereford, after 6m turn L at Burley Gate onto A417 towards Leominster. After approx 2m take 3rd R to Lower Hope. After ½m garden on L. Disabled parking available.* **Sun 14 Apr, Sun 19 May, Sun 8 Sept (2-5). Adm £7.50, chd £2. Light refreshments.**
Outstanding five acre garden with wonderful seasonal variations. Impeccable lawns with herbaceous borders, rose gardens, white garden, Mediterranean, Italian and Japanese gardens. Natural streams, man-made waterfalls, bog gardens. Woodland with azaleas and rhododendrons with lime avenue to lake with wild flowers and bulbs. Glasshouses with exotic plants and breeding butterflies. Tickets bought on the gate will be cash only. Wheelchair access to most areas.

♿ ❀ 🐕 ☕

20 **LOWER HOUSE FARM**
Vine Lane, Sutton, Tenbury Wells, WR15 8RL. Mrs Anne Durston Smith, 07891 928412, adskyre@outlook.com, www.kyre-equestrian.co.uk. *3m SE of Tenbury Wells; 8m NW of Bromyard. From Tenbury take A4214 to Bromyard. After approx 3m turn R into Vine Lane, then R fork to Lower House Farm.* **Sun 14 Apr, Sun 5 May, Sun 16 June (11-4). Adm £5, chd free. Light refreshments. Visits also by arrangement Apr to Sept for groups of 12+.**
Award-winning country garden surrounding C16 farm-house (not open) on working farm. Herbaceous borders, roses, box-parterre, productive kitchen and cutting garden, spring garden, ha-ha allowing sweeping views. Wildlife pond. Walkers and dogs can enjoy numerous footpaths across the farm land. There is spectacular autumn colour and dahlias. Home to Kyre Equestrian Centre with access to safe rides and riding events.

GROUP OPENING

21 NEW MARDEN VILLAGE GARDENS

Tremar, Marden, Hereford, HR1 3DX. Ms Angela Sasso.
Village of Marden, Herefordshire. 4m N of Hereford off of the A49. Turn at Moreton-in-Lugg and cont over bridge. From A4103 Aylestone r'about to Sutton St Nicholas for 2m. Turn at Golden Cross Pub and follow signs to Marden. **Sat 3, Sun 4 Aug (12-4). Combined adm £8, chd £2. Light refreshments will be on offer at several of the gardens.** Parking and tickets at Marden Primary School where maps will also be available. 8-10 gardens of varying sizes and types within the Parish inc flower and vegetable gardens, formal and wild gardens, some with wildlife ponds, some gardens with lovely rural views. The new Marden Community Garden will also be inc. Wheelchair access to a few gardens. Please ask for details.

 ♿ ☕ ⁾⁾⁾

---

22 MILLFIELD HOUSE

Eaton Bishop, Hereford, HR2 9QS. Angela & Richard Mainwaring.
4m SW of Hereford. A465 W to B4349 Hay on Wye. Approx 2m L in Clehonger B4349 to Kingstone. 100yds after 40mph sign R into lane 'unsuitable for long or wide vehicles'. Follow yellow signs. **Sat 10, Sun 11 Aug (11-5). Adm £5, chd free. Home-made teas. Coffee and cakes also available. Visitors are welcome to picnic in the field.** 1½ acre informal country garden shared with wildlife. The terrace and vegetable garden are enclosed by pergolas and espalier fruit trees. Mixed borders of trees, shrubs and perennials create their own tapestry with plenty of self-sown plants to surprise and inspire us! Grass paths connect the borders, ponds and a wildflower meadow and native hedges and trees enclose and divide the different areas.

✳ ☕ ⛩ ⁾⁾⁾

Ivy Croft

23 ◆ MOORS MEADOW GARDENS

Collington, Bromyard, HR7 4LZ. Ros Bissell, 01885 410318, moorsmeadow@hotmail.co.uk, www.moorsmeadow.co.uk. *4m N of Bromyard, on B4214. ½m up lane follow yellow arrows.* **For NGS: Mon 25 Mar, Mon 15 Apr, Mon 20 May, Mon 17 June, Mon 15 July, Mon 12 Aug (10-5). Adm £8, chd £2. For other opening times and information, please phone, email or visit garden website.**

Multi award winning, inspirational seven acre organic hillside garden with a vast amount of species, many rarely seen; emphasis on working with nature, a wildlife haven. Intriguing features and sculptures, a delight for the garden novice as well as the serious plantsman. Wander through fernery, grass garden, extensive shrubberies, herbaceous beds, meadow, dingle, pools and kitchen garden. Huge range of unusual and rarely seen plants from around the world. Unique home-crafted sculptures.

•))

24 OLD GROVE

Llangrove, Ross-On-Wye, HR9 6HA. Ken & Lynette Knowles. *Between Ross & Monmouth. 2m off A40 at Whitchurch. Disabled parking at house otherwise follow signs for parking in nearby field.* **Sun 25 Aug (2-6). Adm £5, chd free. Home-made teas.**

1½ acre garden plus two fields. South west facing with unspoilt views. Lots of mixed beds with plenty of late summer colour and many unusual plants. Large collection of dahlias and salvias; wildlife pond, masses of pots; interesting trees inc a new 15ft tree sculpture. Seating throughout and a large well fenced area where visiting canines can stretch their legs. Wheelchair access, gentle slopes, some steps but accessible.

&. 🐕 ☕ 🏕

25 NEW 30 ORCHARD GREEN

Marden, Hereford, HR1 3ED. Sara Edwards. *6m N of Hereford, 10m S of Leominster. 1½m From A49. At A49 Wellington take Marden turn, go over level crossing and river bridge. Approx 150m, 2nd bungalow on —*

R What3Words app - positions. *risen.flopping.* **Sat 7, Sun 8 Sept (11-4). Adm £4, chd free. Light refreshments.**

Only four years old, RHS Gold Medal winning designer Sara Edwards' small back garden accommodates her eclectic collection of unusual plants, chosen because of their interesting foliage. Features inc a sunken firepit surrounded by a lush green canopy, inc a three headed tree fern; two ponds with a small stream, and a hexagonal cedar pergola trained with various evergreen climbers.

❀ 🅳 ☕ •))

26 ◆ PERRYCROFT

Jubilee Drive, Upper Colwall, Malvern, WR13 6DN. Gillian & Mark Archer, 07858 393767, info@perrycroft.co.uk, www.perrycroft.co.uk. *Between Malvern & Ledbury. On B4232 between British Camp & Wyche cutting. Park in Gardiners Quarry pay & display car park on Jubilee Dr. Short walk to the garden.* **For NGS: Sun 22 Sept (1-5). Adm £5, chd free. Home-made teas. For other**

Archways

opening times and information, please phone, email or visit garden website.

Perrycroft is an Arts and Crafts house designed by CFA Voysey in 1895. Situated high on the Malvern Hills, with magnificent views to the south and west accross Herefordshire and into Wales, the garden has been developed over the past 24 years. Yew and box hedges, topiary, mixed and herbaceous borders, shrubs and roses, meadows, ponds and woodland combine to create a relaxed and varied garden with traditional and contemporary planting styles.

27 ◆ THE PICTON GARDEN
Old Court Nurseries, Walwyn Road, Colwall, WR13 6QE. Paul, Meriel & Helen Picton, 01684 540416, oldcourtnurseries@btinternet.com, www.autumnasters.co.uk. *3m W of Malvern. On B4218 (Walwyn Rd) N of Colwall Stone. Turn off A449 from Ledbury or Malvern onto the B4218 for Colwall.* **For NGS: Sun 25 Feb, Fri 15 Mar (11-4); Fri 19 Apr, Fri 17 May, Sat 15 June, Wed 17 July, Wed 14 Aug, Mon 16 Sept, Mon 14 Oct (11-5). Adm £5, chd free. 2025: Fri 21 Feb. For other opening times and information, please phone, email or visit garden website. Donation to Plant Heritage.**

1½ acres west of Malvern Hills. Bulbs and a multitude of woodland plants in spring. Interesting perennials and shrubs in August. In late September and early October colourful borders display the National Plant Collection of Michaelmas daisies, backed by autumn colouring trees and shrubs. Many unusual plants to be seen, inc more than 100 different ferns and over 300 varieties of snowdrop. National Plant Collection of autumn-flowering asters and an extensive nursery that has been growing them since 1906. Also as of 2023 the National Collection of Polypodium (hardy cvs).

28 POOLE COTTAGE
Coppett Hill, Goodrich, Ross-on-Wye, HR9 6HX. Jo Ward-Ellison & Roy Smith. *5m from Ross on Wye, 7m from Monmouth. Above Goodrich Castle in Wye Valley AONB. Goodrich signed from A40 or take B4234 from Ross. NOTE: No parking at garden or on lane. Use HR9 6HX for village parking. A shuttle service is available to garden or a 10-15 mins walk from village.* **Sun 14 July (10.30-5). Adm £5, chd free. Home-made teas.**

A modern country garden in keeping with the local natural landscape. Home to designer Jo Ward-Ellison the two acre garden is predominately naturalistic in style with a contemporary feel. A long season of interest with grasses and later flowering perennials. Some steep slopes, steps and uneven paths. Features inc a small orchard, a pond loved by wildlife and kitchen garden with fabulous views.

29 ◆ RALPH COURT GARDENS
Edwyn Ralph, Bromyard, Hereford, HR7 4LU. Mr & Mrs Morgan, 01885 483225, ralphcourtgardens@aol.com, www.ralphcourtgardens.co.uk. *1m from Bromyard. From Bromyard follow the Tenbury road for approx 1m. On entering the village of Edwyn Ralph take 1st turning on R towards the church.* **For NGS: Sat 16, Sun 17 Mar, Sat 20, Sun 21 July, Sat 5, Sun 6 Oct, Sat 16, Sun 17 Nov (10-5). Adm £14, chd £10. Light refreshments. For other opening times and information, please phone, email or visit garden website.**

All tickets must be purchased through the garden website or at the gate. 14 amazing gardens set in the grounds of a gothic rectory. A family orientated garden with a twist, incorporating an Italian Piazza, an African Jungle, Dragon Pool, Alice in Wonderland and the elves in their conifer forest and our new section 'The Monet Garden'. These are just a few of the themes within this stunning garden. Overlooking the Malvern Hills 120 seater Licensed Restaurant. Offering a good selection of daily specials, delicious Sunday roasts, afternoon tea and our scrumptious homemade cakes. All areas ramped for wheelchair and pushchair access.

30 REVILO
Wellington, Hereford, HR4 8AZ. Mrs Shirley Edgar, 01432 830189, shirleyskinner@btinternet.com. *6m N of Hereford. On A49 from Hereford turn L into Wellington village, pass church on R. Then just after barn on L, turn L up driveway in front of The Harbour, to furthest bungalow.* **Visits by arrangement 13 Apr to 14 Sept for groups of 10 to 25. Adm £5, chd free. Home-made teas.**

⅓ acre garden surrounding bungalow inc mixed borders, meadow and woodland areas, scented garden, late summer bed, gravelled herb garden and kitchen garden. Flower arranger's garden. Wheelchair access to all central areas of the garden from the garage side.

31 ◆ RHODDS FARM
Lyonshall, Kington, HR5 3LW. Richard & Cary Goode, 01544 340120, cary.goode@russianaeros.com, www.rhoddsfarm.co.uk. *1m E of Kington. From A44 take small turning S just E of Penrhos Farm, 1m E of Kington. Continue 1m, garden straight ahead (a little further than SatNav sends you).* **For NGS: Sun 21 July (11-5). Adm £7, chd free. Home-made teas. For other opening times and information, please phone, email or visit garden website.**

Created by the owner, a garden designer, over the past 18 years, the garden contains an extensive range of interesting plants. Formal garden with dovecote and 100 white doves, mixed borders, double herbaceous borders of hot colours, large gravel garden, three ponds, arboretum, perennial and wildflower meadows and 13 acres of woodland. A natural garden that fits the setting with magnificent views. Interesting and unusual trees, shrubs and perennials. A natural garden on a challenging site. A number of sculptures by different artists. No pesticides used.

47,000 people affected by cancer were reached by Maggie's centres supported by the National Garden Scheme over the last 12 months

Aulden Farm

© Carole Drake

32 SHEEPCOTE

Putley, Ledbury, HR8 2RD. Tim & Julie Beaumont. *5m W of Ledbury off the A438 Hereford to Ledbury Rd. Passenger drop off; parking 200 yds.* **Sun 26 May (1-5.30). Adm £5, chd free. Light refreshments.**

A ⅓ acre garden taken in hand from 2011 retaining many quality plants, shrubs and trees from earlier gardeners. Topiary holly, box, hawthorn, privet and yew formalise the varied plantings around the croquet lawn and gravel garden; beds with heathers, azaleas, lavender surrounded by herbaceous perennials and bulbs; small ponds; kitchen garden with raised beds. Art exhibition for Anya Beaumont will be taking place on the day. Anya is a visual artist working across mediums. The physical environment and its influence have been a significant factor in her practice. If any pieces are sold, a percentage will be given as a donation to the National Garden Scheme.

33 SHUTTIFIELD COTTAGE

Birchwood, Storridge, WR13 5HA. Mr & Mrs David Judge, 01886 884243, judge.shutti@btinternet.com. *15m E of Hereford. Turn L off A4103 at Storridge opp the church to Birchwood. After 1¼ m L down steep tarmac drive signposted to Shuttifield Cottage (150 yards).* **Visits by arrangement 1 Apr to 29 Sept. Adm £5, chd free. Home-made teas.**

Superb position and views. Unexpected three acre plantsman's garden, extensive herbaceous borders, many unusual trees, shrubs, perennials, colour themed for all year interest. Anemones, magnolias, bluebells, rhododendrons, azaleas and camellias in the spring. Large old rose garden with many spectacular climbers. Small deer park, and walks in a 20 acre wood containing wildlife ponds and wildflowers.

34 SOUTHBOURNE & PINE LODGE

Dinmore, Hereford, HR1 3JR. Graham & Lavinia Sole & Frank Ryding. *8m N of Hereford; 8m S of Leominster. From Hereford on A49, turn R at bottom of Dinmore Hill towards Bodenham, gardens 1m on L. From Leominster on A49, L onto A417, 2m turn R & through*

Bodenham, following NGS signs to garden. **Sat 4, Sun 5 May (11-5). Adm £5, chd free. Home-made teas. Visitors are welcome to bring their own picnics and enjoy the gardens at their leisure.**
Southbourne has panoramic views over Bodenham Lake SSSI to the Black Mountains and Malvern Hills. Mature herbaceous beds, shrubs and terraced lawns have been visited by returning NGS guests for a decade. In spring, bluebells, rhododendrons, brooms and a Judas tree star. Pine Lodge is a woodland of over two acres, with extensive paths, featuring most of England's native trees is accessed from Southbourne.

35 ◆ STOCKTON BURY GARDENS
Kimbolton, HR6 0HA. Raymond G Treasure, 07880 712649, twstocktonbury@outlook.com, www.stocktonbury.co.uk. *2m NE of Leominster. From Leominster to Ludlow on A49 turn R onto A4112. Gardens 300yds on R.* **For NGS: Wed 3 Apr (11-4.30). Adm £9, chd £5. Home-made teas in Tithe Barn Café. For other opening times and information, please phone, email or visit garden website.**
Superb, sheltered four acre garden with colour and interest from Apr until the end of Sept. Extensive collection of plants, many rare and unusual set amongst medieval buildings. Features pigeon house, tithe barn, grotto, cider press, auricula theatre, Roman hoard, pools, secret garden, garden museum and rill, all surrounded by countryside. Garden and Café open Wed-Sun. Partial wheelchair access. An able bodied companion is advisable for wheelchair users.

36 THE VINE
School Lane, Tarrington, HR1 4EX. Richard & Tonya Price. *Between Hereford & Ledbury on A438. In Tarrington village, S of the A438. Park as directed. Disabled parking only at house.* **Sat 3 Aug (2-6). Adm £5, chd free. Cream teas.**
Mature, traditional garden in peaceful setting with stunning views of the surrounding countryside. Consisting of various rooms with mixed and herbaceous borders. Secret garden in blue, yellow and white, croquet lawn with C18 summerhouse, temple

garden with ponds, herb and nosegay garden, kitchen garden around greenhouse on the paddock. Cornus avenues with obelisk and willow bower.

37 WAINFIELD
Peterstow, Ross-On-Wye, HR9 6LJ. Nick & Sue Helme. *From the A49 between Ross-on-Wye & Hereford. Take the B4521 to Skenfrith/ Abergavenny. Wainfeild is 50yds on R.* **Sat 17, Sun 18, Sat 24, Sun 25 Feb, Sat 27, Sun 28 Apr, Sun 26, Mon 27 May, Sat 29, Sun 30 June (10-4). Adm £5, chd free. Home-made teas.**
Three acre informal, wildlife garden inc rose garden, fruit trees, climbing roses and clematis. Delightful pond with waterfall. Honeysuckle, snowdrops and aconites a plenty. In spring, tulips, bluebells, crocuses and grasses followed by lush summer planting. Fruit walk with naturalised cowslips all set in an open area of interesting, unusual mature trees and sculptures. Wheelchair access on even ground.

38 WELL HOUSE
Garway Hill, Hereford, HR2 8RT. Mrs Betty Lovering. *12m SW Hereford A465 from Hereford turn L at Pontrilas onto B4347 turn 1st R & immed L signed Orcop & Garway Hill, 3m to Bagwyllydiart then follow signs.* **Sat 22, Sun 23 June (10.30-4.30). Adm £5, chd free. Light refreshments.**
Hillside garden, approx an acre with views over Orcop on Garway Hill. This garden has been created from scratch since 1998 on a steep bank with steps and narrow paths and is ongoing with nature in mind. Herbaceous beds, mature trees, shrubs, wide collection of acers and unusual plants, veg garden, polytunnel, bog garden seating areas, on a working small holding with Dutch Spotted Sheep. Lovely views lots of seating. Secret areas.

39 WESTON HALL
Weston-under-Penyard, Ross-on-Wye, HR9 7NS. Mr P Aldrich-Blake, 01989 562597, aldrichblake@btinternet.com. *1m E of Ross-on-Wye. On A40 towards Gloucester.* **Visits by arrangement Apr to Sept for groups of 5 to 30. Adm £5, chd free. Light**

refreshments.
Six acres surrounding Elizabethan house (not open). Large walled garden with herbaceous borders, vegetables and fruit, overlooked by Millennium folly. Lawns and mature and recently planted trees and shrubs, with many unusual varieties. Orchard, ornamental ponds and lake. Four generations in the family, but still evolving year on year. Wheelchair access to walled garden only.

40 WHITFIELD
Wormbridge, HR2 9BA. Mr & Mrs Edward Clive. www.whitfield-hereford.com. *8m SW of Hereford. The entrance gates are off the A465, Hereford to Abergavenny road, ½ m N of Wormbridge. Postcode for SatNav HR2 9DG.* **Sun 24 Mar, Sun 16 June (2-5). Adm £5.50, chd free. Home-made teas.**
The Whitfield Estate has been a supporter of the National Gardens Scheme for over 50 years with extensive parkland and woodland walks. Our woodland has a grove of coastal redwood trees planted in 1851. Wildflowers, ponds, walled garden, many flowering magnolias (species and hybrids). We also have a wonderful ginkgo tree planted in1780. Partial access for wheelchair users, some gravel paths and steep slopes. Dogs on leads welcome.

152,684 people were able to access guidance on what to expect when a person is dying through the National Garden Scheme support for Hospice UK this year

SHROPSHIRE

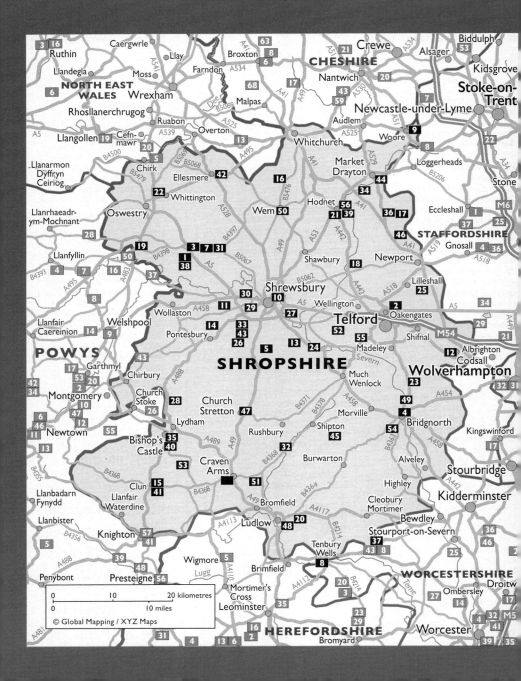

VOLUNTEERS

County Organiser
Andy Chatting
07546 560615
andy.chatting@ngs.org.uk

Treasurer
Elaine Jones 01588 650323
elaine.jones@ngs.org.uk

Volunteers Co-ordinator
Sheila Jones 01743 244108
smaryjones@icloud.com

Publicity
Douglas Wood 07704 683095
douglas.woods@ngs.org.uk

Facebook/Twitter
Vicky Kirk 01743 821429
vicky.kirk@ngs.org.uk

Instagram
John Butcher 07817 443837
butchinoz@hotmail.com

Booklet Co-ordinator
Martin Clifford-Jones
01630 639746
stellaandmartin@ngs.org.uk

Assistant County Organisers
Angela Woolrich
angelawoolrich@hotmail.co.uk

Fiona Chancellor 01952 507675
fiona.chancellor@ngs.org.uk

Jane Wood 01691 839564
jane.liz.wood@gmail.com

Stella Clifford- Jones
01630 639746
pomona_scj@hotmail.com

 @Shropshire NGS

 @shropshireNGS

 @shropshirengs

OPENING DATES

All entries subject to change. For latest information check **www.ngs.org.uk**
Map locator numbers are shown to the right of each garden name.

February

Snowdrop Opening

Sunday 11th
Millichope Park — 32

April

Wednesday 3rd
Hundred House Hotel — 23

Saturday 6th
NEW Cherry Tree Arboretum — 9

Sunday 14th
Edge Villa — 14

Saturday 20th
NEW Upper Farm Garden — 52

Sunday 21st
NEW Upper Farm Garden — 52

Saturday 27th
Ruthall Manor — 45

Sunday 28th
Ruthall Manor — 45
Westwood House — 54

May

Wednesday 1st
Hundred House Hotel — 23

Sunday 5th
Millichope Park — 32
Oteley — 42

Wednesday 8th
Neen View — 37

Saturday 11th
NEW Cherry Tree Arboretum — 9

Sunday 12th
The Ferns — 15
Henley Hall — 20
Longden Manor — 26

Wednesday 15th
◆ Goldstone Hall Gardens — 17

Neen View — 37

Saturday 18th
Ruthall Manor — 45
Tower House — 51

Sunday 19th
Brownhill House — 7
Longner Hall — 27
NEW Riverside — 44
Ruthall Manor — 45

Tuesday 21st
Brownhill House — 7

Saturday 25th
Beaufort — 2
◆ Burford House Gardens — 8

Sunday 26th
◆ Burford House Gardens — 8
◆ Walcot Hall — 53

Monday 27th
◆ Walcot Hall — 53

June

Saturday 1st
Horatio's Garden — 22

Sunday 2nd
The Old Vicarage, Clun — 41
Stanley Hall Gardens — 49

Friday 7th
NEW Lilleshall Home Farm — 25

Saturday 8th
The Leasowes, Cound — 24
Ruthall Manor — 45

Sunday 9th
The Bramleys — 5
Eaton Mascott Hall — 13
Ruthall Manor — 45

Wednesday 12th
◆ Goldstone Hall Gardens — 17

Friday 14th
Four Winds — 16

Saturday 15th
NEW ◆ David Austin Roses — 12
Four Winds — 16
Windy Ridge — 55

Sunday 16th
NEW ◆ David Austin Roses — 12
The Mount — 35
The Old Vicarage, Bishops Castle — 40
Windy Ridge — 55

Thursday 20th
NEW Upper Farm Garden — 52

Friday 21st
 Upper Farm Garden | 52

Saturday 22nd
Grooms Cottage | 18
1 Scotsmansfield | 47
The Secret Gardens at
  Steventon Terrace | 48

Sunday 23rd
Grooms Cottage | 18
The Mill House | 31

Tuesday 25th
Brownhill House | 7

Friday 28th
12 Colley Close | 10

Saturday 29th
48 Bramble Ridge | 4

Sunday 30th
17 Mortimer Road | 34
Riverside | 44

July

Wednesday 3rd
Hundred House Hotel | 23

Saturday 6th
Ruthall Manor | 45

Sunday 7th
◆ Hodnet Hall Gardens | 21
Ruthall Manor | 45
Sambrook Manor | 46

Wednesday 10th
◆ Goldstone Hall Gardens | 17

Saturday 13th
Lower Brookshill | 28

Sunday 14th
Lower Brookshill | 28
1 Mount Pleasant Cottages | 36

Thursday 18th
Appledore | 1
Offcot | 38

Friday 19th
Appledore | 1
Offcot | 38

Saturday 20th
Appledore | 1
Offcot | 38

August

Sunday 4th
Moat Hall | 33

Saturday 10th
Upper Farm Garden | 52

Sunday 11th
The Ferns | 15
Upper Farm Garden | 52

Wednesday 14th
◆ Goldstone Hall Gardens | 17

Sunday 18th
Edge Villa | 14

Saturday 31st
◆ Burford House Gardens | 8

September

Sunday 1st
◆ Burford House Gardens | 8

Wednesday 4th
Hundred House Hotel | 23

Thursday 5th
◆ Wollerton Old Hall | 56

Wednesday 11th
◆ Goldstone Hall Gardens | 17

Sunday 15th
Riverside | 44

Saturday 21st
Cherry Tree Arboretum | 9

Sunday 22nd
Sunningdale | 50

October

Saturday 5th
Upper Farm Garden | 52

Sunday 6th
Upper Farm Garden | 52

Thursday 10th
Appledore | 1
Offcot | 38

Friday 11th
Appledore | 1
Offcot | 38

Saturday 12th
Appledore | 1
Offcot | 38
The Paddock | 43

Sunday 13th
Millichope Park | 32

Saturday 26th
Cherry Tree Arboretum | 9

By Arrangement

Arrange a personalised garden visit with your club, or group of friends, on a date to suit you. See individual garden entries for full details.

Bramble Cottage | 3
48 Bramble Ridge | 4
Brownhill House | 7
Cruckfield House | 11
Edge Villa | 14
The Ferns | 15
Four Winds | 16
Grooms Cottage | 18
Gwynt Newydd | 19
Hundred House Hotel | 23
The Leasowes, Cound | 24
107 Meadowbout Way | 29
Merton | 30
Moat Hall | 33
17 Mortimer Road | 34
The Mount | 35
1 Mount Pleasant Cottages | 36
Neen View | 37
The Old Rectory, Hodnet | 39
The Old Vicarage, Clun | 41
Ruthall Manor | 45
Sunningdale | 50
Tower House | 51

Cherry Tree Arboretum

THE GARDENS

1 APPLEDORE
Kynaston, Kinnerley, Oswestry, SY10 8EF. Lionel Parker. *Just off A5 on Wolfshead r'about (at Oswestry end of Nesscliffe bypass) towards Knockin. Then 1st L towards Kinnerley. Follow NGS signs from this road.* **Thur 18, Fri 19, Sat 20 July, Thur 10, Fri 11, Sat 12 Oct (10-4). Adm £7, chd free. Home-made teas.**
Appledore adjoins neighbouring garden Offcot. It has gone through extensive changes and is managed by Tom Pountney from Offcot. Both gardens are opening together this year so that visitors can see a developing 'edible garden' with six large beds for a wide range of fruit and vegetables, all grown organically. To encourage pollinators, the garden also has a wildlife pond and a small wildflower meadow.

2 BEAUFORT
Coppice Drive, Moss Road Wrockwardine Wood, Telford, TF2 7BP. Mike King, www.carnivorousplants.uk.com. *Approx 2m N from Telford town centre. From Asda Donnington, turn L at lights on Moss Rd, 1/3 m, turn L into Coppice Drive. 4th Bungalow on L with solar panels.* **Sat 25 May (10-5). Adm £5, chd free. Light refreshments. Teas, coffees, soft drinks and cakes available.**
Donation to Plant Heritage.
If carnivorous plants are your thing, then come and visit our National Collection of Sarracenia (pitcher plants); also over 100 different Venus flytrap clones (*Dionaea muscipula*), Sundews (*Drosera*) and Butterworts (*Pinguicula*) - over 6000 plants in total. Large greenhouses at Telford's first carbon negative house; a great place to visit - kids will love it! Visitors are asked to wear a face covering in the greenhouses, please. Regret, greenhouses are not wheelchair accessible.

3 NEW BRAMBLE COTTAGE
Shotatton, Ruyton XI Towns, Shrewsbury, SY4 1JG. Brigette and Adam Wilson, 07739 182315, brigette.wilson14@gmail.com. *1m W of Ruyton Village towards Shotatton.* **Visits by arrangement May to Oct.**
Bramble Cottage is a mainly topiary garden created and looked after by us for the last 26 years. We have box parterres and a formal rose garden as well as yew topiary. It is a ³⁄₄ of an acre site in Shropshire with a yew topiary avenue, lots of box balls and new topiary in development. In addition, we have yew, box and beech hedges and all things topiary.

4 48 BRAMBLE RIDGE
Bridgnorth, WV16 4SQ. Heather, 07572 706706, heatherfran48@gmail.com. *From Bridgnorth N on B4373 signed Broseley. 1st on R Stanley Ln, 1st R Bramble Ridge. From Broseley S on B4373, nr Bridgnorth turn L into Stanley Ln, 1st R Bramble Ridge.* **Sat 29 June (11-5.30). Adm £5, chd free. Light refreshments.**
Visits also by arrangement Apr to Sept for groups of 20 to 30.
Steep cottage-style garden with many steps; part wild, part cultivated, terraced in places and overlooking the Severn Valley with views to High Rock and Queens Parlour. The garden features shrubs, perennials, wildlife pond, summerhouse and, in the wilderness area, wildflowers, fruit trees and a sandstone outcrop. I love my garden very much and am looking forward to sharing it with other people.

5 THE BRAMLEYS
Condover, Shrewsbury, SY5 7BH. Toby & Julie Shaw. *3m S of Shrewsbury. Through Condover towards Dorrington. Pass village hall follow road round, cross the bridge, in approx 100 metres there is a drive on L. Parking limited, please park at school & walk down to garden.* **Sun 9 June (11-5). Adm £6, chd free. Home-made teas.**
A large country garden extending to two acres with a variety of trees and shrubs, herbaceous borders and a woodland with the Cound Brook flowing through. A courtyard oasis welcomes you as you enter the garden with far reaching views over open countryside. Wheelchair access around most of the garden, although not for the woodland area.

7 BROWNHILL HOUSE
Ruyton XI Towns, SY4 1LR. Roger & Yoland Brown, 01939 261121, brownhill@eleventowns.co.uk, www.eleventowns.co.uk. *9m NW of Shrewsbury on B4397. On the B4397 in the village of Ruyton XI Towns.* **Sun 19, Tue 21 May, Tue 25 June (10-6.30). Adm £5, chd free. Pre-booking essential, please visit www.ngs.org. uk for information & booking.**
Home-made teas. Visits also by arrangement 15 Apr to 14 July.
A unique two acre hillside garden with many steps and levels bordering River Perry. Visitors can enjoy a wide variety of plants and styles from formal terraces to woodland paths. The Good Garden Guide said 'It has to be seen to be believed'. The lower areas are for the sure-footed while the upper levels with a large kitchen garden and glasshouses have many places to sit and enjoy the views. Kit cars on show.

National Garden Scheme gardens are identified by their yellow road signs and posters. You can expect a garden of quality, character and interest, a warm welcome and plenty of home-made cakes!

8 ◆ BURFORD HOUSE GARDENS

Burford House, Burford, Tenbury Wells, WR15 8HQ. British Garden Centres, 01584 810777, pbenson@britishgardencentres.com, www.britishgardencentres.com/burford-house-garden-centre. *1m W of Tenbury Wells on A456. Follow signs for Burford House Garden Centre off the A456.* **For NGS: Sat 25, Sun 26 May, Sat 31 Aug, Sun 1 Sept (10-4.30). Adm £5, chd £5. Cream teas in Burford House. Cafe open nearby on site for breakfast, lunch & teas. For other opening times and information, please phone, email or visit garden website.**

The garden is being restored by the Garden Angels (volunteers) under the leadership of the newly appointed Head Gardener. Four acres of sweeping lawns bordered by the River Teme, and serpentine borders, set in the beautiful Teme Valley, around an elegant Georgian House (open for teas). Designed by the late, great plantsman, John Treasure and featuring over 100 varieties of clematis in addition to a myriad of plants in wonderful combinations and colours. Garden centre offers a comprehensive range of plants, gifts and outdoor leisure. Well behaved dogs on lead welcomed.

9 NEW CHERRY TREE ARBORETUM

Cherry Tree Lane, Woore, CW3 9SR. John & Liz Ravenscroft, cherrytreearboretum.org. *1/2m M of Woore on the Nantwich Road. Off the A51 Nantwich Rd in Woore, just N of the village centre. Signs directing you along Cherry Tree Ln to its end.* **Sat 6 Apr, Sat 11 May, Sat 21 Sept, Sat 26 Oct (10.30-4). Adm £10, chd free. Pre-booking essential, please visit www.ngs.org.uk for information & booking. Light refreshments.**

Cherry Tree Arboretum was created in 2006 on 50 acres of unspoilt, lightly-farmed pastureland scattered with mature oaks by John and Liz Ravenscroft. It is located on a hilly area overlooking the Cheshire plain with views to the Pennines in the north, the Peckforton Hills to the northwest and the Breiddons to the southwest on the Welsh borders. The garden is a showcase of specimen trees with magnolias, peonies, dahlias, lilacs, deciduous azaleas and

North American oaks throughout. A series of trails and paths run between meadows and native wildflowers in the arboretum. Many of the trees are rare and unusual. It also contains 19 of England's Champion Trees and a staggering 793 Champion Trees in Shropshire. It is not usually open to the public and it is a privilege to have it added to the NGS portfolio.

10 12 COLLEY CLOSE

Shrewsbury, SY2 5YN. Kevin & Karen Scurry. *Heading down Telford Way from the police stn take the 2nd exit off the r'about onto Oswell Rd. Take the 1st R into Colley Cl.* **Evening opening Fri 28 June (4-9). Adm £4, chd free. Light refreshments. A selection of cakes and drinks available.**

This garden has three ponds inc a large koi pond and waterfall, wildlife pond and goldfish pond all surrounded by interesting planting. A large collection of specimen bonsai trees accent the koi pond giving an oriental feel to the garden. The front garden has a large collection of grasses. Good wheelchair access and many seating areas to view the garden from different angles.

11 CRUCKFIELD HOUSE

Shoothill, Ford, SY5 9NR. Geoffrey Cobley, 01743 850222, geoffcobley541@btinternet.com. *5m W of Shrewsbury. A458 from Shrewsbury, turn L towards Shoothill.* **Visits by arrangement 1 June to 3 Aug. Adm £10, chd free. Tea & cakes only available to larger groups.**

An artist's romantic three acre garden, formally designed, informally and intensively planted with a great variety of unusual herbaceous plants. Nick's garden, with many species' trees, shrubs and wildflower meadow, surrounds a lake with bog and moisture-loving plants. Ornamental kitchen garden. Rose and peony walk. Courtyard fountain garden, large shrubbery and extensive clematis collection. Extensive topiary, and lily pond.

12 NEW ◆ DAVID AUSTIN ROSES

Bowling Green Lane, Albrighton, Wolverhampton, WV7 3HB. Jo Knight, www.davidaustinroses.co.uk. *On Shrops border in Albrighton. 8m NW of Wolverhampton. Brown tourist signs will provide directions from M54 J3, from Wolverhampton on the A41 or from Shifnal on the A464. The entrance to the Plant Centre is on Old Worcester Rd, immed off Bowling Green Ln.* **For NGS: Sat 15, Sun 16 June (9-5). Adm £10, chd free. Light refreshments in the Garden Room or dine in the onsite restaurant. For other opening times and information, please visit garden website.**

Be part of an exclusive summer open weekend at the world-renowned, award-winning gardens of David Austin Roses. Soak up the scent of their six themed gardens and experience over 700 beautiful rose varieties, which inc the National Collection of English Roses. The David Austin open weekend runs in partnership with Stoke-based potter Emma Bridgewater and the duos 'Bring Me Sunshine' charity mug adorned with the vibrant sunshine-coloured namesake rose. Visitors will be treated to live music, garden games and typically English tea-time treats amongst the roses. Meander through the new plant centre shopping area and much-loved gift shop to take home a piece of the magic of David Austin.

13 EATON MASCOTT HALL

Eaton Mascott, Cross Houses, Shrewsbury, SY5 6HG. Mr W. Blum Gentilomo. *7m S of Shrewsbury. About 7m S of Shrewsbury on A458 2nd R past Cross Houses, thereafter follow signs.* **Sun 9 June (11-4.30). Adm £5, chd free. Home-made teas.**

A six acre garden consisting of 1½ acre walled garden with extensive rose collection. Emphasis on symmetry with pergolas, water features and cross views. Bamboo walk and acer collection, specimen trees. 4½ acre woodland garden with walks and glimpses of parkland and surrounding countryside, plus ferns, azaleas and rhododendrons. Wheelchair access possible if accompanied by helper.

Lilleshall Home Farm

© David Austin

⬛14 EDGE VILLA

Edge, nr Yockleton, Shrewsbury, SY5 9PY. Mr & Mrs W F Neil, 01743 821651, billfneil@me.com. *6m SW of Shrewsbury. From A5 take either A488 signed to Bishops Castle or B4386 to Montgomery for approx 6m then follow NGS signs.* **Sun 14 Apr, Sun 18 Aug (2-5). Adm £5, chd free. Home-made teas. Visits also by arrangement 14 Apr to 18 Aug for groups of 10+.**
Two acres nestling in South Shropshire hills. Self-sufficient vegetable plot. Chickens in orchard, foxes permitting. Large herbaceous borders. Dewpond surrounded by purple elder, irises, candelabra primulas and dieramas. Large selection of fragrant roses. Wendy house for children. Extensive plant and book sales in aid of NGS charities. Visitors can stay in the garden for as long as they like. Some gravel paths.

♿ 🐄 ❀ 🚗 ☕))

⬛15 THE FERNS

Newport Street, Clun, SY7 8JZ. Andrew Dobbin, 01588 640064, andrew.clun@outlook.com. *Enter Clun from Craven Arms. Take 2nd R signed into Ford St. At T-junc turn R for parking in the Memorial Hall car park (100 yds). Retrace steps to T-junc. The Ferns is on L.* **Sun 12 May, Sun 11 Aug (12-6). Adm £5, chd free. Visits also by arrangement 31 Aug to 18 Oct for groups of up to 20.**
A formal village garden of ¾ acre, approached via a drive lined with crab apple and pear trees. On the right is the autumn garden, giving fine views of the surrounding hills. From the front courtyard garden a path leads through double herbaceous borders full of late summer colour, to further rooms, of yew, beech and box. There is also a rear courtyard with tender exotics. Lily pond and statuary. Refreshments available in Clun.

🐄 ☕

The National Garden Scheme searches the length and breadth of England, Wales, Northern Ireland and the Channel Islands for the very best private gardens

L6 FOUR WINDS

Gilberts Lane, Whixall, Whitchurch, SY13 2PR. Lynne Beavan, lynne.beavan@googlemail.com. *3m N of Wem. B5476 through Quina Brook turn L onto Coton Park/ Gilbert's Ln. Follow road bearing L at junc. From Whitchurch: B5476 turn R past Bull & Dog take 1st L past social centre then L Gilbert's Ln.* **Fri 14, Sat 15 June (10.30-4). Adm £5, chd free. Home-made teas. Homemade cakes and scones. Gluten free options available. Visits also by arrangement in June for groups of up to 20.**

About an acre garden backed by 150 year old oak trees. The six year old garden planted by the owner, is looking more mature and with many new features. Fruit trees, ornamental trees, silver birches, shrub beds, hedges, pergolas with roses and wisteria, perennial beds. A wildlife area with natural pond. A peaceful but colourful garden to wander in. Easy parking in field. Not all of the garden is wheelchair accessible. Some paths too narrow, uneven lawn.

   ♿ 🐕 ❄ ☕))

L7 ◆ GOLDSTONE HALL GARDENS

Goldstone, Market Drayton, TF9 2NA. John Cushing, 01630 661202, enquiries@goldstonehall.com, www.goldstonehall.com. *5m N of Newport on A41. From Shrewsbury A53, R for A41 Hinstock & follow brown signs & yellow NGS signs.* **For NGS: Wed 15 May, Wed 12 June, Wed 10 July, Wed 14 Aug, Wed 11 Sept (11-5). Adm £8, chd free. Home-made teas. For other opening times and information, please phone, email or visit garden website.**

Five acres with highly productive beautiful kitchen garden. Unusual vegetables and fruits - alpine strawberries, heritage tomatoes, salad, chillies, celeriac. Roses in Walled Garden from May; double herbaceous in front of old English garden wall at its best July and August; sedums and roses stunning in September. Winner of the prestigious Good Hotel Guide's Editor's Choice Award for Gardens. Lawn aficionados will enjoy the stripes. Extensive kitchen garden, box hedge growing sign. Majority of garden can be accessed on gravel and lawns.

   ♿ 🚗 🚌 ☕))

L8 GROOMS COTTAGE

Waters Upton, Telford, TF6 6NP. Joanne & Andi Butler, 07484 236893, joanneharding1@yahoo.co.uk, www.instagram.com/groomscottagegarden. *No parking at the property due to restricted access. Parking available on the verge opp the church or in*

Upper Farm Garden

the village hall car park. **Sat 22, Sun 23 June (11-4). Adm £5, chd free. Home-made teas. Visits also by arrangement June to Aug for groups of up to 40. Please discuss refreshments when booking.**
A cottage garden around ½ an acre in size comprising mixed herbaceous borders and an abundance of English roses. Highlights inc water features, pergolas, oriental garden, hosta garden, alpine and herb beds and a productive vegetable garden and greenhouse. Many established trees and shrubs and shady plant area. New "secret garden" should be ready for opening in 2024. Some gravel areas not accessible for wheelchair users. Parking on the road, with access down the tarmac drive.

19 NEW **GWYNT NEWYDD**
3 Penygarreg Rise, Pant, Oswestry, SY10 8JR. Douglas and Jane Wood, 07967 283721, douglas.woods@ngs.org.uk. *5m S of Oswestry. A483 S from Oswestry towards Welshpool. Follow signs when in Pant Village, turning opp shop.* **Visits by arrangement 27 July to 31 Aug for groups of 10 to 20. Parking very restricted, car share if possible. Adm £5, chd free. Home-made teas.**
Average size garden to the side and rear of detached bungalow in a quiet close. Acer trees, borders with mixed herbaceous perennials, cannas, hostas, ferns, phlox, greenhouse with succulents. Small area with raised vegetable beds, fruit trees and ornamental trees.

20 **HENLEY HALL**
Henley, Ludlow, SY8 3HD. Helen & Sebastian Phillips, www.henleyhallludlow.com. *2m E of Ludlow. 1½ m from A49. Take A4117 signed to Clee Hill & Cleobury Mortimer. On reaching Henley, the gates to Henley Hall are on R when travelling towards Clee Hill.* **Sun 12 May (10-5). Adm £6, chd free. Home-made teas. Coffee and homemade cakes available.**
Henley Hall offers a mixture of formal and informal gardens. The historic elements inc a formal lawn, stone staircase with balustrades, a ha-ha and an ornate stone arched bridge with decorative weirs over the river Ledwyche, created in 1874. Other highlights inc walkways along the banks of the river and woodland

paths. The listed Orangery will serve as a 'pop-up' tearoom at the garden opening. Some parts of the garden are accessible by wheelchair.

21 ◆ **HODNET HALL GARDENS**
Hodnet, Market Drayton, TF9 3NN. Sir Algernon & The Hon Lady Heber-Percy, 01630 685786, secretary@hodnethall.com, www.hodnethallgardens.org. *5½ m SW of Market Drayton. 12m NE Shrewsbury. At junc of A53 & A442. Tickets available on the gate, on the day.* **For NGS: Sun 7 July (11-5). Adm £9, chd free. Light refreshments in the Garden Restaurant. For other opening times and information, please phone, email or visit garden website.**
The 60+ acres of Hodnet Hall Gardens are amongst the finest in the country. There has been a park and gardens at Hodnet for many hundreds of years. Magnificent forest trees, ornamental shrubs and flowers planted to give interest and colour from early spring to late autumn. Woodland walks alongside pools and lakes, home to abundant wildlife. Productive walled kitchen garden and historic dovecot. Maps are available to show access for our less mobile visitors.

22 **HORATIO'S GARDEN**
The Robert Jones & Agnes Hunt Orthopaedic Hospital, Gobowen, Oswestry, SY10 7AG. Horatio's Garden, www.horatiosgarden.org.uk. *From A5 follow signs to Orthopaedic Hospital; park in Visitor Car Park A by hospital. Once parked, facing main hospital entrance turn R at mini r'about & follow yellow NGS signs to entrance gate.* **Sat 1 June (12-4). Adm £5, chd free. Home-made teas.**
Beautifully designed by Bunny Guinness and delightfully planted, Horatio's Garden Midlands opened to great acclaim in September 2019. Partly funded by the National Garden Scheme, the garden offers a therapeutic place of peace for patients, their loved ones and NHS staff spending time in the Midland Centre for Spinal Injuries. Featuring raised beds, beautiful specimen trees, multi-purpose garden room, gorgeous glasshouse, and a pretty rill running the length of the garden,

this is a horticultural sanctuary like no other. Very good wheelchair access throughout.

23 **HUNDRED HOUSE HOTEL**
Bridgnorth Road, Norton, Telford, TF11 9EE. Henry Phillips, 01952 580240, reservations@ hundredhouse.co.uk, www.hundredhouse.co.uk. *10 mins from Ironbridge, Shropshire. Situated on the A442 in the village of Norton. Midway between Bridgnorth & Telford.* **Wed 3 Apr, Wed 1 May, Wed 3 July, Wed 4 Sept (11-4). Adm £5, chd free. Light refreshments. Coffee, cakes and three menus on offer in our restaurant. Please see our website for details. Visits also by arrangement 2 Jan to 30 Dec for groups of 15 to 50.**
An acre of gardens crafted over 35+ years, complete with sculptures, stonework and working herb and kitchen garden. From March onwards, you will find over 5000 bulb flowers inc tulips, hyacinths, daffodils, alliums, blossoming trees and dancing pond flowers. Summer brings a variety of flowers, inc David Austin roses, giant agapanthus, dahlias, clary, foxgloves, fuchsias and arum lilies. Please see website for restaurant booking and information.

24 **THE LEASOWES, COUND**
Cound, Shrewsbury, SY5 6AF. Robert & Tricia Bland, 07802 667636, rjbbland1@outlook.com. *7m SE of Shrewsbury. On the A458 SE of Shrewsbury, 500m to the E of the Riverside Inn adjoining Oakleys, the lawnmower business.* **Sat 8 June (10-4.30). Adm £6, chd free. Home-made teas. Visits also by arrangement 15 Mar to 30 Nov for groups of 15 to 25. No refreshments available for groups. Riverside Pub is close by.**
Within the super structure of mature larches and interconnected ponds, a wide range of rhododendrons and azaleas have been planted as well as shade appreciating trees and shrubs over 10 acres. A large offering of roses of all descriptions provide colour throughout the formal gardens.

25 **NEW** **LILLESHALL HOME FARM**
The Incline, Lilleshall, Newport, TF10 9AP. Connie Sansom. *Follow signs for Lilleshall National Sports Centre, our entrance is off the sports centre drive, which will be signposted.* **Fri 7 June (10-4). Adm £5, chd free. Light refreshments.**
A beautiful country farmhouse garden with far-reaching views across the Shropshire countryside. The garden is split into several areas inc the walled back garden, pool garden and patio, tennis court lined with hydrangeas, pergola, formal rose beds, herbaceous border, croquet lawn, pond, orchard, greenhouse and veg patch. Home farm is also home to horses, sheep, chickens, a goat and a pig. There will also be a small plant sale. There is a wheelchair accessible route around the garden, but it will involve some areas of grass and gravel.

26 **LONGDEN MANOR**
Plealey, SY5 0XL. Karen Lovegrove. *From Shrewsbury take C150 Longden Rd. On entering Longden Village, opp The Tankerville Arms & Village Shop on L, turn R into Manor Ln.* **Sun 12 May (10-4). Adm £5, chd free. Home-made teas.**
Large estate garden with lots of character and interest: woodland walks and grass paths; humorous topiary; wide variety of specimen trees; rhododendrons and azaleas; wildflowers; restored water garden; panoramic vistas of surrounding countryside; holly garden. Also, giant Jenga, skittles and croquet - a great place for all the family to visit. Topiary trail for children inc giraffe, pelican, otter, kingfisher, shark, gorilla and a goose.

27 **LONGNER HALL**
Atcham, Shrewsbury, SY4 4TG. Mr & Mrs R L Burton, www.longner.co.uk. *4m SE of Shrewsbury. From M54 follow A5 to Shrewsbury, then B4380 to Atcham. From Atcham take Uffington Rd, entrance ¼ m on L.* **Sun 19 May (2-5). Adm £6, chd free. Home-made teas.**
A long drive approach through parkland designed by Humphry Repton. Walks lined with golden yew through extensive lawns, with views over the Severn Valley. Borders containing roses and herbaceous

shrubs, also an ancient yew wood. Enclosed one acre walled garden open to NGS visitors. Mixed planting, garden buildings, tower and game larder. Short woodland walk around old moat pond which is not suitable for wheelchairs.

28 **LOWER BROOKSHILL**
Nind, nr Lydham, SY5 0JW. Patricia & Robin Oldfield, 01588 650137, robin.oldfield@live.com. *3m N of Lydham on A488. Take signed turn to Nind & after ½ m sharp L & follow narrow road for another ½ m.* **Sat 13, Sun 14 July (1-5). Adm £6, chd free. Cream teas.**
Ten acres of hillside garden and woods at 950ft within the AONB. Begun in 2010 from a derelict and overgrown site, cultivated areas now rub shoulders with the natural landscape using fine borrowed views over and down a valley. Inc brookside walks, a 'pocket' park, four ponds (inc a Monet lily pond), mixed borders and lawns, cottage garden and wildflowers. Lovely picnic spots. Cash only at gate.

29 **NEW** **107 MEADOWBOUT WAY**
Bowbrook, Shrewsbury, SY5 8QB. Sue and Mark Smith, 07736 837427, sue1706@outlook.com. *2m S of Shrewsbury. On the estate follow Squinter Pip Way until you see Meadowbout Way on R. You will see the NGS sign at the end of the straight section.* **Visits by arrangement 15 June to 8 Sept for groups of up to 12. Adm £6, chd free. Light refreshments.**
Our oasis is a small town garden completed in a tropical style. There are several examples of plants native to other shores but which are happy in the space we have created. With over 200 plants inc tree ferns, bananas, palm trees and cottage garden plants arranged around a variety of seating areas, our visitors have a perpetual sense of being on holiday. Direct access to the garden via a side gate.

30 **MERTON**
Shepherds Lane, Bicton, Shrewsbury, SY3 8BT. David & Jessica Pannett, 01743 850773, jessicapannett@hotmail.co.uk.

3m W of Shrewsbury. Follow B4380 from Shrewsbury past Shelton for 1m. Shepherd's Ln turn L garden signed on R. Or from A5 bypass at Churncote r'about, turn towards Shrewsbury, 2nd turn L is Shepherds Ln. **Visits by arrangement June to Sept for groups of up to 25. Discuss refreshments when booking. Adm £5, chd free.**
Mature ½ acre botanical garden with a rich collection of trees and shrubs inc unusual conifers from around the world. Hardy perennial borders with seasonal flowers and grasses plus an award winning collection of hosta varieties in a woodland setting. Outstanding gunneras in a waterside setting with moisture loving plants. Wheelchair access over level paths and lawns.

31 **THE MILL HOUSE**
Mill Lane, Ruyton XI Towns, Shrewsbury, SY4 1LR. Debbie Sargent & Jeffrey Ewin. *SE of Ruyton X1Towns. Mill Ln can be found on leaving the village just before Platt Bridge. Parking in Mill Ln, 7 mins walk from garden. Disabled parking at the house.* **Sun 23 June (2-5). Adm £5, chd free. Home-made teas.**
Four acre garden situated alongside the River Perry. Herbaceous borders inc roses, peonies and climbers. Terrace, sloping lawns, and unusual trees in a naturalised woodland. Ancient mill pond. Vegetable garden. Wildlife friendly. Uneven ground and some sloping pathways. Adjacent to Arboretum with national collection of Betula.

32 **MILLICHOPE PARK**
Munslow, SY7 9HA. Mr & Mrs Frank Bury, www.millichopepark.com. *8m NE of Craven Arms. Off B4368 Craven Arms to Bridgnorth Rd. Nr Munslow then follow yellow signs.* **Sun 11 Feb (2-5); Sun 5 May (2-6); Sun 13 Oct (2-5). Adm £6, chd free. Regret no refreshments in February.**
Historic landscape gardens covering 14 acres with lakes and cascades dating from C18, formal terraces, woodland walks and wildflowers. Snowdrops feature in February, bluebells in May, and autumn colours in October. Please note, we regret the Walled Garden and Wildegoose Nursery will not be opening jointly on these days.

The Leasowes, Cound

33 MOAT HALL
Annscroft, Shrewsbury,
SY5 8AZ. **Martin & Helen Davies,
01743 860216, helenatthefarm@
hotmail.co.uk.** *3m S of Shrewsbury.
Take the Longden road from
Shrewsbury to Hook a Gate. Our
lane is 2nd on R after Hook a Gate
& before Annscroft. Single track lane
with passing places for ½m.* **Sun
4 Aug (1-5). Adm £6, chd free.
Home-made teas. Visits also by
arrangement 24 Feb to 28 Sept.**
An acre garden around an old
farmhouse within a dry moat. Well
organised and extensive kitchen
garden, fruit garden and orchard for
self-sufficiency. Colourful herbaceous
borders; stumpery; raised cut flower
borders; ⅔ acre pond nearby with
oak gazebo; many interesting stone
items inc troughs, cheese weights,
staddle stones some uncovered in
the garden. Plenty of seating areas
on the lawns for enjoying the garden.

Wheelchair access: mostly lawn with
one grass and one concrete ramp;
kitchen garden has 2' wide paved
paths. Paved path to the pond and
gazebo.

♿ 🐕 ✳ 🚗 ☕))

34 17 MORTIMER ROAD
Buntingsdale, Market Drayton,
TF9 2EP. **Martin & Stella
Clifford-Jones, 07484 327979,
stellaandmartin@ngs.org.uk.**
*What3Words app - undivided.
orbited.apprehend. Access only via
Tern Hill A41. N on A41, as you enter
Tern Hill take first R into Hedley Way,
or going S turn L into Hedley Way
after mobile home sales site.* **Sun
30 June (2-5). Adm £5, chd free.
Home-made teas. Visits also by
arrangement Apr to Oct.**
A wildlife-friendly garden with
plantaholic owners. There are two
ponds, a small meadow, a raised
alpine bed and a huge range of plants
to give year round interest. Most
importantly, there are several delightful
places to sit whilst enjoying your tea
and cake. Wheelchair access to some
of the garden with one small step
linking the two sections.

♿ ✳ ☕))

*The National Garden
Scheme donated
£3,403,960 to our nursing
and health beneficiaries
from money raised at
gardens open in 2023*

35 THE MOUNT

Bull Lane, Bishops Castle, SY9 5DA. Heather Willis, 07779 314609, adamheather@btopenworld.com. *Off A488 Shrewsbury to Knighton Rd. At top of the town, 130 metres up Bull Ln on R. No parking at property. Free parking in Bishops Castle.* **Sun 16 June (1.30-5.30). Adm £6, chd free. Open nearby The Old Vicarage, Bishops Castle. Visits also by arrangement 1 Apr to 29 Sept for groups of 5+.**
An acre of garden that has evolved over 24 years, with four lawns, a rose bed in the middle of the drive with pink and white English roses, and herbaceous and mixed shrub borders. There are roses planted throughout the garden and in the spring daffodils and tulips abound. Two large beech trees frame the garden with a view that sweeps down the valley over fields and then up to the Long Mynd. Wheelchair access easy to most parts of the garden itself, but not to WC which is in the house up steps.

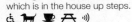

36 1 MOUNT PLEASANT COTTAGES

Lockley Wood, Market Drayton, TF9 2LS. Chris & Clive Brown, 01630 661470, chrisbrownemk@yahoo.co.uk. *Lockley Wood, near Hinstock. From Newport turn off A41 at Hinstock. Follow A529. At x-roads in Lockley Wood turn L. Garden 1st property on R. From Market Drayton, A529 towards Newport. In Lockley Wood turn R at x-roads.* **Sun 14 July (2-5). Adm £5. Home-made teas. Visits also by arrangement 15 June to 26 July for groups of up to 30.**
The garden extends to $\frac{1}{5}$ acre, situated in a rural location. The main garden comprises a long border and island beds with cottage style planting, all colour themed to flow throughout the seasons. Box and yew punctuate the planting. Other features inc a fish pond and productive vegetable plot. The back garden is planted predominantly with shade tolerant plants.

37 NEEN VIEW

Neen Sollars, Cleobury Mortimer, DY14 9AB. Ian & Chris Ferguson, 07485 795079, chrisianfurg@gmail.com. *3m from the Market Town of Cleobury Mortimer. From A456 past Mamble, turn R at Neen Sollars, follow lane to Live & Let Live for parking. From Cleobury take the Tenbury Rd, turn L & L again then up the hill to Neen View gardens.* **Wed 8, Wed 15 May (12-5). Adm £5, chd free. Refreshments at pub. Regret, cash only. Visits also by arrangement Apr to June.**
A woodland garden with stunning panoramic views of the Clee Hills and Teme Valley. Mature trees inc: azaleas, camellias and rhododendrons. Wildlife ponds and wildflower meadow. There are plenty of seats to enjoy the views. Walking around you will find a ruined bothy and Japanese stream garden.

The Old Rectory, Hodnet

38 OFFCOT
Kynaston, Kinnerley, SY10 8EF.
Tom Pountney. *Just off A5 on Wolfshead r'about (at Oswestry end of Nesscliffe bypass) towards Knockin. Then take the 1st L towards Kinnerley. Follow NGS signs from this road.* **Thur 18, Fri 19, Sat 20 July, Thur 10, Fri 11, Sat 12 Oct (10-4). Adm £7. Home-made teas.**
A cottage garden with lots of winding pathways leading to different focal points. The garden is packed with a wide range of evergreen and deciduous trees and shrubs and underplanted with herbaceous perennials. There is a natural looking pond with a running stream feeding into it. A haven for wildlife. So many different areas to see and enjoy inc the garden bar.

39 THE OLD RECTORY, HODNET
Hearne Lane, Hodnet, Market Drayton, TF9 3NG.
Sarah Riley, 01630 685671, rileys55@icloud.com. *¼ m NW of the village of Hodnet. SatNav takes you to the end of Hearne Ln. Bear L, on the single track road, up the hill towards the trees.* **Visits by arrangement 15 Feb to 15 Sept for groups of up to 20. Adm £6, chd free. Tea.**
Set in farmland, 3 ½ acres of gardens, created over 45 years by John and Elizabeth Ravenscroft, surrounding the Grade II listed old rectory. Formal gardens, a walled garden, man-made stream, large pool with stepping stones, lawns and wilder wooded areas. Collections of azaleas, magnolias, peonies. New owners (4 years) are enjoying editing and developing the garden.

40 THE OLD VICARAGE, BISHOPS CASTLE
Church Lane, Bishops Castle, SY9 5AF. **Helen & Jerry Robinson.** *Nr the junc of Church St & Kerry Ln, directly behind St John's Church. Pedestrian access through the main gate on Church Ln or through the garden gate to the rear of St John's churchyard.* **Sun 16 June (1-6). Adm £6, chd free. Home-made teas. Open nearby The Mount.**
Extending to just over 1 ½ acres, the gardens inc lawns surrounded by perennial beds and mature shrubs, a pond, orchard, rose garden and a romantic ruin, remains of the lost C13

church. Tending toward the wild, the garden is full of colour; foxgloves, wisteria, rhododendron, alliums and ornamental trees. Sales by local artists and craftsmen throughout the garden. Level access over gravel drive and lawns.

41 THE OLD VICARAGE, CLUN
Vicarage Road, Clun, SY7 8JG.
Peter & Jay Upton, 01588 640775, jay@salopia.plus.com. *16m NW of Ludlow. Over bridge at Clun heading towards Knighton (parking in public car park by bridge); walk up to church, turn L into Vicarage Rd; house on R next to church.* **Sun 2 June (2-5). Adm £5, chd free. Visits also by arrangement May & June for groups of up to 30.**
A revived, old vicarage garden: a slow retrieval and recovery revealing a wealth of features and plants chosen by plantsmen vicars: buddleia globosa fascinates bees and butterflies; glorious oriental poppies fascinate visitors. 'The Tree', an enormous Leyland cypress (5th biggest girth in the world); the most dramatic feature is a formal wisteria allee with alliums - a symphony of mauve and purple.

42 OTELEY
Ellesmere, SY12 0PB. **Mr RK Mainwaring, www.oteley.com.** *1m SE of Ellesmere. Entrance out of Ellesmere past Mere, opp Convent nr to A528/495 junc.* **Sun 5 May (11-4). Adm £6, chd free. Light refreshments.**
Explore 10 acres running down to The Mere with stunning views. Walled kitchen garden, architectural features, many old interesting trees. Rhododendrons, azaleas, wild woodland walk and views across Mere to Ellesmere. First opened in 1927 when the National Garden Scheme started.

43 THE PADDOCK
Annscroft, Shrewsbury, SY5 8AN.
Ian Ross. *On road from Annscroft to Hanwood/Plealey 200 yds from the Xrds. Parking is at The Farriers SY5 8AN - on the road from Annscroft to Exfords Green.* **Sat 12 Oct (11-5). Adm £6, chd free. Home-made teas.**
A mini arboretum in which 70 trees are tagged - some of which are rare. The collection inc 12 different acers

and a cluster of six Gingko bilobas. A waterfall cascades through three levels. As the new owner since 2001, I see myself as the custodian of an impressive small garden. Wheelchair access is available by paths and grass to most of the garden.

44 NEW RIVERSIDE
Berrisford Road, Market Drayton, TF9 1JH. **Mrs Susan Harrison.** *Market Drayton. Enter Market Drayton on Newcastle Rd , turn into Great Hales St and then L into Berrisford Rd.* **Sun 19 May, Sun 30 June, Sun 15 Sept (12-5). Adm £5, chd free. Home-made teas.**
The garden is ¾ acre, with different planting areas. We have hydrangeas, hostas, woodland walk, hot garden and herbaceous borders with white garden with loggia. Plus an old and large wisteria and a very old climbing rose. Gravel drive but mainly level paths.

45 RUTHALL MANOR
Ditton Priors, WV16 6TN. **Mr & Mrs G T Clarke, 01746 712608, clrk608@btinternet.com.** *7m SW of Bridgnorth. At Ditton Priors Church take road signed Bridgnorth, then 2nd L. Garden 1m.* **Sat 27, Sun 28 Apr, Sat 18, Sun 19 May, Sat 8, Sun 9 June, Sat 6, Sun 7 July (12.30-5.30). Adm £7, chd free. Home-made teas. Visits also by arrangement 2 Apr to 30 Sept for groups of 15 to 50.**
Offset by a mature collection of specimen trees, the garden is divided into intimate sections, carefully linked by winding paths. The front lawn flanked by striking borders, extends to a gravel, art garden and ha-ha. Clematis and roses scramble through an eclectic collection of wrought-iron work, unique pottery and secluded seating. Designed and planted by present owners since 1960. A stunning horse pond with primulas, iris and bog plants. Jigsaw puzzle sale. Wheelchair access to most areas of garden.

46 SAMBROOK MANOR
Sambrook, TF10 8AL. Mrs
E Mitchell, 01952 550256,
eileengran@hotmail.com . *Between
Newport & Tern Hill, 1m off A41. In
the village of Sambrook.* **Sun 7 July
(12-5). Adm £5, chd free. Home-
made teas.**
Deep, colourful, well-planted borders
offset by sweeping lawns surrounding
an early C18 manor house (not open).
Wide ranging herbaceous planting
with plenty of roses to enjoy; the
arboretum below the garden, with
views across the river, has been
further extended with new trees.
The waterfall and Japanese garden
are now linked by a pretty rill. Lovely
garden to visit for all the family.
Wheelchair access to most areas.
Woodland area may be difficult.

47 1 SCOTSMANSFIELD
Burway Road, Church Stretton,
SY6 6DP. Peter Vickers & Hilary
Taylor. *Scotsmansfield is on L,
c.200m up Burway Rd (quite steep).
Approach Church Stretton from A49.
At Sandford Rd/ High St jct, turn R
& then L, up Burway Rd. No parking.
Easthope Rd car park available SY6
6BL. Shuttle bus running from here.*
**Sat 22 June (11-5). Adm £5, chd
free. Light refreshments.**
Terraced garden of ¾ acre, renewed
over a decade after long neglect.
Attached to E wing of 'Scotsmansfield'
(not open), built 1908. Celebration of
favourite plants, with colour, shape,
texture, scent, light, shade and plentiful
wildlife. Trees, fernery, lily pond, mixed
borders, yew hedges, lavish roses.
Areas of tranquillity and intimacy,
occasions of drama and long views of
surrounding woods and hills. Partial

access via steep gravelled paths to
some areas. Wheelchair users will
need support from a competent and
fit assistant.

GROUP OPENING

**48 THE SECRET GARDENS AT
STEVENTON TERRACE**
Steventon Terrace, Steventon New
Road, Ludlow, SY8 1JZ. Kevin &
Carolyn Wood. *Gardens are located
behind row of terraced cottages.
Easily accessible from A49; on-street
parking; Park & Ride stops outside
the garden.* **Sat 22 June (12.30-
4.30). Combined adm £5, chd
free. Home-made teas. Ice cream
also available.**
Discover some very secret gardens
hidden behind a row of Victorian
terraced cottages in Ludlow. A ½
acre south facing garden that has
been developed over 30 years. It has
been divided into different sections
which inc a rose garden, herbaceous
borders, koi fish, chickens, polytunnel
and greenhouse and a Mediterranean
garden.

49 STANLEY HALL GARDENS
Bridgnorth, WV16 4SP. Mr & Mrs M
J Thompson. *½ m N of Bridgnorth.
Leave Bridgnorth by N gate B4373;
turn R at Stanley Ln. Pass Golf
Course Club House on L & turn L at
Lodge.* **Sun 2 June (2-5.30). Adm
£5, chd free. Home-made teas.**
Regency and later landscaped garden
with rhododendrons, woodland walks,
fish ponds and fine trees in parkland
setting. Dower House (Mr and Mrs C
Wells): four acres of specimen trees,
contemporary sculpture and walled
vegetable garden South Lodge (Mr
Tim Warren): Hillside cottage garden.
Wheelchair access to the main
gardens.

50 SUNNINGDALE
9 Mill Street, Wem, SY4 5ED. Mrs
Susan Griffiths, 01939 236733,
sue.griffiths@btinternet.com. *Town
centre. Wem is on B5476. Parking in
car park at Barnard St. The property
is opp the purple house below the
church. Some on-street parking on
High St. Coaches can drop off at
the main gate.* **Sun 22 Sept (11-3).
Adm £4, chd free. Visits also by
arrangement Feb to Oct for groups**

Tower House

of 6 to 60. Refreshments can be ordered in advance.

A ½ acre town garden. Wildlife haven for a variety of birds inc nesting gold crests. A profusion of excellent nectar rich plants means that butterflies and other pollinators are in abundance. Interesting plantings with carefully collected rare plants and unusual annuals means there is always something new to see. Large perennial borders, with exotic climbers, designed as an all year-round garden. Koi pond and natural stone waterfall rockery. Antique and modern sculpture. Sound break yew walkway. Wheelchair access the garden is on the level but with several steps mostly around the pond area; paths are mainly gravel or flags; flat lawn.

51 TOWER HOUSE
Bache, Craven Arms, SY7 9LN. Lady Spicer, 01584 861692, nicspicer@yahoo.com. *7m NW of Ludlow. B4365 Ludlow to Much Wenlock. Turn L after 3m (Bache, Burley). Garden at top of hill after 1½m. B4368 Craven Arms to Bridgnorth. Turn R at Xrds after 1½m immed fork L, garden after ¾m.* **Sat 18 May (11-5.30). Adm £5, chd free. Home-made teas. Visits also by arrangement 1 Apr to 15 July.**
A folly built in 1838 with a two acre garden created by the present owner over 50 years. On a perfect site with views over the Corve Dale, with veg, herbaceous borders, a small parterre and pond. Wheelchair access a little rough in the wood.

52 [NEW] UPPER FARM GARDEN
Rushton, Telford, TF6 5AG. Pete & Paul Turpin-Ottley. *3m from M54 Wellington. Exit 7 M54 take Little Wenlock/Wrekin turn. In 1m at bollards R for Uppington. In 2m at junc, turn L for Eaton Constantine. In ½ m R for Charlton Hill. See NGS signs on your L for Garden and Parking.* **Sat 20, Sun 21 Apr (11-4); Thur 20, Fri 21 June (1-8); Sat 10, Sun 11 Aug (11-6); Sat 5, Sun 6 Oct (11-4). Adm £6. Home-made teas.**
Farmhouse Garden with views of the Wrekin and the Stretton Hills. Comprising several garden 'rooms' connected by gravelled walkways interspersed with ample seating opportunities. Unusual features inc a raised scree terrace, a rose pergola and bed with 40 varieties of English

---

shrub roses, a two sided herbaceous walk, an elevated viewing deck, a cactus house and self-sufficient allotment beds.

53 ◆ WALCOT HALL
Lydbury North, SY7 8AZ. Mr & Mrs C R W Parish, 01588 680570, enquiries@walcothall.com, www.walcothall.com. *4m SE of Bishop's Castle. B4385 Craven Arms to Bishop's Castle, turn L by The Powis Arms in Lydbury North.* **For NGS: Sun 26, Mon 27 May (1.30-5). Adm £5, chd free. Home-made teas. For other opening times and information, please phone, email or visit garden website.**
Arboretum planted by Lord Clive of India's son, Edward in 1800. Cascades of rhododendrons and azaleas amongst specimen trees and pools. Fine views of Sir William Chambers' Clock Towers, with lake and hills beyond. Walled kitchen garden, dovecote, meat safe, ice house and mile-long lakes. Russian wooden church, grotto and fountain, tin chapel. Relaxed borders and rare shrubs. Lakeside replanted and water garden at western end re-established. Outstanding Ballroom where excellent teas are served.

54 WESTWOOD HOUSE
Oldbury, Bridgnorth, WV16 5LP. Hugh & Carolyn Trevor-Jones. *Take the Ludlow Rd (B4364) out of Bridgnorth. Past the Punch Bowl Inn, turn 1st L, Westwood House signed on R.* **Sun 28 Apr (2-5). Adm £5, chd free. Home-made teas.**
A country garden, well designed and planted around the house, particularly known for its tulips and use of colour. Sweeping lawns offset by deeply planted mixed borders; pool garden and lawn tennis court; kitchen and cutting garden, with everything designed to attract wildlife for organic growth. Far reaching views of this delightful corner of the county and woodland walks to enjoy. Reasonable wheelchair access but there are gravel paths and some steps.

55 WINDY RIDGE
Church Lane, Little Wenlock, TF6 5BB. George & Fiona Chancellor. *2m S of Wellington. Follow signs for Little Wenlock from N (J7, M54) or E (off A5223 at*

Horsehay). Parking signed. Do not rely on SatNav. **Sat 15, Sun 16 June (12-5). Adm £7, chd free. Home-made teas.**
Universally admired for its structure, inspirational planting and balance of texture, form and all-season colour, the garden more than lives up to its award-winning record. Developed over 35 years, 'open plan' garden rooms display over 1000 species (mostly labelled) in a range of colour-themed planting styles, beautifully set off by well-tended lawns, plenty of water and fascinating sculpture. Workshops on Garden Design, Planting and Maintenance will be held during the summer. For further information email fiona.chancellor@ngs.org.uk. Wheelchair access via some gravel paths but help available.

56 ◆ WOLLERTON OLD HALL
Wollerton, Market Drayton, TF9 3NA. Lesley & John Jenkins, 01630 685760, info@wollertonoldhallgarden.com, www.wollertonoldhallgarden.com. *4m SW of Market Drayton. On A53 between Hodnet & A53-A41 junc. Follow brown signs.* **For NGS: Thur 5 Sept (11-5). Adm £9, chd £1. Light lunches available from 12.00; afternoon tea and cream teas from 14.00. For other opening times and information, please phone, email or visit garden website.**
Four acre garden created around C16 house (not open). Formal structure creates variety of gardens each with own colour theme and character. Planting is mainly of perennials many in their late summer/early autumn hues, particularly the asters. Ongoing lectures by gardening personalities, designers and technical experts. Mondays (not B/Hols)Tuesdays and Wednesdays reserved for garden club visits. Partial wheelchair access.

Our donation to Marie Curie this year equates to 17,496 hours of nursing care

STAFFORDSHIRE
Birmingham & West Midlands

VOLUNTEERS

County Organiser
Anita & David Wright
01889 441049
davidandanita@ngs.org.uk

County Treasurer
Brian Bailey
01902 424867
brian.bailey@ngs.org.uk

Publicity
Ruth & Clive Plant
07591 886925
ruthandcliveplant@ngs.org.uk

Booklet Co-ordinator
Ruth Plant
07591 886925
ruthandcliveplant@ngs.org.uk

Assistant County Organisers
Fiona Horwath
07908 918181
fiona.horwath@ngs.org.uk

Alison & Peter Jordan
01785 660819
alisonandpeterjordan@ngs.org.uk

Ken & Joy Sutton
07791 041189
kenandjoysutton@ngs.org.uk

✕ @NGSStaffs
f @StaffordshireBirminghamand
WestMidlandsNationalGardenScheme

OPENING DATES

All entries subject to change.
For latest information check
www.ngs.org.uk

Map locator numbers are
shown to the right of each
garden name.

February

Snowdrop Opening

Sunday 18th
5 East View Cottages   9

March

Thursday 21st
23 St Johns Road   26

Sunday 24th
Millennium Garden   20

Sunday 31st
'John's Garden' at Ashwood
  Nurseries   17

April

Thursday 18th
23 St Johns Road   26

May

Saturday 4th
Springfield Cottage   29

Sunday 12th
Millennium Garden   20

Thursday 16th
23 St Johns Road   26

Sunday 19th
10 Paget Rise   24

Thursday 23rd
The Secret Garden   27

Sunday 26th
Butt Lane Farm   4
12 Meres Road   19
The Old Dairy House   22

Monday 27th
The Old Dairy House   22
NEW Westview   33

June

Sunday 2nd
Courtwood House   7
Hamilton House   14
The Pintles   25
12 Waterdale   31
19 Waterdale   32

Thursday 6th
The Secret Garden   27

Saturday 8th
14 Longbow Close   18

Sunday 9th
Ashcroft and Claremont   1
The Bungalow, Wood Farm   3
33 Gorway Road   11

Wednesday 19th
Bankcroft Farm   2

Thursday 20th
23 St Johns Road   26

Friday 21st
Yarlet House   35

Sunday 23rd
Cheadle Allotments   5
5 East View Cottages   9
NEW Westview   33

Wednesday 26th
Bankcroft Farm   2
5 East View Cottages   9

Friday 28th
The Secret Garden   27

Saturday 29th
Hammerwich House Farm   15
Yew Trees   37

Sunday 30th
Hammerwich House Farm   15
Izaak Walton Farm   16
12 Waterdale   31
19 Waterdale   32
Yew Trees   37

July

Thursday 4th
Yew Tree Cottage   36

Saturday 6th
Fifty Shades of Green   10

Sunday 7th
The Bungalow, Wood Farm   3
Fifty Shades of Green   10
NEW Snails Place   28
76 Station Street   30

Thursday 11th
Yew Tree Cottage 36

Saturday 13th
Springfield Cottage 29
Yew Trees 37

Sunday 14th
The Bungalow, Wood Farm 3
NEW Westview 33
The Wickets 34
Yew Trees 37

Tuesday 16th
The Old Vicarage 23

Thursday 18th
Yew Tree Cottage 36

Sunday 21st
Grafton Cottage 12
NEW Snails Place 28
Yew Tree Cottage 36

Sunday 28th
Grafton Cottage 12

August

Thursday 1st
Grafton Cottage 12

Saturday 10th
Colour Mill 6
Yew Trees 37

Sunday 11th
Grafton Cottage 12
Yew Trees 37

Sunday 18th
12 Meres Road 19

Saturday 24th
Fifty Shades of Green 10

Sunday 25th
Fifty Shades of Green 10
Grafton Cottage 12
The Wickets 34

Monday 26th
NEW Westview 33

September

Sunday 1st
Monarchs Way 21

October

Sunday 20th
◆ Dorothy Clive Garden 8

February 2025

Sunday 16th
5 East View Cottages 9

By Arrangement

Arrange a personalised garden visit with your club, or group of friends, on a date to suit you. See individual garden entries for full details.

Butt Lane Farm 4
Colour Mill 6
5 East View Cottages 9
Fifty Shades of Green 10
33 Gorway Road 11
Grafton Cottage 12
22 Greenfield Road 13
Monarchs Way 21
The Pintles 25
23 St Johns Road 26
19 Waterdale 32
The Wickets 34
Yew Tree Cottage 36
Yew Trees 37

Grafton Cottage

© Marianne Majerus

THE GARDENS

GROUP OPENING

1 ASHCROFT AND CLAREMONT
Stafford Road, Eccleshall, ST21 6JP. *7m W of Stafford. J14 M6. At Eccleshall end of A5013 the garden is 100 metres before junction with A519. On street parking nearby. Note: Some SatNavs give wrong directions.* **Sun 9 June (2-5). Combined adm £5, chd free. Home-made teas at Ashcroft.**

ASHCROFT
Gillian Bertram.

26 CLAREMONT ROAD
Maria Edwards.

Weeping limes hide Ashcroft, a one acre garden of green tranquillity, rooms flow seamlessly around the Edwardian house. Covered courtyard with lizard water feature, sunken herb bed, kitchen garden, greenhouse, wildlife boundaries home to five hedgehogs increasing yearly. Deep shade border, woodland area and ruin with stone carvings and stained glass sculpture. Claremont is a master class in clipped perfection. An artist with an artist's eye has blurred the boundaries of this small Italianate influenced garden. Overlooking the aviary, a stone lion surveys the large pots and borders of vibrant planting, completing the Feng-Shui design of this beautiful all seasons garden. Tickets, teas and plants available at Ashcroft. Partial wheelchair access at Claremont.

2 BANKCROFT FARM
Tatenhill, Burton-on-Trent, DE13 9SA. Mrs Penelope Adkins. *2m NW of Burton-on-Trent. 1m NW of Burton upon Trent take Tatenhill Rd off A38 on Burton/Branson flyover, 1m 1st house on L after village sign. Parking on farm.* **Wed 19, Wed 26 June (1.30-4.30). Adm £4, chd free.**
Lose yourself for an afternoon in our 1½ acre organic country garden. Arbour, gazebo and many other seating areas to view ponds and herbaceous borders, backed with shrubs and trees with emphasis on structure, foliage and colour.

Productive fruit and vegetable gardens, wildlife areas and adjoining 12 acre native woodland walk. Picnics welcome. Gravel paths.

3 THE BUNGALOW, WOOD FARM
Great Gate, Nr Tean, Stoke-on-Trent, ST10 4HF. Mrs Dorothy Hurst. *Staffordshire. Arrive in Great Gate & follow yellow signs.* **Sun 9 June, Sun 7, Sun 14 July (11.30-5). Adm £5, chd free. Light refreshments. Tea, coffee & cakes for sale also available gluten free & dairy free cakes.**
Unique 1 acre country cottage garden with stunning views of the Weaver Hills surrounded by farm land, the garden inc a Thai theme underground temple with water feature, a relaxing Japanese area also an area with a New Zealand and Mediterranean vibe all with varied planting, as you wander around you will find plenty of quiet and tranquil seating. It is an experience that will lift your spirits.

4 BUTT LANE FARM
Butt Lane, Ranton, Stafford, ST18 9JZ. Pete Gough, 07975 928968, claire-pickering@hotmail.co.uk, www.facebook.com/buttlanefmopengarden. *6m W of Stafford. Take A518 to Haughton, turn R Station Rd (signed Ranton) 2m turn L at Butt Ln. Or from Great Bridgeford head W B5405 for 3m. Turn L Moorend Ln, 2nd L Butt Ln.* **Sun 26 May (10-4). Adm £5, chd free. Light refreshments inc home made pizza & cakes. Visits also by arrangement June & July for groups of 15 to 50. Parking suitable for mini bus and coach parties.**
Entering from unspoilt farmland through small wooded area into multi award winning garden. The lawns are surrounded by varying floral beds, fruit and vegetable gardens. Different areas of interest can be found, greenhouse courtyard, outside kitchen and glass topped well. Many arts and craft stalls, classic motor vehicle display and live music. Wide selection of craft stalls and displays/demonstrations to be in attendance along side classic motor vehicles. Finalist, Midlands, The English Garden Magazine's The Nation's Favourite Gardens 2023.

5 CHEADLE ALLOTMENTS
Delphouse Road, Cheadle, Stoke-on-Trent, ST10 2NN. Cheadle Allotment Association. *On the A521 1m to the W of Cheadle town centre.* **Sun 23 June (1-5). Adm £5, chd free. Home-made teas inc in the adm price.**
The allotments, which were opened in 2015, are located on the western edge of Cheadle (Staffs). There are 29 plots growing a variety of vegetables, fruits and flowers. A new addition in 2019 was a community area, with an adjacent wildlife area. A small orchard is currently being developed. Wheelchair access on all main paths.

6 COLOUR MILL
Winkhill, Leek, ST13 7PR. Jackie Pakes, 07967 558917, jackie.pakes@icloud.com. *7m E of Leek. Follow A523 from either Leek or Ashbourne, look for NGS signs on the side of the main rd which will direct you down to Colour Mill.* **Sat 10 Aug (1.30-5). Adm £5, chd free. Home-made teas. Visits also by arrangement 17 June to 23 Aug.**
1½ acre south facing garden, created in the shadow of a former iron foundry, set beside the delightful River Hamps. Informal planting in a variety of rooms surrounded by beautiful 7ft beech hedges. Large organic vegetable patch complete with greenhouse and polytunnel. Maturing trees provide shade for the interesting seating areas. River walk through woodland and willows. Herbaceous borders and woodland beside the River Hamps.

7 COURTWOOD HOUSE
3 Court Walk, Betley, CW3 9DP. Mike Reeves. *6m S of Crewe. On A531 toward Keele & Newcastle under Lyme or from J16 off M6, pickup A531 off A500 on Nantwich rd, into village by Betley Court.* **Sun 2 June (12-5). Adm £5, chd free. Home-made teas.**
Small L-shaped, walled garden, which is designed as a walk-through sculpture. Mainly shrubs with ceramic and metal structures and water features, hidden spaces and numerous seating areas, with strong shapes and effects utilising a wide range of materials, inc a synthetic lawn. Small art gallery with acrylic and oil paintings by owner for sale.

⑧ ◆ DOROTHY CLIVE GARDEN
Willoughbridge, Market Drayton, TF9 4EU. Willoughbridge Garden Trust, 01630 647237, info@dorothyclivegarden.co.uk, www.dorothyclivegarden.co.uk. *3m SE of Bridgemere Garden World. From M6 J15 take A53 W bound, then A51 N bound midway between Nantwich & Stone, near Woore.* **For NGS: Sun 20 Oct (10-3.30). Adm £7, chd £2. Home-made teas in the Tearooms. Afternoon Tea can be pre-booked. For other opening times and information, please phone, email or visit garden website.**
12 informal acres, inc superb woodland garden, alpine scree, gravel garden, fine collection of trees and spectacular flower borders. Renowned in May when woodland quarry is brilliant with rhododendrons. Waterfall and woodland planting. Laburnum Arch in June. Creative planting has produced stunning summer borders. Large Glasshouse. Spectacular autumn colour. Much

to see, whatever the season. The Dorothy Clive Tearooms will be open throughout the weekend during winter for refreshments, lunch and afternoon tea. Open all week in summer. Plant sales, gift room, picnic area and children's activities for a wide age range. Wheelchairs (inc electric) are available to book through the website. Disabled parking is available. WC on both upper and lower carparks.

♿ 🐕 ✳ 🚐 ☕ 📶

⑨ 5 EAST VIEW COTTAGES
School Lane, Shuttington, nr Tamworth, B79 0DX. Cathy Lyon-Green, 01827 892244, cathyatcorrabhan@hotmail.com, www.ramblinginthegarden.wordpress.com. *2m NE of Tamworth. From Tamworth, Amington Rd or Ashby Rd to Shuttington. From M42 J11, B5493 for Seckington & Tamworth. Pink house nr top of School Ln. Parking signed, overspill at Wolferstan Arms.* **Sun 18 Feb (12-4); Sun 23 June**

(1-5); Wed 26 June (12-4). Adm £4, chd free. Home-made teas. 2025: Sun 16 Feb. Visits also by arrangement in June for groups of up to 30. Open by arrangement in February and June.**
Deceptive, quirky plantlover's garden, full of surprises and always something new. Informally planted themed borders, cutting beds, woodland and woodland edge, stream, water features, sitooterie, folly, greenhouses and many artefacts. Roses, clematis, perennials, potted hostas. Snowdrops and witch hazels in Feb. Seating areas for contemplation and enjoying home-made cake. 'Wonderful hour's wander'.

🐕 ✳ ☕

⑩ FIFTY SHADES OF GREEN
20 Bevan Close, Shelfield, Walsall, WS4 1AB. Annmarie & Andrew Swift, 07963 041402, annmarie.1963@hotmail.co.uk, www.facebook.com/50SOGTheSwifts. *Walsall. M6 J10 take A454 to Walsall for 1.6m, L*

Hammerwich House Farm

at Lichfield St for ⅓m, L onto A461 Lichfield Rd for 2m, at Co-op T-lights turn L onto Mill rd then follow yellow signs. Parking limited, some in Broad Ln. **Sat 6, Sun 7 July (10.30-5.30); Sat 24 Aug (12-9); Sun 25 Aug (11-9). Adm £3.50, chd free. Home-made teas. Visits also by arrangement 25 May to 26 Oct.** The unique garden took several years to create and landscape. Distinctive areas inc 2 ponds linked by a stream, stone waterfall, many unique water features, places to sit, watch and relax. Wildlife encouraged and welcomed. The planting style is varied inc architectural plants, unusual foliage and textures, over 55 trees and plant collections. Calm garden full of surprises, intrigue and discovery.

11 33 GORWAY ROAD

Walsall, WS1 3BE. Gillian Brooks, 07972 615501, Brooks.gillian@gmail.com. *M6 J9 turn N onto Bescot Rd, at r'about take Wallows L (A4148), in 2m at r'about, 1st exit Birmingham Rd, L to Jesson Rd, L to Gorway Rd.* **Sun 9 June (10.30-3.30). Adm £3.50, chd free. Home-made teas. Visits also by arrangement 2 May to 31 Aug.** Cottage style Edwardian house garden. Late spring bulbs and roses. Willow tunnel, pond and rockery. Garden viewing is over flat grass and paths. Wheelchair access through garage.

12 GRAFTON COTTAGE

Bar Lane, Barton-under-Needwood, DE13 8AL. Margaret & Peter Hargreaves, 01283 713639, marpeter1@btinternet.com. *6m N of Lichfield. Leave A38 for Catholme S of Barton, follow sign to Barton Green, L at Royal Oak, ¼m.* **Sun 21, Sun 28 July, Thur 1, Sun 11, Sun 25 Aug (1-5). Adm £5, chd free. Home-made teas. Visits also by arrangement 20 June to 20 Aug. Min group adm £100 if less than 20 visitors. Donation to Alzheimer's Research UK.** Designed by the gardeners to create a picturesque cottage garden. Roses climbing over trellis, arches laden with clematis. Hollyhocks adorn the front, cottage annuals play a big part. A range of salvias, dahlias and unusual perennials. Colour themed borders, stream, parterre and more has attracted visitors for over 30 years. New vegetable plot. Finalist,

Midlands, The English Garden Magazine's The Nation's Favourite Gardens 2023.

13 22 GREENFIELD ROAD

Stafford, ST17 0PU. Alison & Peter Jordan, 01785 660819, alisonandpeterjordan@ngs.org.uk. *3m S of Stafford. Follow the A34 out of Stafford towards Cannock. 2nd L onto Overhill Rd. 1st R into Greenfield Rd.* **Visits by arrangement 8 May to 28 July for groups of 5 to 25. Home-made teas.** Suburban garden, working towards all round interest. In spring bulbs and stunning azaleas and rhododendrons. June onwards perennials and grasses. A garden that shows being diagnosed with Parkinson's needn't stop you creating a peaceful place to sit and enjoy. You might be able to catch a glimpse of Pete's model railway running. Flat garden but with some gravelled areas.

14 HAMILTON HOUSE

Roman Grange, Roman Road, Little Aston Park, Sutton Coldfield, B74 3GA. Philip & Diana Berry, www.hamiltonhousegarden.co.uk. *3m N of Sutton Coldfield. Follow A454 (Walsall Rd) & enter Roman Rd, Little Aston Park. Roman Grange is 1st L after church but enter rd via pedestrian gate.* **Sun 2 June (2-5). Adm £6, chd free. Light refreshments. Pimms available.** ½ acre north facing English woodland garden in a tranquil setting, making the most of challenging shade, providing a haven for birds and other wildlife. Large pond with a stone bridge, pergolas, water features, box garden with a variety of roses. Interesting collection of rhododendrons, clematis, hostas, ferns, old English roses and stunning artworks in the garden. Join in for tea and cakes, listening to live music and admire the art of the garden.

15 HAMMERWICH HOUSE FARM

Hall Lane, Hammerwich, Burntwood, WS7 0JP. Donna Harvey-Bailye. *3m from Lichfield Staffordshire. Follow Hall Ln from Muckley corner for 1½ m, gateway is just after church Ln on L. Continue through gate and parking is on L past house.* **Sat 29, Sun 30 June**

(11-4.30). Adm £5, chd free. Cream teas, chilled drinks, home-made ice cream. Gardens in the grounds of an 1807 Staffordshire Farmhouse inc a large wildlife pond and an extensive collection of Roses. The garden has a greenhouse and vegetable garden to explore along with open fields overlooking Hammerwich Church to picnic in.

16 IZAAK WALTON FARM

Cresswell Lane, Cresswell, Stoke-on-Trent, ST11 9RE. Mr Mark & Mrs Veronica Swinnerton. *Entrance, Off Cresswell Old Ln, 100 metres from railway Xing.* **Sun 30 June (11-4). Adm £4, chd free. Light refreshments inc home made cakes & deli boards.** Izaak Walton Farm garden has lots of small interesting areas. Flower borders, gravel gardens, shaded areas, vegetables and fruit trees, beautiful bug hotel made from a wine rack and oak pagoda. Water fountain and small greenhouse with cacti's. Interesting children's den, lawn and gravel paths and small grass meadow. Plenty of seating to enjoy light lunches or tea and cake.

17 'JOHN'S GARDEN' AT ASHWOOD NURSERIES

Ashwood Lower Lane, Ashwood, nr Kingswinford, DY6 0AE. John Massey, www.ashwoodnurseries.com. *9m S of Wolverhampton. 1m past Wall Heath on A449 turn R to Ashwood along Doctor's Ln. At T-junc turn L. Garden entrance off main car park at Ashwood Nurseries.* **Sun 31 Mar (10-4). Adm £7.50, chd free.** A stunning private garden adjacent to Ashwood Nurseries, it has a huge plant collection and many innovative design features in a beautiful canalside setting. There are informal beds, woodland dells, a stunning rock garden, a unique ruin garden, an Anemone pavonina meadow and wildlife garden. Fine displays of bulbs and spring-flowering plants and a notable collection of malus and amelanchier. Tearoom, Garden Centre and Gift Shop at adjacent Ashwood Nurseries. Coaches are welcome by appointment only. Disabled access difficult if very wet. Sorry no disabled access to the wildlife garden.

18 14 LONGBOW CLOSE
Stretton, Burton upon Trent,
DE13 0XY. Debbie & Gavin
Richards. *3m NW of Burton upon
Trent in the village of Stretton. From
A38 turn off at A5121 (Burton N)
Follow signs to Stretton turning into
Claymills Rd, then L to Church Rd,
R into Bridge St & R into Athelstan
Way. Please park on Athelstan Way.*
**Sat 8 June (11-4). Adm £3, chd
free. Home-made teas.**
A plantwoman's garden with exotic
evergreens, gorgeous smelling roses,
a flower-filled sunny patio where
refreshments can be enjoyed and a
welcoming front garden. Its design
features planting of herbaceous
perennials, climbers and evergreen
trees with a mauve, pink and purple
colour theme.

19 12 MERES ROAD
Halesowen, B63 2EH.
Nigel & Samantha Hopes,
www.hopesgardenplants.co.uk.
*4m from M5 J3. Follow the A458
out of Halesowen heading W for 2m,
L turn onto Two Gates Ln just after
Round of Beef pub, this becomes
Meres Rd. House is on R.* **Sun 26
May, Sun 18 Aug (10-3). Adm
£3.50, chd free. Home-made teas.
Donation to Plant Heritage.**
A little oasis in the heart of the
Black Country, with stunning views
across to Shropshire. The borders
are filled with interest and colour
throughout the year. A small family
garden, designed for young children
and plantaholics alike, a National
Collection of Roscoea (hardy gingers),
with a passion for Snowdrops,
Hellebores, Epimedium, Bearded Iris,
Cyclamen and Kniphofia.

20 MILLENNIUM GARDEN
London Road, Lichfield,
WS14 9RB. Carol Cooper. *1m S
of Lichfield. Off A38 along A5206
towards Lichfield ¼ m past A38
island towards Lichfield. Park in field
on L. Yellow signs on field post.* **Sun
24 Mar, Sun 12 May (1-5). Adm £4,
chd free. Home-made teas.**
Two acre garden with mixed spring
bulbs in the woodland garden. In May
the laburnum walk and wisteria arch
are in full bloom in this English country
garden. Designed with a naturalistic
edge and with the environment in
mind. A relaxed approach creates a
garden of quiet sanctuary with the
millennium bridge sitting comfortably,
with surroundings of lush planting and
mature trees. Well-stocked borders
give shots of colour to lift the spirit
and the air fills with the scent of
wisterias and climbing roses. A stress
free environment awaits you at the

Yew Tree Cottage

Millennium Garden. Park in field then follow the footpath round garden. Some uneven surfaces.

21 MONARCHS WAY
Park Lane, Coven, Wolverhampton, WV9 5BQ. Eileen & Bill Johnson, 07785 934085, snappy_eileen@hotmail.com, www.monarchsway-garden. co.uk. *From Port Ln (main road between Codsall & Brewood) turn E onto Park Ln. Monarchs Way is on the sharp bend on Park Ln. Limited parking, (further parking is available at other end of Park ln).* **Sun 1 Sept (11-4). Adm £6, chd free. Light refreshments. Visits also by arrangement May to Oct for groups of 6 to 16. We invite groups with garden based interests.**
The owners bought a 1¾ acre bare, treeless blank canvas in 2010 with grass around 3ft high! Since then they have designed a Tudor folly and jungle hut, built a pergola, excavated a lily pond with bog garden created a cottage garden, orchard, and vegetable garden. They have planted hundreds of conifer, evergreen, fruit and flowering trees, roses, hydrangeas, perennials and designed numerous flower beds. Wheelchair access is easy for most of the garden, on arrival request side gate for access. Minibuses can be accepted.

22 THE OLD DAIRY HOUSE
Trentham Park, Stoke-on-Trent, ST4 8AE. Philip & Michelle Moore. *S edge of Stoke-on-Trent. Next to Trentham Gardens. Off Whitmore Rd. Please follow NGS signs or signs for Trentham Park Golf Club. Parking in church car park.* **Sun 26, Mon 27 May (1-5). Adm £4.50, chd free. Home-made teas.**
Grade II listed house which originally formed part of the Trentham Estate forms backdrop to this 2 acre garden in parkland setting. Shaded area for rhododendrons, azaleas plus expanding hosta and fern collection. Mature trees, 'cottage garden', long borders and stumpery. Narrow brick paths in vegetable plot. Large courtyard area for teas. Wheelchair access - some gravel paths but lawns are an option.

23 THE OLD VICARAGE
Fulford, nr Stone, ST11 9QS. Mike & Cherry Dodson. *4m N of Stone. From Stone A520 (Leek). 1m R turn to Spot Acre & Fulford, turn L down Post Office Terrace, past village green/Pub towards church. Parking signed on L.* **Tue 16 July (12-5). Adm £5, chd free. Home-made teas.**
1½ acres of formal sloping garden around Victorian house. Sit on the terrace or in the summerhouse to enjoy home-made cakes and tea amongst mature trees, relaxed herbaceous borders, roses and a small pond. Move to the organic vegetable garden with raised beds, fruit cage and very big compost heaps! In complete contrast, easy walk around the natural setting of a 2 acre reclaimed lake planted with native species designed to attract wildlife. Waterfall, jetty, fishing hut, acer and fern glade plus arboretum provide more interest. Children will enjoy meeting the chickens and horses. A garden of contrasts, with easy formality around the Victorian house and the accent on very natural planting around the lake, managed for wildlife and sustainability. Wheelchair access to most areas.

24 10 PAGET RISE
Paget Rise, Abbots Bromley, Rugeley, WS15 3EF. Mr Arthur Tindle. *4m W of Rugeley 6m S of Uttoxeter & 12m N of Lichfield. From Rugeley: B5013 E. At T-junc turn R on B5014. From Uttoxeter take the B5013 S then B5014. From Lichfield take A515 N then turn L on B5234. In Abbots Bromley follow NGS yellow signs.* **Sun 19 May (11-4). Adm £3, chd free.**
This medium sized split level garden has a strong Japanese influence. Rhododendrons and a wide range of flowering shrubs. Many bonsai-style Acer trees in shallow bowls occupy a central gravel area with stepping stones. The rear of the garden has a woodland feel with a fairy dell under the pine tree. A gem of a garden! Arthur hopes visitors will be inspired with ideas to use in their own garden. Arthur is a watercolour artist and will be displaying a selection of his paintings for sale.

25 THE PINTLES
18 Newport Road, Great Bridgeford, Stafford, ST18 9PR. Peter & Leslie Longstaff, 01785 282582, peter.longstaff@ngs.org.uk. *About 2 m from M6 J14. From J14 M6 take A5013 towards Eccleshall, in Great Bridgeford turn L onto B5405 after 600 metres turn L onto Great Bridgeford Village Hall car park. The Pintles is opp the hall main doors.* **Sun 2 June (1-5). Adm £3.50, chd free. Home-made teas inc gluten free & reduced sugar options. Visits also by arrangement 2 June to 30 June for groups of 15 to 30. Car parking for small coaches.**
Located in the village of Great Bridgeford this traditional semi-detached house has a medium sized wildlife friendly garden designed to appeal to many interests. There are two greenhouses, 100s of cacti and succulents, vegetable and fruit plot, wildlife pond, weather station and hidden woodland shady garden. Plenty of outside seating to enjoy the home-made cakes and refreshments. Steps or small ramp into main garden.

26 23 ST JOHNS ROAD
Rowley Park, Stafford, ST17 9AS. Colin & Fiona Horwath, 07908 918181, fiona_horwath@yahoo.co.uk. *½ m S of Stafford Town Centre. Just a few mins from J13 M6, towards Stafford. After approx 2m on the A449, turn L into St. John's Rd after bus-stop.* **Thur 21 Mar, Thur 18 Apr, Thur 16 May, Thur 20 June (2-5). Adm £4, chd free. Home-made teas. Visits also by arrangement 28 Mar to 21 June for groups of 20 to 50.**
Pass through the black and white gate of this Victorian house into a part-walled gardener's haven. Bulbs, alpines and shady woodlanders in Spring and masses of unusual herbaceous plants and climbers. Numerous Japanese maples. Many spots to sit in sun or shade. Steps and gravel in places. Gardener is keen Hardy Plant Society member and sows far too many seeds, so always something good for sale. The outdoor kitchen and revolving summerhouse are great for refreshments. Plenty of places to sit and enjoy the myriad of plants.

27 THE SECRET GARDEN

3 Banktop Cottages, Little Haywood, ST18 0UL. Derek Higgott & David Aston. *5m SE of Stafford. A51 from Rugeley or Weston signed Little Haywood A513 Stafford Coley Ln, Back Ln R into Coley Gr. Entrance 50 metres on L.* **Thur 23 May, Thur 6, Fri 28 June (11-4). Adm £5, chd free. Home-made teas.**
Wander past other gardens and through the evergreen arch to a fantasy for the eyes and soul. Stunning garden approx ½ acre, created over the last 30+yrs. Strong colour theme of trees and shrubs, underplanted with perennials and 1000 bulbs. Laced with clematis, roses and a laburnum tunnel. Other features include water and a warm bothy for inclement days.

28 🆕 SNAILS PLACE

Victoria Street, Yoxall, Burton-on-Trent, DE13 8NG. Paul Shum. *Parking can be found in the village car park between Hadley St and St Peters Way. Garden is 2min walk away, turn L onto Victoria St at the Golden Cup.* **Sun 7, Sun 21 July (10.30-4.30). Adm £4, chd free. Home-made teas.**
A 2½ acre garden with herbaceous borders, a large lake, and a wildlife area. A small woodland walk can also be found here. Wheelchair accessible but is on grass so can make for a hard push.

29 SPRINGFIELD COTTAGE

Kiddemore Green Road, Bishops Wood, Stafford, ST19 9AA. Mrs Rachel Glover. *A5 to Telford from Gailey Island. Turn L at sign for Boscobel House. Follow Ivetsey Bank Rd to Bishop's Wood. Turn 1st L Old Coach Road past church 2nd white cottage on L.* **Sat 4 May, Sat 13 July (11-4). Adm £2, chd free. Home-made teas inc vegan options.**
Newly designed and landscaped plant enthusiasts cottage garden with unusual planting in areas, a tropical area inc Gunera's, Cannas, Hedichiums and palms, a rose garden, a herb garden and an established vegetable garden with large greenhouse. Fantastic views of the south Staffordshire countryside from all sides of the garden. Disabled parking for two cars, flat garden area and WC facilities.

♿ ❀ 🍵 ♫))

30 76 STATION STREET

Cheslyn Hay, Walsall, WS6 7EE. Mr Paul Husselbee. *Located on B4156. Limited on road parking.* **Sun 7 July (11.30-5). Adm £4, chd free. Home-made teas.**
40 yrs of gardening on this site has produced a hosta filled courtyard which leads to a Mediterranean patio, steps down to small area with folly, formal gardens area with stream, gated courtyard then finally find the secret garden. A quirky garden with a surprise round every corner.

31 12 WATERDALE

Compton, Wolverhampton, WV3 9DY. Colin & Clair Bennett. *1½ m W of Wolverhampton city centre. From Wolverhampton Ring Rd take A454 towards Bridgnorth for 1m. Waterdale is on the L off A454 Compton Rd West.* **Sun 2, Sun 30 June (11.30-5). Combined adm with 19 Waterdale £6, chd free.**
A riot of colour welcomes visitors to this quintessentially English garden. The wide central circular bed and side borders overflow with classic summer flowers, inc the tall spires of delphiniums, lupins, irises, campanula, poppies and roses. Clematis tumble over the edge of the decked terrace, where visitors can sit among pots of begonias and geraniums to admire the view over the garden.

🍵

32 19 WATERDALE

Compton, Wolverhampton, WV3 9DY. Anne & Brian Bailey, 01902 424867, m.bailey1234@btinternet.com. *1½ m W of Wolverhampton city centre. From Wolverhampton Ring Rd take A454 towards Bridgnorth for 1m. Waterdale is on L off A454 Compton Rd West.* **Sun 2, Sun 30 June (11.30-5). Combined adm with 12 Waterdale £6, chd free. Home-made teas. Visits also by arrangement 4 June to 24 July for groups of 10 to 35.**
A romantic garden of surprises, which gradually reveals itself on a journey through deep, lush planting, full of unusual plants. From the sunny, flower filled terrace, a ruined folly emerges from a luxuriant fernery and leads into an oriental garden, complete with tea house. Towering bamboos hide the way to the gothic summerhouse and mysterious shell grotto.

33 🆕 WESTVIEW

Straight Mile, Calf Heath, Wolverhampton, WV10 7DW. Mr David Wright. *3m E of Cannock. Leave A5 on to Four Crosses Ln. Go under M6 motorway, garden is ¼ m on L.* **Mon 27 May, Sun 23 June, Sun 14 July, Mon 26 Aug (10.30-4). Adm £3.50, chd free. Light refreshments.**
Walking into the garden you are greeted by borders of mainly perennial plants. As you continue through you move to a Japanese themed area with a large collection of bonsai trees. Learn about how to prepare bonsai plants from David as you relax and practice your zen with tea and cake.

34 THE WICKETS

47 Long Street, Wheaton Aston, ST19 9NF. Tony & Kate Bennett, 01785 840233, ajtonyb@talktalk.net. *8m W of Cannock, 10m N of Wolverhampton, 10m E of Telford. M6 J12 W towards Telford on A5; 3m R signed Stretton; 150yds L signed Wheaton Aston; 2m L; over canal, garden on R or at Bradford Arms on A5 follow signs.* **Sun 14 July, Sun 25 Aug (1.30-4.30). Home-made teas. Visits also by arrangement 1 July to 1 Sept.**
Around an ex-Police Station, this garden is full of ideas to copy and use in your own garden! The front has cottage garden beds, grasses and fernery. The rear areas inc a gothic garden, succulent theatre, dry stream, clock golf and even a cricket match. Located on the edge of the village opposite The Hartley Pub, there are beautiful walks through the countryside and along the canal. Wheelchair access - two single steps in garden and two gravel paths.

♿ 🍵

35 YARLET HOUSE

Yarlet, Stafford, ST18 9SD. Mr & Mrs Nikolas Tarling. *2m S of Stone. Take A34 from Stone towards Stafford, turn L into Yarlet School & L again into car park.* **Fri 21 June (10-1). Adm £4, chd free. Light refreshments. Donation to Staffordshire Wildlife Trust.**
Four acre garden with extensive lawns, walks, lengthy herbaceous borders and traditional Victorian box hedge. Water gardens with fountain and rare lilies. Sweeping views across Trent Valley to Sandon. New

Monarchs Way

peaceful Japanese garden completed in 2021. Victorian School Chapel and War Memorial. Garden Chess Board. Boules pitch. Yarlet School Art Display. Gravel paths.

36 YEW TREE COTTAGE
Podmores Corner, Long Lane, White Cross, Haughton, ST18 9JR. Clive & Ruth Plant, 07591 886925, pottyplantz@aol.com. *4m W of Stafford. Take A518 W Haughton, turn R Station Rd (signed Ranton) 1m, then turn R at Xrds ¼ m on R.* **Every Thur 4 July to 18 July (11-4). Sun 21 July (2-5). Adm £5, chd free. Home-made teas. Visits also by arrangement 5 July to 26 July. Donation to Plant Heritage.**
Hardy Plant Society member's garden brimming with unusual plants. Year-round interest inc meconopsis, trillium and other shade lovers. ½ acre inc gravel, borders, veg and plant sales. National Collection Dierama featured on BBC Gardeners' World flowering first half July. Covered vinery for tea if weather is unkind, seats in the garden for sunny days. A series of different areas and interests. Cottage garden, shade garden, and National Collection of Dierama (Angel's Fishing

Rods) in a rural location with a working vegetable garden. A garden for plantaholics. Find us on facebook at 'Dierama Species in Staffordshire'. Partial wheelchair access, grass and paved paths, some narrow and some gravel.

37 YEW TREES
Whitley Eaves, Eccleshall, Stafford, ST21 6HR. Mrs Teresa Hancock, 07973 432077, hancockteresa@gmail.com. *7m from J14 M6. Situated on A519 between Eccleshall (2.2m) & Woodseaves, (1m). Traffic cones & signs will highlight the entrance.* **Sat 29, Sun 30 June, Sat 13, Sun 14 July, Sat 10, Sun 11 Aug (10-4). Adm £4, chd free. Pre-booking essential, please visit www. ngs.org.uk for information & booking. Home-made teas inc locally made cakes. Visits also by arrangement June to Aug for groups of up to 30.**
One acre garden divided into rooms by mature hedging, shrubs and trees enjoying views over the surrounding countryside. Large patio area with containers and seating. Other features inc pond, topiary, vegetable plot, hen

run and wildlife area. During June and July there are 8 acres of natural wildflower meadow to enjoy before it is cut for hay.

In 2023, National Garden Scheme funding for Perennial supported a helpline service which provided advice, information and frontline support to around 800 people working in horticulture

WARWICKSHIRE
& West Midlands

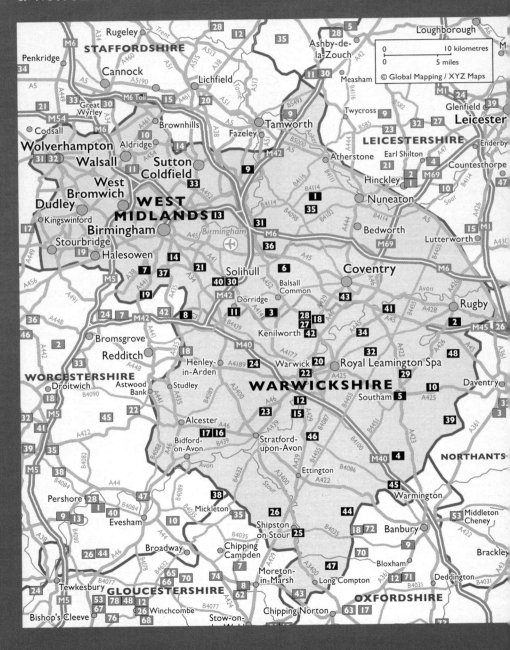

VOLUNTEERS

County Organiser
Liz Watson
01926 512307
liz.watson@ngs.org.uk

County Treasurer
Ian Roberts
01926 864181
ian.roberts@ngs.org.uk

Publicity
Lily Farrah
07545 560298
lily.farrah@ngs.org.uk

Social Media
Jenny Edwards
07884 177889
jenny.edwards@ngs.org.uk

Booklet Co-ordinator
Hazel Blenkinsop
07787 005290
hazel.blenkinsop@ngs.org.uk

Booklet Co-ordinator
James Coleman
07746 561570
james.coleman@ngs.org.uk

Assistant County Organisers
Jane Cerone
01827 873205
jane.cerone@ngs.org.uk

Jane Redshaw
07803 234627
jane.redshaw@ngs.org.uk

Isobel Somers
07767 306673
ifas1010@aol.com

 @WarwickshireNGS
 @WarksNGS
 @warwickshirengs

OPENING DATES

All entries subject to change. For latest information check **www.ngs.org.uk**

Extended openings are shown at the beginning of the month

Map locator numbers are shown to the right of each garden name.

February

Snowdrop Openings

Saturday 17th
◆ Hill Close Gardens   22

Sunday 18th
Fieldgate   18
2 St Nicholas Avenue   42

March

Every Saturday and Sunday from Saturday 30th
◆ Bridge Nursery   10

Friday 29th
◆ Bridge Nursery   10

April

Every Saturday and Sunday
◆ Bridge Nursery   10

Monday 1st
◆ Bridge Nursery   10

Saturday 20th
Broadacre   11

Sunday 21st
Anya Court Care Home   2

May

Every Saturday and Sunday
◆ Bridge Nursery   10

Sunday 5th
◆ Castle Bromwich Hall
  Gardens   13

Monday 6th
◆ Bridge Nursery   10

Friday 10th
Priors Marston Manor   39

Sunday 12th
 Beech Hurst   5
Cats Whiskers   14

Saturday 18th
6 Canon Price Road   12

Sunday 19th
 Beech Hurst   5
6 Canon Price Road   12

Saturday 25th
Ilmington Gardens   26

Sunday 26th
Ilmington Gardens   26
Pebworth Gardens   38

Monday 27th
Bridge House   9
◆ Bridge Nursery   10
Pebworth Gardens   38

June

Every Saturday and Sunday
◆ Bridge Nursery   10

Saturday 1st
 Clay Barn   16

Sunday 2nd
 Clay Barn   16

Friday 7th
Priors Marston Manor   39

Saturday 8th
6 Canon Price Road   12
Priors Marston Manor   39

Sunday 9th
6 Canon Price Road   12
Holywell Farm   24
Honington Gardens   25
Styvechale Gardens   43

Saturday 15th
Hall Green Gardens   21
Packington Hall   36

Sunday 16th
Admington Hall
Hall Green Gardens   21
Kenilworth Gardens   28
Maxstoke Castle   31
8 Rectory Road   40
Whichford & Ascott Gardens   47

Sunday 23rd
Berkswell Gardens   6
Marie Curie Hospice Garden   30
Warmington Gardens   45

Sunday 30th
Ansley Gardens   1
15 New Church Road   33

July

Every Saturday and Sunday
◆ Bridge Nursery — 10

Thursday 4th
Anya Court Care Home — 2

Saturday 6th
◆ Ryton Organic Gardens — 41
Tysoe Gardens — 44

Sunday 7th
Anya Court Care Home — 2
Avon Dassett Gardens — 4
Bournville Village — 7
Tysoe Gardens — 44

Friday 12th
NEW ◆ Kenilworth Castle — 27

Saturday 13th
6 Canon Price Road — 12
Wellesbourne Allotments — 46

Sunday 14th
6 Canon Price Road — 12
128 Green Acres Road — 19
Old Arley Gardens — 35

Saturday 20th
Guy's Cliffe Walled Garden — 20

August

Every Saturday and Sunday
◆ Bridge Nursery — 10

Sunday 25th
Cedar House — 15

Monday 26th
◆ Bridge Nursery — 10

September

Every Saturday and Sunday
◆ Bridge Nursery — 10

Saturday 7th
8 Rectory Road — 40
◆ Ryton Organic Gardens — 41

Friday 13th
Priors Marston Manor — 39

Saturday 14th
Priors Marston Manor — 39

October

Saturday 26th
◆ Hill Close Gardens — 22

By Arrangement

Arrange a personalised garden visit with your club, or group of friends, on a date to suit you. See individual garden entries for full details.

Avening — 3
10 Avon Carrow, Avon Dassett Gardens — 4
NEW Beech Hurst — 5
Brackencote — 8
Bridge House — 9
Broadacre — 11
6 Canon Price Road — 12
Cedar House — 15
The Croft House — 17
36 Ferndale Road, Hall Green Gardens — 21
Fieldgate — 18
128 Green Acres Road — 19
The Hill Cottage — 23
19 Leigh Crescent — 29
The Motte — 32
Oak House — 34
Paul's Oasis of Calm — 37
Priors Marston Manor — 39
8 Rectory Road — 40
NEW Woolscott Barn — 48

Clay Barn

THE GARDENS

ADMINGTON HALL
Admington, Shipston-on-Stour,
CV36 4JN.
house@admingtonhalluk.com
01608 698 234. *6m NW of Shipston-on-Stour. From Ilmington, follow signs to Admington. Approx 2m, turn R to Admington by Polo Ground. Continue for 1m.* **Sun 16 June (11-4) last entry 3pm. Adm £8, chd free. Home-made teas.**
A continually evolving 10 acre garden with an established structure of innovative planning and planting. A wide ranging collection of fine and mature specimen trees provide the essential core structure to this traditional country garden. Features inc a lush broad lawn, orchard, water garden, large walled garden, wildflower meadows and extensive modern topiary. Wheelchair access to most of the garden sometimes on gravel paths.

GROUP OPENING

1 ANSLEY GARDENS
Ansley, CV10 0QR. *Ansley is situated W of Nuneaton, adjacent to Arley. Ansley is directly off the B4114. Tickets are available from the car park or in individual gardens.* **Sun 30 June (1.30-6.30). Combined adm £6, chd free. Home-made teas. Cream teas & home-made cakes in specified gardens.**

25 BIRMINGHAM ROAD
Pat & David Arrowsmith.

79 BIRMINGHAM ROAD
Stephen Shaw.

HOOD LANE FARM
James Morley - David & Lindsay Kearns, 07973 960712, hoodlanefarm@outlook.com, www.hoodlanefarm.co.uk.

5 MARY CAROLL CLOSE
Derek Greedy.

NEW 6 MARY CAROLL CLOSE
Mrs Tracy Barnes.

NEW THE OLD CHAPEL
Ms Teresa Fraser.

THE OLD POLICE HOUSE
Mike & Hilary Ward.

1 PARK COTTAGES
Janet & Andy Down.

Ansley is a small ex-mining village situated in north Warwickshire. The eight gardens open as a selection of different styles and offerings and this year there are two new gardens opening, from a very small traditional cottage garden crammed with flowers and pots to larger gardens and those maximising the amazing views of the countryside. There is one with a lush tropical feel, a country garden with mature plants and ancient roses and one boasting a glamping pod complete with large grounds to get lost in! One of the new gardens is contemporary with an eclectic mix of quirky ornaments and easy care surfaces. Six of the gardens are in the village with the opportunity to walk across the fields on public footpaths to the other two if you are able. (There is parking available at both if not!). The local Norman church will be open and the Morris Dancing Group will be entertaining visitors during the day.

2 ANYA COURT CARE HOME
286 Dunchurch Road, Rugby, CV22 6JA. Hallmark Care Homes, www.hallmarkcarehomes.co.uk/care-homes-in-warwickshire. *Opp Sainsbury's on Dunchurch Rd. If the car park is busy, please use their car park as an alternative. Please go to Anya Court reception, who will guide you to the garden.* **Sun 21 Apr, Thur 4, Sun 7 July (10-4). Adm £5, chd free. Cream teas. Entry includes light refreshments & cream teas. Additional donations welcomed for cakes.**
Anya Court has a large wooded garden consisting of a number of sensory herbaceous perennial planting schemes. There is also a fruit and vegetable garden grown by the residents of the home and a colourful annual bedding and basket display. Due to the number of trees, our garden is a good example of dry shade and drought tolerant planting for anyone requiring inspiration. Fully accessible to wheelchairs.

3 AVENING
Oldwich Lane East, Kenilworth, CV8 1NR. Helen Jones, 07894 321919, hello@mygardenoasis.co.uk, www.mygardenoasis.co.uk. *8 m SE of Solihull & 5 m W of Kenilworth. Avening is at the end of College Ln, a short single-track lane off Oldwich Ln E which runs between Chadwick End and Fen End.* **Visits by arrangement Apr to Sept. Adm £5, chd free.**
Designed in 2009, this is a ¾ acre garden oasis in the West Midlands. It has been designed to attract wildlife and has a typical cottage garden feel. Features inc 2 ponds joined by a waterfall, wildflower meadow, wide mixed shrub/herbaceous border with a stepping stone path running through it and small vegetable plot. There are no steps in the garden, although some of the paths are unsuitable for wheelchairs.

GROUP OPENING

4 AVON DASSETT GARDENS
Avon Dassett, CV47 2AE. *7m N of Banbury. From M40 J12 turn L & L again onto the B4100, following signs to Herb Centre & Gaydon. Take 2nd L (signed) into bottom end of village. Please park in cemetery car park at top of hill or where signed.* **Sun 7 July (2-6). Combined adm £7, chd free. Home-made teas. The Yew Tree pub will be open for lunch and throughout the afternoon.**

10 AVON CARROW
Anna Prosser, 07468 602078, annapross40@gmail.com.
Visits also by arrangement Mar to Sept for groups of 5 to 20.

DASSETT HOUSE
Mrs Sarah Rutherford, dassettdwelling@gmail.com.

THE EAST WING, AVON CARROW
Christine Fisher & Terry Gladwin.

HILL TOP FARM
Mr D Hicks.

THE OLD RECTORY
Lily Hope-Frost.

SINCLAIR WITH THE SNUG
Mrs Deb Watts.

Pretty Hornton stone village sheltering in the lee of the Burton Dassett hills, well wooded with parkland setting and The Old Rectory mentioned in Domesday Book. Wide variety of gardens inc cottage, gravel and tropical gardens. Range of plants inc alpines, herbaceous, perennials, roses, climbers and shrubs. The gardens are on/off the main road through the village. We would be grateful if visitors could park in designated areas and not along the main road in the village. For 2024, we hope to run a shuttle service from top to bottom of the village. Plant sales, homemade teas, historic church open, and lunch available at the Yew Tree village pub, recently purchased by the Community, visit www.theyewtreepub.co.uk for details. Wheelchair access to most gardens.

  ♿ 🐕 ❀ ☕))

5 NEW **BEECH HURST**
3 Warwick Road, Southam, CV47 0HN. Michael and Sharon Mitchell, 01926 817559, michael@fmmitchell.net. *On R, ¼ to ½ m down Warwick Rd from A425 from Leamington Spa.* **Sun 12, Sun 19 May (2-5). Adm £5, chd free. Visits also by arrangement 12 Feb to 30 June for groups of 6 to 20.**
Beech Hurst is a Regency House with an established 1¼ acre garden inc lawns, woodland areas, many mature and some historic trees, established shrubs, herbaceous borders and a recently added Japanese-inspired garden with a raked gravel bed and a variety of flowering cherries, acers, rhododendrons, azaleas and camellias. It also has a fine display of late winter and springtime bulbs.

♿))

GROUP OPENING

6 **BERKSWELL GARDENS**
Berkswell, Coventry, CV7 7BB. Gordon Clark. *7m W of Coventry. A452 to Balsall Common & follow signs to Berkswell. Tickets & maps available at each garden. Car necessary to visit all gardens.* **Sun 23 June (11-6). Combined adm £7, chd free. Light refreshments.**

2 AGRICULTURAL COTTAGES
Mrs Jane Edwards.

EMSCOT BARN
Mr Leigh & Mrs Sarah Mayers.

HOLLY OAK
Jane Bostock.

NEW **1 MONS AVENUE**
Mrs Tracy Vernum-Cooke.

SPENCER'S END
Gordon Clark & Nicola Content.

THE TOWER HOUSE
Penny & David Stableforth.

YEW TREE BARN
Angela & Ken Shaw.

Berkswell is a beautiful village dating back to Saxon times with a C12

Norman church and has several C16 and C17 buildings inc the pub. In 2014/15 the village was awarded Gold in the RHS Britain in Bloom campaign, plus a special RHS award in 2014 for the Best Large Village in the Heart of England. The gardens provide great variety with fine examples of small and large, formal and informal, wild, imaginatively planted herbaceous borders and productive vegetable gardens. Something for everyone and plenty of ideas to take home. Also open to visitors is the C12 Norman church and garden.

🐕 ❀ ☕))

GROUP OPENING

7 **BOURNVILLE VILLAGE**
Birmingham, B30 1QY. Bournville Village Trust, www.bvt.org.uk. *Bournville. Gardens spread across 1,000 acre estate. Walks of up to 30 mins between some. Map available on the day. Parking: Bournville Garden Centre, (B30 2AE) & Rowheath Pavilion, (B30 1HH).* **Sun 7 July (11-5). Combined adm £7, chd free. Light refreshments at various locations.**

5 BLACKTHORN ROAD
Mr & Mrs Andrew Christie.

103 BOURNVILLE LANE
B30 1LH. Mrs Jennifer Duffy.

52 ELM ROAD
Mr Glenn & Mrs Jackie Twigg.

21 HIGH HEATH CLOSE
Dr Faint & Ms Dorward.

32 KNIGHTON ROAD
B31 2EH. Mrs Anne Ellis & Mr Lawrence Newman.

MASEFIELD COMMUNITY GARDEN
Mrs Sally Gopsill, www.masefieldcommunitygarden.wordpress.com.

Bournville Village is showcasing six gardens. Bournville is famous for its large gardens, outstanding open spaces and of course its chocolate factory in a garden! We have a garden railway amongst bonsai, a considered recycling garden, a long garden with surprises at each glance, a small garden for easy maintenance, a little changed original style garden and a community garden. Free information sheet/map available on the day. Gardens spread across the 1,000 acre estate, with walks of up to 30

minutes between sites. For those with a disability, full details of access are available on the NGS website. Visitors with particular concerns with regards to access are welcome to call Bournville Village Trust on 0300 333 6540 or bvt.org.uk. A map will be available to download from www.bvt.org.uk nearer to the date and will be available on the day. Music, singing and food available across a number of sites.

♿ ❀ ☕))

8 **BRACKENCOTE**
Forshaw Heath Road, Earlswood, Solihull, B94 5JU. Mr & Mrs Sandy Andrews, 07710 107000, mjandrews53@hotmail.com. *From J3 M42 take exit signed to Forshaw Heath. At T-junc, turn L onto Forshaw Heath Rd, signed to Earlswood. Garden approx ½ m on the L, before you get to Earlswood Nurseries.* **Visits by arrangement May to July for groups of up to 20. Adm £5, chd free. Light refreshments.**
A beautiful country garden with stunning wildflower meadow, full of orchids in spring and early summer. The 1¼ acre plot is surrounded by mature trees, with herbaceous borders enclosing a large circular lawn. Beyond this, the garden inc a brick and turf labyrinth, a rockery, a pond and bog garden as well as a large raised vegetable plot and garden buildings.

❀ ☕

9 **BRIDGE HOUSE**
Dog Lane, Bodymoor Heath, B76 9JD. Mr & Mrs J Cerone, 01827 873205, janecerone@btinternet.com. *5m S of Tamworth. From A446 at Belfry Island take A4091 to Tamworth, after 1m turn R onto Bodymoor Heath Ln & continue 1m into village, parking in field opp garden.* **Mon 27 May (2-5). Adm £5, chd free. Home-made teas. Visits also by arrangement 4 May to 30 Sept for groups of 6 to 25.**
One acre garden surrounding converted public house. Divided into smaller areas with a mix of shrub borders, azalea and fuchsia, herbaceous and bedding, orchard, kitchen garden with large greenhouse. Pergola walk, arch to formal garden with big fish pool, pond, bog garden and lawns. Some unusual carefully

Brackencote

© James Kerr

chosen trees. Kingsbury Water Park and RSPB Middleton Lakes Reserve located within a mile.

10 ◆ BRIDGE NURSERY
Tomlow Road, Napton, Southam, CV47 8HX. Christine Dakin, 01926 812737, chris.dakin25@yahoo.com, www.bridge-nursery.co.uk. *3m E of Southam. Brown tourist sign at Napton Xrds on A425 Southam to Daventry Rd.* **For NGS: Fri 29 Mar (10-4). Every Sat and Sun 30 Mar to 29 Sept (10-4). Mon 1 Apr, Mon 6, Mon 27 May, Mon 26 Aug (10-4). Adm £3.50, chd free. For other opening times and information, please phone, email or visit garden website.**
Clay soil? Don't despair. Here is an acre of garden with an exciting range of plants which thrive in hostile conditions. Grass paths lead you round borders filled with many unusual plants, a pond and bamboo grove complete with panda! A peaceful haven for wildlife and visitors. A visitor commented 'it is garden that is comfortable with itself.' Tea/ coffee and biscuits gladly provided on request. Group visits welcome. The ground can be unsuitable for wheelchairs after a lot of rain.

11 BROADACRE
Grange Road, Dorridge, Solihull, B93 8QA. John Woolman, 07818 082885, jw234567@gmail.com, www.broadacregarden.org. *Approx 3m SE of Solihull. On B4101 opp The Railway Inn. Plenty of parking.* **Sat 20 Apr (2-6). Adm £6, chd free. Home-made teas. Visits also by arrangement.**
Broadacre is a semi-wild garden, managed organically. Attractively landscaped with pools, lawns and trees, beehives, vegetable area and adjoining stream and wildflower meadows. Dorridge cricket club is on the estate. Lovely venue for a picnic. Dogs and children are welcome. Excellent country pub, The Railway Inn, at the bottom of the drive.

12 6 CANON PRICE ROAD
Nursery Meadow, Barford, CV35 8EQ. Mrs Marie-Jane Roberts, 07775 584336. *1m from Warwick. From A429 turn into Barford. Park on Wellesbourne Rd & walk into Nursery Meadow by red phone box. No 6 is R in 1st close. Disabled parking by house.* **Sat 18, Sun 19 May (2-4.30). Adm £3.50, chd free. Sat 8, Sun 9 June, Sat 13, Sun 14 July (2-4.30). Adm £5, chd free. Home-made teas in the garden room. Visits also by arrangement 20 Apr to 20 July.**
Unexpectedly large and mature garden with colour themed shrub and perennial plants immaculately grown. Separate areas for cut flowers, herbs, vegetables and 19 types of fruit, some fan trained. Spectacularly colourful patio pots, a small delightful rockery, pond and wildlife garden. There are many seating areas throughout. Cash only for plant sale. Access via a single slab path that joins a wide path through the garden.

13 ◆ CASTLE BROMWICH HALL GARDENS

Chester Road, Castle Bromwich, Birmingham, B36 9BT. Castle Bromwich Hall & Gardens Trust, 0121 749 4100, cbhallgardens@gmail.com, www. castlebromwichhallgardens.org.uk. *4m E of Birmingham centre. 1m J5 M6 (exit N only).* **For NGS: Sun 5 May (10.30-4.30). Adm £6, chd £3. Cream teas. For other opening times and information, please phone, email or visit garden website.**

10 acres of restored C17/18 walled gardens attached to a Jacobean manor (now a hotel), with a further 30 acres of historic parkland and nature reserve. Formal yew parterres, wilderness walks, summerhouses, holly maze, espaliered fruit and wild areas. Cream Tea in a Box, cafe and picnics all season. Paths are either lawn or rough hoggin - sometimes on a slope. Most areas generally accessible, rough areas outside the walls difficult when wet.

14 CATS WHISKERS

42 Amesbury Rd, Moseley, Birmingham, B13 8LE. Dr Alfred & Mrs Michele White. *Opp back of Moseley Hall Hospital. Past Edgbaston Cricket ground straight on at r'about & up Salisbury Rd.*

Amesbury Rd, 1st on R. **Sun 12 May (12-5). Adm £6, chd free. Light refreshments inc cake, wine & soft drinks.**

A plantsman's garden developed over the last 40 years but which has kept its 1923 landscape. The front garden, whilst not particularly large, is full of interesting trees and shrubs; the rear garden is on three levels with steps leading to a small terrace and further steps to the main space. At the end of the garden is a pergola leading to the vegetable garden and greenhouse.

15 CEDAR HOUSE

Wasperton, Warwick, CV35 8EB. Mr D Burbidge, 07836 532914, david.burbidge@burbidge.org.uk, www.cedarhousegardens.co.uk. *5 m from Warwick. Turn off A429 into Wasperton. There is only 1 rd in the village. Continue for approx ½ mile.* **Sun 25 Aug (1-5.30). Adm £8, chd free. Home-made teas at Wasperton Village Hall. Visits also by arrangement Apr to Nov for groups of 15 to 25.**

Six acre former vicarage gardens, mature and exciting. Colourful herbaceous borders, collection of mature acer palmatum, walled garden, water meadow garden, woodland glade and walk with mix of young and mature specimen trees, inc two

notable vintage trees, tranquil grass and bamboo area leading to the swimming pool garden. Several seating areas to enjoy the beautiful and peaceful setting. Interesting walks across the fields to the River Avon, Charlecote and Hampton Lucy. Cedar House is close to Warwick and Stratford upon Avon. Some gravel and woodchip paths.

16 NEW CLAY BARN

Redhill, Alcester, B49 6NQ. Louise Darby. *4m equidistant between Stratford-upon-Avon and Alcester off A46. Hidden behind Redhill Farmyard, use Piston Club car park via main entrance. Short walk to Clay Barn from back of car park. Disabled parking only at Clay Barn.* **Sat 1, Sun 2 June (11-4). Adm £3, chd free. Home-made teas.**

An artist rather than a gardener, Louise has created her garden from a field over the last 25 years, with intuitive planting in heavy clay stony ground. A formal garden with round lawn, local stone paving and walled beds and a shady vine covered arbour. Also a wild area with pond, plant varieties to encourage birds, bees and butterflies and a live willow arbour. Natural stone paving and gravelled paths - assistance can be provided.

Maxstoke Castle

17 THE CROFT HOUSE
Haselor, Alcester, B49 6LU. Isobel & Patrick Somers, 07767 306673, ifas1010@aol.com. *6m W of Stratford-upon-Avon, 2m E of Alcester, off A46. From A46 take Haselor turn. From Alcester take old Stratford Rd, turn L signed Haselor, then R at Xrds. Garden in centre of village. Please park considerately.* Visits by arrangement 25 May to 9 June for groups of up to 30. Bookings at short notice welcome. Adm £4, chd free. Home-made teas.
Almost an acre of trees, shrubs and herbaceous borders densely planted with a designer's passion for colour and texture. Hidden areas invite you to linger. Gorgeous scented wisteria on 2 sides of the house. Organically managed, providing a haven for birds and other wildlife. Frog pond, treehouse, small vegetable plot and a few venerable old fruit trees from its days as a market garden.

18 FIELDGATE
Fieldgate Lane, Kenilworth, CV8 1BT. Liz & Bob Watson, 01926 512307, liz.watson@ngs.org.uk. *Fieldgate is at the very bottom of Fieldgate Ln, on the corner next to the T-lights. Parking available at Abbey Fields car park & limited street parking on High St & Fieldgate Ln.* Sun 18 Feb (12-4). Adm £3, chd free. Home-made teas in St Nicholas Church. Open nearby 2 St Nicholas Avenue. Adm to both gardens £5. Opening with Kenilworth Gardens on Sun 16 June. Visits also by arrangement 1 May to 15 Sept for groups of 5 to 30.
Fieldgate is a 1/4 acre town garden with lawns, herbaceous borders and formal ponds. It was remodelled by the owners in 2002 and has matured nicely. The borders contain a wide variety of plants and are colourful throughout summer and late into September with asters and dahlias. A small woodland area was created in 2021 planted with shade lovers, ferns and many snowdrops some of which are unusual. Kenilworth Castle is close by and there are pleasant walks in Abbey Fields. The Millennium Walk, starting at the castle is an hour's walk through the Warwickshire countryside around the shore of the now drained Kenilworth Castle mere.

19 128 GREEN ACRES ROAD
Kings Norton, Birmingham, B38 8NL. Mr & Mrs Mark Whitehouse, 07860 310854, m.k.whitehouse@btinternet.com. *From the M42 J2 take the A441 towards Birmingham take the 2nd exit at r'about continue along the A441 for 3m Green Acres Rd is on the R next to Spar.* Sun 14 July (10.30-4). Adm £3, chd free. Light refreshments. Visits also by arrangement 16 June to 31 July for groups of 6 to 16.
A small garden with lots of character full of interest and abundance of colour, inc various seating areas to enjoy different aspects and views. The garden has many different types of perennials, hostas, roses and dahlias. A fish pond, water feature plus many more points of interest. To access the garden, please follow signs to enter the garden from the rear.

20 GUY'S CLIFFE WALLED GARDEN
Coventry Road, Guy's Cliffe, Warwick, CV34 5FJ. Sarah Ridgeway, www.guyscliffewalledgarden.org.uk. *Behind Hintons Nursery in Guy's Cliffe. Guy's Cliffe is on the A429, between N Warwick & Leek Wootton.* Sat 20 July (10.30-3.30). Adm £4, chd free. Home-made teas.
A Grade II listed garden of special historic interest, having been the kitchen garden for Guy's Cliffe House. The garden dates back to the mid-1700s. Restoration work started 10 yrs ago using plans from the early C19. The garden layout has already been reinstated and the beds, once more, planted with fruit, flowers and vegetables inc many heritage varieties. Part of the Peach House is being restored. The sunken Melon house is visible but not yet restored so not accessible. Original C18 walls. Fernery. Exhibition of artefacts discovered during restoration. 'No Dig' approach to all gardening activities Lots of signs describe different parts of the garden. Wheelchair access through entrance of Hintons Nursery and paths through garden. WC with disabled access.

GROUP OPENING

21 HALL GREEN GARDENS
Hall Green, Birmingham, B28 9LB. *Off A34, 4m from city centre, 6m from M42, J4.* Start at 638 Shirley Road B28 9LB. Sat 15, Sun 16 June (1.30-5.30). Combined adm £6, chd free. Home-made teas at 111 Southam Road.

36 FERNDALE ROAD
Mrs E A Nicholson, 01217 774921. Visits also by arrangement 31 Mar to 30 Sept for groups of up to 30.

NEW 284 ROBIN HOOD LANE
Mrs Margaret Smith.

638 SHIRLEY ROAD
Dr & Mrs M Leigh.

111 SOUTHAM ROAD
Ms Val Townend & Mr Ian Bate.

NEW 65 WOODFORD GREEN ROAD
Mrs Maxine Chapman.

Five very different suburban gardens in leafy Hall Green with its beautiful mature trees and friendly residents. Our visitors love the unique atmosphere in each garden. It is such a perfect way to share a relaxing early summer saunter and pause for refreshments served by our brilliant catering team. We look forward to seeing you! 36 Ferndale Rd: Florist's large suburban garden, ponds and waterfalls, and fruit garden. 111 Southam Rd: Mature garden with well defined areas inc ponds, white garden, rescue hens and a majestic cedar. 638 Shirley Rd: Large garden with herbaceous borders, cutting patch, vegetables and greenhouses. 65 Woodford Green Rd: Much loved, small garden abounding in charming old teapots, bottle edging, and worn-out hiking boots now used as planters. 284 Robin Hood Lane: Beautifully landscaped, terraced garden rich in colour and interest, featuring numerous clematis.

22 ◆ HILL CLOSE GARDENS

Bread and Meat Close, Warwick, CV34 6HF. Hill Close Gardens Trust, 01926 493339, hello@hcgt.org.uk, www.hillclosegardens.com. *Town centre. Follow signs to Warwick racecourse. Entry from Friars St onto Bread & Meat Cl. Car park by entrance next to racecourse. 2 hrs free parking. Disabled parking outside the gates.* **For NGS: Sat 17 Feb, Sat 26 Oct (11-4). Adm £6, chd £1. A choice of light refreshments are available. For other opening times and information, please phone, email or visit garden website. Donation to Plant Heritage.**

Restored Grade II Victorian leisure gardens comprising 16 individual hedged gardens, 8 brick summerhouses. Herbaceous borders, heritage apple and pear trees, C19 daffodils, over 100 varieties of snowdrops, many varieties of asters and chrysanthemums. Heritage vegetables. Plant Heritage border, auricula theatre, and Victorian style glasshouse. Children's garden. Wheelchair available. Please phone to book in advance.

23 THE HILL COTTAGE

Kings Lane, Snitterfield, Stratford-upon-Avon, CV37 0QA. Gillie & Paul Waldron, 07895 369387, info@thehillcottage.co.uk, www.thehillcottage.co.uk. *5 mins from M40, J15. Take A46 to Stratford. 1m take 2nd exit at r'about. 1m take L into Kings Ln, through S bends, house on R. Or from village, up White Horse Hill, R at T-junc, over A46, R into Kings Ln, 2nd on L.* **Visits by arrangement Apr to Sept for groups of up to 20. Adm £6, chd free. Refreshments are £3.50pp.**

High on a ridge overlooking orchards and golf course with fabulous views to distant hills, this 2¼ acre garden, full of surprises, offers varied planting; sunny gravel with exotic specimens; cool, shady woodland with relaxed perennial groups; romantic green oak pond garden and stone summerhouse; pool with newts and dragonflies. Traditional glasshouse in walled kitchen garden with raised beds. Access to all the upper areas inc walled kitchen garden & orchard.

24 HOLYWELL FARM

Holywell, Shrewley, Warwick, CV35 7BH. Antony & Bindy Harper. *7 m N of Stratford-upon-Avon & 5 m W of Warwick. In Claverdon turn off A4189 Henley-Warwick rd, signed Shrewley & The Ardencote. After ½ m fork L off sharp R bend signed Holywell. What3words app - scanner. cars.positives.* **Sun 9 June (11-5). Adm £7, chd free. Home-made teas.**

The gardens at Holywell Farm extend to 2 acres of lawn, large flower beds, and a cutting garden, with open views across the fields beyond. The beds are filled with mostly herbaceous plants and the planting scheme of this large cottage garden has been strictly governed by colour. There is an extensive pergola covered with climbers that winds its way through the main cluster of planting.

GROUP OPENING

25 HONINGTON GARDENS

Honington, Shipston-on-Stour, CV36 5AA. *1½ m N of Shipston-on-Stour. Take A3400 towards Stratford-upon-Avon, then turn R signed Honington.* **Sun 9 June (1.30-5.30). Combined adm £6, chd free. Home-made teas.**

THE GARDEN HOUSE
Mr & Mrs Andrew Sadleir.

HONINGTON HALL
B H E Wiggin.

MALT HOUSE RISE
Mr P Weston.

THE OLD COTTAGE
Donna Elliott.

THE OLD HOUSE
Mrs D Beaumont.

ORCHARD HOUSE
Mr & Mrs Monnington.

THE ORCHARD, HOME FARM
Mr Guy Winter.

ROSE COTTAGE
Mr & Mrs Andrew Sadleir.

SHOEMAKERS COTTAGE
Christopher & Anne Jordan.

C17 village, recorded in Domesday, entered by old toll gate. Ornamental stone bridge over the River Stour and interesting church with C13 tower and late C17 nave after Wren. 9 contrasting gardens. One with extensive lawns and fine mature trees with river and garden monuments.

A small, colourful and well-stocked garden, a developing garden with a hint of Japan, a typical cottage garden fit for a chocolate box cover, a 1 acre garden with informal mixed flower and vegetable beds. A secluded walled country garden with mixed perennial and annual planting, a structured cottage garden formally laid out with box hedging. A partially walled cottage garden with herbaceous borders. A traditional orchard with mown pathways and active beehives. Entrance Payments by Cash please. Teas on the Village Green at Honington are a special feature of the afternoon. Some of the smaller gardens have only partial wheelchair access.

GROUP OPENING

26 ILMINGTON GARDENS

Ilmington, CV36 4LA. *8m S of Stratford-upon-Avon. 8m N of Moreton-in-Marsh. 4m NW of Shipston-on-Stour off A3400. 3m NE of Chipping Campden.* **Sat 25, Sun 26 May (12.30-5.30). Combined adm £10, chd free. Cream teas in Ilmington Community Shop, Upper Green on Saturday, and at the Village Hall on Sunday. Donation to Shipston Home Nursing.**

THE BEVINGTONS
Mr & Mrs N Tustain.

THE DOWER HOUSE
Mr & Mrs M Tremellen.

FROG ORCHARD
Mr & Mrs Jeremy Snowden.

GRUMP COTTAGE
Mr & Mrs Martin Underwood.

ILMINGTON MANOR
Mr Martin Taylor.

NEW MEADOW VIEW
Mr Geoff Davis.

OLD FOX HOUSE
Rob & Sarah Beebee.

RAVENSCROFT
Mr & Mrs Clasper.

STUDIO COTTAGE
Sarah Hobson.

Ilmington is an ancient hillside Cotswold village 2m from the Fosse Way with 2 good pubs. Start at Ilmington Manor (next to the Red Lion Pub); wander the 3 acre gardens with fish pond and then walk to the upper green to see the Old Fox House gardens and on to Grump Cottage. Next go up Grump St to Ravenscroft's large, sculpture filled, sloping vistas commanding the hilltop. Walk to nearby Frog Lane to view the garden of Frog Orchard. Then go on to the Bevingtons many-chambered cottage garden at the bottom of Valanders Lane, by the church and manor ponds, and finally visit the Dower House and Meadow View in Back Street. The traditional Ilmington Morris Dancers will be performing in the village on Sunday.

638 Shirley Road, Hall Green Gardens

27 NEW ◆ **KENILWORTH CASTLE**
Castle Green, Kenilworth, CV8 1NG. English Heritage. *In Kenilworth off A46. Clearly signposted from the town centre, off B4103.* **For NGS: Evening opening Fri 12 July (5.30-8). Adm £15. Pre-booking essential, please phone 07721 813442, email alison. makosch@english-heritage.org. uk or visit www.english-heritage. org.uk/visit/places/kenilworth-castle/events for information & booking. For other opening times and information, please phone, email or visit garden website.**
English Heritage in partnership with the National Garden Scheme is offering you the chance to visit gardens of Kenilworth Castle in the early evening when the site is closed to the public. At this exclusive event, you will meet the head gardener for a tour of the gardens, discover how the gardens are managed and experience the tranquillity and colourful planting of this historic garden.
✿ ☕ 🚻

GROUP OPENING

28 **KENILWORTH GARDENS**
Kenilworth, CV8 1BT. *Fieldgate Ln, off A452. Parking available at Abbey Fields or in town. Street parking is available except on Clarendon Ave and Spring Ln. Tickets & maps at all gardens. Transport is necessary to visit all the gardens.* **Sun 16 June (12-5.30). Combined adm £7, chd free. Home-made teas in St Nicholas Parochial Hall.**

BEEHIVE HILL ALLOTMENTS
Kenilworth Allotment Association.

30 CLARENDON ROAD
Mr & Mrs Craddock.

34 CLARENDON ROAD
Barrie & Maggie Rogers.

FIELDGATE
Liz & Bob Watson.
(See separate entry)

14C FIELDGATE LANE
Sandra Aulton.

9 LAWRENCE GARDENS
Leo Lewis & Judith Masson.

23 LINDSEY CRESCENT
Mr John & Mrs Ruth Titley.

38 LINDSEY CRESCENT
Mrs Christine Poole.

2 ST NICHOLAS AVENUE
Mr Ian Roberts.
(See separate entry)

1 SIDDELEY AVENUE
Clare Wightman, www.instagram.com/ wightmanclare.

2 SIDDELEY AVENUE
Mr Simon & Mrs Celia Christie.

NEW **69 SPRING LANE**
Mr Chris Coton & Mr Nick Wood.

TALISMAN SQUARE COMMUNITY GARDEN
Discovery Properties and Cobalt Estates. www.facebook.com/ FriendsofTalismanSquare.

TREE TOPS
Joanna & George Illingworth.

NEW **1 VICARAGE GARDENS**
Mr Clive & Mrs Fran Dutson.

14 WHITEHEAD DRIVE
James Coleman.

Kenilworth was historically a very important town in Warwickshire. It has one of England's best castle ruins, Abbey Fields and plenty of pubs and good cafes. The 16 gardens open this year are spread out around the town. There are small, medium and large gardens with great variety - formal, relaxed and cottage styles with trees, shrubs, herbaceous borders, ponds and many wildlife friendly features - plus plenty of vegetables at the allotments. Several of the gardens have won Gold in the Kenilworth in Bloom garden competition. Abbey Fields is an attractive park in the old part of town close to Kenilworth Castle and the Millennium Walk, starting here is an hour's walk through the Warwickshire countryside around the now drained Kenilworth Castle mere.

The Garden House, Honington Gardens

is on Castle Ln (adjacent to the golf course). **Sun 16 June (11-5). Adm £10, chd £7. Teas, home made cakes and savoury options will be available on site. Donation to other charities.**

Five acres of garden and grounds with roses, herbaceous plants, shrubs and trees in the courtyard and immediate surroundings of this C14 moated castle. Tea and cakes; plant and gift stalls. Wheelchair access to the garden but not into the house.

  ♿ ❀ ☕

32 THE MOTTE

School Lane, Hunningham, Leamington Spa, CV33 9DS. Margaret & Peter Green, 01926 632903, margaretegreen100@gmail.com. *5m E of Leamington Spa. 1m NW off B4455 (Fosse Way) at Hunningham Hill Xrds.* **Visits by arrangement May to Aug for groups of up to 20. Adm £5, chd free. Home-made teas.**

Plant lover's garden of about 1/3 acre, well-stocked with unusual trees, shrubs and herbaceous plants. Set in the quiet village of Hunningham with views over the River Leam and surrounding countryside. The garden has been developed over the last 21yrs and inc woodland, exotic and herbaceous borders, raised alpine bed, troughs, pots, wildlife pond, fruit and vegetable plot. Wheelchair access to front and upper rear garden.

  ♿ 🐐 ☕

29 19 LEIGH CRESCENT

Long Itchington, Southam, CV47 9QS. Tony Shorthouse, 01926 817192, tonyshorthouse19@gmail.com. *Off the Stockton Rd in Long Itchington village.* **Visits by arrangement 23 June to 30 Sept for groups of 5 to 10. Adm £5, chd free. Tea.**

Discover a tropical garden where dappled sunlight filters through the green canopy above and sounds of a waterfall fill the air. A tropical garden, hidden in a Warwickshire village, densely packed with rare and unusual species, many raised from seed.

 🐐 ☕

30 MARIE CURIE HOSPICE GARDEN

Marsh Lane, Solihull, B91 2PQ. Mrs Do Connolly, www.mariecurie. org.uk/westmidlands. *Close to J5 M42 to E of Solihull Town Centre. M42 J5, travel towards Solihull on* A41. *Take slip toward Solihull to join B4025 & after island take 1st R onto Marsh Ln. Hospice on R. Some onsite parking - plenty for blue badge holders.* **Sun 23 June (11-4). Adm £4, chd free. Light refreshments at the hospice bistro in addition to garden tea and cakes.**

The gardens contain two large, formally laid out patients' gardens, indoor courtyards, a long border adjoining the car park and a wildlife and pond area. Children's games. The volunteer gardening team hope that the gardens provide a peaceful and comforting place for patients, their visitors and staff.

  ♿ 🐐 ❀ ☕ ⋑))

31 MAXSTOKE CASTLE

Castle Lane, Coleshill, B46 2RD. Mr G M Fetherston-Dilke, www.maxstoke.com. *Located in between Birmingham and Coventry. 2½ m E of Coleshill. The Castle drive*

33 15 NEW CHURCH ROAD

Sutton Coldfield, B73 5RT. Owen & Lloyd Watkins. *4½ m NW of Birmingham city centre. Take A38M then A5127 to 6 Ways r'about, take 2nd exit then bear L Summer Rd then Gravelly Ln over Chester Rd to Boldmere Rd, 5th R New Church Rd.* **Sun 30 June (1-5). Adm £4, chd free. Home-made teas.**

A garden changing and evolving over 15 yrs, never standing still. An extended pond and bridge take centre stage with a recently added stream. Different areas inc a small stumpery, a dry shade area, large herbaceous borders, tree ferns and rockery and woodland area. Raised vegetable beds, chickens and a composting system. Wheelchair access is available, although some areas may not be accessible. Several steps, portable ramps available.

34 OAK HOUSE
Waverley Edge, Bubbenhall, Coventry, CV8 3LW. Helena Grant, 07731 419685, helena.grant@btinternet.com. *15 mins from Leamington Spa via the Oxford Rd/A423 & the Leamington Rd/ A445 & the A46. Spaces for 5 cars only.* **Visits by arrangement May to Oct for groups of up to 10. Adm £5, chd free. Tea & cakes can be provided for a charge of £3.00 per person.**
Tucked away next to Waverley Wood, Oak House enjoys a walled garden that has been landscaped and extended over 30 years. The garden is split on 2 levels with seating areas allowing for relaxed appreciation of every aspect of the garden, with peaceful places to sit, ponder and enjoy. A focal point is the large terracotta urn, over 60 years old, which delivers vertical interest and the summerhouse and arbour which face each other diagonally across the garden. The curved borders have a wide range of planting creating distinct areas which surround the lawn. There are over 80 different plant varieties giving year-round interest and creating a haven for birds and wildlife. Wheelchair access only on level path which runs round the house.

GROUP OPENING

35 OLD ARLEY GARDENS
Coventry, CV7 8FT. *Enter Ansley Ln via B'ham Rd or Rectory Rd. Parking at the School. Transport may be required to visit all gardens.* **Sun 14 July (2-6). Combined adm £5, chd free. Light refreshments in local church.**

NEW **1 ELM GROVE**
Ms Jane Taylor.

NEW **HOLLYCROFT**
Mr Lewis Hodges.

NEW **17 ST WILFREDS COTTAGES**
Miss Vanessa-Jayne Eady.

21 ST WILFREDS COTTAGES
Miss Jo Carter.

32 ST WILFREDS COTTAGES
Mr Ronald Whiting.

35 ST WILFREDS COTTAGES
Mrs Justine Clee.

THE SCHOOL HOUSE
Mrs Pauline McAleese.

NEW **17 SPINNEY CLOSE**
Mr David Cox.

Old Arley is an ancient village which appears in the Domesday book. More recently it was a small mining community and St Wilfreds Cottages were built in 1907 to accommodate the mine's supervisors and their families. The gardens around the village vary in style and size and the planting is varied, ranging from traditional cottage to more contemporary styles. This year there are a number of new gardens and walking the route is 1½ miles so transport may be necessary. Hood Lane Farm garden will also be open to visit and serving refreshments.

36 PACKINGTON HALL
Meriden, nr Coventry, CV7 7HF. Lord & Lady Guernsey, www.packingtonestate.co.uk. *Midway between Coventry & B'ham on A45. Entrance 400yds from Stonebridge r'about towards Coventry. For SatNav please use CV7 7HE or What3words app - dreamers.mandolin.portfolio.* **Sat 15 June (2-5). Adm £7.50, chd free. Home-made teas.**
Packington is the setting for an elegant Capability Brown landscape. Designed from 1751, the gardens inc a serpentine lake, impressive Cedars of Lebanon, Wellingtonias and a 1762 Japanese bridge. There is also a millennium rose garden, wildflower meadow, mixed terrace borders, and a newly restored walled garden. Home-made teas on the terrace or in The Pompeiin Room if wet. Wheelchair access is possible but please note there are no paths in the garden. The gravelled terrace, where teas are served, is easily accessible.

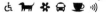

37 PAUL'S OASIS OF CALM
18 Kings Close, Kings Heath, Birmingham, B14 6TP. Mr Paul Doogan, 01214 446943, gardengreen18@hotmail.co.uk. *4m from city centre. 5m from M42 J4. Take A345 to Kings Heath High St then B4122 Vicarage Rd. Turn L onto Kings Rd then R to Kings Cl.* **Visits by arrangement for groups of up to 15. Adm £3, chd free.**
Garden cultivated from nothing into a little oasis. Measuring 18ft x 70ft. It's small but packed with interesting and unusual plants, water features and seven seating areas. The council land in front of the house has been cultivated.

GROUP OPENING

38 PEBWORTH GARDENS
Stratford-upon-Avon, CV37 8XZ. www.pebworth.org/pebworth-open-gardens---national-garden-scheme. *7m SW of Stratford-upon-Avon. For parking & SatNav please use CV37 8XN.* **Sun 26, Mon 27 May (1-5). Combined adm £7, chd free. Home-made teas at Pebworth Village Hall. Coffee and soft drinks also available. Home-made cakes served by The Pebworth and District W.I.**

BROADLEAF FARM
Alix and Ben Hay.

FELLY LODGE
Maz & Barrie Clatworthy.

ICKNIELD BARN
Sheila Davies.

JASMINE COTTAGE
Ted & Veronica Watson.

THE KNOLL
Mr & Mrs K Wood.

MAPLE BARN
Richard & Wendi Weller.

MEON COTTAGE
David & Sally Donnison.

THE MOUNT
Mr & Mrs J Ilott.

NEW **THE OLD POST OFFICE**
Mr Donald Hewlitt.

ORCHARD WILLOW
Mr Roy Bowron.

PEBWORTH ALLOTMENTS
Les Madden.

Pebworth is a delightful village with thatched cottages and properties young and old. There are a variety of garden styles from cottage gardens to modern, walled and terraced gardens. Pebworth is topped by St Peter's Church which has a large ring of 10 bells, unusual for a small rural church. This year we have 7 gardens and the Pebworth Allotments opening, with scrumptious tea and cakes provided by the Pebworth WI in the village hall. The Pebworth Allotments have only been in existence a few years and residents have lovingly tended to them. Some of the Allotmenteers are real characters so do visit and have a chat, they have a wealth of knowledge. Pebworth has been featured on TV a number of times. Partial wheelchair access in some gardens. Ramp available for village hall.

39 PRIORS MARSTON MANOR

The Green, Priors Marston, CV47 7RH. Dr & Mrs Mark Cecil, 07931 461550, matthew.a.j90@gmail.com. *8m SW of Daventry. Off the A361 between Daventry & Banbury at Charwelton. Follow signs to Priors Marston, approx 2m. Arrive at T-junc with a war memorial on R. The manor will be on your L.* Fri 10 May, Fri 7, Sat 8 June, Fri 13, Sat 14 Sept (10-4). Adm £7, chd free. Tea, coffee & home-made cakes. Visits also by arrangement May to Sept for groups of 10+.

Arrive in Priors Marston village and explore the manor gardens. Greatly enhanced by the present owners to relate back to a Georgian manor garden and pleasure grounds. Wonderful walled kitchen garden provides seasonal produce and cut flowers for the house. Herbaceous flower beds and a sunken terrace with water feature by William Pye. Lawns lead down to the lake and estate around which you can walk amongst the trees and wildlife with stunning views up to the house. Regional Winner, Midlands, The English Garden Magazine's The Nation's Favourite Gardens 2023 Partial wheelchair access. Entrance through gravel courtyard.

40 8 RECTORY ROAD

Solihull, B91 3RP. Nigel & Daphne Carter, 07527 475759, npcarter@blueyonder.co.uk. *Located in the town centre: off Church Hill Rd, turn into Rectory Rd, bear L down the rd, house on the R 100 metres down.* Sun 16 June (11-6). Adm £4, chd free. Home-made teas. Evening opening Sat 7 Sept (7-10.30). Adm £4. Wine. Visits also by arrangement 16 June to 7 Sept for groups of 10 to 40.

Stunning town garden divided into areas with different features. A garden with unusual trees and intensively planted borders. Walk to the end of the garden and step into a Japanese themed garden complete with pond, fish and traditional style bridge. Sit on the shaded decking area. A garden to attract bees and butterflies with plenty of places to relax. Japanese themed features and stunning Moon gate.

41 ♦ RYTON ORGANIC GARDENS

Wolston Lane, Ryton on Dunsmore, Coventry, CV8 3LG. Garden Organic, 02476 303517, www.gardenorganic.org.uk. *5m SE of Coventry. From A45 take the exit signed Wolston with brown tourist signs for Ryton Gardens.* For NGS: Sat 6 July, Sat 7 Sept (1-5). Adm £5, chd free. Light refreshments. For other opening times and information, please phone or visit garden website.

Garden Organic's inspirational and sustainable demonstration garden at Ryton contains a wonderful fruit and vegetable potager, together with several large ornamental flowerbeds. Packed full of ideas for gardens of all sizes, it features a large glasshouse, polytunnel, composting area, water features, no-dig and container gardens plus two National Plant Collections.

42 2 ST NICHOLAS AVENUE

Kenilworth, CV8 1JU. Mr Ian Roberts. Sun 18 Feb (12-4). Adm £3, chd free. Home-made teas in St Nicholas Church. Open nearby Fieldgate. Adm to both gardens £5. Opening with Kenilworth Gardens on Sun 16 June.

The garden has been developed over the past 30 years. It has been transformed from an overgrown uninteresting patch to a mature and varied garden containing a wide selection of plants inc a collection of Snowdrops. It contains many features inc. mixed borders, ponds, rockery, structures, mature trees and shrubs. All areas are interconnected by paths so the garden can be enjoyed at leisure.

GROUP OPENING

43 STYVECHALE GARDENS

Knoll Drive, Coventry, CV3 5DE. www.styvechale-gardens.wixsite.com/ngs2020. *The gardens are located on the S side of Coventry close to A45. Tickets & map available on the day from John Paul II Room, St Thomas More Church Knoll Dr Coventry CV3 5DE.* Sun 9 June (11-5). Combined adm £5, chd free.

11 BAGINTON ROAD
Ken & Pauline Bond.

NEW **105 BAGINTON ROAD**
Parmjit and Jasbinder Dhugga.

164 BAGINTON ROAD
Fran & Jeff Gaught.

59 THE CHESILS
John Marron.

66 THE CHESILS
Ami Samra & Rodger Hope.

96 THE CHESILS
Rebecca & Barry Preston.

102 THE CHESILS
Mary & Peter Kinsella.

16 DELAWARE ROAD
Val & Roy Howells.

An eclectic mix of lovely, mature suburban gardens. Enjoy their variety from kitchen garden to a touch of the exotic, restful gardens to a riot of colourful borders. Roses, water features, ponds, shady areas and more. Something for everyone and plenty of ideas for you to take home. One of the gardens was awarded garden of the year by a national newspaper. Relax in the gardens where a warm friendly welcome will await you. Plant sales and refreshments in some gardens. Additional gardens will be open on the day.

GROUP OPENING

44 TYSOE GARDENS

Tysoe, Warwick, CV35 0TR. *W of A422, N of Banbury (9m). E of A3400 & Shipston-on-Stour (4m). N of A4035 & Brailes (3m). Please park on the village Recreation Ground beside the Old Fire Stn CV35 0FF.* Sat 6, Sun 7 July (2-6). Combined adm £7, chd free. Home-made teas at Garden Cottage.

GARDEN COTTAGE & WALLED KITCHEN GARDEN
Sue & Mike Sanderson, www.twkg.co.uk.

NEW **1 JEFFS CLOSE**
Miss Lucy Locke.

NEW **SUNNYSIDE**
Ms Jennifer Cawood.

Tysoe, an original Hornton stone village stands on the North East foothills of the Cotswolds below Edge Hill. You can be sure that Tysoe will offer a happy atmosphere, some terrific gardens, a pleasant walk round the village and a jolly good tea can be had at Garden Cottage. With gardens both large and small, three gardens are open this year. Sunnyside is a recently renovated medium sized garden, 1 Jeff's Close is a small modern garden with interesting terracing and lots of pots. Garden Cottage and walled kitchen garden first opened 8 years ago but has undergone many changes over the years, recent additions are a secret garden and a rill. Contactless payment available at Garden Cottage for entrance. For all plants and teas, cash please.

GROUP OPENING

45 WARMINGTON GARDENS
Banbury, OX17 1BU. *5m NW of Banbury. Take B4100 N from Banbury, after 5m turn R across short dual carriageway into Warmington. From N take J12 off M40 onto B4100.* **Sun 23 June (1-5). Combined adm £6, chd free. Home-made teas at village hall.**

GOURDON
Jenny Deeming.

GREENWAYS
Tim Stevens.

HILL COTTAGE, SCHOOL LANE
Mr Mike Jones.

LANTERN HOUSE
Peter & Tessa Harborne.

THE MANOR HOUSE
Mr & Mrs G Lewis.

THE ORCHARD
Mike Cable.

SPRINGFIELD HOUSE
Jenny & Roger Handscombe, 01295 690286, jehandscombe@btinternet.com.

1 THE WHEELWRIGHTS
Ms E Bunn.

Warmington is a charming historic village, mentioned in the Domesday Book, situated at the NE edge of the Cotswolds in a designated AONB. There is a large village green with a pond overlooked by an Elizabethan Manor House (not open). There are other historic buildings inc St Michael's Church, The Plough Inn and Springfield House all dating from the C16 or before. There is a mixed and varied selection of gardens to enjoy during your visit to Warmington. These inc the formal knot gardens and topiary of The Manor House, cottage and courtyard gardens, terraced gardens on the slopes of Warmington Hill and orchards containing local varieties of apple trees. Some gardens will be selling homegrown plants. WC at village hall, along with

delicious home-made cakes, and hot and cold drinks.

46 WELLESBOURNE ALLOTMENTS
Kineton Road, Wellesbourne, Warwick, CV35 9NE. Wellesbourne Allotments, www. wellesbourneallotments.co.uk. *5m E of Stratford-upon-Avon. On L of Kineton Rd (B4086) E of Wellesbourne, 400 metres from shops in precinct.* **Sat 13 July (1-4). Adm £5, chd free. Light refreshments.**
Visit Wellesbourne Allotments dating back from 1838. View and explore over 126 working Plots on our beautiful seven acre site. The site has been featured on BBC's Country File and is listed as an asset of community value. See how allotments contribute to mental health and wellbeing and how it can help people living with dementia. Impressive vegetables, delicious fruits and beautiful flowers abound on the site offering interest to novice and experienced gardeners of all ages. A large, lush and lovely rural site growing a huge range of crops. Meet enthusiastic gardeners and sample delicious homemade teas. Plants and produce for sale, scarecrows, children's activities, a landscaped Dementia-friendly plot, music, refreshments. Wheelchair access limited. Hard surface entrance and roadway only.

GROUP OPENING

47 WHICHFORD & ASCOTT GARDENS
Whichford & Ascott, Shipston-on-Stour, CV36 5PG. *6m SE of Shipston-on-Stour. For parking please use CV36 5PG. There is parking by the church. Parking also available at Wood House.* **Sun 16 June (1.30-5). Combined adm £7, chd free. Home-made teas.**

ASCOTT LODGE
Charlotte Copley.

ASCOTT RISE
Carol & Jerry Moore.

BELMONT HOUSE
Robert & Yoko Ward.

LENTICULARS
Mrs Diana Atkins.

THE OLD RECTORY
Peter & Caroline O'Kane.

PLUM TREE COTTAGE
Janet Knight.

THE WHICHFORD POTTERY
Jim & Dominique Keeling, www.whichfordpottery.com.

WOOD HOUSE
Mr and Mrs G James.

The gardens in this group reflect many different styles. The 2 villages are in an AONB, nestled within a dramatic landscape of hills, pasture and woodland, which is used to picturesque effect by the garden owners. Fine lawns, mature shrubs and interesting planting will all enrich your visit to our beautiful gardens. Many incorporate the inventive use of natural springs, forming ponds, pools and other water features. Classic cottage gardens contrast with larger and more classical gardens which adopt variations on the traditional English garden of herbaceous borders, climbing roses, yew hedges and walled enclosures. Partial wheelchair access as some gardens are on sloping sites.

48 NEW WOOLSCOTT BARN
Woolscott, Rugby, CV23 8DB. Neil Higginson, 07836 511495, neilnrhigginson@btinternet.com, www.instagram.com/neilhiggison. *2 m from Dunchurch. Take the A45 S from Dunchurch towards Daventry until R turn for Grandborough. After 1 m, go round a big bend & past manor house. Woolscott barn is 400m after manor house on L.* **Visits by arrangement Feb to Sept. Limited parking max 7 cars. Minibuses welcome. Coaches by arrangement. Adm £6, chd free.**
A plantsman's garden set in 1½ acres a great variety of plants. Large areas of shade plantings. Over 300 different snowdrops, anemone nemorosa, erythroniums, ferns and geraniums. A dwarf conifer rockery with a range of choice bulbs and herbaceous borders. Vegetable beds. Autumn brings mass plantings of Cyclamen to the party. There is a large area dedicated to propagation of more unusual plants. Everyone is welcome but because parking is limited please contact the owner to check there is space available before you visit. Gravel drive and hard paths suitable for wheelchairs around some of the garden.

WORCESTERSHIRE

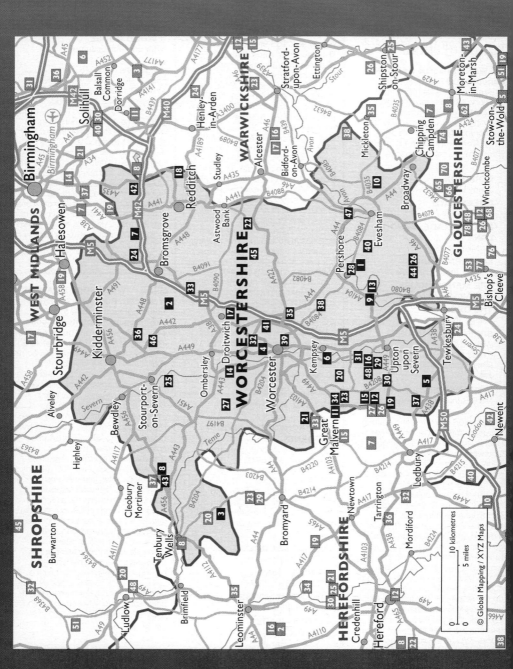

VOLUNTEERS

County Organiser
David Morgan
01214 453595
meandi@btinternet.com

County Treasurer
Doug Bright
01886 832200
doug.bright@ngs.org.uk

Publicity
Pamela Thompson
01886 888295
peartree.pam@gmail.com

Social Media
Brian Skeys
01684 311297
brian.skeys@ngs.org.uk

Booklet Co-ordinator
Steven Wilkinson & Linda Pritchard
01684 310150
steven.wilkinson48412@gmail.com

Assistant County Organisers
Andrea Bright
01886 832200
andrea.bright@ngs.org.uk

Brian Bradford
07816 867137
bradf0rds@icloud.com

Lynn Glaze
01386 751924
lynnglaze@cmail.co.uk

Philippa Lowe
01684 891340
philippa.lowe@ngs.org.uk

Stephanie & Chris Miall
0121 445 2038
stephaniemiall@hotmail.com

Rachel Pryke
rachelgpryke@btinternet.com

David & Sandra Traynor
sandraanddavid.traynor@ngs.org.uk

f @WorcestershireNGS

X @WorcsNGS

OPENING DATES

All entries subject to change. For latest information check **www.ngs.org.uk**
Map locator numbers are shown to the right of each garden name.

February

Snowdrop Openings

Wednesday 14th
Brockamin | 6

Sunday 18th
Brockamin | 6
Warndon Court | 41

March

Friday 15th
◆ Little Malvern Court | 19

Sunday 17th
Brockamin | 6

Thursday 21st
◆ Cotswold Garden Flowers | 10

Friday 22nd
◆ Little Malvern Court | 19

April

Monday 1st
The Dell House | 12

Sunday 7th
Overbury Court | 26
◆ Spetchley Park Gardens | 35

Saturday 13th
The Alpine Garden Society | 1
The Walled Garden & No. 53 | 39

Sunday 14th
Brockamin | 6

Wednesday 17th
The Walled Garden & No. 53 | 39

Thursday 18th
◆ Cotswold Garden Flowers | 10

Saturday 20th
◆ Whitlenge Gardens | 46

Sunday 21st
◆ Whitlenge Gardens | 46

Saturday 27th
Winchester House | 47

Sunday 28th
Winchester House | 47

May

Wednesday 1st
The Dell House | 12

Saturday 4th
The Alpine Garden Society | 1

Sunday 5th
Nimrod, 35 Alexandra Road | 23
◆ White Cottage & Nursery | 45

Monday 6th
Nimrod, 35 Alexandra Road | 23

Saturday 11th
Cowleigh Park Farm | 11

Sunday 12th
Oak Tree House | 24
Pear Tree Cottage | 27

Monday 13th
19 Winnington Gardens | 48

Wednesday 15th
The Alpine Garden Society | 1

Thursday 16th
◆ Cotswold Garden Flowers | 10

Saturday 18th
Madresfield Court | 20
Oak Tree House | 24
Warndon Court | 41
Winchester House | 47

Sunday 19th
2 Brookwood Drive | 7
Rothbury | 34
Winchester House | 47

Saturday 25th
Ravelin | 29

Sunday 26th
1 Church Cottage | 9
Millbrook Lodge | 21
Ravelin | 29
Rothbury | 34
NEW Summercoombe | 37
Whitcombe House | 44
◆ White Cottage & Nursery | 45

Monday 27th
1 Church Cottage | 9
Ravelin | 29
Rothbury | 34

June

Saturday 1st
Eckington Gardens   13

Sunday 2nd
Eckington Gardens   13

Wednesday 5th
The Dell House   12

Saturday 8th
Hanley Swan NGS Gardens   16
Pershore Gardens   28
◆ White Cottage & Nursery   45

Sunday 9th
Birtsmorton Court   5
Hanley Swan NGS Gardens   16
Pershore Gardens   28
Warndon Court   41

Friday 14th
Cowleigh Park Farm   11

Saturday 15th
NEW Elm Hill Cottage   14
◆ Whitlenge Gardens   46

Sunday 16th
NEW Elm Hill Cottage   14
3 Oakhampton Road   25
◆ Whitlenge Gardens   46

Thursday 20th
◆ Cotswold Garden Flowers   10

Saturday 22nd
NEW Bank Farm   3
Rest Harrow   30
The River School   32
Walnut Cottage   40
◆ White Cottage & Nursery   45

Sunday 23rd
NEW Bank Farm   3
2 Brookwood Drive   7
NEW Holly Cottage   18
Rest Harrow   30
NEW Summercoombe   37
Walnut Cottage   40

Saturday 29th
5 Beckett Drive   4

Sunday 30th
5 Beckett Drive   4
Hiraeth   17
3 Oakhampton Road   25

July

Wednesday 3rd
The Dell House   12

Saturday 6th
Wharf House   43

Sunday 7th
Millbrook Lodge   21
◆ Spetchley Park Gardens   35
Wharf House   43

Sunday 14th
3 Oakhampton Road   25

Thursday 18th
◆ Cotswold Garden Flowers   10

Saturday 27th
NEW Cherry Tree Barn   8
NEW Weatheroak and Wythall
Gardens   42

Sunday 28th
3 Oakhampton Road   25
Rothbury   34
NEW Weatheroak and Wythall
Gardens   42

August

Saturday 10th
Nimrod, 35 Alexandra Road   23

Sunday 11th
Nimrod, 35 Alexandra Road   23

Thursday 15th
◆ Cotswold Garden Flowers   10

Sunday 18th
Hiraeth   17

Monday 19th
19 Winnington Gardens   48

Saturday 24th
◆ Morton Hall Gardens   22

Sunday 25th
3 Oakhampton Road   25
Pear Tree Cottage   27

Monday 26th
3 Oakhampton Road   25

Saturday 31st
Rest Harrow   30

September

Sunday 1st
Rest Harrow   30

Saturday 14th
Ravelin   29
◆ Whitlenge Gardens   46

Sunday 15th
Ravelin   29
Rhydd Gardens   31
◆ Whitlenge Gardens   46

Thursday 19th
◆ Cotswold Garden Flowers   10

Sunday 22nd
Brockamin   6

October

Saturday 5th
Ravelin   29

Sunday 6th
Ravelin   29

Thursday 17th
◆ Cotswold Garden Flowers   10

By Arrangement

Arrange a personalised garden visit with your club, or group of friends, on a date to suit you. See individual garden entries for full details.

The Alpine Garden Society   1
Badge Court   2
5 Beckett Drive   4
Birtsmorton Court   5
Brockamin   6
2 Brookwood Drive   7
NEW Cherry Tree Barn   8
1 Church Cottage   9
Cowleigh Park Farm   11
The Dell House   12
Eckington Gardens   13
The Folly   15
Hanley Swan NGS Gardens   16
Hiraeth   17
Joe's Garden, Weatheroak and
Wythall Gardens   42
Millbrook Lodge   21
Nimrod, 35 Alexandra Road   23
Oak Tree House   24
3 Oakhampton Road   25
Overbury Court   26
Pear Tree Cottage   27
NEW The Pond House, Weatheroak
and Wythall Gardens   42
Pump Cottage, Weatheroak and
Wythall Gardens   42
Ravelin   29
Rest Harrow   30
Rhydd Gardens   31
NEW Summercoombe   37
The Tynings   38
Warndon Court   41
Wharf House   43
Whitcombe House   44
19 Winnington Gardens   48

THE GARDENS

◻ THE ALPINE GARDEN SOCIETY

Avon Bank, Wick, Pershore,
WR10 3JP. The Alpine Garden
Society, 01386 554790,
ags@alpinegardensociety.net,
www.alpinegardensociety.net.
Wick, ½m from Pershore town. Take
Evesham Rd from Pershore over the
River Avon, cont for ½m & turn R for
Pershore College, the garden is the
1st entrance on the L. **Sat 13 Apr,
Sat 4, Wed 15 May (11-4). Adm
£4, chd free. Light refreshments.
Visits also by arrangement 8 Apr
to 26 Sept for groups of 10+.**
Inspirational small garden next to
the Alpine Garden Society office.
The garden shows a wide range of
alpine plants that are easy to grow in
contemporary gardens over a long
season. Visitors can see different
settings to grow alpines, inc rock
and tufa, scree, a dry Mediterranean
bed, shade and sunny areas, also a
dedicated alpine house, and many pots
and troughs with alpines and small
bulbs. Volunteers will be on hand on
open days to provide more information,
and planting demonstrations will be
available on some dates. The garden
slopes gently upwards with gravel paths
which are accessible to wheelchairs
with some assistance.

◨ BADGE COURT

Purshull Green Lane, Elmbridge,
Droitwich, WR9 0NJ. Stuart &
Diana Glendenning, 01299 851216,
dianaglendenning1@gmail.com.
5m N of Droitwich Spa. 2½m from
J5 M5. Turn off A38 at Wychbold
down side of the Swan Inn. Turn
R into Berry Ln. Take next L into
Cooksey Green Ln. Turn R into
Purshull Green Ln. Garden is on L.
**Visits by arrangement 3 June to
26 July for groups of 6 to 30. Adm
£6, chd free. Tea, coffee and juice
is available plus a large slice of
home-made cake for £4.**
The 2½ acre garden is set against the
backdrop of a C16 house (not open).
There is something for all gardeners
inc mature specimen trees, huge
range of clematis and roses, lake with
waterfall, stumpery, topiary garden,
walled garden, Mediterranean Garden,
specialist borders, long herbaceous
border, large potager vegetable garden
and Japanese Garden.

◼ NEW BANK FARM

Kyre, Tenbury Wells, WR15 8QD.
Jennifer Grigg. 4 m from Tenbury
Wells. If coming from Bromyard Rd,
drive past Kyre Park - Bank Farm is
then 2nd drive on R. **Sat 22, Sun
23 June (1-5). Adm £5, chd free.
Home-made teas.**
Bank Farm's garden is ½ an acre
of terraced, densely planted mixed
borders and beds set in farmland
with some unusual trees, a water
feature, meadow-in-progress and a
lovely setting with views. Part of the
black and white house (not open)
dates from 1660. Trees inc Catalpa,
Eucryphia, Heptacodium, Cornus
controversa. There are several seating
areas. There is step-free access to
the whole garden. Paths may be
muddy or wet and there are slopes.

◪ 5 BECKETT DRIVE

Northwick, Worcester, WR3 7BZ.
Jacki & Pete Ager, 01905 451108,
agers@outlook.com. 1½m N of
Worcester city centre. A cul-de-sac
off the A449 Ombersley Rd directly
opp Grantham's Autocare Garage.
1m S of the Claines r'about on A449
& just N of Northwick Cinema on
Ombersley Rd. **Sat 29, Sun 30 June
(1-5). Adm £5, chd free. Home-
made ice cream on sale. Visits
also by arrangement 1 June to 4
Aug for groups of 10 to 40.**
An extraordinary town garden on the
northern edge of Worcester packed
with different plants and year-round
interest guaranteed to give visitors
ideas and inspiration for their own
gardens. Over 20 years visitors have
enjoyed the unique and surprising
features of this garden which has
many planting schemes for a variety
of situations.

◻ BIRTSMORTON COURT

Birtsmorton, nr Malvern,
WR13 6JS. Mr & Mrs N G K Dawes,
rosaliedawes@btinternet.com. 7m
E of Ledbury. Off A438 Ledbury/
Tewkesbury rd. **Sun 9 June
(2-5.30). Adm £8, chd free.
Home-made teas. Visits also by
arrangement 14 Apr to 15 Sept for
groups of 20 to 40.**
10 acre garden surrounding beautiful
medieval moated manor house (not
open). White garden, built and planted
in 1997 surrounded on all sides
by old topiary. Potager, vegetable
garden and working greenhouses, all

beautifully maintained. Rare double
working moat and waterways inc
Westminster Pool laid down in Henry
VII's reign to mark the consecration
of the knave of Westminster Abbey.
Ancient yew tree under which
Cardinal Wolsey reputedly slept in the
legend of the Shadow of the Ragged
Stone.

◺ BROCKAMIN

Old Hills, Callow End, Worcester,
WR2 4TQ. Margaret Stone,
01905 830370, stone.brockamin@
btinternet.com. 5m S of Worcester.
½m S of Callow End on the B4424,
on an unfenced bend, turn R into
the car park signed Old Hills. Walk
towards the houses keeping R. **Wed
14 Feb (1-4); Sun 18 Feb (11-4);
Sun 17 Mar, Sun 14 Apr, Sun 22
Sept (1-4). Adm £5, chd free.
Home-made teas. Visits also by
arrangement 15 Feb to 15 Oct for
groups of 10+. Donation to Plant
Heritage.**
1½ acre plantsman's garden situated
next to common land. Informal
mixed borders with a wide variety of
hardy perennials where plants are
allowed to self seed. Large collection
of snowdrops. Plant Heritage
National Collections of Pulmonarias,
Symphyotrichum novae-angliae and
some hardy geraniums. Unusual
plants for sale. Open for snowdrops
in Feb, daffodils and pulmonarias in
March and April, geraniums in June
and asters in September. Seasonal
pond/bog garden and kitchen garden.
Teas with home-made cakes and
unusual plants for sale. An access
path reaches a large part of the
garden.

*100 inpatients and
their families are
being supported at the
newly opened Horatio's
Garden Wales, thanks
to the National Garden
Scheme donations*

7 2 BROOKWOOD DRIVE

Barnt Green, Birmingham, B45 8GG. Mr Mike & Mrs Liz Finlay, 07721 746369, liz@lizfinlay.com. *5m N of Bromsgrove. Please park courteously in local roads or in village. Brookwood Dr is on R towards top of Fiery Hill Rd approx. ¼m from station. Press the access button to open security gates if closed.* **Sun 19 May, Sun 23 June (10-4). Adm £5, chd free. Home-made teas. Refreshments £5 per person inc a choice of cakes and unlimited drinks. Visits also by arrangement 1 Apr to 15 Sept for groups of 8 to 25.**

A multi-themed mature garden with numerous water features and colourful borders. There is a formal white garden, wildlife pond and cutting garden surrounded by large rhododendrons which give a colourful display in late spring. Parking on Brookwood Drive for disabled only.

  ♿ ✿ ☕))

8 NEW CHERRY TREE BARN

Southnett, Mamble, Kidderminster, DY14 9JT. Mr Ian & Mrs Julie Stackhouse, Stackhouse571@ btinternet.com. *12m W of Kidderminster on the A456. Nearest motorway M5 J6. A456 from Kidderminster, past Mamble village approx 1m, garden on L up a track off main road. A456 from Tenbury Wells, past Broombank. Garden on R up a track off main road, follow signs.* **Sat 27 July (11-4). Adm £5, chd free. Home-made teas. Visits also by arrangement 18 May to 31 Aug for groups of 10 to 30. Discuss refreshments when booking.**

The garden has been planted out with a wide variety of trees and shrubs providing year-round interest. The main event are the herbaceous beds filled with a riot of colour from May onwards. There are two ponds, a bog garden inc stumpery, a rose bed, gravel garden, two azalea beds and a small woodland area. The rear garden offers wonderful views of the surrounding countryside.

✿ ☕))

9 1 CHURCH COTTAGE

Church Road, Defford, WR8 9BJ. John Taylor & Ann Sheppard, 01386 750863, ann98sheppard@ btinternet.com. *3m SW of Pershore. A4104 Pershore to Upton Rd, turn into Harpley Rd, Defford. Don't go up Bluebell Ln as directed by SatNav, black & white cottage at side of church. Parking in village hall car park.* **Sun 26, Mon 27 May (1-5). Adm £5, chd free. Home-made teas. Visits also by arrangement 1 May to 15 Sept for groups of 10 to 30. Charge inclusive of tea and cake for by arrangement visits.**

True countryman's ⅓ acre cottage garden. Japanese style feature with 'dragons den'. Specimen trees, rare and unusual plants, water features, perennial garden, vegetable garden, poultry, streamside bog garden. New features in progress. Wheelchair access to most areas, narrow paths may restrict access to some parts.

♿ 🐴 ✿ ☕))

10 ◆ COTSWOLD GARDEN FLOWERS

Sands Lane, Badsey, Evesham, WR11 7EZ. Mr Bob Brown, 01386 833849, info@cgf.net, www.cgf.net. *Sands Ln is the last road on the L when leaving Badsey for Wickhamford. Garden is nearly ½m down lane.* **For NGS: Thur 21 Mar, Thur 18 Apr, Thur 16 May, Thur 20 June, Thur 18 July, Thur 15 Aug, Thur 19 Sept, Thur 17 Oct (11-4). Adm £5, chd free.**

Stone House Cottage Gardens

© Michael Warren

Light refreshments. For other opening times and information, please phone, email or visit garden website.

The garden consists of one acre of stockbeds with many thousands of kinds of plants many of which are unusual and rare. Guided tours are available on NGS open days. Please note this is a working nursery. This garden is proud to provide plants for the National Garden Scheme's Show Garden at Chelsea Flower Show 2024.

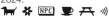

11 COWLEIGH PARK FARM

Cowleigh Road, Malvern, WR13 5HJ. John & Ruth Lucas, 01684 566750, info@cowleighparkfarm.co.uk, www.cowleighparkfarm.co.uk. *On the edge of Malvern. Leaving Malvern on the B4219 the driveway for Cowleigh Park Farm is on the R just before the derestrict speed sign. Coming from the A4103 we are on the L just after the 30mph sign.* **Sat 11 May (2-5). Home-made teas. Evening opening Fri 14 June (5-9.30). Light refreshments. Adm £6, chd free. Evening opening will inc hot drinks. Feel free to bring your own alcoholic drinks and glasses. Visits also by arrangement 25 Mar to 22 Sept.**

The 1½ acre garden at Cowleigh Park Farm surrounds a Grade II listed timber framed former farmhouse (not open). Whilst no longer a farm, the property has views to adjacent orchards and inc lawns, spring fed ponds, a waterfall and stream. The focus in established beds and borders is to be wildlife and bee friendly. The garden contains multiple seating areas and a summerhouse. The whole garden can be viewed from wheelchair accessible places but some parts have steep grassy slopes that may not be accessible by wheelchair.

12 THE DELL HOUSE

2 Green Lane, Malvern Wells, WR14 4HU. Kevin & Elizabeth Rolph, 01684 564448, kande@dellhousemalvern.uk, www.dellhousemalvern.uk. *What3words app - remember.shrub. robot. 2m S of Gt Malvern Behind former church on corner of Wells Rd & Green Ln. Small car park for those pre-booked. Approach downhill from Wells Rd. Do not use Postcode in*

SatNav. **Mon 1 Apr, Wed 1 May (12-5); Wed 5 June, Wed 3 July (2-8). Adm £5, chd free. Pre-booking essential, please visit www.ngs. org.uk for information & booking. Light refreshments. Visits also by arrangement for groups of up to 20. Small numbers welcome at short notice.**

Two acre wooded hillside garden of the 1830s former rectory, now a B&B. Peaceful and natural, the garden contains many magnificent specimen trees inc a Wellingtonia Redwood. Informal in style with meandering bark paths, spectacular tree carvings, historic garden buildings, 16mm garden railway and a paved terrace with outstanding views. Partial wheelchair access with good views from the level paved terrace. Parking is on gravel. Sloping bark paths, some quite steep.

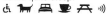

GROUP OPENING

13 ECKINGTON GARDENS

Hilltop, Nafford Road, Eckington, WR10 3DH. Group Coordinator Richard Bateman, 01386 750819. *2 gardens - 1 in Upper End, 1 close by in Nafford Rd. A4104 Pershore to Upton & Defford, L turn B4080 to Eckington. In centre, by war memorial turn L into New Rd (becomes Nafford Rd).* **Sat 1, Sun 2 June (11-5). Combined adm £7, chd free. Light refreshments at Mantoft. Visits also by arrangement May to Sept for groups of 5 to 30. Please liaise with garden owners for refreshments.**

HILLTOP FARM
Richard & Margaret Bateman.

MANTOFT
Mrs Tupper.

Two diverse gardens set in/close to lovely village of Eckington. Hilltop: one acre garden with sunken garden/ pond, rose garden, herbaceous borders, interesting topiary inc cloud pruning and formal hedging to reduce effect of wind and having 'windows' for views over the beautiful Worcestershire countryside. Sculptures made by owner. Vegetable yurt (added 2018) has been successful in allowing pollination and preventing damage to young plants. New treehouse for 2024. Mantoft: Wonderful ancient thatched cottage

with 1½ acres of magical gardens. Fishpond with ghost koi, Cotswold and red brick walls, large topiary, treehouse with seating, summerhouse and dovecote, pathways, vistas and stone statues, urns and herbaceous borders. Featured in Cotswold Life - should not be missed.

14 NEW ELM HILL COTTAGE

Sinton Green, Hallow, Worcester, WR2 6NU. Mr Michael & Mrs Tina Boughey. *4m NW of Worcester. Off A443. Take road to Sinton Green (Dark Ln). Continue for 1m and at 2nd Xrds, turn R at the green, then follow NGS signs. Press button if gates do not open.* **Sat 15, Sun 16 June (1.30-5). Adm £5, chd free. Home-made teas. Gluten and dairy free cake available.**

Charming ¼ acre cottage garden surrounded by fields with views of Worcestershire. Mixed herbaceous planting, white borders, paved area with nod to the Mediterranean, a potted eucalyptus is surrounded by a selection of beds and pots overflowing with colour. Two espalier apples lead to borders with hardy geraniums, alliums, delphiniums, salvias, roses, peonies, clematis, iris, weigelas. Small veg area. A raised sitting area with views of the lakes, plus many more places to sit and not only enjoy the garden but also admire the views of the Worcestershire countryside. There is a public footpath by the house if you would like to extend your visit. The area at the front of the house is laid to gravel. There is access by car to the start of the garden.

Our donation in 2023 has enabled Parkinson's UK to fund 3 new nursing posts this year, directly supporting people with Parkinson's

🔢15 THE FOLLY

87 Wells Road, Malvern, WR14 4PB. David & Lesley Robbins, 01684 567253, lesleycmedley@btinternet.com. *1½ m S of Great Malvern & 9m S of Worcester. Approx 8m from M5 via J7 or J8. Situated in Malvern Wells on A449, 0.7m N of B4209 & 0.2m S of Malvern Common. Parking off the main road is available on lay-by or side road opp the Common.* **Visits by arrangement 29 Apr to 30 June for groups of up to 25. Additional refreshments can be requested on booking tea. Cash preferred for refreshments.**
A hillside garden in Malvern with three terraces and views over the Severn Vale. The first level has a potager with greenhouse, the second is a formal terrace and courtyard by the house, and the third is landscaped to create small cottage and scree gardens, stumpery and pergola under mature cedars. Planting inc climbers, spring plants and shrubs, roses, acers, hostas, succulents and ferns. The terraces all have seating and are linked by both steps and winding paths. Garden art set amongst the plants and trees provides added interest.

☕))

GROUP OPENING

🔢16 HANLEY SWAN NGS GARDENS

Hanley Swan, WR8 0DJ. Group Co-ordinator Brian Skeys, 01684 311297, brimfields@icloud.com, www.brimfields.com. *5m E of Malvern, 3m NW of Upton upon Severn, 9m S of Worcester & M5. From the B4211 towards Great Malvern & Guarlford (Rhydd Rd) turn L to Hanley Swan continue to Orchard Side WR8 0EA for entrance tickets & maps.* **Sat 8, Sun 9 June (1-5). Combined adm £7.50, chd free. Light refreshments at 19 Winnington Gardens. Visits also by arrangement 10 June to 20 Sept for groups of 10 to 20.**

MEADOW BANK

Mrs Lesley Stroud & Mr Dave Horrobin, 01684 310917, djhorrobin@gmail.com.

ORCHARD SIDE

Mrs Gigi Verlander, 01684 310602, gigiverlander@icloud.com.

THE PADDOCKS

Mr & Mrs N Fowler.

19 WINNINGTON GARDENS

Brian & Irene Skeys. (See separate entry)

20 WINNINGTON GARDENS

Mr & Mrs Sauntson.

YEW TREE COTTAGE

Mr & Mrs Read.

Entrance tickets from Orchard Side, a country garden with unusual items in the garden. A large koi pond sits just in front of the peaceful Zen Den to sit and contemplate. The Paddocks, a wildlife garden with ponds, a tadpole nursery, mixed borders, new greenhouse with cacti and succulents. Meadowbank, a modern interpretation of a traditional cottage garden. Cottage garden plants, grasses and bamboos, dahlias. Moving towards a more sustainable way of gardening. 20 Winnington Gardens has an octagonal greenhouse, four water features surrounded by a manicured lawn, colourful beds. Returning this year after building a new patio and entertainment area. Yew Tree Cottage, a C17 black and white cottage (not open) within a cottage garden, vegetables, borders with field views at rear. 19 Winnington Gardens, a garden of rooms. Mixed borders enclosed with climbing roses, a small oriental garden, fruit trees, herbs, pelargonium collection, irises, collection of vintage garden tools. Six enthusiastic garden owners gardening in different styles with wildlife and sustainability becoming more important. Some new designed areas. Plant sales and teas.

🐄 ✿ 🚌 ☕))

🔢17 HIRAETH

30 Showell Road, Droitwich, WR9 8UY. Sue & John Fletcher, 07752 717243, sueandjohn99@yahoo.com. *1m S of Droitwich. On The Ridings estate. Turn off A38 r'about into Addyes Way, 2nd R into Showell Rd, 500yds on R. Follow the yellow signs.* **Sun 30 June, Sun 18 Aug (1.30-4.30). Adm £4, chd free. Home-made teas. Visits also by arrangement 3 June to 30 Sept for groups of up to 30.**
⅓ acre gardens. The front has three barrels of ericaceous plants. A conifer bed, hydrangeas and a 300+ year old olive tree, monkey puzzle, acers,

silver birch and various shrubs. The centre features a large piece Forest of Dean rock at one entrance. The rear garden has an oasis of colour created by numerous trees inc acers, weeping willow and weeping birch. A rose and hosta bed on one side and a fernery on the other. Various stone statues and metal sculptures on display containing a variety of animals inc an alligator or crocodile (we're not sure which!). A local minister has described the garden as 'a haven on the way to heaven'. Partial wheelchair access.

♿ ✿ 🅿

🔢18 NEW HOLLY COTTAGE

Gorcott Hill, Beoley, Redditch, B98 9EW. Mr Robin & Mrs Julie Boyce. *3m S of J3 M42. Take slip road from A435 (signed Ullenhall). Gorcott Hill is on the E side of A435, a no through road. Follow NGS signs to car parking.* **Sun 23 June (11-4). Adm £5, chd free. Light refreshments. Tea, coffee and a selection of cakes available.**
½ acre garden that contains a cottage garden border, jungle area, formal garden, rose borders, small orchard, Mediterranean area with grapes, figs, olives and lavender, and all continually evolving. A pond for wildlife, and many seating areas. Our miniature donkeys look forward to seeing you, along with the chickens.

🅿))

🔢19 ◆ LITTLE MALVERN COURT

Little Malvern, WR14 4JN. Mrs T M Berington, littlemalverncourt@hotmail.com, www.littlemalverncourt.co.uk. *3m S of Malvern. On A4104 S of junction with A449.* **For NGS: Fri 15, Fri 22 Mar (2-5). Adm £6, chd free. Light refreshments only. For other opening times and information, please email or visit garden website.**
10 acres attached to former Benedictine Priory, magnificent views over Severn Valley. Garden rooms and terrace around house designed and planted in early 1980s; chain of lakes; wide variety of spring bulbs, flowering trees and shrubs. Notable collection of old fashioned roses. Topiary hedge and fine trees. Regional Finalist, The English Garden's The Nation's Favourite Gardens 2019. Partial wheelchair access.

♿ 🅳 🅿))

20 MADRESFIELD COURT

Madresfield, Malvern, WR13 5AJ. Trustees of Lord Beauchamp's 1963 Settlement, www.madresfieldestate.co.uk. *2m E of Malvern. Entrance ½m S of Madresfield village, just outside Malvern.* **Sat 18 May (1-4). Adm £10, chd £5. Light refreshments.** Gardens mainly laid out in 1865, based on three avenues of oak, cedar and lombardy poplar, within and around which are specimen trees and flowering shrubs. Meadows within the avenues covered in daffodils, and later, fritillaries, bluebells, cowslips etc. Recent rhododendron plantings. Holly hedge enclosure with 100m walk of peonies and irises, next to a crescent tunnel of pollarded limes. Overall a parkland garden of approx 60 acres. Tarmac main drive interspersed with gravel and grass paths.

21 MILLBROOK LODGE

Millham Lane, Alfrick, Worcester, WR6 5HS. Andrea & Doug Bright, andreabright@hotmail.co.uk. *11m from M5 J7. A4103 from Worcester to Bransford r'about, then Suckley Rd for 3m to Alfrick Pound. Turn L at sign for Old Storridge - No Through Road.* **Sun 26 May, Sun 7 July (1-5). Adm £6, chd free. Home-made teas. Visits also by arrangement 1 May to 8 Sept for groups of 15 to 40.** 3½ acre garden and woodland developed by current owners over 27 years. Large informal flowerbeds planted for year-round interest, from spring flowering bulbs, camellias, hostas, rhododendrons and magnolias through to asters and dahlias. Pond with stream and bog garden. Fruit and vegetable garden and gravel garden. Peaceful setting in an area of outstanding natural beauty and near a nature reserve.

22 ◆ MORTON HALL GARDENS

Morton Hall Lane, Holberrow Green, Redditch, B96 6SJ. Mrs A Olivieri, morton.garden@mhcom.co.uk, www.mortonhallgardens.co.uk. *In centre of Holberrow Green, at a wooden bench around a tree, turn up Morton Hall Ln. Follow NGS signs to gate opp Morton Hall Farm.* **For NGS: Sat 24 Aug (10-5). Adm £11, chd free. Pre-booking essential, please phone 01386 791820, email morton.garden@mhcom.co.uk or visit www.mortonhallgardens.co.uk for information & booking. Light refreshments inc gluten-free & vegetarian options. For other opening times and information, please phone, email or visit garden website.** Perched atop an escarpment with breathtaking views, hidden behind a tall hedge, lies a Georgian country house with a unique garden of outstanding beauty. A garden for all seasons, it features one of the country's largest fritillary spring meadows, sumptuous herbaceous summer borders, a striking potager, a majestic woodland rockery and an elegant Japanese Stroll Garden with tea house. Tulip Festival on first May bank holiday weekend. Visits by appointment from April to September. All visits must be pre-booked via the Morton Hall Garden website. For NGS Open Day, click on the yellow banner on the Morton Hall Gardens homepage. Pre-booking closes at 10 am on 24.08.24.

Elm Hill Cottage

23 NIMROD, 35 ALEXANDRA ROAD

Malvern, WR14 1HE. Margaret & David Cross, 01684 569019, margaret.cross@ifdev.net. *From Worcester A449. From Malvern Link, pass train stn, ahead at T-lights, 1st R into Alexandra Rd. From Great Malvern, go through Link Top T-lights (junc with B4503), 1st L.* **Sun 5, Mon 6 May, Sat 10, Sun 11 Aug (10.30-5). Adm £5, chd free. Home-made teas. Visits also by arrangement 5 May to 31 Aug.**
Overlooked by the Malvern Hills, the garden is on two levels with mature horse chestnuts, western red cedars, wildlife pond, small wildflower meadow, shady woodland area, cottage garden, Japanese garden, rockeries and a New Zealand influenced area. An arbour inspired by Geoff Hamilton, also a treehouse and den for accompanied children. Elgar wrote some of the Enigma variations in a bell tent here. With help, the garden can be accessed by wheelchair, there are few steps but gravel paths and gradients. If advised we can offer closer parking.

24 OAK TREE HOUSE

504 Birmingham Road, Marlbrook, Bromsgrove, B61 0HS. Di & Dave Morgan, 01214 453595, meandi@btinternet.com. *On main A38 midway between M42 J1 & M5 J4. Park in old A38 - R fork 250 yds N of garden or small area in front of Miller & Carter Pub car park 200 yds S or local roads.* **Sun 12, Sat 18 May (1.30-5). Adm £4, chd free. Home-made teas. Visits also by arrangement May to Aug for groups of 10 to 35.**
Plantswoman's cottage garden overflowing with plants, pots and interesting artifacts. Patio with spring colour, azaleas, rhododendrons and acers, small pond and waterfall. Plenty of seating, separate wildlife pond, water features, rear open vista. Scented plants, hostas, dahlias, alpines and lilies. Conservatory with art by owners. Also: 'Wynn's Patch' - part of next door's garden being maintained on behalf of the owner.

25 3 OAKHAMPTON ROAD

Stourport-on-Severn, DY13 0NR. Sandra & David Traynor, 07970 014295, traynor@clickspeedphotography.co.uk. *Between Astley Cross Inn & Kings Arms. From Stourport take A451 Dunley Rd towards Worcester. In 1 m turn L into Pearl Ln. 4th R into Red House Rd, past the Kings Arms Pub, & next L to Oakhampton Rd. Extra parking at Kings Arms Pub.* **Sun 16, Sun 30 June, Sun 14, Sun 28 July, Sun 25, Mon 26 Aug (10-5.30). Adm £5, chd free. Home-made teas. Visits also by arrangement 15 June to 31 Aug.**
Beginning in March 2016 the plan was to create a garden with a decidedly tropical feel to inc palms from around the world, with tree ferns, bananas and many other strange and unusual plants from warmer climes that would normally be considered difficult to grow here as well as a pond and small waterfall. Not a large garden but you'll be surprised what can be done with a small space. Home-made cakes using eggs and honey from the neighbours whose bees visit the garden flowers.

26 OVERBURY COURT

Overbury, GL20 7NP. Sir Bruce Bossom & Penelope Bossom, 01386 725111, gardens@overburyenterprises.co.uk. *5m NE of Tewkesbury. Overbury signed off A46. Turn off village road beside the church. Park by the gates & walk up the drive. What3words app - cars.blurs.crunches.* **Sun 7 Apr (10-4). Adm £5, chd free. Visits also by arrangement Apr to Sept for groups of 10 to 30.**
A 10 acre historic garden, at the centre of a picturesque Cotswold village, nestled amongst Capability Brown inspired Parkland. The Garden compromises vast formal lawns skirted by a series of rills and ponds which reflect the ancient plane trees that are dotted throughout the garden. The south side of the house has a formal terrace with mixed borders and yew hedging, overlooking a formal lawn with a reflection pool and yew topiary. Running parallel to the pool is a long mixed border which repeats its colours of silver and gold down to the pool house. Some slopes, while all the garden can be viewed, parts are not accessible to wheelchairs.

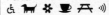

27 PEAR TREE COTTAGE

Witton Hill, Wichenford, WR6 6YX. Pamela & Alistair Thompson, 01886 888295, peartree.pam@gmail.com, www.peartreecottage.me. *13m NW of Worcester & 2m NE of Martley. From Martley, take B4197. Turn R into Horn Ln then 2nd L signed Witton Hill. Keep L & Pear Tree Cottage is on R at top of hill.* **Sun 12 May (11-5). Home-made teas. Sun 25 Aug (12-9.30). Wine. Adm £5, chd free. Sun 25 Aug - Homemdae teas with wine & Pimms after 6pm. Visits also by arrangement May to Aug. Come & celebrate an occasion. Picnics allowed. Artists welcome.**
A Grade II listed black and white cottage (not open) south west facing gardens with far-reaching views across orchards to Abberley Clock Tower. The ¾ acre garden comprises gently sloping lawns with mixed and woodland borders, shade and plenty of strategically placed seating. The garden exudes a quirky and humorous character with the odd surprise and even a Shed of the Year Runner Up. New for 2024 is a lovingly created tile path which twists through a fernery and is made from recycled roof tiles edged with Victorian blue edging tiles. 12 May 2024 - bumper plant sale in aid of local charities. Partial wheelchair access.

GROUP OPENING

28 PERSHORE GARDENS

Pershore, WR10 1BG. Group Co-ordinator Sarah charlton, www.visitpershore.co.uk. *On B4084 between Worcester & Evesham, & 6m from J7 on M5. There is also a train stn to N of town.* **Sat 8, Sun 9 June (1-5). Combined adm £7.50, chd free. Refreshments at selected gardens as indicated on the map/description sheet.**
Most years about 20 gardens open in Pershore. This small town has been opening gardens as part of the NGS for 50 years, almost continuously. Some gardens are surprisingly large, well over an acre, while others are courtyard gardens. All have their individual appeal and present great variety. The Abbey and the River Avon are some of the many points of interest in this market town. Tickets,

which take the form of a map and garden descriptions, are valid for both days. They can be purchased a week before the event at 'Blue' in Broad Street or at the Town Hall. On the weekend they can be bought at Number 8 Community Arts Centre in the High Street and any open garden. Gardens are open all over the town inc Bridge Street, Broad Street, Newlands, Defford Road, Station Road, Cherry Orchard, Priest Lane and Hunter Rise. Refreshments available at Holy Redeemer School and in Number 8 Community Arts Centre.

29 RAVELIN
Gilberts End, Hanley Castle, WR8 0AS. Mrs Christine Peer, 01684 310215, cvpeer55@btinternet.com. *From Worcester/Callow End B4424 or from Upton B4211 to Hanley Castle. Then B4209 to Hanley Swan. From Malvern B4209 to Hanley Swan. At pond/Xrds turn to Welland. ½m turn L opp Hall, to Gilberts End.* **Sat 25, Sun 26, Mon 27 May, Sat 14, Sun 15 Sept, Sat 5, Sun 6 Oct (1-5). Adm £5, chd free. Home-made teas. Visits also by arrangement Apr to Oct.**
Interesting to plant lovers, gardeners and flower arrangers alike, this 60 year old ever evolving ½ acre garden with unusual plants full of colour and texture in all seasons with views overlooking fields and the Malvern Hills. Year-round interest provided by a wide variety of hellebores, hardy geraniums, aconitum, heucheras, Michaelmas daisies, grasses and dahlias and a 55 year old silver pear tree. Thought to be built on medieval clay pottery works in the royal hunting forest. Garden containing herbaceous and perennial planting with gravel garden, woodland area, pond, summerhouse and plenty of seating areas around the garden. A quiz for children.

30 REST HARROW
California Lane, Welland, Malvern, WR13 6NQ. Mr Malcolm & Mrs Anne Garner, 01684 310503, anne.restharrow@gmail.com. *4.6m S of Gt Malvern In un-adopted California Ln off B4208 Worcester Rd. From Gt Malvern A449 towards Ledbury, L onto Hanley Rd/B4209 signed Upton. After about 1m R (Blackmore Park Rd/B4209). After 1m R onto B4208. After ⅓m R (California Ln). Garden 300 yds on L.* **Sat 22, Sun 23 June, Sat 31 Aug, Sun 1 Sept (1.30-5). Adm £6, chd free. Light refreshments. Visits also by arrangement 15 June to 7 Sept for groups of 15 to 30.**
1½ acres developed over 17 years with five acre wildflower meadow, woodland and stunning borrowed views of Malvern Hills. Colourful and diverse flower beds, unusual plants, roses, alstroemeria, stocks and shrubs. Potager kitchen garden, fruit trees and rustic trellis made from our own pollarded trees. Sit, relax, enjoy the views or stroll down through the wildflower meadow to the wetland border area. Wheelchair access in garden but unsuitable down in field.

31 RHYDD GARDENS
Worcester Road, Hanley Castle, Worcester, WR8 0AB. Bill Bell & Sue Brooks, 01684 311001, NGS@Rhyddgardens.co.uk, www.rhyddgardens.co.uk. *2Km N of Hanley Castle. Gates 200m N of layby on B4211.* **Sun 15 Sept (12-5). Adm £5, chd free. Home-made teas. Visits also by arrangement. Please check for available dates.**
Two walled gardens and a 60 ft greenhouse from the early 1800s set in six acres with wonderful views of the entire length of the Malvern ridge. One Walled garden is set out with formal paths and borders bounded by box hedging. We have planted fruit trees in espaliers and cordons as they would have been when the garden was first set out and have a nature area with walks and some woodland. Teas and homemade cakes on the lawn, or in the greenhouse if inclement weather. Self-guided tour leaflets available. Wheelchair access to the main walled garden with grass and paving paths. Parking near gates can be arranged in advance.

32 THE RIVER SCHOOL
Oakfield House, Droitwich Road, Worcester, WR3 7ST. Worcester Christian Education Trust, www.riverschool.co.uk. *2.4m N of Worcester City Centre on A38 towards Droitwich. At J6 M5, take A449 signed for Kidderminster, turn off at 1st turning marked for Blackpole. Turn R to Fernhill Heath & at T-junc with A38 turn L. The school is ½m on R.* **Sat 22 June (10.30-3.30). Adm £5, chd free. Light refreshments in the Lewis Room near garden entrance.**
A former Horticultural College garden being brought back to life. For 35 years after WW2 it was known as Oakfield Teacher Training College for Horticulture. It now features a Forest School, apiary, wildlife pond, and children's vegetable plots within a walled garden. It has many uncommon trees and shrubs with others coming to light as we develop the estate.

33 ◆ RIVERSIDE GARDENS AT WEBBS
Wychbold, Droitwich, WR9 0DG. Webbs of Wychbold, 01527 860000, www.webbsdirect.co.uk. *2m N of Droitwich Spa. 1m N of M5 J5 on A38. Follow tourism signs from M5.* **For opening times and information, please phone or visit garden website.**
2½ acres. Themed gardens inc colour spectrum, tropical and dry garden, rose garden, vegetables, National Collection of Harvington Hellebores, seaside garden, bamboozeleum and self-sufficient garden. The New Wave garden is a natural wildlife area inc seasonal interest with grasses and perennials. We have recently extended the pathways and incorporated our new Woodland Walk, watch out for the Troll! There are willow wigwams and wooden tepees made for children to play in, a bird hide, the Hobbit House and beehives which produce honey for our own food hall. Our New Wave Garden and new Woodland Walk (2022) has had new paths installed and wheelchair accessible.

Our donation to the Army Benevolent Fund supported 608 individuals with front line services and horticultural related grants in 2023

34 ROTHBURY

5 St Peter's Road, North Malvern, WR14 1QS. John Bryson, Philippa Lowe & David, www.facebook.com/RothburyNGS. *7m W of M5 J7 (Worcester). What3words app - departure.repaid.trip. Turn off A449 Worcester to Ledbury Rd at B4503, signed Leigh Sinton. Almost immed take the middle road (Hornyold Rd). St Peter's Rd is ¼m uphill, 2nd R.* **Sun 19, Sun 26 May (12.30-5.30); Mon 27 May (10-5.30); Sun 28 July (12.30-5.30). Adm £5, chd free. Home-made teas. Gluten free options.**

Set on slopes of Malvern Hills, ⅓ acre plant-lovers' garden surrounding Arts and Crafts house (not open), created by owners since 1999. Herbaceous borders, rockery, pond, small orchard. Siberian irises in May, roses in June and magnificent *Eucryphia glutinosa* in July. A series of hand-excavated terraces accessed by sloping paths and steps. Views and seats. Partial wheelchair access. One very low step at entry, one standard step to main lawn and one to WC. Decking slope to top lawn. Dogs on leads.

35 ♦ SPETCHLEY PARK GARDENS

The Estate Office, Spetchley Park, Worcester, WR5 1RS. Mr Henry Berkeley, 01905 345106, enquiries@spetchleygardens.co.uk, www.spetchleyparkestate.co.uk. *2m E of Worcester. On A44, follow brown signs.* **For NGS: Sun 7 Apr, Sun 7 July (10.30-5). Adm £10, chd £5. For other opening times and information, please phone, email or visit garden website.**

Surrounded by glorious countryside lays one of Britain's best kept secrets. Spetchley is a garden for all tastes and ages, containing one of the biggest private collections of plant varieties outside the major botanical gardens and weaving a magical trail for younger visitors. Spetchley is not a formal paradise of neatly manicured lawns or beds but rather a wondrous display of plants, shrubs and trees woven into a garden of many rooms and vistas. Plant sales, gift shop and coffee shop serving homemade treats, and picnics during the open season. Gravel paths, and grassed areas.

36 ♦ STONE HOUSE COTTAGE GARDENS

Church Lane, Stone, DY10 4BG. Louisa Arbuthnott, 07817 921146, louisa@shcn.co.uk, www.shcn.co.uk. *2m SE of Kidderminster. Via A448 towards Bromsgrove, next to church, turn up drive.* **For opening times and information, please phone, email or visit garden website.**

A beautiful and romantic walled garden adorned with unusual brick follies. This acclaimed garden is exuberantly planted and holds one of the largest collections of rare plants in the country. It acts as a shop window for the adjoining nursery. Open Thursday to Sat mid April to late August 10-5. This garden is proud to provide plants for the National Garden Scheme's Show Garden at Chelsea Flower Show 2024. Partial wheelchair access.

37 [NEW] SUMMERCOOMBE

Golden Valley, Castlemorton, Malvern, WR13 6AA. Mr David Mellor & Mrs Emma Prior, 01684 833481, emmavictoriaprior@gmail.com. *Off B4208, turn into road for Golden Valley. Keep going down Golden Valley, bearing slightly L down a small hill. Summercoombe is opp the thatched cottage.* **Sun 26 May, Sun 23 June (11-4). Adm £5, chd free. A selection of hot and cold drinks and home-made cakes (glutten free & vegan options). Visits also by arrangement for groups of up to 10. Also in Jan/Feb for snowdrops.**

One acre cottage garden at the base of the Malverns, a living legacy to those who have lovingly tended it and it continues to evolve reflecting the passion and creativity of previous owners fortunate enough to call it home. Meticulously planned and planted this quiet sanctuary is unlike any other with tranquil seating areas, specimen trees and over 30 varieties of roses entwined with shrubs and perennials. There are some handmade miniature buildings, fruit trees and a walled garden, home to a busy vegetable patch.

38 THE TYNINGS

Church Lane, Stoulton, Worcester, WR7 4RE. John & Leslie Bryant, 01905 840189, johnlesbryant@btinternet.com. *5m S of Worcester; 3m N of Pershore. On the B4084 between M5 J7 & Pershore. The*

Tynings lies beyond the church at the extreme end of Church Ln. Ample parking. **Visits by arrangement June to Sept. Adm £6, chd free. Admission inc light refreshments.**

Acclaimed plantsman's ½ acre garden, generously planted with a large selection of rare trees and shrubs. Features inc specialist collection of lilies, many unusual climbers and rare ferns. The colour continues into late summer with cannas, dahlias, euonymus and tree colour. Surprises around every corner. Lovely views of adjacent Norman Church and surrounding countryside. Plants labelled and plant lists available.

GROUP OPENING

39 THE WALLED GARDEN & NO. 53

Rose Terrace, Worcester, WR5 1BU. Julia & William Scott. *Entry tickets from either garden. Close to the city centre, ½m from the Cathedral. Via Fort Royal Hill, off London Rd. Park on 1st section of Rose Terrace or surrounding streets & walk 20 yds down track to The Walled Garden.* **Sat 13, Wed 17 Apr (1-5). Combined adm £5, chd free. Tea at The Walled Garden only.**

53 FORT ROYAL HILL
Professor Chris Robertson MBE.

THE WALLED GARDEN
William & Julia Scott.

The C19 Walled Kitchen Garden is formal in layout, with relaxed planting. A peaceful historic garden in the city with a focus on chemical free planting especially herbs and their uses. Bees and a bee garden. Seating areas around the garden in shade and in the sun. No 53 a very small part-walled garden divided into three 'rooms', inc shade tolerant planting, a tranquil, 'secret' garden with containers and bee-friendly planting.

40 WALNUT COTTAGE

Lower End, Bricklehampton, Pershore, WR10 3HL. Mr Richard & Mrs Janet Williams. *2½m S of Pershore on B4084, then R into Bricklehampton Ln to T-junc, then L. Cottage is on R.* **Sat 22, Sun 23 June (2-5). Adm £6, chd free. Wine.**

1½ acre garden with views of Bredon Hill, designed into rooms, many created with high formal hedging of beech, hornbeam, copper beech and yew. There is a small 'front garden' with circular gravel path, well-stocked original garden area with pond and arches to the side of the house. Magnolia garden with several species and magnificent tree garden with specimens from around the world. Over 200 roses, in colour themed beds, climbing over a pergola or up trees, greenhouse, raised fish pond and metal stairway leading to roof-based viewing platform surrounded by roses. The garden continues to evolve with plenty of seating and interesting artefacts.

The Alpine Garden Society

41 WARNDON COURT

St Nicholas Lane, Worcester, WR4 0SL. Drs Rachel & David Pryke, 07944 854393, rachelgpryke@btinternet.com.
½ m from J6 of M5, Worcester N. St Nicholas Ln is off Hastings Dr. **Sun 18 Feb (12-3). Adm £5, chd free. Sat 18 May, Sun 9 June (12-4). Adm £6, chd free. Home-made teas in St Nicholas Church Barn. For snowdrop opening we will offer hot chocolate & Welsh cakes. Visits also by arrangement 17 May to 12 Sept for groups of 8+.** Warndon Court is a two acre family garden surrounding a Grade II listed farmhouse (not open) featuring a circular route with formal rose gardens, terraces, two ponds, pergolas, topiary (inc a scruffy dragon), pretty summerhouse, a potager and woodland walk along the dry moat and through the secret garden. It has bee-friendly wildlife areas and is home to great-crested newts and slow worms. Grade I listed St Nicholas Church will also be open to visitors. There will be an exhibition of original paintings, cards for sale and display of vintage cars. The gardens around the house can be accessed over lawns and down a slight slope to the potager. Disabled parking by the house.

♿ 🐎 ✳ 🍵))

GROUP OPENING

42 NEW WEATHEROAK AND WYTHALL GARDENS

Hill Lane, Alvechurch, Birmingham, B48 7EQ. Barry and Sue Knee.
3m E of Alvechurch1.5m N of J3

M42. A435 N 3rd L Hill Ln. A435 S at r'about take 4th exit to Middle Ln. 1st L Chapel Ln then R Hill Ln. To Joe's: From A435 r'about take Station Rd,1st L to School Dr, L into Meadow Rd. **Sat 27, Sun 28 July (12-4). Combined adm £10, chd free. Home-made teas at Pond House.**

JOE'S GARDEN
Joe Manchester.

NEW THE POND HOUSE
Mr Mark & Mrs Tracey Bemrose.

PUMP COTTAGE
Barry and Sue Knee.

Three different inspirational gardens with planting, creative features and artifacts. Pond House, 1½ acres of developing garden around 1915 Arts and Crafts inspired house (not open). Artistic innovation/creative use of reclaimed materials. Split level topiary garden with herbaceous borders leads to large natural wildlife pond and woodland walk. Lawns with mixed shrub borders. Countryside views. Pump cottage, described as a secret wonderland, surprises at every turn. C19 cottage (not open) rural setting. Enchanting, romantic one acre plantaholic's garden. Colourful shrub/herbaceous borders, rockery, fernery, seven water features and natural wildlife pond. Many unusual plants inc shade lovers. Joe's garden, described as one of the most unusual suburban gardens dedicated to woodland/shade loving plants. Expect the unexpected with many tropical/non native plant species! Meander through the garden under the majestic pine, eucalyptus and silver birch. Sit and enjoy the peaceful surroundings.

43 WHARF HOUSE

Newnham Bridge, Tenbury Wells, WR15 8NY. Gareth Compton & Matthew Bartlett, 01584 781966, gco@no5.com, www.wharf-house-gardener.blog/. *Off A456 in hamlet of Broombank, between Mamble & Newnham Bridge. Follow signs. Do not rely on SatNav.* **Sat 6, Sun 7 July (10-5). Adm £7, chd free. Home-made teas. Visits also by arrangement 20 May to 5 July.**

Two acre country garden, set around an C18 house and outbuildings (not open). Mixed herbaceous borders with colour theming: white garden, bright garden, spring garden, canal garden, long double borders, intimate courtyards, a scented border, stream with little bridge to an island, vegetable garden. The garden is on several levels, with some uneven paths and only partial wheelchair access.

🐾 ✿ ☕))

44 WHITCOMBE HOUSE

Overbury, Tewkesbury, GL20 7NZ. Faith & Anthony Hallett, 01386 725206, faith.hallett1@gmail.com. *9m S of Evesham, 5m NE Tewkesbury. Leave A46 at Beckford to Overbury (2m). Or B4080 from Tewkesbury through Bredon/Kemerton (5m). Or small lane signed Overbury at r'about junc A46, A435 & B4077. Approx 5m from J9 M5.* **Sun 26 May (2-5). Adm £5, chd free. Home-made teas. Visits also by arrangement Apr to Sept for groups of up to 50. Refreshments for any time of day, inc teas and evening wine/nibbles.**

One acre of colour from April to Sept in a peaceful Cotswold stone walled shrub and herbaceous garden with mature and young trees inc beech, and Catalpa. Spring fed gravel brook bordered by primula. Pastel colours merge with cool white and blue and later hot colours turn to mellow yellow. Lavender and lots of roses. Secret corners, arches, vines, figs, a vegetable parterre and benches for relaxation. C18 Listed Cotswold stone house (not open). Lovely village of Overbury with St Faith's Church dating from Norman times. Wheelchair access up gravel path through iron gate at south entrance. Also by double wooden gates at back of house by prior arrangement.

♿ 🐾 ✿ 🚗 ☕))

45 ◆ WHITE COTTAGE & NURSERY

Earls Common Road, Stock Green, Inkberrow, B96 6SZ. Mr & Mrs S M Bates, 01386 792414, smandjbates@outlook.com, www.whitecottage.garden. *2m W of*

Inkberrow, 2m E of Upton Snodsbury. A422 Worcester to Alcester, turn at sign for Stock Green by Red Hart Pub, 1½m to T- junction, turn L, 500 yds on the L. **For NGS: Sun 5, Sun 26 May, Sat 8, Sat 22 June (11-4.30). Adm £5, chd free. Home-made teas. Refreshments on a commercial basis. For other opening times and information, please phone, email or visit garden website.**

Two acre garden with large herbaceous and shrub borders, island beds, stream and bog area. Spring meadow with 1000s of snakes head fritillaries. Formal area with lily pond and circular rose garden. Alpine rockery and new fern area. Large collection of interesting trees inc Nyssa sylvatica, Parrotia persica, and Acer 'October Glory' for magnificent autumn colour and many others. New Iris bed. Nursery and Garden open most Thursdays (10.30-5), please check before visiting. For further information please phone, email or visit garden website and Facebook page.

♿ ✿ 🚗 ☕

46 ◆ WHITLENGE GARDENS

Whitlenge Lane, Hartlebury, DY10 4HD. Mr & Mrs K J Southall, 01299 250720, keith.southall@creativelandscapes.co.uk, www.whitlenge.co.uk. *5m S of Kidderminster, on A442. A449 Kidderminster to Worcester L at T-lights, A442 signed Droitwich, over island, ¼m, 1st R into Whitlenge Ln. Follow brown signs.* **For NGS: Sat 20, Sun 21 Apr, Sat 15, Sun 16 June, Sat 14, Sun 15 Sept (10-4.30). Adm £5.95, chd £2.95. Light refreshments in the adjacent tea rooms. Full menu from salads to hot meals, pies etc. Always a special of the day. For other opening times and information, please phone, email or visit garden website.**

Three acre show garden of professional garden designer inc large variety of trees, shrubs etc. Features inc a twisted brick pillar pergola, 2½ metres diameter solid oak moon gate set into reclaimed brickwork, and a four turreted, mini moated castle folly with vertical wall planter set between two water falls, then walk through giant gunnera leaves into the Fairy Garden. There is a full size standing stone circle, a 400 sq metre turf labyrinth and a children's play/pet corner. Extensive plant nursery, Gift shop and large tearoom. Wheelchair access on a mix of hard paths, gravel paths and lawn.

♿ ✿ 🚗 ☕))

47 WINCHESTER HOUSE

Abbey Manor Park, The Squires, Evesham, WR11 4HQ. Dave and Tricia Alesbury. *Nr Twyford, edge of Evesham. Top of Greenhill (A4184) turn into The Squires (no through road), fields on R, 1st turn on L, 2nd house in on L. Please park on The Squires on orchard side only. Disabled parking on drive.* **Sat 27, Sun 28 Apr, Sat 18, Sun 19 May (1-5). Adm £5, chd free. Home-made teas.**

A one acre family garden developed over 20 years, divided into two areas by an original Victorian wall, which formed part of Abbey Manor grounds. Formal planting surrounds the house with a landscaped wood beyond the wall. A wide variety of shrubs, perennials, native and ornamental trees are on display designed around two ponds, a stream and a striking tiered water feature. Patio area and path around house is paved. Brick ramp to woodland area, paved path to greenhouse and top patio, rest of woodland area is grass path.

♿ ✿ ☕))

48 19 WINNINGTON GARDENS

Hanley Swan, Hanley Swan, WR8 0DJ. Brian & Irene Skeys, 01684 311297, brimfields@icloud.com, www.brimfields.com. *5m E of Malvern, 3m NW of Upton upon Severn, 9m S of Worcester & M5. Yellow arrows from the village Xrds.* **Mon 13 May, Mon 19 Aug (11-3). Adm £3, chd free. Savouries and Cream Teas. Opening with Hanley Swan NGS Gardens on Sat 8, Sun 9 June. Visits also by arrangement 14 May to 20 Sept for groups of up to 20.**

19 Winnington Gardens is a small wildlife-friendly garden, planted in a series of garden rooms, for year-round interest from daffodils to dahlias. There is a redesigned green and white garden plus roses and clematis cover an archway to a mixed border enclosed with shrubs, clematis and climbing roses. New iris beds for this year along with more drought tolerant planting. This is a small garden managed to be environment and wildlife-friendly. A no-dig garden, the owner has been experimenting with peat free compost for three years and now testing reduced fertiliser inputs to help control plant disease. There are several seats in the garden where you can sit enjoy the surroundings and observe the birds on the feeders.

🐾 ✿ ☕))

Bedfordshire
Cambridgeshire
Essex
Hertfordshire
Norfolk
Suffolk

EAST OF ENGLAND

Above: Beth Chatto's Plants & Gardens, Essex

EAST OF ENGLAND

The East region stretches from landlocked Bedfordshire near the centre of the country, through Hertfordshire and Cambridgeshire to the adjoining counties of Essex, Suffolk and Norfolk which create a great sweep of the east coast, from the Thames to the Wash.

Predominantly rural other than Hertfordshire's metropolitan edge along the north of greater London, it does not have huge centres of population. But it does have the historic cities of Ely and Norwich which are elevated by their great medieval cathedrals and the university city of Cambridge with its array of world-famous architecture. The topography is gentle and much of the region is as Noel Coward famously said of Norfolk, 'very flat.' But there are large swathes of spectacularly unspoilt countryside that today remain thinly populated, and where a visit to a garden often becomes a voyage of discovery. Gardeners have to work round the low annual rainfall which sometimes combines with extreme summer heat to create challenging conditions, but as with all gardening, there are always compensations such as spring coming early and then summer warmth to boost flowering displays.

Above, from top: Holm House, Suffolk; Old Manor Farmhouse, Norfolk

Below: 28 Fishpool Street, Hertfordshire

BEDFORDSHIRE

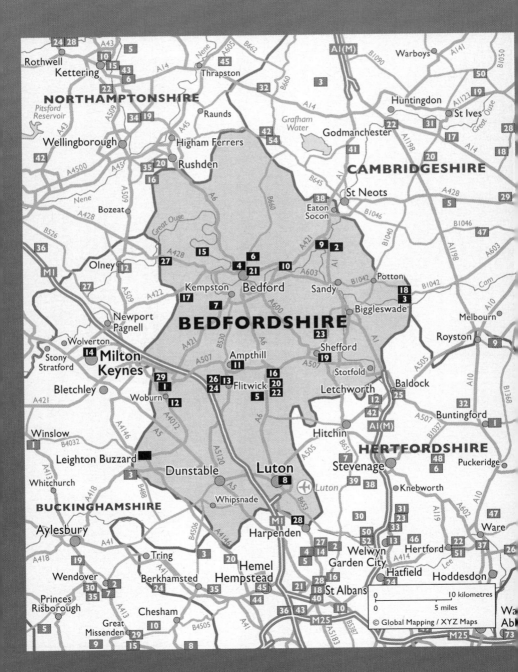

NORTHAMPTONSHIRE

Pitsford
Reservoir

CAMBRIDGESHIRE

BEDFORDSHIRE

HERTFORDSHIRE

BUCKINGHAMSHIRE

Rothwell
Kettering
Thrapston
Wellingborough
Raunds
Higham Ferrers
Rushden
Bozeat
Olney
Kempston
Bedford
Sandy
Potton
Biggleswade
Newport
Pagnell
Wolverton
Stony
Stratford
Milton
Keynes
Bletchley
Woburn
Flitwick
Ampthill
Shefford
Stotfold
Letchworth
Baldock
Melbourn
Royston
Buntingford
Winslow
Leighton Buzzard
Dunstable
Luton
Hitchin
Stevenage
Knebworth
Puckeridge
Whitchurch
Aylesbury
Tring
Whipsnade
Harpenden
Ware
Wendover
Berkhamsted
Hemel
Hempstead
Welwyn
Garden City
Hertford
Hoddesdon
Princes
Risborough
Chesham
St Albans
Hatfield
Great
Missenden

Warboys
Huntingdon
St Ives
Godmanchester
St Neots
Eaton
Socon
Grafham
Water

Luton

0   10 kilometres
0   5 miles
© Global Mapping / XYZ Maps

VOLUNTEERS

Acting County Organiser
Indi Jackson
07973 857633
indi.jackson@ngs.org.uk

County Treasurer
Colin Davies
07811 022211
colin.davies@ngs.org.uk

Booklet Co-ordinators
Indi Jackson
(as above)

Alex Ballance
alexballance@yahoo.co.uk

Press Officer
Vacant position

Talks
Christopher Bamforth Damp
chrisdamp@mac.com

Photographer
Venetia Barrington
venetiajanesgarden@gmail.com

Assistant County Organisers
Alex Ballance
(as above)

Natalie Jeffs
natalie.jeffs@ngs.org.uk

Sunitha Verghis
suniverghis@hotmail.com

Facebook
Indi Jackson
(as above)

 @bedfordshire.ngs

 @NGSBeds

 @ngsbedfordshire

OPENING DATES

All entries subject to change. For latest information check
www.ngs.org.uk
Map locator numbers are shown to the right of each garden name.

February

Snowdrop Openings

Sunday 11th
◆ The Manor House, Stevington 15

Sunday 18th
◆ King's Arms Garden 11

April

Saturday 20th
22 Elmsdale Road 7

Sunday 21st
22 Elmsdale Road 7

Saturday 27th
Steppingley Village Gardens 24

Sunday 28th
Steppingley Village Gardens 24

May

Sunday 12th
204 Hart Lane 8

Saturday 18th
Church Farm 5

Sunday 19th
Church Farm 5
The Old Rectory, Wrestlingworth 18

Sunday 26th
Steppingley Village Gardens 24

Monday 27th
Steppingley Village Gardens 24

June

Sunday 2nd
Ash Trees 1
Southill Park 23
80 West Hill 29

Sunday 9th
NEW Hill Farm House 9

Sunday 16th
Turvey Village Gardens 27

Sunday 30th
NEW 12 Queen Elizabeth Close 19

July

Sunday 7th
The Round Cottage 20

Sunday 14th
Lindy Lea 13

Friday 19th
Bedford Heights 4

Sunday 21st
204 Hart Lane 8

Saturday 27th
NEW Beck House 3

Sunday 28th
NEW Beck House 3

August

Friday 2nd
◆ The Walled Garden 28

Sunday 4th
Silsoe Village Gardens 22

Saturday 17th
1a St Augustine's Road 21

Monday 26th
15 Douglas Road 6

September

Sunday 1st
NEW Nine Ashes 17

Sunday 8th
Howbury Hall Garden 10

Saturday 14th
40 Leighton Street 12

October

Sunday 20th
Newbury Farm Arboretum 16

Saturday 26th
Townsend Farmhouse 26

Sunday 27th
◆ King's Arms Garden 11

By Arrangement

Arrange a personalised garden visit with your club, or group of friends, on a date to suit you. See individual garden entries for full details.

12 Queen Elizabeth Close

THE GARDENS

1 ASH TREES
Green Lane, Aspley Guise, Milton Keynes, MK17 8EN. John & Teresa. *About 10m from Milton Keynes and 2m from J13 M1. Green Ln is off Wood Ln. Yellow signs indicate where to turn. Some on-road parking in Wood Ln. Disabled or mobility parking only at house.* **Sun 2 June (12-5). Combined adm with 80 West Hill £7, chd free. Home-made teas at 80 West Hill. Adm to Ash Trees only, £5.00.**
Medium sized, secluded village garden, walled in with borrowed treescape and hidden in a private lane. Herbaceous borders, shrubs, trees, bulbs, and fruit inc apricot and peach. There is a unique garden arch sculpture created for a Hampton Court show garden. Seats in quiet spots amongst the plants. Children and wheelchairs welcome as are dogs on leads. Garden is flat with reasonable access for wheels and walkers.

2 1C BAKERS LANE
Tempsford, Sandy, SG19 2BJ. Juliet & David Pennington, 01767 640482, juliet.pennington01@gmail.com. *1m N of Sandy on A1 & Station Rd is on the E side. Bakers Ln is 300 yds down Station Rd on L.* **Visits by arrangement. Adm £6, chd free.**
This is a garden for all seasons with interesting and unusual plants. It comes to life with a winter border planted with colourful cornus and evergreen shrubs, underplanted here with snowdrops and hellebores. Gravel areas are carpeted with miniature cyclamen. It develops through the seasons culminating in early autumn with a spectacular show of sun-loving herbaceous plants. Plant sale: exotic and unusual plants. No refreshments but visitors are welcome to bring a picnic to enjoy in the garden. Regret, no dogs. Much of the garden can be accessed by wheelchair.

3 NEW BECK HOUSE
Water End, Wrestlingworth, Sandy, SG19 2HA. Donal & Victoria McKenna. *Halfway between Cambridge & Bedford. From High St, Wrestlingworth turn into Water End (opp 8 and 10 High St). Garden at far end of Water End.* **Sat 27, Sun 28 July (2-5.30). Adm £8, chd free. Home-made teas.**
A 2 ½ acre garden created over 39 years with various formal and informal areas divided by hedges and shrub borders. Features inc topiary yew avenue, circular dahlia garden with small pond, parterre with English roses, herbaceous borders, white, courtyard, herb and vegetable gardens, rose and clematis pergola walk. Woodland garden. Wheelchair accessible but there are some slopes to access upper part of garden.

4 BEDFORD HEIGHTS
Brickhill Drive, Bedford, MK41 7PH. Graham A Pavey, www.grahamapavey.co.uk. *N Bedford. Park in main car park, not at Travelodge.* **Fri 19 July (11-3). Adm £5, chd free. Light refreshments in the Bistro Cafe.**
Originally built by Texas Instruments, a Texan theme runs throughout the building and gardens. The entrance simulates an arroyo or dry riverbed, and is filled with succulents and cacti, plus a mixture of grasses and herbaceous plants, many of which are Texan natives. There are also three courtyard gardens, where less hardy plants thrive in the almost frost-free environment. No wheelchair access to two of the courtyards but can be viewed from a platform.

5 CHURCH FARM
Church Road, Pulloxhill, Bedford, MK45 5HD. Sue & Keith Miles, 07941 593152. *Parking by kind permission of The Cross Keys Pub, Pulloxhill High St, MK45 5HB (approx 500yds from garden). Yellow signs from the Cross Keys to Church Rd & past parish church.* **Sat 18, Sun 19 May (2-5). Adm £7, chd free. Visits also by arrangement June to Aug for groups of 10 to 20. Adm £11.00 inc tour with tea or coffee and home-made cakes.**
Mixed colourful planting to the rear of the house leading to a long sunny border of drought tolerant plants and large topiary subjects. Beyond the farmyard is a wildlife pond, small kitchen garden and wildflower orchard with a rose walk. Cut flower area and countryside views. Livestock may be present in adjoining fields. Regret, no dogs.

6 15 DOUGLAS ROAD
Bedford, MK41 7YF. Peter & Penny Berrington. *B660 Kimbolton Rd, turn into Avon Dr, R into Tyne Cres, & Douglas Rd on R.* **Mon 26 Aug (2-5). Adm £5, chd free. Home-made teas.**
This medium sized town garden has a series of outdoor rooms, separated by hedges, fences and arches. There is seating for visitors to relax and enjoy the peace and seclusion. A circular cottage garden with a central decorative fire pit, separated by plum and apple trees from vegetables and herbs grown in raised beds. The pond is home to newts, snails and 'Brickhill' frogs. Wheelchair access to most parts of the garden.

7 22 ELMSDALE ROAD
Wootton, Bedford, MK43 9JN. Roy & Dianne Richards, 07305 252444, roy.richards60@ntlworld.com. *Follow signs to Wootton, turn R at The Cock Pub, follow to Elmsdale Rd.* **Sat 20, Sun 21 Apr (1.30-5). Adm £5, chd free. Home-made teas. Visits also by arrangement Apr to Sept.**
Topiary garden greets visitors before they enter a genuine Japanese Feng Shui garden inc bonsai. Large collection of Japanese plants, Koi pond, lily pond and a Japanese Tea House. The garden was created from scratch by the owners about 20 years ago and has many interesting features inc Japanese lanterns and a Kneeling Archer terracotta soldier from China. Free flying parrot.

8 204 HART LANE
Luton, LU2 0JH. Alison Bilcock. *Street parking only.* **Sun 12 May, Sun 21 July (2-5). Adm £5, chd free. Home-made teas.**
A small gem, with year-round seasonal plants, mature shrubs, a relaxing water feature and multiple seating areas to enjoy the garden with a cream tea. There are hidden animals for children to find, something for all the family. Home-made jams and preserves for sale.

In 2023, our donations to Carers Trust meant that 26,118 unpaid carers were supported across the UK

9 NEW HILL FARM HOUSE
51 High Street, Roxton, MK44 3ED. Anna and Julian Chillingworth. *S of St Neots. At the A1, Black Cat r'about follow road signs to Roxton. Park on Roxton High St.* **Sun 9 June (2-5). Adm £6, chd free. Home-made teas.**

Our one acre garden contains a variety of spaces which offer a haven for wildlife while also providing a tranquil escape for humans. We welcome you to wander through the clematis pergola into the woodland white garden, to pause and listen to the splash of water falling through rocks in the Japanese courtyard and to spot newts hiding under waterlilies in the pond. Nearly all the garden has wheelchair access.

&. ☕))

10 HOWBURY HALL GARDEN
Howbury Hall Estate, Renhold, Bedford, MK41 0JB. Julian Polhill & Lucy Copeman, www.howburyfarmflowers.co.uk. *Leave A421 at A428/Gt Barford exit towards Bedford. Entrance to house & gardens ½m on R. Parking in field.* **Sun 8 Sept (2-5). Adm £6, chd free. Home-made teas.**

A late Victorian garden with mature trees, sweeping lawns and herbaceous borders. The large walled garden is a working garden, where one half is dedicated to growing a large variety of vegetables whilst the other is run as a cut flower business. Large collection dahlias in September. There are also several varieties of Bedfordshire heritage apple trees and an avenue of pears. Gravel paths and lawns may be difficult for smaller wheelchairs.

&. ☕))

11 ◆ KING'S ARMS GARDEN
Brinsmade Road, Ampthill, Bedford, MK45 2PP. Ampthill Town Council, www.ampthill-tc.gov.uk/ amenities/kings-arm-garden. *Free parking in Waitrose car park limited time. Entrance opp Market Square Cafe, down King's Arms Path, 2nd gate on the R.* **For NGS: Sun 18 Feb, Sun 27 Oct (2-4). Adm £5, chd free. Light refreshments. For other opening times and information, please visit garden website.**

Small woodland garden of about 1½ acres created by plantsman, the late William Nourish. Trees, shrubs, bulbs and many interesting collections throughout the year. Since 1987, the garden has been maintained by 'The Friends of the Garden' on behalf of Ampthill Town Council. Charming woodland garden with mass plantings of snowdrops and early spring bulbs. Beautiful autumn colours in October. Wheelchair friendly path running around most of the garden.

&. 🐾 ✿ ☕))

12 40 LEIGHTON STREET
Woburn, MK17 9PH. Ron & Rita Chidley. *500yds from centre of village L side of road. Very limited on road parking outside house.* **Sat 14 Sept (2-5). Adm £5, chd free. Home-made teas.**

Large cottage style garden in three parts. There are several 'rooms' with interesting features to explore and many quiet seating areas. There are perennials, climbers, vegetables, shrubs, trees and two ponds with fish. In late summer and autumn there is an abundance of colour from dahlias, fuchsias, grasses and late flowering roses. Many pots of unusual and tender plants.

✿ ☕))

13 LINDY LEA
Ampthill Road, Steppingley, Bedford, MK45 5AW. Roy & Linda Collins. *Next to Steppingley Hospital. Park in hospital car park.* **Sun 14 July (2-5). Adm £6, chd free. Home-made teas.**

Set within an acre, this garden is a haven for wildlife with two water features, cottage garden style perennial plantings, a variety of shrubs and mature trees. There is also a vegetable garden and a sunny terrace furnished with pots and climbers. Wheelchair access: some paths may be difficult to negotiate.

&. ✿ ☕))

14 1 LINTON CLOSE
Heelands, Milton Keynes, MK13 7NR. Pat & John Partridge, 01908 220571, pip1941@icloud.com. *From H4 Dansteed Way, take Stainton Dr, Linton Close is 3rd R.* **Visits by arrangement 2 Apr to 29 Sept for groups of up to 6. The adm inc light refreshments. Adm £10, chd free.**

Small town garden developed over 30 years from heavy clay and builder's rubble. Gravel garden with sedum and dwarf conifer collection at the front. The back garden is mainly planted with hardy evergreen shrubs and divided into four main areas for structure - pots and perennials provide year-round interest and colour. We are attempting to garden more sustainably. Sorry, garden is not suitable for wheelchairs.

☕))

15 ◆ THE MANOR HOUSE, STEVINGTON
Church Road, Stevington, Bedford, MK43 7QB. Kathy Brown, 01234 822064, info@kathybrownsgarden.com, www.kathybrownsgarden.com. *5 m NW of Bedford. Off A428 through Bromham. If using SatNav please enter entire address, not just postcode.* **For NGS: Sun 11 Feb (10.30-3.30). Adm £8.50, chd free. Pre-booking essential, please visit www.ngs.org.uk for information & booking. Home-made teas. For other opening times and information, please phone, email or visit garden website.**

The Manor House Garden features avenues of white stemmed Himalayan birches, eucalyptus and metasequoia. Topiary forms a major interest with a snaking dragon, tiered hollies, a jury scene etc. Paths are lined with colourful cornus, rubus, viburnum, honeysuckle and sarcococca. Grass borders swish and sway, aconites and snowdrops play their part too. Garden featured on Gardeners' World, 'Winter Specials'. 85% of the garden accessible for wheelchair users. Disabled WC available.

&. ☕))

16 NEWBURY FARM ARBORETUM
Ampthill Road, Silsoe, Bedford, MK45 4HB. Bruce Liddle. *On the edge of Silsoe Village, along Ampthill Rd.* **Sun 20 Oct (12-4). Adm £5, chd free. Opening with Silsoe Village Gardens on Sun 4 Aug.**

This private four acre arboretum was started over 30 years ago by Maurice and Carol Clarke. Enjoy a stroll through the collection of over 90 trees, planted against a backdrop of rolling Bedfordshire farmland, as well as a recently constructed gravel garden. Bruce Liddle now manages the collection alongside the adjacent plant nursery.

&. ✿))

Beck House

17 NEW ▶ NINE ASHES
West End, Stagsden, Bedford, MK43 8SY. Penny Mowle. *From A422, follow signs to West End Stagsden and pick up yellow arrow signs.* Sun 1 Sept (2-5). Adm £5, chd free. Home-made teas.

1½ acres of garden landscaped into six areas. A small woodland area, a parterre filled with verbena and four conical conifers. Espalier striped pear trees feature on the back walled area with a wisteria to the front of the wall and a mixed cottage garden border. A separate vegetable garden inc raised beds of herbs and soft fruit. Views of wheat and barley fields. Short gravel entrance, wheelchair access to most of the garden.

18 THE OLD RECTORY, WRESTLINGWORTH
Church Lane, Wrestlingworth, Sandy, SG19 2EU. Josephine Hoy, 01767 631204, hoyjosephine@hotmail.co.uk. *Wrestlingworth. Garden is at top of Church Ln, which is well signed, behind the church.* Sun 19 May (2-5). Adm £8, chd free. Visits also by arrangement Apr to June.

A four acre garden full of colour and interest. The owner has a free style of gardening sensitive to wildlife. Beds overflowing with tulips, alliums, bearded iris, peonies, poppies, geraniums and much more. Beautiful mature trees and many more planted in the last 30 years inc a large selection of betulas. Gravel gardens, box hedging and clipped balls, woodland garden and wildflower meadows. Wheelchair access may be restricted to grass paths.

19 NEW ▶ 12 QUEEN ELIZABETH CLOSE
Shefford, SG17 5LE. Kasey Brock. *Turn off Ivel Rd into Queen Elizabeth Rd and follow round to L.* Sun 30 June (2-6). Adm £5, chd free.

A small town garden with a jungle like feel. This garden is all about foliage, with the emphasis on leaf shapes and textures, some more unusual and quirky than others. The whole garden has been designed to make you feel like you've been transported to somewhere far more exotic.

»))

20 THE ROUND COTTAGE
36 Ampthill Road, Silsoe, Bedford, MK45 4DX. Peter & Jane Gregory. *Within Silsoe village on Ampthill Rd. From A6 enter Silsoe village, from Bedford take the 1st R after village sign. From Luton take 2nd L after church. Garden is 500m on R.* Sun 7 July (1-5). Adm £6, chd free. Home-made teas. Opening with Silsoe Village Gardens on Sun 4 Aug.

This is a pretty cottage garden surrounding an 1820's thatched cottage. Traditional flower beds where perennials mix with exotics from around the world and a sprinkling of annuals. A large pond with waterfall, a Victorian style greenhouse, thatched play house, art studio and summerhouse. Vegetable and fruit area and small shady walkway. The cottage has a deep lit well. Two classic cars on display. Activities for children. Discovery activity worksheets available. The vegetable area and shady walk are inaccessible by wheelchair.

21 1A ST AUGUSTINE'S ROAD
Bedford, MK40 2NB. Chris Bamforth Damp, 01234 353730, chrisdamp@mac.com. *St Augustine's Rd is on L off Kimbolton Rd as you leave the centre of Bedford.* **Sat 17 Aug (12-4.30). Adm £6, chd free. Home-made teas. Visits also by arrangement July to Sept.**
A colourful town garden with herbaceous borders, climbers, a greenhouse and a pond. Planted in cottage garden style with traditional flowers, the borders overflow with late summer annuals and perennials inc salvias and rudbeckia. The pretty terrace next to the house is lined with ferns and hostas. The owners also make home-made chutneys and preserves which can be purchased on the day. The garden is wheelchair accessible.

👩‍🦽 ✿ ☕))

GROUP OPENING

22 SILSOE VILLAGE GARDENS
Alder Wynd, Silsoe, Bedford, MK45 4GQ. *Access to the village is via the A6 or the A507. Once in the village follow the yellow signs.* **Sun 4 Aug (10-5). Combined adm £8, chd free. Home-made teas at Round Cottage.**

10 ALDER WYND
David & Frances Hampson, 01525 861356, mail@davidhampson.com.
Visits also by arrangement June to Sept for groups of up to 20.

NEWBURY FARM ARBORETUM
Bruce Liddle.
(See separate entry)

THE ROUND COTTAGE
Peter & Jane Gregory.
(See separate entry)

The historic village of Silsoe dates back to the Viking era, but is best known today as the home of Wrest Park. 10 Alder Wynd is a small modern garden, constructed nine years ago and has been the runner up in two national gardening awards. A wide range of seasonal perennials, trees and shrubs give this garden year-round appeal. Notable for its collection of giant hostas, ferns, exotic perennials and cannas. Round Cottage, which is thatched, dates to the 1820s and is surrounded by a

pretty cottage garden. Traditional style flower beds have perennials mixed with exotics from around the world plus a sprinkle of annuals. Large Koi pond with waterfall, Victorian style greenhouse. There is a deep lit well. The Arboretum at Newbury Farm is a private four acre arboretum, started over 30 years ago by Maurice and Carol Clarke. Enjoy a stroll through the collection of over 90 trees, planted against a backdrop of rolling Bedfordshire farmland. There is also a recently constructed gravel garden. The gardens are short drive away from each other.

👩‍🦽 ✿ ☕))

23 SOUTHILL PARK
Southill, nr Biggleswade, SG18 9LL. Mr & Mrs Charles Whitbread. *On the outskirts of the village of Southill, 5m from the A1.* **Sun 2 June (2-5). Adm £6, chd free. Cream teas.**
Southill Park first opened its gates to NGS visitors in 1927 as one of the inaugural NGS gardens. This is a large garden with mature trees and flowering shrubs, herbaceous borders, a formal rose garden, sunken garden, ponds and kitchen garden. It is on the south side of the 1795 Palladian house. The parkland was designed by Lancelot 'Capability' Brown. A large conservatory houses the tropical collection.

👩‍🦽 🐕 ✿ ☕))

GROUP OPENING

24 STEPPINGLEY VILLAGE GARDENS
Steppingley, Bedford, MK45 5AT. *Follow signs to Steppingley, pick up yellow signs from village centre.* **Sat 27, Sun 28 Apr (2-5). Combined adm £8, chd free. Sun 26, Mon 27 May (12-5). Combined adm £10, chd free. Home-made teas at Townsend Farmhouse. Also Hot Dogs at 21 Church End for May openings.**

NEW 21 CHURCH END
Christine and Steve Ovenden.
Open on Sun 26, Mon 27 May

NEW THE CROFT
Stephen Cook.
Open on Sun 26, Mon 27 May

MIDDLE BARN
John & Sally Eilbeck.
Open on all dates

NEW 1 PARK FARM COTTAGE
Tim & Tally Clift.
Open on Sun 26, Mon 27 May

NEW 4 PEAKES END
Pauline & Bruce Henninger.
Open on Sun 26, Mon 27 May

37 RECTORY ROAD
Bill & Julie Neilson.
Open on Sun 26, Mon 27 May

TOP BARN
Tim & Nicky Kemp.
Open on all dates

TOWNSEND FARMHOUSE
Hugh & Indi Jackson.
Open on all dates
(See separate entry)

Steppingley is a picturesque Bedfordshire village on the Greensand Ridge, close to Ampthill, Flitwick and Woburn. Although a few older buildings survive, most of Steppingley was built by the 7th Duke of Bedford between 1840 and 1872. Eight gardens in the village offer an interesting mix of planting styles and design to inc pretty courtyards, cottage garden style perennial borders, ponds, a Victorian well, glasshouses, an orchard, vegetable gardens, a herb garden, wildlife havens and country views. Livestock inc chickens, ducks and fish.

✿ ☕))

26 TOWNSEND FARMHOUSE

Rectory Road, Steppingley, Bedford, MK45 5AT. **Hugh & Indi Jackson.** *Follow directions to Steppingley village and pick up yellow signs from village centre.* **Evening opening Sat 26 Oct (5.30-8.30). Adm £10, chd free. Pre-booking essential, please visit www.ngs.org.uk for information & booking. Home-made savouries and cakes. Opening with Steppingley Village Gardens on Sat 27, Sun 28 Apr, Sun 26, Mon 27 May.**

Country garden with tree lined driveway and several perennial borders. Pretty cobbled courtyard with a glasshouse housing large selection of house plants. A Victorian well 30 metres deep, viewed through a glass top. Large wildlife pond and a newly created grotto. A spectacular evening of lanterns, diya lamps and flower rangoli in late October.

GROUP OPENING

27 TURVEY VILLAGE GARDENS

High Street, Turvey, Bedford, MK43 8EP. *Follow arrow signs from village centre. Parking in field behind Chantry House.* **Sun 16 June (2-5). Combined adm £8, chd free. Home-made teas in medieval church of All Saints.**

CHANTRY HOUSE
Sheila & Anthony Ormerod.

GABLE END
Chris & Wendy Knell.

7 THE GREEN
Paul & Rosemary Gentry.

PEPPERS
Liz & Mark Upex.

The historic village of Turvey lies beside the River Great Ouse and is recorded in Domesday Book of 1086 as a parish in the Hundred of Willey. Four gardens in the village offer a varied mix of design and interest. Chantry House is a 1½ acre garden, approached by a drive bounded by mature yew and box cloud hedges where the medieval church of All Saints overlooks the garden at this point. A south facing lawn is flanked by high rose covered walls and interspersed by herbaceous beds. 7 The Green is an informal village garden. A wide terrace with comfortable seating and a myriad of planted pots overlooks a central lawn and flowerbeds which slope down to flowering cherries and a view of pasture and mature trees. Gable End is a medium-sized garden consisting of four distinct areas. A range of planting inc fruit and vegetables are enjoyed here. Peppers is a small, informal village garden with mixed planting aimed at attracting wildlife and achieving year-round interest. Wheelchair access via gravel paths and few shallow distanced steps.

28 ◆ THE WALLED GARDEN

Luton, LU1 4LF. **Luton Hoo Estate,** 01582 721443, office@lutonhooestate.co.uk, www.lutonhooestate.co.uk. *From A1081 turn into West Hyde Rd. After 100 metres turn L through black gates, follow signs to Walled Garden.* **For NGS: Fri 2 Aug (11-3). Adm £7, chd free. Light refreshments at Woodyard Coffee Shop.** For other opening times and information, please phone, email or visit garden website.

The five acre Luton Hoo Estate Walled Garden was designed by Capability Brown and established by noted botanist and former Prime Minister, Lord Bute, in the late 1760s. The Walled Garden is now the focus of an incredible volunteer project and continues to be researched, restored, repaired and re-imagined for the enjoyment of all. Unique service buildings inc a vinery, fernery and propagation houses. Exhibition of Victorian tools. Uneven surfaces reflect the age and history of the site.

29 80 WEST HILL

Aspley Guise, Milton Keynes, MK17 8DX. **James & Helen Scott,** www.thegardenco.co.uk/residential/modern-sanctuary/. *6m SE of Milton Keynes; close to Jn13 of the M1. Leave junc 13 of M1. 2m W towards Woburn Sands. On West Hill, turn R onto Ln marked 80-92. No parking ex for disabled visitors; please park at Cricket Club (next R on West Hill).* **Sun 2 June (12-5). Combined adm with Ash Trees £7, chd free. Home-made teas. Adm to 80 West Hill only £5.00.**

Contemporary front and rear gardens to complement a modern house within a walled garden plot. The rear garden is based on strong geometry with naturalistic planting inc several bespoke features. The front garden feels more organic, with various uses of natural stone and planting to suit some dry sunny spots as well as woodland shade. Winner of three National Awards inc a Design Excellence Award. Features inc fire pit area, water feature, glasshouse, secluded seating area. There is careful use of Yorkshire stone illustrating the journey from boulder to slab.

Hill Farm House

CAMBRIDGESHIRE

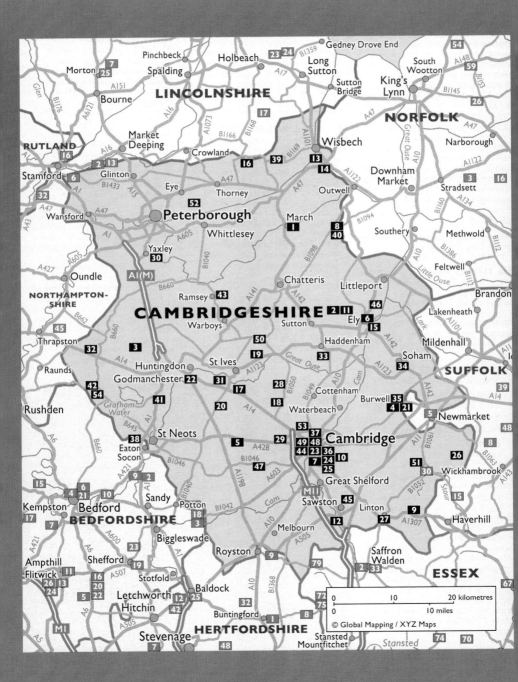

VOLUNTEERS

County Organiser
Jenny Marks 07956 049257
jenny.marks@ngs.org.uk

Deputy County Organiser
Pam Bullivant 01353 667355
pam.bullivant@ngs.org.uk

County Treasurer
Jackie Hutchinson 01954 710950
jackie.hutchinson@ngs.org.uk

Booklet Coordinator
Jenny Marks (As above)

Publicity
Penny Miles 07771 516448
penny.miles@ngs.org.uk

Social Media
Hetty Dean
hetty.dean@ngs.org.uk

Assistant County Organisers
Claire James 07815 719284
claire.james@ngs.org.uk

Jacqui Latten-Quinn 07941 279571
jacqui.quinn@ngs.org.uk

Penny Miles (As above)

Jane Pearson 07890 080303
jane.pearson@ngs.org.uk

Barbara Stalker 07800 575100
barbara.stalker@ngs.org.uk

Carolyn Thompson 01353 778640
carolyn.thompson@ngs.org.uk

Annette White 01638 730876
annette.white@ngs.org.uk

f National Garden Scheme Cambs

X @GardenCambs

cambsngs

OPENING DATES

All entries subject to change. For latest information check **www.ngs.org.uk**
Extended openings are shown at the beginning of the month. Map locator numbers are shown to the right of each garden name.

January

Every day from Wednesday 3rd
Robinson College   44

February

Snowdrop Openings

Every day
Robinson College   44
Sunday 18th
Clover Cottage   9
Sunday 25th
Clover Cottage   9

March

Every day
Robinson College   44
Sunday 3rd
Clover Cottage   9
Sunday 24th
Kirtling Tower   26
Sunday 31st
Netherhall Manor   34

April

Every day to Friday 12th
Robinson College   44
Saturday 13th
Heath Fruit Farm   19
Tuesday 16th
Trinity Hall - Wychfield Site   49
Sunday 21st
Trinity College Fellows' Garden 48

May

Every Friday, Saturday and Sunday
23A Perry Road   41
Sunday 5th
Chaucer Road Gardens   7
Netherhall Manor   34
Newnham Farmhouse   35
Monday 6th
Chaucer Road Gardens   7
Saturday 18th
Fenstanton   17
Sunday 19th
Fenstanton   17
Saturday 25th
Coveney & Wardy Hill Gardens   11
Sunday 26th
Cambourne Gardens   5
Coveney & Wardy Hill Gardens   11
Island Hall   22
Linton Gardens   27
Molesworth House   32
Willow Holt   52
Monday 27th
Willow Holt   52

June

Every Friday, Saturday and Sunday
23A Perry Road   41
Sunday 2nd
38 Chapel Street   6
Clover Cottage   9
Duxford Gardens   12
Ely Open Gardens   15
Saturday 8th
Cottage Garden   10
Sunday 9th
NEW Buckworth Gardens   3
Burwell Village Gardens   4
Clover Cottage   9
Isaacson's   21
Madingley Hall   29
◆ The Manor, Hemingford Grey   31
5 Nelsons Lane   33
The Old Rectory   39
Saturday 15th
NEW 1 Station Cottage   46
Sunday 16th
NEW 1 Station Cottage   46

Saturday 22nd
Little Oak 28

Sunday 23rd
NEW Christchurch Village Gardens 8
Little Oak 28
Toft Gardens 47
Westley Waterless Gardens 51

Saturday 29th
NEW Bramble Lodge 2
NEW Nuffield Road Allotments 37
Twin Tarns 50
Wrights Farm 54

Sunday 30th
NEW Bramble Lodge 2
Elm House 14
Green End Farm 18
King's College Fellows'
Garden and Provost's Garden 23
Kirtling Tower 26
Twin Tarns 50
Wrights Farm 54

July

**Every Friday, Saturday
and Sunday**
23A Perry Road 41

Every day from Monday 8th
Robinson College 44

Saturday 6th
38 Kingston Street 24
NEW 73 Kingston Street 25
38 Norfolk Terrace Garden 36

Sunday 7th
NEW Hilton West 20
38 Norfolk Terrace Garden 36
Sawston Gardens 45

Sunday 14th
Old Farm Cottage 38

Saturday 20th
Preachers Passing 42

Sunday 21st
Preachers Passing 42

August

**Every Friday, Saturday
and Sunday**
23A Perry Road 41

**Every day until Friday 9th,
and then from
Wednesday 28th**
Robinson College 44

Sunday 4th
Netherhall Manor 34
Newnham Farmhouse 35

Sunday 11th
Netherhall Manor 34

Wednesday 14th
◆ Elgood's Brewery Gardens 13

Saturday 17th
NEW Bramble Lodge 2

Sunday 18th
NEW Bramble Lodge 2

Saturday 31st
Wrights Farm 54

September

**Every Friday, Saturday and
Sunday to Sunday 8th**
23A Perry Road 41

Every day
Robinson College 44

Sunday 1st
Wrights Farm 54

Saturday 14th
Ramsey Walled Garden 43

Sunday 22nd
NEW The Old School House 40

October

Every Monday to Friday
Robinson College 44

November

Every day
Robinson College 44

December

**Every day
until Friday 20th**
Robinson College 44

By Arrangement

Arrange a personalised garden visit
with your club, or group of friends,
on a date to suit you. See individual
garden entries for full details.

Beaver Lodge 1
NEW Bramble Lodge 2
Bustlers Cottage, Duxford
Gardens 12
38 Chapel Street 6
Church Lane House, Westley
Waterless Gardens 51
Church View, Westley Waterless
Gardens 51
Clover Cottage 9
Cottage Garden 10
Drovers 11
Fenleigh 16
Isaacson's 21
67 Main Street, Yaxley 30
The Manor House, Fenstanton 17
Molesworth House 32
Netherhall Manor 34
Newnham Farmhouse 35
The Old Rectory 39
NEW 1 Station Cottage 46
Twin Tarns 50
Upwater Lodge, Chaucer Road
Gardens 7
The Windmill 53

*47,000 people affected
by cancer were
reached by Maggie's
centres supported by
the National Garden
Scheme over the last
12 months*

Clover Cottage

THE GARDENS

◐ BEAVER LODGE

Henson Road, March, PE15 8BA.
Mr & Mrs Nielson-Bom,
01354 656185,
beaverbom@gmail.com. *A141
to Wisbech Rd into March, L into
Westwood Ave, at end, R into
Henson Rd, property on R opp sch
playground.* **Visits by arrangement
2 May to 30 Sept for groups
of up to 30. Suitable for some
wheelchairs please call to
discuss arrangements, some
areas may be difficult. Adm £7.50,
chd free. Light refreshments.**
An impeccable oriental garden with
more than 120 large and small
bonsai trees, acers, pagodas, oriental
statues, water features and pond
with koi carp, creating a peaceful
and relaxing atmosphere. Described
by visitors as an oasis of peace and
tranquility.

◱ NEW BRAMBLE LODGE

Gravel End, Coveney, Ely,
CB6 2DN. Mrs Kathryn
Kerridge, 07956 854091,
kerridgek@gmail.com. *3.5m NW of
Ely. From A142 or A10 Ely Bypass
Follow signs for Coveney. Garden*
is off Gravel End, behind 10a. **Sat
29, Sun 30 June, Sat 17, Sun
18 Aug (2-5). Adm £5, chd free.
Light refreshments. Visits also by
arrangement 1 June to 7 Sept for
groups of 10+.**
Bramble lodge is hidden from the
road with panoramic views of open
farmland and large fen skies. A
medium sized garden, it has been
designed and built entirely from
scratch over 15 years by the owners
from a bramble, nettle and rubble
field on the site of an old pig farm.
It has swirling borders filled with
familiar favourites and some unusual
species of perennials, shrubs, roses
and hydrangeas. Mainly lawn, except
secret garden which is gravel.

GROUP OPENING

◳ NEW BUCKWORTH GARDENS

Buckworth, Huntingdon,
PE28 5AN. *10 min drive from the
A1/A14 interchange (Brampton
Hut). From A1, at Alconbury Weston
turn onto Buckworth Rd. Follow for
2.2m, then take L to Buckworth.
Follow this for ½ m into the village.
From A14 come off at Spaldwick.
Parking signed.* **Sun 9 June (12-5).
Combined adm £7, chd free. Light
refreshments.**

KHUSUSI
Mrs Justine Harding.

NEW MANOR LODGE
Neil and Kathryn Broe.

NEW 2 NEW COTTAGES
Carol Greed.

Three gardens opening together
for the first time with extensive
views of surrounding countryside.
At Khusasi, the ½ acre garden has
relaxed wildlife-friendly planting that
is sympathetic to its setting and inc
a small perrenial meadow. Variety
of mature trees, ferns, hostas and
euphorbias. Natural ornamentation
inc a water feature created from local
stones, and tree stumps. Manor
Lodge extend over four acres of
which two are paddocks. Lambs
often graze here along with the
resident brood of hens. The gardens
comprise lawns, small orchard,
herbaceous and rose borders,
walled garden, pond and extensive
vegetable areas with polytunnel.
2 New Cottages is set behind a
Victorian semi-detached cottage.
It has evolved over 30 years and
features a range of mature shrubs
and trees, herbaceous borders,
flowering perennials, garden
ornamentation, wildlife friendly
planting, vegetable growing area.

73 Kingston Street

GROUP OPENING

4 BURWELL VILLAGE GARDENS

High Street, Burwell, CB25 0HB. *10m NE of Cambridge, 4m NW of Newmarket via the B1102/ B1103.* Sun 9 June (12-5). Combined adm with Isaacson's £8, chd free. Home-made teas at Isaacson's.

9 THE BRIARS
Ms Marianne Hall and Mr Tony Hollyer.

NEW **3 FIELD VIEW**
Mr & Mrs Farrow.

NEWNHAM FARMHOUSE
Mr and Mrs Quentin Cooke.
(See separate entry)

3 ROMAN CLOSE
Mrs Dove.

SPRING VIEW
Colin Smith.
NPC

3 Roman Close has a small, pretty modern cottage garden, with roses perennials and annuals. Pots and hanging baskets. Spring View has the National Collection of Yucca, for the specialist plantsman huge diversity of form and sizes, drought tolerant planting plus other species. 9 The Briars is environmentally friendly with a pond, flowers and vegetables, featuring a living wall. Newnham Farmhouse has a walled garden surrounding a C16 thatched cottage, with over 50 Japanese acers. Packed borders and a wildflower lawn, not just grass. Ponds front and back and a few interesting sculptures. See also Isaacsons' separate listing; a plantsman's garden of striking diversity in a series of different zones and incorporating medieval plants, in the grounds of a clunch stone former lodging range dating from 1340. 3 Field View is a new build lockdown garden with modern planting and design, secluded entertaining areas and borrowed vistas, wildflowers and young trees.

GROUP OPENING

5 CAMBOURNE GARDENS

Great Cambourne, CB23 6AH. *8m W of Cambridge on A428. From A428: take Cambourne junc into Great Cambourne. From B1198, enter village at Lower Cambourne & drive through to Great Cambourne.*

Follow yellow signs via either route to start at any garden. Sun 26 May (11-5). Combined adm £7.50, chd free. Home-made teas at 13 Fenbridge.

13 FENBRIDGE
Lucinda & Tony Williams.

14 GRANARY WAY
Jackie Hutchinson.

88 GREENHAZE LANE
Darren & Irette Murray.

128 GREENHAZE LANE
Fran & John Panrucker.

128 JEAVONS LANE
Mr Tim Smith.

8 LANGATE GREEN
Steve & Julie Friend.

5 MAYFIELD WAY
Debbie & Mike Perry.

43 MONKFIELD LANE
Penny Miles.

A unique and inspiring modern group, all created from new build in just a few years. This selection of eight demonstrates how imagination and gardening skill can be combined in a short time to create great effects from unpromising and awkward beginnings. The grouping inc foliage gardens with collections of carnivorous pitcher plants and hosta; a suntrap garden for play, socialising and colour; gardens with ponds, a vegetable plot and many other beautiful borders showing their owners' creativity and love of growing fine plants well. Cambourne is one of Cambridgeshire's newest communities, and this grouping showcases the happy, vibrant place our village has become. Superb examples of beauty and creativity in a newly built environment.

6 38 CHAPEL STREET

Ely, CB6 1AD. Peter & Julia Williams, 01353 659161, peterrcwilliams@btinternet.com. *Entering Ely from Cambridge (A10), pass Cathedral Green (on your R) take 1st L (Downham Rd) towards Ely College. Chapel St is 1st R. Alternatively enter Chapel St from Lynn Rd (300yds).* Sun 2 June (12-6). Combined adm with Ely Open Gardens £10, chd free. Visits also by arrangement Apr to Sept for groups of 5 to 35. Parking available only by prior

arrangement on forecourt for up to 4 cars.
Approx ½ acre, level, with many unusual plants. Year-round interest. Secluded back garden with gravel garden, well-stocked colourful rockery, herbaceous borders raised vegetable beds, soft fruit and fruit trees (inc large quince, fig); pergolas with many climbing roses. Numerous pots on terraces. Front garden has a wide variety of roses, flowering *Prunus*, *Philadelphus*, judas tree. Secluded and tranquil level garden near city centre. Wide variety of unusual plants, year round. Well-established quince often producing 500 or more fruits. Of special note cut-leaf elder, *Solanum rantonetti*, *Viburnum hillieri winton*.

GROUP OPENING

7 CHAUCER ROAD GARDENS

Cambridge, CB2 7EB. *1m S of Cambridge. Off Trumpington Rd (A1309), nr Brooklands Ave junc. Parking available at MRC Psychology Dept on Chaucer Rd.* Sun 5, Mon 6 May (2-5). Combined adm £8, chd free. Home-made teas at Upwater Lodge.

11 CHAUCER ROAD
Mark & Jigs Hill.

12 CHAUCER ROAD
Mr & Mrs Bradley.

16 CHAUCER ROAD
Mrs V Albutt.

UPWATER LODGE
Mr & Mrs George Pearson, 07890 080303, jmp@pearson.co.uk.
Visits also by arrangement 7 May to 21 July.

Chaucer Road Gardens are fine examples of large Edwardian gardens tucked away on the south side of Cambridge. They are all very different in size and character, some with glimpses of a bygone age. There are magnificent old trees, fine lawns, ponds and a water meadow with river frontage and rare breed sheep. Planting is varied, sometimes unusual, and in constant flux. Cakes made with garden fruit where possible. Swings and climbing ropes. Wheelchair access consists of some gravel areas and grassy paths with fairly gentle slopes.

GROUP OPENING

8 NEW CHRISTCHURCH VILLAGE GARDENS

Christchurch, Wisbech, PE14 9PQ. *5m E of March, 10m N of Ely on the Cambridgeshire/Norfolk border. Midway between March and Welney.* **Sun 23 June (2-5). Combined adm £7, chd free. Home-made teas at Christchurch Community Centre with a donation to the National Garden Scheme.**

NEW THE GREEN
Pauline Hutchins.

NEW OAKLANDS
Sandra Kay.

NEW THE OLD SCHOOL HOUSE
Philippa Pearson.
(See separate entry)

NEW SANDHURST
Stuart Turner.

The Old School House is a developing plantswoman's and designer's garden with traditional and contemporary planting, many perennials, a sunny walled border and shady borders. The Green is a traditional cottage garden with small trees, a summerhouse, roses and mixed planting. Sandhurst is a large country garden begun over 30 years ago with island beds, inspired by Alan Bloom's garden at Bressingham, Norfolk. Perennials inc 50 different hardy geraniums, 60 *Hemerocallis* and 70 hostas. Oaklands has cottage garden style planting with shrubs and many perennials including many hostas and hardy geraniums. There's a water feature, two raised beds for vegetables, a greenhouse and patio. Some gravel paths and small level changes, generally all gardens can be accessed.

---

2 CLOVER COTTAGE

50 Streetly End, West Wickham, CB21 4RP. Mr Paul & Mrs Shirley Shadford, 07538 569191, shirleyshadford@live.co.uk. *3m from Linton, 3m from Haverhill & 2m from Balsham. From Horseheath turn L, from Balsham turn R, thatched cottage opp triangle of grass next to old windmill.* **Sun 18, Sun 25 Feb, Sun 3 Mar (2-4). Adm £3, chd free. Sun 2, Sun 9 June (12-4.30). Adm £3.50, chd free. Home-made teas.**

Visits also by arrangement 18 Feb to 30 June.
In winter find a flowering cherry tree, borders of snowdrops, aconites, *Iris reticulata*, hellebores and miniature *Narcissus* throughout the packed small garden which has inspiring ideas on use of space. Pond and arbour, raised beds of fruit and vegetables. In summer arches of roses and clematis, hardy geraniums, delightful borders of English roses and herbaceous plants. Snowdrops, hellebores and spring flowering bulbs for sale for the February opening, plants also for sale in June.

---

10 COTTAGE GARDEN

79 Sedgwick Street, Cambridge, CB1 3AL. Rosie Wilson, 07805 443818, liccycat@icloud.com. *Cambridge City. Off Mill Rd, S of the railway bridge.* **Sat 8 June (2-6). Adm £4, chd free. Visits also by arrangement 31 May to 31 Aug for groups of 15 to 30.**
Small, long, narrow and planted in the cottage garden style with over 40 roses, some on arches and growing through trees. Particularly planned to encourage wildlife with small pond, mature trees and shrubs. Perennials and some unusual plants interspersed with sculptures.

GROUP OPENING

11 COVENEY & WARDY HILL GARDENS

Coveney, Ely, CB6 2DN. *From A142 or A10 Ely bypass, follow signs for Coveney. For Wardy Hill from A142 sp Witcham.* **Sat 25, Sun 26 May (1-5). Combined adm £7, chd free. Home-made teas.**

DROVERS
Mr David Guyer, 07859 917947, guyer100@yahoo.co.uk.
Visits also by arrangement 25 May to 29 Sept for groups of up to 30.

NEW 1A THE GREEN
Mrs Kate Bullen.

HAWTHORN COTTAGE
Lesley & Philip Wenn.

THE HEY CHAPEL
Mr Peter Ross.

2 SCHOOL LANE
Mrs Jane McCartney.

NEW TOADS ACRE
Ms Naomi Laredo.

Six medium sized gardens, in the fenland parish of Coveney overlooking Ely cathedral: School Lane, a plantsman's garden, with year-round interest and unusual plants, patio, rock garden and veg plot. Nearby, Hawthorn Cottage, a cottage garden of bee friendly herbaceous borders, roses, wildlife pond and bonsai in a shaded patio. Do visit the floral displays in the church. In Wardy Hill, Hey Chapel has winding paths to view the cathedral and a splendid veg garden, down through a series rooms of arched roses and wildlife ponds. On the Green 1a, is a new build house and garden with a more modern feel of arbours, interesting herbaceous borders and water feature. Across the Green is Toadsacre, ⅔ acres of Heritage Orchard and mature tree walks with a Potage terrace, all to the gentle strains of a live quartet. Drovers is based on a Chinese pleasure garden philosophy but with English naturalist planting that wanders by a wildlife pond, beneath mature trees to a rose garden and potted terrace.

GROUP OPENING

12 DUXFORD GARDENS

Duxford, CB22 4RP. *Most gardens are close to the centre of the village of Duxford. S of the A505 between M11 J10 & Sawston. Parking at CB22 4PT.* **Sun 2 June (2-6). Combined adm £7, chd free. Home-made teas at Bustlers Cottage (cream teas) and in St Peter's Church (in aid of church roof).**

BUSTLERS COTTAGE
John & Jenny Marks, 07956 049257, jenny.marks@ngs.org.uk.
Visits also by arrangement 3 June to 31 July for groups of 10 to 25.

5 GREEN STREET
Jenny Shaw.

OLD LACEYS
Dr G Hinks.

THE RECTORY
Mr David Baker.

31 ST PETER'S STREET
Mr David Baker.

Several village gardens of different sizes and characters. 5 Green Street is an enclosed garden which was planted to be easily managed and require little maintenance without compromising on colour and interest. 31 St Peter's Street, on a steep slope, is filled with colour and surprises, and also has a dry rockery in front of the house. Bustlers Cottage has an acre of cottage garden inc vegetable garden, many trees and places to sit and enjoy. Stop here and try a home-made cream tea and buy some plants. In St John's Street, the garden at number 38, Old Laceys, has cottage garden planting with some interesting formal touches, inc a cloud pruned *Pyracantha*. Opposite Old Laceys a grass maze has been mown into the lawn at the Rectory. Wheelchair access, some gravel paths and a few steps, mostly avoidable.

13 ◆ ELGOOD'S BREWERY GARDENS

North Brink, Wisbech, PE13 1LW. Elgood & Sons Ltd, 01945 583160, info@elgoods-brewery.co.uk, www.elgoods-brewery.co.uk. *1m W of town centre. Leave A47 towards Wisbech Centre. Cross river to North Brink. Follow river & brown signs to brewery & car park beyond.* **For NGS: Wed 14 Aug (11-4). Adm £5, chd free. For other opening times and information, please phone, email or visit garden website.** Approx four acres of peaceful garden featuring 250 year old specimen trees providing a framework to lawns, lake, rockery, herb garden and maze. Wheelchair access to visitor centre and most areas of the garden.

14 ELM HOUSE

Main Road, Elm, Wisbech, PE14 0AB. Mrs Diana Bullard. *2½ m SW of Wisbech. From A1101 take B1101, signed Elm, Friday Bridge. Elm House is ⅓ m on L.* **Sun 30 June (2-5). Adm £5, chd free. Light refreshments.** Elm House has a lovely walled garden with arboretum, many rare trees and shrubs, mixed perennials and a three acre flower meadow. Children and guide dogs welcome. Most paths suitable for wheelchair users. Uneven surfaces in meadow.

Elgood's Brewery Gardens

GROUP OPENING

15 ELY OPEN GARDENS

Chapel Street, Ely, CB6 1AD. www.elyopengardens.com. *14m N of Cambridge. Parking at Barton Rd, The Grange Council Offices, St.Mary's St, Brays Ln and Newnham St. All in easy reach of most gardens. Map on website or from elyopengardens.com.* **Sun 2 June (12-6). Combined adm with 38 Chapel Street £10, chd free. Light refreshments at Ely Methodist Church and 1 Merlin Drive.**

THE BISHOP'S HOUSE
The Bishop of Ely.

42 CAMBRIDGE ROAD
Mr & Mrs J Switsur.

12 CHAPEL STREET
Ken & Linda Ellis.

5B DOWNHAM ROAD
Mr Christopher Cain.

1 MERLIN DRIVE
Dr Chris Wood.

1 ROBINS CLOSE
Mr Brian & Mrs Ann Mitchell.

A delightful and varied group of gardens in an historic cathedral city: The Bishop's House, adjoining Ely Cathedral, has mixed planting and formal rose garden bordered by wisteria. 12 Chapel Street, a small town garden, shows varied gardening interests, from alpines to herbaceous plants and shrubs and a railway! 1 Merlin Drive and 1 Robins Close are modern estate gardens. The former has a collection of subtropical plants, and ferns, the latter has raised beds, vegetables and a small dry garden. 5b Downham Road a small garden shows how careful planting can create a tranquil garden in a challenging plot. 42 Cambridge Road is a long garden with many features, from fig trees at one end to a town vegetable plot at the other. There are many features to enjoy here, and it's well worth a visit. Wheelchair access to areas of most gardens.

FENLEIGH

Inkerson Fen, off Common Rd, Throckenholt, PE12 0QY. Jeff & Barbara Stalker, 07800 575100, barbara.stalker@ngs.org.uk. *Half way between Gedney Hill & Parson Drove. Postcode for SatNav takes you within 200mtrs, follow NGS signage.* **Visits by arrangement May to Sept for groups of 5 to 30. Please call to discuss larger groups. Adm inc light refreshments. Adm £7, chd free.**
A fish pond dominates this large garden surrounded with planting. Patio with pots and raised beds, Undercover BBQ area. Small wooded area, polytunnels and corners of the garden for wildlife.

GROUP OPENING

 FENSTANTON

Huntingdon, PE28 9JW. *Situated between Cambridge and Huntingdon just off the A1307. All 4 gardens are in the centre of the village: just look for the church spire. There is a public car park next to the church, a 2 min walk away.* **Sat 18, Sun 19 May (1-5). Combined adm £6, chd free. Home-made teas.**

5 CHURCH LANE
Mrs Jan Stone.

 **IVY COTTAGE**
Corinne & Michael King.

THE MANOR HOUSE
Lynda Symonds & Nigel Ferrier, 07768 274456, ginger5098@icloud.com. **Visits also by arrangement.**

 **WIMPOLE HOUSE**
Bob & Mary Henderson.

Four contrasting gardens, two large and two small, set around the oldest houses in the village. Ivy Cottage garden is a beautiful example of a mature cottage garden with a wide variety of unusual plants. Wimpole House has a delightful selection of roses, mature trees and shrubs and a pond brimming with life. The Manor House has a more formal garden wrapped around the building with a winding path between well stocked borders. Church Lane is a hidden garden packed with ferns, hostas and traditional cottage plants. Fenstanton is famous for links to Capability Brown and his family. Whilst in Fenstanton you can visit Brown's memorial in the parish church and the grave stone of one of the country's most famous landscape gardeners. Delicious home made teas can be enjoyed in the United Reformed Church, set in the centre of the village, a two minute stroll from all four gardens.

 GREEN END FARM
Over Road, Longstanton, Cambridge, CB24 3DW. Sylvia Newman, www.sngardendesign.co.uk. *From A14 head towards Longstanton. At r'about take 2nd exit, at next r'about turn L. Garden 200 metres on L.* **Sun 30 June (11-4). Adm £5, chd free. Light refreshments.**
A developing garden that's beginning to blend well with the farm. An interesting combination of new and established spaces executed with a design eye. An established orchard with beehives; two wildlife ponds. An outside kitchen and social space inc pool, productive kitchen and cutting garden. Doves, chickens, bees and sheep complete the picture.

Elm House

19 HEATH FRUIT FARM
The Heath, Bluntisham, Huntingdon, PE28 3LQ.
Rob and Mary Bousfield.
www.heathfruitfarm.co.uk. *4 m N of St Ives Cambs. Drive out of Bluntisham at Wood End; garden on R after water towers. If you come from St Ives to Wheatsheaf Xroads take The Heath on your R. Garden on L after a few bends.* **Sat 13 Apr (10-2). Adm £4, chd free. Home-made teas.**
A traditional orchard of 25 acres, boasting a range of apples, pears, apricots, plums, gages and cherries. Visit for a tour in the spring to behold a magnificent array of blossom and buzzing bees, while brown hares gambol around in springtime madness. Guided tours on the hour focusing on fruit growing, wildlife and the history of a Cambridgeshire orchard. Dogs allowed but must be kept on a lead. We are looking forward to welcoming you to our orchard. Bring your wellies and waterproofs just in case.

GROUP OPENING

20 NEW HILTON WEST
Chapel Close, Hilton, Huntingdon, PE28 9NS. James Hughes. *5m SW of St Ives. Gardens are mainly on W side of B1040 in centre of village.* **Sun 7 July (2-6). Combined adm £7, chd free. Light refreshments at the Village Hall and the Prince of Wales Pub.**

NEW 8 GRAVELEY WAY
Beverley and Bill Williams Smith.

NEW MOAT HOUSE
Jane and Roy Philips.

NEW THE PRINCE OF WALES
Emma Northwood & Simon Perry.

27 SCOTTS CRESCENT
Mrs Sandy Monk.

NEW SHERWOOD HOUSE
James Hughes & Neil Ainley.

NEW 12 WESTBROOK
Janet Taylor.

Six contrasting gardens, inc the private garden at the village pub, not usually open to visitors, from large to small, and showing a variety of different styles and planting. The well established garden at 27 Scotts Crescent is full of unusual varieties of many plants. The garden at Sherwood House has been

developed over five years, with modern design features and a long view across the neighbouring fields.

21 ISAACSON'S
6 High Street, Burwell, CB25 0HB. Dr Richard & Dr Caroline Dyer, 01638 601742, richard@familydyer.com. *10m NE of Cambridge, 4m NW of Newmarket. Behind a tall yew hedge with topiary, & grass triangle, at the S end of the village where Isaacson Rd turns off the High St. Approx 400 yds S of the church.* **Sun 9 June (12-5). Combined adm with Burwell Village Gardens £8, chd free. Home-made teas. Visits also by arrangement 22 Apr to 30 June for groups of 15 to 30. Type of refreshment inc in the adm.**
Warmed and sheltered by the medieval walls of a C14 house (the oldest in Burwell) the garden is richly diverse in format and planting. There are 'theatres' (auricula, pinks), hints of Snowdonia, the Mediterranean, and a French potager, Anglesey Abbey in the snowdrop season and much else. Throughout there are many interesting, unusual and rare plants. Around each corner a new vista surprises.

22 ISLAND HALL
Godmanchester, PE29 2BA. Grace Vane Percy, 01480 459676, enquire@islandhall.com, www.islandhall.com. *1m S of Huntingdon (A1). 15m NW of Cambridge (A14). In centre of Godmanchester next to free Mill Yard car park.* **Sun 26 May (10.30-4.30). Adm £5.50, chd free. Home-made teas.**
Three acre grounds, tranquil riverside setting with mature trees. Chinese bridge over Saxon mill race to embowered island with wildflowers. Garden restoration begun in 1983 to mid C18 formal design, with box hedging, clipped hornbeams, parterres, topiary, beautiful vistas over the borrowed landscape of Portholme. The ornamental island has been replanted with Princeton elm avenue (*Ulmus americana*).

23 KING'S COLLEGE FELLOWS' GARDEN AND PROVOST'S GARDEN
Queen's Road, Cambridge, CB2 1ST. Provost & Scholars of King's College, tinyurl.com/kingscol. *In Cambridge, the Backs. Entry by gate at junc of Queen's Rd & West Rd or at King's Parade. Parking at Lion Yard, short walk, or some pay & display places in West Rd & Queen's Rd.* **Sun 30 June (10.45-4.15). Adm £6, chd free. Home-made teas.**
Fine example of a Victorian garden with rare specimen trees. Rond Pont entrance leads to a small woodland walk, herbaceous and sub-tropical borders, rose pergola, kitchen/allotment garden and orchard. The Provost's garden opens with kind permission, offering a rare glimpse of an arts and crafts design. Chance to view the new wildflower meadow created on the former Great Lawn. Wheelchair access to garden over gravel paths. Tickets available to purchase at the college's shop in King's Parade.

24 38 KINGSTON STREET
Cambridge, CB1 2NU. Wendy & Clive Chapman. *Central Cambridge. Off Mill Rd, W of railway bridge.* **Sat 6 July (2-5). Combined adm with 73 Kingston Street £5, chd free. Open nearby 38 Norfolk Terrace Garden.**
A tiny courtyard garden with contrasts between deep shade and sunlit areas. Raised beds and pots of various sizes with a range of perennial and annual planting. Please note there is a small step into garden.

25 NEW 73 KINGSTON STREET
Cambridge, CB1 2NU. Ed Pearson & Karina Michel. *Off Mill Rd, Cambridge. Enter via Hooper St. Back gate is a short walk from the front of the house. Just follow the signs.* **Sat 6 July (2-5). Combined adm with 38 Kingston Street £5, chd free. Home-made teas. Open nearby 38 Norfolk Terrace Garden.**
A contemporary, sunken urban space, this patio garden contains a small pond and tiered planters and pots with naturalistic planting. The focal point is a Himalayan birch tree offering shade for the concrete benches. Hints of Mexican planting add an interesting accent in a cosy sanctuary.

26 KIRTLING TOWER
Newmarket Road, Kirtling, CB8 9PA. The Lord & Lady Fairhaven. *6m SE of Newmarket. From Newmarket head towards village of Saxon St, through village to Kirtling. Turn L at the war memorial; the road is signed to Upend & the entrance is signed on the L.* **Sun 24 Mar, Sun 30 June (11-4). Adm £6, chd free. Light refreshments.** Large formal gardens surrounding Kirtling Tower (not open). Large moat, ornamental Walled Garden, Cloisters Rose Garden, Cutting and Vegetable Garden. Secret and Summer Gardens, young arboretum and pinetum. Set in 25 acres of park land with extensive views of surrounding countryside. Large swathes of *Narcissus, Tulipa sylvestris* and Fritillaria in spring. Roses, *Camassias* and stunning herbaceous borders in summer. Classic cars in June. Craft and Plant stalls for both openings. Many of the paths and routes around the garden are grass - they are accessible by wheelchairs, but can be hard work if wet.

GROUP OPENING

27 LINTON GARDENS
Linton, CB21 4HS. Chris Tyler-Smith and Yali Xue. *On A1307 between Cambridge & Haverhill, parking at Linton Village College* **Sun 26 May (2-6). Combined adm £8, chd free. Home-made teas in the Maltings Courtyard at 94 High Street.**

14 HIGH STREET
Chris Tyler-Smith and Yali Xue.

94 HIGH STREET
Rosemary Wellings.

20 MILL LANE
Tom and Katy Meeks.

QUEENS HOUSE
Michael & Alison Wilcockson.

Several gardens in the village of Linton. Near the top of the High Street, close to the junction with the A1307, 14 High Street, is a garden where most of the planting is white. The entrance belies the size of the garden, much of which is designed with wildlife in mind. Next door is Queens House, with garden 'rooms' separated by hedging and graced by statuary reflecting the age of the house. Follow the path in front of the church to reach the cottage garden at 20 Mill Lane is full of colour as well as abundant edible produce. The garden behind the Gallery Above at 94 High Street is small and perfectly formed, and accessed via a courtyard where teas are served. Some on-street parking throughout the village, and in the car park next to the Health Centre, reached from Coles Lane.

28 LITTLE OAK
66 Station Road, Willingham, Cambridge, CB24 5HG. Mr & Mrs Eileen Hughes, www.littleoak.org.uk/garden. *4m N of A14 J25 nr Cambridge. Easy to find on the main road in the village. Driveway parking for disabled use only.* **Sat 22, Sun 23 June (11-5). Adm £5.50, chd free. Home-made teas.** An acre garden displaying many different areas and planting schemes with a range of annual, herbaceous and perennial beds, productive kitchen garden, fruit trees and ponds. An ideal place to spend time and relax with a cup of tea and homemade cake. We have a shepherds hut and weather permitting there will be wood turning and model railway. Main garden is wheelchair accessible.

29 MADINGLEY HALL
Cambridge, CB23 8AQ. University of Cambridge, 01223 746222, reservations@madingleyhall.co.uk, www.madingleyhall.co.uk. *4m W of Cambridge. 1m from M11, J13. Located in the centre of Madingley village. Entrance adjacent to mini r'about.* **Sun 9 June (2.30-5.30). Adm £6, chd free. Home-made teas at St Mary Magdalene Church, in the grounds of Madingley Hall.** C16 Hall (not open) set in eight acres of attractive grounds landscaped by Capability Brown. Features inc landscaped walled garden with hazel walk. Historic meadow, topiary, mature trees and wide variety of hardy plants.

30 67 MAIN STREET, YAXLEY
Peterborough, PE7 3LZ. Mrs Karen Woods, 07787 864426, karenandstevewoods@yahoo.co.uk. *S of Peterborough, approx 3m from J16 on A1. On entering Yaxley, turn R into Dovecote Ln. At the bottom, turn L onto Main St. Find us approx 1m on R.* **Visits by arrangement 11 May to 23 Aug for groups of 10 to 20. Adm inc tea, coffee and homemade biscuits. Adm £8, chd free.** An acre working organic cottage garden providing something for the kitchen and vase year-round. Seasonal cut flowers grown in raised beds and traditional borders. Allotment style vegetable garden. Paddock with fruit trees and views over the fen to the rear. Chickens for eggs. Wreath workshops and flower demonstrations available, please email for more details.

31 ◆ THE MANOR, HEMINGFORD GREY
Hemingford Grey, PE28 9BN. Mrs D S Boston, 01480 463134, diana_boston@hotmail.com, www.greenknowe.co.uk. *4m E of Huntingdon. Off A1307. Parking for NGS opening day only, in field off double bends between Hemingford Grey & Hemingford Abbots. This will be signed. Entrance to garden via small gate off river towpath.* **For NGS: Sun 9 June (11-5). Adm £6, chd free. Home-made teas. For other opening times and information, please phone, email or visit garden website.** Garden designed by author Lucy Boston, surrounds C12 manor house on which Green Knowe books based (house by appt). Three acres 'cottage' garden with topiary, snowdrops, old roses, extensive collection of irises inc Dykes Medal winners and Cedric Morris var., herbaceous borders with scented plants. Meadow with mown paths. Enclosed by river, moat and wilderness. Variety of annuals for late flowering. Gravel paths throughout. Wheelchair users are encouraged to use the lawns.

32 MOLESWORTH HOUSE
Molesworth, PE28 0QD. John & Gilly Prentis, 07771 918250, gillyprentis@gmail.com. *10m W of Huntingdon off the A14. Next to the church in Molesworth.* **Sun 26 May (2-6). Adm £5, chd free. Home-made teas. Visits also by arrangement for groups of up to 20.** Molesworth House is an old three acre rectory garden with everything that you'd both expect and hope for,

given its Victorian past. There are surprising corners to this traditional take on a happy and relaxed garden - come and see for yourself. A humble gem awaits your discovery. Accessible to wheelchair users, although there is some gravel.

33 5 NELSONS LANE
Haddenham, Ely, CB6 3UH. Mr Peter Wilson, haddenhamgardener.tumblr.com. *10m N of Cambridge and 7m from Ely. From A10 N of Cambridge, take A1123 at Stretham.Follow for 2½ m to Haddenham, bearing L just before water tower as you enter the village. L at bottom of hill. No parking at all in Nelsons Ln.* **Sun 9 June (12-5). Adm £4, chd free. Home-made teas.**
Extending to ½ acre the garden has been created from scratch over 16 years and inc numerous areas from the central herbaceous borders surrounded by yew hedges to a hidden slate garden, vegetable and fruit beds and wild areas to support nature. A long range of traditional buildings houses summerhouse and potting sheds for tender edibles such as peppers and chilies.

34 NETHERHALL MANOR
Tanners Lane, Soham, CB7 5AB. Timothy Clark, 01353 720269, timothy.r.clark@btinternet.com. *6m Ely, 6m Newmarket. Enter Soham from Newmarket, Tanners Ln 2nd R 100yds after cemetery. Enter Soham from Ely, Tanners Ln 2nd L after War Memorial.* **Sun 31 Mar, Sun 5 May, Sun 4, Sun 11 Aug (2-5). Adm £4, chd free. Home-made teas. Visits also by arrangement Mar to Aug.**
Unusual garden appealing to those with historical interest in individual collections of plant groups: March-old primroses, daffodils, Victorian double flowered hyacinths and first garden hellebore hybrids. May-old English tulips, Crown Imperials. Aug-Victorian *Pelargonium, Heliotrope, Calceolaria,* Red list for Plant Heritage. Margery Fish's Country Gardening and Mary McMurtrie's Country Garden Flowers, Historic Plants 1500-1900. Author's books for sale. Wheelchair access good as it is a flat garden.

35 NEWNHAM FARMHOUSE
16 Low Road, Burwell, CB25 0EJ. Mr and Mrs Quentin Cooke, 07802 857150, q.cooke@ntlworld.com. *The thatched house opp Casburn Ln. Parking on the street outside.* **Sun 5 May, Sun 4 Aug (1-5). Adm £6, chd free. Opening with Burwell Village Gardens on Sun 9 June. Visits also by arrangement 1 Mar to 1 Nov. Discuss refreshments when booking.**
The garden surrounds a C16 grade II listed thatched cottage. It is to a good extent walled and split into the front and back. All told, the site is about ⅓ of an acre. The garden has over 60 Japanese Acers, a magnificent walnut tree, and mature silver birch. The borders are packed and aim to provide all year seasonal interest, and a lawn that is filled with wildflowers rather than just grass. There are ponds front and back and a few interesting sculptures to be discovered. The garden can be accessed by wheelchair, but a bit of a hard push over a gravel drive to access the back garden.

36 38 NORFOLK TERRACE GARDEN
Cambridge, CB1 2NG. John Tordoff & Maurice Reeve. *Central Cambridge. A603 East Rd turn R into St Matthews St to Norfolk St, L into Blossom St & Norfolk Terrace is at the end.* **Sat 6, Sun 7 July (11-5). Adm £3, chd free. Home-made teas.**
This lavish Moroccan style paved courtyard garden, in the middle of the city, has masses of colour in raised beds and pots, backed by oriental arches. The ornamental pool defined by its patterned tiles offers the soothing splash of water. There will be a display of recent paintings by John Tordoff and handmade books by Maurice Reeve.

37 NEW NUFFIELD ROAD ALLOTMENTS
Nuffield Road, CB4 1TF, Cambridge, CB4 1TF. NRAS, www.nuffieldroadallotments.com. *East Chesterton, Cambridge. Nuffield Rd Allotments are adjacent to the bus-way to Cambridge N Stn, and can be accessed by bike/foot from its cycle path. Car access from Green End Rd then Nuffield Rd, parking in Nuffield Rd.* **Sat 29 June (2-5). Adm £5, chd free.**
Almost all of the 83 allotments and the two community gardens will be open for visitors in this enclosed site which extends to over two hectares in a residential and commercial part of the city. Visitors will be able to speak to some of the allotment holders.

38 OLD FARM COTTAGE
Staploe, St Neots, PE19 5JA. Sir Graham & Lady Fry. *Approx 1m W of St Neots. Going S on Great North Rd in St Neots, turn R into Duloe Rd. Under A1 through Duloe village. Follow the road to Staploe. Last house on the L.* **Sun 14 July (1-5). Adm £5, chd free. Tea.**
Terraced and formal flower beds surrounding a thatched house and leading to three acres of orchard, grassland, woodland and wetland maintained for wildlife. Present owners have planted some non-native trees, inc ornamental cherries, loquat, *Metasequoia,* ginkgo, *Pawlonia* and monkey puzzle, extended the area of native woodland and created a wildflower meadow. Wheelchair access: Gravel, uneven ground and one steep slope.

The National Garden Scheme's final instalment to support the building of the Y Bwthyn NGS Macmillan Specialist Palliative Care Unit in Wales, enabled 270 inpatients to be supported this year

39 THE OLD RECTORY
312 Main Road, Parson
Drove, Wisbech, PE13 4LF.
Helen Roberts, 07818 070641,
yogahelen@talk21.com. *SW of
Wisbech. From Peterborough on A47
follow signs to Parson Drove, L after
Thorney Toll. From Wisbech follow
the B1166 through Leverington
Common.* **Sun 9 June (11-4). Adm
£5, chd free. Home-made teas.
Visits also by arrangement 1 May
to 21 July for groups of 10+.**
This garden represents the personality
of this Georgian house (not open),
classical and formal at the front and
friendly and a bit crazy at the back.
A walled cottage style of about an
acre with an abundance of plants
and roses leading onto wildflower
meadows with walking paths. There
are also three ponds each one also
with a different personality.

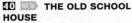

**40 NEW THE OLD SCHOOL
HOUSE**
Church Road, Christchurch,
Wisbech, PE14 9PQ. Philippa
Pearson. *10m N of Ely on the
Cambridgeshire/Norfolk border.
Midway between March and Welney.*
**Sun 22 Sept (2-5). Adm £5, chd
free. Opening with Christchurch
Village Gardens on Sun 23 June.**
Medium sized plantswomen's garden
with established shrubs and many
perennials. A mixture of traditional
planting, a sunny courtyard garden
area with containers, contemporary-
style planting in the rear garden and
a shady border. The sunny walled
border has dahlias at their peak in late
summer, and is lined with trained fruit
trees and climbing roses. The garden
is still being developed. Some slight
level changes and shallow steps.

&

41 23A PERRY ROAD
Buckden, St Neots, PE19 5XG.
David & Valerie Bunnage. *5m
S of Huntingdon on A1. From A1
Buckden r'about take B661, Perry
Rd approx 300yds on L.* **Every Fri,
Sat and from Sun 3 May to 8 Sept
(2-4). Adm £5, chd free. Pre-
booking essential, please visit
www.ngs.org.uk for information
& booking.**
Approx an acre of many garden
designs inc Japanese, interlinked by
gravel paths. Plantsmans garden,
155 acers and unusual shrubs.

Quirky with interesting features some
narrow paths. Regret, not suitable for
wheelchairs. WC available.

42 PREACHERS PASSING
55 Station Road, Tilbrook,
Huntingdon, PE28 0JT. Keith &
Rosamund Nancekievill. *Tilbrook
4½m S of J16 on A14. Station Rd in
Tilbrook can be accessed from the
B645 or B660. Preachers Passing
faces the small bridge over the
River Til at a sharp bend in Station
Rd with All Saints church behind it.*
**Sat 20, Sun 21 July (10-5). Adm
£5, chd free. Home-made teas.
Homemade cakes, ice cream and
soft drinks also available.**
A ¾ acre garden fits into its pastoral
setting. Near the house, parterre,
courtyard and terrace offer formality;
but beyond, prairie planting leads
to a wildlife pond, rock gardens,
meadow, stumpery, rose garden and
copse. Enjoy different views from
arbour, honeysuckle-covered swing or
scattered benches. Deciduous trees
and perennials give changing colour.
Here are open spaces and hidden
places.

Toads Acre, Coveney and Wardy Hill Gardens

43 RAMSEY WALLED GARDEN
Wood Lane, Ramsey,
Huntingdon, PE26 2XD. Ramsey
Abbey Walled Garden CIO,
www.ramseywalledgarden.org.
Just N of Ramsey Town Centre.
Follow B1096 out of Ramsey. Just
after last house on R, turn R opp
cemetery. Take track to Ramsey
Rural Museum. Park under trees.
See map on Ramsey Walled Garden
website. **Sat 14 Sept (2-5). Adm**
£5, chd free. Home-made teas
at Ramsey Rural Museum. The
Museum is volunteer run. Parking
is close by.
A Victorian Walled Garden, located
within the grounds of Ramsey Abbey,
has been restored by volunteers and
is an enchanting secret in the heart
of Ramsey. Dating back to 1840,
this one acre garden is dedicated
to growing fruit, vegetables and
flowers. Features inc a magnificent
33m glasshouse, an apple tunnel
planted with Cambridgeshire varieties,
a dahlia border and a collection of
Salvias. The garden is wheelchair
accessible but is 450m from the car
parking area along a grass path.
Motorised buggies can access the
garden.
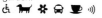

44 ROBINSON COLLEGE
Grange Road, Cambridge,
CB3 9AN. Warden and Fellows,
www.robinson.cam.ac.uk/
about-robinson/gardens/national-
gardens-scheme. *Garden at main*
Robinson College site, report to
Porters' Lodge. There is only on-
street parking. **Daily weekdays**
10-4, weekends 2-4 from Fri 3
Jan. Closed Sat 13 April - Sun
7 July, Sat 10 - Tues 27 Aug,
Sat 21 -Sun 31 Dec. Pre-booking
essential, please visit www.
ngs.org.uk for information &
booking. Light refreshments at
the Robinson College Red Brick
Cafe Bar.
10 original Edwardian gardens
linked to central wild woodland
water garden focused on Bin Brook,
with small lake at heart of site,
giving a feeling of park and informal
woodland, while keeping the sense of
older more formal gardens beyond.
Mature stately trees frame central
wide lawn running down to the lake.
Much original planting is still intact.
More recent planting inc herbaceous
borders and commemorative
trees. No picnics. Children must be
accompanied at all times. Tickets
must be booked on line in advance.

Please collect guidebook from
Porters' Lodge. In 2024 essential
building maintenance will affect part
of the gardens, and some of the
suggested garden walking route may
not be accessible. Occasionally parts
or all of the gardens may be closed
for safety reasons involving work by
contractors and maintenance staff.
Regret no dogs. Ask at Porters'
Lodge for wheelchair access.

GROUP OPENING

45 SAWSTON GARDENS
Sawston, CB22 3HY. *5m SE of*
Cambridge. Midway between Saffron
Walden & Cambridge on A1301.
Sun 7 July (1-5). Combined adm
£6, chd free. Home-made teas
in Mary Challis Garden, 68 High
Street. Refreshments served from
1.30-4.00pm.

NEW 20 LONDON ROAD
Linda and David Ambrose.

♦ MARY CHALLIS GARDEN
A M Challis Trust Ltd,
01223 560816,
chair@challistrust.org.uk,
www.challistrust.org.uk.

11 MILL LANE
Tim & Rosie Phillips.

22 ST MARY'S ROAD
Ann & Mike Redshaw.

10 WYNEMARES
Mr Lee Kirby.

Five gardens in this large South
Cambs village. 11 Mill Lane is an
attractive C16/C19 house with
an impressive semi-circular front
lawn edged with roses and mixed
borders, and a secluded sun-dappled
garden at the rear. The two acre
Mary Challis Garden has a tranquil
setting in the heart of the village,
with extensive lawns, wildflower
meadow, herbaceous borders,
orchard, vegetable beds, vinehouse
and beehives. 22 St Mary's Road
has a large wildlife friendly garden
overlooking SSSI meadows at the
rear, featuring colourful borders,
gravel beds, herb garden, wooded
ditch, pond, fruit trees and beehives.
10 Wynemares presents colourful
and creative plantings in a small
developing garden. New to this group
of gardens, the long rear garden at 20
London Road had a design makeover
in 2023, with winding gravel paths

and plants chosen to encourage
wildlife. Nearly all parts of the gardens
are accessible by wheelchair, with the
exception of 20 London Rd.

46 NEW 1 STATION COTTAGE
Lynn Road, Chettisham,
Ely, CB6 1RX. Mr James
Montgomery, 01353 661894,
jslmont@gmail.com. *3km N of*
Ely centre on Lynn Rd to Littleport.
4.5km S of Littleport. Take Lynn Rd
N out of Ely, through Chettisham and
go over level x-ing. Immed N of level
x-ing turn into layby for parking. **Sat**
15, Sun 16 June (1-6). Adm £5,
chd free. Home-made teas. Visits
also by arrangement Feb to Oct
for groups of 6 to 50.
Our garden is a hidden gem made up
of a formal garden with herbaceous
borders, a small pond, sheds, a
rockery and gravel bed. There are
four acres of wildflower meadow,
vegetable garden, wildlife pond, log
cabin and woodland apiary in a long
plot alongside the railway. It was
an area of sidings, but has been a
garden for the last 30 years, and
we have actively managed it since
2006 for wildlife. Dogs welcome on
leads. The formal area of garden
is accessible to wheelchairs and
scooters. The meadows have mown
paths which are uneven. Driveway to
house is uneven.

The National Garden
Scheme donated
£3,403,960 to our
nursing and health
beneficiaries from
money raised at
gardens open in
2023

GROUP OPENING

47 TOFT GARDENS
Toft, Cambridge, CB23 2RY. *8m W of Cambridge. Park on main road or near church & follow yellow signs.* **Sun 23 June (12-5). Combined adm £6, chd free. Cream teas in Toft People's Hall.**

21 COMBERTON ROAD
Mr Sheppard.

NEW 2 EVERSDEN CLOSE
Annie Wilkinson-Fenn.

THE GIG HOUSE
Jane Tebbit.

MANOR COTTAGE
Mrs Mary Paxman.

Three wonderful cottage gardens and a newly planted garden in Toft. The Gig House: cottage garden with roses, clematis, perennials, cut flower beds and vegetables. Also, plants for natural dyes, dry beds, wildflowers, a small wildlife pond, tiny orchard and plenty of places to sit. Manor Cottage: cottage garden extended and developed by the current owner over 30 yrs. Herbaceous borders, vegetable garden, greenhouse and orchard covering an acre, as well as a paddock and two wooded areas. Borders extended and replanted in 2020 when various grasses, salvias and alliums were added. 21 Comberton Road: the basic concept was conceived before moving in, calling on a wide range of sources and experiences. Four zones in 0.18 acres, 123 taxa, 450 plants; just one afternoon to view this newly planted garden. 2 Eversden Close: perennials & annuals with a pond to encourage nature and a vegetable/fruit growing area set around a 1970's bungalow.

48 TRINITY COLLEGE FELLOWS' GARDEN
Queen's Road, Cambridge, CB3 9AQ. Master and Fellows of Trinity College, www.trin.cam. ac.uk/about/gardens. *Short walk from city centre. At the Northampton St/Madingley Rd end of Queen's Rd. Close to Garret Hostel Ln.* **Sun 21 Apr (1-4). Adm £4, chd free. Light refreshments. Special dietary requirements are catered for.** Interesting historic garden of about eight acres with impressive specimen trees, mixed borders, drifts of spring bulbs and informal lawns with notable influences throughout from Fellows over the years. Across the gently flowing Bin Brook to Burrell's Field, you will find some modern planting styles and plants nestled amongst the accommodation blocks in smaller intimate gardens. Members of the Gardens Department will be on hand to answer any questions and serve homemade cakes and drinks. Plant sales are also available. Wheelchair access - some gravel paths.
♿ ❄ ☕ ⁝))

49 TRINITY HALL - WYCHFIELD SITE
Storey's Way, Cambridge, CB3 0DZ. The Master & Fellows, www.trinhall.cam.ac.uk/about/gardens/. *1m NW of city centre. Turn into Storey's Way from Madingley Rd (A1303) & follow the yellow signs. Limited on-road parking is available.* **Tue 16 Apr (11-2). Adm £5, chd free. Light refreshments in the Sports Pavilion.** A beautiful, large garden that complements the interesting and varied architecture. The Edwardian Wychfield House and its associated gardens contrast with the recent, contemporary development located off Storey's Way. Majestic trees, tulips and spring flowers on the cherry mound, shady under storey woodland planting and established lawns work together to provide an inspiring garden. Plant sale, tea and cakes. Some gravel paths and steps.
♿ ❄ ☕ ⁝))

50 TWIN TARNS
6 Pinfold Lane, Somersham, PE28 3EQ. Michael & Frances Robinson, 07938 174536, mikerobinson987@btinternet.com. *Easy access from the A14. 4m NE of St Ives. Turn onto Church St. Pinfold Ln is next to the church. Please park on Church St as access is narrow & limited.* **Sat 29, Sun 30 June (1-6). Adm £5, chd free. Cream teas. Visits also by arrangement May to Aug for groups of up to 25.** One acre wildlife garden with formal borders, kitchen garden and ponds, large rockery, mini woodland, wildflower meadow (June/July). Topiary, rose walk, greenhouses. Character bridge, veranda and treehouse. Adjacent to C13 village church.
♿ ❄ ☕ ⁝))

GROUP OPENING

51 WESTLEY WATERLESS GARDENS
Westley Waterless, CB8 0RL. *10m E of Cambridge, 5m S of Newmarket. All gardens are near the entrance to Church Ln. Parking along the Main St and part way up Church Ln.* **Sun 23 June (12.30-5.30). Combined adm £7, chd free. Home-made teas at Church Lane House.**

CHURCH LANE HOUSE
Dr Lucy Crosby, lucycrosby.vet@gmail.com. Visits also by arrangement June to Sept. Church View may also be available to visit.

CHURCH VIEW
Diana Hall, 07974 667298, boohall@icloud.com. Visits also by arrangement June to Sept. Church Lane House may also be available to visit.

NEW 41 MAIN STREET
Maurice Biggins.

Church Lane House is just under an acre in size, comprising a wildlife pond, herbaceous borders, cut flowers, dye plants, orchard wildflower meadow, Victorian style greenhouse and kitchen garden, plus chickens, guinea pigs and bees. This is a family friendly garden with plenty of seating areas to take in the views. Church View is a country garden which inc a small flower farm. There are many old fashioned scented roses, both shrub and climbing, plus herbaceous borders, raised growing beds and two polytunnels. The garden features a wildlife pond and flowering plant-filled pots. The farm growing area changes season by season. No. 41 is a contemporary garden inspired by Piet Oudolf and Beth Chatto. Designed for wildlife, with year-round interest, including Prairie style borders, pond, topiary and kitchen gardens. Wheelchair access is mostly on grass and some paving areas.
♿ ❄ ☕ ⁝))

52 WILLOW HOLT
Willow Hall Lane, Thorney, Peterborough, PE6 0QN. Angie & Jonathan Jones. *4m E of Peterborough. Turn S from A47 between Thorney and Eye. Sign post Willow Holt. Go 1.8m, we are on the R.* **Sun 26, Mon 27 May (11-5). Adm £5, chd free. Tea.**

Two acres, part farm field and part old gravel diggings were combined as a building plot in 1960. In 1992 the current owners began a thirty year transformation from nettle bed and local tip to a peaceful garden of mature trees, wildflower meadow, wildlife ponds, bridges, scrap metal sculptures and a varied and impressive collection of plants and shrubs. Largely accessible for wheelchair users with assistance.

  ♿ ❀ ☕ ⛽ ⏺)))

53 THE WINDMILL

10 Cambridge Road, Impington, CB24 9NU. Pippa & Steve Temple, 07775 446443, mill.impington@ntlworld.com, www.impingtonmill.org. *2½ m N of Cambridge. Off A14 at J32, B1049 to Histon, L into Cambridge Rd at T-lights, follow Cambridge Rd round to R, the Windmill is approx 400yds on L.* **Visits by arrangement Mar to Oct. Adm £7.50, chd free. Light refreshments inc coffee, tea, wine and nibbles by arrangement.**
A previously romantic wilderness of 1½ acres surrounding windmill, now filled with bulbs, perennial beds, pergolas, bog gardens and herb bank. Secret paths and wild areas with thuggish roses maintain the romance. Millstone seating area in smouldering borders contrasts with the pastel colours of the remainder of the garden. Also 'Pond Life' seat, 'Tree God' fountain and amazing compost area. The Windmill (an C18 smock on C19 tower on C17 base on C16 foundations) is being restored.

  ♿ ❀ 🚗 ☕

54 WRIGHTS FARM

Tilbrook Road, Kimbolton, Huntingdon, PE28 0JW. Russell & Hetty Dean. *13m SW of Huntingdon. ¼ m W of Kimbolton on the B645. Do not follow sat nav.* **Sat 29, Sun 30 June, Sat 31 Aug, Sun 1 Sept (11-4). Adm £6, chd free. Home-made teas.**
Rural setting taking advantage of countryside views. Varied borders with bee and butterfly friendly planting. Formal walled vegetable garden with raised beds, potting shed and greenhouses. Mediterranean style courtyard with dry garden. Newly designed and planted front garden with tropical greenhouse. New courtyard garden to annexe with raised borders and green roof seating area. Predominantly flat, but with some gravel surfaces.

  ♿ 🐕 ❀ ☕ ⏺)))

20 London Road, Sawston Gardens

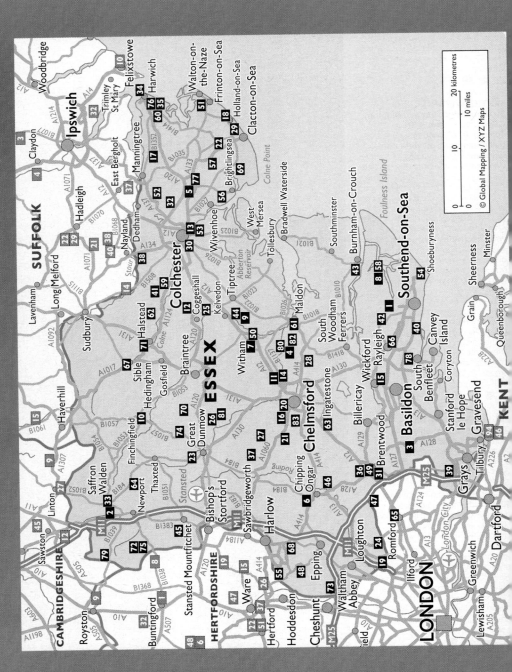

ESSEX

VOLUNTEERS

County Organiser
Susan Copeland
07534 006179
susan.copeland@ngs.org.uk

Deputy County Organiser
Victoria Kennedy 07801 039688
victoria.kennedy@ngs.org.uk

County Treasurer
Richard Steers
07392 426490
steers123@aol.com

**Publicity & Social Media
Co-ordinator**
Debbie Thomson
07759 226579
debbie.thomson@ngs.org.uk

**Publicity & Social Media
Assistant**
Alan Gamblin 07720 446797
alan.gamblin@ngs.org.uk

Booklet Co-ordinator
Doug Copeland 07483 839387
doug.copeland@ngs.org.uk

Assistant County Organisers
Tricia Brett 01255 870415
tricia.brett@ngs.org.uk

Avril & Roger Cole-Jones
01245 225726
randacj@gmail.com

Lesley Gamblin 07801 445299
lesley.gamblin@ngs.org.uk

Frances Vincent 07766 707379
frances.vincent@ngs.org.uk

Talks
Ed Fairey 07780 685634
ed@faireyassociates.co.uk

County Photographer
Caroline Cassell 07973 551196
caroline.cassell@ngs.org.uk

OPENING DATES

All entries subject to change. For latest information check **www.ngs.org.uk**
Extended openings are shown at the beginning of the month.
Map locator numbers are shown to the right of each garden name.

January

Sunday 28th
♦ Green Island | 32

February

Snowdrop Openings

Wednesday 14th
Dragons | 21

Friday 16th
Ulting Wick | 80

Saturday 17th
Horkesley Hall | 38

Sunday 18th
Grove Lodge | 33

Sunday 25th
Brookfield | 11
Grove Lodge | 33

March

Saturday 2nd
♦ Beth Chatto's Plants & Gardens | 5

Wednesday 27th
Ulting Wick | 80

April

Every Thursday
Barnards Farm | 3

Every Thursday and Friday
Feeringbury Manor | 25

Sunday 14th
2 Cedar Avenue | 15

Sunday 28th
Bucklers Farmhouse | 12
♦ Green Island | 32
Peacocks | 63
Ulting Wick | 80
Writtle University College | 83

May

Every Thursday
Barnards Farm | 3

Every Thursday and Friday
Feeringbury Manor | 25

Sunday 5th
The Mount | 55

Monday 6th
Furzelea | 28

Sunday 12th
Blake Hall | 6
NEW Cannock Mill Cohousing Gardens | 13
NEW Connaught House | 18
NEW 9 Gainsford Avenue | 29

Sunday 19th
Longyard Cottage | 48
May Cottage | 51

Wednesday 22nd
NEW ♦ St Osyth Priory | 69

Thursday 23rd
Oak Farm | 59

Sunday 26th
Bassetts | 4
Chippins | 17
The Gates | 31
Laurel Cottage | 45

June

Every Thursday
Barnards Farm | 3

Every Thursday and Friday
Feeringbury Manor | 25

Saturday 1st
Brookfield | 11
Isabella's Garden | 40

Sunday 2nd
Brookfield | 11
Furzelea | 28
Isabella's Garden | 40
Jankes House | 41
1 Whitehouse Cottages | 82

Tuesday 4th
Braxted Park Estate | 9
Caynton Cottage | 14

Wednesday 5th
Caynton Cottage	14
8 Dene Court	20

Thursday 6th
Caynton Cottage	14

Saturday 8th
Allways	1
Fairwinds	24
Thatched Cottage	77

Sunday 9th
Oak Farm	59
Over Hall	62
Saling Hall	70
Silver Birches	73
Thatched Cottage	77

Friday 14th
NEW Old Timbers	61

Saturday 15th
NEW The Garden Studio	30
NEW 30 Queens Road	66

Sunday 16th
NEW The Garden Studio	30
NEW 30 Queens Road	66
Sheepcote Green House	72
NEW Spa Cottage	75
Walnut Tree Cottage	81

Tuesday 18th
NEW 160 Chignal Road	16
8 Dene Court	20
Dragons	21
NEW Moynes Farm	57

Wednesday 19th
NEW Moynes Farm	57

Saturday 22nd
NEW 17 Elm Road	22

Sunday 23rd
2 Cedar Avenue	15
Fudlers Hall	27
NEW 83 Harwich Road	35
The Mount	55
Peacocks	63
NEW Stowford House	76
Two Cottages	79

Tuesday 25th
NEW 4 Boarded Row	8
NEW 4 New Row	58

Wednesday 26th
Keeway	43

Saturday 29th
Brick House	10
Mikri Ellada	54
18 Pettits Boulevard, RM1	65

Sunday 30th
Barnards Farm	3
Chippins	17
Keeway	43
18 Pettits Boulevard, RM1	65
Two Cottages	79

July

Every Thursday
Barnards Farm	3

Every Thursday and Friday
Feeringbury Manor	25

Tuesday 2nd
8 Dene Court	20

Wednesday 3rd
Little Myles	46
Long House Plants	47

Saturday 6th
9 Malyon Road	50
Pear Trees	64

Sunday 7th
262 Hatch Road	36
9 Malyon Road	50
Pear Trees	64
Two Cottages	79

Wednesday 10th
Little Myles	46
Oak Farm	59

Thursday 11th
Ulting Wick	80

Saturday 13th
NEW The Folly	26
207 Mersea Road	53
69 Rundells - The Secret Garden	68

Sunday 14th
NEW The Folly	26
Furzelea	28
Harwich Gardens	34
1 Whitehouse Cottages	82

Tuesday 16th
NEW 160 Chignal Road	16
8 Dene Court	20
Dragons	21

Saturday 20th
9 Malyon Road	50

Sunday 21st
262 Hatch Road	36
9 Malyon Road	50
NEW The Old Rectory	60
291 Thundersley Park Road	78

Monday 22nd
291 Thundersley Park Road	78

Wednesday 24th
8 Dene Court	20

Saturday 27th
Isabella's Garden	40

Sunday 28th
The Delves	19
Isabella's Garden	40

August

Every Thursday
Barnards Farm	3

Sunday 4th
The Mount	55

Wednesday 7th
Long House Plants	47

Sunday 11th
Elmbridge Mill	23

Tuesday 13th
8 Dene Court	20

Friday 16th
NEW Old Timbers	61

Saturday 24th
207 Mersea Road	53

Sunday 25th
207 Mersea Road	53

Monday 26th
Ulting Wick	80

Wednesday 28th
8 Dene Court	20

Friday 30th
Ulting Wick	80

Saturday 31st
NEW 30 Queens Road	66

September

Every Thursday to Thursday 12th
Barnards Farm	3

Every Thursday and Friday
Feeringbury Manor	25

Sunday 1st
Barnards Farm	3
Laurel Cottage	45
NEW 30 Queens Road	66

Wednesday 4th
Long House Plants	47

Saturday 7th
Loxley House	49
Moverons	56
18 Pettits Boulevard, RM1	65

Stowford House

THE GARDENS

1 ALLWAYS

14 St Andrews Road, Rochford, SS4 1NP. Ms Liz Grant. *Traverse down St Andrews Rd. The blue house can be found 100m on the R.* **Sat 8 June (11-4). Adm £5, chd free. Light refreshments inc teas, coffees, cold drinks & home-made cakes.**

A cottage style garden of a grade two listed 1930's home. A mature wisteria greets visitors on the front of the cottage. The rear garden has an area of lawn flanked by perennial borders with a viburnum arch leading to an attractive pond with Monet style bridge, pebbled beach area and a mature Indian Bean tree. A new wildlife pond and bog garden has been created in 2022 in the woodland area. After recently discovering some old steps leading down to the diverted River Roach, a new woodland area will be open for 2024

2 NEW ◆ AUDLEY END HOUSE

Off London Road, Saffron Walden, CB11 4JF. English Heritage. *1m W of Saffron Walden on B1383 (M11 exit 8 or 10).* **For NGS: Evening opening Wed 18 Sept (5.30-7.30). Adm £15. Pre-booking essential, please phone 07721 813442, email alison.makosch@english-heritage.org.uk or visit www. english-heritage.org.uk/visit/ places/audley-end-house-and-gardens/events/ for information & booking. Light refreshments. The café will be open where you may purchase refreshments before the start of the tour. For other opening times and information, please phone, email or visit garden website.**

Sweeping C18 parkland wraps around C19 formality in the parterre. Explore the enchanting Elysian Garden and the 'Capability' Brown landscape setting for the house, still featuring many of its original trees. The tour will take in the kitchen garden where fruit trees are still full of fresh produce and autumn harvests of pumpkins and squash.

3 BARNARDS FARM

Brentwood Road, West Horndon, CM13 3FY. Bernard & Sylvia Holmes & The Christabella Charitable Trust, 07504 210405, vanessa@barnardsfarm.eu, www.barnardsfarm.eu. *What3words app - tulip.folds.statue. 5m S of Brentwood. On A128 1½ m S of A127 Halfway House flyover. From junc continue S on A128 under the railway bridge. Garden on R just past bridge. Please use postcode CM13 3FY.* **Every Thur 4 Apr to 12 Sept (11-4.30). Adm £10, chd free. Light refreshments. Sun 30 June, Sun 1 Sept (1-5.30). Adm £14, chd free. Pre-booking essential, please visit www.ngs.org.uk for information & booking. Visits also by arrangement Feb to Oct for groups of 30+.**

So much to explore! Climb the Belvedere for the wider view and take the train for a woodland adventure. Spring bulbs and blossom, summer beds and borders, ponds, lakes and streams, walled vegetable plot. 'Japanese garden', sculptures grand and quirky enhance and delight. See the new Talia-May Avenue and Angel sculptures. Sorry, no dogs except guide dogs. Ample free parking. Barnards Miniature Railway rides (BMR): Separate charges apply. Sunday extras: Bernard's Sculpture tour 2.30pm Car collection. 1920s Cycle shop. Archery. Model T Ford Rides. Season Tickets cost £30. Aviators welcome (PPO). Picnics welcome. Wheelchair accessible WC. Golf Buggy tours available.

4 BASSETTS

Bassetts Lane, Little Baddow, Chelmsford, CM3 4BZ. Mrs Margaret Chalmers, 07940 179572, magschalmers@btinternet.com. *1m down, Tofts Chase becomes Bassetts Ln. Yellow house on L, wooden gates, red brick wall. From Spring Elms Ln go down Bassetts Ln, L at the bottom of the hill. Cont for ¼ m.* **Sun 26 May (10-5). Adm £5, chd free. Visits also by arrangement 3 June to 13 Oct.**

A two acre garden, tennis court, swimming pool surrounding an early C17 house (not open)with plants for year-round interest set on gently sloping ground with lovely distant views of the Essex countryside. Shrub borders and mature ornamental trees, an orchard and two natural

ponds. Many places to sit and relax. No refreshments but bring a picnic and enjoy the views. Please check wheelchair access with garden owner.

5 ◆ BETH CHATTO'S PLANTS & GARDENS

Elmstead Market, Colchester, CO7 7DB. Beth Chatto's Plants & Gardens, 01206 822007, customer@bethchatto.co.uk, www.bethchatto.co.uk. *¼ m E of Elmstead Market. On A133 Colchester to Clacton Rd in village of Elmstead Market.* **For NGS: Sat 2 Mar, Wed 9 Oct (10-4). Adm £13.50, chd free. Light refreshments at Chatto's Tearoom. Inc sandwiches, paninis, soup, salads, cakes, hot & cold beverages. For other opening times and information, please phone, email or visit garden website.**

Internationally famous gardens, inc dry, damp, shade, reservoir and woodland areas. The result of over 60 years of hard work and application of the huge body of plant knowledge possessed by Beth Chatto and her husband Andrew. Visitors cannot fail to be affected by the peace and beauty of the garden. Beth is renowned internationally for her books, her gardens and her influence on the world of gardening and plants. Please visit website for up to date visiting details and pre-booking. Picnic area available in the adjacent field. Disabled WC and parking. Wheelchair access around all of the gardens on gravel or grass.

6 BLAKE HALL

Bobbingworth, CM5 0DG. Mr & Mrs H Capel Cure, www.blakehall.co.uk. *10m W of Chelmsford. Just off A414 between Four Wantz r'about in Ongar & Talbot r'about in N Weald. Signed on A414.* **Sun 12 May (10.30-4). Adm £6, chd free. Home-made teas in C17 barn.**

25 acres of mature gardens within the historic setting of Blake Hall (not open). Arboretum with broad variety of specimen and spectacular ancient trees. Lawns overlooking countryside. With its centuries old wisteria, alliums, tulips and spring blossom, May is a wonderful time of the year to visit the gardens at Blake Hall. Some gravel paths.

7 BLUNTS HALL
Blunts Hall Drive, Witham,
CM8 1LX. Alan & Lesley
Gamblin, 07720 446797,
alan.gamblin@ngs.org.uk. *Blunts
Hall Drive is off of Blunts Hall Rd.*
**Visits by arrangement 12 Feb to
23 Aug for groups of 10 to 30.
No visits between Feb 22- Mar
9. Weekdays only after Mar 9th.
Adm £10, chd free. Home-made
teas. Discuss refreshments when
booking.**
Restored three acre Victorian garden.
Courtyard garden and terrace leading
down to lawns with re-instated
parterre surrounded by herbaceous
borders. Orchard with old and new
fruit trees and vegetable plot. Listed
Ancient Monument. Woodland walk
around spring-fed pond. Fernery.
Steps lead down to front lawns
recently planted with a yew avenue.
Snowdrops and aconites in early
spring. Specimen trees.

❀ ☕))

8 NEW **4 BOARDED ROW**
East End, Paglesham, Rochford,
SS4 2EN. Anna Watson. *East End,
Paglesham 5m NE of Rochford.
Park at the field opp the Plough
and Sail Pub, walk past the red*
*phone box, through the white gate,
down the private road and the
garden is on your L.* **Tue 25 June
(11-4.30). Combined adm with 4
New Row £5, chd free. Teas will
be available in the Mission Hall
which is a couple of mins from
car park. It will be clearly signed.**
A very small cottage style garden, with
brick path, raised vegetable beds,
summerhouse and patio overlooking
a small wildlife pond and winding path
with borders leading to a patio by
the house. Lots of insect life. Sit on
the patio or in the summerhouse and
enjoy the tranquillity.

☕

Ulting Wick

© Marcus Harpur

9 BRAXTED PARK ESTATE
Braxted Park Road, Great
Braxted, Witham, CM8 3EN.
Mr Duncan & Mrs Nicky Clark,
www.braxtedpark.com. *A12 N,*
by-pass Witham. Turn L to Rivenhall
& Silver End by pub called the Fox
(now closed) At T junc turn R to Gt
Braxted & Witham. Follow brown
sign to Braxted Pk (NOT Braxted
Golf Course). Down drive to Car
Park. **Tue 4 June (10-3.30). Adm**
£7.50, chd £5. Cream teas in
the Orangery. Light lunches and
afternoon tea available.
Idyllic Braxted Park, a prestigious
events venue, welcomes gardeners
to enjoy its tranquil surroundings.
Extensive borders of perennials,
shrubs and roses abound. Walled
Garden features themed gardens
radiating from the central fountain
and parasol mulberry trees. Themes
inc a Black and White Garden,
Italian Garden and English Garden,
each containing a wealth of planting
inspiration. A native wildflower
meadow extends from the house (not
open) towards the lake. The Orangery
will be open for Ploughmans lunches
and of course the obligatory cake,
by the slice and to 'take home'. Tea,

coffee or a glass of wine available.
Head Gardener, Andrea Cooper, will
be on hand to answer questions and
guided tours for a further donation of
£5pp payable upon the day.

& ✿ 🚗 ☕))

10 BRICK HOUSE
The Green, Finchingfield,
CM7 4JS. Mr Graham & Mrs
Susan Tobbell. *9m NW of Braintree.*
Brick House in the centre of the
picturesque village of Finchingfield,
at the Xrds of the B1053 & B1057
in rural NW Essex. **Sat 29 June**
(2-6). Adm £6, chd free. Home-
made teas. Coffee, soft drinks,
bottled water & a variety of cakes
available.
This recently renovated period
property and garden covers 1½
acres, with a brook running through
the middle. The garden features
contemporary sculptures, and several
distinct planting styles; most notably
a hidden scented cottage-style
garden, a crinkle-crankle walled area
with an oriental feel and some rather
glorious high summer herbaceous
borders inspired by the New Perennial
Movement. Modern marble sculptures

by Paul Vanstone add drama and
contrast to the soft landscaping.
Garden is professionally designed to
be a calming space.

🐾 🐈 ☕))

11 BROOKFIELD
Church Road, Boreham, CM3 3EB.
Bob & Linda Taylor. *4m NE*
Chelmsford. Take B1137 Boreham
village, turn R into Church Rd at Lion
Inn. In approx ¼m turning on R after
The Chase marked 58-76 Church
Rd. Pedestrians & disabled access
only - please park & walk down. **Sun**
25 Feb (11-4); Sat 1, Sun 2 June
(2-5). Adm £5, chd free. Home-
made teas.
The gardens and meadow at
Brookfield cover over three acres.
Come in February to enjoy snowdrops
and other early spring delights and in
June island beds and a wall border
inc many roses amongst perennials,
whilst the meadow is bright with
buttercups. Other features inc pond,
shrub bank and a stunning vegetable
garden with raised beds and a soft
fruit area. Wheelchair access to main
part of garden. Partial access to
meadow.

& ✿ ☕))

4 New Row

12 BUCKLERS FARMHOUSE
Buckleys Lane, Coggeshall, Colchester, CO6 1SB. Ann Bartleet, ann@bartleet.co.uk. *1½ m E of Coggeshall. 1m N of A120 via Salmons Ln.* **Sun 28 Apr (1.30-4.30). Adm £6, chd free. Home-made teas. Refreshments can be taken outside or in the traditional Essex Barn. Visits also by arrangement 1 May to 15 June.**
Traditional country garden, with blowsy borders, yew hedges, topiary and a little knot garden. A very tranquil, magical place, with two ponds and a pool. In the spring we have about 1,000 tulips. Later, there is a terrace full of succulents, almost no room for sitting! This two acre garden has been created by the owners over the last 50 years. There is gravel, but about 50% of the garden is accessible with a wheelchair.

&. ✿ ☕

13 NEW CANNOCK MILL COHOUSING GARDENS
Old Heath Road, Colchester, CO2 8AA. Cannock Mill Cohousing, cannockmillcohousing.co.uk/. *In SE Colchester. Cannock Mill is easily visible on Old Heath Rd. On road parking, just over 1m from Colchester city centre. On S1 and S9 bus routes (Scarletts Rd stop).* **Sun 12 May (11-4). Adm £5, chd free. Home-made teas.**
With an emphasis on biodiversity, our two acre sloping site inc both wild and cultivated areas, some private but mostly communal areas, some terraced, some flat, rain gardens, deep green roofs and porous roads as part of a SuDS scheme, grasses - some mown, some not - with flowers, fruit and vegetables all grown for our community meals, as well as a large mill pond and an embryonic bog garden.

✿ ☕))

14 CAYNTON COTTAGE
Church Road, Boreham, Chelmsford, CM3 3EF. Les & Lynn Mann. *4m NE Chelmsford. Take B1137 Boreham Village, turn into Church Rd at the Lion Inn. 50mtrs on L.* **Tue 4, Wed 5, Thur 6 June (1-5). Adm £4, chd free. Home-made teas. Gluten free cakes, decaf tea and coffee and a selection of fruit teas also available.**
A traditional cottage garden designed and planted by the owners since 2013 from a neglected and overgrown plot surrounding a C15 thatched cottage

(not open). Planted with a good selection of shrubs and perennials for maximum all year interest with a small wildlife pond and dry stream. It is ever changing as the plants grow and mature to fill the space, with new features added each season.

✿ ☕))

15 2 CEDAR AVENUE
Wickford, SS12 9DT. Mr Chris Cheswright. *Off Nevendon Rd, 5 mins from Wickford High St. From Basildon on A132 turn 1st R onto Nevendon Rd at BP r'bout, R onto Park Dr, 2nd R Cedar Ave.* **Sun 14 Apr, Sun 23 June (11-4). Adm £6, chd free. Light refreshments. Homemade cakes and pastries.**
A large town garden with a dry front garden, pots arranged on a large patio with bulbs followed by tropical style planting. Collections of hostas, succulents, carnivorous plants, alpines, hardy *Bromeliads* and *Coleus* are on display in appropriate seasons outdoors and in greenhouses. Planting of trees, perennials, grasses with spring bulbs in the lawn. Areas for wildlife and a pond. Access via side of house. The majority of the garden is accessible via a flat lawn area.

&. ✿ ☕))

16 NEW 160 CHIGNAL ROAD
Chelmsford, CM1 2JD. Johanna Chapman. *W of Chelmsford take A1060, Roxwell Rd. R at t-lights into Chignal Rd we are on the R in the set of semi-detached bungalows not far past Melbourne Ave.* **Tue 18 June, Tue 16 July (12-4). Combined adm with 8 Dene Court £6, chd free. Light refreshments. Open nearby Dragons.**
A relatively new garden transformed from a rough piece of grass. The five year old garden goes from floral and leafy planting slowly transforming into vegetables and back to the green hues, benefiting from well thought out seating areas to enjoy the garden throughout the seasons. Wisteria covered deck area, summerhouse and a small greenhouse. The garden inc a small pond.

☕

17 CHIPPINS
Heath Road, Bradfield, CO11 2UZ. Kit & Ceri Leese, 01255 870730, ceriandkit@gmail.com. *3m E of Manningtree. Take A137 from Manningtree Stn turn L opp garage. Take 1st R towards Clacton. At*

Radio Mast turn L into Bradfield continue through village. Bungalow opp primary sch on R. **Sun 26 May, Sun 30 June (11-4). Adm £5, chd free. Visits also by arrangement 25 May to 31 July for groups of 5 to 35.**
Artist's and plantaholics' paradise packed with interest. Hostas, Iris and *Astrantia* in spring. Stream and wildlife pond with Horace the Huge! Summer is an explosion of colour with daylilies, rambling roses, Salvias and Canna. An abundance of tubs, hanging baskets and anything else that can fit a petunia plant. Kit is a landscape artist and printmaker, pictures always on display. Afternoon tea with delicious homemade cakes is also available for small parties (min of 5) on specific days if booked in advance.

&. ✿ 🚗 ☕))

18 NEW CONNAUGHT HOUSE
45 The Esplanade, Holland on Sea, Clacton-on-Sea, CO15 5TU. Jacquie Dixon. *Last but one house on The Esplanade. Located at Holland Haven facing the sea. Blue badge parking. Car park is 0.2m away, although some parking on front lawn.* **Sun 12 May (11-4). Combined adm with 9 Gainsford Avenue £5, chd free.**
A small coastal garden facing the North Sea in Holland on Sea, Essex. This is a private and secluded garden with sun-trap seating areas, pond, hexagonal greenhouse, dry garden/shingle planted herbaceous perennial borders, shady garden, circular lawn, pergola, feature Cotinus tree and brick built patio detail. Seafront location with beach promenade 20 metres away.

🐕 D))

152,684 people were able to access guidance on what to expect when a person is dying through the National Garden Scheme support for Hospice UK this year

19 THE DELVES

37 Turpins Lane, Chigwell, IG8 8AZ.
Fabrice Aru & Martin Thurston,
02085 050739, martin.thurston@
talktalk.net. *Between Woodford &
Epping. Chigwell, 2m from N Circular
Rd at Woodford, follow the signs for
Chigwell (A113) through Woodford
Bridge into Manor Rd & turn L, Bus
275 & W14.* **Sun 28 July, Sun 15
Sept (11-6.30). Adm £4, chd free.
Visits also by arrangement 1 May to
27 Oct for groups of up to 10.**
An unexpected hidden, magical, part-
walled garden showing how much
can be achieved in a small space. An
oasis of calm with densely planted
rich, lush foliage, tree ferns, hostas,
topiary and an abundance of well
maintained shrubs complemented by
a small pond and three water features
designed for year-round interest.

20 8 DENE COURT

Chignall Road, Chelmsford,
CM1 2JQ. Mrs Sheila Chapman,
01245 266156. *W of Chelmsford
(Parkway). Take A1060 Roxwell
Rd for 1m. Turn R at T-lights into
Chignall Rd. Dene Court 3rd exit
on R. Parking in Chignall Rd.* **Wed
5 June (12-4). Adm £4, chd free.
Tue 18 June (12-4). Combined
adm with 160 Chignal Road £6,
chd free. Open nearby Dragons.
Tue 2 July (12-4). Adm £4, chd
free. Tue 16 July (12-4). Combined
adm with 160 Chignal Road £6,
chd free. Open nearby Dragons.
Wed 24 July, Tue 13, Wed 28 Aug
(12-4). Adm £4, chd free. Visits
also by arrangement 5 June to 28
Aug for groups of 10 to 50.**
Beautifully maintained and designed
as a compact garden. Owner is
well-known RHS gold medal-winning
exhibitor (now retired). Circular lawn,
long pergola and walls festooned with
roses and climbers. Large selection
of unusual clematis. Densely-planted
colour coordinated perennials add
interest from June to Sept in this
immaculate garden.

21 DRAGONS

Boyton Cross, Chelmsford,
CM1 4LS. Mrs Margot
Grice, 01245 248651,
margot@snowdragons.co.uk.
*3m W of Chelmsford. On A1060.
½ m W of The Hare Pub.* **Wed 14
Feb (11-3). Light refreshments.
Tue 18 June, Tue 16 July (11-4).
Open nearby 8 Dene Court. Adm
£5, chd free. Refreshments only**

available for by arrangement
visits and Feb opening. **Visits also
by arrangement 7 Feb to 15 Oct
for groups of 10+.**
Galanthus are a passion. A
plantswoman's ¾ acre garden,
planted to encourage wildlife.
Sumptuous colour-themed borders
with striking plant combinations,
featuring specimen plants, fernery,
clematis and grasses. Meandering
paths lead to ponds, patio, scree
garden and small vegetable garden.
Two summerhouses, one overlooking
stream and farmland.

22 NEW 17 ELM ROAD

Little Clacton, Clacton-On-Sea,
CO16 9LP. Stephen Matthews &
Martin Picker. *4m from Clacton
On Sea. From the A133 at Weeley
r'about, take 1st exit B1033. On next
r'about take 3rd exit Weeley By Pass
B1441. Follow road for 2.6m. Turn R
onto Elm Rd. On road parking.* **Sat
22 June (11-4). Adm £4, chd free.
Home-made teas. Coffee and a
selection of cakes also available.**
A compact country garden beautifully
maintained as a modern take on a
cottage style garden. Deep borders
of herbaceous plants, grasses,
roses, ferns, shrubs and trees. Many
unusual. An area of succulents and
cacti, fruit trees and vegetables. A
goldfish pond and aviary with canaries
and finches. Set in a village location
surrounded by fields.

*In 2023 we
awarded over
£260,000 in
Community Garden
Grants, supporting
86 community
garden projects*

23 ELMBRIDGE MILL

Little Easton, Dunmow, CM6 2HZ.
Cilla Swan. *Little Easton. N of Great
Dunmow, B184.* **Sun 11 Aug (12-4).
Adm £5, chd free. Home-made
teas.**
This beautiful and tranquil garden
last opened for the National Garden
Scheme in 2008. A romantic, country
garden full of topiary, unusual plants
and specimen trees. Elmbridge Mill
(not open) with mill stream, one side
flowing under the house, and the River
Chelmer on the other. Explore the
orchard, productive vegetable garden
and walk down to the mill pond.

24 FAIRWINDS

Chapel Lane, Chigwell
Row, IG7 6JJ. Sue & David
Coates, 07731 796467,
scoates@forest.org.uk. *2m SE of
Chigwell. Grange Hill Tube turn R at
exit, 10-15 mins walk uphill. Nr M25
J26. From N Circular Waterworks
r'about, signed Chigwell. Fork R
for Manor/Lambourne Rd. Park in
Lodge Close Car Park. 2 blue badge
holders can park by the house.
Please display blue badge.* **Sat 8
June (2-5). Adm £5, chd free.
Home-made teas. Visits also
by arrangement 5 Feb to 6 Sept
for groups of 10 to 20. Adm inc
refreshments.**
Gravelled front garden and three
differently styled back garden spaces
with planting changes every year.
Established wildflower meadow in
main lawn. Meander, sit, relax and
enjoy. Beyond the rustic fence, lies
the wildlife pond and vegetable plot.
Planting influenced by Beth Chatto,
Penelope Hobhouse, Christopher
Lloyd and Piet Oudolf. Happy
insects in bee house, bug houses,
log piles and bantam hens. Newts
in pond. There be dragons a plenty.
Wheelchair access via wood chip
paths in woodland. May require
assistance.

25 FEERINGBURY MANOR

Coggeshall Road, Feering,
CO5 9RB. Mr & Mrs Giles
Coode-Adams, 01376 561946,
seca@btinternet.com. *Between
Feering & Coggeshall on Coggeshall
Rd, 1m from Feering village.* **Every
Thur and Fri 4 Apr to 26 July (10-
4). Every Thur and Fri 5 Sept to
11 Oct (10-4). Adm £6, chd free.
Visits also by arrangement 4 Apr
to 11 Oct for groups of up to 30.**

Donation to Feering Church.
There is always plenty to see in this peaceful 10 acre garden with two ponds and River Blackwater. Jewelled lawn in early April then spectacular tulips and blossom lead on to a huge number of different and colourful plants, many unusual, culminating in a purple explosion of michaelmas daisies in late Sept. No wheelchair access to arboretum, steep slope.

♿ 🐕 ⛴

26 NEW **THE FOLLY**
Braintree Road, Felsted, Dunmow, CM6 3DN. Miss Claudine Nuss, claudine10@btinternet.com. *10 m N of Chelmsford off the B1417 next to Felsted Preparatory Sch.* **Evening opening Sat 13 July (6-10). Sun 14 July (11.30-4). Adm £6, chd free. Cakes, tea and coffee. Wine and Pimm's also available (13th July only). Visits also by arrangement 20 July to 21 July for groups of 10 to 20.**
This is a small garden which has a mix between classic English country border alongside a more formal Italian element at the rear of the garden after the lawned area. There are many seating areas in both sunny spots and in shady areas. The garden benefits from privacy created by large trees in neighbouring gardens. A very old olive tree imported from Italy is the main focus in the formal area. The garden is on one level and easily accessible for wheelchairs.

♿ 🍵 »)

27 **FUDLERS HALL**
Fox Road, Mashbury, CM1 4TJ. Mr & Mrs A J Meacock. *7m NW of Chelmsford. Chelmsford take A1060, R into Chignal Rd. ½ m turn L to Chignal St James. Approx 5m, 2nd R into Fox Rd signed Gt Waltham. Fudlers From Gt Waltham. Take Barrack Ln for 3m.* **Sun 23 June (2-5). Adm £6, chd free. Home-made teas.**
Award winning, romantic two acre garden surrounding C17 farmhouse with lovely views. Many long herbaceous borders, ropes and pergolas festooned with rambling, perfumed, old fashioned roses. The entire garden has been designed and planted by the current owners over 45 years and is now a quintessential example of an English country garden. Wheelchair access, gravel drive and 30ft path to level lawns. Wonderful views across Chelmer Valley. Two new flower beds, many roses. 500 year old yew tree.

Wheelchair access: gravel farmyard and 30ft path to gardens, all of which is level lawn.

♿ 🚗 🍵

28 **FURZELEA**
Bicknacre Road, Danbury, CM3 4JR. Avril & Roger Cole-Jones, 01245 225726, randacj@gmail.com. *4m E of Chelmsford, 4m W of Maldon. S off A414 in Danbury. At village centre S into Mayes Ln. 1st R. Past Cricketers Pub, L on to Bicknacre Rd. Use NT car park on L. Garden 50 m on R, or parking 200 m past on L. Use NT Common paths from back of car park.* **Mon 6 May, Sun 2 June, Sun 14 July, Sun 15 Sept (11-5). Adm £6, chd free. Home-made teas. Visits also by arrangement 15 Apr to 1 Oct for groups of 15 to 50.**
Country garden of just under an acre designed, planted and maintained over time to showcase the seasons with colour, scent, texture and form. Paths lead through archways and box hedging to lawns and flowerbeds amassed with seasonal planting of shrubs, roses, and herbaceous perennials, bulbs and dahlias. Tulips, Salvias and grasses of particular interest along with many unusual plants. Black and White Garden plus exotics and many unusual plants add to the visitors interest. Short walk to Danbury Country Park and Lakes and short drive to RHS Hyde Hall Plants and metal plant supports are for sale.

✿ 🚗 🍵 »)

29 NEW **9 GAINSFORD AVENUE**
Clacton-On-Sea, CO15 5AT. Zoe Pink. *Close to the Eastcliff playing fields. A133 from Colchester. Next r'about after Tesco, take L onto St. Johns Rd. Approx 1m, turn R on to Holland Rd and L on to Gainsford Ave. Street parking.* **Sun 12 May (11-4). Combined adm with Connaught House £5, chd free. Home-made teas.**
A compact sun trap garden situated in the residential area of Gainsford Avenue. This 1950's semi-detached bungalow has been lovingly renovated, along with the garden in 2021. The garden is a 'lawn-free' garden, with herbaceous perennials, trees, features and multiple patios. Planted in colours of pink, purple and green-grey, the garden is alive with bee and butterfly activity. There are steps into the main garden, but it is all viewable from the main patio.

♿ 🐕 Ⓓ 🍵 »)

30 NEW **THE GARDEN STUDIO**
30 Gladwin Road, Colchester, CO2 7HS. Andrea & Kevin, www.andreaparsons.co.uk. *1m from Colchester centre. The Garden Studio is easily found with postcode. There is plenty of street parking.* **Sat 15, Sun 16 June (10.30-5). Adm £5, chd free. Light refreshments. Home-made cakes, teas & cold drinks.**
This beautiful south facing town garden has evolved over the years from family garden to studio garden. A backdrop of large trees in the neighbouring gardens frames the view, beech hedges and clipped yew makes the garden feel more extensive than it is. A stunning artists studio is hidden amongst rich planting, shade and sun loving plants surround focal points and lovely sitting areas. There is wheelchair access to all areas of the garden.

♿ ✿ Ⓓ 🍵 »)

31 **THE GATES**
London Road Cemetery, London Road, Brentwood, CM14 4QW. Ms Mary Yiannoullou, www.frontlinepartnership.org. *At the rear of the cemetery. Enter the Cemetery (opp Tesco Express). Drive to the rear of the cemetery, our garden is on L. Limited parking within but plenty on the surrounding roads.* **Sun 26 May (11-3). Adm £4, chd free. Home-made teas at tea hut with covered seating and indoor shop with seating. A selection of home-made cakes and bacon rolls.**
A horticultural project that offers local citizens, inc vulnerable adults, an opportunity to develop new skills within a horticultural setting. Greenhouses and allotments for raising bedding plants, educational workshops and growing fruit and vegetables. Walks through the Woodland Dell and Sensory area. Large variety of plants and produce for sale. Our ethos is reclaim and recycle - everything on site has been sustainably built, modified and planted by the team. The site has many features, inc: four large greenhouse used for propagation and sales; numerous seating areas of interest; the Dingley Dell; the apiary and a shop/tearoom. Areas accessed via slopes and ramps.

♿ ✿ 🍵 »)

32 ◆ **GREEN ISLAND**
Park Road, Ardleigh, CO7 7SP.
Fiona Edmond, 01206 230455,
greenislandgardens@gmail.com,
www.greenislandgardens.co.uk.
*3m NE of Colchester. From Ardleigh
village centre, take B1029 towards
Great Bromley. Park Rd is 2nd on
R after level Xing. Garden is last on
L.* **For NGS: Sun 28 Jan, Sun 28
Apr, Sun 13 Oct (11-4). Adm £9,
chd £2.50. Light refreshments.**
Light lunches, cream teas, cakes,
ice creams all available in the
tearoom. Picnics welcome in the
car park area only. **2025: Sun 2
Feb.** For other opening times and
information, please phone, email or
visit garden website. Donation to
Plant Heritage.
A garden for all seasons, highlights
inc bluebells, azaleas, autumn colour,
winter *Hamamelis* and snowdrops.
A plantsman's paradise. Carved
within 20 acre mature woodland are
huge island beds, Japanese garden,
terrace, gravel, seaside and water
gardens, all packed with rare and
unusual plants. Flat and easy walking
or pushing wheelchairs. Ramps at
entrance and tearoom. Disabled
parking and WC.

33 **GROVE LODGE**
3 Chater's Hill, Saffron
Walden, CB10 2AB. Chris
Shennan, 01799 522271,
cds.2022@icloud.com. *Approx 10
mins walk from town centre. Facing
The Common on E side, about
100 yds from the turf maze. Note:
Chater's Hill is one way.* **Sun 18,
Sun 25 Feb (2-5). Adm £6, chd
free. Home-made teas. Visits also
by arrangement 2 Jan to 20 Dec.
Groups of any size are welcome
throughout the year.**
A large walled garden close to the
town centre with unusually high
biodiversity (e.g. 17 species of
butterfly recorded) close to the turf
maze and Norman castle. Semi-
woodland on light free-draining chalk
soil allows bulbs, hellebores and
winter-flowering shrubs to thrive.
Two ponds, topiary, orchard and
small vegetable garden blend some
formality with informal areas where
wildlife thrives. A profusion of winter
aconites, snowdrops, other bulbs
and spring blossom. Lots of seating
from which to enjoy the garden.
Garden appeared in 2023 Feb
edition of Garden Answers magazine.
Wheelchair access via fairly steep
drive leading to terrace from which
the garden may be viewed.

GROUP OPENING

34 **HARWICH GARDENS**
Harwich, CO12 3NH. *Centre of Old
Harwich. Car park on Wellington
Rd (CO12 3DT) within 50 metres
of St Helens Green. Street parking
available.* **Sun 14 July (11-4).
Combined adm £5, chd free.
Light refreshments inc tea, coffee
and cake served all day at 8 St.
Helens Green.**

63 CHURCH STREET
Sue & Richard Watts.

42 KINGS QUAY STREET
Mrs Elizabeth Crame.

QUAYSIDE COURT
Dave Burton.

8 ST HELENS GREEN
Frances Vincent.

The gardens all within walking
distance in the historical town of
Harwich. 8 St Helens Green, just
100metres from the sea. A small
town garden with roses, dahlias,
hydrangeas mixed with perennials,
small fruit trees and pots. 63
Church Street is a long, narrow
walled courtyard with shrubs,

Furzelea

climbers, perennials and a small vegetable garden packed into the garden. Architectural features inc an Elizabethan window with original glass. Quayside Court, a community garden, unusually boasts a sunken garden hidden from view at the end of the car park which features a pond, vegetable patch, roses and climbers. 42 Kings Quay Street courtyard garden recently landscaped. Raised brick beds incorporate established plants such as a grape vine, David Austin roses, tree peony and a combination of edible and ornamental plants. There will be an art display at 8 St. Helens Green with commission to the National Garden Scheme on any purchases.

✻ ☕))

35 NEW 83 HARWICH ROAD
Little Oakley, Nr Harwich, Harwich, CO12 5JA. Ken and Kay Dalby.
From Colchester direction, take the A120 to Ramsey r'about. Take the B1352 up the hill. At church, turn R into Mayes Ln. At end turn R, 83 Harwich Rd is approx 200 metres on R. **Sun 23 June (10.30-4). Combined adm with Stowford House £6, chd free. Tea.**
Family cottage garden with a mix of fruit trees, shrubs, flowers and vegetables, growing in an organised jumble. Two small greenhouses for salad crops and two small ponds. Lawn and patio area.

☕))

36 262 HATCH ROAD
Pilgrims Hatch, Brentwood, CM15 9QR. Mike & Liz Thomas.
2m N of Brentwood town centre. After passing the Brentwood Centre on Doddinghurst Rd, turn R into Hatch Rd. 262 is the 4th house on the R. **Sun 7, Sun 21 July (11.30-4.30). Adm £5, chd free. Home-made teas. All cakes are homemade.**
A formal frontage with lavender. An eclectic rear garden of around an acre divided into 'rooms' with themed borders, several ponds, three greenhouses, fruit and vegetable plots and oriental garden. There is also a secret white garden, spring and summer wildflower meadows,Yin and Yang borders, a folly and an exotic area. There is plenty of seating to enjoy the views and a cup of tea and cake.

& ✻ ☕

37 HEYRONS
High Easter, Chelmsford, CM1 4QN. Mr Richard Wollaston, 01245 231428, richard.wollaston@gmail.com. *½m outside High Easter towards Good Easter. Via High Easter: through village, turn L ¼m on R. Via Good Easter: After 2m on L ½ way up hill before the village. Via Leaden Roding: After 2m turn L over bridge. ¼ m on L.* **Visits by arrangement Apr to July for groups of 10 to 30. Adm £10, chd free. Home-made teas.**
A garden of four parts originally created for family enjoyment within and around an ancient, restored farmyard. An Essex barn and brick farm buildings surround an intensely planted walled garden. A terraced area with mature trees, herbaceous and shady beds leads up to a rose garden. Beyond is an open area with grass beds, tennis court, big skies, a small meadow and fine views over Essex countryside. Wheelchair on gravel driveway can be difficult, but drop off access can be arranged on request.

& ☕

38 HORKESLEY HALL
Vinesse Road, Little Horkesley, Colchester, CO6 4DB. Mr & Mrs Johnny Eddis, 07808 599290, horkesleyhall@hotmail.com, www.airbnb.co.uk/rooms/10354093.
6m N of Colchester City Centre. 2m W of A134, 10 mins from A12. On Vinesse Rd, look for the grass triangle with tree in middle, turn into Little Horkesley Church car park. Go to very far end - access is via low double black gates. **Sat 17 Feb (1-4.30). Adm £6, chd free. Light refreshments in St Peter & St Paul's Church for Feb opening. Soups, home-made cakes, sausage rolls and hot drinks. Visits also by arrangement for groups of 10 to 20.**
Magical parkland, traditional English garden setting with eight acres of romantic garden surrounding classical house overlooking lake. Major 20ft balancing stones sculpture. Exceptional trees. A developing snowdrop collection and winter walk. Over 50 varieties of Iris from disbanded National Collection. Walled garden. Charming enclosed swimming pool garden to relax with teas. Excellent plant stall. We hope to have a talk on snowdrops in the church by renowned Galanthophile,

Chris Wiley, followed by our open garden and teas to remember Brooke, who was a special friend of the garden. Partial wheelchair access to some areas with easy access to tea area with lovely views over lake and garden. Some gravel paths and slopes.

& 🐎 ✻ 🚗 🛏 ☕))

39 61 HUMBER AVENUE
South Ockendon, RM15 5JW. Mr Greg & Mrs Kasia Purton-Dmowski, 07711 721629, kasia.purtondmowski@gmail.com.
M25- J31 to Thurrock Services, or Grays from A13, at r'about take exit onto Ship Ln to Aveley. Turn R then 2nd exit at r'about onto Stifford Rd/ B1335. Take Foyle Dr to Humber Ave. **Visits by arrangement May to Oct for groups of 10 to 20. Home-made teas. Gluten free refreshments available.**
A suburban garden close to Nature Reserve, (30m x 14m) featuring an old cherry tree from the orchard of the famous Belhus Mansion. The garden features abundant large borders planted heavily with herbaceous plants, small trees, roses, lilies, and ornamental grasses with oriental senses mixed with a traditional English feel with shady areas with hostas, tree ferns and Japanese style plants. The owners are interested in design and are members of Sogetsu International School. Original arrangements will be on display during open day.

& 🐎 ✻ ☕

The National Garden Scheme searches the length and breadth of England, Wales, Northern Ireland and the Channel Islands for the very best private gardens

40 ISABELLA'S GARDEN

42 Theobalds Road,
Leigh-On-Sea, SS9 2NE.
Mrs Elizabeth Isabella Ling-Locke,
01702 714424,
ling_locke@yahoo.co.uk. *Take A13
towards Southend on Sea. As you
pass 'Welcome to Leigh-on-Sea'
sign, turn R at T- lights onto Thames
Dr then L onto Western Rd. Carry on
0.6m then R onto Theobalds Rd.* **Sat
1, Sun 2 June, Sat 27, Sun 28 July
(12-4.30); Sun 22 Sept (11.30-5).
Adm £5, chd free. Home-made
teas. Wide range of homemade
cakes inc gluten free and vegan
options, and cream teas. Visits
also by arrangement 27 May to 26
July for groups of 10 to 30.**
This enchanting town garden is
bursting with a profusion of colour
from early spring through to the
autumn months. Roses, clematis,
agapanthus, herbaceous plants,
alpines, pots with unusual succulents
and cacti fill every corner of this
garden. There is a wildlife pond, water
features as well as other garden
features which are to be found hiding
within the shrubbery and throughout
the garden. This garden is situated in
Leigh on Sea, and just a five min walk
from the cockle sheds of Old Leigh
and Leigh railway station. Wheelchair
access to the vast majority of the
garden, there are steps near to the
house.
& ✿ ☕ ᵛ⁾⁾

41 JANKES HOUSE

Jankes Green, Wakes Colne,
Colchester, CO6 2AT. Bridget
Marshall. *8m NW of Colchester.
From A1124 Halstead Rd turn R
at Wakes Colne opp village shop
to Station Rd. Take 2nd R after stn
entrance into Jankes Ln. House
signed. Parking on grass verge.* **Sun
2 June (12-4). Adm £5, chd free.
Home-made teas.**
A ½ acre traditional English country
garden with amazing rural views.
Garden has been artistically created
by owner. Beautiful mixed borders
featuring roses, clematis and
architectural shrubs. *Camassia* in wild
grass area. Many young specimen
trees. Dry garden. Delightful pond
and patio area. Vegetable garden
and small orchard. Intimate places to
sit and relax. Garden owner's artistic
cards and home-made preserves
for sale. Wheelchair access to whole
garden.
& ✿ ☕ ᵛ⁾⁾

42 KAMALA

262 Main Road, Hawkwell,
Hockley, SS5 4NW. Karen
Mann, 07976 272999,
karenmann10@hotmail.com.
*3m NE of Rayleigh. From A127 at
Rayleigh Weir take B1013 towards
Hockley. Garden on L after White
Hart Pub & village green.* **Visits by
arrangement 22 July to 30 Aug.
Adm £6, chd free. Home-made
teas.**
Spectacular herbaceous borders
which sing with colour as displays
of Salvia are surpassed by dahlia
drifts. Gingers, *Brugmansia*, various
bananas, bamboos and *Canna*
add an exotic note. Grasses sway
above the blooms, giving movement.
Rest in the rose clad pergola while
listening to the two Amazon parrots
in the aviary. The garden features an
RHS accredited dahlia named 'Jake
Mann'. Trees and shrubs inc acers,
Catalpa aurea, Cercis 'Forest Pansy'
and a large unusual *Sinocalycanthus*
(Chinese Allspice) a stunning, rare
plant with fantastic flowers.

43 KEEWAY

Ferry Road, Creeksea,
nr Burnham-on-Crouch,
CM0 8PL. John & Sue
Ketteley, 01621 782083,
sueketteley@hotmail.com. *2m W
of Burnham-on-Crouch. B1010 to
Burnham on Crouch. At town sign
take 1st R into Ferry Rd signed
Creeksea & Burnham Golf Club &
follow NGS signs.* **Wed 26, Sun
30 June (2-5). Adm £5, chd free.
Home-made teas. Visits also by
arrangement 19 June to 12 July for
groups of 10+.**
Large, mature country garden with
stunning views over the River Crouch.
Formal terraces surround the house
with steps leading to sweeping lawns,
mixed borders packed full of bulbs
and perennials, formal rose and herb
garden with interesting water feature.
Further afield there are wilder areas,
paddocks and lake. A productive
greenhouse, vegetable and cutting
gardens complete the picture.
& ✿ ☕

44 KELVEDON HALL

Kelvedon, Colchester,
CO5 9BN. Mr & Mrs Jack
Inglis, 07973 795955,
v_inglis@btinternet.com. *Near
Colchester. Take Maldon Rd direction
Great Braxted from Kelvedon High
St. Go over R Blackwater bridge
& bridge over A12. At T-junc turn
R onto Kelvedon Rd. Take 1st L,
sign for KH, a single gravel road
3/4m.* **Visits by arrangement 15
Apr to 28 June for groups of 20
to 40. By arrangement visits on
weekday afternoons only. Adm
£8, chd free. Home-made teas
in the Courtyard Garden or the
Pool Walled Garden - weather
permitting. Hot drinks and
homemade cakes provided.
Please discuss allergies in
advance.**
Varied six acre garden surrounding
a gorgeous C18 house. A blend
of formal and informal spaces
interspersed with modern sculpture.
Pleached hornbeam and yew and box
topiary provide structure. A courtyard
walled garden juxtaposes a modern
walled pool garden, both providing
season long displays. Herbaceous
borders offset an abundance of roses
around the house. Lily covered ponds
with a wet garden.
✿ Ⓓ ☕

45 LAUREL COTTAGE

88 The Street, Manuden,
CM23 1DS. Stewart and Louise
Woskett. *Approx 3m N of Bishop's
Stortford. From B/Stort along Rye St.
At the Mountbatten Restaurant r'about
continue straight on to Hazel End Rd.
In ½m turn L to stay on Hazel End
Rd. Continue past Yew Tree pub. Gdn
is last cottage on R.* **Sun 26 May,
Sun 1 Sept (1-5). Adm £5, chd free.
Home-made teas.**
A romantic, quintessential cottage
garden. Features intimate pathways
meandering through borders with
an abundance of cottage garden
favourites and one or two surprises,
rustic charm and an ancient Yew tree.
Seating areas to sit and enjoy fragrant
borders. Hidden treasures enhance
this characterful and quirky garden.
Created in just five years from a very
neglected plot. Parking at community
centre car park adjacent to cottage
and playing field.
☕ ᵛ⁾⁾

46 LITTLE MYLES

Ongar Road, Stondon Massey,
CM15 0LD. Judy & Adrian Cowan.
*1½m SE of Chipping Ongar. Off
A128 at Stag Pub, Marden Ash,
towards Stondon Massey. Over
bridge, 1st house on R after 'S'
bend. 400yds Ongar side of Stondon
Church.* **Wed 3, Wed 10 July (1.30-
5). Adm £5, chd free. Home-made
teas.**

A three acre romantic garden that has shifted its emphasis to providing an abundance of nectar-rich flowers for struggling bees and butterflies. The Herb garden full of vipers bugloss, marjoram, borage and roses. Meandering paths pass full borders, themed hidden gardens, hornbeam pergola, sculptures and tranquil benches. Crafts and handmade herbal cosmetics for sale. Explorers sheet and map for children. New expanded flower meadow full of colourful nectar-rich flowers for bees and butterflies. Gravel paths. No disabled WC available.

♿ ✿ ☕

47 LONG HOUSE PLANTS
Church Road, Noak Hill, Romford, RM4 1LD. Tim Carter, www.longhouse-plants.co.uk. *3½ m NW of J28, M25. Take A1023 Brentwood. At 1st T-lights, turn L to South Weald. After 0.8m turn L at T-junc. Travel 1.6m & turn L, over M25. ½ m turn R into Church Rd, nursery opp church. Disabled Car Parking. This route keeps out of ULEZ.* **Wed 3 July, Wed 7 Aug, Wed 4 Sept (11-4). Adm £7, chd £3. Home-made teas.**
A beautiful garden - yes, but one with a purpose. Long House Plants has been producing homegrown plants for more than 10 years and here is a chance to see where it all begins! With wide paths and plenty of seats carefully placed to enjoy the plants and views. It has been thoughtfully designed so that the collections of plants look great together through all seasons. Paths are suitable for wheelchairs and mobility scooters. Disabled WC in nursery. Two cobbled areas not suitable.

♿ ✿ 🚐 ☕

48 LONGYARD COTTAGE
Betts Lane, Nazeing, Waltham Abbey, EN9 2DA. Jackie & John Copping. *Nr Harlow, Essex. The garden is. 3½ m S of Harlow & is midway between M25 junc Waltham Abbey and M11 junc (15mins approx by car from either to Betts Ln). Opp red telephone box.* **Sun 19 May (11-4). Adm £5, chd free. Home-made teas.**
Longyard Cottage is an interesting ¾ of an acre garden situated within yards of an SSSI site, a C11 church, a myriad of footpaths. This conceptual garden is based on a 'journey' and depicted through the use of paths which take you through three distinct

areas, with its own characteristics. It's a tactile, semi wild garden.

☕

49 LOXLEY HOUSE
49 Robin Hood Road, Brentwood, CM15 9EL. Robert & Helen Smith. *1m N of Brentwood town centre. On A128 N towards Ongar turn R at mini r'about onto Doddinghurst Rd. Take the 1st road on L into Robin Hood Rd. 2 houses before the bend on L.* **Sat 7, Sun 8 Sept (11-3). Adm £4, chd free. Home-made teas. Homemade cakes and coffees also available.**
On entering the rear garden you will be surprised and delighted by this town garden. A colourful patio with pots and containers. Steps up onto a lawn with circular beds surrounded by hedges, herbaceous borders, trees and climbers. Two water features, one a Japanese theme and another with ferns in a quiet seating area. The garden is planted to offer colour throughout the seasons.

☕ ‣))

50 9 MALYON ROAD
Witham, CM8 1DF. Maureen & Stephen Hicks. *Car park at bottom of High St opp Swan Pub. 5 min walk from car park cross High St by pedestrian x-ing onto River Walk. Follow path, take 1st R turn into Luard Way, Malyon Rd straight ahead.* **Sat 6, Sun 7, Sat 20, Sun 21 July (10.30-4). Adm £4, chd free. Light refreshments inc tea, coffee, cakes, sausage rolls and soft drinks.**
Large town garden with mature trees and shrubs made up of a series of garden rooms. Flower beds, pond, summerhouse and greenhouse giving all year interest. Plenty of places to sit and relax with paths that take you on a tour of the garden. A quiet hidden place not expected in a busy town. Our garden is a hidden oasis, where you can escape from the hustle and bustle of busy life. On the edge of town, close to the Witham's rambling Town River Walk.

✿ ☕

51 MAY COTTAGE
19 Walton Road, Kirby-Le-Soken, Frinton-On-Sea, CO13 0DU. Julie Abbey, 07885 875822, jools.abbey@hotmail.com. *Kirby-Le-Soken, Essex, CO13 0DU. On the B1034, 2m before Walton on Naze. 1/4m after the Red Lion pub and on*

L hand side. **Sun 19 May (11-4). Adm £5, chd free. Home-made teas. Visits also by arrangement 20 May to 30 June for groups of 6 to 14.**
A quintessential English country garden divided into separate areas with three ponds, a stream and a small waterfall. A variety of planting often grown from cuttings. Follow path down to Bakers Oven, a building over 100 years old. A picket gate leads to a secret garden with a winding path, and an area only planted in 2020 leads to a summerhouse. The garden is full of interesting artefacts.

🐾 ☕))

52 MAYFIELD FARM
Hungerdown Lane, Ardleigh, CO7 7LZ. Ed Fairey & Jennifer Hughes, 01206 230883, jen@faireyassociates.co.uk. *3½ m NE of Colchester. From Ardleigh village centre continue on the A137 to Manningtree. 3rd R, Tile Barn Ln. R again Hungerdown Ln. 500yds garden on R.* **Visits by arrangement 25 Mar to 11 Oct for groups of 10 to 40. Adm £10, chd free. Home-made teas. Adm inc tea & cake. Guided tour with the Garden Owner.**
Mayfield Farm is a seven acre garden which only a few years ago was largely a field, with a huge glasshouse and polytunnels. Now filled with many beautiful beds and borders, we have also created a secret garden and planted yew hedging for topiary. Over a 100,000 bulbs have been planted in the garden during the past few years to create a wonderful spring display. Always a new and exciting project being undertaken! Mostly flat but areas of gravel, grass and paddock for parking.

♿ ☕

Our donation in 2023 has enabled Parkinson's UK to fund 3 new nursing posts this year, directly supporting people with Parkinson's

53 **207 MERSEA ROAD**
Colchester, CO2 8PN. Kay and
Rod, klawrence61@gmail.com. *S
part of Colchester. From the town
centre drive 2m up Mersea Rd.
Garden on the L side of the rd past
the cemetery & mini r'about on the
B1025.* **Sat 13 July, Sat 24, Sun
25 Aug (11-4). Adm £4, chd free.
Home-made teas. Home-made
cake & soft drinks also available.
Visits also by arrangement for
groups of 15+. During school
holidays only.**
The garden is 185ft long divided into
sections. There is a decking area
with pots leading to a unique fountain
made from waste slates. A circular
lawn is surrounded by herbaceous
perennials, annuals, trees and shrubs
with cabin. Behind the cabin are ferns
perennials and bee hive. Beyond is a
patio with pergola, patio, pond, long
raised beds with subtropical planting,
veg beds and hens. Most of the
garden is accessible (grass paths).
Regret, no large motorised chairs.

54 **MIKRI ELLADA**
39 Wakering Avenue,
Shoeburyness, Southend-On-
Sea, SS3 9BE. Wendy Adlington.
*Shoeburyness 3m E of Southend
Town Centre on A13. Roadside
parking available on Wakering Ave
& surrounding roads. Public toilets
available at nearby East Beach.* **Sat
29 June (11-5). Adm £5, chd free.
Home-made teas. Vegan and
gluten free cakes available.**
A small well-established town garden
with an interesting use of space,
creating several garden rooms.
Seating areas capture the sun as it
moves across the garden. Lush green
foliage of palm and cordyline contrast
with established ceanothus, olive
and fig trees. Wisteria and grapevine
clambers over the 'Greek Taverna'
(our own little bit of Greece!).

55 **THE MOUNT**
Epping Road, Roydon,
Harlow, CM19 5HT. David &
Liz Davison, 07711 231555,
david.t.davison@gmail.com. *2m
W of Harlow in Roydon Village. Pass
the High St, garden approx 500yds
on R. Look for a board & yellow
balloons on black bollards most sat
navs take you to our drive. Parking
on-site except for Dec opening.*
**Sun 5 May, Sun 23 June, Sun 4
Aug (11-4). Light refreshments.**

Evening opening Fri 13 Dec
(5-7). Wine. Adm £7, chd free.
Tea, coffee, soft drinks and
homemade cakes for sale. Mulled
wine at Christmas lights event.
Visits also by arrangement Apr to
Aug for groups of 10 to 50. Cars
and minibuses can park onsite,
coaches drop visitors at gate.
The garden is set in a total of eight
acres. Three acres of formal gardens
and five acres woodland planted in
2003. The formal gardens are divided
into nine separate areas. The lawns
are edged with mixed planting for
different seasons from snowdrops,
spring bulb displays through the
summer plants and shrubs. There
are many surprising statues and
sculptures throughout the grounds.
Over 100 statues and works of art.
I-spy sheets for children. Fantastic
Christmas lights and Santa grotto
in December. The whole site can
be accessed by wheelchairs and
scooters.

56 **MOVERONS**
Brightlingsea, CO7 0SB.
Lesley & Payne Gunfield,
lesleyorrock@me.com,
www.moverons.co.uk. *7m SE
of Colchester. At old church turn
R signed Moverons Farm. Follow
lane & garden signs for approx 1m.
Some SatNavs take you the wrong
side of the river.* **Sat 7, Sun 8 Sept
(10.30-5). Adm £5.50, chd free.
Home-made teas. Visits also
by arrangement July to Sept for
groups of 10+.**
Tranquil four acre garden in touch
with its surroundings and stunning
estuary views. A wide variety of
planting in mixed borders to suit
different growing conditions. Large
natural ponds, plenty of seating
areas, sculptures and barn for rainy
day teas! Our Reflection pool garden
and courtyard have been completely
redeveloped. Magnificent trees
some over 300 years old give this
garden real presence. Sculpture and
Art Exhibition Most of the garden is
accessible by wheelchair via grass
and gravel paths. There are some
steps and bark paths.

57 NEW **MOYNES FARM**
Wick Road, Great Bentley,
Colchester, CO7 8RA.
Veronica Strucelj and
Jim Carr, 07538 604947,
verostrucelj@icloud.com.

*9m SE from Colchester towards
Clacton on Sea. 2m from Great
Bentley, between Aingers Green
and Weeley Heath.* **Tue 18, Wed 19
June (12-4). Adm £6, chd free.
Home-made teas. Refreshments
inc hot and cold drinks and
home-made cakes. Visits also
by arrangement Apr to Sept for
groups of 10 to 30.**
A traditional, large country garden
and two acre woodland, opening
for the first time for the National
Garden Scheme. Vibrant planting,
mature trees, shrubs and perennials.
A formal courtyard area with box
parterre maze, rose garden, wildlife
pond, parkland. Pottery workshop
and kiln. For transport enthusiasts a
Routemaster London bus and four
military tanks will be on display.

58 NEW **4 NEW ROW**
Waterside Road, East End
Paglesham, Rochford, SS4 2EP.
Dave Kennedy. *5m NE of Rochford.
Turn R at the Shepherd and Dog
pub and follow road. Park in the field
opp the Plough and Sail pub. Follow
Waterside Rd (to the L of the of the
pub) after 100 yds turn R then follow
the signs.* **Tue 25 June (11-4.30).
Combined adm with 4 Boarded
Row £5, chd free.**
Located behind a former oysterman's
cottage c1875, this long, narrow
garden surprisingly offers a range
of garden rooms, planted with silver
birch, roses, clematis, salvia and
various herbaceous plants. The
garden also contains a summerhouse,
a fish pond, a grapevine and climbing
roses. It all comes together to make a
peaceful, tranquil garden.

100 inpatients and
their families are
being supported at the
newly opened Horatio's
Garden Wales, thanks
to the National Garden
Scheme donations

The Delves

59 OAK FARM

Vernons Road, Wakes Colne, Colchester, CO6 2AH. Ann & Peter Chillingworth. *6m NW of Colchester. Vernons Rd off A1124, half way between Ford St & Chappel. From Colchester, 3rd R after Ford St; Oak Farm is 200m up on R. From Halstead, 2nd L after Chappel viaduct.* **Thur 23 May, Sun 9 June, Wed 10 July, Sun 8 Sept (2-5). Adm £5, chd free. Home-made teas.**
Informal farmhouse garden of about an acre on an exposed site. Garden designed to make most of stunning views across Colne Valley to S and W, framed to N by listed house and farmyard. Trees, shrubs, borders, roses and secret garden at best in early and mid summer. Prairie garden, salvias and dahlias come into their own in late summer/early autumn. Mainly accessible by wheelchair avoiding a few steps. Wheelchair access can be gained to most of the garden although there are steps in places.

60 NEW THE OLD RECTORY

Rectory Road, Little Oakley, Harwich, CO12 5LB. Nicky and Jim Coates. *2.5 m SW of Harwich. From Harwich take Oakley Rd/B1414 until*

The Cherry Tree Pub. Turn R into Rectory Rd immed before pub. From Colchester A120 towards Harwich. Turn R at The Maltings, Ramsey and follow NGS signs. **Sun 21 July (11-4). Adm £4, chd free. Home-made teas. Coffee and homemade cakes also available.**
A mature garden of a Grade II listed Georgian Old Rectory rescued from dilapidation over the last ten years. The garden is just over 1½ acres and comprises a small wild wooded area, herbaceous borders in a partly walled garden, a large greenhouse next to a vegetable and cutting garden and an orchard area with a more recent border containing grasses and later flowering perennials.

61 NEW OLD TIMBERS

Church Street, Maldon, CM9 5HW. Margaret McCaskie and Stanley Goulding. *Black timbered building, opp St Mary's church. Public car parking on High St E, Edward Brights Cl, CM9 5RU or Promenade Park, Park Dr, CM9 5JQ.* **Fri 14 June, Fri 16 Aug (11-4.30). Adm £5, chd free. Light refreshments.**
The white shingled spire of St Mary's church, provides historic atmosphere

to this weatherboarded house and large walled garden. Raised vegetable garden beds, lawns, wisteria and rose clad pergola, a pond, several colour themed beds and herbaceous border, can all be admired from several seated areas. Pretty summerhouse, a working area with shed, greenhouse and plants for sale. The majority of garden features can be viewed by a wheelchair user.

62 OVER HALL

Overhall Hill, Colne Engaine, Colchester, CO6 2HW. Mrs Jane Lambert. *1m E of Colne Engaine. From B1124 Earls Colne to White Colne turn onto Colne Park Rd and continue to Countess Cross. Take L Overhall Hill. Garden on L.* **Sun 9 June (12-4). Adm £5, chd free. Home-made teas.**
A large country house garden surrounding a Georgian House (not open) with sloping gardens down to a large pond and extended countryside views across the Colne Valley. The formal walled garden has an unusual crinkle crankle wall and thatched garden pavilion. Vegetable-fruit garden in raised beds and greenhouse. Historic trees and a woodland walk. Garden on a slope so not all areas wheelchair accessible.

Moynes Farm

underplanted with spring bulbs. Rear garden features mature oak tree and many other trees. A garden allotment boasts a wide range of soft fruit and seasonal vegetables. There are herbaceous borders, raised beds. Patio and seating to enjoy a hot drink and home-made cake. Pear Trees is a garden committed to benefit insects and birds. From the gravel drive there is a concrete path to rear garden. No steps.

&. ✿ ☕))

65 18 PETTITS BOULEVARD, RM1

Rise Park, Romford, RM1 4PL. Peter & Lynn Nutley. *From M25 take A12 towards London, turn R at Pettits Ln junc then R again into Pettits Blvd or Romford Stn. 103 or 499 bus to Romford Fire Stn & follow yellow signs.* Sat 29, Sun 30 June, Sat 7, Sun 8 Sept (12-5). Adm £4.50, chd free. Tea.

The garden (80ft x 23ft) is on three levels with an ornamental pond, patio area with shrubs and perennials, many in pots. Large eucalyptus tree leads to a woodland themed area with many ferns and hostas. There are agricultural implements and garden ornaments giving a unique and quirky feel to the garden. Tranquil seating areas situated throughout.

&. 🐕 ✿ ☕

66 NEW 30 QUEENS ROAD

Rayleigh, SS6 8JX. Natasha Gallop, nmathewsuk@gmail.com, www.instagram.com/gal. inthegarden. *1.6m from Rayleigh Weir. Head 0.7m along High Rd, turn R at r'about onto Eastwood Rd, A1015, continue for 1m then turn L onto Queens Rd.* Sat 15, Sun 16 June, Sat 31 Aug, Sun 1 Sept (11-5). Adm £5, chd free. Home-made teas. Visits also by arrangement 10 June to 30 June for groups of 10 to 20. Midweek visits between 11am - 2:30pm.

A medium sized family garden with seperate zones. The front of the garden is a space for children to play. The back has a colourful jungle border filled with banana plants and exotic perennials surrounding a hop covered pergola. A cottage garden with roses, shrubs and homegrown annuals. A main seating area sits amongst vibrant planting inc grasses, rudbeckias and salvias.

🐕 ✿ 🚗 ☕))

&. ✿ ☕
63 PEACOCKS

Main Road, Margaretting, CM4 9HY. Phil Torr, phil.torr@btinternet.com. *Margaretting Village Centre. From Margaretting x-roads go 100yds in the direction of Ingatestone. Entrance gates are on the L, set back from the road. What3words app - visual. global.film.* Sun 28 Apr, Sun 23 June (11-4). Adm £5, chd free. Visits also by arrangement 24 Apr to 3 July for groups of 15 to 60. Inc refreshments and optional garden tour lasting approx 45 mins. Donation to St Francis Hospice.

A 10 acre varied garden ideal for picnics with several seating areas. Specimen trees. Restored horticultural buildings. Series of garden rooms inc Walled Paradise Garden, Garden of Reconciliation (*Alhambra fusion*), a parterre. Long herbaceous/mixed border. Sunken dell and waterfall. Temple of Antheia on the banks of a lily lake. Large areas for wildlife inc woodland walk, nuttery and orchard. Traditionally managed large wildflower

meadow. There are many places to sit with a picnic, we encourage visitors to bring their picnic hampers, whatever size. Display of old Margaretting postcards. Garden sculpture. Most of garden is wheelchair accessible.

&. 🚗 🚏

64 PEAR TREES

Elder Street, Wimbish, Saffron Walden, CB10 2XA. Mrs Julie Bayliss, 07929 802373, peartrees.jb@gmail.com. *Between Saffron Walden & Thaxted. Elder St is a hamlet of Wimbish, also signed Carver Barracks, Turn R off B184 from Saffron Walden or L from Thaxted. Pear Trees is opp entrance to Carver Barracks.* Sat 6, Sun 7 July (1-5). Adm £5, chd free. Home-made teas. Home-made cakes & cheese scones. Visits also by arrangement 15 Mar to 30 June for groups of 5 to 15.

Pear Trees is a south facing garden nearly ½ acre with open views across farmland to Rowney Woods. Front garden has mixed fruit trees

67 ROOKWOODS
Yeldham Road, Sible Hedingham, CO9 3QG. Peter & Sandra Robinson, 07770 957111, sandy1989@btinternet.com, www.rookwoodsgarden.com. *8m NW of Halstead. Entering Sible Hedingham from direction of Haverhill on A1017 take 1st R just after 30mph sign. Coming through SH from the Braintree direction turn L just before the 40mph leaving the village.* **Visits by arrangement 10 May to 27 Sept. Plenty of parking spaces. Adm £12, chd free. Home-made teas.**
Rookwoods is a tranquil garden where you can enjoy a variety of mature trees, herbaceous borders, a shrubbery, pleached hornbeam rooms and a walk through an ancient oak wood. Discover our work-in-progress wildflower bed, along with a buttercup meadow. There is no need to walk far. You can come and linger over tea, under a dreamy wisteria canopy while enjoying views across the garden. Wheelchair access over gravel drive.

68 69 RUNDELLS - THE SECRET GARDEN
Harlow, CM18 7HD. Mr & Mrs K Naunton, 07981 882448, k_naunton@hotmail.com. *3m from J7 M11. A414 exit T-lights take L exit Southern Way, mini r'about 1st exit Trotters Rd leading into Commonside Rd, after shops on left 3rd L into Rundells.* **Sat 13 July (2-5). Adm £3.50, chd free. Home-made teas. Visits also by arrangement June to Aug for groups of 8+.**
69 Rundells is a very colourful, small town garden packed with a wide variety of shrubs, perennials, herbaceous and bedding plants in over 200 assorted containers. Hard landscaping on different levels has a summerhouse, various seating areas and water features. Various small secluded seating areas. A small fairy garden has been added to give interest for younger visitors. The garden is next to a large allotment and this is open to view with lots of interesting features inc a bee apiary. Honey and other produce for sale (conditions permitting).

69 [NEW] ◆ ST OSYTH PRIORY
West Field Lane, St. Osyth, Clacton-On-Sea, CO16 8GW. 01206 430160, info@stosythpriory.co.uk, www.stosythpriory.co.uk. *5m from Colchester. W of the village of St Osyth. Best access by car from Mill St into West Field Ln. Follow signs for parking.* **For NGS: Wed 22 May (12-4). Adm £6, chd free. Home-made teas in the beautifully restored Darcy House. For other opening times and information, please phone, email or visit garden website.**
The St Osyth Priory Estate can trace its history back almost 1,400 years. It is recognised as a Registered Park and Garden County Wildlife Site, featuring historic lakes, woodland, tree lined avenues and ancient reed beds. Magnificent wisteria, Walled Garden, box parterre, Rose Garden, lavender hedging and herbaceous borders. Explore the gardens undergoing restoration.

70 SALING HALL
The Street, Great Saling, Braintree, CM7 5DT. Matthew & Jennifer O'Connell. *Parking at The Salings Millenium Hall (CM7 5DW). 1st R turn on entry into Great Saling from the S, with a short walk N through Great Saling village to Saling Hall.* **Sun 9 June (10-5). Adm £8, chd free. Tea & cakes available.**
Opened for NGS by Hugh and Judy Johnson until 2011, and now undergoing an ambitious programme of works by new owners. This special 12-acre Grade II listed garden combines an historic ornamental walled garden with a large surrounding park, predominantly an arboretum full of rare trees, with orchard, wildflower meadow and water garden. June sees the final flushes of spring on the trees and the abundant roses in the gardens at their peak.

71 SANDY LODGE
Howe Drive, Hedingham Road, Halstead, CO9 2QL. Emma & Rick Rengasamy, 07899 920002, emmarengasamy@gmail.com. *8m NE of Braintree. Turn off Hedingham Rd into Ashlong Grove. Parking is in Ashlong Grove. Visitors will then walk up Howe Dr which is approx 200 metres up a slight incline.* **Sun 8 Sept (11-5). Adm £5, chd free. Home-made teas. Visits also by arrangement May to Sept for groups of 15 to 40.**
A stunning garden with views over Halstead; there is something to see every day. A ¾ acre garden created over 12 years. Enter our gravel Bee Border, and wander through the Winter Wedding border to the Woodlands Walk and on to the meadow. Stroll across to double borders and long border with flowing prairie planting up towards cabin and BBQ. Lots of seating. Winners of the Ideal Home Best Readers Garden Award 2021, published in Ideal Home August 2022. Featured in Essex Life Magazine.

72 SHEEPCOTE GREEN HOUSE
Sheepcote Green, Clavering, Saffron Walden, CB11 4SJ. Jilly & Ross McNaughton, info@thehabitatgarden.co.uk, www.thehabitatgarden.co.uk. *Sheepcote Green. Midway between Clavering & Langley.* **Sun 16 June (1-5). Combined adm with Spa Cottage £7, chd free. Home-made teas. Visits also by arrangement May to Sept for groups of 15 to 25. Guided tours & talks on pond creation and restoration available.**
An atmospheric old country garden, set in the three acre grounds of a former farmhouse, undergoing a gentle reawakening by the current owners with wildlife in mind. Featuring herbaceous beds with structure lent by clipped hedging, a sunken vegetable garden housed in a 1930s swimming pool, new formal and wildlife ponds, bug hotels, orchard, woodland and meadow areas. Views of Georgian windmills. Partial wheelchair access due to gravel driveway and uneven paths.

Our donation to Marie Curie this year equates to 17,496 hours of nursing care

73 SILVER BIRCHES

Quendon Drive, Waltham Abbey, EN9 1LG. Frank & Linda Jewson, 01992 714047, linda.jewson@ngs.org. *M25, J26 to Waltham Abbey. At T-lights by McD turn R to r'about. Take 2nd exit to next r'about. Take 3rd exit (A112) to T-lights. L to Monkswood Ave follow yellow signage.* **Sun 9 June (12-5). Adm £5, chd free. Home-made teas. Coffee and homemade cakes also available. Visits also by arrangement May to Sept for groups of up to 20.**

The garden boasts three lawns on the two levels. This surprisingly secluded garden has many mixed borders packed with colour. Mature shrubs and trees create a short woodland walk. Crystal clear water flows through a shady area of the garden. Chimney Pots for sale. There are areas which would not be suitable for wheelchairs.

&♿ ❀ ☕&

74 SNARES HILL COTTAGE

Duck End, Stebbing, CM6 3RY. Pete & Liz Stabler, 01371 856565, petestabler@gmail.com. *Between Dunmow & Bardfield. On B1057 from Great Dunmow to Great Bardfield, ½m after Bran End on L.* **Visits by arrangement Apr to Sept for groups of 8+. Adm £6, chd free. Home-made teas.**

A 'quintessential English garden' - Gardeners' World. Our quirky 1½ acre garden has surprises round every corner and many interesting sculptures. A natural swimming pool is bordered by romantic flower beds, herb garden and Victorian folly. A bog garden borders woods and leads to silver birch copse, beach garden and 'Roman' temple. We have a shepherds hut and numerous water features. There will be classic cars on display.

🚗 ☕ &

75 NEW SPA COTTAGE

Sheepcote Green, Clavering, Saffron Walden, CB11 4SJ. Mr & Mrs John Rigley. *1m outside Clavering village. Turn into Sheepcote Green and take R turn after 150 metres, into gravel lane. Garden is at end of lane.* **Sun 16 June (1-5). Combined adm with Sheepcote Green House £7, chd free. Home-made teas at Sheepcote Green House, served on the lawn.**

Nestled next to farmland in rural Essex, the main garden is split into three areas, a haven for wildflowers around a small orchard of apple and plum trees, a central extensive lawn and well stocked beds softly planted with a cottage feel, also a vegetable garden amongst dahlia beds. Our rear garden to the cottage has well stocked beds with lawn and beautiful patio of York stone porcelain slabs.

& ☕

76 NEW STOWFORD HOUSE

99 Harwich Road, Little Oakley, Harwich, CO12 5JA. Kim and Steve Lane, 07887 951575, kimlanew@hotmail.com. *3m NW of old Harwich; 17m E of Colchester; 23m S of Ipswich. A120 towards Harwich. At Ramsey r'about take 3rd exit. At top of hill turn R opp church down Mayes Ln. Continue to T-junc beside village shop. Turn R and 200 metres Stowford House on R.* **Sun 23 June (10.30-4). Combined adm with 83 Harwich Road £6, chd free.**

In this evolving garden we aim to inc as many different elements as we can, to create interest. The woodland walk leads to a tropical area; the swimming pool area encompasses a hot border; the orchard is bordered by a camellia walk. We have a parterre at present but the box moth caterpillars are getting the better of it so that may become a cutting garden. The patio, orchard and main garden are wheelchair accessible, though not the pool area.

& 🐕 🛏 ☕ ⠺)

77 THATCHED COTTAGE

Main Road, Frating, Colchester, CO7 7DJ. Elaine Craig-Bennett and Robin Buck. *6m E of Colchester. Located on the A133 between The King's Arms pub and The Village Hall (parking) opp*

Silver Birches

Haggar's Ln. **Sat 8, Sun 9 June (12-4). Adm £5, chd free. Home-made teas in Frating Village Hall.** A thatched cottage garden with many varieties of old and David Austin roses interplanted with a wide range of perennials. Several pathways through arches, weave through the garden taking you past a gazebo, a summerhouse and a bridged pond. Raised brick beds host a variety of common and unusual plants. There are many planted pots and hanging baskets. Art Sale in Village Hall.

78 291 THUNDERSLEY PARK ROAD

Benfleet, SS7 1AH. Mr John & Mrs Janet Fenner. *A13 take a R turn at the top of Bread & Cheese Hill. Private Road.* **Sun 21, Mon 22 July (12-5). Adm £6, chd free. Cream teas.** This interesting garden set on a steep Essex hill is full of hidden treasures. The owner, Janet Fenner has created different garden rooms, inc Chinese, a dry Mediterranean garden, a 'Ravello' bed, a sunken garden and an English garden. A variety of large patios have added interest with large topiary plants, hanging baskets and beautiful annuals that add bursts of colour.

79 TWO COTTAGES

Church Road, Chrishall, SG8 8QT. Michelle Thomas, 07929 218639, mrdhthomas@hotmail.co.uk. *7m W of Saffron Walden. Continue on B1039, take R turn to Chrishall. Bury Ln leading into Church Rd. Two Cottages is 1st L after 30mph limit sign.* **Sun 23, Sun 30 June, Sun 7 July (12-4). Adm £5, chd free. Light refreshments. Visits also by arrangement 19 May to 15 Sept for groups of 5 to 20.**
Magic lurks within this charming 1½ acre garden, evolved over 30 years. Many treasures hidden amongst a variety of planting. Over 215 roses showcased in island borders. Meandering lawn paths lead through wisteria walkway to find three miniature Shetland ponies keen to show off to guests. Tranquil seating areas, teas, cakes and gifts for sale in 'The Shed' shop. The perfect place to buy unusual gifts. Large smoking dragon, once on display at Hampton Court garden show. Superb views over countryside to village church. Shepherds hut.

80 ULTING WICK

Crouchmans Farm Road, Ulting, Maldon, CM9 6QX. Mr & Mrs B Burrough, 07984 614947, philippa.burrough@btinternet.com, www.ultingwickgarden.co.uk. *3m NW of Maldon. Take R turning to Ulting off B1019 as you exit Hatfield Peverel by a green. Garden on R after 2m. Sat Nav can drop short - carry on.* **Fri 16 Feb, Wed 27 Mar (11.30-2). Adm £15. Pre-booking essential, please visit www.ngs.org.uk for information & booking. Light refreshments. Sun 28 Apr, Thur 11 July, Mon 26, Fri 30 Aug (2-5). Adm £7.50, chd free. Home-made teas. For Feb and Mar openings homemade soup and rolls will be offered as well as homemade cakes. Visits also by arrangement 12 Feb to 1 Oct for groups of 15 to 50. Groups receive an introductory talk upon arrival. Donation to All Saints Ulting Church.**
Listed black barns provide backdrop for vibrant and exuberant planting in eight acres. Snowdrops, *Narcissus* tulips, flowing innovative spring planting, herbaceous borders, pond, mature weeping willows, kitchen garden, dramatic late summer beds with zingy, tender, exotic plant combinations. Drought tolerant perennial and mini annual wildflower meadows. Woodland. Many plants propagated in-house. Unusual plants for sale. Beautiful walks along the River Chelmer from the garden. Some gravel around the house but main areas of interest are accessible for wheelchairs.

81 WALNUT TREE COTTAGE

Cobblers Green, Felsted, Dunmow, CM6 3LX. Mrs Susan Monk, susan_monk@hotmail.com. *B1417 brings you into Felsted from both ends of the village then turn into Causeway End Rd, ½m down the road you will see a yellow sign on your L to turn R into the paddock.* **Sun 16 June (11-4). Adm £6, chd free. Home-made teas. Visits also by arrangement 1 Apr to 1 Oct for groups of 6 to 12.**
A traditional cottage garden framed by wonderful views over the Essex countryside and planted with well-stocked flower borders and lawns that slope gently down to a natural pond. A productive garden borders the well maintained paddock where chickens and guinea fowl roam. Large patio and other seating areas provide a place to relax and appreciate the garden. There is a path that makes most of the garden accessible for wheelchairs.

82 1 WHITEHOUSE COTTAGES

Blue Mill Lane, Woodham Walter, CM9 6LR. Mrs Shelley Rand. *In between Maldon & Danbury, short drive from A12. A414 through Danbury. Signs to Woodham Walter, turn L go past The Anchor. Continue through the village. R into Blue Mill Ln. Parking in the top paddock, and a drop-off point near garden.* **Sun 2 June, Sun 14 July (10-3.30). Adm £5, chd free. Home-made teas.**
Nestled betwixt farmland in rural Essex, is our small secret garden, that has a wonderful charm to it. Bordered by three acres of paddocks with grazing horses, a little plot of loveliness wraps around our Victorian cottage, roses and grape smother the porch in June. A meandering lawn takes you through beds and borders softly planted with a cottage feel, a haven for wildlife and people alike. Dean Harris, a local artist blacksmith, will have a pop-up forge, making and selling metal garden accessories.

83 WRITTLE UNIVERSITY COLLEGE

Writtle, CM1 3RR. Writtle University College, www.writtle.ac.uk. *4m W of Chelmsford. On A414, near Writtle village. Parking available on the main campus (student car park).* **Sun 28 Apr (10-4). Adm £5, chd free.**
Writtle University college has 15 acres of informal lawns with naturalised bulbs and wildflowers. Large tree collection, mixed shrubs, herbaceous border, dry/ Mediterranean borders, seasonal bedding and landscaped glasshouses. All gardens have been designed and built by our students studying a wide range of horticultural courses. Wheelchair access: some gravel, however majority of areas accessible to all. Well behaved dogs on lead please.

HERTFORDSHIRE

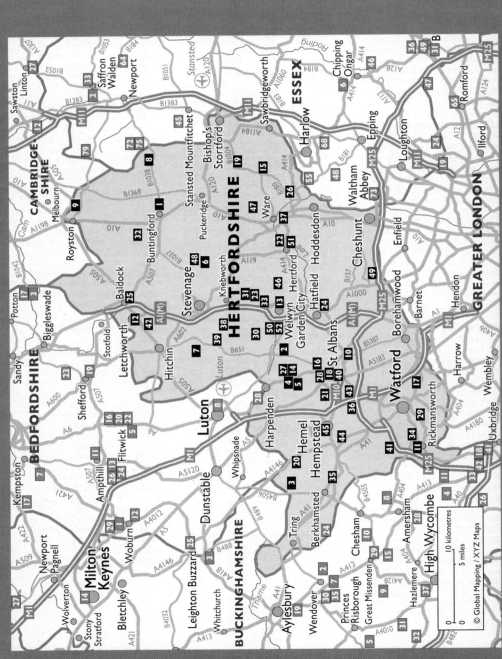

VOLUNTEERS

County Organisers
Bella Stuart-Smith 07710 099132
bella.stuart-smith@ngs.org.uk

Kate Stuart-Smith 07551 923217
kate.stuart-smith@ngs.org.uk

County Treasurer
Peter Barrett 01442 393508
peter.barrett@ngs.org.uk

Publicity
Shubha Allard
shubha.allard@ngs.org.uk

Photography
Lucy Standen 07933 261347
lucy.standen@ngs.org.uk

Julie Meakins 07899 985324
meakinsjulie@gmail.com

Photography & Story Telling
Anna Marie Felice 07500 306273
annamarie.felice@gmail.com

Social Media - Facebook
Anastasia Rezanova
anastasia.rezanova@ngs.org.uk

Social Media - Twitter
Mark Lammin 07966 625559
mark.lammin@ngs.org.uk

Social Media - Instagram
Rebecca Fincham
rebecca.fincham@ngs.org.uk

Radio
Lucy Swift
lucy.swift@ngs.org.uk

Booklet Coordinator
Janie Nicholas 07973 802929
janie.nicholas@ngs.org.uk

New Gardens
Julie Wise 07759 462330
julie.wise@ngs.org.uk

Assistant County Organisers
Parul Bhatt
parul.bhatt@ngs.org.uk

Tessa Birch 07721682481
tessa.birch@ngs.org.uk

Kate de Boinville
kdeboinville@gmail.com

Barbara Goult 07712 131414
barbara.goult@ngs.org.uk

Jennifer Harmes
jenny.harmes@ngs.org.uk

Kerrie Lloyd-Dawson 07736 442883
kerrie.lloyddawson@ngs.org.uk

Sarah Marsh 07813 083126
sarah.marsh@ngs.org.uk

OPENING DATES

All entries subject to change.
For latest information check
www.ngs.org.uk
Extended openings are shown
at the beginning of the month.
Map locator numbers are
shown to the right of each
garden name.

February

Snowdrop Openings

Saturday 3rd
Walkern Hall   48

Sunday 4th
Walkern Hall   48

Tuesday 6th
◆ Benington Lordship   6

Wednesday 7th
8 Gosselin Road   22

Friday 9th
8 Gosselin Road   22

Wednesday 14th
8 Gosselin Road   22

Sunday 18th
Serendi   42

Friday 23rd
1 Elia Cottage   15

Sunday 25th
1 Elia Cottage   15

March

Wednesday 13th
8 Gosselin Road   22

Saturday 16th
◆ Hatfield House West Garden   24

Saturday 23rd
Walkern Hall   48

Sunday 24th
Walkern Hall   48

April

Wednesday 10th
8 Gosselin Road   22

Sunday 14th
Alswick Hall   1

Wednesday 24th
The Mill House   33

Saturday 27th
The Mill House   33

Sunday 28th
Hill House   26
The Mill House   33
◆ St Paul's Walden Bury   39

May

**Every day from Saturday
11th to Sunday 19th**
42 Falconer Road   17

Sunday 5th
Patchwork   35
Pie Corner   36

Wednesday 15th
Rustling End Cottage   38

Friday 17th
Rustling End Cottage   38

Saturday 18th
The Manor House, Ayot St
Lawrence   30

Sunday 19th
◆ Ashridge House Gardens   3

Alswick Hall

THE GARDENS

1 ALSWICK HALL

Hare Street Road, Buntingford, SG9 0AA. Mike & Annie Johnson, www.alswickhall.com/gardens. *1m from Buntingford on B1038. From the S take A10 to Buntingford, drive into town & take B1038 E towards Hare St Village. Alswick Hall is 1m on R.* **Sun 14 Apr, Sun 15 Sept (12-4). Adm £8, chd free. Light refreshments. Licensed bar, barbeque, teas and home-made cakes.**

Listed Tudor House with five acres of landscaped gardens set in unspoiled farmland. Two well established natural ponds with rockeries. Herbaceous borders, shrubs, woodland walk and wildflower meadow with a fantastic selection of daffodils, tulips, camassias and crown imperials. Later in the year, enjoy the spectacular Dahlia beds and late season planting, formal beds and orchard. A plant stall and various trade stands as well as children's face painting. Good access for wheelchair users with lawns and wood chip paths. Slight undulations.

2 AMWELL COTTAGE

Amwell Lane, Wheathampstead, AL4 8EA. Colin & Kate Birss, www.instagram.com/amwellcottage. *½m S of Wheathampstead. From St Helen's Church, Wheathampstead turn up Brewhouse Hill. At top L fork (Amwell Ln), 300yds down lane, park in field opp.* **Sun 9 June (2-5). Adm £5, chd free. Home-made teas.**

Informal garden of approx 2½ acres around C17 cottage. Large orchard of mature trees, with billows of cow parsley in spring, laid out with paths. Extensive lawns with borders, framed by tall yew hedges and old brick walls. Daffodils early in the year. Many roses in beds, borders and a tunnel. Stone seats with views, woodland pond, greenhouse, vegetable garden with raised beds and fire-pit area. Wheelchair access via gravel drive.

3 ◆ ASHRIDGE HOUSE GARDENS

Berkhamsted, HP4 1NS. EF Corporate Education Ltd, 01442 843491, tickets@ashridge.hult.edu, www.ashridgehouse.org.uk.

4m N of Berkhamsted. 1m S of Little Gaddesden. Please use HP4 1NS with Sat Navs. What3words app - fenced.liquid.reverses. **For NGS: Sun 19 May (10-5). Adm £7.50, chd free. Light refreshments at Bakehouse Café. Ashridge House & Bakehouse only accepts payments by card. Dine inside & out in the courtyard, for both light refreshments & substantial meals.** For other opening times and information, please phone, email or visit garden website.

The Grade II* gardens were designed by Humphry Repton, in 1813, and modified by Sir Jeffry Wyatville. The 190 acres inc formal gardens, a large lawn area leading to avenues of trees and arboretum. In May, highlights of the garden inc the azaleas and Rhododendron Avenue and spring bedding displays. Once a monastic site then home to Henry VIII and his children. One of Repton's finest gardens with influences from the Bridgewater dynasty, comprising colourful formal bedding, a rosary, shrubberies and breathtaking views. Free garden introduction talks available on the day. The main garden features, cafe and toilets are accessible via wheelchair.

4 2 BARLINGS ROAD

Harpenden, AL5 2AN. Liz Machin. *1m S of Harpenden. Take A1081 S from Harpenden, after 1m turn R into Beesonend Ln, bear R into Burywick to T-junc. Turn R and follow signs.* **Evening opening Sat 29 June (5-8). Adm £5, chd free. Wine.**

This garden has been developed over many years to provide a haven of privacy and peace in an urban setting. Mature trees, shrubs, climbers and perennials with interesting leaf form give year-round structure/interest. Island beds invite inspection from several perspectives. The tranquil courtyard garden uses plants from a limited colour palette. A shady corner and formal pond add extra interest.

5 BEESONEND HOUSE

Beesonend Lane, Harpenden, AL5 2AB. John & Sarah Worth. *Turn off A1081(turn R from Harpenden & L from St Albans). Keep L up Beesonend Ln, past cottages & derelict stables on the L. Beesonend House is on L next to white stones.* **Sun 19 May (11-4). Adm £5, chd free.**

Light refreshments.
There are four garden areas. The East Garden is lawned with herbaceous borders, pleached hedges, a Japanese-themed border and a eucalyptus tree. The South Garden has herbaceous borders and a semi-mature Lebanese cedar. The South-West Garden has a pond and orchard. The North Garden has a circular lawn, with pots, roses and a herbaceous border. There is a vegetable garden and a greenhouse.

6 ◆ BENINGTON LORDSHIP

Stevenage, SG2 7BS. Mr & Mrs R Bott, 01438 869668, garden@beningtonlordship.co.uk, www.beningtonlordship.co.uk. *4m E of Stevenage. In Benington Village, next to church. Signs off A602.* **For NGS: Tue 6 Feb (11-4). Cream teas in February, served in onsite tea room. In May, refreshments in parish hall adjacent to garden. Sun 26 May (2-5). Adm £8, chd £4.** For other opening times and information, please phone, email or visit garden website.

A seven acre site with ruin of C12 Norman keep and C19 neo Norman folly. Highlights inc spectacular snowdrops and spring bulbs; formal rose garden; walled kitchen garden with vegetables, bantams, and wildflower meadow; orchard with perennial meadow; lake; unspoilt panoramic views over surrounding parkland. Recent replanting of main border with plants resistant to climate change and wildlife friendly. As the garden is on a slope and paths are uneven so there is only partial wheelchair access. Accessible WC available in parish hall.

In 2023, National Garden Scheme funding for Perennial supported a helpline service which provided advice, information and frontline support to around 800 people working in horticulture

7 BRAMBLEY HEDGE

1 Chequers Lane, Preston, Hitchin, SG4 7TX. Lynda & Steve Woodward. *3m S of Hitchin. From A602, Three Moorhens r'about take exit to Gosmore, pass through Gosmore and continue for about 2m into Preston. Chequers Ln is 1st on R, by white fence.* **Sun 2 June (12.30-5.30). Adm £4, chd free. Home-made teas.** Brambley Hedge covers an area of approx ¼ acre. The front garden is mainly set to shrubs and small trees. The rear garden is sections or 'rooms' planted in a cottage style, with around 40 varieties of roses, popular and some less common perennials. There is also a vegetable plot and numerous pots for annuals. The owner is a keen amateur wood turner and some of his work will be on show. The paths are mainly flat and level, some may be slightly narrow.

8 BRENT PELHAM HALL

Brent Pelham, Buntingford, SG9 0HF. Alex & Mike Carrell. *From Buntingford take the B1038 E for 5m. From Clavering take the B1038 W for 3m.* **Sun 23 June (1-4). Adm £8, chd free. Home-made teas in the Estate Office.** Surrounding a beautiful Grade I listed property, the gardens consist of 12 acres of formal gardens, redesigned in 2007 by the renowned landscaper Kim Wilkie. With two walled gardens, a potager, walled kitchen garden, greenhouses, orchard and a new double herbaceous border, there is lots to discover. The further 14 acres of parkland boast lakes and wildflower meadows. All gardened organically. Access by wheelchair to most areas of the garden, inc paths of paving, gravel and grass.

9 BURLOES HALL

Newmarket Road, Royston, SG8 9NE. Lady Newman, www. burloeshallweddings.co.uk. *1m N of Royston. From M11/A505 turn L on Newmarket Rd. 200yds 1st turning on L Burloes Hall or B1329 from Barley to Royston, turning on L signed Burloes Farm.* **Sat 31 Aug, Sun 1 Sept (11-5). Adm £6, chd free. Home-made teas.** Formal gardens with deep colourful mixed herbaceous borders. Bountiful Nepeta and white roses. Handsome beech trees and mature yew hedges with extensive lawns.

10 ◆ THE CELEBRATION GARDEN

North Orbital Road, St Albans, AL2 1DH. Aylett Nurseries Ltd, 01727 822255, info@aylettnurseries.co.uk, www.aylettnurseries.co.uk. *The Celebration Garden is adjacent to Garden Centre. Aylett Nurseries is on the E-bound carriageway of A414, S of St Albans, between Park St r'about & London Colney r'about. Turn L on entry & drive through green gates at end of car park.* **For NGS: Daily Fri 30 Aug to Sun 15 Sept (10-4). Adm by donation. Light refreshments. Tea Tent offering sandwiches, cakes and ice creams with hot and cold drinks. Larger choice available in the Seasons Café. For other opening times and information, please phone, email or visit garden website.** The Celebration Garden is accessed through our famous dahlia field. More dahlias are planted in the garden itself with other herbaceous plants and shrubs. There is also a wildflower border with insect hotel and a willow tunnel. The garden is open all year to visit during the garden centre opening hours. It is especially spectacular from July to early autumn when some 5,000 dahlias are in flower. Annual Autumn Festival held in September. Refreshments available all year round in Seasons Café situated in the Garden Centre. Wheelchair access to the Celebration Garden via grass paths.

11 NEW 38 THE CLUMP

Rickmansworth, WD3 4BQ. Rupert & Fiona Wheeler, 01923 776858, rupert_wheeler@sky.com. *1m W of Rickmansworth. From junc 18 of the M25, drive towards Rickmansworth for about 350 yards, turn R into The Clump. No. 38 is about 350 yards on the R.* **Visits by arrangement May to Oct for groups of 5 to 20. February Snowdrop visits also available. Adm £5, chd free. Light refreshments.** A plantsman's garden containing unusual trees and shrubs on the edge of a wood. The shrubs and trees in the middle garden surround a pond and create an air of relaxing tranquillity. The rear garden is the setting for modern sculptures. There is also a collection of cacti.

12 10 CROSS STREET

Letchworth Garden City, SG6 4UD. Renata & Colin Hume, 01462 673544, renata@cyclamengardens.com, www.cyclamengardens.com. *Nr town centre. From A1(M) J9 signed Letchworth, across 2 r'abouts, R at 3rd, across next 3 r'abouts L into Nevells Rd, 1st R into Cross St.* **Visits by arrangement Jan to Nov for groups of 10 to 30.** A garden with mature fruit trees is planted for interest throughout the year. The structure of the garden evolved around three circles- two grass lawns and a wildlife pond. Mixed borders connect the different levels of the garden

13 35 DIGSWELL ROAD

Welwyn Garden City, AL8 7PB. Adrian & Clare de Baat, 01707 324074, adrian.debaat@ntlworld.com, www.adriansgarden.org. *½m N of Welwyn Garden City centre. From the Campus r'about in city centre take N exit just past the library into Digswell Rd. Over the White Bridge, 200yds on L.* **Sun 28 July (2-5.30); Sun 22 Sept (1.30-4.30). Adm £5, chd free. Home-made teas. Visits also by arrangement July to Oct for groups of 10 to 20. Adm inc tea or coffee and cake.** Town garden of around a ⅓ acre with naturalistic planting inspired by the Dutch garden designer, Piet Oudolf. The garden has perennial borders plus a small meadow packed with herbaceous plants and grasses. The contemporary planting gives way to the exotic, inc a succulent bed and under mature trees, a lush jungle garden inc bamboos, bananas, palms and tree ferns. Daisy Roots Nursery will be selling plants. Grass paths and gentle slopes to all areas of the garden.

14 EASTMOOR LODGE

East Common, Harpenden, AL5 1DA. Ekaterina and Julian Gilbert, 07966 665794, kate2304@yahoo.com. *1m S of Harpenden, turn L onto Limbrick Rd. After 400 yds, turn R onto East Common Rd. After 100 yds turn L. The house is the 3rd on the L. For parking use the car park opp Bamville Cricket club.* **Sat 22 June (12-4). Adm £5, chd free. Home-made teas. Visits also by**

arrangement 6 May to 31 Aug for groups of 8 to 20.
Beautiful modern garden of half an acre featuring an extensive collection of David Austin roses, various perennials, dwarf azaleas, rhododendrons and beautiful hydrangeas, within a woodland setting of giant redwood and other conifer trees. Not suitable for wheelchairs due to steps.

15 1 ELIA COTTAGE
Nether Street, Widford, Ware, SG12 8TH. Margaret & Hugh O'Reilly, 01279 843324, hughoreilly56@yahoo.co.uk. *B1004 from Ware towards Much Hadham. Travel down dip towards Much Hadham, at Xroad take R into Nether St. 8m W of Bishop's Stortford on B1004 through Much Hadham at Widford sign turn L. B180 from Stanstead Abbots.* **Fri 23, Sun 25 Feb (12.30-5.30). Adm £5, chd free. Light refreshments. Visits also by arrangement 23 Feb to 30 Sept.**
A ⅓ acre garden reflecting the seasons. Snowdrops, hellebores and crocus welcome visitors in spring. These are followed in June by clematis and roses. There is a pond, cascade water features, stream with Monet-style bridge. Plenty of seats and two summerhouses. Steep nature of garden and uneven paths means we are sorry no wheelchair access. New ½ acre wildflower meadow opposite.

16 NEW 49 ELLIS FIELDS
St Albans, AL3 6BG. Karen Blain. *Situated at the far end of Ellis Fields.* **Sun 7 July (12-5). Adm £4, chd free. Home-made teas. Coffee and cakes also available.**
A small tranquil urban garden, with both front and back gardens for viewing. Lots of structural evergreen plants and seasonal planting. There are lots of bee and bird friendly summer flowers, and copious numbers of hydrangeas! Painted wooden arches and pathways lead you to raised decked seating areas to enjoy the plants. Wheelchair access via a side gate. The garden should be mostly accessible to all. There are two short steps to slightly higher levels.

17 42 FALCONER ROAD
Bushey, Watford, WD23 3AD. Mrs Suzette Fuller, 07714 294170, suzettesdesign@btconnect.com. *M1 J5 follow signs for Bushey. From London A40 via Stanmore towards Watford. From Watford via Bushey Arches, through to Bushey High St, turn L into Falconer Rd, opp St James church.* **Daily Sat 11 May to Sun 19 May (12-6). Adm £4, chd free. Light refreshments. Visits also by arrangement Feb to May for groups of up to 10.**
Enchanting, magical and unusual Victorian style space. Bird cages and chimney pots feature, plus a walk through conservatory with many plants. Children so very welcome.

In 2023, our donations to Carers Trust meant that 26,118 unpaid carers were supported across the UK

Eastmoor Lodge

18 28 FISHPOOL STREET
St Albans, AL3 4RT. Jenny & Antony Jay, www.instagram.com/jenjay.fishpool. *28 is at the Cathedral end of Fishpool St. Entrance to the garden is through the Lower Red Lion car park.* **Evening opening Fri 21 June (6-8). Wine. Sun 23 June (2-5). Home-made teas. Evening opening Fri 19 July (6-8). Wine. Adm £7, chd free.** Sculpted box, yew hedging and a C17 Tripe House feature strongly in this tranquil oasis set in the vicinity of St Albans Cathedral. Gravel paths lead to a lawn surrounded by late flowering sustainable herbaceous perennial borders and a relaxed woodland retreat. Imaginative planting in all areas offer unique perspectives. Plants are on sale. Not suitable for wheelchairs due to differing levels.
✿ ☕ ᐁ))

19 GABLE HOUSE
Church Lane, Much Hadham, SG10 6DH. Tessa & Keith Birch. *Situated in the picturesque & historic village of Much Hadham. Follow signs to the church. Continue around the R bend & past several white cottages. Gable House driveway is immed on R. Please park in the High St.* **Sun 7 July (12-4). Adm £5, chd free.** Enjoy this colourful and walled village garden of just under an acre. Surrounding the house on three sides, the design is both formal and naturalistic, with structural clipped evergreens and sweeping abundant herbaceous borders. The planting displays an emphasis on strong colour and varied texture. Features inc a woodland walk, a wildlife pond and a cutting garden. Matched funding of all sales goes to Brain Tumour Research. Wheelchair access, level with easy access.
♿ 🐴 ✿ ☕ ᐁ))

20 15 GADE VALLEY COTTAGES
Dagnall Road, Great Gaddesden, Hemel Hempstead, HP1 3BW. Bryan Trueman. *3m N of Hemel Hempstead. Follow B440 N from Hemel Hempstead. Through Water End. Go past turning for Great Gaddesden on L. Park in village hall car park on R. Gade Valley Cottages on R (short walk).* **Sun 26 May, Sun 21 July (1.30-5). Adm £5, chd free. Home-made teas.** Medium sized sloping rural garden. Patio, lawn, borders and pond. Paths lead through a woodland area

emerging by wildlife pond and sunny border. A choice of seating offers views across the beautiful Gade Valley or quiet shady contemplation with sounds of rustling bamboos and bubbling water. Many acers, hostas and ferns in shady areas. *Hemerocallis*, dahlias, iris, *Crocosmia* and phlox found in sun.
✿ ☕

21 GORHAMBURY HOUSE
Gorhambury, St Albans, AL3 6AH. Viscount and Viscountess Grimston, www.gorhamburyestate.co.uk. *Please use AL3 6AE in SatNavs to take you to the correct gate. Parking will be in a field close to the house.* **Wed 22 May (10-3). Adm £12, chd free. Pre-booking essential, please visit www.ngs.org.uk for information & booking. Home-made teas.** Gorhambury House garden was laid out in the 1820s and has evolved over the generations. The current owners have engaged Tom Stuart-Smith to do the design and planting plans and this blends with the older elements that are still in place. In May and June there are some wonderful rhododendrons, camellias, flowering shrubs and trees as well as formal lawns, wildflower meadows and historic topiary. Gravel paths and grass with a wheelchair accessible WC.
♿ ✿ Ⓓ ☕

22 8 GOSSELIN ROAD
Bengeo, Hertford, SG14 3LG. Annie Godfrey & Steve Machin, www.daisyroots.com. *Take B158 from Hertford signed to Bengeo. Gosselin Rd 2nd R after White Lion Pub.* **Wed 7, Fri 9, Wed 14 Feb, Wed 13 Mar, Wed 10 Apr (1-4). Adm £5, chd free.** Daisy Roots nursery garden acts as trial ground and show case for perennials and ornamental grasses grown there. Over 250 varieties of snowdrop in February, deep borders packed with perennials and grasses later in the year. Small front garden with lots of foliage interest. Regret no dogs.
✿

23 GREENWOOD HOUSE
2a Lanercost Close, Welwyn, AL6 0RW. David & Cheryl Chalk. *1½ m E of Welwyn village, close to J6 on A1(M). Off B197 in Oaklands. Opp North Star pub turn into Lower Mardley Hill. Park here unless you*

are disabled as there is very limited parking at house (10 min walk up). Take Oaklands Rise to top of the hill & take L fork. **Sun 30 June (2-5). Adm £5, chd free. Home-made teas. Coffee, soft drinks and a selection of cakes also available.** Secluded garden of ⅓ acre surrounds our contemporary home and backs on to a beautiful ancient woodland. Garden has been transformed over the last 14 years, with mature trees providing a natural backdrop to the many shrubs, Japanese maples and perennials which provide interest and colour throughout the seasons. Access to rear garden across pebble paths and some steps.
✿ ☕ ᐁ))

24 ◆ HATFIELD HOUSE WEST GARDEN
Hatfield, AL9 5HX. The Marquess of Salisbury, 01707 287010, r.ravera@hatfield-house.co.uk, www.hatfield-house.co.uk. *Pedestrian entrance to Hatfield Park is opp Hatfield train stn. From here you can obtain directions to the gardens. Free parking is available, please use AL9 5HX with a SatNav.* **For NGS: Sat 16 Mar (11-4). Adm £12, chd £6. For other opening times and information, please phone, email or visit garden website. Donation to a charity to be nominated by Lady Salisbury.** Visitors can enjoy the spring bulbs in the lime walk, sundial garden and view the famous Old Palace garden, childhood home of Queen Elizabeth I. The adjoining woodland garden is at its best in spring with masses of naturalised daffodils and bluebells. Beautifully designed gifts, jewellery, toys and much more can be found in the Stable Yard shops. Visitors can also enjoy relaxing at the Coach House Kitchen Restaurant which serves a variety of delicious foods throughout the day. There is a good route for wheelchairs around the West garden and a plan can be picked up at the garden kiosk.
♿ 🚌 ☕ ᐁ))

25 NEW HIGH CLOSE
41 High Street, Baldock, SG7 6BG. Tevor and Edita Conway, 07775 662977, conway.trevor1@gmail.com. *North Hertfordshire. Next door to The Cock pub and behind Finesse Interiors.* **Visits by arrangement 1 June to 21 July for groups of**

Mill End Farmhouse

up to 30. **Adm £5, chd free. Light
refreshments. Tea, coffee, wine
and cakes available.**
Set behind an historic C17 house
(not open) and within a walled
garden, this hidden gem is just a
few moments from the bustling
market street in Baldock. A semi
formal, contemporary walled garden,
landscaped in the early 1980s, was
updated in 2020 by Daniel Shea
design. Wheelchair access to most of
the garden.

26 HILL HOUSE
**Stanstead Abbotts, Ware,
SG12 8BX. Mr & Mrs J M
Pilkington.** *Nr Stanstead Abbotts
from A10 turn E on to A414; then
B181 for Stanstead Abbotts; L at
end of High St, garden 1st R past
Church.* **Sun 28 Apr (12-4). Adm
£5, chd free. Light refreshments.**
A nine acre hilltop garden and
woodland. Many species of roses,

herbaceous border, water garden,
woodland walks and blossoming
orchards. Lovely view over Lea Valley.
Wheelchair access is possible, but
garden has gravel paths and steep
contours.

27 8 KINGCROFT ROAD
**Southdown, Harpenden, AL5 1EJ.
Zia Allaway, www.ziaallaway.com.**
*1½ m S of Harpenden town centre.
From Harpenden take the St Albans
Rd A1081 S. At 1st r'about turn
L onto Southdown Rd. Continue
straight over 3 r'abouts to Grove
Rd. Take the 3rd turning on R to
Coleswood Rd. Take 1st turning on
L.* **Evening opening Sun 25 Aug
(5.30-8.30). Wine. Mon 26 Aug
(2-6). Home-made teas. Adm £4,
chd free.**
Beautiful mature town garden
designed by garden writer and
designer in a contemporary informal
style, with small pond and pebbled

beach area, gravel garden, a wide
range of summer bulbs, herbaceous
perennials and shrubs, mature trees,
shady borders, greenhouse, and
inspirational container displays. A
small courtyard features flower-filled
window boxes and fruit in raised
beds.

National Garden Scheme
gardens are identified by
their yellow road signs
and posters. You can
expect a garden of quality,
character and interest, a
warm welcome and plenty of
home-made cakes!

28 16 LANGLEY CRESCENT

St Albans, AL3 5RS. Jonathan Redmayne. *½ m S of St Albans city centre. J21a M25, follow B4630. At mini-r'about by King Harry Pub turn L. At big r'about turn R along A4147, then R at mini-r'about. Langley Cres is 2nd L.* **Evening opening Fri 5 July (5-8). Wine. Sat 6 July (2.30-5.30). Home-made teas. Adm £5, chd free.**

A compact walled garden set on a slope with a wide range of unusual herbaceous perennials, shrubs and trees, both edible and ornamental, and a gentle ambience. The rear garden is divided into two parts; the lower section comprises extensive herbaceous beds inc a collection of *Phlomis* and leads to a secluded area for quiet contemplation beside a wildlife pond surrounded by rambling roses. Fruit trees, herbaceous borders for pollinators, glasshouse and plant propagation also feature. Access by wheelchair to most areas of the garden, inc paved paths, grass and brick terrace beside pond. Garden is on a slope.

&. ✿ 🍵))

29 12 LONGMANS CLOSE

Byewaters, Watford, WD18 8WP. Mark Lammin, 07966 625559, mark.lammin@ngs.org.uk, www. instagram.com/hertstinytropicalgarden. *Leave M25 J18 (A404) & follow Rickmansworth/Croxley Green then A412 to Watford. Follow signs for Watford & Croxley Business Parks & then NGS signs. Park on neighbouring roads if you can.* **Sat 3, Sun 4 Aug (2-6). Adm £4, chd free. Home-made teas. Home-made cakes also available. Visits also by arrangement 6 July to 1 Sept for groups of up to 10. By arrangement visits are available most evenings until September.**

Hertfordshire's Tiny Tropical Garden. See how dazzling colour, scent, lush tropical foliage, trickling water and clever use of pots in a densely planted small garden can transport you to the tropics. Stately bananas and canna rub shoulders with delicate lily and roses amongst a large variety of begonia, hibiscus, ferns and houseplants in a tropical theme more often associated with warmer climes. The garden is beside beautiful walks along the Grand Union Canal and on the Croxley Boundary Walk (signposted). Croxley Common Moor is a very short level stroll away with acres of open moor land, woods and river.

🍵))

30 THE MANOR HOUSE, AYOT ST LAWRENCE

Welwyn, AL6 9BP. *4m W of Welwyn. 20 mins J4 A1M. Take B653 Wheathampstead. Turn into Codicote Rd follow signs to Shaws Corner. Parking in field, short walk to garden. A disabled drop-off point is available at the end of the drive.* **Sat 18, Sun 19 May (11-5). Adm £8, chd free. Home-made cakes, tea and coffee.**

A six acre garden set in mature landscape around Elizabethan Manor House (not open). A one acre walled garden inc glasshouses, fruit and vegetables, double herbaceous borders, rose and herb beds. Herbaceous perennial island beds, topiary specimens. Parterre and temple pond garden surround the house. Gates and water features

20 St Stephens Avenue, St Stephens Avenue Gardens

© Mike Howes

by Arc Angel. Garden designed by Julie Toll. Produce for sale. Regional Finalist, The English Garden Magazine's The Nation's Favourite Gardens, 2023 The drop off point is 5 min walk from the garden.

 ♿ ✱ Ⓓ ☕))

🔳 43 MARDLEY HILL
Welwyn, AL6 0TT. Kerrie Lloyd Dawson & Pete Stevens, www. agardenlessordinary.blogspot. co.uk. *5m N of Welwyn Garden City. On B197 between Welwyn & Woolmer Green, on crest of Mardley Hill by bus stop. Please consider our neighbours and other road users when parking.* **Mon 27 May (1-5). Adm £5, chd free. Home-made teas.**
An unexpected garden created by plantaholics and packed with unusual plants. Focus on foliage and long season of interest. Various areas: alpine bed; sunny border; deep shade; white-stemmed birches and woodland planting; naturalistic stream, pond and bog; chicken house and potted vegetables; potted exotics. Seating areas on different levels. Homegrown plants for sale. Featured in Garden News and Garden Answers. This garden is proud to provide plants for the National Garden Scheme's Show Garden at Chelsea Flower Show 2024.

✱ ☕))

🔳 NEW MILL END FARMHOUSE
Mill End, Sandon, Buntingford, SG9 0RP. John and Jane Davies, 07739 864312, john.davies@camlad.org.uk. *2m W of Buntingford. From S, E and N; Turn off A10 towards Sandon and proceed 1½m and Mill End Farmhouse is on the L. From W; Proceed through Sandon towards Buntingford.* **Sat 8, Sun 9 June (11-4). Adm £6, chd free. Home-made teas. Visits also by arrangement May to Sept for groups of up to 20. Refreshments can be arranged at booking.**
A large garden around a C16 farmhouse, completely renovated since 2020, designed by Julie Toll. The 1½ acre garden is set out in several themes, prairie, woodland, pond and shrub areas, with wild flower meadows in the garden and surrounding four acre paddock. Designated car parking next to the garden.

 ♿ 🐑 ✱ Ⓓ ☕))

🔳 THE MILL HOUSE
31 Mill Lane, Welwyn, AL6 9EU. Sarah & Ian Marsh, www. instagram.com/the_mill_house_ garden/. *Old Welwyn. J6 A1M approx ¾m to garden, follow yellow arrows to Welwyn Village.* **Wed 24, Sat 27, Sun 28 Apr (2-5.30). Adm £5, chd free. Home-made teas.**
An abundance of over 2,000 colourful tulips will greet you as you enter over the mill stream bridge which leads to this romantic walled garden full of spring planting which set off this listed Mill House. Ancient apple and box trees under planted with tulips and Narcissi within which nestles a box parterre and vegetable planters, magnolia tree and colourful terrace. Live Music at the weekend. Regional Finalist, The English Garden's The Nation's Favourite Gardens 2021. Wheelchair access, some gravel and uneven paths.

 ♿ ✱ ☕))

🔳 MORNING LIGHT
7 Armitage Close, Loudwater, Rickmansworth, WD3 4HL. Roger & Patt Trigg, 01923 774293, roger@triggmail.org.uk. *From M25 J18 take A404 towards Rickmansworth, after ¾m turn L into Loudwater Ln, follow bends, then turn R at T-junc & R again into Armitage Close. Limited parking for cars.* **Sun 21 July (1-5). Adm £5, chd free. Light refreshments. Tea, coffee and biscuits. Visits also by arrangement May to Sept for groups of up to 20.**
South facing plantsman's garden, densely planted with mainly hardy and tender perennials and shrubs in a shady environment. Astilbes and phlox prominently featured. The garden inc island beds, pond, chipped wood paths and a raised deck. Tall perennials can be viewed advantageously from the deck. Large conservatory (450 sq. ft) stocked with sub-tropicals.

✱ ☕))

🔳 PATCHWORK
22 Hall Park Gate, Berkhamsted, HP4 2NJ. Jean & Peter Block, 01442 864731, patchwork2@btinternet.com. *3m W of Hemel Hempstead. Entering E side of Berkhamsted on A4251, turn L 200yds after 40mph sign.* **Sun 5 May, Sun 18 Aug (2-5). Adm £5, chd free. Light refreshments. Visits also by arrangement Apr to Oct for groups of 5 to 30.**
¼ acre garden with lots of year-round colour, interest and perfume, particularly on opening days. Sloping site containing rockeries, two small ponds, herbaceous borders, island beds with bulbs in spring and dahlias in summer, roses, fuchsias, hostas, begonias, patio pots and tubs galore - all set against a background of trees and shrubs of varying colours. Seating and cover from the elements.

🐑 ✱ ☕

🔳 PIE CORNER
Millhouse Lane, Bedmond, WD5 0SG. Bella & Jeremy Stuart-Smith, 07710 099132, piebella1@gmail.com, www. instagram.com/piecornergarden/. *Near Watford, Hemel Hempstead & St Albans. 1½m from J21. 3m from J20 of M25. J8 of M1. Go to the centre of Bedmond. Millhouse Ln is opp the shops. Entry is 50m down Millhouse Ln. Parking in field.* **Sun 5 May (2-5). Adm £6, chd free. Home-made teas. Visits also by arrangement 10 Feb to 25 Sept for groups of 15+.**
A garden designed to complement the modern classical house. Formal borders near the house, pond, views across a large lawn, punctuated with wildflowers to the valley beyond. More informal shrub plantings with bulbs edge the woodland. A dry gravel garden leads through more meadow planting to the vegetable garden. Enjoy blossom, tulips, wild garlic, bluebells and young rhododendron in late spring. Early spring bulbs inc masses of snowdrops and daffodils followed by lovely shrubs, perennials and wild roses. Wheelchair access to all areas on grass or gravel paths except the formal pond where there are steps. There are some steep grassy slopes.

 ♿ ✱ ☕))

Our 2023 donation to the Queen's Nursing Institute now helps support over 2,500 Queen's Nurses working in the community in England, Wales, Northern Ireland, the Channel Islands and the Isle of Man

37 THE PINES
58 Hoe Lane, Ware, SG12 9NZ.
Peter Laing. *Approx ½ m S of Ware centre. At S (top) end of Hoe Ln, close to Hertford Rugby Club (car parking) and opp Pinewood Sch. Look for prominent white gateposts with lions.* **Sun 26 May, Sun 29 Sept (2-5.30). Adm £5, chd free. Tea.**
Plantsman's garden with many unusual plants, created by present owner over 30 years. An acre, on an east to west axis so much shade, sandy soil over chalk but can grow ericaceous plants. Front garden formal with fountain. Main garden mature trees, herbaceous borders and island beds. Features inc gravel garden, pergola and obelisk with moss rose "William Lobb". Among many specimen trees, the rare Kashmir cypress. Wheelchair access unless recent heavy rain.

♿ ☕ 🔉

38 RUSTLING END COTTAGE
Rustling End, Codicote, SG4 8TD.
Julie & Tim Wise, www.instagram.com/juliewise2018. *1m N of Codicote. From B656 turn L into '3 Houses Ln' then R to Rustling End. House 2nd on L.* **Wed 15 May (2-5.30). Home-made teas. Evening opening Fri 17 May (5.30-8.30). Wine. Adm £5, chd free.**
Meander through our wildflower meadow to a cottage garden with contemporary planting. Behind lumpy hedges explore a garden managed for wildlife. Natural planting provides an environment for birds, small mammals and insects. Our terrace features drought tolerant low maintenance plants. A flowery mead surrounds the formal pond and an abundant floral vegetable garden provides produce for the summer. Hens in residence. www.rustlingend.com.

✿ ☕ 🔉

39 ♦ ST PAUL'S WALDEN BURY
Whitwell, Hitchin, SG4 8BP. The Bowes Lyon family, 01438 871218, stpaulswalden@gmail.com, www.stpaulswaldenbury.co.uk. *5m S of Hitchin. On B651; ½ m N of Whitwell village. From London leave A1(M) J6 for Welwyn (not Welwyn Garden City). Pick up signs to Codicote, then Whitwell.* **For NGS: Sun 28 Apr, Sun 19 May, Sun 30 June (2-6). Adm £7.50, chd free. Home-made teas. For other opening times and information, please phone, email or visit garden website. Donation to St Paul's Walden Charity.**
Spectacular formal woodland garden, Grade I listed, laid out 1720, covering over 50 acres. Long rides lined with clipped beech hedges lead to temples, statues, lake and a terraced theatre. Seasonal displays of daffodils, cowslips, irises, magnolias, rhododendrons, lilies. Wildflowers are encouraged. This was the childhood home of the late Queen Mother. Children welcome. Dogs on leads. Pre-booking available online at ngs.org.uk. Good wheelchair access to part of the garden. Steep grass slopes in places.

♿ 🐎 🚗 ☕ 🍽 🔉

GROUP OPENING

40 ST STEPHENS AVENUE GARDENS
St Albans, AL3 4AD. *1m S of St Albans City Centre. From A414 take A5183 Watling St. At mini r'about by St Stephens Church/King Harry Pub take B4630 Watford Rd. St Stephens Ave is 1st R.* **Sun 30 June, Sun 1 Sept (2.30-5.30). Combined adm £7, chd free. Home-made teas.**

20 ST STEPHENS AVENUE
Heather & Peter Osborne.

30 ST STEPHENS AVENUE
Carol & Roger Harlow.

Only five doors apart, these two town gardens have been developed in totally different but equally inspiring ways, from an innovative drought tolerant front garden full of Achilleas, Eryngiums and self seeding perennials, to paths winding through borders packed with richly scented roses, clematis, flowering shrubs and hardy plants. The garden at no 20 has been a labour of love since 1993. A series of 'rooms' entices visitors to explore. Specimen trees and fragrant climbers blur the boundaries and provide peaceful seclusion. Colourful patio containers, hostas, wildlife pond, seating in sun and shade, home-made cakes and teas served in the conservatory, WC. The graveled front at no 30 leads round to a sunken garden used as an outdoor kitchen to enjoy the fruits of a productive allotment. Clipped box, beech and hornbeam in the back garden provide a cool backdrop for the strong colours of the double herbaceous borders. A gate beneath an apple arch frames the view to the park behind. Plants for sale at June opening only.

✿ ☕ 🔉

41 SARRATT COMMUNITY GARDEN
The Green, Sarratt, Rickmansworth, WD3 6AT.
Flo Garvey, m.facebook.com/sarrattcommunitygarden/. *Directly behind Sarratt Post Office Stores, in the centre of Sarratt Village.* **Sun 19 May (11-4). Adm £5, chd free. Home-made teas.**
A thriving, productive community garden, growing fruit, veg and cut flowers for local people. This garden is run on organic principles, with a passion for the environment and education. There will be refreshments available, and there is space to sit for around 30 people. Parking is available in the village (extra in the KGV playing fields if needed), though walking and cycling are encouraged.

✿ ☕ 🔉

42 SERENDI
22 Hitchin Road, Letchworth Garden City, SG6 3LT. Valerie, 07548 776809, valerie.aitken22@gmail.com, www.instagram.com/serendigarden/. *1m from city centre. A1M J9 signed Letchworth on A505. At 2nd r'about take 1st exit Hitchin A505. Straight over T-lights. Garden 1m on R.* **Sun 18 Feb (11-4.30). Adm £5, chd free. Light refreshments. Visits also by arrangement 7 Apr to 31 Oct for groups of 10 to 25.**
Massed snowdrops and other spring bulbs. Many different areas within a well designed garden: silver birch grove, a 'dribble of stones', rill, contemporary knot garden, gravel area with alliums. Later in the year an abundance of roses climbing five pillars, perennials, grasses and dahlias. A greenhouse for over wintering, a Griffin glasshouse with, *Tibochina, Aeoniums, Pelargoniums* and more. Wheelchair access via gravel entrance, driveway and paths.

♿ 🐎 ✿ ☕ 🔉

Our donation to the Army Benevolent Fund supported 608 individuals with front line services and horticultural related grants in 2023

42 Falconer Road

GROUP OPENING

43 SERGE HILL GARDENS
Serge Hill Lane,
Bedmond, WD5 0RT.
www.tomstuartsmith.co.uk. ½m
E of Bedmond. Go to Bedmond &
take Serge Hill Ln, where you will be
directed past the lodge & down the
drive. Parking is in a large field. **Sun
2 June (1-5). Combined adm £15,
chd free. Pre-booking essential,
please visit www.ngs.org.uk for
information & booking. Home-
made teas.**

THE BARN
Sue & Tom Stuart-Smith, www.
tomstuartsmith.co.uk/our-work/
toms-garden.
Ⓓ

NEW THE PLANT LIBRARY
Tom & Sue Stuart-Smith,
www.sergehillproject.co.uk.
Ⓓ

SERGE HILL
Kate Stuart-Smith.

Three large country gardens a short
walk from each other. Tom and Sue
Stuart-Smith's garden at The Barn
has an enclosed courtyard with tanks
of water, herbaceous perennials
and shrubs tolerant of generally dry
conditions. To the north there are
views over the five acre wildflower
meadow. The West Garden is a series
of different gardens overflowing with
bulbs, herbaceous perennials, and
shrubs. There is also an exotic prairie
planted from seed in 2011. The Plant
Library is a collection of over 1000
herbaceous plants first planted in
2021. Next door at Serge Hill, there
is a lovely walled garden with a large
Foster and Pearson greenhouse,
orderly rows of vegetables, and
disorderly self-seeded annuals and
perennials. The walls are crowded
with climbers and shrubs. From here
you emerge to a meadow, a mixed
border and a wonderful view over the
ha-ha to the park and woods beyond.
This garden is proud to provide plants
for the National Garden Scheme's
Show Garden at Chelsea Flower
Show 2024. Follow the gardens on
Instagram: @tomstuartsmith
@suestuartsmith @katestuartsmith
@tomstuartsmithstudio.
✳ ☕ ⋙

GROUP OPENING

44 SUNNYSIDE RURAL TRUST TRAIL
Two Waters Road, Hemel
Hempstead, HP3 9BY. Sunnyside
Rural Trust Charity,
www.sunnysideruraltrust.org.uk/.
*The entrance & car park to
Sunnyside Hemel Hempstead are
found off the Two Waters Rd, behind
the K2 restaurant accessed by the
rd to its L.* **Sat 29 June (10-4).
Combined adm £7.50, chd free.**
Home-made teas at Hemel Food
Garden and Northchurch sites.
The cafes offer hot & cold drinks,
cakes & snacks from the farm
shop. The Sunnyside Up cafe
has vegetarian and vegan lunch
options.

SUNNYSIDE RURAL TRUST-BERKHAMSTEAD
HP4 2PP

SUNNYSIDE RURAL TRUST-HEMEL HEMPSTEAD
HP3 9BY

SUNNYSIDE RURAL TRUST-NORTHCHURCH
HP3 9BY

Sunnyside Rural Trust is a therapeutic
horticultural charity and social
enterprise, which supports young
people and adults with learning
disabilities with training and
employment in SW Hertfordshire.
The three, six acre gardens are
located along the Bulbourne valley,
just off the A4251 and close to the
Chilterns AONB. The Northchurch
site is a market garden using 'no
dig' methods, nature trail with wildlife
pond and small animal farm whilst
at Sunnyside Berkhamsted there
is a vegetable growing area and
extensive cane and espalier fruit
garden, with a woodland and hazel
coppice, each busy with wildlife. The
3rd site - Hemel Food Garden is a
Green Flag award winning site that
is also a plant nursery growing peat
free perennial and annual bedding
for domestic and commercial clients.
They have an orchard, quiet garden
space and market garden, growing
a wide range of vegetables for their
own use. For a day out why not
drop in to all three sites under a
combined ticket. A select range of
perennial plants, veg seedlings and
herb plants will be available for sale
as well as homemade chutneys and
jams from our own produce. This

garden is proud to provide plants for
the National Garden Scheme's Show
Garden at Chelsea Flower Show
2024. Assisted wheelchair access
where there are woodland and grass
paths.
♿ 🐄 ✳ ☕ ⋙

45 9 TANNSFIELD DRIVE
Hemel Hempstead, HP2 5LG.
Peter & Gaynor Barrett,
01442 393508,
peteslittlepatch@virginmedia.
com, www.peteslittlepatch.co.uk.
*Approx. 1m NE of Hemel Hempstead
town centre & 2m W of J8 on M1.
From M1 J8, cross r'about to
A414 to Hemel Hempstead. Under
footbridge, cross r'about then 1st
R across dual c'way to Leverstock
Green Rd. On to High St Green. L
into Ellingham Rd then follow signs.*
**Sun 7 July, Sun 4 Aug (1.30-4.30).
Adm £4, chd free. Home-made
teas. Visits also by arrangement
17 June to 18 Aug for groups of
10 to 15.**
A town garden to surprise. Dense
planting together with the ever-
present sound of water, create an
intimate and welcoming oasis of calm.
Narrow paths divide, leading visitors
on a voyage of discovery of the
garden's many features. The owners
regularly experiment with the planting
scheme which ensures the 'look' of
the garden changes from year to year.
Dense planting together with simple
water features, stone statues, metal
sculptures, wall art and mirrors can
be seen throughout the garden. As
a time and cost saving experiment
all hanging baskets are planted with
hardy perennials most of which are
normally used for ground cover.
✳ ☕ ⋙

46 NEW TEWIN GREENS
Hertford Rd, Welwyn,
AL6 0JB. Lloyd Harrison,
www.tewingreens.co.uk. *Set within
the grounds of Tewinbury farm. Head
to the main entrance then follow
signs to the main carpark.* **Sun 4
Aug (11-3). Adm by donation.
Refreshments available from
Tewinbury farm.**
Tewin Greens is a market garden
set within the beautiful grounds of
Tewinbury Farm in Hertfordshire. We
grow seasonal vegetables, fruit and
flowers using no chemicals, minimum
till and organic principles for the local
community as well as providing fresh
produce to the chefs at Tewinbury as

well as other local establishments. www.instagram.com/tewingreens.

47 THUNDRIDGE HILL HOUSE
Cold Christmas Lane, Ware,
SG12 0UE. Christopher &
Susie Melluish, 01920 462500,
c.melluish@btopenworld.com. *2m
NE of Ware. ³⁄₄ m from Maltons off
the A10 down Cold Christmas Ln,
crossing the bypass.* **Sun 16 June
(2-5.30). Adm £5, chd free. Cream
teas. Visits also by arrangement
Apr to Oct for groups of 15+.**
Well established garden of approx
2¹⁄₂ acres; good variety of plants,
shrubs and roses, attractive hedges.
Visitors often ask for the unusual
yellow only bed, 'A most popular
garden to visit'. Wonderful views
in and out of the garden especially
down to the Rib Valley to Youngsbury
and the ruined Tower of St Mary and
All Hallows church. Youngsbury was
visited briefly by Lancelot 'Capability'
Brown. Dogs on leads welcome. A
level garden with paved, gravel and
grass areas.

🚻 🐕 ☕ 🪑))

48 WALKERN HALL
Walkern, Stevenage, SG2 7JA.
Mrs Kate de Boinville. *4m E of
Stevenage. Turn L at War Memorial
as you leave Walkern, heading for
Benington (immed after small bridge).
Garden 1m up hill on R.* **Sat 3, Sun
4 Feb, Sat 23, Sun 24 Mar (12-4).
Adm £5, chd free. Home-made
teas. Warming home-made soup,
coffee and cakes also available.**
Walkern Hall is essentially a winter
woodland garden. Set in eight acres,
the carpet of snowdrops and aconites
is a constant source of wonder in
Jan- Feb. This medieval hunting park
is known more for its established
trees such as the tulip trees and a
magnificent London plane tree which
dominates the garden. Following on in
March and April is a stunning display
of daffodils and other spring bulbs.
There is wheelchair access but quite
a lot of gravel. No disabled WC.

🚻 ❀ 🚗 ☕))

49 WARRENWOOD
39 Firs Wood Close, Potters Bar,
EN6 4BY. Val & Peter Mackie.
*Potters Bar, High Street (A1000)
fork R towards Cuffley, along the
Causeway. Immed before the
T-lights/ Chequers pub, R down
Coopers Ln Rd. ¹⁄₂ m on L Firs Wood*

Close. **Sun 23 June (11-5). Adm
£5, chd free. Home-made teas.
Fantastic selection of home-
made cakes.**
Situated within Northaw Park, a three
acre garden made up of a woodland
area, a field inc a wildflower meadow
and a more formal ¹⁄₂ acre around
the house. Raised vegetable beds
and Victorian greenhouse. Choice
of seating areas inc a breeze house,
sunken fire pit area and colourful patio
benches under the pergola covered
with wisteria. Tranquil views up to
Northaw village. Wheelchair access
is flat from road to back garden and
then on grass.

🚻 🐕 ❀ ☕))

50 WATEREND HOUSE
Waterend Lane, Wheathampstead,
St Albans, AL4 8EP. Mr & Mrs
J Nall-Cain, 07736 880810,
sj@nallcain.com. *2m E of
Wheathampstead. Approx 10 mins
from J4 of A1M. Take B653 to
Wheathampstead, past Crooked
Chimney Pub, after ¹⁄₂ m turn R
into Waterend Ln. Cross river,
house is immed on R.* **Visits by
arrangement Feb to Oct for
groups of 20 to 25. Home-made
teas and a personalised tour of
the garden await you. Adm £12.
Refreshments inc in adm.**
A hidden garden of four acres sets off
an elegant Jacobean Manor House
(not open). Steep grass slopes and
fine views of glorious countryside.
Large quantities of spring bulbs,
formal flint-walled garden. Roses,
peonies and irises in the summer.
Formal beds and lots of colour
throughout the year. Mature specimen
trees, ponds, formal vegetable garden
and chickens. A meditation garden
surrounded by a gallery of hornbeam.
Take a peak at a row of elephants! A
woodland path lined with hellebores.
Hilly garden. Wheelchair access to
lower gardens only.

🚻 ☕))

51 NEW 30 WEST STREET
West Street, Hertford, SG13 8EZ.
Barry and Sophy Lennon. www.
sophylennon.co.uk. *West Street,
Hertford. As you walk from town
into West St, 30 is opp the Black
Horse Pub. West St has limited
parking, please use town car park
or Sainsbury's and walk.* **Evening
opening Wed 12 June (5-8). Adm
£5. Wine. Sat 15 June (10- 12). Adm
£5, chd free. Home-made teas.**
Family garden divided into zones

leading to the riverside. Entrance
into the courtyard (roses, perennials,
small veg patch) with seating under
a pergola. Steps to lawn with
island beds containing grasses and
perennials. Rose arch to a slightly
wilder area, and finally riverside deck
with planted banks. Garden designed
and built by current owners. Planting
design to attract bees and wildlife.
Not suitable for children under 12.

☕))

52 THE WHITE COTTAGE
Waterend Lane,
Wheathampstead,
St Albans, AL4 8EP.
Sally Trendell, 01582 834617,
sallytrendell@me.com,
www.instagram.com/trendellsally.
*2m E of Wheathampstead. Approx
10 mins from J5 A1M Take B653
to Wheathampstead. Soon after
Crooked Chimney pub turn R into
Waterend Ln, garden 300yds on
L. Parking in field opp.* **Evening
opening Fri 28 June (5-9). Adm
£5, chd free. Wine. Soft drinks
and nibbles available.**
Idyllic riverside garden of over an
acre adjacent to the River Lea which
widens to form the garden boundary.
A mix of cottage garden, naturalistic
and wild areas make this a haven for
wildlife which I love to share with my
Airbnb guests as well as the public in
support of NGS and other charities. A
perfect place to relax with a glass of
wine on a summer's evening - bring a
picnic too.

🚻 🐕 ❀ 🪑 ☕ 🏕))

The National
Garden Scheme's
final instalment to
support the building
of the Y Bwthyn NGS
Macmillan Specialist
Palliative Care Unit
in Wales, enabled
270 inpatients to be
supported this year

NORFOLK

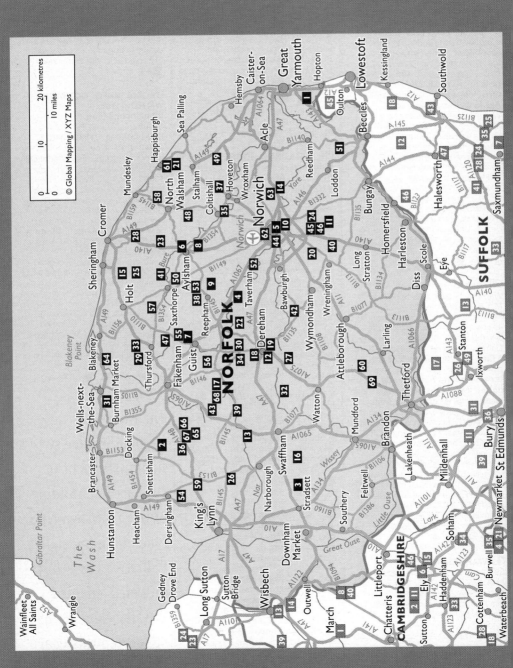

VOLUNTEERS

County Organiser
Julia Stafford Allen
01760 755334
julia.staffordallen@ngs.org.uk

County Treasurer
Andrew Stephens OBE
07595 939769
andrew.stephens@ngs.org.uk

Publicity
Julia Stafford Allen
07778 169775
julia.staffordallen@ngs.org.uk

Social Media
Kenny Higgs 07791 429052
kenny.higgs@ngs.org.uk

Photographer
Simon Smith 01362 860530
simon.smith@ngs.org.uk

**Booklet Co-ordinator
and Group Talks**
Juliet Collier 07986 607170
juliet.collier@ngs.org.uk

New Gardens Organiser
Fiona Black 01692 650247
fiona.black@ngs.org.uk

Group Talks & Visits
Graham Watts 01362 690065
graham.watts@ngs.org.uk

Assistant County Organisers
Jenny Clarke 01508 550261
jenny.clarke@ngs.org.uk

Nick Collier 07733 108443
nick.collier@ngs.org.uk

Sue Guest 01362 858317
guest63@btinternet.com

Sue Roe 01603 455917
sueroe8@icloud.com

Retty Wace 07876 648543
retty.wace@ngs.org.uk

☐ @ngsnorfolk
☒ @Norfolkngs
☐ @norfolkngs

OPENING DATES

All entries subject to change.
For latest information check
www.ngs.org.uk
Map locator numbers are
shown to the right of each
garden name.

February

Snowdrop Openings

Sunday 4th
Lexham Hall   39
Saturday 10th
Horstead House   35
Sunday 11th
Horstead House   35
Lexham Hall   39
Sunday 18th
Bagthorpe Hall   2
Monday 19th
◆ Raveningham Hall   51
Thursday 22nd
NEW Old Hall Farmhouse   47
Saturday 24th
NEW Old Hall Farmhouse   47
Sunday 25th
Chestnut Farm   15

March

Saturday 2nd
◆ Hindringham Hall   29
Saturday 16th
◆ East Ruston Old Vicarage   21
Sunday 24th
Gayton Hall   26
◆ Mannington Estate   41

April

Sunday 14th
Chestnut Farm   15

May

Sunday 5th
Wretham Lodge   69
Monday 6th
Wretham Lodge   69

Sunday 12th
Barton Bendish Hall   3
Holme Hale Hall   32
Tuesday 14th
◆ Stody Lodge   57
Sunday 19th
Blickling Lodge   6
Sunday 26th
Ferndale   24
Lexham Hall   39
Warborough House   64

June

Sunday 2nd
Oulton Hall   50
The Norfolk Hospice, Tapping
House   59
Tuesday 4th
Erpingham House Farm   23
Wednesday 5th
Erpingham House Farm   23
Thursday 6th
Erpingham House Farm   23
Sunday 9th
Booton Hall   9
Elsing Hall Gardens   22
High House Gardens   27
NEW Wensum Farmhouse   65
NEW Wensum House   66
NEW The White Cottage   67
Saturday 15th
Home Farmhouse   33
Sunday 16th
Bolwick Hall   8
Home Farmhouse   33
Manor House Farm, Wellingham   43
Saturday 22nd
47 Norwich Road   45
51 Norwich Road   46
Sunday 23rd
Broadway Farm   12
27 St Edmunds Road   52
Swafield Hall   58
Monday 24th
Swafield Hall   58
Friday 28th
Silverstone Farm   56
Sunday 30th
Kerdiston Manor   38
Walcott House   61

Beck House

THE GARDENS

1 ACRE MEADOW

New Road, Bradwell, Great Yarmouth, NR31 9DU. Mr Keith Knights, 07476 197568, kk.acremeadow@gmail.com, www.acremeadow.co.uk. *Between Bradwell & Belton in arable surroundings. Take Belton & Burgh Castle turn (New Rd) from r'about at Bradwell on A143 Great Yarmouth to Beccles Rd. 400yds on R, drive in wide gateway. For SatNav use NR31 9JW. What3words app - notes.encodes.flip.* **Sun 25 Aug (10-4). Light refreshments. Mon 26 Aug (10-4). Adm £5, chd free. Pre-booking essential, please visit www.ngs.org.uk for information & booking. Home-made cakes, tea & coffee. Visits also by arrangement 18 July to 30 Sept for groups of 8+.**
Dramatic, intensely planted mix of exotic and other late season plants, complementary and contrasting combinations of foliage and flowers, building into a hot colour and dark foliage crescendo. Alive with insects on sunny days. Planting inc *Brugmansia*, dahlias, tall grasses, herbaceous perennials, *Aeoniums*, and lots of cannas. Separate areas inc tea garden and wildlife pond. Disabled access good throughout. No mobility scooters allowed in main garden.

& ✿ 🚗 ☕

2 BAGTHORPE HALL

Bagthorpe, Bircham, King's Lynn, PE31 6QY. Mr & Mrs D Morton. *3½ m N of East Rudham, off A148. Take turn opp The Crown in East Rudham. Look for white gates in trees, slightly set back from the road. Other direction: triangle of grass, continue length of field, white gates on L.* **Sun 18 Feb (11-4). Adm £5, chd free. Light refreshments.**
A delightful circular walk which meanders through a stunning display of snowdrops naturally carpeting a woodland floor, and then returning through a walled garden.

🐐 ✿ 🚗 ☕ ⬤)))

3 BARTON BENDISH HALL

Fincham Road, Barton Bendish, King's Lynn, PE33 9DL. The Barton Bendish Gardening Team. *5m E of Downham Market off A1122. On entering Barton Bendish follow* yellow signs to field parking. **Sun 12 May (11-5). Adm £6.50, chd free. Home-made teas.**
Traditional country estate garden of 10 acres set within farmland. Woodland drive, orchard, south facing terrace, lawns with herbaceous borders. Informal area around pond. Walled kitchen garden with soft fruits, espaliered fruit trees, vegetables, herbs, cut flowers and glasshouse full of scented pelargoniums. Partial wheelchair access.

& ✿ ☕

4 NEW BECK HOUSE

Lyng Easthaugh Road, Weston Longville, Norwich, NR9 5LP. Chris & Wendy Fitch. *11m NW of Norwich, near Lenwade (Gt Witchingham). From either A47 at Honingham or A1067 at Lenwade, turn onto the B1535. Follow this road until you reach Lyng Easthaugh Rd. Follow until you reach Beck House.* **Sun 8 Sept (10.30-4.30). Adm £5, chd free. Home-made teas. and** savouries.
A ¾ acre garden surrounded by open countryside, tirelessly updated over the past four years by the current owners. Bordered by shallow streams, feeding a large natural pond with Japanese inspired plants. There are Mediterranean borders, woodland walkway, flower garden, yew hedge, kitchen garden, patio areas with seating and lots of vertical interest with pergolas and specimen trees. Garden is fairly level and mainly grassed with gravel area at entrance.

& ✿ ☕ ⬤)))

Broadway Farm

152,684 people were able to access guidance on what to expect when a person is dying through the National Garden Scheme support for Hospice UK this year

5 BISHOP'S HOUSE

Bishopgate, Norwich, NR3 1SB. The Bishop of Norwich, www. dioceseofnorwich.org/gardens. *Located in the city centre near the Law Courts & The Adam & Eve Pub. Parking available at town centre car parks inc one by the Adam & Eve pub.* **Sun 7 July (1-4.30). Adm £5, chd free. Home-made teas.** A four acre walled garden dating back to the C12. Extensive lawns with specimen trees. Borders with many rare and unusual shrubs. Spectacular herbaceous borders flanked by yew hedges. Rose beds underplanted with hosta, meadow labyrinth, organic kitchen garden, herb garden and bamboo walk. Popular plant sales. Wheelchair access over gravel paths and some slopes.

6 BLICKLING LODGE

Blickling, Norwich, NR11 6PS. Michael & Henrietta Lindsell, nicky@lindsell.co.uk. *½m N of Aylsham. Leave Aylsham on Old Cromer rd towards Ingworth. Over hump back bridge & house is on R.* **Sun 19 May (12-5). Adm £6, chd free. Home-made teas. Visits also by arrangement 19 May to 27 Sept for groups of 10 to 40. Discuss refreshments when booking.** Georgian house (not open) set in 17 acres of parkland inc cricket pitch, mixed border, walled kitchen garden, yew garden, woodland, and water garden.

7 BLUEBELL BARN

Lyng Hall Lane, Wood Norton, Dereham, NR20 5BJ. Rose and Phil Tweedie. *9m SW of Holt. 9 m E of Fakenham. Take B1110 to Holt from Guist. Ignore the Xrds for Wood Norton and take next R onto Rectory Rd. Drive to the 30 mph signs, take next L onto gravel rd. Bluebell Barn is 1st L.* **Sun 4 Aug (11-5). Adm £4, chd free. Pre-booking essential, please visit www.ngs.org.uk for information & booking.** Garden and meadow in total covering two and a half acres and newly planted by the current owners over the last four years. Colourful herbaceous borders with some specimen trees surround a circular lawn in the formal part of the garden. Informal meadow area with mown pathways through. Limited parking.

8 BOLWICK HALL

Marsham, NR10 5PU. Mr & Mrs G C Fisher. *8m N of Norwich off A140. From Norwich, heading N on A140, just past Marsham take 1st R after Plough Pub, signed 'By Road' then next R onto private drive to front of Hall.* **Sun 16 June (1-5). Adm £6, chd free. Home-made teas.** Landscaped gardens and park surrounding a late Georgian hall. The original garden design is attributed to Humphrey Repton. The current owners have rejuvenated the borders, planted gravel and formal gardens and clad the walls of the house in old roses. Enjoy a woodland walk around the lake as well as as stroll through the working vegetable and fruit garden with its double herbaceous border. Please note that most of the paths are gravel.

9 BOOTON HALL

Church Road, Booton, Norwich, NR10 4NZ. Piers & Cecilia Willis. *1m E of Reepham. Drive out of Reepham east on Norwich Rd, after 1m turn L into Church Rd. After 500 metres turn L through white wooden gates just after bendy road sign on L.* **Sun 9 June (11-5). Adm £6, chd free. Home-made teas.** Walled garden with formal layout and tiered lawns re-designed eight years ago and attached to C17/18 hall. Lawns between the house and parkland meadows, shrub beds, pond planting, small orchard and short woodland walk. Parking in one of the meadows close to drive entrance, prior drop-off by house possible in extremis. Wheelchair access, but some gravel quite deep, and some steps, so will require energetic help.

GROUP OPENING

10 NEW BRACONDALE GARDENS

Norwich, NR1 2BB. Mr Andrew Sankey. *From County Hall r'about, heading towards the City Centre on Bracondale, turn L at Conesford Dr. Parking at County Hall and then a short walk.* **Sun 21 July (10.30-4.30). Combined adm £7, chd free. Light refreshments on the green next to 1 Woodside Cottages.**

NEW 14 CONESFORD DRIVE
Mr Andrew Sankey.

NEW 18 CONESFORD DRIVE
Mrs Pauline McLean.

1 WOODSIDE COTTAGES
Wayne Waith.

A warm welcome awaits you at these three attractive compact town gardens a short walk apart and each with a different character. 1 Woodside Cottages: A very pretty, small cottage garden packed with colourful plants both ornamental and edible and even the resident chickens are decorative. Fruit trees and vegetables grow side by side with perennial and annual flowers and a small pond supports a multitude of frogs each spring. 18 Conesford Drive: This professionally designed and planted garden lies at the back of a 1960s modernist house. Restrained planting of herbaceous flowering plants, climbers and small shrubs give the garden a Japanese feel and a small pool contains white flowering waterlilies. 14 Conesford Drive: Lush planting of fruit, vegetables and flowers welcome you at the side of this 1960s modernist house leading to a densely planted cottage garden of carefully selected perennials and climbers.

11 BRICK KILN HOUSE

Priory Lane, Shotesham, Norwich, NR15 1UJ. Jim & Jenny Clarke, 07748 655815, jennyclarke985@gmail.com. *6m S of Norwich. From Shotesham, All Saints church Priory Ln is 200m on R on Saxlingham Rd.* **Sun 4 Aug (10-4). Adm £6, chd free. Home-made teas. Visits also by arrangement June to Sept for groups of up to 35.** Two acre country garden with a large terrace, lawns and colourful herbaceous borders. There is a contemporary designed pergola garden, sculptures and a stream running through a diversely planted wood. Easy access to brick path.

12 BROADWAY FARM

The Broadway, Scarning, Dereham, NR19 2LQ. Michael & Corinne Steward, 07881 691899, corinneasteward@gmail.com. *16m W of Norwich. 12m E of Swaffham. From A47 W take a R into Fen Rd, opp Drayton Hall Ln. From A47 E*

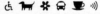

take L into Fen Rd, then immed L at T-junc, immed R into The Broadway. **Sun 23 June (11-5). Adm £5, chd free. Home-made teas. Visits also by arrangement 10 June to 10 Aug for groups of 10 to 40.**
A ½ acre cottage garden surrounding a C14 clapboard farmhouse. Colourful herbaceous borders with a wide range of perennial and woody plants and a well planted pond, providing habitat for wildlife. A plantswoman's garden.

GROUP OPENING

13 CASTLE ACRE GARDENS
King's Lynn, PE32 2AN. 4 m N of Swaffham off A1065. Car park in field below Tudor Lodgings. **Sun 21 July (10.30-4.30). Combined adm £10, chd free. Light refreshments homebaked at Tudor Lodgings.**

NEW EGERTON HOUSE
Tim and Sally Hubbard.

HIGHFIELD HOUSE
David & Jackie Moss.

ORMONDE HOUSE
Anthony & Elizabeth Wright.

TUDOR LODGINGS
Gus & Julia Stafford Allen, 01760 755334, julia.staffordallen@ngs.org.uk. **Visits also by arrangement June to Sept.**

Castle Acre is an attractive historic Norman village with a bailey gate, castle, earthworks, parish church and priory. Set in the countryside of West Norfolk, there is a bookshop, pub, tearoom, shop and playground. The four delightful gardens that vary in planting, size, style and structure, will provide visitors with much interest and inspiration. Tudor Lodgings, has a two acre garden that fronts a C15 house and incorporates part of the Norman earthworks. C18 dovecote, topiary, and lawns, with borders of shrubs, perennials and grasses, a productive fruit cage and cutting garden. The wild area has a pond, ducks and chickens. Just up the road is Ormonde House, a small walled rear garden facing south with mixed shrubs, perennials, and annuals. Situated in Back Lane, the ¾ acre garden at Highfield House, was begun over 30 years ago and has well planted herbaceous borders, vegetable area, gravel garden and pond with wildflower meadow. Nearby Egerton House is packed with both shade and

sun loving plants, patio with pots, a pond and productive vegetable garden.

14 NEW CHARNWOOD
7 Postwick Lane, Brundall, Norwich, NR13 5RD. Vicci and Martin Hine. 5m E of Norwich. From A47 take Brundall exit. Proceed along Cucumber Ln to T-junc and turn R onto Postwick Ln. Charnwood is on the L. **Sun 18 Aug (10-4). Adm £5, chd free. Home-made teas.**
A summer garden which has been evolving over the last three years. It has mixed and herbaceous borders, topiary, a small vegetable garden, a wildlife garden with pond and inc a greenhouse, terrace and pots. Its southerly aspect overlooks the Yare valley.

15 CHESTNUT FARM
Church Road, West Beckham, Holt, NR25 6NX. Mr & Mrs John McNeil Wilson, 01263 822241, judywilson100@gmail.com. 2½ m S of Sheringham. From A148 opp Sheringham Park entrance. Take the road signed 'By way To West Beckham', about ¾ m to the garden by village sign. N.B. SatNav will take you to the pub. **Sun 25 Feb (11-4); Sun 14 Apr (11-5). Adm £5, chd free. Light refreshments. Gluten free options available. Visits also by arrangement 25 Feb to 28 July for groups of 10 to 30.**
Mature three acre garden developed over 60 years with collections of many rare and unusual plants and trees. 100+ varieties of snowdrops, drifts of crocus with seasonal flowering shrubs. Later, wood anemones, fritillary meadow, wildflower walk, pond, small arboretum, croquet lawn and colourful herbaceous borders. In May the handkerchief tree, cercis, camassias and early roses. Always something new. Wheelchair access tricky if wet.

16 COBWEB COTTAGE
51 Shingham, Beachamwell, Swaffham, PE37 8AY. Sue Bunting, 01366 328428, susannahbunting@btinternet.com. 5m from Swaffham. Shingham is next to Beachamwell. The cottage is 1st on the L after the Shingham village sign. **Sun 25 Aug (10-5). Adm £4.50, chd**

free. Cream teas. Visits also by arrangement Apr to Sept for groups of 5 to 50.
A small cottage garden on the edge of the village with mixed borders, a sunken greenhouse, pergola, and a wildlife pond. There is also a large productive ornamental kitchen garden with bees, chickens, treehouse, prairie planting and fruit cage. Plants for sale.

17 NEW COKESFORD FARM
Tittleshall, King's Lynn, PE32 2RQ. Charles & Sara Foster. 6m S of Fakenham. ½ m SE of Tittleshall village, on the Stanfield Rd. Parking available. **Sun 28 July (2-5). Combined adm with Woodford Lodge £6.50, chd free.**
Farmhouse garden of about two acres. Well planted mixed borders surround lawn and ha-ha, with extensive rural views and lake. Parterre, vegetable garden, informal orchard, and short woodland walk.

18 DALE FARM
Sandy Lane, Dereham, NR19 2EA. Graham & Sally Watts, 01362 690065, grahamwatts@dsl.pipex.com. 16m W of Norwich. 12m E of Swaffham. From A47 take B1146 signed to Fakenham, turn R at T-junc, ¼ m turn L into Sandy Ln (on before pelican Xing). **Sun 28 July (10.30-5). Adm £6, chd free. Home-made teas. Visits also by arrangement 10 June to 21 July for groups of 15 to 45.**
A two acre plant lovers' garden with a large spring-fed pond. Over 1000 plant varieties in exuberantly planted borders with sculptures. Also, gravel, vegetable, nature and waterside gardens. Collection of 150 hydrangeas. Swing Band music during the day, some grass paths and gravel drive. Wide choice of plants for sale and wood sculptures exhibition.

The National Garden Scheme donated £3,403,960 to our nursing and health beneficiaries from money raised at gardens open in 2023

19 DUNBHEAGAN
Dereham Road, Westfield,
NR19 1QF. Jean & John
Walton, 01362 696163,
jandjwalton@btinternet.com. *2m
S of Dereham. From Dereham turn
L off A1075 into Westfield Rd by
the Vauxhall garage/Premier food
store. Straight ahead at Xrds into
lane which becomes Dereham Rd.
Garden on L.* **Sun 21 July (1-5).
Adm £5, chd free. Home-made
teas. Visits also by arrangement
20 June to 27 July for groups of
10+.**
Relax and enjoy the garden where
the rare and unusual rub shoulders
with the more recognisable plants in
densely planted beds and borders
in this ever-changing plantsman's
garden. Lots of paths to explore.
A riot of colour all summer. Lots of
seating. Wheelchair access via gravel
driveway.

20 NEW **EAST CARLETON
MANOR**
Rectory Road, East Carleton,
Norwich, NR14 8JY. Clive
Chapman. *4m S of Norwich.
Entrance is at the junc of Scott's Hill
and Rectory Rd in East Carleton.*
**Sat 26 Oct (10-4). Adm £10, chd
free. Pre-booking essential,
please visit www.ngs.org.uk for
information & booking. Home-
made teas.**
A 10 acre garden designed and
planted in the 1960's for autumn
colour, with many interesting trees
and shrubs. There is a summerhouse,
with a knot garden, a walled garden
with a hydrangea border, a moon gate
and Italian garden. Water circulates
through smaller ponds into a lake with
water lilies. Wheelchair access along
slightly uneven gravel paths. Some
areas have steps.

In 2023 we awarded
over £260,000 in
Community Garden
Grants, supporting
86 community garden
projects

**21 ◆ EAST RUSTON OLD
VICARAGE**
East Ruston, Norwich,
NR12 9HN. Alan Gray & Graham
Robeson, 01692 650432, office@
eastrustonoldvicarage.co.uk,
www.eastrustonoldvicarage.co.uk.
*3m N of Stalham. Turn off A149 onto
B1159 signed Bacton, Happisburgh.
After 2m turn R 200yds N of East
Ruston Church (ignore sign to East
Ruston).* **For NGS: Sat 16 Mar, Sat
19 Oct (12-5.30). Adm £13, chd
£2. Light refreshments. For other
opening times and information,
please phone, email or visit garden
website.**
Large garden with traditional borders
and modern landscapes. Discover
our various types of gardens inc
walled, rose and exotic gardens,
topiary and box parterres. We have
water features, Mediterranean garden,
fruit cage and containers to die for
in spring and summer. Cornfield and
meadows, vegetable and cutting
gardens, parkland and heritage
orchard, in all 32 acres. Rare and
unusual plants abound.

22 ELSING HALL GARDENS
Elsing Hall, Hall Road, Elsing,
NR20 3DX. Patrick Lines & Han
Yang Yap, www.elsinghall.com.
*6km NW of Dereham. From A47
take the N Tuddenham exit. From
A1067 take the turning to Elsing
opp the Bawdeswell Garden Centre.*
**Sun 9 June (10-4). Adm £8, chd
free. Home-made teas. Picnics
allowed in the car park.**
C15 fortified manor house (not open)
with working moat. 10 acre gardens
and 10 acre park surrounding the
house. Significant collection of old
roses, walled garden, formal garden,
marginal planting, ginko avenue,
viewing mound, moongate, interesting
pinetum and terraced garden. Please
note that there are very limited WC
facilities available.

23 ERPINGHAM HOUSE FARM
Erpingham, Norwich, NR11 7QD.
Buffy Willcox. *Turn off the A140 into
Erpingham, signposted for caravans
and camping. Continue ½ m along
the road and up a track lined with
lime trees.* **Evening opening Tue
4, Wed 5, Thur 6 June (6-8).
Adm £15, chd free. Pre-booking
essential, please visit www.ngs.
org.uk for information & booking.
Wine.**

The varieties of peonies grown have
been carefully chosen to fill the whole
season from early May to late June,
with a generous selection of colours
and beautiful scents. The peonies
here benefit from being field grown in
full sun and rich grade II loam soil and
have been a successful part of the
diversification on the farm.

24 FERNDALE
14, Poringland Road, Upper
Stoke Holy Cross, Norwich,
NR14 8NL. Dr Alan & Mrs
Sheila Sissons, 01508 494222,
asissons@hotmail.com. *4m
S of Norwich. From Norwich or
Poringland on B1332, take Stoke Rd
at Railway Tavern r'about. Ferndale
is 0.7m on L. Parking on road.* **Sun
26 May, Sun 28 July (11-4). Adm
£4, chd free. Light refreshments.
Visits also by arrangement 19 May
to 18 Aug for groups of 6 to 20.**
⅓ acre garden, paved area with
seating surrounded by borders of
shrubs and flowers. A pond with
water feature. In the second area is
more seating plus apple trees, soft
fruit, vegetable plot, greenhouse and
herb bed. Shingled area with water
feature, rose arbour and low semi-
circular wall planted with flowers.
There will be a craft stall and there
may be an accordionist playing.
Wheelchair access via 1m wide paved
passageway to garden.

25 FIDDIAN'S FOLLY
Upwood Farm, North Barningham,
Norwich, NR11 7LA. Dick & Debbie
Fiddian, fiddiansfollies.uk. *N
Barningham. Follow SatNav. Gardens
will be signed from N Barningham
& Baconsthorpe.* **Sun 11 Aug
(10-5). Adm £6, chd free. Light
refreshments.**
The garden at Upwood Farm
(affectionally known as Fiddian's
Follies), has been described as quirky,
full of surprises and generally very
different to usual herbaceous borders,
rose beds and sweeping lawns. There
are several follies, lovingly created
with brick and stone elements, in and
around what was once an old quarry.
The garden, set in three acres, boasts
wonderful unspoilt views.

Cokesford Farm

26 GAYTON HALL

Gayton, King's Lynn, PE32 1PL.
Viscount & Viscountess Marsham.
*6m E of King's Lynn. Off the B1145.
At village sign take 2nd exit off Back
St to entrance.* **Sun 24 Mar (12-5).
Adm £6, chd free. Home-made
teas.**
This rambling semi-wild garden,
has over two miles of paths which
meander through lawn, streams,
bridges and woodland. Primulas,
astilbes, hostas, lysichiton and
gunnera grow along the water's edge.
There is a good display of spring
bulbs and a variety of unusual trees
and shrubs, many labelled, have been
planted over the years. Wheelchair
access to most areas via gravel and
grass paths.

27 HIGH HOUSE GARDENS

Blackmoor Row, Shipdham,
Thetford, IP25 7PU.

Sue & Fred Nickerson. *6m SW
of Dereham. Take the airfield
or Cranworth Rd off A1075 in
Shipdham. Blackmoor Row is
signed.* **Sun 9 June, Sun 8 Sept
(12-5). Adm £6, chd free. Home-
made teas.**
Three acre plantsman's garden
developed and maintained by the
current owners, over the last 40
years. Garden consists of colour
themed herbaceous borders with
an extensive range of perennials,
box edged rose and shrub borders,
woodland garden, pond and bog
area, orchard and small arboretum.
Plus large vegetable garden.
Wheelchair access via gravel paths.

28 HIGHVIEW HOUSE

Norwich Road, Roughton,
Norwich, NR11 8NA. Graham
& Sarah Last, 07976 066896,
grahamrc.last@gmail.com. *On*

*A140 approx ½m N off Roughton
village mini r'abouts. Highview
House is on the R after the layby,
travelling N of Roughton.* **Visits by
arrangement 15 June to 30 Sept
for groups of 20 to 80. Any time
of day subject to availability inc a
talk by the owners. Adm £10, chd
free. Light refreshments.**
Two acre garden featuring a large
range of herbaceous borders. Long
season of interest through to first
frost with a large range of perennial
plants maintained by the owners.
Over 200 salvia varieties feature
through the planting of over12,000
plants attracting masses of bees and
butterflies. Acer trees, interesting
garden structures, water feature.
Suitable in most parts for wheelchairs.
Wheelchair access, park on the main
driveway with access to pathway.
Some slopes will need to be
accommodated.

29 ◆ HINDRINGHAM HALL
Blacksmiths Lane, Hindringham, NR21 0QA. Mr & Mrs Charles Tucker, 01328 878226, hindhall@btinternet.com, www.hindringhamhall.org. *7m from Holt/ Fakenham/ Wells. Turn off A148 at Crawfish Pub towards Hindringham. Drive 2m. Enter village of Hindringham. Turn L into Blacksmiths Ln after village hall.* **For NGS: Sat 2 Mar (10-4). Adm £8, chd free. Light refreshments inc hot soup and sausage rolls as well as tea, coffee and cakes. For other opening times and information, please phone, email or visit garden website.**
A garden surrounding a Grade II Tudor Manor House (not open) enveloped by a complete medieval moat plus three acres of fishponds. Working walled vegetable garden, Victorian nut walk, formal beds, bog and stream gardens. Something of interest throughout the year. Daffodils, spring wild garden, hellebore and primula, roses and clematis. Third in the 2020 Historic House Garden of the Year Award. Wheelchair access via gravel paths.
& ✿ 🚐 🛏 ☕))

30 HOE HALL
Hall Road, Hoe, Dereham, NR20 4BD. Mr & Mrs James Keith, 01362 693169, vrkeith@hoehall.co.uk. *The garden is next to Hoe church.* **Visits by arrangement 15 May to 30 June for groups of up to 30. Tour of garden and refreshments inc in adm. Adm £10, chd free.**
The main visual is a walled garden featuring a long white wisteria walk. This is set in the grounds of a Georgian rectory surrounded by parkland. The garden was redesigned in 1990 to incorporate climbers and herbaceous plants, with box parterres replacing the kitchen garden. There are espaliered fruit trees, and an old swimming pool with water lilies. Seating area and WC available in the walled garden.
& 🚐 ☕

31 HOLKHAM WALLED GARDEN
Holkham Hall, Wells-Next-The-Sea, NR23 1AB. Holkham Estate, www.holkham.co.uk. *Within the Holkham Estate. Drive through the main entrance and follow signs in the park to walled garden.* **Evening opening Wed 4 Sept (6-8). Adm**
£22, chd free. Pre-booking essential, please visit www.ngs.org.uk for information & booking. Wine.
C18 Walled garden approx 6½ acres divided into six distinct areas which inc ornamental, exotic, kitchen, cutting flower glasshouse area and vineyard. Recent extensive restoration to glasshouses and Samuel Wyatt Vinery. A newly planted maze and plenty of autumn colour. Wheelchair access via gravel paths. Two mobility scooters available.
& 🐕 ☕

32 HOLME HALE HALL
Holme Hale, Swaffham, Thetford, IP25 7ED. Mr & Mrs Simon Broke. *2m S of Necton off A47. 1m E of Holme Hale village on Bradenham Rd.* **Sun 12 May, Sun 18 Aug (12-4). Adm £8, chd free. Light refreshments.**
Walled kitchen garden designed by Arne Maynard and replanted in 2016-17. Soft palette of herbaceous plants inc some unusual varieties and provide a long season of interest. Greenhouse, vegetables, trained fruits, roses and topiary. 130 year old wisteria. Wildlife friendly with wildflower meadow and renovated island pond. Historic buildings with a dry garden formed from crushed concrete and rubble. Wheelchair access to most areas.
& 🐕 ✿ 🚐 ☕))

33 HOME FARMHOUSE
91 The Street, Hindringham, NR21 0PS. Rachel & John Hannyngton. *Hindringham is between the villages of Binham & Thursford. From A148 between Fakenham & Holt, turn N at The Crawfish pub.* **Sat 15, Sun 16 June (10-5). Adm £6, chd free. Home-made teas.**
An imaginative, informal two acre garden, developed over the past 25 years with orchard, working potager, herbaceous borders, 'white' courtyard, Piet Oudolf-style perennial and grass border, wildflower meadow and woodland walk.
✿ ☕))

34 HONEYSUCKLE WALK
Litcham Road, Gressenhall, Dereham, NR20 4AR. Simon & Joan Smith, 01362 860530, simon.smith@ngs.org.uk. *17m W of Norwich. Follow B1146 & signs to Gressenhall Rural Life Museum then*
follow Litcham Rd into Gressenhall village. We are the 4th house on the L after passing the 30mph sign. **Visits by arrangement 15 June to 7 Aug for groups of 10 to 20. Adm inc refreshments. Adm £10, chd free.**
Two acre woodland garden with two ponds, river and stream, 80 ornamental trees and a collection of 400 different hydrangeas, many of which are rare. Enjoy a woodland walk, which is accessed by ¼ m grass track. Hosta plants for sale.
🐕 ✿))

35 HORSTEAD HOUSE
Mill Road, Horstead, Norwich, NR12 7AU. Mr & Mrs Matthew Fleming, 07771 655637, horsteadsnowdrops@gmail.com. *6m NE of Norwich on North Walsham Rd, B1150. Down Mill Rd opp the Recruiting Sergeant pub.* **Sat 10, Sun 11 Feb (11-3). Adm £5, chd free. Home-made teas. Visits also by arrangement 1 Feb to 18 Feb.**
Stunning display of beautiful snowdrops carpet the woodland setting with winter flowering shrubs. Another beautiful feature is the dogwoods growing on a small island in the River Bure, which flows through the garden. There is also a small walled garden. Wheelchair access to main snowdrop area.
& 🐕 🛏 ☕))

36 ◆ HOUGHTON HALL WALLED GARDEN
Bircham Road, Houghton, King's Lynn, PE31 6TY. The Cholmondeley Gardens Trust, 01485 528569, info@houghtonhall.com, www.houghtonhall.com. *11m W of Fakenham. 13m E of King's Lynn. Signed from A148.* **For opening times and information, please phone, email or visit garden website.**
The award-winning, five acre walled garden, beautifully divided into different areas designed by the Bannermans, inc a kitchen garden with espalier fruit trees, glasshouses, a Mediterranean garden, rose parterre, wisteria pergola and a spectacular double-sided herbaceous border. Many antique statues, fountains and contemporary sculptures. Gravel and grass paths. Electric buggies available in the walled garden.
& ✿ 🚐 ☕

37 ◆ HOVETON HALL GARDENS

Hoveton Hall Estate, Hoveton, Norwich, NR12 8RJ. Mr & Mrs Harry Buxton, 01603 784297, office@hovetonhallestate.co.uk, www.hovetonhallestate.co.uk. *8m N of Norwich. 1m N of Wroxham Bridge. Off A1151 Stalham Rd. Follow brown tourist signs.* For NGS: Sun 18 Aug (10.30-5). Adm £9, chd £4.50. Picnics are allowed for garden patrons only. For other opening times and information, please phone, email or visit garden website.

Explore the 15 acre gardens and woodlands taking you through the seasons. Mature walled herbaceous and kitchen gardens. Informal woodlands and lakeside walks. Nature spy activity trail for our younger visitors. A varied events programme runs throughout the season. Please visit our website for more details. Light lunches and afternoon tea from our on site Garden Kitchen Cafe. The gardens are accessible to wheelchair users. We offer a reduced entry price for wheelchair users and their carers.

38 KERDISTON MANOR

Kerdiston, Norwich, NR10 4RY. Philip & Mararette Hollis. *1m from Reepham. Turn at Bawdswell garden centre towards Reepham. After 3.8m turn L Smugglers Rd leaving Reepham surgery on L. Take L into Kerdiston Rd 1½m house on R.* Sun 30 June (11-5). Adm £6, chd free. Light refreshments.

A two acre tranquil garden surrounding Manor House (not open) that has been developed by the owners for over 30 years. Mature trees, colourful herbaceous borders, dell garden, potager style vegetable plot, pond, a 15 acre wild meadow walk and wonderful thatched C18 barn. Wheelchair access to teas and terrace over looking garden.

39 LEXHAM HALL

nr Litcham, PE32 2QJ. Mr & Mrs Neil Foster, www.lexhamestate.co.uk. *6m N of Swaffham off B1145. 2m W of Litcham.* Sun 4, Sun 11 Feb (11-4). Adm £6, chd free. Sun 26 May, Wed 17 July (11-5). Adm £8, chd free. Home-made teas. Donation to East Lexham Church (Feb only).

Parkland with lake and river walks surround C17/18 Hall (not open). Formal garden with terraces, roses and mixed borders. Traditional working kitchen garden with crinkle-crankle wall. Year-round interest; woods and borders carpeted with snowdrops in February, rhododendrons, azaleas, camellias and magnolias in the three acre woodland garden in May, and July sees the walled garden borders at their peak.

40 THE LONG BARN

Flordon Road, Newton Flotman, Norwich, NR15 1QX. Mr & Mrs Mark Bedini. *6m S of Norwich along A140. Leave A140 in Newton Flotman towards Flordon. Exit Newton Flotman & approx 150 yds beyond 'passing place' on L, turn L into drive. Note that SatNav often does not bring you to destination.* Sun 28 July (10.30-4.30). Adm £6, chd free. Home-made teas.

Beautiful informal garden with ha-ha creating infinity views across ancient parkland. Strong Mediterranean influence with plenty of seating in large paved courtyard with pollarded plane trees. Unusual wall-sheltered group of four venerably gnarled olive trees, figs and vines, then herbaceous borders, tiered lawns merging northwards into woodland garden. Walks through parkland to the River Tas - serene. Wheelchair drop off at front of house. Gradual lawn slope accesses upper tier of garden. WC requires steps.

41 ◆ MANNINGTON ESTATE

Mannington, Norwich, NR11 7BB. Lady Walpole, 01263 584175, admin@walpoleestate.co.uk, www.manningtonestate.co.uk. *18m NW of Norwich. 2m N of Saxthorpe via B1149 towards Holt. At Saxthorpe/Corpusty follow signs to Mannington.* For NGS: Sun 24 Mar (11-4.30). Adm £8, chd free. Light refreshments in the Garden Tearooms. Home-made locally sourced food with home-made teas. For other opening times and information, please phone, email or visit garden website.

Explore 20 acres of gardens which feature shrubs, lake and trees, period garden and sensory garden. Extensive countryside walks and trails from the garden. There is also a moated manor house and Saxon church with C19

follies. We have wildflowers and birds a plenty. Wheelchair access via gravel paths. One steep slope.

42 MANOR FARM, COSTON

Coston Lane, Coston, Wymondham, NR9 4DT. Mr & Mrs J D Hambro, 07554 584471. *10m W of Norwich. Off B1108 Norwich-Watton Rd. Take B1135 to Dereham at Kimberley. After 300yds sharp L bend, go straight over to Coston Ln. Garden on L. What3words app - onions.croak.springing.* Visits by arrangement Feb to Nov for groups of 20 to 50. Tour of garden with head gardener and teas inc. Weekdays preferred. Adm £12, chd free. Home-made teas.

Wonderful five acre country garden set in larger estate. Several small garden rooms with both formal and informal planting. Climbing roses, walled kitchen garden, white, grass and late summer themes, classic herbaceous and shrub borders, box parterres and large areas of wildflowers. Large collection of sculptures dotted round the garden. Dogs welcome. Something for everyone. Wheelchair access via some gravel paths. A few steps.

43 MANOR HOUSE FARM, WELLINGHAM

Fakenham, King's Lynn, PE32 2TH. Robin & Elisabeth Ellis, 01328 838227, libbyelliswellingham@gmail.com, www.manor-farm.co.uk. *½m off A1065 7m W from Fakenham & 8m E. Swaffham. By the Church.* Sun 16 June (11-5). Adm £7, chd free. Home-made teas.

Charming four acre country garden surrounds an attractive farmhouse. Formal quadrants, 'hot spot' of grasses and gravel, small arboretum, pleached lime walk, vegetable parterre and rose tunnel. Unusual walled 'Taj' garden with old-fashioned roses, tree peonies, lilies and formal pond. A variety of herbaceous plants. Small herd of Formosan Sika deer. Picnics allowed.

44 NORTH LODGE
51 Bowthorpe Road, Norwich,
NR2 3TN. Bruce Bentley & Peter
Wilson. *1½ m W of Norwich City
Centre. Turn into Bowthorpe Rd off
Dereham Rd, garden150m on L.
By bus: 21, 22, 23, & 24 from city
centre, Old Catton, Heartsease,
Thorpe & most of W Norwich.
Parking available outside & room for
bikes.* **Sun 21, Sun 28 July (11-5).
Adm £5, chd free. Home-made
teas. Cakes inc gluten-free and
vegan.**
Magical town garden surrounding
Victorian Gothic Cemetery Lodge.
Strong structure and vistas inc a
classical temple, oriental water
gardens, formal ponds linked with
winding pathways with a surprise
around every corner! Original
25m-deep well. Predominantly
herbaceous planting. Carnivorous
and succulent collection in hand-built
conservatory. House extension won
architectural award. Slide show of
house and garden history. Wheelchair
access possible but difficult. Sloping
gravel drive followed by steep, narrow
ramp.
♿ ❀ ☕))

45 47 NORWICH ROAD
Stoke Holy Cross, Norwich,
NR14 8AB. Anna & Alistair Lipp.
*Heading S through Stoke Holy Cross
on Norwich Rd, garden on R down
private drive. No parking at property.
Parking at sports ground car park on
L of Long Ln, 500 yds to garden.* **Sat
22 June (11-5). Combined adm
with 51 Norwich Road £6, chd
free. Home-made teas.**
Medium sized, west facing garden
developed over 25 years with views
over Tas Valley and water meadows.
Vine and rose covered pergola, gravel
beds, terrace with raised beds and
shading magnolias, large greenhouse
with exotic plants. Small wildflower
meadow and informal pond. Gravel
driveway to brick paths with slope.
Majority of garden accessible for
wheelchair users.
♿ ❀ ☕))

46 51 NORWICH ROAD
Stoke Holy Cross, Norwich,
NR14 8AB. Mrs Vivian Carrington.
*5m S of Norwich. Heading S through
Stoke Holy Cross on Norwich Rd,
garden on R down private drive.
No parking at property. Parking
at sports ground car park on L of
Long Ln, 500 yds to garden.* **Sat 22
June (11-5). Combined adm with**

47 Norwich Road £6, chd free.
Home-made teas at 47 Norwich
Road.
The garden has a variety of
perennials, roses and annuals at
the front with an asparagus bed
and vegetables to the side and rear.
There are cold frames and a small
greenhouse. Behind the house there
are further flower beds and a small
lawn. Wheelchair access at the front
and rear of garden.
♿ ❀ ☕))

**47 NEW OLD HALL
FARMHOUSE**
Little Wood Lane, Swanton
Novers, Melton Constable,
NR24 2RE. John and Jane-Ann
Walton, www.instagram.com/
jane_ann_walton. *From B1110 Guist/ Holt Rd turn
into Swanton Novers village. Turn
into Church Ln, past the church and
downhill.* **Thur 22, Sat 24 Feb (11-1
& 2-4). Adm £10. Pre-booking
essential, please visit www.ngs.
org.uk for information & booking.
Light refreshments.**
Enjoy a morning or afternoon visit to
this charming garden full of snowdrop
cultivars, hellebores and other winter
flowering plants. The owner will
welcome you and give an introduction
to collecting and growing snowdrops.
❀ ☕

48 OLD MANOR FARMHOUSE
The Hill, Swanton Abbott,
Norwich, NR10 5EA. Drs Paul
and Sian Everden, 07768 376621,
info@hostebarn.com. *Just outside
Swanton Abbott on N Norfolk Coast.
From Swanton Abbott take Long
Common Ln until you see the car
park sign on The Hill.* **Sat 13, Sun
14 July (9.30-5). Adm £5, chd free.
Home-made teas. Visits also by
arrangement June to Aug.**
Originally a field surrounding a
derelict C17 listed Farmhouse (not
open). Winning the 1991 Graham
Allen Conservation Award, the
garden structure, sympathetic to the
Dutch style of the house was laid
down. Closed knot garden of box
surrounded by pleached hornbeam,
pollarded plane trees, beech and yew
hedges divide areas and flank walks,
herbaceous borders and lawns,
clematis and rose walk to potager
and paddock. Regional Finalist, The
English Garden Magazine's The
Nation's Favourite Gardens, 2023
🐕 🚗 🚌 ☕ 🧺))

**49 THE OLD RECTORY,
CATFIELD**
School Road, Catfield, Great
Yarmouth, NR29 5DA. Penny
Middleditch, 07887 584790,
penny.middleditch@me.com.
*A149 to Catfield. ½ m from Catfield
village centre turn R by Post Office
& L at T junc opp Church.* **Visits by
arrangement Mar to May. Adm
£5, chd free. Home-made teas.**
A three acre garden surrounding
former Rectory with gate to adjoining
C14 Church. A further 15 acres of
Glebe land and paddocks providing
circular walk beside small lake and
through orchards, woodland and
extensive cutting garden. Heavily
planted for all year interest but in
spring masses of different species
narcisi, species tulips, hellebores,
fritillaries and anemone. Wheelchair
access from field into main gardens
surrounding house.
♿ 🐕 🚗 🚌 ☕

50 OULTON HALL
Oulton, Aylsham, NR11 6NU.
Bolton Agnew. *4m NW of Aylsham.
From Aylsham: take B1354. After 4m
turn L for Oulton Chapel, Hall ½ m
on R. From B1149 (Norwich/Holt
Rd): take B1354, next R, Hall ½ m
on R.* **Sun 2 June (1.30-5). Adm £6,
chd free. Home-made teas.**
C18 manor house (not open) and
clocktower set in six acre garden with
lake and woodland walks. Chelsea
designer's own garden- herbaceous,
Italian, bog, water, wild, verdant,
sunken and parterre gardens all
flowing from one tempting vista to
another. Developed over 25 years
with emphasis on structure, height
and texture, with a lot of recent
replanting in the contemporary
manner.
♿ 🐕 ❀ ☕ 🧺

51 ◆ RAVENINGHAM HALL
Raveningham, Norwich,
NR14 6NS. Sir Nicholas &
Lady Bacon, 01508 548480,
sonya@raveningham.com,
www.raveningham.com. *14m SE
of Norwich. 4m from Beccles off
B1136.* **For NGS: Mon 19 Feb
(2-4). Adm £22, chd free. Pre-
booking essential, please visit
www.ngs.org.uk for information &
booking. Home-made teas inc in
adm.** For other opening times and
information, please phone, email or
visit garden website.
Join Sir Nicholas Bacon for a guided

walk around the many varieties of snowdrops in the gardens and parkland of Raveningham Hall. There is a restored Victorian conservatory, walled kitchen garden, herbaceous boarders, newly planted stumpery, an arboretum est after 1987 gale and Millennium lake.

52 27 ST EDMUNDS ROAD

Taverham, Norwich, NR8 6NY. Alan Inness & Sue Collins. *6m N of Norwich, just off the Fakenham Rd A1067. Coming from Norwich on A1067, drive through the village of Drayton. Carry on up hill to Taverham, turn L into Roeditch Dr. The property will then be on your R at T-junc.* **Sun 23 June (11.30-4). Adm £5, chd free. Light refreshments. Homemade cakes, quiche and sausage rolls.** ½ acre garden featuring part woodland setting and view over the Wensum valley. The garden has undergone substantial redevelopment over the past 14 years as it was originally two separate gardens. Redevelopment has inc the addition of vine covered pergola, two summerhouses, herbaceous borders, small vegetable plot with greenhouse and potting shed. Recently added Island beds. Plant sales.

53 SALLE PARK

Salle, Reepham, NR10 4SF. Sir John White, www.sallepark.co.uk. *1m NE of Reepham. Off B1145, between Cawston & Reepham.* **Sun 14 July (10-4). Adm £6, chd free. Home-made teas in The Orangery.** Fully productive Victorian kitchen garden with original vine houses, double herbaceous borders, ice house, and Norfolk Heritage fruit orchard. Third year of no-dig. Formal Georgian pleasure gardens with yew topiary, rose gardens and lawns and freshly planted Orangery. Wheelchair access via some bark chip paths.

54 ◆ SANDRINGHAM GARDENS

Sandringham Estate, Sandringham, PE35 6EH. His Majesty The King, 01485 545408, visits@sandringhamestate.co.uk, www.sandringhamestate.co.uk.

Sandringham is 6m NE of King's Lynn and is signposted from the A148 Fakenham Rd and the A149 Hunstanton Rd. The Royal Park's postcode for SatNav is PE35 6AB. **For opening times and information, please phone, email or visit garden website.**

Set in 25 hectares (60 acres) and enjoyed by the British Royal Family and their guests when in residence, the more formal gardens are open from April- October. The grounds have been developed in turn by each Monarch since 1863 when King Edward VII and Queen Alexandra purchased the Estate. Topiary Garden, Cottage Garden and Historic Trees. Gravel paths are not deep, some long distances. Please contact us or visit the website for an Accessibility Guide.

Our donation in 2023 has enabled Parkinson's UK to fund 3 new nursing posts this year, directly supporting people with Parkinson's

Charnwood

55 SEVERALS GRANGE
Holt Road B1110, Wood Norton,
NR20 5BL. Jane Lister,
01362 684206,
hoecroft@hotmail.co.uk. *8m S of
Holt, 6m E of Fakenham. 2m N of
Guist on L of B1110. Guist is situated
5m SE of Fakenham on A1067
Norwich Rd.* **Sun 11 Aug (1-5).
Adm £6, chd free. Pre-booking
essential, please visit www.ngs.
org.uk for information & booking.
Home-made teas.**
The gardens surrounding Severals
Grange are a perfect example of
how colour, shape and form can be
created by the use of foliage plants,
from large shrubs to small alpines.
Movement and lightness are achieved
by interspersing these plants with a
wide range of ornamental grasses,
which are at their best in late summer.
Splashes of additional colour are
provided by a variety of herbaceous
plants. Wheelchair access via some
gravel paths but help can
be provided.

56 SILVERSTONE FARM
North Elmham, Dereham, NR20 5EX.
George Carter, 01362 668130,
george@georgecartergardens.
co.uk, www.georgecartergardens.
co.uk. *Nearer to Gateley than N
Elmham. From N Elmham church
head N to Guist. Take 1st L onto
Great Heath Rd. L at T-junc. Take 1st
R signed Gateley, Silverstone Farm is
1st drive on L by a wood.* **Evening
opening Fri 28 June (6-8). Adm
£6.50, chd free. Wine.**
Garden belonging to George Carter
described by the Sunday Times as
'one of the 10 best garden designers
in Britain'. 1830s farmyard and formal
gardens in two acres. Inspired by C17
formal gardens, the site consists of a
series of interconnecting rooms with
framed views and vistas designed in
a simple palette of evergreens and
deciduous trees and shrubs such
as available in that period. Books by
the owner for sale. Level site, mostly
wheelchair accessible.

57 ◆ STODY LODGE
Melton Constable,
NR24 2ER. Mr & Mrs Charles
MacNicol, 01263 860572,
enquiries@stodyestate.co.uk,
www.stodylodgegardens.co.uk.
*16m NW of Norwich, 3m S of Holt.
Off B1354. Signed from Melton
Constable on Holt Rd. For SatNav*
*NR24 2ER. Gardens signed as you
approach.* **For NGS: Tue 14 May
(1-5). Adm £9, chd free. Home-
made teas. Refreshments provided
by selected local and national
charities. For other opening times
and information, please phone,
email or visit garden website.**
Spectacular gardens with one
of the largest concentrations of
rhododendrons and azaleas in East
Anglia. Created in the 1920s, the
gardens also feature magnolias,
camellias, a variety of ornamental
and specimen trees, late daffodils
and bluebells. Expansive lawns and
magnificent yew hedges. Woodland
walks and four acre water garden
filled with over 2,000 vividly-coloured
azalea mollis. Wheelchair access
to most areas of the garden. Some
gravel paths with uneven ground.

58 SWAFIELD HALL
Knapton Road, Swafield, North
Walsham, NR28 0RP. Tim
Payne & Boris Konoshenko,
www.swafieldhall.co.uk. *Swafield
Hall is approx 1/2 m along Knapton
Rd (also called Mundesley Rd) from
its start in the village of Swafield. You
need to add about 300 yds to the
location given by most SatNavs.* **Sun
23, Mon 24 June (10-5). Adm £6,
chd free. Home-made teas.**
C16 Manor House with Georgian
additions (not open) set within four
acres of gardens inc a parterre and
various rooms inc a summer garden,
orchard, cutting garden, pear tunnel,
secret oriental garden (with nine
flower beds based on a Persian
carpet), the Apollo Promenade of
theatrical serpentine hedging, a duck
pond and woodland walk. The whole
garden is accessible by wheelchair.

**59 THE NORFOLK HOSPICE,
TAPPING HOUSE**
Wheatfields, Hillington,
King's Lynn, PE31 6BH.
www.norfolkhospice.org.uk.
*Wheatfields is in Hillington off Station
Rd, B1153. From the A148, take the
turning into Station Rd, B1153 towards
Grimston. Wheatfields is 1st turning on
the R. The Hospice is located straight
ahead at the end of the road.* **Sun 2
June (9-1). Adm £4.50, chd free.
Light refreshments.**
The Hospice garden has been created
and maintained by a team of volunteers.
The site was purpose built and formally
opened in 2016. The gardens are still
being developed but many areas are
well established and provide a peaceful
and tranquil backdrop to patients,
visitors and staff alike. Set in grounds
of approx two acres there is a variety of
cottage garden plants, perennials and
shrubs. There is a vegetable plot, the
produce of which is used by the kitchen
team and wildlife area with pond. Full
wheelchair access means that our
garden space is available for all to enjoy.

60 NEW VICARAGE HOUSE
Vicarage Road, Great Hockham,
Thetford, IP24 1PE. Richard and
Katie Darby, 07976 814450,
info@vicaragehousenorfolk.com,
www.vicaragehousenorfolk.com. *7m
NE of Thetford, 6m S of Watton. L off
A11,onto A1075 towards Watton. R
into Great Hockham, L at village green
and L into Vicarage Rd. Penultimate
house on R.* **Sat 7 Sept (10.30-4.30);
Sun 8 Sept (11-4). Adm £5, chd
free. Home-made teas. Visits also
by arrangement 1 June to 1 Oct for
groups of up to 20.**
Six acre garden with walled garden,
gravel garden, sunken garden, cutting
garden and small arboretum. Further
cottage-style long borders around house
and pool house. Pool House garden
with box-edged beds and fruit trees.
Avenue of yew drums with trained white
hornbeam. Semi-circle of yew. Garden
has developed over the last 35 years.

61 WALCOTT HOUSE
Walcott Green, Walcott,
Norwich, NR12 0NU. Nick &
Juliet Collier, 07986 607170,
julietcollier1@gmail.com. *3m N of
Stalham. Off the Stalham to Walcott
Rd (B1159).* **Sun 30 June (10-5).
Adm £6, chd free. Home-made
teas. Visits also by arrangement in
July for groups of 15 to 30.**
A 12 acre site with over an acre of
formal gardens based on model C19
Norfolk farm buildings. Woodland and
damp gardens, arboretum, vistas with
tree lined avenues, woodland walks.
Wheelchair access, small single steps
to negotiate when moving between
gardens in the yards.

62 33 WALDEMAR AVENUE
Hellesdon, Norwich, NR6 6TB.
Sonja Gaffer & Alan Beal,
www.facebook.com/
Hellesdontropicalgarden.

Near Norwich Airport. Waldemar Ave is situated approx 400 yds off Norwich ring road towards Cromer on A140. **Sun 4 Aug, Sun 1 Sept (10-5). Adm £5, chd free. Home-made teas. Coffee, cakes and sausage rolls also available.**
A surprising and large suburban garden of many parts with an exciting mix of exotic and tropical plants combined with unusual perennials. A quirky palm-thatched Tiki hut is an eye catching feature. There is a wonderful treehouse draped in plants. You can sit by the pond which is brimming with wildlife and rare plants. A large collection of succulents will be on show and there will be plants to buy. This garden is about big leaves and foliage textures and colours. A wildlife pond snuggles beneath the big leaves. Wheelchair access. Surfaces are mostly of lawn and concrete and are on one level.

63 THE WALLED GARDEN, LITTLE PLUMSTEAD
Old Hall Road, Little Plumstead, Norwich, NR13 5FA. Little Plumstead Walled Garden Community Shop & Cafe, thewalledgardenshop.co.uk. *On arriving in Little Plumstead follow signs to The Walled Garden.* **Evening opening Wed 10 July (6-8). Adm £10, chd free. Pre-booking essential, please visit www.ngs. org.uk for information & booking. Light refreshments in the cafe.**
Richard Hobbs will be taking two guided walks for 20 people around the recently restored Victorian walled garden with heritage apples and pears on beautifully restored brick walls. There are cutting beds, herbaceous and shrub areas together with a Victorian style glasshouse. There is a newly planted alpine area, a stumpery a range of herbs and some rare and unusual plants. Good wheelchair access throughout.

64 WARBOROUGH HOUSE
2 Wells Road, Stiffkey, NR23 1QH. Mr & Mrs J Morgan. *13m N of Fakenham, 4m E of Wells-Next-The-Sea on A149 in the centre of Stiffkey village. Parking is available onsite & is signed at garden entrance (A149). Coasthopper bus stops outside garden. Do not park on the main road as this causes congestion.* **Sun 26 May (11-5). Adm £6, chd free. Home-made teas.**
A seven acre garden on a steep chalk slope, surrounding C19 house (not

open) with views across the Stiffkey valley and to the coast. Woodland walks, formal terraces, shrub borders, lawns, wildflower areas and walled garden create a garden of contrasts. Garden slopes steeply in parts. Paths are gravel, bark chip or grass. Disabled parking allows access to garden nearest the house and teas.

65 NEW WENSUM FARMHOUSE
Pockthorpe, Nr West Rudham, King's Lynn, PE31 8SZ. The Earl and Countess of Romney. *In Pockthorpe village. Take road to Pockthorpe off A148 in West Rudham. Go down lane for 1/2 m. Bear L at village sign and Wensum Farm house is 100 yds on L. Parking in field.* **Sun 9 June (1-5). Combined adm with The White Cottage £6, chd free. Home-made teas. Open nearby Wensum House.**
Two acres planted in 2014 which inc a walled cottage style garden with mixed shrubs, perennial plants and bulbs surrounding the farmhouse, and an adjoining wild meadow with mown grass paths, two small ponds, species trees and shrubs set in pasture grass. Restored Shepherds Hut.

66 NEW WENSUM HOUSE
Station Road, East Rudham, King's Lynn, PE31 8SU. Sue and Tony Dessent. *Off A148 Fakenham/ Kings Lynn. Turn behind Crown pub onto Station Rd. House on L at corner of Broomsthorpe Rd. Disabled parking only on driveway. Parking available at playing fields on School Rd.* **Sun 9 June (1-5). Adm £5.50, chd free. Open nearby Wensum Farmhouse.**
Historic Georgian house and garden previously owned by doctors attending Royal family at Sandringham. Garden is approx two acres with lawned areas, mature trees and woodland areas. Main walled garden comprises box hedge pathways, large cottage style herbaceous borders, rose arches and a small stream running through. Seating areas, summerhouse and greenhouse.

67 NEW THE WHITE COTTAGE
Pockthorpe, West Rudham, King's Lynn, PE31 8TD. Ian & Amanda McCallum. *Take A148 to West Rudham and take road signed Pockthorpe. Parking at*

Wensum Farmhouse. **Sun 9 June (1-5). Combined adm with Wensum Farmhouse £6, chd free. Home-made teas at Wensum Farmhouse. Open nearby Wensum House.**
Surrounded by fields, this newly renovated garden is in its infancy and has been designed by the present owners. Planted in 2021 little remains of the original garden and the planting lends itself to a more naturalistic approach. Influenced by designers such as Nigel Dunnett and Noel Kingsbury plants mingle with each other and at this early stage many are very much still on trial.

68 NEW WOODFORD LODGE
Tittleshall, King's Lynn, PE32 2PF. Martin Webster and The Revd. Hilary De Lyon. *2m N of Litcham, between Swaffham and Fakenham. Follow signs from A1065 Weasenham Woods.* **Sun 28 July (2-5). Combined adm with Cokesford Farm £6.50, chd free. Home-made teas.**
An acre garden around C17 farmhouse with Georgian brick front (not open). Comprises 10 small garden areas inc 80ft rose walk, labyrinth, herb parterre, rill, walled pool garden and raised vegetable beds. Variety of colourful planting with use of leaf colour and texture to create contrast. Many pots give a flexible and changing display.

69 WRETHAM LODGE
East Wretham, IP24 1RL. Mr Gordon Alexander & Mr Ian Salter, 01953 498997, grdalexander@btinternet.com. *6m NE of Thetford. A11 E from Thetford, L up A1075, L by village sign, R at Xroads then bear L.* **Sun 5, Mon 6 May (11-5). Adm £7, chd free. Visits also by arrangement.**
A 10 acre garden surrounding former Georgian rectory (not open). In spring masses of species tulips, hellebores, fritillaries, daffodils and narcissi; bluebell walk and small woodland walk. Topiary pyramids and yew hedging lead to double herbaceous borders. Shrub borders and rose beds (home of the Wretham Rose). Traditionally maintained walled garden with fruit, vegetables and perennials.

SUFFOLK

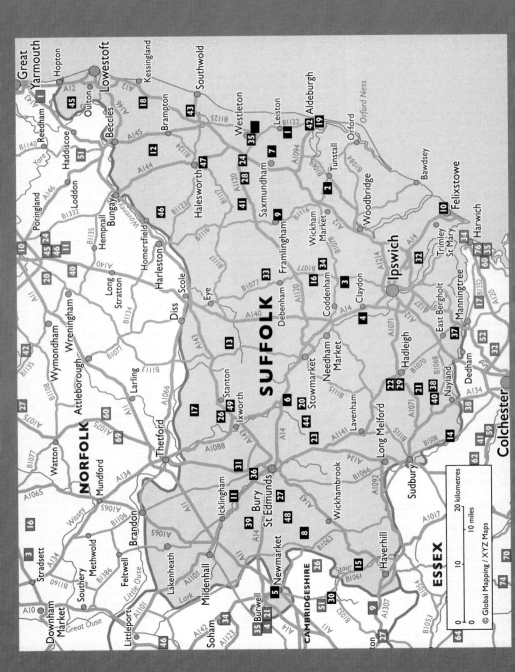

VOLUNTEERS

County Organiser
Jenny Reeve
01638 715289
jenny.reeve@ngs.org.uk

County Treasurer
Julian Cusack
01728 649060
julian.cusack@ngs.org.uk

Publicity
Jenny Reeve
(as above)

Social Media
Barbara Segall
01787 312046
barbara.segall@ngs.org.uk

Booklet Co-ordinator
Michael Cole
07899 994307
michael.cole@ngs.org.uk

Assistant County Organisers
Michael Cole
(as above)

Gillian Garnham 01394 448122
gill.garnham@ngs.org.uk

Mark Hedderwick 01787 249736
ahedderwick@btinternet.com

Wendy Parkes 01473 785504
wendy.parkes@ngs.org.uk

Barbara Segall
(as above)

Peter Simpson 01787 249845
peter.simpson@ngs.org.uk

[f] @SuffolkNGS
[X] @SuffolkNGS
[O] @suffolkngs

OPENING DATES

All entries subject to change.
For latest information check
www.ngs.org.uk
Map locator numbers are
shown to the right of each
garden name.

February

Snowdrop Openings

Sunday 11th
◆ Blakenham Woodland Garden 4

Sunday 18th
Gable House 12
Great Thurlow Hall 15

April

Monday 1st
NEW Porters Lodge 39

Sunday 7th
Great Thurlow Hall 15
◆ The Place for Plants, East
  Bergholt Place Garden 37

Sunday 28th
◆ Blakenham Woodland Garden 4
◆ The Place for Plants, East
  Bergholt Place Garden 37

May

Sunday 5th
◆ Fullers Mill Garden 11

Sunday 19th
The Priory 40

Saturday 25th
◆ Wyken Hall 49

Sunday 26th
Acer House 1
◆ Wyken Hall 49

June

Sunday 2nd
Great Thurlow Hall 15
NEW Mansard House 26

Wednesday 5th
◆ Somerleyton Hall Gardens 45

Friday 7th
Helmingham Hall 16

Sunday 9th
Ashe Park 2
Berghersh Place 3
Lillesley Barn 22
Magnolia House 24
Moat House 27
Oakley Cottage 28
Old Gardens 29
The Old Rectory, Ingham 31
The Old Rectory, Nacton 32
Smallwood Farmhouse 44

Sunday 16th
28 Double Street 9
Holm House 20
2 Holmwood Cottages 21
5 Parklands Green 36
Wenhaston Grange 47

Sunday 23rd
Great Bevills 14
NEW The Old Vicarage 33

Wednesday 26th
◆ The Red House 42

Sunday 30th
Reydon Grange 43
Squires Barn 46

July

Thursday 4th
NEW Brampton Manor Care
  Home 5

Saturday 6th
Foxgrove & Maynell House 10

Sunday 7th
Otley Hall 34

Sunday 14th
NEW Wolfe Hall 48

Sunday 21st
Heron House 19
The Old Rectory, Brinkley 30

August

Saturday 3rd
Gislingham Gardens 13

Sunday 4th
Gislingham Gardens 13
The Old Rectory, Ingham 31

Wednesday 14th
◆ The Red House 42

*Our donation to Marie
Curie this year equates
to 17,496 hours of
nursing care*

The Old Vicarage

THE GARDENS

1 ACER HOUSE

15 Haylings Grove, Leiston, IP16 4DU. Andrew & Linda Barks. *Haylings Gr is on the S outskirts of Leiston off the B1069. On entering Haylings Gr follow the road to the end where you will see 15 Haylings Gr, which is a white house with a glass porch.* **Sun 26 May (12-4). Adm £5, chd free. Home-made teas. Coffee and cake will also be served.**
A ⅓ acre garden with acers, topiary and pond water feature with fish. The acers form the structure of the garden along with topiary, trees and shrubs.

2 ASHE PARK

Ivy Lodge Road, Campsea Ashe, Woodbridge, IP13 0QB. Mr Richard Keeling. *Using the postcode in SatNav will bring you to the entrance to Ashe Park on Ivy Lodge Rd. Drive through entrance signed Ashe Park, past the gate cottage on L & follow signs to car park.* **Sun 9 June (10.30-5). Adm £7, chd free.**
An old 12 acre garden comprised of different areas; a large yew hedge, ancient cedars of Lebanon, canal and other water features. Walled garden and wild areas. Garden planted in ruins of old house. Partial wheelchair access, some gravel paths and steps.

3 BERGHERSH PLACE

Witnesham, Ipswich, IP6 9EZ. Mr & Mrs T C Parkes, 01473 785504, wendyparkes@live.com. *N of Witnesham village, B1077 double bends. Farm entrance, concrete drive, approx 1m S of Ashbocking Xrds. Entrance on sharp bend so please drive slowly. Turn in between North Lodge & Berghersh House.* **Sun 9 June (12-5). Adm £5, chd free. Home-made teas. Gluten-free refreshments available. Visits also by arrangement 1 June to 25 June for groups of 5+. Parking available in concrete farmyard.**
Peaceful walled and hedged gardens surround elegant Regency house (not open) among fields with a pretty view of the Fynn Valley. Circular walk with mature native trees, a mound, three ponds, bog area and orchard paddock. Informal family garden with shrub and perennial beds. Many varieties of roses, some trained on to old farm buildings. Garden created over last 30 years by current owner. Parking for elderly and disabled available. Most areas are accessible, but paths are thick grass, so difficult to push manual wheelchairs.

4 ◆ BLAKENHAM WOODLAND GARDEN

Little Blakenham, Ipswich, IP8 4LZ. M Blakenham, info@blakenhamfarms.com, www.blakenhamwoodlandgarden.org.uk. *4m NW of Ipswich. Follow signs at Little Blakenham, 1m off B1113.* **For NGS: Sun 11 Feb, Sun 28 Apr (10-4). Adm £5, chd £3. Home-made teas. For other opening times and information, please email or visit garden website.**
Beautiful six acre woodland garden with variety of rare trees and shrubs, Chinese rocks and a landscape spiral form. Lovely in spring with snowdrops, daffodils and camellias followed by magnolias and bluebells. Woodland Garden open from 1 March to 28 June. Suffolk Punch Horses, Tosier Artisan Chocolate Stall.

5 NEW BRAMPTON MANOR CARE HOME

Fordham Road, Newmarket, CB8 7AQ. Mr Carl Roberts, www.boutiquecarehomes.co.uk/care-homes-suffolk/brampton-manor. *1m S of junc 37 on A14 or ½m N of Newmarket High St.* **Thur 4 July (1.30-4). Adm £4, chd free. Light refreshments.**
Brampton Manor Care Home's gardens are focused on health and wellbeing of residents living with dementia and residential care needs. With sweeping accessible pathway and a variety of interesting horticultural features the garden inc mature trees, a resident run allotment, beautiful lawn, bedding plants and raised planters. The gardens are lovingly maintained by residents and the team. On our open day we will be hosting a community event with a variety of activities and entertainment to enjoy. Fully accessible garden with step free access throughout Brampton Manor.

6 BRIDGES

The Street, Woolpit, Bury St Edmunds, IP30 9SA. Mr Stanley Bates & Mr Michael Elles. *Through green coach gates marked Deliveries. From A14 take slip road to Woolpit, follow signs to centre of village. Road curves to R. Bridges is on L & covered in Wisteria & opp Co-op.* **Sun 25 Aug (11-5). Adm £5, chd free. Home-made teas.**
C15 Grade II terraced house in the centre of a C12 Suffolk village with walled garden to the rear of the property. Additional land was acquired 20 years ago, and this garden was developed into formal and informal planting. The main formal feature is the Shakespeare Garden featuring the bust of Shakespeare, and the 'Umbrello' a recently constructed pavillion in an Italianate design. Usually a Wind Quintet playing in the main garden.

7 BY THE CROSSWAYS

Kelsale, Saxmundham, IP17 2PL. Mr & Mrs William Kendall, miranda@bythecrossways.co.uk. *2m NE of Saxmundham, just off Clayhills Rd. ½m N of town centre, turn R to Theberton on Clayhills Rd. After 1½m, 1st L to Kelsale, turn L immed after white cottage.* **Visits by arrangement in Sept. Adm by donation.**
A three acre wildlife garden designed as a garden within a working organic farm where wilderness areas lie next to productive beds. Large semi-walled vegetable and cutting garden and a spectacular crinkle-crankle wall. Extensive perennial planting, grasses and wild and uneven areas. The garden is mostly flat, with paved or gravel pathways around the main house, a few low steps and extensive grass paths and lawns.

100 inpatients and their families are being supported at the newly opened Horatio's Garden Wales, thanks to the National Garden Scheme donations

8 DIP-ON-THE-HILL
Ousden, Newmarket,
CB8 8TW. Geoffrey & Christine
Ingham, 07947 309900,
gki1000@cam.ac.uk. *5m E of
Newmarket; 7m W of Bury St
Edmunds. From Newmarket: 1m
from junc of B1063 & B1085. From
Bury St Edmunds follow signs for
Hargrave. Parking at village hall.
Follow yellow NGS sign at the end
of the lane. Visits by arrangement
June to Sept for groups of up to
15. Adm £5, chd free. Tea.*
Approx an acre in a dip on a south
facing hill based on a wide range of
architectural/sculptural evergreen
trees, shrubs and groundcover:
pines; grove of *Phillyrea latifolia*;
'cloud pruned' hedges; palms; large
bamboo; ferns; range of *Kniphofia*
and *Croscosmia*. Visitors may wish to
make an appointment when visiting
gardens nearby.

9 28 DOUBLE STREET
Framlingham, IP13 9BN. Mr &
Mrs David Clark, 01728 720161,
clarkdn@btinternet.com. *250yrds
from Market Hill (main square)
Framlingham opp Church Entrance.
Leave square from top L into Church
St. Double St is 100yds on R. Car
parking in main square & near to
Framlingham Castle. Sun 16 June
(11-5). Adm £5, chd free. Light
refreshments. Visits also by
arrangement June to Sept for
groups of 10 to 25.*
A town garden featuring roses together
with a wide range of perennials and
shrubs. Conservatory, greenhouse,
gazebo, summerhouse and terrace
full of containers all add interest to the
garden. Good views of Framlingham's
roofscape. Wheelchair access via fine
shingle drive with two ramps.

**10 FOXGROVE & MAYNELL
HOUSE**
High Road East, Felixstowe,
IP11 9PU. Ms Nicki Bain. *Suffolk.
Enter Felixstowe on A154. At
r'about take 1st exit then R turn
into Beatrice Ave. L turn to High Rd
East. Garden halfway down on R.
Parking in surrounding roads. Sat 6
July (2-5). Adm £4, chd free. Light
refreshments.*
Over two acres of landscaped
gardens surround Foxgrove and
Maynell House: two care homes
in attractive Victorian buildings,
formally part of Felixstowe College.

The garden is beautifully maintained
and contain mature trees, shrubs,
roses, herbaceous borders, lawn and
colourful pots and baskets. Maynell
has a lovely veranda and large
terrace. Cakes made by the chefs
will be served with afternoon tea and
musical accompaniment. Felixstowe
college memorabilia will be available
to view. Access to all via paved areas.

11 ◆ FULLERS MILL GARDEN
West Stow, IP28 6HD.
Perennial, 01284 728888,
fullersmillgarden@perennial.org.uk,
www.fullersmill.org.uk. *6m NW of
Bury St Edmunds. Turn off the A1101
(Bury to Mildenhall Rd) signposted
West Stow Anglo Saxon Village.
Continue for 1½m and the entrance
is clearly marked. Follow yellow signs
on all major routes. For NGS: Sun
5 May, Sun 6 Oct (11-5). Adm £7,
chd free. Light refreshments.
Tea, coffee, cake and ice creams.
For other opening times and
information, please phone, email or
visit garden website.*
An enchanting and tranquil seven acre
creation on the banks of the River
Lark. It combines a beautiful light
dappled woodland with a plantsman's
collection of unusual shrubs,
perennials, lilies and marginal plants. It
is a garden of truly year-round interest.
Tour our garden, and be inspired by
our cards, gifts, bulbs and plants.
Some uneven surfaces, grassed areas,
proximity to water and sloping ground
limit disabled access to some areas.

12 GABLE HOUSE
Halesworth Road, Redisham,
Beccles, NR34 8NE.
Brenda Foster, 01502 575298,
gablehouse@btinternet.com. *5m
S of Beccles. Signed from A144
Bungay/Halesworth Rd. Sun 18 Feb
(11-4). Adm £5, chd free. Light
refreshments. Soup lunches
available.*
We have a large collection of
snowdrops, cyclamen, hellebores and
other flowering plants for the February
opening. Many bulbs and plants will
be for sale. Greenhouses contain rare
bulbs and tender plants. We have a
wide range of unusual trees, shrubs,
perennials and bulbs collected over
the last 50 years.

GROUP OPENING

13 GISLINGHAM GARDENS
Mill Street, Gislingham, IP23 8JT.
*4m W of Eye. Gislingham 2½m
W of A140. 9m N of Stowmarket,
8m S of Diss. Disabled parking at
Ivy Chimneys. Parking limited to
disabled parking at Chapel Farm
Close. Sat 3 Aug (11-4.30); Sun 4
Aug (11.30-4.30). Combined adm
£5, chd free. Home-made teas at
Ivy Chimneys. Wide range of tea,
coffee & cordials; home-made
cakes, a gluten free offering &
some savouries.*

12 CHAPEL FARM CLOSE
Ross Lee.

IVY CHIMNEYS
Iris & Alan Stanley.

Two varied gardens in a picturesque
village with a number of Suffolk
timbered houses. Ivy Chimneys is
planted for year-round interest with
ornamental trees, some topiary, exotic
borders and fishpond set in an area
of Japanese style. Wisteria draped
pergola supports a productive vine.
Also a separate ornamental vegetable
garden. Small orchard on front lawn.
New: 12 Chapel Farm Close is a tiny
garden, exquisitely planted and an
absolute riot of colour despite the
garden's size, the owner has planted
a *Catalpa*, a *Cornus Florida Rubra*
and many unusual plants. It is a fine
example of what can be achieved in
a small space. Wheelchair access
to Ivy Chimneys. Access for smaller
wheelchairs only at 12 Chapel Farm
Close.

*Our donation to the
Army Benevolent
Fund supported 608
individuals with front
line services and
horticultural related
grants in 2023*

Mansard House

14 GREAT BEVILLS
Sudbury Road, Bures, CO8 5JW.
Mr & Mrs G T C Probert. *4m S of Sudbury. Just N of Bures on the Sudbury road B1508.* **Sun 23 June (2-5.30). Adm £5, chd free. Home-made teas.**
Overlooking the Stour Valley the gardens surrounding an Elizabethan manor house are formal and Italianate in style with Irish yews and mature specimen trees. Terraces, borders, ponds and woodland walks. A short drive away from Great Bevills visitors may wish to also see the C13 St Stephen's Chapel with wonderful views of the Old Bures Dragon recently re-created by the owner. Woodland walks give lovely views over the Stour Valley. There is also a recently created wildflower meadow with mown paths. Wheelchair access via gravel paths.
♿ 🐕 👝 ☕ 💷

15 GREAT THURLOW HALL
Great Thurlow, Haverhill, CB9 7LF.
Mr & Mrs George Vestey. *12m S of Bury St Edmunds, 4m N of Haverhill. Great Thurlow village on B1061 from Newmarket; 3½ m N of junc with A143 Haverhill/Bury St Edmunds rd.* **Sun 18 Feb (1-4). Light refreshments. Sun 7 Apr, Sun 2 June (2-5). Home-made teas. Adm £5, chd free.**
13 acres of beautiful gardens set around the River Stour. Masses of snowdrops in late winter are followed by daffodils and blossom around the riverside walk in spring. Herbaceous borders, rose garden and extensive shrub borders come alive with colour from late spring onwards, there is also a large walled kitchen garden and arboretum. Also open is the Curwen Print Study Centre, Art Studios and Gallery, located adjacent to Great Thurlow Hall will also be open to all garden visitors. Artists will be demonstrating fine art printmaking skills.
♿ 🐕 ☕ 💷 ›))

16 HELMINGHAM HALL
Helmingham, Stowmarket,
IP14 6EF. Helmingham Events,
www.helmingham.com. *From A14 take junc 51 onto A140. Take 1st R onto Needham Rd (B1078). After 1½ m, turn L onto Church Rd then R onto High St. R turn on Stonewall Hill towards Gosbeck. At end of Gosbeck Rd, turn L. Garden on L.* **Fri 7 June (10-5). Adm £8, chd £4. Light refreshments at Wright's Cafe.**
It is hard to exaggerate the effect this beautiful park, with red deer and spectacular moated Hall in mellow patterned red brick with its famous gardens will have on the visitor. The whole combines to give an extraordinary impression of beauty and tranquillity. A classic parterre flanked by hybrid musk roses lies before a stunning walled kitchen garden with exquisite herbaceous borders and beds of vegetables interspersed by tunnels of sweet peas, runner beans and gourds. On the other side lies a herb and knot garden behind which is a rose garden of unsurpassable beauty.
♿ 🐕 🚗 ☕ 💷 ›))

17 HELYG
Thetford Road, Coney Weston, Bury St Edmunds, IP31 1DN. Jackie & Briant Smith, 01359 220106, briant. broadsspirituality@gmail.com. *6m E of Thetford. From Barningham Xrds/shop turn off the B1111 towards Coney Weston & Knettishall Country Park. After approx 1m Helyg will be found on L behind some large willow trees. Visits by arrangement Apr to Sept for groups of 10 to 25. Adm £5, chd free. Light refreshments.*
A garden that combines planting and novel ideas to stimulate interest, with many seats for relaxation. There are different areas with their own character, naturalised spring bulbs,many hostas, roses, rhododendrons, camellias, irises, buddleias, fuchsias, azaleas, herbs, vegetables and exotics. Raised beds, three ponds and four water features supplement the plants and a recently added 'dry garden'. Most of the garden is wheelchair accessible.

18 HENSTEAD EXOTIC GARDEN
Church Road, Henstead, Beccles, NR34 7LD. Andrew Brogan, www.hensteadexoticgarden.co.uk. *Equal distance between Beccles, Southwold & Lowestoft approx 5m. 1m from A12 turning after Wrentham (signed Henstead) very close to B1127.* Sun 25 Aug (11-4). Adm £5, chd £1. Home-made teas. Also available are coffees, local delicatessen made cakes, home made cheese scones & sausage rolls.
A two acre exotic garden featuring 100 large palms, 20+ bananas and giant bamboo, some of biggest in the UK. Streams, 20ft tiered walkway leading to Thai style wooden covered pavilion. Mediterranean and jungle plants around three large ponds with fish. Unique garden buildings, waterfalls, rock walkways, different levels and a Victorian grotto. Wheelchair access to parts of garden.

19 HERON HOUSE
Priors Hill Road, Aldeburgh, IP15 5EP. Mr & Mrs Jonathan Hale, 07968 906715, jonathanrhhale@aol.com. *At the SE junc of Priors Hill Rd & Park Rd. Last house on Priors Hill Rd on S side, at the junc where it rejoins Park Rd.*

Sun 21 July (2-5). Adm £5, chd free. Tea in conservatory. Visits also by arrangement Apr to Oct.
Two acres with superb views over the North Sea, River Alde and marshes. Unusual trees, herbaceous beds, shrubs and ponds with a waterfall in large rock garden, and a stream and bog garden. Some half hardy plants in the coastal microclimate. Partial wheelchair access.

20 HOLM HOUSE
Garden House Lane, Drinkstone, Bury St Edmunds, IP30 9FJ. Mrs Rebecca Shelley. *7m SE of Bury St Edmunds. Coming from the E exit A14 at J47, from W J46. Follow signs to Drinkstone, then Drinkstone Green. Turn into Rattlesden Rd & look for Garden House Ln on L. 1st house on L.* Sun 16 June (10-4.30). Adm £8, chd free. Light refreshments.
Approx 10 acres inc orchard and lawns with mature trees and clipped holm oaks; formal garden with topiary, parterre and mixed borders; rose garden; woodland walk with hellebores, camellias, rhododendrons and bulbs; lake set in wildflower meadow; cut flower garden with greenhouse; large kitchen garden with impressive greenhouse; Mediterranean courtyard with mature olive tree.

21 2 HOLMWOOD COTTAGES
Bower House Tye, Polstead, Colchester, CO6 5BZ. Neil Bradfield, 07887 516054, scuddingclouds2@gmail.com. *3m W of Hadleigh. Just off A1071, Hadleigh to Sudbury Rd, (ignore Polstead signs). At The Brewers Arms, turn off A1071 onto Bower House Tye. Cottage 100yds along this road.* Sun 16 June, Sun 29 Sept (11-5). Adm £5, chd free. Visits also by arrangement Apr to Oct for groups of 5 to 35. Not opening July & August. Donation to Plant Heritage.
Plantsman's garden with many unusual plants. Hot, sunny borders and areas of dappled shade planted to explore flower colour, foliage, texture, form, autumn interest and design principles. Rich variety of perennials, grasses, species and shrub roses, ferns and woodland plants, matrix and gravel planting. Plus summerhouse, several seats and a part of the National Collection

Engleheart Narcissus. Wheelchair access along narrow paths and slightly uneven ground. Please note: there are two steps.

22 LILLESLEY BARN
The Street, Kersey, Ipswich, IP7 6ED. Mr Karl & Mrs Bridget Allen, 07939 866873, bridgetinkerseybarn@gmail.com, www.instagram.com/bridgets_ suffolk_garden. *In village of Kersey, 2m NW Hadleigh. Driveway is 200m above 'The Bell' pub. Lillesley Barn is situated behind 'The Ancient Houses'. Parking is on street.* Sun 9 June (11-5). Combined adm with Old Gardens £6, chd £2.50. Home-made teas. Coffee and home-made cakes also available. Visits also by arrangement 1 May to 21 Sept for groups of up to 40.
Dry gravel garden (inspired by the Beth Chatto Garden) inc variety of Mediterranean plants, ornamental grasses and herbs. Large herbaceous borders, pleached hornbeam hedge, rose arbours and small orchard. The garden contains various species of trees inc birch, amelanchier and willow in less than an acre of garden bordered on two sides by fields.

23 THE LODGE
Bury Road, Bradfield St Clare, Bury St Edmunds, IP30 0ED. Christian & Alice Ward-Thomas, 07768 347595, alice.baring@btinternet.com, www. instagram.com/alicewardthomas. *4m S of Bury St Edmunds. From N: turn L up Water Ln off A134, at Xrds, turn R & go exactly 1m on R. From S: turn R up Ixer Ln, R at T-junc, ½m on R. Before post box on R & next door to Lodge Farm. Visits by arrangement May to Sept. Refreshments may be possible depending on group size.*
A self-made country garden, surrounded by beautiful parkland established from blank canvas over 20 years but recently remodelled. Gravel garden inc alpines and rockery, herbaceous borders, courtyard rose garden, large late summer perennial garden, veg garden, tulip and wildlife meadows, extensive grassland with mown paths. Ground uneven but wheelchair access is possible.

24 MAGNOLIA HOUSE
Yoxford, IP17 3EP. Ian Patterson.
4m N of Saxmundham. White house in centre of Yoxford on A1120, next to Griffin pub. **Sun 9 June (2-5). Adm £5, chd free. Home-made teas.**
A romantic walled garden, originally designed by Mark Rumary, tucked behind a pretty C18 village house. The garden is divided elegantly into rooms and planted to provide year-round colour, scent and both horticultural and wildlife interest. It inc a formal paradise garden, with quatrefoil pond, twin cypresses, hibiscus and fig, and a library garden, full of ferns, peonies and species roses.

26 NEW MANSARD HOUSE
Low Street, Bardwell, Bury St Edmunds, IP31 1AR. Tom Hoblyn, www.thomashoblyn.co.uk. *From N: Go towards Bardwell (A1430). Mansard House is approx ¼ m from the church on the R. From S: Take A1088 to Thetford. Follow signs to Bardwell. Mansard House is on the L approx ¼ m after Knox Ln.* **Sun 2 June (12-6). Adm £6, chd free.**
A naturalistic 2½ acre garden surrounded by water meadows and wet woodland, complete with woodland planting and wildflower meadows. Beds of Benton End iris and peonies lead to the house. Surrounding the house is a productive crinkle-crankle walled kitchen garden, small herbaceous border and Mediterranean gravel garden. The latter demonstrates what can be grown in the driest county in the UK. Partial wheelchair access.

27 MOAT HOUSE
Little Saxham, Bury St Edmunds, IP29 5LE. Mr & Mrs Richard Mason, 01284 810941, suzanne@ countryflowerssuffolk.com. *2m SW of Bury St Edmunds. Leave A14 at J42- leave r'about towards Westley. Through Westley village at Xroads. R towards Barrow/Saxham. After 1.3m turn L down track and follow signs.* **Sun 9 June (1-5). Adm £6, chd free. Home-made teas. Visits also by arrangement in June for groups of 20+.**
Set in a two acre historic and partially moated site. This tranquil, mature garden has been developed over 20 years. Bordered by mature trees the garden has various sections inc a sunken garden, rose and clematis arbours, herbaceous borders with hydrangeas and alliums, small arboretum. A Hartley Botanic

greenhouse erected and parterre have been created. Secluded and peaceful setting and wonderful fencing. Each year the owners enjoy new garden projects.

28 OAKLEY COTTAGE
Chapel Street, Peasenhall, Saxmundham, IP17 2JD. Mr Robin Brooks. *Centre of Peasenhall Village. On the A1120 in the centre of the village of Peasenhall, next door to the Weavers Tearooms.* **Sun 9 June (12-5.30). Adm £5, chd free. Home-made teas.**
This little cottage garden is divided into five small areas - a formal-ish courtyard with *lonicera nitida* instead of box, two lawns, a vegetable plot, lots of soft fruit and an apprentice rose garden. *Persicaria*, hardy geraniums, honesty, gaura, foxgloves, monardas in the borders. Pergolas and associated climbers. Mostly flat with a few low steps, but grass and gravel to be negotiated.

29 OLD GARDENS
The Street, Kersey, Ipswich, IP7 6ED. Mr & Mrs David Anderson, 01473 828044, davidmander15@gmail.com. *10m W of Ipswich. Up hill, approx 100m from The Bell Inn Pub. On the same side of the road.* **Sun 9 June (11-5). Combined adm with Lillesley Barn £6, chd £2.50. Home-made teas at Lillesley Barn. Visits also by arrangement 1 May to 21 Sept for groups of up to 40.**
Entered from The Street, a natural garden with wildflowers under a copper beech tree. To the rear, a formal garden designed by Cherry Sandford with a sculpture by David Harbour. Flat garden, suitable for wheelchair users.

Dip-on-the-Hill

© Carole Drake

30 THE OLD RECTORY, BRINKLEY
Hall Lane, Brinkley, CB8 0SB. Mr & Mrs Mark Coley. *Hall Ln is a turning off Brinkley High St. At the end of Hall Ln, white gates on the R.* Sun 21 July (1.30-6). Adm £5, chd free. Homemade teas in Brinkley Village Hall.
Two acre garden started in 1973 when there was nothing there except a few large trees and snowdrops. Interesting trees planted since inc a large *Liriodendron* (tulip tree) planted in 1975. In the spring, many snowdrops, helebores and winter flowering shrubs. Mixed herbaceous borders with roses, interesting perennials and pockets of annuals grown from seed. Traditional potager with box hedges. Partial wheelchair access.

31 THE OLD RECTORY, INGHAM
Ingham, Bury St Edmunds, IP31 1NQ. Mr J & Mrs E Hargreaves. *5m N of Bury St Edmunds & A14. Parking signed, close to Ingham church.* Sun 9 June, Sun 4 Aug (11-4). Adm £4, chd free. Cream teas. Range of home-made cakes and scones. Variety of teas, coffee and soft drinks.
Come and enjoy teas, scones and cakes in a lovely setting of the large gardens of a Georgian rectory. Formal parterre, lawns, and a wide variety of mature trees inc weeping willows and a wellingtonia. We are building a vibrant display of colours, inc dahlias, geraniums and more, in insect-friendly borders; alliums and roses in June, and a lavender walk in August. Children friendly. Wheelchair access through 1m wide gate.

32 THE OLD RECTORY, NACTON
Nacton, IP10 0HY. Mrs Elizabeth & Mr James Wellesley Wesley, 01473 659673, tizyww@gmail.com. *3m from Ipswich close to N side of the Orwell Estuary. The garden is down the road to Nacton from the 1st A14 turn off after Orwell bridge going SE. Parking on Church Rd opp Old Rectory driveway. This will be signed.* Sun 9 June (10.30-5). Adm £5, chd free. Home-made teas.
Visits also by arrangement 15 Apr to 30 Sept for groups of up to 25.
Just under two acres of garden divided into areas for different seasons: mature trees and herbaceous borders, ample spring bulbs and blossom. Light soil so many self sown flowers. Damp

area with emphasis on foliage (rheum, darmera, rodgersia, hydrangea). Still a work in progress after 34 years. We're looking at how to bring in more butterflies and deal with very dry conditions in most of the garden. Regional Winner, The English Garden Magazine's The Nation's Favourite Gardens 2023 Most areas are wheelchair accessible, however grassy slopes and levels.

33 NEW THE OLD VICARAGE
Church Lane, Kenton, Stowmarket, IP14 6JH. Mr Vic Woodgate. *Take Rishangles Rd out of Debenham. ½ m on R turn into Bellwell Ln. Follow road for 1m. Car Park on L Kenton Field and Old Vicarage 200 metres on R.* Sun 23 June (11-5). Adm £6, chd free. Home-made teas in Kenton Field. Coffee and cakes also available.
A new garden to the scheme with ample village parking. For 30 years the garden has been developed to inc a wild walk, concealed garden, specimen trees and shrubs, formal beds, garden statuary and a delightful orangery.

34 OTLEY HALL
Hall Lane, Otley, Ipswich, IP6 9PA. Mr Stephen & Mrs Louisa Flavell, www.otleyhall.co.uk. *Take Chapel Rd past the Otley village Post Office. After 250 yds take 1st L onto Hall Ln.* Sun 7 July (10-4). Adm £5.50, chd free. Light refreshments at Marthas Barn Cafe (please reserve). Tea tent offering coffee and tea in the garden, also a stocked bar.
The 10 acres of both formal and informal gardens at Otley Hall are managed with an eye to nature. There are stew ponds and woodland to explore. The gardens features three Elizabethan Garden recreations by Sylvia Landsberg. Marthas Barn Cafe has varied recipes using fresh seasonal produce. Booking in advance advised.

35 PAGET HOUSE
Back Road, Middleton, Saxmundham, IP17 3NY. Julian & Fiona Cusack, 01728 649060, julian.cusack@btinternet.com. *From A12 at Yoxford take B1122 towards Leiston. Turn L after 1.2m at Middleton Moor. After 1m enter Middleton & drive straight ahead into*

Back Rd. Turn 1st R on Fletchers Ln for car park. Visits by arrangement 1 Apr to 15 Sept for groups of up to 30. Guided tours and talks available. Light refreshments. Dietary requirements can be catered for by prior arrangement. The garden is designed to be wildlife friendly with wild areas meeting formal planting.There is an orchard and vegetable plot. There are areas of woodland, laid hedges, a pond supporting amphibians and dragonflies, wildflower meadow and an abstract garden sculpture by local artist Paul Richardson. In 2024 we will be making changes designed to increase our resilience to drought. We record over 40 bird species each year and a good showing of butterflies, dragonflies and wildflowers inc orchids. Wheelchair access: gravel drive and mown paths. Parking on drive by prior arrangement.

36 5 PARKLANDS GREEN
Fornham St Genevieve, Bury St Edmunds, IP28 6UH. Mrs Jane Newton, newton.jane@talktalk.net. *2m NW of Bury St Edmunds off B1106. Plenty of parking on the green.* Sun 16 June (11-4). Adm £5, chd free. Home-made teas.
Visits also by arrangement 1 Apr to 1 Oct for groups of up to 50. 1½ acres of gardens developed since the 1980s for all year interest. There are mature and unusual trees and shrubs and riotous herbaceous borders. Explore the maze of paths to find four informal ponds, a treehouse, the sunken garden, greenhouses and woodland walks.

37 ◆ THE PLACE FOR PLANTS, EAST BERGHOLT PLACE GARDEN
East Bergholt, CO7 6UP. Mr & Mrs Rupert Eley, 01206 299224, sales@placeforplants.co.uk, www.placeforplants.co.uk. *2m E of A12, 7m S of Ipswich. On B1070 towards Manningtree, 2m E of A12. Situated on the edge of E Bergholt.* For NGS: Sun 7, Sun 28 Apr (2-5); Sun 6 Oct (1-4). Adm £9, chd free. Home-made teas. For other opening times and information, please phone, email or visit garden website.
A 20 acre woodland garden originally laid out at the turn of the last century by the present owner's great grandfather. Full of many fine trees and shrubs, many

seldom seen in East Anglia. A fine collection of camellias, magnolias and rhododendrons, topiary, and the National Collection of deciduous Euonymus. This garden is proud to provide plants for the National Garden Scheme's Show Garden at Chelsea Flower Show 2024. Partial wheelchair access in dry conditions. Advisable to call before visiting.

&. ❀ 🚗 [NPC] ☕ ୬)

38 POLSTEAD MILL
Mill Lane, Polstead, Colchester, CO6 5AB. Mrs Lucinda Bartlett, 07711 720418, lucyofleisure@hotmail.com, instagram.com/polsteadmill. *Between Stoke by Nayland & Polstead on the River Box. From Stoke by Nayland take road to Polstead. Mill Ln is 1st on L & garden is 1st on R.* Visits by arrangement 18 May to 21 Sept for groups of 10 to 50. Adm £7, chd free. Home-made teas. Range of refreshments available inc cream teas and light lunches.
The garden has been developed since 2002, it has formal and informal areas, a wildflower meadow and a large productive kitchen garden. The River Box runs through the garden and there is a mill pond, which gives opportunity for damp gardening, while the rest of the garden is arid and is planted to minimise the need for watering. Partial wheelchair access.

&. ❀ ☕

39 NEW PORTERS LODGE
Cavenham, IP28 6DB. Mr Craig Wyncoll. *5m W of Bury St Edmunds. 1m SW of Cavenham on the road to Kentford.* Mon 1 Apr (10-4). Adm £5, chd free. Home-made teas.
An unusual and interesting garden designed as a series of interlocked spaces which are enlivened by fountains and ponds, statuary and surrounded by a mature wood with glades and two acres of walks. Individual areas are linked to the inner garden by an acre of semi-formal lawns and mixed borders. Architectural 'follies' culminating in a pavilion which houses a unique water organ playing music by Haydn.

&. 🐕 ☕ ୬)

40 THE PRIORY
Stoke by Nayland, Colchester, CO6 4RL. *7m N of Colchester. Entrance off B1068, 250 metres NW of Stoke by Nayland.* Sun 19 May (2-5). Adm £5, chd free. Home-made teas.

Beautiful nine acre garden with fine views over Constable countryside; lawns sloping down to small lakes and water garden. A large variety of fine trees, rhododendrons and azaleas with mixed borders and walled garden with a 75-foot long ornamental greenhouse. Wide variety of plants and an extensive vegetable garden with raised beds, and fruit cages. Wheelchair access over most of garden, some steps.

&. 🐄 ❀ 🚗 ☕

41 THE PRIORY, LAXFIELD ROAD
Badingham, Woodbridge, IP13 8LS. Mr Nick Smith. *A1120 to Badingham. At White Horse pub, turn in Low St. ¼ m R into Mill Rd. Uphill for ¾ m. L at post box onto Laxfield Rd. ½ m past Priory Cottage, follow yellow NGS signs.* Sun 25 Aug (11-5). Adm £6, chd free. Home-made teas. Coffee and home-made cakes also available.
Designed by Frederic Whyte, Chelsea Gold Medal winner, we wanted to create a garden with a contemporary feel, clear structure and focused on a refined palette of plants. A kitchen garden with raised vegetable beds, a rose garden and perennial borders. A half moon lawn is framed by clusters of flowering trees whilst formal drifts of agapanthus, hydrangeas and white roses are set against the house. Live music (piano and violin) and classic cars on display.

☕ ୬)

42 ◆ THE RED HOUSE
Golf Lane, Aldeburgh, IP15 5PZ. Britten Pears Arts, 01728 451700, info@brittenpearsarts.org, www.brittenpearsarts.org/visit-us/the-red-house. *Top of Aldeburgh, approx. 1m from the sea. From A12, take A1094 to Aldeburgh. Follow the brown sign directing you towards the r'about, take 1st exit: B1122 Leiston Rd. Golf Ln is 2nd L, follow sign to 'The Red House'.* For NGS: Wed 26 June, Wed 14 Aug (11-4). Adm £5, chd free. Light refreshments. For other opening times and information, please phone, email or visit garden website.
The former home of the renowned British composer Benjamin Britten and partner, the tenor Peter Pears. The five acre garden provides an atmospheric setting for the house they shared and contain many plants loved by the couple. Mixed

herbaceous borders, kitchen garden, meadows, contemporary planting and mature trees. The Red House inc the collections left by the men and the archive holds an extraordinary wealth of material documenting their lives. The garden offers a peaceful setting to this beautiful corner of Suffolk. For museum opening times, see website. Wheelchair access: brick, concrete, gravel paths and grass. Some areas are uneven. Wheelchair available on request.

&. 🐄 ☕ ୬)

43 REYDON GRANGE
Mardle Road, Wangford, Beccles, NR34 8AU. Aileen and Bill Irving. *2m W of Southwold.* Sun 30 June (11-4). Adm £5, chd free. Home-made teas. Coffee, cakes and biscuits also available.
The approx three acre garden consists mainly of a series of mixed herbaceous and shrub borders, orchards, a rose garden, dwarf box cloud hedge, kitchen garden, lawns and a pond. We have been developing a romantic and colour co-ordinated style to the garden, with a number of internal vistas and grouping plants according to their environmental needs. There is also a six acre wild meadow.

🐄 ❀ ☕ 🪑 ୬)

44 SMALLWOOD FARMHOUSE
Smallwood Green, Bradfield St George, Bury St Edmunds, IP30 0AJ. Mr & Mrs P Doe, 01449 736127, philipdoe142@btinternet.com. *S of A14, E of A134 on Bradfield St George to Felsham Rd. Disregard sign to Smallwood Green & follow the NGS yellow signage.* Sun 9 June (11-4). Adm £5, chd free. Light refreshments. Visits also by arrangement 20 May to 28 June for groups of 12 to 30.
The garden is a combination of traditional cottage planting and contemporary styles. At its heart, a C16 farmhouse provides the backdrop to a number of old English roses, a profusion of clematis and honeysuckle, and a variety of perennials. There are two natural ponds, a Mediterranean garden and productive kitchen garden, whilst paths wind through an ancient meadow and orchard. Partially wheelchair accessible, although not suitable in damp or wet weather.

&. 🐄 ❀ ☕ ୬)

45 ◆ SOMERLEYTON HALL GARDENS

Somerleyton, NR32 5QQ. Lord Somerleyton, 01502 734901, visitors@somerleyton.co.uk, www.somerleyton.co.uk. *5m NW of Lowestoft. From Norwich take the B1074, 7m SE of Great Yarmouth (A143). Coaches should follow signs to the rear W gate entrance.* **For NGS: Wed 5 June (11-4). Adm £9.95, chd free. Home-made teas. For other opening times and information, please phone, email or visit garden website.**

Beautiful gardens of 12 acres contain a wide variety of magnificent specimen trees, shrubs, borders and plants providing colour and interest throughout the year. Sweeping lawns and formal gardens combine with majestic statuary and original Victorian ornamentation. Highlights inc the Paxton glasshouses, pergola, walled garden and yew hedge maze. House and gardens remodelled in 1840s by Sir Morton Peto. House created in Anglo-Italian style with lavish architectural features and fine state rooms. Most areas of the gardens are wheelchair accessible. Path surfaces are gravel, stone and can be difficult.

46 SQUIRES BARN

St Cross South Elmham, Harleston, IP20 0PA. Stephen & Ann Mulligan. *6m W of Halesworth, 6m E of Harleston & 7m S of Bungay. On New Rd between St Cross & St James. Parking in field opp. Yellow signs from A143 and other local roads.* **Sun 30 June (10.30-4). Adm £5, chd free. Home-made teas. Refreshments inc gluten free, vegan options and ice creams.**

A garden of three acres with views over surrounding countryside. Raised vegetable beds, an orchard, greenhouse and fruit cage. There is also a large ornamental pond with water lilies, fish and waterfall. A wildflower mound, island beds of mixed planting and a range of mature and younger trees. A recent addition is a swimming pool area. Plant stall, art exhibition and a brass band will play at the opening. The garden is largely grass with some slight slopes. Seating is available across the garden. One single flight of steps can be bypassed.

47 WENHASTON GRANGE

Wenhaston, Halesworth, IP19 9HJ. Mr & Mrs Bill Barlow. *Turn SW from A144 between Bramfield & Halesworth. Take the single track road (signed Walpole 2) Wenhaston Grange is approx ½m, at the bottom of the hill on L.* **Sun 16 June (11-4). Adm £5, chd free. Teas and light refreshments.**

Over three acres of varied gardens on a long established site which has been extensively landscaped and enhanced over the last 20 years. Long herbaceous borders, old established trees and a series of garden rooms created by beech hedges. Levels and sight lines have been carefully planned. The vegetable garden is now coming on nicely and there is also a wildflower meadow and woodland garden.

48 NEW WOLFE HALL

Barrow, Bury St Edmunds, IP29 5EZ. Mr & Mrs Mark and Joanne Howard, www.instagram.com/lifeatwh. *Follow signs for Wolfe Hall Grain Store for parking. Walk back along the lane to the stable entrance on your L. WC is available but it is not wheelchair accessible.* **Sun 14 July (10-4). Adm £6, chd free. Home-made teas. Coffee and home-made cakes also available.**

Wolfe Hall is a C16 house and former ecclesiastical retreat in 5½ acres. Mark and Jo have changed the grounds from mostly horse paddock to gardens. The gardens inc an established orchard, a veg plot, pond, a new orchard of heritage apple and various statuary. Some 1½ acres of perennials and grasses loosely based on Piet Oudolf's planting style. Generally wheelchair accessible. Garden uneven, with areas of gravel. Not suitable in wet weather.

49 ◆ WYKEN HALL

Stanton, IP31 2DW. Sir Kenneth & Lady Carlisle, 01359 250262, shop@wykenvineyards.co.uk, www.wykenvineyards.co.uk. *9m NE of Bury St Edmunds. Along A143. Follow signs to Wyken Vineyards on A143 between Ixworth & Stanton.* **For NGS: Sat 25, Sun 26 May (10-5). Adm £5, chd free. For other opening times and information, please phone, email or visit garden website.**

Four acres around the old manor. The gardens inc knot and herb gardens, old-fashioned rose garden, kitchen and wild garden, nuttery, pond, gazebo and maze; herbaceous borders and old orchard. Woodland walk and vineyard nearby. Restaurant (booking 01359 250287), shop and vineyard. Farmers' Market Sat 9am- 1pm.

Berkshire
Buckinghamshire
Hampshire
Isle of Wight
Kent
London
Oxfordshire
Surrey
Sussex

SOUTH EAST

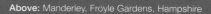

Above: Manderley, Froyle Gardens, Hampshire

SOUTH EAST

Some 900 gardens, or more than 25% of the National Garden Scheme total, open in the cluster of counties in the South East of England including London.

The merging landscapes have some common themes: the chalk hills of the Chilterns, the Berkshire Downs, the North and South Downs and the Isle of Wight; the coastline which includes some of the country's most revered landmarks such as the White Cliffs of Dover and the Needles; and plentiful rivers from the mighty Thames to the chalk streams of Hampshire. But from Oxfordshire and Buckinghamshire through Berkshire to Hampshire and the Isle of Wight, then Surrey, East and West Sussex and Kent, there are subtle graduations of the countryside - interspersed with thriving towns, the ancient cathedral cities of Canterbury and Winchester and the university sophistication of Oxford – which provide for a wide range of soil types and gardens. Greater London is a unique area for the National Garden Scheme, for the sheer density with which the conurbation is dotted with often tiny gardens. But while many parts of the region are busy and densely populated, much of the South East confirms that in England you are never far from rural seclusion while London confirms that gardens are equally – in some ways more – important in an urban setting.

Above, from top: Ichi-Coo Park, Surrey; Spitalfields Gardens, London

Below: Bramley, Sussex

BERKSHIRE

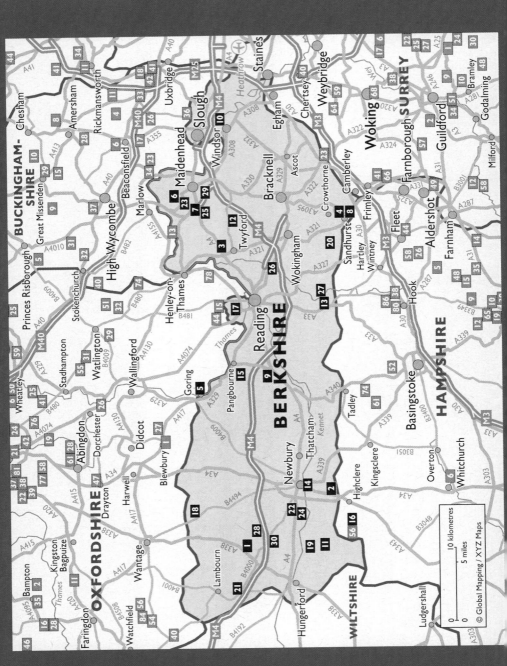

VOLUNTEERS

County Organiser
Heather Skinner
01189 737197
heather.skinner@ngs.org.uk

County Treasurer
Carolyn Clark
07701 016961
carolyn.clark@ngs.org.uk

Booklet Co-ordinator
Heather Skinner
(as above)

Assistant County Organisers
Claire Fletcher
claire.fletcher@ngs.org.uk

Carolyn Foster
07768 566482
candrfoster@btinternet.com

Rebecca Thomas
01491 628302
rebecca.thomas@ngs.org.uk

Bob Weston
01635 550240
bob.weston@ngs.org.uk

f @BerksNationalGardenScheme

X @BerksNGS

@nationalgardenschemeberkshire

OPENING DATES

All entries subject to change.
For latest information check
www.ngs.org.uk
Map locator numbers
are shown to the right
of each garden name.

January

Thursday 18th
St Timothee   23

February

Snowdrop Openings

Wednesday 7th
◆ Welford Park   28

March

Saturday 16th
Stubbings House   25

Sunday 17th
Stubbings House   25

Thursday 21st
St Timothee   23

April

Sunday 7th
NEW The Grange   12

Sunday 14th
The Old Rectory, Farnborough   18
Rookwood Farm House   22

Wednesday 24th
Rooksnest   21

Thursday 25th
Malverleys   16

May

Saturday 11th
Stubbings House   25

Sunday 12th
The Old Rectory, Farnborough   18
Stubbings House   25

Sunday 19th
Chaddleworth   5

Sunday 26th
Rookwood Farm House   22

June

Sunday 2nd
Swallowfield Village Gardens   27

Wednesday 5th
61 Sutcliffe Avenue   26

Saturday 8th
NEW The Forbury   11

Sunday 9th
13 Broom Acres   4
NEW Dorset Cottage   8
NEW The Forbury   11
NEW Pye Hill House   20
Stockcross House   24

Wednesday 12th
NEW Pye Hill House   20

Sunday 16th
Wickham House   30

Wednesday 19th
Malverleys   16

Sunday 23rd
13 Broom Acres   4
NEW Dorset Cottage   8

Wednesday 26th
The Old Rectory, Farnborough   18
Rooksnest   21

July

Tuesday 2nd
Wembury   29

Wednesday 3rd
Eton College Gardens   10

Sunday 7th
Ashbrook   1
Island Cottage   14

Sunday 14th
6 Beverley Gardens   3
Deepwood Stud Farm   7

Sunday 21st
13 Broom Acres   4
NEW Oakland   17

Friday 26th
Wembury   29

Wednesday 31st
The Old Rectory, Farnborough   18

August

Friday 16th
6 Beverley Gardens 3

Sunday 18th
Belvedere 2
Stockcross House 24

Tuesday 20th
Wembury 29

Sunday 25th
13 Broom Acres 4
NEW The Grange 12
Rookwood Farm House 22

September

Sunday 8th
Deepwood Stud Farm 7

February 2025

Wednesday 5th
◆ Welford Park 28

By Arrangement

Arrange a personalised garden visit with your club, or group of friends, on a date to suit you. See individual garden entries for full details.

Ashbrook 1
Belvedere 2
13 Broom Acres 4
Compton Elms 6
Deepwood Stud Farm 7
NEW Dorset Cottage 8
Handpost 13

Island Cottage 14
Lower Bowden Manor 15
The Old Rectory Inkpen 19
NEW Pye Hill House 20
Rooksnest 21
St Timothee 23
Stockcross House 24
Wembury 29

47,000 people affected by cancer were reached by Maggie's centres supported by the National Garden Scheme over the last 12 months

Pye Hill House

THE GARDENS

1 ASHBROOK
Wantage Road, Great Shefford, Hungerford, RG17 7DA. Jackie & Roger Frith, 07584 598189, jackiefrith2468@gmail.com. *5m NE of Hungerford. From M4 (J14) follow A338 towards Wantage for 2m into Great Shefford. Ashbrook is on R opp Station Rd. From Wantage on A338, Ashbrook is on L. Free parking in Station Rd & other roads nearby.* **Sun 7 July (10-4). Adm £4, chd free. Light refreshments. Visits also by arrangement in July for groups of 10 to 30.**
A long narrow garden, full of interest, divided into three areas running down to the river. Front garden inc roses, shrubs, dahlias, tubs and baskets. The middle garden is a very wet garden with mixed herbaceous borders and planting to suit such conditions. Lower garden has a small pond, two greenhouses, vegetable plots and exhibition chrysanthemums, the river Lambourn is at the bottom of this garden.

2 BELVEDERE
Garden Close Lane, Newbury, RG14 6PP. Noushin Garrett, 07500 925270, noushin.garrett@gmail.com. *7m S of M4 J13. Take A34 exit Highclere/Wash Common, then A343 towards Newbury. Sorry, due to narrow lane no parking at garden. Parking at St George's Church, Wash Common RG14 6NU with 600 metres walk to garden.* **Sun 18 Aug (1.30-4). Adm £5, chd free. Visits also by arrangement 15 June to 14 July.**
A garden of 2½ acres consisting of herbaceous borders, rose garden, fruit trees with woodland, bamboo and rhododendron walks. A formal parterre garden with dahlias.

3 6 BEVERLEY GARDENS
Wargrave, Reading, RG10 8ED. Patricia Vella & Jon Black. *A4 from Maidenhead take B477 to Wargrave, turn R into Silverdale Rd. A4 from Reading take A321 into Wargrave, turn R at lights, ¼ m turn L into Silverdale Rd, Beverley Gardens is on R.* **Sun 14 July, Fri 16 Aug (12-4). Adm £4, chd free. Home-made teas.**

The main garden has primarily exotic and Mediterranean planting with small paths through some of the beds, inviting you to take a closer look. This leads into a kitchen garden with greenhouse, chickens and ducks. There is a small woodland garden with stumpery and fire pit. The garden has plenty of places to sit and relax. Wheelchair access over gravel drive leading to a level garden with some bark paths. No access through main beds.

4 13 BROOM ACRES
Sandhurst, GU47 8PN. Sunil Patel, 07974 403077, garden@sunilpatel.co.uk, www.sunilpatel.co.uk. *Between Crowthorne & Sandhurst. From Crowthorne/Sandhurst road turn E into Greenways, then 1st R into Broom Acres. Street parking.* **Sun 9, Sun 23 June (1-5). Combined adm with Dorset Cottage £7, chd free. Sun 21 July, Sun 25 Aug (1-5). Adm £5, chd free. Home-made teas on all dates, but at Dorset Cottage on 23 June. Visits also by arrangement 1 June to 21 Sept for groups of 15+.**
A spellbinding ¼ acre, suburban, romantic style garden with shrubbery, exotics, specimen trees, scented climbers and mixed herbaceous borders. Densely planted and decadently flowering, a feast for all the senses. Come for the garden, stay for the magic and discover why romance remains compelling, timeless and enduring.

5 CHADDLEWORTH
Streatley, Reading, RG8 9PR. Susan & Simon Carter, 07711 420586, www.chaddleworthbedandbreakfast.com. *Just off A329 leaving Streatley towards Wallingford. From T-lights in Streatley take A329 towards Wallingford. Pass L turn for A417. Take next R signed Cleeve Court, then Chaddleworth is 1st on R along lane.* **Sun 19 May (11-4). Adm £5, chd free. Home-made teas.**
Chaddleworth's gardens surround the house on all four sides with a variety of garden styles. A 60ft wisteria, late flowering tulips and other spring bulbs should be a highlight in May. Several lawned areas with different borders, small herbaceous, ornamental grasses, wildflower and wild orchid areas, vegetables and small cutting

garden. A few stalls to browse and home-made teas for sale. Mostly wheelchair accessible with some gravel.

6 COMPTON ELMS
Marlow Road, Pinkneys Green, Maidenhead, SL6 6NR. Alison Kellett, kellettaj@gmail.com. *Situated at end of gravel road located opp & in between Berkshire Aesthetics & The Golden Ball Pub & Kitchen on the A308.* **Visits by arrangement 18 Mar to 5 Apr for groups of 15 to 40. Adm £10, chd free. Light refreshments inc.**
A delightful spring garden set in a sunken woodland, lovingly recovered from clay pit workings. The atmospheric garden is filled with snowdrops, primroses, hellebores and fritillaria, interspersed with anemone and narcissi under a canopy of ash and beech.

7 DEEPWOOD STUD FARM
Henley Road, Stubbings, nr Maidenhead, SL6 6QW. Mr & Mrs E Goodwin, 01628 822684, ed.goodwin@deepwood.co. *2m W of Maidenhead. M4 J8/9 take A404M N. 2nd exit for A4 to Maidenhead. L at 1st r'about on A4130 Henley, approx 1m on R.* **Sun 14 July, Sun 8 Sept (2-5). Adm £6, chd free. Home-made teas. Visits also by arrangement Mar to Oct for groups of 10+.**
4 acres of formal and informal gardens within a 25 acre stud farm. Formal rose garden with fountain; walled herbaceous border with windows through which to admire the views and horses, two rock gardens and hot plant terrace. Small lake with Monet style bridge and pergola. Several neo-classical follies and statues. A planted woodland area with a winding path.

In 2023, our donations to Carers Trust meant that 26,118 unpaid carers were supported across the UK

The Grange

10 ETON COLLEGE GARDENS
Eton, Windsor, SL4 6DB. Eton
College. *½ m N of Windsor. Parking
signed off B3022, Slough Rd. Walk
from car park across playing fields to
entrance.* **Wed 3 July (12-4.30). Adm
£7, chd free. Tea, coffee & cakes.**
A rare chance to visit a group of
central College gardens surrounded
by historic school buildings, inc
Luxmoore's garden on a small island
in the Thames reached across two
attractive bridges. Also, an opportunity
to explore the fascinating Eton College
Natural History Museum, the Museum
of Eton Life and one or two other
private gardens. Sorry, the gardens
are not suitable for wheelchairs due to
gravel, steps and uneven ground.
☕ 🔊

11 NEW THE FORBURY
Forbury Lane, Kintbury,
Hungerford, RG17 9SU. Joel
Loader, www.instagram.com/
theforbury. *4½ m E of Hungerford,
1m S of Kintbury. No parking
at garden but close to Kintbury
Cemetery at junction of Forbury Ln
with Pebble Hill. Please park along
Inkpen Rd.* **Sat 8, Sun 9 June (1-5).
Adm £7, chd free. Pre-booking
essential, please visit www.ngs.
org.uk for information & booking.
Two hour timed slots at 1pm &
3pm. Home-made teas.**
A stunning new naturalistic garden
designed by Andy Sturgeon. Set on a
hillside in 5 acres, Andy has created
flow through the sloping plot using
steps and gently curving paths to link
the functional areas with a pond and
the wooded boundary. Year-round
interest is provided by stylish planting.
For AirBnB accommodation contact
07879 680898.
🚶 🐕 ▣ 🛏 ☕

12 NEW THE GRANGE
The Street, Waltham St. Lawrence,
Reading, RG10 0JJ. Ruth Talbot.
*Between Maidenhead & Reading,
1m from A4. From A4 at Hare
Hatch, take turning to Waltham St
Lawrence, cross railway line & into
village. Parking at village hall. Garden
is next to The Bell pub.* **Sun 7 Apr,
Sun 25 Aug (1-5). Adm £5, chd
free. Home-made teas.**
An atmospheric garden of almost 2
acres, blending formal and natural
planting styles. A parterre blends
seamlessly towards a natural swimming
pond, with a vegetable garden and
orchard beyond. Features inc spring
bulbs, borders with herbaceous

8 NEW DORSET COTTAGE
22 Albion Road, Sandhurst,
GU47 9BP. Sarah & Paul
Merrill, 01252 873530,
sarah.merrill@yahoo.co.uk.
*Albion Rd is N off Yorktown Rd in
Sandhurst. Turning is opp Boots
chemist. Street parking is tricky,
please park in Sandhurst Library car
park in The Broadway GU47 9BL (5
min walk).* **Sun 9, Sun 23 June (1-
5). Combined adm with 13 Broom
Acres £7, chd free. Home-made
teas at 13 Broom Acres (9 June)
& Dorset Cottage (23 June). Visits
also by arrangement 19 Aug to 6
Sept for groups of 10 to 20.**
Discover this attractive suburban
secret garden behind a pretty
red brick cottage. Inviting paths
weave around a curving island bed
surrounded by long borders packed
with interesting plants reflecting the
passion of its owner. Features inc rose
and clematis covered arches, pots
with gunnera, figs, hostas and ferns.
Towering palms, acers and magnolia
trees offer shelter and seclusion.
Wheelchair users can access most of
the garden via a grass path.
♿ ☕ 🔊

**9 ♦ ENGLEFIELD HOUSE
GARDEN**
Englefield, Theale, Reading,
RG7 5EN. Lord & Lady
Benyon, 01189 302504, peter.
carson@englefield.co.uk,
www.englefieldestate.co.uk. *6m
W of Reading. M4 J12. Take A4
towards Theale. 2nd r'about take
A340 to Pangbourne. After ⅙ m
entrance on the L.* **For opening
times and information, please
phone, email or visit garden
website.**
The 12 acre garden descends
dramatically from the hill above the
historic house through woodland
where mature native trees mix with
rhododendrons and camellias. Drifts
of spring and summer planting are
followed by striking autumn colour.
Stone balustrades enclose the lower
terrace with lawns, roses and mixed
borders. A stream meanders through
the woodland. Open every Monday
from Apr-Sept (10am-6pm) and
Oct-Mar (10am-4pm). Please check
the Englefield Estate website for any
changes before travelling. Wheelchair
access to some parts of the garden.
♿ 🚗

perennials, grasses and gravel planting and a new stumpery. Numerous benches for moments of quiet reflection. Step-free access with some areas of gravel and uneven paving.

 ♿ ✿ ☕ ♪))

🔟 HANDPOST

Basingstoke Road, Swallowfield, Reading, RG7 1PU. Faith Ramsay, 07801 239937, faith@mycountrygarden.co.uk, www.mycountrygarden.co.uk. *From M4 J11, take A33 S. At 1st T-lights turn L on B3349 Basingstoke Rd. Follow road for 2¾ m, garden on L, opp Barge Ln. Parking for 12 cars max.* **Visits by arrangement 22 Apr to 21 Sept for groups of 12 to 30. Confirmed numbers required min 7 days before visit. Adm £12, chd free. Home-made teas inc. Donation to Thrive.**

4 acre designer's garden with many areas of interest. Features inc four lovely long herbaceous borders attractively and densely planted in different colour sections, a formal rose garden, an old orchard with a grass meadow, pretty pond and peaceful wooded area. Large variety of plants, trees and a productive fruit and vegetable patch. Largely wheelchair accessible with some gravel areas.

 ♿ ✿ ☕

🔟 ISLAND COTTAGE

West Mills, Newbury, RG14 5HT. Karen Swaffield, karen@lockisland.com. *7m from M4 J13. Park in town centre car parks. Walk past St Nicholas Church or between Côte Restaurant & Holland & Barrett to canal. 200yds to swing bridge & follow signs. Limited side road parking.* **Sun 7 July (2-5). Adm £4, chd free. Home-made teas. Visits also by arrangement 2 June to 29 Sept for groups of 6 to 25.**

A pretty, small waterside garden set between the River Kennet and the Kennet and Avon Canal. Interesting combinations of colour and texture to look at rather than walk through, although visitors are welcome to do that too. A deck overlooks a sluiceway towards a lawn and border. Started from scratch in 2005 and mostly again after the floods of 2014. Trying high planters this year. Home-made teas unless very wet weather. Carrot cake a must!

☕ ♪))

🔟 LOWER BOWDEN MANOR

Bowden Green, Pangbourne, RG8 8JL. Juliette & Robert Cox-Nicol, 07552 217872, robert.cox-nicol@orange.fr. *1½ m W of Pangbourne. Directions provided on booking.* **Visits by arrangement 9 Jan to 19 Dec for groups of 6 to 50. Guided visits. Adm £9, chd free. Teas with cake by prior request.**

A 7 acre designer's garden with stunning views and where structure predominates. Specimen trees show contrasting bark and foliage. A marble 'Pan' plays to a pond with boulders and boulder shaped evergreens. Versailles planters with standard topiaries line a rill. A stumpery leads to the orchard's carpet of daffodils and later a wave of white hydrangeas. Steps and gravel, but most areas accessible. Dogs welcome on leads.

 ♿ 🐕 🚗 ☕

🔟 MALVERLEYS

Fullers Lane, East End, Newbury, RG20 0AA. *A34 S of Newbury, exit signed for Highclere. Directions will be emailed prior to opening. Gate opens 30 mins before each tour.* **Thur 25 Apr, Sun 19 June (10.30-4.30). Adm £17.50, chd free. Pre-booking essential, please visit www.ngs.org.uk for information & booking. Visits start promptly at 10.30am, 1pm & 3pm with guided tour by Head Gardener. Tea or coffee inc.**

10 acres of dynamic gardens which have been developed over the last 12 yrs to inc magnificent mixed borders and a series of contrasting yew hedged rooms, hosting flame borders, a cool garden, a pond garden and new stumpery. A vegetable garden with striking fruit cages sit within a walled garden, also encompassing a white garden. Meadows open out to views over the parkland. Sorry, due to steps and uneven paths, the garden is not suitable for wheelchairs.

☕

🔟 OAKLAND

134 Kidmore Road, Caversham, Reading, RG4 7NB. Erica & Peter Cuthbertson. *2m N of Reading. N from Caversham Bridge, turn L on Church Rd A4074, then R on St Annes Rd & L on Priest Hill. Follow ½ m along The Mount & Kidmore Rd, garden on R. Parking in side roads or in Albert Rd Car Park RG4 7PR (8 min walk). Disabled parking in drive.*

Sun 21 July (10.30-4). Adm £4.50, chd free. Home-made teas.

A contemporary garden showcasing what can be achieved in a young garden, in the heart of suburbia. A tranquil oasis with an attractive water feature, seating areas, outdoor kitchen, wildflower meadow, pergola and a 'Wizard of Oz' path. Planting to attract bees and butterflies. A calming garden with contrasting areas facing different aspects. Mostly wheelchair accessible with some gravel and a grassy slope.

 ♿ 🐕 Ⓓ ☕ ♪))

🔟 THE OLD RECTORY, FARNBOROUGH

nr Wantage, OX12 8NX. Mr & Mrs Michael Todhunter. *4m SE of Wantage. Take B4494 Wantage-Newbury road, after 4m turn E at sign for Farnborough. Approx 1m to village, Old Rectory on L.* **Sun 14 Apr, Sun 12 May (2-5); Wed 26 June, Wed 31 July (11-4). Adm £5, chd free. Home-made teas. Donation to Farnborough PCC.**

In a series of immaculately tended garden rooms inc herbaceous borders, arboretum, secret garden, roses, vegetables and bog garden. There is an explosion of rare and interesting plants, beautifully combined for colour and texture. With stunning views across the countryside, it is the perfect setting for the 1749 rectory (not open), once home of John Betjeman, in memory of whom John Piper created a window in the local church.

✿ 🚗 ☕

🔟 THE OLD RECTORY INKPEN

Lower Green, Inkpen, RG17 9DS. Mrs C McKeon, 07850 678239, oldrectoryinkpen@gmail.com. *4m SE of Hungerford. From centre of Kintbury at the Xrds, take Inkpen Rd. After ½ m turn R, then go approx 3m, passing Crown & Garter Pub, then Inkpen Village Hall on L side.* **Next to St Michael's Church. Visits by arrangement June to Sept for groups of up to 30. Adm £10, chd free. Light refreshments inc.**

On a gentle hillside with views of the Inkpen Hill, the Old Rectory offers a peaceful setting for this pretty 5 acre garden. Originally an historic 1½ hectare formal garden to the south of the C17 Rectory, it is on a gentle slope surrounded by later additions of a walled kitchen garden, herbaceous borders, pleached lime walks and a recently cultivated wildflower meadow.

☕

20 NEW **PYE HILL HOUSE**
Jubilee Road, Finchampstead,
Wokingham, RG40 3RU.
Rachael & Peter Coles,
pyehillgarden@gmail.com. *4m
S of Wokingham. Garden located
off Jubilee Rd, approx ½ m S of
Finchampstead Surgery. Please
follow NGS signs.* **Sun 9, Wed 12
June (10.30-4.30). Adm £5, chd
free. Pre-booking essential,
please visit www.ngs.org.
uk for information & booking.
Home-made teas. Visits also by
arrangement 12 May to 18 Aug for
groups of 12 to 30. Car sharing is
preferable.**
A stylish mature garden over several
acres. Paths weave enticingly through
a sloping landscape which combines
drifts of perennials and grasses,
ornamental shrubs, jungle inspired
planting and specimen trees. Features
inc wildflower and Mediterranean
banks, lime, amelanchier and pinus
walks, natural pond, stumpery, holly
tree terrace with topiary and rose and
clematis obelisks.

☕))

21 **ROOKSNEST**
Ermin Street, Lambourn
Woodlands, RG17 7SB.
Rooksnest Estate, 07787 085565,
gardens@rooksnest.net. *2m S of
Lambourn on B4000. From M4 J14,
take A338 Wantage Rd, turn 1st L
onto B4000 (Ermin St). Rooksnest
signed after 3m.* **Wed 24 Apr, Wed
26 June (11-3.30). Adm £6, chd
free. Light refreshments. Visits
also by arrangement 1 Apr to 27
June.**
Approx 10 acre, exceptionally fine
traditional English garden. Rose
garden, herbaceous garden, pond
garden, herb garden, fruit, vegetable
and cutting garden and glasshouses.
Many specimen trees and fine shrubs,
orchard and terraces. Garden mostly
designed by Arabella Lennox-Boyd.
Limited WC facilities. Most areas have
step free wheelchair access, although
surfaces consist of gravel and mowed
grass.

♿ 🐕 🅳 ☕))

22 **ROOKWOOD FARM HOUSE**
Stockcross, Newbury, RG20 8JX.
The Hon Rupert & Charlotte Digby,
www.rookwoodhouse.co.uk. *3m W
of Newbury. M4 J13, A34(S). After
3m exit for A4(W) to Hungerford. At
2nd r'about take B4000 towards
Stockcross, after approx ¾ m turn R
into Rookwood.* **Sun 14 Apr, Sun 26
May, Sun 25 Aug (11-4.30). Adm
£5, chd free. Home-made teas &
light refreshments.**
This exciting valley garden, a work
in progress, has elements all visitors
can enjoy. A rose covered pergola,
fabulous tulips, giant alliums, join a
jungle garden with cannas, bananas
and echiums. A kitchen garden
features a parterre of raised beds,
which along with a bog garden and
colour themed herbaceous planting,
all make Rookwood well worth a visit.
WC available.

🚗 🚐 ☕

23 **ST TIMOTHEE**
Darlings Lane, Pinkneys Green,
Maidenhead, SL6 6PA. Sarah
& Sal Pajwani, 07976 892667,
pajwanisarah@gmail.com. *1m N
of Maidenhead. M4 J8/9 to A404M,
3rd exit onto A4 to Maidenhead. L
at 1st r'about to A4130 Henley Rd.
After ½ m turn R onto Pinkneys Dr.
At Pinkneys Arms pub turn L into
Lee Ln. Follow NGS signs.* **Talk &
Walk Events: Thur 18 Jan, Thur
21 Mar (10.30-12.30). Adm £16,
chd free. Pre-booking essential,
please visit www.ngs.org.uk for
information & booking. Visits also
by arrangement 9 Jan to 25 Apr
for groups of 10 to 50, with fully
illustrated slideshow talks about
the garden.**
Talk & Walk events on Thur 18 Jan:
The Winter Garden, and Thur 21
Mar: The Joy of Spring Bulbs start
promptly with an illustrated slideshow
talk and home-made teas followed by
time to explore the garden. A 2 acre
country garden planted for year-round
interest with a variety of different
colour themed borders each featuring
a wide range of hardy perennials,
bulbs, shrubs and ornamental
grasses. Also inc a box parterre,
wildlife pond and rose terrace
together with areas of long grass and
beautiful mature trees, all set against
the backdrop of a 1930s house. This
garden is proud to provide plants for
the National Garden Scheme's Show
Garden at Chelsea Flower Show
2024.

♿ ❀ 🚗 🅳 ☕))

24 **STOCKCROSS HOUSE**
Church Road, Stockcross,
Newbury, RG20 8LP. Susan &
Edward Vandyk, 01488 608810,
Info@stockcrosshousegarden.
co.uk. *3m W of Newbury. M4 J13,
A34(S). After 3m exit A4(W) to
Hungerford. At 2nd r'about take
B4000, 1m to Stockcross, 2nd L into
Church Rd. Coach parking available.*
**Sun 9 June, Sun 18 Aug (11-4).
Adm £6, chd free. Home-made
teas. Visits also by arrangement
20 May to 1 Sept for groups of 20
to 40.**
Romantic 2 acre garden set around a
former rectory (not open). Deep mixed
borders with emphasis on strong,
complementary colour combinations.
Large orangery, wisteria and clematis
clad pergola, folly with pond reflecting
the church tower. Croquet lawn
and pavilion. Naturalistic planting
and pond on lower level. Small
stumpery, fernery and kitchen
garden. Plants from garden for sale.
Partial wheelchair access with some
gravelled areas.

♿ ❀ ☕))

25 **STUBBINGS HOUSE**
Stubbings Lane, Henley
Road, Maidenhead,
SL6 6QL. Mr & Mrs D Good,
www.stubbingsnursery.co.uk.
*Located on the outskirts of
Maidenhead, just mins from the M4
J8/9 & M40 J4. From A404(M) W
of Maidenhead, exit at A4 r'about
& follow signs to Maidenhead. At
the small r'about turn L towards
Stubbings. Take the next L onto
Stubbings Ln.* **Sat 16, Sun 17 Mar,
Sat 11, Sun 12 May (10-4). Adm
£4, chd free. Light refreshments
(additional charges apply).**
Parkland garden accessed via
adjacent retail plant centre and
café. Set around C18 Grade II listed
house (not open), home to Queen
Wilhelmina of Netherlands in WW2.
Large lawn with ha-ha and woodland
walks. Notable trees inc historic
cedars and araucaria. March brings
an abundance of daffodils and in
May a 60 metre wall of wisteria.
Attractions inc a C18 icehouse and
access to adjacent NT woodland. On
site licenced café offering breakfast,
snacks, cream teas and seasonal
lunches. Wheelchair access to a level
site with firm gravel paths.

♿ 🐕 ❀ ☕ ☕

26 **61 SUTCLIFFE AVENUE**
Earley, Reading, RG6 7JN. Sue
& Dave Wilder. *3m SE of Reading.
Road: On Wokingham Rd (A329)
from E, pass Showcase Cinema,
then L at Nisa (Meadow Rd), then
R into Sutcliffe Ave; from W, turn R
at Nisa. Train: Earley Stn, then 10
min walk.* **Wed 5 June (10-5). Adm**

£3.50, chd free. Home-made teas. A characterful urban wildlife friendly garden being imaginatively rewilded. The garden offers the relaxing sense of a walk in the countryside. An inviting path winds past wildflower islands, through a rose covered arch, to a pollinators paradise garden and small pond. Tree trunks creatively recycled and a chicken run are added features. Wheelchair access to the bottom of garden.

GROUP OPENING

27 SWALLOWFIELD VILLAGE GARDENS

The Street, Swallowfield, RG7 1QY. *5m S of Reading. From M4 J11 take A33 S. At 1st T-lights turn L on B3349 signed Swallowfield. In village follow signs for parking. Buy tickets & map in Swallowfield Medical Practice (SMP) car park, opp Crown Pub.* **Sun 2 June (2-5.30). Combined adm £8, chd free. Home-made teas at Brambles.**

BIRD IN HAND HOUSE
Margaret McDonald.

BRAMBLES
Sarah & Martyn Dadds.

BRIERLEY HOUSE
Jean & Richard Trinder.

5 CURLYS WAY
Carolyn & Gary Clark.

LAMBS FARMHOUSE
Eva Koskuba.

NORKETT COTTAGE
Jenny Spencer.

SUVIKUJA
Catherine Glover & Richard Hoyle.

Swallowfield is offering seven gardens to visit this yr with four gardens in the village itself and three just outside. The four village gardens can be reached on foot from the village parking with the three outside the village requiring a car or bicycle. Each garden is different and provides its own character and interest. Swallowfield nestles in the countryside by the Blackwater and Loddon rivers with an abundance of wildlife and lovely views. See website for info about individual gardens. Plants for sale. Wheelchair access to many gardens, however some have gravel drives, slopes and uneven ground.

28 ◆ WELFORD PARK

Welford, Newbury, RG20 8HU. **Mrs J H Puxley, 01488 608691, snowdrops@welfordpark.co.uk, www.welfordpark.co.uk.** *6m NW of Newbury. M4 J13, A34(S). After 3m exit for A4(W) to Hungerford. At 2nd r'about take B4000, after 4m turn R signed Welford. Entrance on Newbury-Lambourn road.* **For NGS: Wed 7 Feb (11-4). Adm £12, concessions £10, chd £5. Light refreshments. For 2025: Wed 5 Feb. For other opening times and information, please phone, email or visit garden website.**

One of the finest natural snowdrop woodlands in the country and a wonderful display of hellebores, galanthus cultivars, winter flowering shrubs throughout the extensive gardens. This is an NGS 1927 pioneer garden on the River Lambourn set around Queen Anne House (not open). Also, the stunning setting for Great British Bake Off. Tickets can be purchased at the gate or via the Welford Park website. Refreshments in large tent serving light lunches, home-made cakes, hot and cold drinks. WC's. Child friendly and dogs welcome on leads. Coach parties please book in advance. Paths are as wheelchair friendly as possible, please watch for signs to avoid damp areas and deep wood chip paths.

29 WEMBURY

Altwood Close, Maidenhead, SL6 4PP. **Carolyn Foster, 07768 566482, candrfoster@btinternet.com.** *W side of Maidenhead, S of A4. M4 J8/9, then A404M J9B, 3rd exit to A4 to Maidenhead, R at 1st r'about, 2nd L onto Altwood Rd, then 5th R, follow NGS signs.* **Tue 2, Fri 26 July, Tue 20 Aug (10.30-4). Adm £4.50, chd free. Pre-booking essential, please visit www.ngs.org.uk for information & booking. Home-made teas. Two hour timed slots at 10.30am & 2pm. Visits also by arrangement July & Aug for groups of 10 to 20.**

A wildlife friendly, plant lover's cottage garden with borders generously planted with bulbs, perennials, grasses and shrubs for successional interest for every season. Productive vegetable garden and greenhouses. Many pots and baskets with seasonal annuals and tender perennials especially salvias.

30 WICKHAM HOUSE

Wickham, Newbury, RG20 8HD. **Mr & Mrs James D'Arcy.** *7m NW of Newbury or 6m NE of Hungerford. From M4 J14, take A338(N) signed Wantage. Approx ¾ m turn R onto B4000. Drive through Wickham. Entrance 100yd uphill on R. From Newbury take B4000, house on L 75yds past the Wickham speed limit sign.* **Sun 16 June (11-3.30). Adm £5.50, chd free. Home-made teas, gammon rolls & a variety of cakes.**

In a beautiful country house setting, this exceptional ½ acre walled garden was created from scratch in 2008. Designed by Robin Templar-Williams, the different rooms have distinct themes and colour schemes. Delightful arched clematis and rose walkway. Wide variety of trees, planting, pots brimming with colour and places to sit and enjoy the views. Separate cutting and vegetable garden. Wheelchair access over gravel paths.

National Garden Scheme gardens are identified by their yellow road signs and posters. You can expect a garden of quality, character and interest, a warm welcome and plenty of home-made cakes!

BUCKINGHAMSHIRE

VOLUNTEERS

County Organiser
Maggie Bateson
01494 866265
maggiebateson@gmail.com

County Treasurer
Tim Hart
01494 837328
timgc.hart@btinternet.com

Publicity
Sandra Wetherall
01494 862264
sandracwetherall@gmail.com

Social Media
Stella Vaines
07711 420621
stella@bakersclose.com

Booklet Co-ordinator
Maggie Bateson
(as above)

Assistant County Organisers
Judy Hart
01494 837328
judy.elgood@gmail.com

Mhairi Sharpley
01494 782870
mhairisharpley@btinternet.com

Stella Vaines
(as above)

f @BucksNGS

X @BucksNGS

OPENING DATES

All entries subject to change.
For latest information check
www.ngs.org.uk
Map locator numbers are
shown to the right of each
garden name.

March

Sunday 10th
Wind in the Willows   42

Wednesday 20th
Montana   24

Sunday 31st
Overstroud Cottage   29

April

Sunday 14th
Long Crendon Gardens   22

Sunday 21st
Overstroud Cottage   29

Sunday 28th
Abbots House   1

May

Monday 6th
Turn End   38

Sunday 12th
The Plough   30
◆ Stoke Poges Memorial
  Gardens   36

Monday 13th
◆ Ascott   3

Tuesday 14th
Red Kites   31

Wednesday 15th
Montana   24

Sunday 19th
NEW Foscote Manor   14
Overstroud Cottage   29

Saturday 25th
◆ Nether Winchendon House   25

Sunday 26th
Higher Denham Gardens   18
◆ Nether Winchendon House   25
The Plough   30

Monday 27th
Glebe Farm   16

June

Sunday 2nd
Tythrop Park   39
The White House   41

Saturday 8th
Acer Corner   2
◆ Cowper & Newton Museum
  Gardens   12

Sunday 9th
Acer Corner   2
Bledlow Manor   5
18 Brownswood Road   6
◆ Cowper & Newton Museum
  Gardens   12
Overstroud Cottage   29

Thursday 13th
NEW Cornfield Cottage   11

Saturday 15th
St Michaels Convent   33

Sunday 16th
Long Crendon Gardens   22

Wednesday 19th
The Walled Garden, Wormsley 40

Saturday 22nd
Chiltern Haven   10
Old Park Barn   27

Sunday 23rd
Old Park Barn   27

July

Sunday 7th
Chiltern Forage Farm   9
Fressingwood   15

Tuesday 9th
Red Kites   31

Sunday 14th
Old Keepers   26

Wednesday 17th
Montana   24

Saturday 20th
Howe Farm Flowers   20

August

Wednesday 7th
Danesfield House   13

Sunday 25th
NEW Springfield Farm   35

September

Saturday 28th
Horatio's Garden   19

October

Saturday 12th
Acer Corner   2

Sunday 13th
Acer Corner   2

By Arrangement

Arrange a personalised garden visit with your club, or group of friends, on a date to suit you. See individual garden entries for full details.

Kingsbridge Farm

THE GARDENS

1 ABBOTS HOUSE
10 Church Street, Winslow, MK18 3AN. Mrs Jane Rennie, 01296 712326, jane@renniemail.com. *9m N of Aylesbury. A413 into Winslow. From town centre take Horn St & R into Church St, L fork at top. Entrance through door in wall, Church Walk. Parking in town centre & adjacent streets.* Sun 28 Apr (12-5). Adm £5, chd free. Home-made teas. Visits also by arrangement May & June for groups of 6 to 16.
Behind red brick walls a ¾ acre garden on four different levels, each with unique planting and atmosphere. Lower lawn with white wisteria arbour and pond, upper lawn with rose pergola and woodland, pool area with grasses, Victorian kitchen garden and wild meadow. Spring bulbs in wild areas and woodland, many tulips in Apr, remaining areas peak in June/July. Water feature, sculptures and many pots. Rennie's Winslow Cider and Cider Lush available. Partial wheelchair access only due to steps to garden levels. Guide dogs and medical-aid dogs only.

2 ACER CORNER
10 Manor Road, Wendover, HP22 6HQ. Jo Naiman, 07958 319234, jo@acercorner.com, www.acercorner.com. *3m S of Aylesbury. Follow A413 into Wendover. L at clock tower r'about into Aylesbury Rd. R at next r'about into Wharf Rd, continue past schools on L, garden on R.* Sat 8, Sun 9 June, Sat 12, Sun 13 Oct (2-5). Adm £4, chd free. Visits also by arrangement 1 May to 20 Oct for groups of up to 20.
Garden designer's garden with Japanese influence and large collection of Japanese maples. The enclosed front garden is Japanese in style. Back garden is divided into three areas; patio area recently redesigned in the Japanese style, densely planted area with many acers and roses, also a corner which inc a productive greenhouse and interesting planting. There are over 70 acers in the garden.

3 ◆ ASCOTT
Ascott Estate, Wing, Leighton Buzzard, LU7 0PP. The National Trust, info@ascottestate.co.uk, www.ascottestate.co.uk. *2m SW of Leighton Buzzard, 8m NE of Aylesbury. Via A418. Buses: 150 Aylesbury to Milton Keynes, 250 Aylesbury & Milton Keynes. Access is via the visitors entrance, use postcode LU7 0ND.* For NGS: Mon 13 May (11.30-5). Adm £8, chd £3. Pre-booking essential, please visit national-trust-ascott. checkfront.com/reserve for information & booking. Light refreshments. NT members are required to pay to enter the Gardens on NGS days. For other opening times and information, please email or visit garden website.
Combining Victorian formality with natural planting and modern design. Terraced lawns with specimen and ornamental trees and panoramic views to the Chilterns. Naturalised bulbs, mirror image herbaceous borders and impressive topiary inc a unique box and yew sundial. Ascott House is closed on NGS Days. The Pavilion Tearoom will be open until 15 mins before closing, serving a range of hot and cold refreshments. Pathways are gravel and grass. Manual wheelchairs are available to use for your visit, please contact the Estate Office to reserve in advance.

4 BEECH HOUSE
Long Wood Drive, Jordans, nr Beaconsfield, HP9 2SS. Sue & Ray Edwards, 01494 875580, raychessmad@hotmail.com. *From A40, L to Seer Green & Jordans for approx 1m, turn into Jordans Way on R, Long Wood Dr 1st L. From A413, turn into Chalfont St Giles, straight ahead until L signed Jordans, 1st L Jordans Way.* Visits by arrangement. Adm £5, chd free.
2 acre plantsman's garden built up over the last 36 yrs with a wide range of flowering and foliage plants in a variety of habitats providing a show all yr. Bulbs, perennials, shrubs, roses and grasses provide continuous interest. Trees planted for their flowers, foliage, ornamental bark and autumn display. Two attractive meadows combine long flowering season in a wildlife friendly environment. Meadow gardens established over 30 yrs always attract attention and discussion. Wheelchair access dependent upon weather conditions.

5 BLEDLOW MANOR
Off Perry Lane, Bledlow, nr Princes Risborough, HP27 9PA. Lord & Lady Carrington, www.carington.co.uk/gardens. *9m NW of High Wycombe, 3m SW of Princes Risborough. ½m off B4009 in middle of Bledlow village. For SatNav use postcode HP27 9PA.* Sun 9 June (2-5). Adm £8, chd free. Home-made teas.
The present garden covering around 12 acres inc the walled kitchen garden crisscrossed by paths with vegetables, fruit, herbs and flowers. The sculpture garden, the replanted granary garden with fountain and borders, as well as the individual paved gardens and parterres divided by yew hedges and more. The Lyde water garden formed out of old cress beds fed by numerous springs. Partial wheelchair access via steps or sloped grass to enter gardens.

6 18 BROWNSWOOD ROAD
Beaconsfield, HP9 2NU. John & Bernadette Thompson, 07879 282191, tbernadette60@gmail.com. *From New Town turn R into Ledborough Ln, L into Sandleswood Rd, 2nd R into Brownswood Rd.* Sun 9 June (2-5.30). Adm £4, chd free. Visits also by arrangement 28 Mar to 26 Sept for groups of up to 35.
A plant filled garden designed by Barbara Hunt. A harmonious arrangement of arcs and circles introduces a rhythm that leads through the garden. Sweeping box curves, gravel beds, brick edging and lush planting. A restrained use of purples and reds dazzle against a grey and green background.

152,684 people were able to access guidance on what to expect when a person is dying through the National Garden Scheme support for Hospice UK this year

7 CEDAR HOUSE

Bacombe Lane, Wendover,
HP22 6EQ. Sarah Nicholson,
01296 622131, sarahhnicholson@
btinternet.com. *5m SE Aylesbury.
From Gt Missenden take A413 into
Wendover. Take 1st L before row
of cottages, house at top of lane.
Parking for 10 cars only.* **Visits by
arrangement 17 Feb to 9 Sept for
groups of 10 to 30. Adm £5, chd
free. Home-made teas.**
A plantsman's garden in the Chiltern
Hills with a great variety of trees,
shrubs and plants. A sloping lawn
leads to a natural swimming pond
with wild flowers inc native orchids.
A lodge greenhouse and a good
collection of half-hardy plants in
pots. Local artist's sculptures can be
viewed. Picnics welcome on prior
request. Wheelchair access over
gentle sloping lawn.

& ✿ ☕ 🔥

8 CHESHAM BOIS HOUSE

85 Bois Lane, Chesham Bois,
Amersham, HP6 6DF. Julia
Plaistowe, 01494 726476,
plaistowejulia@gmail.com,
www.cheshamboishouse.co.uk.
*1m N of Amersham-on-the-Hill.
Follow Sycamore Rd (main shopping
centre road of Amersham), which
becomes Bois Ln. Do not use
SatNav once in lane as you will be
led astray.* **Visits by arrangement
Mar to Aug. Adm £6, chd free.
Home-made teas.**
3 acre beautiful garden with
primroses, daffodils and hellebores
in early spring. Interesting for most of
the yr with lovely herbaceous borders,
rill with small ornamental canal, walled
garden, old orchard with wildlife pond,
and handsome trees some of which
are topiary. It is a peaceful oasis.
Wheelchair access via gravel at front
of house.

& ✿ 🚐 ☕

9 CHILTERN FORAGE FARM

Spring Coppice Lane,
Speen, Princes Risborough,
HP27 0SU. Emma Plunket,
www.plunketgardens.com. *Follow
signs to gate at top of the hill & park
in field; trainers or walking shoes
for uneven ground.* **Sun 7 July
(2.30-5). Adm £5, chd free. Light
refreshments.**
Tours at 2.30pm and 4pm of this
project under development in
attractive hillside setting. Pasture
being restored to hay meadows and
planted with fruit. Tips for foraging,

encouraging wild flowers and creation
of wildlife habitats. On calm sunny
day great for spotting butterflies and
moths. Enjoy cool drinks in shady
seating and share our identification
tips, survey findings and field guides.

🅳 ☕))

10 CHILTERN HAVEN

Pednor, Chesham, HP5 2SX.
Mrs Clare Waters & Mr Jonathan
Waters. *2m W of Chesham, 3m E of
Great Missenden. Chesham/Great
Missenden turn off B485 to Little
Hundridge Ln. 1m R at T-junction,
R & parking on R. From Chesham
Chartridge Ln, turn L to Westdean
Ln, then R to Pednor Bottom, after
1½m parking on R.* **Sat 22 June
(2-5). Adm £5, chd free. Home-
made teas.**
A country garden over 1½ acres with
a wide range of flowering and foliage
plants. Bulbs, perennials, roses,
shrubs and trees have been chosen
to provide continuous interest, with
colour concentrated in purple, pink,
blue and lemon. The lawns around
the house have deep, curving borders
with sunny and shady aspects.
There is also a wildlife pond, old
orchard, small vegetable garden and
greenhouse.

✿ ☕))

11 NEW CORNFIELD COTTAGE

Roberts Lane, Chalfont St Peter,
Gerrards Cross, SL9 0QR. Stewart
Walker. *In the hamlet of Horn Hill,
1½m from the centre of Chalfont
St Peter. Take Rickmansworth Ln
to Horn Hill Village Hall, turn R into
Roberts Ln. Cornfield Cottage is 300
metres on L. Limited car parking opp
the house & at Horn Hill Village Hall.*
**Thur 13 June (2-5). Adm £4.50,
chd free. Home-made teas.**
A beautiful rural garden in a quiet
country lane. The borders are
planted with scented roses and bee
and butterfly friendly flowers inc
honeysuckle, delphiniums and sweet
peas. Seating areas provide enjoyable
views of the garden at different times
of the day. A natural arch leads to
a paddock with a small vegetable
garden, orchard, wildflower beds
and wood with a seasonal spring
fed pond. Disabled parking opp the
house or on the drive can be booked.
The entrance gate to the garden is
800mm wide.

& ☕))

12 ✦ COWPER & NEWTON MUSEUM GARDENS

Orchard Side, Market Place,
Olney, MK46 4AJ. Cowper
and Newton Museum,
01234 711516, house-manager@
cowperandnewtonmuseum.org.uk,
www.cowperandnewtonmuseum.
org.uk. *5m N of Newport Pagnell. 12m
S of Wellingborough. On A509. Please
park in public car park in East St.* **For
NGS: Sat 8, Sun 9 June (11-4.30).
Adm £4, chd free. Home-made
teas. For other opening times and
information, please phone, email or
visit garden website.**
The tranquil Flower Garden of C18
poet William Cowper, who said
'Gardening was of all employments,
that in which I succeeded best', has
plants introduced prior to his death in
1800, many mentioned in his writings.
The Summerhouse Garden with
Cowper's 'verse manufactory', now a
Victorian Kitchen Garden, has new and
heritage vegetables organically grown,
also a herb border and medicinal
plant bed. Features inc lacemaking
demonstrations and local artists
painting live art on both days. Georgian
dancers on Sun 9 June. Wheelchair
access on mostly hard paths.

& ✿ ☕))

13 DANESFIELD HOUSE

Henley Road, Marlow, SL7 2EY.
Danesfield House Hotel, www.
danesfieldhouse.co.uk. *3m from
Marlow. On the A4155 between
Marlow & Henley-on-Thames. Signed
on the LHS Danesfield House Hotel
& Spa.* **Wed 7 Aug (10-4). Adm £5,
chd free. Pre-booking essential,
please phone 01628 891010 or
email amoorin@danesfieldhouse.
co.uk for information & booking.**
The gardens at Danesfield were
completed in 1901 by Robert Hudson,
the Sunlight Soap magnate who built
the house. Since the house opened
as a hotel in 1991, the gardens have
been admired by several thousand
guests each yr. However, in 2009
it was discovered that the gardens
contained outstanding examples of
pulhamite in both the formal gardens
and the waterfall areas. The 100 yr
old topiary is also outstanding. Part of
the grounds inc an Iron Age fort. Tour
with Head Gardener at 10.30am and
1.30pm only (max 30 per tour) and
lunch and afternoon tea must also
be pre-booked. Wheelchair access
on gravel paths through parts of the
garden.

& 🛏 ☕))

Red Kites

14 NEW FOSCOTE MANOR

Foscott, Buckingham, MK18 6AE.
Kate Pryke. *Just outside Maids
Moreton, NE of Buckingham. The
postcode takes you to a small hamlet
of cottages. For Foscote Manor,
continue across the cattle grid into
the fields & you will see the gates
of the Manor House.* **Sun 19 May
(2-5). Adm £6, chd free. Home-
made teas.**
A restored walled kitchen garden with
vegetables, fruit, herbs and flowers
as the centre piece of this 40 acre
estate. The surrounding waterway is
bordered by a wildflower meadow,
attracting heron, egret and kingfisher.
Behind the walled garden, the back
drive leads to ancient woodland
sprouting a carpet of spring bulbs,
and the lake which is home to
Canada geese, swans and heron.

15 FRESSINGWOOD

Hare Lane, Little Kingshill, Great
Missenden, HP16 0EF. John &
Maggie Bateson. *1m S of Great
Missenden, 4m W of Amersham.
From the A413 at Chiltern Hospital,
turn L signed Gt & Lt Kingshill. Take
1st L into Nags Head Ln. Turn R
under railway bridge, then L into
New Rd & continue to Hare Ln.* **Sun
7 July (2-5.30). Adm £5, chd free.
Home-made teas.**
Thoughtfully designed and structured
garden with year-round colour
and many interesting features inc
herbaceous borders, a shrubbery with
ferns, hostas, grasses and hellebores.
Small formal garden, pergolas with
roses and clematis. A variety of
topiary and small garden rooms. A
central feature incorporating water
with grasses. Large bonsai collection.

16 GLEBE FARM

Lillingstone Lovell,
Buckingham, MK18 5BB. Mr
David Hilliard, 01280 860384,
thehilliards@talk21.com,
www.sites.google.com/site/
glebefarmbarn. *Off A413, 5m N of
Buckingham & 2m S of Whittlebury.
From A5 at Potterspury, turn off A5
& follow signs to Lillingstone Lovell.
From A413 Lillingsone Lovell is
situated between Lillingstone Dayrell
& Whittlebury.* **Mon 27 May (1.30-5).
Adm £4, chd free. Home-made
teas. Visits also by arrangement
for groups of 6 to 10. Mon, Tues,
Thurs (1.30-5) in June only.**
A large cottage garden with an
exuberance of colourful planting
and winding gravel paths, amongst
lawns and herbaceous borders on
two levels. Ponds, a wishing well,
vegetable beds, a knot garden, a

Foscote Manor

small walled garden and an old tractor feature. Everything combines to make a beautiful garden full of surprises.

17 HALL BARN
Windsor End, Beaconsfield, HP9 2SG. Fred Farncombe, fred@hallbarnestate.co.uk. *½m S of Beaconsfield. Lodge gate 300yds S of St Mary & All Saints' Church in Old Town centre. Please do not use SatNav.* **Visits by arrangement 12 Feb to 16 Oct. Adm £6, chd free. Home-made teas provided for groups of 10+.**
Historical landscaped garden laid out between 1680-1730 for the poet Edmund Waller and his descendants. Features 300 yr old cloud formation yew hedges, formal lake and vistas ending with classical buildings and statues. Wooded walks around the grove offer respite from the heat on sunny days. One of the original NGS garden openings of 1927.

GROUP OPENING

18 HIGHER DENHAM GARDENS
Higher Denham, UB9 5EA. *6m E of Beaconsfield. Turn off A412, approx ½ m N of junction with A40 into Old Rectory Ln. After 1m enter Higher Denham straight ahead. Tickets for all gardens at community hall, 70yds into the village.* **Sun 26 May (2-5). Combined adm £6, chd free. Home-made teas in village hall. Donation to Higher Denham Community CIO (Garden Upkeep Fund).**

11 ASHCROFT DRIVE
Robert Brooks.

NEW **31 LOWER ROAD**
Mark Scanlon.

5 SIDE ROAD
Jane Blyth.

WIND IN THE WILLOWS
Ron James.
(See separate entry)

At least four gardens will open in the delightful Misbourne chalk stream valley, and Wind in the Willows also opens separately in March. Wind in the Willows has over 350 shrubs and trees, informal woodland and wild gardens inc riverside and bog plantings and a collection of 80 hostas and 12 striped roses in 3 acres. A new water lily pond has been created within the river. 'Really different' was a typical visitor comment.

The garden at 5 Side Road is medium sized with lawns, borders and shrubs, and many features which children will love. A big conifer has been removed and the area replanted for greater interest. 31 Lower Road is a small back garden on three levels leading down to the River Misbourne. 11 Ashcroft Drive a unique and not to be missed garden laid out in a Persian style stocked with typical Persian plants. The garden is a 5 min drive away from the other three. In May the owner of Wind in the Willows will lead optional guided tours of the garden starting at 2.30pm and 4pm. Tours generally last approx 1 hour. Partial wheelchair access.

19 HORATIO'S GARDEN
National Spinal Injuries Centre (NSIC), Stoke Mandeville Hospital, Mandeville Road, Stoke Mandeville, Aylesbury, HP21 8AL. Amy Moffett, www.horatiosgarden.org.uk. *The closest car park to Horatio's Garden is at Stoke Mandeville Hospital, Car Park B, opp Asda (charges may apply).* **Sat 28 Sept (2-5). Adm £5, chd free. Home-made teas in the garden room.**
Opened in Sept 2018, Horatio's Garden at the National Spinal Injuries Centre, Stoke Mandeville Hospital is designed by Joe Swift. The fully accessible garden for patients with spinal injuries has been part funded by the NGS. The beautiful space is cleverly designed to bring the sights, sounds and scents of nature into the heart of the NHS. Everything is high quality and carefully designed to bring benefit to patients who often have lengthy stays in hospital. The garden features a contemporary garden room, designed by Andrew Wells as well as a stunning Griffin Glasshouse. We also have a wonderful wildflower meadow. Please come along and meet the Head Gardener and volunteer team and taste our delicious tea and home-made cake! The garden is fully accessible, having been designed specifically for patients in wheelchairs or hospital beds.

20 HOWE FARM FLOWERS
Ashendon Road, Dorton, Aylesbury, HP18 0NY. Mrs Amber Partner, www.howefarmflowers.com. *If using SatNav, please make sure it takes you to Dorton & not the nearby village of Westcott.* **Sat 20 July (2-5). Adm £4, chd free. Home-made teas.**

Howe Farm Flowers is a flower farm located in the beautiful Buckinghamshire countryside. We have one main cutting field, approx an acre in size, which is dedicated to our weddings, events and wholesale. We also have a ¼ acre cut flower garden where we welcome our PYO flowers visitors, and two large polytunnels. We use the no dig method and avoid using chemicals and pesticides. Gravel path easily accessible by wheelchairs leading to the flower field.

21 KINGSBRIDGE FARM
Steeple Claydon, MK18 2EJ. Mr & Mrs Tom Aldous, 01296 730224. *3m S of Buckingham. Halfway between Padbury & Steeple Claydon. Xrds signed to Kingsbridge Only.* **Visits by arrangement Mar to July for groups of 6+. Adm £7, chd free. Home-made teas in our cosy, converted barn.**
Stunning and exceptional 6 acre garden, ever evolving! Main lawn is enclosed by softly curving, colour themed herbaceous borders with gazebo, topiary, clipped yews, pleached hornbeams leading to ha-ha and countryside beyond. A natural stream with bog plants and nesting kingfishers, meanders serenely through shrub and woodland gardens with many walks. A garden always evolving, to visit again and again.

GROUP OPENING

22 LONG CRENDON GARDENS
Long Crendon, HP18 9AN. *2m N of Thame. Park in the village as there is no parking at individual gardens.* **Sun 14 Apr, Sun 16 June (2-6). Combined adm £6, chd free. Home-made teas in Church House, High St (Apr) & St Mary's Church (June).**

BAKER'S CLOSE
Mr & Mrs Peter Vaines.
Open on Sun 14 Apr

BARRY'S CLOSE
Mr & Mrs Richard Salmon.
Open on Sun 14 Apr

BRINDLES
Sarah Chapman.
Open on Sun 16 June

COP CLOSE
Sandra & Tony Phipkin.
Open on all dates

25 ELM TREES
Carol & Mike Price.
Open on all dates

43 HIGH STREET
James & Laura Solyom.
Open on Sun 16 June

MANOR HOUSE
Mr & Mrs West.
Open on Sun 14 Apr

TOMPSONS FARM
Mr & Mrs T Moynihan.
Open on Sun 16 June

Five gardens open Sun 14 Apr. Baker's Close: 1000s of daffodils, tulips, shrubs and wild area, Barry's Close: spring flowering trees, borders and water garden, Cop Close: daffodils, tulips, borders and bog garden, 25 Elm Trees: cottage style organic garden planted to encourage wildlife, and Manor House: a large garden with views to the Chilterns, two ornamental lakes, a variety of spring bulbs and shrubs. Five gardens open Sun 16 June. Brindles: organic garden with natural swimming pool, beehives, roses and vegetable garden, Cop Close: mixed borders, vegetable garden, wildflower bank and damp garden, The Smithy, 43 High Street: cottage style front garden designed by a local garden designer, Tompsons Farm: a large woodland garden with large lake and herbaceous borders, and 25 Elm Trees: cottage style organic garden planted to encourage wildlife and all round colour. Partial wheelchair access only at Barry's Close and Manor House in April, Tompson's Farm and Manor Farm Bungalow in June.

&. 🐕 ❀ ☕))

23 MAGNOLIA HOUSE
Grange Drive, Wooburn Green, Wooburn, HP10 0QD. Elaine & Alan Ford, 01628 525818, lanfordesigns@gmail.com, www.sites.google.com/site/lanforddesigns. *On A4094 2m SW of A40 between Bourne End & Wooburn. From Wooburn Church, direction Maidenhead, Grange Dr is on L before r'about. From Bourne End, L at 2 mini r'abouts, then 1st R.* **Visits by arrangement 24 Feb to 14 July for groups of up to 25. Larger groups on request. Visits can be combined with The Shades, next door. Adm £6, chd free. Home-made teas.**
½ acre garden with mature trees inc large magnolia. Cacti, fernery, stream, water wheel, two ponds, greenhouses, aviary, 10,000 snowdrops, hellebores, bluebells and over 60 varieties of hosta. Small Japanese style area. Child friendly. Constantly being changed and updated. Partial wheelchair access.

&. 🐕 ❀ 🚗 🏠 ☕

24 MONTANA
Shire Lane, Cholesbury, HP23 6NA. Diana Garner *3m NW of Chesham. From Wigginton turn R after Champneys, 2nd R onto Shire Ln. From Cholesbury turn on to Cholesbury Rd by cricket club, 1st L is Shire Ln. Montana ½ m down on LHS by footpath sign.* **Wed 20 Mar, Wed 15 May, Wed 17 July (11-2). Adm £4, chd free. Pre-booking essential, please phone 01494 758347 or email montana@cholesbury.net for information & booking. Home-made teas. Visits also by arrangement Mar to July for groups of up to 35.**
A peaceful large woodland garden planted by the owner with rare and unusual flowering trees, shrubs, perennials and loads of bulbs. Shade loving herbaceous plants, kitchen garden and meadow with apiary. Gate leads to old brickyard, now 3 acre mixed deciduous wood: level paths, large fernery planted in a clay pit, acers and an avenue of thousands of daffodils. Lots of seats to enjoy the quiet. An unmanicured garden high in the Chiltern Hills. Surrounding fields have been permanent pasture for more than 100 yrs. Covered open barn for teas in wet weather. The majority of paths in the garden and wood are wheelchair friendly.

&. 🐕 ☕))

25 ◆ NETHER WINCHENDON HOUSE
Nether Winchendon, nr Aylesbury, HP18 0DY. Mr Robert Spencer Bernard, 01844 290101, Contactus@netherwinchendonhouse.com, www.nwhouse.co.uk. *6m SW of Aylesbury, 6m from Thame. Approx 4m from Thame on A418, turn L to Cuddington, turn L at Xrds, downhill turn R & R again to parking by house.* **For NGS: Sat 25, Sun 26 May (2-5.30). Adm £4, chd free. Pre-booking essential, please visit www.ngs.org.uk for information & booking. Home-made teas in village church. For other opening times and information, please phone, email or visit garden website.**
Nether Winchendon House has fine, and rare trees set in an inspiring and stunning landscape with parkland. The south lawn runs down to the River Thame. A Founder NGS Member (1927). Enchanting and romantic Mediaeval and Tudor House, one of the most romantic of the historic houses of England and listed Grade I. Dogs on leads welcome. Picturesque small village with an interesting church.

&. 🐕 🚗 🏠 ☕

26 OLD KEEPERS
Village Lane, Hedgerley, SL2 3UY. Rob Cooper. *Parking in village hall on Kiln Ln, postcode SL2 3UU.* **Sun 14 July (1-4.30). Adm £5, chd free. Cream teas.**
Described by visitors as 'a real gardener's garden', we are a fairly new 1½ acre garden set around a Grade II listed former brickmaker's cottage (not open), with borders packed full of perennials, a meadow and small orchard that's a haven for wildlife, with over 20 different types of butterfly spotted in 2023. We designed the garden ourselves, and we've made the most of the beautiful views across the garden and village, with strategically positioned benches and perching spots to enjoy, perfect with a coffee and cake!

🐕 ☕))

Cornfield Cottage

27 OLD PARK BARN

Dag Lane, Stoke Goldington, MK16 8NY. Emily & James Chua, 07833 118903, emilychua51@yahoo.com. *4m N of Newport Pagnell on B526. Park on High St. A short walk up Dag Ln. Accessible parking for 4 cars nr garden via Orchard Way. Please contact us for coach parking details.* **Sat 22, Sun 23 June (1.30-5). Adm £5, chd free. Home-made teas. Visits also by arrangement 8 June to 8 July for groups of 10 to 40. Refreshments and a short introduction to the garden on request.**

A garden of almost 3 acres made from a rough field over 25 yrs ago. A series of terraces cut into the sloping site create the formal garden with long and cross vistas, lawns and deep borders. The aim is to provide interest throughout the yr with naturalistic planting and views borrowed from the surrounding countryside. Beyond this is a wildlife pond, stream, meadow and woodland gardens. Partial wheelchair access.

28 ORCHARD HOUSE

Tower Road, Coleshill, Amersham, HP7 0LB. Mrs Jane Livesey, 07740 100342, jane.livesey88@ btinternet.com. *Approx 2m from Amersham. From Amersham Old Town take the A355 to Beaconsfield. Appox ¾ m along this road at top of hill, take 1st R into Tower Rd. Parking in cricket club grounds.* **Visits by arrangement 15 Apr to 12 May. Adm £15, chd free. Home-made teas inc.**

5 acre garden inc two large ponds with wild flowers around the perimeter and a small wood area with orchids in late spring. Profusion of spring bulbs and a winding boardwalk through a bog garden. Raised beds featuring tulips and picking garden. Wheelchair access with sloping lawn.

29 OVERSTROUD COTTAGE

The Dell, Frith Hill, Great Missenden, HP16 9QE. Mr & Mrs Jonathan Brooke, 01494 862701, susanmbrooke@outlook.com. *½ m E Great Missenden. Turn E off A413 at Great Missenden onto B485 Frith Hill to Chesham Rd. White Gothic cottage set back in lay-by, 100yds uphill on L. Parking on R at church.* **Sun 31 Mar, Sun 21 Apr, Sun 19 May, Sun 9 June (2-5). Adm £4, chd free. Cream teas at parish church. Visits also by arrangement for groups of 15 to 20.**

Artistic chalk garden on two levels. Collection of C17/C18 plants inc auriculas, hellebores, bulbs, pulmonarias, peonies, geraniums, herbs and succulents. Many antique species and rambling roses. Potager and lily pond. Blue and white ribbon border. Cottage was once C17 fever house for Missenden Abbey. Features inc a garden studio with painting exhibition (share of flower painting proceeds to NGS).

30 THE PLOUGH
Chalkshire Road, Terrick,
Aylesbury, HP17 0TJ. John &
Sue Stewart. *2m W of Wendover.
Entrance to garden & car park signed
off B4009 Nash Lee Rd. 200yds E
of Terrick r'about. Access to garden
from field car park.* **Sun 12, Sun
26 May (1-5). Adm £5, chd free.
Home-made teas.**
Formal garden with open views to
the Chiltern countryside. Designed
as a series of outdoor rooms around
a listed former C18 inn (not open),
inc border, parterre, vegetable and
fruit garden and a recently planted
organic orchard. Delicious home-
made teas in our barn and adjacent
entrance courtyard. Jams and apple
juice made with fruits from the garden
for sale. Cash only please.

31 RED KITES
46 Haw Lane, Bledlow
Ridge, HP14 4JJ. Mag &
Les Terry, 01494 481474,
lesterry747@gmail.com. *4m S
of Princes Risborough. Off A4010
halfway between Princes Risborough
& West Wycombe. At Hearing Dogs
sign in Saunderton turn into Haw Ln,
then ¾m on L up the hill.* **Tue 14
May, Tue 9 July (2-5). Adm £5, chd
free. Home-made teas. Visits also
by arrangement 1 May to 13 Sept
for groups of 20+. Smaller groups
wishing to visit encouraged to join
another group.**
This Chiltern hillside garden of 1½
acres is planted for year-round
interest and has superb views.
Lovingly and beautifully maintained,
there are several different areas
to relax in, each with their own
character. Wildflower orchard, mixed
borders, pond, vegetables, woodland
area and a lovely hidden garden.
Many climbers used in the garden
which changes significantly through
the seasons.

32 ROBIN HILL
Water End, Stokenchurch,
High Wycombe, HP14 3XQ.
Caroline Renshaw & Stuart
Yates, 07957 394134, info@
cazrenshawdesigns.co.uk. *2m
from M40 J5 Stokenchurch. Turn off
A40 just S of Stokenchurch towards
Radnage, then 1st R to Waterend
& then follow signs.* **Visits by
arrangement 27 May to 15 Sept
for groups of 15 to 30. Adm £5,
chd free. Home-made teas.**

Relaxed designer's garden at the start
of The Chilterns. Informal cottage
garden/prairie style with a variety of
trees, woodland edge plants, shade
borders, shrubs, perennials and grass
borders blending into pastureland,
now restored to beautiful long grass
meadow. Mature cherry orchard,
chickens, vegetable garden. Planting
constantly evolving to better suit our
changing climate and benefit wildlife.
Wheelchair access over mainly flat
and lawned garden, but no paths.

33 ST MICHAELS CONVENT
Vicarage Way, Gerrards
Cross, SL9 8AT. Sisters of the
Church, stmichaelsconvent.
sistersofthechurch.org. *15 min walk
from Gerrards Cross Stn. 10 mins
from East Common buses. Parking
in nearby street, limited parking at
St Michael's.* **Sat 15 June (2-4.30).
Adm by donation. Cream teas.**
St Michael's Convent is home to the
Sisters of the Church and the Society
of the Precious Blood. The garden
is a place for quiet, reflection and to
gaze upon beauty, and inc a walled
garden with vegetables, labyrinth and
pond, a shady woodland dell and a
chapel. Enjoy the colourful borders,
beds and mature majestic trees.
Come and see and spend time being!

34 THE SHADES
High Wycombe, HP10 0QD.
Pauline & Maurice Kirkpatrick,
01628 522540. *On A4094 2m SW
of A40 between Bourne End &
Wooburn. From Wooburn Church,
direction Maidenhead, Grange Dr is
on L before r'about. From Bourne
End, L at 2 mini r'abouts, then 1st
R.* **Visits by arrangement 24 Feb
to 14 July for groups of up to 25.
Combined visit with Magnolia
House.**
The Shades drive is approached
through mature trees, areas of
shade loving plants, beds of shrubs,
60 various roses and herbaceous
plants. The rear garden with natural
well surrounded by plants, shrubs
and acers. A green slate water
feature and scree garden with alpine
plants completes the garden. Light
refreshments at Magnolia House.
Partial wheelchair access.

35 SPRINGFIELD FARM
66 Chalkshire Road, Butlers Cross,
Aylesbury, HP17 0TR. Allan &
Annabel Westray. *In Chalkshire Rd,
there will be a sign opp the lane in
to the property, beside Chalkshire
Cottages. What3Words app -
attention.encroach.sporting. Parking
in mowed paddock.* **Sun 25 Aug (2-
5). Adm £5, chd free. Home-made
teas (cash only).**
A bridge with pond leads you to this
2½ acre garden divided into rooms
by beech hedging. Rose garden
with mainly David Austin roses,
herbaceous borders, shrub borders,
orchard and vegetable garden.
Wheelchair access over level site with
no steps.

36 ♦ STOKE POGES
MEMORIAL GARDENS
Church Lane, Stoke
Poges, Slough, SL2 4NZ.
Buckinghamshire Council,
01753 523744, memorial.
gardens@buckinghamshire.gov.
uk, www.buckinghamshire.gov.uk.
*1m N of Slough, 4m S of Gerrards
Cross. Follow signs to Stoke Poges
& from there to the Memorial
Gardens. Car park opp main
entrance, disabled visitor parking
in the gardens. Weekend disabled
access through churchyard.* **For
NGS: Sun 12 May (1-4.30). Adm
£6, chd free. Home-made teas.
For other opening times and
information, please phone, email or
visit garden website.**
Unique 22 acre Grade I registered
garden constructed 1934-9 with a
contemporary garden extension.
Rock and water gardens, sunken
colonnade, rose garden, 500 individual
gated gardens, beautiful mature trees
and newly landscaped areas. Guided
tours every hour. Guide dogs only.

37 1 TALBOT AVENUE
Downley, High Wycombe,
HP13 5HZ. Mr Alan
Mayes, 01494 451044,
alan.mayes2@btopenworld.com.
*From Downley T-lights off West
Wycombe Rd, take Plomer Hill turn
off, then 2nd L into Westover Rd,
then 2nd L into Talbot Ave.* **Visits by
arrangement 1 May to 13 Sept for
groups of up to 20. Adm £4, chd
free. Tea.**
A Japanese garden, shielded from the
upper garden level by Shoji screens.

A winding path leads you over a traditional Japanese bridge by a pond and waterfall, inviting you through a moon gate to reveal a purpose built tea house, all surrounded by traditional Japanese planting inc maples, cherry blossom trees, azaleas and rhododendrons. Ornamental grasses and bamboo complement the hard landscaping with feature cloud tree and checkerboard garden path.

38 TURN END

Townside, Haddenham, Aylesbury, HP17 8BG. Margaret & Peter Aldington, turnendgarden@gmail.com, www.turnend.org.uk. *3m NE of Thame, 5m SW of Aylesbury. Exit A418 to Haddenham. Turn at Rising Sun pub into Townside. See Turn End's website for parking info for this event. Street parking very limited. Please park with consideration for residents.* **Mon 6 May (2-5). Adm £6, chd free. Pre-booking essential, please visit www.ngs. org.uk for information & booking. Home-made teas (cash only).** Grade II registered. Series of garden rooms, each with a different planting style enveloping architect's own Grade II* listed house (not open). Dry garden, formal box garden, sunken gardens, mixed borders, mixed borders along curving lawn, all framed by ancient walls and mature trees. Bulbs, irises, wisteria, roses, ferns and climbers. Courtyards with pools, pergolas, secluded seating and Victorian coach house. Open artist's studio.

39 TYTHROP PARK

Kingsey, HP17 8LT. Nick & Chrissie Wheeler. *2m E of Thame, 4m NW of Princes Risborough. Via A4129, at T-junction in Kingsey turn towards Haddenham, take L turn on bend. Parking in field on L.* **Sun 2 June (2-5.30). Adm £8, chd free. Home-made teas.**
10 acres of garden surrounds a C17 Grade I listed manor house (not open). This large and varied garden blends traditional and contemporary styles, featuring pool borders rich in grasses with a green and white theme, walled kitchen and cutting garden with large greenhouse at its heart, box parterre, deep mixed borders, water feature, rose garden, wildflower meadow and many old trees and shrubs.

SPECIAL EVENT

40 THE WALLED GARDEN, WORMSLEY

Wormsley, Stokenchurch, High Wycombe, HP14 3YE. Wormsley Estate. *Leave M40 at J5. Turn towards Ibstone. Entrance to estate is ¼ m on R. NB: 20mph speed limit on estate. Please do not drive on grass verges.* **Wed 19 June (10-3). Adm £8, chd free. Pre-booking essential, please visit www.ngs. org.uk for information & booking. Home-made teas.**
The Walled Garden at Wormsley Estate is a 2 acre garden providing flowers, vegetables and tranquil contemplative space for the family. For many yrs the garden was neglected until Sir Paul Getty purchased the estate in the mid 1980s. In 1991 the garden was redesigned and has changed over the yrs, but remains true to the original brief. Wheelchair access to grounds, but no WC facilities.

41 THE WHITE HOUSE

Village Road, Denham Village, UB9 5BE. Mr & Mrs P G Courtenay-Luck. *3m NW of Uxbridge, 7m E of Beaconsfield. Signed from A40 or A412. Parking in Village Rd. The White House is in centre of village, opp St Mary's Church. Chiltern Line Train Stn, Denham.* **Sun 2 June (2-5). Adm £7, chd free. Home-made teas.**
Well established 6 acre formal garden in picturesque setting. Mature trees and hedges with River Misbourne meandering through lawns. Shrubberies, flower beds, rockery, rose garden and orchard. Large walled garden. Herb garden, vegetable plot and Victorian greenhouses. Wheelchair access with gravel entrance and paved path into gardens.

42 WIND IN THE WILLOWS

Moorhouse Farm Lane, Off Lower Road, Higher Denham, UB9 5EN. Ron James, 07740 177038, r.james@company-doc.co.uk. *6m E of Beaconsfield. Turn off A412, approx ½ m N of junction with A40 into Old Rectory Ln. After 1m enter Higher Denham straight ahead. Take lane next to the community centre & Wind in the Willows is the 1st house on L.* **Sun 10 Mar (2-5). Adm £5, chd free. Tea in the community hall. Opening with Higher Denham Gardens on Sun 26 May. Visits also by arrangement Mar to Sept for groups of 10+. Donation to Higher Denham Community CIO (Garden Upkeep Fund).**
3 acre wildlife friendly, year-round garden, comprising informal woodland and wild gardens, separated by streams lined by iris, primulas and astilbe. Over 350 shrubs and trees, many variegated or uncommon, marginal and bog plantings inc 80 hostas and a bed of stripy roses. Stunning was the word most often used by visitors. 'Best private garden I have visited in 20 yrs of NGS visits' said another. Although unlikely to be seen on busy open days, 65 species of bird and 13 species of butterfly have been seen in and over the garden, which is also home to the now endangered water vole (Water Rat in the book Wind in the Willows), frogs and toads. Wheelchair access over gravel paths and spongy lawns.

The National Garden Scheme's final instalment to support the building of the Y Bwthyn NGS Macmillan Specialist Palliative Care Unit in Wales, enabled 270 inpatients to be supported this year

HAMPSHIRE

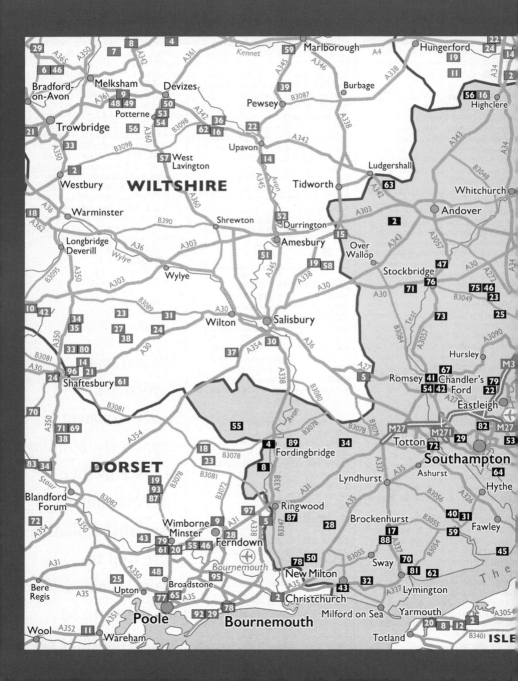

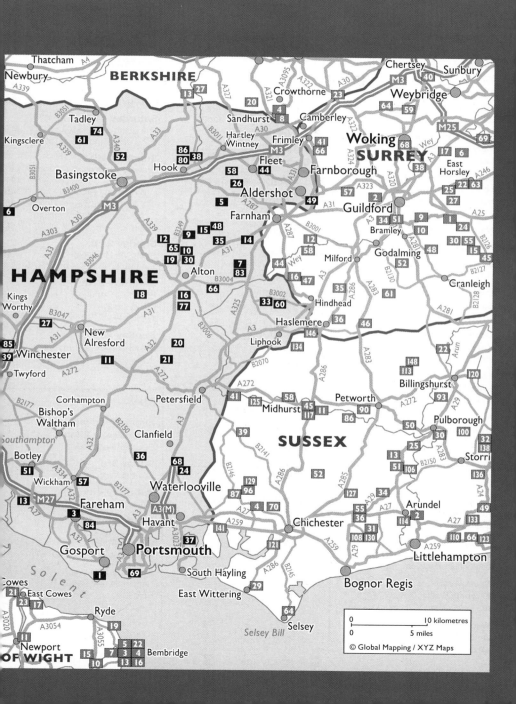

VOLUNTEERS

County Organiser
Mark Porter 07814 958810
markstephenporter@gmail.com

County Treasurer
Fred Fratter 01962 776243
fred@fratter.co.uk

Publicity
Pat Beagley 01256 764772
pat.beagley@ngs.org.uk

Social Media - Facebook
Mary Hayter 07512 639772
mary.hayter@ngs.org.uk

Social Media - Twitter
Louise Moreton 07943 837993
louise.moreton@ngs.org.uk

Booklet Co-ordinator
Mark Porter (as above)

Assistant County Organisers

Victoria Murray 07877 757858
victoria.murray@ngs.org.uk

Central
Sue Cox 01962 732043
suealex13@gmail.com

Central West
Kate Cann 01794 389105
kategcann@gmail.com

East
Linda Smith 01329 833253
linda.ngs@btinternet.com

North
Cynthia Oldale 01420 520438
c.k.oldale@btinternet.com

North East
Lizzie Powell 07799 031044
lizziepowellbroadhatch@gmail.com

North West
Adam Vetere 01635 268267
adam.vetere@ngs.org.uk

South
Barbara Sykes 02380 254521
barandhugh@aol.com

South West
Elizabeth Walker 01590 677415
elizabethwalker13@gmail.com

West
Jane Wingate-Saul 01725 519414
jane.wingatesaul@ngs.org.uk

OPENING DATES

All entries subject to change.
For latest information check
www.ngs.org.uk

Extended openings are shown at the beginning of the month.

Map locator numbers are shown to the right of each garden name.

February

Snowdrop Openings

Sunday 4th
◆ Chawton House   16

Saturday 10th
NEW Woodend Gardens   87

Sunday 11th
Little Court   46
NEW Woodend Gardens   87

Monday 12th
Little Court   46

Wednesday 14th
The Down House   27

Sunday 18th
Little Court   46

Monday 19th
Little Court   46

Wednesday 21st
The Down House   27

Sunday 25th
Bramdean House   11

March

**Every Wednesday from
Wednesday 20th**
Beechenwood Farm   5

Sunday 10th
Bere Mill   6

Sunday 31st
Little Court   46

April

Every Wednesday
Beechenwood Farm   5

Monday 1st
Little Court   46

Sunday 7th
Pylewell Park   62

Thursday 11th
Crawley Gardens   23

Saturday 13th
The Island   41
NEW Lord Wandsworth College   48

Sunday 14th
Crawley Gardens   23
The Island   41
Lepe House Gardens   45
NEW Lord Wandsworth College   48
Old Thatch & The Millennium
    Barn   58

Sunday 21st
Southsea Gardens   69
Terstan   76

Saturday 27th
Brick Kiln Cottage   12
Manor Lodge   51
Twin Oaks   79

Sunday 28th
Manor Lodge   51
◆ Spinners Garden   70
Twin Oaks   79

May

**Every Wednesday to
Wednesday 22nd**
Beechenwood Farm   5

Friday 3rd
Bluebell Wood   10

Saturday 4th
Bluebell Wood   10

Sunday 5th
The Cottage   22
Pylewell Park   62
Walhampton   81

Monday 6th
Beechenwood Farm   5
Bere Mill   6
The Cottage   22

Saturday 11th
◆ Alverstoke Crescent Garden 1

Sunday 12th
The Cottage 22
The House in the Wood 40
[NEW] 4 Stannington Crescent 72
Tylney Hall Hotel 80

Monday 13th
The Cottage 22

Saturday 18th
146 Bridge Road 13
21 Chestnut Road 17

Sunday 19th
146 Bridge Road 13
21 Chestnut Road 17
The Dower House 26
Little Court 46
[NEW] 4 Stannington Crescent 72

Monday 20th
Little Court 46

Saturday 25th
Spitfire House 71

Sunday 26th
Amport Gardens 2
Endhouse 29
King John's Garden 42
The Nelson Cottage 54
Shalden Park House 65
Southsea Gardens 69
Spitfire House 71
Twin Oaks 79

Monday 27th
Amport Gardens 2
Beechenwood Farm 5
Bere Mill 6
Endhouse 29
King John's Garden 42
The Nelson Cottage 54
Twin Oaks 79

Tuesday 28th
Endhouse 29

Thursday 30th
[NEW] Old Channel Hill
Farmhouse 55

June

Every day from Thursday 6th to Tuesday 11th
Appleyards 4

Saturday 1st
Ferns Lodge 32
Froyle Gardens 35
Ladybower 44
Winchester College 85

Sunday 2nd
Ferns Lodge 32
Froyle Gardens 35
◆ The Hospital of St Cross 39
Ladybower 44
Winchester College 85

Saturday 8th
21 Chestnut Road 17
Frey Elma 33
Perrymead 60

Sunday 9th
21 Chestnut Road 17
Frey Elma 33
Old Thatch & The Millennium
Barn 58
Perrymead 60
Tylney Hall Hotel 80

Thursday 13th
Stockbridge Gardens 73

Saturday 15th
Church House 18
[NEW] Kingfishers Care Home 43
[NEW] Old Channel Hill
Farmhouse 55
1 Povey's Cottage 61

Sunday 16th
Bramdean House 11
Church House 18
Fritham Lodge 34
[NEW] Kingfishers Care Home 43
1 Povey's Cottage 61
Stockbridge Gardens 73

Thursday 20th
Crawley Gardens 23

Friday 21st
Redenham Park House 63

Saturday 22nd
Twin Oaks 79
Yew Hurst 89

Sunday 23rd
Broadhatch House 14
Crawley Gardens 23
Terstan 76
Twin Oaks 79
Wicor Primary School
Community Garden 84

Monday 24th
Broadhatch House 14

Tuesday 25th
Broadhatch House 14

Thursday 27th
Mill House 52

Saturday 29th
26 Lower Newport Road 49

Sunday 30th
Longstock Park Water Garden 47
26 Lower Newport Road 49
Mill House 52

July

Every Wednesday to Wednesday 17th
[NEW] 8 Tucks Close 78

Thursday 4th
Tanglefoot 75

Saturday 6th
[NEW] Mountbatten Hospice 53
15 Rothschild Close 64

Sunday 7th
[NEW] Mountbatten Hospice 53
15 Rothschild Close 64
Tanglefoot 75

Friday 12th
Fairweather's Nursery 31

Saturday 13th
Angels Folly 3
Fairweather's Nursery 31
Southsea Gardens 69

Sunday 14th
Angels Folly 3
1 Wogsbarne Cottages 86

Monday 15th
1 Wogsbarne Cottages 86

Thursday 18th
Tanglefoot 75

Saturday 20th
Hook Cross Allotments 38

Sunday 21st
Bleak Hill Nursery & Garden 8
Hook Cross Allotments 38
Tanglefoot 75
Terstan 76

Monday 22nd
Bleak Hill Nursery & Garden 8

Saturday 27th
Angels Folly 3

Sunday 28th
Angels Folly 3

August

Thursday 1st
The Down House 27

Sunday 4th
The Homestead 37
NEW The Old Rectory, Wickham 57
South View House 68

Saturday 10th
Angels Folly 3
Church House 18
Twin Oaks 79

Sunday 11th
Bleak Hill Nursery & Garden 8
Church House 18
Twin Oaks 79

Monday 12th
Bleak Hill Nursery & Garden 8

Saturday 17th
Wheatley House 83

Sunday 18th
Wheatley House 83

Sunday 25th
The Thatched Cottage 77

Monday 26th
Bere Mill 6
Bleak Hill Nursery & Garden 8
The Thatched Cottage 77

Saturday 31st
NEW Woodend Gardens 87
Woodpeckers Care Home 88

September

Sunday 1st
NEW Woodend Gardens 87
Woodpeckers Care Home 88

Saturday 7th
Bumpers 15
15 Rothschild Close 64

Sunday 8th
Bramdean House 11
Bumpers 15
15 Rothschild Close 64
Terstan 76

Sunday 15th
Tadley Place 74

Friday 20th
Redenham Park House 63

February 2025

Sunday 16th
Little Court 46

Monday 17th
Little Court 46

Sunday 23rd
Little Court 46

Monday 24th
Little Court 46

By Arrangement

Arrange a personalised garden visit with your club, or group of friends, on a date to suit you. See individual garden entries for full details.

Angels Folly 3
Appleyards 4
Beechenwood Farm 5
Bere Mill 6
Binsted Place 7
Blounce House 9
Brick Kiln Cottage 12
Broadhatch House 14
Bumpers 15
Clover Farm 19
Colemore House Gardens 20
Coles 21
The Cottage 22
Crookley Pool 24
The Deane House 25
The Down House 27
Durmast House 28
Endhouse 29
Fairbank 30
Ferns Lodge 32
Hambledon House 36
The Homestead 37
The Island 41
Lepe House Gardens 45
Little Court 46
Manor Lodge 51
The Old Rectory 56
1 Povey's Cottage 61
15 Rothschild Close 64
Silver Birches 66
Spitfire House 71
Tanglefoot 75
Terstan 76
The Thatched Cottage 77
Twin Oaks 79
Westward 82
Wheatley House 83

Hook Cross Allotments

Fairbank

© Leigh Clapp

THE GARDENS

1 ◆ ALVERSTOKE CRESCENT GARDEN
Crescent Road, Gosport,
PO12 2DH. Gosport
Borough Council, www.
alverstokecrescentgarden.co.uk.
*1m S of Gosport. From A32 &
Gosport follow signs for Stokes Bay.
Continue alongside bay to small
r'about, turn L into Anglesey Rd.
Crescent Garden signed 50yds on
R.* **For NGS: Sat 11 May (10-4).
Adm by donation. Home-made
teas. For other opening times and
information, please visit garden
website.**
Restored Regency ornamental
garden designed to enhance fine
crescent (Thomas Ellis Owen 1828).
Trees, walks and flowers lovingly
maintained by community and council
partnership. A garden of considerable
local historic interest highlighted by
impressive restoration and creative
planting. Adjacent to St Mark's
churchyard, worth seeing together.
Heritage, history and horticulture,
a fascinating package. Plant sale.
Green Flag Award.

  ♿ 🐕 ✿ ☕ 🏕

GROUP OPENING

2 AMPORT GARDENS
Amport, SP11 8AY. *3m SW of
Andover. Turn off the A303 signed
East Cholderton from the E, or
Thruxton village from the W. Follow
signs to Amport. Car parking in
field next to Amport village green.*
**Sun 26, Mon 27 May (2-5.30).
Combined adm £6, chd free.
Home-made teas.**

BRIDGE COTTAGE
John & Jenny Van de Pette.
CORNER COTTAGE
15 Sarson. Ms Jill McAvoy.

Amport is a pretty village with the Pill
Hill Brook running through it. Visitors
have two gardens to enjoy. Bridge
Cottage, a 2 acre haven for wildlife
with the banks of the trout stream
and lake planted informally with drifts
of colour, a large vegetable garden,
fruit cage, small mixed orchard
and arboretum with specimen
trees. Corner Cottage is a delightful
cottage garden with a serpentine
gravel path winding between gravel
borders, clipped box hedging and
old-fashioned roses. Very popular
large plant sale at Bridge Cottage.
Preserves and chutneys for sale,
along with an artist selling cards (10%
to NGS). Choc ices for sale at Bridge
Cottage (100% to NGS). Amport
has a lovely village green, so come
early and bring a picnic, or stay for
the cream tea in a marquee. Partial
wheelchair access to Corner Cottage.

🔳 ANGELS FOLLY

15 Bruce Close, Fareham, PO16 7QJ. Teresa & John Greenwood, 07545 242654, tgreenwood65@outlook.com, www.facebook.com/angelsfolly. *¾m NNE of Fareham Town Centre. M27 W leave J10 under M27 bridge in the RH-lane, do a U-turn. At r'about, take 3rd exit, across T-lights. 1st R Miller Dr. 2nd R Somervell Dr. 1st R Bruce Cl.* **Sat 13, Sun 14, Sat 27, Sun 28 July (10.30-5). Adm £4, chd free. Home-made teas. Evening opening Sat 10 Aug (4.30-9.30). Adm £6, chd free. Wine. Visits also by arrangement 12 July to 1 Sept for groups of 5 to 30.**
The garden has a number of secluded areas each with their own character inc a Mediterranean garden, decking with raised beds and a seating area with a living wall. An arched folly, bench and fish pond leads to a raised planting bed and fireplace adjacent to a summerhouse. There is a wide range of colourful plants, hanging baskets and a lower secluded decked area with a planted gazebo and statue.

🐄 ✳ ☕ »)

🔳 APPLEYARDS

Bowerwood Road, Fordingbridge, SP6 3BP. Bob & Jean Carr *½m from Fordingbridge on B3078. After church & houses, 400yds on L as road climbs after bridge. Parking for 8 cars only. No parking on narrow road.* **Daily Thur 6 June to Tue 11 June (12-6). Adm £5, chd free. Pre-booking essential, please phone 01425 657631 or email bob.carr.rtd@gmail. com for information & booking. Home-made teas. Visits also by arrangement 13 Apr to 4 Aug for groups of 10 to 50.**
2 acre south facing garden overlooking pasture, restored over last 6 yrs. Sloping lawns and paths though wooded sections with massed daffodils and bluebells in spring. Newly planted rhododendrons in wooded area. Herbaceous beds, two mature rose beds, shrubberies, two wildlife ponds, orchard, sloping rockery beds, soft fruit cages and greenhouse.

🔳 BEECHENWOOD FARM

Hillside, Odiham, Hook, RG29 1JA. Mr & Mrs M Heber-Percy, 07944 162419, beechenwood@gmail.com. *5m SE of Hook. Turn S into King St from Odiham High St. Turn L after cricket ground for Hillside. Take 2nd R after 1½m, modern house ½m.* **Every Wed 20 Mar to 22 May (2-5). Mon 6, Mon 27 May (2-5). Adm £5, chd free. Home-made teas. Visits also by arrangement 13 Mar to 26 May.**
Opening for the 40th yr, this 2 acre garden with many parts. Lawn meandering through woodland with drifts of spring bulbs. Rose pergola with steps, pots with spring bulbs and later aeoniums. Fritillary and cowslip meadow. Walled herb garden with pool and exuberant planting. Orchard inc white garden and hot border. Greenhouse and vegetable garden. Rock garden extending to grasses, ferns and bamboos. Shady walk to belvedere. 8 acre copse of native species with grassed rides. Assistance available with gravel drive and avoidable shallow steps.

🐄 🐄 ✳ ☕

🔳 BERE MILL

London Road, Whitchurch, RG28 7NH. Rupert & Elizabeth Nabarro OBE, 07703 161074, rupertnab@gmail.com, www. beremillfarm.co.uk/garden. *9m E of Andover, 12m N of Winchester. In centre of Whitchurch, take London Rd at r'about. Uphill 1m, turn R into Bere Mill Ln & follow signs for parking in field on L. Drop off at house for the elderly & disabled only.* **Sun 10 Mar, Mon 6, Mon 27 May, Mon 26 Aug (12-5). Adm £8, chd free. Home-made teas. Visits also by arrangement 4 Feb to 30 Sept. Fixed charge of £450 for the attending group.**
Garden built around early C18 mill on idyllic isolated stretch of the River Test, east of Whitchurch. Gardens have been built incrementally over 30 yrs with extensive bulb planting; herbaceous and Mediterranean borders with magnolia, irises, and tree peonies; summer and autumn borders; a traditional orchard and two small arboretums, one specialising in Japanese shrubs and trees. The garden aims to complement the natural beauty of the site and to incorporate elements of oriental garden design and practice. Unfenced and unguarded rivers and streams. Wheelchair access unless very wet.

🐄 🐄 ✳ 🚗 ☕ 🗲 »)

🔳 BINSTED PLACE

River Hill, Binsted Road, Binsted, Alton, GU34 4PQ. Max & Catherine Hadfield, 01420 23146, catherine. hadfield1@icloud.com. *At eastern edge of Binsted Village on Binsted Rd. 1m from Jolly Farmer Pub in Blacknest. 1½m from A325. Parking limited, but safe on-road parking outside the property.* **Visits by arrangement 3 June to 13 Sept for groups of up to 30.**
Binsted Place, a C17 farmhouse with attractive local stone outbuildings, is surrounded by a series of garden rooms covering approx 1½ acres, enclosed by yew hedges and old walls. It is very traditional in style and inc many roses, pergolas, herbaceous borders, lily pond and a productive vegetable garden and orchards. Step free disabled access to most of the garden.

🐄 🐄 ✳ ☕ »)

🔳 BLEAK HILL NURSERY & GARDEN

Braemoor, Bleak Hill, Harbridge, Ringwood, BH24 3PX. Tracy & John Netherway, www.bleakhillplants.co.uk. *2½m S of Fordingbridge. Turn off A338 to Ibsley. Go through Harbridge village to T-junction at top of hill, turn R for ¼m.* **Sun 21 July (2-5); Mon 22 July (11-3); Sun 11 Aug (2-5); Mon 12 Aug (11-3); Mon 26 Aug (2-5). Adm £4, chd free. Home-made teas. No refreshments on 22 July & 12 Aug, welcome to bring a picnic.**
Enjoy this ¾ acre garden, pass through the moon gate to reveal the billowing borders contrasting against a seaside scene with painted beach huts and a boat on the gravel. Herbaceous borders complemented by a spectacular tropical border fill the garden with colour wrapping around a pond and small stream. Greenhouses with cacti and sarracenias. Vegetable patch and small wildflower meadow. Small adjacent nursery.

✳ ☕ 🗲

🔳 BLOUNCE HOUSE

Blounce, South Warnborough, Hook, RG29 1RX. Tom & Gay Bartlam, 07788 911184, tomb@thbartlam.co.uk. *In hamlet of Blounce, 1m S of South Warnborough on B3349 from Odiham to Alton.* **Visits by arrangement 15 June to 8 Sept. Home-made teas.**
A 2 acre garden surrounding a classic

Queen Anne house (not open). Mixed planting to give interest from spring to late autumn. Herbaceous borders with a variety of colour themes. In late summer an emphasis on dahlias, salvias and grasses.

ⅠO BLUEBELL WOOD
Stancombe Lane, Bavins, New Odiham Road, Alton, GU34 5SX. Mrs Jennifer Ospici, www.bavins.co.uk. *On the corner of Stancombe Ln & the B3349 2½ m N of Alton.* **Fri 3, Sat 4 May (11-4). Adm £10, chd free. Light refreshments.**
Unique 100 acre ancient bluebell woodland. If you are a keen walker you will have much to explore on the long meandering paths and rides dotted with secluded seats. The wood is very challenging for those with mobility problems. Refreshments will be served in an original rustic building and inc soups using natural woodland ingredients.

ⅠⅠ BRAMDEAN HOUSE
Bramdean, Alresford, SO24 0JU. Mr & Mrs E Wakefield, garden@bramdeanhouse.com, www.instagram.com/bramdean_house_garden. *4m S of Alresford; 9m E of Winchester; 9m W of Petersfield. In centre of village on A272. Entrance opp sign to the church. Parking is signed across the road from entrance.* **Sun 25 Feb (1-3); Sun 16 June (1-4); Sun 8 Sept (1-3.30). Adm £6.50, chd free. Home-made teas. Donation to Bramdean Church.**
Beautiful 5 acre garden best known for its mirror image herbaceous borders, its 1 acre walled garden, its carpets of spring bulbs, and a large and unusual collection of plants and shrubs giving year-round interest. Features inc fine snowdrops, a large collection of old fashioned sweet peas, an expansive collection of nerines, a boxwood castle and the nation's tallest sunflower 'Giraffe'. Visits also by arrangement for groups of 5+ (non-NGS). Assistance dogs only.

Ⅰ2 BRICK KILN COTTAGE
The Avenue, Herriard, nr Alton, RG25 2PR. Barbara Jeremiah & Kay Linnell, 01256 381301, barbara@klca.co.uk. *4m NE of Alton, nr Lasham Gliding Club. A339 Basingstoke to Alton, 7m out of Basingstoke turn L along The Avenue, past Lasham Gliding Club on R, then past Back Ln on L & take next track on L, one field later.* **Sat 27 Apr (11-3). Adm £6, chd free. Home-made teas. Visits also by arrangement 16 Apr to 26 May for groups of 10+.**
A garden visit designed especially for grandparents to bring their grandchildren to see this enchanted bluebell woodland garden. The 2 acre garden with a perimeter woodland path inc treehouse, pebble garden, billabong, stumpery, ferny hollow, bug palace, waterpool, shepherd's hut and a traditional cottage garden filled with herbs. The garden is maintained using eco-friendly methods as a haven for wild animals, butterflies, birds, bees and English bluebells. Children's reading area. Wildlife friendly garden in a former brick works. A haven in the trees. Gallery of textiles.

Beechenwood Farm

© Leigh Clapp

■3 146 BRIDGE ROAD

Sarisbury Green, Southampton, SO31 7EJ. Audrey & Jonathan Crutchfield. *4m W of Fareham. On A27 between Chapel Rd & Glen Rd. Free car parking by kind permission of the United Reformed Church on Chapel Rd.* **Sat 18 May (12.30-5); Sun 19 May (12-4). Adm £4, chd free. Home-made teas.**
A long, tranquil cottage garden that rambles away from the bustling A27, offering secret rooms, richly filled shrub borders, patios, lawns, nooks, arbours, mirrors, stained glass, statues and a bubbling pond. Inviting resting spots are hidden, allowing visitors a place to pause, relax and enjoy our partnership with nature.
&. ❋ ☕))

■4 BROADHATCH HOUSE

Bentley, Farnham, GU10 5JJ. Bruce & Lizzie Powell, 07799 031044, lizziepowellbroadhatch@gmail. com. *4m NE of Alton. Turn off A31 (Bentley bypass) through village, then L up School Ln. R to Perrylands, after 400yds drive on R.* **Sun 23, Mon 24, Tue 25 June (2-5). Adm £5, chd free. Home-made teas. Visits also by arrangement 15 May to 30 June.**
3½ acre garden set in lovely Hampshire countryside with views to Alice Holt. Divided into different areas by yew hedges and walled garden. Focussing on as long a season as possible we have heavy clay. Two reflective pools help break up lawn areas; lots of flower borders and beds; mature trees. Working greenhouses and vegetable garden. Wheelchair access with gravel paths and steps in some areas.
&. ❋ ☕ ☕))

■5 BUMPERS

Sutton Common, Long Sutton, Hook, RG29 1SJ. Stella Wildsmith, 07766 754993, sfw@staxgroup.com. *From Long Sutton, turn up Copse Ln, opp duck pond. Follow lane for 1½m to top of steep hill, house on L. SatNav will take you to the back entrance of Lord Wandsworth College, keep going!* **Sat 7, Sun 8 Sept (2-5). Adm £5, chd free. Home-made teas. Visits also by arrangement 2 May to 2 Oct for groups of up to 30.**
Large country garden with beautiful views spread over 2 acres with mixed herbaceous and shrub borders and laid out in a series of individual areas. Some interesting sculptures and water features with informal paths through the grounds and a number of places to sit and enjoy the views. Visitors with wheelchairs, please park at front of house.
&. ❋ ☕))

■6 ♦ CHAWTON HOUSE

Chawton, Alton, GU34 1SJ. Chawton House, 01420 541010, info@chawtonhouse.org, www.chawtonhouse.org. *2m S of Alton. Take the Gosport Rd opp Jane Austen's House museum towards St Nicholas Church. Property is at the end of this road on the L. Parking is signed at the end of the road & in Chawton village.* **For NGS: Sun 4 Feb (10-3.30). Adm £6, chd £4. Light refreshments. For other opening times and information, please phone, email or visit garden website.**
Snowdrops and spring flowering bulbs are scattered through this 15 acre listed English landscape garden. Sweeping lawns, wilderness, terraces, fernery and shrubbery walk surround the Elizabethan manor house. The walled garden designed by Edward Knight surrounds a rose garden, borders, orchard, vegetable garden and Elizabeth Blackwell herb garden based on her book 'A Curious Herbal' of 1737-39. Hot and cold drinks, wine, light lunches, cream teas, home-made cakes and local ice creams are available in our tea shed on the main drive and in The Old Kitchen Tearoom at the house.
🐑 🚗 ☕))

■7 21 CHESTNUT ROAD

Brockenhurst, SO42 7RF. Iain & Mary Hayter, www.21-chestnut-rdgardens.co.uk. *New Forest. Please use village car park. Limited parking for those less mobile in road. Leave M27 J2, follow Heavy Lorry Route. Mainline station less than 10 min walk.* **Sat 18, Sun 19 May, Sat 8, Sun 9 June (11.30-5). Adm £5, chd free. Home-made teas.**
A ⅓ acre in a central village location. Behind the hedge awaits the owner designed garden full of colour, scent and full of inspirational ideas for gardening in sun, shade, wet or dry areas. Experience nature inspired formal, naturalistic, and themed areas with statues, fairies, ponds, and a productive fruit and vegetable area. Paintings, plants and bug boxes usually available for sale (% to NGS).
🐑 ❋ ☕))

■8 CHURCH HOUSE

Trinity Hill, Medstead, Alton, GU34 5LT. Mr Paul & Mrs Alice Beresford. *5m WSW of Alton. From A31 Four Marks follow signs to Medstead for 1½m to village centre, turn R into Church Ln/Trinity Hill. From N on A339, R at Bentworth Xrds & continue via Bentworth to Medstead.* **Sat 15 June (1.30-6); Sun 16 June (2-6); Sat 10 Aug (1.30-6); Sun 11 Aug (2-6). Adm £5, chd £1. Home-made teas.**
A colourful 1 acre garden, set within a wide variety of mature trees and shrubs. Long, sweeping, colour themed mixed borders give lots of ideas for planting in sun and shade. Contrasting features and textures throughout the garden are enhanced by interesting sculptures. Espaliered fruit trees, a woodland area, small greenhouse and roses in different settings all contribute to this much loved garden. For further information see Facebook, search Church House Garden Medstead. Wheelchair access via gravel drive to flat lawned garden. No access to some paths and patio.
&. ❋ ☕))

■9 CLOVER FARM

Shalden Lane, Shalden, Alton, GU34 4DU. Tom & Sarah Floyd, 01420 86294. *Approx 3m N of Alton in the village of Shalden. Take A339 out of Alton. After approx 2m turn R up Shalden Ln. At top, turn sharp R next to church sign.* **Visits by arrangement 20 May to 13 Sept for groups of 15 to 50. Adm £10, chd free. Tea & cake inc.**
3 acre garden with far-reaching views. Herbaceous borders and sloping lawns down to reflection pond, wildflower meadow, lime avenue, rose and kitchen garden, and ornamental grass area.
&. 🐑 🚗 ☕

■20 COLEMORE HOUSE GARDENS

Colemore, Alton, GU34 3RX. Mr & Mrs Simon de Zoete, 01420 588202, simondezoete@gmail.com. *4m S of Alton, off A32. Approach from N on A32, turn L in to Shell Ln, ¼m S of East Tisted. Go under bridge, keep L until you see Colemore Church. Park on verge of church.* **Visits by arrangement 15 May to 1 Oct for groups of 10 to 40. Adm £10, chd free.**
4 acres in lovely unspoilt countryside, featuring rooms containing many unusual plants and different aspects

with a spectacular arched rose walk, water rill, mirror pond, herbaceous and shrub borders. Newly designed by David Austin roses, an octagonal garden with 25 different varieties. Explore the interesting arboretum, grass gardens and thatched pavilion. Every yr the owners seek improvement and the introduction of new, interesting and rare plants. We propagate and sell plants, many of which can be found in the garden. Some are unusual and not readily available elsewhere. For private visits, we endeavour to give a conducted tour and try to explain our future plans, rationale and objectives.

21 COLES
Basing Dean, Privett, Alton, GU34 3PH. Mike & Shuna MacKillop-Hall, 07423 541105, mikemackillophall@gmail.com. *6m NW of Petersfield. From Petersfield, come up Bell Hill/Stoner Hill & turn L at top of hill via High Cross. From Winchester on A272 turn L at West Meon Xrds on to A32, after 2m turn R at The Angel.* **Visits by arrangement Apr to Nov for groups of 10 to 40. Talk & walk (2-3 hrs) & refreshments inc. Adm £15, chd free.**
Country Life called it 'a great post-war garden'; historic 25 acre creation being renovated. Dazzling spring rhododendrons and azaleas with bluebells, Japanese acers among ancient oak woodland and arboretum for autumn colour, Koi, wildlife and Japanese ponds, lawns and contemporary beds of grass and perennials around stunning modern house (not open). Easy access around the house. An all terrain wheelchair is needed for the whole garden.

22 THE COTTAGE
16 Lakewood Road, Chandler's Ford, Eastleigh, SO53 1ES. Hugh & Barbara Sykes, 02380 254521, barandhugh@aol.com. *Leave M3 J12, follow signs to Chandler's Ford. At King Rufus on Winchester Rd, turn R into Merdon Ave, then 3rd road on L.* **Sun 5, Mon 6, Sun 12, Mon 13 May (1.30-5.30). Adm £5, chd free. Home-made teas. Visits also by arrangement Apr & May.**
The house was built in 1905, but the ¾ acre garden has been designed, planted and cared for since 1950 by two keen garden

loving families. Azaleas, camellias, trilliums and erythroniums under old oaks and pines. Herbaceous cottage style borders with many unusual plants for year-round interest. Bog garden, ponds, kitchen garden. Bantams, bees and birdsong with over 35 bird species noted. Wildlife areas. NGS sundial for opening for 30 yrs. Childrens' quiz. 'A lovely tranquil garden', Anne Swithinbank. Hampshire Wildlife Trust Wildlife Garden Award. Honey from our garden hives for sale.

GROUP OPENING

23 CRAWLEY GARDENS
Crawley, Winchester, SO21 2PR. F J Fratter, 01962 776243, fred@fratter.co.uk. *5m NW of Winchester. Between B3049 (Winchester - Stockbridge) & A272 (Winchester - Andover). Parking throughout village & in field at Tanglefoot.* **Thur 11, Sun 14 Apr, Thur 20, Sun 23 June (2-5.30). Combined adm £10, chd free. Home-made teas in the village hall.**

BAY TREE HOUSE
Julia & Charles Whiteaway.
Open on all dates

LITTLE COURT
Mrs A R Elkington.
Open on all dates
(See separate entry)

PAIGE COTTAGE
Mr & Mrs T W Parker.
Open on all dates

TANGLEFOOT
Mr & Mrs F J Fratter.
Open on Thur 20, Sun 23 June
(See separate entry)

Crawley is a pretty period village nestling in chalk downland with thatched houses, C14 church and village pond. The spring gardens are Bay Tree House, Little Court and Paige Cottage; all of the gardens are open in the summer; providing varied seasonal interest with traditional and contemporary approaches to landscape and planting. Most of the gardens have beautiful country views and other gardens can be seen from the road. Bay Tree House has bulbs, wildflowers, a Mediterranean garden, pleached limes, a rill and contemporary borders of perennials and grasses. Little Court is a 3 acre

country garden with carpets of spring bulbs, herbaceous borders and a large meadow. Paige Cottage is a 1 acre traditional English garden surrounding a period thatched cottage (not open) with bulbs and wild flowers in spring and old climbing roses in summer. Tanglefoot has colour themed borders, herb wheel, kitchen garden, Victorian boundary wall supporting trained fruit and a large wildflower meadow. Plants from the garden for sale at Little Court and Tanglefoot.

24 CROOKLEY POOL
Blendworth Lane, Horndean, PO8 0AB. Mr & Mrs Simon Privett, 02392 592662, jennyprivett@icloud.com. *5m S of Petersfield, 2m E of Waterlooville, off the A3. From Horndean up Blendworth Ln between bakery & hairdresser. Entrance 200yds before church on L with white railings.* **Visits by arrangement May to Sept for groups of 10+.**
Here the plants choose where to grow. Californian tree poppies elbow valerian aside to crowd round the pool. Verbena 'Bampton' obstructs the way to the door. This is a plantsman's garden with borders full of colour and unusual shrubs and tender perennials, salvias thrive in this warm and sheltered garden. *Pandorea jasminoides, Justicia* and *Ageratum* share the greenhouse with the tomatoes. Hellebores bloom under the trees, a 100 yr old wisteria rampages along pergolas, walls and terraces.

The National Garden Scheme donated £3,403,960 to our nursing and health beneficiaries from money raised at gardens open in 2023

25 THE DEANE HOUSE

Sparsholt, Winchester, SO21 2LR. Mr & Mrs Richard Morse, 07774 863004, chrissiemorse7@gmail.com. *3½m NW of Winchester. Turn off A3049 Stockbridge Rd, onto Woodman Ln, signed Sparsholt. Turn L at 1st cottage on L, cream with green gables, come to top of the drive. Plentiful parking. Do not follow SatNav.* **Visits by arrangement 5 Feb to 14 Sept for groups of 10+. Home-made teas, lunches, wine & canapés.**
A beautiful 4 acre rural garden, overlooking Woodman vineyard, nestled on a gentle south facing slope, landscaped to draw the eye from one gentle terraced lawn to another with borders merging with the surrounding countryside and vines. Featuring a good selection of specimen trees, a walled garden, prairie planting and herbaceous borders. Millennium avenue of tulip trees. Water features and sculptures. Sorry, no dogs. Tour of Woodman vineyard can be arranged. Although the garden is on the side of a hill there is always a path to avoid steps.

26 THE DOWER HOUSE

Church Lane, Dogmersfield, Hook, RG27 8TA. Anne-Marie & Richard Revell. *3½m E of Hook. Turn N off A287. For SatNav please use RG27 8SZ.* **Sun 19 May (2-4.30). Adm £5, chd free. Home-made teas.**
6 acres inc bluebell wood with large and spectacular collection of rhododendrons, azaleas, magnolias and other flowering trees and shrubs; set in parkland with fine views over 20 acre lake.

27 THE DOWN HOUSE

Itchen Abbas, SO21 1AX. Jackie & Mark Porter, 07814 958810, markstephenporter@gmail.com. *5m E of Winchester on B3047. 5th house on R after the Itchen Abbas village sign, if coming on B3047 from Kings Worthy. 500 metres on L after The Plough pub if coming on B3047 from Alresford.* **Wed 14, Wed 21 Feb (1-4.30). Adm £10, chd free. Home-made teas inc. Pre-booking essential, please visit www.ngs.org.uk for information & booking. Thur 1 Aug (2-5). Adm £6, chd free. Home-made teas. Visits also by arrangement 12 Feb to 8 Mar for groups of 10+.**
A 2 acre garden laid out in rooms overlooking the Itchen Valley, adjoining the Pilgrim's Way. In winter come and see garden structure, snowdrops, aconites and crocus, plus borders of dogwoods, willow stems and white birches. In summer, a terrace of agapanthus and succulents, pleached hornbeams, rope-lined fountain garden, formal box-edged potager, a yew lined avenue and walks in adjoining meadows.

&. 💷))

28 DURMAST HOUSE

Bennetts Lane, Burley, BH24 4AT. Mr & Mrs P E G Daubeney, 01425 402132, philip@daubeney.co.uk, www.durmasthouse.co.uk. *5m SE of Ringwood. Off Burley to Lyndhurst Rd, nr White Buck Hotel, C10 road.* **Visits by arrangement 31 Mar to 31 Aug for groups of 10 to 50. Adm £8, chd free. Cream teas.**
Designed by Gertrude Jekyll, Durmast has contrasting hot and cool colour borders, formal rose garden edged with lavender and a long herbaceous border. Many old trees, Victorian rockery and orchard with beautiful spring bulbs. Rare azaleas; Fama, Princeps and Gloria Mundi from Ghent. Features inc rose bowers with rare French roses; Eleanor Berkeley, Psyche and Reine Olga de Wurtemberg. Many old trees inc cedar and Douglas firs. Wheelchair access on stone and gravel paths.

&. 🐎 🔆 🚗 🚌 💷))

29 ENDHOUSE

6 Wimpson Gardens, Southampton, SO16 9ES. Kevin Liles, 02380 777590, k.liles1@virginmedia.com. *West Southampton. Exit M271 at J1 toward Lordshill. At 2nd r'about, turn R into Romsey Rd towards Shirley. After ½m turn R at Xrds into Wimpson Ln, 3rd on R Crabwood Rd (additional parking). Wimpson Gardens 4th on R.* **Sun 26, Mon 27, Tue 28 May (1-4). Adm £4, chd free. Home-made teas. Visits also by arrangement 18 May to 30 June for groups of 10 to 15.**
Award-winning urban oasis of linked garden areas inc small secret garden. Best in spring and summer months, but rich year-round plant interest with tree ferns, palms, acers and wisteria. Deep herbaceous borders planted with hostas, grasses, agapanthus and alstroemerias. Significant exhibition of gallery quality sculpture and ceramics.

🔆 💷))

30 FAIRBANK

Old Odiham Road, Alton, GU34 4BU. Jane & Robin Lees, 01420 86665, j.lees558@btinternet.com. *1½m N of Alton. From S, past Sixth Form College, then 1½m beyond road junction on R. From N, turn L at Golden Pot & then 50yds turn R. Garden 1m on L before road junction.* **Visits by arrangement May to Sept for groups of up to 30. Adm £5, chd free. Home-made teas.**
The planting in this large garden reflects our interest in trees, shrubs, fruit and vegetables. A wide variety of herbaceous plants provide colour and are placed in sweeping mixed borders that carry the eye down the long garden to the orchard and beyond. Near the house (not open), there are rose beds and herbaceous borders, as well as a small formal pond. There is a range of acers, ferns and unusual shrubs and 50 different cultivars of fruit, together with a large vegetable garden. Wheelchair access with uneven ground in some areas.

&. 🚗 💷

31 FAIRWEATHER'S NURSERY

Hilltop, Beaulieu, SO42 7YR. Patrick Fairweather, 01590 612113, info@fairweathers.co.uk, www.fairweathers.co.uk. *Hilltop Nursery. 1½m NE of Beaulieu village on B3054. Please leave plenty of time, the guided tour will start promptly at 10.30am.* **Fri 12, Sat 13 July (10.30-12.30). Adm £10, chd free. Pre-booking essential, please visit www.ngs.org.uk for information & booking. Light refreshments.**
Fairweather's hold a specialist collection of over 400 agapanthus grown in pots and display beds, inc AGM award-winning agapanthus trialled by the RHS. Patrick Fairweather will give a guided tour of the nursery at 10.30am with a demonstration of how to get the best from agapanthus and companion planting. Open nearby Patrick's Patch at Fairweather's Garden Centre, High Street, Beaulieu.

&. 🐎 🔆 💷

32 FERNS LODGE

Cottagers Lane, Hordle, Lymington, SO41 0FE. Sue Grant, 07860 521501, sue.grant@fernslodge.co.uk, www.fernslodge.co.uk. *Approx 5½ m W of Lymington. From Silver St turn into Woodcock Ln, 100 metres to Cottagers Ln, parking in field by opp garden. From A337 turn into Everton Rd & drive approx 1½ m, Cottagers Ln on R.* **Sat 1, Sun 2 June (2-5). Adm £5, chd free. Home-made teas & cream teas. Visits also by arrangement 1 Apr to 27 Sept for groups of 5 to 20.**

Bustling, 4 acre wildlife garden filled with scent, colour and mature trees inc ½ acre cottage garden around a Victorian lodge, full of sweet peas, foxgloves, clematis, roses, agapanthus and salvia. Brick paths wind through this garden with plentiful seating areas, perfect for a cup of tea. The large garden is in restoration with a Woodpecker greenhouse, tree ferns, masses of new planting and 3D art. Wheelchair access to many areas.

33 FREY ELMA

Church Lane, Headley, Bordon, GU35 8PJ. Christine Leonard. *Nr Grayshott. Coming from Alton on B3002. Pass Headley Church on L, take 1st turn L onto Curtis Ln, then 2nd turning L onto Church Ln. Frey Elna is 1st house on L. Please follow signs.* **Sat 8, Sun 9 June (11-5). Combined adm with Perrymead £10, chd free. Home-made teas.**

⅓ acre divided into four rooms. Enter by the front gate to the welcome garden in blue and yellow, through an archway to the main herbaceous and shrub garden; pass through the next archway to the vegetable garden and greenhouse; final stop is the entertaining room with conservatory, gazebo, patio and where tea and cakes are served. Wheelchair access to all areas.

34 FRITHAM LODGE

Fritham, SO43 7HH. Sir Chris & Lady Powell. *6m N of Lyndhurst. 3m NW of M27 J1 (Cadnam). Follow signs to Fritham.* **Sun 16 June (2-4). Adm £5, chd free. Home-made teas.**

A walled garden of 1 acre in the heart of the New Forest, set within 18 acres surrounding a house that was originally a Charles I hunting lodge (not open). Herbaceous and blue and white mixed borders, pergolas and ponds. A box hedge enclosed parterre of roses, fruit and vegetables. Visitors will enjoy the ponies, donkeys, sheep and old breed hens on their meadow walk to the woodland and stream.

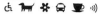

GROUP OPENING

35 FROYLE GARDENS

Lower Froyle, Froyle, GU34 4LG. *Midway between Alton & Farnham just off the A31. Access to Froyle from A31 between Alton & Farnham at Bentley, or at Hen & Chicken Inn. Park at Recreation Ground in Lower Froyle GU34 4LG. Map provided. Additional signed parking in Upper Froyle.* **Sat 1, Sun 2 June (1.30-6). Combined adm £10, chd free. Home-made teas in the village hall & picnics welcome on the recreation ground in Lower Froyle.**

ALDERSEY HOUSE
Nigel & Julie Southern.

DAY COTTAGE
Nick & Corinna Whines.

2 HIGHWAY COTTAGE
Faith Richards & Gordon Mitchell.

NEW MANDERLEY
Mrs Lorna Bailey.

OLD BREWERY HOUSE
Vivienne & John Sexton. **D**

OLD COURT
Sarah & Charlie Zorab.

NEW 1 TURNPIKE COTTAGES
Ms Pam Walls.

WALBURY
Ernie & Brenda Milam.

WARREN COTTAGE
Gillian & Jonathan Pickering.

A warm welcome awaits as Froyle Gardens open their gates once again, enabling visitors to enjoy a wide variety of types of garden, all of which have undergone further development since last year and will be looking splendid. There are two new gardens to explore in Upper Froyle. Froyle (the Village of the Saints) has many old and interesting buildings. Our gardens harmonise well with the surrounding landscape and most have spectacular views. The gardens themselves are diverse with rich planting. You will see greenhouses, water features, vegetables, roses, clematis and wildflower meadows. Lots of ideas to take away with you, along with plants to buy and delicious teas served in the village hall. Close by is a playground with a zip wire where children can let off steam. There is also an exhibition of richly embroidered historic vestments in the Church in Upper Froyle (separate donation). The gardens are well spread out so wear comfortable shoes! No wheelchair access to Day Cottage and 1 Turnpike Cottages, and on request at Warren Cottage. Gravel drive at 2 Highway Cottage.

36 HAMBLEDON HOUSE

East Street, Hambledon, PO7 4RX. Capt & Mrs David Hart Dyke, 02392 632380, dianahartdyke@gmail.com. *8m SW of Petersfield, 5m NW of Waterlooville. In village centre, driveway leading to house in East St. Do not go up Speltham Hill even if advised by SatNav.* **Visits by arrangement Apr to Oct for groups of 10 to 40. Home-made teas.**

3 acre partly walled plantsman's garden for all seasons. Large borders filled with a wide variety of unusual shrubs and perennials with imaginative plant combinations culminating in a profusion of colour in late summer. Hidden, secluded areas reveal surprise views of garden and village rooftops. Planting a large central area, which started in 2011, has given the garden an exciting new dimension.

The National Garden Scheme searches the length and breadth of England, Wales, Northern Ireland and the Channel Islands for the very best private gardens

37 THE HOMESTEAD
Northney Road, Hayling Island, PO11 0NF. Stan & Mary Pike, 02392 464888, jhomestead@aol.com, www.homesteadhayling.co.uk. *3m S of Havant. From A27 Havant & Hayling Island r'about, travel S over Langstone Bridge & turn immed L into Northney Rd. Car park entrance on R after Langstone Hotel.* **Sun 4 Aug (2-5.30). Adm £5, chd free. Home-made teas. Visits also by arrangement July to Sept for groups of 12+.**
1¼ acre garden surrounded by working farmland with views to Butser Hill and boats in Chichester Harbour. Trees, shrubs, colourful herbaceous borders and small walled garden with herbs, vegetables and trained fruit trees. Large pond and woodland walk with shade-loving plants. A quiet and peaceful atmosphere with plenty of seats to enjoy the vistas within the garden and beyond. Extensive range of plants for sale. Wheelchair access with some gravel paths.

& 🐕 ❀ � 🍵 »))

38 HOOK CROSS ALLOTMENTS
Reading Road, Hook, RG27 9DB. Hook Allotment Association. *Northern edge of Hook village on B3349, Reading Rd. 900 metres N of A30 r'about. Concealed entrance track is on RHS at foot of hill opp a farm entrance, straight after turns to B & M Fencing & Searle's Ln.* **Sat 20, Sun 21 July (1-5). Adm £4, chd free. Light refreshments.**
5¼ acre community run allotments overlooking Hook village. More than 100 plots showcasing different vegetables, fruit and flower growing styles. Plot holder demonstrations of how to grow your own. Community orchard, wildflower meadow, beetle banks, wildlife friendly gardening information. Plants and refreshments for sale.

🐕 ❀ 🍵 »))

39 ◆ THE HOSPITAL OF ST CROSS
St Cross Road, Winchester, SO23 9SD. The Hospital of St Cross & Almshouse of Noble Poverty, 01962 851375, porter@hospitalofstcross.co.uk, www.hospitalofstcross.co.uk. *½ m S of Winchester. From city centre take B3335 (Southgate St & St Cross Rd) S. Turn L immed before The Bell Inn. If on foot follow riverside path S from Cathedral & College, approx 20 mins.* **For NGS: Sun 2 June (2-5). Adm £5, chd free. Light refreshments in the Hundred Men's Hall in the Outer Quadrangle. Open nearby Winchester College. For other opening times and information, please phone, email or visit garden website.**
The Medieval Hospital of St Cross nestles in water meadows beside the River Itchen and is one of England's oldest almshouses. The tranquil, walled Master's Garden, created in the late C17 by Bishop Compton, now contains colourful herbaceous borders, old-fashioned roses, interesting trees and a large fish pond. The plant beds in the Compton Garden were repositioned and replanted in 2023. The Hundred Men's Hall tearoom and the Porter's Lodge gift shop will be open. Wheelchair access, but surfaces are uneven in places.

& ❀ 🍵 »))

40 THE HOUSE IN THE WOOD
Beaulieu, SO42 7YN. Victoria Roberts. *New Forest. 8m NE of Lymington. Leaving the entrance to Beaulieu Motor Museum on R (B3056), take next R signed Ipley Cross. Take 2nd gravel drive on RH-bend, approx ½ m.* **Sun 12 May (1.30-5). Adm £6, chd free. Cream teas.**
Peaceful 12 acre woodland garden with continuing progress and improvement. Very much a spring garden with tall, glorious mature azaleas and rhododendrons in every shade of pink, orange, red and white, interspersed with acers and other woodland wonders. A magical garden to get lost in with many twisting paths leading downhill to a pond and a more formal layout of lawns around the house (not open). Used in the war to train the Special Operations Executive.

🐕 🚗 🍵

41 THE ISLAND
Greatbridge, Romsey, SO51 0HP. Mr & Mrs Christopher Saunders-Davies, 01794 512100, ssd@littleroundtop.co.uk. *1m N of Romsey on A3057. Entrance at bridge. Follow drive 100yds. Car park on RHS.* **Sat 13, Sun 14 Apr (2-5). Adm £8, chd free. Home-made teas. Visits also by arrangement Apr to Aug for groups of 15 to 20.**
6 acres both sides of the River Test. Fine display of daffodils, tulips, spring flowering trees and summer bedding. The main garden has herbaceous and annual borders, fruit trees, rose pergola, lavender walk and extensive lawns. An arboretum planted in the 1930s by Sir Harold Hillier contains three ponds, shrubs and specimen trees providing interest throughout the yr. No dogs allowed. Disabled WC.

& 🍵 »))

42 KING JOHN'S GARDEN
Romsey, SO51 7NG. Friends of King John's Garden & Test Valley Borough Council, www.facebook.com/KingJohnsGarden. *Central Romsey. Parking: please use Lortemore Place public car park.* **Sun 26, Mon 27 May (10.30-4.30). Combined adm with The Nelson Cottage £6, chd free. Home-made teas.**
Listed C13 house (not open Sunday). Historic community garden planted with plants available before 1700. Small wildflower meadow. Award-winning Victorian garden and north courtyard with water features, fountains and pump. Paved path and fountain courtyard.

& ❀ 🍵 »))

43 NEW KINGFISHERS CARE HOME
The Meadows, New Milton, BH25 7FJ. Chris Marsh, www.coltencare.co.uk/kingfishers/your-garden. *New Forest. W on A337 from Lymington to New Milton. L opp fish & chip shop down Southern Rd, 1st R into The Meadows. Park in allocated car parking spaces or on Southern Rd.* **Sat 15, Sun 16 June (11-5). Adm £4, chd free. Home-made teas. Dietary requirements catered for.**
This colourful and vibrant care home garden offers wide winding paths to stroll to its various points of interest inc herbaceous borders, a lavender avenue, pergola, greenhouse, vegetable patch and the recent addition, a fascinating water feature. Residents are very involved in the garden, planning and propagating plants, and building habitats for all our fauna. The garden truly offers something for everyone.

& 🐕 ❀ 🍵 🪑 »))

44 LADYBOWER

47 Connaught Road, Fleet, GU51 3LR. **Muriel Pratt.** *Central Fleet. Exit J4A of M3 & follow directions to Fleet, pass train station & turn L at 2nd T-lights on to Kings Rd, Connaught Rd is 3rd on the R. Parking at Ark Veterinary Surgery, 41 Connaught Rd (50 metres).* **Sat 1, Sun 2 June (2-5). Adm £5, chd free. Home-made teas inc gluten free option.**

This garden of over 1/4 of an acre was created 9 yrs ago. Over three terraces it has a large acer bed, several herbaceous borders and a large pond surrounded by rockery. Still developing it is a lovely oasis of peace and calm in the centre of a thriving market town. Floral displays from roses, rhododendrons, salvias, with an additional collection of hostas. Wheelchair access over flat patio and slopes to two of the three terraces. Parking on drive by prior arrangement, 07743 899494.

45 LEPE HOUSE GARDENS

Lepe, Exbury, Southampton, SO45 1AD. **Michael & Emma Page, 07882 640981, emma.page@lepe.org.uk, www.lepe.org.uk.** *New Forest. 1/2 m from Lepe Country Park, 2m from Exbury Gardens. Entrance to drive through gates on S-side of Lepe Rd. What3words app - belong.nurses. highlight.* **Sun 14 Apr (1-5). Adm £10, chd free. Light refreshments inc. Visits also by arrangement 17 Apr to 30 June for groups of 10 to 25. Groups are asked to prepay by BACS.**

This 12 acre spring woodland garden was laid out in 1893. An embarkation point for D-Day, the lighthouse in the garden now marks the entrance to the Beaulieu River. Distinct areas inc walled garden with camellias, coastal walk overlooking the Solent, woodland with mature magnolias and rhododendrons, arboretum with drifts of spring bulbs, wildlife ponds plus formal areas with a wishing well. This garden is proud to provide plants for the National Garden Scheme's Show Garden at Chelsea Flower Show 2024.

46 LITTLE COURT

Crawley, Winchester, SO21 2PU. **Mrs A R Elkington, 01962 776365, elkslc@btinternet.com.** *5m NW of Winchester. Crawley village lies between B3049 (Winchester - Stockbridge) & A272 (Winchester - Andover), 400yds from either pond or church.* **Sun 11, Mon 12, Sun 18, Mon 19 Feb (2-4.30); Sun 31 Mar, Mon 1 Apr, Sun 19, Mon 20 May (2-5.30). Adm £5, chd free. Home-made teas in the village hall. 2025: Sun 16, Mon 17, Sun 23, Mon 24 Feb. Opening with Crawley Gardens on Thur 11, Sun 14 Apr, Thur 20, Sun 23 June. Visits also by arrangement 10 Feb to 31 July.**

This sheltered naturalistic garden is one for all seasons, and is specially exciting in spring. It is mature and exuberant with contrasting areas, a traditional walled kitchen garden and free-range bantams. In July there are many butterflies in the meadow of wild flowers. Several seats throughout with good views, it is an oasis of peace and tranquillity. Sorry, no dogs. Plants grown in the garden for sale.

Lepe House Gardens

47 LONGSTOCK PARK WATER GARDEN

Leckford, Stockbridge, SO20 6EH. Leckford Estate Ltd, part of John Lewis Partnership, www.leckfordestate.co.uk. *4m S of Andover. From Leckford village on A3057 towards Andover, cross the river bridge & take 1st turning L signed Longstock.* **Sun 30 June (10.30-2.30). Adm £10, chd £5.** Famous water garden with extensive collection of aquatic and bog plants set in 7 acres of woodland with rhododendrons and azaleas. A walk through the park leads to National Collections of *Buddleja* and *Clematis viticella*; arboretum and herbaceous border at Longstock Park Nursery. Refreshments at Longstock Park Farm Shop and Nursery (last orders at 3.30pm). Assistance dogs only.

48 NEW LORD WANDSWORTH COLLEGE

Long Sutton, Hook, RG29 1TB. Lord Wandsworth College. *3m S of Odiham. SatNav will take you to the College's main gates. From here our visitor car park is clearly signed.* **Sat 13, Sun 14 Apr (11-3). Adm £3.50, chd free. Home-made teas.** Lord Wandsworth College is set in 1200 acres of rolling farmland and wooded valleys. The main college campus is set around formal lawns with mature paper bark maples, cedar trees, cherry trees, and magnolias. The herbaceous borders are planted with an array of tulips, daffodils, and alliums. A South African inspired border runs the full length of the new science centre.

49 26 LOWER NEWPORT ROAD

Aldershot, GU12 4QD. Pete & Angie Myles. *Nr to the Aldershot junction of the A331. Parking is normally available with the factory opp 'Jondo' & the Salvation Army. Signage in place on the day if available. We are 100 metres away from the McDonalds drive through.* **Sat 29, Sun 30 June (11-4). Adm £3, chd free. Light refreshments.** A T-shaped town garden full of ideas, split into four distinct sections; a semi-enclosed patio area with pots and water feature; a free-form lawn with a tree fern, perennials, bulbs and shrubs and over 200 varieties of hosta; secret garden with a 20ft x 6ft raised pond, exotic planting backdrop and African carvings; and a potager garden with vegetables, roses, cannas and plant storage, and sales.

50 ◆ MACPENNYS WOODLAND GARDEN & NURSERIES

Burley Road, Bransgore, Christchurch, BH23 8DB. Mr & Mrs T M Lowndes, 01425 672348, office@macpennys.co.uk, www.macpennys.co.uk. *6m SE of Ringwood, 5m NE of Christchurch. From Crown Pub Xrd in Bransgore take Burley Rd, following sign for Thorney Hill & Burley. Entrance ½ m on R.* **For opening times and information, please phone, email or visit garden website.** 4 acre woodland garden originating from worked out gravel pits in the 1950s, offering interest year-round, but particularly in spring and autumn. Attached to a large nursery that offers for sale a wide selection of homegrown trees, shrubs, conifers, perennials, hedging plants, fruit trees and bushes. Tearoom offering home-made cakes, afternoon tea (pre-booking required) and light lunches, using locally sourced produce wherever possible. Nursery closed Christmas through to the New Year. Partial wheelchair access on grass and gravel paths. Can be bumpy with tree roots and, muddy in winter.

51 MANOR LODGE

Brook Lane, Botley, Southampton, SO30 2ER. Gary & Janine Stone, 07870 189321, manorlodge@globalnet.co.uk. *6m E of Southampton. From A334 to the W of Botley village centre, turn into Brook Ln. Manor Lodge is ½ m on the R. Limited disabled parking. Continue past Manor Lodge to parking (signed).* **Sat 27, Sun 28 Apr (2-5). Adm £4.50, chd free. Home-made teas. Visits also by arrangement Apr to Oct for groups of 12 to 38.** Close to Manor Farm Country Park, this mid-Victorian house (not open), set in 1½ acres is the garden of an enthusiastic plantswoman. A garden still in evolution with established areas and new projects, a mixture of informal and formal planting, woodland and wildflower meadow areas, large established and new specimen shrubs and trees. Perennials and planting combinations for year-round interest. Largely flat with hard paving, but some gravel and grass to access all areas.

52 MILL HOUSE

Vyne Road, Sherborne St John, Basingstoke, RG24 9HU. Harry & Devika Clarke. *2m N of Basingstoke. From Basingstoke take the A340 N. 400 metres beyond the hospital, turn R for Sherborne St John. Go through, past a red phone box & 400 metres up a hill. As it crests, on L, take track to Mill House.* **Thur 27, Sun 30 June (2-6). Adm £5, chd free. Home-made teas.** Set in a private valley, the 3 acres of domestic fruit, vegetables, wild flowers and casual planting are arranged around a power generating watermill. Sustainability and low maintenance lie at its heart, to fit with modern life. Open views, set with mature trees and livestock, give a tranquil sense of space, with moving and static water framed in an undulating landscape. Partial wheelchair access. Park in car park and follow disabled access signs.

53 NEW MOUNTBATTEN HOSPICE

Botley Road, West End, Southampton, SO30 3JB. Mountbatten Hampshire Hospice, www.mountbatten-hampshire.org.uk. *On Moorgreen NHS site. The hospice is 1st L. Free parking on the day.* **Sat 6, Sun 7 July (1-4). Adm by donation. Light refreshments.** The gardens, tended by dedicated volunteers, are a mixture of shrubs, ornamental grasses, annual and perennial flowers with several bug houses. There are areas of lawn where patients, visitors and staff can enjoy social connections and quiet contemplation, with some lawns left uncut for wildlife and flowers to flourish together with pollinators.

54 THE NELSON COTTAGE

68 Cherville Street, Romsey, SO51 8FD. Margaret Prosser. *Next to Great Bridge Motors in Romsey.* **Sun 26, Mon 27 May (10.30-4.30). Combined adm with King John's Garden £6, chd free.** Formally one of the many public houses in Romsey. A ½ acre garden with a variety of perennial plants and shrubs, and a wild grass meadow bringing the countryside into the town. Wheelchair access with one step on entry into the garden.

55 NEW ▶ OLD CHANNEL HILL FARMHOUSE
North End, Damerham, Fordingbridge, SP6 3HA. Carolyn Andrews & Phil Tandy. *3m W of Fordingbridge. Turn off the A338, go through Fordingbridge & Sandleheath into Damerham & follow the yellow signs.* **Thur 30 May, Sat 15 June (1-5). Adm £4, chd free. Home-made teas.**
A mature garden divided into different areas of interest; main lawn bounded by perennial borders, wild meadow area, small stumpery, gravel area and a pergola seating area covered in vines and roses. Each area has different styles of planting with mature hedging. Old thatched privy and summerhouse.

56 THE OLD RECTORY
East Woodhay, Newbury, RG20 0AL. David & Victoria Wormsley, 07801 418976, victoria@wormsley.net. *6m SW of Newbury. Turn off A343 between Newbury & Highclere to Woolton Hill. Turn L to East End, continue ¾ m beyond East End. Turn R, garden opp St Martin's Church.* **Visits by arrangement 1 Apr to 1 Oct for groups of 20+. Adm £12, chd free. Home-made teas inc.**
A classic English country garden of about 2 acres surrounding a Regency former rectory (not open). Formal lawns and terrace provide tranquil views over parkland. A large walled garden with topiary and roses, full of interesting herbaceous plants and climbers for successional interest. Also a Mediterranean pool garden, orchard, wildflower meadow and fruit garden. Explore and enjoy.

57 NEW ▶ THE OLD RECTORY, WICKHAM
Southwick Road, Wickham, Fareham, PO17 6HR. Neville Craig. *2m N of M27 on A32 to Alton. E from village for 300 metres on B2177 to Southwick. 1st house on R before bend.* **Sun 4 Aug (1-5). Adm £5, chd free. Tea.**
This 5 acre garden surrounds a house built c1700. About a century later it was apparently gifted/sold to the Winchester Diocese. Since 2000 the owners have developed it in the Capability Brown style, exploiting its open aspect and mature trees. The sloping site allows for four interconnected ponds, providing

different habitats, and an acre of rewilding meadow surrounded by uncut hedges.

♿ ☕ 🪑

GROUP OPENING

58 OLD THATCH & THE MILLENNIUM BARN
Sprats Hatch Lane, Winchfield, Hook, RG27 8DD. www.old-thatch.co.uk. *3m W of Fleet. 1½ m E of Winchfield Stn, follow NGS signs. Turning to Sprats Hatch Ln is opp the The Barley Mow pub.* **Sun 14 Apr, Sun 9 June (2-6). Combined adm £5, chd free. Home-made teas. Pimms if hot & mulled wine if cool.**

THE MILLENNIUM BARN
Mr & Mrs G Carter.

OLD THATCH
Jill Ede.

Who could resist visiting Old Thatch, a chocolate box thatched cottage (not open), featured on film and TV, a smallholding with a 5 acre garden and woodland alongside the Basingstoke Canal (unfenced). A succession of spring bulbs, a profusion of wild flowers, perennials and homegrown annuals pollinated by our own bees and fertilised by the donkeys, who await your visit. Over 30 named clematis and rose cultivars. Children enjoy our garden quiz, adults enjoy tea and home-made cakes. Arrive by narrow boat! Trips on 'John Pinkerton' may stop at Old Thatch on NGS days www.basingstoke-canal.org. uk. Also Accessible Boating shuttle from Barley Mow wharf, approx every 45 mins (entrance to the garden is an additional cost). Signed parking for Blue Badge holders: please use entrance by the red telephone box. Paved paths and grass slopes give access to the whole garden.

♿ 🐕 ✳ ☕ 🔊

59 ◆ PATRICK'S PATCH
Fairweather's Garden Centre, High Street, Beaulieu, SO42 7YB. Patrick Fairweather, 01590 612307, info@fairweathers.co.uk, www.fairweathers.co.uk. *SE of New Forest at head of Beaulieu River. Leave M27 at J2 & follow signs for Beaulieu Motor Museum. Go up the one-way High St & park in Fairweather's car park on the L.*

For opening times and information, please phone, email or visit garden website.
Productive fruit and vegetable garden with a full range of vegetables, trained top, soft fruit and herbs. The garden is used as an educational project for primary school children and young people with additional needs. Maintained by volunteers, primary school children and a head gardener. We run the Potting Shed Club, a series of fun educational gardening sessions for children. Open daily. Refreshments available at Steff's Kitchen. Wheelchair access on gravelled site.

♿ ✳ ☕

60 PERRYMEAD
May Close, Headley, GU35 8LR. Helen & Anne Kempster. *From Crabtree Ln (B3002), turn into Liphook Rd. About 500yds along Liphook Rd is May Cl which is a dirt track by the side of the allotments.* **Sat 8, Sun 9 June (11-5). Combined adm with Frey Elma £10, chd free.**
A garden built for wildlife. Mixed borders of perennials, grasses, trees and shrubs chosen for bees, birds and butterflies. Bug boxes, nest boxes and feeders. Walk over the bridge to the wildlife pond and explore our wildlife seating area. Wander round the garden and find nooks and crannies, sitting areas, patios and secret spaces where you can relax and enjoy the peace of this tranquil garden.

🐕 🔊

In 2023, National Garden Scheme funding for Perennial supported a helpline service which provided advice, information and frontline support to around 800 people working in horticulture

Hambledon House
© Leigh Clapp

61 1 POVEY'S COTTAGE
Stoney Heath, Baughurst,
Tadley, RG26 5SN. Jonathan &
Sheila Richards, 01256 850633,
smrichards3012@icloud.com,
www.facebook.com/
onepoveyscottage. *Between
villages of Ramsdell & Baughurst,
10 min drive from Basingstoke. Take
A339 out of Basingstoke, direction
Newbury. Turn R off A339 towards
Ramsdell, then 4m to Stoney Heath.
Pass under overhead power cables,
take next L into unmade road &
Povey's is 1st on the R.* **Sat 15, Sun
16 June (1-5). Adm £5, chd free.
Home-made teas. Visits also by
arrangement 26 May to 15 Aug for
groups of 10 to 30.**
Herbaceous borders, trees and
shrubs, a small orchard area,
greenhouses, fruit cage, vegetable
garden and a small wildflower
meadow area. Beehives in one corner
of the garden and chickens in another
corner. A feature of the garden is
an unusual natural swimming pond.
Plants and home-made bee pottery

for sale. Wheelchair access across flat
grassed areas, but no hard pathways.
& ✿ ☕ ⊲»)

62 PYLEWELL PARK
South Baddesley, Lymington,
SO41 5SJ. Lady Elizabeth
Teynham. *Coast road 2m E of
Lymington. From Lymington follow
signs for Car Ferry to Isle of Wight,
continue for 2m to South Baddesley.*
**Sun 7 Apr, Sun 5 May (2-5). Adm
£5, chd free.**
A large parkland garden laid out
in 1890. Enjoy a walk along the
extensive informal grass and
moss paths, bordered by fine
rhododendron, magnolia and azalea.
Wild daffodils bloom in March and
carpets of bluebells in late April
and May. Large lakes feature giant
gunnera and are home to magnificent
swans. Distant views across the
Solent to the Isle of Wight. Pylewell
House and surrounding garden is
private. Glasshouses, swimming pool
and other outbuildings are not open
to visitors. Lovely day out for families

and dogs. Bring your own tea or
picnic and wear suitable footwear for
muddy areas.
🐕 ⊲»)

63 REDENHAM PARK HOUSE
Redenham Park, Andover,
SP11 9AQ. Lady Clark. *Approx
1½ m from Weyhill on the A342
Andover to Ludgershall road.* **Fri 21
June, Fri 20 Sept (10-1). Adm £6,
chd free. Light refreshments at
pool house.**
Redenham Park built in 1784. The
garden sits behind the house (not
open). The formal rose garden is
planted with white flowered roses.
Steps lead up to the main herbaceous
borders, which peak in late summer.
A calm green interlude, a gate
opens into gardens with espaliered
pears, apples, mass of scented
roses, shrubs and perennial planting
surrounds the swimming pool. A door
opens onto a kitchen garden.
✿ 🚗 ☕ ⊲»)

64 15 ROTHSCHILD CLOSE

Southampton, SO19 9TE. Steve Campion, 07968 512773, Spcampion10@gmail.com, www.instagram.com/tropical_plant_geezer69. *3m from M27 J8. From M27 J8 follow A3025 towards Woolston. After cemetery r'about L to Weston, next r'about 2nd exit Rothschild Cl.* **Sat 6, Sun 7 July, Sat 7, Sun 8 Sept (11-5). Adm £3.50, chd free. Pre-booking essential, please visit www.ngs.org.uk for information & booking. Home-made teas. Visits also by arrangement 1 July to 29 Sept for groups of 5 to 12.**

Small, 8 metre x 8 metre, modern city garden incorporating family living with lush tropical foliage. A large range of unusual tropical style plants inc tree ferns, bananas, cannas, gingers and dahlias. The garden has flourished over the last 7 yrs into a tropical oasis with many plants grown from seeds and cuttings. Tropical plant enthusiasts do come to have a cuppa in the jungle! Adjacent to the River Solent and Royal Victoria Country Park.

65 SHALDEN PARK HOUSE

The Avenue, Shalden, Alton, GU34 4DS. Mr & Mrs Michael Campbell. *4½m NW of Alton. B3349 from Alton or M3 J5 onto B3349. Turn W at Kapadokya Restaurant (formerly The Golden Pot pub) signed Herriard, Lasham, Shalden. Entrance ¼m on L. Disabled parking on entry.* **Sun 26 May (2-5). Adm £5, chd free. Home-made teas.**

Shalden Park House welcomes you to our 4 acre garden to enjoy a stroll through the arboretum, herbaceous borders, rose garden, kitchen garden and wildlife pond. Refreshments will be served from the pool terrace.

66 SILVER BIRCHES

Old House Gardens, East Worldham, nr Alton, GU34 3AN. Jenny & Roger Bateman, 07464 696245/01420 88307, jennyabateman@gmail.com. *2m E of Alton off B3004. Turn L signed Wyck & Binstead, then 1st R into Old House Gardens.* **Visits by arrangement May to Aug for groups of 10 to 30. Adm £5, chd free. Home-made teas.**

½ acre garden featured in ITV's 'Love Your Garden' with Alan Titchmarsh in May 2023. Winding paths lead through colourful mixed borders to fish pond, stream, rockery and summerhouse. Rose garden with arbour. Planting designed for year-round colour and interest using foliage as well as flowers. Many sitting areas and some unusual plants. Partial wheelchair access.

67 ◆ SIR HAROLD HILLIER GARDENS

Jermyns Lane, Ampfield, Romsey, SO51 0QA. Hampshire County Council, 01794 369318, info.hilliers@hants.gov.uk, www.hants.gov.uk/hilliergardens. *2m NE of Romsey. Follow brown tourist signs off M3 J11, or off M27 J2, or A3057 Romsey to Andover.* **For opening times and information, please phone, email or visit garden website.**

Established by the plantsman Sir Harold Hillier, this 180 acre garden holds a unique collection of 12,000 different hardy plants from across the world. It inc the famous Winter Garden, Magnolia Avenue, Centenary Border, Himalayan Valley, Gurkha Memorial Garden, Magnolia Avenue, spring woodlands, Hydrangea Walk, fabulous autumn colour, 14 National Collections and over 600 champion trees. The Centenary Border is one of the longest double mixed border in the country, a feast from early summer to autumn. Celebrated Winter Garden is one of the largest in Europe. Electric scooters and wheelchairs for hire (please pre-book). Accessible WC and parking. Registered assistance dogs only.

68 SOUTH VIEW HOUSE

60 South Road, Horndean, Waterlooville, PO8 0EP. James & Victoria Greenshields, www.youtube.com/@Southview_House_Exotic_Garden. *Between Horndean & Clanfield. From N A3 towards Horndean, R at T-junction to r'about. From S A3, B2149 to Horndean, continue on A3 N to r'about, 1st exit into Downwood Way, 3rd L into South Rd. House is 3rd on R. Park in road.* **Sun 4 Aug (1-5). Adm £4, chd free. Light refreshments.**

A ½ acre site with formal cottage garden to the front and exotic/tropical style garden to the rear. The front inc a large herbaceous border, small woodland garden and formal topiary. The cleverly designed garden to the rear features tropical style planting with many palms, bananas, cannas and many unusual plants. Features inc pond, summerhouse, bar and chicken coop. Well worth a visit. Garden is accessed along a gravel drive on a gentle slope.

GROUP OPENING

69 SOUTHSEA GARDENS

Southsea, Portsmouth, PO4 0PR. Ian & Liz Craig, 07415 889648, ian.craig1@mac.com. *Parking in Craneswater School, St Ronan's Rd, off Albert Rd. Follow signs from Albert Rd or Canoe Lake on seafront.* **Sun 21 Apr, Sun 26 May (2-5.30). Combined adm £5, chd free. Evening opening Sat 13 July (5-8). Combined adm £6, chd free. Home-made teas (Apr & May) & Wine (July) at 28 St Ronan's Avenue.**

> **NEW** **35 GAINS ROAD**
> Leeann Roots.

> **NEW** **67 GAINS ROAD**
> Lyn & Ian Payne.

> **28 ST RONAN'S AVENUE**
> Ian & Liz Craig,
> www.28stronansavenue.co.uk.

Three town gardens in adjacent roads within easy walking distance, off St Ronan's Road. Victorian houses (not open) where the owners have created peaceful green spaces about 700 metres from Southsea promenade. 35 and 67 Gains Road are small gardens designed and planted with artistic flair by the owners, inc ferns, bamboo and sculpture. The creative gardeners are keen plantspeople and have made the very most of the limited space in both front and rear gardens with planting of an exceptional standard. 28 St Ronan's Avenue (145ft by 25ft) is divided into different areas inc a wildflower meadow and pond. Agaves and echeverias grow in drier sandy parts. Planting is a mixture of traditional and tender plants inc puya, echiums, and tree ferns. Tulips feature in April and alliums in May and June. Recycled items are used to create sculptures.

70 ◆ SPINNERS GARDEN

School Lane, Pilley, Lymington, SO41 5QE. Andrew & Vicky Roberts, 07545 432090, info@spinnersgarden.co.uk, www.spinnersgarden.co.uk. *New Forest. 1½m N of Lymington off A337.* **For NGS: Sun 28 Apr (1.30-5). Adm £6, chd free. Cream teas. For other opening times and information, please phone, email or visit garden website.**

Peaceful woodland garden overlooking the Lymington valley with many rare and unusual plants. Drifts of trilliums, erythroniums and anemones light up the woodland floor in early spring. The garden continues to be developed with new plants added to the collections and the layout changed to enhance the views over a pond and small arboretum. The house was rebuilt in 2014 to reflect its garden setting. Andy will take groups of 15 on tours of the hillside with its woodland wonders and draw attention to the treats at their feet.

71 SPITFIRE HOUSE

Chattis Hill, Stockbridge, SO20 6JS. Tessa & Clive Redshaw, 07711 547543, tessa@redshaw.co.uk. *2m from Stockbridge. Follow the A30 W from Stockbridge for 2m. Go past the Broughton/Chattis Hill Xrds, do not follow SatNav into Spitfire Ln, take next R to the Wallops & then immed R again to Spitfire House.* **Sat 25 May (2-5); Sun 26 May (12-4). Adm £5, chd free. Home-made teas on 25 May only. Picnics welcome on 26 May. Visits also by arrangement in June for groups of up to 30.**

A country garden situated high on chalk downland. On the site of a WW11 Spitfire assembly factory with Spitfire tethering rings still visible. This garden has wildlife at its heart and inc fruit and vegetables, a small orchard, wildlife pond, woodland planting and large areas of wildflower meadow. Wander across the downs to be rewarded with extensive views. Wheelchair access with areas of gravel and a slope up to wildflower meadow.

72 NEW 4 STANNINGTON CRESCENT

Totton, Southampton, SO40 3QB. Brian & Julia Graham. *From M271, at r'about take 2nd exit over causeway, then L for Totton. At Totton central r'about take 2nd exit, Salisbury Rd. Stannington Cres, 1st R immed after Memorial Car Park. Park in road or car park.* **Sun 12, Sun 19 May (1.30-5.30). Adm £3.50, chd free. Home-made teas.**

1930s town house (not open) in 100ft x 50ft plot. A garden of two parts reflecting Brian's passion for nature and Julia's wish for a normal garden. Wildlife area with pond, grasshopper bank and small wild grass meadow. Hedgehog boxes, bat box, numerous bird boxes and bug hotels to encourage wildlife. Wisteria, ferns and mixed planting borders.

GROUP OPENING

73 STOCKBRIDGE GARDENS

Stockbridge, SO20 6EX. *9m W of Winchester. On A30, at the junction of A3057 & B3049. All gardens & parking on High St.* **Thur 13, Sun 16 June (2-5). Combined adm £10, chd free.**

NEW FISHMORE HOUSE
Clare & Richard Hills.

THE OLD RECTORY
Robin Colenso & Chrissie Quayle.

SHEPHERDS HOUSE
Kim & Frances Candler.

TROUT COTTAGE
Mrs Sally Milligan.

Four gardens will open this yr in Stockbridge, offering a variety of styles and character. Trout Cottage is a small walled garden, inspiring those with small spaces and little time to achieve tranquillity and beauty. Full of approx 180 plants flowering for almost 10 months of the yr. The Old Rectory has a partially walled garden with formal pond, fountain and planting near the house (not open) with a stream-side walk under trees, many climbing and shrub roses and a woodland area. Shepherds House on Winton Hill with herbaceous borders, a kitchen garden and a belvedere overlooking the pond. New this year, Fishmore House is a 6 yr old garden on a ¾ acre plot. The key elements of design being planting, water and a borrowed landscape. Designed for accessibility incorporating bound gravel paths and no steps. Surrounded by the River Test with seating available to enjoy the views and large, sweeping herbaceous borders. Wheelchair access to all gardens. Gravel path at Shepherds House.

&.))

74 TADLEY PLACE

Church Lane, Baughurst, Tadley, RG26 5LA. Lyn & Ronald Duncan. *10 min drive from Basingstoke, nr Tadley.* **Sun 15 Sept (2-5). Adm £7, chd free. Light refreshments.**

Tadley Place is a Tudor manor house (not open) dating from the C15. The gardens surround the house and inc formal areas, a large kitchen garden and access to a bluebell wood with a pond.

🍵))

75 TANGLEFOOT

Crawley, Winchester, SO21 2QB. Mr & Mrs F J Fratter, 01962 776243, fred@fratter.co.uk. *5m NW of Winchester. Between B3049 (Winchester - Stockbridge) & A272 (Winchester - Andover). Lane beside Crawley Court (Arqiva). For SatNav use SO21 2QA. Parking in adjacent mown field.* **Thur 4, Sun 7, Thur 18, Sun 21 July (2-5.30). Adm £5, chd free. Self-service teas. Opening with Crawley Gardens on Thur 20, Sun 23 June. Visits also by arrangement 18 June to 25 July.**

Developed by owners since 1976, Tanglefoot's ½ acre garden is a blend of influences, from Monet-inspired rose arch and small wildlife pond to Victorian boundary wall with trained fruit trees. Highlights inc a raised lily pond, herbaceous bed (a riot of colour later in the summer), herb wheel, large productive kitchen garden and unusual flowering plants. In contrast to the garden, a 2 acre field with views over the Hampshire countryside has been converted into walk-through spring and summer wildflower meadows with mostly native trees and shrubs. The meadow contains plenty of ox-eye daisy, bedstraw, scabious, vetch, knapweed, bees, butterflies and much more; it has delighted many visitors. Visitors can picnic in the field, but there are no facilities. Plants from the garden for sale. Wheelchair access with narrow paths in vegetable area.

&. 🐾 ✿ 🍵))

76 TERSTAN

Longstock, Stockbridge, SO20 6DW. Penny Burnfield, paburnfield@gmail.com, www. pennyburnfield.wordpress.com. ¾ m N of Stockbridge. From Stockbridge (A30) turn N to Longstock at bridge. Garden ¾ m on R. **Sun 21 Apr, Sun 23 June, Sun 8 Sept (2-5). Adm £5, chd free. Home-made teas. Visits also by arrangement Apr to Sept for groups of 10+.**

A garden for all seasons, developed over 50 yrs into a profusely planted, contemporary cottage garden in peaceful surroundings. There is a constantly changing display in pots, starting with tulips and continuing with many unusual plants. Features inc gravel garden, water features, cutting garden, showman's caravan and live music. Wheelchair access with some gravel paths and steps.

♿ 🐕 ❀ � 🍵

77 THE THATCHED COTTAGE

Church Road, Upper Farringdon, Alton, GU34 3EG. Mr David & Mrs Cally Horton, 01420 587922, dwhorton@btinternet.com. 3m S of Alton off A32. From A32, take road to Upper Farringdon. At top of the hill turn L into Church Rd, follow round corner, past Masseys Folly (large red brick building) & we are the 1st house on the R. **Sun 25, Mon 26 Aug (2-5). Adm £6, chd free. Home-made teas. Visits also by arrangement June & July for groups of 15 to 50. Donation to Cardiac Rehab.**

A 1½ acre garden hidden behind a C16 thatched cottage (not open). Borders burst with cottage garden plants and a pond provides the soothing sound of water. A pergola of roses, clematis and honeysuckle leads to many fine specimen trees. A productive garden with fruit trees, fruit cage and raised vegetable beds. Enjoy the wildflower area and gypsy caravan. Fully accessible by wheelchair after a short gravel drive.

♿ 🐕 ❀ 🍵))

78 NEW 8 TUCKS CLOSE

Bransgore, Christchurch, BH23 8ND. Bob Sawyer. 5m NE of Christchurch. 3m from Christchurch on A35, turn towards Bransgore at the Cat & Fiddle for 2m past shops & follow yellow signs. From B3347 follow Derritt Ln for 2m then turn R on to Brookside. **Every Wed 3 July to 17 July (11-5). Adm £4, chd free.**

A small garden measuring 12 metres x 12 metres is full of interest and ideas showing what can be achieved in a small space. The two greenhouses contain arisaema, pelargoniums and seasonal plants. The borders have mature trees and shrubs underplanted with perennials, half-hardy plants such as hedychium and annuals add to the overall effect. Also on display are some of Bob's paintings.

79 TWIN OAKS

13 Oakwood Road, Chandler's Ford, Eastleigh, SO53 1LW. Syd & Sue Hutchinson, 07876 715046, syd@sydh.co.uk, www.facebook. com/twinoaksngs. Leave M3 J12. Follow signs to Chandlers Ford onto Winchester Rd. After ½ m turn R into Hiltingbury Rd. After approx ½ m turn L into Oakwood Rd. **Sat 27, Sun 28 Apr, Sun 26, Mon 27 May, Sat 22, Sun 23 June, Sat 10, Sun 11 Aug (1-5). Adm £4.50, chd free. Home-made teas. Visits also by arrangement 25 Apr to 13 Aug for groups of 10+.**

Evolving suburban water garden. Enjoy spring colour from azaleas, rhododendrons and bulbs, then summer colour from perennials, water lilies and tropical plants. A lawn meanders between informal beds and ponds, and bridges lead to a tranquil pergola seating area overlooking a wildlife pond. A rockery is skirted by a stream and a waterfall tumbles into a large lily pond, home to dragonflies. Aviary. The property entrance has a short gravel drive and has proven to be suitable for mobility scooters and wide tyred wheelchairs.

♿ 🐕 ❀ 🍵))

80 TYLNEY HALL HOTEL

Ridge Lane, Rotherwick, RG27 9AZ. Elite Hotels, 01256 764881, sales@tylneyhall.com, www.tylneyhall.co.uk. 3m NW of Hook. From M3 J5 via A287 & Newnham, M4 J3 via B3349 & Rotherwick. **Sun 12 May, Sun 9 June (10-5). Adm £5, chd free. Cream teas in the Chestnut Suite from 12pm.**

Large garden of 66 acres with extensive woodlands and beautiful vista. Fine avenues of wellingtonias; rhododendrons and azaleas, Italian garden, lakes, large water and rock garden, dry stone walls originally designed with assistance of Gertrude Jekyll. Partial wheelchair access.

♿ 🐕 🚗 🏛 🍵

81 WALHAMPTON

Beaulieu Road, Walhampton, Lymington, SO41 5ZG. Walhampton School Trust Ltd. 1m E of Lymington. From Lymington follow signs to Beaulieu (B3054) for 1m & turn R into main entrance at 1st school sign, 200yds after top of hill. **Sun 5 May (2-6). Adm £6, chd free. Tea. Donation to St John's Church, Boldre.**

Glorious walks through large C18 landscape garden surrounding magnificent mansion (now a school). Visitors will discover three lakes, serpentine canal, climbable prospect mount, period former banana house and orangery, fascinating shell grotto, plantsman's glade and Italian terrace by Peto (c1907), drives and colonnade by Mawson (c1914) with magnificent views to the Isle of Wight. David Hill will give a talk at the Mercury fountain, followed by a guided tour, every hour from 2.15pm to 5.15pm. Wheelchair access with gravel paths and some slopes. Regret, no dogs allowed.

♿ 🍵

82 WESTWARD

11 Ridgemount Avenue, Bassett, Southampton, SO16 7FP. Russ & Jan Smith, 02380 767112, russjsmith@btinternet.com. 3m N of Southampton city centre. From end of M3 J14 continue down A33 to 2nd r'about & head back to M3. Ridgemount Ave 2nd on L. **Visits by arrangement 8 Apr to 20 Sept. Adm £4.50, chd free. Home-made teas.**

Very colourful ¼ acre garden with diverse selection of planting in summer inc lilies, heucheras, acers, clematis and hydrangeas. Many baskets and containers full of summer colour. Hosta border, vegetable garden, summerhouse, Koi pond, waterfall and wildlife pond. Large collection of aeoniums, echeverias and cacti. New raised water feature in front garden. Wheelchair access through garage.

♿ 🐕 ❀ 🚗 🍵

In 2023 we awarded over £260,000 in Community Garden Grants, supporting 86 community garden projects

83 WHEATLEY HOUSE
Wheatley Lane, Kingsley, Bordon, GU35 9PA. Mrs Michael Adlington, 01420 23113, adlingtons36@gmail.com. *4m E of Alton, 5m SW of Farnham. Between Binsted & Kingsley. Take A31 to Bentley, follow sign to Bordon. After 2m, R at The Jolly Farmer Pub towards Binsted, 1m L & follow signs to Wheatley.* **Sat 17, Sun 18 Aug (1.30-5). Adm £6, chd free. Home-made teas. Visits also by arrangement Apr to Oct for groups of 10+.**
Situated on a rural hilltop with panoramic views over Alice Holt Forest and the South Downs. The owner admits to being much more of an artist than a plantswoman, but has had great fun creating this 1½ acre garden full of interesting and unusual planting combinations. The sweeping mixed borders and shrubs are spectacular with colour throughout the season, particularly in late summer. The black and white border, now with bright red accents, is very popular with visitors. Plants for sale. Selection of home-made, local crafts in the barn and a variety of artwork and sculptures in the garden. Wheelchair access with care on lawns, good views of garden and beyond from terrace.

& ✿ ☕ ⁕))

84 WICOR PRIMARY SCHOOL COMMUNITY GARDEN
Portchester, Fareham, PO16 9DL. Louise Moreton, www.wicor.hants.sch.uk. *Halfway between Portsmouth & Fareham on A27. Turn S at Seagull Pub r'about into Cornaway Ln, 1st R into Hatherley Dr. Entrance to school is almost opp. Parking on site, pay at main gate.* **Sun 23 June (12-4). Adm £4, chd free. Home-made teas.**
As shown on BBC Gardeners' World in 2017. Beautiful school gardens tended by pupils, staff and community gardeners. Wander along Darwin's path to see the coastal garden, Jurassic garden, orchard, tropical bed, stumpery, wildlife areas, allotments and apiary, plus one of the few camera obscuras in the south of England. Wheelchair access to all areas over flat ground.

& 🐎 ✿ ☕ ⁕))

85 WINCHESTER COLLEGE
College Street, Winchester, SO23 9NA. The College, www.winchestercollege.org. *Entrance to the College is via the Porter's Lodge on College St, a short walk from Winchester City Centre. Note there is very limited parking nr the college.* **Sat 1 June (11-4.30); Sun 2 June (11-4). Adm £10, chd free. Light refreshments in the Warden's Garden.**
See the historic gardens of Winchester College. These inc the main quad with herb garden, herbaceous borders and splendid climbing hydrangea; War Cloister designed by Herbert Baker, Bethesda a soft cottage style garden; Meads a stunning walled cricket ground surrounded by magnificent plane trees; and the Warden's Garden with Regency border, chalk stream and wilder woodland area.

☕ ♪))

86 1 WOGSBARNE COTTAGES
Rotherwick, RG27 9BL. Miss S & Mr R Whistler. *2½ m N of Hook. M3 J5, M4 J11, A30 or A33 via B3349.* **Sun 14, Mon 15 July (2-5). Adm £4, chd free. Home-made teas.**
Small traditional cottage garden with a 'roses around the door' look, much photographed for calendars, jigsaws and magazines. Mixed flower beds and borders. Vegetables grown in abundance. Ornamental pond and alpine garden. Views over open countryside to be enjoyed whilst you take afternoon tea on the lawn. Join us as we celebrate our 40th year of opening for NGS. Wheelchair access with some gravel paths.

& ✿ ☕

GROUP OPENING

87 NEW WOODEND GARDENS
Woodend Road, Crow, Ringwood, BH24 3DG. *Ringwood 2½ m. Take the Christchurch Rd (B3347) from Ringwood, after ⅓ m turn L onto Moortown Ln (signed Burley), after 1m Woodend Rd is on the L. Last house in road.* **Sat 10, Sun 11 Feb (11-4); Sat 31 Aug, Sun 1 Sept (11-5). Combined adm £8, chd free. Light refreshments.**

 HOLLYHURST
Mary Reddyhoff.
 TROLLS MEAD
Sheila Lister.

Trolls Mead is a 1 acre garden with interest throughout the yr, whether newly planted, in full bloom or left in its natural state with seed heads to create an architectural display or simply for the birds to appreciate. The wooded area and lake is still under construction but all are welcome to explore. The bottom meadow with its mown paths has SSSI status with natural wild flowers inc wild orchids. Hollyhurst is a 2 acre site of mature trees, shrubs and herbaceous perennials, which are generally resistant to deer, has been created on a freely draining acid soil. Ponds and small sculptures augment the vistas.

✿ ☕

88 WOODPECKERS CARE HOME
Sway Road, Brockenhurst, SO42 7RX. Chris Marsh. *New Forest. Signed from A337 Lymington to Brockenhurst road. Sway Rd to Brockenhurst centre. L then R past petrol station, then school & Woodpeckers on R.* **Sat 31 Aug, Sun 1 Sept (11-5). Adm £5, chd free. Home-made teas with dietary options.**
A vibrant and colourful garden surrounds our care home. We have active involvement from our residents who enjoy the wide paths, whether in a wheelchair or strolling on foot. The courtyard area, small orchard and woodland, all look particularly beautiful in spring and late summer with views through neighbouring fields. An amazing bug house, chainsaw sculpture and vibrant plantings will wow you!

& 🐎 ✿ ☕ 🪑 ⁕))

89 YEW HURST
Blissford, Fordingbridge, SP6 2JQ. Mr & Mrs Henry Richardson. *1m E of Fordingbridge in the New Forest. From Fordingbridge B3078 towards Brook. After approx 1m take R turn to Blissford. Downhill to water splash & Yew Hurst is 3rd house on the L after splash.* **Sat 22 June (10-5). Adm £5, chd free. Home-made teas.**
Set in a beautiful position in the New Forest this is the home of a keen gardener and plant lover. This small garden is filled with a glorious and extensive display of herbaceous perennials, roses and shrubs and a small area of wild flowers. The garden surrounds the house so that each area has its own character and there is a natural flow from one part to another.

D ☕

Bluebell Wood

ISLE OF WIGHT

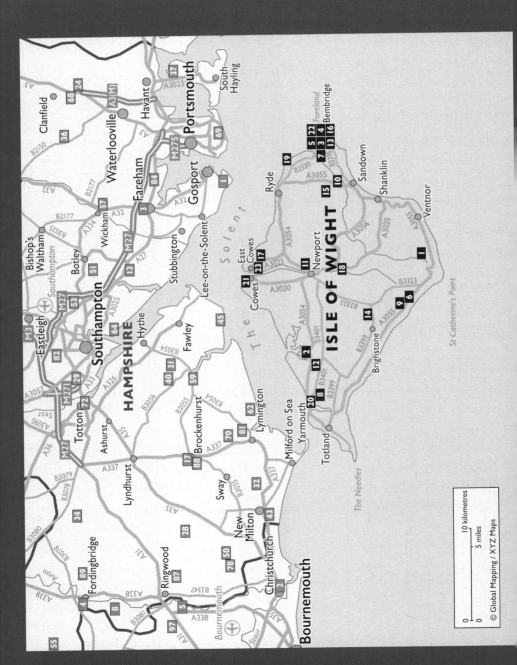

VOLUNTEERS

County Organiser
Jane Bland 01983 874592
jane.bland@ngs.org.uk

County Treasurer
Sally Parker 01983 612495
sally.parker@ngs.org.uk

Booklet Co-ordinator
Jane Bland (as above)

Booklet Advertising
Joanna Truman 01983 873822
joanna_truman@btinternet.com

Assistant County Organisers
Sally Parker
(as above)

Joanna Truman
(as above)

@iow_ngs

OPENING DATES

All entries subject to change.
For latest information check
www.ngs.org.uk

Map locator numbers are
shown to the right of each
garden name.

April

Sunday 14th
NEW Good Robins   9

May

Sunday 19th
Goldings   8
Morton Manor   10
Thorley Manor   20

June

Sunday 2nd
East Dene   6
NEW Elmslie House   7
NEW Norcott House   13
Northcott Manor Gardens   14

Saturday 8th
Rookley Gardens   18

Sunday 9th
East Cliff   5
Rookley Gardens   18

Wednesday 12th
NEW ◆ Osborne House   17

Sunday 16th
Darts   3
Yew Tree Lodge   22

Saturday 22nd
Ashknowle House   1

Sunday 23rd
Ashknowle House   1

Saturday 29th
NEW Mountbatten Hospice   11

Sunday 30th
NEW Mountbatten Hospice   11

July

Sunday 21st
Dove Cottage   4

August

Saturday 3rd
1 Union Road   21

Sunday 11th
Crab Cottage   2
Morton Manor   10
◆ Nunwell House   15

September

Sunday 22nd
NEW Good Robins   9

By Arrangement

Arrange a personalised garden visit
with your club, or group of friends,
on a date to suit you. See individual
garden entries for full details.

Crab Cottage   2
Morton Manor   10
Ningwood Manor   12
Northcourt Manor Gardens   14
NEW Oak House   16
Salterns Cottage   19
1 Union Road   21
NEW 163 York Avenue   23

National Garden
Scheme gardens are
identified by their
yellow road signs
and posters. You can
expect a garden of
quality, character
and interest, a warm
welcome and plenty of
home-made cakes!

THE GARDENS

1 ASHKNOWLE HOUSE

Ashknowle Lane, Whitwell, Ventnor, PO38 2PP. Mr & Mrs K Fradgley. *4m W of Ventnor. Take the Whitwell Rd from Ventnor or Godshill. Turn into unmade lane next to Old Rectory, ignore the no motor vehicles sign. Field parking. Disabled parking at house.* **Sat 22, Sun 23 June (12-4). Adm £5, chd free. Home-made teas.**
The mature garden of this Victorian house (not open) has great diversity inc woodland walks, water features, colourful beds and borders. The large, well maintained kitchen garden is highly productive and boasts a wide range of fruit and vegetables grown in cages, tunnels, glasshouses and raised beds. Diversely planted and highly productive orchard inc protected cropping of strawberries, peaches and apricots. Propagation areas for trees, shrubs and crops.

2 CRAB COTTAGE

Mill Road, Shalfleet, PO30 4NE. Mr & Mrs Scott, 07768 065756, mencia@icloud.com. *4½ m E of Yarmouth. At New Inn, Shalfleet, turn into Mill Rd. Continue 400yds to end of metalled road, drive onto unmade road through open NT gates. After 100yds pass Crab Cottage on L. Park opp on grass.* **Sun 11 Aug (11-5). Adm £4, chd free. Home-made teas. Visits also by arrangement May to Sept.**
1¼ acres on gravelly soil. Part glorious views across croquet lawn over Newtown Creek and Solent, leading through wildflower meadow to hidden water lily pond, secluded lawn and woodland walk. Part walled garden protected from westerlies with mixed borders, leading to terraced sunken garden with ornamental pool and pavilion, planted with exotics, tender shrubs and herbaceous perennials. Croquet, plant sales and excellent tea and cake. Wheelchair access over gravel and uneven grass paths.

3 DARTS

Darts Lane, Bembridge, PO35 5YH. Joanna Truman. *Up the hill from Bembridge Harbour, turn L after the Co-op down Love Ln & take 1st L. The house is painted grey.*

Sun 16 June (12.30-5). Combined adm with Yew Tree Lodge £7, chd free. Home-made teas at Yew Tree Lodge.
Classic walled garden with roses, climbers, shrubs, two large raised vegetable beds and running water feature. Access to garden via two raised steps and three steps up to top garden.

4 DOVE COTTAGE

Swains Lane, Bembridge, PO35 5ST. Mr James & Mrs Alex Hearn. *Head E on Lane End Rd, passing Lane End Court Shops on L. Take 3rd turning on L onto Swains Ln. Dove Cottage is on R.* **Sun 21 July (12.30-4). Adm £6, chd free. Light refreshments.**
An enclosed garden with lawn and woodland area. A central path leads through the woodland setting which has mature variegated shrubs and perennials, leading to the swimming pool area and tennis court.

5 EAST CLIFF

Love Lane, Bembridge, PO35 5NH. Kate & Ian Cheshire. *Disabled parking only. No on site parking as Love Ln cannot cope with two-way traffic, please park locally.* **Sun 9 June (11-2). Adm £8, chd free. Home-made teas.**
The garden is situated in Bembridge overlooking the sea. It is on a 15 acre plot with the lawn and garden covering about 8 acres. The garden was designed by Arabella Lennox Boyd in 2016. She has created rooms within the garden, they inc a white rose garden and a walled cottage garden and to the rear of the house there are six large herbaceous beds. We also have a wildflower meadow. Plants for sale. Cash preferred on the day! Last admission 1.30pm.

6 EAST DENE

Atherfield Green, Ventnor, PO38 2LF. Marc & Lisa Morgan-Huws. *From A3055 Military Rd, turn into Southdown. At end of road turn L on to Atherfield Rd & the garden is ahead on the R.* **Sun 2 June (11-4). Adm £4, chd free. Light refreshments.**
Planted from 2 acres of farmland in the 1970s, the garden is structured around a variety of mature trees. Taken over by brambles and nettles

prior to our arrival 8 yrs ago, the garden is continuing to be developed, whilst still being a haven for wildlife. Occupying a windswept coastal location with areas of woodland, fruit trees, mature pond and informal planting. Alpacas. Level wheelchair access over unmade ground.

7 NEW ELMSLIE HOUSE

49 Foreland Road, Bembridge, PO35 5XN. Dorian Campbell & Nigel Maclean. *From centre of village turn L into Foreland Rd. No. 49 is on the corner of Foreland Rd & Northclose Rd, on the L & shortly before zebra crossing.* **Sun 2 June (12.30-4.30). Combined adm with Norcott House £7, chd free. Home-made teas.**
The garden as it is now, was created in 2013 with the help of Cotswold garden designer, Katie Lukas. The Edwardian house (not open) stands back from the road, being screened by a row of flowering pear and crab apple trees, shrubs and a mature herbaceous border. The garden around the house is laid to lawn, flanked by ornamental trees, clematis, flower borders, rose beds and a wisteria clad pergola.

8 GOLDINGS

Thorley Street, Thorley, Yarmouth, PO41 0SN. John & Dee Sichel. *E of Yarmouth. Follow directions for Thorley from Yarmouth/Newport road or from Wilmingham Ln. Then follow NGS signs. Parking shared with Thorley Manor.* **Sun 19 May (2-5). Combined adm with Thorley Manor £5, chd free. Home-made teas at Thorley Manor.**
A country garden with many focuses of interest. A newly planted orchard already producing cider apples in large amounts. A small, but productive vegetable garden and a well maintained lawn with shrub borders and roses. A microclimate has been created by the adjustment of levels to create a series of terraced areas for planting.

Goldings

© Lucy Hooper

2 NEW GOOD ROBINS
Atherfield Road, Atherfield,
Ventnor, PO38 2LQ. Chris & Dianne
Davis. *2m S from The Crown,
Shorwell; via Farriers Way, Corve
Hill, Park Ln, Atherfield Rd. 3m NW
from The Wight Mouse, Chale via
Military Rd, Southdown, Atherfield
Rd. 9m W of Ventnor via Niton &
Mili Rd. What3words app - bonnet.
applauded.frogs. Parking in nearby
field. Blue Badge holders only on
site.* **Sun 14 Apr, Sun 22 Sept
(11-5). Adm £6, chd free. Light
refreshments.**
In spring the bulbs and blossoms
are amazing. A variety of interesting
trees and shrubs inc numerous acers,
hydrangeas and a new apple orchard
have been planted, a process which
continues. There are two ponds
featuring water lilies and irises, and a
connecting constructed stream. Four
varied island beds, a wild meadow
area and two raised vegetable beds
have been added.
🚍 ☕ ·))

10 MORTON MANOR
Morton Manor Road, Brading,
Sandown, PO36 0EP. Mr & Mrs
G Godliman, 07768 605900,
patricia.godliman@yahoo.co.uk.
*Off A3055, 5m S of Ryde, just out
of Brading. At Yarbridge T-lights
turn into The Mall. Take next L into
Morton Manor Rd.* **Sun 19 May, Sun
11 Aug (11-4). Adm £5, chd free.
Light refreshments. Visits also by
arrangement Apr to Oct.**
A colourful garden of great plant
variety. Mature trees inc many
acers with a wide variety of leaf
colour. Early in the season a display
of rhododendrons, azaleas and
camellias and later many perenials,
hydrangeas and hibiscus. Ponds,
sweeping lawns, roses set on a sunny
terrace and much more to see in
this extensive garden surrounding a
picturesque C16 manor house (not
open). Wheelchair access over gravel
driveway.
🚍 🐕 ✳ 🚗 ☕ ·))

**11 NEW MOUNTBATTEN
HOSPICE**
Halberry Lane, Newport,
PO30 2ER. Mountbatten Isle of
Wight, www.mountbatten.org.uk.
*5 mins from Newport. Halberry Ln is
off the A3054 Fairle Rd from either
Newport or Ryde. Or from Staplers
Rd take Cross Ln to Halberry Ln.
Bus 9 from Ryde or Newport. Bus
5 from East Cowes.* **Sat 29, Sun
30 June (1-4). Adm by donation.
Light refreshments.**
An award-winning Chelsea Garden
is part of Mountbatten Isle of Wight's
beautiful outside space. Designed
by Greenfingers and opened by Alan
Titchmarsh in 2016, the tranquil
gardens are lovingly tended to by
dedicated volunteers. Complementing
a variety of flowers and features,
the gardens offer a space for social
connections, quiet contemplation,
reflection and a backdrop for outdoor
events. Mountbatten Café on site
offering a range of home-made light
lunches, cakes, snacks and drinks.
🚍 🐕 ✳ ☕ ·))

Darts

Home-made teas. Visits also by arrangement 30 Mar to 15 Oct for groups of 5 to 50. Introductory talk & tour.
15 acre garden surrounding large C17 manor house (not open). Boardwalk along jungle garden. Stream and bog garden. A large variety of plants enjoying the different microclimates. Large collection of camellias and magnolias. Woodland walks. Tree collection. Salvias and subtropical plantings for autumn drama. Productive 1 acre walled kitchen garden. Numerous shrub roses. Picturesque wooded valley around the house. Bathhouse and snail mount leading to terraces. A plantsman' garden. Wheelchair access on main paths only, some paths are steep and uneven, and the terraces are hilly.

15 ♦ NUNWELL HOUSE
Coach Lane, Brading,
PO36 0JQ. Mr & Mrs S Bonsey,
info@nunwellhouse.co.uk,
www.nunwellhouse.co.uk. *3m S of Ryde. Signed off A3055 as you arrive at Brading from Ryde & turn into Coach Ln.* **For NGS: Sun 11 Aug (1-4.30). Adm £5, chd free. Home-made teas. For other opening times and information, please email or visit garden website.**
6 acres of tranquil and beautifully set formal and shrub gardens, and old-fashioned shrub roses prominent. Exceptional Solent views over historic parkland and Brading Haven from the terraces. Small arboretum and walled garden with herbaceous borders. House developed over 5 centuries and full of architectural interest.

16 NEW OAK HOUSE
Lane End Road, Bembridge,
PO35 5SZ. Dee Cuddigan,
07932 612558, dee@interchill.com. *At the Birdham Hotel turn down Lane End Rd towards Lifeboat Stn. After ½ m Oak House is on L after long black fence (Lane End House). Off road parking at front of property.* **Visits by arrangement 1 Apr to 14 July for groups of up to 10. Adm £7.50, chd free. Tea.**
Interesting late spring garden extending through three areas inc camellias, *Phillyrea latifolia* and hoheria. There is a small area of scented azaleas and rhododendron. A walled potager containing summer vegetables and herbs.

12 NINGWOOD MANOR
Station Road, Ningwood, nr
Newport, PO30 4NJ. Nicholas & Claire Oulton, 07738 737482, claireoulton@gmail.com. *Nr Shalfleet. From Newport, turn L opp the Horse & Groom Pub. Ningwood Manor is 300-400yds on the L. Please use 2nd set of gates.* **Visits by arrangement 1 May to 30 Aug for groups of up to 30. Adm £5. Light refreshments.**
A 3 acre, landscaped country garden divided into several areas: a walled courtyard, croquet lawn, white garden and kitchen garden. They flow into each other, each with their own gentle colour schemes; the exception to this is the croquet lawn garden which is a riot of colour, mixing oranges, reds, yellows and pinks. Much new planting has taken place over the last few yrs. The owners have several new projects underway, so the garden is a work in progress. Features inc a vegetable garden with raised beds and a small summerhouse, part of which is alleged to be Georgian. Please inform us at time of booking if wheelchair access is required.

13 NEW NORCOTT HOUSE
5 Norcott Drive, Bembridge,
PO35 5TX. Diana Bown. *The entrance to Norcott House is off Foreland Rd, directly opp the turning to Swains Rd.* **Sun 2 June (12.30-4.30). Combined adm with Elmslie House £7, chd free. Home-made teas.**
The Norcott garden is approx ½ acre and is predominantly planted with spring plants, roses and hydrangeas in several borders. It is surrounded by mature lime, horse chestnut and holm oak trees that were planted when the house had a 5 acre garden. There is a summerhouse and several sunny spots to sit and enjoy the garden. An oasis in the middle of the village. Wheelchairs access through the gates in Norcott Drive.

14 NORTHCOURT MANOR GARDENS
Main Road, Shorwell,
Newport, PO30 3JG. Mr & Mrs J Harrison, 01983 740415, john@northcourt.info, www.northcourt.info. *4m SW of Newport. On entering Shorwell from Newport, entrance at bottom of hill on R. If entering from other directions head through village in direction of Newport. Garden on the L, on bend after passing the church.* **Sun 2 June (11.30-5). Adm £7, chd free.**

17 NEW ◆ OSBORNE HOUSE

York Avenue, East Cowes,
PO32 6JY. English Heritage. *1m
SE of East Cowes. For SatNav use
postcode PO32 6JT.* **For NGS:
Evening opening Wed 12 June
(5.30-8). Adm £15. Pre-booking
essential, please phone 07721
813442, email alison.makosch@
english-heritage.org.uk or visit
www.english-heritage.org.uk/
visit/places/osborne/events
for information & booking.
Light refreshments available in
café prior to the tour. For other
opening times and information,
please phone, email or visit garden
website.**
A garden fit for a Queen: Explore the
family home of Queen Victoria and
Prince Albert on the Isle of Wight and
discover their love of the gardens
here. Wander amongst the ornate
terraces and the spectacular bedding
displays, the productive Victorian
walled garden, all set within the
historic wider parkland featuring trees
planted by Prince Albert, and even a
private beach.

❀ ☕

GROUP OPENING

18 ROOKLEY GARDENS

Rookley, Newport, PO30 3BJ.
*4m S of Newport. From the main
Newport to Sandown road, take
turning for Rookley at Blackwater.*
**Sat 8, Sun 9 June (11-4).
Combined adm £6, chd free.
Home-made teas at Oakdene.**

OAKDENE
Mr Tim Marshall.

OLD SCHOOL COTTAGE
Mr Nigel Palmer.

THE OLD STABLES
Mrs Susan Waldron.

A varied group of gardens diverse in
size, design and interest. Set within
the area of Rookley Village, these
gardens are in a well kept and lively
village. Features inc grassy pathways
with colourful borders and places to
rest, to beautiful designs displaying
a riot of colour, shape and form, plus
fruit and vegetables, wild flowers and
bees.

19 SALTERNS COTTAGE

Salterns Road, Seaview,
PO34 5AH. Susan & Noël
Dobbs, 01983 612132,
sk.dobbs@icloud.com. *E of Ryde.
Enter Seaview from W via Springvale,
Salterns Rd links the Duver Rd with
Bluett Ave.* **Visits by arrangement
Apr to Sept for groups of 5 to 20.
Wine & canapés or tea, coffee,
biscuits & cake on request.**
A glasshouse, a potager, exotic
borders and fruit trees are some of
the many attractions in this 40 metre
x 10 metre plot. Salterns Cottage
is a listed building built in 1640
and was bought in 1927 by Noël's
grandmother Florence, married to
Bram Stoker the author of Dracula.
The garden was created by Susan
in 2005 when she sold her school.
Flooding and sandy soil poses a
constant challenge to the planting.
The greenhouse and potager all
raised to cope with floods. Visitors
welcome to see garden renovation in
progress.

🐕 ❀ ☕

20 THORLEY MANOR

Thorley, Yarmouth, PO41 0SJ. Mr
& Mrs Blest. *1m E of Yarmouth.
From Bouldnor take Wilmingham Ln,
house ½ m on L.* **Sun 19 May (2-5).
Combined adm with Goldings £5,
chd free. Tea.**
Mature informal gardens of over 3
acres surrounding manor house (not
open). Garden set out in a number of
walled rooms, perennial and colourful
self-seeding borders, shrub borders,
lawns, large old trees and an unusual
island lawn, all seamlessly blending
into the surrounding farmland. The
delightful cottage garden of Goldings
is open, a short walk away.

♿ 🐕 ❀ ☕

21 1 UNION ROAD

Cowes, PO31 7TW. Mr & Mrs B
Hicks, georgeous1@gmail.com.
*Old Town. Take the Cowes Rd
(A3020) as far as Northwood T-lights
(by the car garage). Bear L & follow
signs for Northwood House. Parking
at Northwood House, PO31 8AZ,
then 3 min walk.* **Sat 3 Aug (11-5).
Adm £5, chd free. Home-made
teas. Visits also by arrangement
8 Apr to 22 Sept for groups of 5
to 50.**
A small, south facing town garden
with views of the Solent and plenty
of sea air. Planting is tropical and
takes full advantage of the many
hours of sunshine. A combination

of unusual plants from drier, arid
environments, with lush planting in
the zones towards the bottom of the
garden. Specimen trees and beautiful
walled garden area. A pond featuring
wildlife and Mediterranean planting.
Working area of the garden features
grapevines and olive, apple, fig, citrus
and walnut trees. A living agapanthus
wall and finally, a herb wall within the
outdoor kitchen. Garden designed
by Helen Elks-Smith in 2019.
Refreshments made from our garden
and allotment produce.

🐕 ❀ ☕))

22 YEW TREE LODGE

Love Lane, Bembridge, PO35 5NH.
Jane Bland. *On the Bembridge
circular one-way system, take 1st L
after Co-op into Love Ln. Darts is on
the L, Yew Tree Lodge is facing you
when Love Ln turns sharply to the R.*
**Sun 16 June (12.30-5). Combined
adm with Darts £7, chd free.
Home-made teas.**
Yew Tree Lodge garden is flanked by
mature oak trees and well established
gardens, its main axis being north
south. It is divided into separate areas
which take into account available
natural light and soil type. I have been
gardening here for 10 yrs, during this
time the garden has altered a great
deal. As well as flowering plants there
is a vegetable garden, fruit cages
and a cool greenhouse. Wheelchair
access over paved path connecting
the front and back gardens and
paved access to decking area.

♿ ❀ ☕))

23 NEW 163 YORK AVENUE

East Cowes, PO32 6BD. Mr
Roy Dorland, 07768 107779,
roydorland@hotmail.co.uk.
*Approach East Cowes through
Wippingham by the A3021. Pass
Barton Manor on R & continue past
Osborne House on R. York Ave on
L. Ample roadside parking on LHS.*
**Visits by arrangement May to
Sept for groups of 10 to 20. Adm
£5, chd free. Home-made teas.**
Situated near Osborne House, this
large colourful garden is packed with
unusual hardy perennials and many
lovely trees and shrubs. On the terrace
is a large date palm, and beyond the
main garden there are tropical plants
and ferns. You then pass through a
gate into a small meadow. There are
plenty of seats with tables throughout
this relaxing garden.

❀ ☕

KENT

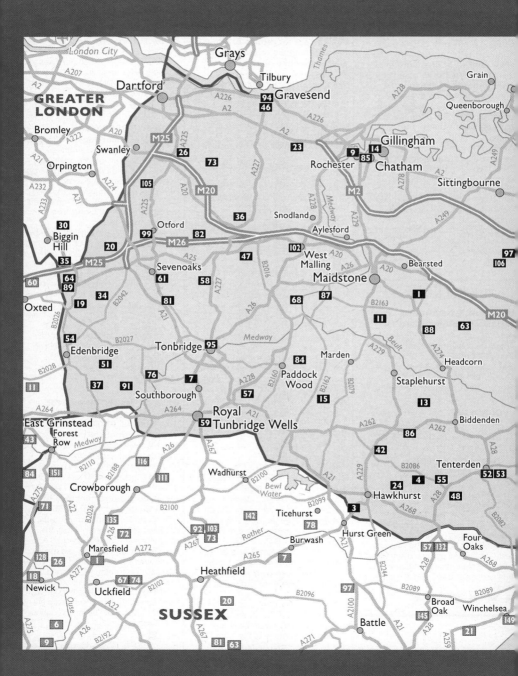

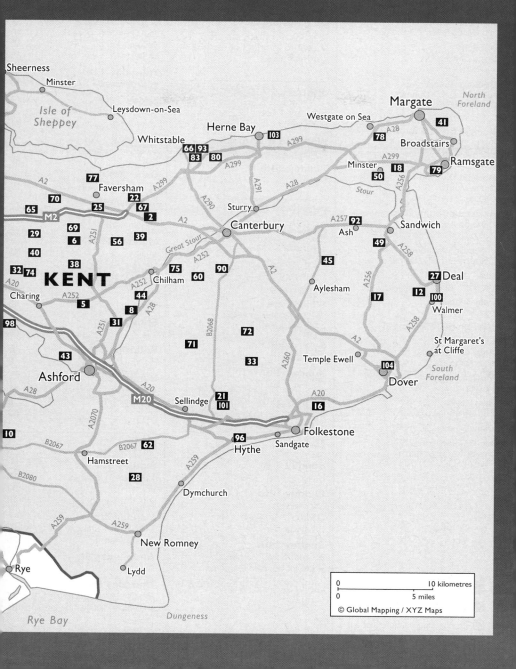

Sheerness

Minster

Isle of Sheppey

Leysdown-on-Sea

Whitstable

Herne Bay

Westgate on Sea

Margate

North Foreland

41

A28

78

Broadstairs

103

A299

A299

Minster

18

A299

A256

Ramsgate

79

A2

77

Faversham

A299

66 **93**

83 **80**

A299

Stour

70

22

65

M2

25

67

A290

Sturry

A291

A28

A257

92

Sandwich

2

A2

Canterbury

Ash

49

A258

29

69

A251

56

39

Great Stour

6

45

A256

40

A252

75

90

A2

17

32 **74**

38

KENT

A252

Chilham

60

Aylesham

A258

27 Deal

Charing

A252

5

B2068

Temple Ewell

12 **100**

Walmer

A20

98

44

A28

8

72

A2

St Margaret's at Cliffe

A251

31

71

33

A260

104

South Foreland

43

Ashford

M20

21

101

A20

Dover

16

A28

Sellindge

96

Folkestone

A2070

10

B2067

B2067

62

Hythe

Sandgate

Hamstreet

A259

28

B2080

A259

Dymchurch

A259

A259

New Romney

Rye

Lydd

Rye Bay

Dungeness

0		10 kilometres
0		5 miles

© Global Mapping / XYZ Maps

VOLUNTEERS

County Organiser
Jane Streatfeild 01342 850362
janestreatfeild@btinternet.com

County Treasurer
Andrew McClintock 01732 838605
andrew.mcclintock@ngs.org.uk

Publicity
Susie Challen
susie.challen@ngs.org.uk

Booklet Advertising
Nicola Denoon-Duncan
01233 758600
nicola.denoonduncan@ngs.org.uk

Booklet Co-ordinator
Ingrid Morgan Hitchcock
01892 528341
ingrid@morganhitchcock.co.uk

Booklet Distribution
Diana Morrish 07831 432528
diana.morrish@ngs.org.uk

Assistant County Organisers
Deborah Anderson
deborah.anderson@ngs.org.uk

Jacqueline Anthony 01892 518879
jacquelineanthony7@gmail.com

Clare Barham 01580 241386
clarebarham@holepark.com

Pam Bridges
pam.bridges@ngs.co.uk

Mary Bruce 01795 531124
mary.bruce@ngs.org.uk

Andy Garland
andy.garland@bbc.co.uk

Virginia Latham 01303 862881
virginia.latham@ngs.org.uk

Sian Lewis
sian.lewis@ngs.org.uk

Diana Morrish (as above)

Nicola Talbot 01342 850526
nicola@falconhurst.co.uk

f @KentNGS

X @NGSKent

@nationalgardenschemekent

OPENING DATES

All entries subject to change.
For latest information check
www.ngs.org.uk

Map locator numbers are
shown to the right of each
garden name.

January

Sunday 21st
Spring Platt   88

Wednesday 24th
Spring Platt   88

Sunday 28th
Spring Platt   88

February

Snowdrop Openings

Thursday 1st
Spring Platt   88

Saturday 3rd
Knowle Hill Farm   63

Sunday 4th
Knowle Hill Farm   63
Spring Platt   88

Saturday 10th
Copton Ash   25

Sunday 18th
Copton Ash   25

Sunday 25th
◆ Doddington Place   29

March

Sunday 3rd
Haven   50

Sunday 17th
Copton Ash   25
Godmersham Park   44
Stonewall Park   91

Sunday 24th
◆ Great Comp Garden   47
◆ Mount Ephraim Gardens   67

April

Monday 1st
◆ Cobham Hall   23
Copton Ash   25

Sunday 7th
Balmoral Cottage   4
Frith Old Farmhouse   40
Haven   50
Nettlestead Place   68

Thursday 11th
◆ Boldshaves   10

Friday 12th
Oak Cottage and Swallowfields
Nursery   71

Saturday 13th
◆ Godinton House & Gardens   43
The Knoll Farm   62
Oak Cottage and Swallowfields
Nursery   71

Sunday 14th
Copton Ash   25
◆ Hole Park   55

Monday 15th
◆ Hever Castle & Gardens   51

Sunday 21st
Balmoral Cottage   4
Bilting House   8
Frith Old Farmhouse   40

Friday 26th
NEW 6 Marine Parade   66

Saturday 27th
Bishopscourt   9

Sunday 28th
◆ Boughton Monchelsea Place   11
Eagleswood   32
Haven   50

May

Sunday 5th
1 Brickwall Cottages   13
NEW 1 Fox Cottages   39
Frith Old Farmhouse   40

Monday 6th
1 Brickwall Cottages   13
Copton Ash   25

Wednesday 8th
The Old Rectory, Otterden   74

Thursday 9th
The Old Rectory, Otterden   74
◆ Riverhill Himalayan Gardens   81

Friday 10th

Oak Cottage and Swallowfields Nursery	71

Saturday 11th

Avalon	2
◆ Godinton House & Gardens	43
Oak Cottage and Swallowfields Nursery	71

Sunday 12th

Avalon	2
Haven	50
The Orangery	75
43 The Ridings	80
Stonewall Park	91

Wednesday 15th

Great Maytham Hall	48
◆ Hole Park	55

Friday 17th

◆ Squerryes Court	89

Saturday 18th

◆ Beech Court Gardens	5
Little Gables	64
Tankerton Gardens	93

Sunday 19th

◆ Beech Court Gardens	5
Bilting House	8
Copton Ash	25
Frith Old Farmhouse	40
Little Gables	64
St Clere	82

Wednesday 22nd

◆ Doddington Place	29

Sunday 26th

The Coach House	22
Haven	50
Old Bladbean Stud	72
Windy Ridge	104

Monday 27th

The Coach House	22
Eagleswood	32
Falconhurst	37

June

Sunday 2nd

◆ Belmont	6
West Malling Early Summer Gardens	102

Saturday 8th

Avalon	2
Elham Gardens	33
The Garden Gate	41
NEW Hospice in the Weald	57
◆ Ightham Mote	58
Little Gables	64

Sunday 9th

Avalon	2
Downs Court	31
Elham Gardens	33
Godmersham Park	44
Haven	50
Little Gables	64
Nettlestead Place	68
Old Bladbean Stud	72

Monday 10th

Norton Court	70

Tuesday 11th

Norton Court	70

Wednesday 12th

Balmoral Cottage	4
◆ Hole Park	55

Thursday 13th

◆ Goodnestone Park Gardens	45
◆ Mount Ephraim Gardens	67
◆ Riverhill Himalayan Gardens	81

Friday 14th

◆ Godinton House & Gardens	43

Saturday 15th

Bishopscourt	9
Brompton Village Gardens	14
Falconhurst	37
95 High Street	52
NEW 99 High Street	53
Ivy Chimneys	59
Stable House, Heppington	90
Walmer Gardens	100

Sunday 16th

Brewery Farmhouse	12
Brompton Village Gardens	14
Chevening	20
Downs Court	31
95 High Street	52
NEW 99 High Street	53
Stable House, Heppington	90
Walmer Gardens	100
◆ The World Garden at Lullingstone Castle	105

Wednesday 19th

Great Maytham Hall	48

Saturday 22nd

NEW Court Lodge	26

Sunday 23rd

Downs Court	31
NEW Farriers Cottage	38
Old Bladbean Stud	72

Friday 28th

Pheasant Barn	77

Saturday 29th

69 Capel Street	16
Pheasant Barn	77
Sir John Hawkins Hospital	85

Sunday 30th

Bidborough Gardens	7
69 Capel Street	16
Deal Town Gardens	27
Haven	50
Pheasant Barn	77
Sir John Hawkins Hospital	85
Smiths Hall	87
Torry Hill	97
Yokes Court	106

July

Monday 1st

Pheasant Barn	77

Wednesday 3rd

Pheasant Barn	77

Thursday 4th

◆ Knole	61
Pheasant Barn	77

Friday 5th

Hoppickers East	56

Saturday 6th

NEW Chapel Farmhouse	17
Eureka	35

Sunday 7th

NEW Chapel Farmhouse	17
Eureka	35
Goddards Green	42
Gravesend Garden for Wildlife	46
NEW 2 Highfields Road	54
NEW Lynsted Community Kitchen Garden	65
NEW New Barns Farm	69
Old Bladbean Stud	72
Pheasant Barn	77

Monday 8th

Pheasant Barn	77

Wednesday 10th

Tonbridge School	95

Sunday 14th

◆ Boughton Monchelsea Place	11
Haven	50
◆ Quex Gardens	78

Tuesday 16th

Avalon	2

Friday 19th

Hoppickers East	56

Sunday 21st

Old Bladbean Stud	72
Sweetbriar	92

Tuesday 23rd

NEW ◆ Down House	30

Saturday 27th

The Orangery	75
Topgallant	96

Sunday 28th

The Orangery	75
Topgallant	96

August

Friday 2nd

Hoppickers East	56

Saturday 3rd

Eureka	35
NEW 1 Fox Cottages	39
Grove Manor	49
Hoppickers East	56
Knowle Hill Farm	63

Sunday 4th

Eureka	35
Grove Manor	49
Haven	50
Knowle Hill Farm	63

Saturday 10th

Avalon	2
NEW Thames House	94

Sunday 11th

Avalon	2
NEW Thames House	94

Friday 16th

Hoppickers East	56

Sunday 18th

Chapel House Estate	18
Sweetbriar	92

Friday 23rd

NEW 6 Marine Parade	66

Sunday 25th

Haven	50
White Horses	103

Wednesday 28th

◆ Doddington Place	29

Saturday 31st

Ivy Chimneys	59

September

Wednesday 4th

◆ Emmetts Garden	34

Sunday 8th

The Copper House	24
NEW 2 Highfields Road	54
Ramsgate Gardens	79
The Silk House	84
◆ Sissinghurst Castle Garden	86

Wednesday 11th

◆ Chartwell	19

Thursday 12th

◆ Goodnestone Park Gardens	45

Sunday 15th

Sweetbriar	92

Wednesday 18th

◆ Penshurst Place & Gardens	76

Friday 20th

◆ Godinton House & Gardens	43

Saturday 21st

45 Seymour Avenue	83

Sunday 22nd

◆ Doddington Place	29
Haven	50
45 Seymour Avenue	83

Sunday 29th

◆ Mount Ephraim Gardens	67

October

Sunday 13th

◆ Hole Park	55

Sunday 20th

Haven	50

Sunday 27th

◆ Great Comp Garden	47

November

Sunday 10th

Haven	50

February 2025

Sunday 2nd

Copton Ash	25

Sunday 16th

Copton Ash	25

By Arrangement

Arrange a personalised garden visit with your club, or group of friends, on a date to suit you. See individual garden entries for full details.

Arnold Yoke	1
Avalon	2
Badgers	3
Boundes End, Bidborough Gardens	7
Brewery Farmhouse	12
1 Brickwall Cottages	13
Cacketts Farmhouse	15
Churchfield	21
The Coach House	22
The Copper House	24
Copton Ash	25
NEW Court Lodge	26
Dean House	28
Downs Court	31
Eagleswood	32
Eureka	35
NEW Fairseat Manor	36
Frith Old Farmhouse	40
The Garden Gate	41
Goddards Green	42
Godmersham Park	44
Gravesend Garden for Wildlife	46
Haven	50
NEW 2 Highfields Road	54
Kenfield Hall	60
Knowle Hill Farm	63
Norton Court	70
The Old Rectory, Fawkham	73
The Old Rectory, Otterden	74
The Orangery	75
Pheasant Barn	77
43 The Ridings	80
45 Seymour Avenue	83
Spring Platt	88
NEW Thames House	94
Tram Hatch	98
Troutbeck	99
West Court Lodge	101
Woodlea, Grams Road, Walmer Gardens	100

100 inpatients and their families are being supported at the newly opened Horatio's Garden Wales, thanks to the National Garden Scheme donations

THE GARDENS

◻ ARNOLD YOKE

Back Street, Leeds, Maidstone, ME17 1TF. Richard & Patricia Stileman, 07968 787950, richstileman@btinternet.com. *5m E of Maidstone. Fm M20 J8 take A20 Lenham R to B2163 to Leeds. Through Leeds R into Horseshoes Ln, 1st R into Back St. House ¾ m on L. From A274 follow B2163 to Langley L into Horseshoes Ln 1st R Back St.* **Visits by arrangement 13 May to 9 Sept for groups of 10 to 20. Entry price inc tea and cake, plus talk and tour of the garden. Adm £10.**
The garden is really a ½ acre 'room', bounded by a yew hedge to the South; an ivy 'wall' to the West; a rock garden to the North; and the house to the East. There is a paradise garden and pond in the middle, and profusely planted borders on the South and West sides. The planting aims for innovative combinations and follows a succession that yields colour from March to October. Framework of yew and box hedging. Water featuring in paradise garden. Extensive planting of small trees of special interest. Borders planted to offer interest from March to October. Wheelchair access from the car park and around most parts of the garden.

&. ☕))

◻ AVALON

57 Stoney Road, Dunkirk, ME13 9TN. Mrs Croll, avalongarden8@gmail.com. *4m E of Faversham, 5m W of Canterbury, 2½ m E of J7 M2. M2 J7 or A2 E of Faversham take A299, first L, Staplestreet, then L, R past Mt Ephraim, turn L, R. From A2 Canterbury, turn off Dunkirk, bottom hill turn R, Staplestreet then R, R. Park in side roads.* **Sat 11, Sun 12 May, Sat 8, Sun 9 June, Tue 16 July, Sat 10, Sun 11 Aug (11- 4.30). Adm £6, chd free. Visits also by arrangement May to Aug for groups of 5 to 30. Parking is limited, mainly on local roads, so car sharing is preferable.**
½ acre edge of woodland garden, for all seasons, on north west slope, something round every corner, views of surrounding countryside. Collections of roses, hostas and ferns plus rhododendrons, shrubs, trees, vegetables, fruit, unusual plants and flowers. Planted by feeling, making it a reflective space and plant lovers' garden. Plenty of seating for taking in the garden and resting from lots of steps. Wide variety of plants and planting zones. Friendly chickens. Borrowed countryside landscape and views across Thames estuary.

🐐 ✿ 🪑))

◻ BADGERS

Bokes Farm, Horns Hill, Hawkhurst, Cranbrook, TN18 4XG. Bronwyn Cowdery, 01580 754178, cowderyfamily@btinternet.com. *On the border of Kent & E Sussex. In centre of Hawkhurst, follow A229 in the direction of Hurst Green. Pass the The Wealden Advertiser. At sharp L bend turn R up Horns Hill. Drive slowly up Horns Hill.* **Visits by arrangement 21 Aug to 25 Sept for groups of 8 to 25. Adm £5, chd free. Home-made teas.**
The garden comes into its own from end of August, when the Tropical Garden is in full growth. There is also a walled Italian style garden, small Japanese area and woodland with ponds and a waterfall. The Tropical Garden has a wide variety of Palms, Bananas, Gingers, Eucomis and Dahlias and has a network of paths threading through for you to explore and immerse yourself in the Tropics.

✿ ☕

43 The Ridings

© Leigh Clapp

4 BALMORAL COTTAGE
The Green, Benenden, Cranbrook, TN17 4DL. Charlotte Molesworth, thepottingshedholidaylet@gmail.com. *Few 100 yds down unmade track to W of St George's Church, Benenden.* **Sun 7, Sun 21 Apr (12-5). Wed 12 June (12-5), open nearby Hole Park. Adm £6, chd £2.50. Light refreshments at Hole Park (separate additional price).**
An owner created and maintained garden now 40 yrs mature. Varied, romantic and extensive topiary form the backbone for mixed borders. Vegetable garden, organically managed. Particular attention to the needs of nesting birds and small mammals lend this artistic plantswoman's garden a rare and unusual quality. No hot borders or dazzling dahlias here.

5 ◆ BEECH COURT GARDENS
Canterbury Road, Challock, Ashford, TN25 4DJ. Chloë & Garth Oates, www.beechcourtgardens.co.uk. *5m N of Ashford, Faversham 6m, Canterbury 9m. W of Xrds A251/A252, off the Lees.* **For NGS: Sat 18, Sun 19 May (11-4.30). Adm £5, chd free. For other opening times and information, please visit garden website.**
Beech Court Gardens are well established, planted in the 1930s. Exceptional collection of Acers and Rhododendron, along with numerous firs, oaks and pines. Many rare and unusual trees grow here and are home to many species of bird. The Gardens have been enhanced with island beds, climbing roses and hydrangeas. Please visit the gallery on our website.

6 ◆ BELMONT
Belmont Park, Throwley, Faversham, ME13 0HH. Harris (Belmont) Charity, 01795 890202, administrator@belmont-house.org, www.belmont-house.org. *4½ m SW of Faversham. A251 Faversham-Ashford. At Badlesmere, brown tourist signs to Belmont.* **For NGS: Sun 2 June (11-4). Adm £7, chd free. Light refreshments inc home-made cakes. For other opening times and information, please phone, email or visit garden website.**
Belmont House is surrounded by large formal lawns that are landscaped with fine specimen trees, a pinetum and a walled garden containing long borders, wisteria and large rose border. Across the drive there is a second walled kitchen garden, restored in 2001 to a design by Arabella Lennox-Boyd inc vegetable and herbaceous borders, hop arbours and walls trained with a variety of fruit.

GROUP OPENING

7 BIDBOROUGH GARDENS
Bidborough, Tunbridge Wells, TN4 0XB. *3m N of Tunbridge Wells, between Tonbridge & Tunbridge Wells W off A26. Take B2176 Bidborough Ridge signed to Penshurst. Take 1st L into Darnley Drive, then 1st R into St Lawrence Ave, no. 2.* **Sun 30 June (1-5). Combined adm £7, chd free. Home-made teas at Boundes End inc gluten & dairy free options. Donation to Hospice in the Weald.**

BOUNDES END
Carole & Mike Marks, 01892 542233, carole.marks@btinternet.com, www.boundesendgarden.co.uk. **Visits also by arrangement 23 June to 30 Aug for groups of up to 20.**

4 THE CRESCENT
Mrs Ann Tyler.

DARNLEY LODGE
Frances & Carl Stick.

SHEERDROP
Mr John Perry.

The Bidborough gardens (collect garden list from Boundes End, 2 St Lawrence Avenue) are in a small village at the heart of which are The Kentish Hare pub (book in advance), the church, village store and primary school. Partial wheelchair access, some gardens have steps. Please phone if you have access queries.

8 BILTING HOUSE
nr Ashford, TN25 4HA. Mr John Erle-Drax. *5m NE of Ashford. A28, 5m E from Ashford, 9m S from Canterbury. Wye 1½ m.* **Sun 21 Apr, Sun 19 May (1-5.30). Adm £7, chd free. Home-made teas.**
6 acre garden with ha-ha set in beautiful part of Stour Valley. Wide variety of rhododendrons, azaleas and ornamental shrubs. Woodland walk with spring bulbs. Mature arboretum with recent planting of specimen trees. Rose garden and herbaceous borders.

9 BISHOPSCOURT
24 St Margaret's Street, Rochester, ME1 1TS. *Central Rochester, nr castle & cathedral. On St Margaret's St at junc with Vines Ln.* **Sat 27 Apr, Sat 15 June (11-2). Adm £5, chd free. Home-made teas.**
Bishopscourt has been home to Bishops of Rochester since 1920 with the walled garden providing a secluded oasis. The garden has been continuously developed for over a decade with lawns, mature trees, hedging, rose garden, gravel garden, mixed herbaceous borders, meadow, glasshouse, vegetable garden and secret garden with a raised 'lookout' offering views of the castle and the river.

10 ◆ BOLDSHAVES
Woodchurch, Kent, nr Ashford, TN26 3RA. Mr & Mrs Peregrine Massey, 01233 860283, masseypd@hotmail.co.uk, www.boldshaves.co.uk. *Between Woodchurch & High Halden off Redbrook St. From centre of Woodchurch, with church on L & Bonny Cravat/Six Bells pubs on R, 2nd L down Susan's Hill, then 1st R after ½ m before L after a few 100 yrds to Boldshaves. Straight on past oast on L.* **For NGS: Thur 11 Apr (2-6). Adm £7.50, chd free. Home-made teas in the Cliff Tea House (weather permitting), otherwise in the Barn. For other opening times and information, please phone, email or visit garden website. Donation to Kent Minds.**
7 acre garden developed over past 30 yrs, partly terraced, south facing, with wide range of ornamental trees and shrubs, walled garden, Italian garden, Diamond Jubilee garden, Camellia Dell, herbaceous borders (inc flame bed, red borders and rainbow border), vegetable garden, bluebell walks in April, woodland and ponds; wildlife haven renowned for nightingales and butterflies. Home of the Wealden Literary Festival. Grass paths & slope.

1 Brickwall Cottages

© Marianne Majerus

☷ ◆ BOUGHTON MONCHELSEA PLACE

Church Hill, Boughton Monchelsea, Maidstone, ME17 4BU. Mr & Mrs Dominic Kendrick, 01622 743120, mk@boughtonplace.co.uk, www.boughtonplace.co.uk. *4m SE of Maidstone. For SatNav use ME17 4HP. What3words app - couch.blocks. picked. From Maidstone follow A229 S for 3½ m to T-lights at Linton Xrds, turn L onto B2163, house 1m on R; or take J8 off M20 & follow Leeds Castle signs to B2163, house 5½ m on L.* **For NGS: Sun 28 Apr, Sun 14 July (2-5.30). Adm £5, chd £1. Home-made teas. Cash payment only. For other opening times and information, please phone, email or visit garden website.**

150 acre estate mainly park and woodland, spectacular views over own deer park and the Weald. Grade I manor house (not open). Courtyard herb garden, intimate walled gardens, box hedges, herbaceous borders, orchard. Planting is romantic rather than manicured. Terrace with panoramic views, bluebell woods, wisteria tunnel, David Austin roses, traditional greenhouse and kitchen garden. Visit St. Peter's Church next door to see the huge stained glass Millennium Window designed by renowned local artist Graham Clark and the tranquil rose garden overlooking the deer park of Boughton Place.

✿ ☕ ☕

☲ BREWERY FARMHOUSE

182 Mongeham Road, Great Mongeham, Deal, CT14 9LR. Mr David & Mrs Maureen Royston-Lee, 07966 202243, david@davidroystonlee.com. *On the corner of Mongeham Rd & Northbourne Rd. Opp the village green, with a white picket fence at the front of the house, entrance to the gardens are through the Brewery yard at the back of the house - entrance on Northbourne Rd.* **Sun 16 June (11-4). Adm £6, chd free. Light refreshments. Visits also by arrangement 1 June to 2 Aug for groups of 5 to 35.**

An established country walled garden divided into a series of 'rooms'. Roses, clematis, poppies abound in herbaceous borders and against walls and trellises. With water features, fruit tree pergola and a Chinese pagoda. There is a gravel drive and one step up into the garden.

♿ ☕ ⟂))

☳ 1 BRICKWALL COTTAGES

Frittenden, Cranbrook, TN17 2DH. Mrs Sue Martin, 01580 852425, suemartin41@icloud.com, www.geumcollection.co.uk. *6m NW of Tenterden. E of A229 between Cranbrook & Staplehurst & W of A274 between Biddenden & Headcorn. Park in village & walk along footpath opp school.* **Sun 5, Mon 6 May (2-5). Adm £6, chd free. Home-made teas. Visits also by arrangement 15 Apr to 2 June for groups of up to 30. Donation to Plant Heritage.**

The garden is a secluded oasis in the centre of the village. It is filled with a wide range of plants, inc many trees, shrubs, perennials and over 100 geums which make up the National Collection. In an effort to attract more wildlife some areas of grass have been left unmown, and a new butterfly and moth 'meadow' was created during lockdown to replace the main nursery area. Some paths are narrow and wheelchairs may not be able to reach far end of garden.

♿ 🐕 ✿ ☕ NPC ☕

GROUP OPENING

14 BROMPTON VILLAGE GARDENS
Garden Street and Prospect Row, Brompton, Gillingham, ME7 5AL. Jennifer Jones. *Brompton is between Chatham & Gillingham A231 - Dock Rd next to Historic Dockyard. At r'about take A231 Wood St, opp. RSME Barracks enter Mansion Row, 1st L Garden St. Road parking in village.* **Sat 15, Sun 16 June (2-5). Combined adm £5, chd free. Home-made teas at 26 Garden Street. Home made cakes, cream teas, tea and coffee.**

26 GARDEN STREET
Mrs Lissie Larkin.

7 PROSPECT ROW
Ms Elaine Fowler.

16 PROSPECT ROW
Jennifer Jones.

NEW 19 PROSPECT ROW
Karen and Neil Fabian Burgess.

Brompton Village Gardens has 4 small town gardens, redesigned by their owners, opening in 2 adjacent streets in historic Brompton. 16 Prospect Row is a plantswoman's garden full of planting to encourage wildlife and with unusual planting. 19 Prospect Row is an elegant Italianate garden. 7 Prospect Row was completely redesigned from scratch after extensive building works and a photographic display shows before and after transformation photos. The planting is now maturing into an elegant colourful garden with a variety of plants complemented by seating areas. 26 Garden Street is a colourful English country garden full of classic planting with summerhouse and relaxed seating areas.
✿ ☕))

15 CACKETTS FARMHOUSE
Haymans Hill, Horsmonden, TN12 8BX. Mr & Mrs Lance Morrish, 07831 432528, diana.morrish@hotmail.co.uk. *Take B2162 from Horsmonden towards Marden. 1st R into Haymans Hill, 200yds 1st L, drive immed to R of Little Cacketts.* **Visits by arrangement June & July for groups of 15 to 30.**
1½ acre garden surrounding C17 farmhouse (not open). Walled garden, bog garden and ponds, woodland garden with unusual plants, bug hotel. 4 acre hayfield with self planted wildflowers.
♿ 🐾 🐕 ☕

16 69 CAPEL STREET
Capel-Le-Ferne, Folkestone, CT18 7LY. John & Jenny Carter. *Take B2011 from Folkestone towards Dover. Past Battle of Britain Memorial on R & then take first L into Capel Street. 69 is 400yds on L.* **Sat 29, Sun 30 June (10-4). Adm £5, chd free. Home-made teas.**
A contemporary urban cottage garden. A clever use of traditional and modern planting providing colour throughout the seasons. A rectangular garden where straight lines have been diffused by angles and planting. Space is provided for vegetables for self sufficiency. A quiet location occasionally amplified by a passing Spitfire. Walking distance to the famous Battle of Britain Memorial and pleasant walks along the White Cliffs of Dover. Garden access for wheelchairs can be achieved via the garage.
♿ 🐾 🐕 ☕

17 NEW CHAPEL FARMHOUSE
Lower Street, Tilmanstone, Deal, CT14 0HY. Nigel Watts and Tanuja Pandit. *4m North of Dover. Exit the A256 at the Tilmanstone r'about then take immediate R to Dover Rd. Garden is 100 yds down Chapel Rd which is on the L past the Plough and Harrow. Parking available on Dover Rd.* **Sat 6, Sun 7 July (12-6). Adm £5, chd free. Home-made teas.**
Recently established small garden designed by Kristina Clode on three sides of a semi-detached listed farmhouse. It is divided into a number of separate spaces in a courtyard style front garden, a Japanese style garden with pond, a formal lawn area, deep herbaceous borders, a meadow with fruit trees and a formal vegetable garden. Emphasis on sustainability and friendliness to wildlife. Wheelchair access via rear gate. Front garden and adjacent pond area is not accessible by wheelchair but can be viewed from other parts.
♿ Ⓓ ☕))

18 CHAPEL HOUSE ESTATE
Thorne Hill, Ramsgate, CT12 5DS. Chapel House Estate, www.chapelhouseestate.co.uk. *3m W of Ramsgate. From Canterbury take A253 towards Ramsgate, from Sandwich take A256 towards Ramsgate. At Sevenscore r'about take slip road turn R, Cottington Rd, follow Chapel House Estate signs.* **Sun 18 Aug (1-5). Adm £6, chd £3. Cream teas at the Walled Courtyard. The No 9 Restaurant will be open please book through www.chapelhouseestate.co.uk/ no-9-restaurant-courtyard.**
Beautifully proportioned and designed garden show-casing established grasses, mixed perennials and unusual shrubs all set within an architectural framework of clipped yew. Coffee, tea and cakes served from the Walled Courtyard. 35 acre estate, with Arts and Craft style gardens, a wild apple orchard and C13 Chapel House. Helipad just off the Orchard.
🐕 ✿ 🚗 ☕))

19 ✦ CHARTWELL
Mapleton Road, Westerham, TN16 1PS. National Trust, 01732 868381, chartwell@ nationaltrust.org.uk, www. nationaltrust.org.uk/chartwell. *4m N of Edenbridge, 2m S of Westerham. Fork L off B2026 after 1½m.* **For NGS: Wed 11 Sept (10-4). Adm £8, chd free. Light refreshments. For other opening times and information, please phone, email or visit garden website.**
Informal gardens on hillside with glorious views over Weald of Kent. Water features and lakes together with red brick wall built by Sir Winston Churchill, former owner of Chartwell. Lady Churchill's rose garden. Avenue of golden roses runs down the centre of a must see productive kitchen garden. Hard paths to Lady Churchill's rose garden and the terrace. Some steep slopes and steps.
♿ 🐾 🐕 ✿ 🚗 ☕

20 CHEVENING
nr Sevenoaks, TN14 6HG. The Board of Trustees of the Chevening Estate, www.cheveninggardens.com. *4m NW of Sevenoaks. Turn N off A25 at Sundridge T-lights on to B2211; at Chevening Xrds 1½m turn L.* **Sun 16 June (2-5). Adm £10, chd £1. Home-made teas. Local ice**

cream, picnic area.

The pleasure grounds of the Earls Stanhope at Chevening House are today characterised by lawns and wooded walks around an ornamental lake. First laid out between 1690 and 1720 in the French formal style, in the 1770s a more informal English design was introduced. In the early C19 lawns, parterres and a maze were established, a lake was created from the ornamental canal and basin, and many specimen trees were planted to shade woodland walks. Expert-guided group tours of the park and gardens can sometimes be arranged with the Estate Office when the house is unoccupied. Gentle slopes, gravel paths throughout.

21 CHURCHFIELD

Pilgrims Way, Postling, Hythe, CT21 4EY. Chris & Nikki Clark, 01303 863558/07415 263413, coulclark@hotmail.com. 2m NW of Hythe. From M20 J11 turn S onto A20. 1st L after ½m on bend take road signed Lyminge. 1st L into Postling. **Visits by arrangement Mar to Oct for groups of up to 35. Combined with West Court Lodge. Home-made teas.**
At the base of the Downs, springs rising in this garden form the source of the East Stour. Two large ponds are home to wildfowl and fish and the banks have been planted with drifts of primula, large leaved herbaceous bamboo and ferns. The rest of the 5 acre garden is a Kent cobnut platt and vegetable garden, large grass areas and naturally planted borders and woodland. Postling Church open for visitors.

22 THE COACH HOUSE

Kemsdale Road, Hernhill, Faversham, ME13 9JP. Alison & Philip West, 07801 824867, alison. west@kemsdale.plus.com. 3m E of Faversham. At J7 of M2 take A299, signed Margate. After 600 metres take 1st exit signed Hernhill, take 1st L over dual carriageway to T-junc, turn R & follow yellow NGS signs. **Sun 26, Mon 27 May (11-5). Adm £7, chd free. Cream teas. Visits also by arrangement 4 May to 30 Sept. Refreshments can be supplied with prior arrangement at an agreed price.**
The ¾ acre garden has views over surrounding fruit-producing farmland. Sloping terraced site and island beds with year-round interest, a pond room, herbaceous borders containing bulbs, shrubs, perennials and a tropical bed. The different areas are connected by flowing curved paths. Unusual planting on light sandy soil where wildlife is encouraged. Some garden accessible to wheelchairs but some slopes. Seating available in all areas.

23 ◆ COBHAM HALL

Brewers Road, Cobham, DA12 3BL. Estates Manager: Jeroen Allen. Commercial Manager: Louis Glynn-Williams, 01474 823371 www.cobhamhall.com. 3m W of Rochester, 8m E of M25 J2. Entrance drive is off Brewers Rd, 50 metres E from Cobham/Shorne A2 junction. Closest train stn: Sole St (2.8m) or Ebbsfleet International (6.8m). **For NGS: Mon 1 Apr (2-5). Adm £5, chd free. Cream teas in the Gilt Hall. For other opening times and information, please visit garden website.**
Landscaped for the 4th Earl of Darnley by Humphrey Repton, the gardens inc extensive tree planting, The Gothic Dairy, The Pump House and some of the classical garden buildings are also being renovated for all our visitors. The grounds yield many delights for the lover of nature, especially in Spring, when the gardens and woods are resplendent with daffodils, narcissi and a myriad of rare bulbs. Film location for The Crown (Season 5 and 6), Wild Child (2008), Junior Bake Off, Bleak House, Agent Cody Banks 2, Hetty Feather and others. Gravel and slab paths throughout the gardens. Land uneven with many slopes. Stairs and steps in Main Hall. Please call in advance to ensure assistance.

Our donation in 2023 has enabled Parkinson's UK to fund 3 new nursing posts this year, directly supporting people with Parkinson's

24 THE COPPER HOUSE

Hinksden Road, Benenden, Cranbrook, TN17 4LE. Eleanor Cochrane, 07710 614 962, eleanor. cochrane@btinternet.com. Located close to Hinksden Dairy. **Sun 8 Sept (11-3). Adm £5, chd free. Pre-booking essential, please visit www.ngs.org.uk for information & booking. Home-made teas. Visits also by arrangement 20 May to 22 Sept for groups of 5+.**
The Copper House garden is a modern flower garden successively planted to provide interest and colour throughout the season. Mixed planting of annuals, perennials, bulbs and shrubs. Small wildflower meadow and orchard. Three small ponds to encourage wildlife. Recently renovated woodland ponds. Mixed borders, views, gravel garden, water features.

25 COPTON ASH

105 Ashford Road, Faversham, ME13 8XW. Drs Tim & Gillian Ingram, 01795 535919, coptonash@yahoo.co.uk, www.coptonash.co.uk. ½m S of A2, Faversham on A251. On A251 Faversham to Ashford rd. Opp E bound J6 with M2. Parking possible beyond Aldi in Tettenhall Way. A251 single yellow lines are Mon to Fri restrictions, so available at weekends. **Sat 10, Sun 18 Feb (12-4); Sun 17 Mar, Mon 1, Sun 14 Apr, Mon 6 May (12-5). Sun 19 May (12-5), open nearby Beech Court Gardens. Adm £5, chd free. Home-made teas. 2025: Sun 2, Sun 16 Feb. Visits also by arrangement 12 Feb to 30 June for groups of up to 30. Coaches to offload at the entrance, park in town and return to collect.**
Garden grown out of a love and fascination with plants. Contains wide collection inc many rarities and newly introduced species raised from wild seed. Special interest in woodland flowers, snowdrops and hellebores with flowering trees and shrubs of spring. Refreshed Mediterranean plantings to adapt to a warming climate. Raised beds with choice alpines and bulbs. Alpine and dryland plant nursery. Gravel drive, shallow step by house and some narrow grass paths.

Eagleswood

© Leigh Clapp

26 NEW ▶ **COURT LODGE**
Horton Road, Horton Kirby,
Dartford, DA4 9BN. Louise Cannon
and Tristan Ward, 07957 183290,
louisecannon@btinternet.com. *9m
north of Sevenoaks, 5m south of
Dartford. Court Lodge is in Horton
Kirby village off Horton Rd: white
gates, next to St Mary's Church.
Please look out for parking and
entrance signs. Farningham Rd
nearest railway stn (15-20 min walk).*
**Sat 22 June (2-5.30). Adm £8,
chd free. Home-made teas. Visits
also by arrangement 24 June to
20 Sept for groups of 10 to 20.
Teas to be paid in advance for by
arrangement visits. Donation to
Local Church.**
Beautifully situated on the River
Darenth, beyond the old farmyard
and C18 dovecote, are gardens
evolved over 4 generations. Mature
trees and an elegant lawn lead down
to the river. Behind old yew hedges
lie a secluded white garden, kitchen
garden, a renovated rose walk, and
bee loving mixed borders. There is
a walled Italian Garden and also a
wild bank to meander through. Well
behaved dogs on leads allowed.
We may have a stall for homemade/

grown plants and veg surplus on the
day. 20% of all money raised will go
to St Mary's Church.

GROUP OPENING

27 **DEAL TOWN GARDENS**
Deal, CT14 6EB. *Signs from all
town car parks, maps & tickets at
all gardens.* **Sun 30 June (10-4).
Combined adm £5, chd free.**

61 COLLEGE ROAD
Andrew Tucker.

4 GEORGE ALLEY
Lyn Freeman & Barry Popple.

16 ST ANDREW'S ROAD
Martin Parkes & Paul Green.

5 ST PATRICK'S CLOSE
Chris & Geoff Hobbs-East.

14 SUTHERLAND ROAD
Joan Bull.

88 WEST STREET
Lyn & Peter Buller.

Start from any town car park (signs
from here). 88 West Street: A non
water cottage garden with perennials,
shrubs, clematis and roses and

shade garden. 4 George Alley: A
pretty alley leads to a secret garden
with courtyard, leading to a vibrant
cottage garden with summerhouse.
16 St Andrew's Road: A tropical
themed walled urban garden with
large sun-drenched borders, lawn
and family seating area. 5 St Patrick's
Close: South-facing, rented garden,
featuring roses, herbs and scented
flowers in a range of containers and
pots. The summerhouse hosts a OO
gauge railway which extends into
the garden. 14 Sutherland Rd: Three
small gardens in one with intense
planting for all year interest and
support for wildlife.61 College Rd:
Small garden filled with colour and a
profusion of plants.

28 **DEAN HOUSE**
Newchurch, Romney
Marsh, TN29 0DL. Jaqui
Bamford, 07480 150684,
jaquibamford@gmail.com.
*Between the village of Newchurch
& New Romney. Bilsington Xrds SE
towards New Romney. 2.9m to S
bend. Garden R after bend. New
Romney leave A259 NE on St Marys*

Rd. 3.7m. Garden on L. **Visits by arrangement 17 June to 22 Sept. Adm £5, chd free. Tea.**

A garden created over 20 yrs, from an old farmyard, featuring mature trees, shady areas, wildlife pond, paths, secluded sitting areas, sun-drenched gravel beds and herbaceous borders designed for pollinators. Extensive views across Romney Marsh. Visitors can explore the field to which the garden leads to see a rewilding project in its infancy. Large collection of cacti and succulents. The garden planting attracts a number of different bumblebee species inc one of the rarer species - the Ruderal bumblebee. Photos of the garden and surrounding area in different seasons are on display throughout the garden. Prints can be made up to order. Wheelchair must be operable on flat gravel and grass areas. Stepping stone paths and some seating will not be accessible.

29 ◆ DODDINGTON PLACE
Church Lane, Doddington, Sittingbourne, ME9 0BB.
Mr & Mrs Richard Oldfield,
07596 090849, enquiries@doddingtonplacegardens.co.uk, www.doddingtonplacegardens.co.uk. *6m SE of Sittingbourne. From A20 turn N opp Lenham or from A2 turn S at Teynham or Ospringe (Faversham), all 4m.* **For NGS: Sun 25 Feb, Wed 22 May, Wed 28 Aug, Sun 22 Sept (11-5). Adm £9, chd £3. Light refreshments. For other opening times and information, please phone, email or visit garden website.**

10 acre garden, wide views; trees and cloud clipped yew hedges; woodland garden with azaleas and rhododendrons; Edwardian rock garden; formal garden with mixed borders. A flint and brick late C20 gothic folly; newly installed at the end of the Wellingtonia walk, a disused pinnacle from the southeast tower of Rochester Cathedral. Snowdrops in February. Chelsea Fringe Events. This garden is proud to provide plants for the National Garden Scheme's Show Garden at Chelsea Flower Show 2024. Wheelchair access possible to majority of gardens except rock garden.

30 [NEW] ◆ DOWN HOUSE
Luxted Road, Downe, BR6 7JT.
English Heritage, 07721 813442, alison.makosch@english-heritage.org.uk. *Luxted Rd, Downe. Off A21or A233. Down House is within ULEZ. Visit TFL's website to check if vehicle meets the emission requirements. If not, charges may apply.* **For NGS: Evening opening Tues 23 July (5.30-8). Adm £15. Pre-booking essential, please phone 07721 813442, email alison.makosch@english-heritage.org.uk or visit www.english-heritage.org.uk/visit/places/home-of-charles-darwin-down-house for information & booking. For other opening times and information, please phone, email or visit garden website.**

Discover Charles Darwin's 'living laboratory' at Down House, the family home where he developed many of his ground-breaking ideas on evolution and natural selection. Tread the same paths as Darwin along the sandwalk and marvel at the collection of carnivorous plants in the glasshouses, in the beautiful surroundings of the Kent countryside.

31 DOWNS COURT
Church Lane, Boughton Aluph, Ashford, TN25 4EU. Mr Bay Green, 07984 558945, bay@baygee.com. *4m NE of Ashford. From A28 Ashford or Canterbury, after Wye Xrds take next turn NW to Boughton Aluph Church signed Church Ln. Fork R at pillar box, garden only drive on R. Park in field. Disabled parking in drive.* **Sun 9, Sun 16, Sun 23 June (2-5). Adm £5, chd free. Visits also by arrangement 25 May to 21 July.**

3 acre downland garden on alkaline soil with fine trees, mature yew and box hedges, mixed borders. Shrub roses and rose arch pathway, small parterre. Sweeping lawns and lovely views over surrounding countryside.

32 EAGLESWOOD
Slade Road, Warren Street, Lenham, ME17 2EG. Mike & Edith Darvill, 01622 858702, mike.darvill@btinternet.com. *Approx 12m E of Maidstone. E on A20 nr Lenham, L into Hubbards Hill for approx 1m then 2nd L into Slade Rd. Garden 150yds on R. Coaches permitted by prior arrangement.* **Sun 28 Apr, Mon 27 May (11-5). Adm £5, chd free. Light refreshments. Visits also by arrangement Apr to Oct for groups of 5+. Donation to Demelza House Hospice.**

2 acre plant enthusiasts garden. Wide range of trees and shrubs (many unusual), herbaceous material and woodland plants grown to give year-round interest.

GROUP OPENING

33 ELHAM GARDENS
High Street, Elham, CT4 6TD. www.elhamgardeningsociety.org.uk. *10m S of Canterbury, 6m N of Hythe. Enter Elham from Lyminge (off A20) or Barham (off A2). Car parking in various locations as signposted inc the Village Hall & weather permitting, the Primary Sch Grounds in New Rd.* **Sat 8, Sun 9 June (12-4.30). Combined adm £10, chd free. Home-made teas in the Old Vicarage Garden, available between 2.00-4.30.**

Elham has a thriving community of keen amateur gardeners, many of whom will open their delightful gardens again, along with others, opening their beautiful and interesting gardens for the first time. They all provide a wide range of style and size. Nearly all the gardens are within walking distance of each other with two a short drive having parking available. This picturesque village provides an idyllic setting with its beautiful Grade I listed St Mary's church at its centre, situated in glorious countryside within the Elham Valley Area of Outstanding Natural Beauty. The Elham Food & Craft Festival will be in The Square and St Mary's Church between 11am - 2pm on Sunday 9 June. There will be a plant stall in the Vicarage Garden.

Our donation to Marie Curie this year equates to 17,496 hours of nursing care

34 ◆ EMMETTS GARDEN
Ide Hill, Sevenoaks, TN14 6BA.
National Trust, 01732 751507,
emmetts@nationaltrust.org.
uk, www.nationaltrust.org.uk/
emmetts-garden. *5m SW of
Sevenoaks. 1½m S of A25 on
Sundridge-Ide Hill Rd. 1½m N of
Ide Hill off B2042.* **For NGS: Wed
4 Sept (10-4). Adm £8, chd free.
Light refreshments in the Old
Stables. For other opening times
and information, please phone,
email or visit garden website.**
5 acre hillside garden, with the highest
tree top in Kent, noted for its fine
collection of rare trees and flowering
shrubs. The garden is particularly
fine in spring, while a rose garden,
rock garden and extensive planting
of acers for autumn colour extend
the interest throughout the season.
Hard paths to the Old Stables for
light refreshments and WC. Some
steep slopes. Volunteer driven buggy
available for lifts up steepest hill.
  ċ ⩋ ✿ ⌂ ☕

35 EUREKA
Westerham Hill, TN16 2HR.
Gordon & Suzanne Wright,
07860 276184/01959 570848,
sb.wright@btinternet.com. *Park
at Westerham Heights Garden
Centre TN16 2HW off A233, 200m
from Eureka. Parking at house for
those with walking difficulties.* **Sat
6, Sun 7 July, Sat 3, Sun 4 Aug
(11-4). Adm £5, chd free. Light
refreshments inc hot/cold drinks
and home made cakes. Visits
also by arrangement 6 May to 30
Aug for groups of 20+. Parking at
Westerham Heights Garden Centre
TN16 2HW.**
Approx 1 acre garden with a blaze of
colourful displays in perennial borders
and the eight cartwheel centre beds.
Sculptures, garden art, chickens,
lots of seating and stairs to a viewing
platform. Many quirky surprises at
every turn. 100s of annuals in tubs
and baskets, a David Austin shrub
rose border and a free Treasure Trail
with prizes for all children. Garden
art inc 12ft Blacksmith's made red
dragon, a horse's head carved out
of a 200yr old yew tree stump and a
10ft dragonfly on a reed. Wheelchair
access to most of the garden.
  ċ ✿ ⌂ ☕

36 NEW FAIRSEAT MANOR
Vigo Road, Fairseat, Sevenoaks,
TN15 7LU. Robert and Anne-Marie
Nelson, 01732 822256, anne.

marie.nelson@btinternet.com.
*Fairseat Village. Opp the pond in
Fairseat.* **Visits by arrangement
10 Feb to 10 Mar for groups of
up to 10. Adm £5, chd free. Light
refreshments.**
2 acre mature garden on top of the
North Downs. Extensive spring bulbs
with many varieties of snowdrops.
Rose and perennial borders, sunken
garden with pond, and meadows. All
accessible, with one step to sunken
pond garden. Wheelchair access
through the garage and shed, with no
steps to much of the garden.
  ċ ☕ ⋅))

37 FALCONHURST
Cowden Pound Road, Markbeech,
Edenbridge, TN8 5NR.
Mr & Mrs Charles Talbot,
www.falconhurst.co.uk. *3m SE of
Edenbridge. B2026 at Queens Arms
pub turn E to Markbeech. 2nd drive
on R before Markbeech village.* **Mon
27 May, Sat 15 June (11-5). Adm
£7, chd free. Home-made teas.**
4 acre garden with fabulous views
devised and cared for by the same
family for 170 yrs. Deep mixed
borders with old roses, peonies,
shrubs and a wide variety of
herbaceous and annual plants; ruin
garden; walled garden; interesting
mature trees and shrubs; kitchen
garden; wildflower meadows with
woodland and pond walks. Market
garden, pigs, orchard chickens;
lambs in the paddocks.
  ċ ⩋ ⌂ ☕ ⋅))

38 NEW FARRIERS COTTAGE
Throwley Forstal, Faversham,
ME13 0PJ. Mr Simon Joy. *5m SW
of Faversham. Leave A251 at sign for
Belles Forstal & Throwley. 1st R into
Workhouse Rd, L at the end then
1st R into Almshouse Rd. Farriers
Cottage is on L of the Forstal.* **Sun
23 June (1-4). Adm £5, chd free.**
Four acres of garden and paddocks,
hidden from view behind a narrow
entrance onto the village Forstal.
The formal flower garden to the
back of the house moves through
yew hedges into the kitchen garden
and then through two orchards to
the series of paddocks which are
managed to provide habitat for
pollinators and other insects. No hard
paving or walkways, so can be tricky
in wet weather, but garden and field
on level ground with no steps.
  ċ

39 NEW 1 FOX COTTAGES
Fox Lane, Oversland, Faversham,
ME13 9PG. Rachel & Andrew
Stead. *4m SE of Faversham.
Opposite Foxhill Stud, 1 Fox
Cottages is the house with dragons
on the roof! Oversland is 1 m to
the W of Selling & close to Selling
train stn.* **Sun 5 May (12-4). Adm
£5, chd free. Sat 3 Aug (11-4).
Combined adm with Hoppickers
East £7, chd free. Home-
made teas inc teas, coffees &
homemade cakes.**
Organic cottage garden with relaxed
planting style used in borders,
multiple fruit trees and apple arches
with beautiful Spring blossom, a
meadow in summer and wildlife
pond with dead hedge. Productive
vegetable/cut flower garden with
most grown from seed. Produce
own compost. Certainly not a perfect
garden but one that feeds us and
brings us much joy. Far-reaching
views from the top of the garden.
  ☕ ⋅))

40 FRITH OLD FARMHOUSE
Frith Road, Otterden, Faversham,
ME13 0DD. Drs Gillian &
Peter Regan, 01795 890556,
peter.regan@cantab.net. *½m off
Lenham to Faversham Rd. From A20
E of Lenham follow signs Eastling;.
After 4m L into Frith Rd. From A2
in Faversham turn S (Brogdale Rd);
cont 7m (thro' Eastling), R into Frith
Rd. Limited parking.* **Sun 7, Sun 21
Apr, Sun 5, Sun 19 May (12.30-
4.30). Adm £6, chd free. Visits also
by arrangement 2 Apr to 30 Sept
for groups of up to 40. Please
contact by email for group visits.**
An eclectic collection of plants
growing together as if in the wild,
developed over nearly 50 years.
Several hundred interesting (and
some very unusual) plants. Trees
and shrubs chosen for year-round
appeal. Special interest in bulbs and
woodland plants. Visitor comments -
'one of the best we have seen, natural
and full of treasures', 'a plethora of
plants', 'inspirational', 'a hidden gem'.
Altered habitat areas to increase
the range of plants grown. Areas for
wildlife. Unusual trees and shrubs.
  ✿ ⌂ ☕ ⛪

41 THE GARDEN GATE
Northdown Park, Northdown
Park Road, Margate, CT9 3TP.
The Garden Gate Project
Ltd, 07714 742456, info@
thegardengateproject.co.uk, www.

Balmoral Cottage

© Bennet Smith

thegardengateproject.co.uk.
Located within Northdown Park,
opp Friends Corner on Northdown
Park Rd B2052 between Margate &
Broadstairs, nr Northdown House.
Sat 8 June (1-4). Adm £5, chd
free. Home-made teas. inc wood
fired pizzas with toppings from
the garden will be on sale. Visits
also by arrangement 10 June to
14 June.
The Garden Gate is a community
garden based in Northdown Park,
growing a mixture of plants, flowers
and vegetables using organic
methods. We also have a wildlife
pond, two polytunnels, a shade
house, some coppiced woodland and
a green roof on one of our buildings.
The garden is flat and on one level
with grass or wood chip paths.

42 GODDARDS GREEN
Angley Road, Cranbrook,
TN17 3LR. John & Linde
Wotton, 01580 715507,
jpwotton@gmail.com,
www.goddardsgreengarden.com.
½m SW of Cranbrook. On W of
Angley Rd. (A229) at junction with
High St, opp War Memorial. **Sun**
7 July (12-4). Adm £6, chd free.
Home-made teas. Visits also
by arrangement Apr to Sept for
groups of 10 to 50.
Gardens of about 7 acres,
surrounding beautiful 500+yr old

clothier's hall (not open), laid out
in 1920s and redesigned since
1992 to combine traditional and
modern planting schemes. fountain
and rill, water garden, fern garden,
mixed borders of bulbs, perennials,
shrubs, trees and exotics; birch
grove, grass border, pond, kitchen
garden, meadows, arboretum and
mature orchard; 2 wild acres. Some
slopes and steps, but most areas
(though not the toilets) are wheelchair
accessible. Disabled parking is
reserved near the house.

43 ◆ GODINTON HOUSE &
GARDENS
Godinton Lane, Ashford,
TN23 3BP. The Godinton House
Preservation Trust, 01233 643854,
info@godintonhouse.co.uk,
www.godintonhouse.co.uk. *1½m*
W of Ashford. M20 J9 to Ashford.
Take A20 towards Charing &
Lenham, then follow brown tourist
signs. **For NGS: Sat 13 Apr, Sat 11**
May, Fri 14 June, Fri 20 Sept (1-6).
Adm £8, chd free. Cream teas.
Please check garden website for
tearoom opening times. For other
opening times and information,
please phone, email or visit garden
website.
Twelve acre gardens complement
a magnificent Jacobean house.
Terraced lawns lead to herbaceous
borders, rose garden and a formal

lily pond. Spring highlights inc a
mass of daffodils, while Summer
sees wisteria bloom in the Italian
garden and delphiniums bringing the
walled garden to life. Visit in Autumn
to see the vegetable garden full of
squashes and the beautiful colours
this season brings. Plant Fair (21
April). Delphinium Festival (8 June -
23 June). Partial wheelchair access
to ground floor of house and most of
gardens.

44 GODMERSHAM PARK
Godmersham, CT4 7DT. Mrs
Fiona Sunley, 01227 730293,
ben@godmershampark.com. *5m*
NE of Ashford. Off A28, midway
between Canterbury & Ashford.
Sun 17 Mar, Sun 9 June (1-5).
Adm £8, chd free. Home-made
teas in the Orangery. Visits also
by arrangement Mar to Sept for
groups of 10 to 50.
24 acres of restored wilderness
and formal gardens set around C18
mansion (not open). Topiary, rose
garden, herbaceous borders, walled
kitchen garden and recently restored
Italian and swimming pool gardens.
Superb daffodils in spring and roses
in June. Historical association with
Jane Austen. Also visit the Heritage
Centre. Deep gravel paths.

45 ◆ **GOODNESTONE PARK GARDENS**
Wingham, Canterbury, CT3 1PL.
Julian Fitzwalter, 01304 840107,
office@goodnestone.com,
www.goodnestonepark.co.uk. *6m
SE of Canterbury. Village lies S of
B2046 from A2 to Wingham. Brown
tourist signs off B2046. Use CT3
1PJ for SatNav.* **For NGS: Thur 13
June (9-5); Thur 12 Sept (10-4).
Adm £9, chd £3. Café tel: 01304
695098. For other opening times
and information, please phone,
email or visit garden website.**
One of Kent's outstanding gardens
and the favourite of many visitors.
14 acres with views over parkland.
Something special year-round from
snowdrops and spring bulbs to
the famous walled garden with old
fashioned roses and kitchen garden.
Outstanding trees and woodland
garden with cornus collection and
hydrangeas later. Two arboreta and a
contemporary gravel garden.

46 GRAVESEND GARDEN FOR WILDLIFE
68 South Hill Road, Windmill
Hill, Gravesend, DA12 1JZ.
Judith Hathrill, 07810 550991,
judith.hathrill@live.com. *On
Windmill Hill 0.6m from Gravesend
town centre, 1.8m from A2. From A2
take A227 towards Gravesend. At
T-lights with Cross Ln turn R then L
at next T-lights, following yellow NGS
signs. Park in Sandy Bank Rd or
Rouge Ln.* **Sun 7 July (12-5). Adm
£5, chd free. Home-made teas.
Visits also by arrangement June
to Aug for groups of up to 20.
Weekday afternoons preferred.**
This small cottage garden combines
native wildflowers, perennials,
annuals, herbs, shrubs and grasses
to attract and sustain wildlife
throughout the year. Container
grown vegetables, 3 ponds and a
wildflower-studded lawn with seating
for teas. Photographic display
in summerhouse. Featured on
Gardeners' World in 2022. Information
and leaflets about gardening for
wildlife always available.

47 ◆ **GREAT COMP GARDEN**
Comp Lane, Platt, nr Borough
Green, Sevenoaks, TN15 8QS.
Great Comp, 01732 885094,
office@greatcompgarden.co.uk,
www.greatcompgarden.co.uk. *7m
E of Sevenoaks. 2m from Borough
Green Station. Accessible from M20
& M26 motorways. A20 at Wrotham
Heath, take Seven Mile Lane, B2016;
at 1st Xrds turn R; garden on L
½m.* **For NGS: Sun 24 Mar, Sun
27 Oct (10-5). Adm £9.50, chd
free. For other opening times and
information, please phone, email or
visit garden website.**
Skillfully designed 7 acre garden of
exceptional beauty. Spacious setting
with maintained lawns and paths lead
visitors through plantsman's collection
of trees, shrubs, heathers and
herbaceous plants. Early C17 house
(not open). Magnolias, hellebores and
snowflakes (leucojum), hamamellis and
winter flowering heathers are a great
feature in the spring. A great variety
of perennials in summer inc salvias,
dahlias and crocosmias. Tearoom
open daily for morning coffee, home-
made lunches and cream teas. Most
of garden accessible to wheelchair
users. Disabled WC.

48 GREAT MAYTHAM HALL
Maytham Road, Rolvenden,
Tenterden, TN17 4NE. The
Sunley Group. *3m from Tenterden.
Maytham Rd off A28 at Rolvenden
Church, ½m from village on R.
Designated parking for visitors.* **Wed
15 May, Wed 19 June (1-4). Adm
£8, chd free.**
Lutyens designed gardens famous
for having inspired Frances Hodgson
Burnett to write The Secret Garden
(pre Lutyens). Parkland, woodland
with bluebells. Walled garden with
herbaceous beds and rose pergola.
Pond garden with mixed shrubbery
and herbaceous borders. Interesting
specimen trees. Large lawned area,
rose terrace with far-reaching views.

49 GROVE MANOR
The Street, Woodnesborough,
Sandwich, CT13 0NH. Deborah
Anderson. *1½m SW of Sandwich.
S'wich - Woodnesb. Rd, 1st L after
Woodland Way. C'bury - A257
through Ash/Marshb, 1st R after
Elmwood. Dover/Thanet - A256 via
Foxbrgh Hill, 1st R after Elmwood.
Last bit single lane.* **Sat 3, Sun 4
Aug (11-5). Adm £5, chd free.
Home-made teas.**
Grove Manor, a Victorian farmhouse
is surrounded by natural gardens
reflecting its past. Close to the house
are lawns, herbaceous beds and a
shady fernery. Home to moorhens and
ducks, the farm pond has recently
been dredged and replanted. The
moat is a haven for wildlife and borders
the orchard and composting area (the
engine room). Beyond are the newly
established veg and cutting beds.

50 HAVEN
22 Station Road, Minster,
Ramsgate, CT12 4BZ. Robin
Roose-Beresford, 01843 822594,
robin.roose@hotmail.co.uk. *1 m
E of Manston. Off A299 Ramsgate
Rd, take Minster exit from Manston
r'bout, straight rd, R fork at church
is Station Rd.* **Sun 3 Mar, Sun 7,
Sun 28 Apr, Sun 12, Sun 26 May,
Sun 9, Sun 30 June, Sun 14 July,
Sun 4, Sun 25 Aug, Sun 22 Sept,
Sun 20 Oct, Sun 10 Nov (10-4).
Adm £5, chd free. Visits also by
arrangement 3 Mar to 24 Nov for
groups of up to 20.**
Award winning 300ft garden,
designed in the Glade style, similar to
Forest gardening but more open and
with use of exotic and unusual trees,
shrubs and perennials, with wildlife in
mind, devised and maintained by the
owner, densely planted in a natural
style with stepping stone paths.
Two ponds (one for wildlife, one for
fish with water lilies), gravel garden,
rock garden, fernery, Japanese
garden, cactus garden, hostas and
many exotic, rare and unusual trees,
shrubs and plants inc tree ferns and
bamboos and year-round colour.
Greenhouse cactus garden. Treefern
grove. Many Palms and exotic trees.

51 ◆ **HEVER CASTLE &
GARDENS**
Edenbridge, TN8 7NG. Hever
Castle Ltd, 01732 865224,
info@hevercastle.co.uk,
www.hevercastle.co.uk. *3m SE of
Edenbridge. Between Sevenoaks &
East Grinstead off B2026. Signed
from J5 & J6 of M25, A21, A264.*
**For NGS: Mon 15 Apr (10.30-4.30).
Please check garden website for
2024 admission prices. For other
opening times and information,
please phone, email or visit garden
website.**
Romantic double-moated castle, the
childhood home of Anne Boleyn, set
in 150 acres of formal and natural
landscape. Topiary, Tudor herb
garden, magnificent Italian garden
with classical statuary, sculpture
and fountains. 38 acre lake, yew
and water mazes. Spring is a
wonderful time to view the gardens

as spectacular carpets daffodils welcome visitors and tulips are in full bloom. Partial wheelchair access.

&. 🐕 ✳ 🚐 🚐 ☕ 🪑

52 95 HIGH STREET

Tenterden, TN30 6LB. Judy & Chris Older. *Nearest parking is Bridewell car park - Saturday visitors will have to pay but free on Sundays. Drive to far end. Venue on R.* **Sat 15, Sun 16 June (12-5). Combined adm with 99 High Street £6, chd free.**
Small town house garden divided into 3 rooms. Has developed since June 2021 from a blank canvas, now well-stocked with perennials and summer flowers to capacity. Colourful and traditional. Plenty of seating. Two small steps.

&. 🐕

53 NEW 99 HIGH STREET

Tenterden, TN30 6LB. Mrs Veryan Rahr. *99 High St, Tenterden. Entrance via far end of Bridewell Ln Car Park.* **Sat 15, Sun 16 June (12-5). Combined adm with 95 High Street £6, chd free.**
Narrow Garden with long brick path and 'rooms', seating areas, mainly shaded with interesting planting over 25 years. A few small steps.

&. 🐕 ☕

54 NEW 2 HIGHFIELDS ROAD

Edenbridge, TN8 6JN. Auralucia, auraluciabrook@hotmail.com. *Marlpit Hill / Edenbridge. From the main road B2026, turn onto Swan Ln. Turn into Highfields Rd. 2nd house on the L.* **Sun 7 July (1.30-5). Adm £5. Sun 8 Sept (1.30-5). Adm £5, chd free. Visits by arrangement 15 June to 4 Aug for groups of up to 10. To make an appointment please request only by email.**
The garden is a multi-season, in the hope of attracting wildlife, birds, amphibians, and, of course, humans. A large collection of plants, upcycled pots, abundant ornaments. It has won 1st and 2nd prizes in the last few years in the local district. I hope in your visit you enjoy the sounds, scents, textures, secrecy, relaxation, and diversity in a very small space and an unusual, unique garden.

55 ◆ HOLE PARK

Benenden Road, Rolvenden, Cranbrook, TN17 4JB. Mr & Mrs Edward Barham, 01580 241344, info@holepark.com, www.holepark.com. *4m SW*

of Tenterden. Midway between Rolvenden & Benenden on B2086. Follow brown tourist signs from Rolvenden. **For NGS: Sun 14 Apr, Wed 15 May, Wed 12 June, Sun 13 Oct (11-6). Adm £12, chd £2.50. Light refreshments. Picnics only in picnic site & car park please. For other opening times and information, please phone, email or visit garden website.**
Hole Park is proud to stand amongst the group of gardens which first opened in 1927 soon after it was laid out by my great grandfather. Our 15 acre garden is surrounded by parkland and contains fine yew hedges, large lawns with specimen trees, walled gardens, pools and mixed borders combined with bulbs, rhododendrons and azaleas. Massed bluebells in woodland walk, standard wisterias, orchids in flower meadow and glorious autumn colours make this a garden for all seasons. Wheelchairs are available for loan and may be reserved. Please email info@holepark.com.

&. 🐕 ✳ 🚐 ☕ 🪑))

56 HOPPICKERS EAST

Hogbens Hill, Selling, Faversham, ME13 9QZ. Katherine Pickering. *Signs from HogbensHill. From A251 signed Selling 1m, then NGS signs.* **Fri 5, Fri 19 July, Fri 2 Aug (11-4). Adm £5, chd free. Sat 3 Aug (11-4). Combined adm with 1 Fox Cottages £7, chd free. Fri 16 Aug (11-4). Adm £5, chd free.**
A new garden, started in autumn 2020 on the edge of a field. No dig principles. Emphasis on plants for pollinators and other insects. New this year removed rose border and replaced with dahlias and mixed planting. Flat grass paths.

&. 🐕 ✳ ☕ 🪑

57 NEW HOSPICE IN THE WEALD

Pembury, Maidstone Road Tunbridge Wells, Tunbridge Wells, TN2 4TA. Hospice in the Weald, www.hospiceintheweald.org.uk. *Off A228 onto Maidstone Rd.* **Sat 8 June (11.30-4). Adm £5, chd free. Light refreshments inc tea, coffee, cake and cream teas.**
The Hospice is surrounded by a beautiful garden. The garden has recently undergone a few changes inc the waterfall area which has been completely refurbished with 2 beautiful water features, seating and new planting. A Victorian style greenhouse

has been built, and there are new raised beds made from oak sleepers on the patio, for use by our patients.

&. 🐕 ✳ ☕

58 ◆ IGHTHAM MOTE

Mote Road, Ivy Hatch, Sevenoaks, TN15 0NT. National Trust, 01732 810378, ighthammote@ nationaltrust.org.uk, www. nationaltrust.org.uk/ightham-mote. *Nr Ivy Hatch: 6m E of Sevenoaks; 6m N of Tonbridge; 4m SW of Borough Green. E from Sevenoaks on A25 follow brown sign R along coach road. W from Borough Green on A25 follow brown sign L along coach rd. N from Tonbridge on A227 follow brown sign L along High Cross rd.* **For NGS: Evening opening Sat 8 June (6-8.30). Adm £9, chd free. Light refreshments. Hot & cold drinks, small selection of cakes & biscuits and ice cream. Visitors are welcome to picnic beyond the north lake. For other opening times and information, please phone, email or visit garden website.**
Lovely 14 acre garden surrounding a picturesque medieval moated manor house c1320, open for NGS since 1927. Herbaceous borders, lawns, C18 cascade, fountain pools, courtyards and a cutting garden provide formal interest; while the informal lakes, stream, pleasure grounds, stumpery/fernery, dell and orchard complete the sense of charm and tranquillity. Please check NT Ightham Mote website for access details, access guide available at visitor reception. Assistance dogs only in garden.

&. ✳ 🚐 ☕ 🪑

59 IVY CHIMNEYS

28 Mount Sion, Tunbridge Wells, TN1 1TW. Laurence & Christine Smith. *At the end of Tunbridge Wells High St, with Pizza Express on the corner, turn L up Mount Sion. Ivy Chimneys is a red brick Queen Anne house at the top of the hill on the R.* **Sat 15 June, Sat 31 Aug (1-5). Adm £5, chd free.**
Town centre garden with herbaceous borders and masses of roses set on three levels of lawns all enclosed in an old walled garden. Large veg/ cutting garden and new for 2024 herb garden. Additional August opening will appeal to dahlia lovers. The property is Queen Anne and one of the oldest houses in Tunbridge Wells. Car Parking in public car parks near the Pantiles. Pantiles cafes nearby.

Boughton Monchelsea Place

60 KENFIELD HALL
Kenfield, Petham, Canterbury, CT4 5RN. Barnaby & Camilla Swire, kenfieldhallgarden@gmail.com. *Petham nr Canterbury. Continue along Kenfield Rd, down the hill & up the other side. Pass the farm & look out for signs.* **Visits by arrangement 1 May to 1 Aug. Adm £10, chd free.**
The 8 acre gardens benefit from views within the AONB and its diverse wildlife, consisting of a sunken formal garden, lawns, mixed borders, herbaceous borders, spring bulbs, a Japanese water garden, orchards, an organic vegetable garden with glasshouses, a wildflower meadow, a rose garden and woodland garden.

61 ◆ KNOLE
National Trust Knole, Sevenoaks, TN15 0RP. Lord Robert Sackville-West, 01732 462100, knole@nationaltrust.org.uk, www.nationaltrust.org.uk/knole. *1½ m SE of Sevenoaks. Leave M25 at J5 (A21). Park entrance S of Sevenoaks town centre off A225 Tonbridge Rd (opp St Nicholas Church). For SatNav use TN13 1HX.* **For NGS: Thur 4 July (11-4). Adm £5, chd £2.50. For other opening times and information, please phone, email or visit garden website. Additional parking charges apply.**
Lord Sackville's private garden at Knole is a magical space, featuring sprawling lawns, a walled garden, an untamed wilderness area and a medieval orchard. Access is through the beautiful Orangery, off Green

Court, where doors open to reveal the secluded lawns of the 26 acre garden and stunning views of the house. Last entry at 3.30pm and closes at 4pm. Please book in advance using Knole's website. Refreshments are available in the Brewhouse Café. Bookshop and shop in Green Court. Wheelchair access via the bookshop. Some paths may be difficult for manual wheelchair users. Assistance dogs are allowed in the garden.

62 THE KNOLL FARM
Giggers Green Road, Aldington, Ashford, TN25 7BY. Lord & Lady Aldington. *The Postcode leads to Goldenhurst, our drive entrance is opp & a little further down hill.* **Sat 13 Apr (11-4). Adm £10, chd free. Donation to Bonnington Church.**

10 acres of woodland garden with over 100 camellias, acer japonica, and a growing collection of specimen pines and oaks; bluebell wood; formal elements; Flock of Jacob Sheep around lake; long views across Romney Marsh. Picnics welcome. Paths throughout but the whole garden is on a slope and clay can be slippery.

63 KNOWLE HILL FARM

Ulcombe, Maidstone, ME17 1ES. The Hon Andrew & Mrs Cairns, 078601 77101, elizabeth@ knowlehillfarm.co.uk, www. knowlehillfarmgarden.co.uk. *7m SE of Maidstone. From M20 J8 follow A20 towards Lenham for 2m. Turn R to Ulcombe. After 1½ m, L at Xrds, after ½ m 2nd R into Windmill Hill. Past Pepper Box Pub, ½ m 1st L to Knowle Hill.* **Sat 3, Sun 4 Feb (11-3.30). Light refreshments. Sat 3, Sun 4 Aug (2-5). Home-made teas. Adm £6, chd free. Visits also by arrangement Feb to Sept for groups of up to 25. The narrow lanes leading to the garden are unsuitable for large coaches.**
2 acre garden created over nearly 40 years on south facing slope below the Greensand Ridge. Spectacular views. Snowdrops and hellebores, many tender plants, china roses, agapanthus, salvias and grasses flourish on light soil. Box hedges and topiary lend structure. Lavender ribbons hum with bees. Pool enclosed in small walled white garden. A green garden was completed in 2018. Access only for 35 seater coaches. Some steep slopes.

64 LITTLE GABLES

Holcombe Close, Westerham, TN16 1HA. Mrs Elizabeth James. *Centre of Westerham. Off E side of London Rd A233, 200yds from The Green. Please park in public car park. No parking available at house.* **Sat 18, Sun 19 May, Sat 8, Sun 9 June (1.30-4.30). Adm £5, chd free. Home-made teas.**
½ acre plant lover's garden extensively planted with a wide range of trees, shrubs, perennials etc, inc many rare varieties in the middle of Westerham. Collection of climbing and bush roses. Bog garden. Large greenhouse.

65 NEW LYNSTED COMMUNITY KITCHEN GARDEN

Lynsted Park, Lynsted, Sittingbourne, ME9 0JH. Mrs V R Ross Russell, www. lynstedkitchengarden.com. *15min drive from Faversham or Sittingbourne. Nearest Train - Teynham stn. Postcode ME9 0JH brings you to the start Lynsted Park's drive, please follow signs from there. Lynsted Community Kitchen Garden is on google maps.* **Sun 7 July (11-5). Combined adm with New Barns Farm £8, chd free. Home-made teas.**
This ½ acre community garden is the work of an ever expanding group of local people who grow organic fruit and vegetables together, sharing all aspects of sowing, growing and harvesting. We follow a 'No Dig' approach with soil health, sustainable water management and composting being key elements of the garden. We keep bees and are working hard to improve the biodiversity in the garden. Lynsted Community Kitchen Garden is set in a 7 acre field that is largely left wild but with small areas mown that can be used to sit down and picnic. The garden is sited in a field and in wet ground conditions, we would, regrettably, not advise wheelchairs.

66 NEW 6 MARINE PARADE

Whitstable, CT5 2BQ. Jain Castiau. *There are double yellow lines on both sides of Marine Parade. Parking generally available in Park Ave and Cliff Rd.* **Fri 26 Apr, Fri 23 Aug (11-4). Adm £7. Pre-booking essential, please visit www.ngs. org.uk for information & booking.**
South facing seaside garden, main garden perennial plants and natural pond. Agave patio area, wild pebble seafront garden, large vegetable garden with trained fruit trees.

67 ◆ MOUNT EPHRAIM GARDENS

Hernhill, Faversham, ME13 9TX. Mr & Mrs Dawes, 01227 751496, info@mountephraimgardens.co.uk, www.mountephraimgardens.co.uk. *3m E of Faversham. From end of M2, then A299 take slip rd 1st L to Hernhill, signed to gardens.* **For NGS: Sun 24 Mar, Thur 13 June, Sun 29 Sept (11-5). Adm £8, chd £3. Cream teas in West Wing Tea Room. For other opening times and information, please phone, email or visit garden website.**

Mount Ephraim is a privately-owned family home set in 10 acres of terraced Edwardian gardens with stunning views over the Kent countryside. Highlights inc a Japanese rock and water garden, arboretum, unusual topiary and a spectacular grass maze plus many mature trees, shrubs and spring bulbs. Partial wheelchair access; top part manageable, but steep slope. Disabled WC. Full access to tea room.

68 NETTLESTEAD PLACE

Nettlestead, Maidstone, ME18 5HA. Mr & Mrs Roy Tucker, www.nettlestead-place.co.uk. *6 m W/SW of Maidstone. S off A26 onto B2015 then 1 m on L, Nettlestead Court Farm after Nettlestead Church.* **Sun 7 Apr, Sun 9 June (1.30-4.30). Adm £8, chd free. Light refreshments.**
C13 manor house in 10 acre plantsman's garden. Large formal rose garden. Large herbaceous garden of island beds with rose and clematis walkway leading to a recently planted garden of succulents. Fine collection of trees and shrubs; sunken pond garden, maze of thuja, terraces, bamboos, camellias, glen garden, acer and daffodil lawns. Young pinetum adjacent to garden. Sculptures. Maze and beautiful countryside views. Collection of Shona and other sculptures. Gravel and grass paths. Most of garden accessible (but not sunken pond garden). Large steep bank and lower area accessible with some difficulty.

69 NEW NEW BARNS FARM

Box Lane, Ospringe, Faversham, ME13 0RU. Ms Kresse Wesling. *3 miles SW of Faversham. Just over ½ way up Box Ln (from Stalisfield Rd) on R or just under ½ way down and on L from Eastling Rd.* **Sun 7 July (11-5). Combined adm with Lynsted Community Kitchen Garden £8, chd free.**
This is a wild garden - we have taken a soil first, nothing is a weed approach. The most interesting thing to see is our wetland based waste water treatment system which will be in full flower in July. There are no real boundaries between the wetland and the regenerative vineyard or garden. Straw Bale workshop.

70 NORTON COURT
Teynham, Sittingbourne, ME9 9JU.
Tim & Sophia Steel, 07798 804544,
sophia@nortoncourt.net. *Off A2
between Teynham & Faversham. L
off A2 at Esso garage into Norton
Ln; next L into Provender Ln; L
signed Church for car park.* **Mon
10, Tue 11 June (2-5). Adm £10,
chd free. Home-made teas inc
in admission price. Visits also
by arrangement June & July for
groups of 15 to 25.**
10 acre garden within parkland setting.
Mature trees, topiary, wide lawns and
clipped yew hedges. Orchard with
mown paths through wildflowers.
Walled garden with mixed borders and
climbing roses. Pine tree walk. Formal
box and lavender parterre. Treehouse
in the Sequoia. Church open, adjacent
to garden. Flat ground except for 2
steps where ramp is provided.
♿ ☕))

**71 OAK COTTAGE AND
SWALLOWFIELDS NURSERY**
Elmsted, Ashford, TN25 5JT.
Martin & Rachael Castle. *6m NW of
Hythe. From Stone St (B2068) turn
W opp the Stelling Minnis turning.
Follow signs to Elmsted. Turn L at
Elmsted village sign. Limited parking
at house, further parking at Church
(7mins walk).* **Fri 12, Sat 13 Apr, Fri
10, Sat 11 May (11-4). Adm £6,
chd free. Home-made teas.**
Get off the beaten track and discover
this beautiful ½ acre cottage garden
in the heart of the Kent countryside.
This plantsman's garden is filled with
unusual and interesting perennials,
inc a wide range of salvias. There is a
small specialist nursery packed with
herbaceous perennials. Auriculas
displayed in traditional theatres in
April. Swallowfields Nursery is proud
to provide plants for the National
Garden Scheme's Show Garden at
Chelsea Flower Show 2024.
✲ ☕))

72 OLD BLADBEAN STUD
Bladbean, Canterbury,
CT4 6NA. Carol Bruce,
www.oldbladbeanstud.co.uk. *6m
S of Canterbury. From B2068, follow
signs into Stelling Minnis, turn R onto
Bossingham Rd, then follow yellow
NGS signs through single track
lanes.* **Sun 26 May, Sun 9, Sun 23
June, Sun 7, Sun 21 July (2-6).
Adm £6, chd free. Cream teas.**
Romantic walled rose garden with
90+ old fashioned rose varieties,
tranquil yellow and white garden,

square garden with a tapestry
of self sowing perennials and
Victorian style greenhouse, 300ft
long colour schemed symmetrical
double borders and an organic fruit
garden. Maintained entirely by the
owner, the gardens were designed
to be managed as an ornamental
ecosystem. Please see the garden
website for more information.
Regional Winner, South East, The
English Garden Magazine's The
Nation's Favourite Gardens 2023
✲ ☕

**73 THE OLD RECTORY,
FAWKHAM**
Valley Road, Fawkham, Longfield,
DA3 8LX. Karin & Christopher
Proudfoot, 01474 707513,
keproudfoot@gmail.com. *1m S of
Longfield. Midway between A2 & A20,
on Valley Rd 1½m N of Fawkham
Green, 0.3m S of Fawkham church,
opp sign for Gay Dawn Farm/Corinthian
Sports Club. Parking on drive only.
Not suitable for coaches.* **Visits by
arrangement in Feb for groups of
up to 20. Small numbers welcome,
but may be put together to make
one larger group . Adm £6, chd free.
Home-made teas.**
1½ acres with impressive display
of long-established naturalised
snowdrops and winter aconites;
collection of over 130 named
snowdrops. Garden developed
around the snowdrops over 40yrs,
inc hellebores, pulmonarias and
other early bulbs and flowers, with
foliage perennials, shrubs and trees,
also natural woodland. Gentle slope,
gravel drive, some narrow paths.
♿ ✲ ☕))

**74 THE OLD RECTORY,
OTTERDEN**
Bunce Court Road, Faversham,
ME13 0BY. Mrs Gry Iverslien,
07734 538272, gry@iverslien.com.
*North Downs. Postcode takes you
to Bunce Ct. We are 600 yds further
on just past Cold Harbour Ln.* **Wed
8, Thur 9 May (10-4). Adm £10,
chd free. Pre-booking essential,
please visit www.ngs.org.uk for
information & booking. Entrance
fee inc tea/coffee and cakes.
Visits also by arrangement 1 Apr
to 27 Sept for groups of 5 to 30.**
4 acre woodland garden with
numerous large Rhododendrons and
Camellias, mass of spring bulbs with
a formal rose garden, cutting garden
and large hydrangea beds throughout
the garden. The garden also has a

large wildlife pond and a variety of
trees of interest, pots of tulips and
narcissus in the spring accompanied
with lots of spring flowering plants.
♿ ☕

75 THE ORANGERY
Mystole, Chartham, Canterbury,
CT4 7DB. Rex Stickland &
Anne Prasse, 01227 738348,
rex.mystole@btinternet.com. *5m
SW of Canterbury. Turn off A28
through Shalmsford St. In 1½m
at Xrds turn R downhill. Continue,
ignoring roads on L & R. Ignore drive
on L (Mystole House only). At sharp
R bend in 600yds turn L into private
drive.* **Sun 12 May (1-6); Sat 27,
Sun 28 July (1-5). Adm £5, chd
free. Home-made teas. Visits also
by arrangement 16 Mar to 30 Sept
for groups of 8 to 50.**
1½ acre gardens around C18
orangery, now a house (not open).
Magnificent extensive herbaceous
border and impressive ancient
wisteria. Large walled garden with a
wide variety of shrubs, mixed borders
and unusual specimen trees. Water
features and intriguing collection
of modern sculptures in natural
surroundings. Splendid views from
the terrace over ha-ha to the lovely
Chartham Downs. Ramps to garden.
♿ 🚧 ✲ 🚐 ☕

**76 ◆ PENSHURST PLACE &
GARDENS**
Penshurst, TN11 8DG. Lord &
Lady De L'Isle, 01892 870307,
contactus@penshurstplace.
com, www.penshurstplace.com.
*6m NW of Tunbridge Wells. SW of
Tonbridge on B2176, signed from
A26 N of Tunbridge Wells.* **For NGS:
Wed 18 Sept (10-5). Adm £13,
chd £8. Light refreshments at
The Porcupine Pantry. For other
opening times and information,
please phone, email or visit garden
website.**
11 acres of garden dating back to
C14. The garden is divided into a
series of rooms by over a mile of yew
hedge. Profusion of spring bulbs,
formal rose garden and famous
peony border. Woodland trail and
arboretum. Year-round interest. Toy
museum. Some paths not paved and
uneven in places; own assistance will
be required. 2 wheelchairs available
for hire.
♿ ✲ 🚐 ☕ 🍽))

77 PHEASANT BARN
Church Road, Oare, ME13 0QB.
Paul & Su Vaight, 07843 739301,
suvaight46@gmail.com. *2m NW
of Faversham. Entering Oare from
Faversham, turn R at Three Mariners
pub towards Harty Ferry. Garden
400yds on R, before church. Parking
on roadside.* **Fri 28, Sat 29, Sun
30 June, Mon 1, Wed 3, Thur 4,
Sun 7, Mon 8 July (11-5). Adm £7,
chd free. Pre-booking essential,
please visit www.ngs.org.uk for
information & booking. Visits also
by arrangement 15 May to 9 July
for groups of up to 16.**
Series of smallish gardens around
award-winning converted farm
buildings in beautiful situation
overlooking Oare Creek. Main garden
is nectar rich planting in formal design
with a contemporary twist inspired
by local landscape. Also vegetable
garden, dry garden, water features,
mowed paths in wildflower meadow,
fruit trees, late summer perennial beds
and grass labyrinth. Kent Wildlife Trust
Oare Marshes Bird Reserve within
1m. Two village inns serving lunches/
dinners, booking recommended. Cafe
by the Creek.

78 ◆ QUEX GARDENS
Quex Park, Birchington, CT7 0BH.
Powell-Cotton Museum,
01843 842168, enquiries@
powell-cottonmuseum.org,
www.powell-cottonmuseum.org.
*3m W of Margate. Follow signs for
Quex Park on approach from A299
then A28 towards Margate, turn R
onto B2048 Park Lane. Quex Park is
on L.* **For NGS: Sun 14 July (11-
4). Adm £3.50, chd £2.50. Light
refreshments in Felicity's Café &
Quex Barn. For other opening times
and information, please phone,
email or visit garden website.**
10 acres of woodland and gardens
with fine specimen trees unusual in
Thanet, spring bulbs, wisteria, shrub
borders, old figs and mulberries,
herbaceous borders. Victorian walled
garden with cucumber house, long
glasshouses, cactus house, fruiting
trees. Peacocks, dovecote, chickens,
bees, woodland walk, wildlife pond,
children's maze, croquet lawn, picnic
grove, lawns and fountains. Head
Gardener and team will be available
on the day for a chat and to answer
questions. Garden almost entirely flat
with tarmac paths. Sunken garden
has sloping lawns to the central pond.

GROUP OPENING

79 RAMSGATE GARDENS
Ramsgate, CT11 9PX. Anne-Marie
Nixey. *Enter Ramsgate on A299,
continue on A255. At r'about take
2nd exit London Rd. Continue for
less than 1m to the r'about and turn
L onto Grange Rd or straight ahead
down West Cliff Rd.* **Sun 8 Sept (12-
5). Combined adm £5, chd free.**
Home-made teas.

104 GRANGE ROAD
Anne-Marie Nixey.

NEW **1 VALE SQUARE**
Jo Anne Webster.

NEW **2 VALE SQUARE**
Peter Ansley.

NEW **3 VALE SQUARE**
Jessica Pennington.

NEW **4 VALE SQUARE**
Mr Ray & Mrs Jeanette Holmes.

NEW **5 VALE SQUARE**
Mr Tracy & Mrs Matt Warden.

NEW **6 VALE SQUARE**
Stephen Davies.

NEW **7 VALE SQUARE**
Mr Peter & Mrs Carol De Rosa.

NEW **8 VALE SQUARE**
Mr Rob & Mrs Suzanne Clay.

NEW **9 VALE SQUARE**
Stephanie Dove.

NEW **10 VALE SQUARE**
Mr Graham & Mrs Alyson Brett.

NEW **16 VALE SQUARE**
Jocelyn McCarthy.

NEW **17 VALE SQUARE**
Fiona Paveley.

NEW **51 VALE SQUARE**
Bindi Holding.

12 WEST CLIFF ROAD
Brian Daubney.

Evolving gardens in the beautiful, yet
windy, coastal town of Ramsgate
showing different sized plots and
how to make unique gardens out of
them. Varied planting from traditional
roses and bedding plants to a range
of vegetables and fruit trees, as well
as use of recycled and sustainable
materials and incorporating traditional
family areas. Vale square gardens
highlight what can be achieved in
front gardens only.

80 43 THE RIDINGS
Chestfield, Whitstable, CT5 3QE.
David & Sylvie Buat-Menard,
01227 500775, sylviebuat-
menard@hotmail.com. *Nr
Whitstable. From M2 heading E cont
onto A299. In 3m take A2990. From
r'about on A2990 at Chestfield, turn
onto Chestfield Rd, 5th turning on L
onto Polo Way which leads into The
Ridings.* **Sun 12 May (11-4). Adm
£5, chd free. Light refreshments
inc tea/coffee and biscuits/cakes.
Visits also by arrangement 12 May
to 11 Aug for groups of 8 to 15.**
Featured on Gardeners' World June
2021. Winner of Kent Life amateur
gardener of the year 2018. Delightful
small garden brimming with interesting
plants both in the front and behind
the house. Many different areas. Dry
gravel garden in front, raised beds with
alpines and bulbs and borders with
many unusual perennials and shrubs.
The garden ornaments are a source of
interest for visitors. The water feature
will be of interest for those with a tiny
garden as planted with carnivorous
plants. Many alpine troughs and raised
beds as well as dry shade and mixed
borders all in a small space.

**81 ◆ RIVERHILL HIMALAYAN
GARDENS**
Riverhill, Sevenoaks, TN15 0RR.
The Rogers Family, 01732 459777,
info@riverhillgardens.co.uk,
www.riverhillgardens.co.uk. *2m
S of Sevenoaks on A225. Leave
A21 at A225 & follow signs for
Riverhill Himalayan Gardens.* **For
NGS: Thur 9 May, Thur 13 June
(10-5). Adm £12, chd £7.50. Light
refreshments. Onsite catering
provided by Cafe, Malabar.
For other opening times and
information, please phone, email or
visit garden website.**
Beautiful hillside garden, privately
owned by the Rogers family since
1840. Spectacular rhododendrons,
azaleas and fine specimen trees.
Edwardian Rock Garden with extensive
fern collection, Rose Walk and Walled
Garden with sculptural terracing.
Bluebell walks. Extensive views
across the Weald of Kent. Hedge
maze, adventure playground and den
building. Café serves speciality coffee,
light lunches and cakes. Plant sales
and quirky shed shop selling beautiful
gifts and original garden ornaments.
Disabled parking. Easy access to café,
shop and tea terrace. Accessible WC.

82 ST CLERE
Kemsing, Sevenoaks, TN15 6NL.
Mr Simon & Mrs Eliza Ecclestone,
www.stclere.com. *6m NE of
Sevenoaks. 1m E of Seal on A25,
turn L signed Heaverham. In
Heaverham turn R signed Wrotham.
In 75yds straight ahead marked
Private Rd; 1st L to house. Main
entrance What3words app - trail.
inner.valid.* **Sun 19 May (2-5). Adm
£7.50, chd free. Home-made teas
in the Garden Room.**
4 acre garden, full of interest. Formal
terraces surrounding C17 mansion
(not open), with beautiful views of the
Kent countryside. Herbaceous and
shrub borders, productive kitchen and
herb gardens, lawns and rare trees.
Some gravel paths and small steps.

83 45 SEYMOUR AVENUE
Whitstable, CT5 1SA. Kevin
Tooher, 07962 972882,
sirplantalot@outlook.com. *Near the
centre of Whitstable town & 400yds
from Whitstable stn. Take Thanet
Way off A299 towards Whitstable.
2nd r'about, L into Millstrood Rd,
bottom of hill R into Old Bridge Rd,
Station car park on L & Seymour
Ave on R.* **Sat 21, Sun 22 Sept
(11-4.30). Adm £5, chd free.
Home-made teas. Visits also by
arrangement 8 June to 29 Sept for
groups of 10 to 20.**
Larger than usual town centre garden
- about ¼ acre with wide range of
unusual plants grown on heavy wet
clay with lots of exotics growing in
containers, troughs and pots. Main
driveway gravel but mostly wheelchair
accessible over chip bark paths in the
garden itself.

84 THE SILK HOUSE
Lucks Lane, Rhoden Green, nr
Paddock Wood, Tunbridge Wells,
TN12 6PA. Adrian & Silke Barnwell,
www.silkhousegarden.com.
*Rhoden Green. The Silk House is
½m from Queen St on sharp bend
near Fish Lake. Also approached
from Maidstone Rd. Parking at
house, or in lane when full.* **Sun 8
Sept (11-5). Adm £10, chd £3.
Light refreshments in the garden,
usually served from the tea
house.**
Japanese stroll garden with Koi,
wildlife ponds, canal pond, unusual
acers, flowering cherries, large
bamboos, bonsai, niwaki, topiary
and rare evergreen trees. Zen

area. Secluded and calming. Small
woodland walk, busy kitchen garden,
dry garden and apiary. 2 acres overall.
Designed, built and maintained
entirely by owners. Bonsai classes
and Japanese garden design talks
available for groups. Best Japanese
stroll garden in the South East!
Structural planting looks good
year-round. Picnics welcome for
an additional charitable donation of
£10, please take all your litter home.
Disabled parking - please call us and
we will assist with side access by
request avoiding steps. Some steps,
banks, bridges, deep water ponds.

85 SIR JOHN HAWKINS HOSPITAL
High Street, Chatham, ME4 4EW.
www.hawkinshospital.org.uk.
*On the N side of Chatham High St,
on the border between Rochester
& Chatham. Leave A2 at J1 &
follow signs to Rochester. Pass
Rochester Stn & turn L at main
junc T-lights, travelling E towards
Chatham.* **Sat 29, Sun 30 June
(11-5). Adm £3, chd free. Cream
teas. Farm House Teas and light
refreshments served all day.**
Built on the site of Kettle Hard - part
of Bishop Gundulph's Hospital of St
Bartholomew, the Almshouse is a
square of Georgian houses dating
from the 1790s. A delightful small
secluded garden overlooks the River
Medway, full of vibrant and colourful
planting. A lawn with cottage style
borders leads to the riverside and a
miniature gnome village captivates
small children. Disabled access via
stairlift, wheelchair to be carried
separately.

86 ◆ SISSINGHURST CASTLE GARDEN
Biddenden Road, Sissinghurst,
Cranbrook, TN17 2AB.
National Trust, 01580 710700,
sissinghurst@nationaltrust.org.
uk, www.nationaltrust.org.uk/
sissinghurst-castle-garden. *2m NE
of Cranbrook, 1m E of Sissinghurst
on Biddenden Rd (A262), see
our website for more information.*
**For NGS: Sun 8 Sept (11-5.30).
Adm £17.60, chd £8.80. Light
refreshments in Coffee Shop and
Granary Restaurant. Picnics on
designated area in Vegetable
Garden. For other opening times
and information, please phone,
email or visit garden website.**

Historic, poetic, iconic; a refuge
dedicated to beauty. Vita Sackville-
West and Harold Nicolson fell in love
with Sissinghurst Castle and created
a world renowned garden. More
than a garden, visitors can also find
an Elizabethan tower, see changing
exhibitions, enjoy estate walks and
can picnic in the vegetable garden.
Food and drink and animals are
not allowed in the formal garden.
Free welcome talks and estate
walks leaflets. Café, restaurant, gift,
secondhand book and plant shops
are open from 10am-5.30pm. Some
areas unsuitable for wheelchair
access due to narrow paths and
steps.

87 SMITHS HALL
Lower Road, West Farleigh,
ME15 0PE. Mr and Mrs S Norman.
*3m W of Maidstone. A26 towards
Tonbridge, turn L into Teston Ln
B2163. At T-junction turn R onto
Lower Rd B2010. Opp Tickled Trout
pub.* **Sun 30 June (11-5). Adm
£5, chd free. Home-made teas.
Donation to Heart of Kent Hospice.**
Delightful 3 acre gardens surrounding
a beautiful 1719 Queen Anne House
(not open). Lose yourself in numerous
themed rooms: sunken garden, four
colour deep herbaceous borders,
many roses (300) in formal rose
garden and elsewhere, irises and
peonies plus woodland walk. Please
note that the annual wildflower
meadow is being replaced with a
larger perennial meadow but neither
will be on show in 2024. Some gravel
paths.

88 SPRING PLATT
Boyton Court Road, Sutton
Valence, Maidstone, ME17 3BY.
Mr & Mrs John Millen *5m SE of
Maidstone. From A274 nr Sutton
Valence follow yellow NGS signs.*
**Sun 21, Wed 24, Sun 28 Jan,
Thur 1, Sun 4 Feb (10.30-3).
Adm £5, chd free. Pre-booking
essential, please phone 01622
843383, email j.millen@talktalk.
net or visit www.kentsnowdrops.
com for information & booking.
Light refreshments inc home-
made soup & bread. Visits also by
arrangement 19 Jan to 16 Feb for
groups of 8 to 50.**
1 acre garden with panoramic views
of the Weald. Major reconstruction
taking place but still have approx
500 different varieties of snowdrops

in raised sleeper beds but many more now planted in grass around the garden with spring flowers in borders. An extensive collection of alpine plants in a large greenhouse. Vegetable garden, natural spring fed water feature and a croquet lawn.

89 ◆ SQUERRYES COURT
Squerryes, Westerham, TN16 1SJ. Henry Warde, www.squerryes.co.uk. *½m W of Westerham. Signed from A25.* **For NGS: Fri 17 May (11-5). Adm £8, chd free. Light refreshments. For other opening times and information, please visit garden website.**
15 acres of garden, lake and woodland surrounding beautiful C17 manor house (not open). Lovely throughout the seasons from the spring bulbs to later-flowering borders. Cenotaph commemorating General Wolfe. C18 dovecote. Lawns, yew hedges, ancient trees, parterres, azaleas, roses.

90 STABLE HOUSE, HEPPINGTON
Street End, Canterbury, CT4 7AN. Charlie & Lucy Markes. *2m S of Canterbury, off B2068. 1st R after Bridge Rd if coming from Canterbury, 400m after Granville pub on the L if coming towards Canterbury.* **Sat 15, Sun 16 June (1.30-5.30). Adm £5, chd free. Home-made teas.**
Approx 2 acres of relaxed, informal interlinked gardens surrounding converted Edwardian stable block in lovely setting with views towards the North Downs. Mixed borders with mature shrubs and perennials. Climbing roses, honeysuckle and clematis. Gravel garden, veg garden and walkthrough garden room beneath clocktower. Adjoining 5 acre wildflower meadow. 15 acre vineyard nearby. Disabled parking by arrangement close to garden. Not all areas wheelchair accessible.

91 STONEWALL PARK
Chiddingstone Hoath, nr Edenbridge, TN8 7DG. Mr & Mrs Fleming. *4m SE of Edenbridge. Via B2026. ½ way between Markbeech & Penshurst. Plenty of parking which will be signed.* **Sun 17 Mar, Sun 12 May (2-5). Adm £7, chd free. Home-made teas. Donation**

to MSA & St Mary's Church, Chiddingstone.
Vast amounts of C19 self-seeded daffodils which lead down to a romantic woodland garden in an historic setting, featuring species such as rhododendrons, magnolias and azaleas. In May, bluebells take over the daffodils in abundance. Winding, mossy paths lead you to a range of interesting trees, sandstone outcrops and lakes. Please wear boots and bring walking sticks as the paths can be slippery and muddy during the spring months. The paths are quite steep so care is needed going down towards the lakes.

92 SWEETBRIAR
69 Chequer Lane, Ash, nr Sandwich, CT3 2AX. Miss Louise Dowle & Mr Steven Edney. *8m from Canterbury, 3m from Sandwich. Turn off A257 into Chequer Ln (second turning into Ash from either Sandwich or Canterbury direction) 100 metres from junc on the L.* **Sun 21 July, Sun 18 Aug, Sun 15 Sept (11-4). Adm £5, chd free. Home-made teas.**
Exotic jungle garden of Steve Edney and Louise Dowle, RHS gold medal winners. Average sized back garden transformed into an exotic jungle paradise full of fabulous foliage. A real plantsman's collection of exotics to transport you into a lawn free oasis. 4 national collections plectranthus, persicaria, pseudopanax and dahlias. Wildlife friendly, with 3 small ponds and 2 greenhouses.

GROUP OPENING

93 TANKERTON GARDENS
Tankerton, CT5 2EP. *All four gardens are in Central Tankerton, about 1 m from whitstable. 3 gardens can be accessed via Castle Rd, except Badlesmere Rd which is off Northwood Rd or Tankerton Rd. Gardens are within 10 mins of Whitstable railway stn & close to cafes and WC facilities.* **Sat 18 May (10-5). Combined adm £6, chd free. Local cafes are available in Tankerton High Street, Tower Parade and the Sea Front, within easy reach of all four gardens, including WC facilities.**

17A BADDLESMERE ROAD
Mr Derek Scoones.

NEW 96 QUEENS ROAD
Ms Wendy Cunningham.

12 STRANGFORD ROAD
Sarah Yallop.

NEW 50 SUMMERFIELD AVENUE

The group comprises of 4 very different gardens which are close to each other. 2 are new to the NGS. They are a delightful artists gravel garden newly created by the owner, an inspiring vegetable and fruit garden with ponds. the third is a plant packed cottage garden aimed at attracting pollinators and wildlife.

Brome House, West Malling Early Summer Gardens

94 NEW **THAMES HOUSE**
29 Royal Pier Road, Gravesend, DA12 2BD. Dr Daniel Curran, 07753 605607. *Last house on L in Royal Pier Rd, past the Clarendon Hotel, and up a short set of steps from the pavement.* **Sat 10, Sun 11 Aug (12-5). Adm £5, chd £2. Home-made teas. Visits also by arrangement 1 July to 1 Sept for groups of 10+.**
Three very different outdoor spaces connected by steps. The main terrace, with views over the Thames River, and the western terrace with fish pond, are classically / formally planted to sit harmoniously with the listed building which dominates these areas. The third and largest space is our main garden, a modern styled walled garden with mixed borders, fruit trees and contemporary seating areas.

95 **TONBRIDGE SCHOOL**
High Street, Tonbridge, TN9 1JP. The Governors. *Maps & guides available for visitors. At N end of Tonbridge High St. Parking signed off London Rd (B245 Tonbridge-Hildenborough) in the Tonbridge Sports Centre car park.* **Wed 10 July (10-3). Adm £6, chd free. Cream teas in Smythe Library Garden.**
In front of and behind Tonbridge School you will find five gardens that you can visit. These are: The Boars Head, The Garden of Remembrance, Smythe Library Garden, Skinners Library Garden, and the Barton Science Centre Garden. We hope the Chapel will be open for visits. Cream teas available for purchase. Head Gardener guided tours throughout the day. Plant sales. Toilets on site. All gardens apart from Skinners Library garden can be accessed easily via wheelchair. Skinners Library path is uneven.

&. ✻ 🚗 ☕ 🎋))

96 **TOPGALLANT**
5 North Road, Hythe, CT21 5UF. Mary Sampson. *on the hill above Hythe town. M20 exit 11, take A259 to Hythe, then going towards Folkestone at r'about, take 2nd L up narrow hill signed to Saltwood. L at junc with North Rd. House on L.* **Sat 27, Sun 28 July (1.30-5). Adm £5, chd free. Cream teas in St Leonards Church, Church Road, Hythe.**
A hillside gardens terraced and developed to cope with the prevailing winds and the slope. Topgallant is a secluded Sculptors' garden, with mature trees and shrubs, a wildlife pond. Decking and grass paths wind down through the garden giving glimpses of the sea. Relaxed planting for year-round interest and to encourage wildlife. Ceramics studio open.

🐕 ✻ ☕

97 **TORRY HILL**
Frinsted/Milstead, Sittingbourne, ME9 0SP. Miranda & Arthur Leigh Pemberton. *5m S of Sittingbourne. M20 J8, A20, B2163 (Hollingbourne). R at Xrds (Ringlestone Rd). Frinsted-Doddington, NGS signs. M2 J5, A249 (Maidstone), 1st L (Bredgar), L (Bredgar), R at War Memorial, 1st L (Milstead), NGS signs.* **Sun 30 June (1-5). Combined adm with Yokes Court £10, chd free. Home-made teas. Picnics welcome in garden. Donation to St. Dunstan's Church, Frinsted.**
Spectacular views across the Medway and Thames estuaries frame these C19 landscaped gardens and mid-C20 formal walled gardens. Growing amongst them are specimen trees, wildflower meadows, a rose garden, herbaceous borders and a walled kitchen garden. Some shallow steps. No wheelchair access to rose garden due to very uneven surface but can be viewed from pathway.

&. 🐕 ✻ ☕ 🎋))

98 **TRAM HATCH**
Barnfield Road, Charing Heath, Ashford, TN27 0BN. Mrs P Scrivens, 07835 758388, Info@tramhatch.com. www.tramhatchgardens.co.uk. *10m NW of Ashford. A20 towards Pluckley, over motorway then 1st R to Barnfield. At end, turn L past Barnfield, Tram Hatch ahead.* **Visits by arrangement Apr to Sept for groups of 10 +. Adm £5, chd free. Home-made teas.**
Meander your way off the beaten track to a mature 3 acre garden changing through the seasons. You will enjoy a garden laid out in rooms. Large selection of trees, vegetable, rose and gravel gardens, colourful containers. River Stour and the Angel of the South enhance your visit. Please come and enjoy, then relax in our lovely garden room for tea. Ample parking and WC facilities available. Great River Stour plus other water features. Large variety of trees. Large vegetable garden. The garden is totally flat, apart from a very small area which can be viewed from the lane.

&. 🐕 ✻ ☕

99 **TROUTBECK**
High Street, Otford, Sevenoaks, TN14 5PH. Mrs Jenny Alban Davies, albandavies@me.com. *3m N of Sevenoaks. At W end of village.* **Visits by arrangement 1 June to 14 June for groups of 8 to 20. Adm £10, chd free. Complimentary refreshments.**
3 acre garden surrounded by branches of River Darent which has been developed over 30 years. It combines the informal landscape of the river, a pond and an area of wild meadow with views to the North Downs. The garden has extensive structural planting using box and yew. Knots and topiary shapes are displayed throughout. All main areas of the garden can be accessed by wheelchair.

&. 🐕 ☕

GROUP OPENING

100 **WALMER GARDENS**
Walmer, Deal, CT14 7JG. *All gardens can be accessed from the Dover Rd/A258.* **Sat 15 June (11-4); Sun 16 June (12-4). Combined adm £5, chd free. Light refreshments.**

196 DOWNS ROAD
Sue Turner.

PEMBROKE LODGE, 140 DOVER ROAD
Mrs Jo & Mr Steve Hammond, PembrokeLodge140@gmail.com.
🏠

NEW 75 SALISBURY ROAD
Barry Honeycombe & Richard Gresham.

WOODLEA, GRAMS ROAD
Mr John & Mrs Liz Lellow, 07774 367105, liz@lellow.co.uk. Visits also by arrangement May to Aug for groups of 5 to 15.

The coastal gardens at Walmer showcase a wide variety of horticultural knowledge and garden maturity: newer gardens in their early development demonstrating how planning and design takes shape in a newer garden as well as more established gardens that continue to deliver the beauty and grace that maturity brings. A wide variety of plants can be seen in all gardens, cared for by an enthusiastic and friendly group.

🐕 ✻ 🚗 ☕))

101 WEST COURT LODGE

Postling Court, The Street, Postling, nr Hythe, CT21 4EX. Mr & Mrs John Pattrick, 07814 419638, pattrickmalliet@gmail.com. *2m NW of Hythe. From M20 J11 turn S onto A20. Immed 1st L. After ½m on bend take rd signed Lyminge. 1st L into Postling.* **Visits by arrangement Mar to Oct for groups of up to 35. Combined with Churchfield. Home-made teas in Postling village hall.**
South facing one acre walled garden at the foot of the North Downs, designed in two parts: main lawn with large sunny borders and a romantic woodland glade planted with shadow loving plants and spring bulbs, small wildlife pond. Lovely C11 church will be open next to the gardens.

GROUP OPENING

102 WEST MALLING EARLY SUMMER GARDENS

West Malling, ME19 6LW. *On a20, nr J4 of M20. Park (Ryarsh Lane & Station) in West Malling. Please start your visit either at Brome House or Went House. Parking available at New Barns Cottages.* **Sun 2 June (12-5). Combined adm £8, chd free. Home-made teas at New Barns Cottages. Donation to St Mary's Church, West Malling.**

ABBEY BREWERY COTTAGE
Dr David & Mrs Lynda Nunn.

BROME HOUSE
John Pfeil & Shirley Briggs.

LUCKNOW, 119 HIGH STREET
Ms Jocelyn Granville.

NEW BARNS COTTAGES
Mr & Mrs Anthony Drake.

TOWN HILL COTTAGE
Mr & Mrs P Cosier.

WENT HOUSE
Alan & Mary Gibbins.

West Malling is an attractive small market town with some fine buildings. Enjoy six lovely gardens that are entirely different from each other and cannot be seen from the road. Brome House and Went House have large gardens with specimen trees, old roses, mixed borders, attractive kitchen gardens and garden features inc a coach house, Roman temple, fountain and parterre. Town Hill Cottage is a walled town garden with mature and interesting planting. Abbey Brewery Cottage is a recent jewel-like example of garden restoration and development Lucknow is a closely planted small town garden. Wheelchair access to Brome House and Went House only.

103 WHITE HORSES

Conyngham Road, Beltinge, Herne Bay, CT6 6PT. Dr Tim Waltham. *Conyngham Rd is next to the large Miramar Nursing Home, near the village Co-op. Unrestricted parking in surrounding roads.* **Sun 25 Aug (12-5). Adm £5, chd free.**
A Plantsman's garden replanted and improved for 2024! Smallish front and back garden, front lawn replaced with perennial bed, back garden contains three perennial borders. Situated in a dry and windy position, planting features euphorbia, salvias, sedums, asters, grasses, etc. Humane ways of dealing with nuisance birds and encouraging bees. Cash preferred for plant sale. Refreshments served at environmentally conscious HatHats coffee company, on Reculver sea front.

104 WINDY RIDGE

Dover Road, Guston, Dover, CT15 5EH. Mr David & Mrs Marianne Slater. *1m N of Dover. From Dover Castle take Guston Rd next to Coach Park and follow for ¾m, Windy Ridge on L side. Please use Car Park on opposite side, signposted.* **Sun 26 May (1-5). Adm £5, chd free. Home-made teas.**
Well established series of separate areas in ⅓ acre plot developed since 2008. Shrubs, herbaceous borders, lawns, pergola with wisteria, trees in pots, productive raised beds, soft and top fruit. Self sufficient in water (in most years) due to extensive rain harvesting, gravity fed to vegetable area. Paths smooth but narrow in places with some low steps to some seating areas.

105 ◆ THE WORLD GARDEN AT LULLINGSTONE CASTLE

Eynsford, DA4 0JA. Mrs Guy Hart Dyke, 01322 862114, info@lullingstonecastle.co.uk, www.lullingstonecastle.co.uk. *1m from Eynsford. Over Ford Bridge in Eynsford Village. Follow signs to Roman Villa. Keep Roman Villa immed on R then follow Private Rd to Gatehouse.* **For NGS: Sun 16 June (11-5). Adm £10, chd £5. Light refreshments. For other opening times and information, please phone, email or visit garden website.**
The World Garden is located within the two acre, C18 Walled Garden in the stunning grounds of Lullingstone Castle, where heritage meets cutting-edge horticulture. The garden is laid out in the shape of a miniature map of the world. Thousands of species are represented, all planted out in their respective beds. The World Garden Nursery offers a host of horticultural and homegrown delights, to reflect the unusual and varied planting of the garden. There is also the opportunity on your visit to purchase the new World Garden puzzle showcasing our 'Hot & Spiky' cactus house. Wheelchairs available upon request.

106 YOKES COURT

Coal Pit Lane, Frinsted, Sittingbourne, ME9 0ST. John & Kate Leigh Pemberton. *2.4m from Doddington. Turn off Old Lenham Rd to Hollingbourne. 1st R at Torry Hill Chestnut Fencing, then 1st L to Torry Hill. 1st L into Coal Pit Ln.* **Sun 30 June (1-5). Combined adm with Torry Hill £10, chd free. Home-made teas at Torry Hill House ME9 0SP.**
3 acre garden surrounded by countryside. Hedges and herbaceous borders set in open lawns. Rose beds. New prairie planting. Serpentine walkway through wildflowers. Walled vegetable garden.

In 2023, National Garden Scheme funding for Perennial supported a helpline service which provided advice, information and frontline support to around 800 people working in horticulture

LONDON

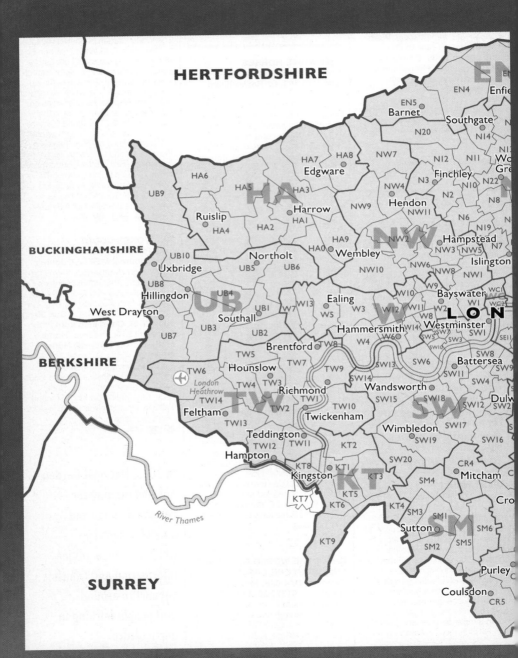

ESSEX

KENT

River Thames

London City

© Global Mapping / XYZ Maps

VOLUNTEERS

County Organiser
Penny Snell
01932 864532
pennysnellflowers@btinternet.com

County Treasurer
Marion Smart
marion.smart@ngs.org.uk

Publicity
Sonya Pinto
07779 609715
sonya.pinto@ngs.org.uk

Booklet Co-ordinator
Sue Phipps
07771 767196
sue@suephipps.com

Booklet Distributor
Joey Clover
joey.clover@ngs.org.uk

Social Media
Sonya Whaley
07941 010005
sonya.whaley@ngs.org.uk

Assistant County Organisers

Central London
Eveline Carn
07831 136069
evelinecbcarn@icloud.com

Clapham & surrounding area
Sue Phipps (as above)

Croydon & outer S London
Christine Murray & Nicola Dooley
07889 888204
christineandnicola.gardens@gmail.com

Dulwich & surrounding area
Clive Pankhurst
07941 536934
alternative.ramblings@gmail.com

E London
Teresa Farnham
07761 476651
farnhamz@yahoo.co.uk

Finchley & Barnet
Debra & Tim Craighead
07415 166617
dcraighead@icloud.com

Hackney
Philip Lightowlers
020 8533 0052
plighto@gmail.com

Hampstead
Joan Arnold
020 8444 8752
joan.arnold40@gmail.com

Islington
Judith Parker
07932 509459
jmfparker@aol.com

**Northwood, Pinner,
Ruislip & Harrow**
Brenda White
020 8863 5877
brenda.white@ngs.org.uk

NW London
Susan Bennett & Earl Hyde
020 8883 8540
suebearlh@yahoo.co.uk

Outer NW London
James Duncan Mattoon
07504 565612

Outer W London
Sarah Corvi
07803 111968
sarah.corvi@ngs.org.uk

SE London
Janine Wookey
07711 279636
j.wookey@btinternet.com

SW London
Joey Clover (as above)

W London, Barnes & Chiswick
Siobhan McCammon
07952 889866
siobhan.mccammon@gmail.com

f @LondonNGS
X @LondonNGS
@londonngs

75 Bampton Road

LONDON GARDENS LISTED BY POSTCODE

Inner London postcodes

E and EC London

Spitalfields Gardens, E1
69 Antill Road, E3
26 College Gardens, E4
Lower Clapton Gardens, E5
43 Roding Road, E5
84 Lavender Grove, E8
London Fields Gardens, E8
17 Greenstone Mews, E11
37 Harold Road, E11
Aldersbrook Gardens, E12
84 Higham Street, E17
28a Worcester Road, E17
83 Cowslip Road, E18
68 Derby Road, E18
The Inner and Middle
 Temple Gardens, EC4

N and NW London

Arlington Square Gardens,
 N1
Barnsbury Group, N1
De Beauvoir Gardens, N1
58 Halliford Street, N1
57 Huntingdon Street, N1
King Henry's Walk Garden,
 N1
7 St Paul's Place, N1
19 St Peter's Street, N1
6 Thornhill Road, N1
66 Abbots Gardens, N2
7 Deansway, N2
12 Lauradale Road, N2
24 Twyford Avenue, N2
4 Atterbury Road, N4
5 Blackthorn Av, Apartment
 5, N7
10 Furlong Road, N7
11 Park Avenue North, N8
77 Muswell Road, Flat 1,
 N10
Princes Avenue Gardens,
 N10
5 St Regis Close, N10
25 Springfield Avenue, N10
94 Brownlow Road, N11
Golf Course Allotments, N11
11 Shortgate, N12
70 Farleigh Road, N16

15 Norcott Road, N16
21 Gospatrick Road, N17
36 Ashley Road, N19
21 Oakleigh Park South,
 N20
20 Hillcrest, N21
Ally Pally Allotments, N22
Railway Cottages, N22
2 Camden Mews, NW1
Garden of Medicinal
 Plants, Royal College of
 Physicians, NW1
36 Park Village East, NW1
28a St Augustine's Road,
 NW1
93 Tanfield Avenue, NW2
Marie Curie Hospice,
 Hampstead, NW3
1A Primrose Gardens, NW3
The Mysteries of Light
 Rosary Garden, NW5
Torriano Community
 Garden, NW5
Highwood Ash, NW7
48 Erskine Hill, NW11
92 Hampstead Way, NW11
5 Hill Close, NW11

SE and SW London

Garden Barge Square
 at Tower Bridge
 Moorings, SE1
The Garden Museum, SE1
Lambeth Palace, SE1
36 Alma Grove, SE1
72 Ewhurst Road, SE4
24 Grove Park, SE5
30 Urlwin Street, SE5
41 Southbrook Road, SE12
13 Waite Davies Road,
 SE12
15 Waite Davies Road,
 SE12
Choumert Square, SE15
Holly Grove Gardens, SE15
Court Lane Group, SE21
103 & 105 Dulwich Village,
 SE21
38 Lovelace Road, SE21
174 Peckham Rye, SE22
86 Underhill Road, SE22
Forest Hill Garden Group,
 SE23
29 Lowther Hill, SE23
39 Wood Vale, SE23
75 Bampton Road, SE23
5 Burbage Road, SE24
South London Botanical
 Institute, SE24
27 Thorpewood Avenue,
 SE26

Cadogan Place South
 Garden, SW1
Eccleston Square, SW1
Spencer House, SW1
31 Trelawn Road, SW2
51 The Chase, SW4
Royal Trinity Hospice, SW4
152a Victoria Rise, SW4
The Hurlingham Club, SW6
1 Fife Road, SW14
40 Chartfield Avenue, SW15
39 Hazlewell Road, SW15
Roehampton Garden
 Society Allotments,
 SW15
31 Ryecroft Road, SW16
61 Arthur Road, SW19
97 Arthur Road, SW19
Paddock Allotments &
 Leisure Gardens, SW20

W and WC London

Rooftopvegplot, W1
Warren Mews, W1
34 Buxton Gardens, W3
41 Mill Hill Road, W3
Zen Garden at Japanese
 Buddhist Centre, W3
Chiswick Mall Gardens, W4
The Orchard, W4
Maggie's West London, W6
27 St Peters Square, W6
Temple Lodge Club, W6
1 York Close, W7
Edwardes Square, W8
57 St Quintin Avenue, W10
Arundel & Elgin Gardens,
 W11
Arundel & Ladbroke
 Gardens, W11
4 Wharton Street, WC1X

Outer London postcodes

37 Crescent Road, BR3
MHA The Wilderness, CR9
Oak Farm/Homestead, EN2
West Lodge Park, EN4
190 Barnet Road, EN5
9 Trafalgar Terrace, HA1
42 Risingholme Road, HA3
4 Manningtree Road, HA4
Horatio's Garden, HA7
53 Lady Aylesford Avenue,
 HA7
26 Hillcroft Crescent, HA9
42 Keynsham Avenue, IG8
7 Woodbines Avenue, KT1
The Watergardens, KT2
15 Catherine Road, KT6
Hampton Court Palace, KT8
5 Pemberton Road, KT8
61 Wolsey Road, KT8
40 Ember Lane, KT10
9 Imber Park Road, KT10
Maggie's, SM2
100 Colne Road, TW2
116 Whitton Road, TW3
Sussex Cottage, TW3
Kew Green Gardens, TW9
Marksbury Avenue Gardens,
 TW9
Ormeley Lodge, TW10
Petersham House, TW10
16 Links View Road, TW12
106 Station Road, TW12
9 Warwick Close, TW12
70 Wensleydale Road,
 TW12
4 Hanworth Road, TW13
Dragon's Dream, UB8
Church Gardens, UB9

51 The Chase

OPENING DATES

All entries subject to change. For latest information check www.ngs.org.uk

March

Sunday 17th
Royal Trinity Hospice, SW4

April

Sunday 14th
Edwardes Square, W8
39 Wood Vale, SE23

Wednesday 17th
39 Wood Vale, SE23

Sunday 21st
84 Lavender Grove, E8
Petersham House, TW10

Thursday 25th
◆ Hampton Court Palace, KT8

Saturday 27th
Maggie's West London, W6

Sunday 28th
Arundel & Ladbroke Gardens, W11
51 The Chase, SW4
37 Crescent Road, BR3
Royal Trinity Hospice, SW4
5 St Regis Close, N10
South London Botanical Institute, SE24
152a Victoria Rise, SW4
The Watergardens, KT2

Tuesday 30th
51 The Chase, SW4

May

Sunday 5th
7 Deansway, N2
42 Risingholme Road, HA3

Monday 6th
King Henry's Walk Garden, N1

Saturday 11th
Maggie's, SM2

Sunday 12th
Eccleston Square, SW1
Highwood Ash, NW7
Horatio's Garden, HA7
27 St Peters Square, W6

Thursday 16th
57 Huntingdon Street, N1

Saturday 18th
The Hurlingham Club, SW6

Sunday 19th
66 Abbots Gardens, N2
Arundel & Elgin Gardens, W11
190 Barnet Road, EN5
Forest Hill Garden Group, SE23
10 Furlong Road, N7
Garden Barge Square at Tower Bridge Moorings, SE1
92 Hampstead Way, NW11
4 Hanworth Road, TW13
5 Hill Close, NW11
Kew Green Gardens, TW9
NEW MHA The Wilderness, CR9
15 Norcott Road, N16
Princes Avenue Gardens, N10
Royal Trinity Hospice, SW4
West Lodge Park, EN4

Monday 20th
Lambeth Palace, SE1

Friday 24th
NEW 36 Alma Grove, SE1

Saturday 25th
Cadogan Place South Garden, SW1
16 Links View Road, TW12
7 St Paul's Place, N1
70 Wensleydale Road, TW12

Sunday 26th
NEW 36 Alma Grove, SE1
36 Ashley Road, N19
NEW 75 Bampton Road, SE23
NEW Holly Grove Gardens, SE15

Kew Green Gardens, TW9
16 Links View Road, TW12
NEW 31 Ryecroft Road, SW16
70 Wensleydale Road, TW12

Monday 27th
36 Ashley Road, N19

Friday 31st
Chiswick Mall Gardens, W4

June

Saturday 1st
41 Southbrook Road, SE12

Sunday 2nd
Barnsbury Group, N1
15 Catherine Road, KT6
40 Chartfield Avenue, SW15
Chiswick Mall Gardens, W4
Choumert Square, SE15
De Beauvoir Gardens, N1
68 Derby Road, E18
NEW 72 Ewhurst Road, SE4
39 Hazlewell Road, SW15
NEW 29 Lowther Hill, SE23
174 Peckham Rye, SE22
1A Primrose Gardens, NW3
19 St Peter's Street, N1
41 Southbrook Road, SE12
NEW Sussex Cottage, TW3
13 Waite Davies Road, SE12
15 Waite Davies Road, SE12
NEW 116 Whitton Road, TW3
61 Wolsey Road, KT8
7 Woodbines Avenue, KT1

Wednesday 5th
5 Burbage Road, SE24

Thursday 6th
The Inner and Middle Temple Gardens, EC4

Saturday 8th
Spitalfields Gardens, E1
Zen Garden at Japanese Buddhist Centre, W3

Sunday 9th
NEW 2 Camden Mews, NW1
26 College Gardens, E4
Dragon's Dream, UB8
103 & 105 Dulwich Village, SE21
40 Ember Lane, KT10
20 Hillcrest, N21
9 Imber Park Road, KT10
NEW 42 Keynsham Avenue, IG8
London Fields Gardens, E8
Marie Curie Hospice, Hampstead, NW3
Marksbury Avenue Gardens, TW9
36 Park Village East, NW1
25 Springfield Avenue, N10
31 Trelawn Road, SW2
Zen Garden at Japanese Buddhist Centre, W3

Saturday 15th
6 Thornhill Road, N1

Sunday 16th
97 Arthur Road, SW19
51 The Chase, SW4
58 Halliford Street, N1
37 Harold Road, E11
Lower Clapton Gardens, E5
21 Oakleigh Park South, N20
Ormeley Lodge, TW10
43 Roding Road, E5
Torriano Community Garden, NW5

Saturday 22nd
Paddock Allotments & Leisure Gardens, SW20
Warren Mews, W1

Sunday 23rd
Ally Pally Allotments, N22
Arlington Square Gardens, N1
1 Fife Road, SW14
Forest Hill Garden Group, SE23
38 Lovelace Road, SE21
4 Wharton Street, WC1X

Saturday 29th
The Mysteries of Light
Rosary Garden, NW5
Sunday 30th
61 Arthur Road, SW19
Court Lane Group, SE21
70 Farleigh Road, N16
5 Pemberton Road, KT8
5 St Regis Close, N10
11 Shortgate, N12
27 Thorpewood Avenue,
SE26

July

Saturday 6th
26 Hillcroft Crescent,
HA9
Rooftopvegplot, W1
Sunday 7th
Aldersbrook Gardens,
E12
[NEW] 69 Antill Road, E3
[NEW] 100 Colne Road,
TW2
83 Cowslip Road, E18
26 Hillcroft Crescent,
HA9
77 Muswell Road, Flat
1, N10
Railway Cottages, N22
Rooftopvegplot, W1
57 St Quintin Avenue,
W10
Monday 15th
Garden of Medicinal
Plants, Royal College
of Physicians, NW1
Thursday 18th
◆ Hampton Court
Palace, KT8
Saturday 20th
[NEW] 4 Atterbury Road,
N4
106 Station Road, TW12
Sunday 21st
[NEW] 4 Atterbury Road,
N4
11 Park Avenue North,
N8
[NEW] Roehampton Garden
Society Allotments,
SW15
57 St Quintin Avenue,
W10
106 Station Road, TW12

93 Tanfield Avenue, NW2
24 Twyford Avenue, N2
Saturday 27th
34 Buxton Gardens, W3
53 Lady Aylesford
Avenue, HA7
Sunday 28th
5 Blackthorn Av,
Apartment 5, N7
34 Buxton Gardens, W3
[NEW] 30 Urlwin Street,
SE5

August

Sunday 4th
94 Brownlow Road, N11
5 St Regis Close, N10
Saturday 10th
9 Warwick Close, TW12
Friday 16th
86 Underhill Road, SE22
Saturday 17th
1 York Close, W7
Sunday 18th
51 The Chase, SW4
[NEW] 84 Higham Street,
E17
4 Manningtree Road,
HA4
86 Underhill Road, SE22
28a Worcester Road,
E17
1 York Close, W7

September

Sunday 1st
Golf Course Allotments,
N11
24 Grove Park, SE5
41 Mill Hill Road, W3
42 Risingholme Road, HA3
Friday 6th
The Orchard, W4
Saturday 7th
9 Trafalgar Terrace, HA1
Sunday 8th
◆ Church Gardens, UB9
12 Lauradale Road, N2
Oak Farm/Homestead,
EN2
Tuesday 10th
◆ The Garden Museum,
SE1

Saturday 14th
Temple Lodge Club, W6
Sunday 15th
Horatio's Garden, HA7
Royal Trinity Hospice,
SW4
Saturday 21st
1A Primrose Gardens,
NW3

October

Sunday 20th
The Watergardens, KT2
West Lodge Park, EN4

By Arrangement

Arrange a personalised
garden visit with your
club, or group of friends,
on a date to suit you. See
individual garden entries
for full details.

8 Almack Road, Lower
Clapton Gardens, E5
36 Ashley Road, N19
[NEW] 75 Bampton Road,
SE23
190 Barnet Road, EN5
5 Burbage Road, SE24
[NEW] 100 Colne Road,
TW2

7 Deansway, N2
40 Ember Lane, KT10
48 Erskine Hill, NW11
21 Gospatrick Road, N17
17 Greenstone Mews,
E11
92 Hampstead Way,
NW11
57 Huntingdon Street, N1
9 Imber Park Road, KT10
12 Lauradale Road, N2
84 Lavender Grove, E8
41 Mill Hill Road, W3
The Mysteries of Light
Rosary Garden, NW5
21 Oakleigh Park South,
N20
1A Primrose Gardens,
NW3
28a St Augustine's Road,
NW1
27 St Peters Square, W6
57 St Quintin Avenue,
W10
5 St Regis Close, N10
41 Southbrook Road,
SE12
93 Tanfield Avenue, NW2
24 Twyford Avenue, N2
9 Warwick Close, TW12
West Lodge Park, EN4
4 Wharton Street, WC1X
61 Wolsey Road, KT8

84 Higham Street

THE GARDENS

66 ABBOTS GARDENS, N2

East Finchley, N2 0JH. Stephen & Ruth Kersley, www.instagram.com/garden_at_66. *8 min walk from rear exit of East Finchley Tube (Northern Line), take Causeway to East End Rd, 2nd L into Abbots Gardens. Buses: 143 stops at Abbotts Gardens, 102, 263 & 234 all go to High Rd.* **Sun 19 May (2-6). Adm £5, chd free. Home-made teas.**

Combination of grass and glass with a calm dramatic atmosphere. Mosaics surround a water feature, home to fish. Fused glass amphorae, feathers and leaves catch the eye amongst grasses, ornamental shrubs and perennials. Rose bedecked archway leads to quiet space with vegetable plot, silver birches and slate pebble fountain. Stephen studied garden design at Capel Manor College; Ruth is a stained glass artist. Also, take a look at the lovely front garden at No. 8 created by Stephen.

GROUP OPENING

ALDERSBROOK GARDENS, E12

Wanstead, E12 5ES. *Empress Ave is a turning off Aldersbrook Rd. Bus 101 from Manor Park or Wanstead Stns. From Manor Park Stn take the 3rd R off Aldersbrook Rd. From Wanstead, drive past St Gabriel's Church, take 6th turning on L.* **Sun 7 July (12-5). Combined adm £10, chd free. Home-made teas at 1 Clavering Road & 4 Empress Avenue.**

19 BELGRAVE ROAD
Gill Usher.

1 CLAVERING ROAD
Theresa Harrison.

39 DOVER ROAD
Brenda Keer.

4 EMPRESS AVENUE
Ruth Martin.

Four different gardens situated on the Aldersbrook Estate between Wanstead Park and Wanstead Flats. 1 Clavering Road is an end of terrace garden where incremental space to the side has been adapted to create a kitchen garden and chicken coop, excess produce is eagerly received by five resident hens. Borders and beds contain a variety of planting. At

4 Empress Avenue a largish garden is divided in two with a cutting bed, soft fruit and wildlife areas inc pond and two mixed borders: one with hot colours and one with white planting. The diverse garden at 19 Belgrave Road is eclectic and busting at the seams with trees and plants. Gill is a ceramicist who uses the plants in her work in her garden studio. Surviving, Edwardian design garden at 39 Dover Road, a new addition to the group this yr.

ALLY PALLY ALLOTMENTS, N22

Alexandra Palace Way, N22 7BB. Peter Campbell. *Entry gate in wooden fence, nr the footpath to Springfield Ave & Garden Centre, look for arrows. Bus W3 to Alexandra Palace Garden Centre stop. Car parking nearby in Dukes Ave, N10. Blue badge holder parking in The Grove. No parking on site.* **Sun 23 June (1-4.30). Adm £5, chd free. Home-made teas.**

Situated on a south facing hillside alongside Alexandra Park, this 140 plot allotment site has the feel of an urban village with spectacular views towards central London and, on a clear day, the North Downs. Its diverse community of gardeners grow fruit, vegetables and flowers with an emphasis on promoting biodiversity. Clearly marked trails will enable you to explore the site and meet plotholders. Plants, produce and used tools on sale. Cash preferred on the day, card reader available for teas and produce.

36 ALMA GROVE, SE1

Bermondsey, SE1 5PY. Alice Jeffries, www.instagram.com/housewithabluedoor. *Between Old Jamaica & Old Kent Rd. Nr Bermondsey Tube (10 min walk). Train: South Bermondsey (15 mins) & London Bridge (20 mins). Buses: 1 (2 mins) & 78 (5 mins).* **Evening opening Fri 24 May (5.30-7.30). Adm £6. Wine. Sun 26 May (2-5). Adm £4.50, chd free. Home-made teas.**

A secluded cottage garden right in the heart of Bermondsey mixing edibles, pollinator friendly planting, annuals and perennials in flower and raised beds. Space saving options for composting, a pond, potting shed and greenhouse, and multiple water containers allowing this small garden (10 x 10 metres) to do much more

than its size suggests. Espresso-based coffee, tea, home-made refreshments inc gluten free and vegan options.

69 ANTILL ROAD, E3

Bow, E3 5BT. Mr William Dowden. *Short walk from Mile End Tube or buses 277, 339, 425 & D6 on Grove Rd.* **Sun 7 July (1-7). Adm £5, chd free. Home-made teas.**

A tropically inspired garden with a range of trees and shrubs. The garden is divided into rooms which show off the elegance of hydrangeas and roses and the lushness of palms, yews and acers. There are several water features and an elegant gazebo. A tranquil place in which to relax with friends and family.

GROUP OPENING

ARLINGTON SQUARE GARDENS, N1

N1 7DP. *South Islington. Off New North Rd via Arlington Ave or Linton St. Buses: 21, 76, 141. 15 min walk from Angel Tube. LTNs operate in this area.* **Sun 23 June (2-5.30). Combined adm £10, chd free. Home-made teas in Arlington Square.**

4 ARLINGTON AVENUE
Helen Nowicka.

15 ARLINGTON AVENUE
Armin Eiber & Richard Armit.

26 ARLINGTON AVENUE
Thomas Blaikie, www.instagram.com/thomas_blaikie.

21 ARLINGTON SQUARE
Alison Rice.

25 ARLINGTON SQUARE
Michael Foley.

30 ARLINGTON SQUARE
James & Maria Hewson.

5 REES STREET
Gordon McArthur & Paul Thompson-McArthur.

Seven early Victorian terraced houses with similar sized small gardens and conditions but with very different garden styles. From a garden designer's exotic contemporary space to an organic wildlife haven, there should be something for all gardeners, whether green-fingered or complete beginners: exotic and unusual plants, gorgeous flowers, lawn paths, hard

4 Atterbury Road

landscaping, composting, rewilding, thrifty up-cycling, fruit, vegetables, herbs, beehives and a wildlife pond. These gardens reflect the diverse tastes and interests of friends who got to know each other through community gardening, helping transform and maintain Arlington Square from a drab and rundown space to an award-winning beautiful and plant-rich public garden which, like the seven private gardens, offers a calm oasis just minutes from the bustle of the City of London.

61 ARTHUR ROAD, SW19
Wimbledon, SW19 7DN. Daniela McBride. *5 mins from St Mary's Church. Tube: Wimbledon Park, then 8 min walk. Train: Wimbledon, 18 min walk.* **Sun 30 June (2-6). Adm £5, chd free. Home-made teas.** This steeply, sloping garden comprises woodland walks filled with flowering shrubs and ferns. Azaleas, rhododendrons and acers bring early season colour. In early summer the focus is the many roses grown around the garden, alongside colourful perennials and a productive herb garden. Partial wheelchair access to top lawn and terrace only, steep slopes elsewhere.

Our donation to the Army Benevolent Fund supported 608 individuals with front line services and horticultural related grants in 2023

97 ARTHUR ROAD, SW19

Wimbledon, SW19 7DP. Tony & Bella Covill. *Wimbledon Park Tube Stn, then 200yds uphill on R.* **Sun 16 June (2-6). Adm £5, chd free. Light refreshments.**
½ acre garden of an Edwardian house (not open). Garden established over 25 yrs with a large variety of mature plants and shrubs, and sloping lawns become a wildflower meadow. Ponds and fountains encourage an abundance of wildlife and a bird haven, and our gravel garden is planted to attract butterflies. A peaceful place with much colour, foliage and texture. Partial wheelchair access.

ARUNDEL & ELGIN GARDENS, W11

Kensington Park Road, Notting Hill, W11 2JD. Residents of Arundel Gardens & Elgin Crescent, www.instagram.com/arundelelgin. *Entrance opp 174 Kensington Park Rd. Nearest tube within walking distance: Ladbroke Grove (5 mins) or Notting Hill (10 mins). Buses: 52, 452, 23, 228 all stop opp garden entrance.* **Sun 19 May (2-6). Adm £5, chd free. Home-made teas.**
A friendly and informal garden square. One of the best preserved gardens of the Ladbroke Estate with mature and rare trees, plants and shrubs laid out according to the original Victorian design of 1862. The larger garden inc a topiary hedge, a rare mulberry tree, a pergola and benches from which vistas can be enjoyed. The central hedged garden is an oasis of tranquillity with extensive and colourful herbaceous borders. All looked after by Gardener, Paul Walsh. Play areas for young children.

ARUNDEL & LADBROKE GARDENS, W11

Kensington Park Road, Notting Hill, W11 2PT. Arundel & Ladbroke Gardens Committee, www.arundelladbrokegardens.co.uk. *Entrance on Kensington Park Rd, between Ladbroke & Arundel Gardens. Tube: Notting Hill Gate or Ladbroke Grove. Buses: 23, 52, 228, 452. Alight at stop for Portobello Market/Arundel Gardens.* **Sun 28 Apr (2-6). Adm £5, chd free. Home-made teas.**
This private communal garden is one of the few that retains its attractive mid-Victorian design of lawns and winding paths. A woodland garden at its peak in spring with rhododendrons, flowering dogwoods, early roses, bulbs, ferns and rare exotics. Live music on the lawn during tea. Playground for small children. Wheelchair access with a few steps and gravel paths to negotiate.

36 ASHLEY ROAD, N19

Crouch Hill, N19 3AF. Alan Swann & Ahmed Farooqui, swann.alan@googlemail.com, www.instagram.com/space36garden. *Between Stroud Green & Crouch End. Tube: Archway or Finsbury Park. Train: Crouch Hill. Buses: 210 or 41 from Archway to Hornsey Rise. W7 from Finsbury Park to Heathville Rd. Car: Free parking in Ashley Rd at weekends.* **Sun 26, Mon 27 May (2-6). Adm £4, chd free. Home-made teas. Visits also by arrangement 13 May to 30 Sept for groups of 8 to 30.**
A lush town garden rich in textures, colour and forms. At its best in late spring as Japanese maple cultivars display great variety of shape and colour whilst ferns unfurl fresh, vibrant fronds over a tumbling stream and, wisteria and clematis burst into flower on the balcony and pergola. A number of microhabitats inc fern walls, bog garden, stream and ponds, rockeries, alpines and shade plantings. Young ferns and plants propagated from the garden for sale. Pop-up café with a variety of cakes, biscuits, gluten free and vegan options, and traditional home-brewed ginger beer. Seating areas around the garden.

NEW 4 ATTERBURY ROAD, N4

Harringay, N4 1SF. Clare & Raj Panjwani. *Harringay Ladder. Closest stations: Harringay Overground, Manor House Tube. Buses 29, 141, 341 to Green Ln, then walk.* **Evening opening Sat 20 July (5-8). Adm £7. Wine. Sun 21 July (2-6). Adm £5. Cream teas.**
Four yrs ago, this garden underwent a complete transformation. Previously, a traditional suburban lawn and border garden, the owners turned it into a lush oasis for practical outdoor living. At its heart lies a serene pond, encircled by a walkway, guiding you through banana palms, kiwis, figs, grapevines and apricots. An ash deck, oak bench cooking area and self-built greenhouse complete it.

NEW 75 BAMPTON ROAD, SE23

SE23 2AX. Max Vickers, 07532 324510, maxvickers.gardens@gmail.com. *7 min walk from Forest Hill Stn, nearest bus stop on Perry Vale.* **Sun 26 May (2-5). Adm £5, chd free. Home-made teas. Visits also by arrangement Apr to Sept for groups of up to 15.**
A small designer's garden, set into a tranquil and tree-lined oasis behind a modernist terrace nr Forest Hill Stn. The garden is defined by strong architectural features inc espaliered crab apples, yew and box topiary, and steel water tanks. Planting is dense and lush in early summer inc peonies, grasses and hostas, before building to an exuberant autumn display.

190 BARNET ROAD, EN5

The Upcycled Garden, Arkley, Barnet, EN5 3LF. Hilde Wainstein, 07949 764007, hildewainstein@hotmail.co.uk. *1m S of A1, 2m N of High Barnet Tube Stn. Garden located on corner of A411 Barnet Rd & Meadowbanks cul-de-sac. Nearest tube: High Barnet, then 107 bus, Glebe Ln stop. Ample unrestricted roadside parking. NB Do not park half on pavement.* **Sun 19 May (1-6). Adm £5, chd free. Home-made teas & gluten free options. Visits also by arrangement 20 May to 15 Sept for groups of 5 to 30.**
Walled garden, 90ft x 36ft with a modern design and year-round interest. Handmade copper pipe trellis divides space into contrasting areas. Herbaceous planting and bulbs drift around trees, shrubs and pond. Kitchen garden with soft fruit and vegetables. Upcycled containers, recycled objects, and home-made sculptures. Gravel garden areas that are never watered. Garden continues evolving as planted areas are expanded. Organic. Home-made jams and plants for sale, all propagated from the garden. Wheelchair access with single steps within garden.

GROUP OPENING

BARNSBURY GROUP, N1

N1 1BX. *Tube: King's Cross, Caledonian Rd or Angel. Train: Caledonian Rd & Barnsbury. Buses: 17, 91, 259 to Caledonian Rd. Buses: 4, 19, 30, 38, 43 to St Mary's Church, Upper St, for Lonsdale Sq.*

Sun 2 June (2-6). Combined adm £12, chd free. Individual garden adm £4 each. Home-made teas at 57 Huntingdon Street.

◆ BARNSBURY WOOD
London Borough of Islington, ecologycentre@islington.gov.uk.

57 HUNTINGDON STREET
Julian Williams.
(See separate entry)

2 LONSDALE SQUARE
Jenny Kingsley.

36 THORNHILL SQUARE
Anna & Christopher McKane.

Discover four contrasting spaces in Barnsbury's Georgian squares. 57 Huntingdon Street is a secluded garden with birches, ferns, perennials, grasses and container ponds to encourage wildlife. 36 Thornhill Square, a 120ft garden with a country atmosphere, is filled with scented roses, clematis, specimen trees and perennials and a new pond attracts wildlife. Bonsai and planters surround the patio. 2 Lonsdale Square is a charming small cobblestoned garden with herbaceous beds and apple trees, structured with box and yew hedges. Climbing roses and star jasmine add delicious scent; planters overflow with lavender and pansies. Barnsbury Wood is London's smallest nature reserve, a hidden gem and one of Islington's few sites of semi-mature woodland, a tranquil oasis of wild flowers and massive trees minutes from Caledonian Road. Wildlife information available. The gardens reveal what can be achieved with the right plants in the right conditions, surmounting difficulties of dry walls and shade. Unusual plants for sale at 36 Thornhill Square.

 ·)))

5 BLACKTHORN AV, APARTMENT 5, N7
Apartment 5, 5 Blackthorn Avenue, N7 8AQ. Juan Carlos Cure Hazzi. *Barnsbury. 6 min walk from Highbury & Islington Stn. Building is on S side of Arundel Square.* **Sun 28 July (11-6). Adm £7. Pre-booking essential, please visit www.ngs. org.uk for information & booking. Light refreshments.**
Small patio garden with beautiful connection with the house. Plenty of colour, texture and year-round interest with lush tropical, subtropical and temperate plants.

 ·)))

94 BROWNLOW ROAD, N11
Bounds Green, N11 2BS.
Spencer Viner. *Tube: Bounds Green, then 5 min walk, direction North Circular. Corner of Elvendon Rd & Brownlow Rd. Buses 299 & 102.* **Sun 4 Aug (2-6). Adm £4, chd free. Light refreshments. Open nearby 5 St Regis Close.**
A small courtyard for meditation created by designer owner, transports the visitor to foreign places of imagination and tranquillity. Features inc reclaimed materials, trees, water, pergola and pleached limes. Pared back simplicity contrasts with newly created prairie planting in front of house on busy main road. Design and horticultural advice available.

5 BURBAGE ROAD, SE24
Herne Hill, SE24 9HJ. Crawford & Rosemary Lindsay, 020 7274 5610, rl@rosemarylindsay.com, www.rosemarylindsay.com. *Nr junction with Half Moon Ln. Herne Hill & N Dulwich Train Stns, 5 min walk. Buses: 3, 37, 40, 68, 196, 468.* **Evening opening Wed 5 June (5.30-8). Adm £7.50, chd free. Wine. Cash only. Visits also by arrangement 1 Mar to 15 June.**
The garden of a member of The Society of Botanical Artists and regular writer for Hortus journal. 150ft x 40ft with large and varied range of plants, many unusual. Herbaceous borders for sun and shade, climbing plants, pots, terraces and lawns. Immaculate topiary. Gravel areas to reduce watering. All the box has been removed because of attack by blight and moth, and replaced with suitable alternatives to give a similar look. A garden that delights from spring through to summer.

34 BUXTON GARDENS, W3
Black&Bold, Acton, W3 9LQ. Alex Buxton. *10-15 min walk from: Acton Town Stn (Piccadilly Line), Acton Main Train Stn, Acton Central Train Stn, West Acton Stn (Central Line).* **Sat 27, Sun 28 July (3-7). Adm £5, chd free. Home-made teas.**
Have you been to the Black & Bold yet? Traditional elements of a garden reimagined at Black & Bold. Darkest reds, purple and copper spill over the rockery, the cottage garden and on the banks of its ponds which are fed by a waterfall, even the smallest meadow is black. Black & Bold the 1000ft square garden which is different, extraordinary and wild!

CADOGAN PLACE SOUTH GARDEN, SW1
Sloane Street, Chelsea, SW1X 9PE. The Cadogan Estate, www.cadogan.co.uk. *Entrance to garden opp 97 Sloane St.* **Sat 25 May (10-4). Adm £5, chd free.**
Many surprises, unusual trees and shrubs are hidden behind the railings of this large London square. The first square to be developed by architect Henry Holland for Lord Cadogan at the end of C18, it was then called the London Botanic Garden. Mulberry trees planted for silk production at end of C17. Cherry trees, wisteria pergola and bulbs are outstanding in spring. Beautiful 300 yr old black mulberry tree (originally planted to produce silk, but incorrect variety!). Area of drought resistant, pollinator plants. This was once the home of the Royal Botanic Garden. Now featuring a bug hotel, children's playground and four wildlife ponds.

NEW 2 CAMDEN MEWS, NW1
Camden Town, NW1 9DB. Annabel & Beverley Rowe. *Arriving by bus, take 29 or 253 to Murray St. Go N for a couple of mins & turn R on Murray St. Take 1st R on Camden Mews & you will see the yellow signs.* **Sun 9 June (3-6). Adm £5, chd free. Light refreshments.**
Twenty yrs ago, two long gardens were turned into one. This resulted in a good sized garden, unusually broad for London and very secluded. Established trees, shrubs and flower beds break up the space so you don't see it all at once. A pool with good marginal planting. Wheelchair access over paved paths. No steps or narrow spaces.

The National Garden Scheme searches the length and breadth of England, Wales, Northern Ireland and the Channel Islands for the very best private gardens

15 CATHERINE ROAD, KT6
Surbiton, KT6 4HA. Malcolm
Simpson & Stefan Gross. *10 min
walk from Surbiton Stn. Public
transport is recommended. Limited
free parking in immed area at
weekends.* **Sun 2 June (12-5).
Combined adm with 7 Woodbines
Avenue £7, chd free.**
A well loved town garden approx 40ft
x 70ft with deep borders of shrubs
and perennial planting, sculptures,
a small folly and a walled area. A
stroll along the river leads you to
7 Woodbines Avenue and allows
visitors to enjoy the gardens along the
Queen's Promenade partly restored
by volunteers.

40 CHARTFIELD AVENUE, SW15
Putney, SW15 6HG. Sally. *10 min
walk from Putney Train Stn & 15
mins from East Putney Tube Stn.
Buses: 14, 37, 93, 85, 39 stop at
end of Chartfield Ave on Putney Hill.
Some free parking at weekends.* **Sun
2 June (2.30-5). Combined adm
with 39 Hazlewell Road £7, chd
free. Light refreshments.**
Fifteen yrs in the making, built and
landscaped on a sloping site, the
garden inc the planting of more than
30 trees. Inspired by the borrowed
landscape with swathes of perennials
around a circular lawn leading to
a more structural feel around the
terrace. Kitchen garden, developing
gravel garden and invisible pergola.
Many shaded seating areas and
places to sit and relax.

51 THE CHASE, SW4
SW4 0NP. Mr Charles
Rutherfoord & Mr Rupert Tyler,
www.charlesrutherfoord.net. *Off
Clapham Common Northside. Tube:
Clapham Common. Buses: 137,
452, 77, 87, 345, 37.* **Sun 28 Apr
(12-5). Evening opening Tue 30
Apr (5.30-8). Sun 16 June, Sun
18 Aug (12-5). Adm £5, chd free.
Light refreshments. Open nearby
152a Victoria Rise & Royal Trinity
Hospice on 28 Apr only.**
Charles, past Chairman of Society
of Garden Designers, and Rupert,
Chairman of NGS, have created the
garden over 40 yrs. Spectacular
in spring when 2500 tulips bloom
among camellias, irises and tree
peonies. Scented front garden.
Rupert's geodetic dome shelters
seedlings, succulents and the
subtropical. Roses, brugmansia,

hibiscus and dahlias later in the
season. New vegetable garden added
in 2023.

GROUP OPENING

CHISWICK MALL GARDENS, W4
Chiswick Mall, Chiswick, W4 2PS.
*By car: Hogarth r'about turn down
Church St or A4 (W), turn L to Eyot
Gardens. Tube: Stamford Brook or
Turnham Green, walk under A4 to
river. Buses: 110, 190, 267, H91.*
**Evening opening Fri 31 May (6-8).
Combined adm £12.50, chd free.
Wine. Sun 2 June (2-5). Combined
adm £15, chd free.**

CEDAR HOUSE
Stephanie & Philippe Camu.
Open on Sun 2 June

FIELD HOUSE
Rupert King,
www.fieldhousegarden.co.uk.
Open on all dates

LONGMEADOW
Charlotte Fraser.
Open on all dates

MILLER'S COURT
Miller's Court Tenants Ltd.
Open on Sun 2 June

THE OLD VICARAGE
Eleanor Fein.
Open on Sun 2 June

NEW ST JOHN'S
George Spalton KC.
Open on Sun 2 June

ST PETERS WHARF
Barbara Brown.
Open on Sun 2 June

SWAN HOUSE
Mr & Mrs George Nissen.
Open on all dates

Gardens on or near the Thames
in historic Old Chiswick. You will
visit a riverside garden in an artist's
community, several large walled
gardens, and a communal garden
on the riverbank with well-planted
borders and lovely views.

CHOUMERT SQUARE, SE15
Choumert Grove, Peckham,
SE15 4RE. The Residents. *Close
to Peckham Car Park. Off Choumert
Grove. Trains from London Victoria,
London Bridge, London Blackfriars,
Clapham Junction to Peckham Rye;
buses 12, 36, 37, 63, 78, 171, 312,*

*345. Free car park in Choumert
Grove.* **Sun 2 June (1-6). Adm £4,
chd free. Savoury items, home-
made teas & Pimms. Donation to
St Christopher's Hospice.**
About 46 mini gardens with maxi
planting in Shangri-la situation that
the media has described as a floral
canyon, which leads to a small
communal secret garden. The day is
primarily about gardens and sharing
with others our residents' love of this
little corner of the inner city, but it is
also renowned for its demonstrable
community spirit and a variety of stalls
and live music. Wheelchair access;
one tiny step to raised paved area in
the communal garden.

◆ CHURCH GARDENS, UB9
Church Hill, Harefield,
Uxbridge, UB9 6DU. Patrick &
Kay McHugh, 01895 823539,
churchgardensharefield@gmail.
com, www.churchgardens.co.uk.
*From Harefield Village, continue for
¼ m down Church Hill. From A40
Uxbridge junction, follow signs to
Harefield. Turn off Church Hill towards
St Mary's Church.* **For NGS: Sun
8 Sept (11-5). Adm £5, chd £2.
Pre-booking preferred, please
visit www.churchgardens.co.uk
for information & booking. Light
refreshments. For other opening
times and information, please
phone, email or visit garden website.**
Harefield's own secret garden.
C17 Renaissance walled gardens
on the outskirts of Harefield inc a
geometrically designed organic
kitchen garden, 60 metre long
herbaceous borders, fruit cage,
alpines, herb garden, vine mount
and an orchard with rare arcaded
wall, dating back to the early 1600s.
Unique opportunity to view ongoing
restoration project. Home-made
cake, tea, coffee and alcohol will be
available throughout the day and light
lunches from 12pm.

26 COLLEGE GARDENS, E4
Chingford, E4 7LG. Lynnette
Parvez. *2m from Walthamstow. 15
min walk from Chingford Train Stn.
Bus 97 from Walthamstow Central
Tube Stn, alight at College Gardens,
then short walk downhill.* **Sun 9
June (2-5). Adm £4, chd free.
Home-made teas.**
Large suburban garden, approx ⅔
acre. Sun terrace leads to established
borders and a variety of climbing

roses. Beyond this, wildlife pond and lawn, small woodland walk with spring plants and wildlife. A further area to the end with raised vegetable beds and a fruit cage.

 100 COLNE ROAD, TW2
Twickenham, TW2 6QE.
Karen Grosch, 020 8893 3660,
info@whettonandgrosch.co.uk,
www.instagram.com/
karensroofgarden. *5 min walk from Twickenham Green. 12 min walk from Twickenham or Strawberry Hill Train Stn. Bus 406, H22 from Richmond Train & Tube Stn, alight Twickenham Green, then short walk. By road, turn off Staines Rd coming from M25/M3 & A416.* **Sun 7 July (11-6). Adm £7. Pre-booking essential, please visit www.ngs.org.uk for information & booking. Light refreshments. Visits also by arrangement 17 June to 6 July for groups of 5 to 6. Please contact for larger groups, weight limitations apply.**
Enchanting first floor roof garden above 1850s workers cottage with converted 1950s studios, and artist workshops to the rear. Wide spiral staircase leads to sheltered garden 9 x 8 metres, intensively planted and fully containerised. A mix of trees, shrubs, climbers, subtle annual perennial plant combinations and new 7 x 10 metre rear extensive roof area with biodiversity mix of sedums and wild flowers. Visits booked during week 17 June-7 July in conjunction with ArtsRichmond Open Studios Festival. Variety of work on show in downstairs studios: painting, prints, ceramics and sculpture.

GROUP OPENING

COURT LANE GROUP, SE21
Dulwich Village, SE21 7EA. *South East London. Buses: P4, 12, 40, 176, 185 to Dulwich Library 37. Train Stn: North Dulwich, then 12 min walk. Ample free parking in Court Ln.* **Sun 30 June (2-5.30). Combined adm £10, chd free. Tea & cakes at 122 Court Lane. Light refreshments at 164 Court Lane.**

122 COURT LANE
Jean & Charles Cary-Elwes.

148 COURT LANE
Mr Anthony & Mrs Sue Wadsworth.

164 COURT LANE
James & Katie Dawes.

No. 164 was recently redesigned to create a more personal and intimate space with several specific zones. A modern terrace and seating area leads onto a lawn with abundant borders and a beautiful mature oak. A rose arch leads to the vegetable beds and greenhouse. No. 122 has a countryside feel, backing onto Dulwich Park with colourful herbaceous borders and unusual plants. No.148 a spacious garden, developed over twenty yrs backs on to Dulwich Park. From the wide sunny terrace surrounded by tall, golden bamboos and fan palms, step down into a garden designed with an artist's eye for colour, form, texture and flow, creating intimate spaces beneath mature trees and shrubs with colourful perennials. Live jazz on the terrace, a children's trail, plant sales and a wormery demonstration at No.122.

83 COWSLIP ROAD, E18
South Woodford, E18 1JN. Fiona Grant. *5 min walk from Central Line tube. Close to exit for A406.* **Sun 7 July (2-6). Adm £5, chd free. Home-made teas.**
80ft long wildlife friendly garden, on two levels at rear of Victorian semi. Patio has a selection of containers with a step down to the lawn past a pond full of wildlife. Flowerbeds stuffed with an eclectic mix of perennials. Ample seating on patio and overspill seating in delightful adjacent garden.

37 CRESCENT ROAD, BR3
Beckenham, BR3 6NF. Myra & Tim Bright. *15 min walk from Beckenham Junction Stn. 227 bus route from Shortlands Stn. Street parking in adjacent roads.* **Sun 28 Apr (2-5.30). Adm £4, chd free. Home-made teas.**
A romantic garden. In spring tulips abound amongst euphorbias and forget-me-nots. In summer, an abundance of geraniums, foxgloves and allium fill the front borders. Go past the potting shed, under the vine arch you arrive in the garden filled with herbaceous plants, roses and clematis, a magnet for bees and butterflies. Gravel paths lead to secret corners with seating.

GROUP OPENING

DE BEAUVOIR GARDENS, N1
100 Downham Road, Hackney, N1 5BE. *Tube stations: Highbury & Islington, then 30 bus; Angel, then 38, 56 or 73 bus; Bank, then 21, 76 or 141 bus. 10 min walk from Dalston Junction Train Stn. Street parking. LTNs operate in this area.* **Sun 2 June (2-6). Combined adm £10, chd free. Home-made teas at 100 Downham Road.**

100 DOWNHAM ROAD
Ms Cecilia Darker.

64 LAWFORD ROAD

72 MORTIMER ROAD
Mr Stephen King.

 1 NORTHCHURCH TERRACE
Joan Ward.

21 NORTHCHURCH TERRACE
Nancy Korman.

Five gardens to explore in De Beauvoir, a leafy enclave of Victorian villas near to Islington and Dalston. The area boasts some of Hackney's keenest gardeners and a thriving garden club. New this year is 1 Northchurch Terrace which has a diverse range of potted shrubs, ferns and flowers. 21 Northchurch Terrace is a walled garden with a formal feel and deep borders which have recently been replanted. 72 Mortimer Road is a secluded romantic garden with colourful and wildflower planting. 100 Downham Road features giant echiums, two green roofs and a pond with a miniature Giverny-style bridge. 64 Lawford Road is a small cottage style garden with old-fashioned roses, espaliered apples and scented plants.

In 2023, our donations to Carers Trust meant that 26,118 unpaid carers were supported across the UK

7 DEANSWAY, N2
East Finchley, N2 0NF. Joan Arnold & Tom Heinersdorff, 07850 764543, joan.arnold40@gmail.com. *Hampstead Garden Suburb. From East Finchley Tube Stn exit along the Causeway to East End Rd, then L down Deansway. From Bishops Ave, head N up Deansway towards East End Rd, close to the top.* **Sun 5 May (12-5.30). Adm £5, chd free. Home-made teas. Visits also by arrangement 17 Feb to 28 July for groups of up to 30.**
A garden of stories, statues, shapes and structures surrounded by trees and hedges. Bird friendly, cottage style with scented roses, clematis, mature shrubs, a weeping mulberry and abundant planting. Containers, spring bulbs and grapevine provide year-round colour. Developing secret, shady and wild woodland area with ferns and hostas. Cakes, gluten free cakes and plants for sale (cash preferred). Wheelchair access through side passage to patio. Assistance may be required with three shallow steps to the lawn and main garden.

68 DERBY ROAD, E18
South Woodford, E18 2PS. Mrs Michelle Greene. *Nearest tube: South Woodford (Central Line). Buses: 20 & 179 to Chelmsford Rd. Close to Epping Forest & the Waterworks r'about.* **Sun 2 June (1-5). Adm £5, chd free. Home-made teas.**
Old fashioned summer garden with two ponds, one for wildlife and one for goldfish. Tiny orchard, vegetable beds and rockery. Highlights inc American pokeweed and Himalayan honeysuckle. Many unusual plants with small plants for sale.

DRAGON'S DREAM, UB8
Grove Lane, Uxbridge, UB8 3RG. Chris & Meng Pocock. *Garden is in a small lane very close to Hillingdon Hospital. Parking available next door. Buses from Uxbridge Tube Stn: U1, U3, U4, U5, U7. Buses from West Drayton: U1, U3.* **Sun 9 June (2-5). Adm £5, chd free. Home-made teas.**
This is an unusual and secluded garden with two contrasting sections divided by a brick shed that has been completely covered by a rampant wisteria and a climbing hydrangea and rose. Other highlights inc rare dawn redwood tree and a huge

Gunnera manicata. More features inc a Romneya poppy, ferns, rose and herb beds, tree peonies, acers and a pond. Refreshments inc home-made cakes, Malaysian curry puffs and café gourmand (tea or coffee, plus bite-sized cakes).

GROUP OPENING

103 & 105 DULWICH VILLAGE, SE21
SE21 7BJ. *Train: North Dulwich or West Dulwich then 10-15 min walk. Tube: Brixton then P4 bus, alight Dulwich Picture Gallery stop. Street parking.* **Sun 9 June (2-5). Combined adm £10, chd free. Home-made teas at 103 Dulwich Village (adm inc tea, coffee & soft drink). Donation to Link Age Southwark.**

103 DULWICH VILLAGE
Mr & Mrs N Annesley.

105 DULWICH VILLAGE
Mr & Mrs A Rutherford.

Two Georgian houses with large gardens, 3 min walk from Dulwich Picture Gallery and Dulwich Park. 103 Dulwich Village is a country garden in London with a long herbaceous border, lawn, pond, roses and fruit and vegetable gardens. 105 Dulwich Village is a very pretty garden with many unusual plants, old-fashioned roses, fish pond and water garden. Amazing collection of plants for sale from both gardens, please bring your own bags (cash preferred). Music provided by the Colomb Street Ensemble Wind Band. Regional Finalist, The English Garden Magazine's The Nation's Favourite Gardens 2023.

ECCLESTON SQUARE, SW1
Pimlico, SW1V 1NP. The Residents of Eccleston Square. www.ecclestonsquaregardens.com. *Off Belgrave Rd, nr Victoria Stn. Parking allowed on Suns.* **Sun 12 May (2-5). Adm £5, chd free. Home-made teas.**
Planned and developed by Thomas Cubitt in the 1830s, the 3 acre garden square is subdivided into sections with noteworthy collections of roses, camellias, ferns and tree peonies. The garden holds the National Collection of *Ceanothus* comprising over 70

species and cultivars, some of which are now rare. Notable important additions of unusual and tender plants are being grown and tested.

EDWARDES SQUARE, W8
South Edwardes Square, Kensington, W8 6HL. Edwardes Square Garden Committee, www.edwardes-square-garden.co.uk. *Tube: Kensington High St & Earls Court. Buses: 9, 10, 27, 28, 31, 49 & 74 to Odeon Cinema. Entrance in South Edwardes Square.* **Sun 14 Apr (12-5). Adm £6, chd free. Home-made teas.**
One of London's prettiest secluded garden squares. 3½ acres laid out differently from other squares with serpentine paths by Agostino Agliothe, an Italian artist and decorator who lived at No.15 from 1814-1820. This quiet oasis is a wonderful mixture of rolling lawns, mature trees and imaginative planting. Children's play area. WC near Holland Park, only a 5 min walk. Wheelchair access through main gate, South Edwardes Square.

40 EMBER LANE, KT10
Esher, KT10 8EP. Sarah & Franck Corvi, 07803 111968, sarah.corvi@ngs.org.uk. *½m from centre of Esher. From the A307, turn into Station Rd which becomes Ember Ln.* **Sun 9 June (1-5). Combined adm with 9 Imber Park Road £6, chd free. Home-made teas. Visits also by arrangement 10 June to 30 Sept for groups of 8 to 25.**
A contemporary family garden designed and maintained by the owners with distinct areas for outdoor living. A 70ft east facing plot where the lawn has been mostly removed to make space for the owner's love of plants and several ornamental trees.

48 ERSKINE HILL, NW11
Hampstead Garden Suburb, NW11 6HG. Marjorie & David Harris, 020 8455 6507, marjorieharris@btinternet.com. *1m from Golders Green. Nr A406 & A1. Tube: Golders Green. H2 Hail & Ride bus from Golders Green to garden, or 13, 102 or 460 buses to Temple Fortune (10 min walk). Free street parking.* **Visits by arrangement 5 May to 31 Aug for groups of 5 to 28. Adm £10, chd free. Tea & cake inc.**

Colourful but restful bird and bee-friendly organic and pesticide free cottage garden, wrapped around 1909 Arts and Crafts artisan's cottage in Hampstead Garden Suburb. Wide sunny borders stuffed with perennials, roses and clematis rampaging up through structures, shrubs and trees. Climber wrapped pergola, container vegetable plot, and greenhouse. Nest box, bee-friendly plants and quirky water feature. Pre-book dairy-free or gluten free cake and soya milk. Wheelchair access to terrace. Narrow paths. Single step from gate with ramp available. Handrail and step to lawn. No wheelchair access to WC.

72 EWHURST ROAD, SE4
Brockley, SE4 1AQ. Anna Crossley. *After the shops, just before the junction to Manwood Rd. Bus: 284 to door. Trains: Crofton Park (8 min walk), Catford or Catford Bridge (12 min walk via Ladywell Fields). Overground to Honor Oak Park (15 min walk).* **Sun 2 June (2-5). Adm £4.50, chd free. Tea, coffee & cake. Open nearby 29 Lowther Hill.**
How do you make small gardens interesting, elegant and functional? This mid-Victorian terraced garden is a masterclass in design. Colour, form, climbing plants and texture are all at play to enable outside rooms to seamlessly flow from inside spaces. An enclosed courtyard sits at the heart of the house whilst the rear garden uses clever design lines to provide an intimate, verdant dining space. Design, form and function in a small urban space.

70 FARLEIGH ROAD, N16
Stoke Newington, N16 7TQ. Mr Graham Hollick. *Short walk from junction of Stoke Newington High St & Amhurst Rd. LTNs operate in this area.* **Sun 30 June (10-6). Adm £4, chd free. Home-made teas.**
A diverse garden in a Victorian terrace with an eclectic mix of plants, many in vintage pots reflecting the owner's interests. A small courtyard leads onto a patio surrounded by pots followed by a lawn flanked by curving borders. At the rear is a paved area with raised beds containing vegetables.

42 Keynsham Avenue

1 FIFE ROAD, SW14
East Sheen, Mortlake, SW14 7EW. **Mr & Mrs J Morgan.** *Bus routes 33, 337 stops are a 15 min walk away on Upper Richmond Rd. Mortlake Train Stn SWT approx 20 mins away. Please note we are at the Christchurch Rd end of Fife Rd. On street parking.* **Sun 23 June (2-6). Adm £5, chd free. Home-made teas.**

Dominated by two large cedar trees the garden has undergone some changes since a redesign in 2013. A maturing oak tree stands in the wild garden with fruit trees and 'dead hedge'. A productive vegetable garden and greenhouse is managed with a no dig regime. Lawn is managed for No Mow May and borders with perennials and shrubs, sunny terrace close to the house.

GROUP OPENING

FOREST HILL GARDEN GROUP, SE23
Forest Hill, SE23 3DE. *Off S Circular Rd (A205) behind Horniman Museum & Gardens. Forest Hill Stn, 10 min walk. Buses 176,185,197, 356, P4.* **Sun 19 May, Sun 23 June (12-5). Combined adm £9, chd free. Home-made teas at 53 Ringmore Rise, Hilltop & 25 Westwood Park. Donation to St Christopher's Hospice & Marsha Phoenix Trust.**

7 CANONBIE ROAD
June Wismayer.
Open on Sun 19 May

[NEW] 75 CANONBIE ROAD
Mary & Ben Bayliss.
Open on Sun 19 May

THE COACH HOUSE, 3 THE HERMITAGE
Pat Rae.
Open on Sun 19 May

HILLTOP, 28 HORNIMAN DRIVE
Frankie Locke.
Open on Sun 19 May

27 HORNIMAN DRIVE
Rose Agnew.
Open on Sun 23 June

35 NETHERBY ROAD
Mr & Mrs K MacLennan.
Open on Sun 23 June

53 RINGMORE RISE
Valerie Ward.
Open on Sun 23 June

25 WESTWOOD PARK
Beth & Steph Falkingham-Blackwell.
Open on Sun 19 May

The leafy suburb of Forest Hill is one of London's best kept secrets. Described by architect Norman Foster as 'a delightful pocket of South London', it is home to the award-winning Horniman Museum and Gardens, with its wholefood cafe, butterfly house and magnificent conservatory an added bonus for visitors. The gardens themselves are all located within easy walking distance of the museum, on what is reputed to be the highest hill in South London. Many boast spectacular views over the city, so you can enjoy your tea and cake while surveying the ever-changing London skyline. The gardens too are ever-changing, particularly as we try to adapt to climate change and the ecological emergency. In these uncertain times, join us for a day of peace, contemplation and cake in our much-loved gardens. Plants for sale at 7 Canonbie Road.

10 FURLONG ROAD, N7
N7 8LS. **Gavin & Nicola Ralston.** *Tube & Train: Highbury & Islington, 3 min walk along Holloway Rd, 2nd L. Furlong Rd runs between Holloway Rd & Liverpool Rd. Buses on Holloway Rd: 21,43, 263, 393; other buses 4, 19, 30.* **Sun 19 May (2-5.30). Adm £5, chd free. Home-made teas.**

A green oasis in the heart of a densely populated area, 10 Furlong Road is an open, sunny garden of considerable size for its urban location. Its owners extensively remodelled the garden in 2019, building on a foundation of trees, shrubs and roses, adding herbaceous planting, seating, winding brick path, pergola, raised vegetable bed and wildflower circle. Plenty of seating dotted around the garden.

GARDEN BARGE SQUARE AT TOWER BRIDGE MOORINGS, SE1
31 Mill Street, SE1 2AX. **Mr Nick Lacey, www.towerbridgemoorings. org.** *5 min walk from Tower Bridge. Mill St off Jamaica Rd, between London Bridge & Bermondsey Stns, Tower Hill also nearby. Buses: 47, 188,* 381, RV1. **Sun 19 May (2-5). Adm £5, chd free. Home-made teas.**

Series of seven floating barge gardens connected by walkways and bridges. Gardens have an eclectic range of plants for year-round seasonal interest. Marine environment: suitable shoes and care needed. Small children must be closely supervised.

♦ THE GARDEN MUSEUM, SE1
5 Lambeth Palace Road, SE1 7LB. **The Garden Museum, 020 7401 8865, info@gardenmuseum.org.uk, www.gardenmuseum.org.uk.** *Lambeth side of Lambeth Bridge. Tube: Lambeth North, Vauxhall, Waterloo. Buses: 507 Red Arrow from Victoria or Waterloo Stns, also 3, 77, 344, C10.* **For NGS: Tue 10 Sept (2-5). Adm £7, chd free. Light refreshments. For other opening times and information, please phone, email or visit garden website.**

At the heart of The Garden Museum is our courtyard garden, designed by Dan Pearson as an 'Eden' of rare plants inspired by John Tradescant's journeys as a plant collector. Taking advantage of the sheltered, warm space, Dan has created a green retreat in response to the bronze and glass architecture, conjuring up a calm, reflective atmosphere. Visitors will also see a permanent display of paintings, tools, ephemera and historic artefacts; a glimpse into the uniquely British love affair with gardens. The Garden Café is an award-winning restaurant. Tours with Head Gardener at 3pm and 4pm. Adm covers access to museum and garden. The museum and garden are accessible for wheelchairs.

GARDEN OF MEDICINAL PLANTS, ROYAL COLLEGE OF PHYSICIANS, NW1
11 St Andrews Place, Regents Park, NW1 4LE. **Royal College of Physicians of London, garden.rcplondon.ac.uk.** *Tubes: Great Portland St & Regent's Park. Garden is one block N of station exits, on Outer Circle opp SE corner of Regent's Park. There is no access via Peto Place.* **Mon 15 July (11-4). Adm £6, chd free.**

We have over 1,000 different plants connected with the history of plants in medicine. These inc plants named after physicians, plants which make modern medicines as well as those used for millennia, plants which cause epidemics, plants used in different medical traditions from all the continents of the world and plants from the College's Pharmacopoeia of 1618. Guided tours will be offered throughout the day by physicians explaining the uses of the plants, their histories and other stories. Books about the plants in the medicinal garden will be on sale alongside free leaflets. All the plants are labelled with their botanical names. Entry to the garden is at far end of St Andrews Place. Accessible paths around the garden. Some slopes. Wheelchair lift for WC. No parking on site.

♿ �))

GOLF COURSE ALLOTMENTS, N11

Winton Avenue, N11 2AR. GCAA Haringey, www. golfcourseallotments.co.uk. *Junction of Winton Ave & Blake Rd. Tube: Bounds Green. Buses: 102, 184, 299 to Sunshine Garden Centre, Durnsford Rd. Through park to Bidwell Gardens. Straight on up Winton Ave. New LTN on Blake Rd, beware cameras. No parking on site.* **Sun 1 Sept (1-4.30). Adm £5, chd free. Pre-booking preferred, cash only on the day. Home-made teas & light lunches.**
Large, long established allotment with over 200 plots, some organic. Maintained by culturally diverse community, growing a wide variety of fruit, vegetables and flowers, enjoyed by bees. With picturesque corners, quirky sheds and tours of best plots. Newly created plot 147, a jewel not to be missed! A visit feels like a holiday in the countryside. Healthy, fresh allotment produce, chutneys, jams and honey for sale (cash only). Wheelchair access to main paths only. Gravel and uneven surfaces. WC inc disabled.

♿ 🐄 ✿ ☕

21 GOSPATRICK ROAD, N17

Tottenham, N17 7EH. Matthew Bradby, 07985 169471, mattbradby@hotmail.com. *London Zone 3. Tube: Turnpike Ln or Wood Green Stns. Train: Bruce Grove Stn. Bus routes: 144, 217, 231, 444 to Gospatrick Rd, or 123, 243 to Waltheof Ave, or 318 to Gt Cambridge Rd.* **Visits by arrangement 1 Mar to 26 June for groups of up to 12. Adm £5, chd free. Light refreshments.**

Diverse 40 metre plot with contrasting areas. A large weeping willow provides shade over fan palms, camellias, ferns and climbers. Fruit and herb garden inc Japanese banana, grapevine, olive, bay and loquat trees. Greenhouse and two ponds. A very tranquil and welcoming garden following organic principles.

🐄 ✿ ☕

17 GREENSTONE MEWS, E11

Wanstead, E11 2RS. Mrs T Farnham, 07761 476651, farnhamz@yahoo.co.uk. *Tube: Snaresbrook or Wanstead, 5 min walk. Buses: 101, 308, W12, W14 to Wanstead High St. Greenstone Mews is accessed via Voluntary Place which is off Spratt Hall Rd.* **Visits by arrangement for groups of up to 8. Adm £5. Tea or coffee inc. Sandwiches & cake on request.**
A 15ft sq slate paved garden. Sunken reused bath was a fish pond now a bog garden! Climbers clothe fences with hardy perennials grown from cuttings, vegetables and herbs in buckets. Height provided by established palm and arch covered with thornless blackberry and a grapevine. Ideas aplenty for small space gardening. Mudlarked rope and wood used for support. Regret, garden unsuitable for children. Wheelchair access through garage but limited turning space.

♿ ✿ ☕ �))

24 GROVE PARK, SE5

Camberwell, SE5 8LH. Clive Pankhurst, www.alternative-planting.blogspot.com. *Chadwick Rd end of Grove Park. Peckham Rye or Denmark Hill Stns, both 10 min walk. Good street parking.* **Sun 1 Sept (11-4.30). Adm £5, chd free. Home-made teas.**
An inspiring exotic jungle of lush, big leafed plants and Southeast Asian influences transport you to the tropics. Huge hidden garden created from derelict land that had been the bottom halves of two neighbouring gardens gives the wow factor and unexpected size. Lawn and lots of hidden corners give spaces to sit and enjoy. Renowned for delicious home-made cake and plant sale.

🐄 ✿ ☕ �))

58 HALLIFORD STREET, N1

Canonbury, N1 3EQ. Jennifer Tripp Black. *Tube: Highbury & Islington or Essex Rd. From Essex Rd, house numbers consecutive on LHS by 3rd speed bump. Overground: Canonbury.* **Sun 16 June (12-5). Adm £4, chd free. Home-made teas. Vegan & full fat cakes. Donation to The Royal Marsden Cancer Charity (Katie's Lymphoedema Fund).**
An English country garden in the heart of Islington. Lush planting: *Cytisus battandieri* 'Yellow Tail' tree, two apple trees, one quince. Bush and climbing roses, tulips, clematis, rhododendrons, exotic palms, cannas, abutilons, heucheras, salvias, cordelines and a hosta collection in pots. Small greenhouse and antique pergola. In summer the front garden welcomes you with special roses and agapanthus.

🐄 ✿ ☕ �))

92 HAMPSTEAD WAY, NW11

Hampstead Garden Suburb, NW11 7XY. Ann & Tom Lissauer, ann.goldman1@gmail.com. *In square set back on Hampstead Way, between Finchley Rd & Meadway. 15 min walk from Golders Green Stn. Buses 13, 102 & 460 on Finchley Rd, stop at Temple Fortune Ln & walk down Hampstead Way to the square.* **Sun 19 May (1.30-5). Adm £5, chd free. Home-made teas. Visits also by arrangement Mar to Sept for groups of up to 6.**
An informal garden, interesting year-round, combining wildlife friendly planting with a passion for plants. Different areas provide a variety of habitats. These inc a wildlife pond and, where there used to be lawns, there are now meadows with mown paths and wild flowers. Shaded and sunny beds offer opportunities to grow a wide range of interesting plants.

✿ ☕ �))

152,684 people were able to access guidance on what to expect when a person is dying through the National Garden Scheme support for Hospice UK this year

Ecclestone Square

SPECIAL EVENT

◆ HAMPTON COURT PALACE, KT8

East Molesey, KT8 9AU. Historic Royal Palaces, www.hrp.org.uk. *Follow brown tourist signs on all major routes. Junction of A308 with A309 at foot of Hampton Court Bridge. Traffic is heavy around Hampton Court. Please leave plenty of time, the tour will start promptly at 6pm & will not be able to wait.* **For NGS: Evening opening Thur 25 Apr, Thur 18 July (6-8). Adm £18, chd free. Pre-booking essential, please visit www.ngs.org.uk for information & booking. Wine. For other opening times and information, please visit garden website. Donation to Historic Royal Palaces.**
Take the opportunity to join special National Garden Scheme private tours after the wonderful historic gardens have closed to the public. Spring walk during the tulip festival and July walk to enjoy the summer bedding in the remarkable gardens of Hampton Court Palace. Wheelchair access over some unbound gravel paths.

4 HANWORTH ROAD, TW13

Feltham, TW13 5AB. Maria Vail. *5 min walk from Feltham Train Stn. Opp Feltham Stn into Hanworth Rd. House on R after the school. Entrance through side gate on Cardinal Rd.* **Sun 19 May (1-4). Adm £4.50, chd free. Home-made teas.**
Appropriately designed garden surrounding a Victorian villa. Pollarded lime trees in the front garden and mature palm trees with colourful under planting. Many tender and unusual Mediterranean plants. Lawn with flower filled urns and pots, rockery and colourful borders. An eclectic mix of plants.

37 HAROLD ROAD, E11

Leytonstone, E11 4QX. Dr Matthew Jones Chesters. *Tube: Leytonstone, exit L subway, 5 min walk. Train: Leytonstone High Road, 5 min walk. Buses: 257 & W14. Parking at station or limited on street.* **Sun 16 June (1-5). Adm £4, chd free. Home-made teas.**
50ft x 60ft pretty corner garden arranged around seven fruit trees. Fragrant climbers, woodland plants and shade-tolerant fruit along north wall. Fastigiate trees protect raised vegetable beds and herb rockery. Long lawn bordered by roses and perennials on one side, prairie plants on the other. Patio with raised pond, palms and rhubarb. Planting designed to produce fruit, fragrance and lovely memories. Garden map with planting plans inc. Adm inc tea and fruit drinks. Home-made cakes, muffins and preserves for sale.

39 HAZLEWELL ROAD, SW15

Putney, SW15 6LS. Kath & Alastair Brown. *12 min walk from Putney Train Stn; 18 mins from East Putney Tube Stn. Buses: 14, 37, 93, 85 & 39 stop on Putney Hill, St John's Ave; 337 stop Putney Leisure Centre. Free parking Suns.* **Sun 2 June (2.30-5). Combined adm with 40 Chartfield Avenue £7, chd free. Light refreshments.**
An 80ft x 40ft town garden with a surprisingly secluded feel provided by the shared landscape of gardens and mature trees. A naturalistic planting scheme of trees, shrubs and perennials in curved beds surround the lawn. The sunny patio, bordered by lavender and climbing roses, looks toward a water feature set in a perennial bed. At the rear a small shady patio is framed by trees and woodland planting.

84 HIGHAM STREET, E17

Walthamstow, E17 6DA. Paula Siqueira & Drew Durham, www.instagram.com/paula.siqueira. *15 min walk from Blackhorse Tube Stn.* **Sun 18 Aug (2-6). Adm £4, chd £1. Light refreshments. Open nearby 28a Worcester Road.**
A low-maintenance garden that will take you on a journey through a wildlife friendly oasis into a small woodland hideaway. The large rainwater pond provides a great contrast to draught tolerant perennial flowers, ornamental grasses, trees and shrubs, all planted with a naturalistic style under a thick layer of gravel mulch. An olive tree set against a 4 metre ivy wall provides a strong focal point. QR codes will be provided to visitors, who will be able to scan with their phones and know more about the plants we've used, the inner workings of the pond rainwater collection and natural filtration, and also take a look at our garden before-and-after photos.

HIGHWOOD ASH, NW7

Highwood Hill, Mill Hill, NW7 4EX. Mrs P Gluckstein. *Totteridge & Whetstone on Northern line, then bus 251 stops outside Rising Sun/ Mill Hill stop. By car: A5109 from Apex Corner to Whetstone. Garden opp The Rising Sun pub at top of hill on the R.* **Sun 12 May (2-6). Adm £6, chd free. Home-made teas.**
Created over the last 60 yrs, this 3¼ acre garden features rolling lawns, two large interconnecting ponds with koi, herbaceous and shrub borders and a modern gravel garden. A country garden in London for all seasons with many interesting plants and sculptures. May should be perfect for the camellias, rhododendrons and azaleas. Partial access for wheelchairs, lowest parts too steep.

5 HILL CLOSE, NW11

Hampstead Garden Suburb, NW11 7JP. Leanne & Winston Newman. *1m N of Golders Green. Off Hampstead Way between Meadway & Willifield Way, also off South Sq. No parking in Hill Cl. Tube: Golders Green then H2 Hail & Ride bus to bottom of Hill Cl.* **Sun 19 May (2-6). Adm £5, chd free. Home-made teas.**
Delightful secluded garden of a unique Arts and Crafts house, where a central cedar tree is bordered by mature oak and poplars. The garden is at its best in the spring before the surrounding trees reach the full extent of their canopies. Planting inc a variety of acers, alliums, lilacs, dicentra, ferns and persicaria. There is a ramp from the road to the front path and to the rear garden.

Our 2023 donation to the Queen's Nursing Institute now helps support over 2,500 Queen's Nurses working in the community in England, Wales, Northern Ireland, the Channel Islands and the Isle of Man

20 HILLCREST, N21
Winchmore Hill, N21 1AT. Gwyneth
& Ian Williams. *North London. Tube:
Piccadilly Line to Southgate, W9 to
Winchmore Hill Green, a short walk
via Wades Hill. Train: Great Northern
Line to Winchmore Hill, turn R
towards the Green, a short walk via
Wades Hill.* **Sun 9 June (1.30-6).
Adm £4, chd free. Home-made
teas.**
This pretty hill garden has a terrace
with ironwork gazebos, wide stone
steps descending to an evergreen
pergola, dappled sunlight and
quiet water feature. Rose arches,
a meandering path and lawn with
shrub and tree borders lead to small
alpine rockeries, a summerhouse,
a miniature wildlife pond and little
garden with fruit trees. Refreshments
inc herbal teas, non-dairy, vegan, and
gluten free options.

26 HILLCROFT CRESCENT, HA9
Wembley Park, HA9 8EE. Gary &
Suha Holmyard, 07773 691331,
garyh@lawyer.com. *½ m from
Wembley Park Stn. If held on
Wembley event day, we can provide
free parking permits. Turn R out of
Wembley Park Stn walking down
Wembley Park Dr, turn L into Manor
Dr, Hillcroft Cres is 2nd on R.* **Sat
6, Sun 7 July (11-5). Adm £5, chd
free. Home-made teas.**
Small cottage front garden with
arched entrance with cloud tree,
wisteria, yucca, canna, hydrangeas,
roses and lilies. Rear garden approx
70ft x 80ft with summerhouse,
arbours and water features. Planting
inc fig, apple, pear, olive, and soft
fruit. Ten different flower beds each
holding its own particular interest
inc lilies, unusual evergreen shrubs,
exotics, clematis and roses. Plenty
of seating around the garden.
Wheelchair access through side gate
via driveway.
&. ✿ ☕ ›)

GROUP OPENING

NEW **HOLLY GROVE GARDENS,
SE15**
Peckham, SE15 5DF. *Peckham
Rye Stn, 3 min walk. Turn L into
Holly Grove & L past Green towards
Bellenden Rd. Buses to Rye Ln,
Peckham 12, 37, 63, 78, 197, 343,
363.* **Sun 26 May (1-5). Combined
adm £5, chd free. Home-made
teas at 29 Holly Grove.**

NEW **26 HOLLY GROVE**
Sally Williams.

NEW **29 HOLLY GROVE**
Jessica Nicholas.

Two very different gardens in a quiet
leafy Peckham road, benefitting from
the shared backdrop of a high wall
along their back acting as an elegant
buffer and offering wind shelter to
create a warm microclimate. No. 26 is
a peaceful, lush green space, framed
by mature trees and bamboo, and
a simple perennial colour palette of
deepest reds and orange, while at
No. 29 grasses and lush evergreens
lead visitors to an enchanting,
informal, relaxed garden with a
distinct cottage feel to it with arching
roses and scrambling clematis.

HORATIO'S GARDEN, HA7
Royal National Orthopaedic
Hospital, Brockley Hill, Stanmore,
HA7 4LP. Horatio's Garden,
www.horatiosgarden.org.uk. *If
driving enter the Hospital via Wood
Ln, Aspire entrance. Park in Aspire
car park & walk back the way you
drove in, taking the L before Wood
Ln exit & follow the signs.* **Sun 12
May, Sun 15 Sept (2-5). Adm
£5, chd free. Home-made teas.
Vegan & gluten free options.**
Opened in Sept 2020, Horatio's
Garden London & South East located
at the Royal National Orthopaedic
Hospital, Stanmore is designed
by Tom Stuart-Smith. The garden
is on one level with smooth paths
throughout ensuring that it is easily
accessible to patients in beds and
wheelchairs. The essential design
features inc a social space, private
areas for patients to seek solitude or
share with a family member or friend,
the calming sound of flowing water, a
garden room and a greenhouse. May
is the perfect time to see the carpet
of tulips and other bulbs. The Head
Gardener Ashley Edwards will be on
hand to answer any plant questions
and give guided tours of this unique
sanctuary. The whole site is designed
for wheelchairs.
&. ✿ Ⓓ ☕ ›)

57 HUNTINGDON STREET, N1
Barnsbury, Islington, N1 1BX.
Julian Williams, 07759 053001,
julianandroman@me.com. *Train:
Caledonian Rd & Barnsbury. Tube:
Kings Cross, Highbury & Islington or
Caledonian Rd. Buses: Caledonian
Rd 17, 91, 259, 274; Hemingford
Rd 153 from Angel.* **Evening
opening Thur 16 May (6-8). Adm
£4, chd free. Wine. Opening with
Barnsbury Group on Sun 2 June.
Visits also by arrangement Mar to
Sept for groups of up to 6.**
A secluded woodland garden room
below an ash canopy and framed
by timber palisade supporting roses,
hydrangea and ivy. An understorey
of silver birch and hazel provides
the setting for shade loving ferns,
perennials and grasses. Oak
pathways offset the informal planting
and lead to a tranquil central space
with bench seating and two container
ponds to encourage wildlife.
☕ ›)

THE HURLINGHAM CLUB, SW6
Ranelagh Gardens, SW6 3PR. The
Members of the Hurlingham Club,
www.hurlinghamclub.org.uk. *Main
gate at E end of Ranelagh Gardens.
Tube: Putney Bridge (110yds). Local
roads have restricted access. No
parking on site.* **Sat 18 May (10-4).
Adm £7, chd free. Pre-booking
essential, please visit www.
ngs.org.uk for information &
booking. Light refreshments.
Card payments only, no cash
accepted.**
Rare opportunity to visit this 42 acre
jewel with many mature trees, 2
acre lake with water fowl, expansive
lawns and a river walk. Capability
Brown and Humphry Repton were
involved with landscaping. The
gardens are renowned for their roses,
herbaceous and lakeside borders,
and stunning bedding displays. The
riverbank is a haven for wildlife with
native trees, shrubs and wild flowers.
Light refreshments on site weather
depending. Free, ticket only, guided
tour at 11am, tickets available at
entrance. Wheelchair and pushchair
access across the site, however
smaller paths in borders are often laid
to woodchip and not as accessible.
&. ☕ ›)

9 IMBER PARK ROAD, KT10
Esher, KT10 8JB. Jane & John
McNicholas, 07867 318655,
jane_mcnicholas@hotmail.com. *½ m
from centre of Esher. From the A307,
turn into Station Rd which becomes
Ember Ln. Go past Esher Train Stn on
R. Take 3rd road on R into Imber Park
Rd.* **Sun 9 June (1-5). Combined
adm with 40 Ember Lane £6, chd
free. Home-made teas.**

Visits also by arrangement 10 June to 30 Sept for groups of 8 to 25.
An established cottage style garden, always evolving, designed and maintained by the owners who are passionate about gardening and collecting plants. The garden is south facing with well-stocked, large, colourful herbaceous borders containing a wide variety of perennials, evergreen and deciduous shrubs, a winding lawn area and a small garden retreat.

SPECIAL EVENT

THE INNER AND MIDDLE TEMPLE GARDENS, EC4
Crown Office Row, Inner Temple, EC4Y 7HL. The Honourable Societies of the Inner & Middle Temples, www.innertemple.org.uk/www.middletemple.org.uk. *Entrance: Main Garden Gate on Crown Office Row, access via Tudor St Gate or Middle Temple Ln Gate. Please note the tour starts promptly at 11.30am.* **Thur 6 June (11.30-3). Adm £55. Pre-booking essential, please visit www.ngs.org.uk for information & booking. Light refreshments.**
Inner Temple Garden is a haven of tranquillity and beauty with sweeping lawns, unusual trees and charming woodland areas. The well known herbaceous border shows off inspiring plant combinations from early spring through to autumn. The award-winning gardens of Middle Temple are comprised of a series of courtyards and a main garden which extends from the Medieval Hall to the Embankment. Adm inc conducted tour of the gardens by Head Gardeners. Light lunch in Middle Temple Hall, please advise of any dietary requirements. Please note this event is not suitable for children. Please advise in advance if wheelchair access is required.

GROUP OPENING

KEW GREEN GARDENS, TW9
Kew, TW9 3AH. *NW side of Kew Green. Tube: Kew Gardens. Train Station: Kew Bridge. Buses: 65, 110. Entrance via riverside.* **Sun 19 May (2-5). Combined adm £8, chd free. Evening opening Sun 26 May (6-8). Combined adm £10, chd** free. Teas in St Anne's Church (19 May). Wine (26 May).

69 KEW GREEN
John & Virginia Godfrey.

71 KEW GREEN
Mr & Mrs Jan Pethick.

73 KEW GREEN
Sir Donald & Lady Elizabeth Insall.

The long gardens run for 100yds from the back of historic houses on Kew Green down to the Thames towpath. Together they cover nearly 1 acre, and in addition to the style and structures of the individual gardens they can be seen as one large space, exceptional in London. The borders between the gardens are mostly relatively low and the trees and large shrubs in each contribute to viewing the whole, while roses and clematis climb between gardens giving colour to two adjacent gardens at the same time.

NEW 42 KEYNSHAM AVENUE, IG8
Woodford Green, IG8 9SZ. Mark Game & Jane Brandon. *Close to the N entrance of The Highams Park. 20 min walk from Highams Park Train Stn or Woodford Tube Stn. 200 metres from 275 bus stop.* **Sun 9 June (2-5). Adm £4. Home-made teas.**
A long and very green suburban garden sloping down from the back of the house towards the mature trees of Epping Forest. Tea house and tranquil area, ferns and bamboos, and roses; raised vegetable beds and greenhouse; herbaceous borders with high hedges; lawn with formal pond and rill; gravel garden. Front garden with steel edged path and cloud pruning.

KING HENRY'S WALK GARDEN, N1
11c King Henry's Walk, N1 4NX. Friends of King Henry's Walk Garden, www.khwgarden.org.uk. *Buses: 30, 38, 56, 141. Behind adventure playground on KHW, off Balls Pond Rd.* **Mon 6 May (2-4.30). Adm £4.50, chd free. Home-made teas. Donation to Friends of KHW Garden.**
Vibrant ornamental planting welcomes the visitor to this hidden oasis leading into a verdant community garden with secluded woodland area, beehives, wildlife pond, wall trained fruit trees, and plots used by local residents to grow their own fruit and vegetables. Live music. Disabled access WC.

53 LADY AYLESFORD AVENUE, HA7
Stanmore, HA7 4FG. Jadon. *About 15 min walk from Stanmore Stn, off Uxbridge Rd, close to St John Church. H12 & 340 bus stops are 5 min walk from garden. Limited free parking nearby.* **Sat 27 July (11.30-5). Adm £5. Light refreshments.**
A compact tropical fusion garden developed over the past 6 yrs, set in a 20 yr old development of a Battle of Britain, RAF base. This delightful gem of a corner garden with water features and a stunning display of plants and flowers, shows what can be achieved, even in a small space. Colours and textures blend effortlessly to create a harmonious space with exceptional attention to detail.

LAMBETH PALACE, SE1
Lambeth Palace Road, SE1 7JU. The Church Commissioners, www.archbishopofcanterbury.org. *Entrance via Main Gatehouse (Morton's Tower) facing Lambeth Bridge. Station: Waterloo. Tube: Westminster, Vauxhall all 10 min walk. Buses: 3, C10, 77, 344, 507.* **Evening opening Mon 20 May (5-8). Adm £6, chd free. Wine.**
Lambeth Palace has one of the oldest and largest private gardens in London. It has been occupied by Archbishops of Canterbury since 1197. Formal courtyard boasts historic White Marseilles fig planted in 1556. Parkland style garden features mature trees, woodland and native planting. There is a formal rose terrace, summer gravel border, scented chapel garden and active beehives. Please note: Gates will open at 5pm, last entry is 7pm and garden closes at 8pm. Garden Tours will be available. Wheelchair access with ramped path to rose terrace. Disabled WC.

12 LAURADALE ROAD, N2

N2 9LU. David Gilbert & Mary Medyckyj, drgilbertprivate@gmail.com, www.davidgilbertart.com/garden. *Muswell Hill / East Finchley. 300 metres from 102 & 234 bus stops. 500 metres from 43 & 134 bus stops. 10 min walk from East Finchley Tube Stn. Look out for NGS signs.* **Sun 8 Sept (1-6). Adm £5, chd free. Home-made teas. Visits also by arrangement.**

Exotic, huge, featuring tropical and Mediterranean zone plants, now maturing well and extended with recent developments. Dramatic, architectural planting inc bananas, large tree ferns and rare palms weave along curving stone paths, culminating in a paradise garden. A modern take on the rockery embeds glacial boulders amid dry zone plants inc many succulents. Sculptures by artist owner.

84 LAVENDER GROVE, E8

Hackney, E8 3LS. Anne Pauleau, 07930 550414, a.pauleau@hotmail.co.uk. *Walk from Haggerston or London Fields Train Stns. The nearest bus stop is the 394 in Lansdowne Dr, just round the corner. LTNs operate in this area.* **Sun 21 Apr (2-5). Adm £4, chd free. Home-made teas. Opening with London Fields Gardens on Sun 9 June. Visits also by arrangement 1 Apr to 16 Oct.**

Courtyard garden with tropical backdrop of bamboos and palms, foil to clipped shrubs leading to wilder area. The cottage garden with mingling roses, lilies, alliums, grasses, clematis, poppies, star jasmine and jasmine. A very highly scented garden with rampant ramblers and billowing vegetation enchanting all senses. Tulips and daffodils herald spring. Fiery crocosmias and dahlias trumpet late summer. Children's quiz offered with prize on completion.

16 LINKS VIEW ROAD, TW12

Hampton Hill, TW12 1LA. Guy & Virginia Lewis. *South West London, nr Richmond & Kingston upon Thames. 5 min walk from Fulwell Stn. On 281, 267, 285 & R70 bus routes.* **Sat 25, Sun 26 May (2-4.30). Adm £5, chd free. Home-made teas. Open nearby 70 Wensleydale Road.**

A surprising garden featuring acers, hostas and fern collection, and other unusual shade loving plants. Many climbing roses, clematis and herbaceous border, and pots of exotic plants. Rockery and folly with shell grotto and waterfall to small pond and bog garden. Lawn and formal pond. Wild area with chickens and summerhouse. Greenhouse with succulent collection. A veranda with pelargonium collection. One very friendly dog. Plants for sale inc many succulents and greenhouse/conservatory plants. Takeaway cake for sale. Wheelchair access with assistance.

29 Lowther Hill

GROUP OPENING

LONDON FIELDS GARDENS, E8
Hackney, E8 3JW. *London Fields. 7 min walk from 149, 242, 243 bus stop, Middleton Rd. 10 mins from 30, 38, 55 stops on Dalston Ln. 7 mins from Haggerston Train Stn or 10 min walk through London Fields from Mare St buses. LTNs operate in this area.* **Sun 9 June (2-6). Combined adm £10, chd free. Home-made teas at 84 Middleton Road.**

84 LAVENDER GROVE
Anne Pauleau.
(See separate entry)

36 MALVERN ROAD
Kath Harris

53 MAPLEDENE ROAD
Tigger Cullinan.

55 MAPLEDENE ROAD
Amanda & Tony Mott.

84 MIDDLETON ROAD
Penny Fowler.

92 MIDDLETON ROAD
Mr Richard & Dr Louise Jarrett.

A fascinating and diverse collection of gardens in London Fields within easy walking distance of each other. At 84 Lavender Grove there are twin south facing gardens, a courtyard with tropical backdrop, and a highly scented, romantic cottage garden. At 36 Malvern Road you will find a little gem of rills and mirrors, and forest pansies. 92 Middleton Road is elegant and serene with a circular theme inc roses, acers and examples of stone lettering. At 84 Middleton Road lies an unusually large secret garden where you can wander down meandering woodland paths and forget you are in London. The other two are north facing with much the same space but totally different styles. 53 Mapledene Road is an established plantaholic's garden in five sections with not a spare unplanted inch. 55 Mapledene Road has a Moorish-inspired terrace leading to a wildlife garden with plants chosen to attract birds, bees and butterflies. A fabulous afternoon to see six such contrasting gardens.

 »))

38 LOVELACE ROAD, SE21
Dulwich, SE21 8JX. José & Deepti Ramos Turnes. *10 min walk from either West Dulwich or Tulse Hill Stns. Buses: 2, 3 & 68.* **Sun 23 June (12-5). Adm £4, chd free. Home-made teas.**
This gem of a garden has an all white front and a wildlife friendly back. The garden slopes gently upwards with curving borders, packed with an informal mix of roses, perennials and annuals. The garden is designed to be an easy to maintain oasis of calm at the end of a busy day. There are several smile inducing features like a dragon, the Cheshire cat and a stream.

 »))

GROUP OPENING

LOWER CLAPTON GARDENS, E5
Lower Clapton, E5 0RL. *12 min walk from Hackney Central, Hackney Downs or Homerton Stns. Buses 38, 55, 106, 242, 253, 254 or 425, alight Lower Clapton Rd or Powerscroft Rd. Street parking.* **Sun 16 June (2-5). Combined adm £7, chd free. Home-made teas at 77 Rushmore Road. Open nearby 43 Roding Road.**

8 ALMACK ROAD
Philip Lightowlers, 07910 850276, plighto@gmail.com.
Visits also by arrangement 30 Mar to 14 Sept for groups of up to 15.

10 ALMACK ROAD
Mr Ben Myhill.

77 RUSHMORE ROAD
Penny Edwards.

Lower Clapton is an area of mid-Victorian terraces sloping down to the River Lea. These gardens reflect their owner's tastes and interests. 10 Almack Road is a long garden with architectural plants like trachycarpus palms and cordylines, a large pond and much Yorkstone and London brick. Next door at No. 8 is a similar space but divided into two rooms, one cool and peaceful the other with hot colours, succulents and greenhouse. 77 Rushmore Road has a fruit and vegetable garden and wildlife pond.

NEW 29 LOWTHER HILL, SE23
Honor Oak, Forest Hill, SE23 1PZ. Marina & Graham Sheen. *10 mins from Honor Oak Stn. 13 mins from Catford Stns. 5 mins from 122,185,171,172 & P4 & P12 buses. Unrestricted street parking.* **Sun 2 June (1.30-5.30). Adm £5, chd free. Home-made teas. Open nearby 72 Ewhurst Road.**
A sloping garden in two parts. Both are about 10 metre square with distinct characters. The front is more formal with a native hedge, clipped box, roses and colourful perennials, annuals and large pots. The back garden is a lush oasis of roses, grasses, euphorbias and geraniums mixed in with fruit trees and a small greenhouse for vegetables. Potted dahlias are a current passion.

 »))

MAGGIE'S, SM2
17 Cotswold Road, Sutton, SM2 5NG. Maggie's Centre, www.maggies.org. *Maggie's at The Royal Marsden is located on the corner of Cotswold Rd via the staff entrance to The Royal Marsden.* **Sat 11 May (10-2). Adm £4, chd free. Home-made teas.**
The garden surrounding the centre is designed by the world-famous Dutch Landscape Architect Piet Oudolf, who envisioned a dynamic landscape. The garden is divided into four interconnected zones. Piet has carefully chosen the plants according to how much sun each zone receives. We have the shaded, woodland, spring and summer zones, creating a powerful experience for the eyes. At 2pm, a free tour of the garden and Q&A with Marc, our gardener and Chris and Toby Marchant from Orchard Dene Nurseries. Chris and Toby grew all the plants and worked with Piet Oudolf in planting out the garden. Wheelchair access over raised paths.

& 🐕 ♨ »))

47,000 people affected by cancer were reached by Maggie's centres supported by the National Garden Scheme over the last 12 months

MAGGIE'S WEST LONDON, W6

Charing Cross Hospital, Fulham Palace Road, Hammersmith, W6 8RF. Maggie's West London, www.instagram.com/maggies. west.london. *Follow Fulham Palace Rd from Hammersmith Stn towards Charing Cross Hospital. The centre is on the corner of the hospital grounds of St Dunstan's Rd, and is painted tomato-orange.* **Sat 27 Apr (10-1). Adm £4, chd free.**

The garden at Maggie's West London was designed by Dan Pearson in 2008. It is now a well established space offering therapy and peace to those affected by cancer each yr. The gardens surround the vivid orange walls of the centre. The path leading to the centre meanders through scented beds and mature trees. Visitors have access to various courtyards with a wonderful array of flora inc fig trees, grapevines and even a mature pink silk mimosa. Maggie's West London won the RIBA Stirling Prize for the best building designed by a British architect when first built. Wheelchair access to ground floor gardens and courtyards. Roof gardens not accessible.

4 MANNINGTREE ROAD, HA4

Ruislip, HA4 0ES. Costas Lambropoulos & Roberto Haddon. *Manningtree Rd is just off Victoria Rd, 10-15 min walk from South Ruislip Tube Stn.* **Sun 18 Aug (2-6). Adm £5, chd free. Home-made teas.**

Compact garden with an exotic feel that combines hardy architectural plants with more tender ones. A feeling of a small oasis inc plants like *Musa Basjoo, Ensete ventricosum* 'Montbeliardii' and a tree fern. Potted Mediterranean plants on the patio inc a fig tree, jasmines and two olive trees. Cakes, savouries, home-made jams and biscuits for sale.

MARIE CURIE HOSPICE, HAMPSTEAD, NW3

11 Lyndhurst Gardens, Hampstead, NW3 5NS. Tracy Annunziato. *North West London. Nearest tube: Belsize Park. Buses: 46, 268 & C11 all stop near the hospice.* **Sun 9 June (2-5). Adm £3.50, chd free. Light refreshments.**

This peaceful and secluded two-part garden surrounds the Marie Curie Hospice, Hampstead. A garden, tended by dedicated volunteers, makes for a wonderful space

for patients to enjoy the shrubs and seasonal colourful flowers. The garden has seating areas for relaxation either in the shade or sunshine with great views of the garden and in company with squirrels running through the trees. Step free access to garden and WC.

GROUP OPENING

MARKSBURY AVENUE GARDENS, TW9

Richmond, TW9 4JE. *Approx 10 min walk from Kew Gardens Tube. Exit westbound platform to North Rd. Take 3rd L into Atwood Ave. Marksbury Ave is 1st R. Buses 190, 419 or R68 stop at S end of road.* **Sun 9 June (2-5). Combined adm £7, chd free. Home-made teas in The Barn Church (corner of Marksbury Ave & Atwood Ave).**

26 MARKSBURY AVENUE
Sue Frisby.

59 MARKSBURY AVENUE
Clarissa & Michael Fletcher.

60 MARKSBURY AVENUE
Gay Lyle.

62 MARKSBURY AVENUE
Sarah Halaka.

NEW 65 MARKSBURY AVENUE
Sue & Richard Gatenby.

Although of similar size, these five neighbouring gardens in Kew are all very different. At No.26 you will find many New Zealand natives. Fruit trees abound with plums, figs, apple, red and black currents, apricots, mulberry, feijoa, loquat and citrus, alongside a delicate chamomile lawn. Over the road at No. 59 the garden has evolved largely through own propagation and self-seeding. Shade is provided from a variety of ornamental trees which lead to a lower patio and small vegetable patch. No. 60 is a typical town garden where visitors can enjoy a fine display of patio roses, flowering shrubs and climbers inc numerous varieties of clematis displayed around a curved lawn. Next door at No. 62 is a family garden, created from scratch in 2018 with a brick edged lawn and yew topiary cones for structure. No.65 is an even newer garden designed in 2021 with symmetrical lines softened by old favourites plus contemporary grasses, cercis and canas.

NEW MHA THE WILDERNESS, CR9

Hall Grange Care Home, 17 Shirley Church Road, Croydon, CR9 5AL. Methodist Homes, www.mha.org. uk/get-involved/the-wilderness. *2m E of Croydon. Situated behind MHA Hall Grange Care Home. The garden is accessed via a green gate to the R of care home & car park (for residents only). Street parking nearby. Buses: 466 & 130 plus 5 min walk.* **Sun 19 May (10-3). Adm £4, chd free. Light refreshments.**

MHA The Wilderness is a reformed heritage garden first created by Rev William Wilks, Vicar of Shirley and former secretary of the Royal Horticultural Society, between 1904 and 1923. In spring/early summer there are mature rhodendrons planted by Wilks, azaleas and Shirley poppies (bred by Wilks). At 2pm Lucy James, Head Gardener, will give a tour of the garden inc its history and development. Accessible path circles the entire garden, though on a slight incline.

41 MILL HILL ROAD, W3

Acton, W3 8JE. Marcia Hurst, marcia.hurst@sudbury-house. co.uk. *Tube: Acton Town, cross zebra crossing on to Gunnersbury Ln, 2nd R to Mill Hill Rd.* **Sun 1 Sept (2-5). Adm £5, chd free. Home-made teas. Visits also by arrangement May to Sept for groups of 5 to 15.**

Surprisingly secluded original garden with varied selection of plants, borders, topiary, lavender hedge and large lawn. Adjoining sunny new garden from 2019 with meadow, pond and gravel garden. Ample seating. Good selection of plants growing in the garden are for sale in pots with planting and growing advice from the knowledgeable plantaholic owner.

77 MUSWELL ROAD, FLAT 1, N10

N10 2BS. Ms Jennifer Granville. *Off Colney Hatch Ln. Highgate Tube then 134 or 43 bus to Queens Ave stop; Bounds Green Tube then 102 or 144 bus to Roseberry Rd stop; Free on street parking on Muswell Rd.* **Sun 7 July (2-6). Adm £5, chd free. Home-made teas.**

The garden is two yrs old, inspired by the bedtime story 'The Little Green Gate' that opens onto Fairy Land, told to the owner by her grandfather. The garden comprises three linked decks, all providing a different mood and experience with a rose arch, wildlife pond and several green gates; bugs encouraged with architect designed bug hotel, fairies sometimes stay too. Sorry, no wheelchair access.

THE MYSTERIES OF LIGHT ROSARY GARDEN, NW5

St Dominic's Priory (the Rosary Shrine), Southampton Road, Kentish Town, NW5 4LB. **Raffaella Morini on behalf of the Church & Priory, 07778 526434, garden@raffaellamorini.com.** *Entrance to the garden is from Alan Cheales Way on the RHS of the church, next to the school.* **Sat 29 June (1-5). Adm £4.50, chd free. Home-made teas. Visits also by arrangement 1 May to 15 Sept.** A walled garden behind the Priory Church of Our Lady of the Rosary and St Dominic, commissioned by the Dominican Friars as a spiritual and meditative space representing the 'Mysteries of Light' of the Holy Rosary. The sandstone path marks out a Rosary with black granite beads, surrounded by flowers traditionally associated with the Virgin Mary: roses, lilies, iris, periwinkle, columbine. The garden is fully accessible with stone path and wheelchair friendly gravel path.

15 NORCOTT ROAD, N16

Stoke Newington, N16 7BJ. **Amanda & John Welch.** *Buses: 67, 73, 76, 106, 149, 243, 393, 476, 488. LTNs operate in this area.* **Sun 19 May (2-6). Adm £4, chd free. Home-made teas.** A large walled garden developed by the present owners over 40 yrs with pond, aged fruit trees and an abundance of herbaceous plants, many available in our plant sale. Bearing in mind the vagaries of climate change (and our ageing) last yr was one of watching or if you like 'wilding'. We like it, though it doesn't seem to mean any less time out there hard at work. We have plenty of room for people to sit, relax and enjoy their tea.

OAK FARM/HOMESTEAD, EN2

Cattlegate Road, Crews Hill, Enfield, EN2 9DS. **Genine & Martin Newport.** *Few mins walk from Crews Hill Stn. Freedom Pass & Oyster Card valid. Follow NGS arrows. Be aware in ULEZ zone. J24 & J25 off M25.* **Sun 8 Sept (12-4). Adm £5, chd free. Home-made teas served in the barn.** In the heart of Crews Hill is our 3 acre garden and meadow. It has been reclaimed over 30 yrs from pig farm to relaxed planting, a haven for wildlife. Walled garden leads to vegetable plot, greenhouse, and orchard. Woodland walk, lawns and stone ornaments. Martin built the house, the brick walls and metal work. Abundant cyclamen in woodland in Sept. Arboretum and lovely country views. Wheelchair access to gardens over grass.

21 OAKLEIGH PARK SOUTH, N20

N20 9JS. **Carol & Robin Tullo, 07909 901731, robin.tullo@btinternet.com.** *Totteridge & Whetstone Tube Stn (Northern Line), 15 min walk or 251 bus. Oakleigh Park Train Stn, 10 min walk. Also buses 34 & 125 from High Rd. Plenty of street parking.* **Sun 16 June (2-6). Adm £5, chd free. Home-made teas. Visits also by arrangement 1 Apr to 28 June for groups of 12 to 20. Mon-Fri in April & June only.** A late spring opening. A mature 200ft garden framed by a magnificent 100 yr old ash tree. Path leads to a pond area fed by a natural spring within landscaped terraced paving. Beyond is a herb and vegetable area, orchard with bulbs and wild flowers and the working part of the garden. A mix of sunny borders, pond marginals and woodland shade areas with seating. Level wheelchair access to terrace and lawn. Path to pond area, but raised levels beyond.

THE ORCHARD, W4

40A Hazledene Road, Chiswick, W4 3JB. **Vivien Cantor.** *10 min walk from Chiswick Mainline Stn & Gunnersbury Tube. Off Fauconberg Rd. Close to junction of A4 & Sutton Court Rd.* **Evening opening Fri 6 Sept (5-7.30). Adm £8, chd free. Wine.** Informal, romantic ¼ acre garden with mature flowering trees, shrubs and imaginative planting in flowing herbaceous borders. Climbers, fern planting, and water features with ponds, a bridge and waterfall in this ever-evolving garden. Exuberant late summer colour with dahlias, annuals and flowering shrubs.

ORMELEY LODGE, TW10

Ham Gate Avenue, Richmond, TW10 5HB. **Lady Annabel Goldsmith.** *From Richmond Park exit at Ham Gate into Ham Gate Ave, 1st house on R. From Richmond A307 after 1½ m, past New Inn on R. At T-lights turn L into Ham Gate Ave.* **Sun 16 June (3-6). Adm £5, chd free. Tea.** Large walled garden in delightful rural setting on Ham Common. Wide herbaceous borders and box hedges. Walk through to orchard with wild flowers. Vegetable garden, knot garden, aviary and chickens. Trellised tennis court with roses and climbers. A number of historic stone family dog memorials. Dogs not permitted.

PADDOCK ALLOTMENTS & LEISURE GARDENS, SW20

51 Heath Drive, Raynes Park, SW20 9BE. **Paddock Horticultural Society.** *Buses 57, 131, 200 to Raynes Park Stn, 7 min walk or bus 163. Bus 152 to Bushey Rd, 7 min walk. Bus 413, 5 min walk from Cannon Hill Ln. Street parking.* **Sat 22 June (12-5). Adm £4, chd free. Light refreshments.** An allotment site not to be missed, over 150 plots set in 5½ acres. Our tenants come from diverse communities growing a wide range of flowers, fruit and vegetables. Some plots are purely organic, others resemble English country gardens. Winner of London in Bloom Best Allotment on four occasions. Plants and produce for sale. Ploughman's lunch available. Wheelchair access over mainly level paved and grass paths.

11 PARK AVENUE NORTH, N8
Crouch End, N8 7RU. Steven Buckley & Liz Roberts. *Buses: 144, W3, W7. Tube: Finsbury Park or Turnpike Lane. Train: Hornsey or Alexandra Palace.* **Sun 21 July (11.30-5.30). Adm £5, chd free. Pre-booking essential, please visit www.ngs.org.uk for information & booking. Home-made teas.**
An award-winning, exotic, 250ft garden, much developed in 2023. Dramatic foliage, spiky and lush, dominates, with the focus on palms, cycads, aloes, agaves, dasylirions, aeoniums, tree ferns, nolinas, bamboos, yuccas, bananas, cacti, puyas and hardy succulents. Trees inc orange, peach, Cussonia spicata and Szechuan pepper. Vegetables grow in oak raised beds and a glasshouse.

36 PARK VILLAGE EAST, NW1
Camden Town, NW1 7PZ. Christy Rogers. *Tube: Mornington Cres or Camden Town, 7 mins. Opp railway, just S of Mornington St bridge. Free parking on Suns.* **Sun 9 June (2-6). Adm £6, chd free. Home-made teas.**
A large peaceful garden behind a sympathetically modernised John Nash house. Relandscaped in 2014, retaining the original mature sycamores and adding hornbeam hedges and orchard from a central large lawn, mixed herbaceous border and rose bank now with a newly planted seating area. Children enjoy an artificial grass slide. Musical entertainment provided by young musicians. Wheelchair access via grass ramp down from driveway to main garden (steeper than wheelchair regulations).

174 PECKHAM RYE, SE22
East Dulwich, SE22 9QA. Mr & Mrs Ian Bland. *Station: Peckham Rye. Buses: 63, 363, 12, 197, 484. Overlooks Peckham Rye Common from Dulwich side.* **Sun 2 June (2.30-5.30). Adm £4, chd free. Home-made teas. Donation to St Christopher's Hospice.**
This oasis, the size of a tennis court has been opening for over 25 yrs and is currently full of contrasting foliage, heights and colours. Among the usual suspects you will find rarer pseudowintera and tetrapanax 'T. Rex', various arisaemas, dracunculus, a baby oven's wattle and a giant fleece flower. The plant sale is very popular or sit on the lawn with a cup of tea and the famed cake selection. Wheelchair access via side alley.

5 PEMBERTON ROAD, KT8
East Molesey, KT8 9LG. Armi Maddison. *Please enter the garden down the side path to R of house.* **Sun 30 June (2-5). Adm £5, chd free. Light refreshments.**
An artist's sheltered and secluded gravel garden, designed alongside our new build in 2015. Many grasses, pink, blue and white planting with occasional pops of bright colour, a galvanised drinking trough with bulrushes and water lilies, a large mature central acer tree, combine with several seating areas to extend the living space into this fabulous outdoor room.

PETERSHAM HOUSE, TW10
Petersham Road, Petersham, Richmond, TW10 7AA. Francesco & Gael Boglione, www.petershamnurseries.com. *Station: Richmond, bus 65 to Dysart. Entry to garden off Petersham Rd, through Petersham Nurseries. Parking very limited on Church Ln.* **Sun 21 Apr (11-4). Adm £7.50, chd free. Light refreshments.**
Broad lawn with large topiary and generously planted double borders. Productive vegetable garden with chickens. Adjoins Petersham Nurseries with extensive plant sales, shop and café serving lunch, tea and cake.

1A PRIMROSE GARDENS, NW3
Hampstead, NW3 4UJ. Debra & Tim Craighead, dcraighead@me.com. *Belsize Park. Convenient from Belsize & Chalk Farm Tube Stns (5 mins) or Swiss Cottage (12 mins). Also buses, 168, 268 & C11. Free parking on Suns.* **Sun 2 June, Sat 21 Sept (2-5.30). Adm £5, chd free. Light refreshments. Visits also by arrangement 13 May to 29 Sept for groups of 10 to 35.**
Hidden oasis in the heart of Belsize Park, cool and relaxing. Planted with various microclimates for surrounding buildings, walls, and desire for privacy. Mirrors help create sense of intrigue. Densely planted for texture: in May, foxglove, allium, clematis, ferns, grasses, and in Sept, gingers, salvia and pennisetum. A restricted colour palette of white, purple and pops of orange throughout the yr. Bird friendly with a sedum rooftop attracting bees and butterflies.

GROUP OPENING

PRINCES AVENUE GARDENS, N10
N10 3LS. Muswell Hill. *Buses: 43 & 134 from Highgate Tube Stn; also W7, 102, 144, 234, 299. Princes Ave opp M&S in Muswell Hill Broadway & The Village Green pub in Fortis Green Rd.* **Sun 19 May (12-6). Combined adm £6, chd free. Home-made teas. Gluten free & vegan options.**

17 PRINCES AVENUE
Patsy Bailey & John Rance.

NEW **26 PRINCES AVENUE**
Tracey Marshall.

In a beautiful Edwardian avenue in the heart of Muswell Hill Conservation Area, two peaceful gardens off the bustling Broadway, both designed for relaxing and entertaining. The gardens are very different. No. 17 is a traditional garden; it is south facing, but shaded by large surrounding trees, inc a ginkgo. The garden features a superb hosta and fern display. No. 26 is a contemporary garden and north facing; it was designed and planted in spring 2023, keeping a number of mature trees and shrubs giving a well established feel. Live music at 17 Princes Avenue by the Secret Life Sax Quartet at 3pm and 4pm. Small step at number No. 17, help available on request.

The National Garden Scheme donated £3,403,960 to our nursing and health beneficiaries from money raised at gardens open in 2023

GROUP OPENING

RAILWAY COTTAGES, N22
2 Dorset Road, N22 7SL. *Nr Alexandra Palace. Tube: Wood Green, 10 min walk. Train: Alexandra Palace, 3 mins. Buses: W3, 184, 3 mins. Free parking in local streets on Suns.* **Sun 7 July (2-5.30). Combined adm £5, chd free. Home-made teas at 2 Dorset Road.**

2 DORSET ROAD
Jane Stevens.

4 DORSET ROAD
Mark Longworth.

14 DORSET ROAD
Cathy Brogan.

22 DORSET ROAD
Mike & Noreen Ainger.

24A DORSET ROAD
Eddie & Jane Wessman.

A row of historical railway cottages, tucked away from the bustle of Wood Green nr Alexandra Palace, takes the visitor back in time. The tranquil country style garden at 2 Dorset Road flanks three sides of the house. Clipped hedges contrast with climbing roses, clematis, honeysuckle, abutilon, grasses and ferns. Trees inc mulberry, quince, fig, apple and a mature willow creating an interesting shady corner with a pond. There is an emphasis on scented flowers that attract bees and butterflies and the traditional medicinal plants found in cottage gardens. No. 4 is a pretty secluded garden (accessed through the rear of No. 2) and sets off the sculptor owners figurative and abstract work. There are three front gardens open for view. No. 14 is an informal, organic, bee-friendly garden, planted with fragrant and useful herbs, flowers and shrubs. No. 22 is nurtured by the grandson of the original railway worker occupant. A lovely place to sit and relax and enjoy the varied planting. No. 24a reverts to the potager style cottage garden with raised beds overflowing with vegetables and flowers. Popular plant sale.

42 RISINGHOLME ROAD, HA3
Harrow, HA3 7ER. Brenda White. *Wealdstone/Harrow Weald. Buses: 258, 340,182,140 Salvatorian College/St Joseph's Catholic Church, Wealdstone. Tube/train: Harrow & Wealdstone Stn (10 min walk or bus). Road opp the Salvatorian College.* **Sun 5 May, Sun 1 Sept (2-5). Adm £5, chd free. Home-made teas.**

A stunning, paved 100ft long garden packed with plants, divided into different themed areas inc a raised bed vegetable garden, a large aviary, beehive and summerhouse. A shady garden that makes the most of every space!

1A Primrose Gardens

43 RODING ROAD, E5
E5 0DN. Ms Tanya Barrett.
Homerton. 6 min walk from Homerton Overground Stn or buses 236, 276, 308 alight nr or on Homerton High St. If coming from Lower Clapton Gardens it is a 10 min walk. **Sun 16 June (2-5). Adm £3, chd free. Open nearby Lower Clapton Gardens.**
A small, west facing Victorian terrace garden with a curved lawn surrounding two mixed borders (one sunny, one semi-shade) of climbers, shrubs, perennials and annuals. Mainly blue, pinks and white inc roses, clematis, salvias and unusual perennial geraniums. Also a patio area with a large number of pots inc scented pelargoniums. An ongoing work in progress as planted only 10 yrs ago. Refreshments are available at Lower Clapton Gardens. There are also lots of wonderful cafés on Chatsworth Rd, a 5 min walk away.

NEW ROEHAMPTON GARDEN SOCIETY ALLOTMENTS, SW15
162 Dover House Road, Putney, SW15 5AR. Roehampton Garden Society, www.roehamptonallotments.co.uk. *Bus: 430, Elmshaw Rd stop. Train: Putney Mainline, Putney High St, then take 430 bus. Street parking.* **Sun 21 July (2-5). Adm £4, chd free. Light refreshments.**
176 allotment plots established in the 1930s, set within the Dover House Estate, a Conservation area in a garden suburb environment. Our plot holders come from diverse communities and grow a wide variety of vegetables, fruit and flowers. Fresh produce and plants will be on sale, as well as refreshments from our Potting Shed located in a lovely floral communal garden. Wheelchair access over mainly level paved paths and uneven grass paths. Accessible WC on site.

ROOFTOPVEGPLOT, W1
122 Great Titchfield Street, W1W 6ST. Miss Wendy Shillam, 07597 438666, coffeeinthesquare@me.com, www.rooftopvegplot.com. *Fitzrovia. Located on the 5th floor, flat roof of a private house. Ring the doorbell marked Shillam & Smith to be let into the building.* **Sat 6, Sun 7 July (11-6). Adm £6, chd £3.**

Pre-booking essential, please visit www.ngs.org.uk for information & booking. Home-made teas.
A nutritional garden with views across London, where fruit and vegetables grow amongst complementary flowers in six inches of soil, in raised beds on a flat roof. Trellis and greenhouse tomatoes. This is a tiny garden, so tours are restricted to six visitors. Home-made cakes, and growing and nutritional tips from Wendy Shillam, a clinical nutritionist and health writer with an extensive knowledge of green nutrition.

ROYAL TRINITY HOSPICE, SW4
30 Clapham Common North Side, SW4 0RN. Royal Trinity Hospice, www.royaltrinityhospice.london/our-gardens. *8 min walk from Clapham Common Tube. Buses: 35, 37, 345, 137, 249 & 322 (137 stops outside).* **Sun 17 Mar, Sun 28 Apr, Sun 19 May, Sun 15 Sept (11-4). Adm £4, chd free. Light refreshments. Open nearby 51 The Chase & 152a Victoria Rise on 28 Apr only.**
Our front gardens feature wisteria, shrubs and trees. The rear landscaped gardens inc two lawns with herbaceous borders either side of a path that leads to the Koi pond. There is lots of year-round colour in the gardens from annuals, perennials, roses and shrubs. In 2023 we added lots of new perennials and shrubs with autumn colours. Wheelchair access via ramps and pathways.

NEW 31 RYECROFT ROAD, SW16
Streatham, SW16 3EW. Chrissy & Pete Silver. *Nr Crown Point. Mainline: Streatham & West Norwood Stns. Buses: 68, 196, 249, 417, & 468 all to Crown Point.* **Sun 26 May (2-5). Adm £5, chd free. Home-made teas.**
Large sunny garden, open aspect with far-reaching views toward the North Downs from a roof terrace. Herbaceous border around a large lawn, vegetable patch, small woodland area, rockery with Mediterranean planting. Old-fashioned roses both front and back. Lovely old Yorkstone paths help to divide the garden into smaller, cosier areas.

28A ST AUGUSTINE'S ROAD, NW1
Camden Town, NW1 9RN. Ricky Patel, rickypatelfilm@gmail.com. *10-12 min walk from Camden Stn, 15 min walk from Kings Cross Stn, 15 min walk from Caledonian Rd Stn.* **Visits by arrangement 15 June to 15 Sept.**
Step from a wide, quiet street into a tropical paradise! This young garden away from busy Camden is only a few yrs old but looking lush and well established thanks to the plants that moved here with the new owner inc bananas, ginger, cannas, tetrapanax and bamboos. A green fingered, self-taught plant lover's garden with an emphasis on impressive foliage and interesting texture.

7 ST PAUL'S PLACE, N1
Islington, N1 2QE. Mrs Fiona Atkins. *50 metres W & N of the junction of St Paul's Rd & Essex Rd in Islington.* **Sat 25 May (12-5.30). Adm £5, chd free. Cream teas.**
The main feature of the walled garden is a pond with natural planting to encourage pollinators and birds. It is a working garden; many of the plants have been grown from seed in the small greenhouse, compost is made from waste and leaves from surrounding trees and water is collected in water butts for the pond. A large terrace features a white wisteria and container planting.

27 ST PETERS SQUARE, W6
British Grove, W6 9NW. Oliver & Gabrielle Leigh Wood, 07810 677478, oliverleighwood@hotmail.com. *Tube to Stamford Brook, exit station & turn S down Goldhawk Rd. At T-lights continue ahead into British Grove. Entrance to garden at 50 British Grove, 100yds on L.* **Sun 12 May (2-6). Adm £6, chd free. Home-made teas. Visits also by arrangement.**
This long, secret space, is a plantsman's eclectic semi-tamed wilderness. Created over the last 12 yrs it contains lots of camellias, magnolias and fruit trees. Much of the hard landscaping is from skips and the whole garden is full of other people's unconsidered trifles of fancy inc a folly and summerhouse.

19 ST PETER'S STREET, N1

N1 8JD. Adrian Gunning. *Angel, Islington. Tube: Angel. Bus: Islington Green.* **Sun 2 June (3-6.30). Adm £5, chd free.**
Charming, secluded town garden with climbing roses, trees, shrubs, climbers, pond, patio with containers and a gazebo with a trompe l'oeil mural.

57 ST QUINTIN AVENUE, W10

W10 6NZ. Mr H Groffman, 020 8969 8292. *Less than 1m from Ladbroke Grove or White City Tube Stn. Buses: 7, 70, 220 all to North Pole Rd.* **Sun 7, Sun 21 July (2-5.30). Adm £5, chd free. Home-made teas. Visits also by arrangement 7 July to 31 Aug.**
Award-winning 30ft x 40ft garden with a diverse selection of plants inc shrubs for foliage effects. Patio with colour themed bedding material. Focal points throughout. Clever use of mirrors and plant associations. New look front garden, new rear patio layout, and new plantings for 2024 with a good selection of climbers and wall shrubs. This yr's special display will feature another inspiring colour theme.

5 ST REGIS CLOSE, N10

Alexandra Park Rd, Muswell Hill, N10 2DE. Mrs S Bennett & Mr E Hyde, 020 8883 8540, suebearlh@yahoo.co.uk. *2nd L in Alexandra Park Rd coming from Colney Hatch Ln. 102 & 299 bus from Bounds Green Tube to St Andrew's Church or 102 from East Finchley. Buses 43 & 143 stop in Colney Hatch Ln. Short walk. Follow NGS signs. Parking on side roads inc coaches.* **Sun 28 Apr, Sun 30 June, Sun 4 Aug (2-6.30). Adm £5, chd free. Home-made teas & gluten free option. Visits also by arrangement Apr to Oct for groups of 10+.**
Cornucopia of sensual delights. Artist's garden famous for architectural features and delicious cakes. Baroque temple, pagodas, Raku tiled mirrored wall conceals plant nursery. American Gothic shed overlooks Liberace terrace and stairway to heaven. Maureen Lipman's favourite garden; combines colour, humour, trompe l'oeil with wildlife friendly ponds, waterfalls, weeping willow, lawns and abundant planting. A unique experience awaits! Unusual architectural features inc

Oriental tea house overlooking carp pond. Mega plant sale and open studio with ceramics and cards (cash only). Gold winner of Haringey in Bloom 2023 'Best Back Garden'. Wheelchair access not suitable for everyone, please check with owners for details.

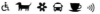

11 SHORTGATE, N12

North Finchley, N12 7JP. Jennifer O'Donovan. *Bus: 326, alight at the green on Southover, follow signs. Tube: Woodside Park, exit from northbound platform, follow signs. Parking: surrounding roads, not in Shortgate.* **Sun 30 June (1.30-5.30). Adm £5, chd free. Home-made teas.**
This corner plot is a spacious and elegant garden. It has sunny herbaceous beds, a neat vegetable patch, shade bearing trees with tranquil seating and a greenhouse busy with plants. Developed over 35 yrs, there wasn't even one tree when the owner arrived.

SOUTH LONDON BOTANICAL INSTITUTE, SE24

323 Norwood Road, SE24 9AQ. South London Botanical Institute, www.slbi.org.uk. *Mainline: Tulse Hill. Buses: 68, 196, 322 & 468 stop at junction of Norwood Rd & Romola Rd.* **Sun 28 Apr (2-5). Adm £5, chd free. Home-made teas. Donation to South London Botanical Institute.**
London's smallest botanical garden is open again after major refurbishment to our building. Spring highlights inc unusual bulbs, ferns, flowering trees and early roses. Wild flowers flourish beside medicinal herbs. Scented, native and woodland plants are featured, growing among rare trees and shrubs. There is a small dye plant bed and a collection of succulents in our greenhouse. Our small cafe will be serving home-made teas.

41 SOUTHBROOK ROAD, SE12

Lee, SE12 8LJ. Barbara Polanski, polanski101@yahoo.co.uk. *Southbrook Rd is situated off S Circular, off Burnt Ash Rd. Train: Lee & Hither Green, both 10 min walk. Bus: P273, 202. Please enter via side access & look out for the balloons!* **Sat 1, Sun 2 June (2.30-5.30). Adm £5, chd free. Home-made teas. Visits also by**

arrangement 15 June to 7 July for groups of 10 to 25.
Developed over 14 yrs, this large garden has a formal layout with wide mixed herbaceous borders full of colour, surrounded by mature trees, framing sunny lawns, a central box parterre and an Indian pergola. Ancient pear trees festooned in June with clouds of white Kiftsgate and Rambling Rector roses. Discover fish and damselflies in two lily ponds. Many sheltered places to sit and relax. Enjoy refreshments in a small classical garden building with interior wall paintings, almost hidden by roses climbing way up into the trees. Orangery, parterre, gazebo and wall fountain. Side access for standard wheelchairs. Gravel driveway and one step.

The National Garden Scheme's final instalment to support the building of the Y Bwthyn NGS Macmillan Specialist Palliative Care Unit in Wales, enabled 270 inpatients to be supported this year

◆ **SPENCER HOUSE, SW1**
27 St James' Place, Westminster, SW1A 1NR. RIT Capital Partners, www.spencerhouse.co.uk. *From Green Park Stn, exit on S side, walk down Queen's Walk, turn L through narrow alleyway. Turn R & Spencer House will be in front of you.* **For opening times and information, please visit garden website.**
Originally designed in the C18 by Henry Holland (son-in-law to Lancelot 'Capability' Brown), the garden was among the grandest in the West End. Restored since 1990 under the Chairmanship of Lord Rothschild, the garden with a delightful view of the adjacent Royal Park, now evokes its original layout with planting suggested by early C19 nursery lists.

GROUP OPENING

SPITALFIELDS GARDENS, E1
E1 6QE. *Nr Spitalfields Market. 10 min walk from Liverpool St Stn, Aldgate East Tube, Shoreditch High St Train Stn.* **Sat 8 June (10-4). Combined adm £12, chd free. Home-made teas at The Rectory (2 Fournier Street), Town House (5 Fournier Street) & 29 Fournier Street.**

30 CALVIN STREET, FLAT 1
Susan Young.

29 FOURNIER STREET
Juliette Larthe.

THE RECTORY, 2 FOURNIER STREET
Jack McCausland.

37 SPITAL SQUARE
Society for the Protection of Ancient Buildings.

Discover a unique selection of secluded gardens in Spitalfields, just a stone's throw from the buzz of Spitalfields Market. The feel of a country garden behind the Church offering fabulous teas and music, a small courtyard garden behind one of the fine French Huguenot houses of the C17, a small paved garden unconstrained by its high boundary walls and another undaunted by the shade of the surrounding tall buildings. Each garden has adapted to its particular urban space with vertical and horizontal beds, inspired planting, pots, statuary and architectural artefacts. The Rectory, 2 Fournier Street is Regional Finalist, The English Garden Magazine's The Nation's Favourite Gardens 2023.

 ))

25 SPRINGFIELD AVENUE, N10
Muswell Hill, N10 3SU. Heather Hampson & Nigel Ragg. *From main r'about in Muswell Hill, down Muswell Hill towards Crouch End. Springfield Ave 1st on L. No. 25 is opp the steps to Grosvenor Gardens.* **Sun 9 June (2-6). Adm £5, chd free. Home-made teas.**
Be pleasantly surprised by this city garden! Magical, packed with colour, fragrance, rambling roses and quirky ideas to stimulate conversation and imagination. A visual delight with three terraces, each with an individual atmosphere that lead to the summerhouse with a backdrop of mature trees. Plenty of spots to sit and enjoy scrumptious tea and cakes. Good plant sale. The summerhouse is somewhere to rest and view the owner's art works for sale in aid of the NGS. NB this is a steep garden, on different levels with uneven steps.

🐎 ✳ 💆))

106 STATION ROAD, TW12
Hampton, TW12 2AS. Diane Kermack. *From Hampton Stn, turn L along Station Rd, past St Theodore's Church, opp the green. Access to garden via the garden gate on the adjacent side road Station Cl.* **Sat 20, Sun 21 July (11-5). Adm £4, chd free. Light refreshments.**
An apiary garden with six busy hives which will be of special interest to beekeepers. Bushy front garden with vegetable plot and perimeter flower bed. Walk through past swimming pool, greenhouses, seating and many pots. Informal back garden featuring many beehives. Pond, chickens and informal flower beds.

💆))

NEW **SUSSEX COTTAGE, TW3**
128 Whitton Road, Hounslow, TW3 2EP. John Meinke. *Hounslow Stn, 5 min walk. 281 bus passes outside. Unrestricted parking on local roads.* **Sun 2 June (1-5). Combined adm with 116 Whitton Road £8, chd free. Home-made teas.**
A surprising garden with a number of unique features, many of which date back to the 1920s. The garden is on several levels, and features a stone bridge, pond and air raid shelter. There are many well established trees which gives the garden a woodland feel. Traditional planting inc roses, lavender, peonies, acanthus and philadelphus.

💆))

93 TANFIELD AVENUE, NW2
Dudden Hill, NW2 7SB. Mr James Duncan Mattoon, 07504 565612. *Nr Dollis Hill, Willesden & Wembley. Nearest station: Neasden (Jubilee line), then 10 min walk; or various bus routes to Neasden Parade or Tanfield Ave.* **Sun 21 July (2-6). Adm £5, chd free. Home-made teas. Visits also by arrangement June to Sept for groups of up to 15.**
Intensely exotic Mediterranean and subtropical paradise garden! Sunny deck with implausible planting and panoramic views of Harrow and Wembley, plunges into incredibly exotic, densely planted oasis of delight, with two further seating areas engulfed by flowers, such as, acacia, colocasia, eryngium, hedychium, plumbago, salvias and hundreds more in vigorous competition! Birds and bees love it! Previous garden was Tropical Kensal Rise (Doyle Gardens), featured on BBC 2 Open Gardens and in Sunday Telegraph. This garden featured in Garden Week and Garden Answers magazine. Steep steps down to main garden.

✳ 💆

TEMPLE LODGE CLUB, W6
51 Queen Caroline Street, Hammersmith, W6 9QL. The Rev. Nigel Lumsden, 020 8748 8388, Booking@templelodgeclub.com, www.templelodgeclub.com/about-us/#history. *Queen Caroline St is opp Broadway Shopping Centre which contains tube & bus stations. Piccadilly, District & Hammersmith & City lines. Buses: 9, 10, 27, 33, 419, 72, H91, 190, 211, 220, 267, 283, 295, 391, Fulham Palace Rd exit. Temple Lodge entrance via Gate Restaurant Courtyard.* **Sat 14 Sept (12-5). Adm £5, chd free. Light refreshments.**
Artist Sir Frank Brangwyn's former home, studio and walled garden. Discover an oasis in the heart of London. Perennials and grasses with long seasons of interest provide changing colour, movement and structure through seasons. Garden designed by Tom Ryder. Old carved stone unearthed and set aside during recent garden renovations are repurposed and are on display. Explore to the rhythmic sound of the flow form water feature. Temple Lodge Club is also a thriving and unique guesthouse and has a vegetarian restaurant (booking recommended). Wheelchair access

through adjacent car park of St Vincent's Care Home. Garden does feature steps and sloped paths.

6 THORNHILL ROAD, N1
Islington, N1 1HW. Janis Higgie. *Barnsbury. Tube: Angel or Highbury & Islington. Train: Caledonian & Barnsbury. Bus: to Liverpool Rd.* **Sat 15 Jun (12-5). Adm £4, chd free. Home-made teas.**
150ft Islington garden, designed and planted over the last 30 yrs. This fully accessible family garden draws inspiration from the owner's antipodean roots. A brick path guides visitors past lawns, raised beds, a water feature, fire bowl and a creative mix of plants from around the globe (inc kowhai and hoheria trees with many shade tolerant plants). This garden has a lot, even the kitchen sink! Completely wheelchair friendly.

27 THORPEWOOD AVENUE, SE26
Sydenham, SE26 4BU. Barbara Nella. *½ m from Forest Hill Stn. Off the S Circular (A205) turning up Sydenham Hill nr Horniman Gardens, or Dartmouth Rd from Forest Hill Stn. Buses: 122, 176, 312 to Forest Hill Library.* **Sun 30 June (1.30-5). Adm £6, chd free. Home-made teas.**
This ½ acre sloping garden blends a cool English woodland look with hotter Mediterranean styles and, with its bamboos and bananas, travels even further afield, all the way to the Antipodes. A particular joy lies in the garden's heart where woodland opens out to reveal a sunny glade packed with alpine delights. Barbara is a compulsive plants person, so come prepared to buy some interesting plants.

TORRIANO COMMUNITY GARDEN, NW5
Torriano Avenue, NW5 2ST. Mrs Elisa Puentes. *Kentish Town. Train station: Camden Road. 10 min walk along Camden Rd to Torriano Ave. Buses: 29, 253. Walk along Torriano Ave & garden is on R opp the primary school.* **Sun 16 June (12-4). Adm £5, chd free. Home-made teas.**
This beautiful 1 acre community garden, designed and built in 2003 by the residents helped by the Army, has amazing features with a variety of flowers. The design of the flower beds have the numbers 2003. This beautiful

space is fully wheelchair accessible and open for all to enjoy even if you do not live on the estate. Our garden is maintained and cleaned by residents and is open all year-round.

9 TRAFALGAR TERRACE, HA1
Harrow, HA1 3EU. George Reeve, www.instagram.com/thehillsjunglegarden. *Harrow-on-the-Hill Stn; 10 min walk via Churchfields & path to Trafalgar Terrace. Free roadside parking on West St; L onto Nelson Rd to end, L to 9 Trafalgar Terrace following NGS signs.* **Sat 7 Sept (1-5). Adm £5, chd free. Pre-booking essential, please visit www.ngs.org.uk for information & booking. Light refreshments.**
Small jungle and tropical themed garden with big leaf plants down to small succulents. The garden is a tranquil space with running water and views up to Harrow's famous St Mary's Church. We look forward to welcoming you to our piece of paradise.

31 TRELAWN ROAD, SW2
SW2 1DH. Mr M Simmons & Mr D Waddock. *Brixton. From Brixton Underground Stn, turn L along Effra Rd towards Sainsbury's. Walk past Halfords & Trelawn Rd is 2nd road on L. Buses 2, 3, 37, 196, 415.* **Sun 9 June (1-5). Adm £4, chd free. Home-made teas inc gluten free & vegan options.**
A small city garden designed to give the illusion of space with a winding path and hidden vistas. Crammed with plants, dominated by perennials, roses, ferns and exotics. There is no lawn, but several seating areas from which to contemplate the space.

24 TWYFORD AVENUE, N2
N2 9NJ. Rachel Lindsay & Jeremy Pratt, 07930 632902, jeremypr@blueyonder.co.uk. *Twyford Ave runs parallel to Fortis Green, between East Finchley & Muswell Hill. Tube: Northern line to East Finchley. Buses: 102, 143, 234, 263 to East Finchley. Buses 43, 134, 144, 234 to Muswell Hill. Buses: 102 & 234 stop at end of road. Garden signed from Fortis Green.* **Sun 21 July (2-6). Adm £4, chd free. Home-made teas. Visits also by arrangement for groups of up to 20.**

Very sunny, 120ft south facing garden, planted for colour. Brick edged borders and many containers packed with traditional herbaceous and perennial cottage garden plants and shrubs. Shady area at rear. Experimental gravel area that is never watered. Some uneven ground. Water feature. Greenhouse. Many places to sit and think, chat or doze. Local honey and bee products on sale.

86 UNDERHILL ROAD, SE22
East Dulwich, SE22 0QU. Claire & Rob Goldie. *Between Langton Rise & Melford Rd. Station: Forest Hill. Buses: P13, 363, 63, 176, 185 & P4.* **Evening opening Fri 16 Aug (7-9.30). Adm £7, chd free. Wine. Sun 18 Aug (2-6). Adm £4.50, chd free. Home-made teas.**
A generous family garden packed with surprises around every corner. Opening for the first time in Aug shows the garden off in its more jungle appearance with hot and spicy tones from the cannas and chocolate sunflowers to the hot pinks of salvias and *Houttuynia cordata*. Lots of variegated foliage to sparkle in the sunshine and the rain; pittosporum, cornus and vinca major. The garden is near The Horniman Garden which is free and within walking distance or a short bus ride.

[NEW] 30 URLWIN STREET, SE5
Camberwell, SE5 0NF. Mrs Judith Gregory. *Close to junction of Albany St & Camberwell Rd. Nearest tube station is Elephant & Castle, 15 min walk. Buses 12,148,176,171, 42, 40, 35, 68, 468. From the bus stop Urlwin St, which is a continuation of Albany St, 5 min walk. Access to garden from private road Horsman St.* **Sun 28 July (2-5). Adm £5, chd free. Home-made teas.**
Lovingly created out of a wilderness over 16 yrs this immaculate garden reflects the elegance of the Georgian house (not open), in a quiet street off busy Camberwell. Structure is key and unusual trees and shrubs are kept well shaped. Water lilies thrive in a goldfish pond with golden Orfe and Shubunkin. An unexpected gate leads to a deeply planted gravel garden. Don't miss the trompe l'oeil corner.

152A VICTORIA RISE, SW4
Clapham, SW4 0NW. Benn Storey, www.instagram.com/thenorthsouthgarden. *South West London. Entry via basement flat. Closest tube Clapham Common. Bus 77, 87, 137, 156, 345, 452.* **Sun 28 Apr (12-5). Adm £4.50, chd free. Open nearby Royal Trinity Hospice.**
In its 8th yr this terraced garden is 21 metres long by 8 metres wide. Planting ranges from the lush greens of the courtyard to the frothy, insect friendly plants of the main level, to the espalier fruit trees and vegetables of the productive levels. A copper beech hedge hides a cozy arbour seat and fire pit at the top of the plot, out of view from surrounding neighbours.

13 WAITE DAVIES ROAD, SE12
Lee, SE12 0NE. Janet Pugh. *Just off A205 South Circular. Lee Train Stn, 11 min walk. Hither Green & Grove Park Stns, 20 min walk. Bus route 261 stops close by. Buses 202 & 160 stop nearby. Usually free roadside parking.* **Sun 2 June (2-5.30). Combined adm with 15 Waite Davies Road £5, chd free. Home-made teas.**
A colourful and welcoming front garden leads you down steps to a bright and peaceful, gently maturing garden. The soft sound of a discreet water feature adds to the calm atmosphere with attractive massed planting in a palette of pinks, purples and creams. Offerings of a rich selection of cream cakes add to the charm.

15 WAITE DAVIES ROAD, SE12
Lee, SE12 0NE. Will Jennings. *Just off the A205 South Circular. Lee Train Stn,11 min walk. Hither Green & Grove Park Stns, 20 min walk. Bus route 261 stops close by. Buses 202 & 160 stop nearby. Usually roadside parking.* **Sun 2 June (2-5.30). Combined adm with 13 Waite Davies Road £5, chd free.**
Hidden behind a Victorian terrace is a tiny yet immaculately presented English garden. A huge Malvern Hills rambling rose gently billows over a willow painted shed, foxgloves spring up beneath a crab apple tree, and box hedging frames the scene. Nearby, the soft pink petals of climbing rose The Generous Gardener nod gracefully over a sunbaked stone patio.

WARREN MEWS, W1
Fitzrovia, W1T 5NQ. Rebecca Hossack. *2 mins from Warren St Tube Stn. Entrance to garden on Warren St, W1T 5NQ.* **Sat 22 June (11-4). Adm by donation. Home-made teas.**
Tucked away behind bustling Tottenham Court Road is the enchanting garden of Warren Mews. On first glance, it is impossible to tell that the plants in this verdant garden have no access to the earth. Warren Mews is a place where pots of paradise flowers, window boxes bursting with geraniums and containers of olive trees rule the street. Eclectic container planting with an Australian influence. The Rebecca Hossack Art Gallery is a 5 min walk away. Mews is fully accessible and entirely cobbled.

9 WARWICK CLOSE, TW12
Hampton, TW12 2TY. Chris Churchman, 07802 470313, cc@cquester.co.uk. *2m W of Twickenham, 2m N of Hampton Court, overlooking Bushy Park. 100 metres from Hampton Open Air Swimming Pool.* **Sat 10 Aug (10.30-5). Adm £4, chd free. Home-made teas. Visits also by arrangement 1 June to 2 Aug for groups of 7 to 20. Bookings must be made a min of 1 month in advance.**
A small suburban garden in South West London. Front garden with espaliered American lime trees, featuring roses, lavender and stipa. Shade garden with rare ferns and herbaceous. Rear garden has recently added canal water feature, rectangular lawn with prairie style plantings crossed with subtropical species. Roof top allotment to garage (the garotment).

THE WATERGARDENS, KT2
Warren Road, Kingston-upon-Thames, KT2 7LF. The Residents' Association. *1m E of Kingston. From Kingston take A308 (Kingston Hill) towards London; after approx ½ m turn R into Warren Rd. No. 57 bus along Coombe Lane West, alight at Warren Rd. Roadside parking only.* **Sun 28 Apr, Sun 20 Oct (1.30-4). Adm £5, chd free.**
Japanese landscaped garden originally part of Coombe Wood Nursery, planted by the Veitch family in the 1860s. Approx 9 acres with ponds, streams and waterfalls. Many rare trees, which in spring and autumn provide stunning colour. For the tree lover this is a must-see garden. Gardens attractive to wildlife. Major renovation and restoration have taken place over the past yrs revealing a hitherto lost lake and waterfall. Restoration works ongoing. Unsuitable for those unsteady on their feet.

70 WENSLEYDALE ROAD, TW12
Hampton, TW12 2LX. Mr Steve Pickering. *9 min walk from Hampton Stn. From Hampton Stn, E on Station Rd towards Oldfield Rd, L onto Tudor Rd, R onto Wensleydale Rd, L to stay on Wensleydale Rd.* **Sat 25, Sun 26 May (1-5). Adm £4, chd free. Open nearby 16 Links View Road.**
Small traditional garden in classic layout with greenhouse, summerhouse, pergolas, patio and rockery with an emphasis on year-round colour. Many evergreen shrubs and perennials. Wisteria over pergola flowers in spring. David Austin Desdemona rose repeat flowering on the patio. Greenhouse containing succulents and many flowering plants. All created by the amateur gardener owners. Wheelchair access only to one section of rear garden, nearest the house.

WEST LODGE PARK, EN4
Cockfosters Road, Hadley Wood, EN4 0PY. Beales Hotels, 020 8216 3904, janegray@bealeshotels.co.uk, www.bealeshotels.co.uk/westlodgepark. *1m S of Potters Bar. On A111. J24 from M25 signed Cockfosters.* **Sun 19 May (2-5); Sun 20 Oct (1-4). Adm £7.50, chd free. Home-made teas. Visits also by arrangement Apr to Oct for groups of 10+.**
Open for the NGS for over 40 yrs, the 35 acre Beale Arboretum consists of over 800 varieties of trees and shrubs inc National Collections of hornbeam cultivars *Carpinus betulus*, Indian bean tree *Catalpa bignonioides*, swamp cypress *Taxodium distichum*. Network of paths through good selection of conifers, oaks, maples and mountain ash, all specimens labelled. Stunning collection within the M25.Guided tours available. Breakfasts, morning coffee and biscuits, afternoon tea, restaurant lunches, light lunches, dinner all served in the hotel. Please see website for details.

4 WHARTON STREET, WC1X
Bloomsbury, WC1X 9PX.
Barbara Holliman, 07733 485324,
jugglingsheep@hotmail.co.uk.
*Bloomsbury/Clerkenwell. Off Kings
Cross Rd. Short walk from Kings
Cross &, Angel & Farringdon Tube.
Buses 19, 38, & 341 to Rosebery
Ave or 73 to Claremont Sq stop on
Pentonville Rd.* **Sun 23 June (2-
5.30). Adm £4.50, chd free. Visits
also by arrangement 23 June to 30
Sept for groups of up to 5.**
Tiny award-winning 16ft x 26ft north
facing garden with shade patio
planted for all year interest.

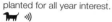 **116 WHITTON ROAD, TW3**
Hounslow, TW3 2EP. Colin Powe.
*5 mins from Twickenham Rugby
Ground. Hounslow Stn, 5 min
walk. Unrestricted parking on local roads.*
**Sun 2 June (1-5). Combined adm
with Sussex Cottage £8, chd
free. Home-made teas at Sussex
Cottage.**
A small, romantic, traditional garden
inspired by Edwardian country gardens.
Approx 85ft long with a manicured
and striped lawn. Planting inc peonies,
myrtle, clematis, old roses, fennel,
lavender, and crab apples. The lawn
is cut using a Ransomes Ajax (one
on display at The Garden Museum).
Hazel features at the end of the garden
and was planted in 1900 (the house is
called Hazeldene).

61 WOLSEY ROAD, KT8
East Molesey, KT8 9EW. Jan & Ken
Heath, janheath61@gmail.com.
*Less than 10 min walk from
Hampton Court Palace & station,
very easy to find.* **Sun 2 June (2-6).
Adm £5, chd free. Home-made
teas. Visits also by arrangement 3
June to 16 June.**
Romantic, secluded and peaceful
garden of two halves designed and
maintained by the owners. Part is
shaded by two large copper beech
trees with woodland planting and
fernery. The second reached through
a beech arch with cottage garden
planting, pond and wooden obelisks
covered with roses. Beautiful octagonal
gazebo overlooks pond, plus an oak
framed summerhouse designed and
built by the owners. Extensive seating
throughout the garden to sit quietly and
enjoy your tea and cake.

39 WOOD VALE, SE23
Forest Hill, SE23 3DS. Nigel
Crawley. *Entrance through Thistle
Gates, 48 Melford Rd. Train stations:
Forest Hill & Honor Oak Park.
Victoria Stn to West Dulwich, then
P4. Buses: 363 Elephant & Castle to
Wood Vale/Melford Rd; 176, 185 &
197 to Lordship Ln/Wood Vale.* **Sun
14 Apr (1-5). Home-made teas.
Evening opening Wed 17 Apr (5-
7). Wine. Adm £5, chd free.**
Diverse garden dominated by a
gigantic perry pear forming part of
one of the East Dulwich orchards.
View our displays of aricula and
pulsatilla. The emphasis in the garden
is on its inhabitants; white comfrey
and pear blossom keeps the bees
busy in the spring. There are clumps
of narcissi around the old apple tree
and pots of hyacinths, fritillary, early
tulips and semponium and other
succulents. Surprising green oasis
in Forest Hill. Close to Sydenham
Woods, Horniman Gardens and
Camberwell Old Cemetery. Level
wheelchair access, but rough terrain
in the lane.

7 WOODBINES AVENUE, KT1
Kingston-upon-Thames, KT1 2AZ.
Mr Tony Sharples & Mr Paul
Cuthbert. *Take K2, K3, 71 or 281
bus. From Surbiton, bus stop
outside Waitrose & exit bus Kingston
University Stop. From Kingston, walk
or bus from Eden St (opp Heals).*
**Sun 2 June (12-5). Combined adm
with 15 Catherine Road £7, chd
free. Light refreshments.**
We have created a winding path
through our 70ft garden with trees,
evergreen structure, perennial flowers
and grasses. Wide herbaceous
borders, an ancient grapevine, a box
hedge topiary garden, large silver
birches and a hot summer terrace
provide contrast.

28A WORCESTER ROAD, E17
Walthamstow, E17 5QR. Mark &
Emma Luggie. *12 min walk from
Blackhorse Road Tube Stn. Just off
Blackhorse Ln. On street parking.*
**Sun 18 Aug (2-6). Adm £4, chd
free. Open nearby 84 Higham
Street.**
Typical Walthamstow terraced back
garden, turned into a lush tropical
oasis of foliage with a small stream
and pond. Small and large leaves mix
with floral accents and varying leaf

textures from ferns, colocasia and
bananas supported by a framework of
larger established trees, jasmine, and
tree ferns. A small gravel path leads
you to a small seating area to reflect,
or sit on the patio and enjoy.

1 YORK CLOSE, W7
Hanwell, W7 3JB. Tony Hulme
& Eddy Fergusson. *By road only,
entrance to York Cl via Church Rd.
Nearest station Hanwell Train Stn.
Buses E3, 195, 207.* **Sat 17, Sun 18
Aug (2-6). Adm £5, chd free.**
Tiny, quirky, prize-winning garden
extensively planted with an eclectic
mix inc hosta collection, and
many unusual and tropical plants.
Plantaholics paradise. Many surprises
in this unique and very personal
garden.

**ZEN GARDEN AT JAPANESE
BUDDHIST CENTRE, W3**
Three Wheels, 55 Carbery Avenue,
Acton, W3 9AB. Reverend Prof K
T Sato, www.threewheels.org.uk/
zen-garden. *Tube: Acton Town, 5
min walk. 200yds off A406.* **Sat 8,
Sun 9 June (2-5). Adm £3.50, chd
free. Matcha tea £3.**
Pure Japanese Zen garden (so no
flowers) with 12 large and small rocks
of various colours and textures, set
in islands of moss and surrounded
by a sea of grey granite gravel raked
in a stylised wave pattern. Garden
surrounded by trees and bushes
outside a cob wall. Oak framed wattle
and daub shelter with Norfolk reed
thatched roof. Talk on the Zen garden
between 3-4pm. Buddha Room open
to public.

*In 2023 we awarded
over £260,000 in
Community Garden
Grants, supporting
86 community garden
projects*

OXFORDSHIRE

VOLUNTEERS

County Organiser
Marina Hamilton-Baillie
01367 710486
marina.hamilton-baillie@ngs.org.uk

Treasurer
Tom Hamilton-Baillie
01367 710486
tom.hamilton-baillie@ngs.org.uk

Talks Co-Ordinator
Priscilla Frost 01608 811818
info@oxconf.co.uk

Dr David Edwards
07973 129473
david.edwards@ngs.org.uk

Social Media- Instagram
Dr Jill Edwards 07971 201352
jill.edwards@ngs.org.uk

Social Media & Marketing
John Fleming 01865 739327
john@octon.scot

Assistant County Organisers
Lynn Baldwin 01608 642754
elynnbaldwin@gmail.com

Dr David Edwards (as above)

Dr Jill Edwards (as above)

Sarah Fernback
sarah.fernback@ngs.org.uk

Penny Guy 01865 862000
penny.theavon@virginmedia.com

Michael & Pat Hougham
01865 890020
gmec@outlook.com

Lyn Sanders
01865 739486
sandersc4@hotmail.com

Paul Youngson 07946 273902
paulyoungson48@gmail.com

 @NGSOxfordshire
 @ngs_oxfordshire
 @ngs_oxfordshire

OPENING DATES

All entries subject to change. For latest information check **www.ngs.org.uk**
Map locator numbers are shown to the right of each garden name.

February

Snowdrop Openings
Sunday 11th
23 Hid's Copse Road | 38
6 High Street | 39
Sunday 25th
Caversfield House | 13
Lime Close | 47

March
Tuesday 12th
◆ Waterperry Gardens | 79
Saturday 23rd
Claridges Barn | 20
Sunday 24th
Claridges Barn | 20

April
Monday 1st
Kencot Gardens | 43
Sunday 7th
Ashbrook House | 1
Buckland Lakes | 11
Magdalen College | 48
Sunday 14th
Sarsden Glebe | 68
Saturday 20th
Central North Oxford Gardens | 14
Claridges Barn | 20
Sunday 21st
Central North Oxford Gardens | 14
Claridges Barn | 20
Lime Close | 47
Upper Bolney House | 78
Saturday 27th
Corpus Christi College | 21
50 Plantation Road | 62

Sunday 28th
◆ Broughton Grange | 9
Corpus Christi College | 21
3 Halliday Lane | 33
NEW 4 Halliday Lane | 34
50 Plantation Road | 62

May
Friday 3rd
Midsummer House | 54
Saturday 11th
◆ Blenheim Palace | 4
Sunday 19th
Church Farm Field | 18
The Priory, Charlbury | 63
Southbank | 72
Westwell Manor | 82
Monday 27th
Barton Abbey | 3

June
Saturday 1st
NEW 93 Church Road | 19
Sunday 2nd
Broughton Poggs & Filkins Gardens | 10
Iffley Gardens | 42
Kidmore House Garden & Vineyard | 44
Steeple Aston Gardens | 73
Tythe Barn | 76
Whitehill Farm | 83
Friday 7th
Midsummer House | 54
Saturday 8th
Claridges Barn | 20
Sunday 9th
Claridges Barn | 20
East Hagbourne Gardens | 27
Failford | 28
Friars Court | 30
Headington Gardens | 36
Langford Gardens | 46
NEW Mill House Garden | 56
116 Oxford Road | 61
Tuesday 11th
Chestlion House | 16
Wednesday 12th
Claridges Barn | 20
Thursday 13th
◆ Stonor Park | 74

Sunday 16th
NEW Maggie's Oxford 49
Old Boars Hill Gardens 58

Wednesday 19th
Rectory Farmhouse 66

Sunday 23rd
Breach House Garden 6
Brize Norton Gardens 7
◆ Broughton Grange 9
Chalkhouse Green Farm 15
The Manor House 50
Rectory Farmhouse 66
Sibford Gardens 70
West Oxford Gardens 81

Sunday 30th
Cumnor Village Gardens 22
Dorchester Gardens 26
Middleton Cheney Gardens 53
Orchard House 60
NEW Shipton Court Water
Gardens 69

July

Friday 5th
Midsummer House 54
Woolstone Mill House 84

Saturday 6th
Stow Cottage Arboretum &
Garden 75

Tuesday 9th
St Edmund Hall 67

Sunday 21st
Merton College Oxford Fellows'
Garden 52

Sunday 28th
◆ Broughton Grange 9
11 Hid's Copse Road 37

August

Friday 2nd
Midsummer House 54

Sunday 4th
113 Brize Norton Road 8

Saturday 24th
Aston Pottery 2

Sunday 25th
Aston Pottery 2
Bolters Farm 5
Kings Cottage 45

Monday 26th
Bolters Farm 5
Kings Cottage 45

September

Sunday 1st
Ashbrook House 1
Southbank 72

Friday 6th
Midsummer House 54

Sunday 8th
◆ Broughton Grange 9
Ham Court 35

Wednesday 11th
Mill Barn 55

Sunday 15th
Old Boars Hill Gardens 58

Tuesday 17th
◆ Waterperry Gardens 79

Sunday 22nd
9 Rawlinson Road 64
11 Rawlinson Road 65

October

Friday 4th
Midsummer House 54

By Arrangement

Arrange a personalised garden visit
with your club, or group of friends,
on a date to suit you. See individual
garden entries for full details.

Ashbrook House 1
Bolters Farm 5
Bush House 12
Carter's Yard, Sibford Gardens 70
Caversfield House 13
Chalkhouse Green Farm 15
Chivel Farm 17
Claridges Barn 20
Dean Manor 23
103 Dene Road 24
Denton House 25
Failford 28
Foxington 29
The Grange 31
Greenfield Farm 32
Hollyhocks 40
Home Close, Garsington 41
Home Close, Sibford Ferris,
Sibford Gardens 70
38 Leckford Road, Central North
Oxford Gardens 14
Lime Close 47
Meadow Cottage 51
Mill Barn 55
Monks Head 57
Old Boars Hill Gardens 58
NEW The Old Rectory, Albury 59
116 Oxford Road 61
Primrose Gardens, Steeple Aston
Gardens 73
Rectory Farmhouse 66
South Newington House 71
Southbank 72
Uplands 77
Wayside 80
Whitehill Farm 83

Maggie's Oxford

THE GARDENS

◻ ASHBROOK HOUSE
Westbrook Street, Blewbury,
OX11 9QA. Mr & Mrs S
A Barrett, 01235 850810,
janembarrett@me.com. *4m SE of
Didcot. Turn off A417 in Blewbury
into Westbrook St. 1st house on
R. Follow yellow signs for parking
in Boham's Rd at west entrance
to the village.* **Sun 7 Apr, Sun 1
Sept (2-5.30). Adm £5, chd free.
Home-made teas. Visits also by
arrangement 8 Apr to 6 Sept.**
The garden where Kenneth Grahame
read Wind in the Willows to local
children and where he took inspiration
for his description of the oak doors
to Badger's House. Come and see,
you may catch a glimpse of Toad
and friends in this 3½ acre chalk and
water garden, in a beautiful spring line
village. In spring the banks are a mass
of daffodils and in late summer the
borders are full of unusual plants.

◻ ASTON POTTERY
Bampton Road, Aston, Bampton,
OX18 2BT. Mr Stephen Baughan,
www.astonpottery.co.uk. *4m S
of Witney. On the B4449 between
Bampton & Standlake.* **Sat 24 Aug
(9.30-4.30); Sun 25 Aug (10-
4.30). Adm £5, chd free. Light
refreshments on-site café.**
6 stunning borders set around Aston
Pottery. 72 metre double hornbeam
border full of riotous perennials. 80
metre long hot bank of alstroemeria,
salvias, echinacea and knifophia.
Quadruple dahlia border with over
600 dahlias, grasses and asters.
Tropical garden with bananas, cannas
and ricinus. Finally, 80 metres of
120 different annuals planted in
four giant successive waves of over
6000 plants. Our gardens are fully
accessible for wheelchair users.
Please note that the paths consist
of a mixture of paving, tarmac and
grass.

◻ BARTON ABBEY
Steeple Barton, OX25 4QS.
Mr & Mrs P Fleming. *8m E of
Chipping Norton. On B4030, ½m
from junc of A4260 & B4030.* **Mon
27 May (2-5). Adm £5, chd free.
Home-made teas.**
15 acre garden with views from house
(not open) across sweeping lawns

and picturesque lake. Walled garden
with colourful herbaceous borders,
separated by established yew hedges
and espalier fruit, contrasts with more
informal woodland garden paths
with vistas of specimen trees and
meadows. Working glasshouses and
fine display of fruit and vegetables.

◻ ◆ BLENHEIM PALACE
Woodstock, OX20 1UL. His
Grace the Duke of Marlborough,
01993 810530, customerservice@
blenheimpalace.com,
www.blenheimpalace.com. *8 m N
of Oxford. The S7 bus runs every 30
mins from Oxford Stn to Blenheim
Palace. The S3 runs hourly from
Chipping Norton and Charlbury to
Blenheim Palace. For bus times visit
stagecoachbus.com.* **For NGS:
Sat 11 May (10-5). Adm £7, chd
£5. For other opening times and
information, please phone, email or
visit garden website.**
Created over the centuries by
esteemed garden designers such
as Henry Wise and Achille Duchêne,
our Formal Gardens reflect a
journey through the styles of the
ages. The Formal Gardens inc the
majestic Water Terraces, the Duke's
Private Italian Garden, the tranquil
Secret Garden with all of its hidden
treasures, the Churchill Memorial
Garden and the beautifully delicate
Rose Garden. The Walled Garden
area inc the Marlborough Maze,
Butterfly House and Blenheim Palace
Adventure Play. Vanbrugh's Grand
Bridge is the focal point of over
2,000 acres of landscaped parkland.
Wheelchair access with some gravel
paths, uneven terrain and slopes.
Dogs permitted on short leads in the
Parkland and East Courtyard only.

◻ BOLTERS FARM
Pudlicote Lane, Chilson, Chipping
Norton, OX7 3HU. Robert & Mandy
Cooper, art@amandacooper.co.uk,
www.instagram.com/
amandacooper684. *Centre of
Chilson village. On arrival in the
hamlet of Chilson, heading N,
we are the last in an old row of
cottages on R. Please drive past &
park considerately on the L in the
lane. Limited parking, car sharing
recommended.* **Sun 25, Mon 26
Aug (2-5). Combined adm with
Kings Cottage £8, chd free. Tea.
Gluten free options and a mug of
tea to stroll around with.**

Visits also by arrangement 3 June
to 26 July for groups of 5 to 20.
If coming in a large bus, parking
needs to be arranged. Donation to
Hands Up Foundation.
A cherished old cottage garden
restored over the last 17 yrs. Tumbly
moss covered walls and sloping
lawns down to a stream with natural
planting and quirky characterful
moments. Running water, weeping
willows, some unusual planting and a
great sense of peace.

◻ BREACH HOUSE GARDEN
High street, Wheatley, Oxford,
OX33 1XU. Liz Parry. *5m E of
Oxford. Breach House entrance
is reached at the rear of The
Manor House.* **Sun 23 June (2-6).
Combined adm with The Manor
House £5, chd free.**
1 acre garden with coppiced hazel
wood walk. Main established area
with extensive shrubs and perennials,
also a more contemporary reflective
space with a wild pond and finally a
long grassed paddock with mowed
paths.

The National
Garden Scheme
searches the length
and breadth of
England, Wales,
Northern Ireland
and the Channel
Islands for the
very best private
gardens

GROUP OPENING

7 BRIZE NORTON GARDENS

Brize Norton, OX18 3LY.
www.bncommunity.org/ngs. *3m SW of Witney. Brize Norton Village, S of A40, between Witney & Burford. Parking at Elderbank Hall. Coaches welcome with plenty of parking nearby. Tickets & maps available at Elderbank Hall & at each garden.* **Sun 23 June (1-6). Combined adm £7.50, chd free.**

BARNSTABLE HOUSE
Mr & Mrs P Butcher.

CHURCH FARM HOUSE
Philip & Mary Holmes,
www.bncommunity.org/ngs.

CLUMBER
Mr & Mrs S Hawkins.

2 ELM GROVE
Rod and Sonja Coles.

GRANGE FARM
Mark & Lucy Artus.

MILLSTONE
Bev & Phil Tyrell.

PAINSWICK HOUSE
Mr & Mrs T Gush.

PILGRIMS
Mr & Mrs Butler.

ROSE COTTAGE
Brenda & Brian Trott.

95 STATION ROAD
Mr & Mrs P A Timms.

STONE COTTAGE
Mr & Mrs K Humphris.

Domesday village on the edge of the Cotswold's offering a number of gardens open for your enjoyment. You can see a wide variety of planting inc ornamental trees and grasses, herbaceous borders, traditional fruit and vegetable gardens. Features inc a Mediterranean style patio, courtyard garden, terraced roof garden, water features; plus gardens where you can just sit, relax and enjoy the day. Plants for sale at individual gardens. A Flower Festival will take place in the Brize Norton St Britius Church. Partial wheelchair access to some gardens.

 ♿ 🐎 ❀ 🚗 ☕

---

8 113 BRIZE NORTON ROAD

Minster Lovell, Witney, OX29 0SQ. **David & Lynn Rogers.** *Approx 2½ m W of Witney. On main village rd (B4447), ½ m N of A40 Witney Bypass intersection on the R. Parking at nearby Scout hut.* **Sun 4 Aug (2-5). Adm £5, chd free. Home-made teas.**
Mixed variety garden of over 1 acre inc quirky features for added interest. Lawns, meadow grass area, small woodland, native mixed hedging, wildlife pond, fish pond, tree ferns, acers, huge mix of plants and trees with emphasis on year-round colour. The whole garden has been developed with wildlife in mind. As seen on Alan Titchmarsh`s `Love Your Garden` June 2023. Gravel and grass surfaces.

♿ ❀ 🚗 ☕ 🌄

9 ◆ BROUGHTON GRANGE

Wykham Lane, Broughton, Banbury, OX15 5DS. S Hester, 07791 747371, enquiries@ broughtongrange.com, www.broughtongrange.com. *¼ m out of village. From Banbury take B4035 to Broughton. Turn L at Saye & Sele Arms Pub up Wykham Ln (one way). Follow road out of village for ¼ m. Entrance on R.* **For NGS: Sun 28 Apr, Sun 23 June, Sun 28 July, Sun 8 Sept (10-5). Adm £12, chd free. Cream teas. For other opening times and information, please phone, email or visit garden website.**
An impressive 25 acres of gardens and light woodland in an attractive Oxfordshire setting. The centrepiece is a large terraced walled garden created by Tom Stuart-Smith in 2001. Vision has been used to blend the gardens into the countryside. Good early displays of bulbs followed by outstanding herbaceous planting in summer. Formal and informal areas combine to make this a special site inc newly laid arboretum with many ongoing projects.

❀ 🚗 🅿 ☕ 🌄 »))

26 Hurst Rise Road, West Oxford Gardens

GROUP OPENING

◨ BROUGHTON POGGS & FILKINS GARDENS

Filkins, nr Lechlade, GL7 3JH. www.filkins.org.uk. *3m N of Lechlade. 5m S of Burford. Just off A361 between Burford & Lechlade on the B4477.* **Sun 2 June (2-6). Combined adm £8, chd free. Home-made teas at Filkins Village Hall.**

ANSTRUTHER
Nicky & Stephen Evans.

BROUGHTON POGGS MILL
Charlie & Avril Payne.

THE CORN BARN
Ms Alexis Thompson.

THE FIELD HOUSE
Peter & Sheila Gray.

FILKINS ALLOTMENTS
Filkins Allotments.

FILKINS HALL
Filkins Hall Residents.

LITTLE PEACOCKS
Colvin & Moggridge.

MERCHANTS COTTAGE
Paul & Corina Floyd.

MUFFITIES
Arthur Parkinson.

PEACOCK FARMHOUSE
Pauline & Peter Care.

PIGEON COTTAGE
Lynne Savege.

PIP COTTAGE
G B Woodin.

THE TALLOT
Ms M Swann & Mr D Stowell.

TAYLOR COTTAGE
Mrs Ronnie Bailey.

12 gardens and flourishing allotments in these beautiful and vibrant Cotswold stone twin villages. Scale and character vary from the grand landscape setting of Filkins Hall, to the small but action packed Pigeon Cottage, Taylor Cottage, Muffities and The Tallot. Broughton Poggs Mill has a rushing mill stream with an exciting bridge; Pip Cottage combines topiary, box hedges and a fine rural view. In these and the other equally exciting and varied gardens horticultural interest abounds. Features inc Swinford Museum of Cotswolds tools and artefacts, and Cotswold Woollen Weavers and Saxon church will be open. Many gardens have gravel driveways, but most are suitable for wheelchair access. Most gardens welcome dogs on leads.

◨◨ BUCKLAND LAKES

nr Faringdon, SN7 8QW. **The Wellesley Family.** *3m NE of Faringdon. Buckland is midway between Oxford (14 m) & Swindon (15 m), just off the A420. Faringdon 3 m, Witney 8 m. Follow yellow signs which will lead you to driveway & car park by St Mary's Church.* **Sun 7 Apr (2-5). Adm £7, chd free. Home-made teas at Memorial Hall. There is a shuttle bus to take visitors to the teas if needed. Donation to Buckland Memorial Hall.**

Descend down wooded path to 2 large secluded lakes with views over undulating historic parkland, designed by Georgian landscape architect Richard Woods. Picturesque mid C18 rustic icehouse, cascade with iron footbridge, thatched boathouse and round house, and exedra. Many fine mature trees, drifts of spring bulbs and daffodils amongst shrubs. Norman church adjoins. Cotswold village. Children must be supervised due to large expanse of unfenced open water.

◨◩ BUSH HOUSE

Wigginton Road, South Newington, Banbury, OX15 4JR. Mr John Ainley, 07503 361050, rojoainley@btinternet.com. *In S Newington on A361 from Banbury to Chipping Norton, take 1st R to Wigginton, Bush House 1st house on the L in Wigginton Rd.* **Visits by arrangement 1 Mar to 29 Nov. Adm inc Bush House and South Newington House with refreshments. Adm £12, chd free. Home-made teas at South Newington House.**

Set in eight acres, over 13 years, a two acre garden has emerged. Herbaceous borders partner dual level ponds and stream. The terrace leads to a walled parterre framed by roses and wisteria. The 'wildflower meadow' (sown 2021) orchard is screened by rose and vine covered wrought iron trellis. Kitchen gardens, greenhouses and fruit cage provide organically grown produce. Stream and interconnecting ponds. Walled parterre and knot garden. 1000 native broadleaved trees planted 2006, 2011 and 2014. Gravel drive, a few small steps, and two gentle grass slopes on either side of the garden.

◨◪ CAVERSFIELD HOUSE

Caversfield, Bicester, OX27 8TQ. Tobias Holst, Head Gardener, 07709 896449, Tobiasholst3@yahoo.dk. *Off the B4100 between Bicester & Aynho.* **Sun 25 Feb (10-3). Adm £8, chd free. Light refreshments. Picnics in wildlife area. Visits also by arrangement for groups of 10+.**

Caversfield House consists of 10 acres of garden, inc herbaceous borders, a walled garden, an orchard and parkland set within a wider 70 acre estate. The estate features a variety of habitats inc an 18 acre wildflower meadow, ponds and a large lake. In early spring carpets of snowdrops, aconites and crocuses light up the ground with a backdrop of topiary and beautiful old trees.

GROUP OPENING

◨◫ CENTRAL NORTH OXFORD GARDENS

50 Plantation Road, Oxford, OX2 6HY. *City gardens situated in parallel streets; in Leckford Rd & Plantation Road. Access from Kingston Rd or Woodstock Rd. Parking in Leckford Rd, Warnborough Rd & Farndon Rd.* **Sat 20 Apr (1.30-5.30). Combined adm £7.50, chd free. Sun 21 Apr (1.30-5.30). Combined adm £10, chd free. Home-made teas at 50 Plantation Road each date. Plants and teas 21 April at 38 Leckford Rd.**

38 LECKFORD ROAD
Dinah Adams, 01865 511996, dinah_zwanenberg@fastmail.com.
Open on Sun 21 Apr
Visits also by arrangement 15 Apr to 20 Oct for groups of up to 10.

41 LECKFORD ROAD
Liz & Mark Jennings.
Open on all dates

50 PLANTATION ROAD
Philippa Scoones.
Open on all dates
(See separate entry)

Three very different town gardens. 50 Plantation Road is a surprisingly wide and deep garden in two parts: lovely trees and planting and lots of pots; and an unusual water feature with stepping stones. Many varieties of tulips. 41 Leckford Road is an exquisitely designed garden for entertaining and relaxing. Hedged with pleached hornbeams are a foreground for lovely spring planting. Every area has vegetation suited to its microclimate. 38 Leckford Road is a protected long walled garden with varying levels of shade and inc rare plants and mature trees.

  ♿ ❀ ☕))

15 CHALKHOUSE GREEN FARM
Chalkhouse Green, Kidmore End, Reading, RG4 9AL. Mr J Hall, 01189 723631, chgfarm@gmail.com, www.chgfarm.com. *2m N of Reading, 5m SW of Henley-on-Thames. Situated between A4074 & B481. From Kidmore End take Chalkhouse Green Rd. Follow yellow signs.* **Sun 23 June (2-6). Adm £4, chd free. Home-made teas. Visits also by arrangement May to Sept for groups of 5 to 15.**
One acre garden and open traditional farmstead. Herbaceous borders, herb garden, shrubs, old fashioned roses, trees inc medlar, quince and mulberries, walled ornamental kitchen garden and cherry orchard. Rare breed farm animals inc British White cattle, Suffolk Punch horses, donkeys, geese, chickens, ducks and turkeys. Plant and jam stall, donkey rides, grass tennis court, trailer rides, farm trail, WWII bomb shelter, heavy horse and bee display. Partial wheelchair access.

  ♿ 🐎 ❀ ☕))

16 CHESTLION HOUSE
Chestlion Lane, Bourton Road, Clanfield, Bampton, OX18 2PA. Louise Johnson. *3m S of Carterton. Chestlion Ln is off A4020 Bourton Rd in the village of Clanfield.* **Tues 11 June (1.30-5). Adm £5, chd free. Home-made teas.**
The garden surrounding the house (not open), has been planted since the new owners took on the house 10yrs ago. The garden to the rear of the house, has approx ³/₄ acre of mixed planting, with many blowsy roses adorning the walls and soft romantic planting in borders. There is a circular meditative garden and a round pond along with a productive kitchen, cutting garden, greenhouse and herb garden. There is a boat house and pond outside the walled

---

area and a newly planted wildflower meadow with a fruit tree avenue and a hornbeam avenue leading to the back entrance.

  ☕))

17 CHIVEL FARM
Heythrop, OX7 5TR. John & Rosalind Sword, 01608 683227, rosalind.sword@btinternet.com. *4m E of Chipping Norton. Off A361 or A44. Parking at Chivel Farm.* **Visits by arrangement. Light refreshments.**
Beautifully designed country garden with extensive views, designed for continuous interest that is always evolving. Colour schemed borders with many unusual trees, shrubs and herbaceous plants. Small formal white garden and a conservatory.

  ♿ 🚗 ☕

18 CHURCH FARM FIELD
Church Lane, Epwell, Banbury, OX15 6LD. Mrs D Castle. *7¹/₂ m W of Banbury on N side of Epwell village.* **Sun 19 May (2-5). Combined adm with Southbank £5, chd free. Light refreshments. Tea & cake in village hall.**
Woodland and an arboretum with wild flowers (planting started 1992). There are over 90 different trees and shrubs within the 4¹/₂ acres. Paths cut through trees for access to various parts of the garden. There is also a lawn tennis court and croquet lawn.

  🐕 ☕

19 NEW 93 CHURCH ROAD
Sandford-on-Thames, Oxford, OX4 4YA. Julie Anderson & Matthew Wilkinson. *A few miles S of Oxford off the A4074 and nr Sandford lock.* **Sat 1 June (2-5). Adm £5, chd free.**
Large garden with different areas. A formal garden set to lawn with mixed shrub and perennial borders, a pond, fruit and vegetable areas, chicken coop, natural woodland area beyond the formal garden leading to bog gardens and a wooden walkway to steps up a short but steep terraced bank to an open area with fruit trees and a further vegetable garden. Wheelchair access in formal gardens and woodland.

  ♿ 🐎 ❀ ☕ 🎋))

---

20 CLARIDGES BARN
Charlbury Road, Chipping Norton, OX7 5XG. Drs David & Jill Edwards, 07973 129473, drdavidedwards@hotmail.co.uk. *3m SE of Chipping Norton. Take B4026 from Chipping Norton to Charlbury after 3 m turn R to Dean, we are 200 metres on the R. Please park on the verge.* **Sat 23, Sun 24 Mar, Sat 20, Sun 21 Apr, Sat 8, Sun 9, Wed 12 June (11-5). Adm £5, chd free. Light refreshments inc coffee & light lunches. Wine is available for evening openings. Visits also by arrangement Mar to Aug.**
3¹/₂ acres of family garden, wood and meadow hewn from a barley field on limestone brash. Situated on top of the Cotswolds, it is open to all weathers, but rewarding views and dog walking opportunities on hand. Large vegetable, fruit and cutting garden, wildlife pond and five cedar greenhouses, all loved by rabbits, deer and squirrel. Herbaceous borders and woodland gardens with gravel and flagged paths, divided by stone walls. Claridges Barn dates back to the 1600s, the cottage 1860s, converted about 35 yrs ago. Plants for sale. Mainly level site with flagstone and gravel paths, flat lawns and some uneven steps. The gravel driveway can be hard work for wheelchair users.

  ♿ 🐎 ❀ 🚗 ☕))

21 CORPUS CHRISTI COLLEGE
Merton Street, Oxford, OX1 4JF. Domestic Bursar, www.ccc.ox.ac.uk. *Just off Oxford High St. Entrance from Merton St.* **Sat 27, Sun 28 Apr (6-10am). Adm £5, chd free. Light refreshments in the Old Lodgings.**
Said by some to have inspired Lewis Carroll, the gates of Corpus conceal winding passageways linking several distinctive quads filled with historical and botanical curiosities like pelican sundials, Kings' gates and "fossil trees". At the rear of the college sits the main garden with its huge copper beech, old town walls, and views over Christ church and its meadows. Wheelchair access with one slope in the garden.

  ♿ ☕

GROUP OPENING

22 CUMNOR VILLAGE GARDENS

10 Leys Road, Cumnor, Oxford, OX2 9QF. *4m W of central Oxford. From A420, exit for Cumnor & follow B4017 into the village. Parking on rd & side rds, behind PO or behind village hall in Leys Rd.* **Sun 30 June (2-5.30). Combined adm £6, chd free. Home-made teas in United Reformed Church Hall, Leys Road.**

19 HIGH STREET
Janet Cross.

10 LEYS ROAD
Penny & Nick Bingham.

NEW 14 LEYS ROAD
Mrs Tracey Iles.

41 LEYS ROAD
Philip & Jennie Powell.

43 LEYS ROAD
Anna Stevens.

These 5 gardens show the wonderful variety of village green space with many different plants, shrubs, trees, vegetables, fruit and wild flowers. One cottage garden has unusual perennials and many shrubs, ferns, trees and vegetables. New this year is a garden full of colour and interest along winding paths. A courtyard garden is cleverly planted for extremes of light and shade highlighted by pops of colour at all levels. At the end of Leys Road are 2 more unique gardens; a picturesque naturalist's garden and small holding complete with thatched cottage (not open), and a more modern style property with a walled garden, ponds, willow with light and shaded walks among plants that delight the imagination and harp music may be played. Wheelchair access to 19 High St also 14, 41 and 43 Leys Road. WC facilities and teas in United Reformed Church Hall.

&. ✿ ☕ ›))

23 DEAN MANOR

Dean, Chipping Norton, OX7 3LD. Mr & Mrs Johnny Hornby, 07786 110561, pippa.hornby@gmail.com. *In Dean, 3 m SE of Chipping Norton. Leaving Chipping Norton follow the A361 for 2 m. At the sharp bend, take the 2nd turning to the R to Dean (there is no rd sign). Follow the lane for 1 m, Dean Manor is R at the next junc.* **Visits by arrangement 1 June to 8 Sept for groups of 10 to 30. Refreshments by arrangement. Adm £8, chd free.**
The gardens at Dean Manor cover approx six acres. Stone walls are home to an abundant and varied selection of climbing/rambling roses, clematis and hydrangeas. The

Tommy's Farm, Old Boars Hill Gardens

formal gardens inc complex yew hedging and herbaceous borders, kitchen and cutting garden, areas of wildflower meadow, an orchard and water gardens make up areas around the house. A spectacular new kitchen and cutting garden designed by Frances Rasch complete with new large glasshouse is currently in development, offering the opportunity to witness the beginnings of a major new chapter in the garden's rich history.

& ✿ ☕ ♫))

24 103 DENE ROAD

Headington, Oxford, OX3 7EQ. Steve & Mary Woolliams, 07778 617616, stevewoolliams@gmail.com. *S Headington, nr Nuffield. Dene Rd accessed from The Slade from the N, or from Hollow Way from the S. Both access roads are B4495. Garden on sharp bend.* Visits by arrangement 6 Apr to 6 Oct for groups of up to 12. Adm £4, chd free. Home-made teas inc hot/cold drinks and cake. A surprising eco-friendly garden with borrowed view over the Lye Valley Nature Reserve. Lawns, a wildflower meadow, pond and large kitchen garden are inc in a downhill sloping 60ft x 120ft site. Fruit trees, soft fruit and mixed borders of shrubs, hardy perennials, grasses and bulbs, designed for seasonal colour. This garden has been noted for its wealth of wildlife inc a variety of birds, butterflies and other insects such as the rare Brown Hairstreak butterfly, the rare Currant Clearwing moth and the Grizzled Skipper.

25 DENTON HOUSE

Denton, Oxford, OX44 9JF. Mr & Mrs Luke, 01865 874440, waveney@jandwluke.com. *Nr Oxford. In a valley between Garsington & Cuddesdon.* Visits by arrangement Feb to Oct. Adm £6, chd free.
Large walled garden surrounds a Georgian mansion (not open) with shaded areas, walks, topiary and many interesting mature trees, large lawns, herbaceous borders and rose beds. The windows in the wall were taken in 1864 from Brasenose College Chapel and Library. Wild garden and a further walled fruit garden.

GROUP OPENING

26 DORCHESTER GARDENS

Dorchester-on-Thames, Wallingford, OX10 7HZ. *Off A4074 or A415 signed to Dorchester. Parking at Old Bridge Meadow, at SE end of Dorchester Bridge. Disabled parking at 26 Manor Farm Rd (OX10 7HZ). Maps available at the car park and at the Co-op in the High St.* Sun 30 June (2-5). Combined adm £10, chd free.

DORCHESTER MANOR HOUSE
Simon & Margaret Broadbent.

26 MANOR FARM ROAD
David & Judy Parker.

6 MONKS CLOSE
Leif & Petronella Rasmussen.

Three contrasting gardens in a historic village close to the medieval abbey, which is now the parish church. 26 Manor Farm Rd (OX10 7HZ) was part of old, larger, partially walled garden, which now has a formal lawn and planting, vegetable garden, greenhouse and several interesting trees. From the yew hedge towards the River Thame is an apple orchard underplanted with spring bulbs. 6 Monks Close (OX10 7JA) is idyllic and surprising. Small spring-fed stream and sloping lawn surrounded by naturalistic planting runs down to monastic fish pond. Bridges over deep pond lead to River Thame. Dorchester Manor House (OX10 7HZ) Two acre garden set around Georgian house (not open) and medieval abbey. Spacious lawn leading to riverside copse of towering poplars with fine views of Dorchester Abbey. Terrace with rose and vine covered pergola around lily pond. Colourful herbaceous borders, small orchard and vegetable garden. Due to deep water at gardens, children should be accompanied at all times. Wheelchair access to 26 Manor Farm Rd and Dorchester Manor House, partial access to other garden. Assistance dogs only.

GROUP OPENING

27 EAST HAGBOURNE GARDENS

East Hagbourne, OX11 9LN. *½ m S of Didcot. Enter village via B4016, or from A417 through West Hagbourne & Coscote. Cycle path 44.* Sun 9 June (1-4). Combined adm £5, chd free. Home-made teas.

BOTTOM BARN
Mr Colin & Dr Jean Millar.

BUCKELS
Felicity Topping.

THE GABLES
Sally & Bill Barksfield.

5 HIGGS CLOSE
Mrs Jenny Smith.

KINGFISHER HOUSE
Robert & Nicola Ainger.

LIME TREE COTTAGE
Jane & Robin Bell.

YEW TREE COTTAGE
Sarah & Jonathan Beynon.

Pretty Domesday village, timber frame and local clunch stone houses. Open every 3 yrs. Follow main road or explore pretty alleyways to visit 9 gardens; new for 2021, 2 Lower Cross Cottages with gravel planting, ferns, shepherds hut and rockery; Bottom Barn, in the shadow of the C12 church with topiary and perennial planting around a converted C18 barn; Lime Tree Cottage with water plants, mature trees and secret garden; Buckels, a sculptured walled garden with cypresses, box, heritage fruit trees and herbs; 5 Higgs Close, a colourful garden with herbaceous borders, small pond and vegetable patch; Kingfisher House, a family garden with mixed herbaceous planting. Little Thatch, a cottage garden with a stream, pond planting, perennials, lavender beds and kitchen garden; The Gables, a garden full of colour with roses, perennials, lavender, box and trees; Yew Tree Cottage, a secluded garden to the front of a thatched cottage (not open) with roses, clematis and honeysuckle. Features inc access to wildflower meadow, plant sales and refreshments, along with a beautiful C12 church. The Fleur de Lys Pub is also open for food and drinks.

28 FAILFORD

118 Oxford Road, Abingdon, OX14 2AG. Miss R Aylward, 01235 523925, aylwardsdooz@hotmail.co.uk. *Entrance is via 116 Oxford Rd. No. 118 is on L of Oxford Rd after Picklers Hill when coming from Abingdon Town, or on R when approaching from the A34 Abingdon N.* Sun 9 June (11-4). Combined adm with 116 Oxford Road £6, chd free. Home-made teas. Visits also by arrangement May to Sept for groups of 10+.

This town garden is an extension of the home divided into rooms both formal and informal. It changes every yr. Features inc walkways through shaded areas, arches, a beach, grasses, fernery, roses, topiaries, acers, hostas and heucheras. Be inspired by the wide variety of planting, many unusual and quirky features, all within an area 570 sq ft.

29 FOXINGTON
Britwell Salome, Watlington, OX49 5LG. Mrs Mary Roadnight, 01491 612418, mary@foxington.co.uk. *1 m from Watlington. On B4009 at Red Lion Pub take turning to Britwell Hill. After 350yds turn into drive on L.* **Visits by arrangement 21 Apr to 29 Sept for groups of 10 to 30. Adm £11, chd free. Home-made teas inc in admission price. Special dietary options by prior request.**
Stunning views to the Chiltern Hills provide a wonderful setting for this impressive garden, remodelled in 2009. Patio, heather and gravel gardens enjoy this view, whilst the back and vegetable gardens are more enclosed. A very large apple tree blew down in the spring of 2022 and has been replaced by a summerhouse. This has resulted in a major revision of the planting. There is an orchard and a flock of white doves. Well behaved dogs are welcome, but they must be kept on a lead at all times as there are many wild animals in the garden, wildflower meadow, wood and neighbouring fields. Wheelchair access throughout the garden on level paths with no steps.

30 FRIARS COURT
Clanfield, OX18 2SU. Charles Willmer, www.friarscourt.com. *4m N of Faringdon. On A4095 Faringdon to Witney rd. ½m S of Clanfield.* **Sun 9 June (2-5). Adm £4, chd free.**
Over three acres of formal and informal gardens with flower beds, borders and specimen trees, lie within the remaining arms of a C16 moat which partially surrounds the large C17 Cotswold stone house. Bridges span the moat with water-lily-filled ponds to the front whilst beyond the gardens is a woodland walk. A museum about Friars Court is located in the old Coach House. A level path goes around part of the gardens. The museum is accessed over gravel.

31 THE GRANGE
1 Berrick Road, Chalgrove, OX44 7RQ. Mrs Vicky Farren, 01865 400883, vickyfarren@mac.com, www.thegrangegardener.com. *12m E of Oxford & 4m from Watlington, off B480. The entrance to The Grange is at the grass triangle between Berrick Rd & Monument Rd, by the pedestrian Xing. GPS is not reliable in the final 200yds.* **Visits by arrangement 1 June to 15 Oct for groups of up to 40. Adm £8, chd free. Light refreshments.**
11 acres of gardens inc herbaceous borders and a large expanse of prairie with many grasses and a wildflower meadow. There is a lake with bridges and a planted island, a dry river bed and a labyrinth. A brook runs through the garden with a further pond, arboretum, old orchard and partly walled vegetable garden. Partial wheelchair access on many grass paths.

32 GREENFIELD FARM
Christmas Common, nr Watlington, OX49 5HG. Andrew & Jane Ingram, 01491 612434, andrew@andrewbingram.com. *4m from J5 M40, 7m from Henley. J5 M40, A40 towards Oxford for ½m, turn L signed Christmas Common. ¾m past Fox & Hounds Pub, turn L at Tree Barn sign.* **Visits by arrangement 20 May to 30 Sept for groups of 5 to 30. Adm £5, chd free.**
10 acre wildflower meadow surrounded by woodland, established 28 yrs ago under the Countryside Stewardship Scheme. Traditional Chiltern chalkland meadow in beautiful peaceful setting with 100 species of perennial wildflowers, grasses and ten species of orchids. ½m walk from parking area to meadow. Opportunity to return via typical Chiltern beechwood.

33 3 HALLIDAY LANE
Oxford, OX2 0FG. John and Viccy Fleming. *3 Halliday Ln, off North Hinksey Ln. From Botley Rd near the A34 Jn (at McDonalds) turn L into N Hinksey Ln. Halliday Ln (private road-no parking) is on R after Botley Cemetery. On-street parking further S on N Hinksey Ln.* **Sun 28 Apr (2-5). Combined adm with 4 Halliday Lane £4, chd free. Home-made teas.**

Small town garden of a new house (not open) recently laid out on the site of old riding stables. Crevice garden at the front planted with more than 400 different alpine plants, a rear garden planted with a rich collection of bulbs, shrubs and perennials for year-round interest, and a narrow strip at the side with fruit, vegetables and greenhouse for propagation.

34 NEW 4 HALLIDAY LANE
Oxford, OX2 0FG. Mr Nathaniel Ward. *Leave the A34 N bound or S bound at Botley Interchange. Follow signs for Oxford. At T-lights opp McDonalds turn R and immed L where you will see an NGS road sign.* **Sun 28 Apr (2-5). Combined adm with 3 Halliday Lane £4, chd free. Home-made teas at 3 Halliday Lane.**
This is a relatively new garden work having started in November 2019 when the house was purchased. The aim was to provide a family space with simple planting to encourage wildlife into the garden.

35 HAM COURT
Ham Court Farm, Weald, Bampton, OX18 2HG. Matthew Rice. *Drive through the village towards Clanfield. The drive is on the R, exactly opp Weald St.* **Sun 8 Sept (2-6.30). Adm £7.50, chd free. Home-made teas.**
Several acres of garden, orchard and paddock surround the last gatehouse fragment of the medieval Bampton Castle, partially moated with walled kitchen garden, a productive greenhouse and farmyard with a variety of farm animals. This project begun by Emma Bridgewater and Matthew Rice is 12 years old so now 'bearing fruit' but will always be in a state of permanent change. Delicious teas and vintage tractors.

Our donation to Marie Curie this year equates to 17,496 hours of nursing care

GROUP OPENING

36 HEADINGTON GARDENS
Old Headington, Oxford, OX3 9BT. *2m E from centre of Oxford. At T-lights in the centre of Headington, travelling towards Oxford, turn R into Old High St. Parking on R in Waitrose car park - gardens further down in Old Headington.* **Sun 9 June (2-6). Combined adm £6, chd free. Home-made teas.**

THE COACH HOUSE
David & Bryony Rowe.

NEW LOWER FARM
Mary Clarkson.

MONCKTON COTTAGE
Julie Harrod & Peter McCarter, 01865 751471, petermccarter@msn.com.

THE OLD POUND HOUSE
Steve & Jane Cowls.

9 STOKE PLACE
Clive Hurst.

10 STOKE PLACE
Tamasin and James Went.

Situated above Oxford, Headington is centred round an old village that is remarkable for its mature trees, high stone walls, narrow lanes and Norman church. The six gardens in Old Headington offer a contrast in styles and formality and there are traces of history: a partially cobbled courtyard for horses, a pound for stray animals, surviving rural surroundings and plaques honouring some of those who have lived here. One garden, Lower Farm, is new this year. Partial wheelchair access to some gardens.

37 11 HID'S COPSE ROAD
Hids Copse Farm House, Cumnor Hill, Oxford, OX2 9JJ. Neil & Valerie Grady. *After 100 yds turn L at T-junc, then fork R after 50 yds.* **Sun 28 July (1.30-5.30). Adm £5, chd free. Home-made teas.**
One acre traditional garden with roses, lawns and mixed borders. The garden is on three levels and accessed by steps or a quite steep path. The woodland areas hold a variety of ferns and hellebores. There is an enchanting children's storytelling area and treehouse, with a mud-kitchen and fire pit in the coppice. The shepherds hut in the paddock catches the late afternoon sun and countryside views.

38 23 HID'S COPSE ROAD
Oxford, OX2 9JJ. Kathy Eldridge. *W of central Oxford, halfway up Cumnor Hill. Turn into Hids Copse Rd from Cumnor Hill. We are the last house on the R before T-junc.* **Sun 11 Feb (2-5). Combined adm with 6 High Street £3, chd free. Opening with West Oxford Gardens on Sun 23 June.**
The garden surrounds a house built in the early 1930s (not open) on a ½ acre plot. Designed to be wildlife friendly, it has a kitchen garden, two ponds with frogs and newts, a wildflower meadow and woodland areas under many trees. Small winding paths lead to areas to sit and contemplate. The planting is dependent on the area within the garden, but a special treat are the snowdrops in early spring.

The Summerhouse, Shipton Court Water Gardens

39 6 HIGH STREET
Cumnor, Oxford, OX2 9PE. Dr
Dianne & Prof Keith Gull. *4m from
central Oxford. Exit to Cumnor
from the A420. In centre of village
opp Post Office. Parking at back
of Post Office.* **Sun 11 Feb (2-5).
Combined adm with 23 Hid's
Copse Road £3, chd free.**
Front, side and rear garden of a
thatched cottage (not open). Front is
partly gravelled and side courtyard has
many pots. Rear garden overlooks
meadows with old apple trees
underplanted with ferns, wildlife pond,
unusual plants, many with black or
bronze foliage, planted in drifts and
repeated throughout the garden.
Planting has mild Japanese influence;
rounded, clipped shapes interspersed
with verticals. Snowdrops feature in
Feb. There are two pubs in the village
serving food; The Bear & Ragged
Staff and The Vine, the former has
accommodation. Wheelchair access to
garden via gravel drive.

40 HOLLYHOCKS
North Street, Islip, Kidlington,
OX5 2SQ. Avril Hughes,
01865 377104/07833 012179,
ahollyhocks@btinternet.com. *3m
NE of Kidlington. From A34, exit
Bletchingdon & Islip. B4027 direction
Islip, turn L into North St.* **Visits by
arrangement 5 Feb to 30 Sept for
groups of up to 25. Visits can be
combined with Monks Head and/
or Bannisters upon request. Adm
£4, chd free. Home-made teas.**
Plantswoman's small Edwardian
garden brimming with year-round
interest, especially planted to
provide winter colour, scent and
snowdrops. Divided into areas
with bulbs, May tulips, herbaceous
borders, roses, clematis, shade and
woodland planting especially trillium,
podophyllum and arisaema, late
summer salvias and annuals give
colour. Large pots and troughs add
seasonal interest and colour.

**41 HOME CLOSE,
GARSINGTON**
29 Southend, Garsington,
OX44 9DH. Mrs M Waud & Dr
P Giangrande, 01865 361394,
m.waud@btinternet.com. *3m SE of
Oxford. N of B480, opp Garsington
Manor.* **Visits by arrangement
Apr to Sept. Please discuss
refreshments when booking. Adm
£5, chd free.**

Two acre garden with listed house
(not open), listed granary and one
acre mixed tree plantation. Unusual
trees and shrubs planted for year-
round effect. Terraces, stone walls
and hedges divide the garden and
the planting reflects a Mediterranean
interest. Vegetable garden, orchard
and woodland garden.

GROUP OPENING

42 IFFLEY GARDENS
Iffley, Oxford, OX4 4EF. *2m S of
Oxford. Within Oxford's ring road,
off A4158 Iffley road, from Magdalen
Bridge to Littlemore r'about, to
Iffley village. Map provided at
each garden.* **Sun 2 June (2-6).
Combined adm £6, chd free.
Home-made teas in Church Hall
and 25 Abberbury Road.**

17 ABBERBURY ROAD
Mrs Julie Steele.

25 ABBERBURY ROAD
Rob & Bridget Farrands.

50 CHURCH WAY
William and Sarah Beaver.

6 FITZHERBERT CLOSE
Eunice Martin.

NEW THE PRIORY
Nanda Pirie.

4A TREE LANE
Pemma & Nick Spencer-
Chapman.

Secluded old village with renowned
Norman church. Visit several gardens
ranging in variety and style. Mixed
family gardens with shady borders and
vegetables. Varied planting throughout
the gardens inc herbaceous borders,
shade loving plants, roses, fine
specimen trees and plants in terracing.
Features inc a small Japanese garden.
Plant sales at several gardens.
Wheelchair access to some gardens.

*Our donation in 2023 has
enabled Parkinson's UK
to fund 3 new nursing
posts this year, directly
supporting people with
Parkinson's*

GROUP OPENING

43 KENCOT GARDENS
Kencot, Lechlade, GL7 3QT. *5m
NE of Lechlade. E of A361 between
Burford & Lechlade.* **Mon 1 Apr
(2-6). Combined adm £6, chd free.
Light refreshments at village hall.**

THE ALLOTMENTS
Amelia Carter Charity.

BELHAM HAYES
Mr Joseph Jones.

THE GARDENS
Mark & Jayne Hodds.

IVY NOOK
Gill & Wally Cox.

MANOR FARM
Henry & Kate Fyson.

WELL HOUSE
Janet & Richard Wheeler.

The 2024 Kencot Gardens group
will consist of five gardens and the
allotments. The Allotments, tended
by nine people, growing a variety of
vegetables, flowers and fruit. Belham
Hayes, mature cottage garden, mixed
herbaceous borders, two old fruit
trees, vegetables. Emphasis on scent
and colour coordination. Manor Farm,
two acre walled garden Grade II C17
house (not open) with bulbs, wood
anemones, fritillaries, mature orchards,
pleached limewalk, clipped 130 year
old yew balls, revolving summerhouse.
A greenhouse with ancient Black
Hamburg vine. Chickens. Well House,
$1/3$ acre garden, mature trees, hedges,
miniature woodland glade, brook with
waterfall. Spring bulbs, rockeries. The
gardens $1/3$ acre garden, two old apple
trees, old well, herbaceous beds. Rear
garden newly planted with perennial
borders and further herbaceous
border, bulbs pots of seasonal flowers.
Ivy Nook, Medium sized garden, mixed
borders with spring bulbs, vegetable
garden, greenhouse, small pond and
magnolia tree. Wheelchair access to
The Allotments, difficult due to step
entrance and narrow paths. Other
gardens maybe difficult due to gravel
and uneven paths.

44 KIDMORE HOUSE GARDEN & VINEYARD

Chalkhouse Green Road, Kidmore End, Reading, RG4 9AR. Mr Stephen & Mrs Niamh Kendall. *6m NNW of Reading, Emma Green/ Reading end of the village. Parking in the field through gate signed Kidmore Vineyard.* **Sun 2 June (2- 6). Adm £6, chd free. Home-made teas in the barn next to the Rose Garden.**

14 acres set in South Oxfordshire landscaped gardens with features inc ha-ha, walled garden with delphiniums, calla lilies and white wisteria, a rose garden and one hectar of vines. Garden sympathetic with a red-brick Queen Anne house (not open). Anecdotally, the large sweet chestnut in the lawn was planted with the house in 1680. Picnics welcome in the field. Partial wheelchair access with gravel pathways and some steps.

45 KINGS COTTAGE

Pudlicote Lane, Chilson, Chipping Norton, OX7 3HU. Mr Michael Anderson. *S end of Chilson village. Entering Chilson from the S, off the B4437 Charlbury to Burford road, 1st house on the L. Please drive past & park considerately in centre of village.* **Sun 25, Mon 26 Aug (2-5). Combined adm with Bolters Farm £8, chd free. Light refreshments.**

An old row of cottages with mature trees and yew hedging. Over the last eight years a new design and planting scheme has been started to reduce the areas of lawn, bring in planting to complement the house (not open) and setting, introduce new borders and encourage wildlife. A work in progress. Partial wheelchair access via gravel drive and grass paths. Moderate slopes, grass and some sections of garden only accessible via steps.

GROUP OPENING

46 LANGFORD GARDENS

Lechlade, GL7 3LF. Lyn Sanders, 01865 739486, sandersc4@ hotmail.com. *6m S of Burford A361 towards Lechlade. 1½ m E of Filkins. Large free car park in village. Coaches welcome on a pre-agreed basis. Map of gardens available.* **Sun 9 June (1-6). Combined adm £8, chd free.**

BAKERY COTTAGE
Mr & Mrs R Robinson.

BAY TREE COTTAGE
Mr & Mrs R Parsons.

BRIDGEWATER HOUSE
Mr & Mrs T R Redston.

CORNER COTTAGE
Scott Trueman & Ian Burrows.

COTSWOLD COTTAGE
Mr & Mrs Tom Marshall.

FAIRCROFT
Penny Gould & Andy Krouwel.

THE GRANGE
Mr & Mrs J Johnston.

KEMPS YARD
Mr & Mrs R Kemp.

LIME TREE COTTAGE
Diane & Michael Schultz.

LOWER FARM HOUSE
Mr & Mrs Templeman.

MEADOW VIEW
Linda Moore.

THE OLD SCHOOL
David Freeman.

PEMBER HOUSE
Mr & Mrs J Potter.

NEW **RIVENDELL**
Mr Mark Skinner.

ROSEFERN COTTAGE
Mrs D Lowden.

SPRINGFIELD
Mr & Mrs M Harris.

STONECROFT
Christine Apperley.

THREEWAYS
Claire & James Mulligan.

THE VICARAGE
Mr & Mrs C Smith.

WELLBANK
Sir Brian & Lady Pomeroy.

WELLBANK COTTAGE
Mr & Mrs S Findlay-Wilson.

WELLBANK HOUSE
Mr Robert Hill.

Langford is a charming small Cotswold village with both the important Grade I listed St Matthew's Church and a splendid pub, The Bell Inn where lunch is available. 22 gardens will be open with a delightful mix from large formal to small cottage gardens. Ancient Cotswold stone walls provide a backdrop for many old variety roses. Our plant stall has a large range of local plants and shrubs and teas available from Pember House.

47 LIME CLOSE

35 Henleys Lane, Drayton, Abingdon, OX14 4HU. M C de Laubarede, mail@mclgardendesign.com, www.mclgardendesign.com. *2m S of Abingdon. Henleys Ln is off main road through Drayton. When visiting Lime Cl, please respect local residents & park considerately.* **Sun 25 Feb, Sun 21 Apr (2-5). Adm £5, chd free. Cream teas. Visits also by arrangement Feb to June for groups of 10+. By arrangement visits also available in autumn. Donation to International Dendrology Society.**

Five acre plantsman's garden with rare trees, shrubs, roses and bulbs. Mixed borders, raised beds, pergola, topiary and shade borders. Herb garden by Rosemary Verey. C16 house (not open). Cottage garden by MCL Garden Design, planted for colour, an iris garden with 100 varieties. Winter bulbs. Arboretum with rare exotic trees and shrubs from Asia and America and new field planted by continents. The garden is flat and mostly grass with gravel drive and paths.

48 MAGDALEN COLLEGE

Oxford, OX1 4AU. Magdalen College, www.magd.ox.ac.uk. *Oxford. Entrance in High St.* **Sun 7 Apr (10-7). Adm £9.50, chd free. Light refreshments in the Old Kitchen Bar.**

60 acres inc deer park, college lawns, numerous trees 150-200 yrs old; notable herbaceous and shrub plantings. Magdalen meadow where purple and white snake's head fritillaries can be found is surrounded by Addison's Walk, a tree lined circuit by the River Cherwell developed since the late C18. Ancient herd of 60 deer. Press bell at the lodge for porter to provide wheelchair access.

49 NEW MAGGIE'S OXFORD

Old Road, Headington, Oxford, OX3 7LE. Pip Dingle, www. maggies.org/our-centres/maggies-oxford. *Opp the Churchill Hospital, parking behind building or in the hospital car park.* **Sun 16 June (11-3). Adm by donation. Light refreshments inc cream teas, home-made cake and tea.**

Our newly created garden was designed by Pip Morrison, which surrounds our cancer support centre.

With the building being on stilts, it is an oasis for shade loving plants. Tree and shrub planting and wildflower seeding strengthen existing communities of plants and offer an evolving habitat for local wildlife. Clare Foster, Garden Editor at House & Garden will be available to answer any questions. Claes Oldenburg Statue on terrace.

50 THE MANOR HOUSE
26 High Street, Wheatley, OX33 1XX. Mark and Juliet Byford. *5 m E of Oxford. Off A40.* **Sun 23 June (2-6). Combined adm with Breach House Garden £5, chd free.**
1½ acre garden of Elizabethan manor house (not open). Formal box walk; herb garden, Lily pond in cottage garden with rose arches, orchard with Medlar and ancient Mulberry trees and a shrubbery with old roses. A romantic oasis in this busy village.

51 MEADOW COTTAGE
Christmas Common, Watlington, OX49 5HR. Mrs Zelda Kent-Lemon, 01491 613779, zelda_kl@hotmail.com. *1m from Watlington. Coming from Oxford M40 to J6. Turn R & go to Watlington. Turn L up Hill Rd to top. Turn R after 50yds, turn L into field.* **Visits by arrangement Feb to Oct. Adm £10, chd free.**
1¾ acre garden adjoining ancient bluebell woods, created by the owner from 1995 onwards. Many areas to explore inc a professionally designed vegetable garden, many composting areas, wildflower garden and pond, old and new fruit trees, many shrubs, much varied hedging and a tall treehouse which children can climb under supervision. Indigenous trees and C17 barn (not open). Come and see the wonderful snowdrops in Feb then stunning aconites during the month of May visit the bluebell woodland. Partial wheelchair access over gravel driveway and lawns.

52 MERTON COLLEGE OXFORD FELLOWS' GARDEN
Merton Street, Oxford, OX1 4JD. Merton College, 01865 276310, www.facebook.com/MertonGardens. *Merton St runs parallel to High St about halfway down.* **Sun 21 July (10-5). Adm £8, chd free.**

Ancient mulberry, said to have associations with James I. Specimen trees, long mixed border, recently established herbaceous bed. View of Christ Church meadow.

GROUP OPENING

53 MIDDLETON CHENEY GARDENS
Middleton Cheney, Banbury, OX17 2ST. *3m E of Banbury. Parking on Main Rd between primary school & library (OX17 2PD) for access to Upper & Lower Middleton. Open garden maps available at the library.* **Sun 30 June (1-6). Combined adm £8, chd free. Home-made teas at Peartree House.**

CROFT HOUSE
Richard & Sandy Walmsley.

6 GLOVERS LANE
Mike Scarlett.

19 GLOVERS LANE
Michael Donohoe & Jane Rixon.

LEXTON HOUSE
Matthew & Diane Tims.

5 LONGBURGES
Mr D Vale.

38 MIDWAY
Margaret & David Finch.

PEARTREE HOUSE
Roger & Barbara Charlesworth.

14 QUEEN STREET
Brian & Kathy Goodey.

2A RECTORY LANE
Debbie Evans.

Large village with C13 church (open) with renowned pre-Raphaelite stained glass. Nine open gardens with a variety of sizes, styles & maturity. Of the smaller gardens, one modern garden contrasts formal features with colour-filled borders and exotic plants, another with flowing curves feels restrained and serene. A mature small front and back garden is planted profusely with a feel of an intimate haven. A garden that has evolved through family use features rooms and dense planting. A steeply-pitched garden on three levels has patio, ponds, herbaceous borders and acer collection. One garden is designed to support nature, providing an environment to attract bird and insects. A stately garden inc a formal terrace surrounded by hedges and fig trees with steps down to secluded lower space and small

vegetable garden. A large garden has colourful cottage planting and vegetable garden. Another has an air of mystery with hidden corners and an extensive water feature weaving its way throughout the garden. Small exhibition 'Introducing Middleton Cheney'.

54 MIDSUMMER HOUSE
Woolstone, Faringdon, SN7 7QL. Penny Spink. *7m W & 7m S of Faringdon. Woolstone is a small village off B4507, below Uffington White Horse Hill. Take rd towards Uffington from the White Horse Pub.* **Fri 3 May, Fri 7 June (2-5). Fri 5 July (2-5), open nearby Woolstone Mill House. Fri 2 Aug, Fri 6 Sept, Fri 4 Oct (2-5). Adm £5, chd free. Home-made teas.**
Midsummer Garden is designed by Justin Spink for his parents, Anthony and Penny Spink, in 2015. In 2018 Mike and Ann Collins continued designing and planting the garden. Over the road there is a newly planted arboretum and nature reserve established 2019. Rare and unusual plants. Picnics welcome in the field opp. Wheelchair access over short gravel drive at entrance.

55 MILL BARN
25 Mill Lane, Chalgrove, OX44 7SL. Pat Hougham, 01865 890020, Gmec@outlook.com. *12m E of Oxford. Chalgrove is 4m from Watlington off B480. Mill Barn is in Mill Ln, W of Chalgrove, 300yds S of Lamb Pub.* **Wed 11 Sept (1.30-5). Adm £4, chd free. Home-made teas. Visits also by arrangement May to Sept for groups of 6 to 40.**
Mill Barn has an informal cottage garden with a variety of flowers throughout the seasons. Rose arches and a pergola lead to a vegetable plot surrounded by a cordon of fruit trees, all set in a mill stream landscape.

56 NEW MILL HOUSE GARDEN

Fernham Road, Uffington, Faringdon, SN7 7RD. Rupert & Julia Lycett Green. *Turn into Fernham Rd by the Tom Brown Museum. After 100 metres, turn into the private road marked 'Grounds Farm', Mill House is the 1st open gate on L.* **Sun 9 June (11.30-5). Adm £4, chd free. Light refreshments inc tea, lemonade and cakes.**

Wonderful setting overlooking the Uffington White Horse and wide views of the Downs. 1 acre garden divided into seasonal rooms connecting around the house. A walled garden leads into a lawned room of box-edged beds and follows into a spring garden and out to a wild growing bank and a rill following the course of the old mill race. Lastly, a vegetable garden with roses and cutting beds. Wheelchair access to central garden and then sloping grass paths to top garden. Exit possible through top stable yard.

57 MONKS HEAD

Weston Road, Bletchingdon, OX5 3DH. Sue Bedwell, 01869 350155, bedwell615@btinternet.com. *Approx 4m N of Kidlington. From A34 take B4027 to Bletchingdon, turn R at Xrds into Weston Rd.* **Visits by arrangement 1 Jan to 29 Nov. Home-made teas. Teas, coffees and home-made cakes.**

Plantaholics' garden for year-round interest. Bulb frame and alpine area, greenhouse. Changes evolving all the time, becoming more of a wildlife garden.

GROUP OPENING

58 OLD BOARS HILL GARDENS

Jarn Way, Boars Hill, Oxford, OX1 5JF. *3m S of Oxford. From S ring road towards A34 at r'about follow signs to Wootton & Boars Hill. Up Hinksey Hill take R fork. 1m R into Berkley Rd to Old Boars Hill.* **Sun 16 June (1.30-5.30). Combined adm £10, chd free. Sun 15 Sept (2-5.30). Combined adm £6, chd free. Home-made teas. Visits also by arrangement 24 Mar to 20 Oct for groups of up to 25.**

BLACKTHORN

Louise Edwards.
Open on Sun 16 June

TALL TREES

David Clark.
Open on Sun 16 June

TANGLEWOOD

Wendy Becker.
Open on Sun 16 June

NEW TOMMYS FARM

Robert and Alison Kirtland.
Open on Sun 15 Sept

WHITSUN MEADOWS

Jane & Nigel Jones.
Open on Sun 15 Sept

YEW COTTAGE

Michael Edwards.
Open on Sun 15 Sept

Gardens located in a wooded conservation area favoured by walkers. Tall Trees is surrounded by pots, more acid soil for Rhododendrons and gravel gardens. Blackthorn (8 acres) has splendid woodland as a backdrop with bright formal borders, herbs, orchard and a large pond Tanglewood is a beautifully designed large, modern garden with many delightful features, a truly family garden. Whitsun Meadows overlooks the Old Golf Course. It is full of year long interest with autumn colour as well as wildflowers and spring displays. Tommy's Farm at the bottom of Old Boars Hill has wonderful views over the hill and a flowing garden with sun loving displays and bulbs in spring. Some gravel and slightly bumpy entrance drive.

59 NEW THE OLD RECTORY, ALBURY

Albury, Thame, OX9 2LP. Mr & Mrs J Nowell-Smith, 01844 339650, Moonowellsmith@gmail.com. *Off A418 Wheatley to Thame road, 5 m from Thame. From Tiddington, turn R onto single track road before 50mph signs.* **Visits by arrangement for groups of up to 30. Refreshments upon request.**

5 acres of extensive herbaceous borders, rose avenue, woodland and lake walk, kitchen and cutting gardens. Surrounded by orchards and the glebe land with some beautiful mature trees with close access to Fernhill Wood, famous for bluebells. There is extensive planting of snowdrops and early bulbs, followed by perpetual roses, and continual herbaceous and annual planting. Sculptures by Andy Goldsworth and Tom Stogdon.

60 ORCHARD HOUSE

Asthall, Burford, OX18 4HH. Dr Elizabeth Maitreyi, 07939 111605, oneconsciousbreath@gmail.com. *3m E of Burford. 1st house on R as you come downhill into Asthall from the A40. There is a small step down from the pedestrian gate onto the driveway. Parking in the village. Please park with consideration.* **Sun 30 June (2-6). Adm £6, chd free. Home-made teas. Tea, home-made cakes and soft drinks are part of our fuindraising effort.**

A five acre garden which was begun eight years ago. Formal borders and courtyard. An English garden finely balanced between the formal and the wild. Beautiful sculptures add to the planting and there is woodland to walk in beyond. If you have been to Orchard House before you can expect to see the hedges and plants all feeling more at home now. Rare breed piglets sometimes to be seen. Dogs on a lead only. If you need accommodation in the area, our lovely 'dacha' is on Airbnb and dinner at the local pub is highly recommended. Wheelchair access with small step onto drive and one step down to garden.

61 116 OXFORD ROAD

Abingdon, OX14 2AG. Mr & Mrs P Aylward, 01235 523925, aylwardsdooz@hotmail.co.uk. *North Abingdon. 116 Oxford Rd is on R if coming from A34 N Abingdon exit, or on L after the Picklers Hill turn if approaching from Abingdon town centre.* **Sun 9 June (11-4). Combined adm with Failford £6, chd free. Home-made teas. Visits also by arrangement May to Sept for groups of 10+.**

This young town garden brings alive the imagination of its creators. It will inspire both the enthusiast and the beginner. Use of recycled materials, lots of colour and architectural plants. A folly and greenhouse is just one of many quirky features. Raised beds, rockeries, specimen plants, beds of roses and hostas. Pushes the boundaries of conventional gardening. There is something for everyone.

62 50 PLANTATION ROAD

Oxford, OX2 6JE. Philippa Scoones. *Central Oxford. N on Woodstock Rd take 2nd L. Coming into Oxford on Woodstock Rd turn R after Leckford Rd. Best to park on Leckford Rd. No disabled parking near house.* **Sat 27, Sun 28 Apr (2-5). Adm £5, chd free. Opening with Central North Oxford Gardens on Sat 20, Sun 21 Apr.**
Surprisingly spacious city garden designed in specific sections. North facing front garden, side alley filled with shade loving climbers. South facing rear garden with hundreds of tulips in spring, unusual trees inc Mount Etna Broom, conservatory, terraced area and secluded water garden with water feature, woodland plants and alpines. Good design ideas for small town garden and 100s of pots that add to the overall atmosphere.

63 THE PRIORY, CHARLBURY

Church Lane, Charlbury, OX7 3PX. Dr D El Kabir & Colleagues. *6m SE of Chipping Norton. Large Cotswold village on B4022 Witney-Enstone Rd, near St Mary's Church.* **Sun 19 May (2-5). Adm £6, chd free.**
1½ acre of formal terraced topiary gardens with Italianate features. Foliage colour schemes, shrubs, parterres with fragrant plants, old roses, water features, sculpture and inscriptions aim to produce a poetic, wistful atmosphere. Formal vegetable and herb garden. Arboretum of over three acres borders the River Evenlode and inc wildlife garden and pond. Partial wheelchair access.

64 9 RAWLINSON ROAD

Oxford, OX2 6UE. Ramnique Lall. *¾ m N of Oxford City Centre. Rawlinson Rd runs between Banbury & Woodstock rds midway between Oxford City Centre & Summertown shops.* **Sun 22 Sept (1-5). Combined adm with 11 Rawlinson Road £7, chd free. Tea.**
Townhouse garden with structured disarray of roses. Terrace of stone inlaid with brick and enclosed by Chinese fretwork balustrade, chunky brick and oak pergola covered with roses, wisteria and clematis; potted topiary. Until autumn the garden is delightfully replete with aconites, lobelias, phloxes, daisies and meandering clematis.

65 11 RAWLINSON ROAD

Oxford, OX2 6UE. Emma Chamberlain. *Central N Oxford. Halfway between Central Oxford & Summertown, off Banbury Rd.* **Sun 22 Sept (1-5). Combined adm with 9 Rawlinson Road £7, chd free. Tea.**
A S facing 120ft walled Victorian town garden created from scratch since 2010. Interesting mix of herbaceous and shrubs with particular interest in late tulips, grasses and unusual plants. Great emphasis on colour and succession planting with paths running through the beds. A riot of asters and autumn colour - if the sun shines the best time of year in our garden.

100 inpatients and their families are being supported at the newly opened Horatio's Garden Wales, thanks to the National Garden Scheme donations

66 RECTORY FARMHOUSE

Church Enstone, Chipping Norton, OX7 4NN. Andrew Hornung & Sally Coles, 01608 677374, giussanese@yahoo.co.uk. *N from Oxford on the A44, Turn R in Enstone to Church Enstone. Parking is on the Little Tew Rd by the church. Proceed through the churchyard, turn R and down the hill. Entrance on unmade road behind The Crown Inn.* **Wed 19, Sun 23 June (1-5). Adm £5, chd free. Tea and cake. There is a pub next door which serves meals and snacks etc. Visits also by arrangement 8 June to 7 July for groups of up to 10.**
A large and very varied garden with a rich mix of formal and informal planting inc fruit trees, soft fruit & vegetable garden. About 100 varieties of rose, particularly climbers; many unusual, some rare plants. The garden inc many different settings, ranging from gravel areas to fruit trees and pondside plantings. More recently developed areas alongside well established plantings.

Gowers Close, Sibford Gardens

© Andrew Lawson

67 ST EDMUND HALL
Queens Lane, Oxford, OX1 4AR.
College entrance is in Queen's Ln, which is off the High St, opp the Examination Schools. **Tue 9 July (10-4). Adm £5, chd free.**
The gardens of St Edmund Hall are on an intimate scale, much used and loved by the college's Fellows and students. The first sight is the college's historic front quad ('the most exquisite of the small Oxford quadrangles' according to Jan Morris) with its double lawn, clambering wisteria, and medieval well. To the left is the graveyard of the medieval church of St Peter in the East, now the college library. The graveyard is thick with snowdrops in February, and behind the church you will find the Broadbent Garden, with its herbaceous planting and overhanging limes. In the more modern part of the college, you will find one of Oxford's new 'green walls', designed to soften and cool the austere concrete of the new part of the historic, central Oxford site.
»)

68 SARSDEN GLEBE
Churchill, Chipping Norton, OX7 6PH. Mr & Mrs Rupert Ponsonby. *Situated between Sarsden and Churchill. Sarsden Glebe is ¼ m S of Churchill on the road to Sarsden. Turn in to the drive by a small lodge.* **Sun 14 Apr (12.30-5). Adm £7.50, chd free. Home-made teas.**
A rectory garden and park laid out by Humphry Repton and his son George. Terraced formal garden; wild garden with spring bulbs and mature oaks; and walled kitchen garden. Wild garden with a sea of blue and white anemone blanda interspersed with fritillaries and daffodils in spring. Most of the garden can be accessed in a wheelchair.
& 🐕 ✱ ☕ »)

GROUP OPENING

69 NEW SHIPTON COURT WATER GARDENS
High Street, Shipton-under-Wychwood, Chipping Norton, OX7 6DG. Mr Richard Polatch. *In Shipton-under-Wychwood. On leaving the cricket club, cross the road and turn L, continue past the entrance to the Jacobean manor house (not open), follow the tall wall. At the end of the wall the entrance is on your R.*

Sun 30 June (11-5). Combined adm £10, chd free. Light refreshments at The Gatehouse. Donation to Local WI.

NEW THE GATEHOUSE
Richard Polatch & Beatrice Foster.
NEW MERE FOLLY
Mr Malcolm & Mrs Maggie McKillop.
NEW THE SUMMERHOUSE
Michael Rosenblum and Lisa Pattenden.

The formal gardens at the Jacobean Shipton Court were extensively remodelled around 1905 by landscape gardeners James Pulham and Son to inc a 60 metre long canal planted with water lilies fed by a cascade from the higher swimming pool to the south. Both pools are surrounded with Yorkstone paving and Cotswold dry stone retaining walls supporting the cascading flower borders. The various levels are linked by stone steps and paths with lawns, extensive topiary and hedges, primarily of yew and box providing evergreen structure throughout the year. Exuberantly planted mixed borders give seasonal colour. Mature trees provide areas for shade tolerant plants and the gardens inc 200 year old mulberry and sequoia trees. The Rose Garden replanted in 2020 is a haven of scent and colour. A 2½ metre high Cotswold stone buttressed retaining wall with stone balls provides the backdrop to a long border of climbers, shrub roses and perennials which provides colour throughout the year. Garden is full of roses.
🐕 ✱ ☕ »)

GROUP OPENING

70 SIBFORD GARDENS
Sibford Ferris, OX15 5RE. *7m W of Banbury. Nr the Warwickshire border, S of B4035, in centre of Sibford Ferris village at T-junc & additional gardens nr the Xrds & Wykham Arms Pub in Sibford Gower. Parking in both villages.* **Sun 23 June (2-6). Combined adm £7, chd free. Home-made teas at Sibford Gower Village Hall (opp the church).**

CARTER'S YARD
Sue & Malcolm Bannister, 01295 780365, sebannister@gmail.com.

Visits also by arrangement May to Sept for groups of 5 to 25. Adm inc a selection of light refreshments.
COPPERS
Mr Andrew & Mrs Chris Tindsley.
GOWERS CLOSE
Philip Hilton.
HOME CLOSE, SIBFORD FERRIS
Graham & Carolyn White, 07711 897902, carolyn@familywhites.co.uk, www.instagram.com/homeclosegardens. **Visits also by arrangement 20 May to 5 July for groups of 10 to 25.**
THE LONG HOUSE
Jan & Diana Thompson.
SHRUBBERY COTTAGE
Nic Durrant.

Two charming small villages of Sibford Gower and Sibford Ferris, off the beaten track with thatched stone cottages. Six contrasting gardens comprising a truly traditional plants woman's cottage garden, a woodland setting with shade garden, a private garden of a renowned landscape architect an Artists garden with planting designed to inspire her works, new for 2024, Gowers Close a beautiful country garden using the natural gradient of divide the garden into different zones that draw your eye and encourage you to explore and the gardens, and lastly the gardens of an early C20 Arts and Crafts house. A fantastic collection bursting with bloom, structural intrigue, interesting planting and some rather unusual plants.
🐕 ✱ ☕ »)

71 SOUTH NEWINGTON HOUSE
South Newington, OX15 4JW. Mr & Mrs David Swan, 07711 720135, claire_ainley@hotmail.com. *6m SW of Banbury. South Newington is between Banbury & Chipping Norton. Take Barford Rd off A361, 1st L after 100yds in between oak bollards. For SatNav use OX15 4JL.* **Visits by arrangement 2 Mar to 29 Nov. Visits arranged for South Newington House and Bush House. Adm £12, chd free.**
A tree lined drive leads to a garden of interest. Herbaceous borders designed for year-round colour. Organic kitchen garden with established beds, rotation and companion planting. Orchard of

fruit trees with a pond for wildlife and hydration for the hives. Walled parterre planted for seasonal colour. A family garden, designed to blend seamlessly into the environment; a warm welcome awaits you. Some gravel paths, otherwise full wheelchair access.

72 SOUTHBANK
Back Lane, Epwell, Banbury, OX15 6LF. Alan Cooper, 01295 780577, alan.cooper2019@gmail.com. *1st bungalow on L after Church Ln on L, steep drive with hand rail. Entrance to garden via Church Ln, signposted.* **Sun 19 May (1-5). Combined adm with Church Farm Field £5, chd free. Sun 1 Sept (1-5). Adm £4, chd free. Home-made teas in the village hall. Visits also by arrangement for groups of up to 12.** Front and back garden evolved over 20 yrs with several mature trees. Very densely planted with many rare and unusual plants. The front inc a rockery, mixed herbaceous border, peony and geranium beds. The back has various borders inc a sub-tropical bed, greenhouse, small vegetable plot and wildflower hedgerow.

GROUP OPENING

73 STEEPLE ASTON GARDENS
Steeple Aston, OX25 4SF. Richard and Daphne Preston. *14m N of Oxford, 9m S of Banbury. ½m E of A4260. Parking at village hall, OX25 4SF.* **Sun 2 June (2-6). Combined adm £7, chd free.**

THE CHURCH ALLOTMENTS
Oxford Diocese.

COMBE PYNE
Chris & Sally Cooper.

THE LONGBYRE
Mr & Mrs V Billings.

THE POUND HOUSE
Mr & Mrs Ray Clarke.

PRIMROSE GARDENS
Richard & Daphne Preston, 01869 340512, richard.preston5@btopenworld.com. **Visits also by arrangement 13 May to 31 July for groups of 10 to 35.**

Steeple Aston, often considered the most easterly of the Cotswold villages, is a beautiful stone-built village with

gardens that provide a wide range of interest. A stream meanders down the hill as the landscape changes from sand to clay. The open gardens inc small floriferous cottage gardens, large landscaped gardens, natural woodland areas, ponds and bog gardens, themed borders and allotments. The gardens provide something for everyone from a courtyard garden to a former walled kitchen garden and so much in between. Primrose Gardens and Longbyre have gravel and many of the gardens are situated on a slope. No wheelchair access to The Church Allotments.

74 ♦ STONOR PARK
Stonor, Henley-on-Thames, RG9 6HF. Lady Ailsa Stonor, 01491 638587, administrator@stonor.com, www.stonor.com. *4 m from Henley on Thames. Stonor is located between the M4 (J8/J9) & the M40 (J6) on the B480 Henley-on-Thames to Watlington rd. If you are approaching Stonor on the M40 from the E, please exit at J6 only.* **For NGS: Thur 13 June (10.30-4). Adm £6.50, chd free. Home-made teas. For other opening times and information, please phone, email or visit garden website.** Nestled within a hidden valley and ancient deer park, you will find the gardens at Stonor, which date back to Medieval times. Visitors love the serenity of our C17 walled, Italianate Pleasure Garden and Old Kitchen Garden beyond. In the four acre walled gardens you'll find a 400ft long herbaceous border, topiary, ancient yews, ponds with water lilies, and beautiful park land views. Medieval Walled Garden 400 ft -long herbaceous border Huge Rosa 'Kiftsgate' which hangs from a vast yew Stunning parkland views Shrubbery.

75 STOW COTTAGE ARBORETUM & GARDEN
Junction Road, Churchill, Chipping Norton, OX7 6NP. Tom Heywood-Lonsdale, www.stowcott.co.uk. *2½m SW of Chipping Norton, off the B4450. Parking: use postcode OX7 6NP & parking will be sign posted from William Smith Cl.* **Sat 6 July (2-5.30). Adm £5, chd free. Home-made teas. Donation to IDS Education Fund.**

The arboretum and garden cover approx 15 acres with extensive views towards Stow-on-the-Wold and beyond. The arboretum began in 2009 and has been extensively developed over the years. There is an array of 650 different trees, particularly oaks as well as sorbus and limes and many magnolias, dogwoods, walnuts, birches and liquidambars. The arboretum began in 2009 and has been extensively developed over the years. There is an array of 500 trees inc different oaks, sorbus and limes as well as many magnolias, dogwoods, walnuts, birches and liquidambars.

76 TYTHE BARN
Guydens Hamlet, Oxford Road Garsington, Oxford, OX44 9AZ. Claire and Dave Parker. *Beyond the Oxford ring road to the E, after Unipart, at the edge of Garsington. Parking is available in the Unipart Car park, about 150 metres from the house. OX4 2PG. Disabled parking, and passenger drop off at Tythe Barn itself (OX44 9AZ).* **Sun 2 June (1.30-5). Adm £4, chd free. Home-made teas. Local honey for sale. Teas and cakes for sale.** ½ acre garden, designed by RHS Chelsea award winner Sarah Naybour. Bee friendly planting in the formal garden leads to woodland area. Oak pergola with roses overlooks the wildlife pond with orchard. Raised vegetable beds behind a mature beech hedge with vintage doorway. 2½ acre wildflower meadow with apiary. Garden is flat and designed to be accessible to wheelchairs. Disabled parking adjacent to the house.

National Garden Scheme gardens are identified by their yellow road signs and posters. You can expect a garden of quality, character and interest, a warm welcome and plenty of home-made cakes!

77 UPLANDS
Old Boars Hill, Oxford, OX1 5JF.
Lyn Sanders, 01865 739486,
sandersc4@hotmail.com. *3m S of
Oxford. From S ring road towards
A34 at r'about follow signs to
Wootton & Boars Hill. Up Hinksey Hill
take R fork. 1m R into Berkley Rd.
Follow rd around 2 bends, garden
opp 3rd bend. Parking in Ln.* **Visits
by arrangement 24 Mar to 20 Oct
for groups of up to 25. Home-
made teas.**
A hidden ½ acre garden with
borrowed views and colour
throughout the year. The long sloping
lawn leads to a sunny formal garden.
There is a wildlife pond inhabited by
great crested and smooth newts in
spring and damselflies and dragonflies
later, plus an extensive range of
perennial plants, spring bulbs, roses,
dahlias, Michaelmas daisies and
clematis. Wheelchair access with
some steps that can be avoided by
using the sloping lawns.

78 UPPER BOLNEY HOUSE
Upper Bolney Road, Harpsden,
Henley-on-Thames, RG9 4AQ.
Anna and Richard Wilson. *2m
S of Henley on Thames, between
Shiplake and Harpsden. Upper
Bolney Rd can be accessed from
Woodlands Rd. Only use the
postcode in Google Maps.* **Sun
21 Apr (11-4). Adm £6, chd £2.
Home-made teas. Cream tea,
cakes, hot and cold drinks.**
The four acre garden has been
extensively developed over the
last 15 years. There are lawns with
herbaceous borders. The terraces
around the house inc planted areas
and yew topiary. Various interesting
areas lie beyond; a rose garden,
wildflower meadow, rhododendron
bed, tropical area, Victorian stumpery,
kitchen garden and greenhouse.
Some garden statuary and several
sitting areas and benches.

South Newington House

79 ◆ **WATERPERRY GARDENS**
Waterperry, Wheatley, OX33 1JZ.
The School of Philosophy and
Economic Science, 01844 339254,
office@waterperrygardens.co.uk,
www.waterperrygardens.co.uk.
*7½m from Oxford city centre.
From E M40 J8, from N M40 J8a.
Follow brown tourist signs. For
SatNav please use OX33 1LA.* **For
NGS: Tue 12 Mar (10-5); Tue 17
Sept (10-5.30). Adm £9.50, chd
free. For other opening times and
information, please phone, email or
visit garden website.**
Eight acres of beautifully landscaped
ornamental gardens featuring a
spectacular 200ft herbaceous border.
New developments underway inc
the replanting of the Mary Spiller
rose garden, planting the new
winter border and creating a new
bluebell copse. The formal garden
is particularly neatly designed and
colourful, with a small knot garden,
herb border and wisteria tunnel.
Newly redesigned walled garden,
river walk, statues and pear orchard.
Riverside walk may be inaccessible to
wheelchair users if very wet.

&♿ ✽ 🚐 [NPC] ☕

80 **WAYSIDE**
82 Banbury Road, Kidlington,
OX5 2BX. Margaret & Alistair
Urquhart, 01865 460180,
alistairurquhart@ntlworld.com. *5m
N of Oxford. On R of A4260 travelling
N through Kidlington.* **Visits by
arrangement June to Sept for groups
of up to 25. Adm £4, chd free.**
¼ acre garden shaded by mature
trees. Mixed border with some rare
and unusual plants and shrubs. A
climber clothed pergola leads past
a dry gravel garden to the woodland
garden with an extensive collection of
hardy ferns. Conservatory and large
fern house with a collection of unusual
species of tree ferns and tender
exotics. Partial wheelchair access.

&♿ ✽ ☕

GROUP OPENING

81 **WEST OXFORD GARDENS**
Cumnor Hill, Oxford, OX2 9HH.
*Take Botley interchange off A34
from N or S. Follow signs for Oxford
& then turn R at Botley T-lights opp
McDonalds & follow National Garden
Scheme yellow signs. Street parking.*
**Sun 23 June (1-5). Combined adm
£7, chd free. Home-made teas at
10 Eynsham Road.**

10 EYNSHAM ROAD
Jon Harker.

22 HID'S COPSE ROAD
Adrienne McKenna.

23 HID'S COPSE ROAD
Kathy Eldridge.
(See separate entry)

 26 HURST RISE ROAD
Mrs Sylvie Thorn.

86 HURST RISE ROAD
Ms P Guy & Mr L Harris.

6 SCHOLAR PLACE
Helen Ward.

New for 2024: 26 Hurst Rise Road - a
beautiful contemporary garden created
by the owners. Shrubs and bee friendly
herbaceous borders and sculptures.
86 Hurst Rise Road, a small garden
abounding in perennials, roses, small
trees and shrubs displayed at different
levels around a circular lawn and path
with sculptural features. 10 Eynsham
Road a New Zealander's take on an
English-style garden inc many rose
varieties, white garden, herbaceous
borders and pond. New for 2024 - 22
Hids Copse Road a large garden
with evergreen shrubs and traditional
herbaceous borders and beds. 23 Hid's
Copse Road, a ½ acre, wildlife friendly
plot under many trees with two ponds,
a wildflower meadow, kitchen garden
and contemplative areas. 6 Scholar
Place, a small garden with a selection
of small trees, shrubs and perennials.
Small pond and an interesting
sculpture. Steps up from the patio lead
to the main garden. Gravel steps at 6
Scholar Place, pebble path at 86 Hurst
Rise Road & sloping gravel driveway at
22 Hids Copse Road.

&♿ ✽ ☕ •))

82 **WESTWELL MANOR**
Westwell, nr Burford, OX18 4JT. Mr
Thomas Gibson. *2m SW of Burford.
From A40 Burford-Cheltenham, turn
L ½m after Burford r'about signed
Westwell. After 1½m at T-junc,
turn R & Manor is 2nd house on L.*
**Sun 19 May (2-6). Adm £5, chd
free. Light refreshments inc tea,
biscuits and cake. Other stands
open in the village. Donation to
Aspire.**
Seven acres surrounding old
Cotswold manor house (not open)
with knot garden, potager, shrub
roses, herbaceous borders, topiary,
earth works, moonlight garden,
auricula ladder, rills and water garden.

✽ ☕

83 **WHITEHILL FARM**
Widford, Burford, OX18 4DT. Mr &
Mrs Paul Youngson, 01993 822894,
paulyoungson48@gmail.com.
*1m E of Burford. From A40 take rd
signed Widford. Turn R at bottom of
hill, 1st house on R with ample car
parking.* **Sun 2 June (2-6). Adm £5,
chd free. Home-made teas. Visits
also by arrangement May to Sept.
Coaches welcome.**
Two acres of hillside gardens and
woodland with spectacular views
overlooking Burford and Windrush
valley. Informal plantsman's garden
built up by the owners over 25 yrs.
Herbaceous and shrub borders,
ponds and bog area, old fashioned
roses, ground cover, ornamental
grasses, bamboos and hardy
geraniums. Large cascade water
feature, pretty tea patio and wonderful
Cotswold views.

🐾 ✽ ☕ 🪑 •))

84 **WOOLSTONE MILL HOUSE**
Woolstone, Faringdon, SN7 7QL.
Mr & Mrs Justin Spink. *7m W
of Wantage. 7m S of Faringdon.
Woolstone is a small village off
B4507, below Uffington White Horse
Hill.* **Fri 5 July (2-5). Adm £5, chd
free. Open nearby Midsummer
House.**
Redesigned by new owner, garden
designer Justin Spink in 2020, this
1½ acre garden has large mixed
perennial beds, and small gravel,
cutting, kitchen and bog gardens.
Topiary, medlars and old fashioned
roses. Treehouse with spectacular
views to Uffington White Horse and
White Horse Hill. C18 millhouse and
barn (not open). Partial wheelchair
access.

&♿ 🚐 ☕ •))

*Our donation to the
Army Benevolent
Fund supported 608
individuals with front
line services and
horticultural related
grants in 2023*

SURREY

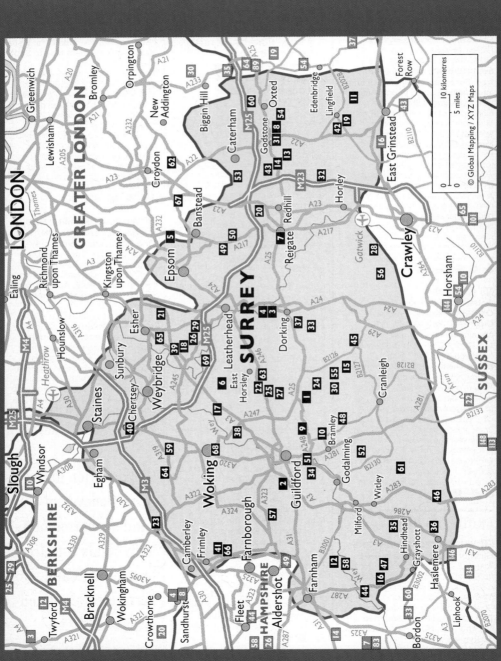

VOLUNTEERS

County Organiser
Clare Bevan
07956 307546
clare.bevan@ngs.org.uk

County Treasurer
Nigel Brandon
020 8643 8686
nbrandon@ngs.org.uk

Booklet Co-ordinator
Annabel Alford-Warren
01483 203330
annabel.alford-warren@ngs.org.uk

Publicity
Sarah Wilson
07932 445868
sarah.wilson@ngs.org.uk

Social Media
Annette Warren
07790 045354
annette.warren@ngs.org.uk

Assistant County Organisers
Jane Allison 07790 476394
jane.allison@ngs.org.uk

Margaret Arnott 01372 842459
margaret.arnott@ngs.org.uk

Jan Brandon 020 8643 8686
janmbrandon@outlook.com

Louise Curtis 07879 426386
louise.curtis@ngs.org.uk

Angela Gilchrist 01306 884613
angela.gilchrist@ngs.org.uk

Joy Greasley 01342 837369
joy@greasley.me.uk

Di Grose 01883 742983
di.grose@btinternet.com

Annie Keighley 01252 838660
annie.keighley12@btinternet.com

Jānis Raubiška 07478 025188
janis.raubiska@ngs.org.uk

Kate Smith 07788 746719
kate.smith@ngs.org.uk

f @surreyngs
✕ @SurreyNGS
◎ @surreyngs

OPENING DATES

All entries subject to change.
For latest information check
www.ngs.org.uk
Extended openings are shown
at the beginning of the month.
Map locator numbers are
shown to the right of each
garden name.

January

Every Wednesday to
Wednesday 17th
Timber Hill | 59

Wednesday 31st
Timber Hill | 59

February

Snowdrop Openings

Every Monday
Timber Hill | 59

Sunday 11th
◆ Gatton Park | 20

Sunday 18th
Shieling | 50

Saturday 24th
NEW Court Lodge Farm | 14

March

Monday 4th
Timber Hill | 59

Monday 11th
Timber Hill | 59

Sunday 17th
Albury Park | 1

Monday 25th
Timber Hill | 59

April

Every day from Monday 1st
to Sunday 7th
◆ Vann | 61

Every day from Monday 29th
◆ Vann | 61

Monday 1st
Moleshill House | 39
Shieling | 50
Timber Hill | 59

Sunday 7th
Coverwood Lakes | 15
Timber Hill | 59

Sunday 14th
Coverwood Lakes | 15
◆ Dunsborough Park | 17

Tuesday 16th
◆ The Sculpture Park | 47

Saturday 20th
11 West Hill | 62

Sunday 21st
Coverwood Lakes | 15
◆ Hatchlands Park | 25
41 Shelvers Way | 49
11 West Hill | 62

Thursday 25th
Lower House | 35

Sunday 28th
Lower House | 35

Monday 29th
Timber Hill | 59

May

Every day from Monday 13th
to Sunday 19th
Chauffeur's Flat | 8

Every Tuesday to Saturday
Crosswater Farm | 16

Every day to Sunday 5th
◆ Vann | 61

Sunday 5th
The Garth Pleasure Grounds | 19
West Horsley Place | 63
Woodpeckers | 68

Monday 6th
Timber Hill | 59

Saturday 11th
Harry Edwards Healing
Sanctuary | 24

Sunday 12th
Coverwood Lakes | 15
The Garth Pleasure Grounds | 19
Westways Farm | 64

Wednesday 15th
NEW Claridge House | 11

Thursday 16th
NEW Claridge House | 11

Friday 17th
NEW Claridge House 11
2 Knott Park House 29
◆ Ramster 46

Saturday 18th
NEW Claridge House 11
Hall Grove School 23
2 Knott Park House 29
NEW Slades Farm 52

Sunday 19th
Chilworth Manor 9
Knowle Grange 30
NEW Slades Farm 52
The Therapy Garden 57
Woodpeckers 68

Monday 20th
Timber Hill 59

Saturday 25th
Monks Lantern 40

Sunday 26th
NEW Ichi-Coo Park 28
◆ Titsey Place Gardens 60

Monday 27th
Fairmile Common Gardens 18
Shieling 50

Friday 31st
Little Orchards 32

June

Every Tuesday to Saturday to Friday 7th
Crosswater Farm 16

Saturday 1st
Bridge End Cottage 6
Cobbetts Corner 12

Sunday 2nd
Little Orchards 32

Saturday 8th
Leigh Place 31
The Old Vicarage 44

Sunday 9th
Leigh Place 31
NEW Logmore Place 33
The Old Rectory 43
The Old Vicarage 44

Tuesday 11th
◆ The Sculpture Park 47

Friday 14th
Ashleigh Grange 4

Saturday 15th
NEW Milton Way House 37

Sunday 16th
◆ Loseley Park 34

Sunday 23rd
The Manor House 36
◆ Titsey Place Gardens 60

Sunday 30th
NEW 48 Woodmansterne Lane 67

July

Sunday 7th
High Clandon Estate Vineyard 27

Sunday 14th
NEW Wrens' Nest Cottage 69

Sunday 21st
◆ Titsey Place Gardens 60

August

Saturday 3rd
The White House 65

Sunday 4th
Grace & Flavour CIC 22
41 Shelvers Way 49
The White House 65

Sunday 11th
Shieling 50

Sunday 18th
Pratsham Grange 45
NEW Shooting Star Children's
Hospices, Christopher's 51
◆ Titsey Place Gardens 60

September

Sunday 1st
Woodpeckers 68

Friday 6th
Little Orchards 32

Sunday 8th
Little Orchards 32
West Horsley Place 63
Woodpeckers 68

Sunday 15th
21 Glenavon Close 21

Sunday 22nd
The Therapy Garden 57

Saturday 28th
Hall Grove School 23

October

Sunday 6th
Albury Park 1
Harry Edwards Healing
Sanctuary 24

Sunday 20th
Coverwood Lakes 15

By Arrangement

Arrange a personalised garden visit
with your club, or group of friends,
on a date to suit you. See individual
garden entries for full details.

29 Applegarth Avenue 2
Ashcombe 3
Ashleigh Grange 4
15 The Avenue 5
Bridge End Cottage 6
Caxton House 7
2 Chinthurst Lodge 10
NEW Claridge House 11
Coldharbour House 13
Coverwood Lakes 15
The Garth Pleasure Grounds 19
Heathside 26
NEW Ichi-Coo Park 28
Lower House 35
NEW Mole End 38
Moleshill House 39
The Nutrition Garden 41
Oaklands 42
The Old Vicarage 44
Shamley Wood Estate 48
41 Shelvers Way 49
Shieling 50
NEW South Wind 53
Southlands Lodge 54
Spurfold 55
Tanhouse Farm 56
Tilford Cottage 58
Westways Farm 64
The White House 65
Wildwood 66
Woodpeckers 68
NEW Wrens' Nest Cottage 69

THE GARDENS

1 ALBURY PARK
Albury, GU5 9BH. Trustees of
Albury Estate. *5m SE of Guildford.
From A25 take A248 towards Albury
for ¼ m, then up New Rd, entrance
to Albury Park immed on L.* **Sun 17
Mar, Sun 6 Oct (2-5). Adm £6, chd
free. Home-made teas.**
14 acre pleasure grounds laid out
in 1670s by John Evelyn for Henry
Howard, later 6th Duke of Norfolk. ¼ m
of terraces, fine collection of trees, lake
and river. Wheelchair access over gravel
path and slight slope.

2 29 APPLEGARTH AVENUE
Guildford, GU2 8LX. Mr Robert
Avenell, robavenell@outlook.com.
*Just off the A3 at Guildford. Follow
directions for The Royal Surrey
Hospital from the A3 along Egerton
Rd. Turn L at the r'about by Kings
College & Applegarth Ave is opp the
shops on Park Barn Estate.* **Visits by
arrangement in June for groups of
up to 10. Weekends only. Adm £6,
chd free. Tea.**
Not a large garden but somewhere to
escape to and relax. The owner's love
of vibrant colours is reflected in the
garden which is full of cherished plants,
glorious blooms and attractive scents.
Walking through a series of outdoor
rooms, you will discover a mixture of
trees, shrubs, herbaceous perennials
and roses. Best seen in early summer.

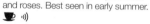

3 ASHCOMBE
Chapel Lane, Westhumble,
Dorking, RH5 6AY. Vivienne &
David Murch, 01306 743062,
murch@ashcombe.org. *2m N of
Dorking. From A24 at Boxhill/Burford
Bridge follow signs to Westhumble.
Through village & take L drive by
ruined chapel (1m from A24). Limited
on site parking for up to 10 cars.*
**Visits by arrangement June to
Sept for groups of 10+. Home-
made teas. Wine for eve visits.**
Rose lovers, 1⅓ acre wildlife friendly,
sloping garden on chalk and flint.
Enclosed ⅓ acre cottage garden with
large borders of roses, delphiniums
and clematis. Amphibian pond.
Secluded decking and patio area with
colourful acers and views over garden
and Boxhill. Gravel bed of salvia and
day lilies. House (not open) surrounded
by banked flower beds and lawn
leading to bee and butterfly garden.

4 ASHLEIGH GRANGE
Off Chapel Lane, Westhumble,
RH5 6AY. Angela & Clive
Gilchrist, 01306 884613,
ar.gilchrist@btinternet.com. *2m N of
Dorking. From A24 at Boxhill/Burford
Bridge follow signs to Westhumble.
Through village & L up drive by
ruined chapel (1m from A24). Sorry
no access for coaches.* **Evening
opening Fri 14 June (5.30-8). Adm
£10, chd free. Wine. Visits also by
arrangement May to July.**
Plant lover's chalk garden on 3½
acre sloping site in charming rural
setting with delightful views. Many
areas of interest inc rockery and water
feature, raised ericaceous bed, prairie
style bank, foliage plants, woodland
walk, fernery and folly. Large mixed
herbaceous and shrub borders
planted for dry alkaline soil and
widespread interest.

5 15 THE AVENUE
Cheam, Sutton, SM2 7QA. Jan &
Nigel Brandon, 020 8643 8686,
janmbrandon@outlook.com. *1m
SW of Sutton. By car: exit A217 onto
Northey Av, 2nd R into The Ave. By
train: 10 min walk from Cheam Stn.
By bus: use 470. Not in ULEZ.* **Visits
by arrangement 1 June to 14 July
for groups of 10 to 50. Adm £10,
chd £3. Light refreshments.**
A contemporary garden designed by
RHS Chelsea Gold Medal Winner,
Marcus Barnett. Four levels divided
into rooms by beech hedging and
columns: formal entertaining area,
contemporary outdoor room, lawn
and wildflower meadow. Over 100
hostas hug the house. Silver birch,
cloud pruned box, ferns, grasses,
tall bearded irises, contemporary
sculptures. Partial wheelchair access,
terraced with steps; sloping path
provides view of whole garden.

6 BRIDGE END COTTAGE
Ockham Lane, Ockham,
GU23 6NR. Clare & Peter
Bevan, 07956 307546,
clare.bevan@ngs.org.uk,
www.bridgeendcottage.co.uk.
*Nr RHS Garden Wisley. At Wisley
r'about turn L onto B2039 to
Ockham/Horsley. After ½ m turn
L into Ockham Ln. House ½ m on*
R. From Cobham go to Blackswan
Xrds. **Sat 1 June (10-5). Adm £6,
chd free. Home-made teas in
the garden room. Visits also by
arrangement 13 May to 31 July for
groups of 10 to 25.**
A 2 acre country garden with different
areas of interest inc perennial borders,
mature trees, pond and streams,
small herb parterre, fruit trees and
a colourful vegetable patch. An
adjacent 2 acre field was sown with
perennial wildflower seed in May 2013
and has flowered each summer since.
There is a lot of interest and much to
be enjoyed in this garden.

7 CAXTON HOUSE
67 West Street, Reigate, RH2 9DA.
Bob Bushby, 07836 201740,
bob.bushby@sky.com. *On A25
towards Dorking, approx ¼ m W
of Reigate. Parking on road or past
Black Horse on Flanchford Rd.* **Visits
by arrangement 8 Apr to 31 Aug
for groups of 10 to 40. Adm £10,
chd free. Light refreshments inc.**
Lovely large spring garden with
arboretum, two well-stocked
ponds, large collection of hellebores
and spring flowers. Pots planted
with colourful displays, plants.
Small Gothic Folly built by owner.
Herbaceous borders with grasses,
perennials and spring bulbs, parterre,
bed with wild daffodils and prairie
style planting in summer, and new
wildflower garden in arboretum.
Wheelchair access to most parts of
the garden. Dogs on leads please.

8 CHAUFFEUR'S FLAT
Tandridge Lane, Tandridge,
RH8 9NJ. Mr & Mrs Richins. *2m E
of Godstone. 2m W of Oxted. Turn
off A25 at r'about for Tandridge. Take
2nd drive on L past church. Follow
arrows to circular courtyard. Do not
use Jackass Ln even if your SatNav
tells you to do so.* **Daily Mon 13
May to Sun 19 May (10-5). Adm
£5, chd free. Home-made teas
(Sat 18 & Sun 19 May only).**
Enter a 1½ acre tapestry of magical
secret gardens with magnificent
views. Touching the senses, all sure
footed visitors may explore the many
surprises on this constantly evolving,
exuberant escape from reality.
Imaginative use of recycled materials
creates an inspired variety of ideas,
while wild and specimen plants reveal
an ecological haven.

9 CHILWORTH MANOR

Halfpenny Lane, Chilworth, Guildford, GU4 8NN. Mia & Graham Wrigley, www. chilworthmanorsurrey.com. *3½ m SE of Guildford. From centre of Chilworth village turn into Blacksmith Ln. 1st drive on R on Halfpenny Ln.* **Sun 19 May (11-5). Adm £7.50, chd free. Pre-booking essential, please visit www.ngs.org.uk for information & booking. Home-made teas.**
The grounds of the C17 Chilworth Manor create a wonderful tapestry, a jewel of an C18 terraced walled garden, topiary, herbaceous borders, sculptures, mature trees and stew ponds that date back a 1000 yrs. A fabulous, peaceful garden for all the family to wander and explore or just to relax and enjoy! Perhaps our many visitors describe it best, 'Magical', 'a sheer delight', 'elegant and tranquil', 'a little piece of heaven', 'spiffing!'. There will be a garden or tree talk at 12.15pm, 1.15pm and 3.15pm. Sorry, dogs are not allowed.
🍵 ᵔ))

10 2 CHINTHURST LODGE

Wonersh Common, Wonersh, Guildford, GU5 0PR. Mr & Mrs M R Goodridge, 01483 535108, michaelgoodridge@ymail.com. *4m S of Guildford. From A281 at Shalford turn E onto B2128 towards Wonersh. Just after Waverley sign, before village, garden on R, via stable entrance opp Little Tangley. No parking for coaches on site.* **Visits by arrangement 1 May to 15 July for groups of 10 to 40. Adm £6, chd free. Home-made teas.**
1 acre enthusiast's atmospheric and tranquil garden divided into rooms with year-round interest. Herbaceous borders, dramatic white garden, specimen trees and shrubs, gravel garden with new water feature, small kitchen garden, fruit cage, two wells, ornamental ponds, herb parterre and millennium rose, iris and hollyhock garden. Wheelchair access with some avoidable gravel paths.
♿ ✿ 🚗 🍵

11 NEW CLARIDGE HOUSE

Dormans Road, Dormansland, Lingfield, RH7 6QH. Meredith Wood, 01342 832150, welcome@claridgehouse.org. uk, www.claridgehouse.org.uk. *From Racecourse Rd, veer R onto Dormans Rd, and follow yellow signs. Claridge House is clearly signed.* **Wed 15, Thur 16, Fri 17, Sat 18 May (11-4). Adm £5, chd free. Visits also by arrangement 15 May to 18 May for groups of 6 to 30. Bookings must be made a min two weeks in advance.**
An established 2 acre woodland garden with a variety of specimen trees and a woodland walk. Two wildflower meadows as well as more formal beds, with many benches to stop for a minute and enjoy. We are as sustainable as possible, using compost created from the Retreat food waste and no pesticides to support nature. We have beehives, bats, hedgehogs and butterflies. Our natural pond has dragonflies, mayflies and newts. Children must be accompanied and supervised. Dogs on leads only. Partial wheelchair access on paths to the formal garden.
♿ ᵔ))

12 COBBETTS CORNER

Tilford, Farnham, GU10 2AJ. Mr Nicholas Faulkner. *3m SE of Farnham. From Farnham take the B3001 towards Elstead, or go through Tilford. Cobbetts Corner is on the corner of Tilford St & Charles Hill (B3001). 2m from Elstead & A3.* **Sat 1 June (2-5.30). Adm £5, chd free. Cream teas.**
Cobbetts Corner has a garden for the owner to relax in, away from the busy world of work. It features colourful borders with minimal maintenance, a productive vegetable garden and greenhouse. It is also home for the owner's chickens together with a pond providing an oasis for wildlife. With a wildflower meadow, the garden is continually evolving to encourage eco diversity.
♿ 🍵 ᵔ))

13 COLDHARBOUR HOUSE

Coldharbour Lane, Bletchingley, Redhill, RH1 4NA. Mr Tony Elias, 01883 742685, eliastony@hotmail.com. *Coldharbour Ln off Rabies Heath Rd, ½ m from A25 at Bletchingley & 1m from Tilburstow Hill Rd. Parking at the house for up to 20 cars.* **Visits by arrangement Apr to Oct for groups of 10+. Adm £8, chd free. Coffee or tea & a slice of something sweet inc.**
This 1½ acre garden offers breathtaking views to the South Downs. Originally planted in the 1920s, it has since been adapted and enhanced. Several mature trees and shrubs inc a copper beech, a

Canadian maple, magnolias, azaleas, rhododendrons, camellias, wisterias, *Berberis* 'Georgei', *Vitex agnus-castus*, fuchsias, hibiscus, potentillas, mahonias, a fig tree and a walnut tree.
🍵

14 NEW COURT LODGE FARM

Church Lane, Bletchingley, Redhill, RH1 4LP. Mr Richard Miles. *Off main A25 in Bletchingley High St. Opp the church, in Church Ln.* **Sat 24 Feb (12-3.30). Adm £5, chd free.**
Beautiful 3 acre woodland garden. Wander at leisure through massed snowdrops and enjoy the serenity of this peaceful location. Refreshments available in the village.
🍵 ᵔ))

15 COVERWOOD LAKES

Peaslake Road, Ewhurst, GU6 7NT. The Metson Family, 01306 731101, farm@coverwoodlakes.co.uk, www.coverwoodlakes.co.uk. *7m SW of Dorking. From A25 follow signs for Peaslake; garden ½ m beyond Peaslake on Ewhurst Rd.* **Sun 7, Sun 14, Sun 21 Apr, Sun 12 May, Sun 20 Oct (11-5). Adm £7, chd free. Light refreshments. Visits also by arrangement 8 Apr to 30 Sept for groups of 20+.**
14 acre landscaped garden in stunning position high in the Surrey Hills with four lakes and bog garden. Extensive rhododendrons, azaleas and fine trees. 3½ acre lakeside arboretum. Marked trail through the 180 acre working farm with Hereford cows and calves, sheep and horses, extensive views of the surrounding hills. Light refreshments inc home produced beef and lamb burgers, gourmet coffee and home-made cakes from the Fillet & Bean Cafe (outdoor mobile kitchen). Sorry, dogs are not allowed.
♿ 🚗 🍵 ᵔ))

16 CROSSWATER FARM

Crosswater Lane, Churt, Farnham, GU10 2JN. David & Susanna Millais, www.rhododendrons.co.uk. *6m S of Farnham, 6m NW of Haslemere. From A287 turn E into Jumps Rd ½ m N of Churt village centre. After ¼ m turn acute L into Crosswater Ln & follow signs for Millais Nurseries.* **Every Tue to Sat 1 May to 7 June (2-4). Adm £6, chd free. Tea & coffee.**
Idyllic 5 acre woodland garden. Plantsman's collection of rhododendrons and azaleas inc rare species collected in the Himalayas

Milton Way House

and hybrids raised by the family. Everything from alpine dwarfs to architectural large leaved trees. Ponds, stream and companion plantings inc sorbus, magnolias and Japanese acers, and many recent new plantings. Woodland garden and specialist rhododendron, azalea and magnolia plant centre. Grass paths may be difficult for wheelchairs after rain.

  ♿ ❀ 🚗 ☕ ⛺))

 17 ♦ DUNSBOROUGH PARK
Ripley, GU23 6AL. Baron & Baroness Sweerts de Landas Wyborgh. *6m NE of Guildford. Entrance via Newark Ln, Ripley, through Tudor-style gatehouses & courtyard up drive. Car park signed. For SatNav use GU23 6BZ.* **For NGS: Sun 14 Apr (11-4). Adm £9, chd free. Pre-booking essential, please visit www.dunsboroughpark.com for information & booking. For queries only, please email events@ dunsboroughpark.com. Charity teas for sale.**
6 acre garden redesigned by Penelope Hobhouse and Rupert

Golby. Garden rooms, lush herbaceous borders, standard wisteria, 70ft ginkgo hedge, potager and 300 yr old mulberry tree. Rose Walk, Italian Garden and Water Garden with folly bridge. Highlights in April's Tulip Festival inc formal borders and a spectacular colourful informal display in the meadow. Wheelchair access over gravel paths and grass, cobbled over folly bridge.

  ♿ ❀ 🚗 ☕ ⛺

GROUP OPENING

 18 FAIRMILE COMMON GARDENS
Portsmouth Road, Cobham, KT11 1BG. *2m NE of Cobham. On A307 Esher to Cobham Rd next to free car park by A3 bridge, at entrance to Waterford Cl.* **Mon 27 May (2-5). Combined adm £12, chd free. Home-made teas at Fairmile Lea.**

23 FAIRACRES
Miranda Filkins.

FAIRMILE LEA
Steven Kay.

MOLESHILL HOUSE
Penny Snell.
(See separate entry)

 SELWORTHY
Steve & Natalie Green.

Four contrasting gardens inc many mature specimen trees. One with new water feature surrounding oak room (not open), vegetables and potager. Another large garden with a castle folly alongside a new and extensive natural pond, sanctuary garden, triffid bed and wilderness mound. The third, a romantic, naturalistic garden on the wild side, much photographed and published. Original features to inspire. New this year is an immaculately maintained plantaholic's family garden. Velvet lawns and colourful borders. Plants for sale at Moleshill House.

❀ ☕))

19 THE GARTH PLEASURE GROUNDS

The Garth, Newchapel Road, Lingfield, RH7 6BJ. Mr Sherlock & Mrs Stanley, hello@thegarth.info, www.thegarth.info. *From A22 take B2028 by the Mormon Temple to Lingfield. The Garth is on the L after 1½m, opp Barge Tiles. Parking: Gun Pit Rd in Lingfield & limited space for disabled at Barge Tiles.* **Sun 5, Sun 12 May (1-5). Adm £8, chd free. Home-made teas. Visits also by arrangement 6 May to 1 Oct for groups of 10 to 40. Bookings must be made via email a min two weeks in advance.**
Mature 9 acre Pleasure Grounds created by Walter Godfrey in 1919, present an idyllic setting surrounding the former parish workhouse refurbished in Edwardian style. The formal gardens, enchanting nuttery, a spinney with many mature trees and a pond attract wildlife. Wonderful bluebells in spring. The woodland gardens and beautiful borders are full of colour and fragrance for year-round pleasure. Many ideas of interest, and large specimen plants inc ancient oak. Picnics are welcome. Wheelchair access to most areas of the garden.

                                        ⧗ 🐑 ❄ 🚗 🛏 ☕ ⛍))

20 ◆ GATTON PARK

Reigate, RH2 0TW. Royal Alexandra & Albert School. *3m NE of Reigate. Entrance off Rocky Ln at main gate of Royal Alexandra & Albert School.* **For NGS: Sun 11 Feb (12-5). Adm £7.50, chd free. Pre-booking preferred, please visit www.gattonpark.co.uk, email events@gatton-park.org.uk or phone 01737 649068 for information & booking. Light refreshments. For other opening times and information, please phone, email or visit garden website.**
Historic 260 acre estate in the Surrey Hills AONB. Capability Brown parkland with ancient oaks. Discover the Japanese garden, Victorian parterre and breathtaking views over the lake. Seasonal highlights inc displays of snowdrops and aconites in Feb. Ongoing restoration projects by the Gatton Trust. Bird hide open to see herons nesting. Free guided tours. A selection of hot and cold drinks, cakes and snacks. Plants for winter interest for sale. Adm: Adults £6.50 pre-book tickets only (£7.50 on the day).

🐑 ❄ 🚗 ☕

Court Lodge Farm

21 21 GLENAVON CLOSE

Claygate, Esher, KT10 0HP. Selina & Simon Botham. *2m SE of Esher. From A3 S exit Esher, R at T-lights. Continue straight through Claygate village, bear R at 2 mini r'abouts. Past church & rec. Turn L at bollards into Causeway. At end straight over to Glenavon Cl.* **Sun 15 Sept (1.30-5.30). Adm £5, chd free. Home-made teas.**

An oasis of plants, natural sculptures and water features created for year-round interest by RHS award-winning garden designer, Selina Botham. The garden, as featured on BBC Gardeners' World, showcases how to design an awkward shaped plot to create a space that can be enjoyed by wildlife and people alike! The garden features an outdoor bath, a pond, water features and a river of naturalistic planting. Free tours by the designer start at 2pm and 3pm alongside a display of design work in her garden studio.

22 GRACE & FLAVOUR CIC

Ripley Lane, West Horsley, Leatherhead, KT24 6JW. Dr Gerard Robbins, www.graceandflavour.org. *Approx halfway between Guildford & Leatherhead, just off the A246. At r'about on A246 in West Horsley, turn L (signed West Horsley & Ripley) into The Street. Follow road for 1/3m. Turn L into Ripley Ln. Garden is 1/3m on L, immed after BUPA Nursing Home.* **Sun 4 Aug (1-4). Adm £5, chd free. Home-made teas.**

Grace & Flavour is a community kitchen garden and 28 allotments. In 2009 it took over a derelict 3 acre walled garden and orchard, part of NT's Hatchlands Estate. It features vegetable beds, soft fruit cages, polytunnels, fruit tree avenue with lavender borders, cut flower beds, wildlife area and pond. It is free of chemicals and pesticides, and has a no dig policy. Wheelchair access to main paths, but not the uneven side paths.

23 HALL GROVE SCHOOL

London Road (A30), Bagshot, GU19 5HZ. Mr & Mrs Graham. *6m SW of Egham. M3 J3, follow A322 1m until sign for Sunningdale A30, 1m E of Bagshot, opp Longacres Garden Centre, entrance at footbridge. Ample car parking.* **Sat 18 May, Sat 28 Sept (2-5). Adm**

£5, chd free. Home-made teas. Formerly a small Georgian country estate, now a co-educational preparatory school. Grade II listed house (not open). Mature parkland with specimen trees. Historical features inc ice house and a recently restored walled kitchen garden with flower borders, fruit and children's vegetable plots. There is also a lake, woodland walks, rhododendrons, azaleas and acers. Live music at 3pm.

24 HARRY EDWARDS HEALING SANCTUARY

Hook Lane, Burrows Lea, Shere, Guildford, GU5 9QG. The Harry Edwards Healing Sanctuary, 01483 202054, alison.mcwhinnie@burrowslea.org.uk, www.harryedwardshealingsanctuary.org.uk. *Close to Shere & Gomshall. From the A25 take the turning to Shere Village & drive through the village. Cross over the railway bridge & turn L into Hook Ln. The Sanctuary is on the R & is clearly signed.* **Sat 11 May, Sun 6 Oct (11-5). Adm £6, chd free. Light refreshments.**

A place of serenity and peace nestled within the Surrey Hills, set in 30 acres of beautiful grounds that inc paddocks, bluebell woods, a rose garden with pond and waterfall, a meditation glade and labyrinth. Spend a while sitting on Cherry Tree Walk and enjoy the stunning Surrey Hills views.

25 ◆ HATCHLANDS PARK

East Clandon, Guildford, GU4 7RT. National Trust, 01483 222482, hatchlands@nationaltrust.org.uk, www.nationaltrust.org.uk/hatchlands-park. *4m E of Guildford. Follow brown signs to Hatchlands Park (NT).* **For NGS: Sun 21 Apr (10-5). Adm £11, chd £5.50. Adm charges subject to change. For other opening times and information, please phone, email or visit garden website.**

Garden and park designed by Repton in 1800. Follow one of the park walks to the stunning bluebell wood in spring (2 1/2 km round walk over rough and sometimes muddy ground). Partial wheelchair access to parkland with rough and undulating terrain, tracks and cobbled courtyard. Mobility scooter booking essential.

26 HEATHSIDE

10 Links Green Way, Cobham, KT11 2QH. Miss Margaret Arnott & Mr Terry Bartholomew, 01372 842459, m.a.arnott@btinternet.com. *1 1/2m E of Cobham. Through Cobham A245, 4th L after Esso garage into Fairmile Ln. Straight on into Water Ln. Links Green Way 3rd turning on L.* **Visits by arrangement. Morning coffee, afternoon tea, or wine & canapés.**

Terraced plants persons garden, designed for year-round interest. Gorgeous planting all set off by harmonious landscaping. Many urns and pots give seasonal displays. Several water features add tranquil sound. Stunning colour combinations excite. Dahlias and begonias a favourite. Beautiful Griffin Glasshouse housing the exotic. Many inspirational ideas. Situated 5 miles from RHS Garden Wisley.

27 HIGH CLANDON ESTATE VINEYARD

High Clandon, East Clandon, GU4 7RP. Sibylla & Bruce Tindale, www.highclandon.co.uk. *A3/Wisley junction, L for Ockham/Horsley for 2m to A246. R for Guildford for 2m, then 100yds past landmark Hatchlands NT, turn L into Blakes Ln, straight uphill through gates High Clandon to vineyard entrance. Extensive parking in our woodland area.* **Sun 7 July (11-4.30). Adm £7.50, chd free. Pre-booking preferred. Cream teas & home-made cakes. Gold awarded English sparkling wine available by the glass & bottle.**

Multi-gold award-winning English sparkling wine vineyard with gardens, 1 acre wildflower meadow with rare butterflies, water features, Japanese garden, truffière, apiary and sculptures. All set in 12 acres of beautiful Surrey Hills, AONB with great vistas and panoramic views to London. Twice winner Cellar Door of Year. Art and Sculptures exhibition with over 180 works of art on show. Pond usually has wild Mallard ducks and ducklings at this time of the year. Access is good; all garden paths are lawns on firm ground based on hard chalky substrate.

28 [NEW] ICHI-COO PARK

Russ Hill Farm, Russ Hill, Charlwood, RH6 0EL. Robin Redmile-Gordon, 07710 045647, robinrgok@gmail.com. *5m E of Gatwick Airport. From A23 N from Gatwick, or A23 S from Horley, or A217 S from Reigate, arrive at Longbridge r'about. Take exit heading E, signed Charlwood. Stay on road all the way.* **Sun 26 May (11-6). Adm £15. Wine. Visits also by arrangement 5 May to 29 Sept for groups of 50 to 99.**
Ichi-Coo Park is unlike any garden you've ever visited. It glories in shapes and shades of green, layered into the hillside, painted onto the natural background of the Sussex Weald. It is an eclectic collection of plants, trees and water, spaces, forms and vistas, habitats and sanctuaries. A place for reflection, for relaxation, oh and a plane spotter's dream.

29 2 KNOTT PARK HOUSE

Wrens Hill, Oxshott, Leatherhead, KT22 0HW. Joanna Nixon. *10 mins from Oxshott village centre. From A244, which is off the A3, or S from Leatherhead take Wrens Hill, next to Bear Pub, continue c200 metres, take R fork, part of 1st big house on L.* **Fri 17, Sat 18 May (10-2). Adm £5, chd free. Light refreshments.**
A south facing terrace with far-reaching views is planted as a bee garden. Steps lead down to a lower area extending to ¼ acre. Wildlife friendly and maintained without pesticides. On four levels, it features pollinator loving plants, trees and shrubs. These inc irises, alliums, sedums, salvias, and many medicinal plants and herbs.

30 KNOWLE GRANGE

Hound House Road, Shere, Guildford, GU5 9JH. Mr P R & Mrs M E Wood. *8m S of Guildford. From Shere (off A25), through village for ¾ m. After railway bridge, continue 1½ m past Hound House on R (stone dogs on gateposts). After 100yds turn R at Knowle Grange sign, go to end of lane.* **Sun 19 May (11-4.30). Adm £7, chd free. Home-made teas on front lawn.**
80 acres undulating landscape. 7 acre gardens. New features recently added. Small knot garden. Double herbaceous border. About seven various garden rooms with French, Japanese and English inspiration. A new clock

tower garden. The one mile bluebell valley unicursal path which snakes through two valleys and a hill, and inc the labyrinth upon a labyrinth. Deep unfenced pools, high unfenced drops.

31 LEIGH PLACE

Leigh Place Lane, Godstone, RH9 8BN. Mike & Liz McGhee. *Take B2236 Eastbourne Rd from Godstone Village. Turn 2nd L onto Church Ln. Follow parking directions.* **Sat 8, Sun 9 June (10-4). Adm £5, chd free. Home-made teas.**
Leigh Place garden has 25 acres on greensand. Part of the Godstone Ponds with SSSI, lakeside paths, walled garden inc cutting garden, orchard and vegetable quadrant with greenhouses. Orchard, beehives and large rock garden. Features inc Edwardian apple arch and historic wisteria. The walled garden has Breedon gravel paths suitable for wheelchairs and pushchairs. Well behaved dogs welcome on leads.

32 LITTLE ORCHARDS

Prince Of Wales Road, Outwood, Redhill, RH1 5QU. Nic Howard, www.instagram.com/nichoward. *A few hundred metres N of the Dog & Duck Pub.* **Fri 31 May, Sun 2 June, Fri 6, Sun 8 Sept (12-4). Adm £6, chd free. Home-made teas.**
A magical, artistic, plantsman's paradise planted for year-round interest using a tapestry of foliage as well as flower interest. The garden is arranged as a series of connected areas that flow between two properties, the old gardener's cottage, and the old stables. Often compared to a mini Petersham Nursery by our visitors; we have a gift shop selling garden paraphernalia and a lovely café area.

33 [NEW] LOGMORE PLACE

Logmore Lane, Westcott, Dorking, RH4 3JN. Jane Clarke. *In between Westcott & Coldharbour. From A25 past the church, turn L into Logmore Ln & Logmore Place is approx ½ m on the R next to Florents Farm. Off road parking in sloping field. Disabled parking in front of house only.* **Sun 9 June (11-4). Adm £7.50, chd free. Light refreshments.**
Established trees, rhododendrons and yew hedges create a framework for the far-reaching views of the Surrey Hills. Small Japanese garden,

walled flower garden, orchard, plus two formal lawns featuring Piet Udolf inspired beds. Walks on the estate inc field tracks, lake with bridges, quiet ancient woodland and stunning views to Ranmore from the trig point. Wheelchair access to terrace and views only. Gravel paths, steps and sloping grass paths to rest of site.

34 ♦ LOSELEY PARK

Guildford, GU3 1HS. Mr & Mrs A G More-Molyneux, 01483 304440/405112, pa@loseleypark.co.uk, www.loseleypark.co.uk. *4m SW of Guildford. For SatNav please use GU3 1HS, Stakescorner Ln.* **For NGS: Sun 16 June (10-4). Adm by donation. Light refreshments in the tea hut in the White Garden. For other opening times and information, please phone, email or visit garden website.**
Delightful 2½ acre walled garden. Award-winning rose garden (over 1000 bushes, mainly old fashioned varieties), extensive herb garden, fruit and flower garden, white garden with fountain and spectacular organic vegetable garden. Magnificent vine walk, herbaceous borders, moat walk, ancient wisteria and mulberry trees.

35 LOWER HOUSE

Bowlhead Green, Godalming, GU8 6NW. Georgina Harvey, 07710 797698, georgina@gharvey.co.uk. *1m from A3 Thursley/Bowlhead Green junction. Using A286 leave at Brook (6m from Haslemere & 3m from Milford). Follow Bowlhead Green & NGS signs for approx 2m. Good parking in field at the property.* **Thur 25 Apr (10.30-5); Sun 28 Apr (1-5). Adm £7, chd free. Home-made teas. Visits also by arrangement 24 Apr to 14 June for groups of 25+.**
Established trees and shrubs shape the layout of the garden creating stunning vistas and quiet areas. Azaleas, rhododendrons, camellias and magnolias are followed by roses to continue the colour until the herbaceous plants bloom. The white topiary garden with fish pond brings calm and the kitchen garden, greenhouses, orchard and fruit cage bring seasonal changes. Alternative routes to avoid steps for wheelchair users and some narrow paths.

36 THE MANOR HOUSE
Three Gates Lane, Haslemere,
GU27 2ES. Mr & Mrs Gerard Ralfe.
NE of Haslemere. From Haslemere
centre take A286 towards Milford.
Turn R after Museum into Three
Gates Ln. At T-Junction turn R into
Holdfast Ln. Car park on R. **Sun 23**
June (10-5). Adm £5, chd free.
Home-made teas.
Described by Country Life as 'The
Hanging Gardens of Haslemere',
the well established Manor House
gardens are tucked away in a valley
of the Surrey Hills. Set in 6 acres, it
was one of Surrey's inaugural NGS
gardens with fine views, an impressive
show of azaleas, wisteria, beautiful
trees underplanted with bulbs,
enchanting water gardens and a
magnificent rose garden.

37 NEW **MILTON WAY HOUSE**
Guildford Road, Westcott,
Dorking, RH4 3PZ. Ingrid Andree
Wiltens. *2m E of Dorking. Access to*
& from the site is from the A25. The
lane is assisted by CCTV to provide
visibility around a blind corner. On
exit L turns only are recommended.
Parking is limited. **Sat 15 June (11-**
4.30). Adm £5.50, chd free. Pre-
booking essential, please visit
www.ngs.org.uk for information
& booking. Timed slots at 11am,
1pm & 3pm. Home-made teas.
A relatively new garden set in the
beautiful Surrey Hills on a sloping
site surrounded by mature trees. For
a small country garden, being just
shy of an acre, it has a wide range of
spaces, inc a lush and green walled
garden, social area where teas will
be available, a vegetable patch,
woodland area and a formal lawn
surrounded by mixed borders of
perennials, grasses and shrubs.

South Wind

38 NEW ▶ MOLE END

10 Farm Lane, Send, Woking, GU23 7AT. Mrs Pat Hutchings, 07810 461144, farm.lane@btinternet.com. *Pass Send Recreation Ground on Sandy Ln, turn L into Farm Ln.* **Visits by arrangement 15 Aug to 15 Sept for groups of 5 to 10. Adm £5, chd free. Tea.**
A tranquil and meditative garden with architectural/jungle planting style that comes to its best in late summer. Lush, bold foliage, striking contrasts and showy specimen plants reflect the owner's love for the unusual. Lots of little quirky creatures are hidden around two ponds in a playful way for visitors to discover.

39 MOLESHILL HOUSE

The Fairmile, Cobham, KT11 1BG. Penny Snell, pennysnellflowers@ btinternet.com, www.pennysnellflowers.co.uk. *2m NE of Cobham. On A307 Esher to Cobham Rd next to free car park by A3 bridge, at entrance to Waterford Cl.* **Mon 1 Apr (2-5). Adm £5, chd free. Light refreshments. Opening with Fairmile Common Gardens on Mon 27 May. Visits also by arrangement Apr to Sept for groups of 10 to 40.**
Romantic disarray. Naturalistic garden on the wild side. Short woodland path leads from dovecote to beehives. Informal planting contrasts with formal topiary, box and garlanded cisterns. Colourful courtyard, conservatory, pond with fountain, pleached avenue, circular gravel garden, gipsy caravan garden, green wall and stumpery. Espaliered crab apples. Chickens and bees. Garden 5 mins from Claremont Landscape Garden, Painshill Park and Wisley, also adjacent to excellent dog walking woods.

40 MONKS LANTERN

Ruxbury Road, Chertsey, KT16 9NH. Mr & Mrs J Granell. *1m NW from Chertsey. M25 J11, signed A320/ Woking. At r'about take 2nd exit A320/ Staines, straight over next r'about. L onto Holloway Hill, R Hardwick La. ½ m, R over motorway bridge, on Almners then Ruxbury Rd.* **Sat 25 May (2-5.30). Adm £6, chd free.**
A delightful garden with borders arranged with colour in mind; silvers and white, olive trees blend together with nicotiana and senecio.

A weeping silver birch leads to the oranges and yellows of a tropical bed with large bottle brush, hardy palms and *Fatsia japonica*. Large rockery and an informal pond. There is a display of hostas, *Cytisus battandieri* and a selection of grasses in an island bed. Aviary with small finches. Workshop with handmade guitars, and paintings. Pond with ornamental ducks and fish. Music and wine. Wheelchairs welcome; two reserved parking spaces at entrance to garden, as gravel drive is not easy.

41 THE NUTRITION GARDEN

156A Frimley Green Road, Frimley Green, Camberley, GU16 6NA. Dr Trevor George RNutr, 07914 917110, t-george@hotmail.co.uk. *2m (5 mins) from J4 of the M3. From M3, follow signs for A331 towards Farnborough, then follow signs to Frimley Green (B3411). The house is down a long drive with telegraph poles at each end, almost opp the recreation ground.* **Visits by arrangement 1 July to 1 Sept for groups of up to 20. Guided tour of the garden and explanation of the plants inc. Adm £5, chd free. Light refreshments.**
A garden designed by a registered nutritionist to produce and display a wide variety of edible plants inc fruits, vegetables, herbs, and plants for infusions. There are trees, shrubs, tubers, perennials and annual plants. Over 100 types of edible plants and over 200 varieties are grown throughout the yr. These inc unusual food plants, heritage varieties and unusual coloured varieties. Tea, coffee, light refreshments and infusions from plants growing in the garden also available. Wheelchair access on paved paths around fruit and vegetable beds. Other areas are step free around uneven grass lawn.

42 OAKLANDS

Eastbourne Road, Blindley Heath, Lingfield, RH7 6LG. Joy & Justin Greasley, 01342 837369, joy@greasley.me.uk. *S of Blindley Heath Village. From M25 take A22 to East Grinstead. Go straight on at Blindley Heath T-lights & after 800yds take sign on L to Nestledown Boarding Kennels. Oaklands is down the lane on the LHS. Limited parking.* **Visits by arrangement July & Aug for groups of 8 to 35. Adm £5, chd free.**

Nestling in woodland, this ½ acre garden has been imaginatively designed from scratch by the enthusiastic owners. There are many areas to enjoy inc Koi pond and bridge, 40 metre curved pergola with climbing plants and hanging baskets, mature specimen trees, large planted pots, folly and colourful herbaceous borders. Many hidden extras to discover and plentiful seating. Level wheelchair access on paths to main features.

43 THE OLD RECTORY

Sandy Lane, Brewer Street, Bletchingley, RH1 4QW. Mr & Mrs A Procter. *Top of village nr The Red Lion pub, turn R into Little Common Ln, then R at Cross Rd into Sandy Ln. Parking nr house, disabled parking in courtyard.* **Sun 9 June (11-4). Adm £5, chd free. Home-made teas.**
Georgian Manor House (not open). Quintessential Italianate topiary garden, statuary, box parterres, courtyard with columns, water features and antique terracotta pots. Much of the 4 acre garden is the subject of ongoing reclamation inc the ancient moat and woodland with fine specimen trees and one of the largest tulip trees in the country. New sunken water garden and tropical garden. Wheelchair access with gravel paths.

44 THE OLD VICARAGE

The Street, Frensham, Farnham, GU10 3DU. Kate Smith, smithkrdr@me.com, www.instagram. com/katesmithgardendesign. *3m S of Farnham, 4m N of Hindhead. Turn off A287 Farnham to Hindhead road at small village green at St Mary's School. Travel along The Street for ½ m, the Old Vicarage is on the RHS, next to St Mary's Church.* **Sat 8 June (10.30-2.30); Sun 9 June (2-5.30). Adm £6, chd free. Home-made teas. Visits also by arrangement 20 May to 16 June for groups of 20 to 40.**
12 acres of garden surrounding the Old Vicarage in Frensham. The garden consists of 2 acres of herbaceous borders and lawns adjacent to the house. Steep slopes lead to the less formal grounds with large pond and the River Wey. Mown paths cut through the water meadows and small woodland.

45 PRATSHAM GRANGE
Tanhurst Lane, Holmbury St Mary, RH5 6LZ. Alan & Felicity Comber. *12m SE of Guildford, 8m SW of Dorking. From A25 take B2126, after 4m turn L into Tanhurst Ln. From A29 take B2126, before Forest Green turn R on B2126 then 1st R to Tanhurst Ln.* **Sun 18 Aug (12.30-5). Adm £6, chd free. Tea.**
5 acre garden overlooked by Holmbury Hill and Leith Hill. Features inc two ponds joined by cascading stream, extensive scented rose and blue hydrangea beds. Also, herbaceous borders, cutting flower garden and two white beds. Partial wheelchair access with some steps, steep slopes (slippery when wet) and gravel paths. Deep ponds and a drop from terrace.

&. ✿ 🍵 ⏺)

46 ◆ RAMSTER
Chiddingfold, GU8 4SN. Mrs Rosie Glaister, 01428 654167, office@ramsterhall.com, www.ramsterevents.com. *12m S of Guildford. Ramster is on A283 1½ m S of Chiddingfold, large iron gates, the entrance is signed from the main road.* **For NGS: Fri 17 May (10-5). Adm £9, chd £3. Light refreshments. For other opening times and information, please phone, email or visit garden website.**
A stunning, mature woodland garden set in over 20 acres, famous for its rhododendron and azalea collection, and its carpets of bluebells in spring. Enjoy a peaceful wander down the grass paths and woodland walk, explore the bog garden with its stepping stones, or relax in the tranquil enclosed tennis court garden. The teahouse, by the entrance to the garden is open every day while the garden is open, serving locally roasted coffee, delicious cakes and fresh sandwiches, home-made quiches and soup. Sculpture Exhibition runs in May. Regional Finalist, The English Garden Magazine's The Nation's Favourite Gardens 2023. Wheelchair access to the Tea House and some paths in the garden.

&. 🐕 ✿ 🚗 🍵 ⏺)

47 ◆ THE SCULPTURE PARK
Tilford Road, Churt, Farnham, GU10 2LB. Eddie Powell, 01428 605453, sian@thesculpturepark.com, www.thesculpturepark.com. *Corner of Jumps & Tilford Rd, Churt.*

Directly opp Bell & The Dragon pub. Use our car park or park in the pub, where refreshments are available. **For NGS: Tue 16 Apr, Tue 11 June (10-5). Adm £10, chd £5. Pre-booking essential, please visit www.ngs.org.uk for information & booking. For other opening times and information, please phone, email or visit garden website.**
This garden sculpture exhibition is set within an enchanting arboretum and wildlife inhabited water garden. You should set aside between 2-4 hrs for your visit as there are 2 miles of trail within 10 acres. Our displays evolve and diversify as the seasons pass with vivid and lush colours of the rhododendrons in May and June, to the enchanting frost in the depths of winter. Approx one third of The Sculpture Park is accessible to wheelchairs. Disabled WC.

&. 🐕 🍵 🧺 ⏺)

48 SHAMLEY WOOD ESTATE
Woodhill Lane, Shamley Green, Guildford, GU5 0SP. Mrs Claire Merriman, 07595 693132, claire@merriman.co.uk. *5m (15 mins) S of Guildford in village of Shamley Green. Entrance is approx ¼ m up Woodhill Ln from centre of Shamley Green.* **Visits by arrangement Mar to Nov. Adm £8, chd free. Teas with gluten free options.**
A relative newcomer, this garden is worth visiting just for the setting! Sitting high on the North Downs, the garden enjoys beautiful views of the South Downs and is approached through a 10 acre deer park. Set within approx 3 acres, there is a large pond and established rose garden. More recent additions inc fire pits, vegetable patch, stream, tropical pergola and terraced wildflower lawn. Wheelchair access to most of garden. Step to access ground level WC.

&. 🐕 🚗 🍵 ⏺)

49 41 SHELVERS WAY
Tadworth, KT20 5QJ. Keith & Elizabeth Lewis, 01737 210707, kandelewis@ntlworld.com. *6m S of Sutton off A217. 1st turning on R after Burgh Heath T-lights heading S on A217. 400yds down Shelvers Way on L.* **Sun 21 Apr, Sun 4 Aug (2-5.30). Adm £5, chd free. Home-made teas. Visits also by arrangement Apr to Sept for groups of 5 to 30.**
In spring a myriad of small bulbs, specialist daffodils and an assortment

of many pots of tulips. Choice perennials follow together with annuals to ensure colour well into Sept. A garden for all seasons.

✿ 🚗 🍵

50 SHIELING
The Warren, Kingswood, Tadworth, KT20 6PQ. Drs Sarah & Robin Wilson, 07932 445868, sarahwilson@doctors.org.uk. *Kingswood Warren Estate. Off A217, gated entrance just before church on S-bound side of dual carriageway after Tadworth r'about. ¾ m walk from station. Parking on The Warren or by church on A217.* **Sun 18 Feb, Mon 1 Apr (11-3); Mon 27 May (2-4); Sun 11 Aug (12-4). Adm £5, chd free. Home-made teas. Visits also by arrangement 25 Feb to 31 Aug for groups of 10 to 30.**
1 acre garden restored to its original 1920s design. Formal front garden with island beds and shrub borders. Unusual large rock garden and mixed borders with collection of beautiful slug free hostas and uncommon woodland perennials and acid loving plants, a new shrub border and a stumpery. Lots for children to do with play area, Wendy house and amazing treehouse. Some narrow paths in back garden. Otherwise, resin drive, grass and paths easy for wheelchairs.

&. 🐕 ✿ 🅿 🍵 🧺 ⏺)

51 NEW SHOOTING STAR CHILDREN'S HOSPICES, CHRISTOPHER'S
Old Portsmouth Road, Artington, Guildford, GU3 1LP. Lucy Hooper. *Situated next to Artington Park & Ride. Christopher's signage shown at entrance. Take 1st exit at the r'about if coming from Guildford or 3rd exit at the r'about if coming from Peasmarsh.* **Sun 18 Aug (12-5). Adm £5, chd free. Tea, coffee & cake.**
Shooting Star Children's Hospices are a leading children's hospice charity supporting over 700 children and their families, across Surrey and West London, 365 days a yr. The gardens at the Guildford Hospice are enjoyed by families year-round, having been specifically designed with the needs of children in mind, from adapted play equipment and sensory trails to tranquil open areas for remembrance and reflection. They are maintained by a dedicated team of volunteer gardeners. Accessible pathway running throughout the garden. Accessible WC on site.

 &. 🍵 ⏺)

Harry Edwards Healing Sanctuary

52 NEW 🚶 **SLADES FARM**
Thorncombe Street, Bramley,
Guildford, GU5 0LT. Edward &
Lulu Hutley. *Take the A281 to*
Bramley, at the r'about turn in to
Snowdenham Ln; Slades Farm is
2½ m. Follow NGS signs. **Sat 18,**
Sun 19 May (12-5). Adm £8, chd
free. Tea & cake.
Slades Farm gardens are
predominantly a woodland garden,
with an abundance of azaleas,
camellias, rhododendrons, gunnera
glades. There are many different
species of trees, home to a variety
of birds and wildlife. Bridges cross
beautiful lakes and streams, but
please take care as the ground
can be uneven and please ensure
children are supervised.

53 NEW 🚶 **SOUTH WIND**
23 Doctors Lane, Chaldon,
Caterham, CR3 5AE.
Mrs Catherine Jones,
opengardenchaldon@gmail.com.
2½ m W of Caterham. Head W on
Rook Ln past Surrey National Golf
Club. After 1m turn R onto Doctors
Ln. Limited parking on Doctors Ln.
Alternative parking on Leazes Ave.

Visits by arrangement 27 June to
6 Sept for groups of 10 to 30. Adm
£5, chd free. Home-made teas.
1⅓ acre garden lovingly transformed
over the last 10 yrs into a peaceful
haven of different garden rooms with
a cottage garden feel. Surefooted
visitors can meander along gravel
paths to the mixed herbaceous
borders, raised vegetable beds, and
orchard. The oak gazebo is a perfect
place to sit whilst listening to the
native birds in the woodland. Sorry,
no dogs allowed.

54 🚶 **SOUTHLANDS LODGE**
Southlands Lane, Tandridge,
Oxted, RH8 9PH. Colin David
& John Barker, 07500 009603,
colin3d@googlemail.com. *3 mins*
from J6 of M25. From Tandridge
Village head S down hill for ¼ m to
T-junction with Southlands Ln. Turn
L along Southlands Ln, approx ¼ m
to Southlands Lodge entrance gate.
Visits by arrangement in Aug for
groups of 12 to 25. Two weeks
prior notice appreciated. Adm £5,
chd free. Home-made teas.
A surprising garden, on the edge of
a woodland, enjoying open views of
adjacent fields. Formal and informal

areas are scaled to complement a late
Georgian gatehouse. Mass planting
offsets selected specimens, mostly
chosen for their pollen and nectar
that helps sustain the resident honey
bees. An enclosed vegetable garden
with greenhouse, a flock of Shetland
sheep and poultry add interest.
Features inc a working apiary of 10
beehives, an insect hotel, and Cayuga
ducks and guinea fowl roam freely
through the property. Home-made
teas can be available, cake will be
gluten free and contain honey, nuts
and dairy. Sorry, no WC facilities.

55 🚶 **SPURFOLD**
Radnor Road, Peaslake,
Guildford, GU5 9SZ. Mr &
Mrs A Barnes, 01306 730196,
spurfold@btinternet.com. *8m SE*
of Guildford. A25 to Shere then
through to Peaslake. Pass village
stores & L up Radnor Rd. **Visits**
by arrangement May & June for
groups of 15 to 30. Sorry, no
coaches due to single track road.
Adm £6, chd free. Home-made
teas or evening wine & nibbles.
2½ acres, large herbaceous and
shrub borders, formal pond with
Cambodian Buddha head, sunken

gravel garden with topiary box and water feature, terraces, beautiful lawns, mature rhododendrons, azaleas, woodland paths, and gazebos. Garden contains a collection of Indian elephants and other objets d'art. Topiary garden and formal lawn area.

56 TANHOUSE FARM
Rusper Road, Newdigate, RH5 5BX. Mrs N Fries, 01306 631334. *8m S of Dorking. On A24 turn L at r'about at Beare Green. R at T-junction in Newdigate, 1st farm on R approx ⅔m. Signed Tanhouse Farm Shop.* **Visits by arrangement. Adm £5, chd free.** Country garden created by owners since 1987. 1 acre of charming rambling gardens surrounding a C16 house (not open). Herbaceous borders, small lake and stream with ducks and geese. Orchard with wild garden with plentiful seats and benches to stop for contemplation.

57 THE THERAPY GARDEN
Manor Fruit Farm, Glaziers Lane, Normandy, Guildford, GU3 2DT. The Therapy Garden General Manager, www.thetherapygarden.org. *SW of Guildford. Take A323 travelling from Guildford towards Aldershot, turn L into Glaziers Ln in centre of Normandy village, opp War Memorial. The Therapy Garden is 200yds on L.* **Sun 19 May, Sun 22 Sept (10-4). Adm £5, chd free. Light refreshments.** The Therapy Garden is a horticulture and education charity that uses gardening to have a positive and significant impact on the lives of people facing challenges in life. In our beautiful and tranquil 2 acre garden we work to change lives for the better and we do this by creating a safe place to enjoy the power of gardening and to connect with nature. We are a working garden full of innovation with an on site shop selling plants and produce. BBQ, light lunches, teas, coffees and cakes are available with a selection of fun family garden related activities to take part in. Wheelchair access over paved pathways throughout most of garden, many with substantial handrails.

58 TILFORD COTTAGE
Tilford Road, Tilford, GU10 2BX. Mr & Mrs R Burn, 01252 795423/07712 142728, rodneyburn@outlook.com. *3m SE of Farnham. From Farnham Stn along Tilford Rd, Tilford Cottage opp Tilford House. Parking by village green.* **Visits by arrangement Apr to Sept for groups of 6 to 40.** Artist's garden designed to surprise, delight and amuse. Formal planting, herb and knot garden. Numerous examples of topiary combine beautifully with the wildflower river walk. Japanese and water gardens, hosta beds, rose, apple and willow arches, treehouse and fairy grotto all continue the playful quality especially enjoyed by children. Local pub within walking distance. Partial wheelchair access to the top half of the garden only.

59 TIMBER HILL
Chertsey Road, Chobham, GU24 8JF. Nick & Lavinia Sealy, 01932 873875, lavinia@chobham.net, www.timberhillgarden.com. *A319 E of Chobham, & nr Woking, Chertsey, Sunningdale & Camberley. 2m from J11 M25, but avoid J10 intersection with A3 Wisley until Jun 2025.* **Every Wed 3 Jan to 17 Jan, Wed 31 Jan (11.30-2.30). Adm £6, chd £1. Every Mon 5 Feb to 26 Feb (11-2.30). Adm £6, chd £1. Mon 4, Mon 11, Mon 25 Mar (11-2.30); Mon 1, Sun 7 Apr (2-4.30); Mon 29 Apr (11-2.30); Mon 6, Mon 20 (11.30-4.30). Adm £7, chd £1. Pre-booking essential, please visit www.ngs.org.uk for information & booking. Self-service refreshments (Jan & Feb). Home-made teas (Mar, Apr & May).** Welcome to 16 acres of informal garden, park and woodland; enticing views to Surrey Hills from the hill. Enjoy winter and spring walks, through witch-hazel and winter honeysuckle, crocus and snowdrops, daffodils/narcissi and spring flowers, then gorgeous bluebells and azaleas and fleeting cherry blossom. Stunning camellias in Feb, March and April. Pretty borders in May. Member of Rhododendron, Camellia and Magnolia Group. Additional dates planned in Jun, Oct and Nov. For further information, please telephone, email or visit garden website.

60 ◆ TITSEY PLACE GARDENS
Titsey, Oxted, RH8 0SA. The Trustees of the Titsey Foundation, 07889 052461, office@titsey.org, www.titsey.org. *3m N of Oxted. A25 between Oxted & Westerham. Follow brown heritage signs to Titsey Estate from A25 at Limpsfield or see website for directions. Please enter via Water Ln & the Pitchfont car park (not Titsey Hill).* **For NGS: Sun 26 May, Sun 23 June, Sun 21 July, Sun 18 Aug (1-5). Adm £7.50, chd £2. Light refreshments. For other opening times and information, please phone, email or visit garden website.** One of the largest surviving historic estates in Surrey. Magnificent ancestral home and gardens of the Gresham family since 1534. Walled kitchen garden and Golden Jubilee rose garden. Etruscan summerhouse adjoining picturesque lakes and fountains. 15 acres of formal and informal gardens. Pedigree herd of Sussex Cattle roam the park. Walks through the estate woodlands are open year-round. Tearoom serving home-made cakes and selling local produce from 12-5pm. Last admission to gardens at 4pm. Dogs on leads allowed in picnic area, car park and woodland walks only. Disabled car parking next to tearoom and accessible WC. There are areas of garden not suited to wheelchairs, please see website for details.

In 2023, National Garden Scheme funding for Perennial supported a helpline service which provided advice, information and frontline support to around 800 people working in horticulture

61 ◆ VANN

Hambledon, Godalming,
GU8 4EF. Caroe Family,
01428 683413, vann@caroe.com,
www.vanngarden.co.uk. *6m S
of Godalming. A283 to Lane End,
Hambledon. Follow yellow Vann
signs for 2m. Please park in the field
as signed, not in road.* **For NGS:
Daily Mon 1 Apr to Sun 7 Apr
(10-4). Daily Mon 29 Apr to Sun
5 May (10-4). Adm £10, chd free.
Cash only on the day. For other
opening times and information,
please phone, email or visit garden
website.**
5 acre, 2* English Heritage registered
garden surrounding house dating back
to 1542 with Arts and Crafts additions
by W D Carõe inc a Bargate stone
pergola. At the front, brick paved
original cottage garden; to the rear a
lake, yew walk with rill and Gertrude
Jekyll water garden. Snowdrops
and hellebores, spring bulbs, and
spectacular fritillaria. Island beds,
crinkle crankle wall, orchard with wild
flowers. Vegetable garden. Also open
for by arrangement visits for individuals
or groups (not for NGS).

62 11 WEST HILL

Sanderstead, CR2 0SB. Rachel
& Edward Parsons. *M25 J6, A22,
3m r'about 4th exit to Succombs
Hill, R to Westhall Rd, at r'about
2nd exit to Limpsfield Rd, r'about
2nd exit on Sanderstead Hill 1m,
sharp R to West Hill. Please park on
West Hill.* **Sat 20, Sun 21 Apr (2-5).
Adm £5, chd free. Home-made
teas. Donation to Croydon Animal
Samaritans.**
A hidden gem tucked away. A
beautiful country cottage style garden
set in 1/2 acre, designed by Sam
Aldridge of Eden Restored. The
garden flows through pathways, lawn,
vegetable and play areas. Flower
beds showcase outstanding tulips,
and informal seating areas throughout
the garden allows you to absorb the
wonderful garden, whilst observing
our rescued chickens and rabbits!

63 WEST HORSLEY PLACE

Epsom Road, West Horsley,
Leatherhead, KT24 6AN.
West Horsley Place Trust,
www.westhorsleyplace.org. *5m E
of Guildford. At r'about on A246 in
West Horsley, turn L (signed West
Horsley & Ripley) into The Street.*

*Follow road for 1/3 m. Turn L into
Ripley Ln. Access after 1/3 m on L via
BUPA Nursing Home entrance.* **Sun
5 May, Sun 8 Sept (10-4). Adm
£10, chd free. Light refreshments
in the Place Farm Barn courtyard.**
West Horsley Place is set within a
380 acre estate. The garden adjacent
to the Manor House dates back
to the C15 and is approx 5 acres,
completely surrounded by a wall
over 300 yrs old. It has an ancient
orchard, rose garden, interestingly
striped formal lawns, an historic box
hedge, many herbaceous borders,
a magnificent white wisteria over
60ft tall and many wildflower areas.
Accessible via a step-free route.
Unpaved and the predominant
surface is turf. Accessible ground floor
WC suitable for wheelchair users.

64 WESTWAYS FARM

Gracious Pond Road,
Chobham, GU24 8HH. Paul &
Nicky Biddle, 01276 856163,
nicolabiddle@rocketmail.com. *4m
N of Woking. From Chobham Church
proceed over r'about towards
Sunningdale, 1st Xrds R into Red
Lion Rd to junction with Mincing Ln.*
**Sun 12 May (10.30-5). Adm £6,
chd free. Home-made teas. Visits
also by arrangement 29 Apr to 7
June for groups of 10 to 50.**
6 acre garden surrounded by
woodlands planted in 1930s
with mature and some rare
rhododendrons, azaleas, camellias
and magnolias, underplanted with
bluebells, lilies and dogwood.
Extensive lawns and sunken pond
garden. Working stables and sand
school. Lovely Queen Anne House
(not open) covered with listed
Magnolia grandiflora. Victorian design
glasshouse. New planting round
garden room.

65 THE WHITE HOUSE

21 West End Lane, West End, Esher,
KT10 8LB. Lady Peteranne Hunt
& Mr David John, 07850 367600,
peajaya@btinternet.com. *From Esher
to Cobham on the old Portsmouth
Rd take the 1st turning on the R into
Hawkshill Way. At T-junction turn R.
We are 5th house on the R.* **Sat 3,
Sun 4 Aug (11-4). Adm £5, chd free.
Light refreshments. Visits also by
arrangement 29 June to 2 Aug for
groups of 5 to 15. Wine & canapés
for eve visits.**

West End has a beautiful village
green, complete with a duck pond,
and nearby is Garsons Farm and the
recently transformed Prince of Wales
public house. Our garden is on several
levels and at the centre is a mature oak
tree. There are many peaceful spots
to rest and contemplate the vibrant
planting, an unusual water feature and
various sculptures. Wheelchair access
on patio only.

66 WILDWOOD

34 The Hatches, Frimley Green,
Camberley, GU16 6HE. Annie
Keighley, 01252 838660, annie.
keighley12@btinternet.com. *3m
S of Camberley. M3 J4 follow A325
to Frimley Green, towards Frimley
Green for 1m. Turn R by the green,
R into The Hatches for on street
parking.* **Visits by arrangement
in June for groups of up to 25.
Contact owner to customise visit
and refreshment options.**
Groups love the hidden surprises
in this romantic cottage garden
with tumbling roses, topiary and
scented *Magnolia grandiflora*. Enjoy
discovering a sensory haven of sun
and shade with wildlife pond, hidden
dell, fernery and loggia. Secret cutting
garden with raised beds, vegetables,
fruit trees and potting shed patio.

67 NEW 48 WOODMANSTERNE LANE

Wallington, SM6 0SW. Joanne
& Graham Winn. *2 1/2 m NE of
Banstead. From A217 head E
on A2022 for 2 1/2 m, turn L onto
Woodmansterne Ln. Plenty of
parking along the road. Do not park
on grass verges (traffic wardens).
What3words app - during.plates.
closes.* **Sun 30 June (12-4). Adm
£6, chd free. Home-made teas.**
Approx 1/3 acre. Part of former
smallholding, converted by garden
designer Joanne Winn and husband
Graham. Built around the original
orchard's fruit trees, the bold, curvy
design is softened by a sumptuous
palette of perennials and grasses.
Pop into the kitchen garden, relax
on the pond's deck amongst darting
dragonflies, take a peek into the
shepherd's hut and enjoy tea and cakes
near the chickens. Partial wheelchair
access; some gravel and narrow paths,
raised deck and boardwalk.

68 WOODPECKERS
Poplar Grove, Woking, GU22 7SD.
Mr Jānis Raubiška, 07478 025188,
janis@grandiflorus.co.uk, www.
instagram.com/grandiflorus.co.uk.
*Next to Woking Leisure Centre.
Please use Woking Leisure Centre
car park (GU22 9BA) & follow signs
for garden entrance. Coach parking
available.* **Sun 5, Sun 19 May, Sun
1, Sun 8 Sept (12-5). Adm £5,
chd free. Cream teas. Donation
to Plant Heritage. Visits also by
arrangement 3 May to 9 Sept for
groups of 10 to 35. Fri, Sat & Mon
around published open days.**
A journey through a horticultural
designer's own garden where plants
take centre stage in succession,
providing year-round colour and
interest. Three rooms, each with a
different planting style and purpose:
vibrant colours in the jewel's
amphitheatre, leafy textures and
pastels in the social room, glasshouse
and grow your own productive area.
Created in 2022, the garden has
sustainability at its heart.

✿ ☕ ♩))

**69 NEW WRENS' NEST
COTTAGE**
Ockham Lane, Cobham,
KT11 1PG. Mrs Patty Robertson
& Mr Fil Towers, 07957 495934,
pattyrobertson45@gmail.com.
*1½ m from Cobham High St. At
Wisley r'about turn L onto B2039
to Ockham/Horsley. After ½ m turn
L into Ockham Ln. House 2m on
R. From Cobham go to Downside
Bridge Rd, turn R into Chilbrook Rd
then turn R. Garden on R.* **Sun 14
July (11-5). Adm £5, chd free.
Home-made teas. Visits also by
arrangement 3 Apr to 31 July for
groups of 6 to 15.**
1½ acre country garden with island
beds of perennials and ancient
bluebell wood. Wildlife friendly with
a butterfly corner, a stream running
the length of the garden, and many
beautiful mature trees. Front garden
with many pots and courtyard. Sunny
sitting areas to enjoy home-made
teas. 2 miles from RHS Wisley.
Wheelchair access to most of garden.

♿ 🐕 ✿ ☕

Slades Farm

SUSSEX

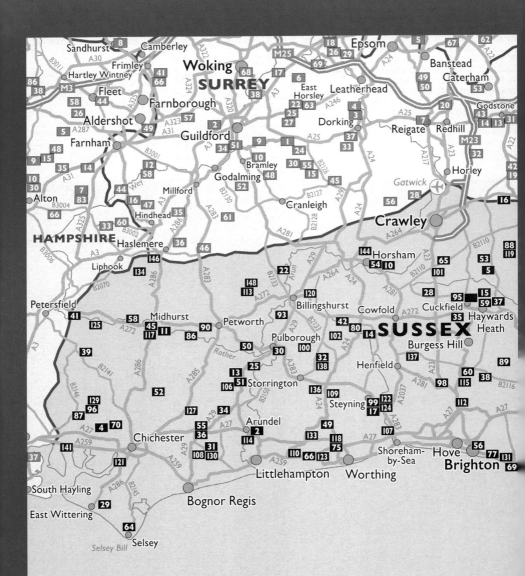

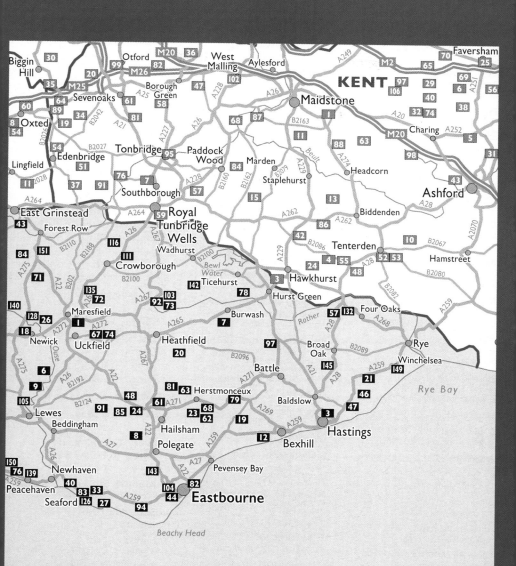

Biggin Hill
30
Otford
99
West Malling
36
Aylesford
Faversham
70
25
82
M20
M26
20
Borough Green
47
A22B
102
A26
KENT
97
106
69
6
56
35
M25
M26
A25
A251
Sevenoaks
64
61
58
A26
Maidstone
29
40
89
M2
M20
65
60
8
54
34
81
68
87
A20
32
74
38
19
B2042
A21
B2163
M20
Charing
A252
Edenbridge
54
A2027
Tonbridge
95
Paddock Wood
11
88
63
98
5
31
Lingfield
51
Marden
Headcorn
43
11
A2028
37
91
76
7
Southborough
57
B2160
B2162
Staplehurst
B2079
A229
13
Ashford
A28
A2070
East Grinstead
43
A264
59
Royal Tunbridge Wells
15
A262
86
Biddenden
10
B2067
Hamstreet
Forest Row
A26
Wadhurst
42
B2086
Tenterden
84
151
116
A261
B2100
Bewl Water
A229
24
4
55
52
53
B2080
71
B2110
B2188
111
Crowborough
B2100
142
Ticehurst
3
Hawkhurst
48
B2082
140
135
72
103
73
78
Hurst Green
57
132
Four Oaks
A259
128
26
92
Burwash
7
Rother
A28
A268
18
1
67
74
Maresfield
A265
Broad Oak
B2089
Rye
Newick
A272
Uckfield
20
Heathfield
97
145
Winchelsea
149
6
A26
B2192
81
63
Herstmonceux
Battle
A271
21
Rye Bay
9
B2124
91
85
24
61
A271
79
Baldslow
46
105
48
23
68
19
A259
3
47
Lewes
8
62
12
Hastings
Beddingham
Hailsham
A259
Bexhill
A27
Polegate
150
76
139
Newhaven
143
A259
Pevensey Bay
40
104
82
Peacehaven
83
33
A259
44
Eastbourne
Seaford
126
27
94

Beachy Head

0		10 kilometres
0	5 miles	

© Global Mapping / XYZ Maps

EAST & MID SUSSEX VOLUNTEERS

County Organiser, Booklet & Advertising Co-ordinator
Irene Eltringham-Willson
01323 833770
irene.willson@btinternet.com

County Treasurer
Andrew Ratcliffe 01435 873310
andrew.ratcliffe@ngs.org.uk

Publicity
Geoff Stonebanks 01323 899296
sussexeastpublicity@ngs.org.uk

Social Media
Nicki Conlon 07720 640761
nicki.conlon@ngs.org.uk

Photographer & Social Media
Lilly Carreras 07763 919602
lilly.carreras@ngs.org.uk

Booklet Distribution
Dr Denis Jones 01323 899452
sweetpeasd49@gmail.com

Assistant County Organisers
Jane Baker 01273 842805
jane.baker@ngs.org.uk

Michael & Linda Belton
01797 252984
belton.northiam@gmail.com

Shirley Carman-Martin
01444 473520
shirley.carmanmartin@ngs.org.uk

Isabella & Steve Cass
07908 123524
oaktreebarn@hotmail.co.uk

Linda Field

Diane Gould 01825 750300
lavenderdgould@gmail.com

Aideen Jones 01323 899452
sweetpeasa52@gmail.com

Dr Denis Jones (as above)

Susan Laing 01892 770168
splaing@btinternet.com

Rosie Pensom 01424 617796
rosie.barry@ymail.com

Sarah Ratcliffe 01435 873310
sarah.ratcliffe@ngs.org.uk

Dianna Tennant 01892 752029
tennantdd@gmail.com

f @SussexNGSEast
X @SussexNGS
@ngseastsussex

WEST SUSSEX VOLUNTEERS

County Organisers, Booklet & Advertising Co-ordinators
Maggi Hooper 07793 159304
maggi.hooper@ngs.org.uk

Meryl Walters 07766 761926
meryl.walters@ngs.org.uk

County Treasurer
Philip Duly 07789 050964
philipduly@tiscali.co.uk

Publicity
Kate Harrison 01798 817489
kate.harrison@ngs.org.uk

Social Media
Claudia Hawkes 07985 648216
claudiapearce17@gmail.com

Photographer
Judi Lion 07810 317057
judi.lion@ngs.org.uk

Talks
Philip Duly (as above)

Booklet Distribution
Lesley Chamberlain 07950 105966
chamberlain_lesley@hotmail.com

Assistant County Organisers
Teresa Barttelot 01798 865690
tbarttelot@gmail.com

Sanda Belcher 01428 723259
sandambelcher@gmail.com

Emma Broda 07739 516178
emma.broda@gmail.com

Lesley Chamberlain (as above)

Patty Christie 01730 813323
pattychristie49@gmail.com

Claudia Hawkes (as above)

Carrie McArdle 01403 820272
carrie.mcardle@btinternet.com

Fiona Phillips 07884 398704
fiona.h.phillips@btinternet.com

Susan Pinder 07814 916949
nasus.rednip@gmail.com

Teresa Roccia 07867 383753
teresa.m.roccia@gmail.com

Diane Rose 07789 565094
dirose8@me.com

f @Sussexwestngs
X @SussexWestNGS
@sussexwestngs

OPENING DATES

All entries subject to change. For latest information check **www.ngs.org.uk**

Extended openings are shown at the beginning of the month.

Map locator numbers are shown to the right of each garden name.

February

Snowdrop Openings

Every Thursday from Thursday 8th
The Old Vicarage   109

Every Thursday and Friday from Thursday 8th
Pembury House   115

Sunday 11th
Sandhill Farm House   125

Thursday 15th
◆ Highdown Gardens   66

Sunday 18th
Manor of Dean   90

Thursday 29th
NEW Crosslands Flower Nursery 31

March

Every Thursday
The Old Vicarage   109

Every Thursday and Friday to Friday 8th
Pembury House   115

Tuesday 5th
NEW Crosslands Flower Nursery 31

Saturday 16th
◆ Nymans   101

Sunday 17th
◆ Bates Green Garden   8
◆ Denmans Garden   36
Manor of Dean   90

Saturday 23rd
Down Place   39
◆ King John's Lodge   78

Sunday 24th
Down Place   39

Friday 29th
Judy's Cottage Garden 75

Saturday 30th
47 Denmans Lane 37

April

Every day from Monday 22nd to Friday 26th
◆ Bateman's 7

Every Thursday
The Old Vicarage 109

Monday 1st
47 Denmans Lane 37
The Old Vicarage 109

Saturday 6th
Butlers Farmhouse 23

Sunday 7th
Butlers Farmhouse 23

Tuesday 9th
Bignor Park 13

Saturday 13th
NEW 5 Coastguard Cottages 27
Rymans 121

Sunday 14th
NEW 5 Coastguard Cottages 27
47 Denmans Lane 37
Penns in the Rocks 116
Rymans 121

Friday 19th
The Garden House 56

Saturday 20th
Peelers Retreat 114
Winchelsea's Secret Gardens 149

Sunday 21st
The Garden House 56
Manor of Dean 90
Newtimber Place 98

Tuesday 23rd
Peelers Retreat 114

Wednesday 24th
Fittleworth House 50

Saturday 27th
Banks Farm 6
The Oast 103
Sandhill Farm House 125
Warnham Park 144

Sunday 28th
Banks Farm 6
◆ Denmans Garden 36
The Oast 103
Sandhill Farm House 125

May

Every Wednesday to Wednesday 15th
Fittleworth House 50

Every Thursday
The Old Vicarage 109

Thursday 2nd
◆ Highdown Gardens 66
◆ Sheffield Park and Garden 128

Saturday 4th
Peelers Retreat 114

Sunday 5th
Stanley Farm 134

Monday 6th
47 Denmans Lane 37

Tuesday 7th
Peelers Retreat 114

Saturday 11th
96 Ashford Road 3
Cookscroft 29

Sunday 12th
Hammerwood House 58
Mountfield Court 97
Penns in the Rocks 116

Tuesday 14th
◆ Borde Hill Garden 15

Saturday 18th
96 Ashford Road 3
NEW The Cottage 30
Forest Ridge 53
Meadow Farm 93

Sunday 19th
Champs Hill 25
47 Denmans Lane 37
Forest Ridge 53
Legsheath Farm 84

Wednesday 22nd
Balcombe Gardens 5
Cupani Garden 33
Lavender Cottage 83

Saturday 25th
96 Ashford Road 3
54 Elmleigh 45
◆ King John's Lodge 78
Peelers Retreat 114
◆ The Priest House 119

Sunday 26th
54 Elmleigh 45
Foxglove Cottage 54
Hollymount 72
◆ King John's Lodge 78
NEW 9 Puttock Way 120

Monday 27th
54 Elmleigh 45
The Old Vicarage 109
NEW 9 Puttock Way 120

Tuesday 28th
Peelers Retreat 114

Friday 31st
NEW Bumble Farm 22
Judy's Cottage Garden 75
Orchard Cottage 111

June

Every Wednesday from Wednesday 12th to Wednesday 19th
Fittleworth House 50

Every Thursday
The Old Vicarage 109

Saturday 1st
NEW Bumble Farm 22
Foxwood Barn 55
◆ Knepp Castle 80
Limekiln Farm 85
Orchard Cottage 111
Skyscape 131
Waterworks & Friends 145

Sunday 2nd
Brickyard Farm Cottage 19
Eastbourne Central Garden Trail 44
Foxwood Barn 55
◆ High Beeches Woodland and Water Garden 65
Limekiln Farm 85
Offham House 105
Orchard Cottage 111
Pangdean Farm 112
Seaford Gardens 126
Skyscape 131

Tuesday 4th
Bignor Park 13

Wednesday 5th
Kemp Town Enclosures: South Garden 77
Kitchenham Farm 79

Friday 7th
Hillside 69
1 Pest Cottage 117

Saturday 8th
Alpines 1
NEW ◆ Farleys Sculpture Garden 48
Harlands Gardens 59
Hoopers Farm 73
Kitchenham Farm 79
The Old Rectory 108

August

Every Thursday
The Old Vicarage 109

Sunday 4th
Penns in the Rocks 116

Tuesday 6th
Kitchenham Farm 79

Wednesday 7th
Fittleworth House 50

Friday 9th
NEW Nyetimber Manor 100

Saturday 10th
Bourne Botanicals 16
Kitchenham Farm 79

Sunday 11th
The Beeches 9
Champs Hill 25

Thursday 15th
Bourne Botanicals 16

Saturday 17th
Holly House 71

Sunday 18th
Bourne Botanicals 16
4 Hillside Cottages 70
Holly House 71
Whitehanger 146

Tuesday 20th
Peelers Retreat 114

Saturday 24th
Butlers Farmhouse 23
Peelers Retreat 114

Sunday 25th
Butlers Farmhouse 23
The Folly 52
Hollymount 72

Monday 26th
Durrance Manor 42
The Old Vicarage 109

September

Every Thursday
The Old Vicarage 109

Sunday 1st
East Grinstead Gardens 43
Malthouse Farm 89

Tuesday 3rd
Bignor Park 13
Peelers Retreat 114

Wednesday 4th
Knightsbridge House 81

Friday 6th
Judy's Cottage Garden 75

Saturday 7th
NEW The Cottage 30
Knightsbridge House 81
Peelers Retreat 114

Sunday 8th
NEW Langney & Willingdon
Garden Trail 82
Parsonage Farm 113
♦ Sussex Prairies 137

Wednesday 11th
Ashling Park Estate 4

Saturday 14th
♦ King John's Lodge 78
Limekiln Farm 85

Sunday 15th
Limekiln Farm 85
Rymans 121

Wednesday 18th
Ashling Park Estate 4

Thursday 19th
Fairlight Hall 47

Saturday 21st
Peelers Retreat 114
Sandhill Farm House 125

Sunday 22nd
Sandhill Farm House 125

Sunday 29th
♦ Bates Green Garden 8
♦ High Beeches Woodland and
Water Garden 65

October

**Every Thursday to
Thursday 10th**
The Old Vicarage 109

Saturday 5th
Peelers Retreat 114

Sunday 27th
♦ Denmans Garden 36

By Arrangement

Arrange a personalised garden visit
with your club, or group of friends,
on a date to suit you. See individual
garden entries for full details.

Alpines 1
The Beeches 9
4 Ben's Acre 10
NEW Berlas 11
Black Barn 14
Bourne Botanicals 16

Brickyard Farm Cottage 19
Brightling Down Farm 20
NEW Broad Street House 21
Butlers Farmhouse 23
Camberlot Hall 24
Champs Hill 25
Colwood House 28
Cookscroft 29
Cosy Cottage, Seaford
Gardens 126
NEW The Cottage 30
Cupani Garden 33
Dale Park House 34
47 Denmans Lane 37
Down Place 39
Driftwood 40
Durrance Manor 42
54 Elmleigh 45
Fairlight End 46
Findon Place 49
Fittleworth House 50
The Folly 52
Foxwood Barn 55
The Garden House 56
4 Hillside Cottages 70
Holly House 71
Hollymount 72
36 Jellicoe Close, Langney &
Willingdon Garden Trail 82
Legsheath Farm 84
Lordington House 87
Luctons 88
Malthouse Farm 89
Manor of Dean 90
Meadow Farm 93
Mill Hall Farm 95
Mitchmere Farm 96
Oaklands Farm 102
Ocklynge Manor 104
Old Cross Street Farm 106
Old Erringham Cottage 107
The Old Rectory 108
The Old Vicarage 109
Orchard Cottage 111
Peelers Retreat 114
6 Plantation Rise 118
Rymans 121
Saffrons 122
Selhurst Park 127
Shepherds Cottage 129
The Shrubbery 130
South Grange 132
Town Place 140
Tuppenny Barn 141
4 Waterworks Cottages,
Waterworks & Friends 145
Whitehanger 146
Winterfield, Balcombe Gardens 5
Wych Warren House 151

THE GARDENS

1 ALPINES

High Street, Maresfield, Uckfield, TN22 2EG. Ian & Cathy Shaw, 07887 825032, Info@shaw.buzz. *1½ m N of Uckfield. Garden approx 150 metres N of Budletts r'about towards Maresfield. Blue Badge parking at garden, other parking in village approx 100 metres from garden.* **Sat 8 June (11-5). Adm £6, chd free. Home-made teas & savouries. Visits also by arrangement for groups of 6+.**
A 1 acre garden put together by the owners to incorporate the ornamental and the edible. Offers riot of colour and scent over many months, especially early summer with large and rampant mixed borders, small orchard, wildflower meadow, fruit cage, vegetable garden, wildlife pond and bog garden. Pretty Victorian style greenhouse. Lots of spots to sit. Wheelchair access largely on grass over one level with a few steps round greenhouse and some gravel paths.

2 ◆ ARUNDEL CASTLE & GARDENS

Arundel, BN18 9AB. Arundel Castle Trustees Ltd, 01903 882173, visits@arundelcastle.org, www.arundelcastle.org. *In the centre of Arundel, N of A27.* **For opening times and information, please phone, email or visit garden website.**
Ancient castle, family home of the Duke of Norfolk. 40 acres of grounds and gardens which inc hot subtropical borders, English herbaceous borders, stumpery, two glasshouses, walled flower and organic kitchen gardens and Fitzalan Chapel white garden.

3 96 ASHFORD ROAD

Hastings, TN34 2HZ. Lynda & Andrew Hayler. *From A21 (Sedlescombe Rd N) towards Hastings, take 1st exit on r'about A2101, then 3rd on L (approx 1m).* **Sat 11, Sat 18, Sat 25 May (1.30-4.30). Adm £3, chd free.**
Small (100ft x 52ft) Japanese inspired front and back garden. Full of interesting planting with many acers, azaleas and bamboos. Over 100 different hostas, many miniature ones.

Also, an attractive Japanese Tea House. New Japanese bridge and pond in lower garden.

4 ASHLING PARK ESTATE

West Ashling, Chichester, PO18 9DJ. Gail Gardner, 01243 967700, contact@ashlingpark.co.uk, www.ashlingpark.co.uk. *Located on the Funtington Rd, 5m W of Chichester. Through the large metal gates onto the private driveway to the vineyard.* **Wed 11, Wed 18 Sept (10-11.30am). Adm £8. Pre-booking essential, please visit www.ngs.org.uk for information & booking. Light refreshments.**
A truly fascinating vineyard tour with wine tasting that starts promptly at 10am. First created in the C19, Ashling Park was cited on the Tithe map and has had a new lease of life when a vineyard was planted in 2017. Pinot Noir, Pinot Meunièr, Chardonnay and Bacchus grape varieties, chef's kitchen garden and beehives.

GROUP OPENING

5 BALCOMBE GARDENS

3m N of Cuckfield on B2036, 3m S of J10A on M23. Individual gardens signed within Balcombe. **Wed 22 May, Sat 22, Sun 23 June (12-5). Combined adm £7.50, chd free. Home-made teas at Stumlet (22 May & 22 June) & at the tea venue for 46 Westup Farm Cottages (23 June).**

STUMLET
Oldlands Avenue, RH17 6LW. Max & Nicola Preston Bell.

46 WESTUP FARM COTTAGES
London Road, RH17 6JJ. Chris & Clare Cornwell.

WINTERFIELD
Oldlands Avenue, RH17 6LP. Sue & Sarah Howe, 01444 811380, sarahjhowe_uk@yahoo.co.uk. Visits also by arrangement 2 Apr to 30 June for groups of up to 50.

Within the Balcombe AONB there are three quite different gardens that are full of variety and interest, which will appeal to plant lovers. Set amidst the countryside of the High Weald, 46 Westup Farm Cottages is a classic cottage garden with

unique and traditional features linked by intimate paths through lush and subtle planting with pollinators and wildlife in abundance. In the village, Winterfield is a country garden packed with uncommon shrubs and trees, herbaceous borders, a summerhouse, pond and wildlife area. At nearby Stumlet the garden is restful, there are places to sit and enjoy a little peace, scent and colour. Redesigned to inc interesting plants for lasting enjoyment by different generations. A garden to watch develop in the future.

---

6 BANKS FARM

Boast Lane, Barcombe, Lewes, BN8 5DY. Nick & Lucy Addyman. *6m N of Lewes. From Barcombe Cross follow signs to Spithurst & Newick. 1st road on R into Boast Ln towards the Anchor Pub. At sharp bend carry on into Banks Farm.* **Sat 27, Sun 28 Apr (11-4). Adm £5, chd free. Home-made teas.**
9 acre garden set in rural countryside. Extensive lawns and shrub beds merge with the more naturalistic woodland garden set around the lake. An orchard, vegetable garden, ponds and a wide variety of plant species add to an interesting and very tranquil garden. Refreshments served outside, so may be limited during bad weather. Wheelchair access to the upper part of garden. Sloping grass paths in the lower part.

7 ◆ BATEMAN'S

Bateman's Lane, Burwash, TN19 7DS. National Trust, 01435 882302, batemans@ nationaltrust.org.uk, www. nationaltrust.org.uk/batemans. *½ m S of Burwash. A265 W from Burwash, 1st turning on L after you leave the village, just before petrol station. Please look out for NT signs. Pick up & drop off points available.* **For NGS: Daily Mon 22 Apr to Fri 26 Apr (10-4.30). Adm £14, chd £7. Light refreshments. For other opening times and information, please phone, email or visit garden website.**
Bateman's is an idyllic spot; a family home loved by Rudyard Kipling. Nestled in a shallow valley, the house and garden were a joy and an inspiration to him, from the formal borders and clipped yew hedges to romantic meadows with the

meandering river flowing through. Highlights inc wild garden carpeted with spring bulbs below flowering trees and shrubs, orchard, vegetable garden, potted tulips, spring flowering borders, working watermill and a dazzling mulberry garden display. On site tearoom offering beverages, cream teas, cakes, hot and cold food. Partly accessible grounds, some uneven paths. Blue Badge parking. Accessible WC. Wheelchairs available to borrow.

8 ◆ BATES GREEN GARDEN
Tye Hill Road, Arlington, BN26 6SH. John McCutchan, 01323 485151, john@bluebellwalk.co.uk, www.batesgreengarden.co.uk. 3½ m SW of Hailsham & A22. Midway between the A22 & A27, 2m S of Michelham Priory. Bates Green is in Tye Hill Rd (N of Arlington village), 350yds S of Old Oak Inn. Ample parking on hard-standing verges. For NGS: Sun 17 Mar, Sun 29 Sept (10.30-4). Adm £7, chd £3. Pre-booking essential, please visit www.ngs.org.uk for information & booking. Home-made soup, cakes & scones, plus light lunches in a large insulated barn. For other opening times and information, please phone, email or visit garden website.
This plantswoman's tranquil garden provides interest through the seasons. Woodland garden created around a majestic oak tree. Colour themed middle garden. Courtyard gardens with seasonal container displays. Front garden a spring and autumn joy with narcissi, primroses, violets then coloured stems and leaves of cornus and salix. Wildlife pond and wildflower meadow. Gardened for nature and wildlife. Spring visitors can walk through a wild daffodil glade leading to the 24 acre ancient oak woodland, home of the Arlington Bluebell Walk. Beatons Wood has been owned by the McCutchan family for 100 yrs and is managed for conservation and diversity. Autumn guests can enjoy spotting the abundant fungi. Wheelchair access to most areas. Mobility scooters to borrow free of charge. Accessible WC.

9 THE BEECHES
Church Road, Barcombe, Lewes, BN8 5TS. Sandy Coppen, 07771 655862, sand@thebeechesbarcombe.com, www.thebeechesbarcombe.com. From Lewes, A26 towards Uckfield for 3m, turn L signed Barcombe. Follow road for 1½ m, turn L signed Hamsey & Church. Follow road for approx ½ m & parking will be in the church car park on LHS. Sun 11 Aug (1-5). Adm £6, chd free. Home-made teas. Visits also by arrangement 16 May to 12 Aug for groups of 10+.
C18 walled garden with cut flowers, vegetables, salads and fruit. Separate orchard and rose garden. Herbaceous borders, a hot border and extensive lawns. A hazel walk is being developed and a short woodland walk. An old ditch has been made into a flowing stream with gunnera, ferns, tree ferns, hostas and a few flowers going into a pond. Wheelchair access without steps, but some ground is uneven.

10 4 BEN'S ACRE
Horsham, RH13 6LW. Pauline Clark, 01403 266912, brian.clark8850@yahoo.co.uk. E of Horsham. A281 via Cowfold, after Hilliers Garden Centre, turn R by Tesco on to St Leonards Rd, straight over r'about to Comptons Ln, next R Heron Way, 2nd L Grebe Cres, 1st L Ben's Acre. Visits by arrangement 3 June to 30 Aug for groups of 10 to 25. Adm £10, chd free. Home-made teas inc. Call to discuss wine & canapé options.
Described as inspirational excellence in design and artistry. A visual delight on different levels, featuring ponds, rockery, summerhouse and arbour. Seating for your teas surrounded by borders full of harmonising perennials, roses, shrubs and more. See how a diverse small space created on different levels can be exciting and inspiring. 5 mins from Hilliers Garden Centre, 15 mins from Leonardslee and NT Nymans. Visit us on YouTube Pauline & Brian's Sussex Garden. Partial wheelchair access, please discuss at time of booking.

11 NEW BERLAS
Park Crescent, Midhurst, GU29 9ED. Mr & Mrs S Curzon-Hope, 07806 701186, suecurzonhope@hotmail.com. From the centre of Midhurst turn R from N or L from S, opp Angel Hotel. Berlas is on the L on Park Cres with lamppost outside. Visits by arrangement 2 May to 13 Oct for groups of 5 to 20. Adm £5, chd free. Home-made teas.
150ft south west facing, sloping town garden, developed over 10 yrs from scratch. Hedges and trees planted, and wildlife pond (2020). Enthusiastic plantswoman, attempting seasonal succession from spring bulbs through to late flowering prairie style planting. Two areas of grass kept as wild meadows. Collection of succulents, echeveria, pelargoniums. Unusual pots and planters.

GROUP OPENING

12 BEXHILL-ON-SEA TRAIL
Bexhill & Little Common. Follow individual NGS signs to gardens from main roads. Tickets & maps at all gardens. Sun 7 July (12-5). Combined adm £7, chd free. Home-made teas & light lunch at Westlands. Light refreshments at De Wilp.

THE CLINCHES
Collington Lane East, TN39 3RJ. Val Kemm.

DE WILP
Collington Lane East, TN39 3RJ. Stuart & Hazel Wood.

ORCHARD COTTAGE
22 Gatelands Drive, TN39 4DP. Pat McCarthy.

NEW **2 RAVENS CLOSE**
TN39 4TG. Jenny & Richard Burton.

NEW **13 THORNBANK CRESCENT**
TN39 3ND. Barbara Echlin.

WESTLANDS
36 Collington Avenue, TN39 3NE. Madeleine Gilbart & David Harding.

De Wilp, a beautiful garden laid to lawn with beds, a large variety of perennial and annual plants, vegetables, a hosta corridor, mature trees and shrubs; light refreshments available. Adjacent to De Wilp, The Clinches is a mature cottage garden surrounded by trees and shrubs, Gaudi inspired steps and a pond with fish, toads and newts. 2 Raven Close (new to trail) has beautifully laid out mixed planting inc roses, an arch with climbers along ropes, and fruit and vegetable beds. Orchard Cottage (returning to trail) is a plantswoman's small garden with climbers on trellis and herbaceous borders. 13 Thornbank Crescent (new to trail) has over 50 specimen fruit trees, a pond, flower and vegetable beds with an emphasis on attracting wildlife to the garden. Westlands (returning to trail), across the road from Thornbank Crescent, is a mature garden with significant range of trees, roses, mixed planting, vegetable and fruit garden, and is the main venue for teas. Parking in adjacent office block. Partial wheelchair access to some gardens.

13 BIGNOR PARK

Pulborough, RH20 1HG. The Mersey Family, www.bignorpark.co.uk. *5m S of Petworth & Pulborough. Well signed from B2138. Nearest villages Sutton, Bignor & West Burton. Approach from the E, directions & map available on website.* **Tue 9 Apr, Tue 4 June, Tue 3 Sept (2-5). Adm £5, chd free. Home-made teas.**
11 acres of peaceful garden to explore with magnificent views of the South Downs. Interesting trees, shrubs, wildflower areas with swathes of daffodils in spring. The walled flower garden has been replanted with herbaceous borders. Temple, Greek loggia, Zen pond and unusual sculptures. Former home of romantic poet Charlotte Smith, whose sonnets were inspired by Bignor Park. Spectacular cedar of Lebanon and rare Lucombe oak. Wheelchair access to shrubbery and croquet lawn. Gravel paths in rest of garden and steps in stables quadrangle.

14 BLACK BARN

Steyning Road, West Grinstead, Horsham, RH13 8LR. Jane Gates, 07774 980819, jane.er.gates@gmail.com. *Between Partridge Green & A24 on Steyning Rd. From A24 follow Steyning Rd signed West Grinstead for 1m, passing Park Ln & Catholic Church on the L, continue round 2 bends, Black Barn is on L. Parking limited so car share appreciated.* **Visits by arrangement 1 Apr to 29 Sept for groups of up to 20. Adm £5, chd free. Home-made teas.**
Black Barn Garden was designed and planted in Jan 2018. The site was cleared and only the mature trees remained. A hedgerow separating the garden from the field was removed and a large pond has been created in the southwest corner. A large gravel garden was created to the south of the barn and a terrace laid. The existing terrace at the back was increased and a large bed was created. Wheelchair access over grass only.

15 ◆ BORDE HILL GARDEN

Borde Hill Lane, Haywards Heath, RH16 1XP. Borde Hill Garden, 01444 450326, info@bordehill.co.uk, www.bordehill.co.uk. *1½m N of Haywards Heath. 20 mins N of Brighton, or S of Gatwick on A23 taking exit 10a via Balcombe.* **For NGS: Tue 14 May (10-5). Adm £12, chd £8. Light refreshments. For other opening times and information, please phone, email or visit garden website.**
Tranquil and picturesque, Borde Hill has been planted with passion by five generations of the Stephenson Clarke family. With rare and fine

Nyetimber Manor

rhododendrons, magnolias, rose borders and champion trees, exploring the 13 outdoor rooms is like travelling around the world in one garden. Wheelchair access to 17 acres of formal garden.

16 BOURNE BOTANICALS

The Bourne, Chesterfield Close, Furnace Wood, Felbridge, East Grinstead, RH19 2PY. Jackie & Andy Doherty *A264 between Copthorne & Felbridge. 1⅛m from Felbridge. Parking in layby RH19 2QF on W bound A264 signed to Furnace Wood. Metrobus 400. Enter Furnace Wood via footpath R of barrier, 8 min walk to Bourne Botanicals.* **Sat 10, Thur 15, Sun 18 Aug (11-5). Adm £8. Pre-booking essential, please phone 07785 562558 or email bournebotanic@outlook. com for information & booking. Home-made teas. Visits also by arrangement in Aug for groups of 15+.**

A lush setting of huge bananas jostling alongside gunnera and arid beds of agave, yucca and cacti. A diverse tropical look garden with a wildlife pond and stream inc bog beds of carnivorous plants. Palms, tree ferns, tetrapanax and many unusual plants and quirky touches all set in an acre of woodland. Features inc a folly and a sunken garden. National Collection holder. Parking at property for disabled badge holders and those with mobility issues only.

 ♿ ✻ NPC ☕ ♪)

17 NEW BRAMBLETYE

25 Maudlyn Park Way, Bramber, Steyning, BN44 3PT. Nicola & Paul Middleton. *4m N of Shoreham-by-Sea. On the eastern edge of Steyning, take Maudlin Ln & turn into Sopers Ln. Take an immed R into Maudlyn Parkway. Brambletye is found on the LHS at the junction to The Ridings.* **Wed 26 June, Wed 3 July (10.30-5). Combined adm with Nightingale House £7, chd free. Home-made teas at Nightingale House.**

A quiet south facing garden on the edge of the South Downs, designed with a prairie effect in mind to attract pollinators and birds. A mix of spring and early summer flowering bulbs, shrubs, herbaceous perennials and roses. There is a small sunken area with raised beds for vegetables and herbs.

 ☕ ♪)

18 BRAMLEY

Lane End Common, North Chailey, Lewes, BN8 4JH. Marcel & Lee Duyvesteyn. *1m S of Sheffield Park NT. From A272 North Chailey mini r'abouts take NE turn to A275 signed Bluebell Railway, after 1m turn R signed Fletching. Bramley is 300yds on R. Free car park opp & roadside parking.* **Fri 14, Sat 15 June (1-5). Adm £6, chd free.**

Rural 1 acre garden. Planting began in 2006 and inc an orchard avenue with wild flowers and long grassed areas and beehives. Vegetable garden, numerous formal and informal ornamental flowerbeds and borders. Planted for strong seasonal effect and structure. Interesting planting and design. SSSI nearby. Home-made teas and English sparkling wine from the Bluebell Vineyard Estate.

 ✻ ☕ ♪)

19 BRICKYARD FARM COTTAGE

Top Road, Hooe, Battle, TN33 9EJ. David & Grace Constable, 07740 407998, dc@constablespublishing.com. *From A269 turn R onto B2095, 2m on R. From A259 turn L onto B2095, 2½m on L. Parking in field adjacent to garden.* **Sun 2 June (11-4.30). Adm £6, chd free. Home-made teas. Visits also by arrangement 1 May to 15 Sept for groups of up to 25.**

A 4 acre garden started 24 yrs ago; stunning views, remarkable brick and stone follies, colourful mixed beds with alstroemeria and roses. Pine rockery surrounds pond. Topiary garden, pinetum, and a rhododendron and azalea walk leads to a planted parterre. Fruit and vegetables in cages. Orchard. Unique items in garden and also metal sculptures, made by garden owners. Rose-filled courtyard front garden where home-made teas will be served. Plentiful seating to admire the Sussex vista.

 ♿

20 BRIGHTLING DOWN FARM

Observatory Road, Dallington, TN21 9LN. Val & Pete Stephens, 07770 807060, valstephens@icloud.com. *1m from Woods Corner. At Swan Pub, Woods Corner, take road opp to Brightling. Take 1st L to Burwash & almost immed, turn into 1st driveway on L.* **Visits by arrangement 3 May to 27 Sept for groups of 12 to 35.**

Preferred days: Mondays or Fridays. Home-made teas inc. The garden has several different areas inc a Zen garden, water garden, walled vegetable garden with two large greenhouses, herb garden, herbaceous borders and a woodland walk. The garden makes clever use of grasses and is set amongst woodland with stunning countryside views. Winner of the Society of Garden Designers award. Most areas of garden can be accessed with the use of temporary ramps.

 ♿ D ☕

21 NEW BROAD STREET HOUSE

Broad Street, Icklesham, Winchelsea, TN36 4AS. Tony & Sally Thorne, 01424 814377, csallythorne@gmail.com. *Halfway between Hastings & Rye, off the A259. From Hastings follow A259 for Icklesham, turn L into Broad St just before village. From Rye, follow A259 through Icklesham, then Broad St on R. Follow yellow signs.* **Sat 20 July (9.30-4.30). Adm £6, chd free. Home-made teas. Visits also by arrangement 26 Apr to 27 Apr for groups of up to 12.**

A big garden, under constant development with wonderful views down the Brede Valley. The garden features a wide variety of trees, a good number of flower beds, a natural pond much loved by wildlife, with a waterfall and viewing bridge. At the beginning of last year, the owners added a large waterfall with associated woodland planting to the front of the property.

 🐾 ☕

22 NEW BUMBLE FARM

Drungewick Lane, Loxwood, Billingshurst, RH14 0RS. Will Carver. *Very well signed in the middle of Drungewick Ln.* **Fri 31 May, Sat 1, Sat 15, Sun 16 June (12-5). Adm £6, chd free. Home-made teas.**

Delightful large country garden. Passionately and imaginatively created by enthusiastic owner over the past 20 yrs. An interesting garden with a series of circular lawns surrounded by borders, full of mass drift, repeat planting of harmonious perennials, roses, shrubs, and more. A newly developed white garden, wisteria pergola, kitchen and cutting garden, fountains and various seating areas.

 ♿ ♪)

23 BUTLERS FARMHOUSE

Butlers Lane, Herstmonceux, BN27 1QH. Irene Eltringham-Willson, 01323 833770, irene. willson@btinternet.com, www.butlersfarmhouse.co.uk. *3m E of Hailsham. Take A271 from Hailsham, go through village of Herstmonceux, turn R signed Church Rd, then approx 1m turn R. Do not use SatNav!* **Sat 6, Sun 7 Apr, Thur 13, Fri 14 June (2-5). Adm £5, chd free. Sat 24, Sun 25 Aug (2-5). Adm £7, chd free. Home-made teas. Visits also by arrangement 29 Mar to 31 Oct. Discuss refreshment options on booking.** Lovely rural setting for 1 acre garden surrounding C16 farmhouse with views of South Downs. Pretty in spring with daffodils, hellebores and primroses. Come and see our meadow in June and perhaps spot an orchid or two. Quite a fun quirky garden with surprises round every corner inc a rainbow border, small pond, Cornish inspired beach corners, a poison garden and secret jungle garden. Plants for sale. Picnics welcome in June and Aug. Live jazz in Aug. Most of garden accessible by wheelchair.

&.🕸️🚌🚐☕🎋))

24 CAMBERLOT HALL

Camberlot Road, Lower Dicker, Hailsham, BN27 3RH. Nicky & Paul Kinghorn, 07710 566453, nickykinghorn@hotmail.com. *500yds S of A22 at Lower Dicker, 4½m N of A27 Drusillas r'about. From A27 Drusilla's r'about through Berwick Stn to Upper Dicker & L into Camberlot Rd after The Plough pub, we are 1m on L. From A22 we are 500yds down Camberlot Rd on R.* **Visits by arrangement July & Aug for groups of 8 to 25. Adm £13, chd £5. Home-made teas.** A 3 acre country garden with a lovely view across fields and hills to the South Downs. Created from scratch over the last 10 yrs with all design, planting and maintenance by the owner. Lavender lined carriage driveway, naturalistic border, vegetable garden, shady garden, 30 metre white border and dahlia garden. Part-walled garden and summerhouse. Wheelchair access over gravel drive and some uneven ground.

&.☕))

25 CHAMPS HILL

Waltham Park Road, Coldwaltham, Pulborough, RH20 1LY. Mrs Mary Bowerman, 01798 831205, info@thebct.org.uk, www.thebct.org.uk. *3m S of Pulborough. On A29 turn R to Fittleworth into Waltham Park Rd, garden 400 metres on R.* **Sun 19 May, Sun 11 Aug (2-5). Adm £5, chd free. Light refreshments. Visits also by arrangement 8 Apr to 13 Sept for groups of 10+.** A natural landscape, the garden has been developed around three disused sand quarries with far-reaching views across the Amberley Wildbrooks to the South Downs. A woodland walk in spring leads you past beautiful sculptures, against a backdrop of colourful rhododendrons and azaleas. In summer the garden is a colourful tapestry of heathers, which are renowned for their abundance and variety.

&.🚌☕))

26 ◆ CLINTON LODGE

Fletching, TN22 3ST. Lady Collum, 01825 722952, garden@clintonlodge.com, www. clintonlodgegardens.co.uk. *4m NW of Uckfield. Clinton Lodge is situated in Fletching High St, N of The Griffin Inn. Off road parking provided, weather permitting. It is important visitors do not park in street. Parking available from 11am.* **For NGS: Thur 20 June (11-5). Adm £7, chd free. Home-made teas from 12pm. No lunches. For other opening times and information, please phone, email or visit garden website. Donation to local charities.** 6 acre formal and romantic garden overlooking parkland with old roses, William Pye water feature, double white and blue herbaceous borders, yew hedges, pleached lime walks, medieval style potager, vine and rose allée, wildflower garden, small knot garden and orchard. Caroline and Georgian house (not open).

🕸️☕))

27 NEW 5 COASTGUARD COTTAGES

Cuckmere Haven, Seaford, BN25 4AR. Mr Daniel Martin. *A259 turn S to Southdown Rd, turn 6th L onto Chyngton Rd edge of golf course, continue to Chyngton Way, at end take the R fork to the top, park & then walk 1m down hill to garden.* **Sat 13, Sun 14 Apr, Sat 15, Sun 16 June (10-5).**

Adm £5, chd free. Home-made teas.
This iconic garden at Coastguard Cottages overlooking the Seven Sisters will be known to many from a distance, but this garden is rarely seen. Nestled on the cliff top in the South Downs National Park with sea views. Planted with native plants and spring bulbs in April and poppies, herbs and acanthus in June it is a perfect setting for the owners sculpture and pottery display. An embryonic vegetable plot and beehives contribute to attracting wildlife to the garden. Note steep cliff drop, children to be supervised at all times.

🐕🐄☕))

28 COLWOOD HOUSE

Cuckfield Lane, Warninglid, RH17 5SP. Mrs Rosy Brenan, 01444 461352. *6m W of Haywards Heath, 6m SE of Horsham. Entrance on B2115 Cuckfield Ln. From E, N & S, turn W off A23 towards Warninglid for ¾ m. From W come through Warninglid village.* **Visits by arrangement May to Sept for groups of 10 to 50. Adm £7, chd free. Light refreshments. Donation to Seaforth Hall, Warninglid.** 12 acres of garden with mature and specimen trees from the late 1800s, lawns and woodland edge. Formal parterre, rose and herb gardens. 100ft terrace and herbaceous border overlooking flower rimmed croquet lawn. Cut turf labyrinth and forsythia tunnel. Water features, statues and gazebos. Pets' cemetery. Giant chessboard. Lake with island and temple. Picnics welcome. Wheelchair access with gravel paths and some slopes.

&.🐄☕🎋

29 COOKSCROFT

Bookers Lane, Earnley, Chichester, PO20 7JG. Mr & Mrs J Williams, 01243 513671, john@cookscroft.co.uk, www.cookscroft.co.uk. *6m S of Chichester. At end of Birdham Straight A286 from Chichester, take L fork to East Wittering B2198. 1m on sharp bend, turn L into Bookers Ln, 2nd house on L. Parking available.* **Sat 11 May (11-4). Evening opening Sat 6 July (4-8). Adm £5, chd free. Light refreshments (May). Wine & cheese (July). Visits also by arrangement for groups of up to 30.** A garden for all seasons which delights the visitor. Started in 1988, it features cottage, woodland and

Japanese style gardens, water features and borders of perennials with a particular emphasis on southern hemisphere plants. Unusual plants for the plantsman to enjoy, many grown from seed. The differing styles of the garden flow together making it easy to wander anywhere. Wheelchair access over grass, bark paths and unfenced ponds.

30 NEW **THE COTTAGE**
Potts Lane, Pulborough,
RH20 2BT. Claire
Denman, 07739 820712,
Claire.denman1@yahoo.co.uk.
Potts Ln is a pedestrian lane off Lower St (A283). The entrance is between two houses next to T-lights. Parking in Lower St public car park.

Sat 18 May, Sat 7 Sept (10-6). Adm £6, chd free. Pre-booking essential, please visit www.ngs. org.uk for information & booking. Two hour timed slots at 10am, 12pm, 2pm & 4pm. Home-made teas. Visits also by arrangement 6 May to 7 Oct for groups of 10 to 20. Home-made teas inc.
A quintessential English cottage garden, jam packed with a mix of perennials and bulbs on a potentially challenging multi layered site. Comprising four distinct rooms inc a small roof terrace, top terrace sitting above the house garden and a vegetable garden built in what was a small swimming pool. This is not a huge garden, however every square inch has been used!

47,000 people affected by cancer were reached by Maggie's centres supported by the National Garden Scheme over the last 12 months

Fairlight Hall

© Judi Lion

31 **CROSSLANDS FLOWER NURSERY**
Barnham Lane, Walberton, Arundel, BN18 0AX. Ben Cross, www.facebook.com/ CrosslandsFlowerNursery. *4m W of Arundel. Midway between Barnham & Walberton down Barnham Ln, signed Crosslands Flower Nursery.* **Thur 29 Feb, Tue 5 Mar (10-12). Adm £10, chd free. Pre-booking essential, please visit www.ngs.org.uk for information & booking. Tea.**
A 2 hr all access tour of a fourth generation, award-winning, sustainably run flower nursery with 3 acres of glasshouses filled to the brim with Sussex grown alstroemeria. There will be an opportunity to purchase flowers at the end of the tour.

32 CUMBERLAND HOUSE
Cray's Lane, Thakeham, Pulborough, RH20 3ER. George & Jane Blunden. *At junction of Cray's Ln & The Street, nr the church.* **Thur 25, Sun 28 July (2-5). Combined adm with Thakeham Place Farm £10, chd free. Home-made teas at Thakeham Place Farm.**
A Georgian village house (not open), next to the C12 church with a beautiful, mature ¾ acre English country garden comprising a walled garden laid out as a series of rooms with well-stocked flower beds, two rare ginkgo trees and yew topiary, leading to an informal garden with vegetable, herb and fruit areas, pleached limes and a lawn shaded by a copper beech tree. Wheelchair access through gate at right-hand side of house.

33 CUPANI GARDEN
8 Sandgate Close, Seaford, BN25 3LL. Dr Denis Jones & Ms Aideen Jones OBE. *From A259 follow signs to Alfriston, E of Seaford. R off Alfriston Rd onto Hillside Ave, 2nd L,1st R & 1st R. Park in adjoining streets. Bus 12A Brighton/ Eastbourne, get off Millberg Rd stop & walk down alley to the garden.* **Wed 22 May (1.30-5). Combined adm, inc home-made teas, with Lavender Cottage £12, chd £5. Pre-booking essential, please phone 01323 899452, email sweetpeasa52@gmail.com or visit www.cupanigarden.com for information & booking. Opening with Seaford Gardens on Sun 2, Sun 30 June. Visits also by**
arrangement 20 May to 4 Aug for groups of 6 to 20. Adm inc teas. Lunch on request.
Cupani is a tranquil haven with a delightful mix of trees, shrubs and perennial border. Courtyard garden, gazebo, summerhouse, water features, sweet pea obelisks and a huge range of plants. See TripAdvisor reviews. The garden has undergone major renovations in 2023/2024 and now inc a gravel garden, some more tropical planting and the old cutting garden has been replaced with planted troughs.

34 DALE PARK HOUSE
Madehurst, Arundel, BN18 0NP. Robert & Jane Green, 01243 814260, robertgreenfarming@gmail.com. *4m W of Arundel. Take A27 E from Chichester or W from Arundel, then A29 (London) for 2m, turn L to Madehurst & follow red arrows.* **Visits by arrangement 20 May to 5 July. Adm £5, chd free. Home-made teas.**
Set in parkland, enjoying magnificent views from the sea. Come and relax in the large walled garden which features an impressive 200ft herbaceous border. There is also a sunken gravel garden, mixed borders, a small rose garden, dreamy rose and clematis arches, an interesting collection of hostas, foliage plants and shrubs, and an orchard and kitchen garden.

GROUP OPENING

35 DEAKS LANE GARDENS
Deaks Lane, Ansty, Haywards Heath. *3m W of Haywards Heath on A272. 1m E of A23. At r'about at junction of A272 & B2036 take exit A272 Bolney, then take immed R onto Deaks Ln. Park at Ansty Village Centre on R, where tickets for gardens are purchased.* **Sun 16 June (12-4). Combined adm £6, chd free. Home-made teas at Ansty Village Centre.**

8 CROUCH FIELDS
RH17 5NW. Danielle & Jason Chapman.

3 LAVENDER COTTAGES
RH17 5AS. Derry Baillieux.

THICKETS
RH17 5AS. Becky & Matt Morgan.

Ansty's garden trail starts at the Village Centre where parking, tickets and maps are available, along with refreshments and plant sale. A walking trail; the owners are keen to tell you about their gardens with plenty of take home ideas. The two gardens on Deaks Lane each bring different designs and feel but are united in attracting pollinators and wildlife. 3 Lavender Cottages is a bee haven with an attractive colourful cottage garden to the front and pretty courtyard to the rear. The planting is particularly well chosen. Two doors down, Thickets has raised beds and an abundance of roses and hydrangeas supplying plenty of bee and butterfly stops. There are seating areas from which to enjoy different aspects of the garden. Some mature trees give a woodland feel. Just 2 mins away is 8 Crouch Fields which offers stylish structure, a rill and beautiful repeat planting. A new garden with a crisp and modern feel to it.

36 ◆ **DENMANS GARDEN**
Denmans Lane, Fontwell, BN18 0SU. Gwendolyn van Paasschen. *5m from Chichester & Arundel. Off A27, ½ m W of Fontwell r'about.* **For NGS: Sun 17 Mar, Sun 28 Apr, Sun 27 Oct (11-4). Adm £9, chd £7. Pre-booking essential, please phone 01243 278950, email office@denmans.org or visit www. denmans.org for information & booking. Light refreshments. For other opening times and information, please phone, email or visit garden website.**
Created by Joyce Robinson, a brilliant pioneer in gravel gardening and former home of influential landscape designer, John Brookes MBE. Denmans is a Grade II registered post-war garden renowned for its curvilinear layout and complex plantings. Enjoy year-round colour, unusual plants, structure and fragrance in the gravel gardens, faux riverbeds, intimate walled garden, ponds and conservatory. On site there is a plant centre with unusual plants for sale, a gift shop and Midpines Café offering breakfast, lunch, afternoon tea and a selection of sweet treats.

37 47 DENMANS LANE
Lindfield, Haywards Heath,
RH16 2JN. Sue & Jim
Stockwell, 01444 459363,
jamesastockwell@aol.com, www.
lindfield-gardens.co.uk/47denmans-
lane. *Approx 1½ m NE of Haywards
Heath town centre. From Haywards
Heath Train Stn follow B2028 signed
Lindfield & Ardingly for 1m. At T-lights
turn L into Hickmans Ln, then after
100 metres take 1st R into Denmans
Ln.* **Sat 30 Mar, Mon 1, Sun 14 Apr,
Mon 6, Sun 19 May (1-5). Adm
£7, chd free. Home-made teas.
Visits also by arrangement Mar to
Sept for groups of 5+. Home-made
teas inc.**
This beautiful and tranquil 1 acre
garden was described by Sussex
Life as a 'garden where plants star'.
Created by the owners over the
past 20 yrs, it is planted for interest
throughout the yr. Spring bulbs are
followed by azaleas, rhododendrons,
roses and herbaceous perennials. The
garden also has ponds, vegetable
and fruit gardens. Extensive choice
of perennial and annual bedding
plants plus home-made jams for sale.
Most of the garden accessible by
wheelchair with some steep slopes.
♿ ❀ 🚗 ☕ ⋙

GROUP OPENING

**38 NEW DITCHLING GARDEN
TRAIL**
Ditchling, nr Hassocks. *Close to
A23, 8m N of Brighton at the junction
of the B2112 & B2116. No on road
parking. Use new car park on B2116,
West St, BN6 8TS. Ideally, follow
signs through churchyard, Church Ln
to High St & maps available at The
Sandrock gardens.* **Sat 6 July (11-
5). Combined adm £8, chd free.
Home-made teas at Meadow
Cottage.**

NEW ASPIN
Farm Lane, BN6 8UN.
Graeme & Lorna Hemsley.

NEW THE BARN
The Sandrock, BN6 8TA.
Jane Traies.

NEW COUM COTTAGE
BN6 8TA. Valerie Winter.

NEW 4 THE DYMOCKS
BN6 8SU. Caroline Senior,
www.instagram.com/potandpen.

NEW MEADOW COTTAGE
24 Beacon Road, BN6 8UL.
Yvonne Hennessy.

NEW SEPTEMBER COTTAGE
The Sandrock, BN6 8TA.
Pamela Roy-Jones.

Set within the South Downs National
Park, Ditchling is a thriving village
dating back to the Anglo-Saxon
period. Today it is still home to artists,
writers and craftspeople, along with
musicians and winemakers. The
museum holds an internationally
important collection of work by
the artists and craftspeople who
were resident over many yrs. The
Horticultural Society was established
in 1822 and is one of the oldest in
the country. The love and passion for
gardening is evident in the gardens
opening. Set within the narrow roads
of Ditchling there will be time to
explore each garden to discover the
different planting and design styles,
from formal to country gardens plus
the smaller gardens packed with
colour and plants, and to talk to the
owners. Each garden has its own
feel, united by a love of bees, birds,
butterflies and wildlife. Maybe even
spot a hedgehog family. Public WC
below the village hall.
❀ ☕ ⋙

Bumble Farm

39 DOWN PLACE

South Harting, Petersfield, GU31 5PN. Mrs David Thistleton-Smith, 01730 825374, selina@downplace.co.uk. *1m SE of South Harting. B2141 to Chichester, turn L down unmarked lane below top of hill.* **Sat 23, Sun 24 Mar, Sun 16, Mon 17 June (1.30-5.30). Adm £5, chd free. Home-made teas & cream teas. Visits also by arrangement for groups of 15+.**
Set on the South Downs with panoramic views out to the undulating wooded countryside. The garden merges seamlessly into its surrounding landscape with rose and herbaceous borders that have been moulded into the sloping ground. There is a well-stocked vegetable garden and walks shaded by beech trees which surround the natural wildflower meadow where various native orchids flourish. The wildflower meadow is covered in natural wild daffodils in April, cowslips in May, and six varieties of wild orchids, plus various other wild flowers from the end of May through to early July. Seeds from the meadow are used to regenerate devastated areas in the South Downs National Park. Substantial top terrace and borders accessible to wheelchairs.

&. ✽ ☕))

40 DRIFTWOOD

4 Marine Drive, Bishopstone, Seaford, BN25 2RS. Geoff Stonebanks & Mark Glassman, 01323 899296, visitdriftwood@gmail.com, www.driftwoodbysea.co.uk. *A259 between Seaford & Newhaven. From Seaford, turn R into Bishopstone Rd, then immed L into Marine Dr, 2nd on R. Only park same side as house please, not on bend beyond the drive.* **Visits by arrangement June & July for groups of up to 30. Adm £6, chd free. Home-made teas or discuss other catering options upon booking.**
Monty Don introduced Driftwood on BBC Gardeners' World in 2016 saying "a small garden by the sea, full of character with inspired planting and design". Filmed for BBC Gardeners' World for the second time in Aug 2023 for broadcast in 2024. Sunday Telegraph said, "Geoff's enthusiasm is catching, he and his amazing garden deserve every visitor that makes their way up his enchanting garden path". Check out the 200 5-star reviews on TripAdvisor, awarded three successive

Certificates of Excellence and three successive Travellers Choice Awards. Selection of Geoff's home-made cakes, all served on vintage china, on trays, in the garden. Sorry, no WC.

🐾 🐕 ☕))

41 DURFORD ABBEY BARN

Petersfield, GU31 5AU. Mr & Mrs Lund. *3m from Petersfield. Situated on the S side of the A272 between Petersfield & Rogate, 1m from the junction with B2072.* **Sat 15, Sun 16 June (1-5.30). Adm £5, chd free. Home-made teas.**
A 1 acre plot with areas styled with cottage garden, prairie and shady borders set in the South Downs National Park with views of the Downs. Plants for sale and small art exhibition. Partial wheelchair access due to quite steep grass slopes.

&. 🐾 ✽ ☕))

42 DURRANCE MANOR

Smithers Hill Lane, Shipley, RH13 8PE. Gordon Lindsay, 01403 741577, galindsay@gmail.com. *7m SW of Horsham. A24 to A272 (S from Horsham, N from Worthing), turn W towards Billingshurst. Approx 1³/₄m, 2nd L Smithers Hill Ln signed to Countryman Pub. Garden 2nd on L.* **Mon 26 Aug (12-6). Adm £8, chd free. Home-made teas. Visits also by arrangement 1 May to 22 Sept for groups of 10 to 30. Home-made teas inc.**
This 2 acre garden surrounding a medieval hall house (not open) with Horsham stone roof, enjoys uninterrupted views over a ha-ha of the South Downs and Chanctonbury Ring. There are many different gardens here, Japanese inspired gardens, a large pond, wildflower meadow and orchard, colourful long borders and vegetable garden. There is also a Monet style bridge over a pond with water lilies.

&. 🐾 ✽ 🚗 ☕))

GROUP OPENING

43 EAST GRINSTEAD GARDENS

7m E of Crawley on A264 & 14m N of Uckfield on A22. For Allotments park at Imberhorne Lane Car Park, disabled parking on site. For 5 Nightingale Cl & 7 Nightingale Cl park on Hurst Farm Rd. Roadside parking at 35 Blount Ave. **Sun 30 June, Sun 1 Sept (1-5). Combined adm £6,**

chd free. Home-made teas at 5 Nightingale Close.

35 BLOUNT AVENUE
RH19 1JJ. Nicki Conlon.
Open on all dates

IMBERHORNE ALLOTMENTS
RH19 1QX. Imberhorne Allotment Association, www.imberhorneallotments.org.
Open on Sun 30 June

5 NIGHTINGALE CLOSE
RH19 4DG. Carole & Terry Heather.
Open on all dates

7 NIGHTINGALE CLOSE
RH19 4DG. Gail & Andy Peel.
Open on all dates

5 Nightingale Close occupies a corner plot. Beautifully landscaped on two levels with wonderful and colourful planting around a naturalistic Koi pond, productive fruit and vegetable area, rose and herbaceous beds, and topiary trees. 7 Nightingale Avenue, contains a fabulous display of roses and gorgeous romantic planting leading down to a stream. The garden also inc a potager and collection of bonsai. 35 Blount Avenue, where contemporary design meets colourful and exuberant planting in this south facing town garden. Colour themed large borders, tropical planting and areas of colour are on show. Dahlias, roses and a variety of interesting perennials feature in the front garden packed with colour. Imberhorne Allotments consist of 80 plots with a diverse range of planting inc grapevines, assorted vegetables, fruit, flowers and a community orchard, well worth a visit with produce on sale. Plant sales at 35 Blount Avenue and 7 Nightingale Close. The Town Council hanging baskets and planting in the High Street are not to be missed and have achieved a Gold Medal from South and South East in Bloom. For steam train fans, the Bluebell Railway starts nearby.

✽ ☕))

GROUP OPENING

44 EASTBOURNE CENTRAL GARDEN TRAIL

Four gardens in Eastbourne town centre, within walking distance of each other, or No. 3 bus. Tickets & trail maps available at each garden. Limited roadside parking, some metered. **Sun 2 June (1-5). Combined adm £7, chd free. Home-made teas.**

51 CARLISLE ROAD
BN21 4JR. E & N Fraser-Gausden, the3growbags.com.

NEW **CHELMSFORD LODGE**
12 Granville Road, BN20 7HE. Jane Stevens.

DITTONS END
Southfields Road, BN21 1BZ. Mrs Frances Hodkinson.

HARDWYCKE
Southfields Road, BN21 1BZ. Lois Machin.

A garden that last opened for NGS in 2005, Chelmsford Lodge, returns to join three other gardens that have regularly opened, to create a central Eastbourne walking trail. 51 Carlisle Road is a secluded, award-winning garden with glorious early summer colour from an abundance of old roses, perennials mixed beds and diverse planting. Dittons End is a lovely well maintained town garden. The 35ft x 20ft back is a pretty garden with a small lawn area and a patio surrounded by a selection of pots and packed borders with lots of colour, while the front is 25ft x 18ft with a compact lawn with colourful borders. Hardwycke is just two houses away with many usual and unusual plants and many shrubs. Chelmsford Lodge's ¾ acre garden has a large lawn with herbaceous borders, a wild garden and a secret garden, a pond, greenhouse, rockery, orchard and many rare trees.

45 54 ELMLEIGH
Midhurst, GU29 9HA. Wendy Liddle, 07796 562275, wendyliddle@btconnect.com. ¼ m W of Midhurst off A272. Parking off road on marked grass area. Reserved disabled parking at top of drive, please phone on arrival for assistance. **Sat 25, Sun 26, Mon 27 May (11-5). Adm £4, chd free. Home-made cakes, cream teas & home-made elderflower cordial. Visits also by arrangement 30 Apr to 30 Sept for groups of 10 to 20.**
⅕ acre property with terraced front garden, leading to a heavily planted rear garden with majestic 120 yr old black pines. Shrubs, perennials, and packed with interest around every corner providing all season colours. Many raised beds, numerous sculptures, vegetables in boxes, a greenhouse, pond and a large collection of tree lilies, growing 6-8ft. Child friendly. Come and

enjoy the peace and tranquillity in this award-winning garden, enjoy our little bit of heaven. Not suitable for large electric buggies.

46 FAIRLIGHT END
Pett Road, Pett, Hastings, TN35 4HB. Chris & Robin Hutt, 07774 863750, chrishutt@fairlightend.co.uk, www.fairlightend.co.uk. 4m E of Hastings. From Hastings take A259 to Rye. At White Hart Beefeater turn R into Friars Hill. Descend into Pett village. **Visits by arrangement 15 May to 15 Sept for groups of 10+. Home-made teas. Donation to Pett Village Hall.**
Gardens Illustrated said 'The 18th century house is at the highest point in the garden with views down the slope over abundant borders and velvety lawns that are punctuated by clusters of specimen trees and shrubs. Beyond and below are the wildflower meadows and the ponds with a backdrop of the gloriously unspoilt Wealden landscape'. Wheelchair access with steep paths, gravelled areas and unfenced ponds.

47 FAIRLIGHT HALL
Martineau Lane, Hastings, TN35 5DR. Mr & Mrs David Kowitz, www.fairlighthall.co.uk. 2m E of Hastings. A259 from Hastings towards Dover & Rye, 2m turn R into Martineau Ln. **Thur 19 Sept (10-4). Adm £10, chd free. Home-made teas. Pre-booking preferred.**
A restored stunning garden in East Sussex. The formal gardens extend over 9 acres and surround the Victorian Gothic mansion (not open). Features semitropical woodland avenues, a huge contemporary walled garden with amphitheatre and two 110 metre perennial borders above and below ha-ha with far-reaching views across Rye Bay. Home-made preserves, vegetables and cut flowers for sale. Pop-up café serving a range of cakes and hot drinks. Most of the garden can be viewed by wheelchair. Please inform us on arrival, so we can direct you to disabled parking.

48 NEW ◆ FARLEYS SCULPTURE GARDEN
Muddles Green, Chiddingly, nr Lewes, BN8 6HW. Farleys House & Gallery Ltd, 01825 872856, www.farleyshouseandgallery.co.uk/sculpture-garden. 9m from Lewes, off A22. Turn L off A22 towards Eastbourne at BP garage at Golden Cross. After 1m turn R at T-junction. Farleys is on R. Free car park. **For NGS: Sat 8 June (10-4.30). Adm £6. Light refreshments. For other opening times and information, please phone or visit garden website.**
Designed as different themed rooms for sculpture, Farleys garden presents our permanent collection of works chosen by photographer Lee Miller and surrealist artist Roland Penrose alongside works by contemporary guest sculptors. Over the yrs, giants, goddesses, mythical African creatures and Roland's own work has populated the garden in the company of work by his artist friends. Farleys is taking part in the NGS for the first time as part of its special 75 yrs celebrations. Also access to Farleys Gallery with two different exhibitions to enjoy. Locally baked cake, light salads and refreshments will be available in Farleys Gallery Café.

49 FINDON PLACE
Findon, Worthing, BN14 0RF. Miss Caroline Hill, 01903 877085, hello@findonplace.com, www.findonplace.com. Directly off A24 N of Worthing. Follow signs to Findon Parish Church & park through the 1st driveway on LHS. **Sun 21 July (2-6). Adm £7, chd free. Pre-booking essential, please visit www.ngs.org.uk for information & booking. Cream teas. Visits also by arrangement May to Sept for groups of 15 to 30.**
Stunning grounds and gardens surrounding a Grade II listed Georgian country house (not open), nestled at the foot of the South Downs. The most glorious setting for a tapestry of perennial borders set off by Sussex flint walls. The many charms inc a yew allee, cloud pruned trees, espaliered fruit trees, a productive ornamental kitchen garden, rose arbours and arches, and a cutting garden.

Brightling Down Farm

50 FITTLEWORTH HOUSE

Bedham Lane, Fittleworth, Pulborough, RH20 1JH. Edward & Isabel Braham, 01798 865074, marksaunders66.com@gmail.com, www.racingandgreen.com. *2m E, SE of Petworth. Midway between Petworth & Pulborough on the A283 in Fittleworth, turn into lane signed Bedham just off sharp bend. Garden is 50yds along on the L. Plenty of car parking space.* **Every Wed 24 Apr to 15 May, Wed 12 June to 19 June, Wed 10 July to 24 July, Wed 7 Aug (2-5). Adm £5, chd free. Home-made teas. Visits also by arrangement 22 Apr to 23 Aug for groups of 8 to 40.**
3 acre tranquil, romantic, country garden with walled kitchen garden growing a wide range of fruit, vegetables and flowers inc a large collection of dahlias. Large glasshouse and old potting shed, mixed flower borders, roses, rhododendrons and lawns. Magnificent 115ft tall cedar overlooks wisteria covered Grade II listed Georgian house (not open). Wild garden, long grass areas and stream.

The garden sits on a gentle slope, but is accessible for wheelchairs and buggies.

51 FIVE OAKS COTTAGE

Petworth, RH20 1HD. Jean & Steve Jackman. *5m S of Pulborough. SatNav does not work! To ensure best route, we provide printed directions, please email jeanjackman@hotmail.com or call 07939 272443.* **Fri 14, Sat 15, Sun 16 June (10-5). Adm £5. Pre-booking essential, please visit www.ngs. org.uk for information & booking. Home-made teas (cash only).**
An acre of delicate jungle surrounding an Arts and Crafts style cottage (not open) with stunning views of the South Downs. Our unconventional garden is designed to encourage maximum wildlife with a knapweed and hogweed meadow on clay attracting clouds of butterflies, plus two small ponds and lots of seating. An award-winning, organic garden with a magical atmosphere.

52 THE FOLLY

Charlton, Chichester, PO18 0HU. Joan Burnett, 01243 811307, joankeirburnett@gmail.com, www.thefollycharlton.com. *7m N of Chichester & S of Midhurst off A286 at Singleton, follow signs to Charlton. Follow NGS parking signs. No parking in lane, drop off only. Parking nr the Fox Goes Free pub.* **Sun 23 June, Sun 21 July, Sun 25 Aug (2-4.30). Adm £5, chd free. Home-made teas. Visits also by arrangement 25 June to 29 Aug.**
Colourful cottage garden surrounding a C16 period house (not open), set in pretty downland village of Charlton, close to Levin Down Nature Reserve. Herbaceous borders well-stocked with a wide range of plants. Variety of perennials, grasses, annuals and shrubs to provide long season of colour and interest. Old well. Busy bees. Art studio open to visitors. Partial wheelchair access with steps from patio to lawn. Visitors with mobility issues can be dropped off at the gate. No dogs.

53 FOREST RIDGE
Paddockhurst Lane, Balcombe, RH17 6QZ. Philip & Rosie Wiltshire, 07900 621838, rosiem. wiltshire@btinternet.com. *3m from M23, J10a. M23 J10a take B2036 to Balcombe. After 2/3m take 1st L onto B2110. After Worth School turn R into Back Ln. After 2m it becomes Paddockhurst Ln. Forest Ridge on R after 2¼m. Ignore SatNav to track!* Sat 18, Sun 19 May (2-5.30). Adm £6, chd free. Home-made teas (cash only).
A charming 4½ acre Victorian garden with far-reaching views, boasting the oldest Atlantic cedar in Sussex. The owners themselves are undertaking a major garden restoration: felling, planting and redesigning areas. Within the garden there is formal and informal planting, woodland dell and mini arboretum. Azaleas, rhododendrons and camellias abound, rare and unusual species. A garden to watch over the coming yrs as the new plantings develop and the newly designed areas grow and flourish. A garden to explore! Please Note: There are several deep-water ponds.

🐕 🛏 🍵))

54 FOXGLOVE COTTAGE
29 Orchard Road, Horsham, RH13 5NF. Peter & Terri Lefevre, www.facebook.com/ FoxgloveCottage1. *East Horsham. At Horsham Stn, over bridge, at r'about 3rd exit (Crawley), 1st R Stirling Way, at end turn L, 1st R Orchard Rd. From A281, take Clarence Rd, at end turn R, at end turn L Orchard Rd. Street parking.* Sun 26 May, Wed 3, Sun 7 July (1-5). Adm £5, chd free. Home-made teas inc vegan, gluten & dairy free cake.
A ¼ acre plantaholic's garden, full of containers, vintage finds and quirky elements. Paths intersect both sunny and shady borders bursting with colourful planting and salvias in abundance! A beach hut summerhouse and deck are flanked by a water feature in a pebble circle. Two additional small ponds encourage wildlife. A surprise at every turn. The end of the garden is dedicated to a plant nursery. A recently added gravel garden for drought tolerant plants with a large, rusty metal arbour, called the Dome! Members of the Hardy Plant Society. A large selection of unusual plants for sale.

 🐕 ✿ 🍵))

55 FOXWOOD BARN
Little Heath Road, Fontwell, Arundel, BN18 0SR. Stephen & Teresa Roccia, 07867 383753, Teresa.m.roccia@gmail.com. *At the junction of Little Heath Rd & Dukes Rd, follow NGS signs. Separate drop off area for wheelchair access.* Sat 1, Sun 2 June (2-5). Adm £6, chd free. Visits also by arrangement June to Aug for groups of 10 to 30. Afternoon or evening visits.
From a green field site 5 yrs ago, this almost 2 acre garden has been developed into different areas inc a wildlife pond, rose and gravel garden, patio areas and a dry riverbed. There are herbaceous borders, wildflower areas and a small orchard and kitchen garden. A separate picnic area adjacent to a paddock with donkeys and ponies.

♿ ✿ 🛏 🍵 🌳))

56 THE GARDEN HOUSE
5 Warleigh Road, Brighton, BN1 4NT. Bridgette Saunders & Graham Lee, 07729 037182, contact@gardenhousebrighton. co.uk, www.gardenhousebrighton. co.uk. *1½m N of Brighton pier, Garden House is 1st L after Xrds, past the open market. Paid street parking. London Road Stn nearby. Buses 26 & 46 stopping at Bromley Rd.* Fri 19, Sun 21 Apr (1-5). Adm £6, chd free. Home-made teas. Visits also by arrangement 15 Mar to 26 Oct for groups of 10 to 30. Tour & Q&A inc.
One of Brighton's secret gardens. We aim to provide year-round interest with trees, shrubs, herbaceous borders and annuals, fruit and vegetables, two glasshouses, a pond and rockery. A friendly garden, always changing with a touch of magic to delight visitors, above all it is a slice of the country in the midst of a bustling city. Plants for sale.

🐕 ✿ 🍵))

57 ♦ GREAT DIXTER HOUSE, GARDENS & NURSERIES
Northiam, TN31 6PH. Great Dixter Charitable Trust, 01797 253107, ticketoffice@greatdixter.co.uk, www.greatdixter.co.uk. *8m N of Rye. Off A28 in Northiam, follow brown signs.* For opening times and information, please phone, email or visit garden website.
Designed by Edwin Lutyens and Nathaniel Lloyd. Christopher Lloyd made the garden one of the most experimental and constantly changing gardens of our time, a tradition now being carried on by Fergus Garrett. Clipped topiary, wildflower meadows, the famous long border, pot displays, exotic garden and more. Spring bulb displays are of particular note. Please see garden website for accessibility information.

♿ ✿ 🚗 🍵 ▣

58 HAMMERWOOD HOUSE
Iping, Midhurst, GU29 0PF. Mr & Mrs M Lakin. *3m W of Midhurst. Take A272 from Midhurst, approx 2m outside Midhurst turn R for Iping. Over bridge, uphill to grassy junction, turn R. From A3 leave for Liphook, follow B2070, turn L for Milland & Iping.* Sun 12 May (1-5). Adm £6, chd free. Home-made teas.
Large south facing garden with lots of mature shrubs inc camellias, rhododendrons and azaleas. An arboretum with a variety of flowering and fruit trees. The old yew and beech hedges give a certain amount of formality to this traditional English garden. Tea on the terrace is a must with the most beautiful view of the South Downs. For the more energetic there is a woodland walk. Partial wheelchair access as garden is set on a slope.

♿ 🐕 ✿ 🍵))

GROUP OPENING

59 HARLANDS GARDENS
Turners Mill Road, Haywards Heath, RH16 1NW. *Gardens within 5 min easy walk from train station & bus stop. Roadside parking is readily available. Park once to visit all gardens.* Sat 8, Sun 9 June (12-4.30). Combined adm £5, chd free. Home-made teas & light refreshments.

27 TURNERS MILL ROAD
Sam & Derek Swanson.

57 TURNERS MILL ROAD
Linda & Steve Mitchell.

NEW **62 TURNERS MILL ROAD**
Philip Rankin & Matthew Kindinger, www.instagram.com/p.a.rankin.

Come and be inspired by our trio of small town gardens and meet our latest newcomer. There will be lots of information on hand and ideas from all the owners who have been busy creating their gardens. They are a mix of different shapes and aspects with a focus on cottage style planting, pretty courtyards, gravel gardens, habitats for wildlife, container gardening, exotic planting schemes and prairie styles. Our popular plant sale will give visitors the opportunity to take home some of what they have seen in the gardens. Please check our Facebook page 'Harlands Gardens' for updated information. There will be a selection of refreshments available inc tea and home-made cake at No. 27 and light refreshments at No. 57.

& ✿ ☕ ◈))

GROUP OPENING

60 HASSOCKS GARDEN TRAIL
Close to A23, 6m N of Brighton, off A273. Between Stonepound Xrds & Keymer, N & S of B2116. Park in free car parks in Hassocks or on road, avoid Parklands Rd. Hassocks Stn nearby. Tickets & map available at each garden & allotments. **Sun 23 June (1-5). Combined adm £5, chd free. Light refreshments at St Edward's Church.**

5 EWART CLOSE
BN6 8FJ. Jeannie & Alex Sheppard.

LODGE HOUSE
Lodge Lane, BN6 8NA.
Jo & Glen Welfare.

PARKLANDS ROAD ALLOTMENTS
Parklands Road, BN6 8LF.
Tony Copeland & Jeannie Brooker.

Two contrasting gardens to suit many interests plus the allotments, along with a small strip of ancient woodland, make up this walkable trail. There is a young modern garden around a new build (not open) and a large wildlife/cottage garden close by, with the allotments a short walk away. The wildlife/cottage garden is wonderful but as can be expected, it is not manicured. There are some trip hazards, uneven steps, low branches and slippery areas, but as you explore this rich habitat the progress made by the owners in just 5 yrs is evident. The 59 allotments are not to be missed, a range of classic vegetables inc some exotic ones are grown. The allotmenteers will show you their plots and answer questions. There are spectacular views across to the Downs to Jack and Jill Windmills. Light refreshments at St Edward's Church, Lodge Lane, BN6 8NT. Public WC at Adastra Park, BN6 8QH and composting WC at allotments. Dogs permitted at allotments only.

✿ ☕ ◈))

GROUP OPENING

61 HELLINGLY PARISH TRAIL
From A267 turn into B2104 & immed L into village, follow signs to gardens. All gardens except Brook Cottage within walking distance. Parking opp church green, in field by Brook Cottage & by Cuckoo Trail. Tickets & maps available on green nr church & at May House. **Sun 16 June (11-5). Combined adm £7, chd free. Lunch & home-made teas at Brook Cottage.**

BROADVIEW
Church Road, BN27 4EX.
Gill Riches.

BROOK COTTAGE
Mill Lane, BN27 4HD. Dr Colin Tourle MBE & Mrs Jane Tourle.

NEW FLINT COTTAGE
Church Lane, BN27 4HA. Emma & Robbie Toothill.

NEW GLOBE COTTAGE
Mill Lane, BN27 4EY. Veronica Lee.

NEW GLOBE PLACE
Mill Lane, BN27 4EY.
Emma & Simon Freedman.

MAY HOUSE
7 The Martlets, BN27 4FA.
Lynda & David Stewart.

NEW POND COTTAGE
Mill Lane, BN27 4EY. Gill Nichols.

PRIORS GRANGE
7 Church Path, BN27 4EZ.
Sylvia Stephens.

Eight gardens in a delightful Sussex village, inc a pretty walled cottage garden with summerhouse and sunny terrace, a garden entered via a bridge over a large pond perfect for wildlife with countryside views and a courtyard, a family garden full of perennials, herbaceous plants, organic vegetables and flowers, a newly remodelled garden bursting with lavender, roses, alliums in a former Victorian school overlooking C12 Church of St Peter and St Paul, another two gardens in the heart of the village, one with a rose-filled front garden leading to a densely planted mature back garden (hosting plant sale) next door to an extensive garden still in development with beautiful trees and roses. On the outskirts an inspiring new-build garden has areas for sun, shade, vegetables, fruit trees, amid sounds of trickling water, and on the other side of the village, a unique garden (serving lunches and teas)

incorporates the River Cuckmere, a sluice gate and a lush mix of perennials and mature trees. Plant sale at Priors Grange. Wheelchair access to some gardens. Dogs on short leads.

& 🐕 ✿ ☕ ◈))

GROUP OPENING

63 HERSTMONCEUX PARISH TRAIL
Follow yellow NGS signs. Tickets & map available at each garden. Ticket covers all gardens. **Sun 23 June (12-5). Combined adm £7, chd free. Light refreshments at Hill House (2-5). Teas (12-5) & BBQ lunch (12-2) at The Windmill.**

THE ALLOTMENTS, STUNTS GREEN
BN27 4PP. Nicola Beart, Herstmonceux Allotments Association.

COWBEECH HOUSE
BN27 4JF. Anthony Hepburn.

NEW THE ELMS
Stunts Green, BN27 4PR.
Sarah Covey.

HILL HOUSE
Windmill Hill, BN27 4RU.
Maureen Madden & Terry Harland.
(See separate entry)

KERPSES
Trollilloes Lane, Cowbeech BN27 4JG.
Lynn & Peter Maguire.

MERRIE HARRIERS BARN
Cowbeech, BN27 4JQ.
Lee Henderson.

THE WINDMILL
BN27 4RT. Windmill Hill Windmill Trust,
www.windmillhillwindmill.org.

Seven gardens inc a historic windmill and allotments. In Cowbeech there are three gardens: Cowbeech House, a place to linger with an exciting range of water features and sculpture in the garden dating back to 1731. Vintage car collection on site to view. Merrie Harriers Barn is a garden with sweeping lawn and open countryside, colourful herbaceous planting and a large pond with places to sit and enjoy the view. Kerpses is a delightful mixture of mature trees, shrubs, herbaceous borders, vegetable garden, ponds and a meadow. In Stunts Green, The Allotments comprise 54 allotments growing a huge variety of traditional and unusual crops. Nearby is The Elms, a working florist's cutting garden. In Herstmonceux, Hill House has abundant roses, trees, shrubs and varied perennials, a greenhouse, and a wildlife pond with water lilies. Plenty of seating areas to sit and reflect and have tea. The historic Windmill is well worth a visit and where you can enjoy a BBQ lunch or tea.

 ))

64 THE HIDDEN GARDEN

School Lane (behind Selsey Library), Selsey, Chichester, PO20 9EH. Paul Sadler. *5m S of Chichester. Park behind Selsey Library or in front of the Academy School on School Ln. You will see The Bridge Support Centre, enter through the gate & The Hidden Garden is behind the centre.* **Sun 30 June (10-4). Adm £5, chd free. Home-made teas.**

The Hidden Garden is a community gardening project encouraging local people to become involved with growing fruit, vegetables, herbs and flowers as well as providing spaces for wildlife to thrive. The garden

is open to people of all ages and abilities, organised by the Selsey Community Forum but looked after by a dedicated group of local volunteers.

65 HIGH BEECHES WOODLAND AND WATER GARDEN

High Beeches Lane, Handcross, Haywards Heath, RH17 6HQ. High Beeches Gardens Conservation Trust, 01444 400589, gardens@highbeeches.com, www.highbeeches.com. *5m NW of Cuckfield. On B2110, 1m E of A23 at Handcross.* **For NGS: Sun 2 June, Sun 29 Sept (1-5). Adm £10, chd £4. Light refreshments. For other opening times and information, please phone, email or visit garden website.**

25 acres of enchanting, landscaped woodland and water gardens with spring daffodils, bluebells and azalea walks, many rare and beautiful plants, an ancient wildflower meadow and glorious autumn colours. Picnic area. National Collection of Stewartias.

66 ◆ HIGHDOWN GARDENS

33 Highdown Rise, Littlehampton Road, Goring-by-Sea, Worthing, BN12 6FB. Worthing Borough Council, 01273 263060, highdown. gardens@adur-worthing.gov.uk, www.highdowngardens.co.uk. *What3words app - quiet.stages. camera. Off the A259 Littlehampton Rd heading E towards Worthing. Turn L up Highdown Rise. Nearest train station: Goring-by-Sea.* **For NGS: Thur 15 Feb (10-4.30); Thur 2 May (10-8). Adm by donation. For other opening times and information, please phone, email or visit garden website.**

Highdown Gardens were created by Sir Frederick Stern. They are home to rare plants and trees, many grown from seed collected by Wilson, Farrer and Kingdon-Ward. A fully equipped glasshouse enables the propagation of this National Plant Collection. A visitor centre shares stories of the plants and people behind the gardens. A new accessible path leads to a sensory garden with a secret sea view. Highdown is also offering Snowdrop Identification tours on the 15th February (not for NGS), for more information and booking please see garden website. Accessible top pathway and lift to visitor centre, see garden website accessibility page for full details.

67 NEW HIGHLANDS

Etchingwood Lane, Framfield, Uckfield, TN22 5SA. Chris Brown, Head Gardener, www.instagram@ thesussexplanthunter. *1½ m E of Uckfield. Leave Uckfield on B2102 (Framfield Rd). Bear L onto Sandy Ln. Turn L at Xrds with Etchingwood Ln. Entrance via field gate in 100 metres on R. Do not use postcode for SatNav, use Highlands.* **Sat 15 June (10-4.30). Adm £9, chd free. Pre-booking essential, please visit www.ngs. org.uk for information & booking. Home-made teas.**

An 8 acre garden set around a house with C15 origins, amid pasture and woodland. Intensively gardened beds near the house inc hot and pink beds and a white garden, are kept vibrant through waves of annuals planted through the perennials. These give way to meadow, orchard, ponds and woodland plantings.

Lodsbridge Mill

68 HILL HOUSE
Windmill Hill, Herstmonceux, BN27 4RU. Maureen Madden & Terry Harland. *4m NE of Hailsham. Opp Windmill Hill PO. Parking for about 6 cars otherwise parking in adjacent streets.* **Sat 29, Sun 30 June (2-5). Adm £5, chd free. Light refreshments. Opening with Herstmonceux Parish Trail on Sun 23 June.**
6 yrs ago the garden was just lawn and a pond which had been filled in. The pond now is a wildlife pond with water lilies, and the garden has three sections divided by a pergola and two arches with climbing roses and honeysuckle. Trees, shrubs and as many perennials as can fit in the flower beds have been planted, and roses abound in the rose bed. A garden very easy to walk around with plenty of seating areas to sit and reflect. Wheelchair access through side gate. No steps in main garden, but steps (not steep) at end of garden to greenhouse and vegetable patch.
&. �֍ ♨))

69 HILLSIDE
The Green, Rottingdean, Brighton, BN2 7HA. Nicky & Dave Boys. *5m E of Brighton on A259. Turn onto High St which becomes The Green. Last house on L before RH-bend, opp Kipling Gardens. Seafront, short & long stay car parks, 5 mins. Frequent buses from Brighton, Eastbourne, Woodingdean.* **Fri 7, Sun 9 June (1-5). Adm £6, chd free.**
Historic Grade II* listed, flint walled garden with C18 barn and gazebo. Large chalk downland garden with naturalistic planting and mown pathways. Relaxed not manicured. Roses, shady trees, birds and bees that will be very active in June, give a secret garden feel. Herbaceous, woodland and poolside planting, willow walk and cottage garden. Behind the barn, ancient trees and beehives fringe a wild meadow with views to the windmill. Hillside honey for sale. Art for sale in barn by local artist in residence, Amanda Davidson.
♨))

70 4 HILLSIDE COTTAGES
Downs Road, West Stoke, Chichester, PO18 9BL. Heather & Chris Lock, 01243 574802, chlock@btinternet.com. *3m NW of Chichester. From A286 at Lavant, head W for 1½m, nr Kingley Vale.* **Sun 9 June, Sun 21 July, Sun 18 Aug (11-4). Adm £5, chd free. Home-made teas. Visits also by**
arrangement 2 June to 18 Aug.
In a rural setting this stunning garden is densely planted with mixed borders and shrubs. Large collection of roses, clematis, fuchsias and dahlias, a profusion of colour and scent in a well maintained garden. Please visit www.ngs.org.uk for pop-up openings in June, July and August.
♨

71 HOLLY HOUSE
Beaconsfield Road, Chelwood Gate, Haywards Heath, RH17 7LF. Mrs Deirdre Birchell, 01825 740484, db@hollyhousebnb.co.uk, www.hollyhousebnb.co.uk. *7m E of Haywards Heath. From Nutley village on A22 turn off at Hathi Restaurant signed Chelwood Gate 2m. Chelwood Gate Village Hall on R, Holly House is opp.* **Sat 17, Sun 18 Aug (2-5). Adm £6, chd free. Home-made teas. Visits also by arrangement 10 May to 13 Sept.**
An acre of English garden providing views and cameos of plants and trees round every corner with many different areas giving constant interest. A fish pond and a wildlife pond beside a grassy area with many shrubs and flower beds. Among the trees and winding paths there is a cottage garden which is a profusion of colour and peace. Exhibition of paintings and cards by owner. Garden accessible by wheelchair in good weather, but it is not easy.
&. ✖ 🚗 🛏 ♨))

72 HOLLYMOUNT
Burnt Oak Road, High Hurstwood, Uckfield, TN22 4AE. Jonathan Hughes-Morgan, 07968 848418, jonnyhughesmorgan@gmail.com. *Exactly halfway between Uckfield & Crowborough, just off the A26. From A26 S of Crowborough or A272 between Uckfield & Buxted, follow sign to High Hurstwood. From N approx 2m down Chillies Ln take 1st L, from S 1½m up Hurstwood Rd take 3rd R, ½m up on L.* **Sun 26 May, Sun 23 June, Sun 21 July, Sun 25 Aug (12-5). Adm £7, chd free. Home-made teas. Visits also by arrangement Apr to Sept for groups of 10+.**
A new 7 acre garden on sloping hillside. Four large ponds, a stream, waterfalls, terraced beds, interesting planting, some tropical, large rhododendrons, wildlife; alpacas, pigs, chickens, ducks, fish. The garden has a great variety of trees,
two greenhouses, shepherds hut, summerhouse, paths, kitchen garden, many decks and wildflower terracing to the rear. Very peaceful setting with great views.
🄳 🛏 ♨))

73 HOOPERS FARM
Vale Road, Mayfield, TN20 6BD. Andrew & Sarah Ratcliffe. *10m S of Tunbridge Wells. Turn off A267 into Mayfield. Parking in the village & field parking at Hoopers Farm, TN20 6BD.* **Sat 8, Sun 9 June (11-5). Adm £6, chd free. Home-made teas. Opening with Mayfield Gardens on Sat 13, Sun 14 July.**
Large south facing garden with colour themed mixed herbaceous planting. Mature trees, flowering shrubs, rose beds and rose arbour, rock garden, secret garden and vegetable plot. New planted area with lots of late season colour. Recent enhancement of lawn area into wildflower meadow. Lovely views. Plant sales by Rapkyns Nursery. Local musicians will entertain in the garden on some of the dates. Regional Finalist, The English Garden Magazine's The Nation's Favourite Gardens 2023. Wheelchair access to most of the garden.
&. ✖ ✖ ♨))

74 THE HUNDRED HOUSE
Pound Lane, Framfield, TN22 5RU. Dr & Mrs Michael Gurney. *4m E of Uckfield. From Uckfield take B2102 through Framfield. 1m from centre of village turn L into Pound Ln, then ¾m on R. Disabled parking close by the entrance gate to the garden.* **Sat 20, Sun 21 July (2-5.30). Adm £7, chd free. Home-made teas.**
Delightful garden with panoramic views, set in the grounds of the historic The Hundred House (not open). Fine stone ha-ha. 1½ acre garden with mixed herbaceous borders, productive vegetable garden, greenhouse, ancient yew tree, pond area with some subtropical plants, secret woodland copse and orchard. Beech hedge, field walk and silver birch (Jacquemontii) grove. Homegrown plants, vegetables and fruit for sale.
&. ✖ ✖ ♨))

75 JUDY'S COTTAGE GARDEN
33 The Plantation, Worthing, BN13 2AE. Mrs Judy Gordon. *Salvington. A24 meets A27 at Offington r'about, turn into Offington Ln, 1st R into The Plantation.*

Fri 29 Mar, Fri 31 May, Fri 6 Sept (10.30-3.30). Adm £5, chd free. Home-made teas.

A beautiful medium sized cottage garden with something of interest all year-round. The garden has several mature trees creating a feeling of seclusion. The informal beds contain a mixture of shrubs, perennials, cottage garden plants and spring bulbs. There are little hidden areas to enjoy, a small fish pond and other water features. There is also a pretty log cabin overlooking the garden.

76 THE JUNGLE GARDEN

144 Rodmell Avenue, Saltdean, Brighton, BN2 8PJ. Sue & Ray Warner. *6m E of Brighton. A259 between Rottingdean & Telscombe, turn into Saltdean (Longridge Ave) at T-lights. Rodmell Ave last turning on R, house ½ m on R. Parking on the road outside the house or adjoining streets.* **Thur 25, Sat 27 July (11-5). Combined adm with Tor Cottage £5, chd free. Home-made teas. Open nearby 33 Wivelsfield Road.**

A fun jungle garden, created in 2012, but completely revamped in 2021. Measuring 65ft x 36ft but appearing larger with winding paths that lead you through lush jungle and insect friendly planting, listen out for jungle sounds and watch out for Tyson, the tiger! Tea and home-made cakes served overlooking the jungle. Exquisite planting of exotic plants.

77 KEMP TOWN ENCLOSURES: SOUTH GARDEN

Lewes Crescent, Brighton, BN2 1FH. Jason Saul, Head Gardener, www.kte.org.uk. *On S coast, 1m E of Brighton Palace Pier, ½ m W of Brighton Marina. 2m from Brighton Stn. Bus No. 7, stop St Mary's Hall. M23/A23 to Brighton Palace Pier; L on A259. 5m S A27 on B2123, R on A259.* **Wed 5 June (12-5). Adm £6, chd free. Pre-booked tickets preferred. Cash ideally on the day. Tours available. No refreshments, good coffee shops nearby.**

Not to be confused with the Secret Garden nearby, this unique historic Grade II listed Regency private town garden is in a spectacular seaside setting. Enduring strong salty winds and thin chalk soil. The garden balances naturalistic planting and a more ordered look, relaxed not manicured. With several distinctive

areas, this wonderful 5 acre garden combines open lawns, meadows, winding paths, trees, herbaceous borders, and a shaded woodland garden. Designed by Henry Phillips, the garden was a central feature of the Regency development of the Kemp Town Estate. Queen Victoria and Edward VII walked in these gardens. Ramped gate entry. Gravel winding paths give access to most of the garden. Relatively steep slopes on main lawn and in the garden tunnel.

78 ◆ KING JOHN'S LODGE

Sheepstreet Lane, Etchingham, TN19 7AZ. Harry Cunningham, 01580 819220, harry@ kingjohnsnursery.co.uk, www.kingjohnsnursery.co.uk. *2m W of Hurst Green. Off A265 nr Etchingham. From Burwash turn L before Etchingham Church, from Hurst Green turn R after church, into Church Ln, which leads into Sheepstreet Ln after ½ m, then L after 1m.* **For NGS: Sat 23 Mar, Sat 25, Sun 26 May, Sat 29, Sun 30 June, Sat 14 Sept (10-5). Adm £5, chd free. Light refreshments. For other opening times and information, please phone, email or visit garden website.**

4 acre romantic garden for all seasons. An ongoing family project since 1987 with new areas completed in 2020. From the eclectic shop, nursery and tearoom, stroll past wildlife pond through orchard with bulbs, meadow, rose walk and fruit according to the season. Historic house (not open) has broad lawn, fountain, herbaceous border, pond and ha-ha. Explore secret woodland with renovated pond and admire majestic trees and 4 acre meadows. Garden is mainly flat. Areas with steps can usually be accessed from other areas. Disabled WC.

79 KITCHENHAM FARM

Kitchenham Road, Ashburnham, Battle, TN33 9NP. Amanda & Monty Worssam. *5m S of Battle. S of Ashburnham Place from A271 Herstmonceux to Bexhill road, take L turn 500 metres after Boreham St. Kitchenham Farm is 500 metres on L.* **Wed 5, Sat 8 June, Tue 6, Sat 10 Aug (2-5). Adm £6, chd free. Home-made teas.**

1 acre country house garden set amongst traditional farm buildings with stunning views over the Sussex

countryside. Series of borders around the house and Oast House (not open). Lawns and mixed herbaceous borders inc roses and delphiniums. A ha-ha separates the garden from the fields and sheep. The garden adjoins a working farm. Wheelchair access to the garden. One step to WC.

80 ◆ KNEPP CASTLE

The Apple Store, nr Knepp Castle, off Pound Lane, West Grinstead, Horsham, RH13 8LJ. Sir Charles & Lady Burrell, www.knepp.co.uk. *8m S of Horsham. Entrance off Pound Ln following NGS signage. Parking on field nr to garden (200 metre walk).* **For NGS: Sat 1 June (10-4). Adm £15, chd free. Pre-booking essential, please visit www.ngs.org.uk for information & booking. Tea. For other opening times and information, please visit garden website.**

The Walled Garden at Knepp has been transformed into a garden for biodiversity. With designers Tom Stuart-Smith and James Hitchmough, we have applied some of the principles we've learned from rewilding the wider landscape to this small, confined space to create a mosaic of dynamic habitats for wildlife. The croquet lawn is now a riot of humps and hollows, hosting almost 1000 species of plants. Lunches available at Knepp Wilding Kitchen, RH13 8NQ.

81 KNIGHTSBRIDGE HOUSE

Grove Hill, Hellingly, Hailsham, BN27 4HH. Andrew & Karty Watson. *3m N of Hailsham, 2m S of Horam. From A22 at Boship r'about take A271, at 1st set of T-lights turn L into Park Rd, new road layout here, so you need to take a L turn approx 150 metres from the lights & drive for 2⅔ m, garden on R.* **Wed 10, Sat 13 July, Wed 4, Sat 7 Sept (2-5). Adm £7.50, chd free.**

Mature landscaped garden set in 5 acres of tranquil countryside surrounding Georgian house (not open). Several garden rooms, spectacular herbaceous borders planted in contemporary style. Lots of late season colour with grasses and some magnificent specimen trees; also partly walled garden. No card machine at this garden (poor phone signal). Wheelchair access to most of garden with gravel paths. Ask to park by house if slope from car park is too steep.

GROUP OPENING

82 NEW LANGNEY & WILLINGDON GARDEN TRAIL

Eastbourne. *Oldfield Rd is in Willingdon off the A2270. Turn W into Broad Rd then L into Oldfield Rd. Jellicoe Cl & Hardy Dr are nr Eastbourne Sovereign Centre. Please note: Not a walking trail.* **Sun 14 July (1-5). Combined adm £5, chd free. Home-made teas. Open nearby 50 Wannock Lane. Sun 8 Sept (1-5). Combined adm £7, chd free. Sorry, no refreshments on 8 Sept, local cafés nearby.**

16 HARDY DRIVE
BN23 6ED. Deb Cornford.
Open on all dates

36 JELLICOE CLOSE
BN23 6DD. Amanda Haines, 07956 322966, polegate@me.com.
Open on all dates
Visits also by arrangement May to Sept. Light refreshments on request.

NEW 23 OLDFIELD ROAD
BN20 9QD. Kathy & Ray Bennett.
Open on Sun 8 Sept

NEW 6 PASHLEY ROAD
BN20 8DU. Janet French.
Open on Sun 14 July

Two new gardens in Willingdon join two other gardens that have opened before to create a new garden trail. The gardens at 36 Jellicoe Close and 16 Hardy Drive are both developed on land reclaimed from the sea. 36 Jellicoe Close has a front and rear garden created over the past 5 yrs on shingle/beach reclaimed land, and is a Mediterranean, cottage-style garden with wildlife, ecology and sustainability at its heart, and a potters studio. 16 Hardy Drive is a small urban back garden packed with plants dominated by a large palm tree and full borders. 23 Oldfield Road is a stunning exotic and tropical garden with hot beds of colour containing cannas, bananas (musa), ginger, palms, *Tetrapanax papyrifer*, gunnera and 70 varieties of succulents inc aeoniums, aloes and agaves. 6 Pashley Road, the tea venue on 14 July only, is a large urban garden backing onto the South Downs with a wide mix of floral shrubs, dahlias, hydrangeas, echium, gingers, a vegetable garden and greenhouse.

83 LAVENDER COTTAGE

69 Steyne Road, Seaford, BN25 1QH. Christina & Steve Machan. *From Bishopstone follow seafront road. Turn L after Martello Tower & go straight. Lavender Cottage is the white house facing you at the end of the road. Car parking in timber yard to R.* **Wed 22 May (1.30-5). Combined adm, inc home-made teas, with Cupani Garden £12, chd £5. Pre-booking essential, please phone 01323 899452 or email Sweetpeasa52@gmail.com for information & booking. Opening with Seaford Gardens on Sun 2 June.**

Flint walled front garden with cottage, coastal and kitchen gardens. The back garden has a terraced bank planted with trees, shrubs and lavenders. Climb the steps to the balcony and enjoy an iconic view of Seaford Head. All the rockeries and gardens contain varied planting throughout the yr. Driftwood sculptures situated around both front and back gardens and quirky features hidden amongst plantings. Partial wheelchair access with some difficult steps and shingle.

&. ⚘ 🍵 🌱

84 LEGSHEATH FARM

Legsheath Lane, nr Forest Row, RH19 4JN. Mr & Mrs Michael Neal, 01342 810230, legsheath@btinternet.com. *4m S of East Grinstead. 2m W of Forest Row, 1m S of Weirwood Reservoir.* **Sun 19 May (2-4.30). Adm £5, chd free. Home-made teas. Visits also by arrangement 27 Apr to 29 Sept for groups of 12 to 60. Donation to Holy Trinity Church, Forest Row.**

Legsheath was first mentioned in Duchy of Lancaster records in 1545. It was associated with the role of Master of the Ashdown Forest. Set high in the Weald with far-reaching views of East Grinstead and Weirwood Reservoir. The garden covers 11 acres with a spring fed stream feeding ponds. There is a magnificent davidia, rare shrubs, embothrium and many different varieties of meconopsis and abutilons.

⚘ 🌼 🍵 🌱))

85 LIMEKILN FARM

Chalvington Road, Chalvington, Hailsham, BN27 3TA. Dr J Hester & Mr M Royle. *10m N of Eastbourne. Nr Hailsham. Turn S off A22 at Golden Cross & follow the Chalvington Rd for 1m. The entrance has white gates on LHS. Disabled*

parking space close to house, other parking 100 metres further along road. **Sat 1, Sun 2 June, Sat 14, Sun 15 Sept (2-5). Adm £7, chd free. Home-made teas in the Oast House.**

The garden was designed in the 1930s when the house was owned by Charles Stewart Taylor, MP for Eastbourne. It has not changed in basic layout since then. The planting aims to reflect the age of the C17 property (not open) and original garden design. The house and garden are mentioned in Virginia Woolf's diaries of 1929, depicting a particular charm and peace that still exists today. Flint walls enclose the main lawn, herbaceous borders and rose garden. Nepeta lined courtyard, Physic garden with talk at 3pm about medicinal plants, informal pond and specimen trees inc a very ancient oak. Many spring flowers and tree blossom. New prairie-style garden. Mostly flat access with two steps up to main lawn and herbaceous borders.

&. ⚘ 🌼 🍵))

86 NEW LODSBRIDGE MILL

Selham, Petworth, GU28 0PL. Helen & David Watson. *Halfway between Petworth & Midhurst. Turn off A272 opp Halfway Bridge towards Selham & after ½ m Lodsbridge Mill will be on the R.* **Sat 6 July (10-6). Adm £8, chd free. Pre-booking essential, please visit www.ngs.org.uk for information & booking. Home-made teas.**

A 20 acre estate in the South Downs National Park with a house (not open) that was a former C18 watermill on the banks of the River Rother, enhanced by mature willows and a timber-decked suspension footbridge. A broad grassy glade is bordered by shrubs and trees, there is also a cottage garden, a disused canal and a belt of mixed mature woodland to explore. A beautiful landscape for gentle walking and taking in the stunning views.

⚘ 🌼 🍵))

87 LORDINGTON HOUSE

Lordington, Chichester, PO18 9DX. Mr & Mrs John Hamilton, 01243 375862, hamiltonjanda@btinternet.com. *7m W of Chichester. On W side of B2146, ½ m S of Walderton, 6m S of South Harting. Enter through white railings on bend.* **Sat 15, Sun 16 June (2-5). Adm £6, chd free. Visits also by arrangement 17 June to 30**

Sept for groups of up to 30.
Early C17 house (not open) and walled gardens in South Downs National Park. Clipped yew, lawns, borders and fine views. Vegetables, fruit and poultry in the kitchen garden. 100+ roses planted since 2008. Trees both mature and young. Lime avenue planted in 1973 to replace elms. Wild flowers in field inside walls, accessible from garden. Gardens overlook Ems Valley, farmland and wooded slopes of South Downs, all in AONB within South Downs National Park. Wheelchair access is possible, but challenging with gravel paths, uneven paving and slopes. No disabled WC.

88 LUCTONS
North Lane, West Hoathly, East Grinstead, RH19 4PP. Drs Hans & Ingrid Sethi, 07787 523510, ingrid@sethis.co.uk. *4m SW of East Grinstead, 6m E of Crawley. In centre of West Hoathly village, nr church, Cat Inn & Priest House. Car parks in village.* **Visits by arrangement 18 May to 29 Sept for groups of 10 to 30. Payment in advance, please. Home-made teas.**
'A garden with everything', 'lots of unusual plants', 'stunning herbaceous borders', are comments of NGS and overseas garden tour visitors. 2 acres of Gertrude Jekyll style garden with herbaceous borders, wildflower orchard, swathes of spotted orchids, pond, roses, chickens, soft fruit, vegetables, herb garden, vine house, greenhouses, croquet lawn and shrubberies.

&

89 MALTHOUSE FARM
Streat Lane, Streat, Hassocks, BN6 8SA. Richard & Helen Keys, 01273 890356, helen.k.keys@btinternet.com. *2m SE of Burgess Hill. From r'about between B2113 & B2112 take Folders Ln & Middleton Common Ln E (away from Burgess Hill); after 1m R into Streat Ln, garden is ½m on R. Please park carefully as signed.* **Sun 1 Sept (2-5.30). Adm £7, chd free. Home-made teas. Visits also by arrangement Apr to Sept for groups of 10 to 40.**
Rural 5 acre garden with stunning views to South Downs. Garden divided into separate rooms; box parterre and borders with glass sculpture, herbaceous and shrub borders, mixed border for seasonal colour and kitchen garden. Orchard

with newly planted wild flowers leading to partitioned areas with grass walks, snail mound, birch maze and willow tunnel. Wildlife farm pond with planted surround. Wheelchair access mainly on grass with some steps (caution if wet).

90 MANOR OF DEAN
Tillington, Petworth, GU28 9AP. Mr & Mrs James Mitford, 07887 992349, emma@mitford.uk.com. *3m W of Petworth just off A272. Car park accessed via New Rd. What3words app - unique.only.novels.* **Sun 18 Feb (2-4); Sun 17 Mar, Sun 21 Apr (2-5). Adm £5, chd free. Home-made teas. Visits also by arrangement 5 Feb to 14 June for groups of 20+.**
Approx 3 acres of traditional English garden with extensive views of the South Downs. Herbaceous borders, early spring bulbs, bluebell woodland walk, walled kitchen garden with fruit, vegetables and cutting flowers. NB under long term programme of restoration, some parts of the garden may be affected.

91 MARCHANTS HARDY PLANTS
2 Marchants Cottages, Mill Lane, Laughton, Lewes, BN8 6AJ. Hannah Fox & Henry Macaulay, www.marchantshardyplants.co.uk. *6m E of Lewes. From Laughton Xrds on B2124 (at Roebuck Inn), head E for ½ m, at Xrds turn S for Ripe down Mill Ln; on R.* **Tue 30, Wed 31 July (10-5). Adm £7, chd free. Pre-booking essential, please visit www.ngs.org.uk for information & booking. Home-made teas.**
Atmospheric 2 acre garden and plant nursery with striking backdrop of the South Downs. Featured on Carol Klein's Great British Gardens TV series, the garden is imaginatively designed and sensitively planted with a rich tapestry of unusual herbaceous plants, and graceful grasses add to the interest. One of the country's leading independent nurseries, the team propagates all their plants. Agapanthus and grasses are a specialty with some developed and cultivated on site. Wheelchair access over grass paths with some slopes.

&

GROUP OPENING

92 MAYFIELD GARDENS
Mayfield, TN20 6AB. *10m S of Tunbridge Wells. Turn off A267 into Mayfield. Parking in the village, TN20 6BE & field parking at Hoopers Farm, TN20 6BD. A detailed map available at each garden.* **Sat 13, Sun 14 July (11-5). Combined adm £7, chd free. Home-made teas at Hoopers Farm & The Oast.**

ABBOTSBURY
Rob & Becky Morris

HOOPERS FARM
Andrew & Sarah Ratcliffe.
(See separate entry)

THE OAST
Mike & Tessa Crowe.
(See separate entry)

SOUTH STREET PLOTS
Val Buddle.

2 SOUTHVIEW VILLAS
Andrew & Clementine Westwood.

Mayfield is a beautiful Wealden village with tearooms, an old pub and many interesting historical connections. The gardens to visit are all within walking distance of the village centre. They vary in size and style with a wide range of shrubs, herbaceous and annual planting and inc wildflower meadows, wildlife ponds, fruit and vegetable plots and a childrens' play area. There are far-reaching, panoramic views over the beautiful High Weald.

93 MEADOW FARM
Blackgate Lane,
Pulborough, RH20 1DF.
Charlie & Ness Langdale,
nesslangdale@icloud.com. *3m N of Pulborough. From Pulborough take A29 N. Just outside Pulborough L into Blackgate Ln signed to Toat. Continue on road for 1½ m. At sign for Scrase Farms keep going straight. Signed parking on R.* **Sat 18 May (2.30-5.30). Adm £5, chd free. Home-made teas. Visits also by arrangement 1 May to 4 Oct for groups of 5 to 25.**
Approx 2 acre garden built from scratch over the last 16 yrs; designed and planted by current owners. Colour themed beds inc double borders, formal pond and green and white shady garden. Pleached hornbeam avenue out to the Sussex countryside. A walled garden provides fruit, cut flowers and vegetables. Orchard with a hazelnut walk. New wildlife swimming pond, bog garden and gravel garden.

94 NEW 40 MICHEL DENE ROAD
East Dean, Eastbourne, BN20 0JU.
Stella Lockyer. *In East Dean village on the A259 between Seaford & Eastbourne. From Seaford on A259, turn L in the centre of East Dene into Michel Dene Rd & continue for about ½ m. From Eastbourne turn R into Michel Dene Rd. 10 min uphill walk from East Dene village car park.* **Fri 21 June (11-4). Adm £5, chd free. Home-made teas.**
A medium sized sloping garden on chalk and flint in the South Downs National Park, with stunning views over the Downs to the sea. Informal flower beds display a love of colour in mainly herbaceous borders. A summerhouse overlooks a wild garden with pond, and a small vegetable plot. Several seating areas nestle in a riot of salvias, grasses, roses, penstemon and other perennial favourites.

95 MILL HALL FARM
Whitemans Green, Cuckfield,
Haywards Heath, RH17 5HX. Kate & Jonathan Berry, 07974 115658,
katehod@gmail.com. *2½ m E of A23, junction with B2115. From S & E take Staplefield Rd, after 300 metres turn R into Burrell Cottages, then L. From W after 30mph & Webster Cottages turn L to Burrell Cottages, then L. Please ignore*

Luctons

SatNav. **Visits by arrangement 15 Apr to 20 Oct. Adm £7, chd free. Home-made teas.**
A 2½ acre north facing, 12 yr old garden with long maturing view sloping down to pond and beyond with lilies, irises and sanguisorba, dragonflies and other wildlife. Long border with ornamental trees, herbaceous plants inc eucryphia, cornus, acer, liquidambar, peonies, daylily, phlox, hollyhock, brunnera, geum and potentillas, and climbing and shrub roses. Victorian underground water cistern (5000 gallons) guarded by a nymph and used for our watering system. Year-round changing colour enhanced by morning light and stunning sunsets. Deep pond. Sloping, uneven lawn and no hard paths. No wheelchair access to WC.

96 MITCHMERE FARM
Stoughton, Chichester, PO18 9JW.
Neil & Sue Edden, 02392 631456,
sue@mitchmere.co.uk. *5½ m NW of Chichester. Turn off the B2146 at Walderton towards Stoughton. Farm is ¾ m on L, ¼ m beyond the turning to Upmarden. Please do not park on verge, follow signs for parking.* **Visits by arrangement Feb to Nov. Light refreshments.**

Min group charge £60. Tea, coffee & biscuits.
1½ acre garden in lovely downland position. Unusual trees and shrubs growing in dry gravel, briefly wet most yrs when the Winterbourne rises and flows through the garden. Coloured stems, catkins, drifts of snowdrops and crocuses. Small collection of special snowdrops. Optional 10 min walk down the long field beside the river, across the sleeper bridge, take the path through the copse with snowdrops up the steps into the new wood, then into the meadow and back to the garden. Wellies advisable. Dogs on short leads. Wheelchair access over gravel and grass.

97 MOUNTFIELD COURT
Robertsbridge, TN32 5JP. Mr & Mrs Simon Fraser. *3m N of Battle. On A21 London-Hastings; ½ m NW from Johns Cross.* **Sun 12 May (2-5). Adm £7, chd free. Home-made teas.**
3 acre wild woodland garden with bluebell lined walkways through exceptional rhododendrons, azaleas, camellias, and other flowering shrubs. Fine trees and outstanding views. Stunning paved herb garden.

98 NEWTIMBER PLACE

Newtimber, BN6 9BU. Andrew & Carol Clay, 07795 346974, andy@newtimberholidaycottages.co.uk, www.newtimberplace.co.uk. *7m N of Brighton. From A23 take A281 towards Henfield. Turn R at small Xrds signed Newtimber in approx 1/2 m. Go down Church Ln, garden is on L at end of lane.* **Sun 21 Apr (2-5.30). Adm £7, chd free. Home-made teas.**
Beautiful C17 moated house (not open). Gardens and woods full of bulbs and wild flowers in spring. Herbaceous border and lawns. Moat flanked by water plants. Mature trees, wild garden, ducks, and fish. Wheelchair access across lawn to parts of garden, tearoom and WC.

99 NIGHTINGALE HOUSE

Twitteninside, Penfold Way, Steyning, BN44 3TW. Lynne Broome. *6m NE of Worthing. Exit r'about on A283 at S end of Steyning bypass into Clays Hill Rd. Turn L at Welcome to Steyning sign then 2nd R into Penfold Way. Park in road & follow NGS signs.* **Wed 26 June, Wed 3 July (10.30-5). Combined adm with Brambletye £7, chd free. Home-made teas.**
Recently redesigned and replanted cottage garden with many perennials and summer annuals. Super new greenhouse and a bespoke metal screen with climbing roses and clematis. The garden is still a work in progress, come and see how it is developing! Wheelchair access to a level garden.

100 NEW NYETIMBER MANOR

Nyetimber Vineyard, Gay Street, Pulborough, RH20 2HH. Eric Heerema, 01798 813989, sally.hughes@nyetimber.com, www.instagram.com/nyetimber. *West Chiltington. The postcode will take you to Lower Jordans Ln. Continue on Gay St & look for the Nyetimber Vineyard sign & gates.* **Fri 9 Aug (9.30-5). Adm £15, chd £7.50. Pre-booking essential, please visit www.ngs.org.uk for information & booking. Timed slots at 9.30am, 11.30am, 1.30pm & 3.30pm. Home-made teas in medieval barn.**
Nestled below the vineyards, The Manor garden at Nyetimber is one that is rarely glimpsed. This garden has everything from extensive herbaceous borders, to orchard, flower and rose garden, and courtyard. A tapestry of topiary, reflected in the lily ponds frame a beautiful view of the South Downs. Extensively redesigned and replanted in 2020, this newly establishing garden is one not to be missed. Cellar door operating for Nyetimber Wine. Wheelchair access to most areas. Some slopes and uneven ground. Disabled WC.

101 ◆ NYMANS

Staplefield Road, Handcross, RH17 6EB. National Trust, 01444 405250, nymans@nationaltrust.org.uk, www.nationaltrust.org.uk/nymans. *4m S of Crawley. On B2114 at Handcross signed off M23/A23 London-Brighton road. Metrobus 271 & 273 stop nearby.* **For NGS: Sat 16 Mar (10-5). Adm £17, chd £8.50. Adm subject to change. Light refreshments. For other opening times and information, please phone, email or visit garden website. Donation to Plant Heritage.**
One of NT's premier gardens with rare and unusual plant collections of national significance. In spring see blossom, bulbs and a stunning collection of subtly fragranced magnolias. The Rose Garden, inspired by Maud Messel's 1920s design, is scented by hints of old-fashioned roses. The comfortable yet elegant house, a partial ruin, reflects the personalities of the creative Messel family. Some level pathways. See full access statement on Nymans website.

102 OAKLANDS FARM

Hooklands Lane, Shipley, Horsham, RH13 8PX. Zsa & Stephen Roggendorff, 01403 741270, zedrog@roggendorff.co.uk. *S of Shipley village. Off the A272 towards Shipley, R at Countryman Pub, follow yellows signs. Or N of A24 Ashington, off Billingshurst Rd, 1st R signed Shipley, garden 2m up the lane.* **Sat 15 June, Sat 13 July (11-5). Adm £6, chd free. Home-made teas. Visits also by arrangement 15 Apr to 27 Sept for groups of up to 25.**
Country garden designed by Nigel Philips in 2010. Oak lined drive leading to the house (not open) and farm opens out to an enclosed courtyard with pleached hornbeam and yew. The herbaceous borders are colourful throughout the yr. Vegetable garden with raised beds and greenhouse with white peach and vine. Wild meadow leading to orchard and views across the fields, full of sheep and poultry. Mature trees. Lovely Louise will be here with her special perennials for sale. Picnics welcome. Wheelchair access over gravel and brick paths, large lawn area and grassy paths.

103 THE OAST

Fletching Street, Mayfield, TN20 6TN. Mike & Tessa Crowe. *10m S of Tunbridge Wells. Turn off A267 into Mayfield. Parking along East St & in the village public car parks. Please do not park outside The Oast in Fletching St as it is very narrow.* **Sat 27, Sun 28 Apr (11-5). Adm £5, chd free. Home-made teas. Opening with Mayfield Gardens on Sat 13, Sun 14 July.**
A south facing, gently sloping 1 acre garden with a lovely view, herbaceous borders and a 1/2 acre wildflower meadow. There is an interesting and varied selection of hardy and half-hardy plants, trees and shrubs, vegetables and fruit. Lots of colour with imaginative planting, a fine display of tulips and spring flowers. Homegrown plants for sale. Local nursery Rapkyns will also be selling plants.

104 OCKLYNGE MANOR

Mill Road, Eastbourne, BN21 2PG. Wendy & David Dugdill, 01323 734121, ocklyngemanor@hotmail.com, www.ocklyngemanor.co.uk. *Close to Eastbourne District General Hospital. Take A22 (Willingdon Rd) towards Old Town, turn L into Mill Rd by Hurst Arms Pub.* **Visits by arrangement Apr & May.**
A hidden oasis behind an ancient flint wall. Informal and tranquil, 1/2 acre chalk garden with sunny and shaded places to sit. Use of architectural and unusual trees. Rhododendrons, azaleas and acers in raised beds. Garden evolved over 20 yrs, maintained by owners. Georgian house (not open), former home of Mabel Lucie Attwell. Wheelchair access over short gravel path before entering garden. Brick path around perimeter.

105 OFFHAM HOUSE
The Street, Offham, Lewes,
BN7 3QE. Mr & Mrs P Carminger &
Mr S Goodman. *2m N of Lewes on
A275. Offham House is on the main
road (A275) through Offham between
the filling station & Blacksmiths Arms.*
**Sun 2 June (1-5). Adm £7, chd
free. Home-made teas.**
Romantic garden with fountains,
flowering trees, arboretum, double
herbaceous border and long peony
bed. 1676 Queen Anne house (not
open) with well knapped flint facade.
Herb garden and walled kitchen
garden with glasshouses, cold frames,
chickens, guinea fowl, sheep and
ducks. A selection of pelargoniums
and other plants for sale.

🐏 ✳ 🍵))

106 OLD CROSS STREET FARM
West Burton, Pulborough,
RH20 1HD. Belinda & David
Wilkinson, 01798 831938,
belinda@westburton.com. *S
of Petworth, nr the Roman Villa
at Bignor. If travelling S on A29,
continue & turn off at signs for
Bignor, Roman Villa. The house
is in the centre of West Burton,
not as indicated by the postcode!
Parking in bottom of field.* **Visits
by arrangement May to Oct for
groups of 20 to 40. Adm £7, chd
£2. Home-made teas.**
A modern garden with a nod to
traditional planting nestled in the
ancient landscape of the South
Downs. Despite its ancient buildings
the garden was only designed and
planted 15 yrs ago and enjoys many
of the contemporary twists not
usually found in such a landscape.
An abundance of mass planting
demonstrates the advantages of a
limited planting palate. An enormous
circular lawn, cloud hedging, an
orchard, cutting garden, transformed
farmyard, modern mass planting,
year-round interest, a cottage garden,
use of hedging, a raised formal pond,
uses of different hard landscaping
materials and planting of over 40
trees. Sorry, no picnics or WC.

✳ 🅳 🍵))

107 OLD ERRINGHAM
COTTAGE
Steyning Road, Shoreham-By-Sea,
BN43 5FD. Fiona & Martin Phillips,
07884 398704, fiona.h.phillips@
btinternet.com. *2m N of Shoreham-
By-Sea. From A27 Shoreham flyover
take A283 towards Steyning. Take
2nd R into private lane. Follow sharp*

LH-bend at top, house on L. **Visits
by arrangement 28 May to 30 June
for groups of 10 to 30. Home-
made teas.**
Plantsman's garden set high on the
South Downs with panoramic views
overlooking the Adur valley. 1⅓
acres with flower meadow, stream
bed and ponds, formal and informal
planting areas with over 600 varieties
of plants. Very productive fruit and
vegetable garden with glasshouses.
Many plants grown from seed and
coastal climate gives success with
tender plants.

🍵))

108 THE OLD RECTORY
97 Barnham Road,
Barnham, PO22 0EQ.
Peter & Alexandra Vining,
theoldrectory97@gmail.com. *8m
E of Chichester. Between Arundel &
Chichester at A27 Fontwell junction,
take A29 road to Bognor Regis.
Turn L at next r'about onto Barnham
Rd. 30 metres after speed camera
arrive at garden.* **Sat 8, Sun 9 June
(10-4). Combined adm with The
Shrubbery £6, chd free. Home-
made teas at The Shrubbery.
Visits also by arrangement 10
June to 15 June for groups of 6
to 20.**
Scratch built in June 2019 after the
300m² garden was removed down to
40cm, then new topsoil and returfed.
By summer 2021 the garden was well
established. Some formal areas and
a range of plants with acers, salvias,
lilies, roses, cypresses and boxes.
New flower bed, new trees and plants
added in 2023. If June 2024 is as
glorious as 2023 then our garden will
be spectacular. No steps. Wheelchair
access through 90cm wide entrance,
please advise if you need disabled
parking.

♿ ✳ 🍵))

109 THE OLD VICARAGE
The Street, Washington,
RH20 4AS. Lady
Walters, 07766 761926,
meryl.walters@me.com, www.
instagram.com/the_old_vicarage_
washington. *2½ m E of Storrington,
4m W of Steyning. From Washington
r'about on A24 take A283 to
Steyning. 500yds R to Washington.
Pass Frankland Arms, R to St Mary's
Church. Car park available, but no
large coaches.* **Every Thur 8 Feb
to 10 Oct (10-5). Pre-booking
essential, please visit www.ngs.
org.uk for information & booking.**

**Adm £7, chd free. Self service
light refreshments on Thurs &
picnics welcome. Mon 1 Apr, Mon
27 May, Sun 30 June, Mon 26 Aug
(10-5). Purchase ticket in advance
or at the gate on the day. Adm £7,
chd free. Home-made teas. Visits
also by arrangement 8 Feb to 10
Oct for groups of 10 to 30.**
Gardens of 3½ acres set around 1832
Regency house (not open). The front
is formally laid out with topiary, wide
lawn, mixed border and contemporary
water sculpture. The rear features
new and mature trees from C19,
herbaceous borders, water garden
and stunning uninterrupted views
of the North Downs. The Japanese
garden with waterfall and pond leads
to a large copse, stream, treehouse
and stumpery. Each yr 2000 tulips are
planted for spring as well as another
2000 snowdrops and mixed bulbs
throughout the garden. WC available.
Wheelchair access to front garden, but
rear garden is on a slope.

♿ 🐏 🍵))

110 OLD WELL COTTAGE
High Street, Angmering,
Littlehampton, BN16 4AG. Mr
N Waters. *Situated nr Angmering
Manor Hotel & almost adjacent to
the top of Weavers Hill in the High
St. Look for the 'mushroom' shape
tree! On road parking only, please be
mindful of residents.* **Sun 30 June
(11-4). Adm £5, chd free. Home-
made teas.**
⅓ acre plot featuring topiary, formal
areas and perennial borders. Framed
within flint walls and surrounding the
C16 to C18 cottage (not open) in
the Angmering Conservation Area.
Splendid holm oak and bay topiary
trees, large espalier apple trees and a
small kitchen garden. Lots of purples,
whites and pinks.

🍵))

111 ORCHARD COTTAGE
Boars Head Road, Boarshead,
Crowborough, TN6 3GR.
Jane Collins, 01892 653444,
collinsjane1@hotmail.co.uk. *6m
S of Tunbridge Wells, off A26. At
T-junction, do not follow SatNav.
Instead, turn L down dead end.
Orchard Cottage is at the bottom of
the hill on LHS.* **Fri 31 May, Sat 1,
Sun 2 June (10-4). Adm £6, chd
free. Home-made teas. Visits also
by arrangement Apr to June for
groups of 5+.**
Mature 1½ acre plantaholic's
garden with a large variety of trees

and shrubs, perennials and bulbs, many unusual. Gardened organically. Mainly colour themed beds, planted informally. Small woodland, meadow and deep pond to encourage wildlife. Kitchen garden with raised beds. Hardy Plant Society member. Access via gravel drive with wide gently sloping grass paths suitable for wheelchairs and mobility scooters. Drop-off in drive by prior arrangement.

& 🐑 ✿ 🚗 ☕ ᴐ)

112 PANGDEAN FARM
London Road, Pyecombe, Brighton, BN45 7FJ. Ian & Nicky Currie, www.pangdean.com. *5m N of Brighton. Leave A23 at Pyecombe, take A273 towards Hassocks. Pangdean signed on E of A23. Please use postcode BN45 7FN for entry to garden.* **Sun 2 June (12-5). Adm £11, chd £4 (chd under 5 free). Pre-booking preferred. Adm inc home-made teas.**
This delightful, sunny walled garden dating from the C17 nestles in the South Downs National Park. Featuring a herb garden that supplies the kitchen, an extensive herbaceous border providing interest over a long period, roses, water feature and a 400 yr old James I mulberry tree. It is very much the late Sue Currie's garden: whenever she entered her garden she smiled! Home-made teas will be served in the garden or the stunning 300 yr old Grade II listed Sussex Barn. Plant sale (cash only). Wheelchair access over lawn and a slight slope. Disabled WC.

& 🐑 ✿ ☕ ᴐ)

113 PARSONAGE FARM
Kirdford, nr Billingshurst, RH14 0NH. David & Victoria Thomas. *5m NE of Petworth. Located between Petworth & Wisborough Green in the village of Kirdford. Opp side of the road from the turn to Plaistow.* **Fri 21 June, Sun 8 Sept (2-6). Adm £8, chd free. Home-made teas (cash only).**
Major garden in beautiful setting developed over 30 yrs with fruit theme and many unusual plants. Formally laid out on grand scale with long vistas. C18 walled garden with borders in apricot, orange, scarlet and crimson. Topiary walk, pleached lime allée, tulip tree avenue, rose borders and vegetable garden with trained fruit. Turf amphitheatre, autumn shrubbery, yew cloisters and jungle walk.

& 🚗 ☕ ᴐ)

114 PEELERS RETREAT
70 Ford Road, Arundel, BN18 9EX. Tony & Lizzie Gilks, 01903 884981, tonygilks9@gmail.com, www.timespanhistoricalpresentations.co.uk. *1m S of Arundel. At Chichester r'about take exit to Ford & Bognor Regis onto Ford Rd. We are situated just before Maxwell Rd on the RHS.* **Sat 20, Tue 23 Apr, Sat 4, Tue 7, Sat 25, Tue 28 May, Sat 8, Tue 18, Sat 22 June, Tue 2, Sat 6 July, Tue 20, Sat 24 Aug, Tue 3, Sat 7, Sat 21 Sept, Sat 5 Oct (2-5). Adm £5, chd free. Home-made teas. Visits also by arrangement Apr to Oct for groups of up to 24.**
This inspirational space is a delight with plenty of shaded areas to sit and relax, enjoying delicious teas. Interlocking beds packed with year-round colour and scent, shaded by specimen trees, inventive water feature inc a rill, raised fish pond, working Victorian fireplace and woodland sculptures.

🐑 🐕 🚗 ☕ ᴐ)

115 PEMBURY HOUSE
Ditchling Road, Clayton, BN6 9PH. Nick & Jane Baker, www.pemburyhouse.co.uk. *6m N of Brighton, off A23. No parking at house. Car park opp church on Underhill Ln off A273. Height restrictor. Follow signs across playing field to footpath by railway to back gate. Good public transport.* **Every Thur and Fri 8 Feb to 8 Mar (10.30-3.30). Adm £11, chd free. Home-made teas inc. Pre-booking essential, please visit www.ngs.org.uk for information & booking. Timed slots at 10.30am & 2pm.**
Depending on the vagaries of the season, hellebores and snowdrops are at their best in Feb and March. It is a country garden, tidy but not manicured. New work always going on. Winding paths give a choice of walks through 3 acres of garden, which is in and enjoys views of the South Downs National Park. Suitable footwear, macs and winter woollies advised. A German visitor observed 'this is the perfect woodland garden'. Year-round interest. Plants for sale. Cash ideally.

🐑 ✿ ☕ ᴐ)

116 PENNS IN THE ROCKS
Groombridge, Tunbridge Wells, TN3 9PA. Mr & Mrs Hugh Gibson, www.pennsintherocks.co.uk. *7m SW of Tunbridge Wells. On B2188 Groombridge to Crowborough road, just S of Xrd to Withyham. For SatNav use TN6 1UX which takes you to the white drive gates, through which you should enter the property.* **Sun 14 Apr, Sun 12 May, Sun 4 Aug (2-6). Adm £7, chd free. Home-made teas.**
Large garden with spectacular outcrop of rocks, 140 million yrs old. Lake, C18 temple and woods. Daffodils, bluebells, azaleas, magnolia and tulips. Old walled garden with herbaceous borders, roses and shrubs. Stone sculptures by Richard Strachey. Part C18 house (not open) once owned by William Penn of Pennsylvania. Cash only on the day please. Restricted wheelchair access. No disabled WC.

& ✿ ☕

117 1 PEST COTTAGE
Carron Lane, Midhurst, GU29 9LF. Jennifer Lewin. *W edge of Midhurst behind Carron Lane Cemetery. Free parking at recreation ground at top of Carron Ln. Short walk on woodland track to garden, please follow signs.* **Fri 7, Sun 9 June (1-5). Adm £4, chd free.**
This edge of woodland, architect's studio garden of approx ¾ acre sits on a sloping sandy site. Designed to support wildlife and biodiversity, a series of outdoor living spaces connected with informal paths through lightly managed areas, creates a charming secret world tucked into the surrounding common land. The garden spaces have made a very small house (not open) into a hospitable family home. Exhibition of architect's projects.

In 2023, our donations to Carers Trust meant that 26,118 unpaid carers were supported across the UK

The Cottage

▮▮8 6 PLANTATION RISE

Worthing, BN13 2AH. Nigel & Trixie Hall, 01903 262206, trixiehall008@gmail.com. *2m from seafront on outskirts of Worthing. A24 meets A27 at Offington r'about. Turn into Offington Ln, 1st R into The Plantation, 1st R again into Plantation Rise. Parking on The Plantation only, short walk up to 6 Plantation Rise.* **Visits by arrangement 14 Mar to 31 Aug for groups of up to 20. Adm £5, chd free. Home-made teas inc. Please advise of specific dietary requirements upon booking.**
Clever use is made of evergreen shrubs, azaleas, rhododendrons and acers enclosing our 70ft x 80ft garden, enhancing the flower decked pergolas, folly and summerhouse which overlooks the pond. Planting inc nine silver birches 'Tristis' which are semi pendula, plus a lovely combination of primroses, anemones and daffodils in spring and a profusion of roses, clematis and perennials in summer. Wheelchair access to patios only with a good view of the garden.

♿ ☕

▮▮9 ◆ THE PRIEST HOUSE

North Lane, West Hoathly, RH19 4PP. Sussex Archaeological Society, 01342 810479, priest@sussexpast.co.uk, www.sussexpast.co.uk. *4m SW of East Grinstead, 6m E of Crawley. In centre of West Hoathly village, nr church & the Cat Inn. Car parks in village.* **For NGS: Sat 25 May, Sat 29 June (10.30-5.30). Adm £3, chd free. Home-made teas. For other opening times and information, please phone, email or visit garden website.**
C15 timber framed farmhouse with cottage garden on acid clay. Large collection of culinary and medicinal herbs in a small formal herb garden and mixed with perennials and shrubs in exuberant borders. Long established yew topiary and espalier apple trees provide structural elements. Traditional fernery and stumpery, recently enlarged with a small, secluded shrubbery and gravel garden. Be sure to visit the fascinating Priest House Museum, adm £1 for NGS visitors.

🐕 ❅ ☕

▮20 NEW 9 PUTTOCK WAY

Billingshurst, RH14 9ZJ. Emma & Simon Parker. *7m SW of Horsham. From the Hilland r'about to the N of Billingshurst, head E along the A272 (Hilland Rd) & take the 1st R turning into the estate (Rhodes Way). Take 2nd R onto Puttock Way.* **Sun 26, Mon 27 May (11-4). Adm £5. Pre-booking essential, please visit www.ngs.org.uk for information & booking. Home-made teas.**
A very small, sloping, new build garden which has been transformed from bare heavy clay into a series of spaces with interesting hard landscaping features. An unexpected cacophony of architectural shapes and textures greets you as you walk through the gate, a true plant lover's paradise. This space shows what can be achieved in a short space of time through hard work and passion.

☕))

▮2▮ RYMANS

Appledram Lane South, Apuldram, Chichester, PO20 7EG. Zarina Chatwin, 07398 102194, zarina.chatwin@gmail.com. *1m S of Chichester. If coming from A27, exit at Fishbourne r'about, following signs to Fishbourne. Take 1st L onto Appledram Lane South, house is 1m S.* **Sat 13, Sun 14 Apr, Sun 23 June, Sun 15 Sept (2-5). Adm £6, chd free. Home-made teas at St Mary's Church, Apuldram. Visits also by arrangement 1 Apr to 3 Oct for groups of 10 to 30.**
Walled and other gardens surrounding C15 stone house (not open); bulbs, flowering shrubs, roses, ponds, and potager. Many unusual and rare trees and shrubs. In late spring the wisterias are spectacular. Hybrid musk roses fill the walled garden in June and in late summer the garden is filled with dahlias, sedums, late roses, sages and Japanese anemones.

🐕 ❅ ☕))

▮22 SAFFRONS

Holland Road, Steyning, BN44 3GJ. Tim Melton & Bernardean Carey, 07850 343516, tim.melton@btinternet.com, www. thetransplantedgardener.uk. *6m NE of Worthing. Exit r'about on A283 at S end of Steyning bypass into Clays Hill Rd. 1st R into Goring Rd, 4th L into Holland Rd. Park in Goring Rd & Holland Rd.* **Visits by arrangement 1 July to 7 Aug for groups of 8 to 30.**
Planted with an artist's eye for contrasts and complementary colours. Vibrant late summer flower beds of salvias, eryngiums, agapanthus, grasses and lilies attract bees and butterflies. A broad lawn is surrounded by borders with maples, rhododendrons, hydrangeas and mature trees interspersed with ferns and grasses. The large fruit cage and vegetable beds comprise the productive area of the garden. One level garden with good access, except in very wet conditions.

♿ 🐕 ❅ ☕

123 ST BARNABAS HOUSE

2 Titnore Lane, Goring-By-Sea, Worthing, BN12 6NZ. St Barnabas Hospices, www.stbh.org.uk. *W of Worthing & just N of the r'about between A259 & A2032. Titnore Ln can be accessed via A27 from N, the A259 from W (Littlehampton) or the A2032 from E (Worthing).* **Sat 29 June (11-4). Adm £5, chd free. Pre-booking essential, please visit www.ngs.org.uk for information & booking. Tea.**
Join one of the accompanied tours through the patient gardens, these will be held throughout the day. After which, take a relaxing wander through the hospice grounds, which have a central courtyard garden like an exotic atrium with seating, water features and abundant foliage from tree ferns, magnolias and katsura trees. Outside a large pond with fountain-aerator adds tranquillity with the sound of running water. Lavender maze, meadow and productive vegetable plot. We've been keeping bees in our gardens since Oct 2021, and our first hive was kindly donated by the Worthing Division of the West Sussex Beekeepers Associations (BKA). Good access to the site, central courtyard, main surrounding gardens and car park.

124 ◆ ST MARY'S HOUSE GARDENS

Bramber, BN44 3WE. Roger Linton & Peter Thorogood, 01903 816205, info@stmarysbramber.co.uk, www.stmarysbramber.co.uk. *1m E of Steyning. 10m NW of Brighton in Bramber village, off A283.* **For NGS: Fri 28, Sat 29 June (2-5). Adm £8.50, chd £5. Home-made teas. For other opening times and information, please phone, email or visit garden website.**
5 acres inc formal topiary, large prehistoric *Ginkgo biloba* and magnificent *Magnolia grandiflora* around enchanting timber-framed medieval house (not open for NGS). Victorian Secret Gardens inc splendid 140ft fruit wall with pineapple pits, Rural Museum, Terracotta Garden, Jubilee Rose Garden, King's Garden and circular Poetry Garden. Woodland walk and Landscape Water Garden. In the heart of the South Downs National Park. WC facilities. Wheelchair access with level paths throughout.

125 SANDHILL FARM HOUSE

Nyewood Road, Rogate, Petersfield, GU31 5HU. Rosemary Alexander. *4m SE of Petersfield. From A272 Xrds in Rogate take road S signed Nyewood & Harting. Follow road for approx 1m over small bridge. Sandhill Farm House on R, over cattle grid.* **Sun 11 Feb (12-4); Sat 27, Sun 28 Apr, Sun 9 June, Sat 21, Sun 22 Sept (2-5). Adm £5, chd free. Home-made teas.**
Front and rear gardens broken up into garden rooms inc small kitchen garden. Front garden with small woodland area, planted with early spring flowering shrubs, ferns and bulbs. White and green garden, large leaf border and terraced area. Rear garden has rose borders, small decorative vegetable garden, red border and grasses border. Snowdrop day on Sun 11th Feb. Home of author and principal of The English Gardening School.

🐎 ✿ D ☕))

GROUP OPENING

126 SEAFORD GARDENS

There are several gardens on the trail, all signed from the A259, the gardens are N & S of this road. NB Not a walking trail. Maps available at each garden. **Sun 2 June (11-5). Combined adm £9, chd free. Sun 30 June (11-5). Combined adm £8, chd free. Light refreshments at 34 Chyngton Road, Cosy Cottage & Marion's pop up teas at Seaford Allotments. Ice cream & soft drinks at Cupani.**

BURFORD
Cuckmere Road, BN25 4DE. Chris Kilsby.
Open on all dates

34 CHYNGTON ROAD
BN25 4HP. Dr Maggie Wearmouth & Richard Morland.
Open on all dates

5 CLEMENTINE AVENUE
BN25 2UU. Joanne Davis.
Open on all dates

NEW 101 CLEMENTINE AVENUE
BN25 2XG. Mr John & Mrs Vanessa Kelly.
Open on Sun 2 June

COSY COTTAGE
69 Firle Road, BN25 2JA. Ernie & Carol Arnold, 07763 196343, ernie.whitecrane@gmail.com, www.facebook.com/CosyCottage69Garden.
Open on all dates
Visits also by arrangement for groups of 6 to 20.

CUPANI GARDEN
8 Sandgate Close, BN25 3LL. Dr Denis Jones & Ms Aideen Jones OBE.
Open on all dates
(See separate entry)

8 DOWNS ROAD
BN25 4QL. Mr Phil & Mrs Julie Avery.
Open on all dates

LAVENDER COTTAGE
69 Steyne Road, BN25 1QH. Christina & Steve Machan.
Open on Sun 2 June
(See separate entry)

MADEHURST
67 Firle Road, BN25 2JA. Martin & Palo.
Open on all dates

SEAFORD ALLOTMENTS
Sutton Drove, BN25 3NQ. Peter Sudell.
Open on Sun 30 June

SEAFORD COMMUNITY GARDEN
East Street, BN25 1AD. Seaford Community Garden.
Open on Sun 2 June

11 gardens open, see dates for each garden. Cosy Cottage, garden over three levels with ponds, flowers, vegetables and shrubs. Madehurst, a garden on different levels with mature planting. Burford, a mature garden with a mix of flowers, vegetables and an auricula theatre. The Community Garden provides a space with flower and vegetable beds for members of the community to come together to share their gardening experience. 34 Chyngton Road is a mature garden of shrubs, trees, herbaceous and vegetable beds. 8 Downs Road, a delightful mix of shrubs, block planted herbaceous beds and vegetables. Lavender Cottage a flint walled garden with a coastal and kitchen garden. Seaford Allotments offer a unique chance to see a variety of planting and colour. A site of 189 well maintained plots with a wildlife area and compost WC. 5 Clementine Avenue, a garden over several levels with agave and succulents and great views over the downs. 101 Clementine Avenue, new garden beautifully planted to attract wildlife and panoramic views over South Downs National Park. Cupani returns to the trail, see individual entry.

🐎 ✿ ☕))

127 SELHURST PARK
Halnaker, Chichester,
PO18 0LZ. Richard & Sarah
Green, 01243 839310, mail@
selhurstparkhouse.co.uk. *8m S of
Petworth. 4m N of Chichester on A285.*
Visits by arrangement 10 June to 26
July for groups of 10 to 30. Adm £6,
chd free. Home-made teas.
Come and explore the varied gardens
surrounding a beautiful Georgian
flint house (not open), approached
by a chestnut avenue. The flint
walled garden has a mature 160ft
herbaceous border with unusual
planting along with rose, hellebore
and hydrangea beds. Pool garden
with exotic palms and grasses
divided from a formal knot and herb
garden by espalier apples. Kitchen
and walled fruit garden. Wheelchair
access to walled garden, partial
access to other areas.
♿ ✿ ☕

**128 ◆ SHEFFIELD PARK AND
GARDEN**
Uckfield, TN22 3QX. National Trust,
01825 790231, sheffieldpark@
nationaltrust.org.uk, www.
nationaltrust.org.uk/sheffieldpark.
*10m S of East Grinstead. 5m NW of
Uckfield; E of A275.* For NGS: Thur
2 May (10-4.30). Adm £14.25, chd
free. Light refreshments. For other
opening times and information,
please phone, email or visit garden
website.
Magnificent, landscaped garden laid
out in C18 by Capability Brown and
Humphry Repton covering 120 acres
(40 hectares). Further development
in the early yrs of this century by its
owner Arthur G Soames. Centrepiece
is original lakes with many rare trees
and shrubs. Beautiful at all times of the
yr, but noted for its spring and autumn
colours. National Collection of Ghent
azaleas. Large number of champion
trees, 87 in total. Light refreshments
available in the Coach House Café and
The Shant. Last entry 4.30pm. Garden
largely accessible for wheelchairs,
please call for information.
♿ 🐴 ✿ 🚗 NPC ☕ 🪑 »)

129 SHEPHERDS COTTAGE
Milberry Lane, Stoughton,
Chichester, PO18 9JJ. Jackie
& Alan Sherling, 07795 388047,
milberrylane@gmail.com, www.
instagram.com/drjackieblackman.
*9⅙ m NW Chichester. Off B2146,
next village after Walderton. Cottage
is nr telephone box & beside
St Mary's Church. No parking*
in lane beside house. Visits by
arrangement May to Aug for
groups of 10 to 30. Adm £10, chd
free. Cream teas.
A compact terraced garden using
the borrowed landscape of Kingley
Vale in the South Downs. The south
facing flint stone cottage (not open) is
surrounded by a Purbeck stone terrace
and numerous individually planted and
styled seating areas. A small orchard
under planted with meadow, lawns,
topiary yew hedges, amelanchier,
cercis and drifts of wind grass provide
structure and year-round interest. Many
novel design ideas for a small garden.
Ample seating throughout the garden to
enjoy the views.
✿ D ☕

130 THE SHRUBBERY
140 Barnham Road, Barnham,
PO22 0EH. John & Ros Woodhead,
johnrosw@sky.com. *Between Arundel
& Chichester. At A27 Fontwell junction
take A29 road to Bognor Regis. Turn
L at next r'about onto Barnham Rd.
After ½ m the garden is 30 metres after*
the speed camera. Sat 8, Sun 9 June
(10-4). Combined adm with The Old
Rectory £6, chd free. Home-made
teas. Visits also by arrangement
10 June to 15 June for groups of 6
to 20.
¼ acre plot with mature trees,
shrubs, wildflower lawn, roses,
agapanthus and dahlias in front
garden leading to walled back garden
of mixed colourful borders, soft
fruit, sculpture and large collection
of hostas. Many colourful pots, wall
baskets and greenhouse. Ideas and
points of interest throughout.
♿ ✿ ☕ »)

131 SKYSCAPE
46 Ainsworth Avenue, Ovingdean,
Brighton, BN2 7BG. Lorna & John
Davies. *From Brighton take A259 coast
road E, passing Roedean School on
L. Take 1st L at r'about to Greenways
& 2nd R into Ainsworth Ave. Skyscape
at the top on R.* No. 52 bus on Sat &
No. 57 on Sun. Sat 1, Sun 2 June
(1-5). Adm £6, chd free. Tea & cakes
served on the patio.

Orchard Cottage

250ft south facing rear garden on a sloping site with fantastic views of the South Downs and the sea. Garden created by owners over past 12 yrs. Orchard, flower beds, wildlife ponds and planting with bees in mind. Small, protected apiary in orchard. Full access to site via purpose built sloping path (not suitable for mobility scooters).

132 SOUTH GRANGE

Quickbourne Lane, Northiam, Rye, TN31 6QY. Linda & Michael Belton, 01797 252984, belton.northiam@gmail.com. *Between A268 & A28, approx ½ m E of Northiam. From Northiam centre follow Beales Ln into Quickbourne Ln, or Quickbourne Ln leaves A286 approx ½ m S of A28 & A286 junction. Disabled parking at front of house.* **Sat 13, Sun 14 July (11-5). Adm £6, chd free. Home-made teas. Light lunches made to order. Visits also by arrangement 1 Mar to 20 Oct for groups of 5+.**
Hardy Plant Society members' garden with wide variety of trees, shrubs, perennials, grasses and pots arranged into a complex garden display for year-round colour and interest. Raised vegetable beds, wildlife pond, water features, orchard, rose arbour, soft fruit cage and living gazebo. House roof runoff diverted to storage and pond. Small area of wild wood. An emphasis on planting for insects. We try to maintain nectar and pollen supplies and varied habitats for most of the creatures that we share the garden with, hoping that this variety will keep the garden in good heart. Home propagated plants for sale. Wheelchair access over hard paths through much of the garden, but steps up to patio and WC.

133 [NEW] SPRINGBOURNE

Rectory Lane, Clapham Village, Worthing, BN13 3UX. Graham & Emily Swain, 07977 925586, info@eartharchitecture.co.uk. *4m N of Worthing. Take A280 via A24 or A27. Clapham Village signed. Park in The Street, please be mindful of residents. Walk down street to Rectory Ln (no vehicle access). Opp the sign for Clapham church.* **Fri 19, Sat 20 July (10-4). Adm £5. Light refreshments (cash only).**
Historic 300 yr old south facing flint walled garden. Designed and planted by a professional garden designer and artist together with his actress

wife Emily. A developing garden divided into different areas inc a large pond with water lilies imported from France, Latour-Marliac. Gently sloping lawns, a small orchard and curved borders with mixed herbaceous and rose planting. The artist's studio will be open.

134 STANLEY FARM

Highfield Lane, Liphook, GU30 7LW. Bill & Emma Mills. *For SatNav please use GU30 7LN which takes you to Highfield Ln & then follow NGS signs. Track to Stanley Farm is 1m.* **Sun 5 May (12-5). Adm £5, chd free. Home-made teas.**
1 acre garden created over the last 15 yrs around an old West Sussex farmhouse (not open), sitting in the midst of its own fields and woods. The formal garden inc a kitchen garden with heated glasshouse, orchard, espaliered wall trained fruit, lawn with ha-ha and cutting garden. A motley assortment of animals inc sheep, donkeys, chickens, ducks and geese. Bluebells flourish in the woods, so feel free to bring dogs and a picnic, and take a walk after visiting the gardens. Wheelchair access via a ramp to view main part of the garden. Difficult access to woods due to muddy, uneven ground.

135 STROODS

Herons Ghyll, Uckfield, TN22 4DB. Geraldine Ogilvy. *Located on A26 opp Clay Studio.* **Wed 12 June (12-4). Adm £10, chd free. Pre-booking essential, please visit www.ngs.org.uk for information & booking. Home-made teas inc.**
Nestled in the beautiful hills of Sussex, the garden is a peaceful space where ancient trees, an orchard and olive grove team carefully with curated herbaceous borders and meandering wildflower meadows, all attracting bees, butterflies and birds. The walled kitchen garden delivers delicious, traditional vegetables, embroidered with flowers and shrubs, plus the occasional wandering chicken.

136 SULLINGTON OLD RECTORY

Sullington Lane, Storrington, Pulborough, RH20 4AE. Oliver & Mala Haarmann. Mark Dixon, Head Gardener, mark@sullingtonoldrectory.com. *Travelling S on A24 take 3rd exit on Washington r'about. Proceed to Xrds on A283 for Sullington Ln & Water Ln. Take L onto Sullington Ln & garden located at the top.* **Thur 18, Fri 19 July (10-4). Adm £10, chd free. Pre-booking essential, please visit www.ngs.org.uk for information & booking. Two hour timed slots at 10am & 2pm. Home-made teas at the Workshop Café, Sullington Manor Farm.**
With a backdrop of stunning views of the South Downs, the naturalistic style of this beautiful country garden sits perfectly into the surrounding landscape. The rarely opened garden inc a potager, orchard, herb garden, established trees and shrubs, a pleached lime walk, new colour themed perennial borders, a profusion of grasses and experimental planting in the moist meadow. Head Gardener will be available for any Q&As. Wheelchair access to most areas.

137 ◆ SUSSEX PRAIRIES

Morlands Farm, Wheatsheaf Road (B2116), Henfield, BN5 9AT. Paul & Pauline McBride, 01273 495902, morlandsfarm@btinternet.com, www.sussexprairies.co.uk. *2m NE of Henfield on B2116 Wheatsheaf Rd (also known as Albourne Rd). Follow Brown Tourist signs indicating Sussex Prairie Garden.* **For NGS: Sun 8 Sept (1-5). Adm £12, chd £6. Home-made teas. For other opening times and information, please phone, email or visit garden website.**
Exciting prairie garden of approx 8 acres planted in the naturalistic style using 60,000 plants and over 1,600 different varieties. A colourful garden featuring a huge variety of unusual ornamental grasses. Expect layers of colour, texture and architectural splendour. Surrounded by mature oak trees with views of Chanctonbury Ring and Devil's Dyke on the South Downs. Permanent sculpture collection and exhibited sculpture throughout the season. Rare breed sheep and pigs. Tropical entrance garden. Woodchip pathway at entrance. Soft woodchip paths in borders not accessible, but flat garden for wheelchairs and mobility scooters. Disabled WC.

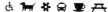

138 THAKEHAM PLACE FARM

The Street, Thakeham, Pulborough, RH20 3EP. Mr & Mrs T Binnington. *3m N of Storrington. The farm is at the E end of The Street, where it turns into Crays Ln. Follow signs down farm drive to Thakeham Place.* **Thur 25, Sun 28 July (2-5). Combined adm with Cumberland House £10, chd free. Home-made teas.**

Set in the middle of a working dairy farm, the garden has evolved over the last 30 yrs. Taking advantage of its sunny position on free draining greensand, the borders are full of sun loving plants and grasses with a more formal area surrounding the farmhouse (not open). Lovely views across the farm to Warminghurst from the orchard.

🐕 ✿ 🍷 »)

139 TOR COTTAGE

8 Tor Road, Peacehaven, BN10 7SX. Julie & Ron Basham. *From A259 coast road at r'about turn N up Sutton Ave, veer R onto Pelham Rise, L onto Glynn Rd, R onto Roderick Ave, then 2nd L onto Tor Rd. Street parking.* **Thur 25, Sat 27 July (11-5). Combined adm with The Jungle Garden £5, chd free. Home-made teas at The Jungle Garden. Open nearby 33 Wivelsfield Road.**

Large, tranquil mature garden surrounds 100 yr old bungalow (not open) with trees, shrubs, plants, bamboos and ornamental grasses. Plenty of colour and different areas inc vegetable garden, rockeries and woodland. There are shady areas and seating in the sun or under the pergola. Art studio and workshop. Plants for sale.

✿ 🍷

140 TOWN PLACE

Ketches Lane, Freshfield, Sheffield Park, RH17 7NR. Anthony & Maggie McGrath, 01825 790221, mcgrathsussex@hotmail.com, www.townplacegarden.org.uk. *5m E of Haywards Heath. From A275 turn W at Sheffield Green into Ketches Ln for Lindfield. 1¾m on L.* **Sun 9, Wed 12, Wed 19, Sun 23, Sun 30 June, Sun 7 July (2-5). Adm £8, chd free. Visits also by arrangement 3 June to 5 July.**

A stunning 3 acre garden with a growing international reputation for the quality of its design, planting and gardening. Set round a C17 Sussex farmhouse (not open), the garden has over 400 roses, herbaceous borders, herb garden, white garden, topiary inspired by the sculptures of Henry Moore, an 800 yr old oak, potager, and a unique ruined Priory Church and Cloisters in hornbeam. Sorry, no dogs allowed, and no refreshments available. Picnics welcome. There are steps, but all areas can be viewed from a wheelchair.

🦽 ✿ 🍱 »)

141 TUPPENNY BARN

Main Road, Southbourne, PO10 8EZ. Maggie Haynes, 01243 377780, contact@tuppennybarn.co.uk, www.tuppennybarn.co.uk. *6m W of Chichester, 1m E of Emsworth. On Main Rd A259, corner of Tuppenny Ln. Disabled parking.* **Sat 6 July (10-3). Adm £6, chd free. Light refreshments. Food intolerances & allergies catered for. Visits also by arrangement 16 Jan to 7 Oct for groups of 12 to 30.**

An iconic, organic smallholding used as an outdoor classroom to teach children about the environment, sustainability and healthy food. 2½ acres packed with a wildlife pond, orchard with heritage top fruit varieties, two solar polytunnels, fruit cages, and raised vegetables, herbs and cut flower garden. Willow provides natural arches and wind breaks. Bug hotel and beehives support vital pollinators. Most of the grounds are accessible for wheelchairs, but undulated areas are more difficult.

🦽 ✿ 🍷 »)

142 WADHURST PARK

Riseden Road, Wadhurst, TN5 6NT. Nicky Browne, www.wadhurstpark.co.uk. *6m SE of Tunbridge Wells. Turn R along Mayfield Ln off B2099 at NW end of Wadhurst. Then turn L at Tidebrook Road & L at Riseden Rd.* **Fri 14, Sat 15 June (10-4). Adm £6, chd free. Home-made teas.**

The naturalistic gardens designed by Tom Stuart-Smith, created on a C19 site, situated within a 2000 acre estate managed organically to enhance its wildlife, cultural heritage and beauty. The gardens invite the wider landscape in with native woodland trees and ground cover, meadows and hedgerows, framing views to hills and lake. We strive to garden with a greater respect for the natural world. Features inc restored Victorian orangery, naturalistic

gardens planted with mainly native species, meadows, potager and log hives. Home-made teas inc vegan and gluten-free cakes, and local produce for sale. Due to uneven paths, please wear sensible shoes. Sorry no dogs. Wheelchair access to main features of garden. Some uneven surfaces over grass, cobbles and steps.

🦽 🅓 🍷 🍱 »)

143 50 WANNOCK LANE

Willingdon, Eastbourne, BN20 9SD. Chris & Nick Ireland. *Between Eastbourne & Polegate on the A2270. From Eastbourne (A2270) turn L into Gorringe Valley Rd, at give way turn R. From Polegate turn R into Gorringe Valley Rd.* **Sun 14 July (1-5). Adm £5, chd free. Open nearby Langney & Willingdon Garden Trail.**

A fully packed front garden with central large rogue Christmas tree. West facing 200ft x 55ft rear garden with a wide selection of shrubs, herbaceous and perennials plus trees. There are two small ponds with fish, vegetable plot and greenhouses. Little nooks and seating areas provide interest and sunny patio. Local cafés nearby.

✿

144 WARNHAM PARK

Robin Hood Lane, Warnham, Horsham, RH12 3RP. Mrs Caroline Lucas. *Turn in off A24 end of Robin Hood Ln, turn immed R by the large poster & follow signs.* **Sat 27 Apr (11-5); Thur 20 June (2-5); Sun 23 June (11.30-5.30). Adm £6, chd free. Soup & home-made teas (27 April & 23 June). Home-made teas (20 June).**

The garden is situated in the middle of a 200 acre Deer Park, which has a very special herd of Red Deer husbanded by the Lucas Family for over 150 yrs. Borders with traditional planting and a kitchen garden that is prolific most of the yr. The rest of the garden comprises different spaces inc a small white garden, a Moroccan courtyard and a walled garden. There is also a woodland walk. Disabled WC. Sorry, no dogs allowed.

🦽 🍷 »)

GROUP OPENING

145 WATERWORKS & FRIENDS
Broad Oak & Brede, TN31 6HG.
*6m N of Hastings. 4 Waterworks
Cottages, Brede, off A28 by church
& opp Red Lion, ¾m at end of
lane. Sculdown, B2089 Chitcombe
Rd, W off A28 at Broad Oak Xrds.
Start at either garden, a map will
be provided.* **Sat 1 June (10.30-4).
Combined adm £6, chd free. Light
refreshments at Sculdown.**

SCULDOWN
TN31 6EX. Mrs Christine Buckland.

4 WATERWORKS COTTAGES
TN31 6HG. Mrs Kristina
Clode, 07950 748097, info@
kristinaclodegardendesign.co.uk,
www.kristinaclodegardendesign.
co.uk.
Visits also by arrangement 3
June to 11 Oct for groups of 10
to 30. Car sharing encouraged
for larger groups.

An opportunity to visit two unique
gardens and discover the Brede Steam
Giants 35ft Edwardian water pumping
engines, and Grade II listed pump
house located behind 4 Waterworks
Cottages. Garden designer Kristina
Clode has created her wildlife friendly
garden at 4 Waterworks Cottages over
the last 14 yrs. Delightful perennial
wildflower meadow, pond, wisteria
covered pergola and mixed borders
packed full of unusual specimens
with year-round interest and colour.
Sculdown's garden is dominated by
a very large wildlife pond formed as a
result of iron-ore mining over 100 yrs
ago. The stunning traditional cottage
(not open) provides a superb backdrop
for several colourful herbaceous
borders and poplar trees. Plants for sale
at 4 Waterworks Cottages. At Brede
Steam Giants, accessible WC available
and assistance dogs only (free entry,
donations encouraged). At Sculdown,
mobility cars to park in flat area at top
of field.

152,684 people were able to access guidance on what to expect when a person is dying through the National Garden Scheme support for Hospice UK this year

Brambletye

146 WHITEHANGER
Marley Lane, Haslemere,
GU27 3PY. Lynn & David
Paynter, 07774 010901,
lynn@whitehanger.co.uk.
*What3words app - barman.funny.
tango. Take A286 Midhurst Rd from
Haslemere & after approx 2m turn
R into Marley Ln (opp Hatch Ln).
After 1m turn into drive shared with
St Magnus Nursing & keep bearing
L through the nursing home.* **Sun
18 Aug (10-4.30). Adm £6.50, chd
£6.50. Pre-booking essential,
please visit www.ngs.org.uk for
information & booking. Tea. Visits
also by arrangement 10 June to 9
Sept for groups of 8 to 35. Final
numbers must be given a week
before visiting & payment made
by BACS.**
Set in 6 acres on the edge of
the South Downs National Park
surrounded by NT woodland, this
rural garden was started in 2012
when a new Huf house (not open)
was built on a derelict site. Now
there are lawned areas with beds
of perennials, a serenity pool with
Koi carp, a wildflower meadow, a
Japanese garden, a sculpture garden,
a woodland walk, a large rockery and
an exotic walled garden.
♿ 🐴 ✻ ☕ ⌭

148 WHITHURST PARK
Plaistow Road, Kirdford, Nr
Billingshurst, RH14 0JW. Mr
Richard Taylor & Mr Rick Englert,
www.whithurst.com. *7m NW of
Billingshurst. A272 to Wisborough
Green, follow sign to Kirdford, turn
R at 1st T-junction through village,
then R again, on Plaistow Rd, look
for the white Whithurst Park sign at
roadside.* **Sun 7 July (10-5). Adm
£5, chd free. Home-made teas.**
13 yr old walled kitchen garden with
many espaliered fruit trees. Herb
beds, vegetable beds, flower borders
and cutting beds. Central greenhouse
and potting shed with interesting
support buildings behind the wall
inc extensive compost area close
to beehives. Sustainability through
permaculture principles. Plants for
sale in courtyard at the front of house.
Teas available on lawn adjacent to the
courtyard. We have plenty of open
lawn around the walled garden and
house which can be used for picnics.
There are also footpaths around the
woodlands surrounding the house
and lake. Wheelchair access via ramp
over 10cm step onto garden paths.
♿ ✻ 🚐 ☕ 🍽 ⌭

GROUP OPENING

**149 WINCHELSEA'S SECRET
GARDENS**
Winchelsea, TN36 4EN. *2m W
of Rye, 8m E of Hastings. Follow
A259 from Rye or Hastings.* **Sat
20 Apr (12-4). Combined adm
£5, chd free. Sat 15 June (11-5).
Combined adm £8, chd free.
Home-made teas at Winchelsea
New Hall.**

BURRIN HOUSE
North Street. Charlotte Beecroft.
Open on Sat 15 June

CLEVELAND PLACE
Sally & Graham Rhodda.
Open on all dates

**NEW   KENT CLOSE
COMMUNAL GARDEN**
Kent Close Residents.
Open on all dates

KING'S LEAP
Philip Kent.
Open on all dates

MAGAZINE HOUSE
Susan Stradling.
Open on Sat 15 June

THE RECTORY
Rev Jonathan & Mrs Shirley Meyer.
Open on Sat 15 June

SOUTH MARITEAU
Robert Holland.
Open on all dates

NEW   STONE WALL
Penny & Nigel West.
Open on all dates

With several properties changing
hands, Winchelsea's offering is
temporarily less extensive than usual,
but we have two fascinating new
gardens joining us this yr. We offer
secret walled gardens, spring bulbs,
roses, herbaceous borders and more,
in the beautiful setting of the Cinque
Port of Winchelsea. Follow signs for
central card payment point or pay
cash at any garden gate. Explore
the town with its magnificent church.
Check winchelsea.com for the latest
information on tours of our famous
medieval cellars. If you are bringing a
coach please contact ryeview@gmail.
com, 01797 226524. Wheelchair
access to four out of five gardens in
April and six out of eight in June.
♿ ✻ 🚐 ☕ ⌭

150 33 WIVELSFIELD ROAD
Saltdean, Brighton, BN2 8FP. Chris
Briggs & Steve Jenner. *From A259
at Saltdean turn onto Arundel Drive
West, continue onto Saltdean Vale.
Take the 6th turning on L, Tumulus
Rd. Take 1st R onto Wivelsfield Rd,
continue up steep hill, No. 33 is on
the R.* **Thur 25, Sat 27 July (11-5).
Adm £6, chd free. Home-made
teas. Open nearby The Jungle
Garden & Tor Cottage.**
The garden, created in 2016,
landscaped during 2017 and planting
started later that yr. Split over three
levels filled with colourful perennials,
annuals, grasses, and succulents
planted in the ground and in
containers. The formal garden leads
onto a wildflower meadow extending
onto the downs, giving spectacular
views of both the ocean and South
Downs National Park. Front garden
revamped in 2023.
🚐 🐴 ✻ ☕ ⌭

151 WYCH WARREN HOUSE
Wych Warren, Forest Row,
RH18 5LF. Colin King &
Mary Franck, 07852 272898,
mlfranck@hotmail.com. *1m S of
Forest Row. Proceed S on A22, track
turning on L, 100 metres past 45mph
warning triangle sign. Or 1m N of
Wych Cross T-lights, track turning on
R. Go 400 metres across golf course
till the end.* **Fri 12 July (2-6). Adm
£5, chd free. Home-made teas.
Visits also by arrangement 18 May
to 20 Sept for groups of 10+. Tour
& refreshments on request.**
6 acre garden in Ashdown Forest,
AONB, much of it mixed woodland.
Perimeter walk all around property.
Delightful and tranquil setting with
plenty of space to roam, and various
aspects of interest providing sensory
and a relaxing visit. Ideal for forest
bathing! Lovely stonework, specimen
trees, three ponds, herbaceous
borders, exotic bed, greenhouse and
always something new on the go!
Plenty of space to roam and explore,
and enjoy the fresh air. Plants for sale
and a great range of chutney and
jams. Dogs on leads and children
welcome. Partial wheelchair access
by tarmac track to the kitchen side
gate.
♿ 🐴 ✻ ☕ ⌭

Channel Islands
Cornwall
Devon
Dorset
Gloucestershire
Somerset, Bristol &
South Gloucestershire
Wiltshire

SOUTH WEST

Above: The Old Rectory, Pulham, Dorset

SOUTH WEST

A holiday destination for so many people, whether to much-loved coastlines stretching from Dorset round Somerset, Devon and Cornwall, or to the scenic uplands of Dartmoor and Exmoor, the Quantocks and the Mendips, our South West region also includes the open spaces and chalk downs of Dorset and Wiltshire and the ever-popular Cotswolds of Gloucestershire. This region also includes the Channel Islands, where gardens first opened for the National Garden Scheme in 2022 and where you can definitely combine some garden visiting with a holiday.

This is predominantly a rural region with many traditional, small-scale farming practices preserved and celebrated, from cut flowers in Cornwall to cheese and apples in Somerset, and dairy produce in Devon. Picturesque villages reveal local characteristics from Dorset thatch to Cotswold stone or Wiltshire chalk and flint. Market towns combine with the unforgettable cathedral cities of Salisbury and Wells, not forgetting glorious Bath with its cathedral-status abbey. Gardens in Devon and Cornwall in particular benefit from the mild, maritime climate created by the Gulf Stream, while often plentiful rain throughout much of the region gives its gardens a feeling of constant abundance. Harsher conditions do exist however, for instance in the open spaces of Salisbury Plain and in the exposed higher Cotswold, but many gardens benefit from a setting of some of England's most glorious and unspoilt countryside and show off a range of horticultural rarities made possible by the mild conditions.

Above, from top: Rodmead Farm, Wiltshire; Skool Beanz Children's Allotment, Somerset & Bristol

Below: The Stables, Gloucestershire

CHANNEL ISLANDS

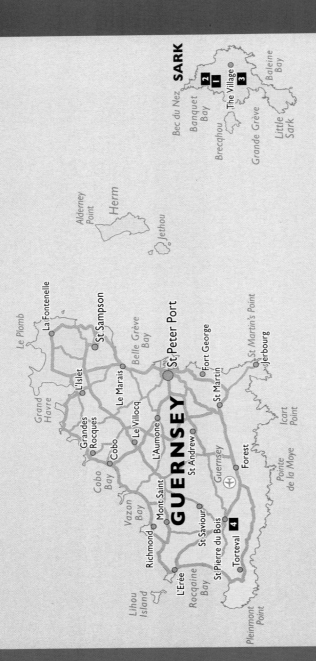

SARK

Bec du Nez

Banquet Bay

2 **1** **3**

The Village

Brecqhou

Grande Grève

Baleine Bay

Little Sark

Herm

Alderney Point

Jethou

Le Plomb

La Fontenelle

St Sampson

Belle Grève Bay

St Peter Port

Fort George

St Martin's Point

St Julerbourg

Grand Havre

L'Islet

Le Marais

St Martin

Grandes Rocques

Le Villocq

L'Aumône

GUERNSEY

St Andrew

Cobo

Cobo Bay

Mont Saint

St Saviour

Guernsey

Forest

Icart Point

Vazon Bay

Richmond

St Pierre du Bois

Torteval **4**

Pointe de la Moye

L'Erée

Rocqaine Bay

Lihou Island

Pleinmont Point

5 kilometres

3 miles

0

0

© Sparrow Publishing

VOLUNTEERS

Area Organiser
Patricia McDermott
patricia.mcdermott@gov.gg

Publicity
Alison Carney
alison.carney@gov.gg

Booklet Coordinator
Ellie Phillips
ellie.phillips@gov.gg

 @National Garden Scheme Guernsey

OPENING DATES

All entries subject to change.
For latest information check
www.ngs.org.uk

Map locator numbers are shown to the right of each garden name.

June

Saturday 8th
NEW ◆ La Seigneurie   1
NEW La Tour   2
Le Grand Dixcart   3

Sunday 9th
NEW La Tour   2
Le Grand Dixcart   3

Saturday 15th
Longfrie House   4

By Arrangement

Arrange a personalised garden visit with your club, or group of friends, on a date to suit you. See individual garden entries for full details.

Longfrie House   4

La Tour

THE GARDENS

1 NEW ◆ **LA SEIGNEURIE**
Sark, Guernsey, GY10 1SF.
Sarah Beaumont, gardens@
laseigneuriedesercq.uk,
www.laseigneuriedesercq.uk.
Follow signs to La Seigneurie, or ask any local for directions. **For NGS: Sat 8 June (9-5). Adm £8, chd £2. Open nearby La Tour. Lunch booking is advisable (01481 832209). For other opening times and information, please email or visit garden website.**
The gardens are a place to relax, unwind and find inspiration. There are 4 diverse acres to explore and an on site café and restaurant to enjoy. The Walled Garden is one of the finest of its kind in the Channel Islands and has regularly won awards for its planting schemes and diversity of flora.

🐾 ✳ ☕ 🪑))

2 NEW **LA TOUR**
Sark, Guernsey, GY10 1SF.
Sébastien & Marie-Agnès
Moerman. *At the north of the Island, following Rue du Fort.* **Sat 8, Sun 9 June (10-4). Adm by donation.**
La Tour is surrounded by hedges of roses, mainly pink and white. In front of the house there is a formal rose garden with roses from David Austin, pink and white. An organic vegetable garden has been created behind the greenhouse. At the back of the house, there is a pond with water lilies surrounded by roses of all colours, also from David Austin.

3 **LE GRAND DIXCART**
Sark, Guernsey, GY10 1SD.
Helen Magell, 01481 832943,
helen@horse.gg. *Next to Stocks Hotel. Take the boat from Guernsey to Sark & follow the signs to Stocks Hotel. Once at the hotel continue up Dixcart Ln towards La Coupee & Le Grand Dixcart will be on your R.* **Sat 8, Sun 9 June (11-3). Adm £5, chd £2.50. Home-made teas.**
The gardens surround an old farmhouse and date from 1565. They are formed into five distinct areas over 2 acres and are cultivated for beauty, wildlife and food. There is a large mandala style permaculture area providing many different vegetables and cutting flowers alongside habitats for wildlife, ponds, lawns, herbaceous borders, two glasshouses, woodland, sculptures and an orchard. Wheelchair access around Sark can be difficult but once you are actually at the gardens there are just grassy slopes and paths.

♿ 🚌 ☕ 🪑))

4 **LONGFRIE HOUSE**
Rue De Longfrie, St Pierre
Du Bois, Guernsey, GY7 9RZ.
Nicola Brink & Carl Jensen,
nicolajensen@icloud.com. *St Pierre, du Bois, Guernsey. Yellow farmhouse opp Longfrie Inn car park.* **Sat 15 June (1-7.30). Adm by donation. Light refreshments. Cakes & sandwiches avail. Visits also by arrangement.**
A country garden that can be enjoyed by all ages. The garden is a haven for friends, family, dogs and birds. The garden is cared for by the owners with the help of a close friend and is divided into 'rooms' or areas to make the most of the sunshine and prevailing weather conditions.

 🐾 ☕))

CORNWALL

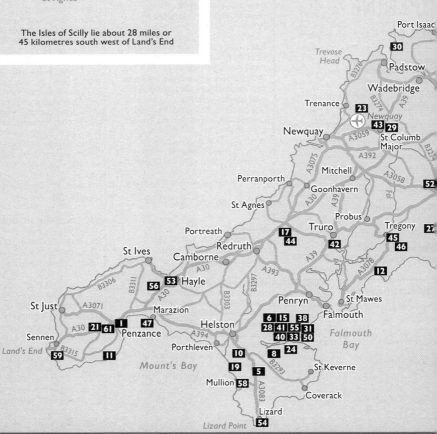

ISLES OF SCILLY

Tresco
St Martin's
Bryher
Hugh Town
St Mary's
St Agnes

The Isles of Scilly lie about 28 miles or
45 kilometres south west of Land's End

Port Isaac
30
Trevose
Head
Padstow
Wadebridge
Trenance
23
Newquay
43 29
Newquay
St Columb
Major
A3059
Mitchell
A392
Perranporth
Goonhavern
A3058
52
St Agnes
Probus
Tregony
27
Portreath
17
Truro
45
Redruth
44
42
46
Camborne
Hayle
12
St Ives
56
53
A30
Penryn
St Mawes
St Just
Falmouth
Marazion
6 15 38
St Austell area
Sennen
21 61 1
47
28 41 55 31
Falmouth
Penzance
40 33 50
Bay
Land's End
59
11
Porthleven
10
8 24
Mount's Bay
19
5
St Keverne
Mullion 58
Coverack
Lizard
54
Lizard Point

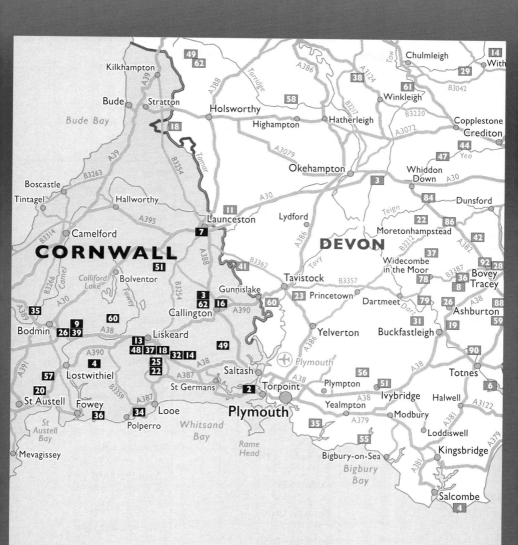

Kilkhampton
Bude
Stratton
49
62
A386
Tow
Chulmleigh
14
With
29
A3124
38
A386
A39
A388
Torridge
A39
Holsworthy
58
Winkleigh
61
B3042
B3220
A3072
Copplestone
Crediton
Bude Bay
Highampton
Hatherleigh
18
Tamar
Boscastle
Tintagel
B3263
A39
Hallworthy
B3254
A3079
Okehampton
3
Whiddon
Down
A30
44
Yeo
47
Camelford
B3314
A395
Launceston
11
7
Lydford
A30
A386
DEVON
Teign
Dunsford
84
A382
42
Moretonhampstead
22
86
51
Colliford
Lake
Bolventor
Fowey
Camel
B3266
A30
A388
B3254
41
B3362
Tavistock
Tavy
B3357
Widecombe
in the Moor
B3212
37
92
28
78
36
8
Bovey
Tracey
35
A389
Bodmin
26
9
39
60
Callington
3
62
16
Gunnislake
A390
60
23
Princetown
Dartmeet
Dart
79
B3387
26
88
Ashburton
59
19
A38
Liskeard
13
48
37
18
32
14
25
22
A38
49
Yelverton
A386
Buckfastleigh
31
A390
Lostwithiel
4
57
St Austell
20
Fowey
36
Looe
34
Polperro
B3359
A387
St Germans
Saltash
2
Torpoint
Plymouth
Plympton
56
A38
Yealmpton
A379
Plymouth
Ivybridge
51
Modbury
35
Halwell
Totnes
6
A3122
A381
Loddiswell
A38
St
Austell
Bay
Mevagissey
Whitsand
Bay
Rame
Head
Bigbury-on-Sea
55
Bigbury
Bay
Kingsbridge
A379
A381
Salcombe
4

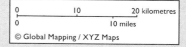

0   10   20 kilometres
0   10 miles
© Global Mapping / XYZ Maps

VOLUNTEERS

County Organiser
Sue Newton 07786 367610
sue.newton@ngs.org.uk

Claire Woodbine 07483 244318
claire.woodbine@ngs.org.uk

County Treasurer
Marie Tolhurst
marie.tolhurst@ngs.org.uk

Publicity
Laura Tucker
laura.tucker@ngs.org.uk

Social Media
Claire Wood 07921 153305
claire.wood@ngs.org.uk

Booklet Co-ordinator
Position vacant Please contact
Claire Woodbine (see above)

Photographer
Keith Tucker
keith.tucker@ngs.org.uk

Assistant County Organisers
Kirsty Angwin
kirsty.angwin@ngs.org.uk

Christopher Harvey Clark
01872 530165
suffree2012@gmail.com

Caroline Cudmore
01726 882325
caroline.cudmore@ngs.org.uk

Sara Gadd 07814 885141
sara.gadd@ngs.org.uk

Sorcha Hitchcox
sorcha.hitchcox@ngs.org.uk

Libby Pidcock 01208 821303
libby.pidcock@ngs.org.uk

Graham Sykes 07719 711683
graham.sykes@ngs.org.uk

f @CornwallNGS
@cornwall.ngs

OPENING DATES

All entries subject to change.
For latest information check
www.ngs.org.uk
Map locator numbers are
shown to the right of each
garden name.

March

Friday 1st
◆ Antony Woodland Garden &
  Woodland Walk   2

Tuesday 5th
◆ Trewidden Garden   61

Thursday 14th
Trevina House   60

Friday 15th
Trevina House   60

Tuesday 19th
NEW Lower Tregamere   29

Wednesday 20th
NEW Lower Tregamere   29

April

Monday 1st
Riverside Cottage   42

Friday 5th
NEW Higher Locrenton   22

Sunday 7th
NEW Higher Locrenton   22

Monday 8th
◆ Pencarrow   35

Thursday 11th
Trevina House   60

Friday 12th
Trevina House   60

Sunday 14th
◆ Boconnoc   4

Saturday 20th
The Lodge   26

Sunday 21st
The Lodge   26
Lower Penbothidnow   28
Rose Morran   43

Tuesday 23rd
Pinsla Garden   39
Riverside Cottage   42

Wednesday 24th
NEW Lower Tregamere   29
Pinsla Garden   39

Thursday 25th
NEW Lower Tregamere   29

Friday 26th
◆ Antony Woodland Garden &
  Woodland Walk   2

Saturday 27th
◆ Chygurno   11

Sunday 28th
◆ Chygurno   11

Tuesday 30th
Pinsla Garden   39
Riverside Cottage   42

May

Wednesday 1st
Pinsla Garden   39

Sunday 5th
Cardinham Gardens   9
East Down Barn   14
NEW Gables   18
Navas Hill House   33
Penmilder   37

Thursday 9th
Trevina House   60

Friday 10th
NEW Higher Locrenton   22
Trevina House   60

Sunday 12th
Cardinham Gardens   9
NEW Higher Locrenton   22
◆ The Japanese Garden   23
South Lea   49
Trebartha Estate Garden and
  Country Garden at Lemarne   51

Monday 13th
◆ The Japanese Garden   23

Tuesday 14th
NEW Lower Tregamere   29
Pinsla Garden   39
Riverside Cottage   42

Wednesday 15th
NEW Lower Tregamere   29
Pinsla Garden   39

Thursday 16th
NEW Treglyn   52

Friday 17th
NEW Treglyn   52

Saturday 18th
NEW The Old Vicarage   34
Trelan   53

Sunday 19th
NEW Lametton Mill 25
Lower Penbothidnow 28
NEW The Old Vicarage 34

Tuesday 21st
Riverside Cottage 42

Thursday 23rd
South Bosent 48

Friday 24th
Bucks Head House Garden 6
South Bosent 48

Sunday 26th
NEW Lametton Mill 25

Wednesday 29th
Gardens Cottage 20
Pendower House 36

Thursday 30th
Gardens Cottage 20

June

Saturday 1st
Trelan 53

Sunday 2nd
Trevesco 58

Tuesday 4th
NEW Gwrythia 21

Wednesday 5th
◆ Kestle Barton 24

Saturday 8th
NEW Tresithney 56

Sunday 9th
Caervallack 8
South Lea 49
NEW Tresithney 56
Trevilley 59

Wednesday 12th
◆ Kestle Barton 24

Thursday 13th
Trevina House 60

Friday 14th
Dobwalls Gardens 13
NEW Higher Locrenton 22
Trevina House 60

Saturday 15th
Dobwalls Gardens 13
Fox Hollow 17

Sunday 16th
NEW Higher Locrenton 22
NEW Mawnan School Nature
Garden 31
Trethew 57

Tuesday 18th
Pinsla Garden 39

Wednesday 19th
◆ Kestle Barton 24
Pinsla Garden 39

Thursday 20th
◆ The Lost Gardens of Heligan ... 27

Friday 21st
Bucks Head House Garden 6

Saturday 22nd
Trelan 53

Sunday 23rd
Crugsillick Manor 12
Firste Park 16
Menheniot Gardens 32

Tuesday 25th
Pinsla Garden 39

Wednesday 26th
Gardens Cottage 20
◆ Kestle Barton 24
Pinsla Garden 39

Thursday 27th
Gardens Cottage 20

Friday 28th
Dobwalls Gardens 13

Saturday 29th
Dobwalls Gardens 13
NEW The Old Vicarage 34
◆ Roseland House 44

Sunday 30th
NEW The Old Vicarage 34
Rose Morran 43
◆ Roseland House 44

July

Wednesday 3rd
◆ Kestle Barton 24

Friday 5th
◆ Antony Woodland Garden &
Woodland Walk 2
Bucks Head House Garden 6
NEW Higher Locrenton 22

Sunday 7th
Anvil Cottage 3
NEW Higher Locrenton 22
NEW Lametton Mill 25
Windmills 62

Wednesday 10th
◆ Kestle Barton 24

Thursday 11th
Trevina House 60

Friday 12th
Trevina House 60

Wednesday 17th
◆ Kestle Barton 24

Thursday 18th
NEW Treglyn 52

Friday 19th
Dobwalls Gardens 13
NEW Treglyn 52

Saturday 20th
◆ Chygurno 11
Dobwalls Gardens 13
Roseland Parc 45

Sunday 21st
◆ Chygurno 11

Wednesday 24th
◆ Kestle Barton 24

Sunday 28th
Byeways 7

Wednesday 31st
◆ Kestle Barton 24

August

Friday 2nd
Bucks Head House Garden 6

Wednesday 7th
◆ Kestle Barton 24

Friday 9th
Dobwalls Gardens 13

Saturday 10th
Dobwalls Gardens 13

Tuesday 13th
NEW Gwrythia 21

Wednesday 14th
◆ Bonython Manor 5
◆ Kestle Barton 24

Wednesday 21st
◆ Kestle Barton 24

Friday 23rd
Bucks Head House Garden 6

Sunday 25th
NEW Lametton Mill 25

Wednesday 28th
◆ Kestle Barton 24

September

Sunday 1st
Gardens Cottage 20
Rose Morran 43

Wednesday 4th
♦ Kestle Barton   24

Friday 6th
Bucks Head House Garden   6

Sunday 8th
Firste Park   16
[NEW] Lametton Mill   25

Wednesday 11th
♦ Kestle Barton   24
South Bosent   48

Thursday 12th
South Bosent   48
Trevina House   60

Friday 13th
Trevina House   60

Wednesday 18th
♦ Kestle Barton   24
[NEW] Lower Tregamere   29

Thursday 19th
[NEW] Lower Tregamere   29
[NEW] Treglyn   52

Friday 20th
[NEW] Treglyn   52

Wednesday 25th
♦ Kestle Barton   24

October

Tuesday 8th
Trevina House   60

Wednesday 9th
Trevina House   60

Friday 11th
♦ Antony Woodland Garden &
Woodland Walk   2

Sunday 20th
Trebartha Estate Garden and
Country Garden at Lemarne   51

By Arrangement

Arrange a personalised garden visit
with your club, or group of friends,
on a date to suit you. See individual
garden entries for full details.

Alverton Cottage   1
Anvil Cottage   3
Bucks Head House Garden   6
Caervallack   8
Carminowe Valley Garden   10
Crugsillick Manor   12
Deviock Farm, Cardinham

Gardens   9
East Down Barn   14
Ethnevas Cottage   15
Garden Cottage   19
Gardens Cottage   20
[NEW] Gwrythia   21
[NEW] Higher Locrenton   22
[NEW] Lametton Mill   25
Lower Penbothidnow   28
Malibu   30
Penwarne   38
Port Navas Chapel   40
Rose Morran   43
Rosevallon Barn   46
South Bosent   48
South Lea   49
Towan House   50
[NEW] Treglyn   52
Trelan   53
Tremichele   54
Trenarth   55
[NEW] Tresithney   56
Trethew   57
Trevilley   59
Trevina House   60
Windmills   62

Mawnan School Nature Garden

THE GARDENS

Trevesco

© Keith Tucker

1 ALVERTON COTTAGE

Alverton Road, Penzance,
TR18 4TG. David & Lizzie
Puddifoot, 07985 735376,
david.puddifoot@gmail.com.
*Next door to YMCA. About 600
metres from Penlee car park
travelling towards A30. Morrab
Gardens are also close to car park.*
**Visits by arrangement May &
June for groups of 6 to 30. Adm
£5, chd free.**
Alverton Cottage is a Grade II listed
Regency house. The garden is modest
in size though large for a Penzance
garden, south facing and sheltered
by mature trees inc elms. Very large
monkey-puzzle tree and holm oak.
Laid out in the 1860s, we have added
a succulent area, fernery and have
cleared and replanted since 2019. In
nearby Morrab Sub-tropical Gardens
the 'Friends' will also welcome
visitors. Off road disabled parking but
wheelchair to garden terrace only.

2 ◆ ANTONY WOODLAND GARDEN & WOODLAND WALK

Ferry Lane, Torpoint, PL11 3AB.
Sir Richard Carew-Pole,
01752 815303, woodlandgarden@
antonyestate.com, www.
antonywoodlandgarden.com. *2m
NW of Torpoint. From the main gate
off A374, proceed along Ferry Lane
past Antony House you will see car
park on R, beneath the trees.* **For
NGS: Fri 1 Mar, Fri 26 Apr, Fri 5
July, Fri 11 Oct (10.30-5). Adm
£9, chd free. Light refreshments.
For other opening times and
information, please phone, email or
visit garden website.**
Antony Woodland Garden is one of the
most beautiful gardens in Cornwall.
It is a haven of serenity and peace,
the perfect place for a pleasant walk,
a picnic, for children to explore and
for those interested in gardening, to
enjoy a magnificent variety of plants.
As an "International Camellia Garden
of Excellence" it holds the National
Collection of *Camellia japonica*. It has
the most stunning array of magnolias,
beautiful walks along the river's edge,
contemporary sculpture and carpets of
wild flowers, waiting to be discovered.

3 ANVIL COTTAGE

South Hill, PL17 7LP. Geoff &
Barbara Clemerson, 01579 362623,
bjclemerson@gmail.com. *3m NW
of Callington. Head N on A388 from
Callington centre. After ½ m L onto
South Hill Rd (signed South Hill),
straight on for 3m. Gardens on R
just before St Sampson's Church.*
**Sun 7 July (1-5). Combined adm
with Windmills £6, chd free.
Home-made teas. Gluten free
refreshments available. Visits also
by arrangement July & Aug for
groups of 8 to 30.**
Essentially, this is a plantsman's
garden. Winding paths lead through a
series of themed rooms with familiar,
rare and unusual plants. Steps lead
up to a raised viewpoint looking west
towards Caradon Hill and Bodmin
Moor. Other paths take you on a
circular route through a rose garden,
hot beds, a tropical area and a secret
garden.

4 ◆ BOCONNOC

Lostwithiel, PL22 0RG.
Fortescue Family, 01208 872507,
events@boconnoc.com,
www.boconnoc.com. *Off A390
between Liskeard & Lostwithiel.
From East Taphouse follow signs
to Boconnoc. Do not rely on Sat
Nav, follow directions on Boconnoc
website.* **For NGS: Sun 14 Apr
(2-5). Adm £6, chd £3. Light
refreshments in stable yard.
For other opening times and
information, please phone, email or
visit garden website.**
20 acres surrounded by parkland
and woods with magnificent trees,
flowering shrubs and stunning views.
The gardens are set amongst mature
trees which provide the backcloth
for exotic spring flowering shrubs,
woodland plants, with newly planted
magnolias, and a fine collection of
hydrangeas. Bathhouse built in 1804,
obelisk built in 1771, house dating
from Domesday, deer park and C15
church.

5 ◆ BONYTHON MANOR
Cury Cross Lanes, Helston,
TR12 7BA. Mr & Mrs Richard
Nathan, 01326 240550,
sbonython@gmail.com,
www.bonythonmanor.co.uk. *5m S
of Helston. On main A3083 Helston
to Lizard Rd. Turn L at Cury Cross
Lanes (Wheel Inn). Entrance 300yds
on R.* **For NGS: Wed 14 Aug (2-4).
Adm £11, chd £2. Tea, coffee,
fruit juices and home-made
cakes. For other opening times
and information, please phone,
email or visit garden website.**
Magnificent 20 acre colour garden
inc sweeping hydrangea drive
to Georgian manor (not open).
Herbaceous walled garden, potager
with vegetables and picking flowers;
3 lakes in valley planted with
ornamental grasses, perennials and
South African flowers. A 'must see'
for all seasons colour.

**6 BUCKS HEAD HOUSE
GARDEN**
Trengove Cross, Constantine,
TR11 5QR. Deborah Baker,
07801 444916,
deborah.fwbaker@gmail.com,
deborahfwbaker.com/home.html.
*5m SW of Falmouth. A394 towards
Helston, L at Edgcumbe towards
Gweek/Constantine. Proceed for
0.8m then L towards Constantine.
Further 0.8m, garden on L at
Trengove Cross.* **Fri 24 May, Fri 21
June, Fri 5 July, Fri 2, Fri 23 Aug,
Fri 6 Sept (2-5). Adm £6, chd free.
Light refreshments. Visits also by
arrangement 21 May to 13 Sept for
groups of up to 25.**
Enchanting cottage and woodland
gardens of native and rare trees,
shrubs and perennials, encouraging
biodiversity. The site of 1½ acres
is on a south facing Cornish hillside
with panoramic views. Protected by
essential windbreak hedging, the
inspiring collection of plants has been
chosen to create intrigue and increase
diversity. During the summer months
art works will be on display.

7 BYEWAYS
Dunheved Road, Launceston,
PL15 9JE. Tony Reddicliffe.
*Launceston town centre. 100yds
from multi-storey car park past
offices of Cornish & Devon Post into
Dunheved Rd, 3rd bungalow on R.*
**Sun 28 July (1-5). Adm £5, chd
free. Light refreshments.**

Small town garden developed over
11 yrs by enthusiastic amateur
gardeners. Herbaceous borders,
rockery. Tropicals inc bananas,
gingers and senecio. Stream
and water features. Roof garden.
Japanese inspired tea house and
courtyard with bridge. Fig tree and
Pawlonia flank area giving secluded
seating. Living pergola. New area
of ponds and water features with
removal of sheds and overgrown
areas.

8 CAERVALLACK
St Martin, Helston, TR12 6DF.
Matt Robinson & Louise
McClary, 01326 221339,
mat@build-art.co.uk, www.
mattrobinsonarchitecture.co.uk.
*5m SE of Helston. Go through
Mawgan village, over 2 bridges, past
Gear Farm shop; go past turning
on L, garden next farmhouse on L.
Parking is in field opp entrance.* **Sun
9 June (1.30-4). Adm £6, chd free.
Tea & home-made cakes; scones,
clotted cream & jam. Visits also
by arrangement 28 Mar to 30 Sept
for groups of 5 to 30. Group visits
are for 1 ½ hours.**
Romantic garden arranged into
rooms, the collaboration between
an artist and an architect. Colour
and form of plants structured by
topiary, hedging and architectural
experiments in cob, brick, slate &
concrete. Grade II listed farmhouse
and ancient orchard. Roses and
wisteria a speciality. 29yrs in the
making. 2 acre field turning into
native grassland/woodland. Arts &
Crafts cob walls and paving; heroic
54ft pedestrian footbridge, 5 sided
meditation studio, cast concrete
ponds and amphitheatre; coppice
and wildflower meadow; mature
orchard and vegetable plot. Topiary
throughout.

GROUP OPENING

9 CARDINHAM GARDENS
Cardinham, Bodmin, PL30 4AY. *5m
NE of Bodmin. From A30 or Bodmin
take A38 towards Plymouth, 1st
L at r'about, past Crematorium &
Cardinham Woods turning. Continue
towards Cardinham village for garden
signs. Maps at each garden.* **Sun
5, Sun 12 May (11-5). Combined
adm £6, chd free. Home-made
teas at Deviock Farm from 11-5**

on 5th May, at Lower Treslea
from 11-5 on 12th May.

DEVIOCK FARM
PL30 4DA. Bernie & Sue
Muir, 01208 821645,
smenhinick@gmail.com.
**Open on Sun 5 May
Visits also by arrangement 5
May to 31 July for groups of 6
to 20.**

LOWER TRESLEA
PL30 4DL. Loraine & Nigel
Pollard.
Open on Sun 12 May

THE OLD SCHOOL HOUSE
PL30 4EA. Mike & Libby Pidcock.
Open on Sun 12 May

PINSLA GARDEN
Mark & Claire Woodbine.
Open on all dates
(See separate entry)

The rural parish of Cardinham on the
south west side of Bodmin Moor has
a wide range of ecosystems as the
moorland merges into woodland and
ancient downs and meadows. May
5th group opening has 2 gardens,
both welcome dogs. Pinsla Garden
with naturalistic planting, stone circle
and vegetable garden in peaceful
woodland, and Deviock Farm, a 2
acre south facing wildlife friendly
garden with many mature trees and
shrubs developed over past five
yrs. Enclosed farmhouse garden,
pond, damp areas, vegetables and
a disused waterwheel pit feature.
On May 12th, 3 gardens are open,
(regret no dogs). Pinsla Garden, The
Old School House and Lower Treslea.
The Old School House is a cottage
garden created in the grounds of a
Victorian school by a passionate and
enthusiastic gardener over 35yrs.
Lower Treslea has a separate good-
sized orchard/vegetable plot. The
garden has been constructed over 20
yrs by the present owners as a haven
for wildlife: herbaceous borders,
roses, magnolias and wisteria.
Picturesque valley on the edge of
Bodmin moor.

**10 CARMINOWE VALLEY
GARDEN**
Tangies, Gunwalloe,
TR12 7PU. Mr & Mrs Peter
Stanley, 01326 565868,
stanley.m2@sky.com. *3m SW of
Helston. A3083 Helston-Lizard rd.
R opp main gate to Culdrose. 1m*

downhill, garden on R. **Visits by arrangement 7 Apr to 2 June for groups of 6 to 30. Adm £6, chd free. Cream teas.**
Overlooking the beautiful Carminowe valley towards Loe Pool, this abundant garden combines native oak woodland, babbling brook and large natural pond with more formal areas. Wildflowers, mown pathways, shrubberies, orchard. Enclosed cottage garden, spring colours and roses in early summer provide great variety and contrast. Gravel paths, slopes.

◆ CHYGURNO
Lamorna, TR19 6XH. Dr & Mrs Robert Moule, 01736 732153, rmoule010@btinternet.com. *4m S of Penzance. Off B3315. Follow signs for The Lamorna Cove Hotel. Garden is at top of hill, past Hotel on L.* **For NGS: Sat 27, Sun 28 Apr, Sat 20, Sun 21 July (2-5). Adm £5, chd free. For other opening times and information, please phone or email.**
Beautiful, unique, 3 acre cliffside garden overlooking Lamorna Cove. Planting started in 1998, mainly southern hemisphere shrubs and exotics with hydrangeas, camellias and rhododendrons. Woodland area with tree ferns set against large granite outcrops. Garden terraced with steep steps and paths. Plenty of benches so you can take a rest and enjoy the wonderful views.

12 CRUGSILLICK MANOR
Ruan High Lanes, Truro, TR2 5LJ. Dr Alison Agnew & Mr Brian Yule, 07538 218201, alisonagnew@icloud.com. *On Roseland Peninsula. Turn off A390 Truro-St Austell road onto A3078 towards St Mawes. Approx 5m after Tregony turn 1st L after Ruan High Lanes towards Veryan, garden is 200yds on R. Limited parking.* **Sun 23 June (11-5). Adm £5, chd free. Tea, coffee, soft drinks, cakes & light lunches. Visits also by arrangement 13 May to 14 Oct for groups of 10 to 50.**
2 acre garden, substantially re-landscaped and planted, mostly over last 12 yrs. To the side of the C17/ C18 house, a wooded bank drops down to a walled kitchen garden and hot garden. In front, sweeping yew hedges and paths define oval lawns and broad mixed borders. On a lower

terrace, the focus is a large pond and the planting is predominantly exotic flowering trees and shrubs. Wheelchair access to the central level of the garden, the house and cafe. Garden is on several levels connected by fairly steep sloping gravel paths.

GROUP OPENING

13 DOBWALLS GARDENS
Dobwalls, Liskeard, PL14 4LR. *In Dobwalls at double mini r'about take road to Duloe. Yellow signs will then direct to both gardens.* **Fri 14, Sat 15, Fri 28, Sat 29 June, Fri 19, Sat 20 July, Fri 9, Sat 10 Aug (1.30-5.30). Combined adm £8, chd free. Home-made teas at South Bosent.**

9 HIGMAN CLOSE
Jim Stephens & Sue Martin.

SOUTH BOSENT
Adrienne Lloyd & Trish Wilson.
(See separate entry)

Two very different gardens within a few minutes drive from each other. 9 Higman Close, a restless, constantly changing, unapologetically busy garden, full of good plants with colour, scent and surprises. Glasshouse overflowing with cacti and succulents, some over 35 yrs old. The garden at South Bosent is currently being developed from farmland. The aim is to create a combination of interesting plants coupled with habitat for wildlife over a total of 9½ acres. Several garden areas, woodland gardens, a meadow, ponds of varying sizes, inc. rill and waterfall. In spring, the bluebell wood trail runs alongside the stream. Partial wheelchair access at 9 Higman Close and main garden accessible at South Bosent.

14 EAST DOWN BARN
Menheniot, Liskeard, PL14 3QU. David & Shelley Lockett, 07803 159662, davidandshelleylockett@ btinternet.com. *S side of village nr cricket ground. Turn off A38 at Hayloft restaurant/railway stn junction & head towards Menheniot village. Follow NGS signs from sharp LH bend as you enter village.* **Sun 5 May (1-4.30). Adm £4, chd free. Home-made teas. Visits also by**

arrangement 1 Apr to 7 June for groups of 12 to 30.
Garden laid down between 1986-1991 with the conversion of the barn into a home and covers almost ½ acre of east sloping land with stream running north-south acting as the easterly boundary. 3 terraces before garden starts to level out at the stream. Garden won awards in the early years under the stewardship of the original owners. Ducks are in residence in the stream so regret no dogs.

15 ETHNEVAS COTTAGE
Constantine, Falmouth, TR11 5PY. Lyn Watson & Ray Chun, 01326 340076, ethnevas@outlook.com. *6m SW of Falmouth. Nearest main roads A39, A394. Follow signs for Constantine. At lower village sign, at bottom of winding hill, turn off on private lane. Garden ¾ m up hill.* **Visits by arrangement Mar to June for groups of 5 to 20. Adm £5, chd free.**
Isolated granite cottage in 2 acres. Intimate flower and vegetable garden. Bridge over stream to large pond and primrose path through semi-wild bog area. Hillside with grass paths among native and exotic trees. Many camellias and rhododendrons. Mixed shrubs and herbaceous beds, wildflower glade, spring bulbs. A garden of discovery with hidden delights.

16 FIRSTE PARK
Winsor Lane, Kelly Bray, Callington, PL17 8HD. Mrs Tina Monahan. *From Callington towards Kelly Bray, just before Swingletree pub, turn R into Station Rd, about ¼ m Firste Park is on the L top of Winsor Lane. Parking signposted in adjoining field.* **Sun 23 June, Sun 8 Sept (11-4). Adm £5, chd free. Light refreshments.**
1950s house with mature trees, flower gardens established about 5 yrs ago with just over 1 acre incorporating a waterfall, pond and lawned areas. Packed with many plants and shrubs inc over 100 named roses, several varieties of hydrangeas and perfumed plants in abundance. There is an outside kitchen area, pergolas, a fruit and vegetable garden with cut flowers which we also use for dried flowers. Most of the garden is accessible but some gravel pathways.

17 FOX HOLLOW
Station Road, Carnhot,
Chacewater, Truro, TR4 8PA.
Adele & Gary Peters-Float. *Enter
Blackwater, take lane next to Citroen
garage signed Chacewater, Station
Rd, 1m on R just before train viaduct.
Ignore SatNav once on this lane.
Park in lane, few extra spaces opp.*
**Sat 15 June (11-4). Adm £5, chd
free. Light refreshments.**
Approx 1 acre garden rediscovered
over 8 yrs by the owners. Lovingly
redesigned so the 4 generations
living here can enjoy. Planted with
herbaceous beds, traditional cottage
flowers, wildflower areas, vegetable
garden and orchard. A garden of
discovery, meandering paths lead
to hidden upcycled treasures and
seating areas with far reaching views.
Greenhouses with many plants. Most
areas accessible to wheelchairs.

18 NEW GABLES
Lodge Hill, Liskeard, PL14 4EL.
Mr Chris Bryant. *1m S of Liskeard
on the B3254.* **Sun 5 May (11-5).
Combined adm with Penmilder
£6, chd free. Home-made teas.**
This pretty garden is being opened as
a tribute to Carol, who sadly passed
away last year from motor neurone
disease. Carol and husband Chris
have lovingly tended the garden
together for many years. The garden
is bursting with colour in spring and
has plenty of places to sit and enjoy
the scents and sounds of nature.
Wheelchair users will be able to
access the front garden and patio
which overlooks the garden.

19 GARDEN COTTAGE
Gunwalloe, Helston, TR12 7QB.
Dan & Beth Tarling, 01326 241906,
bethgunwalloe@gmail.com,
www.gunwalloecottages.co.uk.
*Just beyond Halzephron Inn
at Gunwalloe. Cream cottage
with green windows.* **Visits by
arrangement 18 Mar to 28 Sept.
Adm £5, chd £5. Cream teas.**
Coastal cottage garden. Small garden
with traditional cottage flowers,
vegetable garden, greenhouse and
meadow with far reaching views.
Instagram: seaview_gunwalloe.

20 GARDENS COTTAGE
Prideaux, St Blazey, PL24 2SS.
Sue & Roger Paine, 07786 367610,
sue.newton@btinternet.com,
en-gb.facebook.com/
gardenscottageprideaux/. *1m from
railway Xing on A390 in St Blazey.
Turn into Prideaux Rd opp Gulf
petrol station in St Blazey (signed
Luxulyan). Proceed ½ m. Turn R
(signed Luxulyan Valley and Prideaux)
& follow signs.* **Wed 29, Thur 30
May, Wed 26, Thur 27 June, Sun
1 Sept (2-5). Adm £5, chd free.
Home-made teas. Visits also by
arrangement 27 May to 6 Sept for
groups of 10 to 30.**
A stunning landscape and a variety
of planting styles define this country
garden. Formal and informal areas are
enhanced with sculpture, and with its
abundant herbaceous borders, dry
terraces, courtyard garden, woodland
glade, wildlife pond, beehives,
orchard, fruit garden and a productive
(and beautiful) kitchen garden it's
a plot that feels much bigger than
its one and a half acres. Check our
Facebook page for special events.

21 NEW GWRYTHIA
Sancreed, Penzance, TR20 8QS.
Maggie Feeny, 07840 288916,
maggiefeeny@yahoo.com,
www.maggiefeeny.co.uk. *4m
w of Penzance. From Penzance
A30 to Lands End, at Drift go R at
Xrds to Sancreed, Beacon Ancient
Monument. Go1.7m past Sancreed
sign, go L up track for Gwrythia.
Walkers pay on gate. Visitors in
cars to pre book.* **Tue 4 June, Tue
13 Aug (1.30-5.30). Adm £5, chd
free. Pre-booking essential,
please visit www.ngs.org.uk for
information & booking. Light
refreshments. Visits also by
arrangement 17 June to 9 Aug for
groups of 6 to 15. (Not weekends).
Time 2-5.30pm.**
A 3 acre garden with meadows, two
wildlife ponds, mixed ornamental
borders of grasses, perennials,
annuals and roses. An arch of a
hornbeam hedge leads to a large
vegetable garden, polytunnel, on to
an artist's studio, and down through a
small woodland. Gwrythia is gardened
organically, with plants chosen for
both their attraction to wildlife and
plant lovers alike. The gardener is an
artist with open studio at the end of
May for a week.

22 NEW HIGHER LOCRENTON
St Keyne, Liskeard, PL14 4RN.
Ade & Elise Allen, 01579 342301,
adelise.allen@btinternet.com.
*Nr St Keyne Well, between Looe &
Liskeard. By St Keyne Church, take
the lane to St Keyne Well for ½ m.
Turn L at Well. Higher Locrenton is
100 yds on R. Parking for 8 cars.*
**Fri 5, Sun 7 Apr, Fri 10, Sun 12
May, Fri 14, Sun 16 June, Fri 5
July (2-5). Sun 7 July (2-5), also
open nearby Lametton Mill. Adm
£5, chd free. Light refreshments.
Visits also by arrangement 15 Mar
to 20 Oct for groups of up to 20.**
The garden is set in 2 acres on a
hillside. It has been developed over
the past 30 yrs and is 'plantsman' in
style, featuring a wide variety of trees,
shrubs and perennials. It is informally
divided into a number of beds with
different themes. A key aim has been
to provide interest throughout the year
in terms of atmosphere, form, colour
and scent. Some parts of the garden
can only be accessed via steps or
somewhat steep gradients.

23 ◆ THE JAPANESE GARDEN
St Mawgan, TR8 4ET. Natalie Hore
& Stuart Ellison, 01637 860116,
info@japanesegarden.co.uk,
www.japanesegarden.co.uk. *6m
E of Newquay. St Mawgan village
is directly below Newquay Airport.
Follow brown & white road signs on
A3059 & B3276.* **For NGS: Sun 12,
Mon 13 May (10-6). Adm £6, chd
£3. For other opening times and
information, please phone, email or
visit garden website.**
Discover an oasis of tranquillity in a
Japanese-style Cornish garden, set in
approx 1 acre. Spectacular Japanese
maples and azaleas, symbolic
teahouse, koi pond, bamboo
grove, stroll woodland, zen and
moss gardens. A place created for
contemplation and meditation. Adm
free to gift shop, bonsai and plant
areas. Refreshments available in the
village a short walk from garden. 90%
wheelchair accessible, with uneven,
gravel paths.

24 ◆ KESTLE BARTON
Manaccan, Helston, TR12 6HU.
Karen Townsend, 01326 231811,
info@kestlebarton.co.uk,
www.kestlebarton.co.uk. *10m S
of Helston. Leave Helston on A3083
towards Lizard. At the R'about
take 1st exit onto B3293 & follow*

Gardens Cottage

signs towards St Keverne; after Trelowarren turn L and follow the brown signs for appprox 4m. **For NGS: Every Wed 5 June to 25 Sept (10.30-5). Adm by donation. Modest Tea Room in garden. Cash only honesty box. Tea/ coffee, cakes, ice creams, apple juice from our own orchards. For other opening times and information, please phone, email or visit garden website.**

A delightful garden near Frenchmans Creek, on the Lizard, which is the setting for Kestle Barton Gallery; wildflower meadow, Cornish orchard with named varieties and a formal garden with prairie planting in blocks by James Alexander Sinclair. It is a riot of colour in summer and continues to delight well into late summer. Good wheelchair access & reasonably accessible WC. Dogs on leads welcome.

25 NEW LAMETTON MILL
St Keyne, Liskeard, PL14 4SH. Mr Richard & Mrs Leigh Woods, 07812 103518, lamettonmill@btinternet.com, www.lamettonmill.co.uk. *What 3 Words app ///access.motoring. nicknames. The postcode brings you to our door. If you wish to travel by train we are across the rd from the St Keyne Wishing Well Halt railway stn.* **Sun 19, Sun 26 May (11-4). Sun 7 July (11-4), also open nearby Higher Locrenton. Sun 25 Aug, Sun 8 Sept (11-4). Adm £5, chd free. Tea. Visits also by arrangement 18 May to 15 Sept for groups of up to 30.**

A newly created garden, planted during 2023, on the site of a former mill. Contains a variety of young specimen trees, herbaceous borders, an extensive collection of Intersectional (ITOH) peonies, roses, small pond and water feature. The garden is laid out on different levels on a gently sloping site with several seating areas to relax in sun or shade. There are gravel paths and some steps.

26 THE LODGE
Fletchersbridge, Bodmin, PL30 4AN. Mr Tony Ryde & Dr James Wilson. *2m E of Bodmin. From A38 at Glynn Crematorium r'about take road towards Cardinham & continue down to hamlet of Fletchersbridge. Park at Stable Art on R. Short walk to garden 1st R over river bridge.* **Sat 20, Sun 21 Apr (12.30-5.30). Adm £6, chd free. Home-made teas.**

3 acre riverside garden created since 1998, specialising in trees and shrubs chosen for their flowers, foliage and form, and embracing a Gothic lodge remodelled in 2016, once part of the Glynn estate. Water garden with ponds, waterfalls and abstract sculptures. Magnolias, azaleas, rhododendrons, camellias, prunus and spring bulbs at their peak in mid April. Wheelchair access to gravelled areas around house and along left side of garden.

27 ◆ THE LOST GARDENS OF HELIGAN

Pentewan, St Austell, PL26 6EN. Heligan Gardens Ltd, 01726 845100, heligan.reception@heligan.com, www.heligan.com. *5m S of St Austell. From St Austell take B3273 signed Mevagissey, follow signs.* **For NGS: Thur 20 June (10-12.30). Adm £25, chd free. Pre-booking essential, please visit www.ngs.org.uk for information & booking. For other opening times and information, please phone, email or visit garden website.**

Lose yourself in the mysterious world of The Lost Gardens where an exotic sub-tropical jungle, atmospheric Victorian pleasure grounds, an interactive wildlife project and the finest productive gardens in Britain all await your discovery. This year a limited number of tickets have been made available for a private tour of the Northern Gardens (Productive and Ornamental Gardens). Pls arrive at 10am. At 10.30 Head Gardener, Nicola, will give an introductory talk. The group will be split to tour both gardens, accompanied by Nicola and Chris (from the gardening team), after which visitors can go on to visit the Jungle in their own time and explore. Sturdy footwear is recommended. Wheelchair access to Northern gardens. Armchair tour shows video of unreachable areas. Wheelchairs available at reception free of charge but pre booking advised due to limited availability..

♿ 🐕 ❀ 🚗 NPC ☕

28 LOWER PENBOTHIDNOW

Penbothidno Lane, Constantine, Falmouth, TR11 5AU. Dorothy Livingston, 07785 254975, Dorothy.livingston61@gmail.com. *5m SW of Falmouth. Signs point downhill on Fore St ⅓m & at top of lane, opp Save the Children Shop at bottom of Fore St - 200 metres at end of lane. Park by church or on street. Disabled parking only at property.* **Sun 21 Apr, Sun 19 May (1.30-4.30). Adm £7, chd free. Cream teas. Cold drinks available. Visits also by arrangement 16 Mar to 31 Oct for groups of up to 20. For group visits up to 12 cars can be accommodated on site.**

Hillside garden of about 2 acres with different areas planted in different styles and plant selections, ranging from formal to wildflower meadow. Surrounded by field and woods.

Colour year-round with high point for shrubs and trees in late spring and with herbaceous border, hydrangeas and flowering shrubs in August. Ample outside seating. Plenty to interest a plantsperson. Spring and summer shrubs and flowering trees. Formal garden with clipped hedges and wisteria. Tree fern grove. Southern hemisphere plants. Summer herbaceous border, lawns and sculpture. WCs available. Wheelchair can access drive and main lawns and see over or into most areas of the garden including the formal garden.

♿ 🐕 ☕ 🔊

29 NEW LOWER TREGAMERE

Tregamere, St Columb, TR9 6DN. Annette & Stuart Taylor. *Approx 1m from St Columb Major. Take A30 to Indian Queens then A39 towards Wadebridge. 1½m after Trekenning r'about turn R signed St Columb Major. After ½m turn L signed Tregamere. Follow for ½m. 1st L into drive after bridge.* **Tue 19, Wed 20 Mar, Wed 24, Thur 25 Apr, Tue 14, Wed 15 May, Wed 18, Thur 19 Sept (2-5). Adm £5, chd free.**

An evolving 2½ acre Cornish garden. Bisected by a river, where English formal style juxtaposes with woodland and oriental styles. Walk through tall redwoods and past magnificent old oaks to take in many unusual trees and shrubs. Catch the cherry blossoms in late spring, the colourful acers or the autumnal display of the Katsuras. Experience the air of tranquility the garden evokes.

🪑 🔊

30 MALIBU

Tristram Cliff, Polzeath, Wadebridge, PL27 6TP. Nick Pickles, 07944 414006, nickdpickles@gmail.com. *Travel via Pityme/Rock/Trebetherick past Oystercatcher pub on L. Take 2nd L signed Tristram Caravan Park/Cracking Crab Restaurant. Then L signed Tristram Cliff, up to end house. Free parking for coast & beach.* **Visits by arrangement for groups of up to 25. Hosted by keen cook any variety of refreshments/parties can be catered for. Adm £4, chd free. Cream teas, coffee, cakes & light lunches/suppers offered by prior agreement.**

Just yards away from the Coast Path with stunning views over the beach and Pentire headland, Malibu consists of a sheltered compact

garden to the rear and a general interest front garden. An interesting mix of features, different rockeries and strong focus on succulents, ferns and herbaceous plants. Greenhouse with many plants make this a rounded garden experience. We welcome dogs on leads. Wheelchairs can access the front garden with ease. Rear garden can only be accessed with assistance. Ground floor WC available.

♿ 🐕 ❀ 🚗 🛏 ☕

31 NEW MAWNAN SCHOOL NATURE GARDEN

Shute Hill, Mawnan Smith, Falmouth, TR11 5HQ. Zinnia Swanzy, www.instagram.com/mawnanschoolnature/. *Parking on the school grounds, & outside the main gates. Pls follow signs to the garden from the school gates.* **Sun 16 June (1.30-4.30). Adm £6, chd free. Home-made teas.**

First school garden in Cornwall to open for the NGS. The garden, est. 2021, began with a vision - to teach children how to grow. To see, smell, hear, touch and taste the natural world, learning sustainable gardening skills along the way. A hands-on haven, where everyone can be themselves. Garden features wildlife planting, raised vegetable beds, bee friendly companion planting, espaliered apple trees, wildflower meadow and stumpery. Wheelchair-friendly paths from the parking, right through the main garden. The meadow area at the end has a compacted aggregate path.

♿ ❀ ☕ 🔊

GROUP OPENING

32 MENHENIOT GARDENS

Menheniot Village, PL14 3RZ. *4m SE of Liskeard. From the A38 turn L at the Menheniot junction, drive 1¼m into the village, follow yellow signs to the sports pavilion and collect a comprehensive map of the gardens to be visited.* **Sun 23 June (2-5.30). Combined adm £5, chd free. Home-made teas at the Old School, adjacent to the village green at the end of the tour.**

Menheniot Gardens is a group of 5 gardens and 3 community spaces situated in an attractive old mining village all within a reasonable walking distance from the sports pavilion. They consist of cottage gardens, private gardens and community spaces. There is a wide range of plants and shrubs and a section on rewilding that should interest most visitors. The village has a Holy Well which is a short distance from St Lalluwy's Church which is also a place of interest.

33 NAVAS HILL HOUSE

Bosanval Valley, Mawnan Smith, Falmouth, TR11 5LL. Aline & Richard Turner, 01326 251233, alineturner@btinternet.com. *1½ m from Trebah & Glendurgan Gardens. Head for Mawnan Smith, pass Trebah & Glendurgan Gardens then follow yellow signs. Don't follow SatNav which suggests you turn R before Mawnan Smith.* **Sun 5 May (2-5). Adm £5, chd free. Home-made teas on the terrace. 'All you can eat' £5.00.**

8½ acre elevated valley garden with paddocks, woodland, kitchen garden and ornamental areas. The ornamental garden consists of 3 plantsman areas with specialist trees and shrubs, walled rose garden, water features and rockery. Young and established wooded areas with bluebells, camellia walks and young large leafed rhododendrons. Seating areas with views across wooded valley. There is plenty of parking at the property. The Trengilly Singers will entertain us about 3.30pm. Partial wheelchair access, some gravel and grass paths.

34 NEW THE OLD VICARAGE

Talland, PL13 2JA. Rachel James & Iain Doubleday, oldvicaragetalland@gmail.com, instagram.com/oldvicaragetalland. *Situated next to Talland Church & opp Talland Barton Farm. From Looe follow A387 towards Polperro for 1.2m & take L turn signed 'The Bay' & 'Tencreek'. Follow winding road for 1.2m. Entrance on L, just before Talland Church.* **Sat 18, Sun 19 May, Sat 29, Sun 30 June (2-5). Adm £5, chd free. Light refreshments.**

Vibrant 4 acre south-facing coastal garden, with varied stunning vistas of Talland Bay, the ancient Talland Church and surrounding hills. Mature Monterey pines lead directly to the SW Coast Path. Restoring this historic churchyard garden has been an ongoing labour of love since 2018. Paths and some steep steps

wind through terraced gardens, with seating to rest and enjoy the wonderful views. Special features inc mature Monterrey pines, large magnolia and copper beech, a small vineyard, and recreational facilities inc a tennis lawn, pétanque, and sand pit for younger children. Main garden area around the house is accessed over gravel paths, with an accessible WC.

35 ◆ PENCARROW

Washaway, Bodmin, PL30 3AG. Molesworth-St Aubyn Family, 01208 841369, info@pencarrow.co.uk, www.pencarrow.co.uk. *4m NW of Bodmin. Signed off A389 & B3266. Free parking.* **For NGS: Mon 8 Apr (10-5). Adm £8.75, chd free. Cream teas. For other opening times and information, please phone, email or visit garden website.**

50 acres of tranquil, family-owned Grade II* listed gardens. Superb specimen conifers, azaleas, magnolias and camellias galore. Many varieties of rhododendron give a blaze of spring colour; blue hydrangeas line the mile-long carriage drive throughout the summer. Discover the Iron Age hill fort, lake, Italian gardens and granite rock garden. Dogs welcome, café and children's play area. Gravel paths, some steep slopes.

36 PENDOWER HOUSE

Lanteglos-by-Fowey, PL23 1NJ. Mr Roger Lamb. *Nr Polruan off B3359 from East Taphouse. 2m from Fowey if using the Bodinnick ferry. Parking in NT Lantivet Bay car park. Yellow signs from B3359.* **Wed 29 May (2-5). Adm £5, chd free. Home-made teas.**

Set in the heart of Daphne du Maurier country in its own valley this established garden, surrounding a Georgian rectory, is now undergoing a revival having been wild and neglected for some years. It has formal herbaceous terraces, a cottage garden, orchard, ponds, streams and a C19 shrub garden with a fine collection of azaleas, camellias and rhododendrons plus rare mature specimen trees.

37 PENMILDER

Lodge Hill, Liskeard, PL14 4EL. Chris & Amanda Deegan. *1m S of Liskeard town centre. On 3254 between Liskeard & Duloe . Entrance on L directly opp 'Santa Trees'.* **Sun 5 May (11-5). Combined adm with Gables £6, chd free. Home-made teas.**

Gently sloping lawns, with mature borders and paths leading to a lily pond with plenty of wildlife. There are also natural wooded areas and an apple orchard which is particularly pretty in spring with daffodils, bluebells and primroses. In all about 3 acres. Sadly it is not suitable for wheelchair users due to gravel paths.

38 PENWARNE

Mawnan Smith, Falmouth, TR11 5PH. Mrs R Sawyer, penwarnegarden@gmail.com. *Located approx lm N of Mawnan Smith.* **Visits by arrangement Mar to June for groups of 5 to 25. Adm £10, chd free.**

Originally planted in the late C19, this 12 acre garden inc extensive plantings of camellias, rhododendrons and azaleas. Special features inc large magnolias and a number of fine mature trees inc copper beech, handkerchief tree and Himalayan cedar. The walled garden, believed to be the site of a medieval chapel, houses herbaceous planting, climbing roses and fruit trees. Historic house and gardens with many mature specimens.

The National Garden Scheme's final instalment to support the building of the Y Bwthyn NGS Macmillan Specialist Palliative Care Unit in Wales, enabled 270 inpatients to be supported this year

39 PINSLA GARDEN
Glynn, nr Cardinham, Bodmin,
PL30 4AY. Mark & Claire
Woodbine, www.pinslagarden.
wordpress.com. *3½ m E of Bodmin.
From A30 or Bodmin take A38 towards
Plymouth, 1st L at r'about, go past
Crematorium & Cardinham woods
turning. Continue towards Cardinham
village, up steep hill, 2m on R.* **Tue 23,
Wed 24, Tue 30 Apr, Wed 1, Tue 14,
Wed 15 May, Tue 18, Wed 19, Tue
25, Wed 26 June (9-5). Adm £5,
chd free. Opening with Cardinham
Gardens on Sun 5, Sun 12 May.**
Surround yourself with deep nature.
Pinsla is a tranquil cottage garden
buzzing with insects enjoying the
sheltered sunny edge of a wild wood.
Lose yourself in an experimental
tapestry of naturalistic growing and
self seeding. There are lots of unusual
planting combinations, cloud pruning,
intricate paths, garden art and a stone
circle. Sorry, no teas but you are
welcome to bring your own thermos.
Partial wheelchair access as some
paths are narrow and bumpy.

&. ♞ 🎋 »))

40 PORT NAVAS CHAPEL
Port Navas, Constantine,
Falmouth, TR11 5RQ. Keith Wilkins
& Linda World, 01326 341206,
keithwilkins47@gmail.com. *2m E
of Constantine, nr Falmouth. From
the direction of Constantine, we are
the 2nd driveway on R after the 'Port
Navas' sign.* **Visits by arrangement
for groups of up to 20. Adm £6,
chd free. Light refreshments.**
Japanese style garden set in ¾
acre of woodland, next to the old
Methodist Chapel, with ornamental
ponds and waterfalls, rock
formations, Tsukubai water feature,
granite lanterns, woodland stream,
geodesic dome and Zen garden.
Partial wheelchair access to driveway
and sloping grass areas.

&. ✿ 🍵 🎋

41 ◆ POTAGER GARDEN
High Cross, Constantine,
Falmouth, TR11 5RF. Mr
Mark Harris, 01326 341258,
enquiries@potagergarden.org,
www.potagergarden.org. *5m SW of
Falmouth. From Falmouth, follow signs
to Constantine. From Helston, drive
through Constantine and continue
towards Falmouth.* **For opening times
and information, please phone,
email or visit garden website.**
Potager has emerged from the bramble
choked wilderness of an abandoned
plant nursery. With mature trees which
were once nursery stock and lush
herbaceous planting interspersed with
fruit and vegetables Potager Garden
aims to demonstrate the beauty of
productive organic gardening. There
are games to play, hammocks to laze
in and boules and badminton to enjoy.
Potager café serving vegetarian food all
day. Potager gives an annual donation
to the NGS.

&. 🐴 ✿ 🍵

42 RIVERSIDE COTTAGE
St Clement, Truro, TR1 1SZ. Billa &
Nick Jeans. *1½ m SE of Truro. From
Trafalgar r'about on A39 in Truro,
follow signs for St Clement, up St
Clement Hill. R at top of hill, continue
to car park by river; Riverside
Cottage is first cottage on L.* **Mon
1, Tue 23, Tue 30 Apr, Tue 14,
Tue 21 May (10.30-4.30). Adm by
donation. Tea, coffee & cakes.**
Small wildlife friendly cottage garden
overlooking beautiful Tresillian River.
Wildflower areas, soft fruit and
raised bed vegetable patch. Serious
composting. Wildlife pond, old apple
trees, sloping grassy paths and steps
and plenty of seats affording places to
rest to enjoy views down river. Sadly,
not suitable for wheelchairs.

🐴 🍵 🎋 »))

43 ROSE MORRAN
Talskiddy, St Columb,
TR9 6EB. Peter & Jenny
Brandreth, 07711 517159,
jennybrandreth@yahoo.com. *2 m
N of St Columb Major. From A39
take Talskiddy/St Eval turn. Then
take 2nd R signed Talskiddy & follow
yellow NGS signs.* **Sun 21 Apr, Sun
30 June, Sun 1 Sept (11-5). Adm
£5, chd free. Light refreshments.**

Gwrythia

Visits also by arrangement Apr to Oct for groups of up to 24.

Colour, shape and texture define this North Cornwall garden. The property and gardens extend to about an acre, with grassland, wild areas and Cornish hedges completing the 2 acre plot. Planted over the past 11 yrs there is a mix of shrubs and trees interplanted with perennials to ensure year-round display. Vegetable beds and a polytunnel with tender plants make this a rounded garden visit. There are level areas to view and the whole garden is accessible via grass slopes but some are quite steep. There is one step to the inside WC.

44 ◆ ROSELAND HOUSE
Chacewater, TR4 8QB. Mr & Mrs Pridham, 01872 560451, charlie@roselandhouse.co.uk, www.roselandhouse.co.uk. *4m W of Truro. Park in village car park (100yds) or on surrounding roads.* **For NGS: Sat 29, Sun 30 June (1-5). Adm £5, chd free. Home-made teas. For other opening times and information, please phone, email or visit garden website.**
The 1 acre garden is a mass of summer colour in late June and July when the National collection of *Clematis viticella cvs* is in flower. Other climbing plants abound lending foliage, flower and scent. Situated in the garden is a specialist climbing plant nursery which along with a Victorian conservatory and greenhouse is open. The garden features two ponds and lots of seating areas. Some slopes.

45 ROSELAND PARC
Tregony, Truro, TR2 5PD. Mr Bob Mehen (Head Gardener). *Follow signs for Tregony from the A390. Roseland Parc is situated on the main street, just past the clock tower & Kings Arms pub.* **Sat 20 July (11-3.30). Adm £5, chd free. Home-made teas.**
Set in 7½ acres of wooded grounds, Roseland Parc delivers a varied selection of all that Cornish gardens have to offer. Spring time camellia, rhododendron & magnolia give way to bright summer displays of perennials, tree ferns & exotic planting. A small wildflower meadow and wildlife area with ponds is also featured. Approx half the gardens are accessible for wheelchair users.

46 ROSEVALLON BARN
Tregony, Truro, TR2 5TS. Jenny Ralph, 07971 436344, rosevallon@icloud.com. *From main road in Tregony turn into Cuby Close on opp side of the road from St Cuby. Follow lane for just over 1m, pass Pencoose, then turn R down lane onto farm track.* **Visits by arrangement 24 Apr to 30 Sept for groups of 5 to 10. Adm £5, chd free. Tea.**
Rural setting surrounded by farmland. Converted barn with 3 acres of garden planted by present owners. Small stream and pond fed from spring water, herbaceous borders, shrubs, coppice with snowdrops, bluebells, primroses, fritillary. Vegetables and fruit, wildflower meadow, gravel garden, year-round interest. Bricked drive and accessible grass areas.

47 ◆ ST MICHAEL'S MOUNT
Marazion, TR17 0HS. James & Mary St Levan, www.stmichaelsmount.co.uk. *2½ m E of Penzance. ½ m from shore at Marazion by Causeway.* **For opening times and information, please visit garden website, or www.ngs.org.uk for details of pop up opening date.**
Infuse your senses with colour and scent in the unique sub-tropical gardens basking in the mild climate and salty breeze. Clinging to granite slopes the terraced beds tier steeply to the ocean's edge, boasting tender exotics from places such as Mexico, the Canary Islands and South Africa. This year the St Aubyn Family will be opening the Gardens again but pre booking is essential.Pls visit St Michael's Mount website for details of pop up opening and link to book. Last entry to the garden is 4pm. Laundry lawn, mackerel bank, pill box, gun emplacement, tiered terraces, well, tortoise lawn. Walled gardens, seagull seat.

48 SOUTH BOSENT
Liskeard, PL14 4LX. Adrienne Lloyd & Trish Wilson, 07539 256855, lloydadj@btinternet.com, www.southbosentgardens.co.uk. *2½ m W of Liskeard. From r'about at junction of A390 & A38 take turning to Dobwalls. At mini-r'about R to Duloe, after 1¼ m at Xrds turn R. Garden on L after ¼ m.* **Thur 23, Fri**

24 May, Wed 11, Thur 12 Sept (2-5). Adm £5, chd free. Home-made teas. Opening with Dobwalls Gardens on Fri 14, Sat 15, Fri 28, Sat 29 June, Fri 19, Sat 20 July, Fri 9, Sat 10 Aug. Visits also by arrangement 22 May to 12 Sept.
This garden is an example of work in progress currently being developed from farmland. The aim is to create a combination of interesting plants coupled with habitat for wildlife over a total of 9½ acres. There are several garden areas, woodland gardens, a meadow, ponds of varying sizes, inc a rill and waterfall. In spring, the bluebell wood trail runs alongside the stream. Main garden area accessible. No wheelchair access to bluebell wood due to steps.

49 SOUTH LEA
Pillaton, Saltash, PL12 6QS. Viv & Tony Laurillard, 01579 350629, tonyandviv.laurillard@gmail.com. *Opp Weary Friar pub. 4m S of Callington. Signed from r'abouts on A388 at St Mellion & Hatt, & on A38 at Landrake. Roadside parking. Please do not park in pub car park.* **Sun 12 May, Sun 9 June (1-5). Adm £6, chd free. Home-made teas. Visits also by arrangement 12 May to 30 June for groups of 10+.**
In the front a path winds through interesting landscaping with a small pond and unusual planting. Tropical beds by front door with palms, agave, etc. The back garden, with views over the valley, is a pretty picture in May with spring bulbs and clematis, and attractive mixed borders in June. Lawns are separated by a fair sized fish pond and the small woodland area is enchanting in spring. Plenty of seating. Due to steps, wheelchair access only to front dry garden and rear terrace, from which much of garden can be viewed.

In 2023 we awarded over £260,000 in Community Garden Grants, supporting 86 community garden projects

50 TOWAN HOUSE

Old Church Road, Mawnan Smith, Falmouth, TR11 5HX.
Mr Dave & Mrs Tessa Thomson, 01326 250378, tandd.thomson@btinternet.com. *Approx 5m from Falmouth. On entering Mawnan Smith, fork L at the Red Lion pub. When you see the gate to Nansidwell, turn R into Old Church Rd. Follow NGS signs.* **Visits by arrangement 6 June to 15 Sept for groups of 5 to 20. Adm £6, chd free. Home-made teas.**
Towan House is a coastal garden with some unusual plants and views to St Mawes, St Anthony Head lighthouse and beyond with easy access to the SW coast path overlooking Falmouth Bay. It is approximately 1/4 acre and divided into 2 gardens, one exposed to the north and east winds, the other sheltered allowing tropical plants to flourish such as Hedychium, Tetrapanax and cannas.

 🚻 🐕 ✿ ☕ »))

51 TREBARTHA ESTATE GARDEN AND COUNTRY GARDEN AT LEMARNE

Trebartha, nr Launceston, PL15 7PD. The Latham Family. *6m SW of Launceston. North Hill, SW of Launceston nr junction of B3254 & B3257. No coaches.* **Sun 12 May, Sun 20 Oct (2-5). Adm £8, chd free. Home-made teas.**
Historic landscape gardens featuring streams, cascades, rocks and woodlands, inc fine trees, bluebells, ornamental walled garden and country garden at Lemarne. Ongoing development of C19 American garden and C18 fish ponds. Allow at least 1 hour for a circular walk. Some steep and rough paths, which can be slippery when wet. Stout footwear advised. October opening for autumn colour.

 🐕 ☕

52 [NEW] TREGLYN

Gover Valley, St Austell, PL25 5RD. Mrs Heather Beales, 01726 339040, keith.cats@gmail.com. *1m from St Austell town centre. Sat Nav use PL25 5RB (not D). Keep on Gover Rd which becomes an unmade single track lane (do not veer to R) & follow signs.* **Thur 16, Fri 17 May, Thur 18, Fri 19 July, Thur 19, Fri 20 Sept (1-5). Adm £5, chd free. Teas served on vintage china. Outside seating & small covered area. Visits also by arrangement 19 May to 29 Sept for groups of**
up to 20.
A tranquil woodland garden that celebrates Cornwall's unique industrial heritage. Deep in the Gover Valley on the site of old china clay works this wildlife friendly garden has been lovingly created to make the most of the many historical features. River/woodland walks, spring bluebells, formal planting, bog garden, exotic plant jungle, stumpery, leat fed ponds, secluded seating areas and more. Quarries and Goblins Gold. Remains of industrial heritage accessible. Wheelchair access to lower garden area, lawns and refreshment areas.

 ♿ 🐕 ✿ ☕

53 TRELAN

Wharf Road, Lelant, St Ives, TR26 3DU. Nick Williams, 07817 425157, nick@nickgwilliams.com. *Close to St Uny Church, Lelant. Trelan Gardens are off Wharf Rd which leads to a car park on Dynamite Quay. Car park signed at the end of Wharf Rd & the gardens are 100m down on R.* **Sat 18 May, Sat 1, Sat 22 June (2-6). Adm £6, chd free. Home-made teas. Visits also by arrangement 11 May to 20 July. Large groups are welcome by arrangement.**
Trelan has a distinctly tropical feel. There is a swimming pond surrounded by lush vegetation, an Italianate sunken garden, a fern garden, numerous young trees and countless *Echium pininana*. It is a feast for the eyes.

 🐕 ☕ »))

54 TREMICHELE

Housel Bay, The Lizard, Helston, TR12 7PG. Mike & Helen Painton, 01326 291370, paintonfam@btinternet.com. *On the Lizard peninsular approx 10m from Helston. Follow directions to Lizard village. Park on the village green, parking is by voluntary contribution. Walk along Beacon Terrace & follow signs for Housel Bay Hotel.* **Visits by arrangement 1 Apr to 15 Sept for groups of up to 10. Adm £5, chd free. Tea, coffee, cold drinks, home-made cake & cookies.**
A coastal garden, created in 2016, of approx 1 acre overlooking the Atlantic and the Lizard Lighthouse. It is a steep sloping garden divided into 3 terraces accessed by slopes or steps. A productive kitchen garden, with raised beds and fruit trees.
Greenhouse and cold frames. A wildflower meadow with access to the coast path. Banks have a mix of planting inc hardy exotics.

 🐕 ☕ »))

55 TRENARTH

High Cross, Constantine, Falmouth, TR11 5JN. Lucie Nottingham, 01326 340444, lmnottingham@btinternet.com, www.trenarthgardens.com. *6m SW of Falmouth. Main road A39/A394 Truro to Helston, follow Constantine signs. High X garage turn L for Mawnan, 30yds on R down dead end lane, Trenarth is 1/2 m at end of lane.* **Visits by arrangement 1 Feb to 1 Nov for groups of 5 to 30. Very welcoming garden for art & photographic groups to enjoy. Adm £5, chd free. Light refreshments.**
4 acres round C17 farmhouse in peaceful pastoral setting. Year-round and varied. Emphasis on tender, unusual plants, structure and form. C16 courtyard, listed garden walls, holm oak avenue, yew rooms, vegetable garden, traditional potting shed, orchard, palm and gravel area with close planting inc agapanthus, agave and dierama, woodland area interesting to children. Circular walk down ancient green lane via animal pond to Trenarth Bridge, returning through woods. Abundant wildlife. Bees in tree bole, lesser horseshoe bat colony, swallows, wildflowers and butterflies. Family friendly, children's play area, the Wolery, and plenty of room to run, jump and climb.

 🐕 ✿ 🪑 ☕ 🛝 »))

56 [NEW] TRESITHNEY

Bowl Rock, Lelant, St Ives, TR26 3JE. Caroline Marwood, 07515 339400, carolinemarwood@me.com, www.facebook.com/Tresithney. *At Bowl Rock just off The Old Coach Rd between the A3074 & B3311. A 'Walking Garden' on The St Michael's Way between Carbis Bay & Trencrom Hill. Walkers can pay on the gate. Visitors in cars can pre book. Turn at Bowl Rock, between Lelant & St Ives. Marked with flag.* **Sat 8, Sun 9 June (10.30-4.30). Adm £5, chd free. Pre-booking essential, please visit www.ngs.org.uk for information & booking. Home-made teas. Visits also by arrangement Apr to Sept for groups of up to 15.**
This is a unique 'Walking Garden' on

the ancient St Michael's Way. The garden is approx 1½ acres with a variety of distinct areas, inc a rose garden, potager, fernery, orchard and wild areas. With beautiful views up to Trencrom Hill an Iron Age Hill Fort. Visitors arriving on foot do not need to book but due to limited parking visitors arriving by car must pre-book. Partial wheelchair access by using main path through centre of garden.

57 TRETHEW

Lanlivery, nr Bodmin, PL30 5BZ. Ginnie & Giles Clotworthy, 01208 872612, ginnieclotworthy@ hotmail.co.uk. *3 m W of Lostwithiel. On road between Lanlivery & Luxulyan. 1m from Lanlivery. Yellow signs used on Open day otherwise ask for directions when booking. Do not use SatNav.* **Sun 16 June (1-5). Adm £5, chd free. Home-made teas. Visits also by arrangement 17 June to 23 June for groups of up to 24. Individuals as well as groups are very welcome.** Series of profusely planted and colourful areas surrounding an ancient Cornish farmhouse. Features inc terracing with wisteria and rose covered pergola, gazebo and herbaceous borders within yew and beech hedges, all overlooking orchard with old fashioned roses and pond beyond. Late summer colour with salvias, dahlias and Michaelmas daisies. Magnificent views. Regional Finalist for The English Garden Magazine's The Nation's Favourite Gardens 2023. This is a garden on a hill with flat areas around the house. Uneven drive with gravel.

58 TREVESCO

7 Commons Close, Mullion, Helston, TR12 7HY. Colin Read. *Situated on the W side of Mullion on the road to Poldhu Cove & Cury. ¼ m from village centre car parks.* **Sun 2 June (11-4). Adm £5, chd free. Home-made teas.** This ¼ acre garden has been established over 14 yrs in a sub-tropical style with rare unusual plants inc puya, furcraea, tetrapanax, pseudopanax and several larger feature plants e.g. olive trees, *Phoenix canariensis*, and *Ceanothus arboreus*. Many tender plants have been established without winter protection very successfully due to local climate. There is also a pond.

59 TREVILLEY

Sennen, Penzance, TR19 7AH. Patrick Gale & Aidan Hicks, 01736 871808, trevilley@btinternet.com. *For walkers, Trevilley lies on the footpath from Trevescan to Polgigga & Nanjizal. On Open Day follow the signs into our parking field. If visiting by arrangement, Trevilley lies up a track opposite Trevescan. If you reach a white house, reverse then enter our farmyard by the gate!* **Sun 9 June (2-6). Adm £6, chd free. Home-made teas. Visits also by arrangement 18 May to 30 June for groups of 6 to 40. Min charge for groups smaller than 6 will be £36.** Eccentric, romantic and constantly evolving garden, as befits the intense creativity of its owners, carved out of an expanse of concrete farmyard over 20 yrs. Inc elaborate network of decorative cobbling, pools, container garden, vegetable garden, shade garden, the largely subtropical mowhay garden and both owners' studios but arguably its glory is the westernmost walled rose garden in England. Dogs are welcome on leads. The garden visit can form the climax of enjoying the circular coast path walk from Land's End to Nanjizal and back across the fields. Cream teas also avail in the Apple Tree Cafe in Trevescan. Visitors may leave their cars with us while they walk there across the fields.

60 TREVINA HOUSE

St Neot, Liskeard, PL14 6NR. Kevin & Sue Wright, 07428 102104, kevin@trevina.com, www. facebook.com/TrevinaInCornwall. *1m N of St Neot. From A38 turn off at Halfwayhouse pub. Head up hill to Goonzion Downs. Bear L & keep straight on towards Colliford Lake. From A30 take Colliford Lake/St Neot turning. Head towards St Neot.* **Thur 14, Fri 15 Mar, Thur 11, Fri 12 Apr, Thur 9, Fri 10 May, Thur 13, Fri 14 June, Thur 11, Fri 12 July, Thur 12, Fri 13 Sept, Tue 8, Wed 9 Oct (10.30-5.30). Adm £5, chd free. Home-made teas. Visits also by arrangement Feb to Nov for groups of 5 to 30. Narrow lane and limited parking so please car share wherever possible.** The gardens at Trevina are both old and new. From a Victorian cottage garden with original cobbled paths to rewilded woodland. A trout pond occupies the

site of a medieval fish pond and the site of a Cornish Round. There is a traditional kitchen garden and organic orchard. The gardens have colour and interest year-round, from the first snowdrops, bluebells, apple blossom and ripe apples in October.

61 ◆ TREWIDDEN GARDEN

Buryas Bridge, Penzance, TR20 8TT. Mr Alverne Bolitho - Richard Morton, Head Gardener, 01736 364275, contact@ trewiddengarden.co.uk, www.trewiddengarden.co.uk. *2m W of Penzance. Entry on A30 just before Buryas Bridge. Postcode for SatNav is TR19 6AU.* **For NGS: Tue 5 Mar (10.30-5.30). Adm £9, chd £1. Tearoom open 9:30 - 4:30 serving breakfast to 11:30 & lunch from 12 - 2:30. For other opening times and information, please phone, email or visit garden website.** Trewidden garden is a tranquil oasis & home to a collection of magnolias, camellias, rhododendron, azalea and one of the finest collections of *Dicksonia antarctica* tree ferns in the Northern Hemisphere. 15 acres of woodland garden to explore, walking along unusual twisty paths between banks of extraordinary flowering trees and shrubs. Last entry is 4:30pm.

62 WINDMILLS

South Hill, Callington, PL17 7LP. Sue & Peter Tunnicliffe, 01579 363981, tunnicliffesue@gmail.com. *3m NW of Callington. Head N from Callington A388, after about ½ m turn L onto South Hill Rd (signed South Hill). Straight on for 3m, gardens on R just before church.* **Sun 7 July (1-5). Combined adm with Anvil Cottage £6, chd free. Home-made teas. Gluten free cakes available. Visits also by arrangement July & Aug for groups of 8 to 30.** Next to medieval church and on the site of an old rectory there are still signs in places of that long gone building. A garden full of surprises, formal paths and steps lead up from the flower beds to extensive vegetable and soft fruit area. More paths lead to a pond, past a pergola, and down into large lawns with trees and shrubs and chickens. Partial wheelchair access.

DEVON

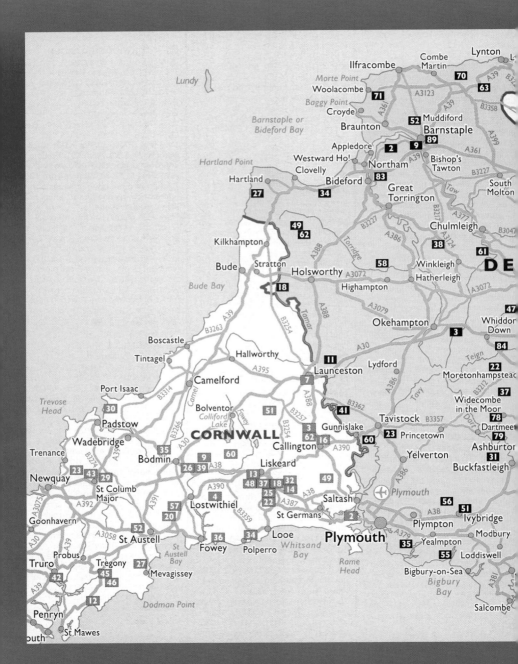

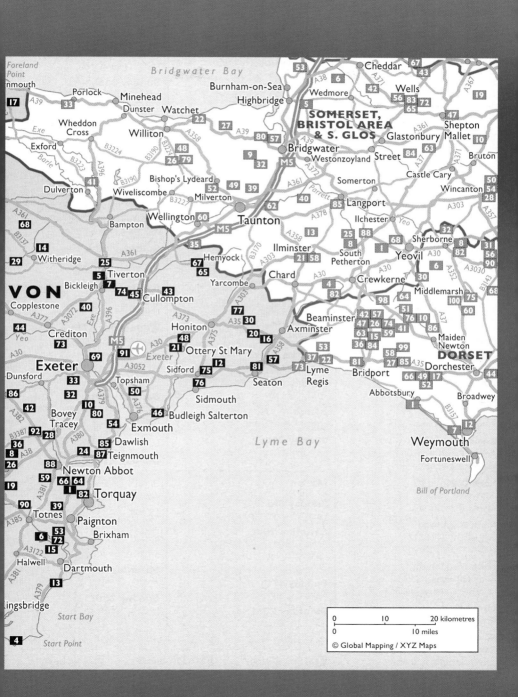

VOLUNTEERS

County Organiser & Central Devon
Miranda Allhusen 01647 440296
Miranda@allhusen.co.uk

County Treasurer
Nigel Hall 01884 38812
nigel.hall@ngs.org.uk

Publicity
Brian Mackness 01626 356004
brianmackness@clara.co.uk

Tracy Armstrong 07729 225549
tracygorsty@aol.com

Paul Vincent 01803 722227
paul.vincent@ngs.org.uk

Booklet Co-ordinator
Anne Sercombe 01626 923170
anne.sercombe@ngs.org.uk

Social Media
Neil Littleales 07722 321838
littleales@ngs.org.uk

Talks
Brian Mackness (see above)

Julia Tremlett 01392 832671
jandjtremlett@hotmail.com

Assistant County Organisers

East Devon
Penny Walmsley 01404 831375
walyp_uk@yahoo.co.uk

Exeter
Jenny Phillips 01392 254076
jennypips25@hotmail.co.uk

Exmoor
Angela Percival 01598 741343
lalindevon@yahoo.co.uk

North Devon
Jo Hynes
hynesjo@gmail.com

North East Devon
Jill Hall 01884 38812
jill22hall@gmail.com

North West Devon
Kerry Littleales 07727 657246
kerry.littleales@ngs.org.uk

Plymouth
Position vacant

South Hams
Sally Vincent 01803 722227
sallyvincent14@gmail.com

South West Devon
Naomi Hindley 07969 792360
naomi.hindley@ngs.org.uk

Torbay
Tracy Armstrong (see above)

West Devon
Jan Gasper 01822 6111304
jan.gasper@ngs.org.uk

OPENING DATES

All entries subject to change. For latest information check **www.ngs.org.uk**
Map locator numbers are shown to the right of each garden name.

February

Snowdrop Openings
Friday 2nd
Higher Cherubeer 38

Friday 9th
Higher Cherubeer 38

Saturday 10th
The Mount, Delamore 56

Sunday 11th
The Mount, Delamore 56

Saturday 17th
Higher Cherubeer 38

Sunday 25th
East Worlington House 29

March

Sunday 3rd
East Worlington House 29

Saturday 16th
Ashley Court 5
Haldon Grange 32
Samlingstead 71

Sunday 17th
Haldon Grange 32

Saturday 23rd
NEW Little Dinworthy 49

Sunday 24th
Chevithorne Barton 25
Heathercombe 37
NEW Little Dinworthy 49
Upper Gorwell House 89

Saturday 30th
Bickham House 10
Haldon Grange 32

Sunday 31st
Haldon Grange 32
Kia-Ora Farm & Gardens 45

April

Monday 1st
Haldon Grange 32
Kia-Ora Farm & Gardens 45

Friday 5th
◆ Marwood Hill Garden 52

Sunday 7th
Andrew's Corner 3

Saturday 13th
Haldon Grange 32
NEW Little Dinworthy 49

Sunday 14th
Haldon Grange 32
Sherwood 73

Wednesday 17th
Haldon Grange 32

Friday 19th
Musselbrook Cottage Garden 58
Pounds 65

Saturday 20th
Musselbrook Cottage Garden 58
Pounds 65
Regency House 67
South Wood Farm 77

Sunday 21st
Andrew's Corner 3
Bickham House 10
Kia-Ora Farm & Gardens 45
NEW Little Dinworthy 49
Musselbrook Cottage Garden 58
Regency House 67
South Wood Farm 77
Whitstone Farm 92

Saturday 27th
Haldon Grange 32

Sunday 28th
Haldon Grange 32

Upper Gorwell House	89
Whitstone Farm	92

May

Wednesday 1st
Haldon Grange	32

Saturday 4th
Bagtor Mill Gardens	8
Greatcombe	31

Sunday 5th
Andrew's Corner	3
Bagtor Mill Gardens	8
Bickham House	10
Greatcombe	31
Heathercombe	37
Kia-Ora Farm & Gardens	45
◆ Mothecombe House	55

Monday 6th
Andrew's Corner	3
Greatcombe	31
Kia-Ora Farm & Gardens	45

Friday 10th
Avenue Cottage	6
Musselbrook Cottage Garden	58

Saturday 11th
Avenue Cottage	6
Haldon Grange	32
Heathercombe	37
Musselbrook Cottage Garden	58
Spitchwick Manor	79
Spring Lodge	80

Sunday 12th
Haldon Grange	32
Heathercombe	37
Musselbrook Cottage Garden	58
Spitchwick Manor	79

Wednesday 15th
Haldon Grange	32

Friday 17th
Sutton Mead	86

Saturday 18th
Bradford Tracey House	14
◆ Goren Farm	30
Haytor Gardens	36
Heathercombe	37
NEW Little Dinworthy	49
NEW Old Glebe	61
Sutton Mead	86

Sunday 19th
Bickham House	10
Bradford Tracey House	14
NEW The Chantry	23
◆ Goren Farm	30
Haytor Gardens	36

Heathercombe	37
NEW Old Glebe	61
Sutton Mead	86
Upper Gorwell House	89

Monday 20th
◆ Goren Farm	30

Tuesday 21st
◆ Goren Farm	30
Heathercombe	37
◆ Hotel Endsleigh	41

Wednesday 22nd
◆ Goren Farm	30
Heathercombe	37

Thursday 23rd
◆ Goren Farm	30
Heathercombe	37

Friday 24th
◆ Goren Farm	30
Heathercombe	37

Saturday 25th
Abbotskerswell Gardens	1
Bulland Farm	19
Dunley House	28
◆ Goren Farm	30
Greatcombe	31
Haldon Grange	32
Heathercombe	37
NEW Old Glebe	61
NEW Rosebarn Gardens	69
Torview	88

Sunday 26th
Abbotskerswell Gardens	1
Andrew's Corner	3
Ashley Court	5
Bulland Farm	19
◆ Cadhay	21
NEW The Chantry	23
Chevithorne Barton	25
Dunley House	28
◆ Goren Farm	30
Greatcombe	31
Haldon Grange	32
Heathercombe	37
Kia-Ora Farm & Gardens	45
NEW Little Dinworthy	49
NEW Old Glebe	61
NEW Rosebarn Gardens	69
Sherwood	73
Torview	88

Monday 27th
Andrew's Corner	3
◆ Cadhay	21
◆ Goren Farm	30
Greatcombe	31
Haldon Grange	32
Kia-Ora Farm & Gardens	45

Heathercombe	37
NEW Old Glebe	61
Sutton Mead	86
Upper Gorwell House	89

Tuesday 28th
◆ Goren Farm	30
Heathercombe	37

Wednesday 29th
◆ Goren Farm	30
Heathercombe	37

Thursday 30th
◆ Goren Farm	30
Heathercombe	37

Friday 31st
◆ Goren Farm	30
Heathercombe	37
Pounds	65

June

Saturday 1st
Breach	16
Brendon Gardens	17
◆ Goren Farm	30
Haldon Grange	32
Heathercombe	37
Pounds	65
Regency House	67
Shutelake	74
Stone Farm	83

Sunday 2nd
Breach	16
Brendon Gardens	17
The Bridge Mill	18
◆ Goren Farm	30
Haldon Grange	32
Heathercombe	37
Regency House	67
Shutelake	74
Stone Farm	83

Monday 3rd
◆ Goren Farm	30

Tuesday 4th
◆ Goren Farm	30

Wednesday 5th
◆ Goren Farm	30

Thursday 6th
◆ Goren Farm	30
Southcombe Barn	78

Friday 7th
◆ Goren Farm	30
Southcombe Barn	78

Saturday 8th
Bramble Torre	15
◆ Goren Farm	30
Heathercombe	37
Higher Orchard Cottage	39
Kentisbeare House	43

Sunday 4th

Barnstaple World Gardens	9
Bickham House	10
Brendon Gardens	17
NEW Chagford Community Gardens	22
Middle Well	53

Saturday 10th

NEW Chagford Community Gardens	22
NEW Rose Ash House	68
Sidmouth Gardens	76

Sunday 11th

NEW Chagford Community Gardens	22
Kia-Ora Farm & Gardens	45
NEW Rose Ash House	68
Sidmouth Gardens	76

Friday 16th

◆ Marwood Hill Garden	52

Saturday 17th

NEW Keymelford House	44
Stone Farm	83

Sunday 18th

Bickham House	10
NEW Keymelford House	44
Stone Farm	83

Friday 23rd

Spring Lodge	80

Sunday 25th

32 Allenstyle Drive	2
Ashley Court	5
◆ Cadhay	21
Higher Cherubeer	38
Kia-Ora Farm & Gardens	45

Monday 26th

◆ Cadhay	21
Kia-Ora Farm & Gardens	45

September

Friday 6th

Pounds	65
Sutton Mead	86

Saturday 7th

Pounds	65
Sutton Mead	86

Sunday 8th

32 Allenstyle Drive	2
Bickham House	10
Kia-Ora Farm & Gardens	45
Littlefield	50
Sutton Mead	86

Saturday 14th

Ash Park	4
South Wood Farm	77

Sunday 15th

Ash Park	4
South Wood Farm	77
Upper Gorwell House	89

Saturday 21st

Little Ash Bungalow	48

Sunday 22nd

Kia-Ora Farm & Gardens	45

October

Saturday 5th

◆ Stone Lane Gardens	84

Saturday 12th

◆ Stone Lane Gardens	84

Sunday 13th

Sherwood	73

Saturday 19th

Dunley House	28
Regency House	67

Sunday 20th

Dunley House	28
Regency House	67

Sunday 27th

Chevithorne Barton	25

February 2025

Friday 7th

Higher Cherubeer	38

Friday 14th

Higher Cherubeer	38

Sunday 23rd

Higher Cherubeer	38

By Arrangement

Arrange a personalised garden visit with your club, or group of friends, on a date to suit you. See individual garden entries for full details.

32 Allenstyle Drive	2
Andrew's Corner	3
Ash Park	4
Avenue Cottage	6
Bickham House	10
Breach	16
Brendon Gardens	17
Byes Reach, Sidmouth Gardens	76
Coombe Meadow	26
Haldon Grange	32

Hall Farm, Brendon Gardens	17
Halscombe Farm	33
Harbour Lights	34
The Haven	35
Heathercombe	37
Higher Cherubeer	38
Higher Orchard Cottage	39
Higher Tippacott Farm, Brendon Gardens	17
Kia-Ora Farm & Gardens	45
Lee Ford	46
Lewis Cottage	47
Little Ash Bungalow	48
Middle Well	53
The Mount, Delamore	56
NEW Old Crebor Farm	60
NEW Old Glebe	61
Pounds	65
Regency House	67
NEW Rudd Cottage	70
Samlingstead	71
Sherwood	73
Shutelake	74
Springfield House	81
Squirrels	82
Stone Farm	83
Stonelands House	85
Sutton Mead	86
Torview	88
NEW Weston House, Sidmouth Gardens	76
Whitstone Farm	92

National Garden Scheme gardens are identified by their yellow road signs and posters. You can expect a garden of quality, character and interest, a warm welcome and plenty of home-made cakes!

THE GARDENS

GROUP OPENING

1 ABBOTSKERSWELL GARDENS

Abbotskerswell, TQ12 5PN. *2m SW of Newton Abbot town centre. A381 Newton Abbot/Totnes rd. Sharp L turn from Newton Abbot, R from Totnes. Field parking at Fairfield. Maps available at all gardens & at Church House.* **Sat 25, Sun 26 May (1-5). Combined adm £7, chd free. Home-made teas at Church House in the village. Teas available from 2pm. Maps and tickets from 1pm.**

ABBOTSFORD
Wendy & Phil Grierson.

ABBOTSKERSWELL ALLOTMENTS
Tasha Mundy.

1 ABBOTSWELL COTTAGES
Jane Taylor.

BRIAR COTTAGE
Peggy & David Munden.

FAIRFIELD
Brian Mackness.

1 FORDE CLOSE
Ann Allen.

NEW PINE TREES LODGE
Gary & Richard.

THE POTTERY
Beverley & Dougal Dubash.

7 WILTON WAY
Vernon & Cindy Stunt.

16 WILTON WAY
Katy & Chris Yates.

For 2024 Abbotskerswell offers nine gardens plus the village allotments; ranging from very small to large, the gardens offer a wide range of planting styles and innovative landscaping. Cottage gardens, terracing, wildflower areas, specialist plants and an arboretum. Ideas for every type and size of garden. Visitors are welcome to picnic in the field or arboretum at Fairfield. Tea and cake served in the historic Church House in the centre of the village. Sales of plants, garden produce, jams and chutneys. Disabled access to three gardens. Partial access to most others.
🦽 ❀ 🚗 ☕ ᭟)

2 32 ALLENSTYLE DRIVE

Yelland, Barnstaple, EX31 3DZ. Steve & Dawn Morgan, 01271 861433, fourhungrycats@aol.com, www.devonsubtropicalgarden.rocks. *5m W of Barnstaple. From Barnstaple take B3233 towards Instow. Through Bickington & Fremington. L at Yelland sign into Allenstyle Rd. 1st R into Allenstyle Dr. Light blue bungalow. From Bideford go past Instow on B3233.* **Sun 25 Aug, Sun 8 Sept (12-5). Adm £5, chd free. Light refreshments. Opening with Barnstaple World Gardens on Sun 4 Aug. Visits also by arrangement 5 Aug to 15 Sept for groups of up to 15.**
Our garden is 30m x 15m and is packed full of all our favourite plants. See our huge bananas, cannas, colocasias, delicate and scented tropical passion flowers, rudbeckias, perennial sunflowers, a wildlife pond and a new large cedar greenhouse. Relax and inhale the heady scents of the garden and rest awhile in the many seating areas.
❀ ☕ ᭟)

3 ANDREW'S CORNER

Skaigh Lane, Belstone, EX20 1RD. Robin & Edwina Hill, 01837 840332, edwinarobinhill@outlook.com, www.andrewscorner.garden. *3m E of Okehampton. Signed to Belstone from A30. In village turn L, signed Skaigh. Follow NGS signs. Garden approx 1/2 m on R. Visitors may be dropped off at house, parking in nearby field.* **Sun 7, Sun 21 Apr, Sun 5, Mon 6, Sun 26, Mon 27 May (2-5). Adm £5, chd free. Cream teas. Visits also by arrangement Feb to May for groups of up to 30.**
Take a walk on the wild side in this tranquil moorland garden. April openings highlight magnolias, trillium and the lovely erythroniums. Early May the maples, rhododendrons and unusual shrubs provide interest, late May brings the Snowdrop Tree, Chilean Firebush and the spectacular blue poppies. Wheelchair access difficult when wet.
🦽 🐾 ❀ ☕ ᭟)

4 ASH PARK

East Prawle, Kingsbridge, TQ7 2BX. Chris & Cathryn Vanderspar, 07739 108493, cvanderspar@btconnect.com. *Take A379 Kingsbridge to Dartmouth, at Frogmore after pub R to East Prawle, after 1.1m L, in 1.4m at Cousins Cross bear R (middle of 3 rds). In village head to Prawle Point.* **Sat 14, Sun 15 Sept (11-5). Adm £6, chd free. Home-made teas. Visits also by arrangement for groups of 8+.**
In a stunning location, with 180° view of the sea, Ash Park nestles at the foot of the escarpment, in 3½ acres of sub-tropical gardens, paths to explore, woodland glades, ponds and hidden seating areas. In September, cannas, hydrangeas, ginger lilies, salvias, aeoniums and dahlias are at their best. At other times there are spectacular displays of lampranthas, agapanthas, camelias and echiums.
🐾 ❀ ☕ ᭟)

5 ASHLEY COURT

Ashley, Tiverton, EX16 5PD. Tara Fraser & Nigel Jones, 07768 878015, hello@ashleycourtdevon.co.uk, www.ashleycourtdevon.co.uk. *1m S of Tiverton on the Bickleigh road (A396). Turn off the A396 to Ashley & then immed L. Take the drive to the L of Ashley Court Lodge Cottage (don't go up Ashley Back Lane where the SatNav will direct you).* **Sat 16 Mar, Sun 26 May, Sun 25 Aug (12.30-4.30). Adm £6, chd free. Speciality teas inc many delicious vegan recipes & cakes containing fruits & vegetables from the walled kitchen garden.**
Ashley Court is a small Regency country house with an historically interesting walled kitchen garden currently undergoing restoration. It is unusually situated in a deep valley and has a frost window and the remains of several glasshouses and cold frames. View the apple loft, root stores, stable buildings, woodland walk and lawns, borders and beautiful mature trees. A walk through discovery and history. The walled garden probably pre-dates the 1805 house as there was previously an older Ashley Court on the other side of the garden. Peculiar features such as a curved garden wall and a frost window make it unusual.
🐾 ❀ 🚗 🛏 ☕ ᭟)

6 AVENUE COTTAGE

Ashprington, Totnes, TQ9 7UT. Mr Richard Pitts & Mr David Sykes, 01803 732769, richard.pitts@btinternet.com, www.avenuecottage.com. *3m SE of Totnes. A381 Totnes to Kingsbridge for 1m; L for Ashprington, into village then L*

by pub. *Garden ¼ m on R after Sharpham Estate sign.* **Fri 10, Sat 11 May (11-5). Pre-booking essential, please visit www.ngs. org.uk for information & booking. Sun 21 July (11-5). Adm £5, chd free. Home-made teas. Visits also by arrangement Apr to Sept for groups of up to 25.**
11 acre woodland valley garden, forming part of the Grade II* Sharpham House Landscape. The garden contains many rare and unusual trees and shrubs with views over the River Dart AONB and Sharpham. Azaleas, hydrangeas and magnolias are a speciality. A spring rises in the garden under a spectacularly large rhododendron feeding two ponds and a small stream running through a meadow with mown paths.

◪ BACKSWOOD FARM
Bickleigh, Tiverton, EX16 8RA. Andrew Hughes, 01884 855005, andrew@backswood.co.uk, www.backswood.co.uk. *2m SE of Tiverton. Take A396 off the A361. Turn L to Butterleigh opp Tesco, L at mini r'about, after 150 yds turn R up Exeter Hill for 2m then 1st R to Bickleigh. After 500 yds turn 1st R into farm entrance.* **Sat 6, Sun 7 July (2-5). Adm £5, chd free. Home-made teas.**
Created with the natural environment at its heart, this evolving 2 acre nature garden provides uniquely designed homes for wildlife. Wander through the flower meadow visiting individually designed rooms with many structures, water features and pools. Seating areas afford stunning views towards Exmoor and Dartmoor. Both native and herbaceous plants have been chosen to benefit insect and bird life. Dogs on leads. WC available.

GROUP OPENING

◪ BAGTOR MILL GARDENS
Ilsington, Newton Abbot, TQ13 9RT. Mark Wills. *Coming from Haytor at Smokey Cross take the road to Bickington & at Birchanger Cross turn R to Bagtor. Coming from Liverton/Ilsington carry on towards Haytor until Smokey Cross & turn L.* **Sat 4, Sun 5 May (10-4). Combined adm £5, chd free. Cream teas.**

BAGTOR MILL
Mark Wills.

LEMON COTTAGE
Phil & Jamie Richards.

Bagtor Mill is a C17 corn mill beside the River Lemon surrounded by a wildlife garden with rhododendrons, camellias, ponds, bluebells and massive gunnera. The 21 acres of ancient woodland that joins the garden in a steep valley setting is a SSSI following an old packhorse track made by charcoal burners. Opposite is Lemon Cottage with a spring-fed pond, a Japanese-inspired garden and 14 acres of woodland with views across Dartmoor. While the main paths are accessible, not all paths in both gardens are.

GROUP OPENING

◪ BARNSTAPLE WORLD GARDENS
Anne Crescent, Little Elche, Barnstaple, EX31 3AF. *32 Allenstyle Dr, from Barnstaple take B3233 towards Instow. Through Bickington & Fremington. L at Yelland sign into Allenstyle Rd. 1st R into Allenstyle Dr. 31 Anne Cres, L off Old Torrington Rd into Phillips Ave then follow signs. 21 Becklake Cl, from A3125 to Roundswell on Westermoor Way.* **Sun 4 Aug (11-4). Combined adm £5, chd free. Light refreshments. Japanese snacks, teas and cakes.**

32 ALLENSTYLE DRIVE
Steve & Dawn Morgan.
(See separate entry)

31 ANNE CRESCENT
EX31 3AF. Mr Gavin Hendry.

21 BECKLAKE CLOSE
EX31 3UZ. Karen & Steve Moss.

Explore 3 very different spaces in lovely N Devon. 31 Anne Crescent: N Devon's Little Elche a small urban L-shaped tropical garden complete with wide variety of palms, agaves, bananas, cacti, tree ferns and delightful pond surrounded by large tree ferns. 32 Allenstyle Drive 30 x 15 metre garden packed full of our favourite plants. See our huge bananas, cannas, colocasias, delicate and scented tropical passionflowers, rudbeckias, perennial sunflowers, a wildlife pond and a new large cedar greenhouse. Relax and inhale the heady scents of the garden and rest awhile in the many seating areas. 21 Becklake Close: All things Japanese.

Haldon Grange

The Old Granary

10 BICKHAM HOUSE

Kenn, Exeter, EX6 7XL. Julia Tremlett, 01392 832671, jandjtremlett@hotmail.com. *6m S of Exeter, 1m off A38. Leave A38 at Kennford Services, follow signs to Kenn, 1st R in village, follow lane for ¾ m to end of no through rd. Only use SatNav once you are in the village of Kenn.* **Mar: Sat 30. Apr: Sun 21. May: Sun 5, Sun 19. June: Sun 23. July: Sun 21. Aug: Sun 4, Sun 18. Sept: Sun 8 (1.30-5). Adm £6, chd free. Home-made teas. Visits also by arrangement 29 Mar to 8 Sept. Small coaches only.**
6 acres with lawns, borders, mature trees. Formal parterre with lily pond. Walled garden with colourful profusion of vegetables and flowers. Palm tree avenue leading to millennium summerhouse. Late summer colour with dahlias, crocosmia, agapanthus etc. Cactus and succulent greenhouse. Pelargonium collection. Lakeside walk. WC, disabled access.

11 NEW THE BLACK FARMER AT WEST KITCHAM FARM

St. Giles-On-The-Heath, Launceston, PL15 9SL. Wilfred Emmanuel-Jones. *A30/Liftondown. Go R. Continue until L to YEAT. Continue to next L. Continue to T junction, go L. Entrance approx 1m on L.* **Sat 27, Sun 28 July (10-4). Adm £6.50, chd free. Pre-booking essential, please visit www. ngs.org.uk for information & booking. Tea, coffee & cake will be available.**
The garden at West Kitcham is a 'work in progress'. The house and garden are set in beautiful countryside with expansive views across farmland to Dartmoor. The garden encompasses a range of old and new beds, with new planting all around the garden which considers our changing climate. Visitors can enjoy the garden, small orchard, vegetable garden and new woodland walk and wildflower areas.

 ))

12 ◆ BLACKBURY HONEY FARM

Southleigh, Colyton, EX24 6JF. Maureen Basterfield, 01404 871600, maureen@basterfield.com, www.blackburyfarm.co.uk. *6m S of Honiton. From Honiton take the Sidmouth rd, A375. Turn L at Hare & Hounds. Straight ahead then turn L after brown sign. From Exeter direction, take A3052 & follow brown signs from Branscombe Cross.* **For NGS: Sat 29 June (10-4). Adm £5, chd free. Tea, coffee, cakes, light lunches, cream teas. Vegetarian & gluten free options usually available. For other opening times and information, please phone, email or visit garden website.**
On a working Honey Farm, a garden for all pollinators, alive with buzzing and fluttering from spring to autumn. Large beds and borders with a wide range of colourful perennials and annuals providing pollen and nectar. Shrubs and trees underplanted with bulbs. Herb garden, polytunnel growing salad and vegetables for the tearoom. 20 acres of wildflower meadows, large apple orchard, plums, damsons, apricots and peaches. Courses and demonstrations available. Apple pressing in the autumn.

13 ◆ BLACKPOOL GARDENS

Dartmouth, TQ6 0RG. Sir Geoffrey Newman, 01803 771801, beach@blackpoolsands.co.uk, www.blackpoolsands.co.uk. *3m SW of Dartmouth. From Dartmouth follow brown signs to Blackpool Sands on A379. Entry tickets, parking, WCs & refreshments available at Blackpool Sands. Sorry, no dogs permitted.* **For opening times and information, please phone, email or visit garden website.**
Carefully restored C19 subtropical plantsman's garden with collection of mature and newly planted tender and unusual trees, shrubs and carpet of spring flowers. Paths and steps lead gradually uphill and above the Captain's Seat offering fine coastal views. Recent plantings follow the southern hemisphere theme with callistemons, pittosporums, acacias and buddlejas.

14 BRADFORD TRACEY HOUSE

Witheridge, Tiverton, EX16 8QG. Elizabeth Wilkinson. *20 mins from Tiverton. The postcode will get you to the Bradford Tracy Lodge a thatched cottage at the bottom of the drive which has 2 bouncing hares on the top. NGS direction signs from Witheridge & Rackenford.* **Sat 18, Sun 19 May (1.30-5). Adm £6, chd free. Tea & home-made cakes served takeaway style to enjoy in the garden or inside.**
A pleasure garden set around a Regency hunting lodge combining flowers with grasses, shrubs and huge trees in a natural and joyful space. It is planted for productivity and sustainability giving harvests of wonderful flowers, fruits, herbs and vegetables (and weeds!). There are beautiful views over the lake, forest walks, deep blowsy borders, an ancient wisteria and an oriental treehouse garden.

15 BRAMBLE TORRE

Dittisham, nr Dartmouth, TQ6 0HZ. Paul & Sally Vincent, www. sallyvincent14@gmail.com. *¾ m from Dittisham. Leave A3122 at Sportsman's Arms. Drop down into village, at Red Lion turn L to Cornworthy. Continue ¾ m, Bramble Torre straight ahead. Follow signs to car park.* **Sat 8, Sun 9, Mon 10 June (2-5). Adm £5, chd free. Cream teas.**
Set in 30 acres of farmland in the beautiful South Hams, the 3 acre garden follows a rambling stream through a steep valley: lily pond, herbaceous borders, roses, camellias, lawns and shrubs, a formal herb and vegetable garden. All are dominated by a huge embothrium glowing scarlet in late spring against a sometimes blue sky! Well behaved dogs on leads welcome. Partial wheelchair access, parts of garden very steep and uneven. Tea area with wheelchair access and excellent garden view.

16 BREACH

Shute Road, Kilmington, Axminster, EX13 7ST. Judith Chapman & BJ Lewis, 01297 35159, jachapman16@btinternet.com. *1½ m W of Axminster off A35. Turn L off the A35 at the War Memorial, continue up Shute Rd, past farm on R & after 150m, Breach is a short walk along a byway to the L. Parking is on Shute Rd.* **Sat 1, Sun 2 June (1.30-5). Adm £6, chd free. Home-made teas. Visits also by arrangement 3 June to 31 Oct for groups of 10 to 30.**
3+ acres with many mature trees, some unusual trees planted recently, e.g. Hoheria, *Cornus mas*, Nyssa. Herbaceous borders, shrubberies, vegetable/fruit area. Bog garden using natural spring and 2 ponds attract dragon flies. Disused shale tennis court has orchids and is being developed as wildflower area. Soil mainly acidic & a band of specimen rhododendrons was planted 12 yrs ago. Development continues. Partial wheelchair access.

GROUP OPENING

17 BRENDON GARDENS

Brendon, Lynton,
EX35 6PU. 01598 741343,
lalindevon@yahoo.co.uk. *1m S
of A39 N Devon coast rd between
Porlock and Lynton.* **Sat 1, Sun 2
June, Sat 3, Sun 4 Aug (12-5).
Combined adm £6, chd free.
Light refreshments at Higher
Tippacott farm. Light lunches,
home-made cakes, inc gluten
free & cream teas. WC. Visits also
by arrangement Apr to Sept. (Hall
Farm & Higher Tippacott Farm
only).**

BARN FARM
Andrew & Debra Hodges.

HALL FARM
Karen Wall, 01598 741604,
kwall741604@btinternet.com.

HIGHER TIPPACOTT FARM
Angela & Malcolm
Percival, 01598 741343,
lalindevon@yahoo.co.uk.

MEADPOOL HOUSE
Gillian Reynolds.

Stunning part of Exmoor National
Park. Excellent walking along river.
Barn Farm: Stylish courtyard garden
on two levels incorporating walls
and old stone buildings. Roses,
shrubs and other cottage garden
flowers and vegetables. Adjoining
paddock with copse and young
orchard of Devon varieties. Hall
Farm: C16 longhouse set in 2 acres
of tranquil mature gardens, with
lake and wild area beyond. Idyllic
setting with views. Rare Whitebred
Shorthorn cattle. Higher Tippacott
Farm: 950ft alt. on moor, facing
south overlooking its own valley
with stream and pond. Interesting
planting on many interconnecting
levels with lawns. Young fruit trees in
meadow. Vegetable patch with sea
glimpse. Lovely views along valley
and up to high moorland. Meadpool
House: Spacious and restful riverside
garden with flat terrain. Interesting
paved areas, borders, trees, feature
walls and a productive gated kitchen
garden. Visit www.ngs.org.uk/
brendon-gardens-ngs-map-2023/
to see a map of the gardens. Plants,
books and bric a brac for sale at
Higher Tippacott Farm. Display of
vintage telephones and toys.

🐄 ✷ 🚗 ☕))

18 THE BRIDGE MILL

Mill Rd, Bridgerule, Holsworthy,
EX22 7EL. Rosie & Alan Beat,
www.thebridgemill.org.uk. *In
Bridgerule village on R Tamar between
Bude & Holsworthy. Between the
chapel by river bridge & church at
top of hill. Garden is at bottom of
hill opp Short & Abbott agricultural
engineers. See website for detailed
directions.* **Sun 2 June (11-5). Adm
£5, chd free. Home-made teas in
the garden with friendly ducks
if the weather is fine, or in the
stable if wet. Plenty of dry seating.
Homemade cakes with organic
tea/ coffee. Gluten free cakes &
dairy alternatives available.**
One acre organic gardens around mill
cottage and restored working water
mill. Cottage garden style planting;
herb garden with medicinal and dye
plants; productive fruit and vegetable
garden, and wild woodland and
water garden behind mill and by the
river Tamar. 16 acre smallholding:
lake and riverside walks, wildflower
meadows, friendly livestock, sheep,
ducks and hens. The historic water
mill was restored to working order
in April 2012 and in 2017 Alan was
awarded a plaque by the Society for
the Protection of Ancient Buildings
for his sympathetic restoration of
the buildings. Exhibition of beautiful
garden embroideries by Linda Chilton
in the white barn. Wheelchair access
to some of gardens plus accessible
WC and baby change facilities.

ᘯ ✷ ☕ ⌖

19 BULLAND FARM

Ashburton, Newton Abbot,
TQ13 7NG. S & L Middleton. *1m
from A38. Exit A38 at Peartree
Cross nr Ashburton and follow signs
directing initially towards Landscove.
Turning R halfway up hill, follow NGS
signs. Expect narrow country lanes.*
**Sat 25, Sun 26 May (10.30-3.30).
Adm £5, chd free. Home-made
teas.**
Once an old cider orchard that had
grown wild, over the last 15 yrs it has
been transformed into a beautiful
and productive garden. Set over 8
acres, it makes the most of wonderful
views over rolling rural countryside.
Designed with wildlife in mind it
encompasses formal areas, prairie
planting, boardwalk water garden,
woodland trail, wildflower meadows
and terraced vegetable garden. Steps
and steep slopes although the central
path of the garden is suitable for
wheelchairs which allows great views

over the countryside and garden.

ᘯ 🐄 ✷ ☕))

20 ◆ BURROW FARM GARDENS

Dalwood, Axminster, EX13 7ET.
Mary & John Benger,
www.burrowfarmgardens.co.uk.
*3½ m W of Axminster. From A35
turn N at Taunton Xrds then follow
brown signs.* **For opening times and
information, please visit garden
website.**
This beautiful 13 acre garden has
unusual trees, shrubs and herbaceous
plants. Traditional summerhouse
looks towards lake and ancient oak
woodland with rhododendrons and
azaleas. Early spring interest and
superb autumn colour. The more
formal Millennium garden features
a rill. Anniversary garden featuring
late summer perennials and grasses.
Café, nursery and gift shop with range
of garden ironwork. Various events
inc spring and summer plant fair and
open air theatre held at garden each
yr. Visit events page on website for
more details.

ᘯ 🐄 ✷ 🚗 ☕

21 ◆ CADHAY

Ottery St Mary, EX11 1QT. Rupert
Thistlethwayte, 01404 813511,
jayne@cadhay.org.uk,
www.cadhay.org.uk. *1m NW of
Ottery St Mary. On B3176 between
Ottery St Mary & Fairmile. From
E exit A30 at Iron Bridge. From
W exit A30 at Patteson's Cross,
follow brown signs for Cadhay.* **For
NGS: Sun: 26, Mon 27 May, Sun
25, Mon 26 Aug (2-5). Adm £5,
chd £1. Cream teas. For other
opening times and information,
please phone, email or visit garden
website.**
Tranquil 2 acre setting for Tudor
manor house. 2 medieval fish ponds
surrounded by rhododendrons,
gunnera, hostas and flag iris. Roses,
clematis, lilies and hellebores
surround walled water garden. 120ft
herbaceous border walk informally
planted. Magnificent display of dahlias
throughout. Walled kitchen gardens
have been turned into allotments and
old apple store is now a tearoom.
Gravel paths.

ᘯ 🐄 🚗 ☕

22 NEW CHAGFORD COMMUNITY GARDENS

Meldon Road, Chagford, Newton
Abbot, TQ13 8BG. Nicky Scott,
wellmoor.org.uk. *Chagford*

Little Dinworthy

Allotments. From Chagford car park walk through play park above car park to gate at the top which takes you to outer allotment gate. Walk along track & the community plot is the first one as you enter the site. **Sat 3, Sun 4, Sat 10, Sun 11 Aug (10-4). Adm £5, chd free. Home-made teas in adjoining Jubilee Fields where there are picnic tables.**

This is a community plot consisting of 'starter' beds for people on the waiting list for an allotment as well as a medicinal herbs bed, a culinary herb bed, several fruit trees and two beds for unusual, mainly perennial plants. Lots of native wild flowers around the plot, a pond, two sheds, a composting area and more. We also have people referred from the local health centre. Our shed and decking area is easily accessed by wheelchair from where you can enjoy the view. The gardens are not very accessible.

23 NEW THE CHANTRY
Marshall Close, Tavistock, PL19 9RB. Jan & Ian Gasper. *1m S of Tavistock town centre along Whitchurch Rd. From Plymouth turn off A386 at signs for Whitchurch. Follow Anderton Ln to end, turn L. Marshall Cl 3rd on R. From N(A386) & town follow rd for 1m. Marshall Cl on L. Park Marshall Cl or Whitchurch Rd.* **Sun 19, Sun 26 May (1.30-4.30). Adm £5, chd free. Home-made teas.**
This is a quiet, modest sized garden, located on the edge of Tavistock. Situated on three levels with two terraces it is set out to make the most of the difficult terrain and maximises space. The many flower beds are filled with perennials, shrubs, ferns and a good collection of shade lovers. In addition we have a patio full of pots, a rill with two small ponds, a fernery and more.

24 NEW CHAO NAN
Forder Lane, Bishopsteignton, Teignmouth, TQ14 9SL. Nicholas & Diane Shaw. *10m N Torquay18m S Exeter on the Teign Estuary. From Teignmouth take the A381 past Otter Garden Centre and turn R into Forder Lane. From Exeter take A380, turn L at the Ware Barton Junction onto A381 then L again at Forder Lane junction.* **Sat 27, Sun 28 July (11-5). Adm £5, chd free. Cream teas. Picnics welcome on the croquet lawn.**
Chao Nan is a ¾ acre garden full of history and life boasting an impressive collection of trees and shrubs with a large sloping lawn which leads you to the various areas of the garden. An ever evolving space designed primarily for wildlife and year-round interest, highlights include an ancient Wisteria, newly installed wildlife pond, herbaceous perennial beds and lavender border.

25 CHEVITHORNE BARTON

Chevithorne, Tiverton,
EX16 7QB. Head Gardener,
chevithornebarton.co.uk. *3m NE of Tiverton. Follow yellow signs from A361, A396 or Sampford Peverell.* **Sun 24 Mar, Sun 26 May, Sun 28 July, Sun 27 Oct (1.30-4.30). Adm £6, chd free. Cream teas.**
Walled garden, summer borders and Robinsonian inspired woodland of rare trees and shrubs. In spring the garden features a large collection of magnolias, camellias, and rhododendrons with grass paths meandering through a sea of bluebells, and grass meadows. Home to National Collection of Quercus (Oaks). Lots of Autumn colour.

26 COOMBE MEADOW

Ashburton, Newton Abbot,
TQ13 7HU. Angela & Mike Walker, 07775 627237,
coombemeadow2016@gmail.com. *Opp Waterleat. Enter Ashburton town centre, turn onto North St. After Victoria Inn, bear R at junction, do not cross bridge to Buckland in the Moor. Follow signs.* **Visits by arrangement Apr to Sept for groups of 6 to 24. Light refreshments included in adm. Adm £12.50, chd £5.**
This lost garden, by a beautiful Dartmoor stream was overgrown and neglected. Since 2016 its mature magnolias, camellias, azaleas and other trees have been rescued. Paths and ponds have been cleared, archaeology preserved, borders created, bridges and terraces repaired and over 15,000 bulbs planted. The meadows contain wild daffodils and bluebells, so in spring the garden is a kaleidoscope of colour. Wheelchair access to front and rear patios only.

27 ◆ DOCTON MILL

Lymebridge, Hartland,
EX39 6EA. Lana & John Borrett, 01237 441369,
docton.mill@btconnect.com,
www.doctonmill.co.uk. *8m W of Clovelly. Follow brown tourist signs on A39 nr Clovelly.* **For NGS: Sun 9 June (11-5). Adm £5, chd free. Cream teas & light lunches available all day. For other opening times and information, please phone, email or visit garden website.**
Situated in a stunning valley location. The garden surrounds the original mill pond and the microclimate created within the wooded valley enables tender species to flourish. Recent planting of herbaceous, stream and summer garden give variety through the season.

28 DUNLEY HOUSE

Bovey Tracey, TQ13 9PW. Mr & Mrs F Gilbert. *2m E of Bovey Tracey on rd to Hennock. From A38 going W turn off slip rd R towards Chudleigh Knighton on B3344, in village follow yellow signs to Dunley House. From A38 eastwards turn off on Chudleigh K slip rd L and follow signs.* **Sat 25, Sun 26 May, Sat 19, Sun 20 Oct (2-5). Adm £6, chd free. Home-made teas.**
9 acre garden set among mature oaks, sequoiadendrons and a huge liquidambar started from a wilderness in mid eighties. Rhododendrons, camellias and over 40 different magnolias. Arboretum, walled garden with borders and fruit and vegetables, rose garden and new enclosed garden with lily pond. Large pond renovated in 2016 with new plantings. Woodland walk around perimeter of property.

Rose Ash House

29 EAST WORLINGTON HOUSE

East Worlington, Witheridge, Crediton, EX17 4TS. Barnabas & Campie Hurst-Bannister. *In centre of E Worlington, 2m W of Witheridge. From Witheridge Square R to E Worlington. After 1½ m R at T-junction in Drayford, then L to Worlington. After ½ m L at T-junction. 200 yds on L. Parking nearby, disabled parking at house.* **Sun 25 Feb, Sun 3 Mar** (1.30-5). Adm £5, chd free. Cream teas in thatched parish hall next to house.

Thousands of purple crocuses feature in this 2 acre garden, set in a lovely position with views down the valley to Little Dart river. These spectacular crocuses have spread over many years through the garden and into the neighbouring churchyard. Walks from the garden across the river and into the woods. Dogs on leads please.

30 ◆ GOREN FARM

Broadhayes, Stockland, Honiton, EX14 9EN. Julian Pady, 01404 881335, gorenfarm@hotmail.com, www.goren.co.uk. *6m E of Honiton, 6m W of Axminster. Go to Stockland television mast. Head 100 metres N signed from Ridge Cross, head E towards Ridge.* **For NGS: Evening openings Sat 18 May to Fri 7 June** (5-9). Adm by donation. **Sat 8, Sun 9 June** (10-9). Adm £5, chd free. Home-made teas. **Evening openings Mon 10 June to Wed 3 July** (5-9). Adm by donation. No refreshments available for evening opening, picnics allowed. For other opening times and information, please phone, email or visit garden website.

50 acres of natural species rich wildflower meadows. Easy access footpaths. Dozens of varieties of wild flowers and grasses. Thousands of orchids from early June and butterflies in July. Georgian house with stunning views of Blackdown Hills. Late season when the meadows are setting seed, ready to be mown, butterflies, beetles and many other insects are in abundance on the grasses and wildflower seed heads. Nature trail with species information signs and picnic tables. Visit the cider museum, walled vegetable garden and greenhouse. Various music events are held throughout the summer. Café serving Cream teas and light refreshments on open weekend only. Partial wheelchair access to meadows. Dogs welcome on a lead only, please clean up after your pet.

31 GREATCOMBE

Greatcombe Gardens & Gallery, Holne, Newton Abbot, TQ13 7SP. Robbie & Sarah Richardson, 07725 314887, sarah@greatcombe.com, www.facebook.com/greatcombegardens. *4m NW Ashburton via Holne Bridge & Holne village. 4m NE Buckfastleigh via Scorriton. Narrow lanes. Large car park adjacent to garden.* **May: Sat 4, Sun 5, Mon 6, Sat 25, Sun 26, Mon 27. June: Sat 15, Sun 16. July: Sat 20, Sun 21** (1-5). Adm £6, chd free. Home-made teas.

This year we're letting our visitors describe the garden! 'A truly beautiful, tranquil garden with unusual plants and exciting use of colour, a garden to visit again and again.' 'Enchanting, magical place, one of our favourites which has given us much inspiration. A real asset to the NGS and fabulous home-made teas by the stream!'. Plant nursery. Artist's studio. Metal plant supports in all sizes.

32 HALDON GRANGE

Dunchideock, Exeter, EX6 7YE. Ted Phythian, 01392 832349, judithphythian@yahoo.com, youtu.be/G0gluYoWncA. *5m SW of Exeter. From A30 through Ide village to Dunchideock 5m. L to Lord Haldon, Haldon Grange is next L. From A38 (S) turn L on top of Haldon Hill follow Dunchideock signs, R at village centre to Lord Haldon.* **Sat 16, Sun 17, Sat 30, Sun 31 Mar, Mon 1, Sat 13, Sun 14, Wed 17, Sat 27, Sun 28 Apr, Wed 1, Sat 11, Sun 12, Wed 15, Sat 25, Sun 26, Mon 27 May, Sat 1, Sun 2 June** (1-5). Adm £6, chd free. Home-made teas. Our visitors are welcome to bring a picnic. **Visits also by arrangement 16 Mar to 2 June for groups of 10+. Access for small coach size only.**

Peaceful, well established 19 acre garden, parts dating back to 1770s. This hidden gem boasts one of the largest collections of rhododendrons, azaleas, magnolias and camellias. Interspersed with mature and rare trees and complemented by a lake and cascading ponds. 6 acre arboretum, large lilac circle, wisteria pergola with views over Woodbury completes this family run treasure.

Plant sale, teas and home bakes (cash only) open at other times. On site car parking. WC available, alcohol wipes and hand gel provided. Strictly no dogs. Wheelchair access to main parts of garden.

33 HALSCOMBE FARM

Halscombe Lane, Ide, Exeter, EX2 9TQ. Prof J Rawlings, jgshayward@tiscali.co.uk. *From Exeter go through Ide to mini r'about take 2nd exit and continue to L turn into Halscombe Lane.* **Visits by arrangement May to Sept. Adm £4, chd free.**

Farmhouse garden created over last 11 yrs. Large collection of old roses and peonies, long and colourful mixed borders, productive fruit cage and vegetable garden all set within a wonderful borrowed landscape.

34 HARBOUR LIGHTS

Horns Cross, Bideford, EX39 5DW. Brian & Faith Butler, 01237 451627, brian.nfu@gmail.com, harbourlightsgarden.org. *8m W of Bideford, 3m E of Clovelly. On main A39 between Bideford and Clovelly, halfway between Hoops Inn & Bucks Cross. There will be a union jack flag & yellow arrow signs at the entrance.* **Sat 22, Sun 23 June** (11-5). Adm £5, chd free. Cream teas, cakes, light lunches, wine all available. **Visits also by arrangement 1 June to 5 Aug for groups of 12 to 40. We can provide teas, light lunches, or evening meals.**

½ acre colourful garden with Lundy views. A garden of wit, humour, unusual ideas, installation art, puzzles, volcano and many surprises. Water features, shrubs, foliage area, grasses in an unusual setting, fernery, bonsai and polytunnel, plus masses of colourful plants. You will never have seen a garden like this! Free leaflet. We like our visitors to leave with a smile! Child friendly. A 'must visit' unique and interactive garden with intriguing artwork of various kinds, original plantings and ideas.

35 THE HAVEN

Wembury Road, Hollacombe, Wembury, South Hams, PL9 0DQ. Mrs S Norton & Mr J Norton, 01752 862149, suenorton1@hotmail.co.uk. *20mins from Plymouth city centre. Use A379 Plymouth to Kingsbridge Rd. At Elburton r'about follow signs to Wembury. Parking on roadside. Bus stop nearby on Wembury Rd. Route 48 from Plymouth.* **Visits by arrangement 18 Mar to 1 May for groups of 10 to 30. Adm £5, chd free. Cream teas.**
½ acre sloping plantsman's garden in South Hams AONB. Tearoom and seating areas. 2 ponds. Substantial collection of large flowering Asiatic and hybrid tree magnolias. Large collection of camellias inc *Camellia reticulata*. Rare dwarf, weeping and slow growing conifers. Daphnes, early azaleas and rhododendrons, spring bulbs and hellebores. Wheelchair access to top part of garden.

GROUP OPENING

36 HAYTOR GARDENS

Haytor, Newton Abbot, TQ13 9XT. Judy Gordon Jones. *300m from Haytor on road to Ilsington. From Bovey Tracey, turn L at red phone box. After approx. 300m Brambly Wood signposted on R. Garden 50m. Haytor House next to this turning. Parking 200m further down the road in field on L.* **Sat 18, Sun 19 May (11-5). Combined adm £7, chd free. Home-made teas at Haytor House.**

BRAMBLY WOOD
Lindsay & Laurie Davidson.

HAYTOR HOUSE
Judy Gordon Jones & Hilary Townsend.

Haytor Gardens offers two very different gardens on the edge of Dartmoor with views across to Torbay and the Teign estuary. The one acre garden at Brambly Wood has been developed over the past 40 yrs with packed herbaceous borders, a pond and extensive planting of rhododendrons, azaleas and camellias looking their best in spring with tranquil seating areas throughout the garden. Visitors are also welcome to view the owners' studios showing artisan pottery and textile work. The ¼ acre garden at Haytor House was

designed along more classical lines as a project for horticultural students in the 1930s and provides distinctive planting within partitioned areas. An inner walled garden with a folly leads to three further distinctive garden 'rooms' with a lily pond, raised beds, mixed herbaceous borders and large shrubs and acers among its many features.

37 HEATHERCOMBE

Manaton, nr Bovey Tracey, TQ13 9XE. Claude & Margaret Pike Woodlands Trust, 01626 354404, gardens@pike.me.uk, www.heathercombe.com. *7m NW of Bovey Tracey. From Bovey Tracey take scenic B3387 to Haytor/ Widecombe. 1.7m past Haytor Rocks (before Widecombe Hill) turn R to Hound Tor & Manaton. 1.4m past Hound Tor turn L at Heatree Cross to Heathercombe.* **Sun 24 Mar, Sun 5, Sat 11, Sun 12, Sat 18, Sun 19 May (1.30-5.30). Every Tue to Sun 21 May to 2 June (1.30-5.30). Sat 8, Sun 9, Sat 15, Sun 16, Sat 22, Sun 23 June (11-5.30). Adm £6, chd free. Self service tea & coffee. Do bring a picnic. Please pay for your tickets in advance where possible via www.ngs.org.uk. Visits also by arrangement 25 Mar to 31 Oct. Donation to Rowcroft Hospice.**
Enjoy our daffodils, extensive bluebells, large collection of colourful rhododendrons, azaleas and many unusual specimen trees and shrubs, wildflower meadow and cottage garden with a leisurely stroll beside streams and ponds and through woodland, 'parkland', gardens and orchard, with many benches and summerhouses where you can sit and enjoy the tranquillity of Heathercombe's natural setting. Disabled reserved parking close to tea room & WC.

38 HIGHER CHERUBEER

Dolton, Winkleigh, EX19 8PP. Jo & Tom Hynes, hynesjo@gmail.com. *2m E of Dolton. From the A3124 between Winkleigh and Dolton turn S towards Stafford Moor Fisheries, take 1st R signed Dolton, garden 500m on L.* **Fri 2, Fri 9, Sat 17 Feb (2.30-4.30); Sun 25 Aug (2-5.30). Adm £5, chd free. Home-made teas. 2025: Fri 7, Fri 14, Sun 23 Feb. Visits also by arrangement 1**

Feb to 20 Oct for groups of 10+. 1¾ acre country garden with gravelled courtyard and paths, raised beds, alpine house, lawns, herbaceous borders, woodland beds with naturalised cyclamen and snowdrops, kitchen garden with large greenhouse and orchard. Winter openings for National Collection of Cyclamen species, hellebores and over 400 snowdrop varieties.

39 HIGHER ORCHARD COTTAGE

Aptor, Marldon, Paignton, TQ3 1SQ. Mrs Jenny Saunders, 01803 551221, jennymsaunders@aol.com, www.facebook.com/ HigherOrchardCottage/. *1m SW of Marldon. A380 Torquay to Paignton. At Churscombe Cross r'about R for Marldon, L towards Berry Pomeroy, take 2nd R into Farthing Lane. Follow for exactly 1m. Turn R at NGS sign & follow signs for parking.* **Sat 8, Sun 9 June (11-5). Adm £5, chd free. Coffee available in the morning. Tea & cakes available from 2pm provided by Marldon Garden Club, if weather permits. Outside seating only. Visits also by arrangement Apr to Sept for groups of up to 20.**
Two acre garden with generous colourful herbaceous borders, wildlife pond, specimen trees and shrubs, productive vegetable beds and grass path walks through wildflower meadows in lovely countryside. Each year we host art and craft installations by local artists and crafters.

40 NEW HIGHLAND HOUSE

Cadbury, Exeter, EX5 5LA. Peter & Cheryl Rees. *Mid-way between Tiverton & Crediton, just off the A3072. Look out for sign to Cadbury Castle on L (if coming from Exeter/ Tiverton) or R (from Crediton). Pass Cadbury church then turn immed L, follow rd for approx ½m.* **Sat 22, Sun 23 June (1-5). Adm £6, chd free. Home-made teas.**
A multi-level garden with mixed herbaceous borders, rose garden, orchard, ponds, cutting garden, vegetable garden, newly established wildflower meadow and a woodland walk, all with far-ranging views over the surrounding countryside. Children's trail. Display of garden sculptures.

41 ◆ HOTEL ENDSLEIGH
Milton Abbot, Tavistock,
PL19 0PQ. Olga Polizzi,
01822 870000,
info@hotelendsleigh.com, www.
hotelendsleigh.com/garden.
7m NW of Tavistock, midway
between Tavistock & Launceston.
From Tavistock, take B3362 to
Launceston. 7m to Milton Abbot then
1st L, opp school. From Launceston
& A30, B3362 to Tavistock. At Milton
Abbot turn R opp school. **For NGS:
Tue 21 May (11-4). Adm £10, chd
free. Light refreshments in hotel
only please pre-book coffee/
lunch/afternoon tea beforehand
due to limited space. For other
opening times and information,
please phone, email or visit garden
website.**
Set in 108 acres, Endsleigh was the
last garden designed by Humphry
Repton in 1814. Today the visitor can
enjoy Repton's vision for the gardens
with its streams, rills, pools and
cascades splashing through valleys of
Champion Trees. Closer to the house,
a 'cottage orne' style hunting lodge,
you will find a 100m herbaceous
border, rose arch, yew walk, and Shell
House.

42 NEW KENNICK BARN
Christow, Exeter, EX6 7NZ.
Libby Woods & Saul Ackroyd,
www.kennickbarn.co.uk.
Nr Kennick Reservoir. From
Moretonhampstead take the Exeter
rd & turn off R at Cossick Cross.
Then follow yellow signs. From the
A38 take the Teign Valley rd & then
turn sharp L uphill after Canonteign.
**Sat 15, Sun 16 June (2-5.30). Adm
£5, chd free. Home-made teas.**
About 1½ acres with a copse, wild
flower meadow and mown labyrinth
on a small field. A small flock of
chickens, vegetable beds and a
greenhouse containing a vine. The
more formal part of the garden near
the house has borders with a mix of
perennials including several varieties
of salvia. Roses and delphiniums are
the early summer stars in the garden.
There is a small wildlife pond.

43 KENTISBEARE HOUSE
Kentisbeare, Cullompton,
EX15 2BR. Nicholas & Sarah
Allan. 2m E of M5 J28 (Cullompton).
Turn off A373 at Post Cross signed
Kentisbeare. After ½ m past cricket
field & main drive on R, entrance to
carpark is through next gate on R.
**Sat 8 June (10.30-4.30); Sun 9
June (10.30-1.30). Adm £6, chd
free. Home-made teas.**
Surrounding the listed former
Kentisbeare rectory, the gardens
have been redesigned and planted
by the present owners in recent
years with various planting themes
that complement the surrounding
countryside. Formal beds, lake walk,
kitchen garden and glasshouse,
recently established wildflower
meadow, orchard. Diverse and
interesting collection of trees, shrubs
and woodland plants.

44 NEW KEYMELFORD HOUSE
Keymelford, Yeoford, Crediton,
EX17 5JG. Mr Mark Flawn. 0.8km
NW of Yeoford. From A30 take exit
for Cheriton Bishop, in village take R
for Yeoford. From A377 turn off opp
Homleigh Garden Centre, follow
signs for recycling centre. By train
leave at Yeoford, 12 mins walk. **Sat
17, Sun 18 Aug (1-5). Adm £5, chd
free. Home-made teas.**
5 acres of gardens and sheep
enclosures surrounding a Grade II*
thatched farmhouse in a mid Devon
valley. The gardens are gradually being
developed and include an enclosed box
edged Potager (vegetables, cut flowers
and fruit), croquet lawn, small orchard,
riverside walk and dell. A spring fed
pond with exotic planting feeds a leat
running through the garden down to
the small river. Wheelchair access to
the Potager is challenging due to steep
slope. All other paths are grass.

45 KIA-ORA FARM & GARDENS
Knowle Lane, Cullompton,
EX15 1PZ. Mrs M B Disney,
01884 32347,
rosie@kia-orafarm.co.uk,
www.kia-orafarm.co.uk. On W side
of Cullompton & 6m SE of Tiverton.
M5 J28, through town centre to
r'about, 3rd exit R, top of Swallow
Way turn L into Knowle Lane, garden
beside Cullompton Rugby Club. **Sun
31 Mar, Mon 1, Sun 21 Apr, Sun 5,
Mon 6, Sun 26, Mon 27 May, Sun 9,
Sun 23 June, Sun 14, Sun 28 July,
Sun 11, Sun 25, Mon 26 Aug, Sun
8, Sun 22 Sept (2-5.30). Adm £4,
chd free. Home-made teas. Teas,
plants & sales not for NGS. Visits
also by arrangement Apr to Sept.
Please state for NGS when booking.**
Charming, peaceful 10 acre garden with
lawns, lakes and ponds. Water features
with swans, ducks and other wildlife.
Mature trees, shrubs, rhododendrons,
azaleas, heathers, roses, herbaceous
borders and rockeries. Nursery avenue,
novelty crazy golf. Stroll leisurely around
and finish by sitting back, enjoying a
traditional home-made Devonshire
cream tea or choose from the wide
selection of cakes!

46 LEE FORD
Knowle Village, Budleigh
Salterton, EX9 7AJ. Mr & Mrs N
Lindsay-Fynn, 01395 445894,
crescent@leeford.co.uk,
www.leeford.co.uk. 3½ m E of
Exmouth. For SatNav use postcode
EX9 6AL. **Visits by arrangement
Apr to Oct for groups of up to 30.
Adm £7.50, chd free. Discounted
entry for 10 or more £7. Morning
coffee & biscuits, morning &
afternoon teas with selection
of cakes or cream teas served
in conservatory. Donation to
Lindsay-Fynn Trust.**
Extensive, formal and woodland
garden, largely developed in
1950s, but recently much extended
with mass displays of camellias,
rhododendrons and azaleas, inc
many rare varieties. Traditional
walled garden filled with fruit and
vegetables, herb garden, bog garden,
hydrangea collection, greenhouses
for ornamentals, conservatory with
pot plants including pelargoniums,
Bougainvilleas and coleus. Direct
access to pedestrian route and
National Cycle Network Route 2
which follows old railway linking
Exmouth to Budleigh Salterton.
Woodland and formal garden are an
ideal destination for cycle clubs or
rambling groups. Formal gardens are
lawn with paths. Moderately steep
slope to woodland garden on tarmac
drive with gravel paths in woodland.

Our donation to
Marie Curie this
year equates to
17,496 hours of
nursing care

47 LEWIS COTTAGE

Spreyton, nr Crediton, EX17 5AA.
Mr & Mrs M Pell and Mr R Orton,
07773 785939, rworton@mac.com,
www.lewiscottageplants.co.uk. *5m
NE of Spreyton, 8m W of Crediton.
From Hillerton X keep stone X to
your R. Drive approx 1½ m, Lewis
Cottage on L, drive down farm track.
From Crediton follow A377 N. Turn
L at Barnstaple X junction, then 2m
from Colebrooke Church.* **Visits by
arrangement 18 May to 8 Sept for
groups of 12 to 24. Adm £5, chd
free. Home-made teas.**
4 acre garden located on SW
facing slope in rural mid Devon.
Evolved primarily over last 30 yrs,
harnessing and working with the
natural landscape. Using informal
planting and natural formal structures
to create a garden that reflects the
souls of those who garden in it, it is
an incredibly personal space that is a
joy to share. Spring camassia cricket
pitch, rose garden, large natural dew
pond, woodland walks, bog garden,
hornbeam rondel, winter garden, hot
and cool herbaceous borders, fruit
and vegetable garden, outdoor poetry
reading room and plant nursery selling
plants mostly propagated from the
garden.

48 LITTLE ASH BUNGALOW

Fenny Bridges, Honiton,
EX14 3BL. Helen & Brian
Brown, 07833 247927,
helenlittleash@hotmail.com, www.
facebook.com/littleashgarden.
*3m W of Honiton. Leave A30 at 1st
turn off from Honiton 1m, Patteson's
Cross from Exeter ½ m & follow
NGS signs.* **Sun 21 July, Sat 21
Sept (1-5). Adm £5, chd free.
Light refreshments. Visits also
by arrangement May to Sept for
groups of 10+.**
Country garden of 1½ acres,
packed with different and unusual
bulbs, herbaceous perennials, trees,
and shrubs. Designed for year-
round interest, wildlife and owners'
pleasure. Naturalistic planting in
colour coordinated mixed borders,
highlighted by metal sculptures,
providing foreground to the view.
Natural stream, pond and damp
woodland area, mini wildlife meadows
and raised gravel/alpine garden.
Grass paths.

49 NEW LITTLE DINWORTHY

Bradworthy, Holsworthy,
EX22 7QX. Melanie & Simon
Osborne, LittleDinworthyGardens.
co.uk. *1½ m NW of Bradworthy. In
Bradworthy Square, head towards
Meddon/Hartland on North Rd. Take
1st L to Dinworthy, & follow yellow
NGS signs. The lane entrance to
Little Dinworthy will be seen on L,
approx 1½ m.* **Sat 23, Sun 24 Mar,
Sat 13, Sun 21 Apr, Sat 18, Sun 26
May, Sat 15, Sun 23 June (10.30-
5.30). Adm £7, chd free. Cream
teas. Selected small range of
additional refreshments.**
A wildlife garden and lake with young
20yr old woodland. A developing
garden with magnolias, flowering
cherries and a variety of different
specimen trees. Wild flowers abound
encouraging multiple species in the
many natural habitats. Around the
house, box and yew topiary add
a touch of fun and solidity to the
profusion of growth. Meadow walks.
Children's woodland trail. Suitable
footwear is recommended due to wet
grass and some muddy paths. Dogs
welcome on leads in garden and
woodland.

50 LITTLEFIELD

Parsonage Way, Woodbury, Exeter,
EX5 1HY. Caryn Vanstone & Bruno
Dalbiez. *15 min from J30 M5 nr
Exeter. Please park cars in the village
& follow signs to a narrow driveway
shared with Summer Lodge. Access
to driveway from Parsonage Way,
opp the stone X on junction with
Pound Lane.* **Sun 8 Sept (11-4).
Adm £5, chd £1. Scones with
cream & home-made jam, homebaked cakes & biscuits. Tea &
coffee.**
Opening for the first time in late
summer. ½ acre eco-garden.
Rescued from derelict land in
2009/10, only 13m wide, 150m long,
divided into herbaceous, shrub and
tree planting, with large vegetable
area, fruit and orchard with chickens
and beehive. Wide variety of plants,
sculptures, unusual ironwork, wildlife
pond all add charm and interest.
Managed using permaculture
techniques. Photo books and other
displays show the evolution of the
garden from its derelict beginnings.
Other displays introduce the visitor
to the key ideas of permaculture and
high-sustainability gardening, with
wildlife and healthy ecosystems at
its heart. The entire garden can be

accessed in a wheelchair, but be
aware that most paths are gravel and
can be soft.

51 ◆ LUKESLAND

Harford, Ivybridge, PL21 0JF.
Mrs R Howell and Mr & Mrs
J Howell, 01752 691749,
lorna.lukesland@gmail.com,
www.lukesland.co.uk. *10m E of
Plymouth. Turn off A38 at Ivybridge.
1½ m N on Harford rd, E side
of Erme valley. Beware of using
SatNavs as these can be very
misleading.* **For opening times and
information, please phone, email or
visit garden website.**
25 acres of flowering shrubs, wild
flowers and rare trees with pinetum
in Dartmoor National Park. Beautiful
setting of small valley around
Addicombe Brook with lakes,
numerous waterfalls and pools.
Extensive and impressive collections
of camellias, rhododendrons,
azaleas and acers; also spectacular
Magnolia campbellii and huge *Davidia
involucrata*. Superb spring and
autumn colour. Open Suns, Weds
and BH (11-5) 10 March - 9 June and
9 Oct - 13 November. Adm £8.00,
under 16s free. Group discount for
parties of 20+. Group tours available
by appointment. Children's trail.

52 ◆ MARWOOD HILL GARDEN

Marwood, nr Guineaford,
Barnstaple, EX31 4EB. Dr J A
Snowdon, 01271 342528, info@
marwoodhillgarden.co.uk,
www.marwoodhillgarden.co.uk.
*4m N of Barnstaple. Turn off
A361 & B3230. Look out for brown
signs. See website for map &
directions. Coach & car park.* **For
NGS: Fri 5 Apr, Fri 16 Aug (10-
4.30). Adm £9.50, chd £5. Garden
Tea Room offers selection of
light refreshments throughout
the day, all home-made or locally
sourced. For other opening times
and information, please phone,
email or visit garden website.**
Home to four National Plant Heritage
collections and numerous Champion
trees, these private valley gardens
span over 20 acres. Showcasing
three stunning lakes, sculptures,
rare trees & shrubs, and colourful
surprises throughout each season.
The gardens, plant nursery and
tearooms are a delight. Partial
wheelchair access.

Regency House

53 MIDDLE WELL

Waddeton Road, Stoke Gabriel, Totnes, TQ9 6RL. Neil & Pamela Millward, 01803 782981, neilandpam72@gmail.com. *A385 Totnes towards Paignton. Turn off A385 at Parkers Arms, Collaton St. Mary. After 1m, turn L at Four Cross.* **Sun 4 Aug (11-5). Adm £6, chd free. Home-made teas. Visits also by arrangement Apr to Oct. Coach access for 35-seater or less. Larger coaches need to park 300m away.**

Tranquil 2 acre garden plus woodland and streams contain a wealth of interesting plants chosen for colour, form and long season of interest. Many seats from which to enjoy the sound of water. Interesting structural features (rill, summerhouse, pergola, cobbling, slate bridge). Heady mix of perennials, shrubs, bulbs, climbers and specimen trees. Late colour. Vegetable garden. Child friendly. Architectural features offset by striking planting. Mostly accessible by wheelchair.

54 2 MIDDLEWOOD

Cockwood, Exeter, EX6 8RN. Cliff & Chris Curd. *1m S of Starcross. A379 from Dawlish, R at Cofton Cross, passing Cofton Holidays. Middlewood ½m on R. A379 from Exeter, turn L at Cockwood Harbour. Turn R, pass The Ship. Park on Church Rd, not in Middlewood.* **Sat 29, Sun 30 June, Sat 6, Sun 7 July (1-5). Adm £5, chd free. Home-made teas.**

Entered via a courtyard, a former market garden on a north facing slope, with steep, uneven paths. View over the Exe. A food production and wildlife garden with a self-sufficiency ethos; greenhouse, polytunnel, fruit cage, raised vegetable beds, wild area, ponds. Productive fruit bushes and trees inc exotics. Steep access path. Not accessible for wheelchair users. Nearby are two well-regarded country/harbourside pubs. Cockwood harbour 300 yards.

55 ♦ MOTHECOMBE HOUSE

Mothecombe, Holbeton, Plymouth, PL8 1LA. Mr & Mrs J Mildmay-White, jmw@flete.co.uk, www.flete.co.uk/gardens/. *12m E of Plymouth. From A379 between Yealmpton & Modbury turn S for Holbeton. Continue 2m to Mothecombe.* **For NGS: Sun 5 May (11-5). Adm £6, chd free. Home-made teas. For other opening times and information, please email or visit garden website.**

Queen Anne House (not open) with Lutyens additions and terraces set in private estate hamlet. Walled gardens, orchard with spring bulbs and magnolias, camellia walk leading through bluebell woods to streams and pond. Mothecombe Garden is managed for wildlife and pollinators. Bee garden with 250 lavenders in 16 varieties. New project to manage adjacent 6 acre meadow as a traditional wildflower pasture. Sandy beach at bottom of garden, unusual shaped large *Liriodendron tulipifera*. Tea, coffee and cake in the garden. Lunches at The Schoolhouse, Mothecombe village. Gravel paths, two slopes.

56 THE MOUNT, DELAMORE
Cornwood, Ivybridge,
PL21 9QP. Mr & Mrs Gavin
Dollard, 01752 837605,
nicdelamore@gmail.com. *Please
park in car park for Delamore Park
Offices not in village. From Ivybridge
turn L at Xrds in Cornwood village
keep pub on L, follow wall on R
to sharp R bend, turn R.* **Sat 10,
Sun 11 Feb (10.30-3.30). Adm
£7.50, chd free. Visits also by
arrangement 10 Feb to 25 Feb.**
Welcome one of the first signs of
spring by wandering through swathes
of thousands of snowdrops in this
lovely wood. Closer to the village
than to Delamore Gardens, paths
meander through a sea of these lovely
plants, some of which are unique to
Delamore and which were sold as
posies to Covent Garden market as
late as 2002. The Cornwood Inn in
the village is now community owned
and open, serving excellent food.
Main house and garden open for
sculpture exhibition every day in May.
🐕 � icons 🚗))

57 MUSBURY BARTON
Musbury, Axminster, EX13 8BB.
Lt Col Anthony Drake. *3m S of
Axminster off A358. Turn E into
village, follow yellow signs. Garden
next to church, parking for 12 cars,
otherwise park on road in village.* **Sat
29, Sun 30 June (1-5). Adm £6,
chd free. Home-made teas.**
This 6 acre garden surrounds a
traditional Devon longhouse. It is
planted with much imagination. There
are many rare and unusual things to
see, inc 2000 roses in beds, some
of them edged with local stone. A
stream in a steep valley tumbles
through the garden. Visit the avenue
of horse chestnuts and the arboretum
with interesting trees. Enjoy the many
vantage points in this unusual garden
with a surprise round every corner.
🐕 ☕

**58 MUSSELBROOK COTTAGE
GARDEN**
Sheepwash, Beaworthy,
EX21 5PE. Richard Coward. *1.3m
N of Sheepwash. SatNav may be
misleading. A3072 to Highampton.
Through Sheepwash. L on track
signed Lake Farm. A386 S of Merton
take rd to Petrockstow. Up hill opp,
eventually L. After 350 yds turn R
down track signed Lake Farm.* **Fri
19, Sat 20, Sun 21 Apr, Fri 10, Sat
11, Sun 12 May, Fri 14, Sat 15,
Sun 16 June, Fri 19, Sat 20, Sun**

**21 July (11-4.30). Adm £5, chd
free.**
1 acre naturalistic/wildlife/
plantsman's/sensory garden on
sloping site which is autism friendly.
Year-round interest with rare and
unusual plants, 13 ponds (koi,
lilies), stream, Japanese garden,
Mediterranean garden, wildflower
meadow, massed bulbs. Ericaceous
plants inc camellias, magnolias,
rhododendrons, acers, hydrangeas.
Grasses/bamboo. Clock golf. Planting
extremely labour intensive as ground
is full of rocks. A mattock soon
became my indispensable tool, even
for planting bulbs. Small nursery (inc
aquatics, water lilies) can be visited by
appointment.
✳ 🪑

GROUP OPENING

59 OGWELL GARDENS
Ogwell, TQ12 6AH. *1½ m SW of
Newton Abbot. Turn R at the r'about
on the Totnes rd. Go straight on up
the hill to the village green. Turn R
between the 2 parts of the green
down to the Memorial Hall for tickets
and a map.* **Sat 8, Sun 9 June
(11-5). Combined adm £7, chd
free. Home-made teas at Ogwell
Memorial Hall, Ogwell, Newton
Abbot. TQ12 6AJ.**

BUTTERCOMBE COTTAGE
Helen Clarke.
NEW **HOLBEAM MILL**
Mr Nick Holdsworth.
ROSELEA
Andy Harper.
RYDON BRAKE
Paul & Pauline Wynter.
4 SUNNY HOLLOW
Paul & Anthea Martin.
WILLOW TREE HOUSE
Dan & Katy Farrell-Wright.
WINDYRIDGE
Rebecca & Tim Flower.
NEW **WYNDHAM CROFT**
Shani & Richard Broome.

The Ogwell group offers eight gardens
of varying styles, inc small cottage
gardens, an historic mill and those
focused on encouraging wildlife, one
with a swimming pond and striking
planting, and large gardens with
ponds, a bonsai collection and other
attractions.
☕))

60 NEW **OLD CREBOR FARM**
Gulworthy, Tavistock, PL19 8HZ.
Yvette & Rob Andrewartha,
01822 614355,
ynndrwrth@gmail.com. *2½ m
SW from Tavistock. From Tavistock
take the A390 towards Gunnislake.
After 2½ m turn L marked Buctor &
Crebor. Past Buctor Farm next on R.*
**Visits by arrangement Apr to Sept
for groups of 6+. Adm £6, chd
free. Light refreshments.**
Traditional cottage planting around a
pretty mid C18 farmhouse with stone
walls, streams, bridges, ponds and
terracing. Wonderful views of the
valley and Dartmoor. Mature wood,
orchard, wisteria, vine and walled
garden. 3 acres of sloping wildflower
meadows with mown paths for a
stroll. Lots of spots to rest and enjoy.
Supporting biodiversity and coping
with climate change a focus.
☕ 🪑

61 NEW **OLD GLEBE**
Eggesford, Chulmleigh, EX18 7QU.
Joanne Court, 07983 736461,
joanne.court0910@gmail.com.
*20m NW of Exeter. Turn S off A377
at Eggesford Stn (halfway between
Exeter & Barnstaple), cross railway
tracks, drive uphill for ³⁄₄ m, turn R into
bridlepath, drive is on the left.* **Sat 18,
Sun 19, Sat 25, Sun 26 May (2-5).
Adm £5, chd free. Home-made
teas. Visits also by arrangement
Mar to Sept for groups of up to 20.
Donation to Friends of Eggesford All
Saints Trust.**
7 acre gardens surrounding Georgian
rectory. Magnificent display of
rhododendrons and azaleas in May.
Many interesting mature trees. Walled
Long Border and new herbaceous
beds. Productive 'no dig' kitchen
and cutting garden. 'Messenger'
greenhouse (1929) being restored.
Small newly planted orchard. Wildflower
meadow with mown paths to gazebo
and suspension bridge. Series of ponds.
🐕 ✳ ☕ 🪑))

In 2023, our donations
to Carers Trust meant
that 26,118 unpaid
carers were supported
across the UK

Hotel Endsleigh

Rudd Cottage

62 NEW **THE OLD GRANARY**
North Road, Bradworthy,
EX22 7QS. Mrs Karen Barclay.
*Make your way to Bradworthy village
square and follow the NGS signs.*
**Sun 23 June (11-5). Adm £5, chd
free. Home-made teas.**
The Old Granary is a barn conversion
with a small four year old garden. It
includes a greenhouse, a log cabin
used as a Bowen Therapy studio and
a small shed. I grow cut flowers at the
rear of the garden for sale, and the
remaining borders are a colourful and
exuberant example of what can be
achieved in a small space. The style
is relaxed and informal, fairly cottagey
with a few quirky twists.
✻ 🍵))

GROUP OPENING

63 **PARRACOMBE GARDENS**
Parracombe, Barnstaple,
EX31 4QL. *Off A39 between
Blackmore Gate & Lynton. Car
parking at Pavilion Stores & Café
EX31 4QL.* **Sat 22, Sun 23 June
(12-5). Combined adm £6, chd**
free. Cream teas, cakes & light
refreshments available in the
Pavilion Stores & Café.

NEW **CHURCH COTTAGE**
Jo & Harry Harrison.

LAUREL HOUSE
Lesley & John Brownlee.

LITTLECLOSE
Julia & Jeremy Holtom.

PARADISE VILLA
Andy Full.

SOUTH HILL HOUSE
Alison Smith & Dave Austin.

Set in the historic Exmoor village of
Parracombe, with its Norman motte
& bailey castle and an ancient C12
church. St Petrock's Church is Grade
I listed, and the churchyard, managed
by volunteers, is set to become
a County Wildlife Site. Church
Cottage is a garden in progress,
with informal cottage-style beds, a
large vegetable & cut-flower area &
a young orchard. Laurel Cottage is a
small gem of a garden, packed with
successional planting & landscape
features. Littleclose has a terraced

garden, roses, a developing orchard
& a lovely view of the motte & bailey
castle. Paradise Villa is a charming
garden with a productive vegetable
area. South Hill House has a walled
front garden & an elegant, cobbled
courtyard leading to the rear garden,
with its herbaceous borders & mature
trees, set beside the river Heddon.
Teas/light lunches and WC at Pavilion
Community Stores & Café. Lunches
available at the Fox & Goose (booking
advised 01598 763239).
🐕 ✻ 🍵))

---

64 ✦ **PLANT WORLD**
St Marychurch Road,
Newton Abbot, TQ12 4SE.
Ray Brown, 01803 872939,
info@plant-world-seeds.com,
www.plant-world-gardens.co.uk.
*2m SE of Newton Abbot. 1½m from
Penn Inn turn-off on A380. Follow
brown tourist signs at end of A380
dual carriageway from Exeter.* **For
opening times and information,
please phone, email or visit garden
website.**
The four acres of landscape gardens

with fabulous views have been called Devon's 'Little Outdoor Eden'. Representing five continents, they offer an extensive collection of rare and exotic plants from around the world. Superb mature cottage garden and Mediterranean garden will delight the visitor. Attractive viewpoint café, picnic area and shop.

65 POUNDS

Hemyock, Cullompton, EX15 3QS. Diana Elliott, 01823 680802, shillingscottage@yahoo.co.uk, www.poundsfarm.co.uk. *8m N of Honiton. M5 J26. From ornate village pump, nr pub & church, turn up rd signed Dunkeswell Abbey. Entrance ½m on R. Park in field. Short walk up to garden on R. Not far from Regency House often open at the same time.* **Fri 19, Sat 20 Apr, Fri 31 May, Sat 1, Fri 14, Sat 15 June, Fri 6, Sat 7 Sept (1-4). Adm £5, chd free. Home-made teas. Visits also by arrangement May to Sept for groups of 10 to 20.**
Cottage garden of lawns, colourful borders and roses, set within low flint walls with distant views. Slate paths lead through an acer grove to a swimming pool, amid scented borders. Beyond lies a traditional ridge and furrow orchard, with a rose hedge, where apple, pear, plum and cherries grow among ornamental trees. Further on, an area of raised beds combine vegetables with flowers for cutting. Some steps, but most of the garden accessible via sloping grass, concrete, slate or gravel paths.

66 THE PRIORY

Priory Road, Abbotskerswell, Newton Abbot, TQ12 5PP. Priory Residents. *2m SW of Newton Abbot town centre. A381 Newton Abbot/Totnes Rd. Sharp L turn from NA. R from Totnes. At mini r'about in village centre turn L into Priory Rd.* **Sat 22, Sun 23 June (1-5). Adm £6, chd free. Light refreshments.**
The Priory is a Grade II* listed building, originally a manor house extended in Victorian times as a home for an Augustinian order of nuns, now a retirement complex of 44 apartments and cottages. The grounds extend to approx 5 acres and include numerous flower borders, a wild flower meadow, an area of woodland with some interesting specimen trees, cottage gardens and lovely views. Small Mediterranean

garden and area of individually owned raised beds and greenhouses. Wheelchair access difficult when wet and some slopes.

67 REGENCY HOUSE

Hemyock, EX15 3RQ. Mrs Jenny Parsons, 07772 998982, jenny. parsons@btinternet.com, www. regencyhousehemyock.co.uk. *8m N of Honiton. M5 J26/27. From Catherine Wheel pub & church in Hemyock take Dunkeswell-Honiton Rd. Entrance ½m on R. Please do not drive on the long grass alongside the drive. Disabled parking (only) at house.* **Sat 20, Sun 21 Apr (2-5). Every Sat and Sun 1 June to 16 June (2-5). Sat 19, Sun 20 Oct (2-5). Adm £6, chd free. Home-made teas. Visits also by arrangement 15 Apr to 31 Oct for groups of 10 to 25.** Jenny will always accompany groups around the garden.
5 acre plantsman's garden approached across a little ford. Many interesting and unusual trees and shrubs. Visitors can try their hand at identifying plants with the very comprehensive and amusing plant list. Plenty of space to eat your own picnic. Walled vegetable and fruit garden, lake, ponds, bog plantings and sweeping lawns. Horses, Dexter cattle and Jacob sheep. A tranquil space to relax in. Gently sloping gravel paths give wheelchair access to the walled garden, lawns, borders and terrace, where teas are served.

68 NEW ROSE ASH HOUSE

Rose Ash, South Molton, EX36 4RB. Caro & Murray Hammick. *5m S of South Molton. Centre of Rose Ash, head W from thatched cottage (signed to Romansleigh) follow red arrow signs. After 150 yards park in field on L. Follow signs to garden. Parking might change if VERY wet.* **Sat 10, Sun 11 Aug (11-4.30). Adm £5, chd free. Cream teas, soft drinks, cakes etc. will be available.**
Informal garden around old house, next to the village green & church, with views to Dartmoor & Exmoor. Fun mixed-borders, rose-arbour, shrubs, interesting trees, uncut grassland & vegetable garden. The local church will be specially decorated for the weekend. Martyn Rix, plant-hunter extraordinaire, will be on-hand to identify any plants

you bring. Melinda Hilliard, a teacher of garden-design, can assist with garden planning. We plan to have an exhibition of landscape oils of Exmoor and North Devon countryside. 10% of proceeds of any sales will go to NGS. Reasonable wheelchair access to the whole garden - there are few steep slopes or steps.

GROUP OPENING

69 NEW ROSEBARN GARDENS

Exeter, EX4 6DY. *Situated in the north of the City off Pennsylvania Rd & Rosebarn Lane nr the University. Rosebarn Ave can be reached on the 'P' bus from the City Centre.* **Sat 25, Sun 26 May (1-5). Combined adm £5, chd free. Home-made teas.**

NEW 7 ROSEBARN AVENUE
Steve & Sue Bloomfield.

NEW 16 ROSEBARN AVENUE
Chris & Jane Read.

NEW 25 ROSEBARN AVENUE
Jenny & Mike Phillips.

NEW 62 ROSEBARN LANE
Clive & Nim Dunkley.

NEW 73 ROSEBARN LANE
Gerry & Lizzy Sones.

Featuring five gardens on a short walking circuit. No. 7 Rosebarn Ave is a traditional 1950's garden with flower borders, pond, wild area and a recently redesigned and planted front garden. No.16 Rosebarn Ave was redesigned in 2022. This landscaped garden features a kitchen garden, pond, summerhouse, herbaceous beds and native trees. No.25 Rosebarn Ave is a typical townhouse garden featuring perennial borders, plant house, potting shed, veg plot and mature apple trees. No.73 Rosebarn Lane, has an interesting landscaped front garden and a tranquil mature back garden divided into 'rooms', a large pond and many specimen trees. No. 62 Rosebarn Lane, has an attractive front garden and small back garden created over the last 10 yrs featuring many shrubs, perennial plants, small pond and fruit trees. Limited wheelchair access in two of the gardens.

70 NEW RUDD COTTAGE
Trentishoe, Parracombe,
Barnstaple, EX31 4PL.
Sally Oxenham & Jonathan
Kelway, 01598 763366,
sal.skipper2@gmail.com. *Valley
2m W of Hunters Inn, between
Combe Martin & Lynmouth. DONT
USE SAT NAV! Road from Rhydda
Bank Cross, 1m W of Hunters Inn,
marked Unsuitable for Motors 1
Mile Ahead. Drive 1m to end.* **Visits
by arrangement Apr to Sept for
groups of up to 15. Adm £5, chd
free. Home-made teas.**
In a peaceful Exmoor valley an informal
and diverse garden blended into
the surrounding rural and woodland
landscape. 1 acre garden and 8
further acres of fields, ponds and
streams to explore, and picnic. Spring
flowers are followed by a succession
of flowering trees and shrubs, mature
rhododendrons, *Cornus kousa* and
perennial plants. There are 30+ shrub
roses plus many others.

71 SAMLINGSTEAD
Near Roadway Corner,
Woolacombe, EX34 7HL. Roland
& Marion Grzybek, 01271 870886,
roland135@msn.com. *1m
outside Woolacombe. Stay on
A361 all the way to Woolacombe.
Passing through town head up
Chalacombe Hill, L at T-junction,
garden 150metres on L.* **Sat 16
Mar, Sat 20 July (10.30-3.30).
Adm £5, chd free. Cream teas
in 'The Swallows' a purpose
built out-building. Hot sausage
rolls (meat & vegetarian), cakes,
tea, coffee & soft drinks will
also be available. Visits also by
arrangement 4 Mar to 5 Oct.**
Garden is within 2 mins of N Devon
coastline and Woolacombe AONB. 6
distinct areas; cottage garden at front,
patio garden to one side, swallows
garden at rear, meadow garden, orchard
and field (500m walk with newly planted
hedgerow). Slightly sloping ground so
whilst wheelchair access is available to
most parts of garden certain areas may
require assistance.

72 SANDRIDGE PARK
Stoke Gabriel, Totnes, TQ9 6RL.
Mark & Rosemary Yallop. *Stoke
Gabriel is 4½m from Totnes on
the A385 via Aish. Sandridge Park
is 1½m from Stoke Gabriel on
Waddeton Rd.* **Sat 8, Sun 9 June**
**(11-5). Adm £6, chd free. Home-
made teas.**
High above the River Dart the
Sandridge Park Estate has a Nash
villa of 1805 at its heart. Close to the
house are formal gardens and ponds,
a newly-built walled kitchen garden
and orchard, and lawns overlooking
the river. There is an extensive
collection of roses and specimen
trees, a fern garden and woodland
walks along the banks of the Dart.
Gravel paths around the house and
some steps in places. Woodland
walks not suitable for wheelchairs.

73 SHERWOOD
Newton St Cyres, Exeter, EX5 5BT.
Nicola Chambers, 07702 895435,
nikkinew2012@yahoo.com,
www.facebook.com/
SherwoodGardensDevon/. *2m
SE of Crediton. Off A377 Exeter to
Barnstaple rd, ¾m Crediton side of
Newton St Cyres, signed Sherwood,
entrance to drive in 1¾m. Do not
follow SatNav once on lane, don't
fork R, just drive straight & keep
going.* **Sun 14 Apr, Sun 26 May,
Sun 23 June, Sun 13 Oct (1-5).
Adm £7.50, chd £3. Pre-booking
essential, please visit www.ngs.
org.uk for information & booking.
Cream teas. Visits also by
arrangement 1 Jan to 30 Dec.**
23 acres, 2 steep wooded valleys.
Wild flowers, spring bulbs, especially
daffodils; extensive collections of
magnolias, camellias, rhododendrons,
azaleas, berberis, heathers, maples,
cotoneasters, buddleias, hydrangeas,
cornus and epimedium. Collections
of magnolias, Knaphill azaleas and
berberis. Regret no dogs. Suitable
footwear required due to areas of
steep terrain.

74 SHUTELAKE
Butterleigh, Cullompton,
EX15 1PG. Jill & Nigel Hall,
01884 38812, jill22hall@gmail.com.
*3m W of Cullompton; 3m S of
Tiverton. Follow signs for Silverton
from Butterleigh village. Take L fork
100yds after entrance to Pound
Farm. Car park sign on L after
150yds. If visiting by arrangement
its a different postcode (EX15
1PR).* **Sat 1, Sun 2 June (11-
4.30). Adm £6.50, chd free. Light
refreshments in the studio barn
if inclement. Snack lunches &
cakes inc GF/Veg. Visits also by
arrangement 30 Apr to 28 Sept for**
groups of 10 to 20.
Shutelake is a working farm. The
garden melds subtly with surrounding
landscape, in the way its terraces
complement the tumbling Devon
countryside. Formal close to the
house, with a Mediterranean feel.
Terraced borders full of warm
perennials in summer. Beyond, a
natural pond teeming with wildlife
feeds the Burn stream. Woodland
paths and sculptures.

75 NEW SIDBURY MILL
Burnt Oak, Sidbury, Sidmouth,
EX10 0RE. Helen Munday. *On
the A375 at the southern end of
Sidbury village. From Honiton
take A375 towards Sidmouth. In
Sidbury pass the church on the L
& continue for ½m. Sidbury Mill
on L. From Sidmouth take A375
towards Honiton. Sidbury Mill brown
signs on R.* **Fri 21, Sun 23 June
(11-4.30). Adm £5, chd free. Light
refreshments. Tea, coffee, cold
drinks & sweet treats. Seating
outside as well as under cover.**
The gardens and grounds of Sidbury
Mill extend to 6 acres. As well as
diversity of plants and trees, it's a
haven for wildlife. The gardens range
from a perennial, rose and shrub
garden, a greenhouse and vegetable
patch, to mature woodland through
which the River Sid flows. A 'woodland
walk' encompasses many elements of
the gardens through which the visitor
will appreciate the plants and wildlife.
Sidbury Mill is a working water mill,
milling wheat grown in our nearby
field. The Strong Wholemeal Flour,
particularly suitable for bread making,
is available in a number of local outlets.
Aspects of the mill can be seen while
viewing the gardens. The garden areas
with the floral borders, greenhouse
and vegetable gardens are accessible.
The woodland walk is mainly flat with
grass paths.

GROUP OPENING

76 SIDMOUTH GARDENS
26 Coulsdon Road, Sidmouth,
EX10 9JP. Lynette Talbot. *Byes
Reach: From Exeter on A3052 turn
R at lights, Sidford Rd A375. ½m
turn L into Coulsdon Rd. Weston
House: A3052, at Bowd Inn turn
onto A3176 After 1.7m R Broadway
(NOT Bickwell Lane) 3rd L Bickwell
Valley. Sharp R onto Boughmore Rd.*

Sat 10, Sun 11 Aug (1.30-5.30).
Combined adm £6, chd free.
Home-made teas. Gluten free,
lactose free cakes available.

BYES REACH
26 Coulsdon Road, Sidmouth,
EX10 9JP. Lynette Talbot &
Peter Endersby, 07767 773374,
latalbot01@gmail.com.
Visits also by arrangement 22
Apr to 31 Aug for groups of 10 to
22. (excluding 10 & 11 Aug).

NEW WESTON HOUSE
Boughmore Road, Sidmouth,
EX10 8SJ. Anna & Peter
Duncan, 07753 818454,
duncannab@gmail.com.
Visits also by arrangement 20
Feb to 30 Sept for groups of 6 to
20. (excluding 10 & 11 Aug).

On the Jurassic Coast World Heritage
Site, Sidmouth has fine beaches,
beautiful gardens and coastal views.
2 contrasting gardens, $\frac{1}{4}$ acre and 1
acre, 1mile apart. Byes Reach: Potager
style vegetable garden, colour-themed
herbaceous borders, rill, ferns, rockery,
hostas. Spring colour of fruit blossom,
spring bulbs - tulips, erythroniums
and alliums. 20m arched walkway.
Seating in niches each with views of
garden. Front hot border. Wheelchair
access. Weston House: A glorious 1
acre east facing hillside garden with
views over the valley, towards the sea.
Developed around beautiful specimen
trees and shrubs, the garden has
been planted to the maximum with
herbaceous perennials and grasses.
Colour, perfume and helping wildlife are
key with areas for quiet contemplation,
The aim is to offer refuge to people and
wildlife and have interest year-round.
The garden is blessed with few frosts,
so a wonderful gardening environment
for its special plants. Regret no
wheelchair access or dogs.

77 SOUTH WOOD FARM
Cotleigh, Honiton, EX14 9HU.
Professor Clive Potter. *3m NE of
Honiton. From Honiton head N on
A30, take 1st R past Otter Valley
Field Kitchen layby. Follow for 1m.
Go straight over Xrds and take first
L. Entrance after 1m on R.* Sat 20,
Sun 21 Apr, Sat 14, Sun 15 Sept
(2-5). Adm £6, chd free. Home-
made teas.
Designed by renowned Arne
Maynard around C17 thatched
farmhouse, country garden

exemplifying how contemporary
design can be integrated into a
traditional setting. Herbaceous
borders, roses, yew topiary, knot
garden, wildflower meadows,
orchards, lean-to greenhouses and a
mouthwatering kitchen garden create
an unforgettable sense of place. Rare
opportunity to visit spring garden in
all its glory with 5000 bulbs inc 2500
tulips and hundreds of camassias in
flower meadow. Gravel pathways,
cobbles and steps.

78 SOUTHCOMBE BARN
Widecombe-in-the-Moor,
Newton Abbot, TQ13 7TU.
Tom Dixon & Vashti Cassinelli,
info@southcombebarn.com,
www.southcombebarn.com. *6m W
of Bovey Tracey. B3387 from Bovey
Tracey after village church take rd
SW for 400yds then sharp R signed
Southcombe, after 200yds pass C17
farmhouse & park on L.* Thur 6, Fri
7, Sat 8, Sun 9, Thur 13, Fri 14,
Sat 15, Sun 16 June (10-4). Adm
£5, chd free. Home-made teas.
Southcombe Barn gardens comprises
5 acres of vibrant wildflower meadows
and flowering trees with mown grass
paths running alongside a gently
babbling stream. There is a new
apothecary garden on the sheltered
hillside with medicinal, dye, culinary,
tea plants and herbs and now buzzing
with new wildlife. Fresh herbal brews,
teas and cakes will be served. Art
exhibition will be open in the gallery.

79 SPITCHWICK MANOR
Poundsgate, Newton Abbot,
TQ13 7PB. Mr & Mrs P Simpson.
*4m NW of Ashburton. Princetown rd
from Ashburton through Poundsgate,
1st R at Lodge. From Princetown
L at Poundsgate sign. Past Lodge.
Park after 300yds at Xrds.* Sat 11,
Sun 12 May, Sat 8, Sun 9 June
(11-4.30). Adm £6, chd free.
Cream teas.
$6\frac{1}{2}$ acre garden with extensive
beautiful views. Mature garden
undergoing refreshment. A variety of
different areas; lower ancient walled
garden with glasshouses, formal rose
garden with fountain, camellia walk
with small leat and secret garden
with Lady Ashburton's plunge pool
built 1773. 2.6 acre vegetable garden
sheltered by high granite walls
housing 9 allotments and lily pond.
Mostly wheelchair access.

80 SPRING LODGE
Kenton, Exeter, EX6 8EY. David &
Ann Blandford. *Between Lyson &
Oxton. Head for Lyson then Oxton.*
Sat 11 May, Fri 23 Aug (10-4).
Adm £5, chd £1. Pre-booking
essential, please visit www.ngs.
org.uk for information & booking.
Light refreshments. Teas, coffee,
soft drinks, cakes & biscuits.
Originally part of the Georgian
pleasure gardens to Oxton House,
the garden at Spring Lodge boasts
a hermit's cave, dramatic cliffs and a
stream which runs under the house.
Built in the quarry of the big house
this $\frac{1}{2}$ acre garden is on many levels,
with picturesque vistas and lush
planting. Pre booking essential due to
restricted parking.

81 SPRINGFIELD HOUSE
Seaton Road, Colyford,
EX24 6QW. Wendy Pountney,
01297 552481. *Starting on A3052
coast rd, at Colyford PO take
Seaton Rd. House 500m on L.
Ample parking in field.* Sat 6 July
(10.30-4.30). Adm £5, chd free.
Home-made teas. Visits also by
arrangement 15 Mar to 1 Oct for
groups of 10 to 30.
1 acre garden with mainly new
planting. Numerous beds, majority
of plants from cuttings and seed
keeping cost to minimum, full of
colour spring to autumn. Vegetable
garden, fruit cage and orchard with
ducks and chickens. Large formal
pond. Wonderful views over River
Axe and path to bird sanctuary, which
is well worth a visit, leads from the
garden.

---

*Our donation in
2023 has enabled
Parkinson's UK to
fund 3 new nursing
posts this year,
directly supporting
people with
Parkinson's*

82 SQUIRRELS
98 Barton Road, Torquay,
TQ2 7NS. Graham & Carol Starkie,
01803 329241, calgra@talktalk.net.
*5m S of Newton Abbot. From
Newton Abbot take A380 to Torquay.
After ASDA store on L, turn L at
T-lights up Old Woods Hill. 1st L into
Barton Rd. Bungalow 200yds on
L. Also could turn by B&Q. Parking
nearby.* **Sat 13, Sun 14 July (2-5).
Adm £5, chd free. Home-made
teas. Visits also by arrangement
in July.**
Plantsman's small town environmental
garden, landscaped with small
ponds and 7ft waterfall. Interlinked
through abutilons to Japanese,
Italianate, Spanish, tropical areas.
Specialising in fruit inc peaches, figs,
kiwi. Tender plants inc bananas,
tree fern, brugmansia, lantanas,
oleanders. Collection of fuchsia,
dahlias, abutilons, bougainvillea.
Environmental and Superclass Gold
Medal Winners. 27 hidden rainwater
storage containers. Advice on free
electric from solar panels and solar
hot water heating and fruit pruning.
Three sculptures. Many topiary birds
and balls. Huge 20ft Torbay palm.
9ft geranium. 15ft abutilons. New
Moroccan and Spanish courtyard with
tender succulents etc.

✿ 🚃 ☕

The National
Garden Scheme
donated £3,403,960
to our nursing and
health beneficiaries
from money raised
at gardens open
in 2023

---

83 STONE FARM
Alverdiscott Rd, Bideford, EX39 4PN.
Mr & Mrs Ray Auvray, 01237 421420,
rayauvray@icloud.com. *1½ m from
Bideford towards Alverdiscott. From
Bideford cross river using Old Bridge
& turn L onto Barnstaple Rd. 2nd R
onto Manteo Way & 1st L at r'about.*
**Sat 1, Sun 2 June, Sat 17, Sun 18
Aug (2-5). Adm £4.50, chd free.
Home-made teas. Visits also by
arrangement for groups of 10 to
20. A talk on organic gardening
practices alongside the visit if
interested.**
2 acre country garden with striking
herbaceous borders, dry stone
wall terracing, white garden, hot
garden and dahlia beds. Extensive
fully organic vegetable gardens
with polytunnels and ⅓ acre walled
garden, together with an orchard with
traditional apples and pears. Some
gravel paths but wheelchair access to
whole garden with some help.

♿ 🐕 ✿ ☕

---

84 ◆ STONE LANE GARDENS
Stone Farm, Stone Lane,
Chagford, TQ13 8JU. Stone Lane
Gardens Charity, 01647 231311,
admin@stonelanegardens.com,
www.stonelanegardens.com.
*Halfway between Chagford & Whiddon
Down, close to A382. 2.3m from
Chagford, 1½ m from Castle Drogo,
2½ m from A30 Whiddon Down via
Long Lane near Sandy Park Inn.* **For
NGS: Sat 5, Sat 12 Oct (10-6). Adm
£7, chd £3.50. Light refreshments
in small tea room and tea garden.
For other opening times and
information, please phone, email or
visit garden website.**
Outstanding and unusual 5 acre
arboretum and water garden on edge
of Dartmoor National Park. Beautiful
National Collection of Betula species
with lovely colourful peeling bark,
from dark brown, reds, orange, pink
and white. Interesting underplanting.
Meadow walks and lovely views.
Summer sculpture exhibition situated
in the garden. Tripadvisor award
winner. Near to NT Castle Drogo and
garden. RHS Partner Garden. Partial
wheelchair access to the gardens.

♿ 🐕 ✿ NPC ☕))

---

85 STONELANDS HOUSE
Stonelands Bridge, Dawlish,
EX7 9BL. Mr Kerim Derhalli
(Owner) Mr Saul Walker (Head
Gardener), 07815 807832,
saulwalkerstonelands@outlook.com.
Outskirts of NW Dawlish. From A380

---

*take junction for B3192 & follow signs
for Teignmouth, after 2m L at Xrds onto
Luscombe Hill, further 2m, main gate
on L.* **Visits by arrangement 1 Apr
to 28 June for groups of 10 to 20.
Weekdays only, morning (10.30am)
& afternoon (2pm) slots. Adm £7,
chd free. Home-made teas. Please
book refreshments through Head
Gardener, separate payment on
the day.**
Beautiful 12 acre pleasure garden
surrounding early C19 property
designed by John Nash. Many
mature specimen trees, shrubs and
rhododendrons, large formal lawn,
recently landscaped herbaceous
beds, vegetable garden, woodland
garden, orchard with wildflower
meadow and riverside walk.
An atmospheric and delightful
horticultural secret. Wheelchair
access to lower area of gardens.
Paths through woodland, meadow
and riverside walk may be unsuitable.

♿ 🐕 D ☕

---

86 SUTTON MEAD
Moretonhampstead, Newton
Abbot, TQ13 8PW. Edward &
Miranda Allhusen, 01647 440296,
miranda@allhusen.co.uk, www.
facebook.com/suttonmeadgarden.
*½ m N of Moretonhampstead on
A382. R at r'about.* **Fri 17, Sat 18,
Sun 19 May, Fri 6, Sat 7, Sun 8
Sept (12-5). Adm £6, chd free.
Home-made teas. Hot soup and
savoury scones. Visits also by
arrangement. Guided tour by the
owners.**
A large garden with splendid views of
Dartmoor. Remote yet only a dozen
miles from Exeter, Okehampton and
Newton Abbot. A constantly colourful
garden. May numerous varieties
of rhododendron, azalea and late
spring bulbs. September hydrangeas,
dahlias, agapanthus and much more.
Mature orchard, productive vegetable
garden, substantial tree planting,
croquet lawn. Wander through tranquil
woodland. Lawns surround a granite
lined pond with a seat at the water's
edge. Elsewhere unusual planting,
grasses, bog garden, granite walls,
rill fed pond, secluded seating and an
unusual concrete gothic greenhouse
all contribute to a garden of variety that
has been developed & constructed
over 45 yrs by the current owners.
Plants from the garden for sale & teas,
cream or otherwise, are a must. Dogs
on leads welcome. Partial access,
there is a gravel drive.

♿ 🐕 ✿ 🚃 ☕))

GROUP OPENING

87 TEIGNMOUTH GARDENS

Lower Coombe Cottage, Coombe Lane, Teignmouth, TQ14 9EX. Tracy & Tim Armstrong. *½ m from Teignmouth town centre. 5m E of Newton Abbot. 11m S of Exeter. Purchase ticket for all gardens at 1st garden visited, a map will be provided showing location of gardens & parking.* **Sat 8, Sun 9 June (1-5). Combined adm £6. Home-made teas at Lower Coombe Cottage.**

21 GORWAY
Mrs Christine Richman.

26 HAZELDOWN ROAD
Mrs Ann Sadler.

LOWER COOMBE COTTAGE
Tim & Tracy Armstrong.

THE ORANGERY
Teignmouth Town Council.

Four gardens, including the beautifully restored Orangery, are opening in the picturesque coastal town of Teignmouth. A wide range of garden styles and sizes can be explored this year from very small but inspiring manicured gardens to large wildlife havens. Features include courtyards, greenhouses, pollinator friendly planting, exotic plants, streams and ponds, fruit and vegetable beds and some stunning sea views. Tickets are valid for both days. Partial wheelchair access at some gardens.

♿ ✺ ⛳))

88 TORVIEW

44 Highweek Village, Newton Abbot, TQ12 1QQ. Ms Penny Hammond, penny.hammond2@ btinternet.com. *On N of Newton Abbot accessed via A38. From Plymouth: A38 to Goodstone, A383 past Hele Park & L onto Mile End Rd. From Exeter: A38 to Drumbridges then A382 past Forches Cross & take next R. Please park in nearby streets.* **Sat 25, Sun 26, Mon 27 May (12-5). Adm £5, chd free. Home-made teas. Visits also by arrangement 1 Apr to 25 Oct for groups of 10 to 25. Refreshments on request.**
Owned by two semi-retired horticulturists: Mediterranean formal front garden with wisteria clad Georgian house and small alpine

house. Rear courtyard with tree ferns, pots/troughs, lean-to 7m conservatory with tender plants and climbers. Steps to 30x20m walled garden - flowers, vegetables and trained fruit. Shade tunnel of woodland plants. Many rare and unusual plants.

✺ ⛳))

89 UPPER GORWELL HOUSE

Goodleigh Rd, Barnstaple, EX32 7JP. Dr J A Marston, www. gorwellhousegarden.co.uk. *¾ m E of Barnstaple centre on Bratton Fleming rd. Drive entrance between 2 lodges on L coming uphill (Bear St) approx ¾ m from Barnstaple centre. Take R fork at end of long drive. New garden entrance to R of house up steep slope.* **Sun 24 Mar, Sun 28 Apr, Sun 19 May, Sun 23 June, Sun 28 July, Sun 15 Sept (2-6). Adm £6, chd free. Cream teas. Visitors are welcome to bring their own picnics.**
Created mostly since 1979, this 4 acre garden overlooking the Taw estuary has a benign microclimate which allows many rare and tender plants to grow and thrive, both in the open and in the walled garden. Several strategically placed follies complement the enclosures and vistas within the garden. Mostly wheelchair access but some very steep slopes at first to get into garden.

♿ 🐔 ✺ ⛳ 🍽))

90 THE WALLED GARDEN

Nelson Coach House, Staverton, Totnes, TQ9 6PA. Chris & Carmen Timpson, www.instagram.com/ thewalled.garden. *8mins from Totnes. From Totnes/Ashburton A384 direction 1st property on R after the Staverton village sign. Parking around village or at pub if you are having lunch there.* **Sun 7 July (11-5). Adm £5, chd free.**
A 1 acre historic walled garden and adjacent orchard undergoing re-imagination since 2018. Productive kitchen garden with peaches and nectarines thriving on the hot wall, dry garden with mature olive trees and drought resistant planting, water rill and paradise pond, orchard and small scale wildflower meadow. Lunch/ refreshments at Sea Trout pub. Top of garden not accessible but dry garden, kitchen garden and orchard are via gravel paths with some slopes.

♿ ✺))

GROUP OPENING

91 WEST CLYST BARNYARD GARDENS

Westclyst, Exeter, EX1 3TR. *From Pinhoe take B3181 towards Broadclyst. At Westclyst T-lights continue straight past speed camera 1st R onto Private Road over M5 bridge, R into West Clyst Barnyard.* **Sat 8, Sun 9 June (1-5). Combined adm £5, chd free. Home-made teas.**

6 WEST CLYST BARNYARD
Alan & Toni Coulson.

7 WEST CLYST BARNYARD
Malcolm & Ethel Hillier.

These gardens have been planted in farmland around a converted barnyard of a medieval farm. There are 2 gardens with a wildflower meadow, wildlife ponds, bog garden, David Austin roses, magnolias and many trees and shrubs. Cars may be driven to the gate of No 7 for disabled access to the gardens but then please park in the car park.

♿ 🐔 ✺ ⛳ 🍽))

92 WHITSTONE FARM

Whitstone Lane, Bovey Tracey, TQ13 9NA. Katie & Alan Bunn, 01626 832258, klbbovey@gmail.com. *½ m N of Bovey Tracey. From A382 turn L opp golf club, after ⅓ m L at swinging sign 'Private road leading to Whitstone'. Follow NGS signs.* **Sun 21, Sun 28 Apr, Sun 28 July (2-5). Adm £6, chd free. Pre-booking essential, please visit www.ngs.org.uk for information & booking. Tea & home-made cakes, gluten free option. Visits also by arrangement 17 Feb to 30 Sept for groups of up to 25. Donation to Plant Heritage.**
Nearly 4 acres of steep hillside garden with stunning views of Haytor and Dartmoor. Snowdrops start in January followed by bluebells throughout the garden. Arboretum planted 45 yrs ago, over 200 trees from all over the world inc magnolias, camellias, acers, alders, betula, davidias and sorbus. Always colour in the garden and wonderful tree bark. Major plantings of rhododendrons and cornus. Late flowering eucryphia (National Collection) and hydrangeas. Display of architectural and metal sculptures and ornaments. Partial access to lower terraces for wheelchair users.

♿ NPC 🛌 ⛳

DORSET

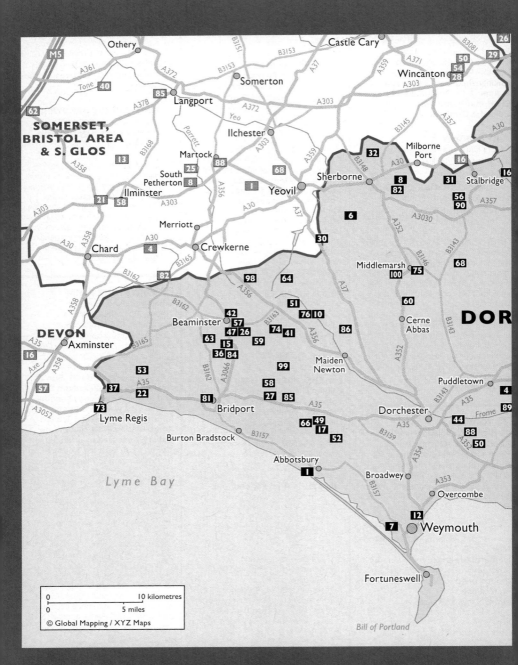

Map labels:

Othery · Castle Cary · M5 · A361 · Tone · Somerton · Wincanton · B3081 · 26 · 29 · 50 · 54 · 28 · A371 · A359 · A303 · A37 · B3153 · B3151 · Langport · 85 · A378 · A372 · Yeo · A303 · 62 · B3145 · A357 · A30 · 40

SOMERSET, BRISTOL AREA & S. GLOS · 13 · B3168 · Martock · 88 · Ilchester · A3591 · Milborne Port · 32 · B3148 · A30 · 16 · 16 · South Petherton · 25 · 8 · A356 · 68 · Sherborne · 8 · 82 · 31 · Stalbridge · Ilminster · 21 · 58 · A303 · 1 · Yeovil · 6 · 56 · 90 · A357 · A358 · Merriott · A30 · A37 · A3030 · A352 · B3143 · 68 · Chard · A30 · 4 · Crewkerne · 30 · Middlemarsh · 100 · 75 · B3146 · A358 · B3162 · 82 · B3165 · 98 · 64 · 60 · A3052 · B3162 · A356 · 51 · Cerne Abbas · DOR · 76 · 10 · DEVON · Beaminster · 42 · 57 · B3163 · 74 · 41 · 86 · A352 · A352 · B3143 · Axminster · 47 · 26 · 59 · A356 · 16 · 63 · 15 · 36 · 84 · 99 · Puddletown · 4 · Axe · A358 · 53 · B3162 · A3066 · Maiden Newton · B3143 · A35 · 89 · 57 · 37 · A35 · 58 · Dorchester · 44 · Frome · 73 · 22 · 81 · Bridport · 27 · 85 · A35 · 88 · 50 · Lyme Regis · Burton Bradstock · B3157 · 66 · 49 · 17 · 52 · B3159 · A354 · A35 · **Lyme Bay** · Abbotsbury · 1 · Broadwey · A353 · B3157 · Overcombe · 12 · Fortuneswell · 7 · Weymouth

Scale:
0 — 10 kilometres
0 — 5 miles
© Global Mapping / XYZ Maps

Bill of Portland

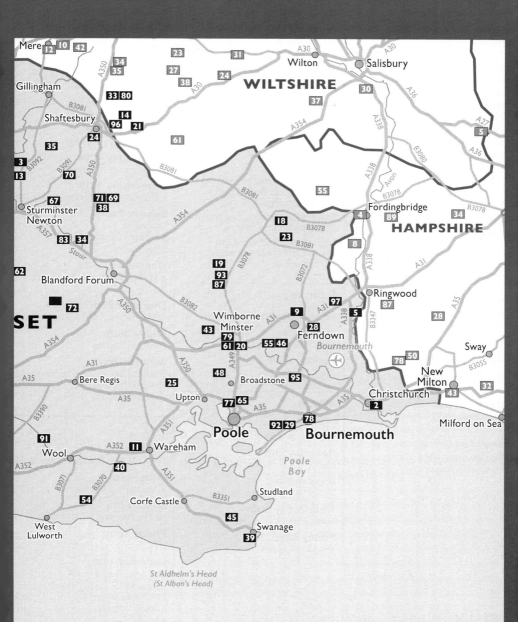

VOLUNTEERS

County Organiser & Social Media
Alison Wright 01935 83652
alison.wright@ngs.org.uk

County Treasurer
Richard Smedley 01202 528286
richard@carter-coley.co.uk

Publicity
Cathy Dalton 07712 139766
cathy.dalton@ngs.org.uk

Booklet Editor
Felicity Perkin 01297 480930
felicity.perkin@ngs.org.uk

Photographers
Jenny Hare 07583 757958
jennyhare@btconnect.com

Christopher Middleton
07771 596458
christophermiddleton@mac.com

Assistant County Organisers

Central East
Tony Leonard 07711 643445
tony.leonard@ngs.org.uk

Joanna Mains 01747 839831
mainsmanor@tiscali.co.uk

North East
Jules Attlee 07837 289964
julesattlee@icloud.com

South East
Mary Angus 01202 872789
mary@gladestock.co.uk

Phil Broomfield 07810 646123
phil.broomfield@ngs.org.uk

North West Central
Suzie Baker 07786 695150
suzie.baker@ngs.org.uk

South East Central
Pip Davidson 07765 404248
pip.davidson@ngs.org.uk

🅕 @National Gardens Scheme Dorset

🅞 @ngsdorset

South West
Christine Corson 01308 863923
christine.corson@ngs.org.uk

Trish Neale 01308 863790
trish.neale@ngs.org.uk

Felicity Perkin (see left)

West Central
Alison Wright (as above)

South Central
Emily Cave 01308 482266
emily.cave@ngs.org.uk

OPENING DATES

All entries subject to change.
For latest information check
www.ngs.org.uk
Extended openings are shown
at the beginning of the month.
Map locator numbers are
shown to the right of each
garden name.

27A Forest Road 29
Knowle Cottage 47
Wincombe Park 96

Monday 13th
24 Carlton Road North 12

Wednesday 15th
Oakdale Library Gardens 65
Wincombe Park 96

Friday 17th
NEW 20 Wicket Road 95

Saturday 18th
NEW Folly Farm Cottage 27
18 Ford Close 28
22 Lancaster Drive 48
Myrtle Cottage 62
NEW The Potting Shed 75
NEW 20 Wicket Road 95

Sunday 19th
NEW Folly Farm Cottage 27
18 Ford Close 28
22 Lancaster Drive 48
Manor Farm, Hampreston 55
Myrtle Cottage 62
The Secret Garden at Serles
House 79
NEW 20 Wicket Road 95

Thursday 23rd
◆ Mapperton House, Gardens &
Wildlands 59

Friday 24th
NEW Pipsford Farm 74

Saturday 25th
18 Ford Close 28
Knitson Old Farmhouse 45
Little Benville House 51

Sunday 26th
Annalal's Gallery 2
◆ Careys Secret Garden 11
18 Ford Close 28
Knitson Old Farmhouse 45
Little Benville House 51
The Manor House, Beaminster 57
The Old Vicarage 70

Monday 27th
Knitson Old Farmhouse 45
The Manor House, Beaminster 57

Wednesday 29th
Deans Court 20

Friday 31st
Mappercombe Manor 58

June

Saturday 1st
Edwardstowe 24
NEW Folly Farm Cottage 27

Sunday 2nd
Edwardstowe 24
NEW Folly Farm Cottage 27
Frankham Farm 30
Mappercombe Manor 58
The Old Rectory, Manston 67
The Old Rectory, Pulham 68
NEW Sheepwash Barn 81

Wednesday 5th
The Old Rectory, Manston 67

Thursday 6th
The Old Rectory, Pulham 68

Saturday 8th
Philipston House 72

Sunday 9th
Hanford School 34
The Old School House 69
Penmead Farm 71
Rampisham Gardens 76
Shillingstone Gardens 83
Utopia 89
Yew Tree House 100

Monday 10th
Oakdale Library Gardens 65

Tuesday 11th
◆ Holme for Gardens 40

Thursday 13th
Farrs 26
The Old School House 69
Penmead Farm 71

Saturday 15th
27A Forest Road 29
The Hollow, Blandford Forum 38
Hooke Farm 41
The Manor House, Beaminster 57

Sunday 16th
22 Avon Avenue 5
27A Forest Road 29
The Hollow, Blandford Forum 38
Hooke Farm 41
The Manor House, Beaminster 57
The Secret Garden at Serles House 79

Tuesday 18th
◆ Littlebredy Walled Gardens 52

Wednesday 19th
The Hollow, Blandford Forum 38

Friday 21st
◆ Athelhampton House Gardens 4

Sunday 23rd
Annalal's Gallery 2
The Chantry 15
Hingsdon 36
Semley Grange 80
Western Gardens 92
Wyke Farm 98

Tuesday 25th
◆ Littlebredy Walled Gardens 52

Wednesday 26th
Deans Court 20

Thursday 27th
NEW Wytherston Farm 99

Sunday 30th
Bembury Farm 6
NEW Corner Cottage 17
Langebride House 49
Slape Manor 84

July

Every Wednesday
The Hollow, Swanage 39

Wednesday 3rd
Bembury Farm 6
Horn Park 42

Friday 5th
◆ Museum of East Dorset 61
Stafford House 88

Saturday 6th
◆ Cranborne Manor Garden 18

Sunday 7th
The Old Rectory, Litton Cheney 66

Wednesday 10th
Lulworth Castle House 54

Sunday 14th
Broomhill 10
◆ Hogchester Farm 37
Manor Farm, Hampreston 55

Saturday 20th
Hilltop 35

Sunday 21st
Hilltop 35

Thursday 25th
Farrs 26

Saturday 27th
Hilltop 35

Sunday 28th
Annalal's Gallery 2
22 Avon Avenue 5
Black Shed 8
Hilltop 35

Our 2023 donation to the Queen's Nursing Institute now helps support over 2,500 Queen's Nurses working in the community in England, Wales, Northern Ireland, the Channel Islands and the Isle of Man

THE GARDENS

◻ ◆ ABBOTSBURY SUBTROPICAL GARDENS

Abbotsbury, Weymouth, DT3 4LA. Ilchester Estates, 01305 871387, info@abbotsbury-tourism.co.uk, www.abbotsburygardens.co.uk. *8m W of Weymouth. From B3157 Weymouth-Bridport, 200yds W of Abbotsbury village.* **For opening times and information, please phone, email or visit garden website.**
30 acres, started in 1760 and considerably extended in C19. Much recent replanting. The maritime microclimate enables this Mediterranean and southern hemisphere garden to grow rare and tender plants. National Collection of Hoherias (flowering Aug in NZ garden). Woodland valley with ponds, stream and hillside walk to view the Jurassic Coast. Open all year except for Christmas week. Partial wheelchair access, some very steep paths and rolled gravel but we have a selected wheelchair route with sections of tarmac hard surface.

◻ ANNALAL'S GALLERY

25 Millhams Street, Christchurch, BH23 1DN. Anna & Lal Sims, www.annasims.co.uk. *Town centre. Park in Saxon Square PCP - exit to Millhams St via alley at side of church.* **Sun 26 May, Sun 23 June, Sun 28 July, Sun 25 Aug, Sun 15 Sept, Sun 24 Nov, Sun 8 Dec (2-4). Adm £3.50, chd free.**
Enchanting 180 yr old cottage, home of two Royal Academy artists. 32ft x 12½ ft garden on 3 patio levels. Pencil gate leads to colourful scented Victorian walled garden. Sculptures and paintings hide among the flowers and shrubs. Unusual studio and garden room. Mural of a life-size greyhound makes the cottage easy to find and adds a smile to people's faces.

◻ ARDHURST

Nash Lane, Marnhull, Sturminster Newton, DT10 1JZ. Mr & Mrs Ed Highnam. *3m N of Sturminster Newton. From A30 E Stour, B3092 3m to Marnhull, Crown Inn on R. Turn R down Church Hill, follow NGS yellow signs. From Sturminster Newton, 3m into Marnhull, turn L down Church Hill, follow yellow signs.* **Sat 24, Sun 25 Aug (1-5.30). Adm £7, chd free. Home-made teas. Wine.**
The garden has been 7 yrs in the making. A plantsman's garden with deep perennial borders, large netted vegetable area, water harvesting, and all work in progress. A riot of colour with salvias, grasses and hot plants in Aug/Sept. All plants for pollination and year-round interest. Tall grasses and varied fruit trees. Parking in field indicated. Parking in driveway for wheelchair access, though driveway is rough & assistance will be needed. Rest of garden laid to lawn, patio at rear for shade.

◻ ◆ ATHELHAMPTON HOUSE GARDENS

Athelhampton, Dorchester, DT2 7LG. Giles Keating, 01305 848363, hello@athelhampton.house, www.athelhampton.co.uk. *Between Poole & Dorchester just off the A35. 5m E of Dorchester well signed off A35 trunk road at Puddletown. Easily reached from A31 Ringwood, & A354 Blandford Forum.* **For NGS the first day of the new season: Wed 20 Mar, Fri 21 June, Sun 22 Sept (10-5); Sat 21 Dec (10-3.30). Adm £12.50, chd free. Coffee, lunches & afternoon tea are available daily. Adm is for garden only. Tickets to visit the house can be bought on the day. For other opening times and information, please phone, email or visit garden website.**
The award-winning gardens at Athelhampton, surround the Tudor manor house, and date from 1891. The Great Court with 12 giant yew topiary pyramids is overlooked by two terraced pavilions. This glorious Grade I architectural garden is full of vistas with spectacular planting, ponds with fountains and the River Piddle flowing past. Wheelchair map to guide you around the gardens. There are accessible toilets in the Visitor Centre. Please see our Accessibility Guide on our website.

◻ 22 AVON AVENUE

Avon Castle, Ringwood, BH24 2BH. Terry & Dawn Heaver, dawnandterry@yahoo.com. *Past Ringwood from E A31 turn L after garage, L again into Matchams Ln, Avon Castle 1m on L. A31 from W turn R into Boundary Ln, then L into Matchams Ln, Avon Ave ½ m on R.* **Sun 5 May, Sun 16 June, Sun 28 July, Sun 25 Aug (12-5). Adm £5, chd free. Tea, coffee & home-made cakes.**
Japanese themed water garden featuring granite sculptures, ponds, waterfalls, azaleas, rhododendrons, cloud topiary and a collection of goldfish and water lilies. Children must be under parental supervision due to large, deep water pond. No dogs please.

◻ BEMBURY FARM

Bembury Lane, Thornford, Sherborne, DT9 6QF. Sir John & Lady Garnier, 01935 873551, dodie.garnier32@gmail.com. *Bottom of Bembury Lane, N of Thornford village. 6m E of Yeovil, 3m W of Sherborne on Yetminster road. Follow signs in village. Parking in field.* **Sun 30 June, Wed 3 July (2-6). Adm £8, chd free. Home-made teas. Visits also by arrangement May to Sept for groups of 10 to 40.**
Created and developed since 1996 this peaceful garden has lawns and large herbaceous borders informally planted with interesting perennials around unusual trees, shrubs and roses. Large collection of clematis; also a pretty woodland walk, wildflower corner, lily pond, oak circle, yew hedges with peacock, clipped hornbeam round kitchen garden and plenty of seating to sit and reflect.

100 inpatients and their families are being supported at the newly opened Horatio's Garden Wales, thanks to the National Garden Scheme donations

7 NEW ◆ **BENNETTS WATER GARDENS**
Putton Lane, Chickerell, Weymouth, DT3 4AF. James Bennetts, 01305 785150, Info@bennettswatergardens.com, www.bennettswatergardens.com. *2m W of Weymouth Harbour on the B3157 to Bridport. Follow the brown signs for 'Water Gardens'. From the A35 at Dorchester take the A354 S to Weymouth & Portland, then take the B3157 W towards Chickerell.* **For NGS: Fri 6 Sept (10-4). Adm £10, chd £4. Light refreshments in Café Monet. Home-made lunches, cakes & cream teas. For other opening times and information, please phone, email or visit garden website.** Bennetts Water Gardens is a main visitor attraction in Dorset. Set over 8 acres the gardens hold the National Plant Collection of Water Lilies with a Claude Monet style Japanese Bridge, Tropical House, Woodland Walks and Museum. Regret no dogs. Partial wheelchair access but during periods of sustained wet weather the gardens are closed to wheelchair users. Pls contact us for further advice.

 🕭 NPC ☕))

8 **BLACK SHED**
Blackmarsh Farm, Dodds Cross, Sherborne, DT9 4JX. Paul & Helen Stickland, www.blackshed.flowers/blog. *From Sherborne, follow A30 towards Shaftesbury. Black Shed approx 1m E at Blackmarsh Farm, on L, next to The Toy Barn. Large car park shared with The Toy Barn.* **Sun 28 July, Sun 25 Aug (1-5). Adm £5, chd free.** Over 200 colourful and productive flower beds growing a sophisticated selection of cut flowers and foliage to supply florists and the public for weddings, events and occasions throughout the seasons. Traditional garden favourites, delphiniums, larkspur, foxgloves, scabious and dahlias alongside more unusual perennials, foliage plants and grasses, creating a stunning and unique display. A warm welcome and generous advice on creating your own cut flower garden is offered. Easy access from gravel car park. Wide grass pathways enabling access for wheelchairs. Gently sloping site.

 🕭 🐕 ❄ 🚗 ☕

9 **BROOK VIEW CARE HOME**
Riverside Road, West Moors, Ferndown, BH22 0LQ. Tracey Tardif, www.brookviewcare.co.uk. *Past village shops, L into Riverside Rd, Brook View Care Home is on R after 100 metres. Parking onsite or nearby roads.* **Sat 17, Sun 18 Aug (11-4.30). Adm £3.50, chd free. Home-made teas. Range of home made cakes, inc dietary options.** Our colourful and vibrant garden is spread over two main areas, one warm and sunny, the other cooler and shadier. A delightful pond area, games lawn and mixed borders, then walking past our greenhouse leads to further gardens and raised beds, in a courtyard setting. Residents will help out with the production of many of our plants, all expertly managed by our gardener.

 🕭 🐕 ❄ ☕))

10 **BROOMHILL**
Rampisham, Dorchester, DT2 0PT. David & Carol Parry, 07775 806 875, carol.parry2@btopenworld. com. *11m NW of Dorchester. From Dorchester A37 Yeovil, 9m L Evershot. From Yeovil A37 Dorchester, 7m R Evershot. Follow signs. From Crewkerne A356, 1½m after Rampisham Garage L Rampisham. Follow signs.* **Sun 21 Apr, Sun 14 July, Thur 8 Aug (2-5). Adm £5, chd free. Home-made teas. Opening with Rampisham Gardens on Sun 9 June. Visits also by arrangement 5 June to 9 Aug for groups of 8 to 45.** A former farmyard transformed into a delightful, tranquil garden set in 2 acres. Clipped box, island beds and borders planted with shrubs, roses, grasses, masses of unusual perennials and choice annuals to give vibrancy and colour into the autumn. Lawns and paths lead to a less formal area with large wildlife pond, meadow, shaded areas, bog garden, late summer border. Orchard and vegetable garden. Gravel entrance, the rest is grass, some gentle slopes.

 🕭 🐕 ❄ 🚗 ☕ ⛱ 🌳

11 ◆ **CAREYS SECRET GARDEN**
Wareham, BH20 7PG. Simon Constantine, 07927 132148, hello@ careyssecretgarden.co.uk, www. careyssecretgarden.co.uk. *We send the exact location once you have booked a ticket. The garden is within a 3m radius of Wareham, (5 min drive from the train stn). 11m*

from Poole & 19m from Dorchester. **For NGS: Sun 26 May, Sun 25 Aug (11-3). Adm £7.50, chd £2.75. Pre-booking essential, please phone 07927 132148, email hello@careyssecretgarden.co.uk or visit www.careyssecretgarden. co.uk for information & booking. Cream teas in the Secret Coffee Shop within the walled garden. For other opening times and information, please phone, email or visit garden website.** Behind a 150 yr old wall, situated just outside of Wareham, sits 3 ½ acres in the midst of transformation. Left untouched for more than 40 yrs, this garden is about to flourish again, with a focus on permaculture and rewilding. Awarded Gold in Dorset Tourism's 'Business of the Year' 2021/2022 and Silver in South West Tourism Awards 'New Business of the Year' 2021/2022. Those with mobility issues are welcome to contact us in advance and we can tailor your visit to your needs accordingly.

 🕭 ❄ ☕

12 **24 CARLTON ROAD NORTH**
Weymouth, DT4 7PY. Anne & Rob Tracey. *8m S of Dorchester. A354 from Dorchester, almost opp Rembrandt Hotel R into Carlton Rd North. From Town Centre follow esplanade towards A354 Dorchester, L into Carlton Rd North.* **Fri 10, Sat 11, Sun 12, Mon 13 May (2-5). Adm £4, chd free. Home-made teas.** Town garden near the sea. Long garden on several levels. Steps and narrow sloping paths lead to beds and borders filled with trees, shrubs and herbaceous plants inc many unusual varieties. A garden which continues to evolve and reflect an interest in texture, shape and colour. Wildlife is encouraged. Raised beds in front garden create a space for vegetable growing.

 ☕))

13 **CARRAWAY BARN**
Carraway Lane, Marnhull, Sturminster Newton, DT10 1NJ. Catherine & Mark Turner, 07905 960281, Carrawaybarn.ngs@gmail.com. *From Shaftesbury A30 & B3092. ½m after The Crown turn R into Carraway Ln. From Sturminster Newton B3092 2.8m turn L into Carraway Ln. Bear R behind 1st house, until in large courtyard.* **Visits by arrangement 3 June to 30 Aug**

for groups of 8 to 40. Mondays to Fridays inc. Adm inc home-made teas. Adm £10, chd free.

Set in 2 acres, around C19 former barn. In recent years, a natural swimming pond, waterfall, late summer borders and pergola have been created. Shady woodland walks, a white border of hydrangeas, hostas and ferns lead to the beautiful established walled garden, where deep borders are planted with roses, peonies, alliums, geraniums and topiary, encircling a water lily pond. Partial wheelchair access; gravelled courtyard and walled garden, gently sloping lawns.

♿ ☕ ⁑))

14 CASTLE RINGS
Donhead St Mary, Shaftesbury, SP7 9BZ. Michael Thomas. *2 m N of Shaftesbury. A350 Shaftesbury/ Warminster road, past Wincombe Business Park. 1st R signed Wincombe & Donhead St Mary.* Sun 25 Aug (2-5). Adm £5, chd free.

Small, long garden in two parts laid out beside an Iron Age hill fort with spectacular views. A formal area with colourful planting and pots is followed by a paved area with steps leading through to a more informal garden. Topiary, roses and clematis on tripods.

15 THE CHANTRY
Chantry Street, Netherbury, Bridport, DT6 5NB. Peter Higginson. *1m S of Beaminster, follow signs for Netherbury. Garden is in centre near church.* Sun 23 June (2-6). Combined adm with Hingsdon £8, chd free. Teas available at Hingsdon.

Set in the middle of the village and within stone walls and hedges, a 1 acre established traditional garden of lawns, trees, shrubs and colourful mixed borders on a gently sloping site, with a formal pond and some new planting.

105 Woolsbridge Road

16 NEW **CHANTRY FARM**
Phillips Hill, Marnhull, Sturminster Newton, DT10 1NU. Ivan & Sue Shenkman, 07767 455089, sueshenkman@mac.com. *Between Shaftesbury & Sherborne. From the A30 turn W at East Stour to Marnhull on the B3092. After the Crown pub turn 2nd R onto New St. After 1m at the L bend Chantry Farm is on the R.* **Sun 18 Aug (1.30-5.30). Adm £8, chd free. Home-made teas. Visits also by arrangement Apr to Sept for groups of 10 to 20.**
Chantry Farm is a new opening and offers a series of gardens surrounding the 16C Farm House and three renovated barns. Designed by Justin Spink there are colourful long borders, walled gardens, swimming pool area, cutting and vegetable gardens. Espalier fruit trees, pleached hornbeam and weeping pears divide the areas. Fields with mown paths and beautiful views. Seating and wheel chair access.

17 NEW **CORNER COTTAGE**
Long Bredy, Dorchester, DT2 9HU. Susan & Colin Dyer. *7m E of Bridport. 8m W of Dorchester. W on A35 from Dorchester, turn L approx 4m from Winterbourne Abbas. 7m E on A35 from Bridport, turn R. Follow road down and turn L at T-junction. Drive along stone wall and turn L up drive to park.* **Sun 30 June (2-5). Combined adm with Langebride House £8, chd free. Home-made teas.**
⅓ of an acre of a structured cottage-style garden inc a productive, attractive kitchen garden, small orchard and deep flower and shrub borders. Well-placed seating areas invite enjoyment of different aspects of the garden and its surroundings. Clipped box, perennials, roses and clematis feature. The aim is to have food, scent and colour on every day of the year.

18 ◆ **CRANBORNE MANOR GARDEN**
Cranborne, BH21 5PP. Viscount & Viscountess Cranborne, 01725 517289, info@cranborne.co.uk, www.cranborne.co.uk. *10m N of Wimborne on B3078. Enter garden via Cranborne Garden Centre, on L as you enter top of village.* **For NGS: Sat 6 July (9.30-5). Adm £6.50, chd £1. Light refreshments at Cranborne Garden Centre (cafe).**

For other opening times and information, please phone, email or visit garden website. Donation to other charities.
Beautiful and historic garden laid out in C17 by John Tradescant and enlarged in C20, featuring several gardens surrounded by walls and yew hedges: blue and white garden, cottage style and mount gardens, water and wild garden. Many interesting plants, with fine trees and avenues. Mostly accessible by wheelchair.

SPECIAL EVENT

19 **CRICHEL HOUSE**
Moor Crichel, Wimborne, BH21 5DT. Mr & Mrs R Chilton Jr. Head Gardener: Mark Lyons. *6m N of Wimborne. From B3078 turn to Witchampton and follow signs through village to gatehouse.* **Thur 25 Apr (1-4). Adm £30, chd free. Pre-booking essential, please visit www.ngs.org.uk for information & booking. Home-made teas.**
60 acre park, 40 acre lake and 3 acre walled garden surrounding Crichel House split into 3 distinctive parts. Mature trees inc exceptional cedars form the backdrop to the Walled Garden which was set out in 1976 and recently over the last 9 yrs. Box hedges and paths lead into herbaceous borders. Lime avenue flanked by orchards, leads to reflecting pond completed by a stone pavilion and 7 individual secret gardens. An average of 100,000 perennial spring bulbs have been plated each yr for the last 5 yrs. The annual display starts early with naturalised snowdrops then leading into daffodils, crocuses and bluebells. Varieties of daffodils inc Mount Hood, White Lion and Carlton to name but a few. A limited number of tickets have been made available for this special one-day event, kindly hosted by the head gardener, Mark Lyons. Meet at the front of the house on the main drive for an introductory talk on the gardens, followed by a guided tour accompanied by Mark and his gardening team who will be available throughout the garden. After visiting the garden, home-made teas will be served in the stable courtyard. Partial wheelchair access. Most of garden can be reached by grass pathways.

20 **DEANS COURT**
Deans Court Lane, Wimborne Minster, BH21 1EE. Sir William Hanham, 01202 849314, info@deanscourt.org, www.deanscourt.org. *Pedestrian entrance (no parking) is on Deans Ct Lane. Vehicle entrance via Poole Road (BH21 1QF).* **Wed 29 May, Wed 26 June (11-4). Adm £7, chd free. Light refreshments at our Deans Court Café on Deans Court Lane. Donation to Friends of Victoria Hospital, Wimborne.**
13 acres of peaceful, partly wild gardens in ancient monastic setting with mature specimen trees, Saxon fish pond, herb garden, orchard and apiary beside River Allen close to town centre. First Soil Association accredited garden, within C18 serpentine walls. The Permaculture system has been introduced here with chemical free produce supplying the Deans Court Café (open) nearby. For disabled access, please contact us in advance of visiting to help us understand your specific needs and work out the best plan. Follow signs within grounds for disabled parking closer to gardens. Deeper gravel on some paths. See website extended description re access.

21 **DONHEAD HALL**
Donhead St Mary, Shaftesbury, SP7 9DS. Paul & Penny Brewer. *4m E of Shaftesbury. A30 towards Shaftesbury. In Ludwell turn R opp brown sign to Tollard Royal. Follow rd for ¾m and bear R at T-junction. Donhead Hall 50 yds on L on corner of Watery Lane, cream gates.* **Sun 15 Sept (2-5). Adm £7, chd free. Home-made teas.**
Walled garden overlooking deer park. The house and garden are built into the side of a hill with uninterrupted views to Cranborne Chase. Martin Lane Fox designed the terracing and advised on the landscaping of the gardens which are on 4 different levels. Large mixed borders and specimen trees, kitchen garden with glasshouses.

22 NEW **DORSET DAHLIAS**
Befferlands Farm, Charmouth, Bridport, DT6 6RD. Anna May, 07950 566986, anna@annamayeveryday.co.uk, www.dorsetdahlias.co.uk. *Approach Berne Ln from the A35 by Charmouth. Approx ½m down*

Berne Ln, Befferlands Farm is on the L. Parking in workshops opp farmhouse. **Sun 15 Sept (1-5). Adm £5, chd free. Refreshments, squash & iced tea will be available in the Dahlia fields/ garden.**

Dorset Dahlias started 8 yrs ago at Befferlands Farm and has since overtaken the kitchen garden and a large patch in one of the farm fields. Dahlias are grown in rows and organised by colour, with up to 80 different varieties grown, and around 600 plants, that bloom from late Jul until late Oct. There are multiple colours from whites and baby pinks through to bright corals, oranges & pinks. The Dahlias grown on the farm are mainly sold wholesale to florists in Dorset, Somerset, Devon and Wiltshire for weddings, parties and other events. Dorset Dahlias also welcomes private enquiries if they have a party or wedding to discuss. Regret no dogs.

23 ◆ EDMONDSHAM HOUSE
Edmondsham, Wimborne, BH21 5RE. Mrs Julia Smith, 01725 517207, julia. edmondsham@homeuser.net. *9m NE of Wimborne. 9m W of Ringwood. Between Cranborne & Verwood. Edmondsham off B3081. Wheelchair access and disabled parking at West front door.* **For NGS: Mon 1 Apr (2-5). Every Wed 3 Apr to 24 Apr (2-5). Every Wed 2 Oct to 23 Oct (2-5). Adm £4, chd £1. Tea, coffee, cake & soft drinks 3.30 to 4.00 pm in Edmondsham House, Weds only. For other opening times and information, please phone or email. Donation to Prama Care.**

Six acres of mature gardens and grounds with trees, rare shrubs, spring bulbs and shaped hedges surrounding C16/C18 house, giving much to explore inc C12 church adjacent to garden. Large Victorian walled garden is productive and managed organically (since 1984) using 'no dig' vegetable beds. Wide herbaceous borders planted for seasonal colour. Traditional potting shed, cob wall, sunken greenhouse. Coaches by appointment only. Some grass and gravel paths.

24 EDWARDSTOWE
50-52 Bimport, Shaftesbury, SP7 8BA. Mike & Louise Madgwick. *Park in town's main car park. Walk along Bimport (B3091) 500 metres, Edwardstowe last house on L.* **Sat 1, Sun 2 June (10.30-4.30). Adm £4, chd free.**

Parts of the garden were extensively remodelled during 2018, a new greenhouse and potting shed have been added, along with changing pathways and the vegetable garden layout. Long borders have been replanted in places with trees managed letting in more light.

25 FALCONERS
89 High Street, Lytchett Matravers, Poole, BH16 6BJ. Hazel & David Dent. *6m W from Poole. Garden is past village hall at end of High St, on L. No parking at the garden, please park considerately in the village.* **Sat 11, Sun 12 May (10.30-4.30). Adm £4, chd free. Home-made teas.**

Behind the gate of 150yr old Falconers Cottage lies a ¼ acre mature garden with some interesting plants. The characterful cottage and garden have been cared for and enhanced by the current custodians. As you wander round the many aspects, inc pond, herbaceous bed, climbers and vegetable plot, you will find restful areas to sit and enjoy this garden in spring. Regrettably unsuitable for wheelchairs.

The National Garden Scheme searches the length and breadth of England, Wales, Northern Ireland and the Channel Islands for the very best private gardens

SPECIAL EVENT

26 FARRS
3, Whitcombe Rd, Beaminster, DT8 3NB. Mr & Mrs John Makepeace, www.johnmakepeacefurniture.com. *Southern edge of Beaminster. On B3163. Car parking in the Square or Yarn Barton Car Park, or side streets of Beaminster.* **Thur 13 June, Thur 25 July (2.30-5). Adm £40. Pre-booking essential, please visit www.ngs.org. uk for information & booking. Cream teas in the house or garden, weather dependent. Donation to Victoria & Albert Foundation.**

Enjoy several distinctive walled gardens, rolling lawns, sculpture and giant topiary around one of Beaminster's historic town houses. John's inspirational grass garden and Jennie's very contrasting garden with an oak fruit cage; a riot of colour. Glasshouse, straw bale studio, geese in orchard. Remarkable trees, planked and seasoning in open sided barn for future furniture commissions. A limited number of tickets have been made available for these two special afternoon openings, hosted by John and Jennie Makepeace. There will be a warm welcome from John at 2.30pm in the main rooms of the house, with a talk on his furniture design and recent commissions. Jennie will then give a guided walk around the gardens followed by a cream tea. Some gravel paths, alternative wheelchair route through orchard.

27 NEW FOLLY FARM COTTAGE
Spyway Road, Uploders, Bridport, DT6 4PH. Neil & Steph Crabb. *On Spyway Road ½m on L from Matravers House, Uploders. ½m on R from The Spyway Inn, Askerswell.* **Sat 18, Sun 19 May, Sat 1, Sun 2 June, Sat 24, Sun 25 Aug (1-5). Adm £6, chd free. Home-made teas.**

An established garden of approx 1 acre with a contemporary twist. The garden has 4 connecting rooms, a main lawn with borders, ornamental trees and rose bed, a large pond area with mature trees, grasses, golden willow & silver pear which leads on to a natural fruit orchard, tennis court, greenhouse and mixed raised bed. Far reaching views of Eggardon Hill and the surrounding fields. The majority of the garden can be enjoyed via wheelchair, there are 3 short steps at the kitchen side entrance of house.

Farrs

© Carole Drake

28 18 FORD CLOSE

Ferndown, BH22 8AA. Carolyn Best. *1m outside of Ferndown town centre toward Ringwood. Just off the A348 heading S toward Ferndown. 1st turning after the Smugglers Haunt pub but before the next r'about. The road is a dead end. Parking available along the length of Ford Close.* **Sat 18, Sun 19, Sat 25, Sun 26 May (12-4.30). Adm £4, chd free. Home-made teas.**
Ever changing gardens and planting surround the property. Smaller front garden and 60ft back garden which extends across 2 levels. The upper level is subdivided with raised beds, of perennial planting, fruit and vegetables and grapevines. The lower level is partially decked and surrounded by potted salvias and other choice plants. Plenty of seating for refreshments.

✿ ☕))

29 27A FOREST ROAD

Poole, BH13 6DQ. Paul James Allen. *Located off the Avenue between Branksome Chine & Westbourne. Turn into Tower Rd W (L from Branksome end, R from*

Westbourne end) then 1st R into Forest Rd. **Sat 11, Sun 12 May, Sat 15, Sun 16 June (10-4). Adm £4, chd free. Teas, coffee & cakes.**
This unusual plantsman's garden comprises of a courtyard style front garden and jungle themed back garden packed full with vibrant unusual plants, many rare and exotic. Over 1800 different types inc over 100 Salvias and 50 Abutilons alone! A plant lover's paradise.

✿ ☕

30 FRANKHAM FARM

Ryme Intrinseca, Sherborne, DT9 6JT. Susan Ross MBE, 07594 427365, neilandsusanross@gmail.com. *3m S of Yeovil. Just off A37 - turn next to Hamish's farm shop signed to Ryme Intrinseca, go over small bridge and up hill, drive is on L.* **Sun 24 Mar, Sun 21 Apr, Sun 2 June, Sun 13 Oct (12-5). Adm £7, chd free. Light refreshments in our newly converted barn (no steps). BBQ with our own farm produced beef, lamb & pork, vegetarian soup, home-made cakes made by village bakers.**

3½ acre garden, created since 1960 by the late Jo Earle for year-round interest. This large and lovely garden is filled with a wide variety of well grown plants, roses, unusual labelled shrubs and trees. Productive vegetable garden. Clematis and other climbers. Spring bulbs through to autumn colour, particularly oaks. Sorry, no dogs. Ramp available for the two steps to the garden. Modern WCs inc disabled.

♿ 🚗 🛏 ☕))

31 FRITH HOUSE

Stalbridge, DT10 2SD. Mr & Mrs Patrick Sclater, 01963 250809, rosalynsclater@btinternet.com. *4m E of Sherborne. Between Milborne Port & Stalbridge. From A30 1m, follow sign to Stalbridge. From Stalbridge 2m and turn W by PO.* **Visits by arrangement May & June for groups of 15+. Adm £10, chd free. Home-made teas included in admission.**

Approached down a long drive with fine views, 5 acres of garden around Edwardian house and self-contained hamlet. Range of mature trees, lakes and flower borders. House terrace edged by rose border and featuring Lutyensesque wall fountain and game larder. Well-stocked kitchen gardens. Woodland walks with masses of bluebells in spring. Garden with pretty walks set amidst working farm. Accessible gravel paths.

32 GLENHOLME HERBS

Penmore Road, Sandford Orcas, Sherborne, DT9 4SE. Maxine & Rob Kellaway, www.glenholmeherbs.co.uk. *3m N of Sherborne. Please see directions on our website & type Glenholme Herbs into Google maps to find us as the postcode will take you to the wrong location.* **Sat 10, Sun 11 Aug (10-4). Adm £4, chd free. Home-made teas.**

Paths meander through large, colourful beds inspired by Piet Oudolf. Featuring a wide selection of herbs and salvias along with grasses, verbena and echinacea. Planted with wildlife in mind and alive with pollinators. The garden also features a beautiful natural swimming pond. A mixture of grass and firm gravel paths.

33 GROVE HOUSE

Semley, Shaftesbury, SP7 9AP. Judy & Peter Williamson, 07976 391723, judy@judywilliamson.net. *N of Shaftesbury on A350 to Warminster. A350 turn to Semley. Grove House approx ½m on L just before railway bridge. From Semley village leave pub on R go under railway bridge (approx ⅓m) Grove House 2nd on R.* **Visits by arrangement 20 May to 31 July for groups of up to 30. Tea or wine by arrangement. Adm £10, chd free.**

Classic English garden divided into rooms. Yew hedges and topiary. Rose garden. Large herbaceous border. Late summer hot garden with grasses. Lawns. Mown walks through specimen trees. Several good places to eat nearby.

34 HANFORD SCHOOL

Child Okeford, Blandford Forum, DT11 8HN. Mrs Hilary Phillips. *From Blandford take A350 to Shaftesbury; 2m after Stourpaine turn L for Hanford. From Shaftesbury take A350 to Poole; after Iwerne Courtney turn R to Hanford. NGS signage from A350 & A357.* **Sun 9 June (2-4.30). Adm £5, chd free.**

Perhaps the only school in England with a working kitchen garden growing quantities of seasonal vegetables, fruit and flowers for the table. The rolling lawns host sports matches, gymnastics, dance and plays while ancient cedars look on. The stable clock chimes on the hour and the chapel presides over it all. Teas in Great Hall (think Hogwarts). What a place to go to school or visit. Several steps/ramp to main house. No wheelchair access to WC.

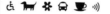

35 HILLTOP

Woodville, Stour Provost, Gillingham, SP8 5LY. Josse & Brian Emerson, www.hilltopgarden.co.uk. *7m N of Sturminster Newton, 5m W of Shaftesbury. On B3092 turn E at Stour Provost Xrds, signed Woodville. After 1¼m thatched cottage on R. On A30, 4m W of Shaftesbury, turn S opp Kings Arms. 2nd turning on R signed Woodville, 100 yds on L.* **Sat 20, Sun 21, Sat 27, Sun 28 July, Sun 11, Sun 18 Aug (2-6). Adm £4, chd free. Home-made teas.**

Summer at Hilltop is a gorgeous riot of colour and scent, the old thatched cottage barely visible amongst the flowers. Unusual annuals and perennials grow alongside the traditional and familiar, boldly combining to make a spectacular display, which attracts an abundance of wildlife. Always something new, the unique, gothic garden loo is a great success.

36 HINGSDON

Netherbury, Bridport, DT6 5NQ. Anne Peck. *Between Bridport & Beaminster. 1½m from A3066 or 1m from B3162 signed to Netherbury.* **Sun 23 June (2-6). Combined adm with The Chantry £8, chd free. Home-made teas at Hingsdon only (not at The Chantry).**

Hingsdon is a hilltop garden of about 2 acres with spectacular panoramic views. There are many unusual shrubs, mostly planted within the last 15 yrs, a mixed border of two halves (cool and hot), rose garden and a large kitchen garden. There is also a small arboretum with an idiosyncratic collection of over 90 trees. The main garden is accessible, although sloping, but the arboretum is too steep for wheelchair access. The kitchen garden has steps.

37 ◆ HOGCHESTER FARM

Axminster Road, Charmouth, Bridport, DT6 6BY. Mr Rob Powell, 07714 291846, rob@hogchester.com. *A35 Charmouth Rd, follow dual carriageway and take turning at signs for Hogchester Farm.* **For NGS: Sun 14 July (9-6). Adm £4, chd £1. Coffee shack serving drinks, cream teas & light refreshments. For other opening times and information, please phone or email.**

Hogchester Farm is a collaboration between those seeking connection with nature and themselves through conservation therapy and the arts. The 75 acre old dairy farm has been largely gifted to nature which has helped to preserve the overflowing abundance of natural life. Having worked closely with the Dorset Wildlife Trust, Hogchester Farm has been able to preserve wild meadows and wilding areas which are filled with local flora and fauna inc wild orchids, foxgloves and primroses. The farm offers something for everyone, making a great family day out. For children there is a giant trampoline in the meadow and a treasure hunt in a stream! You might bump into some of our many free ranging animals, inc rare breed soay sheep and pygmy goats. There will be a talk on the history of Hogchester wildflower meadows and meadows conservation at 2pm.

38 THE HOLLOW, BLANDFORD FORUM

Tower Hill, Iwerne Minster, Blandford Forum, DT11 8NJ. Sue Le Prevost, 01747 812173, sue.leprevost@hotmail.co.uk. *Between Blandford & Shaftesbury. Follow signs on A350 to Iwerne Minster. Turn off at Talbot Inn, continue straight to The Chalk, bear R along Watery Lane for parking in Parish Field on R. 5 min uphill walk to house.* **Sat 15, Sun 16, Wed 19 June (2-5). Adm £4, chd free. Home-made cakes & gluten-free available. Visits also by arrangement 30 Mar to 21 Oct for groups of 10 to 20.**

Hillside cottage garden built on chalk, about ⅓ acre with an interesting variety of plants in borders that line the numerous sloping pathways. Water features for wildlife and well placed seating areas to sit back and enjoy the views. Productive fruit and vegetable garden in converted paddock with raised beds and greenhouses. A high maintenance garden which is constantly evolving. Use of different methods to plant steep banks.

39 THE HOLLOW, SWANAGE

25 Newton Road, Swanage, BH19 2EA. Suzanne Nutbeem, 01929 423662, gdnsuzanne@gmail.com. *½ m S of Swanage town centre. From town follow signs to Durlston Country Park. At top of hill turn R at red postbox into Bon Accord Rd. 4th turn R into Newton Rd.* **Every Wed 3 July to 28 Aug (2-5). Adm £4, chd free. Visits also by arrangement for groups of up to 30.**

Wander in a dramatic sunken former stone quarry, a surprising garden at the top of a hill above the seaside town of Swanage. Stone terraces with many unusual shrubs and grasses form beautiful patterns of colour and foliage attracting butterflies and bees. Pieces of mediaeval London Bridge lurk in the walls. Steps have elegant handrails. WC available. Exceptionally wide range of plants inc cacti and airplants.

40 ◆ HOLME FOR GARDENS

West Holme Farm, Wareham, BH20 6AQ. Simon Goldsack, 01929 554716, simon@holmefg.co.uk, www.holmefg.co.uk. *2m SW Wareham. Easy to find on the B3070 road to Lulworth 2m out of Wareham.*

For NGS: Tue 11 June, Tue 10 Sept (10-5.30). Adm £7, chd free. Cream teas in The Orchard Café. For other opening times and information, please phone, email or visit garden website.

Extensive formal and informal gardens strongly influenced by Hidcote Manor and The Laskett. The garden is made up of distinct rooms separated by hedges and taller planting. Extensive collection of trees, shrubs, perennials and annuals sourced from across the UK. Spectacular wildflower meadows. Grass amphitheatre, Holme henge garden, lavender avenue, cutting garden, pear tunnel, hot borders, white borders, ornamental grasses, unusual trees and shrubs. Grass paths are kept in good order and soil is well drained so wheelchair access is reasonable except immediately after heavy rain.

41 HOOKE FARM

Hooke, Beaminster, DT8 3NZ. Julia Hailes MBE & Jamie Macdonald, www.juliahailes.com. *Coming from Crewkerne, Yeovil or Dorchester, turn R at church & R again after 500 yds, just before pond. From Beaminster or Bridport turn L at Hooke woods, past Hooke Court & L after pond.* **Sat 15, Sun 16 June (10.30-4.30). Adm £8, chd £4. Locally sourced lunch, cream teas & refreshments throughout the day.**

Hooke Farm's 3rd Wilding Weekend shows its transformation into a wildlife haven with bats, butterflies and bee-friendly wildflower meadows. It inc woodlands, ponds, orchard trees, standing stones and a stilted henhouse all interlinked by meandering paths. There will be talks and guided tours on both afternoons, covering different aspects of wilding and environmentally friendly gardening. This will inc butterflies, moths, reptiles, weed control, tree maintenance, grassland management and how to attract insects and birds. We are peat-free. There are areas of the garden that cannot be accessed by wheelchairs but there's still plenty to see if you can manage slopes.

42 HORN PARK

Tunnel Rd, Beaminster, DT8 3HB. Mr & Mrs David Ashcroft. *1½ m N of Beaminster. On A3066 from Beaminster, L before tunnel (see signs).* **Wed 24 Apr, Wed 3 July (2.30-4.30). Adm £5, chd free. Home-made teas.**

Large plantsman's garden with magnificent views over Dorset countryside towards the sea. Many rare and mature plants and shrubs in terrraced, herbaceous, rock and water gardens. Woodland garden and walks in bluebell woods. Good amount of spring interest with magnolia, rhododendron and bulbs which are followed by roses and herbaceous planting, wildflower meadow with 164 varieties inc orchids.

43 ◆ KINGSTON LACY

Wimborne Minster, BH21 4EA. National Trust, 01202 883402, kingstonlacy@nationaltrust. org.uk, www.nationaltrust.org. uk/kingston-lacy. *2½ m W of Wimborne Minster. On Wimborne-Blandford rd B3082.* **For opening times and information, please phone, email or visit garden website.**

35 acres of formal garden, incorporating parterre and sunk garden planted with Edwardian schemes during spring and summer. 5 acre kitchen garden and allotments. Victorian fernery containing over 35 varieties. Rose garden, mixed herbaceous borders, vast formal lawns and Japanese garden restored to Henrietta Bankes' creation of 1910. National Collection of Convallaria and *Anemone nemorosa*. Snowdrops, blossom, bluebells, autumn colour and Christmas light display. Deep gravel on some paths but lawns suitable for wheelchairs. Slope to visitor reception and South lawn. Dogs allowed in some areas of woodland.

44 ◆ KINGSTON MAURWARD GARDENS AND ANIMAL PARK

Kingston Maurward, Dorchester, DT2 8PY. Kingston Maurward College, 01305 215003, events@kmc.ac.uk, www.morekmc.com. *1m E of Dorchester off A35. Follow brown Tourist Information signs.* **For opening times and information, please phone, email or visit garden website.**

Stepping into the grounds you will be greeted with 35 impressive acres of formal gardens. During the late spring and summer months, our National Collection of penstemons and salvias display a lustrous rainbow of purples, pinks, blues and whites, leading you on through the ample hedges and

The Old Rectory, Litton Cheney

stonework balustrades. An added treat is the Elizabethan walled garden, offering a new vision of enchantment. Open early Jan to mid Dec. Hours will vary in winter depending on conditions - check garden website or call before visiting. Partial wheelchair access only, gravel paths, steps and steep slopes. Map provided at entry, highlighting the most suitable routes.

  ♿ 🚗 NPC ☕

45 KNITSON OLD FARMHOUSE
Corfe Castle, Wareham, BH20 5JB. Rachel Helfer, 01929 421681, rjehelfer@gmail.com. *Purbeck. Between Corfe Castle & Swanage. Follow the A351 3m E from Corfe Castle. Turn L signed Knitson. After 1m fork R. We are on L after ¼ m.* **Sat 30, Sun 31 Mar, Mon 1 Apr, Sat 25, Sun 26, Mon 27 May (12-5). Adm £4, chd free. Hot & cold drinks, cakes, sweet/savoury pastries, cream teas available. Visits also by arrangement Feb to Nov for groups of up to 10. Roads here are very** narrow for larger vehicles.
Mature cottage garden nestled under chalk downland. Herbaceous borders, rockeries, climbers and shrubs, evolved and designed over 60 yrs for year-round colour. Wildlife friendly, sustainable kitchen garden inc 20+ different fruits for self-sufficiency. Historical stone artefacts, ancient trees and shrubs are part of the integral design. Level lawn for tea but also uneven sloping paths. Plants are selected for drought tolerance and hardiness. 100+ shrubs, both new and some over 100 yrs old. Vegetables year-round sustain a healthy lifestyle. Points of historical interest inc an ancient side-handled quern, Roman padstones, and a C15 farmhouse. Garden is on a slope, main lawn and tea area are level but there are uneven, sloping paths.

  ♿ 🐕 ❀ ☕ 🏕))

46 ◆ KNOLL GARDENS
Hampreston, Wimborne, BH21 7ND. Mr Neil Lucas, 01202 873931, enquiries@ knollgardens.co.uk, www.knollgardens.co.uk. *2½ m W of Ferndown. Brown tourist signs from all directions, inc from A31. Car park on site.* **For NGS: Fri 20 Sept (10-5). Adm £7.95, chd £5.95. Self-service refreshment facilities. For other opening times and information, please phone, email or visit garden website.**
A unique, naturalistic and calming garden, renowned for its whispering ornamental grasses, it also surprises and delights with an abundance of show-stopping flowering perennials. A stunning backdrop of trees and shrubs add drama to this wildlife and environmentally-friendly garden. On site nursery selling quality plants, with expert advice readily available. Some slopes. Various surfaces inc gravel, paving, grass and bark.

  ♿ ❀ 🚗 NPC ☕

Abbotsbury Gardens

© Carole Drake

47 KNOWLE COTTAGE
No.1, Shorts Lane,
Beaminster, DT8 3BD. Claire
& Guy Fender, 01308 301321,
claire.fender@live.com. *Nr St
Mary's Church. Park in main square
or in main town car park, (disabled
parking on-site) & walk down Church
Lane & R onto single track Shorts
Lane. Entry is through blue gates
after 1st cottage on L.* **Sat 11, Sun
12 May (12-4). Adm £5, chd free.
Visits also by arrangement 1 Apr
to 1 July for groups of 5 to 6.**
Knowle Cottage is a large 1½ acre
garden with 35 metre long south
facing herbaceous border with year-
round colour. Formal rose garden
with circular beds interspersed with
light floral planting and framed on 3
sides with lavender borders. Small
orchard and vegetables in raised beds
in adjacent walled area, with whole
garden leading to small stream, and
bridge to pasture. Beds accessed
from level grass, slope not suitable for
wheelchairs. Limited outside seating
available.

   ﹺ 🚗 ☕ 🌲))

48 22 LANCASTER DRIVE
Broadstone, BH18 9EL. Karen
Wiltshire. *2 mins from Broadstone
village centre. From B3074
Higher Blandford Rd, take first L
onto Springdale Rd, 2nd R onto*
*Springdale Ave, then head straight
on to Lancaster Dr, the house will be
on the R. Park on Lancaster Dr.* **Sat
18, Sun 19 May (12-5). Adm £5,
chd free. Light refreshments.**
360ft natural woodland garden that
is hidden in the heart of Broadstone.
Mature oaks and a natural spring
make up a magical woodland setting
that's left for wildlife to live without
disturbance. New acers have been
planted in the woodland to add
seasonal colour. A new gravel garden
closer to the house with water
features fed from the natural spring.

❄ ☕))

49 LANGEBRIDE HOUSE
Long Bredy, DT2 9HU. *8m W of
Dorchester. S off A35, midway
between Dorchester & Bridport. Well
signed. 1st gateway on L in village.*
**Sun 30 June (2-5). Combined adm
with Corner Cottage £8, chd free.
Home-made teas.**
Lovely herbaceous borders surround
the house, inc peonies and roses in
the summer. An old walled kitchen
garden at the back, filled with fruit
trees and vegetables. A number
of magnificent trees in grounds,
underplanted with copper beech,
magnolias and hydrangeas. Partial
wheelchair access if wet weather.

 ﹺ ☕

50 LEWELL LODGE
West Knighton, Dorchester,
DT2 8RP. Rose & Charles
Joly, 01935 83652,
alison.wright@ngs.org.uk. *3m SE
of Dorchester. Turn off A35 onto
A352 towards Wareham, take West
Stafford bypass, turn R for West
Knighton at T junction. ¾ m turn R
up drive after village sign.* **Visits by
arrangement 1 Apr to 28 July for
groups of 10+.**
Elegant 2 acre classic English garden
designed by present owners over
last 25 yrs, surrounding Gothic
Revival house. Double herbaceous
borders enclosed by yew hedges
with old fashioned roses. Shrub beds
edged with box and large pyramided
hornbeam hedge. Crab apple tunnel,
box parterre and pleached hornbeam
avenue. Large walled garden, many
mature trees and woodland walk.
Garden is level but parking is on
gravel and there are gravel pathways.

 ﹺ ☕))

51 LITTLE BENVILLE HOUSE
Benville Lane, Corscombe,
Dorchester, DT2 0NN. Jo & Gavin
Bacon. *2½ m (6mins) from Evershot
village on Benville Lane. Benville
may be approached from A37, via
Evershot village. House is on L ½ m
after Benville Bridge. Alternatively
from A356, Dorchester to Crewkerne*

road, 1m down on R. **Sat 25, Sun 26 May (11-5). Adm £8, chd £4. Home-made teas.**
Contemporary garden, with landscape interventions by Harris Bugg Studio within a varied ecological ANOB and historic landscape off Benville Lane, mentioned in Thomas Hardy's Tess. Within the curtilage there are new herbaceous borders, woodland planting, walled vegetable and cutting garden, cloud pruned topiary, ha-ha, ornamental and productive trees and moat which is a listed Ancient Monument. Bring a tennis racquet and appropriate footwear to try the tennis court and enjoy the view.

52 ◆ LITTLEBREDY WALLED GARDENS

Littlebredy, DT2 9HL. The Walled Garden Workshop, 01305 898055, secretary@wgw.org.uk, www.littlebredy.com. 8m W of Dorchester. 10m E of Bridport. 1½ m S of A35. NGS days: park on village green then walk 300yds. For the less mobile (and on normal open days) use gardens car park. **For NGS: Tue 18, Tue 25 June (2-6). Adm £6, chd free. Home-made teas. For other opening times and information, please phone, email or visit garden website.**
1 acre walled garden on south facing slopes of Bride River valley. Herbaceous borders, riverside rose walk, lavender beds and potager vegetable and cut flower gardens. Partial wheelchair access, some steep grass slopes. For disabled parking please follow signs to main entrance.

53 LOWER ABBOTTS WOOTTON FARM

Whitchurch Canonicorum, Bridport, DT6 6NL. Clare Trenchard, 01297 560477, claretrenchard@hotmail.co.uk. 5m W of Bridport. Well signed from A35 at Morecombe Lake (2m) & Bottle Inn at Marshwood on B3165 (1½ m). Some disabled off-road parking. **Visits by arrangement May to Sept for groups of 10+. Late afternoon visits from 5pm preferred, but can be flexible. Light savoury snacks with a glass of wine.**
Sculptor owner reflects her creative flair in garden form, shape and colour. Open gravel garden contrasts with main garden consisting of lawns, borders

and garden rooms, making a perfect setting for sculptures. The naturally edged pond provides a tranquil moment of calm and tranquillity, but beware of being led down the garden path by the running hares!

SPECIAL EVENT

54 LULWORTH CASTLE HOUSE

Lulworth Park, East Lulworth, Wareham, BH20 5QS. James & Sara Weld. In the village of E Lulworth enter through the main entrance to Lulworth Castle and Park & follow the signs. **Wed 10 July (10.30-1). Adm £30, chd free. Pre-booking essential, please visit www.ngs.org.uk for information & booking.**
Large coastal garden next to Lulworth Castle with views to the sea. Pleasure grounds surround a walled garden filled with roses and perennials, behind which sits a working kitchen garden. In front of the house the scented walk leads to a wildflower meadow, lavender labyrinth and Islamic garden with rills and fountains. A new wild white garden has been created over the past winter. A limited number of tickets have been made available for this special one-day event, kindly hosted by the owners, James & Sara Weld. Meet at the front the house on the main drive for an introductory talk on the gardens, followed by a guided tour accompanied by Sara and her gardening team. After visiting the garden a set menu lunch will be made available at the nearby Weld Arms from 1pm (not inc in adm price). To make a booking pls visit: https://theweldarms.co.uk or telephone: 01929 400211.

&

55 MANOR FARM, HAMPRESTON

Wimborne, BH21 7LX. Guy & Anne Trehane, 01202 574223, anne.trehane@live.co.uk. 2½ m E of Wimborne, 2½ m W of Ferndown. From Canford Bottom r'about on A31, take exit B3073 Ham Lane. ½ m turn R at Hampreston Xrds. House at bottom of village. **Sat 2 Mar (10-1); Sun 3 Mar (1-4). Light refreshments. Sun 19 May, Sun 14 July, Sun 4 Aug, Sun 1 Sept (1-5). Home-made teas. Adm £5, chd free. Visits also by arrangement 16 May to 31 July for groups of 15 to 30.**

Traditional farmhouse garden designed and cared for by 3 generations of the Trehane family through over 100 yrs of farming and gardening at Hampreston. Garden is noted for its herbaceous borders and rose beds within box and yew hedges. Mature shrubbery, water and bog garden. Excellent plants as usual for sale at openings inc hellebores in March.

56 MANOR FARM, STOURTON CAUNDLE

Stourton Caundle, DT10 2JW. Mr & Mrs O S L Simon. 6m E of Sherborne, 4 m W of Sturminster Newton. From Sherborne take A3030. At Bishops Caundle, L signed Stourton Caundle. After 1½ m, L opp Trooper Inn in middle of village. **Sun 8 Sept (2-5.30). Combined adm with Wagtails £10, chd free. Tea & cake.**
C17 farmhouse and barns with walled garden in middle of village. Mature trees, shrubberies, herbaceous borders, lakes and vegetable garden. Lovingly created over last 50 yrs by current owners. Wheelchair access to lower areas of garden, steps to top areas of garden.

57 THE MANOR HOUSE, BEAMINSTER

North St, Beaminster, DT8 3DZ. Christine Wood. 200yds N of town square. Park in the square or public car park, 5 mins walk along North St from the square. Limited disabled parking on site. **Sun 26, Mon 27 May, Sat 15, Sun 16 June (11-5). Adm £7, chd free. Home-made teas in the Coach House garden.**
Set in heart of Beaminster, 16 acres of stunning parkland with mature specimen trees, lake and waterfall, The Manor House looks forward again to welcoming old and new visitors to enjoy this peaceful garden a haven for wildlife with a woodland walk, wildflower meadow and walled garden 'serendipity'. Ornamental ducks, black swans, pigmy goats, alpaca,chickens and guinea pigs. Partial wheelchair access.

58 MAPPERCOMBE MANOR
Nettlecombe, Bridport, DT6 3SS.
Arthur Crutchley. *4m NE of
Bridport. From A3066 turn E signed
W Milton & Powerstock. After 3m
leave Powerstock on your L, bear R
at Marquis of Lorne pub, entrance
drive 150yds ahead.* **Fri 31 May,
Sun 2 June (1-5). Adm £6, chd
free. Home-made teas.**
Elegant Manor House that was
originally a monks' rest house with
stew pond and dovecote. South
facing gardens on 4 levels with
ancient monastic route and sweeping
views. Approx 4 acres of gardens with
well-planted borders, inc echiums,
salvias and euphorbia. Apart from
stonework and mature trees, garden
mostly replanted in last 25 yrs. Many
old roses and a haven for bees and
butterflies. Dogs on leads. Partial
wheelchair access, gravel and stone
paths, steps. 150 yd walk from car
park, limited parking by house.

SPECIAL EVENT

59 ◆ MAPPERTON HOUSE, GARDENS & WILDLANDS
Mapperton, Beaminster,
DT8 3NR. Viscount & Viscountess
Hinchingbrooke, 01308 862645,
office@mapperton.com,
www.mapperton.com. *6m N of
Bridport. Off A356/A3066. 2m SE
of Beaminster off B3163.* **For NGS:
Thur 23 May (10-4). Adm £40. Pre-
booking essential, please visit
www.ngs.org.uk for information
& booking. Light refreshments
in the Coach House cafe (inc
in admission price). For other
opening times and information,
please phone, email or visit garden
website.**
Terraced valley gardens surrounding
Tudor/Jacobean manor house. On
upper levels, walled croquet lawn,
orangery and Italianate formal garden
with fountains, topiary and grottoes.
Below, C17 summerhouse and
fishponds.Lower garden with shrubs
and rare trees, leading to woodland
and spring gardens. Mapperton is
also home to a spectacular rewilding
project known as Mapperton
Wildlands.A limited number of
tickets have been made available
for a special 1 day rewilding tour on
23rd May. On arrival please meet
at the Coach House Café, where
you will be joined by Ben Padwick,
the ranger at Mapperton. Ben will
give an introductory talk and will be

your guide throughout your visit.
The tour will last for 2 ½ hours
and covers a distance of 2 miles.
Do wear appropriate footwear and
bring waterproofs if it is expected to
rain. Parts of the tour will take you
up steep hills and across uneven
ground, which may be challenging
for anyone less able and with mobility
difficulties. In the gardens there is
partial wheelchair access to the lawn
and upper levels.

60 ◆ MINTERNE GARDEN
Minterne House, Minterne
Magna, Dorchester, DT2 7AU.
Lord Digby, 01300 341370,
enquiries@minterne.co.uk,
www.minterne.co.uk. *2m N of
Cerne Abbas. On A352 Dorchester-
Sherborne road.* **For opening times
and information, please phone,
email or visit garden website.**
As seen on BBC Gardeners' World
and voted one of the 10 prettiest
gardens in England by The Times.
Famed for their display of historic
rhododendrons, azaleas, Japanese
cherries and magnolias in April/
May when the garden is at its peak.
Small lakes, streams and cascades
offer new vistas at each turn around
the 1m horseshoe shaped gardens
covering 23 acres. The season ends
with spectacular autumn colour.
Snowdrops in Feb. Spring bulbs,
blossom and bluebells in April. Easter
trails for children. Over 200 acers
provide spectacular autumn colour
in Sept/Oct, inc Halloween trails for
children. Fireworks at end of October.

61 ◆ MUSEUM OF EAST DORSET
23-29 High Street, Wimborne
Minster, BH21 1HR. Museum of
East Dorset, 01202 882533, info@
museumofeastdorset.co.uk, www.
museumofeastdorset.co.uk.
*Wimborne is just off A31. From W
take B3078, from E take B3073
towards town centre. From Poole
and Bournemouth enter town from
S on A341.* **For NGS: Evening
opening Fri 1 Mar, Fri 3 May, Fri
5 July (6-8.30). Adm £15, chd
free. Pre-booking essential,
please visit www.ngs.org.uk for
information & booking. Light
refreshments in The Tea Room
which opens on to the garden.
For other opening times and
information, please phone, email or**

visit garden website.
Tranquil walled garden tucked away
in the centre of Wimborne. Colourful
herbaceous borders and heritage
orchard trees line the path which
stretches 100m down to the mill
stream. This year we have 3 evening
garden lectures taking place at the
Museum from 6pm to 8.30pm.
Blackshed Flower Farm by Paul
Stickland – Fri 1st March, Deans
Court by Sir William Hanham – Fri 3rd
May, Athelhampton House Gardens
by Owen Davies & Sophy Robertson
– Fri 5th July. Please visit our website
for more details: www.ngs.org.uk.
Wheelchair access throughout the
site.

62 MYRTLE COTTAGE
Woolland, Blandford Forum,
DT11 0ES. Brian & Lynn Baker,
01258 817432, brian.baker15@
btinternet.com. *7m W of Blandford
Forum. Situated at the base of
Bulbarrow Hill, pass the church on
your L, pass the turning to Ibberton
on the R. Myrtle Cottage is on the
R after the Elwood Centre.* **Sat 18,
Sun 19 May (10-5). Adm £4, chd
free. Home-made teas. Visits also
by arrangement 1 Mar to 1 Sept.
Home-made teas.**
A small to medium size segmented
garden, sympathetic to wildlife with
a wildflower meadow and pond,
part flower, part fruit and vegetable,
a mix for everyone. Interesting
hostas in pots and numerous chilli
plant varieties grown from seed in
greenhouse.

63 🆕 NORTH BOWOOD FARMHOUSE
North Bowood, Bridport, DT6 5JL.
Evelina Gregson, 07771 906754,
megregson@googlemail.com. *On
the Broadwinsor to Bridport rd,
turn L signed for North Bowood,
house 1st on L opp farmyard.* **Visits
by arrangement May to Sept for
groups of 10+. Home-made teas
on terrace overlooking the main
garden.**
Traditional English country garden,
deep herbaceous borders surround
the house with whimsical informality.
Box balls provide structure
interspersed with peonies, irises,
acanthus, roses, geraniums, nepeta,
hydrangeas and *Alchemilla mollis*.
Large pond provides a central feature
on the main lawn. Wildflower meadow
at entrance with Michelmas daisies

and fruit trees. Kitchen garden with raised vegetable beds, asparagus and cut flower beds.

64 NORWOOD HOUSE

Corscombe, Dorchester, DT2 0PD. Mr & Mrs Jonathan Lewis, 07836 600185, jonathan.lewis@livegroup.co.uk. *Equidistant between Halstock & Corscombe. 1m from Fox Inn towards Halstock. 1m from national speed limit sign leaving Halstock towards Corscombe. Parking in field off the main drive.* **Visits by arrangement May to Sept for groups of 10+. Home-made teas.**

The gardens of Norwood House combine the controlled chaos of nature with a little formality. The planting is elegant and modern, with box topiary providing formal structure, interspersed with soft planting of verbena, grasses, alchemilla mollis and crocosmia. The East lawn is now filled with a wildflower meadow framed by borders offering subtle floral colour. The borders also inc many varieties of geranium and other perennials and shrubs. In front of the house is a large wildflower meadow and a lake, which offers the most spectacular view. We can assist wheelchair users to access the gardens only some parts of which are inaccessible.

65 OAKDALE LIBRARY GARDENS

Wimborne Road, Poole, BH15 3EF. Oakdale Library Gardens Association, www.facebook.com/Oakdalelibrarygardens/. *Corner of Wimborne Rd & Dorchester Rd. Number 5/6 bus towards Canford Heath. Bus stop directly adjacent to Library. Free parking on site.* **Wed 15 May, Mon 10 June (2-5). Adm by donation. Light refreshments on NGS open days only.**

Award winning gardens comprising of the 'Bookerie' Reading and Rhyme time garden where wildlife is welcomed with bee friendly planting, an insect mansion and pond. Also a Commemorative Garden, a nautical themed garden, herb garden and children's adventure trail. The gardens have been designed and maintained by volunteers. Featured in '111 places in Poole that you shouldn't miss ' by Katherine Bebo. The Bookerie is only open during Library opening hours. Other gardens open at all times.

Plant sales on NGS open days. Full wheelchair access in all the gardens except the children's adventure trail.

66 THE OLD RECTORY, LITTON CHENEY

Litton Cheney, Dorchester, DT2 9AH. Richard & Emily Cave, 01308 482266, emilycave@rosacheney.com. *9m W of Dorchester. 1m S of A35, 6m E of Bridport. Park in village and follow signs.* **Sun 28 Apr, Wed 1 May, Sun 7 July (11-5). Adm £7, chd free. Home-made teas. Visits also by arrangement 30 Apr to 30 Sept.**

Steep paths lead to beguiling 4 acres of natural woodland with many springs, streams, 2 pools one a natural swimming pool planted with native plants. Formal front garden, designed by Arne Maynard, with pleached crabtree border, topiary and soft planting inc tulips, peonies, roses and verbascums. Walled garden with informal planting, kitchen garden, orchard and 350 rose bushes for a cut flower business.

67 THE OLD RECTORY, MANSTON

Manston, Sturminster Newton, DT10 1EX. Andrew & Judith Hussey, 01258 474673, judithhussey@hotmail.com. *6m S of Shaftesbury, 2½m N of Sturminster Newton. From Shaftesbury, take B3091. On reaching Manston go past Plough Inn, L for Child Okeford on R-hand bend. Old Rectory last house on L.* **Sun 2, Wed 5 June (2-5). Adm £8, chd free. Home-made teas. Visits also by arrangement Mar to Sept.**

Beautifully restored 5 acre garden. South facing wall with 120ft herbaceous border edged by old brick path. Enclosed yew hedge flower garden. Wildflower meadow marked with mown paths and young plantation of mixed hardwoods. Well maintained walled Victorian kitchen garden with new picking flower section. Large new greenhouse also installed. Knot garden now well established.

68 THE OLD RECTORY, PULHAM

Dorchester, DT2 7EA. Mr & Mrs N Elliott, 01258 817595, gilly.elliott@hotmail.com, www.instagram.com/theoldrectory_pulham. *13m N of Dorchester. 8m SE of Sherborne. On B3143 turn E at Xrds in Pulham. Signed Cannings Court.* **Sun 2, Thur 6 June, Sun 4, Thur 8 Aug (2-5). Adm £8, chd free. Home-made teas. Visits also by arrangement 1 May to 15 Sept for groups of 10 to 50. Adm £9 (or inc tea & home-made cakes £13).**

Four acres of formal and informal gardens surrounding C18 rectory with splendid views. Yew pyramid allées and hedges, circular herbaceous borders with late summer colour. Exuberantly planted terrace, purple and white beds. Box parterres, mature trees, pond, sheets of daffodils, tulips, glorious churchyard. Ha-ha, pleached hornbeam circle. Enchanting bog garden with stream and islands.10 acres woodland walks. Mostly wheelchair accessible.

69 THE OLD SCHOOL HOUSE

The Street, Sutton Waldron, Blandford Forum, DT11 8NZ. David Milanes. *7m N of Blandford. Turn into Sutton Waldron from A350, continue for 300 yds, 1st house on L in The Street.* **Sun 9 June (2-6); Thur 13 June (1-6). Adm £5, chd free. Also open nearby Penmead Farm.**

Village garden(.8 acre) laid out in last 10 yrs with hornbeam hedges creating 'rooms' inc orchard, secret garden and pergola walkway. Raised bed for growing vegetables. Strong framework of existing large trees, beds are mostly planted with roses and herbaceous plants. Pleached hornbeam screen. A designer's garden with interesting semi-tender plants close to house with benches to sit and relax on. Refreshments available at Penmead Farm nearby in the village, open on same days. Level lawns.

Cranborne Manor Garden

70 THE OLD VICARAGE

East Orchard, Shaftesbury,
SP7 0BA. Miss Tina Wright,
01747 811744, tina_lon@msn.com.
*4½ m S of Shaftesbury, 3½ m N
of Sturminster Newton. On B3091
between 90 degree bend & layby with
defibrillator red phone box. Parking is
on the opp corner towards Hartgrove.*
**Fri 16, Sun 18 Feb, Fri 22, Sun
24 Mar, Fri 26, Sun 28 Apr, Sun
26 May (2-5). Adm £5, chd free.
Home-made teas in garden but
inside if wet weather. Visits also by
arrangement 2 Jan to 3 Dec.**
1.7 acre well established garden
with new additional wildlife garden
including hundreds of different
snowdrops, crocus and many other
bulbs and winter flowering shrubs.
A stream meanders down to a pond
and there are lovely reflections in the
swimming pond, the first to be built in
Dorset. The wildlife garden has been
planted with several unusual trees.

Grotto, old Victorian man pushing
his lawn mower which his owner
purchased brand new in 1866. Pond
dipping, swing and other children's
attractions. Cakes inc gluten free,
and vegans are also catered for. Not
suitable for wheelchairs if very wet.

🚻 🐄 ✿ 🚌 ☕))

71 PENMEAD FARM

The Street, Sutton Waldron,
Blandford Forum, DT11 8PF.
Matthew & Claire Cripps. *5½ m
S of Shaftesbury. From A350 turn
into the village of Sutton Waldron.
Drive through the village & entrance
is approx ¼ m on R after the road
bridge which straddles the stream.*
**Sun 9 June (2.30-6.30); Thur 13
June (3.30-7.30). Adm £5, chd
free. Home-made teas. Also open
nearby The Old School House.
Wine & light refreshments will
be available from 6.30 pm on
Thursday opening.**

Situated on the site of an old brick
works the property is bordered by
over 30 mature oak trees. The garden
comprises a woodland and stream
(Fontmell Brook) walk, meadows,
substantial vegetable garden,
orchard, spring fed pond and small
semi walled garden. Being on clay
soil roses thrive. Views to Pen Hill
and Fontmell Down. Some sloping
paths and can be wet under foot.
Accessible bar steep slope down to
stream and some gravel paths.

♿ ✿ ☕))

72 PHILIPSTON HOUSE

Winterborne Clenston, Blandford
Forum, DT11 0NR. Mark & Ana
Hudson. *SW of Blandford Forum. 2
km N of Winterborne Whitechurch &
1 km S of Crown Inn in Winterborne
Stickland. Park in signed track/field
off road, nr Bourne Farm Cottage.
Enter garden from field.* **Sat 8 June
(2-5.30). Adm £5, chd free. Cream**

teas £5 per person. Please bring cash for refreshments & garden entry.

Charming 2 acre garden with lovely views in Winterborne valley. Many unusual trees, rambling roses, wisteria, mixed borders and shrubs. Sculptures. Rose parterre, walled garden, swimming pool garden, vegetable garden. Stream with bridge over to wooded shady area with cedarwood pavilion. Orchard with mown paths planted with spring bulbs. Sorry, no WC available. Dogs welcome on leads, pls clear up after them. Wheelchair access is good providing it is dry.

73 1 PINE WALK
Lyme Regis, DT7 3LA. Mrs Erika Savory. *Pls park in Holmbush Car Park at top of Cobb Rd.* **Thur 5, Sun 8 Sept (11-4.30). Adm £7.50, chd free. Home-made teas.**
Unconventional ½ acre, multi level garden above Lyme Bay, adjoining NT's Ware Cliffs. Abundantly planted with an exotic range of shrubs, cannas, gingers and magnificent ferns. Apart from a rose and hydrangea collection, planting reflects owner's love of Southern Africa inc staggering succulents and late summer colour explosion featuring drifts of salvias, dahlias, asters, grasses and rudbeckia.

74 NEW PIPSFORD FARM
Beaminster, DT8 3NT. Charlie & Bee Tuke. *2m SE of Beaminster off B3163, 7m N of Bridport. Postcode & SatNav brings you to the main front drive entrance, clearly signed.* **Fri 24 May (2-5). Adm £10, chd free. Pre-booking essential, please visit www.ngs.org.uk for information & booking. Home-made teas in the stable yard. Refreshments included in adm.**
3 acres of formal and informal gardens. Ponds surrounded by mature specimen trees, acers, hydrangeas, ferns and bamboo. Bog garden, with raised walkway. Walled garden with herbaceous beds, pond, pergola covered in apples and productive beds surrounded by Ilex crenata. Cut flower area with paths to greenhouses and fruit cage, surrounded by mature yew hedges.

75 NEW THE POTTING SHED
Middlemarsh, Sherborne, DT9 5QN. Andy Cole & Michele Hounsell, www.therapygarden.co.uk. *7m S of Sherborne, 11m N of Dorchester on the A352 in Middlemarsh. 300 yrds S of The Hunters Moon pub.* **Sat 18 May, Sat 14 Sept (10-4). Adm £4.50, chd free. Cream teas. Gluten free & vegan scones available, freshly picked herbal teas & home-made jams.**
The Potting Shed opened its doors in April 2023. This new 2 acre Wellbeing Nursery, Therapy Garden has been created from scratch to enhance relaxation and tranquillity. The community garden has been planted organically to encourage all forms of wildlife. There is an acre of wildflower meadow, plant nursery and tea garden to explore. It truly is a special place to relax, unwind and be inspired. Partial access, small area of gravel, remainder paved and hard paths plus grass.

GROUP OPENING

76 RAMPISHAM GARDENS
Dorchester, DT2 0PU. 01935 83652, alison.wright@ngs.org.uk. *11m NW of Dorchester. From Dorchester A37 Yeovil, 9m L to Evershot. From Yeovil A37 Dorchester, 7m R Evershot, follow signs. From Crewkerne A356, 1½m after Rampisham Garage L to Rampisham.* **Sun 9 June (12-5). Combined adm £8, chd £4. Home-made teas at Rampisham Manor by the Orangery at the back of the house.**

BROOMHILL
David & Carol Parry.
(See separate entry)

THE OLD RECTORY
Peter & Jenny Thomas.

PUGIN HALL
Tim & Ali Wright, 01935 83652, alison.wright@ngs.org.uk.
Visits also by arrangement May to Sept for groups of 10 +.

RAMPISHAM MANOR
Robert & Camilla Boileau.

1 ROSE COTTAGE
Trevor & Sarah Ball.

ROSEMARY COTTAGE
Nigel & Annika Purkhardt.

This beautiful historic village will host an open garden day for a wide variety of gardens, with 6 gardens opening this year. These will inc some larger gardens with perennial borders, roses and shrubs, as well as an old walled garden more recently developed as a flower garden with topiary, standard trees and soft floral planting. Inc this year for the first time are some new cottage gardens with an array of floral colour, fruit trees and vegetables. Within 2 of these cottage gardens our resident carpenters will have their workshops open with wooden bowls, walking sticks and household items for sale. Access to all 6 gardens for wheelchairs. Gravel pathways and terraced or sloping lawns in some gardens mean wheelchairs can only access part of the garden.

77 NEW 1C RECTORY ROAD
Poole, BH15 3BH. Dave Hutchings, www.instagram.com/goosesquawks/. *5 mins from Poole town centre. The bungalow is behind the main houses on the road down a pedestrian access drive.* **Sun 18 Aug, Sun 8 Sept (11-5). Adm £4, chd £2. Light refreshments.**
An unusual character house and garden. With a passion for maximalist design the house and garden has been designed and built by the owner over the last 5 yrs. Both garden and house are full of objet d'art spanning centuries, there's curiosities to see in every corner.

In 2023, National Garden Scheme funding for Perennial supported a helpline service which provided advice, information and frontline support to around 800 people working in horticulture

78 RUSSELL-COTES ART GALLERY & MUSEUM

East Cliff, Bournemouth, BH1 3AA. Phil Broomfield, 07810 646123, russellcotes@bcpcouncil.gov. uk, www.russellcotes.com. *On Bournemouth's East Cliff Promenade. Situated next to the Royal Bath Hotel, 2 mins walk from Bournemouth Pier. The closest car park is Bath Road Sth. Parking also available on the cliff top.* **Visits by arrangement Apr to Oct for groups of 6 to 15. Adm £3, chd free.**

Enjoy a private garden tour of this sub-tropical garden sited on the cliff top, overlooking the sea, full of a wide variety of plants from around the globe. East Cliff Hall was the home of Sir Merton and Lady Annie Russell-Cotes. The garden was restored allowing for modern access with areas retaining original 1901 design conceived by the founders such as the ivy clad grotto and Japanese influence. The Russell-Cotes Café serves a delicious range of light lunches, teas, coffees, and cakes. Some gravel paths and no wheelchair access to terrace.

&. ♨

79 THE SECRET GARDEN AT SERLES HOUSE

47 Victoria Road, Wimborne, BH21 1EN. Chris & Bridget Ryan. *Centre of Wimborne. On B3082 W of town, very near hospital, Westfield car park 300yds. Off road parking close by.* **Sun 19 May, Sun 16 June (1-4.30). Adm £5, chd free. Sandwiches, cakes, tea, coffee etc. Donation to Wimborne Civic Society and The Arts' Society.**

The former home of the late Ian Willis, who lived here for just under 40 yrs. Alan Titchmarsh described this amusingly creative garden as 'one of the best 10 private gardens in Britain'. The ingenious use of unusual plants complements the imaginative treasure trove of garden objets d'art. Wheelchair access to garden only. Narrow steps may prohibit wide wheelchairs.

&. ✿ ⊟ ♨

80 SEMLEY GRANGE

Semley, Shaftesbury, SP7 9AP. Mr & Mrs Reid Scott. *From A350 take turning to Semley, continue along road & under railway bridge. Take 1st R up Sem Hill. Semley Grange is*

1st on L - parking on green. **Sun 23 June (12-5). Adm £5, chd free.**
Large garden recreated in last 10 yrs. Herbaceous border, lawn and wildflower meadow intersected by paths and planted with numerous bulbs. The garden has been greatly expanded by introducing many standard weeping roses, new mixed borders, pergolas and raised beds for dahlias, underplanted with alliums. Numerous fruit and ornamental trees introduced over last 10 yrs.

&. ✿

81 NEW SHEEPWASH BARN

Symondsbury, Bridport, DT6 6HH. Charles Chesshire, www.charleschesshire.co.uk. *From A 35, head through Symondsbury past Shear Plot on R, down hill & the garden is on R, or from Bridport take Symondsbury Estate rd to Mill Lane & the garden is on L.* **Sun 2 June, Sun 8 Sept (1-5). Adm £5, chd free. Home-made teas.**

Set in heavenly Dorset countryside, the half acre garden is composed of an intricate web of gravel paths weaving between deep and colourful borders to create an intimate experience for the extensive collection of new and unusual plants, especially Itoh peonies and hydrangeas. At the heart of the garden is a Japanese styled koshi-kake 'waiting room', surrounded by dwarf pines, grasses and ferns.

🐾 ✿ ⊟ ♨

82 ♦ SHERBORNE CASTLE

New Rd, Sherborne, DT9 5NR. Mr E Wingfield Digby, www.sherbornecastle.com. *½ m E of Sherborne. On New Rd B3145. Follow brown signs from A30 & A352.* **For opening times and information, please visit garden website.**

40+ acres. Grade I Capability Brown garden with magnificent vistas across surrounding landscape, inc lake and views to ruined castle. Herbaceous planting, notable trees, mixed ornamental planting and managed wilderness are linked together with lawn and pathways. Short and long walks available. Partial wheelchair access, gravel paths, steep slopes, steps.

&. 🐾 ⊟ 🞐

GROUP OPENING

83 SHILLINGSTONE GARDENS

Shillingstone, DT11 0SL. Caroline Salt. *4m W of Blandford Forum. The village lies on the A357 between Blandford Forum and Sturminster Newton. Parking at Shillingstone House, additional parking & access to WC at Church Centre.* **Sun 9 June (10-4). Combined adm £7, chd free. Home-made teas at Shillingstone Church Centre, Main Rd, Shillingstone DT11 0SW**

CHERRY COTTAGE
Lal & Gloria Ratnayake.

SHILLINGSTONE HOUSE
Michael & Caroline Salt.

Both gardens are in the centre of this pretty village which lies close to the River Stour with Hambledon Hill as a backdrop. The larger garden has some magnificent trees, traditional borders, old brick walls supporting multiple rambling roses and an old fashioned walled kitchen garden mixing vegetables, fruit and flowers. Nearby a cottage garden packed with exotic plants, Bonsai, pond, fruit and herbs and beds of perenials and annuals. Wheelchair access to Shillingstone House garden only.

&. ✿ 🞐 ⅔))

84 SLAPE MANOR

Netherbury, Bridport, DT6 5LH. Paul Mulholland & Tarsha Finney, 07534 676148, info@slapemanor.com. *1m S of Beaminster. Turn W off A3066 to Netherbury. House ½m S of Netherbury on back rd to Bridport signed Waytown.* **Sun 21 Apr, Sun 30 June (1-5). Adm £9, chd free. Home-made teas. Visits also by arrangement Feb to Dec for groups of 5+.**

River valley garden in a process of transformation. Spacious lawns, wildflower meadows, and primula fringed streams leading down to a lake. Walk over the stream with magnificent hostas, gunneras and horizontal *Cryptomeria japonica* 'Elegans' around the lake. Admire the mature wellingtonias, ancient wisterias, rhododendrons and planting around the house. Kitchen garden renovation underway. Slape Manor is one of the inspirations behind Chelsea 2022 Gold medal winning and Best in Show Garden

Bennetts Water Gardens

designed by Urquhart and Hunt with Rewilding Britain. Mostly flat with some sloping paths and steps. Ground is often wet and boggy.

85 SOUTH EGGARDON HOUSE
Askerswell, Dorchester, DT2 9EP. Buffy Sacher, 07920 520280, buffysacher@gmail.com. *From Dorchester on A35 turn R for Askerswell. Through village at T junction. Go straight over. From Bridport on A35 take 1st turning to Askerswell. Pass Spyway Inn on R. Turn next L.* **Visits by arrangement May to Sept for groups of 5+.**
acres of formal and informal gardens designed around a 2000 yr old yew tree and lake. Water garden with streams pond and lake. Woodland walk, orchard, wild garden, large herbaceous borders filled with roses and perennials. Ornamental kitchen garden and vegetable garden.

86 STABLE COURT
Chalmington, Dorchester, DT2 0HB. Jenny & James Shanahan, 01300 321345, jennyshanahan8@gmail.com. *10m N of Dorchester. From A37 travel towards Cattistock & Chalmington for 1½ m. R at triangle to Chalmington. ½ m house on R, red letter box at gate. From Cattistock take 1st turn R then next L at triangle.* **Visits by arrangement 1 May to 28 Sept for groups of 10 to 25. Home-made teas by request.(Adm £10 with refreshments included). Adm £6, chd free.**
This exuberant garden was begun in 2010. Extending to about 1½ acres, it is naturalistic in style with a shrubbery, gravel garden, wild garden and pond where many trees have been planted and which are maturing wonderfully. Overflowing with roses scrambling up trees, over hedges and walls. More formal garden closer to house with lawns and herbaceous borders. Lovely views over Dorset countryside. Exhibition of paintings in studio. Gravel path partway around garden, otherwise the paths are grass, not suitable for wheelchairs in wet weather.

87 STADDLESTONES
14 Witchampton Mill, Witchampton, Wimborne, BH21 5DE. Annette & Richard Lockwood, 01258 841405, richardglockwood@yahoo.co.uk. *5m N of Wimborne off B3078. Follow signs through village and park in sports field, 7 mins walk to garden. Limited disabled parking nr garden.* **Visits by arrangement 2 Apr to 2 Oct. Adm £5, chd free. Cream teas.**
A beautiful setting for a cottage garden with colour themed borders, pleached limes and hidden gems, leading over chalk stream to shady area which has some unusual plants. Plenty of areas just to sit and enjoy the wildlife. Wire bird sculptures by local artist. Wheelchair access to first half of garden.

SPECIAL EVENT

88 STAFFORD HOUSE

West Stafford, Dorchester, DT2 8AD. Lord & Lady Fellowes. *2m E of Dorchester in Frome Valley. Follow signs to West Stafford from the West, 1st house on L before you get to the village, green park railings and gate.* **Fri 5 July (10-12.30). Adm £25, chd free. Pre-booking essential, please visit www.ngs. org.uk for information & booking. Home-made elevenses inc cake & biscuits in a gardening theme.**

The gardens at Stafford House include a river walk and tree planting in the style of early C19 Picturesque. Humphry Repton prepared landscape proposals for the garden and the designs were later implemented, they were also included in his famous Red Books. A limited number of tickets have been made available for this private morning opening, hosted by Lord and Lady Fellowes. The morning will inc special home-made elevenses which will be served underneath the turkey oak tree planted in 1633 on the main terrace. There will then be the opportunity to explore the grounds and gardens, finishing at 12.30pm.

89 UTOPIA

Tincleton, Dorchester, DT2 8QP. Nick & Sharon Spiller. *4m SE of Dorchester. Take signs to Tincleton from Dorchester, Puddletown. Pick up garden signs in the village.* **Sun 9 June (1-5). Adm £5, chd £4. Light refreshments.**

Approximately 1/2 acre of secluded, peaceful garden made up of several rooms inspired by different themes. Inspiration is taken from Mediterranean and Italian gardens, woodland space, water gardens. Seating is scattered throughout to enable you to sit and enjoy the different spaces and take advantage of both sun and shade Parking available with ten minute walk or park in village.

90 WAGTAILS

Stourton Caundle, Sturminster Newton, DT10 2JW. Sally & Nick Reynolds. *6m E of Sherborne. From Sherborne take A3030. At Bishops Caundle, L signed Stourton Caundle. After 1 1/2 m in village on R as descending hill, 5 houses before*

Trooper Inn. **Sun 8 Sept (2-5.30). Combined adm with Manor Farm, Stourton Caundle £10, chd free. Home-made teas at Manor Farm a short walk away.**

Contemporary Arne Maynard inspired garden of almost 3 acres, with wildflower meadows, orchards, kitchen garden and lawns, linked by a sweeping mown pathway, studded with topiary, divided by box, yew and beech hedging. Landscaped and planted over last 10 yrs by current owners, and still work in progress. Wheelchair access over majority of garden and orchards over lawn grade paths. Gentle slopes with grass pathways.

91 ◆ THE WALLED GARDEN

Moreton, Dorchester, DT2 8RH. 01929 405685, info@ walledgardenmoreton.co.uk, walledgardenmoreton.co.uk/. *In the village of Moreton, near Crossways. Look for the brown signs out on the main road.* **For opening times and information, please phone, email or visit garden website.**

The Walled Garden is a beautiful 5 acre landscaped formal garden situated in Moreton, Dorset. The village is close to the historic market town of Dorchester and situated on the River Frome. A wide variety of perennial plants sit in the borders, which have been styled in original Georgian and Victorian designs. Sculpture from various local artists, family area and play park, animal area, and plant shop, plus on site café.

92 WESTERN GARDENS

24A Western Ave, Branksome Park, Poole, BH13 7AN. Mr Peter Jackson, 01202 708388, pjbranpark@gmail.com. *3m W of Bournemouth. From S end Wessex Way (A338) at gyratory take The Avenue, 2nd exit. At T-lights turn R into Western Rd then at bottom of hill L. At church turn R into Western Ave.* **Sun 28 Apr, Sun 23 June (2-5.30). Adm £6, chd free. Home-made teas. Visits also by arrangement 15 Apr to 1 Sept for groups of 20+.**

Created over 40 yrs, a garden of enormous variety with rose, Mediterranean courtyard and woodland gardens, herbaceous borders and cherry tree and camellia walk. Lush foliage and vibrant flowers give year-round colour and interest

enhanced by wood sculpture and topiary. 'This secluded and magical 1acre garden captures the spirit of warmer climes and begs for repeated visits' (Gardening Which?). Plants and home-made jams and chutneys for sale. Wheelchair access to 3/4 garden.

93 WHITE HOUSE

Newtown, Witchampton, Wimborne, BH21 5AU. Mr Tim Read, 01258 840438, tim@witchampton.org. *5m N of Wimborne off B3078. Travel through village of Witchampton towards Newtown for 800m. Pass Crichel House's castellated gates on L. White House is a modern house sitting back from road on L after further 300m.* **Visits by arrangement May to Aug for groups of 8 to 20. Adm includes home-made teas. Adm £10, chd free.**

1 1/2 acre garden set on different levels, with a Mediterranean feel, planted to encourage wildlife and pollinators. Wildflower border, pond surrounded by moisture loving plants, prairie planting of grasses and perennials, orchard. Chainsaw sculptures of birds of prey. Reasonable wheelchair access to all but the top level of the garden.

The National Garden Scheme's final instalment to support the building of the Y Bwthyn NGS Macmillan Specialist Palliative Care Unit in Wales, enabled 270 inpatients to be supported this year

95 NEW 20 WICKET ROAD
Kinson, Bournemouth, BH10 5LT.
Carron Bowen (& Peter Hellawell).
*300 metres SE of Kinson Green.
From Kinson Green (The Hub/
Library): follow Wimborne Rd (A341)
towards Northbourne. Turn R after
shops into Kitscroft Rd, R again into
Bramley Rd; Wicket Rd is second L.
No 20 is on the L.* **Fri 17, Sat 18,
Sun 19 May, Sat 24, Sun 25, Mon
26 Aug (2-5). Adm £5, chd free.
Home-made teas.**
Built around a modern terrace, this
small suburban garden (just 18 x 13
metres) sits on an awkward shaped
plot, over a bed of clay. Set down
from its neighbours, it developed a
habit of flooding. But you'd never
know. 'Borrow, hint, reveal, distract,
attract, conceal' – the design uses
every trick in the gardening handbook
to create a truly memorable space.
Exhibition of the garden's history,
some unusual plants, a unique 'quay'
(for storing run-off water as part of a
hidden drainage system) and an array
of small-scale features. Access is via
the garage through a narrow doorway
(0.66 m / 26'). However, once in the
garden, paths are wide with step-free
route to most areas.

96 WINCOMBE PARK
Shaftesbury, SP7 9AB.
John & Phoebe Fortescue,
www.wincombepark.com. *2m N
of Shaftesbury. A350 Shaftesbury
to Warminster, past Wincombe
Business Park, 1st R signed
Wincombe & Donhead St Mary.* ³/₄ m
on R. **Sun 12, Wed 15 May (2-5).
Adm £8, chd free. Home-made
teas. Dairy & gluten free options
available.**
Extensive mature garden with
sweeping panoramic views from lawn
over parkland to lake and enchanting
woods through which you can
wander amongst bluebells. Garden is
a riot of colour in spring with azaleas,
camellias and rhododendrons in
flower amongst shrubs and unusual
trees. Beautiful walled kitchen garden.
Partial wheelchair access only, slopes
and gravel paths.

**97 NEW 105 WOOLSBRIDGE
ROAD**
Ashley Heath, Ringwood,
BH24 2LZ. Richard & Lynda Nunn.
*A31 W for 2m after Ringwood, R
at Woolsbridge Rd r'about. 1m on
L. A31E, L at W'bridge Rd r'bout.*
*Parking in side roads best due to
cycle lane.* **Sat 17, Sun 18 Aug (11-
4.30). Adm £4, chd free. Home-
made teas.**
Plantsman's garden with paths
meandering through different areas
inc architectural jungle exotics,
bamboos and bananas, a woodland
walkway with rhododendrons, fernery,
grass bed, pond and hot gravel bed.
Several secluded seating areas, lawn
and traditional vegetable patch.

SPECIAL EVENT

98 WYKE FARM
Chedington, Beaminster,
DT8 3HX. Alex & Robert Appleby,
wykefarm.com. *Take the turning
from the A356, opp The Winyards
Gap Inn, away from Chedington,
signed to Halstock. Drive 1m down
the lane and we are the 1st farm
entrance on the L.* **Sun 23 June
(1-5). Adm £25, chd free. Pre-
booking essential, please visit
www.ngs.org.uk for information
& booking. Home-made teas in
the barn by the white courtyard
garden.**
The owners of Wyke Farm, Robert
and Alex Appleby are both fanatical
about rewilding, environmental
conservation and preservation of
the natural habitat. They have lived
at Wyke Farm for almost 20 yrs and
in this time have worked hard to
empathically restore the land to inc
a substantial wildflower meadow at
the front of the house, and a large
lake and woodland area. There are
herbaceous borders and lawns
around the house. There is a rose
garden that leads to the woodland
garden, then a more formal courtyard
garden that leads through the barn to
a kitchen garden. A limited number
of tickets have been made available
for this special 1 day rewilding event.
Meet at the front of the house on the
main drive for an introductory talk
and guided tour with Ecologist, Tom
Brereton, who has supported the
Applebys on their work at Wyke Farm.
The paths are gravel.

SPECIAL EVENT

99 NEW WYTHERSTON FARM
Powerstock, Bridport, DT6 3TQ.
Johnnie & Sophie Boden. *From Mt
Pleasant Xrds go down hill for 1m.
At very bottom where lane bends to
R carry straight on. following sign
for Wytherston Farm only. Carry on
to end of the drive into a yard. From
Powerstock leave village going uphill
with church on R. After 1m take 1st
turning on R for Wytherston Farm.*
**Thur 27 June (2.30-5). Adm £25,
chd free. Pre-booking essential,
please visit www.ngs.org.uk for
information & booking. After the
tour home-made teas will be
served in the barn.**
Johnnie and Sophie Boden bought
Wytherston in 2005. Since then they
and their fantastic team have tried
to encourage wild flowers in both
their garden and in the meadows
surrounding the farm, which makes
for a breathtaking display. They
have also maintained the gardens
around the house, which inc deep
herbaceous borders, roses and formal
topiary structure interspersed with
bright floral colour. A limited number
of tickets have been made available
for this special event, kindly hosted
by Johnnie, who will give a talk and
guided tour through the wildflower
garden and meadows. Please meet
in the Tithe Barn at 2.30pm prompt.
Plenty of parking. Dogs are very
welcome.

100 YEW TREE HOUSE
Hermitage Lane, Hermitage,
Dorchester, DT2 7BB. Anna Vines,
annavinesgardens.co.uk. *7m S of
Sherborne. Turn towards Holnest
off A352, Dorchester-Sherborne
road. Continue 2m to Hermitage.
In Hermitage, new build house on
N side at the western end of village
green.* **Sun 9 June (12-5). Adm £5,
chd free. Home-made teas.**
A recently landscaped and
planted ½ acre plot, surrounding
a new-build eco home. House
and garden designed to connect
harmoniously and sit naturally within
the surrounding rural landscape. The
garden comprises a small kitchen
garden, orchard, Mediterranean
garden, boules court and herbaceous
borders, each providing their own
ambience. Informal perennial borders
enclose terraces around the house.
Photographic display in the barn
within the garden. Gravel driveway.

GLOUCESTERSHIRE

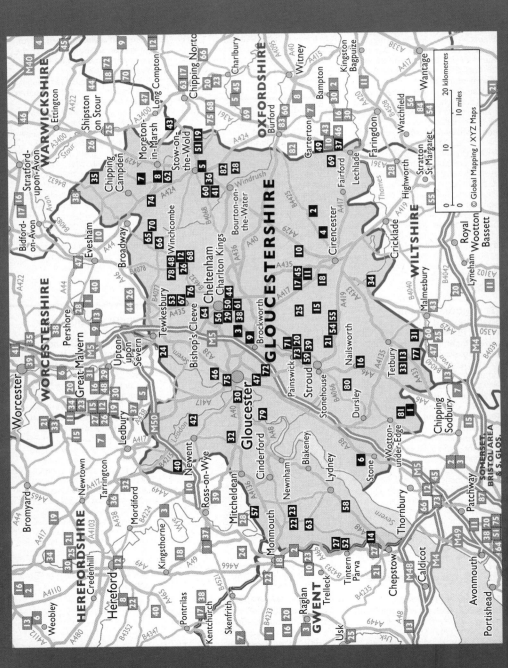

VOLUNTEERS

County Organiser
Vanessa Berridge
01242 609535
vanessa.berridge@ngs.org.uk

County Treasurer
Pam Sissons
01242 573942
pam.sissons@ngs.org.uk

Social Media
Mandy Bradshaw
01242 512491
mandy.bradshaw@ngs.org.uk

Publicity
Ruth Chivers
01452 542493
ruth.chivers@ngs.org.uk

Booklet Coordinator
Vanessa Graham
07595 880261
vanessa.graham@ngs.org.uk

By Arrangement Coordinator
Simone Seward
01242 573733
simone.seward@ngs.org.uk

Assistant County Organisers
Yvonne Bennetts 01242 463151
yvonne.bennetts@ngs.org.uk

Jackie Healy 07747 186302
jackie.healy@ngs.org.uk

Ali James 01869 350654
ali.james@ngs.org.uk

Valerie Kent 01993 823294
valerie.kent@ngs.org.uk

Immy Lee 07801 816340
immy.lee@ngs.org.uk

Sally Oates 01285 841320
sally.oates@ngs.org.uk

Rose Parrott 07853 164924
rosemary.parrott@ngs.org.uk

Liz Ramsay 01242 672676
liz.ramsay@ngs.org.uk

f @gloucestershirengs
X @Glosngs
@ngs_gloucestershire

OPENING DATES

All entries subject to change. For latest information check **www.ngs.org.uk**
Map locator numbers are shown to the right of each garden name.

January

Sunday 28th
Home Farm   32

February

Snowdrop Openings

Monday 5th
Downton House   20

Tuesday 6th
Downton House   20

Sunday 11th
Home Farm   32
Trench Hill   71

Saturday 17th
Cotswold Farm   17

Sunday 18th
Cotswold Farm   17
Trench Hill   71

March

Sunday 10th
Home Farm   32

Sunday 31st
Trench Hill   71

April

Monday 1st
Trench Hill   71

Sunday 7th
◆ Highnam Court   30
Home Farm   32

Sunday 14th
South Lodge   63
◆ Upton Wold   74

Monday 15th
◆ Kiftsgate Court   35

Wednesday 17th
Barnsley House   4

Sunday 21st
Charlton Down House   13

Tuesday 23rd
Wortley House   81

Wednesday 24th
Lords of the Manor Hotel   41

Thursday 25th
Kemble House   34

Sunday 28th
Blockley Gardens   7
Home Farm   32
Pear Tree Cottage   53

May

Wednesday 1st
Daylesford House   19

Sunday 5th
Eastcombe and
    Bussage Gardens   21
◆ Highnam Court   30
Ramblers   58
Trench Hill   71

Monday 6th
Eastcombe and Bussage
Gardens   21
The Gate   26
Trench Hill   71

Saturday 18th
Charingworth Court   12

Sunday 19th
Charingworth Court   12
20 Forsdene Walk   23
11 Hatherley Court Road   29
NEW Milton Cottage   44
Penny Leaze   54
Pontings Farm   55
37 Queen's Road   56

Monday 20th
NEW ◆ Nature in Art
    Museum and Art Gallery   46
Penny Leaze   54
Pontings Farm   55

Sunday 26th
NEW Park House   50
Pasture Farm   51
◆ Stanway Fountain
    & Water Garden   66

Monday 27th
Pasture Farm   51

Wednesday 29th
Brockworth Court   9
Rockcliffe   60

Thursday 30th
Richmond Villages Painswick 59

Friday 31st
NEW 1 Cobden Villas 16
Hookshouse Pottery 33

June

Saturday 1st
NEW 1 Cobden Villas 16
Cotswold Farm 17
Hookshouse Pottery 33
NEW Tower Close 70

Sunday 2nd
Cotswold Farm 17
Madams 42
NEW Tower Close 70
Tuffley Gardens 72

Wednesday 5th
Trench Hill 71

Saturday 8th
Chase End 14
Forthampton Court 24
South Lodge 63

Sunday 9th
Forthampton Court 24
Greenfields, Brockweir Common 27
Hodges Barn 31
◆ Oxleaze Farm 49
◆ Sezincote 62
Stanton Village Gardens 65

Monday 10th
Hodges Barn 31

Wednesday 12th
Oak House 48
Trench Hill 71
Weir Reach 75
NEW White Cottage 78

Thursday 13th
Alderley Grange 1
Richmond Villages Painswick 59

Saturday 15th
Oak House 48
11 Upper Washwell 73
NEW White Cottage 78

Sunday 16th
Weir Reach 75

Monday 17th
Berkeley Castle 6

Tuesday 18th
Wortley House 81

Wednesday 19th
Lords of the Manor Hotel 41
Trench Hill 71

Friday 21st
NEW The Closes 15
Hookshouse Pottery 33

Sunday 23rd
Beechwood Park 5
Blockley Gardens 7
Langford Downs Farm 37
Leckhampton Court Hospice 38

Wednesday 26th
Trench Hill 71

Saturday 29th
Little Orchard 39
11 Upper Washwell 73

Sunday 30th
Little Orchard 39
Moor Wood 45
NEW Park House 50
Pear Tree Cottage 53
NEW Stone Barn, Shutter Lane 67
Woodchester Park House 80

July

Wednesday 3rd
Awkward Hill Cottage 2

Thursday 4th
Charlton Down House 13
Richmond Villages Painswick 59

Friday 5th
Hookshouse Pottery 33

Saturday 6th
Oak House 48
NEW White Cottage 78

Sunday 7th
NEW Badgeworth Manor 3
NEW 39 Fairways Avenue 22
Greenfields, Little Rissington 28
Kirkham Farm 36
NEW 1 Sandy Lane 61
◆ Westonbirt School Gardens 77

Thursday 11th
Charlton Down House 13

Sunday 14th
◆ Cerney House Gardens 11
11 Hatherley Court Road 29
Trench Hill 71

Thursday 18th
Charlton Down House 13

Tuesday 23rd
NEW The Stables 64

Saturday 27th
NEW 1 Cobden Villas 16

Sunday 28th
NEW 1 Cobden Villas 16

August

Sunday 4th
Beechwood Park 5
◆ Highnam Court 30

Monday 5th
NEW ◆ Thyme 69

Tuesday 6th
NEW ◆ Thyme 69

Wednesday 7th
NEW ◆ Thyme 69

Thursday 8th
Charlton Down House 13
◆ The Garden at Miserden 25
Richmond Villages Painswick 59
NEW ◆ Thyme 69

Friday 9th
NEW ◆ Thyme 69

Saturday 10th
39 Neven Place 47

Sunday 11th
39 Neven Place 47
◆ Stanway Fountain & Water Garden 66

Monday 12th
◆ Kiftsgate Court 35

Thursday 15th
Charlton Down House 13

Sunday 18th
◆ Bourton House Garden 8
NEW ◆ Little Orchard Kempley Dymock 40
The Manor 43

Monday 26th
Calmsden Manor 10

Thursday 29th
Charlton Down House 13

Saturday 31st
Cotswold Farm 17
NEW Wicks Green Farm 79

September

Sunday 1st
Cotswold Farm 17
Pontings Farm 55
NEW Wicks Green Farm 79

Monday 2nd
Pontings Farm 55

Sunday 8th
Trench Hill   71
Wyck Rissington Gardens   82
Sunday 15th
The Patch   52
Wednesday 18th
Brockworth Court   9
Lords of the Manor Hotel   41
Friday 20th
◆ Sudeley Castle & Gardens   68

January 2025

Sunday 26th
Home Farm   32

February 2025

Sunday 9th
Home Farm   32
Trench Hill   71
Saturday 15th
Cotswold Farm   17
Sunday 16th
Cotswold Farm   17
Trench Hill   71

By Arrangement

Arrange a personalised garden visit with your club, or group of friends, on a date to suit you. See individual garden entries for full details.

Awkward Hill Cottage   2
Berkeley Castle   6
Brockworth Court   9

Charingworth Court   12
Charlton Down House   13
Chase End   14
Daglingworth House   18
20 Forsdene Walk   23
Greenfields, Brockweir Common 27
11 Hatherley Court Road   29
Home Farm   32
Little Orchard   39
Moor Wood   45
Oak House   48
Pasture Farm   51
The Patch   52
Pear Tree Cottage   53
Radnors   57
South Lodge   63
NEW Tower Close   70
Trench Hill   71
Westaway   76
NEW White Cottage   78
Wortley House   81

Forthampton Court

THE GARDENS

1 ALDERLEY GRANGE

Alderley, GL12 7QT. Alexander & Kezzie Acloque. *2m S of Wotton-under-Edge. The entrance to the house is through a set of black iron gates which will be open on the day.* **Thur 13 June (2-4.30). Adm £12, chd free. Pre-booking essential, please visit www.ngs.org.uk for information & booking. Home-made teas. (included in admission).** Originally designed by Alvilde Lees-Milne in the early 1960's, this quintessentially English garden boasts an abundance of old-fashioned roses. Features include a walled garden, a pleached lime walk, fine trees and a Regency summerhouse.

2 AWKWARD HILL COTTAGE

Awkward Hill, Bibury, GL7 5NH. Mrs Victoria Summerley, 07718 384269, v.summerley@hotmail.com, www.awkwardhill.co.uk. *No parking at property, or on Hawkers Hill or Awkward Hill, which are both narrow lanes. Best to park in village & walk past Arlington Row up Awkward Hill, or up Hawkers Hill from Catherine Wheel pub.* **Wed 3 July (2-6). Adm £5, chd free. Home-made teas. Visits also by arrangement 10 June to 7 Sept for groups of 10 to 30. Owner will give a private tour of the garden to visiting groups.** An ever-evolving country garden in one of the most beautiful villages in the Cotswolds, designed by its owner, an award-winning garden writer, to reflect the local landscape and encourage wildlife. Planting contributes year-round interest with lots of colour and texture. Pond and waterfall, chickens. Wonderful views over neighbouring meadow and woodland, small pond with jetty, 2 sunny terraces and plenty of places to sit and relax, both in sun and shade.

3 NEW BADGEWORTH MANOR

Badgeworth, Cheltenham, GL51 4UL. Mrs Imogen Loxam. *4m SW of Cheltenham. When you reach the village green at the end of Church Ln take the lane to your R. The large black metal driveway gates are then directly ahead of you. There is parking available on site.* **Sun 7 July (1.30-4.30). Adm £5, chd free. Cream teas.** The gardens of Badgeworth Manor are a stunning and carefully designed arrangement planned by the landscape architect John Hill of Sherborne. It comprises a quaint knot garden, two manicured lawns, borders of ornamental raised flower beds, two beautiful ponds, one of which is bordered by beds of roses and two Judas trees. The entire garden is beautifully accented by topiary and lavender. There is a children's play area, a tennis court, and a stunning bougainvillea in the conservatory where tea and cake will be served. There is ample seating around the garden. A short walk across the lane leads you to our wildflower meadow where you can access a brook that runs through woodland. There is wheelchair access to the majority of the garden. However, the wheelchair will initially need to be wheeled over the shingle on the driveway.

4 BARNSLEY HOUSE

Barnsley, Cirencester, GL7 5EE. HALO HM Ltd, 01285 740000, reception@barnsleyhouse.com, www.barnsleyhouse.com. *4m NE of Cirencester. From Cirencester, take B4425 to Barnsley. House entrance on R as you enter village.* **Wed 17 Apr (10-4). Adm £10, chd free. Tea. Afternoon teas can be purchased at the Potager, subject to availability.**

Hookshouse Pottery

The beautiful garden at Barnsley House, created by Rosemary Verey, is one of England's finest and most famous gardens inc knot garden, potager garden and mixed borders in her successional planting style. The house also has an extensive kitchen garden which will be open with plants and vegetables available for purchase. Narrow paths mean restricted wheelchair access but happy to provide assistance.

5 BEECHWOOD PARK

Fosseway, Stow On The Wold, Cheltenham, GL54 1FP. Brio Retirement Living, www.facebook. com/BrioBeechwoodPark. *Head out of Stow towards Bourton on the Water. Pass a BP garage on the R & a cemetery on the L. Beechwood Park be just past this on the L.* **Sun 23 June, Sun 4 Aug (10-4). Adm £5, chd free. Tea, coffee, cake & full bar.**
Five beautifully designed, modern courtyard gardens, plus several residents' gardens, set in a semi-urban community in Stow-on-the-Wold. The gardens and main lawn area with feature pod are set against a contemporary design of Cotswold apartment communities. Full wheelchair access plus disabled WC.

6 BERKELEY CASTLE

Berkeley, GL13 9PJ. Charles Berkeley, 01453 810303, info@berkeley-castle.com, www.berkeley-castle.com. *Halfway between Bristol & Gloucester, 10mins from J13 &14 of M5. Follow signs to Berkeley from A38 & B4066. Visitor entrance L off Canonbury St, just before town centre.* **Mon 17 June (11-5). Adm £8, chd £4. Light refreshments in the new Walled Garden. Visits also by arrangement 3 June to 17 June.**
Unique historic garden of a keen plantsman, with far-reaching views across the River Severn. Gardens contain many rare plants which thrive in the warm microclimate against the stone walls of this medieval castle. Woodland, historic trees and stunning terraced borders. The admission price does not include entrance into the castle.

GROUP OPENING

7 BLOCKLEY GARDENS

Blockley, Moreton-in-Marsh, GL56 9DB. *3m NW of Moreton-in-Marsh. Just off the A44 Morton-in-Marsh to Evesham road.* **Sun 28 Apr, Sun 23 June (1-6). Combined adm £8, chd free. Home-made teas at St George's Hall.**

BLOCKLEY ALLOTMENTS
Blockley & District Allotment Ass, www.blockleyallotments.wixsite. com/blockleyallotments.
Open on Sun 23 June

CHURCH GATES
Mrs Brenda Salmon.
Open on all dates

NEW **CLAREMONT HOUSE**
Linda & Berns Russ.
Open on Sun 23 June

COLEBROOK HOUSE
Mr & Mrs G Apsion, www. instagram.com/colebrook_house_ gardens.
Open on all dates

GARDEN HOUSE
Nick & Ginny Williams-Ellis.
Open on Sun 23 June

THE MANOR HOUSE
Zoe Thompson.
Open on Sun 23 June

THE OLD SILK MILL
Mr D Martell.
Open on all dates

PORCH HOUSE
Mr & Mrs Johnson.
Open on Sun 28 Apr

SNUGBOROUGH MILL
Rupert & Mandy Williams-Ellis.
Open on all dates

WOODRUFF
Paul & Maggie Adams.
Open on all dates

This popular historic Cotswold hillside village has a great variety of high quality, well stocked gardens - large and small, old and new. The delightful spring fed Blockley Brook flows right through the village and some of the gardens, including former water mills and millponds. From some gardens there are wonderful rural views. Children welcome, but close supervision is essential.

8 ♦ BOURTON HOUSE GARDEN

Bourton-on-the-Hill, GL56 9AE. Mr & Mrs R Quintus, 01386 700754, info@bourtonhouse.com, www.bourtonhouse.com. *2m W of Moreton-in-Marsh. On A44.* **For NGS: Sun 18 Aug (10-5). Adm £10, chd free. Light refreshments & home-made cakes in Grade I Listed C16 tithe barn. For other opening times and information, please phone, email or visit garden website.**
Award-winning, 3 acre garden featuring imaginative topiary, wide herbaceous borders with many rare, unusual and exotic plants, water features, unique shade house and many creatively planted pots. Fabulous at any time of year, but magnificent in summer months and early autumn. Walk around a 7 acre pasture, with free printed guide to specimen trees available. 70% access for wheelchairs. Disabled WC.

9 BROCKWORTH COURT

Court Road, Brockworth, GL3 4QU. Tim & Bridget Wiltshire, 01452 862938, timwiltshire@hotmail.co.uk. *6m E of Gloucester. 6m W of Cheltenham. Adj St Georges Church on Court Rd. From A46 turn into Mill Lane, turn R, L, R at T junctions. From Ermin St, turn into Ermin Park, then R at r'about then L at next r'about.* **Wed 29 May, Wed 18 Sept (2-5.30). Adm £6, chd free. Home-made teas. Visits also by arrangement 1 May to 10 Oct for groups of 10 to 40.**
This intense yet informal tapestry style garden beautifully complements the period manor house which it surrounds. Organic, naturalistic, with informal cottage-style planting areas that seamlessly blend together. Natural fish pond, with Monet bridge leading to small island with thatched Fiji house. Kitchen garden once cultivated by monks. Views to Crickley and Coopers Hill. Adjacent Norman church (open). Historic tithe barn, manor house visited by Henry VIII and Anne Boleyn in 1535. Partial wheelchair access.

10 CALMSDEN MANOR

Calmsden, Cirencester, GL7 5ET. Mr M & Mrs J Tufnell. *5m N of Cirencester. Turn to Calmsden off A429 at The Stump pub. On entering the village Manor gates are straight ahead of you.* **Mon 26 Aug (2.30-6.30). Adm £10, chd free. Home-made teas.**

With borders originally designed by Mary Keen, Calmsden Manor is a well loved garden. A treat for plant lovers, design enthusiasts, vegetable growers or those simply looking for a lovely day out. Inc herbaceous borders, a small arboretum, wild grass and flower meadow, and a walled garden. The garden moves with the seasons with stunning early season bulbs, summer borders and late season colour.

 ♿ ❀ ☕ ᐅ))

11 ◆ CERNEY HOUSE GARDENS

North Cerney, Cirencester, GL7 7BX. Mr N W Angus & Dr J Angus, 01285 831300, janet@cerneygardens.com, www.cerneygardens.com. *4m NW of Cirencester. On A435 Cheltenham rd turn L opp Bathurst Arms, follow rd past church up hill, then go straight towards pillared gates on R (signed Cerney House).* **For NGS: Sun 14 July (10-7). Adm £6, chd £1. Home-made teas in The Bothy Tea room. For other opening times and information, please phone, email or visit garden website.**

A romantic English garden for all seasons. There is a secluded Victorian walled garden featuring herbaceous borders overflowing with colour. In the summer the magnificent display of rambling romantic roses comes to life. Enjoy our woodland walk, extended nature trail and new medicinal herb garden. Dogs welcome. Walled garden accessible for electric wheelchairs. Gravel paths and inclines may not suit manual wheelchairs.

♿ 🐕 ❀ 🚌 ☕ 🪑 ᐅ))

12 CHARINGWORTH COURT

Broadway Road, Winchcombe, GL54 5JN. Susan & Richard Wakeford, 07791 353779, susanwakeford@gmail.com, www.charingworthcourtcotswoldsgarden.com. *8m NE of Cheltenham. 400 metres N of Winchcombe town centre on B4632. Limited parking along Broadway Rd. Town car parks in Bull Lane, Chandos St (short stay)* and all day parking (£1) in Back Lane. Map on our website. **Sat 18, Sun 19 May (11-5.30). Adm £5, chd free. Home-made teas. Visits also by arrangement May & June for groups of 10 to 30. Owners can give guided tour of the garden.**

Artistically and lovingly created 1½ acre garden surrounding restored Georgian/Tudor house (not open). Relaxed country style with Japanese influences, large pond, sculpture and walled vegetable/flower garden, created over 25 yrs from a blank canvas. Mature copper beech trees, Cedar of Lebanon and Wellingtonia; and younger trees replacing an earlier excess of *Cupressus leylandii*. Partial access due to gravel paths which can be challenging but several areas accessible without steps. Some disabled parking by house. Ring to book.

♿ 🐕 ☕ ᐅ))

13 CHARLTON DOWN HOUSE

Charlton Down, Tetbury, GL8 8TZ. Neil & Julie Record, cdh.groupbookings@gmail.com. *From Tetbury, take A433 towards Bath for 1½ m; turn R (north) just before the Hare & Hounds, then R again after 200yds into Hookshouse Lane. Charlton Down House is 600yds on R.* **Sun 21 Apr (11-5); Thur 4, Thur 11, Thur 18 July, Thur 8, Thur 15, Thur 29 Aug (1-5). Adm £7, chd free. Home-made teas. Cash payment preferred for refreshments. Visits also by arrangement 1 July to 30 Aug for groups of 20 to 35.**

Extensive country house gardens in 180 acre equestrian estate. Formal terraces, perennial borders, walled topiary garden, enclosed cut flower garden and large glasshouse. Jubilee copse. Rescue animals. Ample parking. Largely flat terrain; most garden areas accessible.

♿ 🐕 🚌 ☕ 🪑 ᐅ))

14 CHASE END

Tidenham Chase, Chepstow, NP16 7JN. Tim & Penny Wright, pennyjwright63@gmail.com. *On the B4228 between Chepstow & St Briavels. 1st house on R after Boughspring Ln, travelling on the B4228 towards St. Briavels. Parking 2nd entrance on R, through gate into top field. No parking on main road.* **Sat 8 June (11-5). Adm £5, chd free. Home-made teas. Visits also by arrangement 20 May to 28 June** for groups of up to 20.

Four acre, south facing, sloping site overlooking the Severn, where soil and wildlife are nurtured with organic and no-dig methods. There are 3 acres of mature wildflower meadows, with orchards and a vineyard, and 1 acre of more formal garden with mature herbaceous borders, trees and shrubs (notably roses), 2 ponds with bog gardens, an area of prairie planting and a greenhouse.

❀ ☕ ᐅ))

15 NEW THE CLOSES

Farm Road, Edgeworth, Stroud, GL6 7JG. Mr & Mrs R Lindemann. *10m NW of Cirencester. From the A419 through Sapperton & past the Daneway pub. Satnav to Edgerton then follow NGS signs. Roads are narrow.* **Fri 21 June (2-5). Adm £10, chd free. Home-made teas. (included in admission).**

The garden is over 2 acres, contrasting rooms, roses, herbaceous beds and a working vegetable garden surrounded by a wide variety of trees and shrubs. Standard roses beside the parterre lead you into the sunken garden. Through the gate and beyond the roses and box you'll go past the hosta and fern bed. From there you reach the water feature to enjoy the peace and tranquility of the garden.

☕ ᐅ))

16 NEW 1 COBDEN VILLAS

Meadow Bank, Walkley Wood, Nailsworth, GL6 0RT. Sue Ratcliffe. *Parking in Nailsworth town centre with a 10 min walk to Shortwood Rd, L at the Britannia pub onto Horsley Rd; R onto Pike Lane. There is very limited on road parking in Pike Lane/Meadow Bank.* **Fri 31 May, Sat 1 June, Sat 27, Sun 28 July (10-4). Adm £5. Tea, coffee & cold drinks.**

Set into a hillside this organic and wildlife friendly garden is divided into distinct areas. A small mixed woodland area provides separation from the adjacent lane with underplanting of shade loving native and unusual plants. Terraced beds and borders adopt cottage garden planting ethos with extensive ground cover and shrubs. A rill and small pond provides a home for frogs and dragonflies. A visitor described the garden as like having a big green hug.

❀ ☕

17 COTSWOLD FARM

Duntisbourne Abbots, Cirencester, GL7 7JS. John & Sarah Birchall, www.cotswoldfarmgardens.org. uk. *5m NW of Cirencester off old A417. From Cirencester L signed Duntisbourne Abbots Services, R and R underpass. Drive ahead. From Gloucester L signed Duntisbourne Abbots Services. Pass Services. Drive L.* **Sat 17, Sun 18 Feb (11-3). Light refreshments. Sat 1, Sun 2 June, Sat 31 Aug, Sun 1 Sept (2-5). Home-made teas. Adm £7.50, chd free. 2025: Sat 15, Sun 16 Feb. Donation to A Rocha.**
This beautiful Arts & Crafts garden overlooks a quiet valley on descending levels with terraces designed by Norman Jewson in the1930s. Enclosed by Cotswold stone walls and yew hedges, the garden has year-round interest inc a snowdrop collection with over 80 varieties. The terraces, shrub garden, herbaceous borders and bog garden are full of scent and colour from spring to autumn. Rare orchid walks. Picnics welcome. Wheelchair access to main terrace only (no wheelchair access to WCs).

18 DAGLINGWORTH HOUSE

Daglingworth, Cirencester, GL7 7AG. David & Henrietta Howard, 07970 122122, ettajhoward@gmail.com. *3m N of Cirencester off A417/419. House with blue gate beside church in centre of Daglingworth, at end of No Through Road.* **Visits by arrangement Apr to Sept for groups of up to 20. Adm £8, chd free. Light refreshments.**
Walled garden, temple, grotto, and pools. Classical garden of 2½ acres, with humorous contemporary twist. Hedges, topiary shapes, herbaceous borders. Pergolas, grass garden, wildflower meadow, woodland, cascade and mirror canal. Sunken garden. Pretty Cotswold village setting beside church. Visitor comment: 'It breaks every rule of gardening - but it's wonderful!'.

19 DAYLESFORD HOUSE

Daylesford, GL56 0YG. Lord & Lady Bamford. *5m West of Chipping Norton. Off A436 between Stow-on-the-Wold & Chipping Norton.* **Wed 1 May (1-5). Adm £8, chd free. Home-made teas.**
Magnificent C18 landscape grounds created in 1790 for Warren Hastings, greatly restored and enhanced by present owners under organic regime. Lakeside and woodland walks within natural wildflower meadows. Large formal walled garden, centred around orchid, peach and working glasshouses. Trellised rose garden. Collection of citrus within period orangery. Secret garden, pavilion, formal pools. Very large garden with substantial distances. The owners of Daylesford House have specifically requested that photographs are NOT taken in their garden or grounds. No dogs allowed except guide dogs. Teas cash only. Partial wheelchair access.

20 DOWNTON HOUSE

Gloucester St, Painswick, GL6 6QN. Ms Jane Kilpatrick. *4m N of Stroud. Entry to garden is via Hollyhock Lane only. Please note: NO cars in Lane. Park in Stamages Lane village car park off A46 below church, or in Churchill Way, 1st L off Gloucester St B4073.* **Mon 5, Tue 6 Feb (10.30-3). Adm £6, chd free. Light refreshments. Coffee & home-made cakes from Lucy and her Horsebox.**
The owner is co-author of 'The Galanthophiles : 160 Years of Snowdrop Devotees' (2018, Orphans Publishing). The walled ⅓ acre garden in the centre of Painswick provides the perfect setting for Jane's collection of Galanthus cultivars. In addition, naturalised drifts of *Galanthus nivalis* and *Galanthus atkinsii* flourish amongst winter-flowering shrubs, cyclamen, Iris reticulata and Polystichum ferns. Steep ramp provides access to path and paved area.

GROUP OPENING

21 EASTCOMBE AND BUSSAGE GARDENS

Eastcombe, Stroud, GL6 7EB. *3m E of Stroud. Maps available on the day from Eastcombe Village Hall GL6 7EB & Redwood GL6 8AZ. On street parking only. Tickets valid Sunday & Monday due to length of trail (2 miles).* **Sun 5, Mon 6 May (1.30-5.30). Combined adm £8, chd free. Light refreshments at Eastcombe Village Hall. Ice creams at Hawkley Cottage.**

CADSONBURY
Natalie & Glen Beswetherick.

17 FARMCOTE CLOSE
John & Sheila Coyle.

20 FARMCOTE CLOSE
Ian & Dawn Sim.

21 FARMCOTE CLOSE
Robert & Marion Bryant.

HAMPTON VIEW
Geraldine & Mike Carter.

HAWKLEY COTTAGE
Helen & Gerwin Westendorp.

12 HIDCOTE CLOSE
Mr K Walker.

HIGHLANDS
Helen & Bob Watkinson.

1 JASMINE COTTAGE
Mrs June Gardiner.

LITTLE DORMERS
Bernadette Scahill.

REDWOOD
Heather Collins.

50 STONECOTE RIDGE
Julie & Robin Marsland.

WHITE HOUSE
Jane & Dave Gandy.

WOODVIEW COTTAGE
Julian & Eileen Horn-Smith.

Medium and small gardens in a variety of styles and settings within this picturesque hilltop village location, with its spectacular views of the Toadsmoor Valley. In addition, one large garden is located in the bottom of the valley, approachable only on foot as are some of the other gardens. Full descriptions of each garden and those with wheelchair access can be found on the National Garden Scheme website. Please show any pre-booked tickets at village hall or Redwood. WC at village hall and Hawkley Cottage. Plants for sale at village hall and some gardens.

47,000 people affected by cancer were reached by Maggie's centres supported by the National Garden Scheme over the last 12 months

22 NEW **39 FAIRWAYS AVENUE**
Coleford, GL16 8RP. Ms Carrie
Wildman. *6m from Monmouth in
Coleford, close to the centre of
town. Off the B4228 (Old Station
Way) which runs from Tutshill into
Coleford and less than 1m from the
library. Please park in the large public
car park. The garden is signed from
there.* **For NGS: Sun 7 July (11-4).
Adm £3, chd free. Tea, coffee,
squash & a selection of home-
made cakes available.**
Beautiful, small town garden with
cottage style planting and an array
of colourful perennials and evergreen
plants.

23 **20 FORSDENE WALK**
Coalway, Coleford, GL16 7JZ.
Pamela Buckland, 01594 837179.
*From Coleford take Lydney/
Chepstow Rd at T-lights. L after
police station ½ m up hill turn L
at Xrds then 2nd R (Old Road)
straight on at minor Xrds then L into
Forsdene Walk.* **Sun 19 May (1-5).
Adm £3.50. Home-made teas.**

Visits also by arrangement May to
Sept for groups of up to 15. Regret
not suitable for children.
Corner garden full of design ideas
to maximise smaller spaces in
interlocking colour themed rooms,
some on different levels, packed with
perennials and grasses. A shady
pergola for ferns and hostas. A small
man-made stream. Vegetables in
containers. Low maintenance gravelled
areas with trees, shrubs & self sown
perennials, plus pots in abundance.

Pontings Farm

24 FORTHAMPTON COURT

Forthampton, Tewkesbury, GL19 4RD. Alan & Anabel Mackinnon. *W of Tewkesbury. From Tewkesbury A438 to Ledbury. After 2m turn L to Forthampton. At Xrds go L towards Chaceley. Go 1m turn L at Xrds.* **Sat 8, Sun 9 June (1.30-4.30). Adm £7, chd free. Home-made teas.**
Charming and varied garden surrounding N Gloucestershire medieval manor house (not open) within sight of Tewkesbury Abbey. Inc borders, lawns, roses and magnificent Victorian vegetable garden. Disabled drop off at entrance, some gravel paths and uneven areas.
& ✿ ☕))

25 ◆ THE GARDEN AT MISERDEN

Miserden, nr Stroud, GL6 7JA. Mr Nicholas Wills, 01285 821303, hello@miserden.org, www.miserden.org. *6m NW of Cirencester. Leave A417 for Birdlip, drive through Whiteway & follow signs for Miserden.* **For NGS: Thur 8 Aug (10-5.30). Adm £10, chd free. Light refreshments at The Glasshouse Café. For other opening times and information, please phone, email or visit garden website.**
A timeless walled garden designed in the C17 with a wonderful sense of peace and tranquillity. Known for its magnificent mixed borders and Lutyens' Yew Walk and quaint grass steps; there is also an ancient mulberry tree, plus enchanting arboretum and stunning views across the Golden Valley. Potting Shed Shop, Glasshouse Café, a variety of workshops, pop-up restaurant. Afternoon Tea experiences in the garden and woodland. Routes around the garden are gravel or grass, there are alternative routes to those that have steps. Disabled WC at the café.
& ✿ 🚗 ☕))

26 THE GATE

80 North Street, Winchcombe, GL54 5PS. Vanessa Berridge & Chris Evans. *Winchcombe is on B4632 midway between Cheltenham & Broadway. Parking behind Library in Back Lane, 50 yds from The Gate. Entry via Cowl Lane.* **Mon 6 May (1-5). Adm £4, chd free. Home-made teas.**
Compact cottage-style garden planted with a colourful display of tulips in spring, and with perennials,

annuals and climbers in the walled courtyard of C17 former coaching inn. Also a separate, productive, walled kitchen garden with espaliers and other fruit trees. Wheelchair access to most areas of the garden; other areas are partially visible from negotiable paths.
& ✿ ☕))

27 GREENFIELDS, BROCKWEIR COMMON

Brockweir, Chepstow, NP16 7NU. Jackie Healy, 07747 186302, jackie@greenfields.garden, www.greenfields.garden. *Located between Chepstow & Monmouth. A446 from M'mouth. Go thru Llandogo, L to Brockweir. From Chepstow, thru Tintern, R to B'weir. Go over bridge, up hill, 1st L, follow lane to fork, L at fork. 1st property on R. No coaches.* **Sun 9 June (1-5). Adm £6, chd free. Home-made teas. Visits also by arrangement 10 June to 23 June for groups of 10 to 40.**
Greenfields is a 1½ acre plantsperson's gem of a garden set in the beautiful Wye Valley AONB. The garden features many mature trees and numerous rare/unusual plants and shrubs planted as discrete gardens. Greenfields is the passion and work of 'Head Gardener' Jackie, who has a long interest in the propagation of plants. Some areas of the garden are not accessible by wheelchair, and the WC is not wheelchair accessible.
& ✿ ☕))

28 GREENFIELDS, LITTLE RISSINGTON

Cheltenham, GL54 2NA. Mrs Diana MacKenzie-Charrington. *On Rissington Rd between Bourton-on-the-Water & Little Rissington, opp turn to Grt Rissington (Leasow Lane). SatNav using postcode does not take you to house.* **Sun 7 July (2-6). Adm £6, chd free.**
The honey coloured Georgian Cotswold stone house sits in 2 acres of garden, created by current owners over last 22 yrs. Lawns are edged with borders full of flowers and flowering bulbs. A small pond and stream overlook fields. Bantams roam freely. Mature apple trees in wild garden, greenhouse in working vegetable garden. Regret no dogs. Partial wheelchair access.
& ☕))

29 11 HATHERLEY COURT ROAD

Cheltenham, GL51 3AQ. Mike & Rosemary Richards, 07884 493823, gaiatraditionalgardeners@gmail.com. *Hatherley. Next to Hatherley Court Road entrance to Hatherley Park.* **Sun 19 May (2-5), open nearby 37 Queen's Road. Sun 14 July (2-5). Adm £5, chd free. Pre-booking essential, please visit www.ngs.org.uk for information & booking. Tea. Visits also by arrangement 19 May to 14 July for groups of up to 20.**
A large urban garden developed over the last 25 yrs by the current owners. Their vision is to create an informal nature lovers' garden where there is tranquillity away from the town and a time for mental refreshment. The space consists of paths, herbaceous border, pond, wildflower spread, silver birch copse and lush green vegetation of the dry river bed. Although the far area of the garden is inaccessible for wheelchairs, the raised decking area gives an overall view of the garden.
& ☕))

30 ◆ HIGHNAM COURT

Highnam, Gloucester, GL2 8DP. Mr R J Head, www.HighnamCourt.co.uk. *2m W of Gloucester. On A40/A48 junction from Gloucester to Ross or Chepstow. At this r'about take exit at 3 o'clock if coming from Gloucester direction. Do NOT go into Highnam village.* **For NGS: Sun 7 Apr, Sun 5 May, Sun 4 Aug (11-5). Adm £6, chd free. Light refreshments. For other opening times and information, please visit garden website. Donation to other charities.**
40 acres of Victorian landscaped gardens surrounding magnificent Grade I house (not open), set out by artist Thomas Gambier Parry. Lakes, shrubberies and listed Pulhamite water gardens with grottos and fernery. Exciting ornamental lakes, and woodland areas. Extensive 1 acre rose garden and many features, inc numerous wood carvings and kitchen garden.
 🐕 ☕ 🪑))

31 HODGES BARN

Shipton Moyne, Tetbury, GL8 8PR. Mr & Mrs N Hornby, www.hodgesbarn.com. *3m S of Tetbury. On Malmesbury side of village.* **Sun 9, Mon 10 June (2-5). Adm £7, chd free. Home-made teas at the Pool House.**
Very unusual C15 dovecote converted into family home. Cotswold stone walls host climbing and rambling roses, clematis, vines, hydrangeas and together with yew, rose and tapestry hedges create formality around house. Mixed shrub and herbaceous borders, shrub roses, water garden, woodland garden planted with cherries and magnolias. Vegetable and picking flower garden.
 ♿ 🐕 ❄ ☕))

32 HOME FARM

Newent Lane, Huntley, GL19 3HQ. Mrs T Freeman, 01452 830210, torillfreeman@gmail.com. *4m S of Newent. On B4216 ½m off A40 in Huntley travelling towards Newent.* **Sun 28 Jan, Sun 11 Feb, Sun 10 Mar, Sun 7, Sun 28 Apr (11-4). Adm £4, chd free. 2025: Sun 26 Jan, Sun 9 Feb. Visits also by arrangement 28 Jan to 5 May.**
Set in elevated position with exceptional views. 1m walk through woods and fields to show carpets of spring flowers. Enclosed garden with fern border, sundial and heather bed. White and mixed shrub borders. Stout footwear advisable in winter. Two delightful cafés within a mile.
🐕 🎋

33 HOOKSHOUSE POTTERY

Hookshouse Lane, Tetbury, GL8 8TZ. Lise & Christopher White, www.hookshousepottery.co.uk. *2½m SW of Tetbury. Follow signs from A433 at Hare & Hounds Hotel, Westonbirt. Alternatively take A4135 out of Tetbury towards Dursley & follow signs after ½m on L.* **Fri 31 May, Sat 1, Fri 21 June, Fri 5 July (1.30-5.30). Adm £5, chd free. Pre-booking essential, please visit www.ngs.org.uk for information & booking. Home-made teas.**
Garden offers a combination of long perspectives and intimate corners. Planting inc wide variety of perennials, with emphasis on colour interest throughout the seasons. Herbaceous borders, woodland garden and flower meadow, water garden containing treatment ponds (unfenced) and flowform cascades.

Sculptural features. Kitchen garden with raised beds, orchard. Run on organic principles. Pottery showroom with hand thrown woodfired pots inc frost proof garden pots. 'Art in the Garden' will feature a small collection of work by artists working in metal, glass, wood and willow, set in idyllic surroundings. Mostly wheelchair accessible.
 ♿ 🐕 ❄ ☕ 🎋))

34 KEMBLE HOUSE

Kemble, Cirencester, GL7 6AD. Jill Kingston. *3m from Cirencester. Approaching Kemble on the A429 from Cirencester, turn L onto School Rd then R onto Church Rd, pass Kemble Church on L. Kemble House is the next house on L.* **Thur 25 Apr (2.30-5). Adm £5, chd free.**
A landscaped garden with many tall lime trees. Herbaceous borders line the lawns. The main one in front of the house is a grass tennis court that was laid in the 1880s. There is a walled garden with many fruit trees and two rose gardens. Two paddocks surround the property with Hebridean sheep. Wheelchair access possible, gravel pathways and some steps.
 ♿ ❄

35 ◆ KIFTSGATE COURT

Chipping Campden, GL55 6LN. Mr & Mrs J G Chambers, 01386 438777, info@kiftsgate.co.uk, www.kiftsgate.co.uk. *4m NE of Chipping Campden. Opp Hidcote NT Garden.* **For NGS: Mon 15 Apr (2-6); Mon 12 Aug (12-6). Adm £11, chd £3.50. Light refreshments. For other opening times and information, please phone, email or visit garden website.**
Magnificent situation and views, many unusual plants and shrubs, tree peonies, hydrangeas, abutilons, species and old-fashioned roses inc largest rose in England, *Rosa filipes* 'Kiftsgate'.
❄ 🚗 🛏 ☕))

36 KIRKHAM FARM

Upper Slaughter, Cheltenham, GL54 2JS. Mr & Mrs John Wills. *On road between Lower Slaughter & Lower Swell. Opp farm buildings on roadside. 1½m W of Fosseway A429 & SW of Stow on the Wold.* **Sun 7 July (11-5). Adm £7, chd free. Home-made teas.**
A country garden overlooking lovely views with several mixed borders that

always have a succession of colour. Gravel gardens, trees and shrubs and a hidden pool garden, raised beds, cutting beds and a developing wildflower bank give plenty of interest. Teas are served in our beautifully restored stone barn. This garden is proud to provide plants for the National Garden Scheme's Show Garden at Chelsea Flower Show 2024. The majority of the garden is accessible.
 ♿ 🐕 ❄ ☕))

37 LANGFORD DOWNS FARM

Langford Downs Farm, nr Lechlade, GL7 3QL. Mr & Mrs Gavin MacEchern. *Access from A361 via layby behind copse - 6m from Burford towards Lechlade on the R OR 2m from Lechlade towards Burford on the L (NOT in Langford).* **Sun 23 June (2-6). Adm £7, chd free. Home-made teas.**
Cotswold house and good sized garden created in 2009, with extensive tree planting, and mixed tree, shrub and herbaceous borders. Traditional hedges comprising arches and windows and crab apple espalier. Extensive cut flower and vegetable garden, interesting courtyard with raised nursery beds. Cotswold pond with natural spring, bug hotels, magic garden and lots of quirky things to see and find! All areas wheelchair friendly.
 ♿ 🐕 ❄ 🚗 ☕

38 LECKHAMPTON COURT HOSPICE

Church Road, Leckhampton, Cheltenham, GL53 0QJ. www.sueryder.org/care-centres/hospices/leckhampton-court-hospice. *2m SW of Cheltenham. From Church Rd take driveway by church signed Sue Ryder Leckhampton Court Hospice & follow parking signs.* **Sun 23 June (11-4). Adm £5, chd free. Light refreshments. Visitors welcome to picnic on our back lawn (bring your own chairs & picnic blankets).**
Set within this Grade II* listed medieval estate, the informal gardens at Leckhampton Court Hospice surround the buildings combining lawns and planted beds. Courtyard garden designed by Peter Dowle, RHS Chelsea gold medal winner. Highlights inc woodland walk around lake and into woodland, numerous protected mature trees and a terrace with magnificent views

across Cheltenham towards Malvern. Features inc a golden maple tree planted by His Majesty King Charles III to commemorate his 70th birthday, a kitchen garden supplying fresh vegetables for patients. Wheelchair access in some areas: from back of reception to Sir Charles Irving terrace; woodland walk; main courtyard.

39 LITTLE ORCHARD
Slad, Stroud, GL6 7QD. Rod & Terry Clifford, 07967 253420, terryclifford.tlc@gmail.com. *2m from Stroud, 10 m from Cheltenham. Last property in Slad village, on L before leaving 30mph speed limit travelling from Stroud to Birdlip on B4070. Sat Nav may not bring you directly to property. Parking on verge opp.* **Sat 29, Sun 30 June (11-5). Adm £5, chd free. Cider tasting available. Visits also by arrangement May to Sept for** groups of 5 to 30. Talk on the evolution of the house, garden & Slad Valley Cider.
One acre garden created from wilderness on a challenging, steeply sloping site using many reclaimed materials, stonework and statuary. Multiple terraces and garden 'rooms' enhanced with different planting styles and water features to complement the natural surroundings. Many seating areas with stunning views. Children's Trail. Cidery offering tastings. Exhibition and sale of local artists' work. Wheelchair access possible but challenging due to the severity of slopes and steps. Please phone for further details.

40 NEW ◆ LITTLE ORCHARD KEMPLEY DYMOCK
Kempley, Dymock, GL18 2BU. Ros Flook. *7m from Ross-on-Wye, 8m from Ledbury. From Ross M50, J3. L B4221, then R for Kempley. After 2.6m, follow NGS signs for parking & garden. From Ledbury B4126, 5.1m turn R B4125, 120m turn L onto Kempley Rd. After 2.1m, follow NGS signs.* **For NGS: Sun 18 Aug (1-5). Adm £5, chd free. Home-made teas.**
Four acre wildlife friendly garden with views over open countryside. Mixing naturalistic planting of native and specimen trees with ornamental borders, rose garden and cottage gardens, all of which can be explored from the large connecting lawns. Year-round interest: several ponds, productive apple orchard, woodland, wildflower meadows, ancient horse chestnut. Disabled parking at house. Wheelchair access restricted to garden areas nearest the house, WC not wheelchair accessible.

Greenfields, Little Rissington

41 LORDS OF THE MANOR HOTEL

Upper Slaughter, Cheltenham, GL54 2JD. Mike Dron (Head Gardener), 01451 820243, reservations@lordsofthemanor. com, www.lordsofthemanor.com. *2m W of Bourton-on-the-Water. From Fosse way follow signs for the Slaughters from close to Bourton-on-the-Water (toward Stow). From B4077 (Stanway Hill rd) coming from Tewkesbury direction, follow signs 2m after Ford village.* **Wed 24 Apr, Wed 19 June, Wed 18 Sept (10-3). Adm £7, chd £5. Light refreshments are available from the hotel, from light snacks to afternoon tea. Pre-booking is essential for afternoon tea.**

Classic Cotswold country garden with a very English blend of semi-formal and informal, merging beautifully with the surrounding landscape. Beautiful walled garden, established wildflower meadow, the River Eye. The herb garden and stunning bog garden were originally designed by Julie Toll around 2012. Wildlife garden, croquet lawn, courtyard and Victorian skating pond. Steps in walled garden & bog garden. Regret that due to the age & layout of the building there are no wheelchair-friendly facilities within the hotel.

♿ 🐕 🛏 ☕))

42 MADAMS

Eden's Hill, Upleadon, Newent, GL18 1EE. Phil & Pauline Cooke, www.upleadon-village.co.uk/ madams-ngs/. *3m ENE of Newent, 10m NNW of Gloucester. Newent Xrds to B4216 Dymock, 1st R Tewkesbury Rd for 2.6m. At Xrds L to Eden's Hill. Gloucester A40 to Ross-on-Wye, R B4215 to Newent, 3.4m R onto Gloucester Rd. 2.8m to Xrds. Limited parking at garden.* **Sun 2 June (2-6). Adm £5, chd free. Home-made teas.**

Two acre country woodland garden with far reaching views. The garden is still developing with a variety of herbaceous and mixed borders, wildflower area with an abundance of common spotted orchids, small formal pond and small veg patch. Mature trees and areas left wild for nature. As parking is limited at garden, pls park in village & walk up Eden's Hill approx 350m through wood (steep in places). Partial wheelchair access possible with gravel on drive, grass slopes and some steps. Some disabled parking at the house.

 ♿ ☕))

43 THE MANOR

Little Compton, GL56 0RZ. Reed Foundation (Charity). *½m from A44 or 2m from A3400. Follow signs to Little Compton, then yellow NGS signs.* **Sun 18 Aug (1-5). Adm £6, chd free. Home-made teas in church yard next door.**

Arts & Crafts garden surrounding Jacobean manor house. Large plant collection, with deer park, meadow and arboreta. Croquet, golf, and tennis free to play. Children, picnics, and dogs very welcome. Arts and Crafts layout, water features, extensive mixed planting and styles, formal lawns, hedges and topiary, unique enclosed setting, sculptures, deer and sheep. Orchard and flower garden (small part of the formal gardens) not accessible by wheelchair. Disabled drop-off at entrance.

♿ 🐕 ☕ 🧺))

44 NEW MILTON COTTAGE

Overbury Street, Charlton Kings, Cheltenham, GL53 8HJ. Jackie Bickell. *Off A40 at Sixways, Charlton Kings. Heading E on A40 Overbury St is on the R just past the pedestrian crossing at Sixways. Heading W, the turning is L just after the Co-op supermarket. Free parking behind Badhams Chemist.* **Sun 19 May (11-5). Adm £4, chd free.**

A secluded and attractive walled garden just a short distance from the busy A40 but a tranquil space planted in cottage garden style. Over 40 yrs, the current owners have transformed a sloping site with terracing, brick retaining walls and a wildlife pond. Extensive container planting adds another dimension to the garden. Due to the sloping site and steps, wheelchair access is NOT possible.

🐕

45 MOOR WOOD

Woodmancote, GL7 7EB. Mr & Mrs Henry Robinson, 07973 688240, henry@moorwoodhouse.co.uk, www.moorwoodroses.co.uk. *3½m NW of Cirencester. Turn L off A435 to Cheltenham at N Cerney, signed Woodmancote 1¼m; entrance in village on L beside lodge with white gates.* **Sun 30 June (2-6). Adm £6, chd free. Home-made teas. Visits also by arrangement 20 June to 3 July for groups of up to 30.**

Two acres of shrub, orchard and wildflower gardens in beautiful isolated valley setting. Holder of National Collection of Rambler Roses.

June 20th to 30th is usually the best time for the roses.

NPC ☕))

46 NEW ◆ NATURE IN ART MUSEUM AND ART GALLERY

Wallsworth Hall, Sandhurst Lane, Twigworth, Gloucester, GL2 9PA. 01452 731422, enquiries@natureinart.org.uk, www.natureinart.org.uk. *3m N of Gloucester on the A38. Satnav postcode: GL2 9PG. The turning to Nature in Art is opp the Twigworth Co-op. There is a ½m drive to the house.* **For NGS: Mon 20 May (10-5). Adm £6.50, chd free. Light refreshments in the main museum building, next to the garden. The Hayward coffee shop serves tea, coffee, light lunches, cakes, snacks, ice creams & cold drinks. Indoor & outdoor seating. For other opening times and information, please phone, email or visit garden website.**

The Nature in Art garden is an expression of the art found in nature. A haven for wildlife with ponds, heritage apple orchard, championing old local varieties and flowerbeds focusing on native plants & aromatic planting. In May, the cow parsley is a main feature, along with primroses and aquilegia. Insect houses and sculptures (plus new ones specially for this opening) nestle in the greenery. Admission gives entry to Garden & Gallery. 2 wheelchairs available to hire, call in advance to book. Majority of garden is wheelchair accessible.

♿ ✱ 🚌 ☕ 🧺))

47 39 NEVEN PLACE

Gloucester, GL1 5NF. Mr Chris & Mrs Jenny Brooker. *Approx 3m N of J12 M5. Follow A38 to Bristol Rd, then into Tuffley Ave, Tuffley Cres, Manu Marble Way to Neven Place. Limited on street parking.* **Sat 10, Sun 11 Aug (10.30-4). Adm £3, chd free. Home-made teas.**

A jungle/exotic small scale garden on a relatively new development, featuring tree ferns, palms, bamboos, bananas, a rill, raised beds and other interesting features.

48 OAK HOUSE

Greenway Lane, Gretton, Cheltenham, GL54 5ER. Paul & Sue Hughes, 01242 603990, ppphug@gmail.com. *In centre of Gretton. Signed Gretton from B4077, approx 3m from A46 Teddington Hands r'about. Greenway Lane 300m R past railway bridge. Parking on main road with short walk to garden.* **Wed 12, Sat 15 June, Sat 6 July (11-4). Combined adm with White Cottage £8, chd free. Home-made teas. Visits also by arrangement 8 Apr to 8 Sept for groups of up to 20.**

One acre secret garden divided into rooms. Gradually developed over the last 30 yrs. Many places to sit and enjoy the scent of honeysuckle, philadelphus and over 50 varieties of roses. Wildflower meadow, gazebo and summerhouse. Formal lily pond and small wildlife pond. Some quirky features. You may even see a fairy.

49 ◆ OXLEAZE FARM

Between Eastleach & Filkins, Lechlade, GL7 3RB. Mr & Mrs Charles Mann, 07786 918502, chipps@oxleaze.co.uk, www.oxleaze.co.uk/garden. *5m S of Burford, 3m N of Lechlade off A361 to W (signed Barringtons). Take 2nd L then follow signs.* **For NGS: Sun 9 June (11-5). Adm £7, chd free. Coffee, tea & home-made cakes available for NGS opening & visiting groups. For other opening times and information, please phone, email or visit garden website.**

Set among beautiful traditional farm buildings, plantsperson's good sized garden created by owners over 35 yrs. Year-round interest; mixed borders, vegetable potager, decorative fruit cages, pond/bog garden, bees, potting shed, meadow, and topiary for structure when the flowers fade. Garden rooms off central lawn with corners in which to enjoy this organic Cotswold garden. Groups welcome by arrangement. This garden is proud to provide plants for the National Garden Scheme's Show Garden at Chelsea Flower Show 2024. Mostly wheelchair access.

50 NEW PARK HOUSE

Thirlestaine Road, Cheltenham, GL53 7AS. Yoko Mathers. *Off A40 through Cheltenham. Street parking nearby. Enter garden through side gate.* **Sun 26 May, Sun 30 June (2-**

5). **Adm £5, chd free. Cream teas.** Award-winning ¼ acre rear garden of a Cheltenham Regency town house includes a striking new Japanese 'Karesansui' Garden. Stones and rocks cascade into a gravel pond. Acers, ornamental pine trees and a sheltered "Machiai" sitting bench complete the scene. Specimen trees are grouped in the lawn. Inviting summerhouse with wisteria walkway. Shrubs and wide herbaceous border frame the garden.

51 PASTURE FARM

Upper Oddington, GL56 0XG. Mr & Mrs John LLoyd, 07850 154095, ljmlloyd@yahoo.com. *3m W of Stow-on-the-Wold. Just off A436, midway between Upper & Lower Oddington.* **Sun 26, Mon 27 May (11-6). Adm £7, chd free. Home-made teas. Visits also by arrangement June to Aug for groups of 10 to 40.**

Informal country garden developed over 40 yrs by current owners. Mixed borders, topiary, orchard and many species of trees. Gravel garden and rambling roses in 'the ruins'. A concrete garden and wildflower area leads to vegetable patch. Large spring-fed pond with ducks. Also bantams, chickens, black Welsh sheep and Kunekune pigs. Public footpath across 2 small fields arrives at C11 church, St Nicholas, with doom paintings, set in ancient woodlands. Truly worth a visit (See Simon Jenkins' Book of Churches). This garden is proud to provide plants for the National Garden Scheme's Show Garden at Chelsea Flower Show 2024. Mostly wheelchair access.

52 THE PATCH

Hollywell Lane, Brockweir, Chepstow, NP16 7PJ. Mrs Immy Lee, 07801 816340, immylee1@hotmail.com, www.thepatchbrockweir.com. *6.7m N of Chepstow & 10.6m S of Monmouth, off A466, across Brockweir Bridge. From Monmouth & Chepstow direction follow satnav to Brockweir Bridge, then yellow signs. From Coleford/Gloucester direction follow SatNav to Hewelsfield Xrds, then yellow signs.* **Sun 15 Sept (1-5). Adm £5, chd free. Home-made teas. Visits also by arrangement 15 Sept to 21 Sept. The garden is not accessible for coaches.**

Rural ¼ acre garden with stunning views across the Wye Valley. The maturing planting of 60+ roses, shrubs, grasses and perennials in a modern English Garden style provides year-round interest. The established borders are linked by meandering grass paths and small seating areas in different parts of the garden. Partial wheelchair access.

53 PEAR TREE COTTAGE

58 Malleson Road, Gotherington, nr Cheltenham, GL52 9EX. Mr & Mrs E Manders-Trett, 01242 674592, mmanderstrett@gmail.com. *4m N of Cheltenham. From A435, travelling N, turn R into Gotherington at garage 1m after Bishop's Cleeve bypass. Garden on L 100yds past Shutter Inn.* **Sun 28 Apr (2-5). Adm £5, chd free. Sun 30 June (2-5). Combined adm with Stone Barn, Shutter Lane £8, chd free. Light refreshments. Tea/coffee & cake available. Visits also by arrangement 24 Mar to 7 July for groups of up to 30.**

Mainly informal country garden of approx ½ acre with pond and gravel garden. Herbaceous borders, trees and shrubs surround lawns and seating areas. Wild garden and orchard lead to greenhouses, vegetable garden and beehives. Spring bulbs, early summer perennials and shrubs particularly colourful. Gravel drive and several shallow steps can be overcome for wheelchair users with prior notice.

54 PENNY LEAZE

Sturmyes Road, France Lynch, Stroud, GL6 8LU. Pam Meecham. *Between Stroud & Cirencester. Limited parking at site. Park at Pontings Farm & follow yellow signs.* **Sun 19, Mon 20 May (1-5). Combined adm with Pontings Farm £10, chd free. Home-made teas.**

The garden is nestled into a south-east facing slope where we have attempted to balance wildness, formal gardening, tiny orchard, and fern collection. With seasonal planting for pollinators and wildlife in mind we also grow fruit, vegetables and cut flowers.

55 PONTINGS FARM

France Lynch, Stroud, GL6 8LX. Mr & Mrs Randall. *Between Stroud & Cirencester. From Old Neighbourhood turn into Abnash, then Burrcombe Rd, follow thru to Highfield Way, R at T junction signed Avenis Green, follow Hillside lane ½ m to village, Pontings Farm on L before post box.* **Sun 19, Mon 20 May (1-5). Combined adm with Penny Leaze £10, chd free. Sun 1, Mon 2 Sept (1-5). Adm £6, chd free. Cream teas.**

One acre accessible hillside garden with views of the Golden Valley and beyond. Bee and wildlife friendly with wildflower meadow, pond and orchard. Raised beds for vegetables and flowers. Our prairie style and gravel gardens thrive in our changing climate of hotter drier summers. The woodland is an ongoing project planted with birch trees, magnolias, Scots pines and hawthorn. There is a short walk of 10 mins between Pontings Farm and Penny Leaze. Directions will be signed through this pretty Cotswold village. Penny Leaze has very limited parking, and the lanes are narrow. Sat Nav can become inaccurate. Parking for both gardens in field, disabled parking at the garden. Majority of the garden is wheelchair/small scooter accessible (not Penny Leaze).

♿ 🐕 ☕ 🏮

56 37 QUEENS ROAD

Cheltenham, GL50 2LX. Geraldine & Richard Pinch. *4 mins walk from Cheltenham Spa train stn. Garden on L as you walk from the stn towards town. Free parking on Queens Rd & Christchurch Rd.* **Sun 19 May (2-5). Adm £4, chd free. Open nearby 11 Hatherley Court Road.**

A wildlife and wildflower-friendly urban garden with many shrubs and climbers. At the front there are shrub borders and a gravel garden. The rear garden slopes upward from the house and is accessed by steps. There are seven ponds, old fruit trees, a vine-house, raised beds planted with perennials and dwarf shrubs, a wild area and a brickery for alpines. Animal sculpture trail for children. Two cafés 5 mins walk away.

🏮))

57 RADNORS

Wheatstone Lane, Lydbrook, GL17 9DP. Mrs Mary Wood, 01594 861690, 07473 959068, woodmary37@gmail.com. *In the Wye Valley on the edge of the Forest of Dean. From Lydbrook, go down through village towards the River Wye. At the T junction turn L into Stowfield Rd. Wheatstone Ln (300m) is 1st turning L after the white cottages. Radnors is at end of lane.* **Visits by arrangement Apr to Sept for groups of up to 10. We offer a guided tour of the garden. Adm £5, chd free. We offer a range of home-made cakes with tea, coffee or fruit juice.**

Five acre hillside woodland garden in AONB on bank above the River Wye. Focus on wildlife with naturalistic planting and weeds, some left for specific insects/birds. It has many paths, a wooded area, wildflower area, flower beds and borders, lawns, stumpery, fernery, vegetable beds and white garden. Of particular interest is the path along a disused railway line, and the summer dahlias.

❀ ☕ 🏕

58 RAMBLERS

Lower Common, Aylburton, Lydney, GL15 6DS. Jane & Leslie Hale. *1½ m W of Lydney. Off A48 Gloucester to Chepstow Rd. From Lydney through Aylburton, out of de-limit turn R signed Aylburton Common, ¾ m along lane.* **Sun 5 May (1.30-5). Adm £5, chd free. Home-made teas.**

Peaceful medium sized country garden with informal cottage planting, herbaceous borders and small pond looking through hedge windows onto wildflower meadow and mature apple orchard. Some shade loving plants and topiary. Large productive vegetable garden. Past winner of The English Garden magazine's Britain's Best Gardener's Garden competition.

❀ ☕

Hodges Barn

59 RICHMOND VILLAGES PAINSWICK

Stroud Road, Painswick, Stroud, GL6 6UL. Richmond Villages/ Bupa. *5m E of Stroud. South of Painswick village on the A46, take R turn into retirement village car park.* **Thur 30 May, Thur 13 June, Thur 4 July, Thur 8 Aug (9-3.30). Adm £5, chd free. Cafe, & if booked in advance restaurant meals.** Situated on the southern slopes of Painswick this 4 acre retirement village boasts formal lawns and borders planted for year-round interest. A varied mix of herbaceous and shrubs, with many areas of interest inc a wildflower meadow with fruit trees that combine to attract an abundance of wildlife. The gardens are a blaze of colour. There are gentle slopes in wildflower meadow and around some areas of the village.

60 ROCKCLIFFE

Upper Slaughter, Cheltenham, GL54 2JW. Mr & Mrs Simon Keswick, www.rockcliffegarden.co.uk. *2m from Stow-on-the-Wold. 1½ m from Lower Swell on B4068 towards Cheltenham. Leave Stow-on-the-Wold on B4068 through Lower Swell. Continue on B4068 for 1½ m. Rockcliffe is well signed on R.* **Wed 29 May (12-5). Adm £7.50, chd free. Home-made teas in car park. Donation to Kate's Home Nursing.**
Large traditional English garden of 8 acres inc pink garden, white and blue garden, herbaceous borders, rose terrace, large walled kitchen garden and greenhouses. Pathway of topiary birds leading up through orchard to stone dovecot Featured in many books and magazines. Overall Winner, The English Garden Magazine's The Nation's Favourite Gardens 2023. 2 wide stone steps through gate, otherwise good wheelchair access. Regret no dogs. .

61 NEW 1 SANDY LANE

Charlton Kings, Cheltenham, GL53 9BS. Linda & Geoff Pratt. *A435 Cirencester Rd out of Cheltenham, R at T-lights into Moorend Rd. Sandy Lane ½ m on at junction with Greenhills Rd. B bus to & from Cheltenham stops at entrance.* **Sun 7 July (2-5). Adm £4, chd free. Home-made teas.**
Third of an acre shady garden on dry

sandy soil with flowering trees and borders planted within the last 3 yrs. Variety of foliage plants and bulbs for year-round interest. Raised stone beds round the patio with alpines and smaller bulbs. Wisterias and climbers clothe 2 pergolas with seating areas.

62 ◆ SEZINCOTE

Moreton-in-Marsh, GL56 9AW. Mrs D Peake, 01386 700444, enquiries@sezincote.com, www.sezincote.co.uk. *3m SW of Moreton-in-Marsh. From Moreton-in-Marsh turn W along A44 towards Evesham; in 1½ m (just before Bourton-on-the-Hill) turn L, by stone lodge with white gate opp Batsford Arboretum.* **For NGS: Sun 9 June (11-5). Adm £9, chd £3. Home-made teas. For other opening times and information, please phone, email or visit garden website. Donation to local school from refreshment money.**
Exotic, oriental water garden by Repton and Daniell, with lake, pools and meandering stream, banked with massed perennials. Large semi-circular orangery, formal Indian garden, fountain, temple and unusual trees of vast size in lawn and wooded park setting. House in Indian manner designed by Samuel Pepys Cockerell. Garden on slope with gravel paths, so not all areas wheelchair accessible.

63 SOUTH LODGE

Church Road, Clearwell, Coleford, GL16 8LG. Andrew & Jane MacBean, 01594 837769, southlodgegarden@ btinternet.com, www.southlodgegarden.co.uk. *2m S of Coleford. Off B4228. Follow signs to Clearwell. Garden on L of castle driveway. Please park on rd in front of church or in village. No parking on castle drive.* **Sun 14 Apr, Sat 8 June (1-5). Adm £4.50, chd free. Home-made teas. Visits also by arrangement 13 Apr to 8 June for groups of 15 to 40.**
Peaceful country garden in 2 acres with stunning views of surrounding countryside. High walls provide a backdrop for rambling roses, clematis, and honeysuckles. Organic garden with large variety of perennials, annuals, shrubs and specimen trees with year-round colour. Vegetable garden, wildlife and formal ponds. Rustic pergola planted with English climbing roses and willow

arbour in gravel garden. Gravel paths and steep grassy slopes. Assistance dogs only.

64 NEW THE STABLES

Hyde Lane, Cheltenham, GL51 9QN. R & Linda Marsh. *10 mins from M5 junction 10. On A4019 at r'about turn NE into Kingsditch Lane leading to Wyman's Lane. Pass under rail bridge into Hyde Lane. Take first L parking opp entrance. Playing fields car park also before bridge.* **Tue 23 July (12-4). Adm £6.**
The garden extends to 0.6 acre on the original stables site and is surrounded by fields. Inspired by the work of Piet Oudolf, the garden consists of large perennial beds which merge into the surrounding landscape. The garden has been developed over the last 3 yrs from a bare site and includes a fully grown native hedge which separates the garden from the newly planted 1 acre wildflower meadow.

»))

GROUP OPENING

65 STANTON VILLAGE GARDENS

Stanton, nr Broadway, WR12 7NE. *3m S of Broadway. Off B4632, between Broadway (3m) & Winchcombe (6m).* **Sun 9 June (1-6). Combined adm £9, chd free. Home-made teas in several gardens around the village. Donation to Village charities.**
A selection of gardens open in this picturesque, unspoilt Cotswold village. Many houses border the street with long gardens hidden behind. Gardens vary, from those with colourful herbaceous borders, established trees, shrubs and vegetable gardens to tiny cottage gardens. Some also have attractive, natural water features fed by the stream that runs through the village. Plants for sale. Free parking. Church also open. The Mount Inn is open for lunch. An NGS visit not to be missed in this gem of a Cotswold village. Regret gardens not suitable for wheelchair users due to gravel drives.

66 ◆ STANWAY FOUNTAIN & WATER GARDEN
Stanway, Cheltenham,
GL54 5PQ. The Earl of Wemyss
& March, 01386 584528,
office@stanwayhouse.co.uk,
www.stanwayfountain.co.uk. *9m NE of Cheltenham. 1m E of B4632 Cheltenham to Broadway rd on B4077 Toddington to Stow-on-the-Wold rd.* **For NGS: Sun 26 May (2-5); Sun 11 Aug (2.30-5). Adm £7, chd £2.50. Home-made teas in Stanway Tearoom. For other opening times and information, please phone, email or visit garden website.**
20 acres of planted landscape in early C18 formal setting. The restored canal, upper pond and fountain have recreated one of the most interesting Baroque water gardens in Britain. Striking C16 manor with gatehouse, tithe barn and church. The garden features Britain's highest fountain at 300ft, and it is the world's highest gravity fountain. It runs at 2.45pm and 4.00pm for 30 mins each time. Partial wheelchair access in garden, some flat areas, able to view fountain and some of garden. House is not suitable for wheelchairs.

67 NEW STONE BARN, SHUTTER LANE
Shutter Lane, Gotherington,
Cheltenham, GL52 9EZ.
Mr Colin & Mrs Penny Weller. *Take A435 Evesham R out of Cheltenham North for approx 4m, turn R at garage onto Malleson Rd. Turn R at Shutters Inn into Shutter Lane. Stone Barn is approx 100yards on L.* **Sun 30 June (11-4). Combined adm with Pear Tree Cottage £8, chd free.**
Cottage-style garden in three sections. Trees shrubs and perennials with small pond at front. Paved mid area with potted plants, olive trees and seat under arch. In back garden two seated areas, herbaceous borders and trees.

68 ◆ SUDELEY CASTLE & GARDENS
Winchcombe, GL54 5JD. Lady Ashcombe, 01242 604244,
enquiries@sudeley.org.uk,
www.sudeleycastle.co.uk. *8m NE Cheltenham, 10 m from M5 J9. SatNavs use GL54 5LP.* **Free parking. For NGS: Fri 20 Sept**
(10-5). Adm £10, chd £6. Light refreshments at The Pavilion and The Old Coach House. For other opening times and information, please phone, email or visit garden website.
Sudeley Castle features 10 magnificent gardens, each with its own unique style and design. Surrounded by striking views of the Cotswold Hills, each garden reflects the fascinating 1000 yr history of the Castle. This series of elegant gardens is set among the Castle and atmospheric ruins and inc a knot garden, Queen's garden and Tudor physic garden. Admission is for garden only. Sudeley Castle remains the only private castle in England to have a queen buried within the grounds - Queen Katherine Parr, the last and surviving wife of King Henry VIII – who lived and died in the castle. A circular route around the gardens is wheelchair accessible although some visitors may require assistance from their companion.

69 NEW ◆ THYME
Southrop Estate, Southrop,
Lechlade, GL7 3PW. Caryn Hibbert, 01367 850174,
enquiries@thyme.co.uk, www.
instagram.com/Thyme.England/. *Pls follow the signs through the village of Southrop towards Lechlade & to our Estate Drive.* **For NGS: Daily Mon 5 Aug to Fri 9 Aug (11-4). Adm £5, chd free. There are 2 restaurants on site that visitors can book, the Ox Barn & The Swan at Southrop. For other opening times and information, please phone, email or visit garden website.**
Situated on the edge of the water meadows, Thyme's carefully managed kitchen gardens ensure abundance from the land while protecting and maintaining the fertile alluvial soil. The garden is productive for much of the year and features a herb garden, cutting gardens and polytunnels to extend the seasons. We grow a large variety of flavoursome and unusual varieties to supply our restaurants.

70 NEW TOWER CLOSE
Snowshill, Broadway, WR12 7JU.
Mr James & Mrs Claire Wright,
claireannewright@gmail.com.
2½ m SW of Broadway. Parking at Snowshill village car park. 50 metres up the hill from Snowshill Manor car park. Take L fork to the top of the road. Follow signs. **Sat 1, Sun 2 June (10.30-4.30). Adm £5, chd free. Home-made teas & ice cream. Visits also by arrangement 3 June to 5 June for groups of 5 to 30.**
Striking views of the Malvern Hills from this 3 acre Cotswold garden positioned at the top of the charming village of Snowshill. Featured in Country Life, the C17 Grade II listed house is surrounded by terraces of garden rooms. Herbaceous borders, espaliered fruit trees & sunken vegetable garden. Plants tumble down the terraces to a romantic stream, ponds, garden features, orchard and meadow.

71 TRENCH HILL
Sheepscombe, GL6 6TZ. Celia & Dave Hargrave, 01452 814306,
celia.hargrave@btconnect.com.
1½ m E of Painswick between the A46 & Sheepscombe. From Cheltenham A46 take 1st turn signed Sheepscombe, follow for approx 1½ m. Or from the Butcher's Arms in Sheepscombe (with it on R) leave village and take lane signed for Cranham. **Sun 11, Sun 18 Feb (11-4); Sun 31 Mar, Mon 1 Apr, Sun 5, Mon 6 May (11-6). Adm £5. Every Wed 5 June to 26 June (2-6). Adm £5, chd free. Sun 14 July, Sun 8 Sept (11-6). Adm £5. Home-made teas. Gluten & dairy free usually available. 2025: Sun 9, Sun 16 Feb. Visits also by arrangement 11 Feb to 14 Sept for groups of up to 35. If coming by coach this must be agreed with the owner.**
Approx 3 acres set in a small woodland with panoramic views. Variety of herbaceous and mixed borders, rose garden, tulips, extensive vegetable plots, wildflower areas, plantings of spring bulbs with thousands of snowdrops and hellebores, woodland walk, two small ponds, waterfall and larger conservation pond. Interesting wooden sculptures, many within the garden. Cultivated using organic principles. Children's play area. Mostly wheelchair accessible but some steps and slopes.

GROUP OPENING

72 TUFFLEY GARDENS
Tuffley Lane, Gloucester, GL4 0DT. Martyn & Jenny Parker. *3m S Gloucester. Follow arrows off St. Barnabas R'about. Cash tickets & maps only from 24 Tuffley Lane. On road parking.* **Sun 2 June (11-4). Combined adm £5, chd £1. Home-made teas at 389 Stroud Road GL4 0DA. Please advise of any allergies on ordering.**
A number of mature suburban gardens of all sizes and styles. Old favourites plus new openers. Lots of colourful flowers, shrubs, trees, baskets and tubs. Circular route of approx one mile. Close to Robinswood Hill Country Park, 250 acres of open countryside and viewpoint, pleasant walks and way-marked trails.

73 11 UPPER WASHWELL
Painswick, Stroud, GL6 6QY. Stella Barber. *Parking in Stamages Lane village car park. From A46 Cheltenham/Stroud rd take B4073 Gloucester St. At the junction turn R into Pullens Rd, then L into Upper Washwell.* **Sat 15, Sat 29 June (10-4). Adm £5, chd free.**
Delightful and secluded. This is a cottage-style garden, including a small pond, gravelled area, and box hedging, small architectural pieces and many interesting nooks and crannies. Come and enjoy this secret garden.

74 ◆ UPTON WOLD
Moreton-in-Marsh, GL56 9TR. Mr & Mrs I R S Bond, www.uptonwold.co.uk. *4½ m W of Moreton-in-Marsh on A44. From Moreton/Stow ½ m past A424 turn R to road into fields then L at mini Xrds. From Evesham 1m past B4081 C/Campden Xrds turn L at end of stone wall to road into fields then as above.* **For NGS: Sun 14 Apr (10-5). Adm £15, chd free. Home-made teas. For other opening times and information, please visit garden website.**
A secret garden of the Cotswolds, Upton Wold has commanding views, yew hedges, herbaceous walks, vegetable, pond and woodland gardens, and a labyrinth. An abundance of unusual and interesting plants, shrubs and trees.

National Collections of Juglans and Pterocarya. A garden of interest to any garden and plant lover. Snowdrop walks from 10 Feb to 3 March. Details on website.

75 WEIR REACH
The Rudge, Maisemore, Gloucester, GL2 8HY. Sheila & Mark Wardle. *3m NW of Gloucester. Turn into The Rudge by White Hart pub. Parking 100yds from garden.* **Wed 12, Sun 16 June (11-5). Adm £5, chd free. Home-made teas.**
Country garden by River Severn. Approx 2 acres with herbaceous beds and mixed borders plus productive fruit and vegetable gardens. Clematis, roses and acers, stone ornaments, small sculptures, bonsai collection. Planted rockery with waterfall and stream connect 2 ponds. Large specimen koi pond borders patio. Meadow with specimen trees leading to river and country views.

76 WESTAWAY
Stockwell Lane, Cleeve Hill, Cheltenham, GL52 3PU. Liz & Ian Ramsay, 07982 605994, lizmramsay@gmail.com. *5m NW of Cheltenham. Off the B4632 Cheltenham to Winchcombe rd at Cleeve Hill. Parking available in the lay-bys at the top of Stockwell Ln on the Cleeve Hill Rd.* **Visits by arrangement 26 Apr to 14 Sept for groups of up to 25. This garden is unsuitable for visitors with limited mobility. Adm £6, chd free. Home-made teas.**
Hillside 1½ acre garden situated on the Cotswold escarpment with spectacular views across the Severn Vale. Interesting solutions to the challenges of gardening on a gradient, reflecting the local topography. Mixed shrub and herbaceous borders, bog garden, orchard, small arboretum and several wildflower areas. Landscaping inc extensive terracing with grass banks.

77 ◆ WESTONBIRT SCHOOL GARDENS
Tetbury, GL8 8QG. Holfords of Westonbirt Trust, 01666 881373, jbaker@holfordtrust.com, www.holfordtrust.com. *3m SW of Tetbury. Please enter through main school gates on A433 - some SatNavs will send you via a side*

entrance where there will be no access - main school gates only please. **For NGS: Sun 7 July (11-4). Adm £7.50, chd free. We offer visitors tea, coffee, soft drinks, water & biscuits throughout the day. For other opening times and information, please phone, email or visit garden website.**
28 acres. Former private garden of Robert Holford, founder of Westonbirt Arboretum. Formal Victorian gardens inc walled Italian garden now restored with early herbaceous borders and exotic border. Rustic walks, lake, statuary and grotto. Rare, exotic trees and shrubs. Beautiful views of Westonbirt House open with guided tours to see fascinating Victorian interior on designated days of the year. Gravelled paths in some areas, grass in others and wheelchair users are limited to downstairs part of the house due to evacuation protocols.

152,684 people were able to access guidance on what to expect when a person is dying through the National Garden Scheme support for Hospice UK this year

78 NEW WHITE COTTAGE

Gretton, Cheltenham, GL54 5HB. Mrs Judith Woodlock, 01242 620474, jandjwoodlock@gmail.com. *Gretton is 2m NW of Winchcombe, & White Cottage is on the western edge of Gretton, on the Gotherington Rd.* **Wed 12, Sat 15 June, Sat 6 July (11-4.30). Combined adm with Oak House £8, chd free. Home-made teas at Oak House with squash & biscuits available at White Cottage. Visits also by arrangement 8 July to 25 July for groups of 5 to 20.**
An 1½ acre garden comprising flower beds and shrubs around the house, a herb garden, a woodland area of native trees, a fernery, a large pond, a small orchard, a fruit and vegetable garden and a wildflower meadow. There are various seats around the garden on the 'cricket pavilion' veranda overlooking the lawn, and steam trains run along the embankment behind the garden. Entry through a side gate allows avoidance of steps.

&. ✿ 🚐 ☕ 🪑

79 NEW WICKS GREEN FARM

Wicks Green, Longney, Gloucester, GL2 3SP. Dianne Evans. *What 3 Words app - broom.almost.messy. From A38 turn into Castle Ln, over Epney Bridge, R at T junction to Longney, at next T junction turn L into Chatter St, follow the lane for approx 1m, Wicks Green Farm will be signed with parking opp gate on hardstanding.* **Sat 31 Aug, Sun 1 Sept (11-4). Adm £5, chd free. Hot drinks, soft drinks & cakes available to purchase Also home-made chutneys & pickles.**
Set in about 1½ acres, Wicks Green Farm has an exceptional garden with further outbuildings, well stocked borders, raised vegetable beds, a natural spring fed pond and an orchard. Some of the pear trees are mature old varieties, as yet to be identified. Parking is available near the house for those with limited mobility.

🐕 ✿ ☕ 🚐

80 WOODCHESTER PARK HOUSE

Nympsfield, Stonehouse, GL10 3UN. Robin & Veronica Bidwell. *Nr Nailsworth. Off the road joining Nailsworth & Nympsfield (Tinkley Ln). Around 3m from Nailsworth, turn R down next turning after the NT Tinkley Gate.* **Sun 30 June (12-5). Adm £6, chd free. Tea.**
This partially walled garden of approx 3 acres incorporates extensive herbaceous borders, a yew walk, a rose covered belvedere overlooking a large pond, a woodland garden, rose walk, vegetable garden and terrace. Wide variety of plants and settings. Wheelchair access to most parts of the garden but there are steep slopes to be negotiated.

&. 🐕 🚐 ☕))

81 WORTLEY HOUSE

Wortley, Wotton-under-Edge, GL12 7QP. Simon & Jessica Dickinson, 01453 843174 / 07899 668984, jessica@wortleyhouse.co.uk. *On Wortley Rd 1m S of Wotton-under-Edge. Grand entrance on L as you enter Wortley coming from Wotton.* **Tue 23 Apr, Tue 18 June (2-5). Adm £15, chd free. Pre-booking essential, please visit www.ngs. org.uk for information & booking. Home-made teas inc in the adm price. Visits also by arrangement 23 Apr to 4 Sept for groups of up to 30.**
A diverse garden of over 20 acres created during the last 30 yrs by the current owners. Inc a walled garden, pleached lime avenues, nut walk, potager, ponds, Italian garden, arbour, shrubberies and wildflower meadows. Strategically placed follies, urns and statues enhance extraordinary vistas. Wheelchair access to most areas, golf buggy also available.

&. ☕ 🪑

GROUP OPENING

82 WYCK RISSINGTON GARDENS

Cheltenham, GL54 2PN. *Nr Stow-on-the-Wold & Bourton-on-the-Water. 1m from Fosse Way A429.* **Sun 8 Sept (1-5). Combined adm £10, chd free. Home-made teas in village hall. Donation to St Laurence's Church Fabric Fund.**

ANSELLS BARN
Andrew & Elizabeth Ransom.

GREENFIELDS FARM
Graham Wild.

LAURENCE HOUSE
Mr & Mrs Robert Montague.

MACES COTTAGE
Tim & Pippa Simon.

NEW THE OLD SCHOOL HOUSE

Mr Simon & Mrs Cheryl Lanyon.

An unspoilt Cotswold village off the beaten track set round a village green and its pond. The gardens are within easy reach of convenient parking and this popular group opening provides an enjoyable afternoon in a perfect Cotswold setting. Gardens included are at various stages of maturity. We have a new garden, the Old Schoolhouse, to add to previously opened gardens which continue to evolve. The much admired Laurence House garden features a maturing wildlife pond, the re-designed Greenfields Farm, a stunning Japanese Garden, Maces Cottage its fine borders and Ansells Barn garden, dating from 2020, now settled in with even more grasses, fruit trees and sculpture. Fantastic feedback from visitors praising, not only the diversity and quality of the gardens, but the superb teas. Leaflet with map and garden details on entry. Plants & garden produce for sale. Beautiful historic church to visit whilst walking between gardens allowing visitors to appreciate the beauty of the historic buildings grouped around the attractive village green and fine views across the Windrush Valley. Wheelchair access available at most gardens and WC in village hall.

&. 🐕 ✿ 🚐 ☕

The National Garden Scheme donated £3,403,960 to our nursing and health beneficiaries from money raised at gardens open in 202

Laurence House, Wyck Rissington Gardens

SOMERSET, BRISTOL AREA
& SOUTH GLOUCESTERSHIRE including BATH

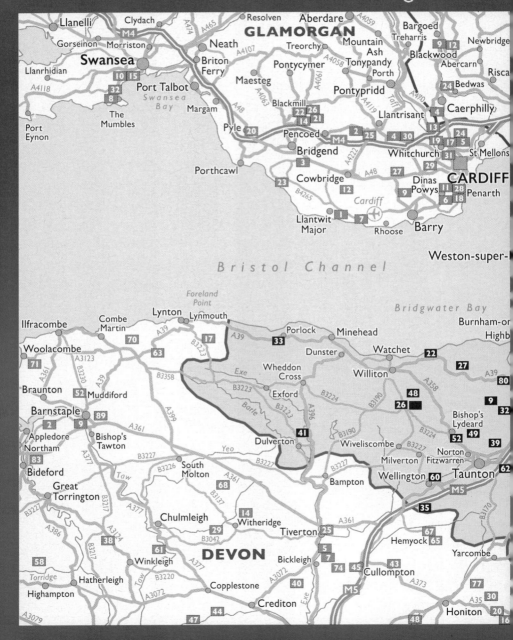

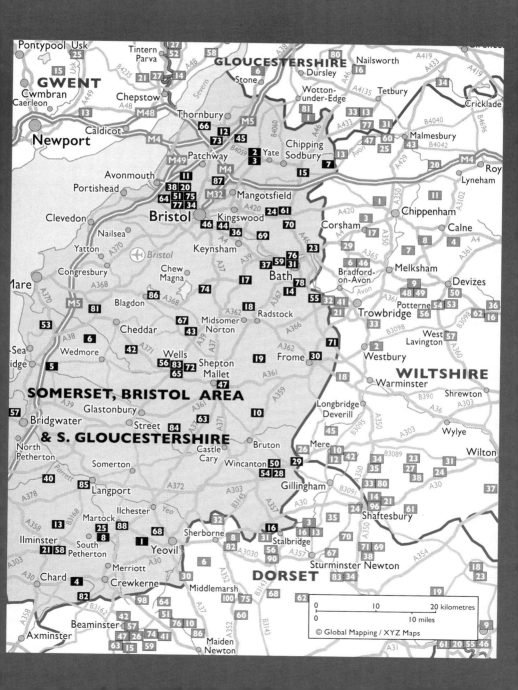

SOMERSET VOLUNTEERS

County Organiser
Laura Howard 01460 282911
laura.howard@ngs.org.uk

County Treasurer
Jill Wardle 07702 274492
jill.wardle@ngs.org.uk

Publicity
Roger Peacock
roger.peacock@ngs.org.uk

Social Media
Janet Jones 01749 850509
janet.jones@ngs.org.uk

Lisa Prior 07773 440147
lisa.prior@ngs.org.uk

Presentations
Dave & Prue Moon
01373 473381
davidmoon202@btinternet.com

Booklet Co-ordinator
John Simmons 07855 944049
john.simmons@ngs.org.uk

Booklet Distributor
Laura Howard (see above)

Assistant County Organisers
Jo Beaumont 07534 777278
jo.beaumont@ngs.org.uk

Marsha Casely 07854 882616
marsha.casely@ngs.org.uk

Kirstie Dalrymple 07772 170537
kirstie.dalrymple@ngs.org.uk

Patricia Davies-Gilbert
01823 412187
pdaviesgilbert@gmail.com

Alyson Holland 07729 059382
alyson.holland@btinternet.com

Janet Jones (as above)

Sue Lewis 07885 369280
sue.lewis@ngs.org.uk

Judith Stanford 01761 233045
judith.stanford@ngs.org.uk

f @nationalgardenschemesomerset

X @SomersetNGS

@ngs_bristol_s_glos_somerset

BRISTOL AREA VOLUNTEERS

County Organiser
Su Mills 01454 615438
su.mills@ngs.org.uk

County Treasurer
Harsha Parmar 07889 201185
harsha.parmar@ngs.org.uk

Publicity
Position vacant

Social Media
Harsha Parmar (see above)

Booklet Co-ordinator
John Simmons 07855 944049
john.simmons@ngs.org.uk

Booklet Distributor
John Simmons (as above)

Assistant County Organisers
Tracey Cruickshank
07956 784838
thallada@icloud.com

Helen Hughesdon
07793 085267
helen.hughesdon@ngs.org.uk

Jeanette Parker
01454 299699
jeanette_parker@hotmail.co.uk

John Burgess
07795 466513

Irene Randow
01275 857208
irene.randow@sky.com

Karl Suchy 07873 588540
karl.suchy@icloud.com

OPENING DATES

All entries subject to change.
For latest information check
www.ngs.org.uk

Extended openings are shown
at the beginning of the month.

Map locator numbers are
shown to the right of each
garden name.

January

Sunday 28th
Rock House   66

February

Snowdrop Openings

Thursday 1st
Elworthy Cottage   26

Sunday 4th
Rock House   66

Tuesday 13th
Elworthy Cottage   26

Thursday 15th
◆ East Lambrook Manor
Gardens   25

Sunday 18th
1 Birch Drive   12

Sunday 25th
Algars Manor   2
Algars Mill   3
Greystones   34

Tuesday 27th
Elworthy Cottage   26

March

Tuesday 5th
◆ Hestercombe Gardens   39

Sunday 17th
Nynehead Court   60
Rock House   66

Saturday 23rd
Forest Lodge   29
Lower Shalford Farm   50

Sunday 24th
Rock House   66

April

Every Thursday from Thursday 11th
Model Farm — 57

Monday 1st
Elworthy Cottage — 26
Stoneleigh Down — 73

Sunday 7th
◆ The Yeo Valley Organic Garden at Holt Farm — 86

Sunday 14th
Watcombe — 81

Wednesday 17th
◆ Greencombe Gardens — 33

Saturday 20th
◆ The Walled Gardens of Cannington — 80

Sunday 21st
NEW ◆ The Cottage Garden at Jordans Courtyard — 21
Fairfield — 27
Glenfield — 31
Greystones — 34
◆ The Walled Gardens of Cannington — 80

Tuesday 23rd
Elworthy Cottage — 26

Saturday 27th
◆ East Lambrook Manor Gardens — 25

Sunday 28th
Algars Manor — 2
Algars Mill — 3
Wayford Manor — 82

May

Every Thursday
Model Farm — 57

Saturday 4th
Hillcrest — 40
Westbrook House — 84

Sunday 5th
Hillcrest — 40
Little Yarford Farmhouse — 49

Monday 6th
Little Yarford Farmhouse — 49

Friday 10th
NEW Valley Spring — 78

Sunday 12th
◆ Milton Lodge — 56
NEW Valley Spring — 78

Thursday 16th
Barford House — 9

Saturday 18th
Forest Lodge — 29
Lower Shalford Farm — 50
NEW Wick Gardens — 85

Sunday 19th
Court House — 22
4 Haytor Park — 38
1 Sunnyside — 75
Watcombe — 81
NEW Wick Gardens — 85
The Yews — 87

Saturday 25th
◆ East Lambrook Manor Gardens — 25
10 Flingers Lane — 28
The Hayes — 37
NEW The Manor — 54

Sunday 26th
10 Flingers Lane — 28
The Hayes — 37
NEW The Manor — 54
NEW Mellowstones — 55

June

Every Thursday
Model Farm — 57

Saturday 1st
Badgworth Court Barn — 6
Japanese Garden Bristol — 44
◆ Stoberry Garden — 72

Sunday 2nd
Badgworth Court Barn — 6
81 Coombe Lane — 20
◆ Stoberry Garden — 72

Tuesday 4th
◆ Hestercombe Gardens — 39

Thursday 6th
Caisson House — 14
Watcombe — 81

Saturday 8th
Hanham Court — 36
NEW New Wood House, 19 The Beacon — 58

Sunday 9th
Church Farm — 17
Hanham Court — 36
4 Haytor Park — 38
Lucombe House — 51
Lydeard House — 52
◆ Milton Lodge — 56

Tuesday 11th
Pennard House — 63

Wednesday 12th
◆ Kilver Court Gardens — 47

Saturday 15th
Batcombe House — 10
Stoneleigh Down — 73

Sunday 16th
Frome Gardens — 30
Penny Brohn UK — 64
Rock House — 66
Stoneleigh Down — 73

Monday 17th
Badminton House — 7

Thursday 20th
◆ Special Plants — 70

Saturday 22nd
The Old Rectory, Doynton — 61
The Rib — 65

Sunday 23rd
NEW ◆ The Cottage Garden at Jordans Courtyard — 21
Nynehead Court — 60

Tuesday 25th
Elworthy Cottage — 26
Trafalgar House — 76

Saturday 29th
Lympsham Gardens — 53
165 Newbridge Hill — 59
NEW Standerwick Court — 71

Sunday 30th
Lympsham Gardens — 53
NEW Mellowstones — 55
165 Newbridge Hill — 59

July

Every Thursday to Thursday 18th
Model Farm — 57

Tuesday 2nd
Elworthy Cottage — 26

Sunday 7th
NEW Barcroft Hall — 8
Honeyhurst Farm — 42
◆ University of Bristol Botanic Garden — 77
Yews Farm — 88

Monday 8th
Honeyhurst Farm — 42

Saturday 13th
Babbs Farm — 5
Court View — 23

Sunday 14th
Babbs Farm   5
Court View   23
◆ Milton Lodge   56

Monday 15th
◆ Berwick Lodge   11

Wednesday 17th
◆ Greencombe Gardens   33

Thursday 18th
◆ Special Plants   70

Saturday 20th
Goathurst Gardens   32

Sunday 21st
Court House   22
Goathurst Gardens   32
Hangeridge Farmhouse   35
Stowey Gardens   74

Tuesday 30th
Elworthy Cottage   26

August

Saturday 3rd
◆ Jekka's Herb Garden &
  Herbetum   45

Friday 9th
John's Corner   46

Saturday 10th
John's Corner   46
The Old Vicarage, Ruishton   62

Sunday 11th
John's Corner   46
The Old Vicarage, Ruishton   62

Thursday 15th
◆ Special Plants   70

Saturday 17th
◆ Stoberry Garden   72

Sunday 18th
◆ Stoberry Garden   72

Saturday 24th
Westbrook House   84

Monday 26th
Elworthy Cottage   26

September

Sunday 1st
Doynton House   24

Sunday 8th
Batcombe House   10
Coleford House   19
Yews Farm   88

Wednesday 11th
◆ Kilver Court Gardens   47

Saturday 14th
10 Flingers Lane   28
◆ The Walled Gardens of
  Cannington   80

Sunday 15th
10 Flingers Lane   28
Skool Beanz Children's
  Allotment   68
◆ The Walled Gardens of
  Cannington   80

Thursday 19th
◆ Special Plants   70

October

Thursday 17th
◆ Special Plants   70

January 2025

Sunday 26th
Rock House   66

February 2025

Sunday 2nd
Rock House   66

By Arrangement

Arrange a personalised garden visit
with your club, or group of friends,
on a date to suit you. See individual
garden entries for full details.

1 Birch Drive

THE GARDENS

1 ABBEY FARM

Montacute, TA15 6UA. Elizabeth McFarlane, 01935 823556, abbey.farm64@gmail.com. *4m from Yeovil. Follow A3088, take slip rd to Montacute, turn L at T-junction into village. Turn R between church & King's Arms (no through rd).* Visits by arrangement 10 May to 28 June for groups of 10 to 30. Adm £8, chd free. Light refreshments. Details on request.

2½ acres of mainly walled gardens on sloping site provide the setting for Cluniac Medieval Priory gatehouse. Interesting plants inc roses, shrubs, grasses, clematis. Herbaceous borders, white garden, gravel garden. Small arboretum. Pond for wildlife - frogs, newts, dragonflies. Fine mulberry, walnut and monkey puzzle trees. Seats for resting.

2 ALGARS MANOR

Station Rd, Iron Acton, BS37 9TB. Mrs B Naish. *9m N of Bristol, 3m W of Yate/Chipping Sodbury. Turn S off Iron Acton bypass B4059, past village green & White Hart pub, 200yds, then over level Xing. No access from Frampton Cotterell via lane; ignore SatNav. Parking at Algars Manor.* Sun 25 Feb (1-4); Sun 28 Apr (1-5). Combined adm with Algars Mill £7, chd free. Tea & biscuits in Feb at Algars Mill. Home-made cakes & drinks in Apr at Algars Manor.

2 acres of woodland garden beside River Frome, mill stream, native plants mixed with collections of 60 magnolias and 70 camellias, rhododendrons, azaleas, eucalyptus and other unusual trees and shrubs. Daffodils, snowdrops and other early spring flowers.

3 ALGARS MILL

Frampton End Rd, Iron Acton, Bristol, BS37 9TD. Mr & Mrs John Wright. *9m N of Bristol, 3m W of Yate/Chipping Sodbury. (For directions see Algars Manor).* Sun 25 Feb (1-4); Sun 28 Apr (1-5). Combined adm with Algars Manor £7, chd free. Tea & biscuits in Feb at Algars Mill. Home-made cakes & drinks in Apr at Algars Manor.

2 acre woodland garden bisected by River Frome; spring bulbs, shrubs; very early spring feature (Feb-Mar) of wild Newent daffodils. 300-400yr-old mill house (not open) through which millrace still runs.

4 AVALON

Moor Lane, Higher Chillington, Ilminster, TA19 0PT. Dee & Tony Brook, 07506 688191, dee1jones@hotmail.com. *Just off the A30 between Crewkerne & Chard. From A30 take turning signed to Chillington opp Swandown Lodges. Take 2nd L down Coley Ln & 1st L Moor Ln. Avalon is the large pink house. Parking limited, so please car share if possible.* Visits by arrangement June & July for groups of up to 40. Adm £5, chd £2. Home-made teas. Gluten & dairy free cakes available if requested in advance.

Secluded hillside garden with wonderful views as far as Wales. The lower garden has large herbaceous borders, a sizeable wildlife pond and 2 greenhouses filled with RSA succulents. The middle garden has mixed borders, wild spotted orchids on the lawn, allotment area and a small orchard. The upper garden has a spring fed watercourse with ponds, and many terraces with different planting schemes. Partial wheelchair access across lower lawns & side paths. Steep slope & gravel paths. Wheelchairs will require to be pushed & attended at all times.

5 BABBS FARM

Westhill Lane, Bason Bridge, Highbridge, TA9 4RF. Sue & Richard O'Brien, www.babbsfarm.co.uk. *1½ m E of Highbridge, 1½ m SSE of M5 exit 22. Turn into Westhill Ln off B3141 (Church Rd), 100yds S of where it joins B3139 (Wells-Highbridge road).* Sat 13, Sun 14 July (2-5). Adm £8, chd free. Home-made teas.

1½ acre plantsman's garden on Somerset Levels, gradually created out of fields surrounding old farmhouse over last 30 yrs and still being developed. Trees, shrubs and herbaceous perennials planted with an eye for form and shape in big flowing borders. Plants for sale if circumstances allow. Many unusual Salvias, especially in late summer. A garden with a restful atmosphere and attractive vistas.

6 BADGWORTH COURT BARN

Notting Hill Way, Stone Allerton, Axbridge, BS26 2NQ. Trish & Jeremy Gibson, www.instagram.com/theoldbarngardeners/. *4m SW of Axbridge. Turn off A38 in Lower Weare, signed Wedmore, Weare. Continue 1.1m, past rd on R (Badgworth Arena). Continue 0.1m, to 'No Footway for 600 yds' sign. Garden & car park will be signed.* Sat 1, Sun 2 June (2-5.30). Adm £5, chd free. Home-made teas.

In this 1 acre plot around old stone barn buildings, a small orchard leads to a part-walled garden with perennial meadow areas and multi-stemmed trees. Gently curving beds are flanked by a more formal oak pergola walk. The planting is a relaxed contemporary mix. In the atmospheric courtyard, planting is more established and leads to an innovative, colourful sand garden in front of the barns. Main garden is level and accessible. Courtyard and drive areas are loose stone chippings and can be difficult for some wheelchairs. No accessible WC.

7 BADMINTON HOUSE

Badminton, GL9 1DB. Duke & Duchess of Beaufort, www.badmintonestate.co.uk. *4m N of M4 J18. From M4 J18, 1st exit onto A46/Bath Rd. Follow signs to Badminton.* Mon 17 June (11-4). Adm £10, chd free. Pre-booking essential, please visit www.ngs.org.uk for information & booking. Refreshments will not be available but picnics are welcome. Last entry 3pm.

Explore the private gardens of the historic Badminton House from the formal beds to the South Garden with its water squares, hedges, beds and borders. Glorious displays of roses and borders of summer colours are combined with herbaceous perennials. The Walled Garden is home to the kitchen garden, providing fruit, vegetables and cut flowers for much of the yr. The greenhouse is used for propagation and houses a fine display of pelargoniums. A limited number of tickets have been made available for this special opening by kind permission of the owners, the Duke and Duchess of Beaufort. We regret no dogs are allowed in the private gardens, with the exception of assistance dogs. The majority of the gardens are accessible to wheelchairs. Accessible WCs.

8 NEW **BARCROFT HALL**
North Street, South Petherton, TA13 5DA. Richard & Tracey Killen. *N side of S Petherton. From A303 drive to centre of S Petherton, through village, R at fork with Methodist Church into North St (St James St), R into Barcroft Ln, follow signs.* **Sun 7 July (11-5). Adm £7, chd free. Home-made teas.**
A lovely 10 acre garden with glorious views over the surrounding countryside. The garden has many features of interest inc formal planting,water and wildlife areas, a kitchen garden and greenhouse, soft fruits and large orchard. Over 1000 trees all set within the extensive lawns and 7 lakes and ponds. Seating areas throughout the gardens and on the beautiful terraces. There is some disabled parking by the main house plus drop off. Some gravel paths and slopes may only be accessible by motorised mobility vehicles.

9 **BARFORD HOUSE**
Spaxton, Bridgwater, TA5 1AG. Donald & Bee Rice. *4½ m W of Bridgwater. Midway between Enmore & Spaxton.* **Thur 16 May (2-5). Adm £6.50, chd free. Home-made teas.**
Secluded walled garden contains wide borders, kitchen garden beds, shrubs and fruits trees. Lawns lead to a 6 acre woodland garden of camellias, rhododendrons, azaleas and magnolias. Stream-side gardens feature candelabra primulas, ferns, foxgloves and lily-of-the-valley among veteran pines and oaks, and some rarer trees. Partial wheelchair access. Some areas of woodland garden inaccessible.

10 **BATCOMBE HOUSE**
Gold Hill, Batcombe, Shepton Mallet, BA4 6HF. Libby Russell, 0207 931 9996, libby@mazzullorusselllandscapedesign.com, www.mazzullorusselllandscapedesign.com. *In centre of Batcombe, 3m from Bruton. Parking between Batcombe House & church at centre of village will be clearly marked.* **Sat 15 June (12-5.30); Sun 8 Sept (2-6). Adm £7.50, chd free. Home-made cream teas & cakes. Visits also by arrangement 18 May to 15 Sept for groups of 15+. Refreshments for groups available by arrangement.**

Plantswoman's and designer's garden of two parts – one a riot of colour through kitchen terraces, potager leading to wildflower orchard; the other a calm contemporary amphitheatre with large herbaceous borders and interesting trees and shrubs. Always changing. Dogs are welcome on a lead. A wide range of interesting, and constantly changing, herbaceous plantings, pots and seasonal displays.

11 ◆ **BERWICK LODGE**
Berwick Drive, Bristol, BS10 7TD. Sarah Arikan, 01179 581590, info@berwicklodge.co.uk, www.berwicklodge.co.uk. *Leave M5 at J17. A4018 towards Bristol West. 2nd exit on r'about, straight on at mini r'about. At next r'about by Old Crow pub do 360° turn back down A4018, follow sign saying BL off to L.* **For NGS: Mon 15 July (11-2.30). Adm £5, chd £2.50. Cream teas. For other opening times and information, please phone, email or visit garden website.**
Berwick Lodge, named Bristol's hidden gem by its customers, is an independent hotel with beautiful gardens on the outskirts of Bristol. Built in 1890, this Victorian Arts & Crafts property is set within 18 acres, of which 4 acres are accessible and offer a peaceful garden for use by its visitors. The gardens enjoy pretty views across to Wales, and continue to evolve. Created by Head Gardener Robert Dunster, an ex Royal gardener who worked for Prince Charles at Highgrove, it features an elegant water fountain, Victorian summerhouse, orchard, wildflower meadow, beehives, pond, plus a thriving house martin colony.

12 **1 BIRCH DRIVE**
Alveston, Bristol, BS35 3RQ. Myra Ginns, 07766 021616, myra.ginns@ngs.org.uk. *14m N of Bristol. Alveston on A38 Bristol to Gloucester. Just before T-lights turn L into David's Lane. At end, L then R onto Wolfridge Ride. Birch Drive 2nd on R.* **Sun 18 Feb (11-2). Adm £5, chd free. Pre-booking essential, please visit www.ngs.org.uk for information & booking. Visits also by arrangement 12 Feb to 24 Feb for groups of up to 12.**
A garden with particular interest in the spring, having a wide range of bulbs in flower, inc unusual named varieties

of anemone, hellebore, hepatica and crocus. The garden's main feature are the snowdrops, collected since 2008. Named varieties, flowering between November and March, will interest snowdrop collectors. The garden will be open to visit and book by arrangement in February of 2025. Five species of Snowdrop to view and many varieties collected for differences in shape, markings, colour and name. Ramp to decked area gives a view of the garden.

13 **BRADON FARM**
Isle Abbotts, Taunton, TA3 6RX. Mr & Mrs Thomas Jones, deborahjstanley@hotmail.com. *Take turning to Ilton off A358. Bradon Farm is 1½ m out of Ilton on Bradon Lane.* **Visits by arrangement for groups of 10+. Adm £7, chd free. Home-made teas.**
Classic formal garden demonstrating the effective use of structure with parterre, knot garden, pleached lime walk, formal pond, herbaceous borders, orchard and wildflower planting.

14 **CAISSON HOUSE**
Combe Hay, Bath, BA2 7EF. Amanda & Phil Honey, amandahoney5@gmail.com, www.caissongardens.com. *3m S of Bath. Take A367 from centre of Bath towards Radstock, at 2nd r'about take 1st exit, follow signs to Combe Hay. 1st L after Wheatsheaf pub, marked No Through Rd. Entrance 1st on R.* **Thur 6 June (11-4). Adm £12, chd free. Pre-booking essential, please visit www.ngs.org.uk for information & booking. Home-made teas.**
This is a wonderfully eclectic and romantic garden set in the most beautiful English countryside around a Georgian house built in 1815. It is a mix of herbaceous borders, topiaries, ponds and rills, a walled garden with fruit trees, greenhouses, flower and vegetable beds.There are wildflower meadows surrounding the garden and the disused Somerset Coal Canal running through the property. Great variety of species and biodiversity, inc native orchids.

Wayford Manor

© Val Corbett

15 CAMERS
Badminton Road, Old Sodbury, Bristol, BS37 6RG. Mr & Mrs Michael Denman, 01454 327929, jodenman@btinternet.com, www.camers.org. *2m E of Chipping Sodbury. Entrance in Chapel Lane off A432 at Dog Inn. Enter through the field gate and drive to the top of the fields to park next to the garden.* **Visits by arrangement 15 May to 13 Sept for groups of 20 to 50. Adm £7. Refreshments by arrangement.** Elizabethan farmhouse (not open) set in 4 acres of constantly developing garden and woodland with spectacular views over Severn Vale. Garden full of surprises, formal and informal areas planted with wide range of species to provide year-round interest. Parterre, topiary, Japanese garden, bog and prairie areas, white and hot gardens, woodland walks. Some steep slopes.

16 CHERRY BOLBERRY FARM
Furge Lane, Henstridge, BA8 0RN. Mrs Jenny Raymond, 01963 362177, cherrybolberryfarm@tiscali.co.uk. *6m E of Sherborne. In centre of Henstridge, R at small Xrds signed Furge Ln. Continue straight up lane, over 2 cattle grids, garden at top of lane on R.* **Visits by arrangement in June for groups of 5+. Adm £5, chd free.**
Designed and maintained by the owner, this 48 yr-old award winning 1 acre garden has been planted for year-round interest with wildlife in mind. Colour themed island beds, shrub and herbaceous borders, unusual perennials, shrubs, old roses and an area of specimen trees. Lots of hidden areas, brilliant for hide and seek! Vegetable and flower cutting garden, greenhouses, nature ponds. Wonderful extensive views. Garden

surrounded by our dairy farm which has been in the family for over 100 years.

17 CHURCH FARM
Stanton Prior, Bath, BA2 9HT. Mr & Mrs A Hardwick. *6 m W of Bath. W onto A39 from A4 out of Bath. Turn L in Marksbury. Located next to the village church.* **Sun 9 June (2-6). Adm £5, chd free. Light refreshments.**
1 ½ acre garden. Planted with roses, clematis, foxgloves, lavenders and mature trees. Beautiful countryside views. Medieval pond with toads, newts, ducks and sometimes a swan. Garden surrounded by our dairy farm which is part of the Duchy of Cornwall Estate.

18 COLDHARBOUR COTTAGE

Radford Hill, Radford, Radstock, BA3 2XU. Ms Amanda Cranston, 01761 470600, amanda.cranston@yahoo.co.uk. *Between Timsbury & Radstock. 8m S of Bath. Please ask for directions when booking.* **Visits by arrangement 6 May to 9 Aug for groups of up to 15.** Access via narrow lane.Limited parking, car sharing advised. **Adm £6, chd £2. Light refreshments. Tea & coffee.** Bath In Bloom Gold Award Winner 2023. Idyllic rural garden set in peaceful countryside. Sublime mix of thoughtful planting, natural areas reflect historical and modern heritage of this secluded acre. Natural hedges and uninterrupted fields form the backdrop to the gentle calm of the design. Glorious spring flowers give way to peonies, lavender and formal rose garden. Romantic arches with climbing roses, clematis, box hedges and chamomile lawn. Deep herbaceous borders, hidden natural areas frame the lawns, home to old fruit trees. Productive kitchen garden adds practicality to this quiet, sensitive space. Two summerhouses, plenty of seating areas. Wheelchair access to grassed areas weather dependent. Some narrow and uneven paths and areas.

♿ ☕

19 COLEFORD HOUSE

Underhill, Coleford, Radstock, BA3 5LU. Mr James Alexandroff. *5m from Frome. Coleford House is opp Kings Head pub in Lower Coleford with black wrought iron gates just before bridge over river. Parking in field 100 metres away.* **Sun 8 Sept (10.30-4). Adm £6, chd free. Home-made teas.** The River Mells flows through this picturesque garden with large lawns, wildflower planting, ornamental pond, woodland, substantial herbaceous borders, walled garden, arboretum/ orchard, kitchen garden, vegetable garden, bat house and orangery. Most of garden is wheelchair friendly.

♿ 🐕 ☕ 🍽 ⌵

20 81 COOMBE LANE

Stoke Bishop, Bristol, BS9 2AT. Karl Suchy, 07873 588540, karl.suchy@icloud.com. *4m from Bristol city centre. J17 of M5, then follow A4018, direction Bristol for approx 2m. Turn R onto Canford Lane A4162. After 0.8m turn L onto Coombe Lane. Destination on R.* **Sun 2 June (12-5). Adm £5, chd free. Home-made teas. Visits also by arrangement 20 May to 28 July for groups of up to 25.** Hidden Victorian walled garden. You'll encounter substantial mixed borders containing traditional and contemporary planting. Large lawns, numerous seating areas, summerhouse and French inspired patio with coppiced lime trees. Parterre and large raised Koi pond surrounded by bananas and tree ferns. Access to parterre and Koi pond might be difficult for wheelchair due to narrow gravel path, main part of garden is accessible.

♿ ❀ ☕ ⌵

Hestercombe

21 NEW ◆ THE COTTAGE GARDEN AT JORDANS COURTYARD

Horton Cross, Ilminster, TA19 9PY. Angie Blackwell, 01460 53020, info@cottageflowersandmore.co.uk, www.cottageflowersandmore.co.uk/. *Jordans Courtyard is signed from Southfields R'about (where A303 & A358 meet outside Ilminster).* **For NGS: Sun 21 Apr, Sun 23 June (9-2). Adm £5, chd free. Home-made teas.** For other opening times and information, please phone, email or visit garden website.

The Cottage Garden at Jordans Courtyard is an immersive experience. Visitors can enjoy the tranquillity of an ambient styled garden room, the beauty of a wildflower meadow, the peace of the woodland style nook and the inspirational seasonal border displays. This walled garden is a little escape from daily life in the heart of Somerset, lovingly transformed in the last 2 years. Angie Blackwell, the owner of Cottage Flowers, will be on hand to talk to visitors about how the garden has been transformed over 2 years from bare earth to what you see today.

22 COURT HOUSE

East Quantoxhead, TA5 1EJ. Mr & Mrs Hugh Luttrell. *12m W of Bridgwater. Off A39, house at end of village past duck pond. Enter by Frog St (Bridgwater/Kilve side from A39). Car park £1 in aid of church.* **Sun 19 May, Sun 21 July (2-5). Adm £6, chd free. Cream teas.**

Lovely 5 acre garden, trees, shrubs (many rare and tender), herbaceous and 3 acre woodland garden with spring interest and late summer borders. Views to sea and Quantocks. Gravel, stone and some mown grass paths.

23 COURT VIEW

Solsbury Lane, Batheaston, Bath, BA1 7HB. Maria & Jeremy Heffer, www.thebathgreenhouse.com. *3m E of Bath. In Batheaston High St take turning on L signed Northend, St Catherine. At top of rise L into Solsbury Lane. Court View is 2nd driveway on L. Public car park in the village.* **Sat 13, Sun 14 July (10.30-4.30). Adm £5, chd free. Home-made teas.**

Two acre south facing gardens with

⅓ acre devoted to cut flowers and foliage. Colourful mix of annuals, biennials and perennials. Spectacular views from terraced lawns, box parterre, small orchard and meadow area. A floral experience for garden lovers, artisan florists, flower arrangers and anyone interested in the revival of beautiful, diverse and locally grown British cut flowers.

24 DOYNTON HOUSE

Bury Lane, Doynton, Bristol, BS30 5SR. Frances & Matthew Lindsey-Clark, Franceslc11@gmail.com. *5m S of M4 J18, 6m N of Bath, 8m E of Bristol. Doynton is NE of Wick (turn off A420 opp Bath Rd) and SW of Dyrham (signed from A46). Doynton House is at S end of Doynton village, opp Culleysgate/Horsepool Lane. Park in signed field.* **Sun 1 Sept (2-6). Adm £7.50, chd free. Home-made teas.** Visits also by arrangement Apr to Sept for groups of 15 to 30.

A variety of garden areas separated by old walls and hedges. Mixed borders, several of which are newly-planted, lawns, wall planting, parterre, rill garden, walled vegetable garden, cottage beds, pool garden, dry gardens, peach house and greenhouse. Bees, chickens and meadow area. We can recommend our local pub, the Cross House, just a short stroll across our parking field. Paths are of hoggin, stone and gravel. The grade of the gravel makes it a hard push in places but all areas are just about wheelchair accessible.

25 ◆ EAST LAMBROOK MANOR GARDENS

Silver Street, East Lambrook, TA13 5HH. Mike Werkmeister, 01460 240328, enquiries@eastlambrook.com, www.eastlambrook.com. *2m N of South Petherton. Follow brown tourist signs from A303 South Petherton r'about or B3165 Xrds with lights N of Martock.* **For NGS: Thur 15 Feb, Sat 27 Apr, Sat 25 May (10-5). Adm £7, chd free. Tea and cake.** For other opening times and information, please phone, email or visit garden website.

The quintessential English cottage garden created by C20 gardening legend Margery Fish. Plantsman's paradise with contemporary and old-fashioned plants grown in a

relaxed and informal manner to create a remarkable garden of great beauty and charm. With noted collections of snowdrops, hellebores and geraniums and the excellent specialist Margery Fish Plant Nursery. Partial wheelchair access.

26 ELWORTHY COTTAGE

Elworthy, Taunton, TA4 3PX. Mike & Jenny Spiller, 01984 656427, mike@elworthy-cottage.co.uk, www.elworthy-cottage.co.uk. *12m NW of Taunton. On B3188 between Wiveliscombe & Watchet.* **Thur 1, Tue 13, Tue 27 Feb, Mon 1, Tue 23 Apr, Tue 25 June, Tue 2, Tue 30 July, Mon 26 Aug (11-4.30). Adm £5, chd free. Home-made teas. Visits also by arrangement Feb to Sept.**

1 acre plantsman's garden in tranquil setting. Island beds, scented plants, clematis, unusual perennials and ornamental trees and shrubs to provide year-round interest. In spring, pulmonarias, hellebores and more than 350 varieties of snowdrops. Planted to encourage birds, bees and butterflies. Lots of birdsong, wildflower areas and developing wildflower meadow, decorative vegetable garden, living willow screen. Seats for visitors to enjoy views of the surrounding countryside. Garden attached to plantsman's nursery, open at the same time.

27 FAIRFIELD

Stogursey, Bridgwater, TA5 1PU. Lady Acland Hood Gass. *7m E of Williton. 11m W of Bridgwater. From A39 Bridgwater to Minehead road turn N. Garden 1½m W of Stogursey on Stringston road. No coaches.* **Sun 21 Apr (2-5). Adm £7, chd £4. Home-made teas.**

Woodland garden with many interesting bulbs inc naturalised anemones, fritillaria with roses, shrubs and fine trees. Paved maze. Views of Quantocks. The ground is flat and should be accessible, around half the paths are grass so may be more difficult when wet.

28 10 FLINGERS LANE

Wincanton, BA9 9LE. Yseult Ogilvie, 07736 609789, yseult@yoarchitecture.com. *Situated on the L side of Flingers Lane to the N of the B3081. Parking available for 4 cars. Additional parking on the High St or around the Memorial Hall.* **Sat 25, Sun 26 May (10-5), open nearby The Manor. Sat 14, Sun 15 Sept (10-4). Adm £5, chd free. Light refreshments. Visits also by arrangement for groups of 5 to 30.**
A secluded third of an acre secret walled garden hidden behind the High Street in Wincanton on a no through road. Box hedges, topiary, a formal kitchen garden with fruit trees, a fernery, glasshouses, and a lawn flanked by herbaceous borders and shrubs. Designed by an architect, the striking layout leads the visitor from one notional 'room' to another.

29 FOREST LODGE

Pen Selwood, BA9 8LL. James & Lucy Nelson, www.forestlodgegardens.co.uk. *1½ m N of A303, 3m E of Wincanton. Leave A303 at B3081 (Wincanton to Gillingham rd), up hill to Pen Selwood, L towards church. ½ m, garden on L - low curved wall and sign saying Forest Lodge Stud.* **Sat 23 Mar, Sat 18 May (11-4). Combined adm with Lower Shalford Farm £10, chd free. Home-made teas. Lavender blue famous carrot cake, brownies & flapjacks. Donation to Well Wessex group of Mental Health charities in Somerset.**
3 acre mature garden with beautiful lake, full of bulbs and flowering trees. Many camellias and rhododendrons from March till May. Lovely views towards Blackmore Vale. Part formal with pleached hornbeam allée and rill, part water garden. Wonderful roses in June. Unusual spring flowering trees such as paulownia, *Davidia involucrata* and many beautiful cornus. Interesting garden sculpture. Good plant interest year-round due to acidic greensand soil (hamamelis, Daphne, magnolia, lovely rhododendrons, camellias and flowering trees in the spring) and south west facing slope. Beautiful in all seasons and good structure which underpins the planting. Wheelchair access to front garden only, however much of garden viewable from there.

GROUP OPENING

30 FROME GARDENS

The Cedars, Frome, BA11 2FF. *15m S of Bath. Card payments at 5 The Cedars; private cul-de-sac off Rodden Rd, S of Vine Tree Inn from Bath, & 46 Nunney Rd; from A362 to Radstock L Badcox (signed) straight to wisteria covered house on R.* **Sun 16 June (1-5). Combined adm £8, chd free. Home-made teas at Highclere, cold drinks at 5 The Cedars.**

9 CATHERSTON CLOSE
BA11 4HR. Dave & Prue Moon.

NEW 5 THE CEDARS
BA11 2FF. Mr I & Mrs K Vincent.

NEW HIGHCLERE
BA11 4DS. Mrs Sally Gregory.

NEW 46 NUNNEY ROAD
BA11 4LE. Ms Lisa Hewer.

61 NUNNEY ROAD
BA11 4LA. Mrs Caroline Toll.

1 TUCKER CLOSE
BA11 5LS. Bev Revie & Tim Cutting.

84 WEYMOUTH ROAD
BA11 1HJ. Amanda Relph.

Welcome to 7 differing town gardens. 84 Weymouth Rd, seasoned NGS opener, garden designed by and celebrating the life of Simon Relph. 61 Nunney Rd, a well-cared for garden, re designed from 2020 by a new owner who considers herself an untidy planter as she falls for plants and then finds the right place for them! 3 new gardens open. Wisteria clad 46 Nunney Rd, currently developed using the no dig organic method to be insect, bird and human friendly. Planted with form, shape and colour in mind. 5 The Cedars is a modern new build with attractive garden, emphasis on wildlife. Colour surrounds a lawn with waterfall. Highclere, large garden, created by the owner's parents, flower borders a riot of colour combine with a mix of trees, shrubs, climbers and veg. 2 gardens return, 1 Tuckers Close, small walled town garden of unusual design planted by the owners with wildlife in mind. Its borders set with decking and slate rather than grass. 9 Catherston Close, where the unexpected awaits the visitor. The garden grew to ⅓ acre, colour themed shrub, herbaceous borders and much more. All very different,

with unusual and interesting styles of design, the planting complements each other in these seven exciting secret town gardens. Very small step from terrace to lawn at 61 Nunney Road; 3 small steps at 84 Weymouth Rd; steps at entrance up to 46 Nunney Road.

31 GLENFIELD

Glenfield, Weston Park, Bath, BA1 4AL. Mrs Sue Haskins. *1m west of Bath city centre, in Weston area. Approach from Weston High St and go up Crown Hill past Old Crown pub on R & into Weston Park - Glenfield is the 3rd house before the end of Weston Park on the R. Parking on nearby streets.* **Sun 21 Apr (10-5). Adm £7, chd free. Home-made teas in the garden.**
One acre town garden created over last 20 yrs by current owner. Formal overall design with a series of rooms with scented and colour themed plants: Spring bulbs, blossom and early perennials, woodland walk, sunken garden, lime walk and annual flower area. Unusual trees, exuberant rose pergola, Mediterranean rockery and alliums. Gravel paths and some steps.

GROUP OPENING

32 GOATHURST GARDENS

Goathurst, Bridgwater, TA5 2DF. *4m SW of Bridgwater, 2½ m W of N Petherton. Parking available at Halswell House. Limited parking at the Temple of Pan.* **Sat 20, Sun 21 July (2-5). Combined adm £7.50, chd free. Home-made teas at Halswell House & The Temple of Pan.**

HALSWELL HOUSE
Mrs Oksana Kadatskaya.

THE LODGE
Sharon & Richard Piron.

OLD ORCHARD
Mr Peter Evered.

THE TEMPLE OF PAN
Peter Strivens & Tessa Shaw.

Four very different gardens in the picturesque village of Goathurst on the edge of the Quantock Hills. The Lodge and Old Orchard are beautiful examples of quintessentially English cottage gardens approx 30 metres apart in

Penny Brohn UK

a rural village setting. The gardens at Halswell Park are a history of garden design in England, with a new knot garden created to reflect an original C16 design. The garden of the Temple of Pan is centred on an C18 baroque folly built as part of the pleasure gardens for Halswell House. The Lodge, Old Orchard and Halswell knot gardens have wheelchair access to most areas. The gardens at The Temple of Pan are steep in some places.

33 ◆ GREENCOMBE GARDENS
Porlock, Minehead,
TA24 8NU. Greencombe
Garden Trust, 01643 862363,
info@greencombe.org,
www.greencombe.org. *W of
Porlock below the wooded slopes
of Exmoor. Take A39 to west end
of Porlock and turn onto B3225
to Porlock Weir. Drive ½m, turn
L at Greencombe Gardens sign.
Go up drive; parking signed.* **For
NGS: Wed 17 Apr, Wed 17 July
(2-6). Adm £7, chd £1. Cream
teas.** For other opening times and
information, please phone, email or
visit garden website. Donation to
Plant Heritage.
Organic woodland garden of
international renown, Greencombe

stretches along a sheltered hillside
and offers outstanding views over
Porlock Bay. Moss-covered paths
meander through a collection of
ornamental plants that flourish
beneath a canopy of oaks, hollies,
conifers and chestnuts. Camellias,
rhododendrons, azaleas, lilies,
roses, clematis, and hydrangeas
blossom among 4 National
Collections. Champion English
Holly tree (*Ilex aquifolium*), one of
the largest and oldest in the UK.
Giant rhododendrons species and
exceptionally large camellias. A
millennium chapel hides in the mossy
banks of the wood. A moon arch
leads into a walled garden.

34 GREYSTONES
Hollybush Lane, Bristol, BS9 1JB.
Mrs P Townsend. *2m N of Bristol
city centre, close to Durdham Down
in Bristol, backing onto the Botanic
Garden. A4018 Westbury Rd, L at
White Tree r'about, L into Saville Rd,
Hollybush Lane 2nd on R. Narrow
lane, parking limited, recommended
to park in Saville Rd.* **Sun 25 Feb,
Sun 21 Apr (11-4). Adm £4.50, chd
free. Home-made teas.**
Peaceful garden with places to sit
and enjoy a quiet corner of Bristol.
Interesting courtyard, raised beds,

large variety of conifers and shrubs
leads to secluded garden of contrasts
- sunny beds with olive tree and
brightly coloured flowers to shady
spots, with acers, hostas and ferns.
Snowdrops, hellebores, spring bulbs,
naturalised daffodils. Small orchard,
espaliered pears. Paved footpath
provides level access to all areas.

35 HANGERIDGE FARMHOUSE
Wrangway, Wellington, TA21 9QG.
Mrs J M Chave, 07812 648876,
hangeridge@hotmail.co.uk. *2m
S of Wellington. Off A38 Wellington
bypass signed Wrangway. 1st L
towards Wellington monument,
over motorway bridge 1st R.* **Sun
21 July (2-5). Adm £3, chd free.
Home-made teas. Visits also by
arrangement 12 May to 4 Aug for
groups of 10 to 20.**
Rural fields and mature trees
surround this 1 acre informal garden
offering views of the Blackdown and
Quantock Hills. Magnificent hostas
and heathers, colourful flower beds,
hydrangeas and roses and a trickling
stream. Relax with home-made
refreshments on sunny or shaded
seating admiring the views and
birdsong.

Hanham Court

36 HANHAM COURT
Ferry Road, Hanham Abbots,
BS15 3NT. Hanham Court Gardens,
www.hanhamcourtgardens.co.uk.
*5m E of Bristol centre, 9m W of
Bath centre. E-A431 from Bath, via
Willsbridge, L at mini r'about, Court
Farm Rd 1m Entrance sharp L bend.
W-A420 from Bristol. A431,1m. R
at mini r'about Memorial Rd 1m
Entrance on Court Farm Rd sharp R
bend.* **Sat 8, Sun 9 June (11-4.30).
Adm £8, chd free. Home-made
teas.**
Hanham Court Gardens is a deeply
romantic and enchanting idyll, hidden
in a rural bowl, containing a rich mix
of bold formal topiary and blowsy
planting, water, woodland, orchard,
meadow and kitchen garden with
emphasis on scent, structure and
romance, set amid a remarkable
cluster of manorial buildings between
Bath and Bristol.

37 THE HAYES
Newton St Loe, Bath, BA2 9BU.
Jane Giddins, 07966 431088,
jeturner@btinternet.com. *From the
Globe Pub on A4 take Pennyquick
which is signed to Odd Down. Take
1st turning R which is just after the
bend. At top of hill turn R then L.* **Sat
25, Sun 26 May (2-5). Adm £7, chd
free. Home-made teas. Visits also
by arrangement 10 May to 30 Sept
for groups of 20+.**
Stunning in all seasons. 1 acre garden
on edge of Duchy of Cornwall village.
Herbaceous borders and formal
lawns and terraces; informal garden
of trees and long grass, bulbs and
meadow flowers; formal potager
and greenhouse; small orchard with
espalier apple trees. Tulips, wisteria,
alliums, foxgloves, gladioli, dahlias,
asters. Wonderful views. All of garden
can be accessed by wheelchair but
some grassy inclines.

38 4 HAYTOR PARK
Bristol, BS9 2LR. Mr & Mrs
C J Prior, 07779 203626,
p.l.prior@gmail.com. *3m NW of
Bristol city centre. From A4162 Inner
Ring Rd take turning into Coombe
Bridge Ave, Haytor Park is 1st on L.
Please no parking in Haytor Park.*
**Sun 19 May (1-5). Combined adm
with 1 Sunnyside £5, chd free.
Home-made teas at 1 Sunnyside.
Sun 9 June (1-5). Adm £4, chd
free. Open nearby Lucombe
House. Visits also by arrangement
May to Aug for groups of 10 to 30.**

A hidden haven of peace and
tranquillity in a city suburb. Full of
unusual objects forming screens and
plant supports. Horticultural interest at
every level for all seasons. Places to
sit and dream, secret paths, spaces
for unusual plants and wildlife. Kids
find the dragons for a prize!

39 ◆ HESTERCOMBE
GARDENS
Cheddon Fitzpaine, Taunton,
TA2 8LG. Hestercombe
Gardens Trust, 01823 413923,
info@hestercombe.com,
www.hestercombe.com. *3m N
of Taunton, less than 6m from J25
of M5. Follow brown daisy signs.
SatNav postcode TA2 8LQ.* **For
NGS: Tue 5 Mar (10-3.30). Adm
£14.50, chd £7.25. Evening
opening Tue 4 June (6-8). Adm
£30. For other opening times and
information, please phone, email or
visit garden website.**
Magnificent Georgian landscape
garden designed by artist Coplestone
Warre Bampfylde, a contemporary
of Gainsborough and Henry Hoare
of Stourhead. Victorian terrace
and shrubbery and an exquisite
example of a Lutyens/Jeykll designed
formal garden; C17 water garden.

Enjoy 50 acres of woodland walks, temples, terraces, pergolas, lakes and cascades. A limited number of tickets have been made available for a private tour of the gardens on the evening of the 4th June. Please arrive promptly at 6pm for a glass of wine, and an introductory talk by Head Gardener, Claire Greenslade, after which there will be the opportunity to explore the gardens, accompanied by Claire. This will be a unique experience to wander the gardens in the early evening when the garden is closed to other visitors. Restaurant and café, restored watermill and barn, contemporary art gallery. Four centuries of garden design. Gravel paths, steep slopes, steps. An all-access route is shown on the guide map, & visitors can pre-book an all-terrain tramper vehicle (5 Mar only).

40 HILLCREST

Curload, Stoke St Gregory, Taunton, TA3 6JA. Charles & Charlotte Sundquist, 01823 490852, chazfix@gmail.com. *At top of Curload. From A358 take A378, L to & through North Curry, L 1/2 m after Willows & Wetlands centre. Hillcrest on R (parking directions). From A361 turn S at Burrowbridge Xrds. Then 1st R follow NGS signs.* **Sat 4, Sun 5 May (1-5). Adm £5, chd free. Home-made teas.** Visits also by arrangement Apr to June for groups of 5 to 30. Guided tour inc but groups welcome to explore on their own.

Boasting stunning views of the Somerset Levels, Burrow Mump and Glastonbury Tor this 6 acre garden offers plenty of interest, inc a standing stone. Enjoy woodland walks, varied borders, flowering meadow and several ponds. There are greenhouses, orchards, a new produce garden and newly built large gravel garden. Garden is mostly level with gentle sloping paths down through meadow. Cashless payments cannot be taken for refreshments or plants. Gravel around refreshment area.

41 HOLLAM HOUSE

Dulverton, TA22 9JH. Annie Prebensen, 01398 323445, annie@hollam.co.uk. *From Dulverton Bridge, go straight & bear R at the chemist. At the garage, Hollam Ln is the 2nd L turning immed after the garage, it is between*

a cottage & music shop. **Visits by arrangement 15 Apr to 27 June for groups of 8 to 30. Teas by prior arrangement. Very limited access for disabled. Adm £7, chd free.** Extending over 5 acres, this sloping Exmoor garden inc ponds, a water garden, woodland planting, borders and meadow areas. There are magnificent mature trees and old rhododendrons. Spring highlights are the thousands of tulips and other bulbs as well as flowering shrubs and trees; magnolia, cornus and viburnum among others. Not suitable for those of limited mobility or small children. No dogs.

42 HONEYHURST FARM

Honeyhurst Lane, Rodney Stoke, Cheddar, BS27 3UJ. Don & Kathy Longhurst, 01749 870322, donlonghurst@btinternet.com, www.ciderbarrelcottage.co.uk. *4m E of Cheddar. From Wells (A371) turn into Rodney Stoke signed Wedmore. Pass church on L and continue for almost 1m. Car park signed. From Cheddar (A371) turn R signed Wedmore, through Draycott to car park.* **Sun 7, Mon 8 July (2-5). Adm £4, chd free. Home-made teas.** Visits also by arrangement 1 Apr to 14 Sept for groups of 10 to 40. 2/3 acre part walled rural garden with babbling brook and 4 acre traditional cider orchard, with views. Specimen hollies, copper beech, paulownia, yew and poplar. Pergolas, arbour and numerous seats. Mixed informal shrub and perennial beds with many unusual plants. Many pots planted with shrubs, hardy and half-hardy perennials. Level, grass and some shingle.

43 NEW IVY COTTAGE

Bell Road, Chewton Mendip, Radstock, BA3 4NX. Gill & Andrew Tindal, 01761 241790, gilltindal@btinternet.com. *6m N of Wells. From Wells, head N on A39. On S edge of Chewton Mendip, turn L at Bathway Xrds. After 500 metres, take an awkward R turn on a LH bend.* **Visits by arrangement 18 May to 29 June for groups of 10 to 20. Parking for 4 cars at the garden. Small layby for 3 cars along lane. Adm £5, chd free. Light refreshments.** In a rural hilltop location, this 1 acre garden surrounds an old cottage. It has different areas of interest

throughout which inc many mixed borders, large wildlife pond, wildflower areas, an orchard, cutting patch, beautiful mature trees and a hovel with exotic-style planting inspired by Great Dixter. We have a gravel drive but the garden itself is almost flat and most areas are accessible.

44 JAPANESE GARDEN BRISTOL

13 Glenarm Walk, Brislington, Bristol, BS4 4LS. Martin Fitton, www.facebook.com/japanesegardenbristol. *A4 Bristol to Bath. A4 Brislington, at Texaco Garage at bottom of Bristol Hill turn into School Rd & immed R into Church Parade. Car park 1st turn on R or proceed to Glenarm Walk.* **Sat 1 June (12-5). Adm £6, chd free. Pre-booking essential, please visit www.ngs.org.uk for information & booking. Home-made teas.**

As you walk through the gate you will be welcomed by Japanese Koi. Then take a step to another level to the relaxing Japanese garden room and tea house surrounded by acers and cloud trees. Walk past Buddha corner into the Bonsai and Zen water feature area. Continue to a Japanese courtyard through a gate to a peaceful Japanese rock garden. There you will find seating to enjoy the serene atmosphere. Please note steps to different levels means the garden is unsuitable for disabled access.

In 2023 we awarded over £260,000 in Community Garden Grants, supporting 86 community garden projects

45 ◆ JEKKA'S HERB GARDEN & HERBETUM
Shellards Lane, Alveston, Bristol, BS35 3SY. Mrs Jekka McVicar, 01454 418878, sales@jekkas.com, www.jekkas.com. *7m N of M5 J16 or 6m S from J14 of M5. 1m off A38 signed Itchington. From M5 J16, A38 to Alveston, past church turn R at junction signed Itchington. M5 J14 on A38 turn L after T-lights to Itchington.* **For NGS: Sat 3 Aug (9.30-4). Adm £10, chd free. Pre-booking essential, please phone 01454 418878, email sales@jekkas.com or visit www. jekkas.com for information & booking. Our herb inspired café will be open offering seasonal herb-based treats, home-made cakes & coffee as well as Jekka's herbal infusions. For other opening times and information, please phone, email or visit garden website.**
Jekka's is home to a living encyclopedia of over 400 different varieties of culinary and medicinal herbs that are displayed in Jekka's Herbetum and Jekka's Herb Garden. Visit Jekka's and browse their collection, buy herb, plants and seeds, visit the farm shop or have some tasty treats from Jekka's café. Wheelchair access possible however terrain is rough from car park to Herbetum.

46 JOHN'S CORNER
2 Fitzgerald Road, Bedminster, Bristol, BS3 5DD. John Hodge. *3m from city centre. South Bristol, off St. John's Lane, Totterdown end. 1st house on R entrance at side of house. On number 91 bus route. Parking in residential street.* **Fri 9, Sat 10, Sun 11 Aug (12-5). Adm £4, chd free. Home-made teas.**
Unusual and interesting city garden with a mixture of exciting plants and features. Ponds, ferns and much more. Eden project style greenhouse with collection of cacti. Not all areas accessible by wheelchair.

47 ◆ KILVER COURT GARDENS
Kilver Street, Shepton Mallet, BA4 5NF. Showering Family, 01749 705279, enquiries@kilvercourt.co.uk, www.kilvercourt.com. *30 mins drive from Bristol & Bath on the A37. Opp Showerings factory on Kilver St. Disabled parking in lower car park.* **For NGS: Wed 12 June, Wed 11 Sept (10-4). Adm £7.50, chd free. Light refreshments in Kilver Court Café. Discount/prepaid vouchers are not valid on National Garden Scheme open days. For other opening times and information, please phone, email or visit garden website.**
Visitors can wander by the millpond, explore the formal and informal gardens and enjoy a replica of the splendid Chelsea Flower Show Gold Medal winning rockery where a gushing recirculated stream flows from pool to pool and waterfalls into the lake. All this set against the stunning backdrop of Charlton Viaduct with the 100m herbaceous flower border beyond. Seek out the famous Babycham. Please note, on site payment is card only. Some slopes, rockery not accessible for wheelchairs but can be viewed from garden.

48 KNOLL COTTAGE
Stogumber, Taunton, TA4 3TN. Elaine & John Leech, 01984 656689, john@Leech45.com, www.knoll-cottage.co.uk. *3m SE of Williton. From A358 follow signs to Stogumber. After 2½m, at T-junction, turn R towards Williton. After ⅓m turn R up narrow lane. Knoll Cottage on L after 100yds.* **Visits by arrangement June to Oct for groups of 5 to 30. Adm £5, chd free. Home-made teas.**
Four acre garden started from fields in 1998. Extensive mixed beds with shrubs, perennials and annuals. Over 80 different roses. Small arboretum area inc many different cornus, rowans, hawthorns, oaks and birches. Pond, large vegetable and fruit areas.

49 LITTLE YARFORD FARMHOUSE
Kingston St Mary, Taunton, TA2 8AN. Mrs D Bradley, 01823 451350, dilly.bradley@gmail.com. *1½m W of Hestercombe, 3½m N of Taunton. From Taunton on Kingston St Mary road. At 30mph sign turn L at Parsonage Ln. Continue 1¼m W, to Yarford sign. Continue 400yds. Turn R up concrete road.* **Sun 5 May (2-5); Mon 6 May (11-4.30). Adm £7, chd free. Cream teas. Visits also by arrangement 7 Apr to 31 Oct.**
Unusual 5 acre garden embracing

C17 house (not open) Natural pond and 90ft water lily pond. A plantsman's garden notable for the aesthetics of its planting especially its 300+ rare and unusual tree cultivars: the best collection of broad leaf and conifer specimens in Western Somerset (link to the full list can be found under Extended Description on NGS website); those trees not available to Bampfylde Warre at Hestercombe in C18. There will be brief guided tree tours at 2.30 and 3.30pm. An exercise in landscaping, contrast planting and creating views both within the garden and without to the vale and the Quantock Hills. Mostly wheelchair access.

50 LOWER SHALFORD FARM
Shalford Lane, Charlton Musgrove, Wincanton, BA9 8HE. Mr & Mrs David Posnett. *Lower Shalford is 2m NE of Wincanton. Leave A303 at Wincanton go N on B3081 towards Bruton. Just beyond Otter Garden Centre turn R Shalford Lane, garden is ½m on L. Parking opp house.* **Sat 23 Mar (10-3); Sat 18 May (10-4). Combined adm with Forest Lodge £10, chd free. Light refreshments.**
Fairly large open garden with extensive lawns and wooded surroundings with drifts of daffodils in spring. Small winterbourne stream running through with several stone bridges. Walled rose/parterre garden, hedged herbaceous garden, mature wisterias in all their glory and several ornamental ponds.

51 LUCOMBE HOUSE
12 Druid Stoke Ave, Stoke Bishop, Bristol, BS9 1DD. Malcolm Ravenscroft, 01179 682494, famrave@gmail.com. *4m NW of Bristol centre. At top of Druid Hill. Turn in Druid Stoke Avenue. Garden on R 300m from junction.* **Sun 9 June (1-5). Adm £4, chd free. Home-made teas. Open nearby 4 Haytor Park. Visits also by arrangement 1 June to 29 Sept for groups of up to 30. Please try to give 3 weeks notice of visit.**
For tree lovers of all ages! In addition to the 260 yr old Lucombe Oak - registered as one of the most significant trees in the UK - there are over 30 mature English trees planted together with ferns and bluebells to create an urban woodland - plus a newly designed Arts & Crafts front

garden. A new path through the woodland provides a behind the scenes look at the garden. Trio of recorder players will entertain visitors. Rough paths in woodland area, 2 steps to patio.

&. ✿ ☕

52 LYDEARD HOUSE
West Street, Bishops Lydeard, Taunton, TA4 3AU. Mrs Vaun Wilkins. *5m NW of Taunton. A358 Taunton to Minehead, do not take 1st 3 R turnings to Bishops Lydeard but 4th signed to Cedar Falls. Follow signs to Lydeard House.* **Sun 9 June (2-5). Adm £5, chd free. Light refreshments.**
4 acre garden with C18 origins and many later additions. Sweeping lawns, lake overhung with willows, canal running parallel to Victorian rose-covered pergola, along with box parterre, chinoiserie-style garden, recent temple folly and walled vegetable garden plus wonderful mature trees. Plants for sale. Children must be supervised because of very deep water. Deep gravel paths and steps may cause difficulty for wheelchairs but most features are accessible by lawn and parking will be available.

&. ✿ ☕))

GROUP OPENING

53 LYMPSHAM GARDENS
Church Road, Lympsham, Weston-super-Mare, BS24 0DT. *5m S of Weston-super-Mare and 5m N of Burnham on Sea. 2m M5 J22. Entrance to all gardens initially from main gates of Manor at junction of Church Rd & Lympsham Rd. Visitors will then receive directions to other gardens.* **Sat 29, Sun 30 June (2-5). Combined adm £5, chd free. Cream teas at Lympsham Manor.**

CHURCH FARM
Andy & Rosemary Carr.

HAWTHORNS
Mrs Victoria Daintree.

LYMPSHAM MANOR
James & Lisa Counsell.

At the heart of the stunning village of Lympsham next to its C15 church are the gardens of two of the village's most historic homes. Lympsham Manor, a 200 yr old gothic rectory manor house with 2 octagonal towers, is set in 10 acres of formal/

semi-formal garden, surrounded by paddocks and farmland. Fully working Victorian kitchen garden and greenhouse, arboretum of trees from all parts of the world, a large pond with a Japanese style bridge (built from oak from the garden), a wildflower area and a beautiful old rose garden. Church Farm has a $\frac{3}{4}$ acre informal English country garden with herbaceous borders, shrub-lined paths, raised beds and a small courtyard garden. In addition visitors will receive a warm welcome to Hawthorns, a short drive to the hamlet of Eastertown, an informal cottage garden with colourful borders and an extensive vegetable garden.

&. 🐕 ✿ ☕))

54 NEW THE MANOR
South Street, Wincanton, BA9 9DL. Anna Hughes. *On the R of South St on the one-way system in central Wincanton, opp Our Lady's Primary School. Parking on the High St or in the Memorial Hall car park. The garden is also known as 'The Dogs'.* **Sat 25, Sun 26 May (10.30-5). Adm £7, chd free. Home-made teas. Open nearby 10 Flingers Lane.**
Hidden and unexpected large walled garden in town centre around seventeenth-century manor house. Developed by the current owners over the last 25 yrs. Yew hedges provide good structure and divide the garden into distinct areas. Formal pond garden. Vegetable garden with box edging. Orchard. Tiny 'lockdown' garden created in 2020. A small number of parking places by the house for disabled use. Wheelchair access is available to the main upper part of the garden.

&. 🐕 ☕))

55 NEW MELLOWSTONES
Staples Hill, Freshford, Bath, BA2 7WL. Mrs Jackie Kennedy. *5m S of Bath. A36 Bath/Warminster rd. Take exit to Freshford; past pub over bridge up Staples Hill to top. Mellowstones is on the R. Parking at Downside Nurseries, 1st L after property (a 15 min walk).* **Sun 26 May, Sun 30 June (11-4). Adm £6, chd free. Home-made cakes & teas.**
Developed over the last 4 yrs, this 1 acre south facing hillside terraced garden is set in woodland, with wonderful views across the Frome valley. The upper level has cottage

garden plants and yew hedges, a quarry kitchen and a grass path through wildflowers to the summerhouse. The Mediterranean terrace has olive trees, a gravel planting area with stepping stones across a corten steel pond. The lower terrace is a formal garden leading to a grass path which extends through the sloping wildflower orchard. Woodland and valley walks. Short distance from the canal.

🐕 D ☕))

56 ♦ MILTON LODGE
Old Bristol Road, Wells, BA5 3AQ. Simon Tudway Quilter, 01749 679341, www.miltonlodgegardens.co.uk. *½ m N of Wells. From A39 Bristol-Wells, turn N up Old Bristol Rd; car park 1st gate on L signed.* **For NGS: Sun 12 May, Sun 9 June, Sun 14 July (2-5). Adm £5, chd free. Home-made teas (cash only). Children 14 & under free entry to garden. Discount/membership/ prepaid vouchers not valid on the National Garden Scheme charity days. For other opening times and information, please phone or visit garden website.**
This garden is a must for garden lovers, well worth a visit. Land transformed into architectural terraces capitalising on views of Wells Cathedral and Vale of Avalon. A Grade II terraced garden restored to its former glory by the owner's parents, who moved here in 1960, replacing the orchard with a collection of ornamental trees, specimen trees and yew hedges. A serene, relaxing atmosphere within the garden succeeds the ravages of two World Wars. Cross over Old Bristol Rd to our 7 acre woodland garden, The Combe, open on NGS days, a natural peaceful contrast to the formal garden of Milton Lodge. Card machine or cash for admission.

✿ ☕))

The National Garden Scheme searches the length and breadth of England, Wales, Northern Ireland and the Channel Islands for the very best private gardens

57 MODEL FARM

Perry Green, Wembdon, Bridgwater, TA5 2BA. Dave & Roz Young, 01278 429953, dave@modelfarm.com, www.modelfarm.com. *4m from J23 of M5. Follow Brown signs from r'about on A39 2m W of Bridgwater.* **Every Thur 11 Apr to 18 July (10-4). Adm £5, chd free. Tea, coffee, squash.**

Four acres of flat gardens to south of Victorian country house. Created from a field in last 14 yrs and still being developed. A dozen large mixed flower beds planted in cottage garden style with wildlife in mind. Wooded areas, mixed orchard, lawns, wildflower meadows and wildlife ponds. Plenty of seating throughout the gardens with various garden sculptures by Somerset artists.

58 NEW NEW WOOD HOUSE, 19 THE BEACON

Ilminster, TA19 9AH. Mr & Mrs Julian Gibbs. *½ m from Ilminster Market Place. Northern outskirts of Ilminster on B3168 (Curry Rivel road), on W side of road.* **Sat 8 June (1.30-5). Adm £5, chd free. Home-made teas.**

Building on an existing design of terraces, paths and some fine mature trees, the garden has been extensively restored over 8 yrs, replanting with several unusual species, inc wild-collected acers, oaks and malus. Formal areas close to the house, with long views, and steep winding paths on both sides leading through unexpected incidents to the bottom of the garden and an orchard.

59 165 NEWBRIDGE HILL

Bath, BA1 3PX. Helen Hughesdon, 07793 085267, thefragrantlife@hotmail.com. *On the western fringes of Bath (A431), 100m on L after Apsley Rd. Several bus routes go to Newbridge Hill.* **Sat 29, Sun 30 June (11-5). Adm £5, chd free. Home-made teas & light lunches. Visits also by arrangement June and Sept for groups of 8 to 20.**

Incorporating 'Sculpture to Enhance a Garden' at its June opening this south facing garden on the edge of the city has unusual and exotic plants, vegetable garden, wildlife pond, greenhouse, treehouse and swing, late summer colour, fabulous views

and a sunny terrace overlooking the garden where light lunches, cream teas and home-made cakes are served. Pieces of sculpture are for sale.

60 NYNEHEAD COURT

Nynehead, Wellington, TA21 0BN. Nynehead Care Ltd, 01823 662481, nyneheadcare@aol.com, www.nyneheadcourt.co.uk. *1½ m N of Wellington. M5 J26 B3187 towards Wellington. R on r'about marked Nynehead & Poole, follow lane for 1m, take Milverton turning at fork, turning into Chipley Rd.* **Sun 17 Mar, Sun 23 June (2-4.30). Adm £6.50, chd free. Tea, coffee, squash & biscuits available. Visits also by arrangement 8 Jan to 16 Dec for groups of 10 to 30. Please contact Head Gardener to book visit on Garden@nyneheadcourt. co.uk.**

Nynehead Court was the home of the Sandford family from 1590-1902. The 14 acres of gardens are noted for specimen trees, and there will be a garden tour with the Head Gardener at 2pm (pls wear suitable footwear). Nynehead is now a private residential care home. The garden combines Victorian formality with natural style further into the parkland inc spring bulbs in managed grassland. A Historic England garden of national importance, Nynehead won a landscape heritage award in 2007 from Taunton Deane Borough Council. Partial wheelchair access: cobbled yards, gentle slopes, chipped paths, liable to puddle during or after rain.

61 THE OLD RECTORY, DOYNTON

18 Toghill Lane, Doynton, Bristol, BS30 5SY. Edwina & Clive Humby, www.tumblr.com/doyntongardens. *At heart of village of Doynton, between Bath & Bristol. Parking in Bury Lane, just after junction with Horsepool Lane. Car parking is signed. Parking is restricted to designated areas.* **Sat 22 June (11-5). Adm £6, chd free. Cream teas.**

Doynton's Grade II listed Georgian Rectory's walled garden and extended 15 acre estate. Renovated over 12 yrs, it sits within AONB. Garden has diversity of modern and traditional elements, fused to create an atmospheric series of garden rooms. Large landscaped kitchen

garden with canal, vegetable plots, fruit cages and treehouse. Bees and a woodland area are also features for a longer stroll.

62 THE OLD VICARAGE, RUISHTON

Church Lane, Ruishton, Taunton, TA3 5LL. Mr & Mrs Andrew Lukes. *5 mins E of M5, J25. Opp St George's Church, Ruishton.* **Sat 10, Sun 11 Aug (12-4). Adm £5, chd £2.50. Home-made teas.**

Traces of the old garden are still in evidence with plenty of new beds incorporated. A terrace overlooks compact formal lawns and walled garden with attractive rope roses, wisteria tunnel and herbaceous beds. Below is a productive vegetable garden and espalier fruit trees. Lawns lead to a wildlife area with pond. At the front, a newly designed driveway and fountain garden frame the house. Shallow gravel paths and level lawns provide access.

63 PENNARD HOUSE

East Pennard, Shepton Mallet, BA4 6TP. Martin Dearden. *5m S of Shepton Mallet on A37. 1m W of A37 Turn R at the top of the hill, or L if coming from the south.* **Tue 11 June (12-5). Adm £5, chd free. Home-made teas.**

Two delightful separate gardens. Both with extensive lawns, mature trees, rose beds, rustic topiary, a Victorian spring fed swimming pool and ponds. Garden layout dates from 1835 when the Napier family enlarged the main house and acquired the house next door. Next door, Pennard Plants, will also open for plant purchasing. On offer is a selection of edible plants, fruit trees, herbs and seeds. The gardens are on a slope, but accessible with assistance.

64 PENNY BROHN UK

Chapel Pill Lane, Pill, BS20 0HH. Penny Brohn UK, www.pennybrohn.org.uk. *4m W of Bristol. Off A369 Clifton Suspension Bridge to M5 (J19 Gordano Services). Follow signs to Penny Brohn UK & to Pill/Ham Green (5 mins).* **Sun 16 June (10-4). Adm £5, chd free. Hot & cold drinks and home-made cakes are available.**

3½ acre tranquil garden surrounds Georgian mansion with many mature trees, wildflower meadow, flower garden and cedar summerhouse. Fine views from historic gazebo overlooking the River Avon. Courtyard gardens with water features. Garden is maintained by volunteers and plays an active role in the Charity's 'Living Well with Cancer' approach. Plants, teas, music and plenty of space to enjoy a picnic. Tours of centre to find out more about the work of Penny Brohn UK. Some gravel and grass paths.

65 THE RIB

St Andrews Street, Wells, BA5 2UR. Paul Dickinson & David Morgan-Hewitt. *Wells City Centre, adjacent to east end of Wells Cathedral & opp Vicars Close. There is absolutely no parking at or very near this city garden. Visitors should use one of the 5 public car parks and enjoy the 10-15 minutes stroll through the city to The Rib.* **Sat 22 June (12-5). Adm £6, chd free.**
The Rib is one of the few houses in England that can boast a cathedral and a sacred well in its garden. Whilst the garden is compact, it delivers a unique architectural and historical punch. Long established trees, interesting shrubs and more recently planted mixed borders frame the view in the main garden. Ancient walled orchard and traditionally planted cottage garden. Lunch, tea and WC facilities available in Wells marketplace or Wells Cathedral. Slightly bumpy but short gravel drive and uneven path to main rear garden. 2-3 steps up to orchard and cottage gardens. Grass areas uneven in places.

66 ROCK HOUSE

Elberton, BS35 4AQ. Mr & Mrs John Gunnery, 01454 413225. *10m N of Bristol. From Old Severn Bridge on M48 take B4461 to Alveston. In Elberton, take 1st turning L and then immed R. SatNav starts at top of village, come down hill to Littleton turning on R, R again.* **Sun 28 Jan, Sun 4 Feb, Sun 17, Sun 24 Mar (11-4); Sun 16 June (12-5). Adm £5, chd free. 2025: Sun 26 Jan, Sun 2 Feb. Visits also by arrangement 2 Jan to 20 Dec.**
Two acre garden. Woodland vistas with swathes of snowdrops and carpets of daffodils, some unusual. Spring flowers, cottage garden plants and climbing roses in season. Old yew tree, maturing cedar tree, pond.

The garden will also be open to visitors on Sunday 26th January and Sunday 2nd February 2025 between 11am and 4pm.

67 ROSE COTTAGE

Smithams Hill, East Harptree, Bristol, BS40 6BY. Bev & Jenny Cruse, 01761 221627, bandjcruse@gmail.com. *5m N of Wells, 15m S of Bristol. From B3114 turn into High St in EH. L at Clock Tower & immed R into Middle St, up hill for 1m. From B3134 take EH rd opp Castle of Comfort, continue 1½ m. Car parking in field opp cottage.* **Visits by arrangement 8 Apr to 30 Apr for groups of up to 30. Adm £5.50, chd free. Home-made teas.**
Organically gardened and planted to encourage wildlife. Bordered by a stream and mixed hedges, our acre of hillside cottage garden is carpeted with seasonal bulbs, primroses and hellebores in spring, roses and hardy geraniums in summer. Plenty of seating areas to enjoy the panoramic views over Chew Valley. Opp our cottage, in the corner of the field, our wildlife area with pond develops with interest. Full of spring colour.

68 SKOOL BEANZ CHILDREN'S ALLOTMENT

Little Sammons Allotments, Chilthorne Domer, BA22 8RB. South Somerset County Council, www.skoolbeanzcic.mystrikingly. com. *Situated between the Carpenters Arms & the village school adjacent to Tintinhull rd. Parking either at pub or at The Rec just off Main St next to the school.* **Sun 15 Sept (11-5). Adm £3, chd free. Home-made tea & cakes.**
Skool Beanz children's gardening club was created by Lara Honnor to encourage children to enjoy gardening. The allotment has a huge cut flower dahlia bed, vegetable area, fruit trees and bushes, a rainwater collecting station, 'Muddy Buddy' compost heap, quiet wildlife garden, secret den, polytunnel and plenty of seating and tables for upcycling garden arts & crafts. Lara contributed to Charles Dowding's No Dig Children's Gardening Book sharing tips she has learnt from Skool Beanz on teaching the joys of gardening to children.

69 SOUTH KELDING

Brewery Hill, Upton Cheyney, Bristol, BS30 6LY. Barry & Wendy Smale, 01179 325145, wendy.smale@yahoo.com. *Halfway between Bristol & Bath. Upton Cheyney lies ½ m up Brewery Hill off A431 just outside Bitton. Detailed directions & parking arrangements given when appt made. Restricted access means pre-booking essential.* **Visits by arrangement Mar to Oct for groups of up to 40. Adm £10, chd free. Home-made teas. Adm price includes refreshments & tour by owner.**
Seven acre hillside garden offering panoramic views from its upper levels, with herbaceous and shrub beds, prairie-style scree beds, orchard, native copses and small, labelled arboretum grouped by continents. Large wildlife pond, boundary stream and wooded area featuring shade and moisture-loving plants. Due to slopes and uneven terrain this garden is unsuitable for disabled access.

70 ◆ SPECIAL PLANTS

Greenway Lane, Cold Ashton, Chippenham, SN14 8LA. Derry Watkins, 01225 891686, derry@specialplants.net, www.specialplants.net. *6m N of Bath. From Bath on A46, turn L into Greenways Lane just before r'about with A420.* **For NGS: Thur 20 June, Thur 18 July, Thur 15 Aug, Thur 19 Sept, Thur 17 Oct (10.30-5). Adm £5, chd free. Home-made teas. For other opening times and information, please phone, email or visit garden website.**
Architect-designed ¾ acre hillside garden with stunning views. Started autumn 1996. Exotic plants. Gravel gardens for borderline hardy plants. Black and white (purple and silver) garden. Vegetable garden and orchard. Hot border. Lemon and lime bank. Annual, biennial and tender plants for late summer colour. Spring fed ponds. Bog garden. Woodland walk. Allium alley. Free list of plants in garden.

71 NEW **STANDERWICK COURT**
Standerwick, Frome, BA11 2PP.
**Mr Guy Monson & Lady Rose
Monson.** *3m from Frome, 12m from
Bath to Beckington. Follow A36 to
Beckington r'about. Take turning
to White Row Farm Shop. Follow
lane in front of farm shop to end,
pass gatehouse, entrance to garden
on L, through black gates, parking
signed.* **Sat 29 June (11-4). Adm
£7.50, chd free. Home-made teas
in the garden at the front of The
Wool House or inside, weather
dependent.**
A hidden gem near the Somerset/
Wilts border. With far reaching views
over the White Horse and Cley Hill
lies a stunning Queen Anne House
nestled in 76 acres of parkland. Ha-ha
and woodland partially surround the
formal gardens recently redesigned
by Mark Lutyens and Catherine
Fitzgerald to inc an Italian inspired
terrace, walled garden with tiki hut,
tennis court, greenhouse and pool
garden. Over the past 7yrs the
surrounding grounds have developed
into a mix of contemporary cottage
garden, formal hedging and lawns
throughout. Do take an enjoyable
stroll up the lime avenue to the
folly, where deer, hares, rabbits and
squirrels gather. Pls supervise children
at all times. Dogs on leads.

72 ◆ **STOBERRY GARDEN**
Stoberry Park, Wells,
BA5 3LD. **Frances & Tim
Young,** 01749 672906,
stay@stoberry-park.co.uk, www.
stoberryparkgarden.co.uk. *½m
N of Wells. From Bristol - Wells on
A39, L into College Rd & immed L
through Stoberry Park, signed.* **For
NGS: Sat 1, Sun 2 June, Sat 17,
Sun 18 Aug (1-5). Adm £5, chd
free. Home-made teas. Discount/
prepaid vouchers not valid on
NGS charity days. For other
opening times and information,
please phone, email or visit garden
website.**
With breathtaking views over Wells
Cathedral, this 5 acre family garden
is planted sympathetically within
its landscape providing stunning
combinations of vistas accented
with wildlife ponds and water
features. In comparison 1½ acre
walled garden, full of interesting
planting. Colour and interest for every
season; spring bulbs, irises, salvias,
a newly planted wildflower area, a
new modern rockery. Interesting

sculpture artistically integrated in the
garden. Gardening is great fun and
the exciting reality is that everyone's
opinions of the way a garden should
look, differ.

73 **STONELEIGH DOWN**
Upper Tockington Road,
Tockington, Bristol, BS32 4LQ.
Su & John Mills. *12m N of Bristol.
On LH side of Upper Tockington
Rd when travelling from Tockington
towards Olveston. Set back from
road up gravel drive. Parking in
village.* **Mon 1 Apr (12-4); Sat 15,
Sun 16 June (12-5). Adm £6, chd
free. Home-made teas.**
Approaching ⅔ acre, the south facing
garden has curved gravel pathways
around an S-shaped lawn that
connects themed areas: exotic border;
summer walk; acers; oriental pond;
winter garden; spring garden. On a
level site, it has been densely planted
with trees, shrubs, perennials and
bulbs for year-round interest. Plenty of
places to sit. Steps into courtyard.

GROUP OPENING

74 **STOWEY GARDENS**
Stowey, Bishop Sutton, Bristol,
BS39 5TL. *10m W of Bath. Stowey
Village on A368 between Bishop
Sutton & Chelwood. From Chelwood
r'about take A368 to Weston-s-
Mare. At Stowey Xrds turn R to car
park, 150yds down lane, ample off
road parking opp Dormers. Limited
disabled parking at each garden
which will be signed.* **Sun 21 July
(2-6). Combined adm £7, chd
free. Home-made teas at Stowey
Mead.**

DORMERS
Mr & Mrs G Nicol.

◆ **MANOR FARM**
Richard Baines & Alison Fawcett,
01275 332297.

STOWEY MEAD
Mr Victor Pritchard.

VICARAGE COTTAGE
Chris & Carrie Edwards.

A broad spectrum of interest and
styles developing year on year. But
there is far more than this in these
gardens; the visitor's senses will be
aroused by the sights, scents and
diversity of these gardens in the tiny,

ancient village of Stowey. There are
flower-packed beds, borders and
pots, roses, topiary, hydrangeas,
exotic garden, many unusual trees
and shrubs, orchards, vegetables,
ponds, specialist sweet peas, lawns,
a large rockery bank and a ha-ha.
Abundant collections of mature trees
and shrubs and ample seating areas,
with glorious views from each garden.
There is something of interest for
everyone, all within a few minutes
walk of car park at Dormers. Plant
sales at Dormers. Well behaved dogs
on short leads welcome. Wheelchair
access restricted in places, many
grassed areas in each garden.

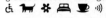

75 **1 SUNNYSIDE**
Stoke Bishop, Bristol, BS9 1BQ.
Mrs Magda Goss. *Approach
via Stoke Hill or Druid Hill,near
shops. Parking on Druid Hill, gate
with sloping gravel drive. This is a
combined opening with Haytor Park.
It is a 20 min walk between the two
gardens or a short drive.* **Sun 19
May (1-5). Combined adm with 4
Haytor Park £5, chd free. Home-
made teas.**
C17 cottage in heart of Stoke Bishop
with part walled, cottage style front
garden. Garden sculptures dominated
by large magnolia, perennials, roses
and spring bulbs. Courtyard garden
with open studio at rear.

76 **TRAFALGAR HOUSE**
29 Sion Hill, Bath, BA1 2UW. **Mrs
Judith Lywood.** *Top of Sion Hill opp
allotments. Only 2 bays available
with free 3 hour parking, otherwise
please park in Victoria Park (pay
by the meter) and walk up the hill.
Please car share where possible.*
**Tue 25 June (9.30-4). Adm £5,
chd free. Pre-booking essential,
please visit www.ngs.org.uk for
information & booking. Home-
made teas. Refreshments cash
only.**
Our garden is a plantsman's garden,
with a background of topiary. My
gardener and I have worked the
last six years with colour, to try and
maintain interest, throughout the
flowering months. The garden has
continual colour throughout the year.
Opposite the front of the house is our
allotment with a glorious view over the
city of Bath. Partial wheelchair access
to main part of garden.

77 ◆ **UNIVERSITY OF BRISTOL BOTANIC GARDEN**
Stoke Park Road, Stoke Bishop, Bristol, BS9 1JG. University of Bristol Botanic Garden, 01174 282041, botanic-gardens@bristol.ac.uk, www.botanic-garden.bristol.ac.uk/. *Located in Stoke Bishop ¼ m W of Durdham Downs & 1m from city centre. After crossing the Downs to Stoke Hill, Stoke Park Rd is 1st on R.* **For NGS: Sun 7 July (10-4.30). Adm £9, chd free. Light refreshments provided by local deli. For other opening times and information, please phone, email or visit garden website. Donation to University of Bristol Botanic Garden.**
Exciting and contemporary award winning Botanic Garden with dramatic displays illustrating collections of Mediterranean flora, rare native, useful plants (inc European and Chinese herbs) and those that illustrate plant evolution. Large floral displays illustrating pollination in flowering plant and evolution. Glasshouses are home to giant Amazon water lily, tropical fruit, medicinal plants, orchids, cacti and unique sacred lotus collection.

Wheelchair available to borrow from Welcome Lodge on request. Wheelchair friendly primary route through garden inc glasshouses, accessible WCs.

& ✿ 🚌 ☕ ⟩⟩

78 NEW **VALLEY SPRING**
Southstoke Road, Bath, BA2 5SP. Liz Bloor. *2m S of Bath. The entrance to Valley Spring is on Southstoke Rd. It is a clearly signed single track road. We have very limited parking & turning, pls park on Southstoke Rd & walk down.* **Fri 10 May (2-5); Sun 12 May (1-5). Adm £8, chd free. Home-made teas.**
Mid-Century modernist house with extensive views over Horsecombe Valley south of Bath looking over 5 acres of garden, meadow and woodland. The garden has been created over the last 6 years to complement distant views, capture spring water that runs through the property and create distinct areas of interest. A new woodland was planted in 2020 and a series of winter beds are being developed.

☕ ⟩⟩

National Garden Scheme gardens are identified by their yellow road signs and posters. You can expect a garden of quality, character and interest, a warm welcome and plenty of home-made cakes!

The Manor

80 ◆ THE WALLED GARDENS OF CANNINGTON

Church Street, Cannington, TA5 2HA. Bridgwater College, 01278 655042, walledgardens@btc.ac.uk, www. canningtonwalledgardens.co.uk. *Part of Bridgwater & Taunton College Cannington Campus, 3m NW of Bridgwater. On A39 Bridgwater-Minehead road, at 1st r'about in Cannington 2nd exit, through village. War memorial, 1st L into Church St then 1st L.* **For NGS: Sat 20, Sun 21 Apr, Sat 14, Sun 15 Sept (10-4). Adm £7.50, chd free. Light refreshments. For other opening times and information, please phone, email or visit garden website.**

Within the grounds of a medieval priory, the Walled Gardens of Cannington are a gem waiting to be discovered! Classic and contemporary features inc hot herbaceous border, blue garden, sub-tropical walk and Victorian style fernery, amongst others. Botanical glasshouse where arid, sub-tropical and tropical plants can be seen. Tearoom, plant nursery, gift shop, also events throughout the year. Gravel paths.

🚶 🐕 ❄ 🚗 ☕

81 WATCOMBE

92 Church Road, Winscombe, BS25 1BP. Peter & Ann Owen, 01934 842666, peterowen449@btinternet.com. *12m SW of Bristol, 3m N of Axbridge. 100 yds after yellow signs on A38 turn L, (from S), or R. (from N) into Winscombe Hill. After 1m reach The Square. Watcombe is on L after 150yds.* **Sun 14 Apr, Sun 19 May, Thur 6 June (2-5.30). Adm £5, chd free. Home-made teas. Gluten-free available. Visits also by arrangement 15 Apr to 11 July.** ³⁄₄ acre mature Edwardian garden with colour-themed, informally planted herbaceous borders. Strong framework separating several different areas; pergola with varied wisteria, unusual topiary, box hedging, lime walk, pleached hornbeams, cordon fruit trees, 2 small formal ponds and growing collection of clematis. Many unusual trees and shrubs. Small vegetable plot. Some steps but most areas accessible by wheelchair with minimal assistance.

♿ 🐕 ❄ 🚗 ☕

82 WAYFORD MANOR

Wayford, Crewkerne, TA18 8QG. Wayford Manor. *3m SW of Crewkerne. Turn N off B3165 at Clapton, signed Wayford or S off A30 Chard to Crewkerne road, signed Wayford.* **Sun 28 Apr (2-5). Adm £6, chd £3. Home-made teas.** The mainly Elizabethan manor (not open) mentioned in C17 for its 'fair and pleasant' garden was redesigned by Harold Peto in 1902. Formal terraces with yew hedges and topiary have fine views over W Dorset. Steps down between spring-fed ponds past mature and new plantings of magnolia, rhododendron, maples, cornus and, in season, spring bulbs, cyclamen and giant echium. Primula candelabra, arum lily and gunnera around lower ponds.

🐕 ❄ ☕))

Wick Manor, Wick Gardens

83 WELLFIELD BARN

Walcombe Lane, Wells, BA5 3AG.
Virginia Nasmyth, 01749 675129.
½m N of Wells. From A39 Bristol
to Wells road turn R at 30 mph sign
into the narrow Walcombe Lane.
Entrance at 1st cottage on R, parking
signed. Visits by arrangement June
& July for groups of 10+. Adm
£5.50, chd free. Please bring your
own picnic.

Our garden is a haven for wildlife.
27yrs ago, a once bustling concrete
farmyard grew into a tranquil ½
acre garden. Planned, created
and still evolving today to provide
enjoyment of colour and form for
year-round enjoyment. Structured
design integrates house, lawn and
garden with the landscape. Wonderful
views, ha-ha, specimen trees, mixed
borders, hydrangea bed, hardy
geraniums and roses. Formal sunken
garden, grass walks with interesting
young and semi-mature trees for
each season. Now tranquillity, sheep
as neighbours, perfect peace. Our
collection of hardy geraniums was
featured on BBC Gardeners' World
with Carol Klein. Moderate slopes in
places, an abundance of grass with
some gravel paths.

84 WESTBROOK HOUSE

West Bradley, BA6 8LS.
Keith Anderson & David
Mendel, 01458 850604,
andersonmendel@aol.com, www.
instagram.com/keithbfanderson.
4m E of Glastonbury; 8m W of Castle
Cary. From A361 at W Pennard
follow signs to W Bradley (2m). From
A37 at Wraxall Hill follow signs to
W Bradley (2m). Sat 4 May, Sat
24 Aug (11-5). Adm £6, chd free.
Visits also by arrangement for
groups of 10+. Donation to West
Bradley Church.

Layout and planting began in 2003
by a garden designer and a painter. 4
acres comprising 3 distinct gardens
around house with exuberant mixed
herbaceous and shrub borders
leading to a meadow and orchard
with wildflowers, masses of spring
bulbs, species roses and lilacs.

GROUP OPENING

85 NEW WICK GARDENS

Wick, Langport, TA10 0NL. Mrs Penny
Horne. Nr Langport. From Langport to
Curry Rivel take R turn at Hurds Hill ¾m
Wick Farm on L before sharp bend.
Or from Burrow Bridge follow road to
Langport. Sat 18 May (12-5); Sun 19
May (12-4). Combined adm £6, chd
free. Light refreshments.

NEW PERHAM HOUSE
Chloe Stickland,
www.gatheringswallows.com.

NEW THE STUDIO HOUSE
Andy Waller.

NEW WICK FARM
Mrs Penny Horne,
www.awakeningsatwick.com.

NEW WICK MANOR
Rachel Spencer.

Four gardens in close proximity with
structure yet informality, lovely planting
and much colour Three gardens on
old sites and one modern converted
from a concrete farmyard. All worth
exploring in this delightful village.

86 ◆ THE YEO VALLEY ORGANIC GARDEN AT HOLT FARM

Bath Road, Blagdon,
BS40 7SQ. Mr & Mrs Tim
Mead, 01761 238155,
visit@yeovalleyfarms.co.uk,
www.yeovalley.co.uk. 12m S of
Bristol. Off A368. Entrance approx
½m outside Blagdon towards
Bath, on L, then follow garden
signs past dairy. For NGS: Sun
7 Apr (10-5). Adm £7, chd £2.
Light refreshments. For other
opening times and information,
please phone, email or visit garden
website.

One of only a handful of ornamental
gardens that is Soil Association
accredited, 6½ acres of contemporary
planting, quirky sculptures, bulbs
in their thousands, purple palace,
glorious meadow and posh vegetable
patch. Great views, green ideas.
Events, workshops and exhibitions
held throughout the year - see website
for further details. Level access to
café. Around garden there are some
grass paths and some uneven bark
and gravel paths. Accessibility map
available at ticket office.

87 THE YEWS

Harry Stoke Road, Stoke Gifford,
Bristol, BS34 8QH. Dr Barbara
Laue & Dr Chris Payne. From A38/
Filton, take A4174 ring road to M32.
L turn at Sainsbury R'about. Straight
across next R'about. After 200 yds,
sharp R turn into Harry Stoke Rd.
Parking in paddock. Sun 19 May
(2-5). Adm £5, chd free. Home-
made teas.

Approx 1 acre, developed by
present owners since 1987. Part of
the old hamlet of Harry Stoke, now
surrounded by housing development.
Formal area with pond, gazebo,
herbaceous borders, clipped box
and yew. 300 yr old yews, wedding
cake tree, magnolias, eucalyptus,
Indian bean tree, gingkoes and more.
Vegetable garden, greenhouse,
orchard and meadow. Spring bulbs
and blossom.

88 YEWS FARM

East Street, Martock, TA12 6NF.
Louise & Fergus Dowding, www.
instagram.com/dowdinglouise.
Turn off main road, Church St, at
Market House/visitor's centre, onto
East St, go past White Hart & PO
on R. Yews Farm 150 yds on R, opp
Foldhill Lane. Turn around if you get
to Nag's Head. Sun 7 July, Sun 8
Sept (1.30-5). Adm £8, chd free.
Home-made teas.

Theatrical planting in large south
facing walled garden, plants selected
for height, form, leaf and texture.
Prolific box topiary. Low maintenance
perennials. High maintenance
pots. Vegetables and cut flowers
grown together. Self seeding hugely
encouraged. Working organic kitchen
garden. Greenhouses bursting with
summer vegetables. Organic orchard
with heritage varieties and active cider
barn. Hens and pigs.

Our donation in 2023
has enabled Parkinson's
UK to fund 3 new
nursing posts this year,
directly supporting
people with Parkinson's

WILTSHIRE

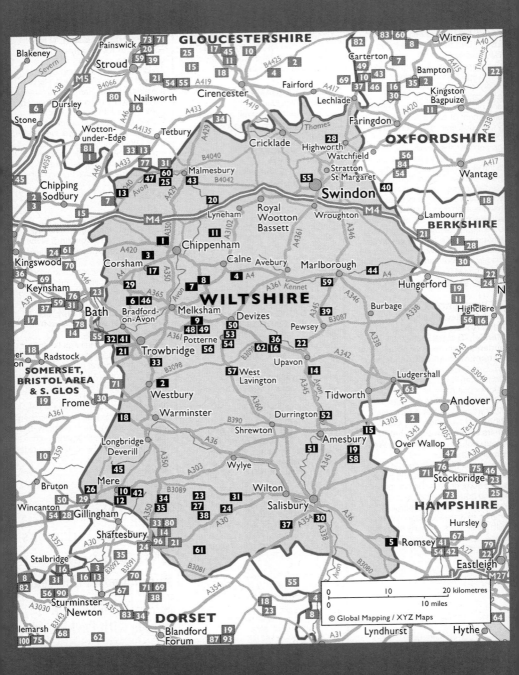

VOLUNTEERS

County Organisers
Ros Ford 07717 135028
ros.ford@ngs.org.uk

Alex Graham 07906 146337
alex.graham@ngs.org.uk

County Treasurer
Tony Roper 01249 447436
tony.roper@ngs.org.uk

Publicity
& Booklet Co-ordinator
Tricia Duncan 01672 810443
tricia.duncan@ngs.org.uk

Social Media
Maud Peters 07595 266299
maudahpeters@gmail.com

Assistant County Organisers
Sue Allen 07785 294153
sue.allen@ngs.org.uk

Sarah Coate 01722 782365
sarah.coate@ngs.org.uk

Annabel Dallas 01672 520266
annabel.dallas@btinternet.com

Andy Devey 07810 641595
andy.devey@ngs.org.uk

Donna Hambly 07760 889277
donna.hambly@ngs.org.uk

Jo Hankey 01722 742472
jo.hankey@ngs.org.uk

Alison Parker 07786 985741
alison.parker@ngs.org.uk

f @WiltshireNGS
◎ @Wiltshirengs

OPENING DATES

All entries subject to change.
For latest information check
www.ngs.org.uk

Map locator numbers are
shown to the right of each
garden name.

Extended openings are shown
at the beginning of the month.

January

Every Thursday
Westcroft 58

Saturday 27th
NEW The Botanic Nursery 6

Sunday 28th
Westcroft 58

February

Snowdrop Openings

Every Thursday
Westcroft 58

Saturday 3rd
Westcroft 58

Sunday 4th
Westcroft 58

Friday 9th
Westcroft 58

Sunday 18th
Westcroft 58

Saturday 24th
Westcroft 58

Sunday 25th
Westcroft 58

March

Thursday 7th
Westcroft 58

Sunday 24th
◆ Corsham Court 17
Fonthill House 23

April

Sunday 7th
◆ Corsham Court 17

Sunday 14th
Brow Cottage 9
Seend House 48

Saturday 20th
NEW The Botanic Nursery 6
◆ Iford Manor Gardens 32

Wednesday 24th
Blackland House 4

Saturday 27th
Wellaway 56

Sunday 28th
Oare House 39
Wellaway 56

May

Wednesday 1st
Blackland House 4

Sunday 5th
Allington Grange 1

Sunday 12th
Cottage in the Trees 19
Manor Farm House 36

Friday 17th
Biddestone Manor 3

Saturday 18th
Winkelbury House 61

Sunday 19th
1 Southview 50
Trymnells 54
◆ Twigs Community Garden 55

Wednesday 22nd
Bowden Park 7

Saturday 25th
Knoyle Place 34
Lower Lye 35
Tristenagh House 53

Sunday 26th
Hyde's House 31
North Cottage 38

Wednesday 29th
Riverside House 44

June

Saturday 1st
Fovant House 24

Wednesday 5th
Whatley Manor 60

Thursday 6th
NEW The Botanic Nursery 6
Cadenham Manor 11

By Arrangement

Arrange a personalised garden visit with your club, or group of friends, on a date to suit you. See individual garden entries for full details.

Blackland House

© Britt Willoughby Dyer

THE GARDENS

1 ALLINGTON GRANGE
Allington, Chippenham,
SN14 6LW. Mrs Rhyddian Roper,
www.allingtongrange.com. *2m W
of Chippenham. Take A420 W from
Chippenham. 1st R signed Allington
Village, entrance I m up lane on L.*
**Sun 5 May (2-5). Adm £7.50, chd
free. Home-made teas.**
Informal country garden around C17
farmhouse (not open) with year-round
interest and a diverse range of plants.
Many early spring bulbs. Mixed
and herbaceous borders. Pergola
underplanted with shade loving plants
and newly developed fountain garden.
Walled potager. Wildlife pond with
natural planting. Many alpine troughs,
and increasing fern collection. Mainly
level with ramp into potager. Dogs
on leads.

2 BEGGARS KNOLL CHINESE GARDEN
Newtown, Westbury, BA13 3ED.
Colin Little & Penny Stirling,
01373 823383, silkendalliance@
talktalk.net. *1m SE of Westbury.
Turn off B3098 at White Horse
Pottery, up hill towards the White
Horse for ³/₄m. Parking at end
of drive for 10-12 cars.* **Visits by
arrangement June & July for
groups of 5 to 20. Adm £6, chd
free. Tea & cake on request.**
A series of Chinese-style garden
rooms, separated by elaborate
gateways inc moongate, with mosaic
paths winding past pavilions, ponds
and many rare Chinese trees, shrubs
and flowers. Relatively new, a tranquil
Islamic-style tiled garden influenced
by NW China. Potager full of flowers
and vegetables. Spectacular views to
the Mendips. Garden tours by owners
included in ticket.

3 BIDDESTONE MANOR
Chippenham Lane, Biddestone,
SN14 7DJ. Andy Smith, Head
Gardener. *On A4 between
Chippenham & Corsham turn N from
A420, 5m W of Chippenham, turn
S.* **Fri 17 May (10.30-4). Adm £8,
chd free. Home-made teas and
cakes.**
Cotswold stone C17 manor house
(not open) with 5 acres of garden
to enjoy. Lake, ponds, streams,
arboretum, vegetable, cutting gardens
and orchard. Formal front garden
featuring box and yew topiary.
Wheelchair access to most parts, a
few steps.

4 BLACKLAND HOUSE
Quemerford, Calne, SN11 8UQ.
Polly & Edward Nicholson,
www.bayntunflowers.co.uk.
*Situated just off A4. Use Google
Maps. Enter the grounds through
the side entrance signed St. Peter's
Church & Blackland Park Deliveries.
Opp The Willows on Quemerford.*
**Wed 24 Apr, Wed 1 May (2-5).
Adm £10, chd free. Pre-booking
essential, please visit www.ngs.
org.uk for information & booking.
Home-made teas. Vegan & gluten
free cakes. Please bring cash for
teas & plants. Donation to Dorothy
House Hospice.**
A wonderfully varied 5 acre garden
adjacent to the River Marden
(house not open). Formal walled
productive and cutting garden,
traditional glasshouses, rose garden
and wide herbaceous borders.
Interesting topiary, trained fruit trees,
historic tulips (including the National
Collection of historic tulips) and
other unusual spring bulbs. Certified
organic with the Soil Association.
Hand-tied bunches of flowers and
Polly's new book 'The Tulip Garden'
will be for sale. Partial wheelchair
access, steps, grass and cobbles,
wooden bridges, deep water.

5 BLUEBELLS
Cowesfield, Whiteparish,
Salisbury, SP5 2RB. Hilary
Mathison, 01794 885738,
hilary.mathison@icloud.com. *SW
of Salisbury. On main A27 road from
Salisbury to Romsey. 1¹/₂m SE of
Whiteparish, on A27, 100-200 m
inside Wiltshire county boundary.*
**Visits by arrangement 23 Mar
to 15 Sept for groups of 5 to 35.
12 cars max (no street parking).
Adm £5, chd free. Home-made
teas. Wine & savoury bites for
evening visits. Please bring cash
for refreshments.**
1¹/₂ acre garden in a rural setting.
Small woodland has carpets of
bluebells in season. Large front
lawn surrounded by borders. Rear
garden faces south and the design is
contemporary to reflect the newly built
house on site. Many tulips in spring
throughout the garden, amongst
the mainly perennial planting. Large
vegetable area, fruit trees, including
espalier trees, 'stepovers' and 2
ponds.

6 NEW THE BOTANIC NURSERY
Coombe Lane, Atworth,
Melksham, SN12 8NU.
Terence & Mary Baker,
www.botanicnursery.co.uk. *1m
outside the village of Atworth, follow
signs for Stonar School. Pls drive
slowly through the school grounds,
following the one way road. Leave
the school grounds through the 2
stone pillars and turn R. Entrance
& car park is 50 metres down the
road.* **Sat 27 Jan, Sat 20 Apr
(11-3). Adm £5, chd free. Tea.
Thur 6, Fri 7, Sat 8 June (11-4).
Combined adm with Rookery
Cottage £10, chd free. Tea, coffee
& posh biscuits. Donation to Plant
Heritage.**
The nursery garden is a haven
where the wildlife that shares our
site abounds. Many rare specimen
evergreen and deciduous trees can
be seen, underplanted with hardy
perennials. A lush green oasis,
shady in the heat of the summer
and pleasant to wander around any
time of the year. Year-round seasonal
interest from winter flowering shrubs
into the colour of summer and foliage
of autumn. Peonies towards end of
May early June, National Collection
of Digitalis (Foxgloves) feature
throughout June. Some narrow
pathways, however most wheelchairs
can get round the grassy garden
area, there is also a gravel area.

7 BOWDEN PARK
Lacock, Chippenham, SN15 2PP.
Bowden Park Estate. *10 mins
S of Chippenham. Entrance via
Top Lodge at top of Bowden Hill,
between A342 at Sandy Lane and
A350 in Lacock.* **Wed 22 May (10-
4). Adm £8, chd free. Home-made
teas. Bowden Hill range of home-
made cakes & refreshments.**
22 acre private garden within
surrounding parkland. Pleasure
garden, water garden, working
kitchen garden with formal lawns
and grotto. Rhododendrons and
azaleas in flower. Extensive views of
surrounding countryside. Dogs on
short leads welcome. Most areas
accessible on tarmac paths & lawns.

8 ◆ BOWOOD WOODLAND GARDENS

Calne, SN11 9PG. The Marquis of Lansdowne, 01249 812102, houseandgardens@bowood.org, www.bowood.org. *3½ m SE of Chippenham. Located off J17 M4 nr Bath & Chippenham. Entrance off A342 between Sandy Lane & Derry Hill Villages. Follow brown tourist signs.* **For opening times and information, please phone, email or visit garden website.**
This 30 acre woodland garden of azaleas, magnolias, rhododendrons and bluebells is one of the most exciting of its type in the country. From the individual flowers to the breathtaking sweep of colour, this is a garden not to be missed. With two miles of meandering paths, you will find hidden treasures at every corner. The Woodland Gardens are 2m from Bowood House and Garden.

9 BROW COTTAGE

Seend Hill, Seend, Melksham, SN12 6RU. James & Alexandra Gray, www.alexandragray.com. *2m W of Devizes on A361. Garden on L when coming from E, at top of Inmarsh Lane, but parking on green in village centre. Footpath along road or via fields as marked by yellow signs.* **Sun 14 Apr (1-5). Combined adm with Seend House £8, chd free. Home-made teas.**
Half acre contemporary cottage garden owned by a garden designer and created over the past 24 yrs. A garden of many harmonious parts inc lawns, well-stocked borders, topiary, potager, sunken pool garden, wildlife pond, short woodland walk, species bulb lawn and canopied dining area. Open with Seend House and connected by a field footpath offering fine views to Salisbury Plain. Shuttle available. Enter from the driveway rather than the pedestrian gate on the main road.

10 BURTON GRANGE

Burton, Mere, BA12 6BR. Sue Phipps & Paddy Sumner, www.suephipps.com. *Take lane, signposted to Burton, on A303 just E of Mere bypass. After 400 yds follow rd past pond and round to L. Go past wall on R. Burton Grange entrance is in laurel hedge on R.* **Sun 9 June (11.30-5). Adm £5, chd free. Home-made teas.**
1½ acre garden, created from scratch since 2014. Lawns, borders, large ornamental pond, some gravel planting, vegetable garden and pergola rose garden, together with a number of wonderful mature trees.

11 CADENHAM MANOR

Foxham, Chippenham, SN15 4NH. Victoria & Martin Nye, garden@cadenham.com, www.cadenham.com. *B4069 from Chippenham or M4 J17, turn R in Christian Malford & L in Foxham. On A3102 turn L from Calne or R from Lyneham at Xrds between Hilmarton & Goatacre. See map www.cadenham. com/contact.* **Thur 6 June (2-7). Adm £10, chd free. Pre-booking essential, please visit www.ngs. org.uk for information & booking. Home-made teas. Visits also by arrangement 1 Apr to 27 Sept for groups of 10 to 40. Lunches, coffees & teas with cake are on offer.**
This glorious French-style 4 acre garden surrounds a listed C17 manor house with moats and a C16 dovecote Its many rooms are furnished with specimen trees, fountains and statues to focus the eye. Known for its stunning displays of old roses, it also has swathes of spring bulbs, wisteria, bearded iris, a water garden in the old canal, plus extensive vegetable and herb gardens.

12 THE CHANTRY

Church Street, Mere, Warminster, BA12 6DS. Mr & Mrs Richard Wilson, instagram.com/ thechantrygarden. *In the centre of Mere, turn down Angel Lane & follow it to the Cemetery Car Park (RHS) & through it into the field at the Chantry. Pedestrian access is via Church St.* **Sat 8, Sun 9 June (11-5). Adm £7.50, chd free. Home-made teas.**
Medieval chantry house with large landscaped gardens (inc cottage and walled gardens) ponds, orchard, fields and woodland. Historical connection with celebrated Dorset poet William Barnes who wrote his most famous work 'My Orchard in Linden Lea' about the garden.

13 CHERRY ORCHARD BARN

Luckington, SN14 6NZ. Paul Fletcher & Tim Guard. *Cherry Orchard Barn is ¾ m before the centre of SN14 6NZ, at a T junction.*
Passing the Barn is ill-advised, as turning rapidly becomes difficult. **Sun 21 July (1.30-5). Adm £5, chd free. Home-made teas.**
Charming 1 acre garden created over past 10 yrs from the corner of a field, with open views of surrounding countryside. Containing 7 rooms, 3 of which are densely planted with herbaceous perennials, each with individual identities and colour themes. The garden is described by visitors as a haven of tranquillity. Largely level access to all areas of garden. Some gravel paths.

14 CHISENBURY PRIORY

East Chisenbury, SN9 6AQ. Mr & Mrs John Manser, 07810 483984, peterjohnmanser@gmail.com. *3m SW of Pewsey. Turn E from A345 at Enford then N to E Chisenbury, main gates 1m on R.* **Sun 16 June (2-6). Adm £5, chd free. Home-made teas. Visits also by arrangement 2 May to 30 June.**
Medieval Priory with Queen Anne face and early C17 rear (not open) in middle of 5 acre garden on chalk. Mature garden with fine trees within clump and flint walls, herbaceous borders, shrubs, roses. Moisture loving plants along mill leat, carp pond, orchard and wild garden, many unusual plants.

15 CHOLDERTON ESTATE

Kingsettle Stud, Cholderton Park, Cholderton, SP4 0DX. Henry & Felicity Edmunds, www.kingsettlestud.co.uk. *Signed from the Cholderton Farm Shop on the A338 (Tidworth to Salisbury rd) near A303 junction.* **Sun 16 June (2-5). Adm £5, chd free. Home-made teas in the courtyard at Kingsettle Stud, the Estate's Grade II listed stable block.**
A striking Victorian walled garden featuring a peony walk dating over 100 yrs old and a working kitchen garden. In the arboretum there is a wildlife garden with a maze and numerous tree species. There are no stairs, but ground is uneven.

16 NEW CONOCK MANOR

Conock, Devizes, SN10 3QQ. Justin Kennedy. *5m SE of Devizes. Conock lies just off the A342 between the turnings for Urchfont & Chirton. Conock Manor is on the*

R side of the lane. What 3 Words app - flap.emeralds.cashiers. **Sat 8 June (11-4). Adm £8, chd free. Teas, coffee, cold drinks, cakes & pastries.**
A relaxed family garden embracing C18 architecture (inc a rustic dairy) and defined by its long, south facing wall. There are lawns and wildflower meadows, mixed borders and climbers, a magnolia grove and a vegetable garden with greenhouse. Evolving under the stewardship of Pip Morrison, the garden utilises a ha-ha to sit comfortably in the surrounding wooded parkland with views out to the surrounding hills and the Alton Barnes chalk-horse. Soft lawn, some gravel paths.

17 ◆ CORSHAM COURT
Corsham, SN13 0BZ. Lord Methuen, 01249 701610, staterooms@corsham-court.co.uk, www.corsham-court.co.uk. *4m W of Chippenham. Signed off A4 at Corsham.* **For NGS: Sun 24 Mar, Sun 7 Apr (2-5.30). Adm £5, chd £2.50. For other opening times and information, please phone, email or visit garden website.**
Park and gardens laid out by Capability Brown and Repton. Large lawns with fine specimens of ornamental trees surround the Elizabethan mansion. C18 bath house hidden in the grounds. Spring bulbs, beautiful lily pond with Indian bean trees, young arboretum and stunning collection of magnolias. Wheelchair (not motorised) access to house, gravel paths in garden.

18 CORSLEY HOUSE
Corsley, Warminster, BA12 7QH. Glen Senk & Keith Johnson. *From Longleat on the A362 towards Frome turning 1st R on Deep Lane. Corsley House is ¼m on R. The parkland entrance, where there is parking, is on R beyond the house.* **Sun 8 Sept (11-5). Adm £10, chd free. Cream teas.**
A garden full of surprises to reflect the eclectic nature of a Georgian home with a secret Jacobean facade. A unique sculpted wave lawn and a truly exceptional walled garden. Many well preserved ancient outbuildings such as a potting and apple storage shed and a granary built on staddle stones. All gloriously overlooking the NT's Cley Hill.

19 COTTAGE IN THE TREES
Tidworth Rd, Boscombe Village, nr Salisbury, SP4 0AD. Karen Robertson. *7m N of Salisbury. Turn L off A338 just before Social Club. Continue past church, turn R after bridge to Queen Manor, cottage 150yds on R.* **Sun 12 May, Sun 16 June (1.30-5). Adm £4, chd free. Home-made teas.**
Enchanting ½ acre cottage garden, immaculately planted with water feature, raised vegetable beds, small wildlife pond and gravel garden. Spring bulbs, hellebores and pulmonarias give a welcome start to the season, with pots and baskets, roses and clematis. Mixed borders of herbaceous plants, collection of geraniums, dahlias, grasses and shrubs giving year-round interest. Large variety of cottage plants for sale, grown from the garden.

Iford Manor Gardens

© Heather Edwards

GROUP OPENING

20 DAUNTSEY GARDENS

Church Lane, Dauntsey, Malmesbury, SN15 4HT. Mr & Mrs Christopher Jerram. *5m SE of Malmesbury. Approach via Dauntsey Rd from Gt Somerford, 1¼ m from Volunteer Inn Great Somerford.* **Sun 16 June (1-5). Combined adm £10, chd free. Home-made teas at Idover House.**

THE COACH HOUSE
Col & Mrs J Seddon-Brown.

DAUNTSEY PARK
Mr & Mrs Giovanni Amati,
01249 721777, enquiries@
dauntseyparkhouse.co.uk.
🛏

THE GARDEN COTTAGE
Miss Ann Sturgis.

IDOVER HOUSE
Mr & Mrs Christopher Jerram.

THE OLD COACH HOUSE
Tony & Janette Yates.

THE OLD POND HOUSE
Mr & Mrs Stephen Love.

THE OLD RECTORY
Mr Christopher &
Mrs Claire Mellor-Hill,
www.theoldrectorydauntsey.com.

This group of 7 gardens, centred around the historic Dauntsey Park Estate, ranges from the Classical C18 country house setting of Dauntsey Park, with spacious lawns, old trees and views over the River Avon, to mature country house gardens and traditional walled gardens. Enjoy the formal rose garden in pink and white, old fashioned borders and duck ponds at Idover House, and the quiet seclusion of The Coach House with its thyme terrace and gazebos, climbing roses and clematis. Here, mop-headed pruned *Crataegus prunifolia* line the drive. The Garden Cottage has a traditional walled kitchen garden with organic vegetables, orchard, woodland walk and yew topiary. Meanwhile the 2 acres at The Old Pond House are both clipped and unclipped! Large pond with lilies and fat carp, and look out for the giraffe and turtle. The Old Coach House is a small garden with perennial plants, shrubs and climbers. The Old Rectory is a 2 acre garden adjoining the River Avon with mature trees, roses and shrubs.

&. ✿ ☕ ✿

21 DUCK POND BARN

Church Lane, Wingfield, Trowbridge, BA14 9LW. Janet & Marc Berlin. *9m SW of Bath. On B3109 from Frome to Bradford on Avon, turn opp Poplars pub into Church Ln. Duck Pond Barn is at end of lane. Big field for parking.* **Sun 30 June (10-5). Adm £5, chd free.** Garden of 1.6 acres with large duck pond, lawns, ericaceous beds, dry bed, orchard, vegetable garden, big greenhouse, wood and wild areas of grass and trees with many wildflowers. Large dry stone wall topped with flowerbeds with rose arbour. 3 ponds linked by a rill in flower garden and large pergola in orchard. Set in farmland and mainly flat. Many interesting and rare succulents.

&. ✿ ☕

22 FALKNERS COTTAGE

North Newnton, Pewsey, SN9 6LA. Anne & John Thompson-Ashby. *3m W Pewsey. SW from Pewsey on A345 direction Salisbury, exit 3 at Woodbridge r'about to Hilcott. Pass farm, next house on sharp L hand bend. Care turning R.* **Sat 31 Aug (1.30-5.30). Adm £6.50, chd free. Cream teas.**
This 5 acre site inc a formal garden with colourful borders, topiary and box framed parterre and courtyard 'rooms' with contemporary sculpture. Behind the thatched barn lies a kitchen garden with hens. There is a meadow with ornamental trees, a small lake with a summerhouse on an island, a woodland, a wildlife pond and a bog garden. A short walk from the meadow is the C13 St James' Church.

☕ ✿

23 FONTHILL HOUSE

Tisbury, SP3 5SA. The Lord Margadale of Islay, www.fonthill.co.uk/gardens. *13m W of Salisbury. Via B3089 in Fonthill Bishop. 3m N of Tisbury.* **Sun 24 Mar (12-5). Adm £8, chd free. Sandwiches, quiches & cakes, soft drinks, tea, coffee and wine.**
Wonderful woodland walks with daffodils, rhododendrons, azaleas, shrubs, bulbs. Magnificent views, formal gardens. The gardens have been extensively redeveloped under the direction of Tania Compton and Marie-Louise Agius. The formal gardens are being continuously improved with new designs, exciting trees, shrubs and plants. Gorgeous

William Pye fountain and other sculptures. Regional Finalist, The English Garden Magazine's The Nation's Favourite Gardens 2023. Partial wheelchair access.

&. 🐴 ☕ ✿

24 FOVANT HOUSE

Church Lane, Fovant, Salisbury, SP3 5LA. Amanda & Noel Flint. *Approx 10m W of Salisbury. 6½ m W of Wilton & 9.3m E of Shaftesbury. Take A30 to Fovant then head N through village and follow signs to St Georges Church.* **Sat 1 June (2-5). Adm £7, chd free. Home-made teas.**
Fovant House is a former Rectory set in about 3 acres of formal garden (house not open). In 2016 the garden was redesigned by Arabella Lennox Boyd. Garden inc 60m herbaceous border, terraces and parterre. A range of mature trees inc cedars, copper beech and lime. Majority of garden has easy wheelchair access subject to ground conditions being dry.

&. 🐴 ✿ 🅓 ☕ ✿

25 FOXLEY MANOR

Foxley, Malmesbury, SN16 0JJ. Richard & Louisa Turnor. *2m W of Malmesbury. 10 mins from J17 on M4. Turn towards Malmesbury/ Cirencester, then towards Norton & follow signs for the Vine Tree, yellow signs from here.* **Sat 15 June (11-4). Adm £7, chd free. Home-made teas.**
Yew hedges divide lawns, borders, rose garden, lily pond and a newer wild area with a natural swimming pond shaded by a liriodendron. Views through large Turkey oaks to farmland beyond. Small courtyard gravel garden. Sculptures are sited throughout the gardens.

🐴 ✿ ☕ ✿

26 GASPER COTTAGE

Gasper Street, Gasper Stourton, Warminster, BA12 6PY. Bella Hoare & Johnnie Gallop, 07812 555 883, bella.hoare@icloud.com, www.youtube.com/channel/ UCgar2Akygp4j3dWNGMI6i0A. *Nr Stourhead Gardens, 4m from Mere. Turn off A303 at B3092 Mere. Follow Stourhead signs. Go through Stourton. After 1m, turn R after phone box, signed Gasper. Parking before house on R, in field. House 2nd on R going up hill.* **Sun 8 Sept (11-5). Adm £6, chd free. Visits also by arrangement 1 May to 15**

Sept for groups of 10 to 30. $1\frac{1}{2}$ acre garden, with stunning rural views. Luxurious planting of late summer blooms including new perennial planting combinations. Orchard with wildlife pond and model railway. Artist's studio surrounded by colour balanced planting and formal pond. Several seating areas. Ornamental grasses, forest garden.
))

27 GOLD HILL
Hindon Lane, Tisbury, Salisbury, SP3 6PZ. Anne Ralphs. *12m W of Salisbury. On Hindon Lane, 500 yds up on R from top of Tisbury High St. From Hindon, on L 500yds after road narrows. Parking down the lane in field beside the garden.* **Sun 16 June (2-5). Adm £6, chd free. Home-made teas in the garden.**
Overlooking the Fonthill Brook the house and garden, which were designed together and are Arts & Crafts inspired, were created on a 1.2 acre derelict builder's yard and field between 2015 and 2017. Formal garden with mixed shrub and perennial planting give interest throughout the year. Sunk garden, rose garden, fruit trees, white walled garden with pond, fountain and parterre beds.
🐕 D ☕))

GROUP OPENING

28 HANNINGTON VILLAGE GARDENS
Hannington, Swindon, SN6 7RP. *Off B4019 Blunsdon to Highworth Rd by the Freke Arms. Park as directed by signs, in the street where possible, or opp Lushill House.* **Sun 16 June (11-5). Combined adm £8, chd free. Home-made teas in Hannington Village Hall.**

CHESTNUT HOUSE
Mary & Garry Marshall.

CHESTNUT VILLA
David Cornish.

GLEBE HOUSE
Charlie & Tory Barne.

NEW HILL TOP BARNS
Mr Alex & Mrs Gill Drummond.

LOWER FARM
Mr Piers & Mrs Jenny Martin.

LUSHILL HOUSE
John & Sasha Kennedy.

QUARRY BANK
Paul Minter & Michael Weldon.

ROSE COTTAGE
Mrs Ruth Scholes.

YORKE HOUSE GARDEN
Mr Miles & Mrs Cath Bozeat.

Hannington has a dramatic hilltop position on a Cotswold ridge overlooking the Thames Valley. A great variety of gardens, from large manor houses to small cottage gardens, many of which follow the brow of the hill and afford stunning views of the surrounding farmland. You will need lots of time to see all that is on offer in this beautiful historic village.
🐕 ✿ ☕))

29 HAZELBURY MANOR GARDENS
Wadswick, Box, Corsham, SN13 8HX. Mr L Lacroix. *5m SW of Chippenham, 5m NE of Bath. From A4 at Box, A365 to Melksham, at Five Ways junction L onto B3109 towards Corsham; 1st L in $\frac{1}{4}$m, drive immed on R.* **Sun 9 June (11-5); Wed 11 Sept (10-4); Sun 15 Sept (11-5). Adm £7.50, chd free. Home-made teas.**
The C15 Manor house comes into view as you descend along the drive and into the Grade II landscaped Edwardian gardens. The extensive plantings that surround the house are undergoing considerable redevelopment by the owners and their head gardener. A wide range of organic horticulture is practiced in 8 acres of relaxed gardens.
🐕 ✿ 🚗 ☕ 🏓))

30 HORATIO'S GARDEN
Duke of Cornwall Spinal Treatment Centre, Salisbury Hospital NHS Foundation Trust, Odstock Road, Salisbury, SP2 8BJ. Horatio's Garden Charity, www.horatiosgarden.org.uk. *1m from centre of Salisbury. Follow signs for Salisbury District Hospital. Please park in car park 10, which will be free to NGS visitors on the day.* **Sat 8 June (2-5). Adm £5, chd free. Tea & delicious cakes, made by Horatio's Garden volunteers, will be served in the Garden Room.**
Award winning hospital garden, opened in Sept 2012 and designed by Cleve West for patients with spinal cord injury at the Duke of Cornwall Spinal Treatment Centre. Built from donations given in memory of Horatio Chapple who was a volunteer at the centre in his school holidays. Low limestone walls, which represent the form of the spine, divide densely planted herbaceous beds. Everything in the garden designed to benefit patients during their long stays in hospital. Garden is run by a Head Gardener and team of volunteers. Designer Cleve West has 9 RHS gold medals.
♿ ✿ 🚗 D ☕))

31 HYDE'S HOUSE
Dinton, SP3 5HH. Mr George Cruddas. *9m W of Salisbury. Off B3089 nr Dinton Church on St Mary's Rd.* **Sun 26 May (2-5). Adm £8, chd free. Home-made teas at Thatched Old School Room with outside tea tables.**
3 acres of wild and formal garden in beautiful situation with series of hedged garden rooms. Numerous shrubs, flowers and borders, all allowing tolerated wildflowers and preferred weeds, while others creep in. Large walled kitchen garden, herb garden and C13 dovecote (open). Charming C16/18 Grade I listed house (not open), with lovely courtyard. Every year varies. Free walks around park and lake. Steps, slopes, gravel paths and driveway.
♿ 🐕 ☕))

32 ◆ IFORD MANOR GARDENS
Bradford-on-Avon, BA15 2BA. Mr Cartwright-Hignett, 01225 863146, info@ifordmanor.co.uk, www.ifordmanor.co.uk. *7m S of Bath. Off A36, brown tourist sign to Iford 1m. From Bradford-on-Avon or Trowbridge via Lower Westwood Village (brown signs). Please note all approaches via narrow, single track lanes with passing places.* **For NGS: Sat 20 Apr (11-4). Adm £9.50. Pre-booking essential, please phone 01225 863146, email info@ifordmanor.co.uk or visit www.ifordmanor.co.uk for information & booking. Enjoy refreshments in Iford's award winning restaurant or in the adjacent café. Children under 10 will not be admitted to the garden. For other opening times and information, please phone, email or visit garden website.**
Harold Peto's former home, this $2\frac{1}{2}$ acre terraced garden provides timeless inspiration. Influenced by his travels, particularly to Italy and Japan, Peto embellished the garden with a collection of classical statuary and architectural fragments. Steep steps link the terraces with pools, fountains, loggias, colonnades, urns and figures, with magnificent rural views across the Iford Valley.
🐕 ✿ 🏠 ☕

33 KETTLE FARM COTTAGE

Kettle Lane, West Ashton, Trowbridge, BA14 6AW. Tim & Jenny Woodall, 01225 753474, trwwoodall@outlook.com. *Kettle Lane is halfway between West Ashton T-lights & Yarnbrook r'about on S side of A350. Garden ½ m down end of lane. Limited car parking.* **Visits by arrangement 17 June to 21 Sept for groups of up to 20. Adm inc home-made teas. Adm £10, chd free.**
Previously of Priory House, Bradford on Avon, which featured on Gardeners' World, September 2017, we have now created a new cottage garden, full of colour and style, flowering from June to Sept. Bring a loved one/friend to see the garden. One or two steps.
⟨symbols⟩

34 KNOYLE PLACE

Holloway, East Knoyle, Salisbury, SP3 6AF. Lizzie de la Moriniere. *Turn off A350 into E Knoyle & follow signs to parking at Lower Lye. Walk 5 mins to Knoyle Place through village following signs.* **Sat 25 May (2-5). Adm £10, chd free. Home-made teas. Open nearby Lower Lye.**
Very beautiful and elegant garden created over 60 years by previous and current owners. Above the house there are several acres of mature rhododendron and magnolia woodland planting. Among the many different areas in this 9 acre garden is a box parterre, rose garden, vegetable garden and, around the house, a recently planted formal garden designed by Dan Combes. Sloping lawns and woodland paths, stone terrace.
⟨symbols⟩

35 LOWER LYE

Holloway, East Knoyle, Salisbury, SP3 6AQ. Belinda & Andrew Scott. *From A350 exit at East Knoyle. Lower Lye is at upper southern end of village, follow signs to house. Parking on L entrance field.* **Sat 25 May (2-5). Adm £10, chd free. Pre-booking essential, please visit www.ngs.org.uk for information & booking. Open nearby Knoyle Place.**
The gardens at Lower Lye are exceptional and were completely reconfigured by the landscape architect Michael Balston 24 yrs ago. An extremely large garden, approx 9 acres placed on the brow of the hill with wonderful views across the valley and the magnificent King Alfred's Tower in the distance. More recently the gardens have been worked on by garden designers Tania Compton and Jane Hurst, who have given improved structure through replanting of the various borders. The gardens have been developed in a simplistic and modern style, which gives a sense of elegance whilst respecting the natural habitat There are numerous modern sculptures and water features placed throughout the garden which are spectacular and provide a number of individual focal points. The gardens inc herbaceous borders, mature trees, a meadow area and a vegetable and cutting garden. Coffee/tea and light refreshments will be served at the beautiful gardens just along the road at Knoyle Place, which will also be open throughout the afternoon.

36 MANOR FARM HOUSE

Manor Farm Lane, Patney, Devizes, SN10 3RB. Mark & Tricia Alsop. *Between Pewsey & Devizes. Take 3rd entrance on L going up Manor Farm Lane from village green. Parking available in paddock.* **Sun 12 May (2-5). Adm £6, chd free. Home-made teas.**
2 acre plantsman's garden originally designed by Michael Balston and updated by us over the past 12 yrs. Lawned areas with borders surrounded by hornbeams and yew hedging, long border and gravel garden by tennis court, formal vegetable garden with buxus parterres and meadow with spring bulbs, box mound and walkway through moisture loving plants. Limited wheelchair access. No WC.
⟨symbols⟩

37 MANOR HOUSE, STRATFORD TONY

Stratford Tony, Salisbury, SP5 4AT. Mr & Mrs Hugh Cookson, 01722 718496, lc@stratfordtony.co.uk, www.stratfordtony.co.uk. *4m SW of Salisbury. Take minor road W off A354 at Coombe Bissett. Garden on S after 1m. Or take minor road off A3094 from Wilton signed Stratford Tony & racecourse.* **Visits by arrangement 1 Feb to 15 Sept. Adm £10, chd free.**
Varied 4 acre garden with year-round interest. Formal and informal areas. Herbaceous borders, vegetable garden, parterre garden, orchard, shrubberies, roses, specimen trees, lakeside planting, winter colour and structure, many original contemporary features and places to sit and enjoy the downland views. Some gravel and uneven paving.
⟨symbols⟩

Manor Farm House

38 NORTH COTTAGE

Tisbury Row, Tisbury, SP3 6RZ. Jacqueline & Robert Baker, 01747 870019, baker_jaci@yahoo.co.uk. *12m W of Salisbury. From A30 turn N through Ansty, L at T-junction, towards Tisbury. From Tisbury take Ansty road. Car park entrance nr junction signed Tisbury Row.* **Sun 26 May, Sun 16 June (11-5). Adm £5, chd free. Home-made light lunches & teas.**

Walk through the vegetables onto mown paths past wild flowers via the pleached limes to the Cottage. Although modest there's great variety, each part of the garden differs in style and feel but remains cohesive. Difficult to describe so do come and see for yourself. Augmented by pottery and woodwork handmade by us. From the intimacy of the garden explore the orchard, coppice, ponds and smallholding. There are also exciting metalwork sculptures, decorations and plant supports by Metal Menagerie. Please see NGS website for extra pop-up open days.

39 OARE HOUSE

Rudge Lane, Oare, nr Pewsey, SN8 4JQ. Sir Henry Keswick. *2m N of Pewsey. On Marlborough Rd (A345).* **Sun 28 Apr, Sun 30 June (2-6). Adm £8, chd free. Home-made teas in the potting shed. Donation to The Order of St John.**

1740s mansion house later extended by Clough Williams Ellis in 1920s (not open). The original formal gardens around the house have been developed over the years to create a wonderful garden full of many unusual plants. Current owner is very passionate and has developed a fine collection of rarities. Garden is undergoing a renaissance but still maintains split compartments each with its own individual charm; traditional walled garden with fine herbaceous borders, vegetable areas, trained fruit, roses and grand mixed borders surrounding formal lawns. The magnolia garden is wonderful in spring with some trees dating from 1920s, together with strong bulb plantings. Large arboretum and woodland with many unusual and champion trees. In spring and summer there is always something of interest, with the glorious Pewsey Vale as a backdrop. Partial wheelchair access.

40 THE OLD VICARAGE

Church Lane, Ashbury, Swindon, SN6 8LZ. Mr David Astor. *In the village of Ashbury, next to the church.* **Sat 8 June (11-4). Adm £5, chd free. Home-made teas.**

Within The Vale of the White Horse, Ashbury is a picturesque village with thatched cottages and a friendly atmosphere. Nestled between the village pub and St Mary's Church is the garden of The Old Vicarage. The garden surrounds the house and is made up of a floriferous walled garden, a wildflower meadow, an extensive kitchen garden, filled with flowers, as well as vegetables, plus more.

41 NEW THE OLD VICARAGE

Lower Westwood, Bradford-on-Avon, BA15 2AF. Mrs Elizabeth Triggs. *SW side of Bradford-On-Avon. Enter Lower Westwood, take the turning opp the New Inn, it is the 2nd house after the church. Parking available outside the church.* **Sun 23 June (2-6). Adm £5, chd free. Home-made teas in the Parish Rooms next door between 2-5pm.**

Large garden (⅔ acre) with lovely views to open countryside. A work in progress - a recently landscaped formal Italianate area with Mediterranean planting, fruit and vegetable garden, small orchard and wild meadow, and a large family area set amongst prairie planting. Flat, some areas of gravel.

42 THE PARISH HOUSE

West Knoyle, Mere, BA12 6AJ. Alex Davies. *From E on A303 take signpost to West Knoyle at petrol station. Continue down hill and past church, take 1st R signed Charnage, continue 1m to end of lane. Parking in field on L.* **Sun 14 July (2-5). Adm £5, chd free. Home-made teas.**

The garden at The Parish House is small and south facing surrounded by hedges protecting it from the exposure of a high wide open landscape beyond. The garden is laid out with gravel to encourage a self-seeding natural look but there are also roses and herbaceous perennials as well. The look is held together with topiary. Beyond this garden there is a larger area of lawn, trees and developing bulb cover (Camassia). Large conservatory greenhouse containing mature Muscat grapevine and pelargoniums. Small vegetable garden. Level but gravel surfaces, some lawn.

43 NEW RIVER BARN

Cowbridge Farm, Swindon Road, Malmesbury, SN16 9LZ. Finn & Nicki Spicer, www.riverbarn.org.uk. *1m SE of Malmesbury. From Malmesbury r'about, take Wootton Bassett road (B4042) for approx ½ m. L immed after Sir Bernard Lovell turning.* **Sun 16 June, Wed 3 July (10-6). Adm £7, chd £3. Home-made teas.**

3 acre garden in a sublime river setting as part of former model farm. Planting commenced 2007 to create an arboretum with specimen trees, wildflower meadows and large wildlife pond. Colourful walled courtyard garden with pond, rose pergola, mosaics and rich planting. Formal terraced lawn, pinetum with prairie style planting, stone circle, fruit and vegetable garden, leading to the River Avon. Dragonflies breeding in wildlife pond. Wildflower areas teeming with butterflies, moths, honey bees, solitary bees and bumblebees. River has swans, ducks, moorhens, dabchicks and kingfishers. Courtyard garden and first third of the main garden is easily accessed by wheelchair.

44 RIVERSIDE HOUSE

Axford, Marlborough, SN8 2HA. Hamish & Susie Watson. *4 m E of Marlborough. Parking for the garden is in the Jubilee Field which is adjacent to Stone Lane. It is then a short walk through a wildflower meadow before arriving at the garden.* **Wed 29 May (11-5). Adm £5, chd free. Light refreshments in the village hall opp house.**

Beautiful wisteria-clad village house (originally a farmhouse) dating back to C16, with William and Mary additions in late C17. Cottage style garden of over 1 acre, with many wild areas, mature trees and herbaceous borders. A charming rose garden and lawns sweeping down to a stream and small pond, with fine views to the south over water meadows to hills beyond.

45 NEW **RODMEAD FARM**
Rodmead, Maiden Bradley, Warminster, BA12 7HP. Angus & Sarah Neish. *8m SW of Warminster. Leave Maiden Bradley (with the church on your L) on the B3092. Drive 300m out of the village, and take the L fork to Rodmead Farm.* **Sun 23 June (2-5.30). Adm £6, chd free.**
Set in the middle of a working farm, the garden has glorious views of surrounding downland. The extensive gardens have been created over the last 25 yrs and have many different areas to explore, from a spectacular new rill, a formal parterre, old farm pond to the wildflower meadow surrounded by traditional farm buildings, all covered by a huge variety of climbing roses.

46 NEW **ROOKERY COTTAGE**
Coombe Lane, Atworth, Melksham, SN12 8NU. Lorraine MacFarlane. *3m from Bradford on Avon, Corsham or Melksham. Follow signs for Stonar School, pls drive slowly through the school grounds & follow yellow signs for car parking at The Botanic Nursery, or overflow car park.* **Thur 6, Fri 7, Sat 8 June (11-4). Combined adm with The Botanic Nursery £10, chd free. Tea, coffee & posh biscuits at The Botanic Nursery.**
Delightful garden evolved by the owners over the past 40 yrs. Meander via the mown paths through beautiful trees and shrubs with unique features, many of which enable the abundance of wildlife. Different areas with gravel, where plants self seed and wild flowers thrive. The planting and artistic use of unusual containers will give you lots of inspiration. Not fully accessible because of uneven paths and different levels.

47 **SCOTS FARM**
Pinkney, Malmesbury, SN16 0NZ. Mr & Mrs Martin Barrow, 07947 792919, ljikob@gmail.com, www.Lawrencebarrow.com. *5m W of Malmesbury on B4040 towards Sherston. Take L at Pinkney Xrds, follow road over a bridge and up a hill.* **Visits by arrangement in July for groups of up to 25. Adm £7, chd free. We offer tea & cake for group visits.**
Across 7 acres a colourful perennial border, a white garden, a Japanese Zen garden, a Mediterranean garden

and follow a path through a wildflower meadow to a pottery studio and koi pond in this haven of tranquillity. Garden ware, pottery and sculptures on display. Most areas are wheelchair accessible although the meadow and Zen garden are via fields with paths mown through.

48 **SEEND HOUSE**
High Street, Seend, Melksham, SN12 6NR. Maud Peters, www.instagram.com/maud_seendgarden/. *In Seend village. Nr church & opp PO. Parking on village green.* **Sun 14 Apr (1-5). Combined adm with Brow Cottage £8, chd free. Sat 15 June (1-5). Combined adm with Seend Manor £10, chd free. Home-made teas at Brow Cottage on 14th April and Seend House on 15th June.**
Seend House is a Georgian house with 6 acres of gardens and paddocks. Framed with yew and box. Highlights inc cloud and rose garden, stream lavender, view of knot garden from above, fountain with grass border, walled garden as well as formal borders. Amazing view across the valley to Salisbury Plain. There is a shuttle bus running between Seend House and Brow Cottage for the April opening.

49 **SEEND MANOR**
High Street, Seend, Melksham, SN12 6NX. Stephen & Amanda Clark, SeendManorGarden.com. *In centre of village, opp village green with car parking for garden visitors.* **Sat 15 June (1-5). Combined adm with Seend House £10, chd free. Home-made teas.**
Created over 20 yrs, a stunning walled garden with 4 quadrants evoking important parts of the owners' lives - England, China, Africa and Italy, with extensive trelliage, hornbeam hedges on stilts, cottage orne, temple, Chinese ting, grotto, fern walk, fountains, parterres, stone loggia and more. Kitchen garden. Folly ruin in woods. Courtyard garden. Extensive walled gardens, water features, garden structures, topiary and hedging and one of the best views in Wiltshire. Many gravel paths, so only wheelchairs with thick tyres.

50 **1 SOUTHVIEW**
Wick Lane, Devizes, SN10 5DR. Teresa Garraud, 01380 722936, tl.garraud@hotmail.co.uk. *From Devizes Market Place go S (Long St). At r'about go straight over, at mini r'about turn L into Wick Ln. Continue to end of Wick Ln. Park in road or roads nearby.* **Sun 19 May (1.30-5), open nearby Trymnells. Sun 15 Sept (2-5). Adm £5, chd free. Visits also by arrangement 13 May to 27 Sept for groups of up to 20. Coffee, tea & biscuits available for small groups.**
An atmospheric and very long town garden, full of wonderful planting surprises at every turn. Densely planted with both pots near the house and large borders further up, it houses a collection of beautiful and often unusual plants, shrubs and trees many with striking foliage. Colour from seasonal flowers is interwoven with this textural tapestry. 'Truly inspirational' is often heard from visitors.

51 **TEASEL**
Wilsford, Amesbury, Salisbury, SP4 7BL. Ray Palmer. *2m SW of Amesbury in the Woodford Valley on western banks of R Avon which runs through the gardens.* **Sun 7 July (11-5). Adm £7, chd free. Tea.**
Extensively developed since 2020, Teasel's 11 acres include long herbaceous borders, a lake and ½ m riverside walk. Recently added potager, shrub border, hoggin pathways through orchard to fruit store, Monet inspired bridge, duck house on small pond, water lilies, specimen trees, chess pavilion and croquet lawn. Enjoy teas on the upper terrace with magnificent views of the garden and river.

52 **TRANTOR HOUSE**
Hackthorne Road, Durrington, SP4 8AS. Mrs Jane Turner, 01980 655101, sjcturner@talktalk.net. *9 m N of Salisbury. Turn off A345 (signed Village Centre) onto Hackthorne Rd. Approx 200 yds on LHS, after old white thatched cottage.* **Sat 8, Sun 9 June (1-5). Adm £4, chd free. Tea, coffee, biscuits & cake. Visits also by arrangement 1 June to 15 June.**
Border Oak timber framed house on country lane surrounded by approx ⅔ acre of both formal and informal gardens. Attractive mixed and herbaceous colour themed borders, rose garden, wildlife pond and stream.

Summerhouse, raised vegetable beds and wildflower meadow. Chickens. Sloping garden with steps.

53 TRISTENAGH HOUSE

Devizes Road, Potterne, Devizes, SN10 5LW. Andrew & Ros Ford, ros.ford@ngs.org.uk. *1m S of Devizes on A360. Pls turn down Byway beside Tristenagh Cottage & post box for car park. Turning will be clearly marked with large yellow signs.* **Sat 25 May (1.30-5.30). Adm £8, chd free. Home-made cakes, inc gluten free options. Visits also by arrangement May & June for groups of 5+.**

Garden of approx 2 acres, created over the past 20 yrs. Island beds with a mixture of herbaceous plants, bulbs, annuals and shrubs. Year-round structure provided by beech and yew hedges, box topiary and by mature beech and Scots pine trees. Small vegetable garden. Some gravelled areas with containers. Good views of valley from terrace. Wheelchair access to most parts of garden on grass paths. Access to terrace limited due to gravel. Some steps.

54 TRYMNELLS

1a Coxhill Lane, Potterne, Devizes, SN10 5PH. Linda Smith. *Coxhill Ln is opp George & Dragon pub. Trymnells is 2nd property on L & is at the top of a gravel drive. Parking at Potterne Village Hall, Some space on drive for those with limited mobility.* **Sun 19 May (12-5). Adm £5, chd free. Home-made teas. Open nearby 1 Southview.**

Trymnells is a relatively new garden which was started approx 6 yrs ago. It is now maturing and has many trees, shrubs, hedges and perennials. The garden is steep and slopes up from the property and reaches a steep bank at the very top. Sleepers, fences, walls and plants have imposed a sense of structure with bulbs and perennials providing wonderful colour.

55 ◆ TWIGS COMMUNITY GARDEN

Manor Garden Centre, Cheney Manor, Swindon, SN2 2QJ. TWIGS, 01793 523294, twigs.reception@gmail.com, www. twigscommunitygardens.org.uk. *From Gt Western Way, under Bruce St Bridges onto Rodbourne Rd. 1st L at r'about, Cheney Manor Industrial Est. Through estate, 2nd exit at r'about. Opp Pitch & Putt. Signs on R to Manor Garden Centre.* **For NGS: Sun 19 May, Sun 21 July (12-4). Adm £3.50, chd free. Home-made teas. For other opening times and information, please phone, email or visit garden website.**

Delightful 2 acre community garden, created and maintained by volunteers. Features inc 7 individual display gardens, ornamental pond, plant nursery, Iron Age round house, artwork, fitness trail, separate kitchen garden site, Swindon beekeepers and the haven, overflowing with wildflowers. Excellent hot and cold lunches available at Olive Tree café within Manor Garden Centre adj to Twigs (pre booking required) 01793 533152. Regional Finalist, The English Garden Magazine's The Nation's Favourite Gardens 2023. Most areas wheelchair accessible. Disabled WC at TWIGS.

Allington Grange

© Lynn Keddie

56 WELLAWAY

Close Lane, Marston, SN10 5SN.
Mrs P Lewis. *5m SW of Devizes.
From A360, Devizes to Salisbury,
R in Potterne just before George &
Dragon pub. Through Worton. L at
end of village signed to Marston,
Close Lane ½ m on L.* **Sat 27, Sun
28 Apr, Sat 14, Sun 15 Sept (1-5).
Adm £6, chd free. Home-made
teas.**

Two acre flower arranger's garden
comprising herbaceous borders,
orchard, vegetable garden,
ornamental and wildlife ponds,
lawns and naturalised areas. Planted
since 1979 for year-round interest.
Shrubberies and rose garden, other
areas underplanted with bulbs or
ground cover. Springtime particularly
colourful with daffodils, tulips and
hellebores. Extensive autumn colour.

57 WEST LAVINGTON MANOR

1 Church Street, West Lavington,
SN10 4LA. Andrew Doman &
Jordina Evins, 07768 773856,
andrewdoman01@gmail.com,
www.instagram.com/
westlavingtonmanor/. *6m S of
Devizes, on A360. House opp White
St, where parking is available. See
more details on Instagram.* **Sat 8
June (11-6). Adm £10, chd free.
We offer an extended lunch
& tea menu inc wines, beer &
other beverages. Seating nr to
refreshment marquee. Visits also
by arrangement. We welcome
groups and students at any time
of the year. Donation to West
Lavington Youth Club and Nestling
Trust.**

A C15 manor house with spectacular
5 acre walled garden, established by
Sir John Danvers, who brought the
Italianate garden to the UK. Delightful
aspects including Laburnum walk,
replanted herbaceous border, an
authentic Japanese garden, new
Mulberry rotunda, orchard with 25
different apple and pear species, an
arboretum with outstanding specimen
trees and lake with duck house.
Partial wheelchair access.

58 WESTCROFT

Boscombe Village, nr
Salisbury, SP4 0AB. Lyn
Miles, 01980 610101 or 07787
852756, lynmiles@icloud.com,
www.westcroftgarden.co.uk.
*7m N/E Salisbury. On A338 from
Salisbury, just past Boscombe &*
District Social Club. Park there or in
field opp house, or where signed on
day. Disabled parking only on drive.
**Every Thur 4 Jan to 7 Mar (11-4).
Sun 28 Jan, Sat 3, Sun 4, Fri 9,
Sun 18, Sat 24, Sun 25 Feb (11-4).
Adm £4, chd free. Home-made
soups & teas, inside or outside.
Visits also by arrangement Jan to
Mar for groups of 15+.**

Whilst overflowing with roses in
June, in Jan and Feb the bones of
this ⅔ acre galanthophile's garden
on chalk are on show. Brick and flint
walls, terraces, rustic arches, gates
and pond add character. Drifts of
snowdrops carpet the floor whilst
throughout is a growing collection of
well over 400 named varieties. Many
hellebores, pulmonarias, grasses and
seedheads add interest. Snowdrops
(weather dependent) and snowdrop
sundries for sale inc greetings cards,
mugs, bags, serviettes, also chutneys
and free range eggs.

59 WESTWIND

Manton Drove, Manton,
Marlborough, SN8 4HL. MG
Campbell-Sharp, 07738 180759,
westwindmanton@gmail.com.
*1m W of Marlborough off A4. In
Manton, bear R past Oddfellows
Arms, then after 180 metres go L
into Manton Drove. House is up the
hill on the R.* **Visits by arrangement
20 Apr to 26 Aug for groups of
up to 15. Adm £7, chd free. Light
refreshments.**

Working in harmony with nature,
inspired by William Robinson,
Westwind is an informal country
garden set in 4 acres inc a 2½
acre meadow and woodland. It is
home to a rich assortment of wildlife
and has an abundance of mature
trees, cottage garden, beds full of
herbaceous plants and the Armillary
Garden which is home to 10 raised
beds stuffed with colour from April to
October.

60 WHATLEY MANOR

Easton Grey, Malmesbury,
SN16 0RB. Christian & Alix
Landolt, 01666 822888,
reservations@whatleymanor.
com, www.whatleymanor.com.
*4m W of Malmesbury. From A429
at Malmesbury take B4040 signed
Sherston. Manor 2m on L.* **Wed 5
June (2-6). Adm £8.50, chd free.
Light refreshments in The Loggia
Garden.**

12 acres of English country gardens
with 26 distinct areas each with
a strong theme based on colour,
scent or style. Original 1920s Arts &
Crafts plan inspired the design and
combines classic style with more
contemporary touches, inc specially
commissioned sculpture. Dogs must
be on a lead at all times. Hotel also
open for lunch and full afternoon tea.

61 WINKELBURY HOUSE

Berwick St John, Shaftesbury,
SP7 0EY. Ian & Carrie Stewart. *5m
E of Shaftesbury. From A30 follow
sign to Berwick St John, after 1½ m
turn L into Woodlands Lane.* **Sat 18
May (2-5). Adm £7.50, chd free.
Home-made teas.**

1½ acres with glorious views
of surrounding countryside. The
garden has evolved over last 6 yrs
to inc kitchen garden with bothy and
greenhouse, mown paths through
informal areas, meadow planted with
spring bulbs, 30m iris border, ha-ha,
wildlife pond and bee friendly planting.

62 WUDSTON HOUSE

High Street, Wedhampton,
Devizes, SN10 3QE. David
Morrison, 01380 840965,
djm@piml.co.uk. *Wedhampton lies
on N side of A342 approx 4m SE of
Devizes. House is set back on East
side of village street at end of drive
lined with a beech hedge.* **Visits by
arrangement 1 June to 15 Sept
for groups of up to 50. No min
numbers, max 50. £10 per visitor
or £15 with light refreshments.**

The garden was started in 2010,
following completion of the house.
It consists of formal gardens round
the house, perennial meadow,
pinetum and arboretum. Nick Macer
and James Hitchmough, who have
pioneered the concept of perennial
meadows, have been extensively
involved in aspects of the garden,
which is still developing.

*Our donation to Marie
Curie this year equates
to 17,496 hours of
nursing care*

Carmarthenshire & Pembrokeshire
Ceredigion
Glamorgan
Gwent
Gwynedd & Anglesey
North East Wales
Powys

WALES/ CYMRU

Above: Llanover, Gwent

WALES/CYMRU

Throughout much of Wales, it seems that every garden you visit has wonderful, panoramic views across stretches of unspoilt and sparsely populated countryside, with which the country is so blessed.

This is as true in the long central and eastern county of Powys as it is further south in Gwent and Glamorgan, in North East Wales or in the counties of Carmarthenshire, Pembrokeshire, Ceredigion, Gwynedd and Anglesey, where the remoteness and sense of space increases as you travel west or north-west. Whether in the valleys of the rivers Severn, Usk and Wye, the mountains of the Bannau Brycheiniog (Brecon Beacons) and Eryri (Snowdonia), or the beaches of the Gower Peninsular and Pembrokeshire, you will find some of the most picturesque landscapes in the United Kingdom. In south and west Wales gardens benefit from a similarly mild, maritime climate to the south-west of England, while in the more upland areas gardens embrace the steep terrain with ingenuity. This is another strongly rural region, particularly since most of the traditional heavy industries of South Wales are now quiet. Cathedrals abound in Wales, from Llandaff and Newport in the south to Bangor and St Asaph's in the north. The most memorable is St David's on Pembrokeshire's west coast, the jewel of Britain's smallest city, where both William the Conqueror and Henry II visited to pray.

Above, from top: Bryngwyn, Ceredigion; House On Stilts, Carmarthenshire & Pembrokeshire

Below: Plas Cadnant Hidden Gardens, Gwynedd

CARMARTHENSHIRE
& PEMBROKESHIRE

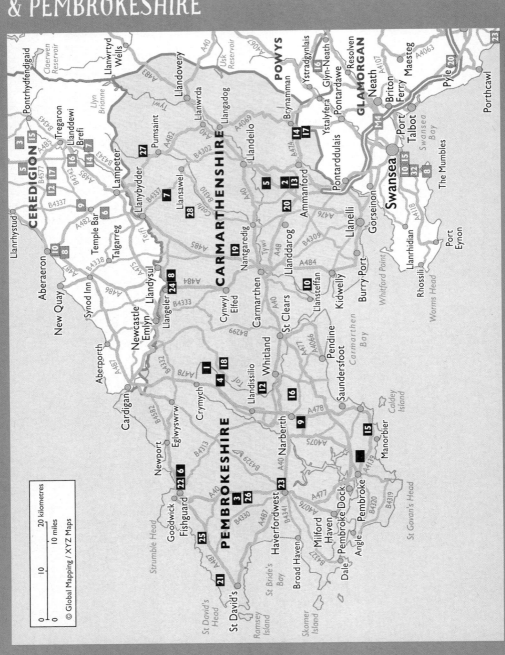

VOLUNTEERS

County Organisers
Jackie Batty
01437 741115
jackie.batty@ngs.org.uk

County Treasurer
Brian Holness
07713 635512
brian.holness@ngs.org.uk

Assistant County Organisers
Elena Gilliatt
01558 685321
elenamgilliatt@hotmail.com

Gayle Mounsey
07900 432993
gayle.mounsey@gmail.com

Mary-Ann Nossent
07985 077022
maryann.nossent@ngs.org.uk

Liz and Paul O'Neill
01994 240717
lizpaulfarm@yahoo.co.uk

Social Media
Mary-Ann Nossent
(as above)

Fran Rumbelow
07862 736341
fran.rumbelow@ngs.org.uk

 @CarmsandPembsNGS
 carmsandpembsngs

OPENING DATES

All entries subject to change.
For latest information check
www.ngs.org.uk
Map locator numbers are
shown to the right of each
garden name.

April

Sunday 7th
Treffgarne Hall | 26

May

Sunday 5th
Treffgarne Hall | 26

Tuesday 7th
Cefn Amlwg | 2
Moelfryn | 13

Sunday 12th
◆ Dyffryn Fernant | 6

Saturday 18th
NEW Cornerstone House | 4

Sunday 19th
Cold Comfort Farm | 3
NEW Cornerstone House | 4
NEW House On Stilts | 10
Norchard | 15

Wednesday 22nd
Cold Comfort Farm | 3

Sunday 26th
Pont Trecynny | 22

Friday 31st
Dwynant | 5

June

Saturday 1st
Dwynant | 5
Skanda Vale Hospice Garden | 24

Sunday 2nd
Dwynant | 5

Tuesday 4th
Cefn Amlwg | 2
Moelfryn | 13
◆ The Perennial | 21

Wednesday 5th
Pont Trecynny | 22

Saturday 8th
Neuadd y Felin | 14

Sunday 9th
Neuadd y Felin | 14

Sunday 16th
Cold Comfort Farm | 3

Saturday 22nd
Pen-y-Garn | 20
West Wales Willows | 28

Sunday 23rd
Cae Bach | 1
NEW Grove of Narberth | 9

Thursday 27th
Pont Trecynny | 22

July

Tuesday 2nd
Cefn Amlwg | 2
Moelfryn | 13

Sunday 7th
Pentresite | 19
Pen-y-Garn | 20
Treffgarne Hall | 26

Sunday 14th
Pont Trecynny | 22

Saturday 27th
Neuadd y Felin | 14

Sunday 28th
Neuadd y Felin | 14

August

Sunday 18th
Cae Bach | 1

Sunday 25th
Pont Trecynny | 22

September

Sunday 1st
◆ Dyffryn Fernant | 6

Sunday 8th
Pentresite | 19

Saturday 21st
◆ The Perennial | 21

Sunday 22nd
NEW Grove of Narberth | 9

By Arrangement

Arrange a personalised garden visit with your club, or group of friends, on a date to suit you. See individual garden entries for full details.

100 inpatients and their families are being supported at the newly opened Horatio's Garden Wales, thanks to the National Garden Scheme donations

Shoals Hook Farm

THE GARDENS

1 CAE BACH

Hermon, Glogue, nr Crymych, Pembrokeshire, SA36 0DS. Liz & Will North, 01239 831663, elizabethmmnorth@gmail.com. *2m SE of Crymych. From Crymych take Hermon Rd at Ysgol Bro Preseli, at T-junc in Hermon, turn L. Cae Bach is 300 yds on R. Disabled parking only at house, other parking signposted in village.* Sun 23 June, Sun 18 Aug (11-5). Adm £4, chd free. Home-made teas. Visits also by arrangement 16 June to 21 July for groups of 5 to 30. Discuss refreshments when booking.

A 1½ acre newly established garden designed to attract wildlife, particularly bees and butterflies. Inc herbaceous borders, ponds, grasses, Japanese garden with rill, rose garden (50 varieties), greenhouse, exotic area, conifer and heather area, wildflower meadow area, vegetable and fruit trees and fruit cage. Most areas wheelchair accessible.

2 CEFN AMLWG

Llandeilo Road, Gorslas, Llanelli, Carmarthenshire, SA14 7LU. Ann & Collin Wearing, 01269 842754, collin.wearing@yahoo.co.uk. *Approx 2m from Cross Hands r'about heading to Llandeilo, From Llandeilo towards Cross Hands on A476 go through Carmel village into Castell y Rhingyll. 1st & 2nd properties on R.* Tue 7 May, Tue 4 June, Tue 2 July (10.30-4.30). Combined adm with Moelfryn £6, chd free. Home-made teas. Visits also by arrangement 1 May to 14 Aug. Teas on request when booking.

The garden provides a mix of neat and tidy manicured lawn and ornamental beds with colour, planted to attract bees and butterflies. A large fish pond, raised vegetable beds, fruit cage and seating areas. A summerhouse allows you to sit and soak in the delights, the lawn leads your eyes to explore the beautifully laid out garden. Cleverly designed structures add interest. See separate entry for description of Moelfryn.

3 COLD COMFORT FARM

Wolfscastle, Haverfordwest, Pembrokeshire, SA62 5PA. Judy & Paul Rumbelow, 07809 560409, judy.rumbelow@gmail.com, www.facebook.com/p/Cold-Comfort-Plants, *7m N of Haverfordwest. Signed off A40 at Wolfscastle. Turn towards Hayscastle at Wolfe Inn. 1m along lane on L.* Sun 19, Wed 22 May, Sun 16 June (11-4). Adm £4, chd free. Home-made teas. Visits also by arrangement May to July for groups of up to 50. For groups we can offer a garden tour in English or Welsh.

Two acres of developing wildflower meadow alongside wrap around farm garden and small plant nursery. Perennial beds, showcasing nursery stock, rockery, gravel garden, raised beds, greenhouses, polytunnel and compost. Welcoming garden under development on sloping plot, full of planting ideas. Outstanding views of the Preseli Mountains.

4 NEW CORNERSTONE HOUSE

Glandwr, Whitland, Carmarthenshire, SA34 0XY. Ruth Swaffield, 01994 419683, ruth.swaff@gmail.com. *3.8m S of Crymych. From Narberth, N on A478 for approx 11 m, turn R at the sign for Glandwr. From Cardigan S on the A478 for approx 11 m turn L, 1m down hill turn R.* Sat 18, Sun 19 May (11-5). Adm £3.50, chd free. Home-made teas. Visits also by arrangement 2 Apr to 30 Sept for groups of up to 30. Discuss refreshments when booking.

A rural sloping garden of an acre which features a pond, small sunken garden and a gravel area, patio and seating areas, and view of hills. A path leads through Wisteria covered pergola and shrubbery to another pergola with hops and climbing roses leading to a sun house. The garden contains many rhododendrons and azaleas. Fruit trees and low hedges separate the fruit cage and vegetable gardens.

5 DWYNANT

Golden Grove, Carmarthenshire, SA32 8LT. Mrs Sian Griffiths *14m E of Carmarthen, 3m from Llandeilo. Take B4300 Llandeilo to Carmarthen. Take L turn to Gelli Aur, pass church & vicarage then 1st R onto Old Coach Rd. Dwynant is approx ¼ m on R.*

Fri 31 May, Sat 1, Sun 2 June (11-6). Adm £4, chd free. Pre-booking essential, please phone 07502 539737 or email sian.41@btinternet.com for information & booking. Cream teas. Visits also by arrangement Apr to Sept for groups of 5 to 20. Discuss refreshments when booking.

A ¾ acre garden set on a steep slope designed to sit comfortably within a verdant countryside environment with beautiful scenery and tranquil woodland setting. A spring garden with lily pond, selection of plants and shrubs inc azaleas, rhododendrons, rambling roses set amongst a carpet of bluebells. Seating in appropriate areas to enjoy the panoramic view and flowers. For accom. go to www.airbnb.co.uk/rooms/31081717.

6 ◆ DYFFRYN FERNANT

Llanychaer, Fishguard, Pembrokeshire, SA65 9SP. Christina Shand & David Allum, 01348 811282, christina@dyffrynfernant.co.uk, www.dyffrynfernant.co.uk. *3m E of Fishguard, then ½ m inland. A487 E, 2m from Fishguard turn R towards Llanychaer. Follow lane for ½ m, entrance on L. Look for yellow garden signs.* For NGS: Sun 12 May, Sun 1 Sept (12-5). Adm £7, chd free. Hot drinks machine in the Library takes card payments. For other opening times and information, please phone, email or visit garden website.

Magical 2.4 ha garden, evolving from wilderness and ancient rocky landscape. Distinctively planted areas leading down to marsh and woodland, against backdrop of the Preselis. RHS Partner Garden. Planting inc: tulips, primulas, *Camassias*, *Wisteria alba*, orchard fruit blossom, roses. Peonies and *Embothrium coccineum*, salvias, dahlias, *Hedychium*, canna, *Colocasia*, *Ricinus*, and ornamental grasses. Gravel paths and some steep slopes make the garden difficult for wheelchair users. Disabled parking near house.

7 GELLI UCHAF

Rhydcymerau, Llandeilo, Carmarthenshire, SA19 7PY. Julian & Fiona Wormald, 01558 685119, thegardenimpressionists@gmail.com, www.thegardenimpressionists.com/visiting-the-garden/. *See garden website for detailed directions. 5m SE of Llanybydder. 1m NW of Rhydcymerau. From the B4337 in Rhydcymerau take minor road opp bungalows. After 300yds turn R up track. Limited parking so essential to phone or email first.* **Visits by arrangement 3 Feb to 7 July for groups of up to 20. See full details at garden website. Discuss refreshments when booking. Adm £5, chd free.** Complementing a C17 Longhouse and 11 acre smallholding this 1½ acre garden is mainly organic. Trees and shrubs are underplanted with hundreds of thousands of snowdrops, crocus, cyclamen, daffodils, with woodland shrubs, clematis, rambling roses, hydrangeas and autumn flowering perennials. Extensive views and seats to enjoy them. Shepherd's hut. Year-round flower interest with naturalistic plantings. Six acres of wildflower meadows, two ponds and stream.

8 GLANDWR

Pentrecwrt, Llandysul, Carmarthenshire, SA44 5DA. Jo Hicks, 01559 363729, leehicks@btinternet.com. *15m N of Carmarthen, 2m S of Llandysul, 7m E of Newcastle Emlyn. On A486. At Pentrecwrt village, take minor road opp Black Horse pub. After bridge keep L for ¼m. Glandwr is on R.* **Visits by arrangement June to Aug. Perfect for small groups. Discuss refreshments when booking. Adm £3.50, chd free.** Delightful one acre enclosed mature garden, with a natural stream. Inc rockery, various flower beds (some colour-themed), many clematis and shrubs. Do spend time in the woodland with interesting trees, shade loving plants and ground cover, surprise paths, and secluded places to hear the bird song.

9 NEW GROVE OF NARBERTH

Molleston, Narberth, Pembrokeshire, SA67 8BX. 01834 860915, reservations@grovenarberth.co.uk, www.grovenarberth.co.uk. *2m S of Narberth. From A40 between Whitland and Haverfordwest, take A4075 towards Tenby. Go past Oakwood Theme Park, turn L on the A4115 towards Templeton. L turn at brown sign for Grove approx 2m later.* **Sun 23 June, Sun 22 Sept (2.30-5.30). Adm £7, chd free. Pre-booking essential, please visit www.ngs.org.uk for information & booking. Please pre-book teas with hotel (cream teas at £10.80 pp).** The garden is framed by ancient oaks and towering beeches, and from our hillside glade you can enjoy views across the rolling Pembrokeshire countryside to the Preseli Hills. 26 acres of woodlands, meadows and gardens, inc an historic walled garden, kitchen garden, and cut flower garden. Extensive woodland walks through the grounds, which inc some steep slopes and undulating paths.

10 NEW HOUSE ON STILTS

Rotten Pill Road, Ferryside, Carmarthenshire, SA17 5TN. Paula & Iain Davies, 07967 125881, paulapdavies@gmail.com, www.instagram.com/paulapdavies/. *9 m SW of Carmarthen. A48 towards Kidwelly, at Llandyfaelog junc turn R towards Ferryside. Follow road until the 'Welcome to Ferryside' sign. Follow NGS signs to garden for drop off only or parking at rugby club (7 min walk).* **Sun 19 May (1-5). Adm £4, chd free. Light refreshments. Visits also by arrangement 20 July to 14 Aug for groups of 10 to 20. Discuss refreshments when booking.** A ⅓ acre garden surrounds a mid century modern house, a garden designed with an artist's eye, subtle colour palette and use of form and texture. A mosaic of different habitats for wildlife, from a large pond at the rear to a dry cockle shell garden to the front, and steps to viewing platforms at different levels. An emphasis on promoting biodiversity, whilst creating a relaxing space for people. Coastal front garden, wildlife pond with viewing deck, bog garden, native hedging summer house (for sheltering from the rain), slopes planted with shrubs, perennials, bulbs and edibles, wild area with log pile etc. Potting shed and propagation area. Compost corner.

12 LLWYNGARREG

Llanfallteg, Whitland, Carmarthenshire, SA34 0XH. Paul & Liz O'Neill, 01994 240717, lizpaulfarm@yahoo.co.uk, www.llwyngarreg.co.uk. *19m W of Carmarthen. A40 W from Carmarthen, turn R at Llandewi Velfrey, 2½ m to Llanfallteg. Go through village, garden ½m further on: 2nd farm on R. Disabled car park in bottom yard on R.* **Visits by arrangement Feb to Nov. Adm £6, chd free. Discuss refreshments when booking.** Llwyngarreg is always changing, delighting plant lovers with its many rarities inc species primulas, many huge bamboos with roscoeas, hedychiums and salvias extending the season through to autumn colour. Trees and rhododendrons are underplanted with perennials. The exotic sunken garden and gravel gardens continue to mature. Springs form a series of linked ponds across the main garden, providing colourful bog gardens. Spot the subtle mobiles and fun constructions hidden around the four acre garden. Wildlife ponds, fruit and vegetables, composting, numerous living willow structures, mobiles, swing, chickens, goldfish. Partial wheelchair access.

13 MOELFRYN

Llandeilo Road, Gorslas, Llanelli, Carmarthenshire, SA14 7LU. Elaine & Graeme Halls, 01269 842754 (Cefn Amlwg). *Approx 2m from Cross Hands r'about heading to Llandeilo. From Llandeilo towards Cross Hands on A476 go through Carmel village into Castell y Rhingyll. 1st & 2nd properties on R.* **Tue 7 May, Tue 4 June, Tue 2 July (10.30-4.30). Combined adm with Cefn Amlwg £6, chd free. Home-made teas. Visits also by arrangement 1 May to 14 Aug. Please book and discuss refreshments with Cefn Amlwg (tour on request).** Organic and environmentally friendly, our garden has a herb labyrinth, cottage garden borders, vegetable beds and tunnels, fruit cages, orchard, small wildflower meadow area, shrubs, small wooded/wild patch, hens, hedgehog house, bug hotels, bird boxes and bat boxes, small pond and bog garden. Interesting arches, compost bins, water butts and a collection of 50 varieties of mints. Seats at every level. Lots of quirky areas and every twist and turn reveals something more. A garden, we are told, that keeps on giving. Mint tasting quiz can be booked in advance. Hen keeping and holding advice can be given. See separate entry for Cefn Amlwg.

🐕 ✳ ☕

14 NEUADD Y FELIN

Neuadd Road, Garnant, Ammanford, Carmarthenshire, SA18 1UF. Terry & Sara Knight. *Garnant. on A474, 5m W of Pontardawe, 5m E of Ammanford. Access to garden entrance is best from Nant Gwinau Rd, turn R as you enter Garnant on A474 from Pontardawe. From Ammanford direction turn L just before you leave Garnant on A474.* **Sat 8, Sun 9 June, Sat 27, Sun 28 July (10.30-4.30). Adm £4.50, chd free. Home-made teas.**
A mature two acre smallholding inc different areas of interest: large garden with sloping perennial beds; rose garden; large dahlia display; mature shrubs and shaded planted areas;40 foot white wisteria pergola; wildlife pond and fish pond; meadow with willow walk; and riverside walk with seated area. Located on the site of an old C14 watermill.

🐕 ✳ ☕))

15 NORCHARD

The Ridgeway, Manorbier, Tenby, Pembrokeshire, SA70 8LD. Ms H Davies. *4m W of Tenby. From Tenby, take A4139 for Pembroke. ½m after Lydstep, take R at Xrds. Proceed down lane for ¾m. Norchard on R.* **Sun 19 May (12-5). Adm £6, chd free. Home-made teas.**
Historic gardens at medieval hall house nestled in tranquil location sheltered by ancient oak woodland. Strong structure with formal and informal areas. Early walled gardens, restored Elizabethan parterre, ornamental kitchen garden, subtropical planting and orangery. 1½ acre orchard of old (many local) varieties. Young arboretum and meadow looking towards grist mill and millpond with moorhens and ducks. Extensive collections of roses, daffodils and tulips. Partial wheelchair access. Access to lower level of the kitchen garden via steps only.

♿ 🐕 ☕

16 THE OLD RECTORY

Lampeter Velfrey, Narberth, Pembrokeshire, SA67 8UH. Jane & Stephen Fletcher, 01834 831444, jane_e_fletcher@hotmail.com. *3m E of Narberth. Next to church in Lampeter Velfrey. Parking in church car park.* **Visits by arrangement 18 Mar to 15 Sept. Teas on request when booking. Adm £4, chd free.**
Behind a formal front garden the woodland garden is a green hollow of historic charm; wildlife welcoming, with ancient and newly planted trees and shrubs. Spring brings snowdrops, daffodils and bluebells to the woodlands. Later rhododendrons, hydrangeas, acers, roses, daisies and geraniums bring pops of colour to the green backdrop. Approx two acres inc veg, ponds and unique garden buildings.

🐕 🚗 🛏 ☕ 🪑

17 PEN Y BRYN

Gwaun Cae Gurwen, Ammanford, Carmarthenshire, SA18 1DY. Helen & Alex Brook, 07551 393030, hjh63@hotmail.co.uk. *8m E of Ammanford off the A474. At railway Xing in GCG drop down into Quarry Place (very small lane, opp CK food store). Go over waterfalls, turn L, follow road round to R & go under low bridge, property on L.* **Visits by arrangement 25 Apr to 27 Oct for groups of up to 15. Teas on request when booking. Adm £4.50, chd free.**
A garden of two halves. Upper formal gardens offering herbaceous borders, a pond and no-dig fruit and veg beds. The woodland is full of ferns and other woodland planting, a pond with marginal planting and several winding paths.

✳ ☕

18 PENCWM

Hebron, Whitland, Carmarthenshire, SA34 0JP. Lorna Brown, 07967 274830, lornambrown@hotmail.com. *10m N of Whitland. From A40 take St Clears exit & head N to Llangynin then on to Blaenwaun. Through village, after speed limit signs take 1st L. Over Xrds, 1¼m then 2nd lane on L marked Pencwm.* **Visits by arrangement Apr to Oct. Teas on request when booking. Adm £4, chd free.**
A secluded garden of about an acre set among large native trees, designed for year-round interest and

for benefit of wildlife. A wide variety of exotic specimen trees and shrubs inc magnolias, rhododendrons, hydrangeas, bamboos and acers. Drifts of bluebells and other spring bulbs and good autumn colour. Inc boggy area and pond with appropriate planting. Wellies recommended at most times.

🐕 🛏 ☕

The National Garden Scheme's final instalment to support the building of the Y Bwthyn NGS Macmillan Specialist Palliative Care Unit in Wales, enabled 270 inpatients to be supported this year

19 PENTRESITE

Rhydargaeau Road,
Carmarthen, SA32 7AJ. Gayle
& Ron Mounsey, 07900 432993,
gayle.mounsey@gmail.com. *4m N
of Carmarthen. Take A485 heading
N out of Carmarthen, once out of
village of Peniel take 1st R to Horeb
& cont for 1m. Turn R at NGS sign,
2nd house down lane.* **Sun 7 July
(11-5), open nearby Pen-y-Garn.
Sun 8 Sept (11-5). Adm £5, chd
free. Home-made teas. Visits also
by arrangement June to Sept.
Teas on request when booking.
Entrance driveway not suitable for
coaches.**
Approx. two acre garden developed
over the last 17 years with extensive
lawns, colour filled herbaceous and
mixed borders, on several levels, a
bog garden and magnificent views of
the surrounding countryside. There
are many unusual trees, shrubs and
herbaceous plants, with an interesting
collection of hydrangeas This garden
is south facing and catches the south
westerly winds from the sea.

20 PEN-Y-GARN

Foelgastell, Cefneithin,
Carmarthen, SA14 7EU.
Mary-Ann Nossent & Mike Wood,
07985 077022,
maryann.nossent@ngs.org.uk,
www.instagram.com/pen_y_garn.
*10m SE Carmarthen, A48 N
from Cross Hands. Take 1st L to
Foelgastell R at T-junc 300 metres
sharp L, 300 metres 1st gateway
on L. A48 S Bot. Gdns turning
r'about R to Porthythyd 1st L before
T junc. 1m 1st R & 300 metres on
L.* **Sat 22 June (10.30-4.30). Sun
7 July (10.30-4.30), open nearby
Pentresite. Adm £4, chd free.
Home-made teas. Visits also
by arrangement June to Aug
for groups of up to 20. Limited
parking for by arrangement days.**
1½ acres set in former limestone
quarry sympathetically developed
to sit within the landscape, with five
distinct areas cultivated herbaceous
borders and wild no mow lawns. A
shady area with woodland planting
and wild ponds; no dig kitchen
garden; terraced borders with shrubs
and herbaceous planting; lawns and
pond. The garden is on several levels
with slopes and steps. Garden is
steep in places.

21 ◆ THE PERENNIAL

Llanrhian Road, St David's,
Pembrokeshire, SA62 6DB.
Dr Pippa Allen, 07398 804148,
perennialgardensandcafe@gmail.
com, www.perennialstdavids.co.uk.
*3m E of St David's on Llanrhian Rd.
Between St David's & Fishguard.*
**For NGS: Tue 4 June, Sat 21 Sept
(11-4.30). Adm £4, chd free. Light
refreshments. For other opening
times and information, please phone,
email or visit garden website.**
An independent, nursery, café and
farm shop with a formal garden at
the centre featuring plants from the
nursery. Polytunnels for salad crops,
veg and cut flowers; developing small
woodland; compost and propagating
areas; coastal/countryside views.
Focus on sustainability, "no dig" and
recycling principles; peat and pesticide
free; member of Pollinators Assurance
Scheme. We want to inspire visitors to
grow plants for food and for pleasure,
whatever their space. On open days
we will make 'behind the scenes'
(e.g. composting areas, salad tunnels)
open to visitors, and 20% profits from
cafe will go to the National Garden
Scheme. Car park and paths with
limestone chips and some grass which
can make access bumpy but garden is
level with no steps.

Pen-y-Garn

22 PONT TRECYNNY

Garn Gelli Hill, Fishguard, Pembrokeshire, SA65 9SR. **Wendy Kinver** *1½ m N of Fishguard. Driving up the hill from Fishguard to Dinas turn R ½ way up the rd & follow signs. SatNav will take you to a lay-by opp the garden. Parking very limited.* **Sun 26 May (10-1); Wed 5 June (1-4); Thur 27 June (12-4); Sun 14 July, Sun 25 Aug (10-1). Adm £5, chd free. Pre-booking essential, please phone 01348 873040 or email wendykinver@icloud.com for information & booking. Visits also by arrangement 26 May to 8 Sept for groups of 10 to 30.**

A diverse garden of 3½ acres. Meander through the meadow planted with native trees, pass the pond and over a bridge which takes you along a path, through an arboretum, orchard and gravel garden and into the formal garden full of cloud trees, exotic plants and pots,which then leads you to the stream and vegetable garden.

23 SHOALS HOOK FARM

Shoals Hook Lane, Haverfordwest, Pembrokeshire, SA61 2XN. **Karen & Robert Hordley, 07712 268899, shoalshook@icloud.com.** *What3words app - clips.november. samplers. From A40 take B4329 to H/west town centre (Prendergast). Before fork with Fishguard Rd, turn L into Back Ln, turn L to Shoals Hook Ln, cont. 1m, property on L.* **Visits by arrangement 15 Apr to 26 Sept for groups of up to 14. Visits from Mon-Thurs only. Discuss refreshments when booking. Adm £5, chd free.**

Approx six acre garden on our smallholding. Designed and made by ourselves over 26 years. Inc flower borders, veg garden, fruit trees, woodland walk, lake garden and specimen trees. Planted for the different seasons and to encourage wildlife. Many spring bulbs at the start of the year, ending with a late summer prairie style grass garden area.

24 SKANDA VALE HOSPICE GARDEN

Saron, Llandysul, Carmarthenshire, SA44 5DY. brotherfrancis@ skandavalehospice.org, www.skandavalehospice.org. *On A484, in village of Saron, 13m N of Carmarthen. Between Carmarthen & Cardigan.* **Sat 1 June (11-4.30). Adm £4, chd free. Home-made teas.**

A tranquil garden of approx an acre, built for therapy, relaxation and fun. Maintained by volunteers, the lawns and glades link garden buildings with willow spiral, wildlife pond, colourful borders, sculptures and stained glass. Planting schemes of blue and gold at entrance inspire calm and confidence, leading to brighter red, orange and white. Hospice facilities open for visitors to view. A garden for quiet contemplation, wheelchair friendly, with lots of small interesting features. Craft stall.

25 STABLE COTTAGE

Rhoslanog, Mathry, Haverfordwest, Pembrokeshire, SA62 5HG. **Mr Michael & Mrs Jane Bayliss, 01348 837712, michaelandjane1954@ michaelandjane.plus.com.** *Between Fishguard and St David's. Heading W on A487, turn R at Square & Compass sign. ½ m, at hairpin take track L. Stable Cottage on L with block paved drive.* **Visits by arrangement 1 Apr to 7 July for groups of up to 15. for groups of up to 15. Parking limited, so car sharing necessary. Cream teas by prior arrangement. Adm £3.50, chd free.**

Garden extends to approx ⅓ of an acre. It is divided into several smaller garden types, with a seaside garden, small orchard and wildlife area, scented garden, small vegetable/ kitchen garden, and two Japanese areas - a stroll garden and courtyard area.

26 TREFFGARNE HALL

Treffgarne, Haverfordwest, Pembrokeshire, SA62 5PJ. **Martin & Jackie Batty, 01437 741115, jmv.batty@gmail.com.** *7m N of Haverfordwest, signed off A40. Go up through village & follow road round sharply to L, Hall ¼ m further on L.* **Sun 7 Apr, Sun 5 May, Sun 7 July (1-5). Adm £5.50, chd free. Home-made teas. Visits also by arrangement Mar to Sept. Teas for groups on request when booking.**

Stunning hilltop location with panoramic views: handsome Grade II listed Georgian house (not open) provides formal backdrop to garden of four acres with wide lawns and themed beds. A walled garden, with double rill and pergolas, planted with a multitude of borderline hardy exotics. Also large scale sculptures, summer border, gravel garden, heather bed and stumpery. Planted for year-round interest. The planting schemes seek to challenge the boundaries of what can be grown in Pembrokeshire. Gravel paths not wheel-friendly, some steps.

27 TY'R MAES

Tyr Maes, Farmers, Llanwrda, Carmarthenshire, SA19 8JP. **John & Helen Brooks, 01558 650541, johnhelen140@gmail.com.** *7m SE of Lampeter. 8m NW of Llanwrda. From Llanwrda 1½ m N of Pumsaint on A482, 1st L after turn to Ffarmers. From Lampeter first R after Springwater Lakes. Garden entrance 30 yds down lane. Please use postcode SA19 8DP with SatNav.* **Visits by arrangement Mar to Oct. Adm £6, chd free. Discuss refreshments when booking.**

A four acre garden with splendid views. Herbaceous and shrub beds – formal design, exuberantly informal planting, full of cottage garden favourites and many unusual plants. Wildlife and lily ponds; fascinating arboretum with over 200 types of tree; particular focus on rhododendron, magnolia and hydrangea cultivars. Gloriously colourful from early spring till late autumn. Wheelchair note: Some gravel paths.

28 WEST WALES WILLOWS

The Mill, Gwernogle, Carmarthen, SA32 7SA. **Justine & Alan Burgess, www.facebook.com/ WestWalesWillows.** *3m from Brechfa. On A40 at Nantgaredig, take B4310 to Brechfa. ½ m after Brechfa, turn L towards Gwernogle. After 2½ m pass Chapel on R, go up steep hill & bear R. Take 1st R turn & The Mill is on the R.* **Sat 22 June (10-4). Adm £4.50, chd free. Light refreshments.**

Located in a scenic valley, halfway up a mountain, the National Plant Collection of *Salix* (willow) is set in a sloping field with grass pathways. Approx 260 varieties are on show, inc varieties for pollinators, autumn colour, bio fuel, hedging and windbreaks. The field also has sample living willow structures on display inc domes, tepee, long arch/tunnel, hedges and a new arbour.

NPC

CEREDIGION

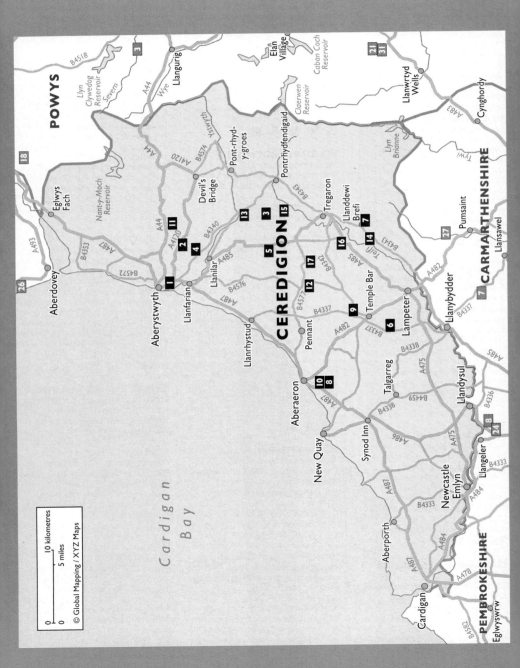

VOLUNTEERS

County Organiser
Stuart Bradley
07757 799553
stustart53@outlook.com

County Treasurer
Elaine Grande
01974 261196
e.grande@zoho.com

Booklet Co-ordinator
Shelagh Yeomans
07796 285003
shelaghyeo@hotmail.com

Publicity
Position vacant

Social Media
Samantha Wynne-Rhydderch
07899 911483
samantha.wynne-rhydderch
@ngs.org.uk

Assistant County Organisers
Gay Acres
01974 251559
gayacres@aol.com

Joanna Kennaugh
07872 451821
joanna.kennaugh@ngs.org.uk

f @Ceredigion Gardens

OPENING DATES

All entries subject to change.
For latest information check
www.ngs.org.uk
Map locator numbers are
shown to the right of each
garden name.

April
Saturday 6th
Bryngwyn — 2

May
Saturday 18th
Llanllyr — 9
Sunday 19th
Bwlch y Geuffordd — 4

June
Saturday 1st
Bryngwyn — 2
Sunday 2nd
Rhos Villa — 14
Monday 3rd
Bryngwyn — 2
Sunday 16th
Ffynnon Las — 8
Sunday 23rd
Llanllyr — 9
Sunday 30th
Ysgoldy'r Cwrt — 17

July
Sunday 7th
Aberystwyth Allotments — 1
Saturday 13th
Penybont — 13
Sunday 14th
Penybont — 13
Sunday 21st
◆ Cae Hir Gardens — 6
Sunday 28th
Yr Efail — 16

August
Monday 26th
Bryngwyn — 2
Wednesday 28th
Bryngwyn — 2

September
Sunday 8th
Tanffordd — 15

By Arrangement
Arrange a personalised garden visit
with your club, or group of friends,
on a date to suit you. See individual
garden entries for full details.

Brynmeheryn — 3
Bwlch y Geuffordd Gardens — 5
Delfryn — 7
Ffynnon Las — 8
Llanllyr — 9
Marlais — 10
Melindwr Valley Bees,
Tynyffordd Isaf — 11
Pencnwc — 12
Penybont — 13
Tanffordd — 15
Yr Efail — 16
Ysgoldy'r Cwrt — 17

In 2023, National Garden Scheme funding for Perennial supported a helpline service which provided advice, information and frontline support to around 800 people working in horticulture

THE GARDENS

1 ABERYSTWYTH ALLOTMENTS

5th Avenue, Penparcau, Aberystwyth, SY23 1QT. Aberystwyth Town Council. *On S side of R.Rheidol on Aberystwyth by-pass. From N or E, take A4120 between Llanbadarn & Penparcau. Cross bridge then take 1st R into Minyddol. Allotments ¼ m on R.* **Sun 7 July (1-5). Adm £5, chd free. Home-made teas.**

There are 47 plots in total on two sites just a few yards from each other. The allotments are situated in a lovely setting alongside River Rheidol close to Aberystwyth. Wide variety of produce grown, vegetables, soft fruit, top fruit, flowers, herbs and a newly created wildlife pond. Car parking available. For more information contact Brian Heath 01970 617112. There will be sample tastings from allotment produce. Grass and gravel paths throughout.

🚾 🐕 ☕

2 BRYNGWYN

Capel Seion, Aberystwyth, SY23 4EE. Mr Terry & Mrs Sue Reeves. *5m E of Aberystwyth on A4120. On the A4120 between the villages of Capel Seion & Pant y Crug. Parking for up to 15 cars available on site. What3words app - elephant.sunflower.forks.*

Sat 6 Apr (1.30-5). Adm £5, chd £1. Sat 1, Mon 3 June, Mon 26, Wed 28 Aug (1.30-5). Adm £5, chd free. Home-made teas.

Traditional wildflower-rich hay meadows managed for wildlife. As a result of conservation work and tree planting, habitat has been restored to such, that numbers and diversity of wildflowers and wildlife have increased. Explore along mown paths. Small orchard containing Welsh heritage apples and pears, option to gather wildflower seeds in August. Wildflower seed sales. Find us on Facebook at 'Wildlife and Photographic Days Aberystwyth'.

🐕 ☕ 🏕

Aberystwyth Allotments

3 BRYNMEHERYN

Tynygraig, Ystrad Meurig, SY25 6AH. **Sharron Johnson, brynmeherynforestry@gmail.com.** *Between Tynygraig and Lledrod. Garden located down a no through road. Follow SatNav to postcode & you will see yellow NGS signs.* **Visits by arrangement 4 July to 20 July. By arrangement on Thursday, Friday and Saturday only. Adm £5, chd free. Light refreshments. Vegan options available.**
We have five acres of gardens separated into different themes. There are three large ponds; the first is purely for wildlife; the second is the tropical area, moss and fernery; the third is a large ornate pond. There is a sunken garden with the most beautiful azaleas in the spring, a vegetable area and bordered back garden, a large grass labyrinth which looks out over the Cambrian Mountains.

❀ ☕ 🚉

4 BWLCH Y GEUFFORDD

New Cross, Aberystwyth, SY23 4LY. **Manuel & Elaine Grande.** *5m SE of Aberystwyth. Off A487 from Aberystwyth, take B4340 to New Cross. Garden on R at bottom of small dip. Parking in lay-bys opp house.* **Sun 19 May (10.30-4.30). Adm £5, chd free. Home-made teas.**
Landscaped hillside 1½ acre garden, fine views of Cambrian Mountains. Embraces its natural features with different levels, ponds, mixed borders merging into carefully managed informal areas. Banks of rhododendrons, azaleas, bluebells in spring. Full of unusual shade and damp-loving plants, flowering shrubs, mature trees, clematis and climbing roses scrambling up the walls of the old stone buildings. Partial wheelchair access only to lower levels around house. Some steps and steep paths further up the hillside.

♿ 🐕 ❀ ☕))

5 BWLCH Y GEUFFORDD GARDENS

Bronant, Aberystwyth, SY23 4JD. **Mr & Mrs J Acres, 01974 251559, gayacres@aol.com, bwlch-y-geuffordd-gardens.myfreesites. net.** *12m SE of Aberystwyth, 6m NW of Tregaron off A485. Take turning opp village sch in Bronant for 1½m then L up ½m uneven track.* **Visits by arrangement. You are welcome to bring a picnic. Adm £5, chd £2.50. Tea.**

1000ft high, three acre, constantly evolving wildlife and water garden. An adventure garden for children. There are a number of themed gardens, inc Mediterranean, cottage garden, woodland, oriental, memorial and jungle. Plenty of seating. Unique garden sculptures and buildings, inc a cave, temple, gazebo, jungle hut, tree-house and willow den. Children's adventure garden, musical instruments, pond dipping, dragon hunt, beautiful lake, temple and labyrinth, treehouse, sculptures, wildlife rich, particularly insects and birds. Gravel paths and some steps. A route that covers the main features, without steps. Chairs with robust wheels can access more.

♿ ☕ 🚉))

6 ◆ CAE HIR GARDENS

Cribyn, Lampeter, SA48 7NG. **Julie & Stuart Akkermans, 01570 471116, caehirgardens@gmail.com, caehirgardens.com.** *5m W of Lampeter. Take A482 from Lampeter towards Aberaeron. After 5m turn S on B4337. Garden on N side of village of Cribyn.* **For NGS: Sun 21 July (10-5). Adm £6, chd £2. Cream teas. For other opening times and information, please phone, email or visit garden website.**
A Welsh Garden with a Dutch History, Cae Hir is a true family garden of unassuming beauty, made tenable by its innovative mix of ordinary garden plants and wildflowers growing in swathes of perceived abandonment. At Cae Hir the natural meets the formal and riotous planting meets structure and form. A garden not just for plant lovers, but also for design enthusiasts. Five acres of fully landscaped gardens. Tearoom serving a selection of homemade cakes and scones and a 'Soup of the Day'. Limited wheelchair access.

🐕 ❀ 🚗 ☕

7 DELFRYN

Pentre Rhew, Llanddewi Brefi, SY25 6SB. **Tim Brock, tim.brock108@gmail.com.** *1m from Llanddewi Brefi village. Take the youth hostel road out of Llanddewi Brefi & after ¼ m take the 1st R. Follow the narrow lane & take the next sharp L. The garden is further up this lane on the R.* **Visits by arrangement June to Sept for groups of up to 10.. Adm £5. Tea.**
Unique fern garden with the Plant

Heritage National Collection of hart's-tongue (*Asplenium scolopendrium*) cultivars. The rock garden is situated on a hillside in Cwm Brefi and the ferns are growing in individual stone circles. There are over a hundred different fern cultivars to see. Access to the collection is via steep steps and rocky paths in a stunning location overlooking Llanddewi Brefi. Guided tour of the fern garden.

NPC ☕

8 FFYNNON LAS

Ffosyffin, Aberaeron, SA46 0HB. **Liz Roberts, 01545 571687, lizhomerent@hotmail.co.uk.** *A short distance off the A487. 1m S of Aberaeron. Turn off A487 opp The Forge Garage in Ffosyffin, 300m up the road take the L turn at the T junc.* **Sun 16 June (12-4). Adm £5, chd free. Home-made teas. Homemade cakes available with hot or cold drinks. Visits also by arrangement June & July. Donation to Pancreatic Cancer Research.**
A two acre garden that has been in the making for over 15 years, Ffynnonlas is a beautiful area that delivers on many different aspects of gardening. There are large lawns, several beds of mature shrubs and flowers. A small lake and two smaller ponds that are separated by a Monet style bridge with lilies. There is a wildflower meadow, a work in progress that has spectacular wild orchids in spring. A rockery with water cascade, vegetable garden with raised beds. For wheelchair users, please note there are grass paths and level ground.

♿ 🐕 ❀ ☕ 🚉

Our donation to the Army Benevolent Fund supported 608 individuals with front line services and horticultural related grants in 2023

9 LLANLLYR

Talsarn, Lampeter, SA48 8QB. Mrs Loveday Gee & Mr Patrick Gee, 01570 470900, lgllanllyr@aol.com. *6m NW of Lampeter. On B4337 to Llanrhystud. From Lampeter, entrance to garden on L, just before village of Talsarn.* Sat 18 May, Sun 23 June (2-6). Adm £5, chd free. Light refreshments. Visits also by arrangement 1 Apr to 29 Sept. Large early C19 garden on site of medieval nunnery, renovated and replanted since 1989. Large pool, bog garden, formal water garden, rose and shrub borders, gravel gardens, rose arbour, allegorical labyrinth and mount, all exhibiting fine plantsmanship. Year-round appeal, interesting and unusual plants. Spectacular rose garden planted with fragrant old fashioned shrub and climbing roses. Specialist Plant Fair by Ceredigion Growers Association. Garden mostly flat for wheelchair users.

10 MARLAIS

Ffosffin, Aberaeron, SA46 0EY. Dr & Mrs David Shepherd, 01545 574916, lymphoedemamidwales@btinternet.com. *Just S of Aberaeron. From Aberaeron take A487 S to Henfynyw and bear L at green bear past bus stop, then L again past single storey cottages. Marlais is then 2nd on R after jctn of Parc Ffos.* Visits by arrangement Apr to July for groups of up to 20. Discuss refreshments when booking. Adm £3.50, chd free. Home-made teas. The garden at Marlais is the smallest NGS garden in Ceredigion and was designed for easy access, no-dig and low maintenance to suit more mature gardeners with some disability. To the front we have a mini-orchard with 20 varieties of top-fruit on dwarfing rootstocks underplanted with bulbs, primroses and cowslips. The rear garden has a paved patio area with raised beds planted with an exceptional variety of unusual shrubs and herbaceous plants. Raised vegetable and soft-fruit beds are screened by trellis with tayberry, loganberry, blackberry, boysenberry and Japanese wineberry. Three pergolas add height, support climbers and provide attractive seating areas. Garden is level but unsuitable for wheelchairs or mobility scooters.

11 MELINDWR VALLEY BEES, TYNYFFORDD ISAF

Capel Bangor, Aberystwyth, SY23 3NW. Vicky Lines, 01970 880534, vickysweetland@googlemail.com. *Capel Bangor. From Aberystwth take L turn off A44 at E end of Capel Bangor. Follow this road round to R until you see sign with Melindwr Valley Bees.* Visits by arrangement 1 June to 4 Aug for groups of 5 to 10. Adm £5, chd free. Home-made teas. Cream teas £5 each. A bee farm dedicated to wildlife with permaculture and forest garden ethos. Fruit, vegetables, culinary and medicinal herbs and bee friendly plants within our wildlife zones. Beehives are situated in dedicated areas and can be observed from a distance. Ornamental and wildflower areas in a cottage garden theme. Formal and wildlife ponds. Vintage tractors and other machinery on show.

12 PENCNWC

Penuwch, Tregaron, SY25 6RE. Ms Andrea Sutton, 01974 821413, andreasutton@uclmail.net. *7m W of Tregaron on B4577. On the B4577, in the corner where the B4576 turns off in direction of Bwlchllan. This turning is opp cottage called Bear's Hill. Driveway to Pencnwc is 100 yds from the Tregaron Road on R.* Visits by arrangement for groups of up to 5. Garden is unsuitable for children. Adm £5. 7½ acre landscape garden 900ft up with view of Irish Sea between long bare hill and treed hill. Stone and slate house is in the centre. Land reaches out in a star shape around, all sloping down to marshland, now holding a large lake with boathouse. Springs are collected into hillside pools that run to the lake. Woodland, wildlife, especially birds. Walks, bridges, dry stone walls and castles, seats. Gorgeous lake. Excellent examples of dry stone walling inc a castle wall.

13 PENYBONT

Llanafan, Aberystwyth, SY23 4BJ. Norman & Brenda Jones, 01974 261737, tobrenorm@gmail.com. *9m SE of Aberystwyth. Ystwyth Valley. 9 m SE of Aberystwyth. B4340 via Trawscoed towards Pontrhydfendigaid. Over stone bridge. ¼ m up hill. Turn R along Lane/Ystwyth Trail past ex forestry*

houses. Sat 13, Sun 14 July (11-5.30). Adm £5, chd free. Home-made teas. Visits also by arrangement 11 May to 1 Sept. Discuss refreshments when booking. Carefully designed hillside country garden next to the Ystwyth Forest overlooking the valley. An acre of interest with continuity of colour and textures from spring bulbs & bluebells, rhododendrons and azaleas through May, roses from June and a Mediterranean summer feel with swathes of lavender, grapevines and lots of different hydrangeas in bright blues, whites and pinks. On the Ystwyth Trail. Designed and landscaped for colour and texture. Seats with stunning views over fields, woodland, valley and hills. Red kites, buzzards and sheep wander. Sloping ground, lawns, gravel paths. Very limited wheelchair access.

14 RHOS VILLA

Llanddewi Brefi, Tregaron, SY25 6PA. Andrew & Sam Buchanan. *From Lampeter take the A485 towards Tregaron. After Llangybi turn R opp junc for Olmarch. The property can be found on the R after 1½ m.* Sun 2 June (10.30-4.30). Adm £5, chd free. Home-made teas. A ¾ acre garden creatively utilising local materials. Secret pathways meander through sun and shade, dry and damp. A variety of perennials and shrubs are inter-planted to create interest throughout the year. A productive vegetable and fruit garden with semi-formal structure contrasts the looser planting through the rest of the garden. Interesting and beautifully crafted pitch cobble paths and walls constructed from local stone.

15 TANFFORDD

Swyddffynnon, Ystrad Meurig, SY25 6AW. Jo Kennaugh & Stuart Bradley, 07872 451821, stustart53@outlook.com. *Swyddffynnon. 1m W of Ystrad Meurig. 5m E of Tregaron. Tanffordd is ¼ m from Swyddffynnon village on the road to Tregaron. Please do not follow SatNav.* Sun 8 Sept (11-4.30). Adm £5, chd free. Home-made teas. Visits also by arrangement May to Sept for groups of up to 20. Wildlife garden, rich in biodiversity, set in a five acre smallholding with

Bwlch y Geuffordd

large pool. The garden inc a small woodland area and beds of shrubs and herbaceous planting containing more unusual plants. Vegetables, polytunnel and poultry enclosures with chickens and ducks. Wander along to meet the friendly donkeys and ponies who share a buttercup filled field in late spring and early summer. Large natural pond with an island. Some unusual shrubs and trees.

✿ ☕ 🪑

16 YR EFAIL
Llanio Road, Tregaron, SY25 6PU. Mrs Shelagh Yeomans, 07796 285003, shelaghyeo@hotmail.com, www.facebook.com/Yr-Efail. *3m SW of Tregaron. On B4578 between Llanio & Stag's Head.* Sun 28 July (10-4.30). Adm £5, chd free. Home-made teas. Visits also by arrangement 11 Feb to 29 Sept for groups of up to 30.

Savour one of the many quiet spaces to sit and reflect amongst the informal gardens of relaxed perennial planting, inc a wildlife pond, shaded areas, bog and gravel gardens. Be inspired by the large productive vegetable plots, three polytunnels and greenhouse. Wander along grass paths through the maturing, mostly native woodland. Enjoy home-made teas incorporating homegrown fruit and vegetables. Seasonal bilingual Unicorn quiz sheet. Seasonal vegetables, flowers and plants for sale. Find us on facebook at 'Yr Efail'. Gravel and grass paths accessible to wheelchairs with pneumatic wheels.

♿ 🐕 ✿ 🚻 ☕ 🪑

17 YSGOLDY'R CWRT
Llangeitho, Tregaron, SY25 6QJ. Mrs Brenda Woodley, 01974 821542, gg.gardening@hotmail.co.uk. *1½ m N of Llangeitho. From Llangeitho, turn L at sch signed Penuwch. Garden 1½ m on R. From Cross Inn take B4577 past Penuwch Inn, R after brown sculptures in field. Garden ¾ m on L.* Sun 30 June (11-5). Adm £5, chd free. Home-made teas. Visits also by arrangement Apr to Oct. Dietary requirements taken into account. One acre hillside garden, with five natural ponds which are a magnet for wildlife. Areas of wildflower meadow, rockery, bog, dry and woodland gardens. Established laburnum walk. Rare trees, large herbaceous beds with ornamental grasses. Azalea and acer collection in shade bed, bounded by a mountain stream, with two natural cascades and magnificent views of the Cambrian Mountains. Large *Iris ensata* and *Iris laevigata* collections in a variety of colours.

🐕 ✿ 🚻 ☕

GLAMORGAN

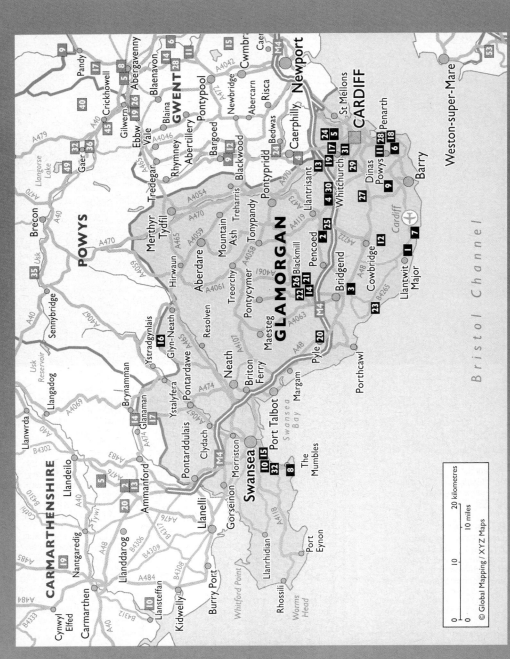

VOLUNTEERS

County Organiser
Rosamund Davies 01656 880048
rosamund.davies@ngs.org.uk

County Treasurer
Steven Thomas 01446 772339
steven.thomas@ngs.org.uk

Publicity
Bernadette Nicholas 07815 449568
bernadette.nicholas@ngs.org.uk

Social Media – Instagram
Sue Deary 01656 720833
suedeary888@gmail.com

Social Media – Facebook
Sarah Boorman 07969 499967
sarah.boorman@ngs.org.uk

Booklet Co-ordinator
Lesley Sherwood 02920 890055
lesley.sherwood@ngs.org.uk

Talks Co-ordinator
Frances Bowyer 02920 892264
frances.bowyer@ngs.org.uk

Health and Gardens Co-ordinator
Miranda Workman 02920 766225
miranda.parsons@talktalk.net

Assistant County Organisers
Cheryl Bass 07969 499967
cheryl.bass@ngs.org.uk

Sol Blytt Jordens 01792 391676
sol.blyttjordens@ngs.org.uk

Sarah Boorman (as above)

Pam Creed
pam.creed@ngs.org.uk

Janet Evans 07961 542452
janetevans54@me.com

Dr. Isabel Graham
isabel.graham@ngs.org.uk

Tony Leyshon 07896 799378
anthony.leyshon@icloud.com

Ceri Macfarlane 01792 404906
ceri@mikegravenor.plus.com

Derek Price 07717 462295
derekprice7@btinternet.com

Rhian Rees 01446 774817
rhian.rees@ngs.org.uk

Marie Robson
mariedrobson@gmail.com

@ @ngsglamorgan

OPENING DATES

All entries subject to change. For latest information check www.ngs.org.uk
Map locator numbers are shown to the right of each garden name.

February
Sunday 11th
Slade 23

April
Saturday 6th
Slade 23
Sunday 7th
Slade 23
Sunday 21st
Hen Felin & Swallow Barns 9
Sunday 28th
Gileston Manor 7

May
Saturday 4th
9 Willowbrook Gardens 32
Sunday 5th
9 Willowbrook Gardens 32
Saturday 18th
Horatio's Garden Cardiff 11
Maggie's Swansea 15
Sunday 19th
NEW Glenview, 140 Langland Road 8
Friday 31st
100 Pendwyallt Road 19

June
Saturday 1st
17 Maes y Draenog 13
100 Pendwyallt Road 19
9 Railway Terrace 21
Sunday 2nd
Hen Felin & Swallow Barns 9
17 Maes y Draenog 13
Sunday 9th
185 Pantbach Road 17
Friday 14th
V21 Community Garden 29

Saturday 15th
Boverton House 1
Penarth Gardens 18
NEW Tal-Y-Fan Farm 26
Sunday 16th
22 Dan-y-Coed Road 5
Penarth Gardens 18
NEW Tal-Y-Fan Farm 26
Saturday 22nd
Boverton House 1
Uplands 27
NEW 64 Western Drive 31
Sunday 23rd
Creigiau Village Gardens 4
NEW 64 Western Drive 31
Sunday 30th
12 Uplands Crescent 28

July
Saturday 6th
Dinas Powys 6
38 South Rise 24
Sunday 7th
Dinas Powys 6
38 South Rise 24
12 Uplands Crescent 28
Sunday 14th
Corntown Gardens 3
Maes-y-Wertha Farm 14
Saturday 20th
Swn y Coed 25
Saturday 27th
Pwyllygarth Farm 20
Sunday 28th
Pwyllygarth Farm 20

August
Sunday 11th
12 Uplands Crescent 28
Sunday 18th
Rose Cottage 22
Waunwyllt 30
Sunday 25th
12 Uplands Crescent 28

September
Sunday 1st
NEW Coed Cae Farm 2
Sunday 15th
NEW Glenview, 140 Langland Road 8

February 2025

Sunday 16th
Slade   23

By Arrangement

Arrange a personalised garden visit with your club, or group of friends, on a date to suit you. See individual garden entries for full details.

In 2023, our donations to Carers Trust meant that 26,118 unpaid carers were supported across the UK

Llandough Castle

THE GARDENS

1 BOVERTON HOUSE
Boverton, Llantwit Major, CF61 1UH. Mr John Wainwright. *Boverton, at the E end of Llantwit Major. Garden entrance is approx 50m E of the Boverton Post Office. Please follow yellow NGS signs.* Sat 15, Sat 22 June (10-4). Adm £4, chd free. Home-made teas.
A walled garden next to the River Hoddnant, recently brought back to use. Formerly an orchard and kitchen garden, the garden has a unique character and has been designed to create a beautiful garden space and encourage wildlife, whilst retaining its unique historic character. There is a raised kerb to enter from the road which may require assistance. Thereafter level grass throughout.
&. 🐕 ☕ •))

2 NEW COED CAE FARM
Llanharan, Pontyclun, CF72 9NH. The Liley Family. *What3words app - reputable.casino.shorthand. 10 min from M4 J34 or J35 on the A473. Turn off A473 at gates/ stone pillars of Llanharan Manor House, approx. 1/2m E of Village of Llanharan. Please follow yellow signs.* Sun 1 Sept (11-5). Adm £6, chd free. Home-made teas.
While it's the garden you come to view, your first instinct will be to stop and admire the panoramic views over the countryside. The gardens are laid out for all seasons, bulbs and herbaceous in shrub borders. Water features with cascades down to a pond, surrounded by mixed borders and trees, offering shade. A native woodland with a large pond offers alternative areas in the gardens. Please ask to park in yard where there is wheelchair access into the garden.
&. 🐕 ☕ 🛏

GROUP OPENING

3 CORNTOWN GARDENS
Corntown, Bridgend, CF35 5BB. *Take B4265 from Bridgend to Ewenny. Take L in Ewenny on B4524 to Corntown follow yellow NGS signs. From A48 take B4524 to Corntown.* Sun 14 July (11-4). Combined adm £5, chd free. Light refreshments.

RHOS GELER
Bob Priddle & Marie D Robson.

Y BWTHYN
Mrs Joyce Pegg.

Y Bwthyn has had over 40 years of hard labour, some guesswork and considerable good luck resulting in a delightful garden. The area at the front of the house is a mixture of hot colour combinations whilst at the rear of this modest sized garden the themes are of a more traditional cottage garden style which inc colour themed borders as well as soft fruit, herbs and vegetables. Rhos Geler's garden has a lavender hedge at the front and subjects to attract butterflies. The main garden area at the back of the house is a long narrow garden that is in a series of themed areas. These inc an herbaceous border, shade loving plants, an Elizabethan style knot garden and a Japanese influenced area. Containers hold a range of subjects inc a collection of sempervivums.
🌺 ☕ 🛏 •))

GROUP OPENING

4 CREIGIAU VILLAGE GARDENS
Maes Y Nant, Creigiau, CF15 9EJ. *W of Cardiff (J34 M4). From M4 J34 follow A4119 to T-lights, turn R by Castell Mynach Pub, pass through Groes Faen & turn L to Creigiau. Follow NGS signs.* Sun 23 June (11-5). Combined adm £7, chd free. Home-made teas at 28 Maes y Nant.

28 MAES Y NANT
Mike & Lesley Sherwood.

26 PARC Y FRO
Mr Daniel Cleary.

WAUNWYLLT
John Hughes & Richard Shaw.
(See separate entry)

Creigiau Village Gardens - three vibrant and innovative gardens. Each quite different, they combine some of the best characteristics of design and planting for modern town gardens as well as cottage gardens. Each has its own forte; Waunwyllt's 1/2 acre is divided into garden rooms; 28 Maes y Nant, cottage garden planting reigns; 26 Parc y Fro is newly planted with wildlife at its heart. Enjoy a warm welcome, home-made teas and plant sales.
🌺 ☕

5 22 DAN-Y-COED ROAD
Cyncoed, Cardiff, CF23 6NA. Alan & Miranda Workman, 07764 614013, miranda.parsons@talktalk.net. *Dan y Coed Rd leads off Cyncoed Rd at the top & Rhydypenau Rd at the bottom. No 22 is at the bottom of Dan y Coed Rd. There is street parking & level access to the R of the property.* Sun 16 June (2-6). Adm £5, chd free. Light refreshments. Visits also by arrangement 1 Apr to 23 Sept for groups of 6 to 20.
A medium sized, much loved garden. Owners share a passion for plants and structure, each year the lawn gets smaller to allow for the acquisition of new features. Hostas, ferns, acers and other trees form the central woodland theme as a backdrop is provided by the Nant Fawr woods. Year-round interest has been created for the owner's and visitor's greater pleasure. There is a wildlife pond, many climbing plants and a greenhouse with cacti, succulents and pelargoniums. There is wheelchair access to the garden patio area only.
&. 🐕 🌺 ☕ •))

Our 2023 donation to the Queen's Nursing Institute now helps support over 2,500 Queen's Nurses working in the community in England, Wales, Northern Ireland, the Channel Islands and the Isle of Man

GROUP OPENING

6 DINAS POWYS

Dinas Powys, CF64 4TL. *Approx 6m SW of Cardiff. Exit M4 at J33, follow A4232 to Leckwith, onto B4267 & follow to Merry Harrier T-lights. Turn R & enter Dinas Powys. Follow yellow NGS signs.* Sat 6, Sun 7 July (11-5). Combined adm £6, chd free. Light refreshments in Nightingale Community Garden, 21 Cardiff Road, West Cliffe, 30 Millbrook Road & 5 Sir Ivor Place. Donation to Dinas Powys Voluntary Concern & Dinas Powys Community Library.

21 CARDIFF ROAD
Rob & Pam Creed.

23 CARDIFF ROAD
Eoghan Conway & David Manfield.

32 LONGMEADOW DRIVE
Julie & Nigel Barnes.

30 MILLBROOK ROAD
Mr & Mrs R Golding.

32 MILLBROOK ROAD
Mrs G Marsh.

NIGHTINGALE COMMUNITY GARDENS
Keith Hatton.

THE POUND
Helen & David Parsons.

32 ST DAVIDS AVENUE

5 SIR IVOR PLACE
Ceri Coles.

WEST CLIFF
Alan & Jackie Blakoe.

There are many gardens to visit in this small friendly village, all with something different to offer. Displays of vegetables and fruit in the community garden, gardens with exuberant planting providing yearlong interest, wildlife ponds, chickens and a mini vineyard. There will also be plants for sale and refreshments in the different gardens. There are many restful and beautiful areas to sit and relax. Good wheelchair access to all gardens apart from 32 St David's Avenue.

7 GILESTON MANOR

Gileston Road, Gileston, Barry, CF62 4HX. Joshua Llewelyn and Lorraine-Garrad Jones, 01446 754029, enquiries@gilestonmanor.co.uk, www.gilestonmanor.co.uk. *Gileston Village. From Cardiff airport take B4265 to Llantwit Major. After 3m turn L at the petrol stn. Go under the bridge, turn R follow yellow NGS signs to Gileston Manor. Situated in the small village.* Sun 28 Apr (11-4). Adm £6, chd free. Tea in our marquee and or Manor House. Light refreshments and alternative drinks available from our Bar. Visits also by arrangement 1 Mar to 20 Dec for groups of up to 60. Groups receive high tea in the Manor House and a tour with head gardener.

Surrounded by beautiful Welsh countryside with breathtaking views across the jurassic coast, you will find our historic nine acre estate. Gileston Manor, in the Vale of Glamorgan has been loved and lived in since 1320 and recently, lovingly renovated and restored by the current owners. There is so much to see and explore and will definitely delight any keen gardener - a perfect blend of old and new. Meet our alpacas, view the house (subject to confirmation on the day), browse plant sales and entertainment provided in our large marquees and Manor House. Discover our church and look inside our many outbuildings that make up our ancient village. Meet our head gardener for Q&A. We have recently added further paths to our estate, allowing wheelchair access from the gravel car park, to all areas of the garden.

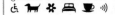

8 NEW GLENVIEW, 140 LANGLAND ROAD

Mumbles, Swansea, SA3 4LU. Mrs Helen Belton. *Central Mumbles, W of Swansea. Access via Underhill Park, vehicles can park in Underhill Park car park. Follow arrows to woodland gate on path near all weather pitch.* Sun 19 May, Sun 15 Sept (1-5). Adm £5, chd free. Home-made teas. Homemade cakes.

Access to the hidden garden of Glenview is via a strip of woodland that borders Underhill Park. After much needed maintenance, this woodland is evolving into a more usable space with the introduction of a large number of newly planted

trees and shrubs. Follow the path up through the woods, steps lead round to the gravel garden, hidden from the road and park, due to the level changes.

GROUP OPENING

9 HEN FELIN & SWALLOW BARNS

Vale of Glamorgan, Dyffryn, CF5 6SU. Janet Evans & Rozanne Lord, 07961 542452, janet.evans54@me.com. *Dyffryn village. 3m from Culverhouse. Cross r'about take the A48 up the hill to st Nicholas, L at T-lights, past Dyffryn. House, R at T-junc & follow the road to big yellow NGS signs.* Sun 21 Apr (11.30-5.30); Sun 2 June (11-6). Combined adm £5, chd free. Visits also by arrangement 18 Mar to 1 Nov.

Yr Hen Felin: Beautiful cottage garden with stunning borders, breathtaking wildflower meadows, oak tree with surrounding bench, 200 year old pig sty, wishing well, secret garden with steps to river, lovingly tended vegetable garden and chickens, sheep and alpacas. Mill stream running through garden with adjacent wildflowers. The Barns: Cross the bridge over the river to enter the Barns garden of about four acres. The area around the house is formal with mixed herbaceous borders, and a rose walk to a small secluded pond. The meandering paths pass small garden rooms and raised beds for vegetables, runs alongside the River Waycock through an orchard of heritage, apple trees, plums, and cherries, and finally through woods, reaches a large pond with water lilies, dragon flies, pontoon with seating and summer house. Teas and cakes are available from the house with seating in the herb garden, and a sale of original water colours. NB Unprotected river access, children must be supervised. Teas and cakes and a water colour sale. Wheelchair access possible to most areas of the two gardens. The bridge has steps and wheelchair access between the gardens is via the lane.

Coed Cae Farm

10 16 HENDY CLOSE
Derwen Fawr, Swansea,
SA2 8BB. Peter & Wendy
Robinson, 07773 711973,
robinsonpete1@hotmail.co.uk.
*Approx 3m W of Swansea. A4067
Mumbles Rd follow sign for Singleton
Hospital. Then R onto Sketty Ln at
mini r'about. Turn L then 2nd R onto
Saunders Way. Follow yellow NGS
signs. Please park on Saunders Way
if possible.* **Visits by arrangement
1 May to 22 Sept for groups
of 6+. Adm £7, chd free. Tea.
Refreshments inc in the adm.**
Originally the garden was covered
with 40ft conifers. Cottage style,
some unusual and mainly perennial
plants which provide colour in spring,
summer and autumn. The garden
is an example of how to plan for all
seasons. Visitors say it is like a secret
garden because there are a number
of hidden places. Plants to encourage
all types of wildlife in to the garden.

**11 HORATIO'S GARDEN
CARDIFF**
University Hospital Llandough,
Penlan Road, Llandough,
CF64 2XX. Owen Griffiths,
www.horatiosgarden.org.uk.
*University Hospital Llandough.
Turn into the University Hospital
Llandough from the main road and
keep going straight. The garden is
raised on the R-hand side of the
road, just past the visitor's car park.*
**Sat 18 May (11-4). Adm £5, chd
free. Pre-booking essential,
please visit www.ngs.org.uk for
information & booking. Light
refreshments in Aroma Cafe
nearby.**
Sarah Price's design was inspired by
the Welsh landscape. The planting inc
valerian, Welsh poppy, field maple,
and crab apples. Circular openings
within the perimeter fence frame the
countryside and sea in the distance.
The fence is covered with climbers
such as clematis, grapes, and roses.
It provides patients, visitors and
staff with a beautiful place to spend

time in the garden year-round. Fully
wheelchair accessible.

12 LLANDOUGH CASTLE
Llandough, Cowbridge, CF71 7LR.
Mrs Rhian Rees, 07802 438299,
rhianedrees@gmail.com. *1½ m
outside Cowbridge. At the T- lights in
Cowbridge turn onto the St Athan Rd.
Continue then turn R to Llandough.
Drive into the village follow the car
park signs. The car park is a 5 min
walk from the gardens.* **Visits by
arrangement 8 Feb to 27 Sept for
groups of 10 to 40.. Adm £9, chd
free. Light refreshments.**
Set within castle grounds and with a
backdrop of an ancient monument,
the 3½ acres of garden inc a potager
with a hint of the Mediterranean,
formal lawns and herbaceous beds,
a wildlife pond with waterfall and a
woodland garden with stumpery and
sculpture. Over 90,000 spring bulbs
have been planted inc snowdrops,
Narcissi and tulips. Potager, wildlife
pond, formal borders, stumpery.

13 17 MAES Y DRAENOG
Tongwynlais, Cardiff, CF15 7JL.
Mr Derek Price, 07717 462295,
derekprice7@btinternet.com. *N of
M4, J32. From M4 , J32, take A4054
into village. R at Lewis Arms pub, up
Mill Rd. 2nd R into Catherine Dr. Park
in signed area (no parking in Maes y
Draenog). Follow signs to garden.* Sat
1, Sun 2 June (12-5). Adm £5, chd
free. Home-made teas. Selection
of cream teas, homemade cakes
and coffee will be available. Visits
also by arrangement 3 June to 9
June for groups of 6 to 15.
A hidden garden, in the shadow of
Castell Coch, fed by a mountain
stream, and a wooden footbridge to a
naturalised, woodland area. There are
wonderful late spring flower displays
set against a woodland backdrop.
Developed over many years with a
wide variety of lavender beds and
herbaceous borders, summerhouse,
patios, greenhouse and vegetable
area. A good variety of plants in
different borders around house. Rear
of house is set against woodland and
fields, while front areas have mature
roses and herbaceous plants, borders.
Not suitable for young children and
partial access for wheelchair users.

14 MAES-Y-WERTHA FARM
Bryncethin, CF32 9YJ. Stella &
Tony Leyshon. *3m N of Bridgend.
Follow sign for Bryncethin, turn R at
Masons Arms. Follow sign for Heol-
y-Cyw garden about 1m outside
Bryncethin on R.* Sun 14 July
(12-7). Adm £7, chd free. Pimms
available and live music all day.
A three acre hidden gem outside
Bridgend. Entering the garden you
find a small Japanese garden fed by
a stream, this leads you to informal
mixed beds and enclosed herbaceous
borders. Ponds and rill are fed by
a natural spring. A meadow with
large lawns under new planting gives
wonderful vistas over surrounding
countryside. Mural in the summerhouse
by contemporary artist Daniel Llewelyn
Hall. His work is represented in the
Royal Collection and House of Lords.
Fresh handmade sandwiches available
and live music all afternoon.

15 MAGGIE'S SWANSEA
Singleton Hospital, Sketty
Lane, Sketty, Swansea,
SA2 8QL. Maggie's Swansea,
www.maggies.org/swansea. *On
the grounds of Singleton Hospital.*

*Next to the Genetic building & close
to the chemotherapy day unit at the
back of the main hospital. Please
follow orange signs for Maggie's.*
Sat 18 May (10-12). Adm £3, chd
free. Light refreshments inc tea,
coffee, squash, cakes & biscuits.
Maggie's Swansea's gardens wrap
around the building, and overlook into
Swansea Bay. The garden, designed
by Kim Wilkie, attracts wildlife,
heightening the natural and tranquil
feel, and there is also a fully functional
allotment. The Centre sits among a
small wooded area, and the wings
of the design also help to shelter the
outside seating areas, meaning that
visitors can enjoy sitting out for as
much of the year as possible. Decking
all the way around the building.

16 NANT MELYN FARM
Seven Sisters, Neath,
SA10 9BW. Mr Craig Pearce,
cgpearce@hotmail.co.uk. *From
J43 on M4 take A465 towards
Neath. Exit for Seven Sisters at
r'about take 3rd exit, 6m for Seven
Sisters you come to Pantyffordd
sign, turn L under low bridge.* Visits
by arrangement June to Aug for
groups of up to 20.. Adm £4.50,
chd free. Light refreshments.
A spacious interesting garden with
many features which inc a stunning
natural waterfall, a meandering
woodland stream covered by
a canopy of entwined trees, a
picturesque Japanese garden,
beautiful lawned areas with winding
pathways.

17 185 PANTBACH ROAD
Rhiwbina, Cardiff, CF14 6AD.
Kate & Glynn Canning. *Situated
½m from Heol-y -Deri in the heart
of Rhiwbina.* Sun 9 June (11.30-5).
Adm £5, chd free. Home-made
teas.
An Urban Retreat in the heart of
Cardiff. The garden, once overgrown
wasteland, turned into an ongoing
lockdown' project in 2020 for owners
Kate and Glynn. Although still in its
infancy, the garden features raised
beds, a formal rose garden and a
central water feature. The winding
path is framed by standard roses,
borders and lawns.

GROUP OPENING

18 PENARTH GARDENS
Penarth, CF64 3HY. *Penarth. Follow
yellow signs to Lower Penarth.*
Sat 15, Sun 16 June (10-5).
Combined adm £6, chd free.
Light refreshments at Seafield
House (18 Clinton Road). Light
refreshments only.

NEW **2 BERKLEY DRIVE**
Ian & Jane Hydon.
Open on all dates

NEW **23 PLYMOUTH ROAD**
Mrs Nicola Griffiths.
Open on Sat 15 June

SEAFIELD HOUSE
Anja Ernest.
Open on all dates

**VICTORIA SQUARE
COMMUNITY GARDEN**
Friends of Victoria Square,
www.friendsofvictoriasquare.org
Open on Sat 15 June

During the Victorian Era, Penarth
was known as the 'Garden by the
Sea'. Come and visit a selection of
traditional and contemporary town
gardens all within walking distance of
each other. There is also a chance to
visit an exciting community garden in
the grounds of All Saints Church.

19 100 PENDWYALLT ROAD
Whitchurch, Cardiff, CF14 7EH.
*Near J32 of M4. Cul de sac on
opp side of road to Village Hotel.
Take narrow road opp side of road
to Whitworth Sq. Go uphill past
blocks of flats (Odet Court and
Greenmeadow Court).* Fri 31 May,
Sat 1 June (12-5). Adm £5, chd
free.
Three large separate areas form the
garden and are planted to encourage
wildlife. Trees inc Japanese maples,
shrubs, grasses and bamboos. Long
pergola. Two huge ponds, one of
which has windows to view the koi.

20 PWYLLYGARTH FARM
Garth Street, Kenfig Hill, Bridgend,
CF33 6EU. Cheryl Bass. *In Kenfig
Hill. Farmhouse directly off main
road in Kenfig Hill. At the Spar follow
yellow signs.* Sat 27 July (10-5);
Sun 28 July (11-4). Adm £5, chd
free. Home-made teas.

Pwllygarth Farm, built by Welsh heiress Emily Charlotte Talbot in 1904 as a working farm. The front and side gardens are a mix of rose gardens, sedum planted walls, raised rockery beds, small woodland garden and a landscaped paved area. The relaxing rear garden offers a Japanese garden, butterfly rockery, summerhouse, reading corner and a wildlife pond incorporating grasses and creative planting. To the rear of the property is a car park area that will feature some classic cars. The garden is wheelchair accessible and there are no steps.

21 9 RAILWAY TERRACE

Heol Laethog, Bryncethin, Bridgend, CF32 9JE. Ms Sue Deary. *Between Bryncethin and Heol Y Cyw. Approx 1m from Bryncethin & just over 2m from Pencoed. Drive along the common road over the railway bridge and follow road by the children's park. Go over a cattle grid then follow yellow signage.* **Sat 1 June (11-5). Adm £3.50. Home-made teas. Tea, coffee, cold drinks with homemade cakes and bakes. Cream teas with homemade jam and clotted cream.**

An old miner's cottage circa 1900 on Coity common with a sloping small south facing garden that has been terraced and has two different levels divided by some steps. There are a number of fruit trees inc apple, pear and fig trees, also magnolias and a palm tree. There are herbaceous borders planted with roses and many other plants. There is a seated area on the top terrace and a rose covered arbour on the lower level and a small water feature with uninterrupted views of the common. The main ethos of the garden is to try and keep it as a cottage garden inc reusing and repurposing various items inc old water tanks for planting and planting vegetables and flowers side by side. Unfortunately, there is no wheelchair access in the front garden. The rear garden could be accessed by wheelchair with caution.

22 ROSE COTTAGE

32 Blackmill Road, Bryncethin, Bridgend, CF32 9YN. Maria & Anne Lalic, scarecrowcottagewales@ gmail.com, www.instagram.com/ scarecrowcottagewales. *1m N of M4 J36 on A4061. Follow A4061 to Bryncethin. Straight on at mini*

r'about for approx 400 metres. Just past Used Car Garage, turn R onto side road at grassed area. Please park considerately. **Sun 18 Aug (1-5). Adm by donation. Light refreshments. Limited availability of gluten free cakes. Visits also by arrangement 18 June to 13 Sept for groups of up to 8.**

If you want a proper garden with manicured borders and Latin plant names, Rose Cottage isn't the place for you. We have a traditional Welsh working cottage garden with jumbled flower beds, a herb yard, seasonal

growing of fruit and vegetables, ideas borrowed from permaculture, no-dig and companion planting to help us with our simple, self-reliant way of life. Our pop up tea room sells tea, coffee and home-made cakes. Maria leads tours around the garden and Anne is a available to give advice on growing and pruning fig trees. Main path and gateways suitable for wheelchairs. Narrower, bark chip paths and grass paths are uneven and care should be taken.

Slade

Penarth Gardens

23 SLADE

Southerndown, CF32 0RP.
Rosamund & Peter Davies,
01656 880048,
rosamund.davies@ngs.org.uk,
www.sladeholidaycottages.co.uk.
*5m S of Bridgend. M4 J35 Follow
A473 to Bridgend. Take B4265 to
St. Brides Major. Turn R in St. Brides
Major for Southerndown, then follow
yellow NGS signs.* **Sun 11 Feb
(1.30-4); Sat 6, Sun 7 Apr (11-5).
Adm £7, chd free. Home-made
teas. 2025: Sun 16 Feb.**
Hidden away, Slade garden is an
unexpected jewel to discover next to
the sea with views overlooking the
Bristol Channel. The garden tumbles
down a valley protected by a belt of
woodland. In front of the house are
delightful formal areas a rose and
clematis pergola and herbaceous
borders. From terraced lawns great
sweeps of grass stretch down the
hill enlivened by spring bulbs and
fritillaries. Heritage Coast wardens
will give guided tours of adjacent
Dunraven Gardens with slide shows
every hour from 2pm (Apr opening
only). Partial wheelchair access.

&. ✿ 🚗 🚌 ☕ ›))

24 38 SOUTH RISE

South Rise, Llanishen, Cardiff,
CF14 0RH. Dr Khalida Hasan. *N
of Cardiff. From Llanishen Village
take Station Rd past train stn and
go R down The Rise. Or further
down onto S Rise directly. Following
yellow signs.* **Sat 6, Sun 7 July
(12-5). Adm £5.50, chd free. Light
refreshments. Cakes & South
Asian savouries (e.g. samosa,
chick pea chaat) available.**
An inner city garden backing on
to Llanishen Reservoir gradually
establishing with something of
interest and colour all year-round.
Herbaceous borders, vegetables
and fruit plants surround central
lawn. Wildlife friendly; variety of
climbers and exotics. In front shrubs
and herbaceous borders to a lawn.
Stepping stones leading to children's
play area and vegetable plot also at
the back. Wheelchair access to rear
from the side of the house.

&. ✿ 🚗 ☕ ›))

25 SWN Y COED

Tyla Garw, Pontyclun, CF72 9HD.
Mair & Owen Hopkin,
07434 096410,
mair.hopkin@icloud.com. *N of
Pontyclun. M4- J34. On A4119
r'about take 1st exit to A473. Go
straight over next r'about. Head*

*through t-lights and L at r'about.
at next r'about 2nd L over Xing
immed R past pub. 1st house on
R after forestry entrance.* **Sat 20
July (11-4). Adm £5, chd free.
Home-made teas inc gluten &
dairy free options. Visits also by
arrangement June & July.**
This family friendly garden started
from a blank canvas 7 years ago,
initially laid to lawn. Raised vegetable
beds were installed and a 75m
natural hedge planted along the side
boundary to encourage wildlife. This
was supplemented with fruit trees,
flower and herb borders to attract
insects. The lawn provides a clearing
to the surrounding forestry attracting
a variety of birds. Disabled parking
on drive. Ramped access to rear
patio and WC. Path adjacent to herb
border also accessible to wheelchair.

&. ✿ ☕ ›))

26 NEW TAL-Y-FAN FARM

Blackmill, Bridgend, CF35 6UD.
Suzanne, 07721 385633,
skchurchill100@hotmail.co.uk.
*Between Llangeinor and Blackmill.
Accessed via A4093 between
Llangeinor & Blackmill. Take turning
opp the hanging sign for the
Llangeinor Arms & follow the yellow
signs. Access is along a private
gravel road crossing the common.*

Sat 15, Sun 16 June (10-5). Adm £5, chd free. Cream teas. Cakes, homemade scones, tea, coffee and cold drinks and snacks.
Elevated country garden with stunning 360 degree views over the Bristol Channel to the Devon coastline. Situated in an isolated location. David Austin roses are the main attraction in the garden it has a parterre and rose arch, surrounded by 180 year old beech trees. There is a large seating area with glass balustrade to enjoy the views. We have pigs, alpaca, chickens, geese and turkeys - I also run a small campsite and glamping in the adjacent paddock. Access onto terrace area with views over the garden and far reaching coastal views.
& 🛏 ☕))

27 UPLANDS
Gwern-y-Steeple, Peterston Super Ely, CF5 6LG. David Richmond. *From the A48 between St Nicholas & Bonvilston take the Peterston Super Ely turning & follow yellow NGS arrow, park at small green near Gwern-y-Steeple sign.* Sat 22 June (12-5). Adm £4, chd free. Light refreshments.
Uplands has a rustic heart within a cottage garden design. The front has vegetables and currant bushes. The back was planted in 2019, on once all grass. There are four main herbaceous borders, young fruit trees, ornamental grasses, ferns, shrubs and roses, with many places to relax and enjoy the garden. Medium sized greenhouse with citrus and fig tree. Several sculptures located around the garden.
🐕 ✳ ☕))

28 12 UPLANDS CRESCENT
Llandough, Penarth, CF64 2PR. Mr Dean Mears, 07910 638682, dean.mears@ntlworld.com. *Head for Llandough Hospital & a small turning head with a Weeping Beech clearly visible in the front garden. Follow NGS signs.* Sun 30 June, Sun 7 July, Sun 11, Sun 25 Aug (2-4.30). Adm £5, chd free. Visits also by arrangement June to Sept for groups of up to 6.
An exotic small garden full of unusual and large plants and a pond. Banana plants, tree ferns, gunnera, *Tetrapanax* and a foxglove tree surround the garden. Ferns, *Phormium, Brunnera, Brugmansia, Cordyline* and giant reed add interest to the garden. An area of potted

tropical plants, *Brugmansia, Canna, Alocasia, Colocasia, Strelitzia* and palms add to the significant variety of exotic plants.
✳))

29 V21 COMMUNITY GARDEN
Sbectrwm, Bwlch road, Cardiff, CF5 3EF. Mr Roy Bailey, www.V21.org.uk. *3m W of central Cardiff. From the A48 turn R onto St Fagans Rd. Continue onto Norbury Rd leading to Finchley Rd & Bwlch Rd.* Fri 14 June (10-4). Adm £4.50, chd free. Home-made teas at the on-site café.
The V21 Community Garden is developed and maintained by people with learning disabilities. The garden is designed to be an accessible learning environment. The garden has a newly developed herbaceous flower border, a Spring garden, a wildlife pond, bog garden and areas for growing fruit & vegetables. There is also a large polytunnel and glasshouse to extend the growing season. Wheelchairs access via main paths.
& 🐕 ✳ ☕))

30 WAUNWYLLT
Pant y Gored, Creigiau, Cardiff, CF15 9NF. John Hughes & Richard Shaw. *Heol Pant y Gored, Creigiau.* Sun 18 Aug (11-5). Adm £5, chd free. Home-made teas. Opening with Creigiau Village Gardens on Sun 23 June.
Waunwyllt is a garden of approx ½ an acre, divided into several 'garden rooms'. Winding paths lead the visitor through a tranquil garden set against a woodland backdrop with many secluded seating areas along the way and something of interest around every corner. Colour coordinated borders and strong design contribute to an attractive and stylish garden.
✳ ☕

31 [NEW] 64 WESTERN DRIVE
64 Western Drive, Cardiff, CF14 2SF. 07511 744976. *Gabalfa Cardiff. A470 - Manor Way W along Birchgrove Rd to Whichchurch. R at t-lights along College Rd. L at r'about, across next r'about to NGS sign. A48 Western Ave past LLandaff, at Tesco lights turn L.* Sat 22 June (10-5); Sun 23 June (1-5). Adm £4, chd free. Light refreshments. Visits also by arrangement 25 May to 30 Aug for groups of up to 10.
Interesting small, town garden in a city

suburb. Pretty garden with something of interest for everyone. Water feature, pebble garden and mixed perennial borders inc species roses, English, rambler and climbing roses. Wildlife pond with small waterfall. Cordon fruit trees. River, sea, garden and hedgerow bird species all visit the garden. Nearby walks and cycle paths. Established hedgerow and trees. Concrete drive access to front garden with concrete path access to back garden. Well behaved dogs on leads.
& 🐕 ✳ ☕

32 9 WILLOWBROOK GARDENS
Mayals, Swansea, SA3 5EB. Gislinde Macphereson, 01792 403268, ngs@ willowgardens.idps.co.uk. *Nr Clyne Gardens. Go along Mumbles Rd to Blackpill. Turn R at Texaco garage up Mayals Rd. At the top of Clyne Park, turn R into Westport Ave. Willowbrook Gardens is 2nd turning on the L as you go up Westport Ave.* Sat 4, Sun 5 May (12.30-5). Adm £5, chd free. Home-made teas. Visits also by arrangement 8 Apr to 31 Oct.
Informal ½ acre mature garden on acid soil, designed to give natural effect with balance of form and colour between various areas linked by lawns; unusual trees suited to small suburban garden, especially conifers and maples; rock and water garden. Sculptures, ponds and waterfall.
& 🐕 ✳ ☕

152,684 people were able to access guidance on what to expect when a person is dying through the National Garden Scheme support for Hospice UK this year

GWENT

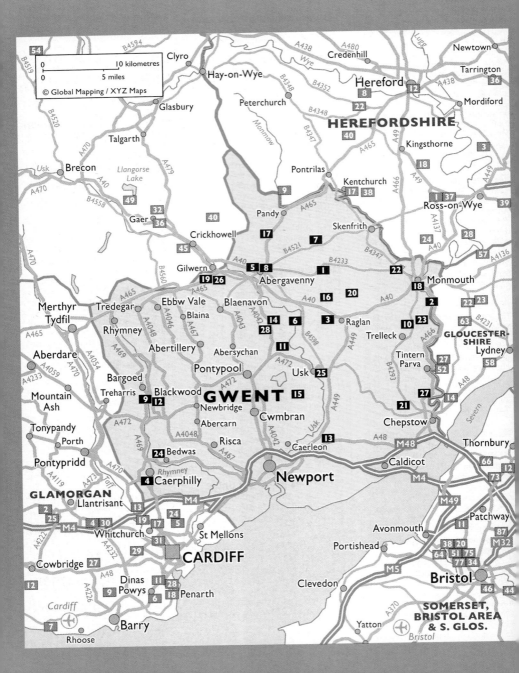

Map Legend Places:

Newtown, Clyro, Credenhill, Hay-on-Wye, Hereford, Tarrington, Mordiford, Glasbury, Peterchurch, HEREFORDSHIRE, Kingsthorne, Talgarth, Pontrilas, Kentchurch, Ross-on-Wye, Brecon, Llangorse Lake, Pandy, Skenfrith, Gaer, Crickhowell, Monmouth, Gilwern, Abergavenny, Merthyr Tydfil, Tredegar, Ebbw Vale, Blaenavon, Raglan, GLOUCESTER-SHIRE, Lydney, Aberdare, Rhymney, Blaina, Trelleck, Abertillery, Abersychan, Tintern Parva, Mountain Ash, Bargoed, Pontypool, Usk, Treharris, Blackwood, GWENT, Tonypandy, Porth, Newbridge, Cwmbran, Chepstow, Pontypridd, Abercarn, Thornbury, Risca, Caerleon, Bedwas, Caldicot, Caerphilly, Newport, GLAMORGAN, Llantrisant, Avonmouth, Patchway, Whitchurch, St Mellons, Portishead, Cowbridge, CARDIFF, Clevedon, Bristol, Dinas Powys, Penarth, Cardiff, Barry, SOMERSET, BRISTOL AREA & S. GLOS., Rhoose, Yatton, Bristol

Scale: 0 — 10 kilometres / 0 — 5 miles
© Global Mapping / XYZ Maps

VOLUNTEERS

County Organiser
Debbie Field
01873 832752 / 07885 195304
wenalltisaf@gmail.com

County Treasurer
David Warren
01873 880031
david.warren@ngs.org.uk

Publicity
Penny Reeves
01873 880355
penny.reeves@ngs.org.uk

Social Media
Roger Lloyd
01873 880030
droger.lloyd@btinternet.com

Booklet Co-Ordinator
Veronica Ruth
07967 157806 / 01873 859757
veronica.ruth@ngs.org.uk

Assistant County Organiser
Suzanne George
01443 837708
philandsuzannegeorge@gmail.com

Tim Haynes
07738 236899
tim.haynes@hotmail.co.uk

Jenny Lloyd
01873 880030 / 07850 949209
jenny.lloyd@ngs.org.uk

Veronica Ruth
(as above)

📘 @gwentngs
✖ @GwentNGS
📷 @gwentngs

OPENING DATES

All entries subject to change.
For latest information check
www.ngs.org.uk

Map locator numbers are
shown to the right of each
garden name.

February

Snowdrop Openings

Saturday 10th
Bryngwyn Manor   3

Sunday 11th
Bryngwyn Manor   3

March

Sunday 24th
Llanover   14

Friday 29th
Bryngwyn Manor   3

Sunday 31st
The Old Vicarage   20

April

Saturday 20th
Longhouse Farm   16

Sunday 21st
Longhouse Farm   16

Saturday 27th
Glebe House   6
Park House   21

Sunday 28th
Glebe House   6

May

Sunday 5th
High Glanau Manor   10

Sunday 19th
Monmouth Gardens   18

Saturday 25th
Hillcrest   12

Sunday 26th
Baileau   1
Hillcrest   12

Monday 27th
Hillcrest   12

June

Sunday 2nd
Wenallt Isaf   26

Tuesday 4th
◆ Wyndcliffe Court   27

Sunday 9th
Long Owl Barn   15

Friday 14th
NEW Chapel Gardens   5

Saturday 15th
NEW Chapel Gardens   5

Sunday 16th
Glen Trothy   7
Highfield Farm   11

Saturday 22nd
Usk Open Gardens   25

Sunday 23rd
Bryngwyn Manor   3
Mione   17
Usk Open Gardens   25

Saturday 29th
NEW Little Caerlicyn   13

Sunday 30th
NEW Little Caerlicyn   13
Mione   17

July

Sunday 7th
NEW The Caerphilly Miners
  Community Centre - Climate
  Change Garden   4
Hillcrest   12
Mione   17

Sunday 14th
The Growing Space Garden   8
Highfield Farm   11

Saturday 20th
14 Gwerthonor Lane   9

Sunday 21st
14 Gwerthonor Lane   9

August

Sunday 4th
Hillcrest   12

Sunday 11th
Highfield Farm   11

Sunday 18th
NEW Neuadd Stone Barn 19

Sunday 25th
Wenallt Isaf 26

September

Sunday 1st
Hillcrest 12

Sunday 8th
Highfield Farm 11

Sunday 29th
NEW Ty Isaf Farm 24

By Arrangement

Arrange a personalised garden visit with your club, or group of friends, on a date to suit you. See individual garden entries for full details.

Birch Tree Well 2
Bryngwyn Manor 3
Highfield Farm 11
Hillcrest 12
NEW Little Caerlicyn 13
Llanover 14
Rockfield Park 22
NEW The Tump 23
Wenallt Isaf 26
Y Bwthyn 28

Highfield Farm

THE GARDENS

1 BAILEAU

Llantilio Crossenny, Abergavenny, NP7 8TA. Sue Wilson & Seb Gwyther. *Nr Llantilio Crossenny. Between Llantilio Crossenny & Treadam. Please follow the yellow NGS signs. What3words app - dislikes.piglet.views.* Sun 26 May (11-5). Adm £5, chd free. Cream teas.

A mature cottage style garden around an ancient farmhouse (not open). Packed with fruit and vegetables, the garden inc a rose walk, a crab apple walk, herbaceous borders, a circular ornamental vegetable garden and an old orchard. Activities for children and dogs welcome. Plenty of spots for a picnic. Views to Blorenge and Sugarloaf Mountains. Baked goods, light lunches, drinks and treats for sale, making creative use of abundant produce from the garden.

2 BIRCH TREE WELL

Upper Ferry Road, Penallt, Monmouth, NP25 4AN. Jill Bourchier, 01600 775327, gillian. bourchier@btinternet.com. *4m SW of Monmouth. Approx 1m from Monmouth on B4293, turn L for Penallt & Trelleck. After 2m turn L to Penallt. On entering village turn L at Xrds & follow yellow signs. Approach lanes are single track & steep.* Visits by arrangement Apr to Sept for groups of 5 to 25. Adm £5, chd free. Tea.

Situated in the heart of the Lower Wye Valley, amongst the ancient habitat of woodland, rocks and streams, these three acres can be viewed from a lookout tower. The garden features bluebells, specialist hydrangeas as well as unusual plants and trees attracting butterflies, bees and insects. An addition this year is the newly planted Reflective Garden with a brookside walk featuring many ferns. For the noble footed only (children welcome under supervision)

3 BRYNGWYN MANOR

Bryngwyn, Raglan, NP15 2JH. Peter & Louise Maunder, 01291 691485, louiseviola@live.co.uk. *2m W of Raglan. SatNav unreliable so please set for Bryngwyn Manor*

House, NP15 2JH. Take B4598 (old Abergavenny - Raglan Rd signed Clytha). Turn S between the two garden centres (opp village hall). House ¼m up lane on L. What3words: fond.haggle.like.* Sat 10, Sun 11 Feb, Fri 29 Mar (11-4). Adm £5, chd free. Pre-booking essential, please visit www.ngs.org.uk for information & booking. Home-made teas. Sun 23 June (11-5). Adm £6, chd free. Cream teas. Visits also by arrangement 20 Jan to 20 July for groups of 12+. Variety of refreshments available. Price dependent on options.

A relaxed three acre garden featuring snowdrops, daffodil walk, mature trees, walled parterre garden, mixed borders, lawns, ponds and shrubbery. Family friendly afternoon out, with children's activities, loads of space to run about, and scrumptious teas. All the garden can be accessed without using the steps, however, ground is uneven and mainly grass paths. Please contact owner with any concerns.

4 NEW THE CAERPHILLY MINERS COMMUNITY CENTRE - CLIMATE CHANGE GARDEN

Watford Road, Caerphilly, CF83 1BJ. Caerphilly Miners Centre for the Community, www. caerphillyminerscentre.co.uk. *Use 'Caerphilly Miners Centre' for Google maps rather than postcode or What3words app - lakes.pushy. bill. From Ystrad Mynach: A469 to Caerphilly follow A468/A469 then 1st exit onto St Cenydd Rd. From Newport M4: Junc 32 take A470 exit Cardiff(N)/Merthyr Tydfil A468 then A469 turn onto Watford Rd.* Sun 7 July (11-4). Adm £4, chd free. Home-made teas.

A climate change garden promoting carbon reduction, biodiversity, health and wellbeing. The front garden has a mini stumpery, wildlife pond planted to encourage sustainability in all weathers and attract local fauna. The aim is a beautiful palette of year-round colour which inc a clematis covered gazebo, cut flower and wildflower borders. A drought resistant rear garden planted with grasses and perennials is being created. Wheelchair accessible paths at top of the front garden. Accessible slope to the rear garden.

GROUP OPENING

5 NEW CHAPEL GARDENS

Chapel Farm House, Pentre Road, Abergavenny, NP7 7BE. Mary Barkham and Gary Smith. *Access via Avenue Rd, Abergavenny. Please follow signs to individual gardens.* Fri 14 June (3-8); Sat 15 June (10-4). Combined adm £8, chd free. Pre-booking essential, please visit www.ngs.org.uk for information & booking. Home-made teas. Refreshments only served at Chapel Farm House.

NEW THE CHAIN, 90 CHAPEL ROAD

Sarah Price. www.sarahpricelandscapes.com.

NEW CHAPEL FARMHOUSE

Mary Barkham and Gary Smith, 07799 540380, marymbarkham@hotmail.com, www.airbnb.co.uk/rooms/50408422.

NEW ROCK VILLA

Veronica Ruth and Rod Cunningham.

These gardens are opening for the first time as Chapel Gardens and have been developed with the same ethos of encouraging wildlife and pollinators. The Chain: A two acre Victorian walled garden created by award winning garden designer, Sarah Price. With a wide range of habitats for wildlife to thrive, this garden is a must see. It has been gardened experimentally over the last nine years and was created especially for the beauty of nature and wildlife. Chapel Farm House: A stunning 1½ acre garden with an ancient orchard and wildlife pond. A wildflower meadow and new prairie garden are spectacular. Chapel Farm House also has formal front and courtyard gardens. Rock Villa: A town garden encircling the house, developed over 25 years, this garden is organically cultivated. With purple beech hedges, roses and clematis, this garden is the very essence of a town garden. Some areas may not be accessible for those with mobility difficulties, such as the Secret Garden at The Chain.

6 GLEBE HOUSE

Llanvair Kilgeddin, Abergavenny, NP7 9BE. Mr & Mrs Murray Kerr.
Midway between Abergavenny (5m) & Usk (5m) on B4598. **Sat 27, Sun 28 Apr (2-6). Adm £6, chd free. Home-made teas.**
Borders bursting with spring colour inc tulips, Narcissi and Camassias. South facing terrace with wisteria and honeysuckle, decorative vegetable garden and orchard densely underplanted with succession of bulbs. Some topiary and formal hedging in $1\frac{1}{2}$ acre garden in wonderful setting of Usk valley AONB. St Mary's church, Llanfair Kilgeddin will also be open to view famous Victorian scraffito murals. Some gravel and gently sloping lawns.

7 GLEN TROTHY

Llanvetherine, Abergavenny, NP7 8RB. Mr & Mrs Ben Herbert.
5m NE of Abergavenny. 6m from Abergavenny off B4521 (Old Ross Rd). **Sun 16 June (2-6). Adm £8, chd £4. Home-made teas.**
Victorian house (not open) in the Scottish Baronial style, set in mature parkland with a small pinetum and arboretum. The walled garden has been renovated over the past 12 years, incorporating blue and white herbaceous borders, a rose garden and ornamental vegetable garden with pear tunnel as well as an Italianate loggia.

8 THE GROWING SPACE GARDEN

Mardy Park Resource Centre, Hereford Road, Mardy, Abergavenny, NP7 6HU. Jim Quinn.
The rear of Mardy Park Resource Centre. 1.4m N of centre of Abergavenny, on the Hereford Rd opp the Crown & Sceptre public house. **Sun 14 July (10-4). Adm £5, chd free. Home-made teas. Coffee and homemade cakes available.**
The gardens are laid out around disabled access paths, herbaceous borders, a prairie-style border, and fruit and veg beds. There is also a tropical border and large raised beds. We have two polytunnels and a small craft and carpentry workshop. The gardens are tended by a hard working team of volunteers of mixed ability and ages from 18 to 96. Adjoining parkland is perfect for a picnic. Good access for wheelchair users. There is

also a hand rail. The garden is on a slight slope.

9 14 GWERTHONOR LANE

Gilfach, Bargoed, CF81 8JT. Suzanne & Philip George. *8m N of Caerphilly. A469 to Bargoed, through the T-lights next to sch then L filter lane at next T-lights onto Cardiff Rd. First L into Gwerthonor Rd, 4th R into Gwerthonor Ln.* **Sat 20, Sun 21 July (11-6). Adm £5, chd free. Light refreshments.**
The garden has a beautiful panoramic view of the Rhymney Valley. A real plantswoman's garden with over 800 varieties of perennials, annuals, bulbs, shrubs and trees. There are numerous rare, unusual and tropical plants combined with traditional and well loved favourites (many available for sale). A pond with a small waterfall adds to the tranquil feel of the garden.

10 HIGH GLANAU MANOR

Lydart, Monmouth, NP25 4AD. Mr & Mrs Hilary Gerrish, 01600 860005, helenagerrish@gmail.com, www.highglanaugardens.com. *4m SW of Monmouth. Situated on B4293 between Monmouth & Chepstow. Turn R into private road, $\frac{1}{4}$m after Craig-y-Dorth turn on B4293.* **Sun 5 May (2-5.30). Adm £6, chd free. Home-made teas.**
Listed Arts and Crafts garden laid out by H Avray Tipping 100 years ago. Original features inc impressive stone terraces with far reaching views over the Vale of Usk to Blorenge, Skirrid, Sugar Loaf and Brecon Beacons. Pergola, herbaceous borders, Edwardian glasshouse, rhododendrons, azaleas, tulips, orchard with wildflowers. Originally open for the NGS in 1927. Garden guidebook by owner, Helena Gerrish, available to purchase. Gardens lovers cottage to rent.

11 HIGHFIELD FARM

Penperlleni, Goytre, NP4 0AA. Dr Roger & Mrs Jenny Lloyd, 01873 880030, jenny.plants@btinternet.com, www.instagram.com/davidrogerlloyd. *4m W of Usk, 6m S of Abergavenny. Turn off the A4042 at Goytre Arms, over railway bridge, bear L. Garden $\frac{1}{2}$m on R. From Usk off B4598, turn L after chain Bridge, then L at Xrds. Garden 1m on L.*

Sun 16 June, Sun 14 July, Sun 11 Aug, Sun 8 Sept (12-4). Adm £7, chd free. Home-made teas. Visits also by arrangement May to Sept for groups of 5 to 40.
Highfield Farm Garden is a celebration of plants. There are over 1400 cultivars, with many rarities, densely planted over three acres and set within the majestic Monmouthshire landscape. It offers an exuberant display across the seasons, providing an intimate, immersive experience with this diverse array of herbaceous, shrubs and trees. Huge sale of plants from the garden. Live music. Art sale. Regional Winner, The English Garden Magazine's The Nation's Favourite Gardens 2023 Access to almost all garden without steps.

12 HILLCREST

Waunborfa Road, Cefn Fforest, Blackwood, NP12 3LB. Mr M O'Leary, 01443 837029, olearymichael18@gmail.com. *3m W of Newbridge. B4254/A469 at T/L head to B'wood. At Xrd take lane ahead, 1st on L at top of hill. A4048/B4251 cross Chartist Bridge, 2nd exit on next 2 r'abouts. End of road turn L & immed R onto Waunborfa. 400m on R.* **Sat 25, Sun 26, Mon 27 May (11-6); Sun 7 July (11-5). Light refreshments. Sun 4 Aug, Sun 1 Sept (11-5). Adm £5, chd free. Visits also by arrangement Apr to Sept.**
A cascade of secluded gardens of distinct character over $1\frac{1}{2}$ acres with a naturalistic approach in some areas. Magnificent, unusual trees, interesting shrubs, perennials and annuals. Choices at every turn, visitors are well rewarded as hidden delights and surprises are revealed. Well placed seats encourage a relaxed pace to fully appreciate the garden's treasures. Tulips in April, glorious blooms of the Chilean firebushes, handkerchief tree and Cornuses in May and many trees in their autumnal splendour. Lowest parts of garden not accessible to wheelchairs.

13 NEW LITTLE CAERLICYN

Caerlicyn Lane, Langstone, Newport, NP18 2JZ. Mrs Katharine Notley, 07793 122936, lc.flowerfarm@gmail.com. *Off the A48 from Newport towards Penhow/Chepstow. Just over 2m from the Coldra r'about (M4 junc 24). Please follow yellow signs up Caerlicken Ln.* **Sat 29, Sun 30 June (10-4.30).**

Adm £5, chd free. Home-made teas. Visits also by arrangement May to Oct for groups of 6 to 15. Adm inc guided tour and homemade teas.

Small flower farm and gardens around renovated Tudor cottage and barn. Three distinct areas with a fourth, woodland walk, in development. Perennials, roses, grape vines and wildflower areas and an ancient mulberry tree plus bees. Protecting and promoting of wildlife is central to this organically developed garden whose owners follow a no dig approach. Amazing views over the Severn Estuary.

14 LLANOVER

Abergavenny, NP7 9EF. Mr & Mrs M R Murray, 07753 423635, elizabeth@llanover.com, www.llanovergarden.co.uk. *4m S of Abergavenny, 15m N of Newport, 20m SW Hereford. On A4042 between Abergavenny & Goytre. At Llanover, turn into the driveway with tall black gates opp the pull-in bus stop.* Sun 24 Mar (2-5). Adm £8, chd free. Home-made teas. Visits also by arrangement May to Oct.

Benjamin Waddington, the direct ancestor of the current owners, purchased the house and land in 1792. Subsequently he created a series of ponds, cascades and rills which form the backbone of the 15 acre garden as the stream winds its way from its source in the Black Mountains to the River Usk. There are herbaceous borders, a drive lined with Narcissi, spring bulbs, wildflowers, a water garden, champion trees and two arboreta. The house (not open) is the birthplace of Augusta Waddington, Lady Llanover, C19 patriot, supporter of the Welsh language and traditions. Delicious home made cakes cooked by fundraisers for Llanover Church. Gravel and grass paths and lawns. No disabled WC.

15 LONG OWL BARN

Coedypaen, Pontypool, NP4 0TB. Mike & Tina Booth, www. instagram.com/michaelbooth1963. *2m W of Usk, 1m from Llandegveth reservoir. Take turning to Coed-y-paen from Llanbadoc or Llangybi then follow yellow signs. From Cwmbran Crematorium, take Tre-Herbert lane towards Llangybi, then L turn to Coed-y-Paen.*

Sun 9 June (11-5). Adm £5, chd free. Light refreshments.

In a rural setting with extensive views, there are meandering paths, colourful borders and wildlife areas with plenty to explore in a little over an acre. Small orchard, ponds, a vegetable plot and greenhouse. Extensive perennial beds full of colour. Sloping ground makes some areas inaccessible

16 LONGHOUSE FARM

Penrhos, Raglan, NP15 2DE. Mr & Mrs M H C Anderson. *Midway between Monmouth & Abergavenny. 4m from Raglan. Off Old Raglan/ Abergavenny rd signed Clytha. At Bryngwyn/Great Oak Xrds turn towards Great Oak - follow yellow NGS signs from red phone box down narrow lane.* Sat 20, Sun 21 Apr (2-5.30). Adm £6, chd free. Home-made teas.

Spacious two acre country garden, colourful borders, interesting trees, shrubs, productive vegetable garden, natural pond, house and barns covered with roses and vines. A roundabout with un-named ancient Perry Pear tree surrounded by bulbs

and seasonal plants. Woodland walk around a series of spring fed ponds with wonderful views of hidden parts of Monmouthshire.

17 MIONE

Old Hereford Road, Llanvihangel Crucorney, Abergavenny, NP7 7LB. Yvonne & John O'Neil. *5m N of Abergavenny. From Abergavenny take A465 to Hereford. Mione is ½m on L - signed Pantygelli.* Sun 23, Sun 30 June, Sun 7 July (10.30-5). Adm £5, chd free. Home-made teas.

Beautiful garden with a wide variety of established plants, many rare and unusual. Pergola with climbing roses and clematis. Wildlife pond with many newts, insects and frogs. Numerous containers with diverse range of planting. Several seating areas, each with a different atmosphere. Enjoy our new benches in a secret hideaway under the pergola. Lovely home-made cakes, biscuits and scones to be enjoyed sitting in the garden or pretty summerhouse.

The Chain, 90 Chapel Road, Chapel Gardens

Baileau

GROUP OPENING

18 MONMOUTH GARDENS
Worcester Street, Monmouth,
NP25 3DF. *Central Monmouth.
Parking at Glendower St (NP25 3DF)
or Monnow St (NP25 3EN). Tickets
available at each garden. Maps
produced to aid visitors. Please
follow signage throughout Monmouth
the to gardens.* **Sun 19 May (11.30-
5.30). Combined adm £10, chd
free. Home-made teas at North
Parade House and St Johns.**

**NEW CORNWALL HOUSE, 58
MONNOW ST**
Jane Harvey and John Wheelock,
www.historichouses.org/house/
cornwall-house/visit/.

NEW 11 THE GARDENS
Mrs Cheryl Cummings, www.
cherylcummingswildgardenwriting.
co.uk/.
D

MANSARD HOUSE
NP25 3HW. Richard & Liz Wills.

THE NELSON GARDEN
Blestium Street,
Monmouth, NP25 3ER.
www.nelsongarden.org.uk.

NORTH PARADE HOUSE
NP25 3PB. Tim Haynes & Lisa
O'Neill.

ST JOHNS
NP25 3DG. Simon & Hilary
Hargreaves.

Six very different town gardens open
under the banner of Monmouth Gardens.
The Nelson Garden dates back to
Roman times, and as the name suggests
has links with Lord Nelson. St Johns,
in Glendower St is a charming walled
garden which has undergone extensive
restoration with a sunken central lawn
and deep herbaceous borders. Entrance
to both these gardens is via Chippenham
Fields. Cornwall House opens with the
group for the first time this year. The
beautiful walled garden and productive
kitchen garden date from the C17.
North Parade House is a hidden gem
with a surprisingly large and secluded
walled garden with mature specimen
trees, herbaceous borders and a kitchen
garden. Another new garden belongs
to garden designer, Cheryl Cummings.
She is re-wilding her garden creating
a tranquil space for visitors. Mansard
House, Vine Acre has spectacular
views of the Black Mountains from this
contemporary garden which features an
architectural planting scheme and striking
sculpture. Range of different gardening
styles in town gardens. Plant sales at the
Nelson Garden. Some gardens may not
be accessed by wheelchair users due to
steps at the entrances.
&. 🐕 ❀ ☕)))

19 NEW NEUADD STONE BARN
Church Road, Gilwern,
Abergavenny, NP7 0HF.
Mrs Katherine Franklin,
www.brambleandbombus.co.uk.
*Out of Gilwern past Llanelly Church.
From the middle of Gilwern, follow
Church Rd, past the Church on
the R and follow the yellow signs.
What3words app - compress.
envelope.sparrows.* **Sun 18 Aug
(11-5). Adm £4, chd free. Home-
made teas.**
Recently established flower farm
which is part of a working farm. The
site is in an Area of Outstanding
Natural Beauty and has breathtaking
views of the three hills surrounding
Abergavenny. A huge array of
perennial and annual flowers are
grown for cutting and sale.
❀ ☕)))

20 THE OLD VICARAGE
Penrhos, Raglan, Usk, NP15 2LE.
Mrs Georgina Herrmann. *3m N of
Raglan. From A449 take Raglan exit,
join A40 & move immed into R lane
& turn R across dual carriageway.
Follow yellow NGS signs.* **Sun 31
Mar (2-5.30). Adm £5, chd free.
Light refreshments.**
Designed by Welsh architect, George
Mair, this unusual Victorian vicarage
(1867, not open) is set in rolling
countryside and is surrounded by
a traditional garden. Lovely all year
but especially in spring with a variety
of trees, shrubs and spring bulbs,
a parterre with a charming gazebo,
kitchen garden, wildlife areas and
ponds make this a garden, always
changing, well worth a visit.
❀ ☕)))

21 PARK HOUSE
School Lane, Itton, Chepstow,
NP16 6BZ. Professor Bruce
& Dr Cynthia Matthews. *Itton
Monmouthshire. From M48 take
A466 Tintern. At 2nd r'about turn L
B4293 After blue sign Itton turn R
Park House is at end of lane. Parking
200m before house. From Devauden
B4293 1st L in Itton.* **Sat 27 Apr
(10-5). Adm £5, chd free.**
Approx one acre garden with large
vegetable areas and many mature
trees, rhododendrons, azaleas,
camellias in a woodland setting.
Bordering on Chepstow Park Wood.
Magnificent views over open country.
🐕)))

22 ROCKFIELD PARK

Rockfield, Monmouth, NP25 5QB.
Mark & Melanie Molyneux,
07803 952027,
melmolyneux@yahoo.co.uk. *On
arriving in Rockfield village from
Monmouth, turn R by phone box. After
approx 400yds, church on L. Entrance
to Rockfield Park on R, opp church,
via private bridge over river.* **Visits
by arrangement Feb to July for
groups of 8+. Limited in 2024 due
to groundworks. Adm £7, chd free.
Home-made teas on the terrace.**
Rockfield Park dates from C17
and is situated in the heart of the
Monmouthshire countryside on the
banks of the River Monnow. The
extensive grounds comprise formal
gardens, meadows and orchard,
complemented by riverside and
woodland walks. Possible to picnic on
riverside walks. Main part of gardens
can be accessed by wheelchair but
not steep garden leading down to river.

23 NEW THE TUMP

Penallt, Monmouth, NP25 4AQ.
Mr Doug and Mrs Sue Hilton,
07899 995822,
bucklandlake@hotmail.com. *3m S
of Monmouth Town. The postcode
brings you to the gate. There is a
bus stop there too. From A40 take
B4293 at 3.5m turn L for Narth and
Whitebrook. follow signs L at .65m.
Same turn is 1.2m N of Trellech on
B4293 on R.* **Visits by arrangement
in June for groups of 5 to 12.
Adm £5, chd free. Home-made
teas. Cakes also available.**
Nine acres of mixed habitat,
sloping meadows surrounded by
mature trees, views, mown paths,
orchard areas, two large ponds,
stream, stone circle and exhibition
of wildlife and wildflower paintings
in art studio. Three years into
rewilding from grazing land to triple
gold award winning gardening for
wildlife. Emphasising the importance
of building up the understory of
grassland and mixed habitat.

24 NEW TY ISAF FARM

Pandy Mawr Road, Bedwas,
Caerphilly, CF83 8EQ. Mrs Linda
Davies, 07429 529161. *3m N of the
centre of Caerphilly. From A468 at
Caerphilly head towards Bedwas and
then Pandy-Mawr Road and follow
NGS yellow signs. The postcode
will take SatNav users to the area,
please then follow the NGS yellow
signs.* **Sun 29 Sept (11-5). Adm £5,
chd free. Light refreshments.**
This garden, on a working farm,
surrounds the Grade II listed sub-
medieval farmhouse and barn. The
garden is being revitalised with the
renovation of beds and development
of areas such as the wildlife pond. The
ancient yew is a magnificent feature as
are the stone walls surrounding areas
of the garden. A naturalistic approach
to planting. Wonderful autumn colour
and far reaching views.

GROUP OPENING

25 USK OPEN GARDENS

Maryport Street, Usk, NP15 1BH.
*Main car park postcode is NP15
1AD. From M4 J24 take A449 for
8m N to Usk exit. Signposts to free
parking around town. Blue badge
parking in main car parks. Map of
gardens provided with ticket.* **Sat
22, Sun 23 June (10-5). Combined
adm £10, chd free. Donation to
local charities.**
Usk's floral public displays are a
wonderful backdrop to the gardens.
Around ten private gardens opening.
Gardeners' Market with interesting
plants. Lovely day out for all the
family with lots of places to eat and
drink inc places to picnic. Wheelchair
accessible gardens and gardens
allowing well-behaved dogs on leads
noted on passport/map available from
the ticket desks at the free car park at
Usk Memorial Hall (NP15 1AD).

26 WENALLT ISAF

Twyn Wenallt, Gilwern,
Abergavenny, NP7 0HP. Tim
& Debbie Field, 07885195304,
wenalltisaf@gmail.com. *3m W of
Abergavenny. Between Abergavenny
& Brynmawr. Leave the A465 at
Gilwern & follow yellow NGS signs
through the village. Do not follow
SatNav. What3words app - sensibly.
gone.connects.* **Sun 2 June, Sun
25 Aug (2-6). Adm £6, chd free.
Home-made teas. Visits also by
arrangement June to Sept for
groups of 8+.**
A hidden gem of nearly three acres
owner designed in sympathy with
its surroundings and the challenges
of being 650ft up on a north facing
hillside. Far reaching views of the
magnificent Black Mountains, mature
trees, Rhododendrons, Viburnum,
spectacular hydrangeas, herbaceous
borders, vegetable garden, small
polytunnel, orchard, chickens, bees.
Child friendly with plenty of space to
run about.

27 ♦ WYNDCLIFFE COURT

St Arvans, NP16 6EY. Mr & Mrs
Anthony Clay, 07710 138972,
sarah@wyndcliffecourt.com,
www.wyndcliffecourt.com. *3m
N of Chepstow. Off A466, turn at
Wyndcliffe signpost coming from
the Chepstow direction.* **For NGS:
Tue 4 June (2-5). Adm £10, chd
free. Pre-booking essential,
please visit www.ngs.org.uk for
information & booking. Home-
made teas. Refreshments inc in
adm. For other opening times and
information, please phone, email or
visit garden website.**
Exceptional, unaltered garden
designed by H. Avray Tipping in 1922.
Arts and Crafts 'Italianate' style. Stone
summerhouse, terracing and ponds.
Yew hedging and topiary, sunken
garden, rose garden, bowling green
and woodland. Walled garden with
new in 2023 Charles III coronation
Renaissance mural and vine shaded
arbour. Rose garden designed by
Sarah Price.

28 Y BWTHYN

Pencroesoped, Llanover,
Abergavenny, NP7 9EL. Jacqui
& David Warren, 01873 880031,
warrens.ybwthyn@gmail.com.
*6m S of Abergavenny, just outside
Llanover. Detailed directions
provided ahead of visit.* **Visits by
arrangement 22 July to 30 Aug
for groups of 8 to 30. We have
parking on grass for up to 12 cars
so car-sharing is recommended.
Home-made teas.**
There's plenty to see in this beautifully
varied 1½ acre garden, with
sweeping vistas across the garden
and the surrounding countryside.
Mixed and late summer borders,
gravel garden, lawns, pond and bog
garden, ornamental kitchen garden
and greenhouse, meadow areas
with mown paths and a magnificent
veteran oak. Small house history
and art exhibitions too. Close to the
Monmouthshire and Brecon Canal.
Most garden routes are step-free.
Some steep grass slopes and narrow
gravel paths. Sorry, no wheelchair
access to the WC.

GWYNEDD & ANGLESEY
GWYNEDD A MÔN

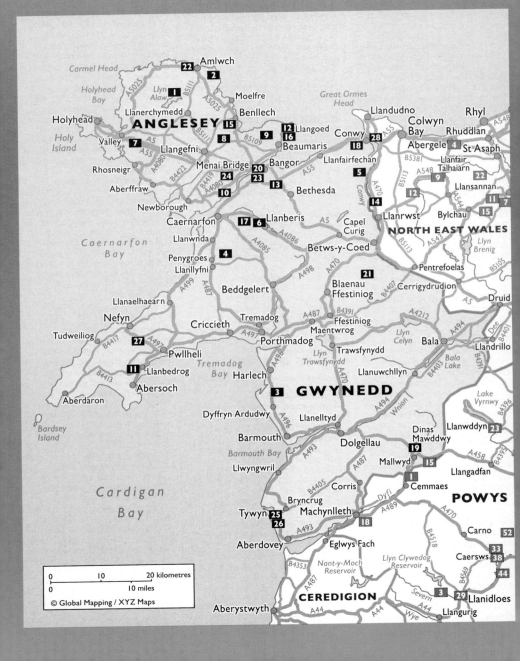

VOLUNTEERS

County Organiser
Kay Laurie
07971 083361
kay.laurie@ngs.org.uk

County Treasurer
Chris Clark
07760 174154
chris.clark@ngs.org.uk

Publicity
Position vacant

Booklet Co-Ordinator
Heather Broughton
07747 737237
heather.broughton@ngs.org.uk

Photographer
Gary Phillips
07742 892743
gary.phillips@ngs.org.uk

Assistant County Organisers
Hazel Bond
07378 844295
hazelcaenewydd@gmail.com

Janet Jones
01758 740296
janetcoron@hotmail.co.uk

Delia Lanceley
01286 650517
delia@lanceley.com

f @gwyneddandangleseyngs
o @ngs.gwyneddandanglesey

OPENING DATES

All entries subject to change. For latest information check www.ngs.org.uk
Map locator numbers are shown to the right of each garden name.

April

Wednesday 24th
◆ Plas Cadnant Hidden Gardens ... 20

Sunday 28th
Cae Newydd ... 1
Maenan Hall ... 14

May

Saturday 4th
Llanidan Hall ... 10

Sunday 5th
NEW Caswallon ... 2
Sunningdale ... 22

Saturday 11th
NEW Mynydd, Cors Goch ... 15

Saturday 18th
NEW Tyn Y Pant ... 27

Sunday 19th
◆ Gardd y Coleg ... 4
NEW Tyn Y Pant ... 27

Saturday 25th
Glan Llyn ... 6

Sunday 26th
Gwaelod Mawr ... 7
Ty Cadfan Sant ... 25

June

Saturday 1st
Sunningdale ... 22

Sunday 2nd
Cae Newydd ... 1

Sunday 16th
NEW Cyplau ... 3
◆ Pensychnant ... 18

Saturday 22nd
Llanidan Hall ... 10
NEW Mynydd, Cors Goch ... 15

Sunday 23rd
Pant Ifan ... 17

Saturday 29th
NEW Caswallon ... 2
Llwydiarth ... 11

Sunday 30th
Llwydiarth ... 11

July

Saturday 6th
Llanidan Hall ... 10
NEW Ty Celyn ... 26

Saturday 13th
NEW Llanddona Village Gardens ... 9

Sunday 14th
◆ Pensychnant ... 18

Sunday 21st
Trefnant Bach ... 24

August

Sunday 4th
Maenan Hall ... 14

Sunday 18th
41 Victoria Drive ... 28

Saturday 31st
Trefnant Bach ... 24

September

Sunday 1st
NEW Llwyn Onn ... 12
NEW The Old School ... 16

Saturday 7th
NEW ◆ Plannwch y Plas ... 19

Saturday 14th
Treborth Botanic Garden, Bangor University ... 23

Sunday 15th
NEW Gwenfro Uchaf ... 8

Sunday 22nd
◆ Gardd y Coleg ... 4

By Arrangement

Arrange a personalised garden visit with your club, or group of friends, on a date to suit you. See individual garden entries for full details.

Gilfach ... 5
Llwydiarth ... 11
Llys-y-Gwynt ... 13
NEW Plasglasgwm ... 21
Ty Cadfan Sant ... 25
NEW Tyn Y Pant ... 27

THE GARDENS

1 CAE NEWYDD
Rhosgoch, Anglesey, LL66 0BG.
Hazel & Nigel Bond. *3m SW of Amlwch. A5025 from Benllech to Amlwch, follow signs for leisure centre & Lastra Farm. Follow yellow NGS signs (approx 3m), car park on L.* **Sun 28 Apr, Sun 2 June (11-4). Adm £5, chd free. Light refreshments.**
An informal country garden of 2½ acres which blends seamlessly into the open landscape with stunning views of Snowdonia and Llyn Alaw. Variety of shrubs, trees and herbaceous areas, large wildlife pond, polytunnel, greenhouses. Collections of fuchsia, pelargonium, cacti and succulents. An emphasis on gardening for wildlife throughout the garden, lots of seating to enjoy this peaceful space. Hay meadow with cut paths, beehives, visitors are welcome to bring a picnic. Garden area closest to house suitable for wheelchairs.

2 NEW CASWALLON
Llaneilian, Amlwch, LL68 9NN.
Julian & Gillian Sandbach. *Mynydd Eilian. From the A5025 take the turning to Pengorffwysfa near Amlwch, the garden will be signed from this village. It is a single track lane.* **Sun 5 May, Sat 29 June (10-4.30). Adm £5, chd free. Home-made teas.**
In 2018 we bought Caswallon, house and garden in complete need of renovation. House now finished our energy is dedicated to restoring the large historic gardens. Under years of undergrowth we have discovered formal gardens, small woodland dells, a walled garden, an ancient well, meandering paths, crumbling drystone walls, steps carved into bedrock, everyday is an adventure, always more to discover.

3 NEW CYPLAU
Llanbedr, LL45 2ND.
Ms Jacqueline Gilleland. *7m NW Barmouth. From Barmouth A496 direct to Llanbedr. From Harlech 3m on A496 to Llanbedr.* **Sun 16 June (12-4.30). Adm £4, chd free. Cream teas.**
A 0.7 acre intensely planted hillside garden created over 23 years.

Twisting pathways with steps lead to small garden areas. Inc topiary, cloud pruned yew, tsunami heather hedge, box and *Ilex crenata*. Multi stemmed and shaped shrubs, ornaments and sculptures. Superb sea views in hillside garden. Vegetable garden with fruits. This garden is a way of living to encourage nature and enjoy peace. Arts and crafts for sale. Relax and listen to choir in the garden.

4 ♦ GARDD Y COLEG
Carmel, LL54 7RL. Pwyllgor Pentref Carmel Village Committee. *Garden at Carmel village centre. Parking on site.* **For NGS: Sun 19 May, Sun 22 Sept (12-4.30). Adm £3, chd free. Tea. For other opening times and information, please visit garden website.**
Approx ½ acre featuring raised beds planted with ornamental and native plants mulched with local slate. Benches and picnic area, wide pathways suitable for wheelchairs. Spectacular views. Garden created and maintained by volunteers. Development of the garden is ongoing. Ramped access for wheelchair users.

5 GILFACH
Rowen, Conwy, LL32 8TS.
James & Isoline Greenhalgh, 01492 650216, isolinegreenhalgh@btinternet.com. *4m S of Conwy. At Xrds 100yds E of Rowen S towards Llanrwst, past Rowen Sch on L, turn up 2nd drive on L.* **Visits by arrangement May to Aug. Adm £4, chd free. Refreshments to be discussed when booking.**
An acre of country garden on south facing slope with magnificent views of the River Conwy and mountains; set in 35 acres of farm and woodland. Collection of mature shrubs is added to yearly; woodland garden, herbaceous border and small pool. Spectacular panoramic view of the Conwy Valley and the mountain range of the Carneddau. Classic cars. Large coaches can park at bottom of steep drive.

6 GLAN LLYN
Llanberis, Caernarfon, LL55 4EL.
Mr Bob Stevens. *On A4086, ½m from Llanberis village. Next door to the Galty-Glyn Hotel (Pizza & Pint Restaurant) opp DMM factory.*

Sat 25 May (10-6). Adm £5, chd free. Light refreshments.
A three acre woodland edge garden inc two acres of woodland, wildlife ponds, stream, wildflower area, raised sphagnum bog garden, two green roofs, three glasshouses for cacti and succulents, Australasian and South African beds, sand bed, many unusual ferns, shrubs and herbaceous perennials. The garden is on fairly steep sloping ground, no wheelchair access to the woodland.

7 GWAELOD MAWR
Caergeiliog, Anglesey, LL65 3YL.
Tricia Coates. *6m E of Holyhead. ½m E of Caergeiliog. From A55 J4. r'about 2nd exit signed Caergeiliog. 300yds, Gwaelod Mawr is 1st house on L.* **Sun 26 May (11-4). Adm £5, chd free. Home-made teas.**
A two acre garden created by owner over 30 years with lake, large rock outcrops and palm tree area. Spanish style patio and wonderful laburnum arch in May which leads to sunken garden and wooden bridge over lily pond with fountain and waterfall. Peaceful Chinese orientated garden offering contemplation. Separate Koi carp pond. Abundant seating throughout. Garden is mainly flat, with gravel and stone paths. No wheelchair access to sunken lily pond area.

8 NEW GWENFRO UCHAF
Lon Gwenfro, Talwrn, Llangefni, LL77 8JD. Ms Karen Hillyer. *4m NE from Llangefni towards Llanbedrgoch and Red Wharf Bay. From Bridge take A5025 towards Amlwch; go through Pentraeth, turn L to Llanbedrgoch after layby; Take 2nd L onto Lon Gwenfro, follow yellow ngs signs 1m to field car park, 400 metres walk to garden.* **Sun 15 Sept (11-5). Adm £5, chd free. Light refreshments. Homemade soup, teas and cakes using garden produce. Gluten and dairy free available.**
2½ acres of formal and informal areas with encroaching nature and great views; wild meadow walks, trees, hedgerows, stream and ducks; a kitchen garden (veg, soft fruit), lean-to greenhouse, orchard and apiary, divided by hedges and stonewall terracing with steps. All paths are mown, with one slate path down slope to house and lawn, teas, seating and firepit. Food and

nature focus not flowers. A collection of 15 apple and pear tree varieties. Honey from the apiary for sale and possibly other garden produce (herbs, juice, fruit) depending on availability. Wheelchair access limited: only house and shed areas have hard pathways (slate gravel). Lawn and grassland which may prove difficult.

GROUP OPENING

9 NEW LLANDDONA VILLAGE GARDENS

Beaumaris, LL58 8TU. Gardens of Llanddona Residents. *3m from Beaumaris take B5109 for 1m turn R at T junc. 2 m to Llanddona. Follow signs for parking in village.* Sat 13 July (11-4). Combined adm £5, chd free. Home-made teas at Owain Glyndwr Pub. Pre-booking for lunch advised. 01248 810710.

Llanddona, one of the highest villages in Anglesey sits between Red Wharf Bay and the Menai Strait. Village garden owners welcome you to visit their Open Gardens. Some gardens need shelter from strong winds but it's a sunny location, with spectacular outlooks. The gardens often have rocky outcrops, but many plants do well. Agapanthus particularly enjoy the climate. A variety of gardens, some small and some quite large will be open with different gardening styles and favourite plants. You may pop in to see some carefully tended vegetables; a smallholding gardened organically with a herd of Golden Guernsey goats and lovely orchard; or a garden with a pottery studio. A map will show you where each garden is located. Most will be within a short walk. A day out with a difference for walking groups. The more accessible gardens will be shown on the map provided on the day. Dogs, if allowed, on short lead. No dogs in some gardens due to livestock.

10 LLANIDAN HALL

Brynsiencyn, LL61 6HJ. Head Gardener. *5m E of Llanfair Pwll. From LlanfairPG follow A4080 towards Brynsiencyn for 4m. After Hooton's farm shop on R take next L, follow lane to gardens.* Sat 4 May, Sat 22 June, Sat 6 July (10-4). Adm £5, chd free. Home-made teas. Donation to CAFOD.

Walled garden of 1¾ acres. Physic and herb gardens, ornamental vegetable garden, herbaceous borders, water features, spring bulb display, many varieties of old roses in June and well established summer perennials. Sheep, rabbits and hens to see. Children must be kept under supervision. Well behaved dogs on leads welcome. Llanidan Church open for viewing. Hard gravel paths and gentle slopes.

11 LLWYDIARTH

Mynytho, Pwllheli, LL53 7RW. David & Anne Mitchell, 07973 968207, anne@wishawcountrysports.com. *Mynytho, Gwynedd. Garden on main road through Mynytho village. 5½ m from Pwllheli 3½ m from Abersoch.* Sat 29, Sun 30 June (12-5). Adm £5, chd free. Home-made teas. Visits also by arrangement May to Sept for groups of 10 to 30.

Just three years ago this garden was an overgrown field, but now with hedges, trees, shrubs, grasses, perennials and roses planted, it is already developing character and interest. A large wildlife pond, filled with aquatic plants and surrounded with tons of sandstone, dug from the field itself, now makes a stunning rockery. There is a lush green Mediterranean style back yard.

12 NEW LLWYN ONN

Penmon Village, Beaumaris, LL58 8SG. Paul Richardson & Pauline Williams. *3m NE of Beaumaris. Pass Beaumaris castle on coast road. After 1.7m turn R to Penmon and follow yellow signs.* Sun 1 Sept (11-4). Combined adm with The Old School £5, chd free. Home-made teas.

The garden benefits from coastal and mountain views, and inc some three acres of deciduous woodland, originally planted by a local estate owner in the C19, mostly with beech. We have protected the remaining old trees, encouraged natural regeneration, and enriched the woodland with some plantings. The garden we created inc lawns, herbaceous borders, and a small wildlife pond.

13 LLYS-Y-GWYNT

Pentir Road, Llandygai, Bangor, LL57 4BG. Jennifer Rickards, 07799 893418, mjrickards@gmail.com. *3m S of Bangor. 300yds from Llandygai r'about at J11, A5 & A55, just off A4244. Follow signs for services (Gwasanaethau). Turn off at No Through Rd sign, 50yds beyond. Do not use SatNav.* Visits by arrangement. Adm £5, chd free. Light refreshments. Tea or coffee and biscuits.

Interesting, harmonious and very varied two acre garden inc magnificent views of Snowdonia. An exposed site inc Bronze Age burial cairn. Winding paths, varied levels planted to create shelter, year-round interest, microclimates and varied rooms. Ponds, bridge and other features use local materials and craftspeople. Wildlife encouraged, well organised compost. Good family garden with visiting peacocks. Parts of the garden are wheelchair accessible.

14 MAENAN HALL

Maenan, Llanrwst, LL26 0UL. The Hon Mr & Mrs Christopher Mclaren. *2m N of Llanrwst. On E side of A470, ¼ m S of Maenan Abbey Hotel.* Sun 28 Apr (10.30-4.30); Sun 4 Aug (10.30-5). Adm £5, chd free. Home-made teas. Donation to Ogwen Valley Mountain Rescue Organisation.

Superbly beautiful four hectares on the slopes of the Conwy Valley. Dramatic views of Snowdonia, set amongst mature hardwoods. Both the upper part, with sweeping lawns, ornamental ponds and retaining walls, and the bluebell carpeted woodland dell contain copious specimen shrubs and trees, many originating at Bodnant. Magnolias, rhododendrons, camellias, pieris, cherries and hydrangeas, amongst many others, make a breathtaking display. Upper part of garden accessible but with fairly steep slopes.

15 NEW ◆ MYNYDD, CORS GOCH
Llanbedrgoch, LL76 8TZ.
Mr Wyn & Mrs Ann Williams.
*2m N of Pentraeth, ½ m N of
Llanbedrgoch next to Cors Goch
nature reserve. From Pentraeth take
L turn to Llanbedrgoch, thru village.
Parking is on R side of road after
¼ m, almost opp short track to
garden. From B5108 turn at sign for
Llanbedrgoch, parking on L.* **Sat 11
May, Sat 22 June (11-4). Adm £5,
chd free. Home-made teas.**
An acre garden planted with trees,
mature shrubs, perennials, heathers
and bulbs. Another three acres
devoted to wildlife inc a pond and a
copse. Wildflower meadow with a
good show of wild orchids.

16 NEW ◆ THE OLD SCHOOL
Penmon Village, Beaumaris,
LL58 8RU. Kay Laurie. *3m NE of
Beaumaris. Pass Beaumaris castle
on coast road, after 1.7m turn R to
Penmon and follow yellow signs.*
**Sun 1 Sept (11-4). Combined
adm with Llwyn Onn £5, chd free.
Home-made teas.**
Created from brambly wilderness
since 2015, the garden is on
unforgiving rocky remains of quarried
stone from building the Old School.
South facing, views of Menai Strait.
Sheltered from westerly winds dry,
free draining soil suits agapanthus;
ginger lilies; salvias and enormous
echiums. Winding paths, steep in
parts, mean accessibility is limited.
Biomass heated greenhouse. An
ongoing project. Sea and Mountain
views. Historic Old School. Use of
recycled materials for structures.

17 ◆ PANT IFAN
Ceunant, Llanrug, Caernarfon,
LL55 4HX. Mrs Delia Lanceley. *2m
E of Caernarfon. From Llanrug take
rd opp old PO between Convenience
Store & Monumental Mason. Straight
across at next Xrds. Then 3rd turn on
L at Xrds. Pant Ifan 2nd house on L.*
**Sun 23 June (11-5). Adm £5, chd
free. Home-made teas.**
A large garden with a mix of formal
and relaxed areas surrounding house
and yard. Fruit and vegetable garden,
ponds, young woodland and fields,
horses, donkeys, and various breeds
of poultry. Wheelchair users can
access yard and teas.

18 ◆ PENSYCHNANT
Sychnant Pass, Conwy, LL32 8BJ.
Pensychnant Foundation; Warden
Julian Thompson, 01492 592595,
jpt.pensychnant@btinternet.com,
www.pensychnant.co.uk. *2½ m
W of Conwy at top of Sychnant
Pass. From Conwy: L at Lancaster
Sq. into Upper Gate St; after 2½ m,
Pensychnant's drive signed on R.
From Penmaenmawr: fork R by
shops, up Sychnant Pass; after
walls at top of Pass, U turn L into
drive.* **For NGS: Sun 16 June, Sun
14 July (11-5). Adm £4, chd free.
Home-made teas. Fair Trade
cakes also available. For other
opening times and information,
please phone, email or visit garden
website.**
Wildlife Garden. Diverse herbaceous
cottage garden borders surrounded
by mature shrubs, banks of
Rhododendrons, ancient and
Victorian woodlands. 12 acre
woodland walks with views of Conwy
Mountain and Sychnant. Woodland
birds. Picnic tables, archaeological trail
on mountain. A peaceful little gem.
Large Victorian Arts and Crafts house
(open) with art exhibition. Partial
wheelchair access, please phone for
advice.

19 NEW ◆ PLANNWCH Y PLAS
Dinas Mawddwy, Machynlleth,
SY20 9JB. Mr Michael Hennessy.
www.facebook.com/p/Plannwch-
Y-Plas. *Dinas Mawddwy,
Machynlleth. Travelling from Mallwyd,
turn in to the village, pass through
and at the Red Lion Pub go straight
accross 200 yds to the garden.
Coming from Dolgellau, turn in to the
village, take the 1st L* **For NGS: Sat
7 Sept (10-4). Adm by donation.
Light refreshments. Tea, coffee
and cakes will be available.
For other opening times and
information, please visit garden
Facebook page.**
A community garden in Dinas
Mawddwy, Gwynedd created to
provide a growing and communal
space where people can work, chat
and relax. Primarily a garden for
production of food and to connect
with nature, the plot has many
raised beds and a large space for
wildflowers. The attached pond and
woodland is a haven for wildlife and
is packed full of native and non native
species of trees and shrubs.

**20 ◆ PLAS CADNANT HIDDEN
GARDENS**
Cadnant Road, Menai Bridge,
LL59 5NH. Mr Anthony
Tavernor, 01248 717174,
plascadnantgardens@gmail.com,
www.plascadnantgardens.co.uk.
*½ m E of Menai Bridge. Take A545
& leave Menai Bridge heading for
Beaumaris, then follow brown tourist
information signs. SatNav not always
reliable.* **For NGS: Wed 24 Apr (12-
5). Adm £9.50. Light refreshments
in our traditional Tea Room.
For other opening times and
information, please phone, email or
visit garden website. Donation to
Wales Air Ambulance.**
Early C19 picturesque garden
undergoing restoration since 1996.
Valley gardens with waterfalls, large
ornamental walled garden, woodland
and early pit house. Also Alpheus
water feature and Ceunant (Ravine)
which gives visitors a more interesting
walk featuring unusual moisture loving
Alpines. Restored area following flood
damage. Guidebook available. Visitor
centre open. Public Garden Winner:
The English Garden Magazine's
The Nation's Favourite Gardens,
2023. Partial wheelchair access.
Some steps, gravel paths and
slopes. Access statement available.
Accessible Tea Room and WC.

21 NEW ◆ PLASGLASGWM
Penmachno, Betws-Y-Coed,
LL24 0PU. Mr & Mrs Peter and
Tamsyn Gallimore, 01690 760181,
office@plasglasgwm.co.uk,
www.plasglasgwm.co.uk. *5m from
Betws y Coed, turn off the A5 at
Conwy Falls Cafe onto the B4406 to
Penmachno. Once in Penmachno,
please follow the Brown Tourism signs
for Plasglasgwm up from the village for
1m.* **Visits by arrangement 5 Apr to 29
Sept for groups of up to 18. Discuss
refreshments when booking.**
Discover a hidden place tucked
away in the foothills of Snowdonia.
Five acres of gardens and grounds
created by the owners over 30 years
at this historic mountain farm. Hedges
of yew, box and beech complement
mixed and herbaceous borders, a re-
introduced orchard, natural woodland
and natural areas. Wander along the
pathways to discover all the secret
corners of this C16 farm holding.
Yew and box hedging, box parterre,
orchard, woodland walks, stream,
bridges, seating areas.

Tyn y Pant

22 SUNNINGDALE

Bull Bay Road, Bull Bay, Amlwch, LL68 9SD. Mike & Gill Cross. *1½ m NW of Amlwch. On A5025 through Amlwch towards Cemaes. Just after the Trecastel Hotel. No parking at house.* **Sun 5 May, Sat 1 June (12-6.30). Adm £5, chd free. Home-made teas.**

A garden in three parts. Headland, overlooking the Irish sea, has cliffs, steps, wildflowers, seating, bird life and sheer drops! Front garden has hedging, raised fishpond, wildlife pond and herbaceous planting. Enclosed rear garden, an oasis for wildlife, plants jostling together and constantly evolving. Lots of seating, many areas separated by paths and arches clothed with plants. Access to ours and our neighbour's private headland and a completely different atmosphere in the rear garden. A 70 year old Laburnum. different gardens within the garden and many paths. Wheelchair access to front garden only.

23 TREBORTH BOTANIC GARDEN, BANGOR UNIVERSITY

Treborth, Bangor, LL57 2RQ. Natalie Chivers, treborth.bangor.ac.uk. *On the outskirts of Bangor towards Anglesey. Approach Menai Bridge either from Upper Bangor on A5 or leave A55 J9 & travel towards Bangor for 2m. At Antelope Inn r'bout turn L just before entering the Menai Bridge.* **Sat 14 Sept (10-1). Adm £4, chd free. Home-made teas inc vegan & gluten free options.**

Owned by Bangor University and used as a resource for teaching, research, public education and enjoyment. Treborth comprises planted borders, species rich natural grassland, ponds, arboretum, Chinese garden, ancient woodland, and a rocky shoreline habitat. Six glasshouses provide specialised environments for tropical, temperate, orchid and carnivorous plant collections. Partnered with National Botanic Garden of Wales to champion Welsh horticulture, protect wildlife and extol the virtues of growing plants for food, fun, health and wellbeing. Wheelchair access to some glasshouses and part of the garden. Woodland path is surfaced but most of the borders only accessed over grass.

24 TREFNANT BACH

Anglesey Bees, Llanddaniel Fab, Gaerwen, LL60 6ET. Dafydd & Dawn Jones, 07816 188573, dafydd@angleseybees.co.uk, www.angleseybees.co.uk. *0.4m from the centre of Llanddaniel Fab. A5 from LlanfairPG, 1½ km W, turn L for Llanddaniel. Village centre, by bus shelter follow signs down farm track. Parking on site. Alternatively park in village & 10 min walk.* **Sun 21 July, Sat 31 Aug (11-5). Adm £5, chd free. Home-made teas.**

Beekeepers' magical 7½ acre wildlife garden with beautiful large spring-fed pond with islands and stream; honeybee friendly woodland and woodland walks; grazed pastures; small garden with herbaceous plants; vegetable raised beds, orchard, soft fruit; fun summerhouse; information

Cyplau

© Gary Phillips

boards; woodland treasure hunt; suitable picnic areas. Apiary and Anglesey Bees centre for beekeeping training and experiences. Local honey for sale. Tree-friendly Shropshire sheep. Very gentle slopes, short-mowed grassed or hard paths. Refreshment area accessible with hard surface. Regret WC unsuitable for wheelchair access.

25 TY CADFAN SANT
National Street, Tywyn, LL36 9DD. Mrs Katie Pearce, 07816 604851, katie@tycadfansant.co.uk. *Tywyn centre. A493 going S & W. L into one way, garden ahead. Bear R, parking 2nd L. A493 going N, 1st R in 30mph zone, L at bottom by garden, parking 2nd L.* Sun 26 May (9.30-4.30). Adm £5, chd free. Cream teas. Pulled pork baps at lunchtime, drinks and cakes. **Visits also by arrangement 30 Mar to 29 Sept. Discuss refreshments when booking.**
Large eco friendly garden. In the front, shrubbery, mixed flower beds and roses surround a mature copper beech. Up six steps the largely productive back garden has an apiary in the orchard, fruit, vegetables, flowers and a polytunnel, plenty of seating. Seasonal produce available, honey, plants and crafts. Partial wheelchair access due to steps to rear garden.

Gilfach

© Gary Phillips

26 NEW TY CELYN
6 Bryn y Paderau, Tywyn, LL36 9LA. Lady Houghton. *0.25m from Tywyn town centre. Off A493 near Ysbyty Tywyn Hospital.* Sat 6 July (11-4). Adm £4, chd free. Light refreshments.
Situated at bottom of a close of 10 modern houses, Ty Celyn is a wrap around garden with the Talyllyn steam railway line running along one boundary. Pond with fish and lillies, rose and clematis arch, shrub borders, large cordylines and mature trees, fruit cage and unusual miniature wheeled greenhouse by L.E. Versha based on a Victoria design. Step free access; level plot.

27 NEW TYN Y PANT
Boduan, Pwllheli, LL53 6DT. Mrs Elizabeth Broadbent, 01758 720587, royandlizbroadbent@hotmail.co.uk.

Off the A497 between Pwllheli and Nefyn. On the A497 travelling from Pwllheli, turn L opp St Buan's Church, (from Nefyn R) after approx 500 metres. Sharp R into our driveway which has the house name clearly displayed. Sat 18, Sun 19 May (11-4.30). Adm £5, chd free. Light refreshments. **Visits also by arrangement June to Sept for groups of up to 20. Adm inc refreshments. Discuss details when booking.**
A sheltered, tranquil, rural garden developing around mature trees, shrubs and ponds. Highlights: veg garden, flower beds, bluebell banks, a mini woodland walk and plenty of places to sit. Emphasis is given to reusing reclaimed materials and gardening organically to fully benefit wildlife and the environment. By growing plants from seeds and

cuttings the garden is constantly changing and maturing. The main garden is wheelchair accessible. there are areas of gravel and paths that may not be suitable.

28 41 VICTORIA DRIVE
Llandudno Junction, LL31 9PF. Allan & Eirwen Evans. *A55 J18. From Bangor 1st exit, from Colwyn Bay 2nd exit, A546 to Conwy. Next r'about 3rd exit then 1st L.* Sun 18 Aug (2-5). Adm £3, chd free. Home-made teas. Homemade cakes also available.
A very interesting small urban garden, offering so many creative ideas inc growing sweet peas and dahlias in a small garden. Come along to see the huge selection of bedding plants shrubs and herbaceous plants.

NORTH EAST WALES

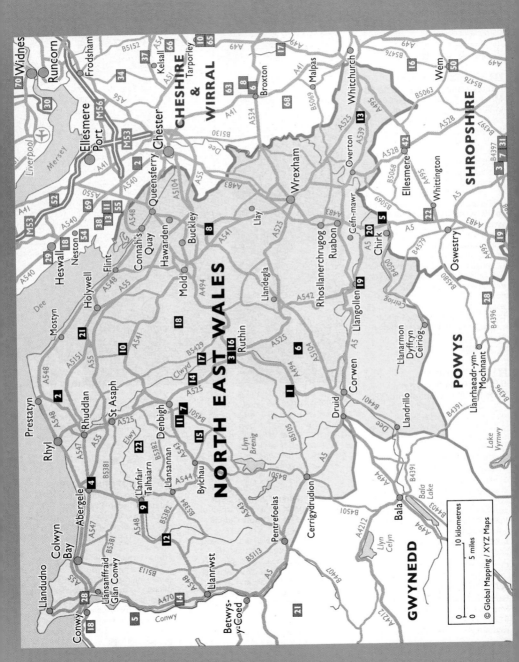

VOLUNTEERS

County Organiser
Jane Moore
07769 046317
jane.moore@ngs.org.uk

County Treasurer
Helen Robertson
01978 790666
helen.robertson@ngs.org.uk

Booklet Co-ordinator
Position vacant
Please email hello@ngs.org.uk for details

Assistant County Organisers
Fiona Bell
07813 087797
bell_fab@hotmail.com

Iris Dobbie
01745 886730
iris.dobbie@ngs.org.uk

Anne Lewis
01352 757044
anne.lewis@ngs.org.uk

Pat Pearson
01745 813613
pat.pearson@ngs.org.uk

@North East Wales NGS

OPENING DATES

All entries subject to change. For latest information check **www.ngs.org.uk**

Map locator numbers are shown to the right of each garden name.

February

Snowdrop Openings

Wednesday 14th
Aberclwyd Manor 1

Wednesday 28th
Aberclwyd Manor 1

March

Wednesday 13th
Aberclwyd Manor 1

Wednesday 27th
Aberclwyd Manor 1

April

Wednesday 10th
Aberclwyd Manor 1

Wednesday 24th
Aberclwyd Manor 1

Saturday 27th
The Laundry 14

Sunday 28th
The Laundry 14

May

Monday 6th
Dibleys Nurseries 6

Wednesday 8th
Aberclwyd Manor 1

Wednesday 15th
NEW Plas Newydd 18

Sunday 19th
Brynkinalt Hall 5
The Homestead 13

Wednesday 22nd
Aberclwyd Manor 1

Saturday 25th
Glasfryn Hall 10

Sunday 26th
Glasfryn Hall 10
Hafodunos Hall 12

Monday 27th
Garthewin 9

June

Wednesday 5th
Aberclwyd Manor 1

Saturday 8th
33 Bryn Twr and Lynton 4

Sunday 9th
33 Bryn Twr and Lynton 4

Wednesday 12th
NEW Plas Newydd 18

Sunday 16th
Gwaenynog 11
Queen Anne Cottage 20

Wednesday 19th
Aberclwyd Manor 1

Friday 21st
◆ Plas Newydd 19

Sunday 23rd
Mysevin 15

Sunday 30th
NEW Bron y Gaer 3
Nantclwyd y Dre 16

July

Wednesday 3rd
Aberclwyd Manor 1

Wednesday 17th
Aberclwyd Manor 1

Wednesday 31st
Aberclwyd Manor 1

August

Wednesday 14th
Aberclwyd Manor 1

Wednesday 28th
Aberclwyd Manor 1

September

Sunday 8th
Brynkinalt Hall 5

Wednesday 11th
Aberclwyd Manor 1

Wednesday 25th
Aberclwyd Manor   1

By Arrangement

Arrange a personalised garden visit with your club, or group of friends, on a date to suit you. See individual garden entries for full details.

The National Garden Scheme donated £3,403,960 to our nursing and health beneficiaries from money raised at gardens open in 2023

The Laundry

THE GARDENS

1 ABERCLWYD MANOR

Derwen, Corwen, LL21 9SF. Mr & Mrs G Sparvoli, 01824 750431, irene662010@live.com. *7m from Ruthin. Travelling on A494 from Ruthin to Corwen. At Bryn SM Service Station turn R, follow sign to Derwen. Aberclwyd gates on L before Derwen. Do not follow SatNav directions.* Wed 14, Wed 28 Feb, Wed 13, Wed 27 Mar, Wed 10, Wed 24 Apr, Wed 8, Wed 22 May, Wed 5, Wed 19 June, Wed 3, Wed 17, Wed 31 July, Wed 14, Wed 28 Aug, Wed 11, Wed 25 Sept (11-4). Adm £5, chd free. Cream teas. **Visits also by arrangement 21 Feb to 25 Sept for groups of 10 to 25.**
A four acre garden on a sloping hillside overlooking the Upper Clwyd Valley. The garden has many mature trees underplanted with snowdrops, fritillaries and cyclamen. An Italianate garden of box hedging lies below the house and shrubs, ponds, perennials, roses and an orchard are also to be enjoyed within this cleverly structured area. Mass of Cyclamen in Sept. Abundance of spring flowers. Mostly flat with some steps and slopes.

2 5 BIRCH GROVE

Woodland Park, Prestatyn, LL19 9RH. Mrs Iris Dobbie, iris.dobbie@ngs.org.uk. *A547 from Rhuddlan turn up The Avenue, Woodland Park after railway bridge 1st R into Calthorpe Dr, 1st L Birch Gr. 10 mins walk from town centre - at top of High St, turn R & L onto The Avenue.* Visits by arrangement 8 May to 11 Sept for groups of 5 to 15. Adm £4, chd free.
The gardens consist of a variety of borders inc woodland, grass, herbaceous, alpine, shrub, drought, tropical and a simulated bog garden with a small pond. The more formal front lawned garden has borders of mixed colourful planting and box balls. A small greenhouse is fully used for propagation. Gravel drive with few steps. Plenty of parking and not far from the beach, Offa's Dyke, and town centre.

3  BRON Y GAER

Castle Street, Ruthin, LL15 1DP. Mr Richard Chamberlain. *120yd up Castle St from the Square on the R.* Sun 30 June (11-4). Combined adm with Nantclwyd y Dre £7, chd free.
A real secret garden. Hidden from the bustle of town, and nestled next door to Nantclwyd y Dre. This garden has beautiful cottage garden planting, a small collection of medicinal herbs and seating by a quiet reflective pool. Wheelchair access good, but please be aware that the garden has two low steps.

4 33 BRYN TWR AND LYNTON

Lynton, Highfield Park, Abergele, LL22 7AU. Mr & Mrs Colin Knowlson & Bryn Roberts & Emma Knowlson-Roberts, 01745 832002, apk@slaters.ltd. *From A55 heading W take slip road into Abergele town centre. Turn L at 2nd set of T-lights signed Llanfair TH, 3rd road on L. For SatNav use LL22 8DD.* Sat 8, Sun 9 June (1-5). Adm £5, chd free. Home-made teas. **Visits also by arrangement in June.**
Bryn Twr is a family garden with children, dogs, chickens, shrubs, roses, pots vegetables and lawn. Lynton completely different, intense cottage style garden: vegetables, trees, shrub, roses, ornamental grasses and lots of pots. Garage with interesting fire engine; classic cars and memorabilia; greenhouse over large water capture system that was part of an old swimming pool.

5 BRYNKINALT HALL

Brynkinalt, Chirk, Wrexham, LL14 5NS. Iain & Kate Hill-Trevor, www.brynkinalt.co.uk. *6m N of Oswestry, 10m S of Wrexham. Come off A5/A483 & take B5070 into Chirk village. Turn into Trevor Rd (beside St Mary's Church). Continue past houses on R. Turn R on bend into Estate Gates. N.B. Do not use postcode with SatNav.* Sun 19 May, Sun 8 Sept (10.30-4.30). Adm £6, chd free. Home-made teas.
A five acre ornamental woodland shrubbery, overgrown until recently, now cleared and replanted, rhododendron walk, historic ponds, well, grottos, ha-ha and battlements, new stumpery, ancient redwoods and yews. Also two acre garden beside Grade II* house (see website for opening), with modern rose and formal beds, deep herbaceous borders, pond with shrub, mixed beds, pleached limes and hedge patterns. Home of the first Duke of Wellington's grandmother and Sir John Trevor, Speaker of House of Commons. Stunning rhododendrons and formal West Garden. Major film location for Lady Chatterley's Lover.

6 DIBLEYS NURSERIES

Cefn Rhydd, Cricor, Llanelidan, Ruthin, LL15 2LG. Rex Dibley, www.dibleys.com. *7m S of Ruthin. Follow brown signs off A525 nr Llysfasi College.* Mon 6 May (10-4). Adm £6, chd free. Light refreshments. We have a very limited area of seating but can provide take-away hot drinks. **Donation to Plant Heritage.**
An eight acre woodland garden with a wide selection of rare and unusual trees set in beautiful countryside. In late spring there is a lovely display of rhododendrons, magnolias, cherries and camellias. Much of our grassland promotes native wildflowers. Our $\frac{3}{4}$ acre commercial glasshouses are open showing a display of streptocarpus and other rare houseplants. Houseplant shop. Partial wheelchair access to glasshouses, uneven ground and steep paths in arboretum and elsewhere.

7 DOLHYFRYD

Lawnt, Denbigh, LL16 4SU. Captain & Mrs Michael Cunningham, 01745 814805, virginia@dolhyfryd.com, dolhyfrydgardens.com. *1m SW of Denbigh. On B4501 to Nantglyn, from Denbigh - 1m from town centre.* Visits by arrangement 27 Jan to 1 Nov for groups of 10+. Light refreshments.
Established garden set in small valley of River Ystrad. Acres of crocuses in late Feb to early Mar. Paths through wildflower meadows and woodland of magnificent trees, shade loving plants and azaleas; mixed borders; walled kitchen garden. Many woodland and riverside birds, inc dippers, kingfishers, grey wagtails. Many species of butterfly encouraged by new planting. Much winter interest, exceptional display of crocuses. Wheelchair users will need to negotiate gravel paths and some steep slopes.

8 DOVE COTTAGE
Rhos Road, Penyffordd, Chester, CH4 0JR. Chris & Denise Wallis, 01244 547539, dovecottage@supanet.com. *6m SW of Chester. Leave A55 at J35 take A550 to Wrexham. Drive 2m, turn R onto A5104. From A541 Wrexham/Mold Rd in Pontblyddyn take A5104 to Chester. Garden opp train stn.* Visits by arrangement 1 July to 1 Sept for groups of 5 to 25. Adm £5, chd free. Tea.
Approx 1½ acre garden, shrubs and herbaceous plants set informally around lawns. Established vegetable area, two ponds (one wildlife), summerhouse. Raised board walk through planted woodland area. The garden has gravel paths.

9 GARTHEWIN
Llanfairtalhaiarn, LL22 8YR. Mr Michael Grime, 01745 720288, michaelgrime12@btinternet.com. *6m S of Abergele & A55. From Abergele take A548 to Llanfair TH & Llanrwst. Entrance to Garthewin 300yds W of Llanfair TH on A548 to Llanrwst. SatNav misleading.* Mon 27 May (2-6). Adm £6, chd free. Home-made teas. Visits also by arrangement 1 Apr to 1 Nov.
Valley garden with ponds and woodland areas. Much of the eight acres have been reclaimed and redesigned providing a younger garden with a great variety of azaleas, rhododendrons and young trees, all within a framework of mature shrubs and trees. Teas in old theatre. Chapel open.

10 GLASFRYN HALL
South Street, Caerwys, Mold, CH7 5AF. Mrs Lise Roberts, orielglasfryn.com. *In Caerwys, Flintshire. Follow the signs for Caerwys either from the A55 N Wales expressway or the A541 Mold - Denbigh Rd. Off the junc on South St & Pen Y Cefn Rd follow signs for Oriel Glasfryn Gallery.* Sat 25 May (10-5); Sun 26 May (10-4). Adm £5, chd £2.50. Light refreshments. Teas, coffees & cake available.
A Victorian villa set in a beautiful Victorian garden with an interesting variety of mature trees and stunning views of the Clwydian hills - croquet lawn, Victorian tea house and pond, walled parterre garden. Sculptures and an art gallery showcasing Welsh Art add a modern and distinctive character to the garden. Teas and coffees available in the grounds from a horsebox cafe. Art gallery and sculpture for sale within garden.

11 GWAENYNOG
Denbigh, LL16 5NU. Major & Mrs Tom Smith. *1m W of Denbigh. On A543, Lodge on L, ¼m drive.* Sun 16 June (2-5). Adm £5, chd free. Home-made teas.
Two acres inc the restored walled garden where Beatrix Potter wrote and illustrated the Tale of the Flopsy Bunnies. Also a small exhibition of some of her work. Long herbaceous borders and island beds, some recently replanted, espalier fruit trees, rose pergola and vegetable area. C16 house (not open) visited by Dr Samuel Johnson during his Tour of Wales. Wheelchair users will need to negotiate grass paths.

12 HAFODUNOS HALL
Llangernyw, Abergele, Conwy, LL22 8TY. Dr Richard Wood. *1m W of Llangernyw. Halfway between Abergele & Llanrwst on A548. Signed from opp Old Stag pub. Parking available onsite.* Sun 26 May (12-5). Adm £6, chd free. Home-made teas in the Victorian conservatory.
Historic garden undergoing restoration after 30 years of neglect, surrounds a Sir George Gilbert Scott Grade I listed Hall, derelict after arson attack. Unique setting with a ½ mile tree-lined drive, formal terraces, woodland walks with ancient redwoods, laurels, yews, lake, streams, waterfalls and a gorge. Wonderful rhododendrons. Most areas around the hall are wheelchair accessible by gravel pathways. Some gardens are set on slopes.

13 THE HOMESTEAD
Horsemans Green, Whitchurch, SY13 3DY. Mr Elwyn & Mrs Jenny Hughes, 01948 830433, jdh53@hotmail.co.uk. *From Wrexham travel 9m on A525 towards Whitchurch & turn R into Horseman's Green. From Whitchurch travel 5m on the A525 & turn L into Horseman's Green.* Sun 19 May (2-5). Adm £5, chd free. Home-made teas. Visits also by arrangement Feb to Sept.
For 20 years we opened The Old Rectory, Llanfihangel Glyn Myfyr, for the National Garden Scheme. We have moved and look forward to inviting visitors to our new garden which has an emphasis on low maintenance, but without losing any of our passion for plants. It has taken three years to reimagine this new garden. We have planted an abundance of acers, magnolias, Cornus species, perennials, bulbs.

14 THE LAUNDRY
Llanrhaeadr, Denbigh, LL16 4NL. Mr & Mrs T Williams, 01745 890515, hello@thelaundryretreat.co.uk, thelaundryretreat.co.uk. *3m SE of Denbigh. Entrance off A525 Denbigh to Ruthin Rd.* Sat 27, Sun 28 Apr (11-4). Adm £6, chd free. Home-made teas.
A chance to see a new garden evolving within an old setting. Terraced courtyard garden, developed since 2009, surrounded by old stone walls enclosing cottage style planting and formal hedging. 10 years ago, work started on the old kitchen walled garden with a view to incorporating it within the whole garden plan. Woodland walk, roses, pleached limes, peonies and herbaceous planting. Some deep gravel areas, may prove difficult for wheelchair users.

15 MYSEVIN
Nantglyn, Denbigh, LL16 5PG. Ms Alex Kerr-Wilson. *4½m SW of Denbigh. From Denbigh B4501 to Nantglyn. Mysevin entrance on R opp footpath sign. What3words app - stay.denoting.hips. Stone gate pillars to 8ft wide drive & bridge.* Sun 23 June (2-5.30). Adm £5, chd free. Home-made teas.
Situated on a wooded hillside over looking lawned gardens, a little rose garden, meadows, interesting herbaceous borders running down to the river Ystrad. To the rear of the house is a green bank inc white garden and ornamental woodland garden. The garden is the essence of peace and serenity, with rare plants and a shell house by Blott Kerr-Wilson. Some steps and gravel paths. Shell House created by Blott Kerr-Wilson. Wheelchair access to front garden on gravel paths.

16 NANTCLWYD Y DRE
Castle St, Ruthin, LL15 1DP.
Denbighshire County Council.
100yds from the square. 100yd along Castle St from the square on the R. Sun 30 June (11-4). Combined adm with Bron y Gaer £7, chd free. Cream teas.
With far-reaching views over Ruthin, this nationally important part-walled garden, Grade II listed on the Cadw Register of Landscapes, Parks and Gardens of Special Historic Interest, may once have been the kitchen garden for Ruthin Castle. Restoration is taking place with borders now displaying a variety of herbaceous plants and medieval herbs. One of the oldest timber framed town houses in Wales and the Lord's garden first mentioned in 1282 is thought to pre-date the structure. Most of the garden is wheelchair accessible but there are steps down to the Lords Garden.

17 PLAS COCH
Llanychan, Ruthin, LL15 1UF.
Sir David & Lady Henshaw, 01824 790985. *Situated on B5429 between villages of Llandyrnog & Llanbedr DC.* Visits by arrangement 31 May to 30 June for groups of 5 to 10. Adm £3.50, chd free.
Well established country garden with deep and varied herbaceous borders, vegetable garden and fruit trees with heritage variety small orchard. Other sections inc small yard garden, pond areas, three seater tybach (outside privy) MG TC 1949, all in the centre of the vale of Clwyd with extensive views towards the Clwydian Hills.

18 NEW PLAS NEWYDD
Pen Line Road, Cilcain, Mold, CH7 5NZ. Mrs Eileen Bigglestone, 01352 741894, plasnewydd.teagarden@mail.com. *If you enter Plas Newydd tea garden on Google maps, it will bring you directly to the garden. Alternatively What3words app - stones.curtail.unfounded.* Wed 15 May, Wed 12 June (11-3). Adm £4, chd free. Pre-booking essential, please visit www.ngs.org.uk for information & booking. Home-made teas.
Small country garden located opposite Moel Famau with spectacular views and established herbaceous borders created over the last 15 years. It has been described by several of our tea garden customers as a hidden gem nestled amongst the Welsh Hills. We now have a shepherds hut sited in the top corner of the garden so you can stay here and enjoy the garden at leisure.

19 ♦ PLAS NEWYDD
Llangollen, LL20 8AW. Denbighshire County Council, 01978 862834, plasnewydd@denbighshire.gov.uk. *Follow brown sign from A5 in Llangollen.* For NGS: Fri 21 June (10-4). Adm by donation. Light refreshments. For other opening times and information, please phone or email.
Plas Newydd was the home of the famous Ladies of Llangollen (1780-1814) who created this picturesque garden which inc a woodland walk to the gothic alcove with a stone font from Valle Crucis Abbey. There is a formal parterre and rose garden, a dell area and a streamside walk along the Cyflymen. Late C19 formal beds and gorsedd stone circle are in front of the house.

20 QUEEN ANNE COTTAGE
Whitehurst Gardens, Chirk, LL14 5AS. Michael Kemp. *A5 from Chirk to Llangollen. 50 metres off Whitehurst r'about, opp Jewson's Building Yard.* Sun 16 June (1-6). Adm £5, chd free. Home-made teas.
Queen Anne Cottage was the banqueting house of Whitehurst Gardens, the original walled garden of Chirk Castle. The Cottage was bought by a professional gardener who has made a beautiful garden around his unique home with a selection of unusual trees, shrubs, herbaceous, woodland, and old roses.

21 SAITH FFYNNON FARM
Downing Road, Whitford, Holywell, CH8 9EN. Mrs Jan Miller-Klein, 01352 711198, jan@7wells.org, www.7wells.co.uk. *1m outside Whitford village. From Holywell follow signs for Pennant Park Golf Course. Turn R just past the Halfway House. Take 2nd lane on R (signed for Downing & Trout Farm) & Saith Ffynnon Farm is the 1st house on R.* Visits by arrangement 16 May to 15 Sept for groups of up to 10. Regret, cash only. Adm £5, chd £2. Light refreshments. Discuss refreshments when booking. Donation to Plant Heritage, North Wales Wildlife Trust.
Wildlife garden of an acre and re-wilded meadows of eight acres, inc ponds, woods, wildflower meadows, butterfly and bee gardens, Medieval herbal, natural dye garden and the Plant Heritage National Collection of Eupatorium. Garden at it's best early Sep to early Oct. Guided walks with the owner, ID charts for children to use, moth trap live catch from the night before. Other wildlife displays depending on the weather. Hard surface from gate to patio and two sections of the garden. No wheelchair access on the damp meadows.

22 TAL-Y-BRYN FARM
Llannefydd, Denbigh, LL16 5DR. Mr & Mrs Gareth Roberts, 01745 540208, falmai@villagedairy.co.uk, www.villagedairy.co.uk. *3m W of Henllan. From Henllan take road signed Llannefydd. After 2½m turn R signed Llaeth y Llan. Garden ½m on L.* Visits by arrangement 1 Apr to 1 Oct. Adm by donation. Home-made teas.
Medium sized working farmhouse cottage garden. Ancient farm machinery. Incorporating ancient privy festooned with honeysuckle, clematis and roses. Terraced arches, sunken garden pool and bog garden, fountains and old water pumps. Herb wheels, shrubs and other interesting features. Lovely views of the Clwydian range. Water feature, new rose tunnel, vegetable tunnel and small garden summerhouse. Wheelchair access to most of the garden.

In 2023 we awarded over £260,000 in Community Garden Grants, supporting 86 community garden projects

POWYS

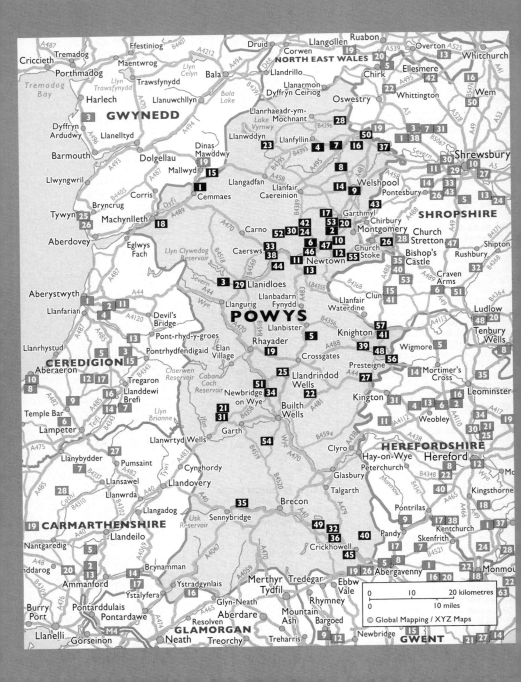

VOLUNTEERS

North Powys County Organiser
Susan Paynton 01686 650531
susan.paynton@ngs.org.uk

County Treasurer
Jude Boutle 07702 061623
jude.boutle@ngs.org.uk

Publicity
Sue McKillop 07753 289701
sue.mckillop@ngs.org.uk

Gill Powell 07968 250364
gill.powell@ngs.org.uk

Simon Quin 07958 915120
simon.quin@ngs.org.uk

Talks
Helen Anthony 07986 061051
helen.anthony@ngs.org.uk

Social Media
Nikki Trow 07958 958382
nikki.trow@ngs.org.uk

Booklet Co-ordinator
Position vacant

Assistant County Organisers
Simon Cain 07958 915115
simon.cain@ngs.org.uk

Elizabeth Fairhead 07824 398840
elizabeth.fairhead@ngs.org.uk

Kate Nicoll 07960 656814
kate.nicoll@ngs.org.uk

Chris Smith 07775 656299
chris.smith@ngs.org.uk

South Powys County Organiser
Christine Carrow 01591 620461
christine.carrow@ngs.org.uk

County Treasurer
Steve Carrow 01591 620461
steve.carrow@ngs.org.uk

Publicity Officer
Gail Jones 07974 103692
gail.jones@ngs.org.uk

f @powysngs
X @PowysNGS
@ @powysngs

OPENING DATES

All entries subject to change. For latest information check
www.ngs.org.uk

Map locator numbers are shown to the right of each garden name.

Extended openings are shown at the beginning of each month

May

Sunday 5th
Garthmyl Hall 20

Saturday 11th
◆ Dingle Nurseries & Garden 14
◆ Gregynog Hall & Garden 24

Sunday 12th
◆ Dingle Nurseries & Garden 14
◆ Gregynog Hall & Garden 24

Saturday 18th
Hill Cottage 25
Rock Mill 47

Sunday 19th
Hill Cottage 25
Rock Mill 47
Treberfydd House 49

Saturday 25th
Bachie Uchaf 4

Sunday 26th
Bachie Uchaf 4
Garregllwyd 19
Llysdinam 34

Monday 27th
Garregllwyd 19

June

Sunday 2nd
NEW Llwyn 30
Llwyn Madoc 31
The Neuadd 40
NEW Parson's Field 42
Tranquility Haven 48

Thursday 6th
Gilwern Barn 21

Saturday 8th
NEW The Malthouse 37
Tremynfa 50

Sunday 9th
NEW The Malthouse 37
Tremynfa 50

Thursday 13th
White Hopton Farm 55

Friday 14th
White Hopton Farm 55

Saturday 15th
Caebardd 8
NEW Forge Village Gardens 18
NEW Plum Tree Cottage 45

Sunday 16th
NEW Forge Village Gardens 18
Hurdley Hall 26
NEW Llwynau Mawr Farm 32
NEW Maes Llechau 36
NEW Plum Tree Cottage 45

Sunday 23rd
Glanoer 22
Llangedwyn Hall 28
Willowbrook 56

Saturday 29th
Ash and Elm Horticulture 3
Lower Wernfigin Barns 35

Sunday 30th
Ash and Elm Horticulture 3
NEW Eve's Garden 16
Lower Wernfigin Barns 35
Tyn-y-Graig 52

July

Every day from
Saturday 27th
◆ Welsh Lavender 54

Thursday 4th
Gilwern Barn 21

Saturday 6th
Cultivate Community Garden 11

Sunday 7th
Felindre Gardens 17
Hurdley Hall 26
Tynrhos 51

Saturday 13th
1 Church Bank 9

Sunday 14th
1 Church Bank 9
The Meadows 38
Monaughty Mill 39

Saturday 20th
1 Glanrafon 23

Sunday 21st
1 Glanrafon 23
Vaynor Park 53

Saturday 27th
Bryn Teg   6
Ponthafren   46

Sunday 28th
Bryn Teg   6
Ponthafren   46

August

Every day to Friday 2nd
◆ Welsh Lavender   54

Thursday 1st
Gilwern Barn   21

Sunday 4th
Bryngwyn Hall   7
The Meadows   38

Saturday 17th
NEW Llanidloes Gardens   29

Sunday 18th
Brookside   5
NEW Llanidloes Gardens   29

Saturday 31st
Aberangell, The Old Coach
House   1

September

**Every day from Saturday 7th
to Sunday 15th**
The Hymns   27

Sunday 1st
Aberangell, The Old Coach
House   1

Thursday 5th
Gilwern Barn   21

Sunday 8th
Cwm-Weeg   13
NEW Eve's Garden   16

Sunday 15th
Willowbrook   56

October

Saturday 5th
◆ Dingle Nurseries & Garden   14

Sunday 6th
◆ Dingle Nurseries & Garden   14

Saturday 19th
◆ Gregynog Hall & Garden   24

Sunday 20th
◆ Gregynog Hall & Garden   24
Tranquility Haven   48

By Arrangement

Arrange a personalised garden visit
with your club, or group of friends,
on a date to suit you. See individual
garden entries for full details.

Aberangell, The Old Coach
House   1
Abernant   2
Brookside   5
Caebardd   8
1 Church Bank   9
NEW Cuckoo Hall   10
Cwm Sidwell   12
Dugoed Bach   15
Glanoer   22
The Hymns   27
Llys Celyn   33
Llysdinam   34
The Meadows   38
The Neuadd   40
No 2 The Old Coach House   41
Pen-y-Bank   43
Plas Dinam   44
NEW Plum Tree Cottage   45
Ponthafren   46
Rock Mill   47
Tranquility Haven   48
Tremynfa   50
Tyn-y-Graig   52
Willowbrook   56
1 Ystrad House   57

Maes Llechau

THE GARDENS

1 ABERANGELL, THE OLD COACH HOUSE

Dolcorsllwyn, Aberangell, Machynlleth, SY20 9AB.
Sue McKillop, 07753 289701, sue58.sm@gmail.com. *On A470 midway beween Dolgellau & Machynlleth. From Mallwyd r'about to Cemmaes Rd, turn R after 3m just after turn for Aberangell village. From Machynlleth, come through Cemmaes and Cwm Llinau. 1m on L.* Sat 31 Aug, Sun 1 Sept (11.30-5). Adm £5, chd free. Home-made teas. Visits also by arrangement 17 May to 30 Aug for groups of 5 to 15. Discuss refreshments when booking. Evening visits available in June & July.
Nestled in the heart of Dyfi Valley this small, cottage style garden is haven for birds and pollinating insects. Narrow paths take you around flower and vegetable beds, to greenhouses, poly tunnel and old stables. Planting is informal with mostly perennials and shrubs. Secluded seating areas allow the visitor to relax and enjoy different aspects of the garden with views down to River Dyfi. Homemade preserves and conserves and local handmade quilted products for sale, with a % going to the NGS. Bilingual garden trail for children. A gravel drive and cobbled area in front of the house leads to a grassy slope into the garden. A few low steps in the garden.

2 ABERNANT

Garthmyl, SY15 6RZ. Mrs B M Gleave, 01686 640494. *1½ m S of Garthmyl. On A483 midway between Welshpool & Newtown (both 8m). Approached over steep humpback bridge with wooden statue of workman. Straight ahead to house & parking.* Visits by arrangement Apr to Aug for groups of up to 12. Adm £4.50, chd free.
A three acre cottage garden with a stunning cherry blossom orchard. Explore our knot garden, formal rose garden, rockery and pond. There are an abundance of shrubs and ornamental trees. Discover our archaic sundials, fossilised wood and stone heads. Wander through an additional nine acres of woodland with borrowed views of the Severn Valley.

3 ASH AND ELM HORTICULTURE

Cae Felyn, Old Hall, Llanidloes, SY18 6PW. Emma Maxwell, www.ashandelmhorticulture.co.uk. *3m from Llanidloes. At Llanidloes Market Hall turn R on Shortbridge St over river & stay on this road for 3m. Garden on L.* Sat 29, Sun 30 June (11-3). Adm £5, chd free. Home-made teas. Range of cakes, seasonal fruit and homemade elderflower cordial.
Diverse five acre market garden; flowers, vegetables, fruit, nuts and plants grown using agroecological techniques that nurture nature. Enjoy wandering through the extensive cut flower garden or explore the one acre orchard, home to a family of barn owls. See wide range of seasonal vegetables growing in the polytunnels, glasshouse and in the field or just relax by one of the wildlife pools. Talks through the day on growing principles. Wheelchair access via grass paths.

4 BACHIE UCHAF

Bachie Road, Llanfyllin, SY22 5NF. Glyn & Glenys Lloyd. *S of Llanfyllin. Going towards Welshpool on A490 turn R onto Bachie Rd after Llanfyllin primary sch. Keep straight for 0.8m. Take drive R uphill at cottage on L.* Sat 25, Sun 26 May (11-5). Adm £5.50, chd free. Home-made teas.
Inspiring and colourful hillside country garden. Gravel paths meander around extensive planting and over streams cascading into ponds. Specimen trees, shrubs, rhododendrons and azaleas aplenty and a vegetable garden. Enjoy the wonderful views from one of the many seats; your senses will be rewarded.

5 BROOKSIDE

Llanbister, Llandrindod Wells, LD1 6TW. Mrs Liz Fairhead, 07824 398840, liz.fairhead@gmail.com. *11m N of Llandrindod Wells. Head N from Llandrindod Wells on A483. After 11m turn R onto minor road signed Llanbister Rd, after 1m turn R signed Heartsease. After approx 1m garden is on R immed before bridge.* Sun 18 Aug (2-5). Adm £5, chd free. Home-made teas. Visits also by arrangement May to Aug for groups of up to 30.
A stream side garden in the Maelienydd. Approx one acre, inc

species rich meadow with mown paths to wander through, colourful herbaceous beds and borders, vegetable plot and small apiary, wetland and woodland plantings. Pollinators, butterflies, birds and amphibians in abundance. The garden combines peace, beauty and colour with rich wildlife in the midst of glorious scenery.

6 BRYN TEG

Bryn Lane, Newtown, SY16 2DP. Novlet Childs, www.instagram.com/dollys_jamaican_garden. *N side of Newtown. From centre Newtown, turn L on B4568 at t-lights then R on Llanfair Caereinion Rd. Turn L Bryn Ln signed Hospital.* Sat 27 July (10-5); Sun 28 July (1-5). Adm £4, chd free. Open nearby Ponthafren.
Amazing exotic, secret Caribbean garden in centre of Newtown planted to remind me of my childhood in Jamaica and an exciting walk through the jungle. High above the head are banana leaves and colourful climbers. A winding path takes you on a journey through a moon gate into another land. Sounds of water fill the air; explosion of colourful intermingling flowers and plants. A huge number of plants on many levels. All shapes, sizes and colours mixed together as found in tropical jungles. Feel transported to another continent. Even in the rain you will get that jungle experience. Regional Finalist, The English Garden Magazine's The Nation's Favourite Gardens, 2023

🐕 ❀ ☕ »)

7 BRYNGWYN HALL

Bwlch-y-Cibau, Llanfyllin, SY22 5LJ. Auriol Marchioness of Linlithgow, www.bryngwyn.com. *3m SE Llanfyllin. From Llanfyllin take A490 towards Welshpool for 3m turn L up drive just before Bwlch-y-Cibau.* Sun 4 Aug (12-5). Adm £7, chd free. Home-made teas.
Stunning grade II* listed nine acre garden with 60 acres parkland design inspired by William Emes. Woodland garden, shrubbery, rose garden, restored herbaceous borders, meadows and serpentine lake. Unusual trees, shrubs and unique Poison Garden.

8 CAEBARDD

Guilsfield, Welshpool, Powys, SY21 9DJ. Sandy Jones, 07816 527344. *9m N Welshpool. From Londis petrol stn on A490 nr Guilsfield, continue towards Llanfyllin for approx 2m & turn L following NGS signs on single track lane.* Sat 15 June (11-5). Adm £5, chd free. Home-made teas. Gluten free and vegan options available. Visits also by arrangement 16 June to 28 July.

Meandering garden with established trees and shrubs circling large pond. Dry stone walls support banks of herbs, herbaceous and wildflowers. Paths lead to hidden Japanese corner with waterfall, bamboos, acers and bridge. Covered seating area. Across farmyard to wild garden full of wildflowers and trees. Several short walks through woodlands and 10 mins hike to top of farm boasts magnificent 360 degree views of Long Mountain, Rodney's Pillar, Shropshire plain, Berwyns. Cadair Berwyn and Allt y Main. Seat at summit to sit and catch your breath. Bring walking shoes. Most of main garden has wheelchair access but paths in wild meadow are too narrow.

9 1 CHURCH BANK

Welshpool, SY21 7DR. Mel & Heather Parkes, 01938 559112, melandheather@live.co.uk. *Centre of Welshpool. Church Bank leads onto Salop Rd from Church St. Follow one way system, use main car park then short walk. Follow yellow NGS signs.* Sat 13, Sun 14 July (12-5). Adm £3.50, chd free. Home-made teas. Visits also by arrangement Apr to Aug for groups of 5 to 30.

An intimate jewel in the town with many interesting plants and unusual features where the sounds of water fill the air. Densely planted garden with Gothic arch and zig zag path leading to shell grotto, bonsai garden and fernery. You can also explore the ground floor of this C17 barrel maker's cottage and walk into a large garden room which houses a museum of tools and motor memorabilia.

10 NEW CUCKOO HALL

Abermule, Montgomery, SY15 6LD. Gill and Cliff Plowes, 01686 630209, gillian.plowes@gmail.com. *3m W of Montgomery. From Newtown A483 N approx 3m, turn R B4386 signposted Abermule/ Clun/ Montgomery. At r'bout take L (B4385) to Montgomery, after 0.2m over bridge immed R towards Llandyssil. Follow yellow signs.* Visits by arrangement May to July for groups of 8 to 12. Adm £6, chd free. Home-made teas.

A 1½ acre garden developed and designed by retired nursery owners and RHS gold medallists, around existing semi mature trees with island beds, mature grasses and shrubs to give permanent structure: series of three wildlife ponds, a streamside garden, rose and clematis pergola, herbaceous borders and small potager garden. Colour co-ordination has been foremost in mind during the design to give a flowing feel. Wheelchair access to the majority of the garden.

11 CULTIVATE COMMUNITY GARDEN

Pendinas, Llanidloes Road, Newtown, SY16 4HX. www.cultivate.uk.com. *A489 W from centre Newtown adjacent to Newtown College & Theatre Hafren.* Sat 6 July (11-4). Adm £4.50, chd free. Light refreshments.

Thriving two acre community garden run by local food hub, Cultivate. Extensive range of vegetables, herbs and fruit growing on communal plots and 'micro-allotments'. Lawns to relax on and wildlife area with pond. Managed by Cultivate volunteers with help from our partners Montgomery Wildlife Trust, Tir Coed and students from Neath Port Talbot college. Look out for the turf-roofed roundhouse, amazing colourful mural, and trained apple trees. Polytunnels and lots of compost heaps. Wheelchair access to main parts of garden, although surfaces may be soft or uneven. Accessible compost toilet.

12 CWM SIDWELL

Kerry, Newtown, SY16 4NA. Jan Rogers, 07772 414783, janetrogers62@hotmail.co.uk. *6m E Newtown. From Newtown take A489. After 4m turn L on B4368. After 1½ m turn R signed Goetre Follow yellow arrows.* Visits by arrangement June to Sept for groups of up to 20. Adm £4, chd free. Home-made teas.

Cottage garden with lovely views brought back from the wilderness over the last couple of years. Roses, sweet peas, herbaceous perennials, vegetable garden and cut flower garden all grown from seed. Pockets of colour whichever way you look. Pond and chickens. Flower and vegetable seedlings for sale.

13 CWM-WEEG

Dolfor, Newtown, SY16 4AT. Dr W Schaefer & Mr K D George, 01686 628992, wolfgang@cwmweeg.co.uk, www.cwmweeg.co.uk. *4½ m SE of Newtown. Off Bypass, take A489 E from Newtown for 1½ m, turn R towards Dolfor. After 2m turn L down asphalted farm track. Do not follow SatNav. Google: Cwm Weeg Gardens.* Sun 8 Sept (2-5). Adm £6, chd free. Home-made teas. Cream teas available.

A two½ acre garden set within 24 acres of wildflower meadows and bluebell woodland with stream centred around C15 farmhouse (open by prior arrangement). Formal garden in English landscape tradition with vistas, grottos, sculptures, stumpery, lawns and extensive borders terraced with stone walls. Translates older garden vocabulary into an innovative C21 concept. Extensive under cover seating area in the large Garden Pavilion. Partial wheelchair access. For further information please see garden website.

14 ◆ DINGLE NURSERIES & GARDEN

Welshpool, SY21 9JD. Mr & Mrs D Hamer, 01938 555145, info@ dinglenurseriesandgarden.co.uk, www.dinglenurseryandgarden. co.uk. *2m NW of Welshpool. Take A490 towards Llanfyllin & Guilsfield. After 1m turn L at sign for Dingle Nurseries & Garden. Follow signs & enter the Garden from adjacent plant centre.* For NGS: Sat 11, Sun 12 May, Sat 5, Sun 6 Oct (9-5). Adm £3.50, chd free. Tea & coffee available. For other opening times and information, please phone, email or visit garden website.

4½ acre internationally acclaimed RHS partner garden on south facing site, sloping down to lakes. Huge variety of rare and unusual trees, ornamental shrubs and herbaceous plants give year-round interest. Set in the hills of mid Wales this beautiful well known garden attracts visitors from Britain and abroad. Plant collector's paradise.

15 DUGOED BACH
Mallwyd, Machynlleth, SY20 9HR.
Katie & Elaine Weston,
07745 529597,
katiewestonuk@gmail.com. *14m N of Machynlleth, 25m W of Welshpool. Directly on A458 1m E of Mallwyd r'about. What3words app - generally. nitrate.drain.* Visits by arrangement 21 June to 30 Sept for groups of up to 20. Car parking limited, so visitors will need to car share. Adm £5, chd £3. Home-made teas.
A rural ¾ acre cottage garden set in Snowdonia National Park with magnificent views. Large variety of plants, and planting themes on a sloping site, with challenging conditions. Orchard, wildflower meadow and ponds provide habitats for wildlife and our own bees. The garden is at its best in late summer with a profusion of roses and other perennials.

16 EVE'S GARDEN
The Old Stackyard, Cefn-Y-Coed, Llansantffraid, SY22 6TB. Emyr Wigley. *2m S Llansantffraid. Across bridge out of Llansantffraid on B4393 in direction of Shrewsbury. Turn R for Deuddwr & follow signs to garden.* Sun 30 June, Sun 8 Sept (11-5). Adm £5, chd free. Home-made teas.
Deep borders filled with roses, fuchsias, pelargoniums, annuals and flowering shrubs surround the house which is itself adorned with pots, hanging baskets and climbing roses. At the back there is a lawn with Japanese maples and a kitchen garden for vegetables, fruit and cut flowers. A homemade greenhouse with tomatoes completes this vibrant garden made in memory of the owner's wife. Plant sale at June opening only. Level paths throughout the garden for wheelchair access.

GROUP OPENING

17 FELINDRE GARDENS
Felindre, Berriew, Welshpool, SY21 8BE. *6m S Welshpool. From Welshpool A483 for approx 4m. Turn R on B4390 straight through Berriew. After1m fork L, cross bridge & take road to R. Follow NGS signs to car park.* Sun 7 July (12-5). Combined adm £6, chd free. Home-made teas at Rivermead.

NEW FELINDRE BUNGALOW
Brian and Joan Hilditch.
2 FELINDRE COTTAGE
Wendy & Richard Rossiter.
NEW GLANLLYN
Sally Turner & Viv Arch.
RIVERMEAD
Kathleen & Mark Harvey.

Four gardens in hamlet of Felindre with its old corn mill on River Rhiew. Spot dippers, kingfishers and otters. Rivermead large riverside garden with dense planting, quirky features and driftwood sculptures; 2 Felindre Cottage compact garden on banks of river with hanging baskets and pots; Felindre Bungalow riverside garden bursting with colour, pots and unusual plants; Glanllyn cottage garden with roses and hollyhocks. Visit the artist Matthew Wood's open studio. www.matthewwoodpaintings.com.

GROUP OPENING

18 NEW FORGE VILLAGE GARDENS
Forge, Machynlleth, SY20 8RN. *1.4m E Machynlleth. From Machynlleth: A489 E for 0.3m. Turn R on Forge Rd for 1.1m. Car parking just over the bridge on L.* Sat 15, Sun 16 June (11-5). Combined adm £7, chd free. Home-made teas at Glanyrafon, but can be taken to the two adjacent gardens.

NEW 1 BONTFAEN
Mrs Stephanie Pickard.
NEW BRONAWEL
Mrs M Sadler.
NEW BRYNGLAS
Mrs J Kirby.
NEW BWYTHYN CYMRAEG
Mrs J Hibbert.
NEW GLANYRAFON
Jane and Colin Lees.
NEW GLAN Y PANDY
Neil and Jane Griffin.

Six delightful gardens in the hamlet of Forge adjacent to the River Dulas. Four established riverside gardens with shrubs, borders and raised beds, one newly developed garden on a small and challenging plot, one very small garden at the bridge. Gardens overlooking the river have historical interest having once been an area with many working mills. Wheelchair access to most areas of some of the riverside gardens. Refreshments at Glanyrafon.

19 GARREGLLWYD
Nantmel, Rhayader, LD6 5PE. Stephanie Morgan. *5m E of Rhayader. From Rhayader take A44 E for 3½m to Nantmel. Turn L by Dolau Chapel signed Abbeycwmhir. Follow lane for 1½m then turn R by red warning triangle signed Garregllwyd. Follow track for ½m.* Sun 26, Mon 27 May (12-5). Adm £5, chd free. Home-made teas.
A three acre landscaped garden at 1000' with stunning panoramic views of mid Wales. Large ponds with abundance of wildlife, unusual specimen trees, daffodils, bluebells, rhododendrons and raised vegetable beds and greenhouses growing seasonal veg. Designed to cope with exposed altitude with minimal maintenance and to encourage wildlife. Variety of seating areas to enjoy the ever changing weather conditions.

20 GARTHMYL HALL
Garthmyl, Montgomery, SY15 6RS. Julia Pugh, 01686 639401, hello@garthmylhall.co.uk, www.garthmylhall.co.uk. *On A483 midway between Welshpool & Newtown (both 8m). Turn R 200yds S of Nag's Head Pub.* Sun 5 May (1-5). Adm £6, chd free. Home-made teas.
Grade II listed Georgian manor house (not open) surrounded by five acres of grounds. 100 metre herbaceous borders, newly restored one acre walled garden with gazebo, circular flowerbeds, lavender beds, wildflower meadow, pond, two fire pits and gravel paths. Fountain, three magnificent cedar of Lebanon and giant redwood. Partial wheelchair access. Accessible WC.

Our donation to Marie Curie this year equates to 17,496 hours of nursing care

The Malthouse

21 GILWERN BARN

Beulah, LD5 4YG. **Mrs Penelope Bourdillon.** *2m N of Beulah. Take B4348 out of Beulah. After ¾ turn L (by blue pole) at t-junc. Follow yellow NGS signs to garden.* **Thur 6 June, Thur 4 July, Thur 1 Aug, Thur 5 Sept (2-5). Adm £5, chd free. Pre-booking essential, please visit www.ngs.org.uk for information & booking. Home-made teas.**
Terraced garden on very challenging site. Situated on a steep rocky hillside in the beautiful and secluded Cammarch Valley, the garden has roses, herbaceous, and shrub borders. Many fine walls and gate posts made of stone and slate found in the garden. The situation, on a steep rocky slope, is fairly dramatic and makes it interesting and the man-made waterfall is quite a feature. Though steep most of garden can be seen from a wheelchair. Easy access to tearoom.

22 GLANOER

Bettws, Hundred House, Llandrindod Wells, LD1 5RP. **Dave & Sue Stone, 07771 767246, stone@glanoer.co.uk.** *Use postcode for SatNav. From A481 take turning to Bettws & Franksbridge by Hundred House Inn. Take L fork signposted Bettws. Glanoer is 1m further along lane on L (past St Mary's Church).* **Sun 23 June (1-5). Adm £6, chd free. Home-made teas. Picnics welcome on the field. Visits also by arrangement May to Sept Discuss refreshments when booking.**
Just over an acre in an alder valley with running brook. Numerous 'rooms' throughout providing seating, vistas and interest; inc an allotment, bluebell wood, wildlife pond, secret garden and water features. Planting for colour and pollination throughout the year for resident bees with over 80 varieties of rose. A young garden created since 2015 on boulder clay from open space. Free-range chickens, beehives, allotment, terraces.

23 1 GLANRAFON

Llanwddyn, Oswestry, SY10 0LU. **Margaret Herbert.** *24m W of Oswestry. From Llanfyllin, follow brown signs to Lake Vyrnwy. Through village of Llanwddyn & turn L across dam then L past Artisans Cafe. Park in public car park by playground. Follow yellow signs to*

garden. **Sat 20, Sun 21 July (1-5). Adm £4.50, chd free.**
An acre of secluded organic garden: mix of wild and cultivated. This steeply sloping, densely planted wildlife garden with hundreds of varieties of shrubs and perennials has been evolving since 2013. Very productive raised veg beds, greenhouse with ornamental and edible crops, fruit cages, mixed borders and large pond. Perfect for garden photographers, picnics and wildlife. Links with RSPB site at Lake Vyrnwy and Montgomery Wildlife Trust. Children's quiz. Wheelchair access to upper and lower levels via access road and separate gate. Car parking strictly for blue badge holders at sculpture park.

24 ◆ GREGYNOG HALL & GARDEN

Tregynon, Newtown, SY16 3PL. **The Gregynog Trust, 01686 650224, enquiries@gregynog.org, www.gregynog.org.** *5m N of Newtown. From Newtown A483 turn L B4389 for Tregynon/ Llanfair Caereinion (car parking charge applies).* **For NGS: Sat 11, Sun 12 May, Sat 19, Sun 20 Oct (10.30-4). Adm by donation with % to NGS. Light refreshments in Courtyard Cafe. For other opening times and information, please phone, email or visit garden website.**
Gardens are Grade I listed due to association with the C18 landscape architect William Emes. Set within 750 acres, a designated National Nature Reserve with SSSI, there is parkland with small lake and traces of a water garden. A mass display of rhododendrons, azaleas and unique yew hedge surround the sunken lawns. Unusual trees, woodland walks and arboretum. Good autumn colour. Wheelchair access via some gravel paths.

25 HILL COTTAGE

North Avenue, Llandrindod Wells, LD1 6BY. **Mr Neville & Mrs Sylvia Clare.** *From Llandod take A483 N for ½ m. Turn L on A4081 at r'about junc of Cadwallader Way & North Ave.* **Sat 18, Sun 19 May (2-5). Adm £5, chd free. Home-made teas.**
A delightful garden in Llandrindod Wells designed by the architect owner over the past 37 years on a formerly derelict ¾ acre site. The

garden contains many mature trees and shrubs, ponds, and a variety of oriental features. There is an authentic Finnish barbecue cabin, a hidden Alice in Wonderland themed area and vegetable plot.

26 HURDLEY HALL

Hurdley, Churchstoke, SY15 6DY. **Simon Cain & Simon Quin.** *2m from Churchstoke. Take turning for Hurdley off A489, 1m E of Churchstoke. Garden is a further 1m up the lane.* **Sun 16 June, Sun 7 July (11-5). Adm £6, chd free. Home-made teas.**
'A glorious Welsh Garden' (Country Life, 2022) set in stunning location. Topiary, herbaceous and mixed borders, ponds and kitchen garden leading to 18 acres of Coronation Meadows, woodland and orchard. Visit in June for wildflower meadows, orchids and roses and July for lavender and colourful herbaceous border.

27 THE HYMNS

Walton, Presteigne, LD8 2RA. **E Passey, 07958 762362, thehymns@hotmail.com, www.thehymns.co.uk.** *5m W of Kington. Take A44 W, then 1st R for Kinnerton. After approx 1m, at the top of small hill, turn L (W).* **Daily Sat 7 Sept to Sun 15 Sept (11-5). Adm £6, chd free. Light refreshments inc tea, coffee & cake, quiches and more. Visits also by arrangement 31 Mar to 30 Sept.**
In a beautiful setting in the heart of the Radnor valley, the garden is part of a restored C16 farmstead, with long views to the hills, and the Radnor Forest. It is a traditional garden reclaimed from the wild, using locally grown plants and seeds, and with a herb patio, wildflower meadows and a short woodland walk. It is designed for all the senses: sight, sound and smell. The September garden opening coincides with Herefordshire Art Week where local artists will be exhibiting. Garden visitors will also be warmly welcomed to the exhibition.

28 LLANGEDWYN HALL
Llangedwyn, Oswestry, SY10 9JW.
Nicholas Williams-Wynn,
llangedwyn.co.uk/. *8m SW of
Oswestry. From Oswestry, A483
S for 3½ m, turn R at Llynclys
x-roads turn W on to the B4396
towards Llanrhaeadr-ym-Mochnant.
Continue approx 5m to the village of
Llangedwyn.* **Sun 23 June (1-5). Adm
£6, chd free. Home-made teas.**
Beautiful four acre formal terraced
garden on three levels, designed and
laid out in late C17 and early C18.
Unusual herbaceous plants, sunken
rose garden, small water garden,
walled kitchen garden and woodland
walk. Partial wheelchair access along
gravel paths.
&. ☕ ⁕))

GROUP OPENING

29 NEW LLANIDLOES GARDENS
Bethel Street, Llanidloes,
SY18 6BS. Lauren Sheldrick. *In
Llanidloes, off A470. Map and tickets
at Compton's Yard (Great Oak St)
and The Hanging Gardens (Bethel
St).* **Sat 17, Sun 18 Aug (11-5).
Combined adm £6, chd free.
Home-made teas at The Hanging
Gardens.**

NEW BURIAL GROUND
ALLOTMENTS
Andi & Meg Clevely.

NEW COMPTON'S YARD
Compton's Yard Charitable Trust.

NEW THE HANGING GARDENS
Fran and Kevin Blockley,
www.thehanginggardens.org.

NEW 42 HIGH STREET
Rose Challands.

NEW MILLENIUM GARDEN
Lynne Evans, www.facebook.
com/llanidloesmillenniumgarden.

NEW OAK SHOP COTTAGE
Mike Rutland.

A trail of interesting gardens in market
town of Llanidloes the first town
on River Severn with its distinctive
C17 black and white timber-framed
houses and Old Market Hall. The
town has a large focus on community
spirit, whole-foods and fair trade. A
mix of public and private gardens inc
two community gardens, allotments,
courtyard and cottage gardens,
two with very productive fruit and
vegetables gardens. On Sat only:
Llanidloes Charter Market, 9am- 2pm.
Stalls inc local produce, crafts and

antiques. Exhibition of quilts by Quilt
Association of Great Britain at Minerva
Arts Centre Gallery.
⁕ ☕ ⁕))

30 NEW LLWYN
Tregynon, Newtown, SY16 3PP.
Bob and Liz Davies. *6m N
Newtown. A483 N 3m turn L B4389
to Tregynon. L at sch, and then
L at church. From Bwlch y ffridd,
up hill 1m then1st R. Follow NGS
yellow arrows.* **Sun 2 June (1-5).
Combined adm with Parson's
Field £5, chd free. Home-made
teas. Fruit punch and Pimms at
the Parson's Field.**
This small, colourful garden is packed
with interest for the inquisitive visitor,
inc pond, paths, hidden places and
kitchen garden. The practical workings
of the garden are very visible: sheds,
compost heaps and the many uses
of old plastic sacks as befits a low
budget project stocked largely from
cuttings, sowing and division. Many
plants are available for sale.
⁕ ☕ ⁕))

31 LLWYN MADOC
Beulah, Llanwrtyd Wells, LD5 4TT.
Patrick & Miranda Bourdillon,
01591 620564, miranda.
bourdillon@gmail.com. *8m W of
Builth Wells. On A483 at Beulah take
road towards Abergwesyn for 1m.
Drive on R. Parking on field below
drive- follow yellow signs.* **Sun 2
June (2-5.30). Adm £6, chd free.
Cream teas.**
Terraced garden in an attractive
wooded valley, overlooking a stunning
lake. Yew hedges and a rose garden
with pergola. The gardens slope
down away from the house and are
at their best when the rhododendrons
and azaleas are out.
🐾 🚪 ☕

32 NEW LLWYNAU MAWR FARM
Cwmdu, Crickhowell, NP8 1RS.
Dr Pauline Ruth. *N of Tretower
on edge of Cwmdu. Travelling N
turn L at the Farmers Arms pub in
Cwmdu, through the village and then
follow the signs to Llwynaumawr.
Llwynaumawr Farm is the 300 year
old barn. Parking will be signposted.*
**Sun 16 June (11-5). Combined
adm with Maes Llechau £7.50,
chd free. Home-made teas.**
Old barn beautifully located on
Beacons Way facing south with
fantastic views of Black Mountains.

Since Oct 2022 Pauline has been
working on an established garden
with productive veg plot, two acre
orchard of rare apples, pears,
plums, damsons, cherry, crabapple
and walnut. Woodland track with
bluebells. Climbing roses, fig and vine.
Borders and wildflower area. Multiple
seating areas to enjoy. Stream,
mown paths, dry stone walling,
arbour, greenhouses, ancient pears,
free range hens, wildflowers and
pollinators. Children's swing.
☕ 🪑

33 LLYS CELYN
Llanwnog, Caersws, SY17 5JG.
Lesley & Tony Geary,
01686 688476,
lesley_geary@hotmail.com. *9m W
of Newtown. From Newtown A489
W to A470, turn R to Machynlleth
& Caersws. After 3m turn R on
B4589. Follow signs. Alternative
route: from Newtown B4589 from
McDonalds direct to Llanwnog.*
**Visits by arrangement June & July
for groups of 5 to 20. Adm £5, chd
free. Home-made teas.**
An evolving one acre garden with
extensive vegetable garden which
inc fruit cage, polytunnel and
greenhouse. Large and intensively
planted herbaceous borders. Wildlife
areas inc bog garden, ponds and
habitats, a haven for re-homed rescue
hedgehogs. Secluded courtyard
garden and rockery. Fabulous views
of the surrounding countryside and
village church steeple.
&. ☕

34 LLYSDINAM
Newbridge-on-Wye, LD1 6NB.
Sir John & Lady Venables-
Llewelyn & Llysdinam
Charitable Trust, 07748 492025,
llysdinamgardens@gmail.com,
llysdinamgardens.org. *5m SW of
Llandrindod Wells. Turn W off A470
at Newbridge-on-Wye; turn R immed
after crossing R Wye; entrance up
hill.* **Sun 26 May (2-5). Adm £5, chd
free. Cream teas. Visits also by
arrangement 15 Jan to 16 Dec.**
Llysdinam Gardens are among the
loveliest in mid Wales, especially
noted for a magnificent display
of rhododendrons and azaleas in
May. Covering some six acres, they
command sweeping views down
the Wye Valley. Successive family
members have developed the
gardens over the last 150 years to inc
woodland with specimen trees, large
herbaceous and shrub borders and

a water garden, all of which provide varied, colourful planting throughout the year. The Victorian walled kitchen garden and extensive greenhouses grow a wide variety of vegetables, hothouse fruit and exotic plants. Limited spaces for booked groups of between 4-10 for guided walk and refreshments at £12pp. Wheelchair access: gravel paths.

35 LOWER WERNFIGIN BARNS

Trallong, Brecon, LD3 8HW. Mark Collins & Alan Loze. *Trallong, Nr Sennybridge, Brecon. A40 W from Brecon, 2nd signpost to Trallong (R). Down, over river, up to Trallong Common then follow yellow signs. A40 E from Sennybridge take 1st sign to Trallong then the same.* Sat 29, Sun 30 June (11-5). Adm £6, chd free. Home-made teas. Coffee, cakes and cream scones available.

A terraced south facing garden with dense planting of herbaceous perennials and shrubs. Rear garden planted with hydrangeas, azaleas and rhododendrons. A newly planted area of woodland and field walk. A small orchard, vegetable and fruit garden, all managed, like the flower garden without chemicals. In front of the house is a large courtyard with formal rill, fishpond and seating areas.

36 NEW MAES LLECHAU

Cwmdu, Crickhowell, NP8 1SB. Drs Douglas and Alison Paton. *5m NW of Crickhowell. Take A40 from Crickhowell towards Brecon after 4½ m turn into the lane on R. After ½ m, Maes Llechau on L. Or from Brecon direction take 1st L off A40 after leaving Bwlch.* Sun 16 June (11-5). Combined adm with Llwynau Mawr Farm £7.50, chd free. Home-made teas. Cakes and savoury options available.

We moved to Maes Llechau, translated as 'field of slate' in 2016 having converted a long-barn into their home. Developed from scratch the 1½ acres of verdant garden inc perennial borders, meadows, orchard, new woodland and vegetable garden. Maes Llechau draws from the borrowed landscape of the Black Mountains.

37 NEW THE MALTHOUSE

Llandrinio, Llanymynech, SY22 6SG. Veronica and Alec White. *On B4393, in Llandrinio Village. Between the Punchbowl Pub and Llandrinio Church. Car park opp entrance drive. Parking for disabled at the house.* Sat 8, Sun 9 June (1-5). Adm £6, chd free. Home-made teas. Open nearby Tremynfa.

Walled kitchen garden dating from the C17, adjacent to Llandrinio Hall (Grade II listed building). Restored and planted by present owners over the last 20 years. A long herbaceous border, vegetable parterres, interesting range of C17 pig sties, fruit trees, beehives, long view to the Breidden Hills. Garden is flat and wheelchair accessible.

38 THE MEADOWS

Carno Road, Caersws, SY17 5JA. Pete & Lesley Benton, 07929 038936, bentlesl@aol.com. *7m W of Newtown. From Newtown A489 for 6m & turn R on A470 thru Caersws & car park on R. Garden on L 200mtrs along. Disabled & drop off point at garden.* Sun 14 July (12-4); Sun 4 Aug (2-5). Adm £4, chd free. Home-made teas. Visits also by arrangement June to Aug for groups of up to 15. Afternoon or evening visits available.

South facing, compact level garden on village edge, originally The Manse. An eclectic mix of areas with different themes. Colourful annuals, perennials and shrubs, many homegrown from seed or cuttings. Over 100 containers, with an emphasis on recycling and upcycling. A number of cosy seating areas to rest a while and take in the scents and colours. Quiz/treasure hunt for kids and adults.

39 MONAUGHTY MILL

Monaughty, Knighton, LD7 1SH. Peter & Shelley Lane. *5m SW Knighton. From Knighton take A488 towards Llandrindod Wells. After 4m turn R B4356 Garden 400m on L.* Sun 14 July (11.30-4.30). Adm £5, chd free. Home-made teas.

C17 converted mill (not open) with approx two acre garden set on banks of River Lugg in stunning position with lovely views of Glogg Hill. Features inc informal herbaceous and shrub borders, pond, small woodland areas, riverside, shady and bog plantings. Discover our unusual rusted iron

'church' sculpture laden with climbers and shrubs.

40 THE NEUADD

Llanbedr, Crickhowell, NP8 1SP. Robin & Philippa Herbert, 01873 812164, philippahherbert@gmail.com. *1m NE of Crickhowell. Leave Crickhowell by Llanbedr Rd. At junc with Great Oak Rd bear L, cont up hill for approx 1m, garden on L. Ample parking.* Sun 2 June (2-6). Adm £6.50, chd free. Home-made teas in the courtyard. Visits also by arrangement 1 May to 1 Sept for groups of up to 12.

Robin and Philippa Herbert have worked in the garden at The Neuadd since 1999 and have planted many unusual trees and shrubs in the dramatic setting of the Bannau Brycheiniog National Park. One of the major features is the walled garden, which has both traditional and decorative planting of fruit, vegetables and flowers. There is also a woodland walk with ponds and streams and a formal garden with flowering terraces. Spectacular views, water feature, rare trees and shrubs and a plant stall and teas. Most of the garden is accessible for wheelchair users, but some steep paths.

41 NO 2 THE OLD COACH HOUSE

Church Road, Knighton, LD7 1ED. Mr Richard & Mrs Jenny Vaughan, 01547 520246, jennifervaughan6210@gmail. com. *Out of Knighton on the A488 road to Clun, take 1st L into Church Rd, enter by courtyard of 1 Ystrad House.* Visits by arrangement 15 June to 30 Sept for groups of up to 25. Combined adm with 1 Ystrad House £6, chd free. Home-made teas at 1 Ystrad House.

The garden at the Old Coach House is a quiet haven of rooms as you move along a winding path edged by the top borders of shrubs, colourful perennials and circular lawns. An archway of climbers leads to the lower lawn, flanked by beech hedging, apple trees, a greenhouse, fruit bushes, vegetable patch, shrubs, hostas and ferns, arriving at a private quiet riverside woodland glade. The garden can be accessed through the side gate for wheelchair users, where the lawns are generally level.

42 NEW PARSON'S FIELD

Tregynon, Newtown, SY16 3EH.
Liz Davies, www.facebook.com/
people/Parsons-Field-Tregynon.
*6m N Newtown. From Newtown
A483, N 3m turn L B4389 to
Tregynon. Park in Community Centre
car park and follow yellow NGS
signs. Disabled access opp church
but with limited on road parking.* **Sun
2 June (1-5). Combined adm with
Llwyn £5, chd free. Home-made
teas at Llwyn. Fruit punch and
Pimms available.**
This community garden has stunning
views across the village and to the
Severn Valley beyond. Until November
2022 it was a 2/3 acre plot of
inaccessible waste church land but
a group of volunteers are turning it
into a tranquil wildlife haven. They are
developing a wildflower meadow, native
woodland, an orchard, raised beds
of soft fruit and a border of pollinator
friendly herbs and shrubs. Path to
garden from the car park is steep.
Wheelchair access from opp the church
leads to the path at top of garden.

&. 🐄 ✿ 🍵 🎋))

43 PEN-Y-BANK

Marton, Welshpool, SY21 8JY. Robin
& Penny Kenward, 01938 580216,
rckenward@btinternet.com. *6m NE
Montgomery. B4386 N side of Marton
turn L on 'S' bend to Marton Hill &
Trelystan. Follow this for1m; do not take
1st R but cont up hill. Entrance is on R.*
Visits by arrangement 13 May to 28
June for groups of 10 to 20. Home-
made teas £4 pp. Max of six cars per
group. Weekday visits only. Adm £6,
chd free.
A five acre, elevated, hillside setting
with beautiful views. Garden is
comprised of a herbaceous garden,
ornamental trees, kitchen garden and
wildflower meadow. The herbaceous
area is very colourful mid-spring to
mid-summer. Several cornus, acer and
betula varieties also *Parrotia, Sorbus,
Quercus* and *Platanus*; the meadow
contains common spotted orchids.
Please mention any food allergies or
intolerances when booking.

✿ 🍵

44 PLAS DINAM

Llandinam, Newtown, SY17 5DQ.
Eldrydd Lamp, 07415 503554,
eldrydd@plasdinam.co.uk,
www.plasdinamcountryhouse.co.uk.
7½ m SW Newtown. on A470. Visits
by arrangement Apr to Oct for groups
of 10+. Please discuss refreshments

at booking. Adm £5, chd free.
12 acres of parkland, gardens, lawns
and woodland set at the foot of
glorious rolling hills with spectacular
views across the Severn Valley. A
host of daffodils followed by one
of the best wildflower meadows in
Montgomeryshire with 36 species of
flowers and grasses inc hundreds of
wild orchids; Glorious autumn colour
with *Parrotias, Liriodendrons, Cotinus*
etc. Millennium wood. From 1884
until recently the home of Lord Davies
and his family (house not open).

&. 🐄 🚻 🚗 🚻 🍵 🎋

45 NEW PLUM TREE COTTAGE

Ffawyddog, Crickhowell, NP8 1PY.
Mr & Mrs Bennett, 07557 396707,
nicholas611@me.com. *1m S
of Crickhowell, Powys. From
Crickhowell cross the river and then
R by Vine Tree. Follow the road into
Llangattock and take the 1st R after
the Horseshoe pub. Follow yellow
signs up hill to Ffawyddog common.*
**Sat 15, Sun 16 June (12-7). Adm
£6, chd free. Home-made teas.
Hot drinks, sandwiches and
cakes will be available.** Visits also
by arrangement 1 May to 30 Oct
for groups of up to 6.
This large cottage garden in the heart
of the Brecon Beacons National Park
is around ¾ acre and comprises a
shaded area, herbaceous borders,
vegetable beds and wilded areas.
Wild orchids grow freely in unmown
grass along with other wild flowers.
The garden is organic and free of
herbicides and pesticides. Well laid
out raised vegetable beds. Large
herbaceous borders with a wide
range of traditional and unusual plants
and shrubs. Uncultivated areas have
been allowed to encourage wildlife.
There is also a large greenhouse used
for raising and growing plants.

✿ 🍵 🎋))

46 PONTHAFREN

Long Bridge Street, Newtown,
SY16 2DY. Ponthafren
Association, 01686 621586,
admin@ponthafren.org.uk,
www.ponthafren.org.uk. *Park in
main car park in town centre, 5
mins walk. Turn L out of car park,
turn L over bridge, garden on L.
Limited disabled parking, please
phone for details.* **Sat 27 July
(10-5); Sun 28 July (1-5). Adm by
donation. Home-made teas. Open
nearby Bryn Teg.** Visits also by
arrangement 3 June to 30 Aug for
groups of 8 to 30.

Ponthafren is a registered charity
that provides a caring community to
promote positive mental health and
well-being for all. Open door policy
so everyone is welcome. Interesting
community garden on banks of River
Severn run and maintained totally by
volunteers: sensory garden with long
grasses, herbs, scented plants and
shrubs, quirky objects. Productive
vegetable plot. Lots of plants for sale.
Covered seating areas positioned
around the garden to enjoy the views.
Partial wheelchair access.

&. 🐄 ✿ 🚗 🍵))

47 ROCK MILL

Abermule, Montgomery,
SY15 6NN. Rufus & Cherry
Fairweather, 01686 630664,
fairweathers66@btinternet.com.
*1m S of Abermule towards Kerry.
Best approached from Abermule
village on B4368 as there is an
angled entrance into field for parking.*
**Sat 18, Sun 19 May (2-5). Adm £6,
chd free. Home-made teas.** Visits
also by arrangement in May for
groups of 10 to 30.
A river runs through this magical
three acre award-winning garden in
a beautiful wooded valley. Colourful
borders and shrubberies, specimen
trees, terraces, woodland walks,
bridges, extensive lawns, fishponds,
orchard, herb and vegetable beds,
roundhouse and remnants of industrial
past (corn mill and railway line) will offer
you much to explore. Child friendly
activities (supervision required) inc
croquet, sunken trampoline, animal
treasure hunt, wilderness trails,
cockleshell tunnel. Sensible shoes and
a sense of adventure recommended.
Much to explore.

✿ 🍵

The National Garden
Scheme's final instalment
to support the building
of the Y Bwthyn NGS
Macmillan Specialist
Palliative Care Unit
in Wales, enabled 270
inpatients to be supported
this year

48 TRANQUILITY HAVEN
7 Lords Land, Whitton, Knighton, LD7 1NJ. Val Brown, 01547 560070, valerie.brown1502@gmail.com. *Approx 3m from Knighton & 5m Presteigne. From Knighton take B4355 after approx. 2m turn R on B4357 to Whitton. Car park on L by yellow NGS signs.* **Evening opening Sun 2 June (4-6). Sun 20 Oct (2-4). Adm £5, chd free. Visits also by arrangement 31 Mar to 31 Dec for groups of up to 30. Discuss refreshments when booking.**
Amazing Japanese inspired garden with borrowed views to Offa's Dyke. Winding paths pass small pools and lead to Japanese bridges over natural stream with dippers and kingfishers. Sounds of water fill the air. Enjoy peace and tranquillity from one of the seats or the Japanese Tea House. Dense oriental planting with *Cornus kousa satomi*, acers, azaleas, unusual bamboos and wonderful cloud pruning.

49 TREBERFYDD HOUSE
Llangasty, Bwlch, Brecon, LD3 7PX. Sally Raikes, sally@treberfydd.com, www.treberfydd.com. *6m E of Brecon. From Abergavenny on A40, turn R in Bwlch on B5460. Take 1st L towards Pennorth & cont 2m along lane. From Brecon, turn L off A40 in Llanhamlach towards Pennorth. Go through Pennorth, 1m on L.* **Sun 19 May (12.30-5.30). Adm £6.50, chd free. Cream teas.**
Grade I listed Victorian Gothic house with 10 acres of grounds designed by W A Nesfield. Magnificent cedar of Lebanon, avenue of mature beech, towering Atlantic cedars, Victorian rockery, herbaceous border and manicured lawns ideal for a picnic. Wonderful views of the Black Mountains. Plants available from Commercial Nursery in grounds - Walled Garden Treberfydd. House tours are an additional £3.00 on the day. Easy wheelchair access to areas around the house, but herbaceous border only accessible via steps.

50 TREMYNFA
Carreghofa Lane, Llanymynech, SY22 6LA. Jon & Gillian Fynes, 01691 839471, gillianfynes@btinternet.com. *Edge of Llanymynech village. From Oswestry, S on A483 to Welshpool. In Llanymynech turn R at Xrds (car wash on corner). Take 2nd R then follow yellow NGS signs. 300yds park signed field, limited disabled parking nr garden.* **Sat 8, Sun 9 June (1-5). Adm £5, chd free. Home-made teas. Open nearby The Malthouse. Gluten free options available. Visits also by arrangement 3 June to 13 June for groups of 10 to 35. Afternoon or evening visits available.**
South facing one acre garden developed over 17 years. Old railway cottage set in herbaceous and raised borders, patio with many pots of colourful and unusual plants. Garden slopes to productive fruit and vegetable area, ponds, spinney, unusual trees, wild areas and peat bog. Patio and seats to enjoy extensive views inc Llanymynech Rocks. Pet ducks on site, Montgomery canal close by. 100s of homegrown plants and home-made jams for sale.

Our donation in 2023 has enabled Parkinson's UK to fund 3 new nursing posts this year, directly supporting people with Parkinson's

51 TYNRHOS
Newbridge-On-Wye, Llandrindod Wells, LD1 6ND. Clare Wilkinson. *1m NW Newbridge-on-Wye. From A470 take B4518 (signed Beulah). After 400yds, cross bridge & turn R for Llysdinam. Proceed up the hill for 1m, Tynrhos is on L.* **Sun 7 July (1.30-5.30). Adm £5, chd free. Home-made teas.**
A ¾ acre family cottage garden lying at approx 800ft with views over the Wye Valley. Mainly herbaceous planting with summer annuals and pots. Vegetable plot with greenhouse leading to orchard, fields and wildlife pond. Cobbled area to terrace. Access to rear garden area over grass. Paths are a mix of gravel and grass – slippery if wet.
&. ✳ ☕

52 TYN-Y-GRAIG
Bwlch y Ffridd, Newtown, SY16 3JB. Simon & Georgina Newson, 07989 855925, simon.newson@yahoo.com. *4m N Caersws. B4568 from Newtown: Turn R after Aberhafesp. At fork bear L past community centre and at x-roads turn R. At fork bear L. After cattle grid take 1st R onto rough track.* **Sun 30 June (11-5). Adm £5, chd free. Home-made teas. Visits also by arrangement 20 May to 23 June for groups of 5 to 10.**
Plants person's garden at 300m with views of surrounding hills, variety of borders and hectare of stunning wildflower meadow managed for biodiversity around large pond and woodland. Garden planted to achieve different moods inc a herb area, bright, white and pastel borders, rose garden, farmyard borders, fernery, fruit trees and vegetable beds. Open studio. Partial wheelchair access. Grass paths, some steps, most can be avoided. Disabled visitors may be dropped off at house.
&. ☕ 🪑

53 VAYNOR PARK
Berriew, Welshpool, SY21 8QE. Mr & Mrs William Corbett-Winder. *5m S Welshpool. Leave Berriew going over bridge & straight up the hill on the Bettws Rd. Entrance to Vaynor Park is on R ¼ m from speed derestriction sign.* **Sun 21 July (1-5). Adm £6, chd free. Home-made teas.**
Beautiful C17 house (not open) with five acre garden. Spectacular long herbaceous borders with cardoons, crambe, geraniums. A box edged rose parterre and banks of hydrangeas; topiary yew birds, box buttresses and spires bring formality. Courtyard with lime green *Hydrangea paniculata* and Annabelle. Explore our woodland garden and orangery. Spectacular views. Home to the Corbett-Winder family since 1720.
&. 🐐 ✳ ☕))

54 ◆ WELSH LAVENDER
Cefnperfedd Uchaf, Maesmynis, Builth Wells, LD2 3HU. Nancy Durham, 01982 552467, farmers@welshlavender.com, www.welshlavender.com. *Approx 4½ m S of Builth Wells & 13m N from Brecon Cathedral off B4520. The farm is 1⅓ m from turn signed Farmers' Welsh Lavender.* **For NGS: Daily Sat 27 July to Fri 2 Aug (10-4). Adm £5, chd free. Pre-booking essential, please visit www.ngs. org.uk for information & booking. Light refreshments. For other opening times and information, please phone, email or visit garden website.**
Jeni Arnold's stylish wild planting of the steep bank above the ever popular wild swimming pond is a riot of colour. Fields of blue lavender peak from mid July to mid August. Walk in the lavender fields, learn how the distillation process works, and visit the farm shop to try body creams and balms made with lavender oil distilled on the farm. Swim in the pond before enjoying coffee, tea and light refreshments. Partial wheelchair access. Large paved area adjacent to coffee, teas and shop area easy to negotiate.
&. 🐐 ✳ ☕ 🪑

55 WHITE HOPTON FARM
Wern Lane, Sarn, Newtown, SY16 4EN. Claire Austin, www. claireaustin-hardyplants.co.uk. *From Newtown A489, E towards Churchstoke for 7m & turn R in Sarn follow yellow NGS signs.* **Thur 13, Fri 14 June (10-4). Adm £7, chd free. Home-made teas.**
Horticulturist and author Claire Austin's private 1½ acre plant collector's garden designed along the lines of a cottage garden with hundreds of different perennials. Front garden mainly full of May blooming perennials, back garden, which is split into various areas, has a June and July garden, a small woodland walk, a Victorian fountain and mixed rose borders. Fabulous views over the Kerry Vale. Stunning peony and iris fields. Wide range of Claire Austin's Hardy Plants for sale at the nursery. Toilet facilities on site. Sloped track to and around garden. Wheelchair users may require assistance.
&. 🐐 ✳ NPC ☕))

56 WILLOWBROOK
Knighton Road, Presteigne, LD8 2ET. Fiona Collins & David Beech, 07867 385694, fm.collins@hotmail.co.uk. *Outskirts of Presteigne on B4355 towards Knighton, turning L just before the bridge.* **Sun 23 June, Sun 15 Sept (12-5). Adm £5, chd free. Home-made teas. Visits also by arrangement 20 May to 30 Sept for groups of 10 to 25.**
Begun in 2013, yew hedges create garden rooms and vistas. Discover the pergola cottage garden planted with climbing roses and wisteria. There is a formal 'Italian' style pond garden and double west facing, late summer 'hot' borders. Rose border, rill, box parterre, sunken garden. Kitchen garden with raised vegetable beds, fruit trees, soft fruit. Greenhouses, cold frames, polytunnel. Wheelchair access via level grass and gravel paths.
&. 🐐 ✳ ☕))

57 1 YSTRAD HOUSE
1 Church Road, Knighton, LD7 1EB. John & Margaret Davis, 01547 528154, jamdavis@ ystradhouse.plus.com. *At junc of Church Rd & Station Rd. Take the turning opp Knighton Hotel (A488 Clun) travel 225yds along Station Rd. Yellow House, red front door, at junc with Church Rd. Enter by side gate in Station Rd.* **Visits by arrangement 15 June to 30 Sept for groups of up to 25. Combined adm with No 2 The Old Coach House £6, chd free. Home-made teas.**
A town garden behind a Regency Villa of earlier origins. A narrow entrance door opens revealing unexpected calm and timelessness. A small walled garden with box hedging and greenhouse lead to broad lawns, wide borders with soft colour schemes and mature trees. More intimate features: pots, urns and pools add interest and surprise. The formal areas merge with wooded glades leading to a riverside walk. Croquet on request. Lawns and gravelled paths mostly flat, except access to riverside walk.
&. 🐐 ✳ 🚗 ☕

NORTHERN IRELAND

Above: Old Balloo House & Barn

NORTHERN IRELAND

In 2022 gardens in Northern Ireland opened in support of the National Garden Scheme and, with gardens opening in the Channel Islands in the same year, extended the charity's area of activity for the first time since its foundation in 1927.

It brought in the country blessed with an enviable landscape of rolling hills and an endlessly enchanting coastline, which includes the revered highlights of the Giant's Causeway and the Mourne Mountains. Its major city, Belfast, has energetically used its shipbuilding heritage as one foundation of a dynamic new existence and remains the country's beating heart. With the Atlantic on one side and the Irish Sea on the other, there is inevitably high rainfall; this combines with a generally mild maritime climate to allow gardens to flourish and nurture some exotic rarities, especially in the readily available sheltered areas around the coast.

Above, from top: 13 Ballynagard Road; Helen's Bay Organic

Below: The Old Methodist Manse

NORTHERN IRELAND

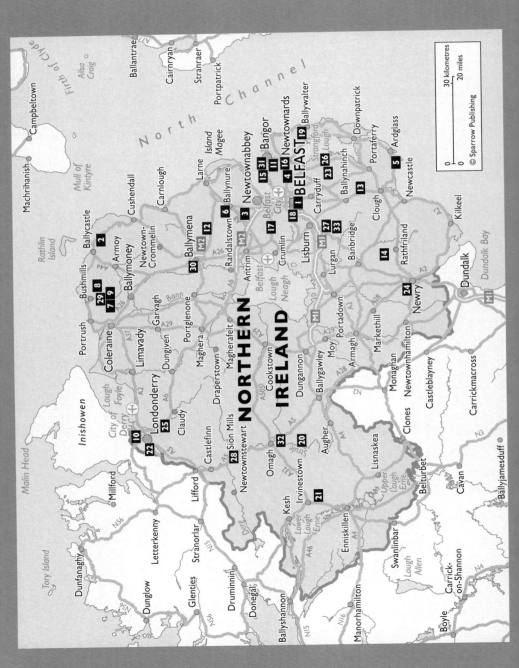

VOLUNTEERS

Area Organiser
Trevor Edwards
07860 231115
trevor.edwards@ngs.org.uk

Area Treasurer
Jackie Harte
07977 537842
jackie.harte@ngs.org.uk

Assistant Area Organisers
Trevor Browne
07788 538284
trevor.browne@ngs.org.uk

Pat Cameron
07866 706825
pat.cameron@ngs.org.uk

Patricia Clements
07470 474527
patricia.clements@ngs.org.uk

Fionnuala Cook
028 4066 9669
fionnuala.cook@ngs.org.uk

Patricia Corker
07808 926779
pat.corker@ngs.org.uk

Ann Fitzsimons
07706 110367
ann.fitzsimons@ngs.org.uk

Will Hamilton
02890 825967
will.hamilton@ngs.org.uk

Rosslind McGookin
07736 524393
rosslind.mcgookin@ngs.org.uk

Sally McGreevy
07871 427025
sally.mcgreevy@ngs.org.uk

Margaret Orr

@ngsnorthernireland
@ngsnorthernireland

OPENING DATES

All entries subject to change.
For latest information check
www.ngs.org.uk
Map locator numbers are
shown to the right of each
garden name.

February

Snowdrop Openings

Saturday 10th
Benvarden Gardens | 7
Billy Old Rectory Peace Garden | 8

Sunday 11th
Benvarden Gardens | 7
Billy Old Rectory Peace Garden | 8

April

Saturday 13th
◆ Brook Hall Estate & Gardens | 10

Sunday 14th
◆ Brook Hall Estate & Gardens | 10

May

Saturday 11th
Clandeboye Estate | 11

Sunday 12th
Clandeboye Estate | 11

Saturday 18th
NEW The Old Methodist Manse | 28

Sunday 19th
NEW The Old Methodist Manse | 28

Saturday 25th
NEW 35 Sheridan Drive | 31
NEW Brockagh Wood | 9

Sunday 26th
NEW 35 Sheridan Drive | 31
NEW Brockagh Wood | 9

June

Saturday 1st
Old Balloo House & Barn | 26

Sunday 2nd
Old Balloo House & Barn | 26

Saturday 8th
Holly House Garden | 17

Sunday 9th
Holly House Garden | 17

Saturday 15th
Billy Old Rectory Peace Garden | 8
NEW Lavender Manor | 21

Sunday 16th
Billy Old Rectory Peace Garden | 8
NEW Lavender Manor | 21

Saturday 22nd
NEW Trillick House | 33

Sunday 23rd
NEW Trillick House | 33

Saturday 29th
NEW Old Barrack House Garden | 27

Sunday 30th
NEW Old Barrack House Garden | 27

July

Saturday 6th
Oak Gardens | 25

Sunday 7th
Oak Gardens | 25

Saturday 13th
Kilcootry Barn | 20

Sunday 14th
Kilcootry Barn | 20

Saturday 20th
NEW ◆ Ballyrobert Gardens | 3

Sunday 21st
NEW ◆ Ballyrobert Gardens | 3

August

Every day from Thursday 8th to Wednesday 14th
NEW Rustic Garden, 14 Woodgrove | 30

Saturday 31st
Helen's Bay Organic | 15

October

Sunday 13th
NEW Horatio's Garden Northern Ireland | 18

By Arrangement

Arrange a personalised garden visit
with your club, or group of friends,
on a date to suit you. See individual
garden entries for full details.

Brook Hall Estate & Gardens

THE GARDENS

1 ADRIAN WALSH BELFAST GARDEN

59 Richmond Park, Stranmillis, Belfast, BT9 5EF. Adrian Walsh, 07808 156856. *From the r'about at Stranmillis College & going along the Stranmillis Rd towards Malone Rd, Richmond Park is the 2nd exit on the L. No 59 is on the L.* **Visits by arrangement June to Oct for groups of up to 25. Adm £5, chd free.**
Described by Shirley Lanigan, in 'The Open Gardens of Ireland', as 'a paradise garden' and 'a veritable sea of plants', this is an imaginatively designed naturalistic city garden that combines a vibrant mix of annuals, perennials, grasses, shrubs and trees set within a formal layout.

2 13 BALLYNAGARD ROAD

Ballyvoy, Ballycastle, BT54 6PW. Tom & Penny McNeill, 07754 190687, pennymcneill@yahoo.co.uk. *3m outside Ballycastle. Drive through Ballycastle, pass hotel on L, 2nd exit at r'about to Cushendall. From Ballyvoy drive ¾ m, Ballynagard Rd is on R. Drive ¾ m. Arrive at 1st bungalow on R.* **Visits by arrangement June to Aug for groups of up to 10. Adm £5.**
A challenging ½ acre site 400 ft above sea level with stunning rural and sea views. Designed to meet prevailing environmental conditions and to protect each section from severe winds. Seasonal planting with mature shrubs and rockery on a terraced site with cosy contrasting rooms with seating area. Regret unsuitable for young children due to steep paths through rockery.

3 NEW ◆ BALLYROBERT GARDENS

154 Ballyrobert Road, Ballyclare, BT39 9RT. Mr Maurice Parkinson, 02893 322952, maurice.parkinson@ballyrobertgardens.com, www.ballyrobertgardens.com. *At the northern edge of Ballyrobert Village, on the B56.* **For NGS: Sat 20 July (11-4); Sun 21 July (2-4). Adm £12, chd free. Pre-booking essential, please visit www.ngs.org.uk for information & booking. Light refreshments. For other opening times and information, please phone, email or visit garden website.**

Ballyrobert Gardens is a uniquely created Ulster Garden. The setting for the garden is a C17 landscape complete with the original cottage, barn and wilding area extending to 16 acres. Sensitively integrating the elements is a six acre garden containing an extensive collection of plants. Appeared in 2016 on BBC TV's Breakfast programme as an exemplar naturalistic garden. Booking essential. Traditional entrance, extensive plant collection, small lake/large pond, large spiral, concentric rings and Bridgid's Cross in the wilding area. Traditional buildings inc the cottage and nearby barn. Stream running through a glen. Access is available for key areas in the garden.

♿ »)

4 BARLEY HOUSE

3 Brooklands Park, Newtownards, BT23 4XY. Miss Gillian Downing, 02891 815263, downingoriginals@gmail.com. *Newtownards, Co. Down. From Dundonald follow A20 to the r'about at Ards Shopping Centre. Take the 1st exit onto Blair Mayne Rd N. Turn L onto Manse Rd. Continue until you reach Brooklands Pk on the L.* **Visits by arrangement May to Aug. Adm £5, chd free.**
A constantly evolving garden with emphasis on roses, trees, shrubs and herbaceous perennials grown to attract birds, bees and butterflies. It has an extensive range of plants and the garden areas have features aimed to enhance and intrigue. It has been artistically planted to give year-round interest. Most of the garden is wheelchair accessible.

♿ ❋ 🚗

5 THE BARN GALLERY AND ROSE GARDENS

49 Rossglass Road South, Killough, Downpatrick, BT30 7RA. Mr Bernard Magennis, 02844 842082, bernardjjmagennis@hotmail.com, www.facebook.com/barngalleryandrosegardens. *2m E of Tyrella Beach. From Clough on A2 6 m. After Minerstown turn R signed St John's Point. From Killough A2 1.8 m turn L. Park opp Our Lady Star of the Sea Church, then 2 min walk. Limited disabled parking at garden.* **Visits by arrangement 18 May to 30 Sept for groups of up to 15. Adm £6, chd free. Home made teas by arrangement.**
The Garden contains circa 300 roses of over 100 varieties. The rose walk leads up hill to a stunning view point across Dundrum Bay to Newcastle, Kilkeel and the Mournes. The downhill route leads through massed dahlias and a white garden to a planting of sunflowers. Original stone built farmyard, fishpond, waterfall, rockery, herbaceous perennials etc. Artist's Studio and Gallery.

☕ »)

6 BEECHMOUNT HOUSE GARDEN

85 Ballyalbanagh Road, Ballyclare, BT39 9SP. Mr David Henderson, 07977 324940, dchenderson2@btopenworld.com. *N of Ballyeaston nr Ballyclare. From Ballyclare town centre take the Rashee Rd after 1.8 m at 5 Corners Guest House fork R onto the Sawmill Rd at junction turn R. Ballyalbanagh Rd is next R.* **Visits by arrangement 20 June to 30 Sept for groups of 15 to 50. Adm £6, chd free.**
A large country garden on all sides of house with herbaceous plants, mixed shrub borders and trees. Lawns and a large elevated rockery offer stunning views of the surrounding Co Antrim countryside.

7 BENVARDEN GARDENS

Benvardin Road, Ballybogy, Ballymoney, BT53 6NN. Hugh Montgomery. *From Ballymoney head toward Portrush, in the village of Ballybogey turn R into the Benvardin Rd after ½ m (before the River Bush) the Gardens are on your R.* **Sat 10, Sun 11 Feb (12-4.30). Adm £5, chd free. Light refreshments.**
The garden at Benvarden enclosed since the C17, when it was most probably a semi-fortified Bawn, built for the purpose of protecting livestock from roaming thieves. Bought by the Montgomery family in the late C18, it was transformed into a modern, for those days, walled garden with the bawn wall faced with brick, the height raised to the present 16ft and paths and beds laid out. From the pond, paths lead to the banks of the River Bush, well-known as the river which leads to the Bushmills Distillery, the world's oldest whiskey, and here the river is spanned by a splendid bridge, built by Robert James Montgomery, who survived the charge of the Heavy Brigade in the Crimean war.

❋ 🚗 »)

8 BILLY OLD RECTORY PEACE GARDEN

5 Cabragh Road, Castlecat, Bushmills, BT57 9YH. Mrs Meta Page. *B/money passes straight at Kilraughts Rd take 2nd R to B66 sign Dervock turn L (B66) sign Bushmills thro Derrykeighan after 2.3 m at Castlecat, R sign Billy ½ m & L - Haw Rd at Church R -Cabragh Rd.* **Sat 10, Sun 11 Feb (1-4). Adm £5, chd free. Sat 15, Sun 16 June (1-5). Adm £5, chd £5. Home-made teas.**
A mature three acre garden on an historic site. Front of the Georgian rectory is a large lawn with mature trees, an ancient well and a developing woodland garden with a small fernery. Rear has another large lawn with contrasting borders of roses, herbaceous, shrubs and pond area. Also kitchen, greenhouse, herb, vegetable and fruit gardens - a large old orchard and area with wildflowers and annuals. Limited refreshments during Snowdrop Opening.

9 NEW BROCKAGH WOOD

47 Benvardin Road, Ballybogy, Ballymoney, BT53 6NN. Mr Shaun Boyd, 07973 682319, shaunboyd2020@gmail.com. *From Ballymoney take road to Portrush. At Ballybogey turn R onto Benvarden Rd. 1½ m on L.* **Sat 25, Sun 26 May (1-5). Visits by arrangement June to Sept. Adm £5, chd free.**
Living better with nature. A rewilding habitat created during lockdown 2020. This 15 acre site inc a two acre pond, native wildflower meadows, marginal plants, water lilies, moorhens, mallard ducks and little grebes. The one mile undulating walk around the perimeter of Brockagh Wood will enrich our lives and help us to reconnect with Mother Nature. Key to a happy and healthy life. Wheelchair access is available to the main pond but not the walk around Brockagh Wood.

10 ◆ BROOK HALL ESTATE & GARDENS

65-67 Culmore Road, Londonderry, BT48 8JE. Mr Gilliland, 02871 358968, info@brookhall.co.uk, www.brookhall.co.uk. *3m N of Derry~Londonderry. From the Culmore r'about off the Foyle Bridge, take the exit towards Moville (A2). Continue on the Culmore Rd (A2)* *for 1m to the entrance on the R.* **For NGS: Sat 13, Sun 14 Apr (2-5). Adm £5, chd free. Light refreshments in the Visitors Centre, check on the day for additional refreshment locations. For other opening times and information, please phone, email or visit garden website.**
Brook Hall Estate & Gardens is a C18 demesne, home to one of the finest private arboretums in the north west of Ireland with unique collections of conifers, rhododendrons, magnolias and camellias. The C17 walled garden on the edge of the River Foyle once used to feed the people of the City of Derry, now home to many of the gardens magnolia and camellia collections. Hard surface paths suitable for wheelchairs and prams through the arboretum and gardens. Please note that some paths may be quite steep.

11 CLANDEBOYE ESTATE

Bangor, BT19 1RN. Mrs Karen Kane, www.clandeboye.co.uk. *Clandeboye Estate Bangor Co Down. Main entrance is off the main Belfast to Bangor A2 circa 2m before Bangor.* **Sat 11, Sun 12 May (2-5). Adm £10, chd free. Pre-booking essential, please visit www.ngs.org.uk for information & booking. Teas, coffees, tray bakes, scones etc. available to purchase in the Banqueting Hall.**
A series of intimate walled gardens adjoin the courtyard and house. These inc the delightful Bee Garden, the Chapel Walk and the intimate Conservatory Garden. Garden features in Shirley Lanigan's ' The Open Gardens of Ireland'.

12 CLAYBURN

30A Ballynulto Road, Glenwherry, Ballymena, BT42 4RJ. Judith & Hugh Jackson, 07539 712991. *What3words app - schematic. composers.remedy. From the A36 Ballymena to Larne Rd, ½ m E of its junc with the B94, turn L onto Ballynulto Rd. The garden is 0.8m on the R.* **Visits by arrangement 15 June to 14 Sept for groups of up to 8. House tours by special arrangement. Adm £5, chd free. Refreshments available by arrangement.**
Clayburn has been transformed from an exposed site in the shadow of Slemish Mt. to become a low maintenance prairie style garden. It has winter interest, shrubs, grasses and insect attracting perennials along with traditional hedging and many dry stone walls. Also incorporated are numerous trees providing both windbreaks and habitat for many bird species.

13 61 CRAWFORDSTOWN ROAD

Drumaness, Ballynahinch, BT24 8LZ. Mr Liam & Mrs Brigid McDonald, 07470 728815. *A24 Ballynahinch to Newcastle, after 2m turn L to Drumaness. Through village, straight at mini r'about onto Crawfordstown Rd. No 61 on L after 1 m. Pass black railings. Garden signed.* **Visits by arrangement May & June. Adm £5, chd free.**
Two acre country garden in which rock is a dominant feature. This has been put to good use creating paths and beds for alpines etc. A recently developed woodland walk contains birch, larch, conifers and oak trees. Roses, hydrangeas, shrubs and perennial plants add to the colour palette. Not all of the garden can be accessed by wheelchair.

14 FORTH COTTAGE GARDEN

67 Lisnacroppan Road, Rathfriland, Newry, BT34 5NZ. Mrs Helen Harper, 02840 651649, helenlharper@yahoo.co.uk. *From A1 take B10 Rathfriland Rd. After 7½ m turn R up steep hill onto Lisnacroppan Rd After 2m garden is on R. Park on R after cottage. From Rathfriland take B10 for 2m & turn L.* **Visits by arrangement May to July for groups of up to 8. Adm £5, chd free.**
Forth Cottage garden is inc in Shirley Lanigan's book "The Open Gardens of Ireland". A cottage garden with three distinct and contrasting areas. Summer emphasis on violas, geraniums, orchids, alpines and drought tolerant plants. There is partial wheelchair access.

15 HELEN'S BAY ORGANIC

Coastguard Avenue, Helen's Bay, BT19 1JY. Mr John McCormick, www.helensbayorganic.com. *Coastguard Ave. off Craigdarragh Rd. Coming from A2 (Main Belfast-Bangor Rd). Drive 200 metres past the railway bridge on Craigdarragh Rd then turn L onto Coastguard Ave. Go over 2 speed bumps & enter 1st farm gate* on L. **Sat 31 Aug (2-5). Adm £5, chd free. Light Tea and/or Coffee by Community Garden Volunteers.** An urban market garden, established in 1991, producing over 50 varieties of organic vegetables for direct retailing. Also hosts a community garden and allotments which inc an extensive range of fruit and vegetables. An ideal space to get ideas to combine flowers, fruit, food and biodiversity in your garden.

🐕 ✻ ☕))

I6 NEW THE HENRY'S GARDEN

5 Aldergrange Avenue, Newtownards, BT23 4FY. Mr Victor & Mrs Roz Henry, 02891 826764, victhenry@aol.com. *From Dundonald follow A20 to r'about at Ards Shopping Centre. Take the 1st exit onto Blair Mayne Rd N. Turn L onto Manse Rd. Turn R to Aldergrange Pk then R into Aldergrange Ave. Turn R to No 5.* **Visits by arrangement 20 May to 31 July for groups of up to 50. Adm £5, chd free.** An abundance of plants and wildlife await you at this multi award winning large urban garden. Tropical ginger lilies and banana plants give the garden an exotic feel. Roses, agapanthus, clematis, succulents give colour and scent. The pond adds more wildlife activity to the garden. A selection of tree ferns tower and flourish, adding interest, texture and a jungle feel to this area of the garden. Partially suitable for wheelchairs.

ょ

I7 HOLLY HOUSE GARDEN

3 Ballyutoag Hill, Nutts Corner, Crumlin, BT29 4UH. Mr Will Hamilton, www.hollyhousegardens.com. *In the hills over looking W Belfast. Crumlin Rd, following signs for Crumlin/Int Airport (A52). After 3m Horseshoe bend, 4m turn L onto Ballyutoag Hill & the garden is the 1st entrance on the R.* **Sat 8, Sun 9 June (2-5). Adm £5, chd free.** Holly House Garden is an area of six acres created out of farmland over the past 20 yrs. The garden comprises woodlands, herbaceous borders and an iris garden where thousands of spring and summer bulbs have been planted. There is an alpine bed, wildlife ponds and a newly planted shrub and woodland garden. Also, in contrast to the traditional parts there is a modern contemporary garden. Partially wheelchair friendly.

ょ ✻ 🚗 ☕))

I8 NEW HORATIO'S GARDEN NORTHERN IRELAND

Musgrave Park Hospital, Stockmans Way, Belfast, BT9 7JB. Mr Matthew Lee, www.horatiosgarden.org.uk/ the-gardens/horatios-garden-northern-ireland. *Off Stockmans Ln, Balmoral. Off Stockmans Ln turn into Stockmans Way - signed Musgrave Park Hospital the garden is to the rear of the Withers Orthopaedic Centre.* **Sun 13 Oct (2-6). Adm £5, chd free.** Horatio's Garden Northern Ireland is a beautiful, accessible, restorative garden located at the heart of the Spinal Cord Injuries Unit (SCIU) at Musgrave Park Hospital in Belfast. Designed by nine-time RHS Chelsea Gold Medal winner Andy Sturgeon, the garden supports people adjusting to life-changing spinal injuries from across the entirety of Northern Ireland. Designed for patients, their friends and families, and NHS staff spending time at the Spinal Cord Injuries Unit (SCIU) at Musgrave Park Hospital in Belfast. Full wheelchair access throughout the garden.

ょ ✻ D ☕))

Brockagh Wood

19 NEW IONA COTTAGE GARDEN

14C Cardy Road, Greyabbey, Newtownards, BT22 2LS. Mr Darren & Mrs Victoria Colville, 07793 672653, victoria.colville@ googlemail.com. *From N'Ards 4 m down P'ferry Rd, turn L onto Mount Stewart Rd. After 3 m, sharp R turn onto Cardy Rd. Immed on R go down concrete lane. Go over 3 speed bumps to 2nd lane, 14C on R.* **Visits by arrangement in June. Adm £5, chd free.**
A relaxed, environmentally friendly country cottage garden which has been under development for the past 9 years. The garden, which inc herbaceous borders, kitchen garden and cut flower garden is pesticide free with wildlife friendly habitats such as pond, log piles, bird boxes and meadow. Some natural exposed rock areas and slightly uneven terrain. Fantail doves fly freely. 2023 In Bloom Competition, Runner up- Garden for Wildlife. Most of the garden has wheelchair access.

20 KILCOOTRY BARN

Fintona, Omagh, BT78 2JF. Miss Anne Johnston, 07761 918951, annejohnston678@btinternet. com. *Situated 2 m from Fintona on the A5 & approx 6 m from Omagh on the L. Google map directions are best found searching for Kilcootry Barn rather than postcode.* **Sat 13, Sun 14 July (1-4). Adm £5, chd free. Light refreshments. Light refreshments provided by Pandora's box.**
A 2½ acre mature cottage garden featuring herbaceous seasonal perennials, water feature, fruit trees, vegetable garden, children's play area, alpacas and ponies in delightful surroundings. Some areas have uneven surfaces.

21 NEW LAVENDER MANOR

61 Salloon Road, Ballinamallard, Enniskillen, BT94 2GH. Vera Cassidy, 07923 802848, veracassidy@hotmail.com, www.lavenderlets.com. *6 m from Enniskillen. Take the A32 from Enniskillen to Ballinamallard, turn L onto the Irvinestown Rd then after 100 yds R onto Salloon Rd. Garden is 1 m on R.* **Sat 15, Sun 16 June (2-5). Adm £5, chd free. Light refreshments.**

A range of well-maintained gardens, accessed via a sweeping avenue with well established trees and a beech hedge. In front of the Manor there are many manicured topiaries and a lush wildlife pond surrounded by a tranquil white garden. To the rear a vibrant herbaceous border leads past a stream to the enchanting woodland garden. Also visit our secluded courtyard and fruit and vegetable garden.

22 NEW 63 LETTERKENNY ROAD

Londonderry, BT48 9XQ. Mr William & Mrs Elma Lynn, 07771 608084, wlynn_geology@hotmail.com. *3 m S of Derry-Londonderry. On Letterkenny Rd (N40). From lower deck Craigavon Bridge turn L to Letterkenny. Pass settlement at Nixon's Corner then ½ m with entrance on R (white gates).* **Visits by arrangement 29 Apr to 31 May for groups of up to 12. Adm £5, chd free.**
A mature garden set in 2½ acres of woodland surrounding a Georgian house c1780. Variety of trees and shrubs most notably a collection of rhododendrons, camellias and azaleas with mature trees, some dating from the construction of the house. Easy access with a network of level gravel or grass paths with a profusion of bluebells in late April/early May. Some remnants of United States naval hospital in the grounds from 1943 to 1945. Owner can provide information on request. Wheelchair access to main features.

23 LINDEN

24 Raffrey Road, Killinchy, Newtownards, BT23 6SF. Alan & Margaret McAteer, 07770 773611. *From the Saintfield Xrds take Todds Hill Rd to Station Rd for 1.6 m then L bend. After 1 m go R & then L at the staggered junc. Go along road signed Killinchy for 1.6 m, Raffrey Rd is on the R.* **Visits by arrangement in June for groups of up to 8. Adm £6, chd free.**
A new (Six years) 2 acre country garden with formal and informal areas. A large rose covered pergola and small parterre and lawn are complemented by year-round colour from perennials, grasses and trees. An orchard of approximately ⅓ acre with apple, pear and damson trees along with a good

mix of soft fruits. Trial planting beds are a feature of the upper garden. There is a large greenhouse. Wheelchair access most areas.

24 THE MCKELVEY GARDEN

7 Mount Charles North, Bessbrook, Newry, BT35 7DW. Mr William & Mrs Hilary McKelvey, 02830 838006. *In the village of Bessbrook. Enter village from junc beside Morrow's Garage, 300 yds up hill past terraced houses turn L through gate.* **Visits by arrangement May to Aug for groups of up to 50. Adm £5, chd free.**
A connoisseurs garden situated in a village setting containing snowdrops, alpine crevice beds, salvias and a large collection of clematis planted among herbaceous and shrub borders. Can also be accessed by a side entrance.

25 OAK GARDENS

219 Glenshane Road, Derry, Londonderry, BT47 3EW. Mr & Mrs Kelly. *4 m from Londonderry. From the A6, slip of for Eglinton/airport, follow brown signs for Faughan Valley Woodlands.* **Sat 6, Sun 7 July (1-5). Adm £5, chd free. Light refreshments.**
Our family garden has been developing on a 2 acre site since 2014.The gardens offer an array of different graded areas encompassing everything from the humble vegetable garden through to the formal gardens with its neoclassical statues and reflective pond. Salvaged pieces sit in unison with a diverse range of planting to create harmonious schemes within each garden area. Flat grass paths.

26 OLD BALLOO HOUSE & BARN

15-17 Comber Road Balloo, Killinchy, Newtownards, BT23 6PB. Ms Lesley Simpson & Miss Moira Concannon, 07484 649767, lsimpsonballoo@gmail.com. *Balloo, Killinchy, Co. Down. Between Comber & Killyleagh on the A22. On the Xrds opp Sofaland shop.* **Sat 1, Sun 2 June (2-5). Adm £5. Visits also by arrangement 3 June to 7 June.**
Restored and newly created, shared, informal gardens around late Georgian house and barn. There is a great variety of trees, shrubs

and perennials but the garden is open in 2024 especially for late rhododendrons and early roses. Part of the garden is not accessible to everyone due to the steep incline, but can be seen from viewing points. Unsuitable for children.

27 NEW **OLD BARRACK HOUSE GARDEN**
7 Main Street, Hillsborough, BT26 6AE. Mr Ken & Mrs Dawn McEntee. *Situated at the bottom of Main St in Royal Hillsborough, opp the Parish Church.* **Sat 29, Sun 30 June (2-5). Adm £5, chd free. Home-made teas.**
Old Barrack House garden is in essence a secret garden, hidden behind the Grade I listed house. Venturing down the alley between the houses you reach the yard and barn, subtly changed and improved to create charming pebbled terraces and garden areas. Dawn's creative instinct is much in evidence. Plants and flowers are chosen for height, form and leaf colour in relation to the ambiance of each area. Most of garden has wheelchair access.

28 NEW **THE OLD METHODIST MANSE**
52 Moyle Road, Newtownstewart, Omagh, BT78 4JT. Mr Uel Henderson, 07864 855315. *100 metres off A5 main Omagh / Strabane Rd in Newtownstewart. Approaching Omagh on A5, Moyle Rd is S of the town Newtownstewart. From Strabane on the A5, bypass Newtownstewart & turn L onto Strahulter Rd which joins Moyle Rd.* **Sat 18 May (11-5); Sun 19 May (2-5). Adm £5, chd free. Visits also by arrangement 13 May to 23 June for groups of 5 to 40.**
When the riverside garden was purchased 50 years ago, the only trees were 10 mature Scots pine and a huge elm predating the house of 1880. Today it is mainly a woodland garden with 120 rhododendrons, azaleas, magnolias, camellias and other acid soil loving plants; betulas, parrotias, malus, ilexs, abutilons and eucryphia. Herbaceous perennials to attract wildlife. Also a vegetable garden and greenhouse. Loose stone driveway. Toilet not wheelchair accessible. Regretfully the glen and the riverside walk are not suitable for wheelchairs.

29 NEW **10 RIVERSIDE ROAD**
Bushmills, BT57 8TP. Mrs Pam Traill, 02820 731219, pmtraill@gmail.com. *1½ m from Bushmills on Riverside Rd, off the B66. Turn L by Drum Lodge, 100 yds further on R beware ramps.* **Visits by arrangement 12 Feb to 16 Sept for groups of up to 10. Parking for 3 cars only. Adm £5, chd free.**
Rambling cottage garden with unusual shrubs, deep borders, woodland spring walk, rockery and arboretum. Springtime is a sea of snowdrops and aconites and May/June see the perennials in the borders at their best.

30 NEW **RUSTIC GARDEN, 14 WOODGROVE**
Ballymena, BT43 5JQ. Mr Colin Agnew. *1½ m N of B'mena on the B'money Rd At r'about turn L onto the Carnburn Rd. Turn R onto the Carniny Rd then L onto the Woodtown Rd. Woodgrove is the 1st cul-de-sac on the R.* **Daily Thur 8 Aug to Wed 14 Aug (10-8). Adm £5, chd free. Light refreshments.**
The Rustic Garden' is a suburban garden bordered to the north by the Antrim countryside. Features inc a small pond and stream with marginal planting and a modest collection of Hydrangea species. Well established trees help to create a natural canopy under which a 'Sunken Fernery' has been developed. Ornamental grasses and Agapanthus thrive in the south facing aspect of the garden. Sunken Fernery, and water feature. Mature ornamental trees.

31 NEW **35 SHERIDAN DRIVE**
Helen's Bay, Bangor, BT19 1LB. Prof Desmond and Mrs Amy Archer. *Located between Bangor and Holywood, Co. Down. A2 to Craigdarragh Rd, Helen's Bay and 2nd L to Sheridan Dr. The garden is on the sea side.* **Sat 25, Sun 26 May (2-5). Adm £5, chd free.**
Two acre garden along Belfast Lough. Developed over 50 years from a challenging site with a stream and small pond, it features Japanese maples, magnolias, azaleas, hydrangeas, unusual trees inc *Cornus controversa* 'Variegata', *Cercidiphyllum japonicum* and *Parrotia persica*.

32 NEW **TATTYKEEL HOUSE GARDEN**
115 Doogary Road, Omagh, BT79 0BN. Mr Hugh & Mrs Kathleen Ward, 02882 249801, tattykeelhouse@hotmail.com, www.tattykeelhouse.com/gardens. *Tattykeel House is approx 2½ m from Omagh on the S side of the A5 Omagh to Ballygawley Rd. There's a sign outside the entrance Tattykeel House & Studio.* **Visits by arrangement May to Aug for groups of 5 to 30. Adm £5, chd free. Refreshments to be arranged at booking.**
A country garden of approximately 1½ acres created over a 30 year period, planted with conifers, shrubs, roses and perennials. There is a sheltered seating area, a Japanese influenced area, interesting features and a collection of well grown climbers on the house. Numerous exciting and significant improvements were carried out in early 2022. Partially suitable for wheelchairs.

33 NEW **TRILLICK HOUSE**
50 Edentrillick Hill, Hillsborough, BT26 6PQ. Mr & Mrs Robert Brown. *S of Hillsborough off the A1 Rd onto the Dromore Rd. Travel on the A1 S side of Hillsborough turn off the A1 Rd at the major junc (signed into Hillsborough) quickly then turn onto the Dromore Rd (heading S) after 1m turn L into Edentrillick Rd.* **Sat 22, Sun 23 June (2-5). Adm £5, chd free. Light refreshments.**
Just outside the heart of Royal Hillsborough, the 4 acre garden combines both native and exotic plantings. Manicured lawns are punctuated with bursts of colour from perennial borders, with secluded nooks. Contains ornate water features and statuesque trees. This garden is not just a visual delight but a sensory experience, with fragrant blooms, rustling leaves, and the gentle hum of pollinators.

The National Garden Scheme donation of £90,000 in 2023 will help fund Horatio's Garden Northern Ireland

Early Openings 2025

Plan your garden visiting well ahead – put these dates in your diary!

Gardens across the country open early – before the next year's guide is published – with glorious displays of colour including hellebores, aconites, snowdrops and carpets of spring bulbs.

Berkshire
Wed 5 February (11-4)
Welford Park

Cheshire & Wirral
Sun 23 February (12.30-4.30)
Bucklow Farm

Devon
Fri 7, Fri 14, Sun 23 February (2.30-4.30)
Higher Cherubeer

Essex
Sun 2 February (11-4)
Green Island

Glamorgan
Sun 16 February (1.30-4)
Slade

Gloucestershire
Sun 26 January,
Sun 9 February (11-4)
Home Farm

Sun 9, Sun 16 February (11-4)
Trench Hill

Sat 15, Sun 16 February (11-3)
Cotswold Farm

Hampshire
Sun 16, Mon 17, Sun 23,
Mon 24 February (2-4.30)
Little Court

Herefordshire
Fri 21 February (11-4)
The Picton Garden

Kent
By arrangement in February
The Old Rectory, Fawkham

Sun 2, Sun 16 February (12-4)
Copton Ash

Northamptonshire
Fri 14, Sat 15, Sun 16 February (11-3)
136 High Street

Somerset, Bristol & South Gloucestershire
Sun 26 January,
Sun 2 February (11-4)
Rock House

Staffordshire & Birmingham
Sun 16 February (12-4)
5 East View Cottages

Yorkshire
Sat 22 February (11-2)
Skipwith Hall

A Big Garden Get-together

Everyone's invited to join our Great British Garden Party – think sunshine, flowers and cake! Gather your friends and family to celebrate summer with a cup of goodwill and host a fundraiser for nursing and health charities.

ngs.org.uk/gardenparty

Visit Scottish gardens open for charity
Explore secret gardens and hidden gems

scotlandsgardens.org

SC049866

✿ Plant Heritage

Nearly seventy gardens that open for the National Garden Scheme are holders of a Plant Heritage National Plant Collection although this may not always be noted in the garden description. These gardens carry the [NPC] symbol.

Plant Heritage, Stone Pine, Wisley, Woking, Surrey, GU23 6QD.
01483 447540, www.plantheritage.org.uk, info@plantheritage.org.uk

Acer (excl. palmatum cvs.)
Blagdon, North East

Alnus
Stone Lane Gardens, Devon

Asplenium scolopendrium cvs.
Delfryn, Ceredigion

Aster & related genera (autumn flowering)
The Picton Garden, Herefordshire

Astilbe
Holehird Gardens, Cumbria
Marwood Hill Garden, Devon

Astrantia
Norwell Nurseries, Norwell Gardens, Nottinghamshire

Betula
Stone Lane Gardens, Devon

Buddleja
Longstock Park Water Garden, Hampshire

Camellia (autumn and winter flowering)
Green Island, Essex

Camellia japonica
Antony Woodland Garden & Woodland Walk, Cornwall

Camellias & Rhododendrons introduced to Heligan pre-1920
The Lost Gardens of Heligan, Cornwall

Carpinus
Sir Harold Hillier Gardens, Hampshire

Carpinus betulus cvs.
West Lodge Park, London

Catalpa
West Lodge Park, London

Ceanothus
Eccleston Square, London

Cercidiphyllum
Sir Harold Hillier Gardens, Hampshire
Hodnet Hall Gardens, Shropshire

Chrysanthemum (Hardy)
Norwell Nurseries, Norwell Gardens, Nottinghamshire
Hill Close Gardens, Warwickshire

Clematis viticella cvs.
Roseland House, Cornwall

Codonopsis & related genera
Woodlands, Lincolnshire

Colchicum
East Ruston Old Vicarage, Norfolk

Convallaria
Kingston Lacy, Dorset

Cornus
Sir Harold Hillier Gardens, Hampshire

Cornus (excl. C. florida cvs.)
Newby Hall & Gardens, Yorkshire

Corylus
Sir Harold Hillier Gardens, Hampshire

Cotoneaster
Sir Harold Hillier Gardens, Hampshire

Cyclamen (excl. persicum cvs.)
Higher Cherubeer, Devon

Daboecia
Holehird Gardens, Cumbria

Daffodil Dispersed Noel Burr Cultivars
Mill Hall Farm, Sussex

Dierama spp.
Yew Tree Cottage, Staffordshire

Digitalis
The Botanic Nursery, Wiltshire

Dionaea
Beaufort, Shropshire

Echium spp. & cvs. from Macaronesian Islands
Renishaw Hall & Gardens, Derbyshire

Erica & Calluna (Sussex heather cvs.)
Nymans, Sussex

Erythronium
Greencombe Gardens, Somerset

Eucalyptus spp.
The World Garden at Lullingstone Castle, Kent

Eucryphia
Whitstone Farm, Devon

Euonymus (deciduous)
The Place for Plants, East Bergholt Place Garden, Suffolk

Eupatorium
Saith Ffynnon Farm, North East Wales

Euphorbia
Firvale Perennial Garden, Yorkshire

Fraxinus
The Lovell Quinta Arboretum, Cheshire

Galanthus
127 Stoke Road, Bedfordshire

Gaultheria (incl Pernettya)
Greencombe Gardens, Somerset

Geranium sanguineum, macrorrhizum & x cantabrigiense
Brockamin, Worcestershire

Geranium phaeum cvs. & primary hybrids
The New Barn, Leicestershire

Geum cvs.
1 Brickwall Cottages, Kent

Hamamelis
Sir Harold Hillier Gardens, Hampshire

OUR
FUTURE
IS
BOTANIC.

KEW IS RESEARCHING AND
PROTECTING PLANTS AND
FUNGI TO HELP SOLVE THE
CLIMATE CRISIS

JOIN | DONATE | DISCOVER

Royal Botanic Gardens
Kew

Cyathea medullaris

Hamamelis cvs.
Green Island, Essex

Heliotropium
Hampton Court Palace, London

Helleborus (Harvington hybrids)
Riverside Gardens at Webbs,
  Worcestershire

Heritage Seed Library (vegetable)
Ryton Organic Gardens, Warwickshire

Hilliers (Plants raised by)
Sir Harold Hillier Gardens, Hampshire

Hoheria
Abbotsbury Gardens, Dorset

Hosta cvs. (Mouse series)
Holehird Gardens, Cumbria

Hypericum sect. Androsaemum & Ascyreia spp.
Holme for Gardens, Dorset

Hypericum spp. & cvs.
Sir Harold Hillier Gardens, Hampshire

Iris ensata
Marwood Hill Garden, Devon

Jovibarba
Fir Croft, Derbyshire

Juglans
Upton Wold, Gloucestershire

Lapageria rosea (& named cvs)
Roseland House, Cornwall

Lewisia
'John's Garden' at Ashwood
  Nurseries, Staffordshire

Ligustrum
Sir Harold Hillier Gardens, Hampshire

Lithocarpus
Sir Harold Hillier Gardens, Hampshire

Malus (ornamental)
Barnards Farm, Essex

Marwood Collection
Marwood Hill Garden, Devon

Meconopsis (large flowered blue spp. & cvs.)
Holehird Gardens, Cumbria

Metasequoia
Sir Harold Hillier Gardens, Hampshire

Narcissus (Engleheart cvs) dispersed
2 Holmwood Cottages, Suffolk

Narcissus cvs. (bred & introduced by Noel Burr)
Mill Hall Farm, Sussex

Nymphaea
Bennetts Water Gardens, Dorset

Paeonia (hybrid herbaceous)
White Hopton Farm, Powys

Pennisetum spp. & cvs. (hardy)
Knoll Gardens, Dorset

Persicaria virginiana
Sweetbriar, Kent

Photinia
Sir Harold Hillier Gardens, Hampshire

Pinus
The Lovell Quinta Arboretum,
  Cheshire
Sir Harold Hillier Gardens, Hampshire

Plectranthus
Sweetbriar, Kent

Polypodium (hardy cvs.)
The Picton Garden, Herefordshire

Polystichum
Holehird Gardens, Cumbria
Greencombe Gardens, Somerset

Pseudopanax
Sweetbriar, Kent

Pterocarya
Upton Wold, Gloucestershire

Pulmonaria cvs.
Brockamin, Worcestershire

Quercus
Chevithorne Barton, Devon
Sir Harold Hillier Gardens, Hampshire

Quercus (Sir Bernard Lovell collection)
The Lovell Quinta Arboretum,
  Cheshire

Rhododendron (Ghent Azaleas)
Sheffield Park and Garden, Sussex

Rhododendron (Kurume Azalea Wilson 50)
Trewidden Garden, Cornwall

Rhus
The Place for Plants, East Bergholt
  Place Garden, Suffolk

Rosa (English roses bred by David Austin)
David Austin Roses, Shropshire

Rosa (rambling)
Moor Wood, Gloucestershire

Roscoea
12 Meres Road, Staffordshire

Salix
West Wales Willows, Carmarthenshire
  & Pembrokeshire

Salvia (tender)
Kingston Maurward Gardens and
  Animal Park, Dorset

Sambucus
Cotswold Garden Flowers,
  Worcestershire

Sarracenia
Beaufort, Shropshire

Saxifraga sect. Ligulatae: spp. & cvs.
Waterperry Gardens, Oxfordshire

Saxifraga sect. Porphyrion subsect. Porophyllum
Waterperry Gardens, Oxfordshire

Sempervivum
Fir Croft, Derbyshire

Sorbus
Ness Botanic Gardens, Cheshire

Sorbus (British endemic spp.)
Blagdon, North East

Stern, Sir Frederick (plants selected by)
Highdown Gardens, Sussex

Stewartia (Asian spp.)
High Beeches Woodland and Water
  Garden, Sussex

Streptocarpus
Dibleys Nurseries, North East Wales

Symphyotrichum (Aster) novae-angliae
Brockamin, Worcestershire

Symphytum
Ryton Organic Gardens, Warwickshire

Taxodium spp. & cvs.
West Lodge Park, London

Toxicodendron
The Place for Plants, East Bergholt
  Place Garden, Suffolk

Tulbaghia spp. & subsp.
Marwood Hill Garden, Devon

Tulipa (historic tulips)
Blackland House, Wiltshire

Vaccinium
Greencombe Gardens, Somerset

Yucca
Spring View, Burwell Village Gardens,
  Cambridgeshire

Society of Garden Designers

The **D** symbol at the end of a garden description indicates that the garden has been designed by a Fellow, Member, Pre-Registered Member, Student or Friend of the Society of Garden Designers.

Fellow of the Society of Garden Designers

Rosemary Alexander FSGD
Roderick Griffin FSGD
Sarah Massey FSGD
Dan Pearson FSGD
Nigel Philips FSGD
Anne-Marie Powell FSGD
James Scott FSGD
Ian Smith FSGD
David Stevens FSGD
Tom Stuart-Smith FSGD
Andy Sturgeon FSGD
Joe Swift FSGD
Robin Templar Williams FSGD
Julie Toll FSGD
Cleve West FSGD

Member of the Society of Garden Designers

Lee Bestall MSGD
Fi Boyle MSGD
Kristina Clode MSGD
Anna Crossley MSGD
Cheryl Cummings MSGD (retired)
Jill Fenwick MSGD
Phil Hirst MSGD
Thomas Hoblyn MSGD
Nic Howard MSGD
Barbara Hunt MSGD (retired)
Melissa Jolly MSGD
Anne Keenan MSGD
Ian Kitson MSGD
Arabella Lennox-Boyd MSGD

Richard Miers MSGD
Robert Myers MSGD
Andrea Parsons MSGD
Chris Parsons MSGD
Joe Perkins MSGD
Emma Plunket MSGD
Debbie Roberts MSGD
Libby Russell MSGD
Charles Rutherfoord MSGD
Sue Townsend MSGD
Lizzie Tulip MSGD
Matthew Wilson MSGD
Rebecca Winship MSGD

Pre-Registered Member

Sara Edwards
Claire Merriman
Sarah Murch
Ian Murray
Zoe Pink
Caz Renshaw
Daniel Shea
Urquhart and Hunt

Student

Ingrid Andree Wiltens
Will Jennings

Friend

Sarah Naybour
Richard Rogers

Acknowledgements

Each year the National Garden Scheme receives fantastic support from the community of garden photographers who donate and make available images of gardens: sincere thanks to them all. Our thanks also to our wonderful garden owners who kindly submit images of their gardens.

Unless otherwise stated, photographs are kindly reproduced by permission of the garden owner.

The 2024 Production Team: Vicky Flynn, Louise Grainger, Vince Hagan, Sarah Hosker, Kay Palmer, Christina Plowman, Helena Pretorius, George Plumptre, Gail Sherling-Brown, Laura Steel, Catherine Swan, Georgina Waters, Anna Wili.

A CIP catalogue record for this book is available from the British Library.

ISBN: 978-1-3999-6997-0

Designed by Level Partnership
Cover designed by lydiafee.co.uk
Maps by Mary Spence © Global Mapping and XYZ Maps
Printed and bound in the United Kingdom by PCP Ltd

WORLD LAND TRUST™
www.carbonbalancedpaper.com
CBP021465